International Directory of
COMPANY
HISTORIES

International Directory of
COMPANY
HISTORIES

VOLUME 117

Editor

Tina Grant

ST. JAMES PRESS
A part of Gale, Cengage Learning

Detroit • New York • San Francisco • New Haven, Conn • Waterville, Maine • London

International Directory of Company Histories, Volume 117

Tina Grant, Editor

Project Editor: Miranda H. Ferrara

Editorial: Virgil Burton, Donna Craft, Louise Gagné, Peggy Geeseman, Julie Gough, Sonya Hill, Keith Jones, Matthew Miskelly, Lynn Pearce, Laura Peterson, Holly Selden

Production Technology Specialist: Mike Weaver

Imaging and Multimedia: John Watkins

Composition and Electronic Prepress: Gary Leach, Evi Seoud

Manufacturing: Rhonda Dover

Product Manager: Jenai Drouillard

For product information and technology assistance, contact us at **Gale Customer Support, 1-800-877-4253.** For permission to use material from this text or product, submit all requests online at **www.cengage.com/permissions.** Further permissions questions can be emailed to **permissionrequest@cengage.com**

Gale
27500 Drake Rd.
Farmington Hills, MI, 48331-3535

LIBRARY OF CONGRESS CATALOG NUMBER 89-190943
ISBN-13: 978-1-4144-4728-5
ISBN-10: 1-4144-4728-0

This title is also available as an e-book
ISBN-13: 978-1-55862-780-2   ISBN-10: 1-55862-780-4
Contact your Gale, a part of Cengage Learning sales representative for ordering information.

BRITISH LIBRARY CATALOGUING IN PUBLICATION DATA
International directory of company histories, Vol. 117
Tina Grant
33.87409

Printed in Mexico
1 2 3 4 5 6 7 14 13 12 11 10

Contents

Preface

The St. James Press series *The International Directory of Company Histories* (*IDCH*) is intended for reference use by students, business people, librarians, historians, economists, investors, job candidates, and others who seek to learn more about the historical development of the world's most important companies. To date, *IDCH* has profiled more than 11,125 companies in 117 volumes.

INCLUSION CRITERIA

Most companies chosen for inclusion in *IDCH* have achieved a minimum of US$25 million in annual sales and are leading influences in their industries or geographical locations. Companies may be publicly held, private, or nonprofit. State-owned companies that are important in their industries and that may operate much like public or private companies also are included. Wholly owned subsidiaries and divisions are profiled if they meet the requirements for inclusion. Entries on companies that have had major changes since they were last profiled may be selected for updating.

The *IDCH* series highlights 25% private and nonprofit companies, and features updated entries on approximately 35 companies per volume.

ENTRY FORMAT

Each entry begins with the company's legal name; the address of its headquarters; its telephone, toll-free, and fax numbers; and its web site. A statement of public, private, state, or parent ownership follows. A company with a legal name in both English and the language of its headquarters country is listed by the English name, with the native-language name in parentheses.

The company's founding or earliest incorporation date, the number of employees, and the most recent available sales figures follow. Sales figures are given in local currencies with equivalents in U.S. dollars. For some private companies, sales figures are estimates and indicated by the abbreviation *est.* The entry lists the exchanges on which the company's stock is traded and its ticker symbol, as well as the company's NAICS codes.

Entries generally contain a *Company Perspectives* box which provides a short summary of the company's mission, goals, and ideals; a *Key Dates* box highlighting milestones in the company's history; lists of *Principal Subsidiaries*, *Principal Divisions*, *Principal Operating Units*, *Principal Competitors*; and articles for *Further Reading*.

American spelling is used throughout *IDCH*, and the word "billion" is used in its U.S. sense of one thousand million.

SOURCES

Entries have been compiled from publicly accessible sources both in print and on the Internet such as general and academic periodicals, books, and annual reports, as well as material supplied by the companies themselves.

CUMULATIVE INDEXES

IDCH contains three indexes: the **Cumulative Index to Companies**, which provides an alphabetical index to companies profiled in the *IDCH* series, the **Index to Industries**, which allows researchers to locate companies by their principal industry, and the **Geographic Index**, which lists companies alphabetically by the country of their headquarters. The indexes are cumulative and specific instructions for using them are found immediately preceding each index.

SPECIAL TO THIS VOLUME

This volume of *IDCH* contains entries on several regional beverage makers, including craft beer brewer Bell's Brewery, Kentucky ginger ale maker Ale-8-One, and the California winery Sebastiani.

SUGGESTIONS WELCOME

Comments and suggestions from users of *IDCH* on any aspect of the product as well as suggestions for companies to be included or updated are cordially invited. Please write:

The Editor
International Directory of Company Histories
St. James Press
Gale, Cengage Learning
27500 Drake Rd.
Farmington Hills, Michigan 48331-3535

St. James Press does not endorse any of the companies or products mentioned in this series. Companies appearing in the *International Directory of Company Histories* were selected without reference to their wishes and have in no way endorsed their entries.

Notes on Contributors

M. L. Cohen
Novelist, business writer, and researcher living in Paris.

Ed Dinger
Writer and editor based in Bronx, New York.

Paul R. Greenland
Illinois-based writer and researcher; author of three books and former senior editor of a national business magazine; contributor to *The Ency-clopedia of Chicago History*, *The Encyclopedia of Religion*, and the *Encyclopedia of American Industries*.

Robert Halasz
Former editor in chief of *World Progress* and *Funk & Wagnalls New Encyclopedia Yearbook*; author, *The U.S. Marines* (Millbrook Press, 1993).

Evelyn Hauser
Researcher, writer and marketing specialist based in Germany.

Frederick C. Ingram
Writer based in South Carolina.

Carrie Rothburd
Writer and editor specializing in corporate profiles, academic texts, and academic journal articles.

Christina M. Stansell
Writer and editor based in Louisville, Kentucky.

Ellen D. Wernick
Writer and editor based in Florida.

List of Abbreviations

€ European euro
¥ Japanese yen
£ United Kingdom pound
$ United States dollar

A

AB Aktiebolag (Finland, Sweden)
AB Oy Aktiebolag Osakeyhtiot (Finland)
A.E. Anonimos Eteria (Greece)
AED Emirati dirham
AG Aktiengesellschaft (Austria, Germany, Switzerland, Liechtenstein)
aG auf Gegenseitigkeit (Austria, Germany)
A.m.b.a. Andelsselskab med begraenset ansvar (Denmark)
A.O. Anonim Ortaklari/Ortakligi (Turkey)
ApS Amparteselskab (Denmark)
ARS Argentine peso
A.S. Anonim Sirketi (Turkey)
A/S Aksjeselskap (Norway)
A/S Aktieselskab (Denmark, Sweden)
Ay Avoinyhtio (Finland)
ATS Austrian shilling
AUD Australian dollar
Ay Avoinyhtio (Finland)

B

B.A. Buttengewone Aansprakeiijkheid (Netherlands)
BEF Belgian franc

BHD Bahraini dinar
Bhd. Berhad (Malaysia, Brunei)
BND Brunei dollar
BRL Brazilian real
B.V. Besloten Vennootschap (Belgium, Netherlands)
BWP Botswana pula

C

C. de R.L. Compania de Responsabilidad Limitada (Spain)
C. por A. Compania por Acciones (Dominican Republic)
C.A. Compania Anonima (Ecuador, Venezuela)
C.V. Commanditaire Vennootschap (Netherlands, Belgium)
CAD Canadian dollar
CEO Chief Executive Officer
CFO Chief Financial Officer
CHF Swiss franc
Cia. Compagnia (Italy)
Cia. Companhia (Brazil, Portugal)
Cia. Compania (Latin America [except Brazil], Spain)
Cie. Compagnie (Belgium, France, Luxembourg, Netherlands)
CIO Chief Information Officer
CLP Chilean peso
CNY Chinese yuan
Co. Company
COO Chief Operating Officer
Coop. Cooperative

COP Colombian peso
Corp. Corporation
CPT Cuideachta Phoibi Theoranta (Republic of Ireland)
CRL Companhia a Responsabilidao Limitida (Portugal, Spain)
CZK Czech koruna

D

D&B Dunn & Bradstreet
DEM German deutsche mark (W. Germany to 1990; unified Germany to 2002)
Div. Division (United States)
DKK Danish krone
DZD Algerian dinar

E

E.P.E. Etema Pemorismenis Evthynis (Greece)
EC Exempt Company (Arab countries)
Edms. Bpk. Eiendoms Beperk (South Africa)
EEK Estonian Kroon
eG eingetragene Genossenschaft (Germany)
EGMBH Eingetragene Genossenschaft mit beschraenkter Haftung (Austria, Germany)
EGP Egyptian pound
Ek For Ekonomisk Forening (Sweden)
EP Empresa Portuguesa (Portugal)

ESOP Employee Stock Options and Ownership
ESP Spanish peseta
Et(s). Etablissement(s) (Belgium, France, Luxembourg)
eV eingetragener Verein (Germany)
EUR European euro

F

FIM Finnish markka
FRF French franc

G

G.I.E. Groupement d'Interet Economique (France)
gGmbH gemeinnutzige Gesellschaft mit beschraenkter Haftung (Austria, Germany, Switzerland)
GmbH Gesellschaft mit beschraenkter Haftung (Austria, Germany, Switzerland)
GRD Greek drachma
GWA Gewerbte Amt (Austria, Germany)

H

HB Handelsbolag (Sweden)
HF Hlutafelag (Iceland)
HKD Hong Kong dollar
HUF Hungarian forint

I

IDR Indonesian rupiah
IEP Irish pound
ILS Israeli shekel (new)
Inc. Incorporated (United States, Canada)
INR Indian rupee
IPO Initial Public Offering
I/S Interesentselskap (Norway)
I/S Interessentselskab (Denmark)
ISK Icelandic krona
ITL Italian lira

J

JMD Jamaican dollar
JOD Jordanian dinar

K

KB Kommanditbolag (Sweden)
KES Kenyan schilling
Kft Korlatolt Felelossegu Tarsasag (Hungary)
KG Kommanditgesellschaft (Austria, Germany, Switzerland)
KGaA Kommanditgesellschaft auf Aktien (Austria, Germany, Switzerland)
KK Kabushiki Kaisha (Japan)
KPW North Korean won
KRW South Korean won
K/S Kommanditselskab (Denmark)
K/S Kommandittselskap (Norway)
KWD Kuwaiti dinar
Ky Kommandiitiyhtio (Finland)

L

L.L.C. Limited Liability Company (Arab countries, Egypt, Greece, United States)
L.L.P. Limited Liability Partnership (United States)
L.P. Limited Partnership (Canada, South Africa, United Kingdom, United States)
LBO Leveraged Buyout
Lda. Limitada (Spain)
Ltd. Limited
Ltda. Limitada (Brazil, Portugal)
Ltee. Limitee (Canada, France)
LUF Luxembourg franc
LYD Libyan dinar

M

mbH mit beschraenkter Haftung (Austria, Germany)
Mij. Maatschappij (Netherlands)
MUR Mauritian rupee
MXN Mexican peso
MYR Malaysian ringgit

N

N.A. National Association (United States)
N.V. Naamloze Vennootschap (Belgium, Netherlands)
NGN Nigerian naira
NLG Netherlands guilder
NOK Norwegian krone
NZD New Zealand dollar

O

OAO Otkrytoe Aktsionernoe Obshchestve (Russia)
OHG Offene Handelsgesellschaft (Austria, Germany, Switzerland)
OMR Omani rial
OOO Obschestvo s Ogranichennoi Otvetstvennostiu (Russia)
OOUR Osnova Organizacija Udruzenog Rada (Yugoslavia)
Oy Osakeyhtiö (Finland)

P

P.C. Private Corp. (United States)
P.L.L.C. Professional Limited Liability Corporation (United States)
P.T. Perusahaan/Perseroan Terbatas (Indonesia)
PEN Peruvian Nuevo Sol
PHP Philippine peso
PKR Pakistani rupee
P/L Part Lag (Norway)
PLC Public Limited Co. (United Kingdom, Ireland)
PLN Polish zloty
PTE Portuguese escudo
Pte. Private (Singapore)
Pty. Proprietary (Australia, South Africa, United Kingdom)
Pvt. Private (India, Zimbabwe)
PVBA Personen Vennootschap met Beperkte Aansprakelijkheid (Belgium)
PYG Paraguay guarani

Q

QAR Qatar riyal

R

REIT Real Estate Investment Trust
RMB Chinese renminbi
Rt Reszvenytarsasag (Hungary)
RUB Russian ruble

S

S.A. Sociedad Anónima (Latin America [except Brazil], Spain, Mexico)
S.A. Sociedades Anônimas (Brazil, Portugal)
S.A. Société Anonyme (Arab countries, Belgium, France, Jordan, Luxembourg, Switzerland)
S.A. de C.V. Sociedad Anonima de Capital Variable (Mexico)
S.A.B. de C.V. Sociedad Anónima Bursátil de Capital Variable (Mexico)
S.A.C. Sociedad Anonima Comer-

cial (Latin America [except Brazil])

S.A.C.I. Sociedad Anonima Comercial e Industrial (Latin America [except Brazil])

S.A.C.I.y.F. Sociedad Anonima Comercial e Industrial y Financiera (Latin America [except Brazil])

S.A.R.L. Sociedade Anonima de Responsabilidade Limitada (Brazil, Portugal)

S.A.R.L. Société à Responsabilité Limitée (France, Belgium, Luxembourg)

S.A.S. Societe Anonyme Syrienne (Arab countries)

S.A.S. Societá in Accomandita Semplice (Italy)

S.C. Societe en Commandite (Belgium, France, Luxembourg)

S.C.A. Societe Cooperativa Agricole (France, Italy, Luxembourg)

S.C.I. Sociedad Cooperativa Ilimitada (Spain)

S.C.L. Sociedad Cooperativa Limitada (Spain)

S.C.R.L. Societe Cooperative a Responsabilite Limitee (Belgium)

S.E. Societas Europaea (European Union Member states

S.L. Sociedad Limitada (Latin America [except Brazil], Portugal, Spain)

S.N.C. Société en Nom Collectif (France)

S.p.A. Società per Azioni (Italy)

S.R.L. Sociedad de Responsabilidad

Limitada (Spain, Mexico, Latin America [except Brazil])

S.R.L. Società a Responsabilità Limitata (Italy)

S.R.O. Spolecnost s Rucenim Omezenym (Czechoslovakia

S.S.K. Sherkate Sahami Khass (Iran)

S.V. Samemwerkende Vennootschap (Belgium)

S.Z.R.L. Societe Zairoise a Responsabilite Limitee (Zaire)

SAA Societe Anonyme Arabienne (Arab countries)

SAK Societe Anonyme Kuweitienne (Arab countries)

SAL Societe Anonyme Libanaise (Arab countries)

SAO Societe Anonyme Omanienne (Arab countries)

SAQ Societe Anonyme Qatarienne (Arab countries)

SAR Saudi riyal

Sdn. Bhd. Sendirian Berhad (Malaysia)

SEK Swedish krona

SGD Singapore dollar

S/L Salgslag (Norway)

Soc. Sociedad (Latin America [except Brazil], Spain)

Soc. Sociedade (Brazil, Portugal)

Soc. Societa (Italy)

Sp. z.o.o. Spólka z ograniczona odpowiedzialnoscia (Poland)

Ste. Societe (France, Belgium, Luxembourg, Switzerland)

Ste. Cve. Societe Cooperative (Belgium)

T

THB Thai baht

TND Tunisian dinar

TRL Turkish lira

TTD Trinidad and Tobago dollar

TWD Taiwan dollar (new)

U

U.A. Uitgesloten Aansporakeiijkheid (Netherlands)

u.p.a. utan personligt ansvar (Sweden)

V

V.O.f. Vennootschap onder firma (Netherlands)

VAG Verein der Arbeitgeber (Austria, Germany)

VEB Venezuelan bolivar

VERTR Vertriebs (Austria, Germany)

VND Vietnamese dong

VVAG Versicherungsverein auf Gegenseitigkeit (Austria, Germany)

W–Z

WA Wettelika Aansprakalikhaed (Netherlands)

WLL With Limited Liability (Bahrain, Kuwait, Qatar, Saudi Arabia)

YK Yugen Kaisha (Japan)

ZAO Zakrytoe Aktsionernoe Obshchestve (Russia)

ZAR South African rand

ZMK Zambian kwacha

ZWD Zimbabwean dollar

A.S. Eesti Mobiltelefon

Valge 16
Tallinn, 19095
Estonia
Telephone: (+372) 639 7130
Fax: (+372) 639 7132
Web site: http://www.emt.ee

Wholly Owned Subsidiary of Eesti Telekom
Founded: 1991
Employees: 597
Sales: $339.7 million (2009 est.)
NAICS: 517212 Cellular and Other Wireless Telecommunications

■ ■ ■

A.S. Eesti Mobiltelefon (EMT) is Estonia's leading mobile telephone services provider. EMT operates the country's most extensive network based on the GSM 900/1800 standard, offering 3G services and since March 2010 super-high-speed 4G service. In addition to its EMT subscription-based mobile service, EMT's brands include prepaid card-based services Simpel and POP. The company also offers a subscription service for students, called YLICOOL. The company had more than 760,000 subscribers in 2010, representing approximately 55 percent of Estonia's total population.

In addition to mobile services, the company operates a network of EMT Esindused retail stores, which sell mobile handsets as well as computers, MP3 players, and other high-tech consumer products. EMT is a wholly owned subsidiary of Eesti Telekom, the leading telecommunications company in Estonia. Eesti Telekom is in turn controlled by TeliaSonera, which holds 60.12 percent, and the Estonian government, which maintains a 24.17 percent stake. Valdo Kalm is EMT's president and CEO. In 2009 the company posted sales of $339.7 million.

ESTONIA'S MOBILE TELEPHONE PIONEER IN 1991

Estonia's telecommunications sector was governed by the Ministry of Communications until the country gained its independence upon the breakup of the Soviet Union. In 1991 the new Estonian government established Eesti Telekom to take over the monopoly operation of the country's fixed-line telephone network.

The new company quickly began developing plans to introduce mobile telephone service into Estonia. For this Eesti Telekom brought in foreign partners, turning to Televerket (later Telia) in Sweden and Post and Telecommunications of Finland (later Sonera). This partnership resulted in the joint venture Eesti Mobiltelefon (EMT), with Telia and Sonera serving as minority shareholders. EMT was the first of a number of co-investments by Telia and Sonera that ultimately led to the creation of TeliaSonera in 2002.

EMT launched its first mobile telephone service based on the NMT 450 analog standard in June 1991. Within a year the company had succeeded in signing up 2,500 subscribers, despite the economic upheavals that accompanied Estonia's transition to a free market economy. Eesti Telekom also adapted to the new market, developing a new structure as a holding

EMT's vision: We are leaders of people-friendly information society. EMT's mission: EMT creates for its customers' opportunities to be successful in a global information society relating to their individual personal needs. EMT's business definition: EMT is a successful and profitable high technology service company operating in the field of telecommunications and information technology. EMT owns and operates telecommunications networks in the domestic Estonian market. EMT develops and markets telecommunication and information technology related services, solutions and environments in Estonia and increasingly for export.

company for its fixed-line business and its stake in EMT. In a later restructuring in 1994, EMT became a joint stock company, with Eesti Telekom, Telia, and Sonera as its three shareholders.

The company continued to expand its mobile network through the first half of the 1990s. The expanded range attracted a growing pool of subscribers, which topped 7,000 by the end of 1993. By then, EMT had also begun developing a parallel network based on the GSM standard, which became the European-wide digital mobile telecommunications standard. The company initially developed a network of GSM support stations, which used the backbone provided by Sonera's GSM network. This provided EMT with the time needed to build its own digital network. When this became operational at the beginning of 1995, EMT discontinued its use of the Finnish network.

MOBILE COMPETITION IN 1995

The launch of GSM services also provided Eesti Telekom and EMT with their first taste of competition. EMT's launch of its GSM 900 service coincided with the launch of a rival service, Radiolinja Eesti (later Elisa Eesti), as the Estonian branch of Elisa Group in Finland. Two years later a third provider, Ritabell (later Tele2 Estonia), became operational as well.

EMT managed to stay ahead of the competition, in part by rapidly deploying its network beyond the core Tallinn market. In November 1995 the company's network extended along the Tallinn-Parnu highway, helping the company build its subscriber base past 30,000 by the end of the year. The opening of the next

leg of EMT's network, connecting Tallinn to Tartu, came early the following year. By the end of 1996 EMT claimed coverage of all of Estonia's main population centers and highways. The company's subscriber base rose accordingly, reaching 50,000.

EMT completed construction of its headquarters in 1997. The company signed on with Iridium that year, a provider of satellite-based mobile connection services, further increasing its coverage and capacity. EMT also boosted its marketing in 1997, creating a new series of subscriber packages offering a range of prices and options. The new flexibility in pricing helped attract the consumer market to the mobile telephone sector for the first time. The company's subscriber numbers doubled by the end of the year.

MOBILE TELEPHONE BOOM IN 1999

The late 1990s witnessed the first true boom in mobile telephone services, as the driving force behind the sector's momentum shifted from the corporate to the consumer market. A key factor in the growing popularity of mobile telephone services was the introduction of a second-generation GSM standard, GSM 1800, which provided greater reliability, clarity, and connectivity. EMT remained the technological leader in Estonia, becoming the first to expand its network to GSM 1800 capability, starting with the Tallinn market in 1998.

The company backed this launch with a new pricing package, called Delta, which featured lower monthly fees and lower per-minute calls. Delta became especially popular for the youth and family markets. The company also added a new brand of prepaid cards called Simpel, which did not require customers to maintain a monthly subscription.

As a result, by the beginning of 1999 EMT's subscriber totals jumped past 150,000, and by June of that year passed the 200,000 mark. The company extended its GSM 1800 network to include Tartu and Parnu soon after. By the end of the year, the company had almost 250,000 customers, representing nearly 18 percent of the total population of Estonia.

Eesti Telekom was privatized in 1999, launching a public offering that ultimately reduced the government's stake in the company to more than 24 percent. Eesti Telekom then once again restructured its holdings, taking 100 percent control of EMT. During this restructuring Telia and Sonera (which merged in 2003) exchanged their stakes in EMT for shares of Eesti Telekom. Telia-Sonera thus emerged as the majority shareholder of Eesti Telekom, and therefore EMT, controlling more than 60 percent of the former Estonian telecommunications monopoly.

KEY DATES

1991: Eesti Mobiltelefon (EMT) is founded with the launch of analog mobile telephone services by Eesti Telekom in partnership with Telia and Sonera.

1995: EMT completes development of its GSM network.

1999: EMT becomes a wholly owned subsidiary of Eesti Telekom.

2005: EMT completes rollout its 3G network and services.

2010: EMT begins testing a 4G network.

EXPANDING SERVICES IN 2000

EMT began expanding its range of mobile-related services at the dawn of the new century. This effort started at the end of 1999, when the company introduced its first GSM phone-based payment service, enabling customers to purchase soft drinks with their telephones from specially equipped vending machines. In 2000 the company debuted its first WAP (wide access protocol) services, providing a number of information services, such as weather forecasts, stock market information, translation, and bill checking, as well as e-mail and directory information services.

As part of this effort the company also developed a number of partnerships. These included an agreement with Privador in 2000 to develop a public key-based security infrastructure in order to secure customer data and information. The group also teamed up with Ericsson Eesti and Tallinn Technical University in a software development project called WAY (for Wireless Application Odyssey). Other partnerships included the creation of a mobile positioning system service with the Estonian State Rescue Service and the launch of mobile protection insurance with insurance brokers Marsh Eesti and Trenwick International.

One service disappeared at the end of 2000, however, when EMT shut down its NMT 450 network, transferring most of its remaining analog subscribers to the new digital networks. By then, the GSM standard had not only become the standard in Europe but had been embraced across most of the world. As a result, operators began developing a series of cross-border partnerships and alliances. The industry was also increasingly marked by a series of high-profile mergers and acquisitions, creating a number of global heavyweight operators.

EMT itself began to look beyond Estonia's borders. In 2001 the company reached an agreement with Latvia's LMT and Lithuania's Omnitel to establish the Baltic Sea Alliance, allowing their customers to access the other companies' networks free of charge. EMT also continued to strengthen its presence in Estonia, adding another 100 relay stations in 2001 to enhance its coverage both in the urban and rural markets. The company also played a major role in bringing Internet access to the country's rural regions, which remained underserved by Eesti Telekom's fixed-line network, launching a high-speed wireless Internet access service.

3G INTRODUCED IN 2003

The company continued to roll out new services, such as MMS (multimedia messaging service) and multi-SMS, which enabled mass messaging via the company's SMS (short messaging service), in 2002. The company, which had already launched MobiKIT, a mobile phone-based security system for automobiles, introduced parking payment using mobile telephones. Soon after, the company launched its m-ticket service in partnership with Estonia's public transportation service company Connex, whereby tickets could be purchased and transmitted by mobile phone. By the beginning of 2003 EMT's subscriber base had climbed past 425,000, and by the end of the year had grown to nearly 500,000.

EMT had also begun developing its 3G, or third-generation, network. The new high-speed technology promised a new era in mobile telecommunications, permitting the transmission of data-intensive applications including video and live television broadcasting services. EMT claimed the lead in this technology in Estonia, initiating its 3G network in September 2003. However, the full-scale rollout of the new high-speed services, hampered in part by a lack of handsets capable of using the technology and a lack of content tailored to the new high-speed standard, was not completed until October 2005.

The promise of new high-speed services, as well as the launch of the hugely popular Apple iPhone, helped stimulate EMT's growth, as it neared 600,000 customers at the end of 2004 and 680,000 by the end of 2005. By 2007 the company claimed more than 759,000 subscribers, representing more than half of the total population of Estonia. The Estonian market also ranked among the highest mobile telephone penetration rates in the world, topping 105 percent (as an increasing number of people owned telephones both for work and personal use) in 2005, and rising to 123 percent by the end of the decade.

With the market reaching the saturation point, EMT's efforts turned toward increasing the array of services. For example, in 2006 the company provided broadcasting services for the Torino, Italy, Winter Olympic Games, in cooperation with Estonian Television. The company extended its 3G network to the Tartu and Parnu markets that year, while also introducing a 3.5G data transmission service, capable of transmitting at 1.8 megabits per second at first, and shortly after at 3.6 Mbps. The company also rolled out a mobile Internet portal, called EMT SurfPort.

INTRODUCING A 4G NETWORK IN 2010

EMT also developed a significant retail presence in Estonia. The company's retail subsidiary, EMT Esindused, had originally focused on selling portable telephones. With the growing saturation of the market, as well as the increasing convergence of telecommunications and other media offerings, EMT's retail operations began expanding its product offering. Beginning in 2006, the company targeted the growth of its retail subsidiary into a full-fledged multimedia retail group, selling high-technology consumer goods such as computers, MP3 players, and digital cameras, as well as portable telephones.

Eesti Telekom restructured its operations again in 2009. As part of that restructuring, meant to streamline Eesti Telekom's operations, EMT merged with its two wholly owned subsidiaries, Mobile Wholesale and EMT Esindused. At the same time, the company continued to extend its 3.5G network, reaching half of Estonia's population by 2007, and nearly all of the country by the end of 2009. This extension allowed EMT to roll out Internet access into areas of the country not connected to the fixed-line network. EMT then developed a new product, called MyEMT, a customizable calling plan combining voice call minutes with Internet connection services.

With revenues reported at $339.7 million for 2009, EMT had become a driving force behind Eesti Telekom, which posted total revenues of more than $550 million at the end of the decade. EMT remained committed to leading Estonia's mobile telecommunications technology. In March 2010 the company launched testing of new 4G technology, promising super-high-speed data transfer rates up to 100 Mbps. The new technology promised the inauguration of a new era for EMT as well as for the telecommunications and multimedia industries.

M. L. Cohen

PRINCIPAL SUBSIDIARIES

OÜ Voicecom (26%); Serenda Invest OÜ (51%).

PRINCIPAL COMPETITORS

Elisa Eesti A.S.; Latvijas Mobilais Telefons SIA; SIA Tele2; Tele2 Eesti A.S.; UAB Omnitel.

FURTHER READING

"AS Eesti Telekom to Initiate Mergers amongst Subsidiaries," *Telecom World Wire*, April 24, 2009.

"Eesti Telekom Offers Personalised Mobile, Internet Plans," *Telecompaper Europe*, May 6, 2009.

"EMT Introduces New Latvian Short Numbers whilst Roaming," *Tarifica Alert*, February 15, 2005.

"EMT Launches Student Card," *Tarifica Alert*, March 28, 2006.

"EMT Offers Cheaper Starter Kit for Prepaid Service," *Tarifica Alert*, September 13, 2005.

"EMT's First 3G Call in Estonia," *Tarifica Alert*, September 23, 2003.

"Levira, EMT Launch Pilot DVB-H Mobile TV Service in Estonia," *Broadcast Engineering*, May 20, 2008.

Agrofert Holding A.S.

Pyselska 2327/2
Prague, 149 00 4
Czech Republic
Telephone: (+420 2) 72 192 111
Fax: (+420 2) 72 192 289
Web site: http://www.agrofert.cz

Joint Stock Company
Founded: 1993 as Agrofert s.r.o.
Employees: 21,000
Sales: CZK 137.32 billion ($6.53 billion) (2009)
NAICS: 551112 Offices of Other Holding Companies

■ ■ ■

Agrofert Holding A.S. is a highly integrated fertilizers-to-foods group controlling more than 250 companies across the Czech Republic and elsewhere in Europe. Agrofert is the leading agricultural company in the Czech Republic and the second-largest producer of fertilizers in Europe. Following its 2009 acquisition of rival Czech group Agropol, the company is also the leading poultry producer in the Czech Republic and one of the largest in Europe.

Agrofert focuses on three primary industries: chemistry, agriculture, and food. The company's chemistry holdings include Lovochemie, the country's leading fertilizer producer; the Precolor chemicals trading group; Deza, a leading producer of tar; specialty chemicals producer Synthesia; and Fatra A.S., one of the largest plastics producers in the Central European region.

In addition to Agropol, Agrofert's agriculture division operates primarily through ZZN, ACHP, and AGRO, which distribute pesticides, fertilizers, and other farm products. The agriculture division also produces and distributes feed, seeds, petroleum products, and liquid fertilizers, as well as providing grain harvesting, processing, and storage services.

Agrofert's food industry division includes Adex, the Czech Republic's leading turkey producer, and consumer food products companies such as Maso and Masna Studena. Agrofert Holding is wholly owned by CEO and Chairman Andrej Babis, who founded the company in 1993. Agrofert Holding's revenues in 2009 were reported to have topped CZK 137 billion ($6.5 billion). These results, however, included only approximately 150 of the companies controlled by Agrofert.

BUILDING A CAREER IN SOVIET ERA CZECHOSLOVAKIA

A native of Slovakia, then part of Czechoslovakia, Andrej Babis moved to Geneva, Switzerland, as a child. In 1969 Babis's father was appointed the Czech Republic's representative to the GATT (General Agreement on Trade and Tariffs) talks then under way in Geneva. The younger Babis attended the city's prestigious College Rousseau. Babis returned to Slovakia to continue his studies at the University of Bratislava's School of Economics. His experience in Geneva, however, was to prove crucial to the creation of his future business empire.

COMPANY PERSPECTIVES

From the beginning of its foundation, Agrofert has successfully interconnected its commercial activities with its strategy to acquire companies, which fall into its sector of commercial interest. Today, the company has major equity ownership in processing, producing, and distributor businesses in the agricultural, food, and chemical industry, which form the foundation of the growing Agrofert group. The strategy of controlled expansion is based on fast and effective restructuring of equity participation and simultaneous strict maintaining of economic prosperity and stability of all interested entities.

Having completed his studies, Babis went to work for Petrimex. This company, founded in 1949, served as the state monopoly for the import of oil and chemicals products to Slovakia, and as a counterpart to the similar Czech company, Chemapol. Both companies were converted to joint stock company status in 1969. The companies' shareholders were also their largest customers. Babis joined Petrimex in the beginning of the 1980s.

Part of the controversy that would later surround Babis came when his name was discovered among a 1982 list of agents working for the Czechoslovakian secret police. Babis later denied working for the secret police, however, telling *Respekt*: "I have never cooperated with the secret police, on the contrary I was interrogated in the year 1982 due to my refusal to purchase the phosphates of low quality in Syria."

Nevertheless, Babis soon rose through the ranks at Petrimex, becoming a managing clerk by 1985. Babis was assigned to Morocco soon after, where he represented Petrimex as well as the interests of a number of other Slovak firms. However, as one former Slovakia counterintelligence officer told *Respekt*: "Morocco was one of the few Arabic countries where the Soviets had minimal influence. Of course they were trying to establish it. It is possible Babis was listed [*sic*] to help them do it."

FOUNDING A CZECH AGRO-CHEM GIANT IN 1993

Babis returned to Slovakia in 1990, soon after Czechoslovakia broke away from the collapsing Soviet Union. Upon his return Babis was handpicked by Petri-

mex's managing director as his successor, taking up the position of deputy manager. By 1993 Babis had joined Petrimex's board of directors.

Babis soon found himself caught up in the changing political situation, leading to the breakup of Czechoslovakia and the founding of Slovakia as an independent republic under Vladimir Meclar. Petrimex came under the control of pro-Meclar supporters, and Babis then found himself assigned to the Czech Republic with orders to set up Petrimex's trading arm there. The new company, which initially focused on the trade in fertilizers, was named Agrofert s.r.o.

Agrofert started out with just four employees. Babis's ambitions quickly extended beyond the trade in fertilizers, however. By 1994 the company had expanded its range of businesses to include the wider agricultural commodities and chemicals sector. Babis soon targeted an entry into fertilizer production, a move viewed with a wary eye by parent company Petrimex, which considered this market too risky.

Petrimex's wariness provided Babis with the window for gaining control of Agrofert. In 1995 Babis turned to a Baar, Switzerland, company called Ost Finanz und Investition (OFI). This company, which appeared to exist only as an address, was said to include a number of Babis's friends from his Geneva school days. The company had also been set up at approximately the same time as Agrofert.

With OFI's aid, Babis led an equity increase at Agrofert, which reincorporated as a Czech company, Agrofert A.S., with a capital of CZK 1 million. Petrimex refused to participate in the equity increase (and unsuccessfully sued to fight it). As a result, OFI gained control of Agrofert. Babis was removed from Petrimex's board of directors soon after. In response, Babis hired away 55 of Petrimex's employees.

BUILDING A BUSINESS EMPIRE

In 1995 Babis created a new company, Precolor A.S., as the vehicle for building Agrofert's chemicals operations. The company also began investing in the Czech agricultural products distribution sector, buying up stakes in ZZN, ACHP, and other major companies in this area. ACHP then provided the company with an entry into the Slovakia trade market, starting in 1996.

As the Czech economy struggled through the transitional years of its newly established free market economy, Babis and Agrofert instituted a strategy of buying poorly run and financial troubled companies at discounted prices. As Babis told the *Financial Times*:

KEY DATES

1993: Andrej Babis establishes Agrofert in the Czech Republic as a subsidiary of Slovakia's Petrimex.
1997: Agrofert acquires Lovochemie.
2003: Babis acquires 100 percent control of Agrofert.
2008: Agrofert enters the dairy sector.
2010: Babis is included on the *Forbes* Rich List.

"We were looking for companies that were cheap and which we thought had big potential. We've always targeted companies in financial difficulties and companies which were not restructured."

The Czech Republic's privatization program provided Babis with many of the company's most important growth opportunities. For example, in 1996 the company succeeded in its bid to take over the former state run chemicals concern Precheza. Acquired through Precolor, the company initially gained a 53.5 percent stake. By 2002 the company had raised its control stake of Precheza above 97 percent.

Agrofert's chemical interests also included Slovakia, where the company created a joint venture with Duslo, a leading producer of fertilizer and compounds for rubber production. Duslo had been founded as a single factory in 1958, before becoming a separate state-owned company in 1969. In 1994 Duslo was privatized as a joint stock company. Agrofert's relationship with Duslo deepened over the years, and by 2005 Agrofert had acquired Duslo outright.

Agrofert marked a new milestone in 1997 when it joined in the equity increase of Lovochemie, gaining control of the Czech Republic's largest manufacturer of ammonia and fertilizers. This deal was completed through Agrobohemie, a 50-50 partnership with Czech chemicals group Unipetrol. Lovochemie originated as a sulfuric acid and superphosphate factory founded in 1904, and had expanded into artificial silk production in 1923. During the 1950s Lovochemie began building up its fertilizer operations, while expanding into other areas, such as nitric acid and calcium ammonium nitrate production.

RESTRUCTURING IN 1997

In 1993 Lovochemie became a joint stock company, with Proferta as its majority shareholder. However, the capital increase at Lovochemie came at a moment when Proferta's financial difficulties barred the company from participating in the increase. As a result, Agrofert gained effective control of the Czech Republic's leading fertilizer group. The deal quickly sparked a controversy because Babis held a seat on the board of directors of Proferta, and was therefore suspected of using his inside knowledge of Proferta's financial situation to orchestrate control of Lovochemie.

An investigation into the deal remained stalled, however, in the next decade. In the meantime, Babis took steps to secure his control over his growing business empire. In 1997 Agrofert created a new subsidiary called Agrofert Holding. The company then launched a restructuring, which resulted in Agrofert Holding taking over all of the operations of Agrofert A.S. The company announced the restructuring as a means of unlocking the value of the company's holdings. It also provided a future vehicle for Babis to gain full control of the company.

The acquisition of Lovochemie permitted Agrofert to achieve a balance between its trading arm and its production arm. The company reinforced this strategy, founding a new Slovakia-based pesticides producer, Chemagro s.r.o, in 1997, followed by a corresponding distribution company, AGFTrading s.r.o in 1998. In 1999 these two companies were merged, representing the first internal merger in the company's short history.

UNIPETROL CONTROVERSY IN 2001

Agrofert concluded a new major acquisition in 1999, completing the privatization of Deza A.S. This company was a major producer of the coal by-products benzol and coking tar, used in the production of asphalt. Deza then took its place alongside Lovochemie and Precheza as a core of Agrofert's rapidly growing chemicals and fertilizers operations.

Agrofert's business interests in the next decade focused on broadening its existing operations, including expanding the company's geographic reach, while also developing its vertical integration. The collapse and subsequent breakup of Chemapol in 1999 enabled Agrofert to acquire that company's AliaChem subsidiary. AliaChem in turn controlled two important Czech chemicals companies. The first of these was Synthesia, a leading European producer of explosives and specialty chemicals. Synthesia was founded in 1920 and was renamed Explosia in 1934, becoming the state-owned VCHZ Synthesia in 1958.

The second company was Fatra Nepajedla, and its subsidiary Technoplast. Fatra was founded in 1935 and claimed to be the Czech Republic's first plastics producer. That company grew into one of the country's largest plastic products group, specializing in floor coverings, waterproofing sheeting systems, PET films and laminates, and other products. Agrofert completed the AliaChem takeover in partnership with Unipetrol in 2001. Agrofert, through Deza, initially acquired Synthesia, while Unipetrol gained control of Fatra and Technoplast.

During 2001 Babis and Agrofert nearly gained control of Unipetrol itself, as Agrofert beat out other contenders for the state run company's privatization. However, the deal quickly devolved into a new controversy for Babis, and the privatization was put on hold.

SECOND UNIPETROL BID IN 2003

By then Agrofert had launched its vertical integration strategy, buying up several major Czech food processing companies, including Maso Plana, Masna Studena, and Adex in 2000, and a cooperation agreement with Kotstelecke Uzenny in 2003. In 2004 Agrofert entered the bakery sector, buying Penama, the Czech Republic's third-largest producer of flour and baked goods.

The company's geographic expansion during this time included the takeover of Istrochem in Slovakia in 2002, and the group's first entry into Germany, with the purchase of a stake in SKW Piesterlitz Holding, also that year. That company had been one of Lovochemie's major ammonia suppliers.

By the dawn of the 21st century, Andrej Babis had earned the nickname as "the richest Czech." Through the next decade, Babis moved to gain control of the company he had founded. In 2001 OFI sold its 50 percent stake in Agrofert to Ameropa, a new and equally mysterious investment group, also based in Switzerland. Ameropa had previously acquired a 5 percent stake in Agrofert, giving it nominal control over Babis's 45 percent.

In 2003, however, Babis bought back 10 percent of the company. Then, in April 2003, Babis quietly purchased all of Ameropa's shares, a shareholder restructuring that came to light only at the beginning of 2004. Babis had launched another bid for Unipetrol during this period in partnership with Poland's PKN Orlen. Under terms of that partnership, PKN agreed to sell Agrofert five of Unipetrol's companies, including Agrobohemie and AliaChem. However, the Unipetrol deal once again became mired in controversy, including charges of bribery and other allegations. By 2005

PKN attempted to renege on its agreement with Agrofert.

FORBES RICH LIST IN 2010

Despite this setback, Agrofert continued to grow strongly through the decade. After completing its takeover of Duslo in 2005, that company was merged into Istrochem. In 2006 the company bought out full control of SKW Piesterlitz. The company completed a new restructuring during this time, which resulted in the merger of Agrofert A.S. into Agrofert Holding. Agrofert also entered a new market in 2006, acquiring, through Precheza, a titanium dioxide factory in Anhui Province, China.

The company added new operations in Germany in 2007 when it bought two companies, Dreha Dresdner and Getreide, which together boasted a total storage capacity of 120,000 metric tons of rapeseed and other grains. The acquisitions were made in order to ensure the raw materials supply for Agrofert's planned biodiesel production facility, to be constructed through Lovochemie.

The second half of the decade saw Agrofert step up its vertical integration effort. This led the company into the dairy sector, with the acquisition of a 54 percent stake in the Milkagro dairy cooperative in October 2008. That company, which focused on the collection and sale of raw milk, also controlled 51 percent of Olma, the Czech Republic's second-largest dairy products group. Following the completion of the Milkagro deal, Agrofert launched the buyout of the remainder of Olma's shares. By March 2010 the company had gained 99.8 percent of Olma.

By then, Agrofert had achieved another milestone when it gained control of one of its major agricultural sector rivals, Agropol. That company, founded in 1997, grew rapidly to become a leading player in the Czech market, with revenues of $738 million and a strong presence in the agrochemicals and fertilizers sector, as well as the poultry processing industry. The addition of Agropol in 2009 helped stabilize Agrofert's own reported revenues. Amid the economic recession, the company's sales had slipped back by 4 percent in 2009, to CZK 137 billion ($ 6.5 billion). This figure, however, included only about 150 of the companies controlled by Agrofert.

Despite the downturn, Babis himself had reason to celebrate. In 2010 Babis was included on the *Forbes* Rich List for the first time. Babis had built Agrofert into one of the Czech Republic's largest companies, and was himself the country's second-wealthiest person.

M. L. Cohen

PRINCIPAL SUBSIDIARIES

ACHP A.S.; Adex A.S.; AGF Osiva A.S.; Agro A.S.; Agrobohemie A.S.; Agrochema A.S.; Agrofert Pigment Co. Ltd. (China); Agrofert Schweiz Holding AG (Switzerland); Agrofert Slovakia A.S.; Agropol Group A.S.; Deza Polska Sp. z o.o.; Deza A.S.; Istrochem Plasty; Maso Plana A.S.; Navos A.S.; Penam Slovakia A.S.; Precheza A.S.; Zeva Chlistovice A.S.; ZZN a.a.

PRINCIPAL DIVISIONS

Chemistry; Agriculture; Food Industry.

PRINCIPAL OPERATING UNITS

Agricultural Commodities and Products for the Nutrition of Animals; Agrochemicals; Animal Production and Selected Food Products; Chemicals; Fuels and Heating Oils; Industrial Fertilizers.

PRINCIPAL COMPETITORS

CGS A.S.; CKD Praha Holding A.S.; Demonta Trade SE; MVV Energie CZ S.R.O.; Promet Group A.S.; Skanska CS A.S.; Skoda Holding A.S.; SPGroup A.S.; Unimex Group, A.S.; VCES Holding S.R.O.; Vitkovice A.S.

FURTHER READING

"Agrofert Holding Set to Acquire Dairies Olma," *Europe Intelligence Wire*, October 3, 2008.

Andress, Mark, "Controversial Empire Builder," *Financial Times*, November 19, 2003, p. 4.

"Babis Has Got Two Billion from PKN," *Access Czech Republic Business Bulletin*, June 29, 2009.

"Czech-Slovak Poultry Giant Emerges as Agrofert's Acquisition of Agropol Cleared," *Feedinfo News Service*, April 2009.

Panayi, Kelly, "Three Czechs on Forbes 'Richest' List," *Prague Post*, March 24, 2010.

Robinson, Simon, "Agrofert Targets Europe in Plan to Grow from Czech Home," *ECN–European Chemical News*, September 13, 2004, p. 8.

Sedleik, Lubomir, "Agrofert Acquires Agropol," *just-food.com*, April 9, 2009.

———, "Agrofert Acquires Controlling Stake in Milkagro," *just-food.com*, January 29, 2009.

Spurny, Jaroslav, "The Richest Czech Keeps a Secret," *Respekt*, May 13, 2002.

Ale-8-One Company
Bottling Company, Inc.

25 Carol Road
Winchester, Kentucky 40391
U.S.A.
Telephone: (859) 744-3484
Fax: (859) 744-7950
Web site: http://ale8one.com

Private Company
Incorporated: 1962
Employees: 81
Sales: $34.6 million (2009 est.)
NAICS: 312111 Soft Drink Manufacturing

■ ■ ■

Based in Winchester, Kentucky, Ale-8-One Bottling Company, Inc., is a privately held regional company whose primary business is the bottling and distribution of the Ale-8-One soft drink. Ale-8-One is a ginger ale variant that features a fruitier taste and more caffeine. For decades it has enjoyed success in Kentucky, where in its home market it has a cult following and outsells national soft drink brands.

The beverage, along with diet Ale-8-One, is available in most of Kentucky (100 out of 120 counties), as well as in portions of southeast Ohio and southwestern Indiana. Longtime devotees of Ale-8-One shun cans and the newer glass bottles, preferring instead the old long-neck returnable bottles. Ale-8-One is also a popular mixer in Kentucky, combined with the state's famous bourbons to create such drinks as the Kentucky Speed Ball and the Kentucky Gentleman, vodka to create the

Tender Lovin', and Seagram's Seven to make Kentucky Beer.

Through licensing agreements, the Ale-8-One label also adorns several foods products, including barbecue sauce, salsa, apple butter, strawberry jam, and candy suckers. These items as well as the soda and miscellaneous merchandise bearing the Ale-8-One logo are available for purchase on the company's Web site and at a shop maintained at the company's main Winchester building that also caters to people taking scheduled tours of the Ale-8-One plant. The company is owned by its President Frank A. Rogers III, a great-nephew of the founder, and his children.

FOUNDER BEGINS BOTTLING SOFT DRINKS: 1902

Ale-8-One's inventor was George Lee (G. L.) Wainscott, the son of a rail conductor in Lexington, Kentucky, who eventually operated a hotel in the smaller city of Winchester. Wainscott started a bottling plant in town in 1902 under the name Wainscott's Distilled Water and began bottling flavored drinks. With the growing popularity of Coca-Cola at the time, Wainscott, like many others, soon developed his own cola. In 1906 he introduced Roxa-Kola, named for his wife, Roxanne. It was distributed to drug stores and soda fountains throughout the United States and Canada. Coca-Cola did not look kindly on any soft drink using "cola" in its name, and in 1926 it sued Wainscott for trademark infringement. Wainscott eventually prevailed, thanks to his spelling of cola with a "k," but in the meantime he developed a drink that would provide a fallback position should he lose in court. It was a new ginger ale.

Wainscott enjoyed travel and it was during a trip to northern Europe in the 1920s that he bought some soda recipes, including one for a ginger ale that likely originated in Germany. Wainscott was also an anglophile who was aware that ginger ale was popular among the richer classes in England, another factor in his decision to introduce a non-cola drink. He experimented with the ginger ale recipe until he had a drink he liked. He did not, however, have a name for it. In 1926 he held one of America's first "name that product" contests, conducted at a county fair. A young girl was the winner when she suggested "a late one," referring to the latest thing in soft drinks. Wainscott made a visual pun out of the name, coining Ale-8-One.

MOVE TO LARGER SITE: 1935

Ale-8-One grew in popularity, so much so that Wainscott focused most of his attention on Ale-8-One and Roxa-Kola. To keep up with demand, he moved his bottling business in 1935 to a larger property, a former livery stable he converted on West Broadway in Winchester. In the meantime, Wainscott took advantage of the repeal of Prohibition in 1933 to truck in beer from Louisville as soon as it became available.

Wainscott continued to head the company until his death in 1944. At that time, stock in the company was split between his second wife, Jane Rogers Wainscott, and the company's employees. When Jane died in 1954, her brother, Frank Allen Rogers Sr., inherited her stake in the business. He then bought out the remaining interest in 1962 and incorporated the company as Ale-8-One Bottling Company, Inc. Around this time, his son, Frank Allen Rogers Jr., joined the company. The younger Rogers was well into his 40s at the time and in the mid-1960s succeeded his father as president of the company, which was struggling. He rescued it from bankruptcy and built a new plant on Carol Road in Winchester in 1965.

Ale-8-One was clearly the flagship product of the company. Roxa-Kola production came to an end in 1968, and over the next six years the other flavored soft drinks were phased out as well. It was also in 1974 that Frank Allen (Buddy) Rogers III became a company executive. His father became chairman in the 1980s and he became the third Rogers to serve as president. He also inherited Ale-8-One's secret recipe and mixed batches of the syrup by hand behind locked doors. He was known to remove labels and wash out the jugs and bottles containing the ingredients to prevent anyone from guessing the elements of the recipe.

FLORIDA OPERATION BEGINS: 1981

Ale-8-One opened a nearby warehouse in 1976 and five years later added a two-story syrup room to the main facility. The additional syrup was needed to meet expansion plans for Ale-8-One. Brothers Williams B. and David B. Spears, Winchester natives, secured an agreement in the early 1980s to distribute the beverage throughout the United States, with the exception of markets in Kentucky, Indiana, and Missouri. They formed Ale-8-One of Florida Inc. in Atlanta and in June 1981 began producing the soda through local bottlers and used a food broker to distribute the product in Florida. The brothers hoped to take Ale-8-One national by 1984, but Ale-8-One failed to extend its popularity beyond its Central Kentucky market.

Ale-8-One also made attempts to diversify its product offerings in the 1980s. An Ale-8-One-flavored jelly was introduced in 1985. It was produced at the behest of Bill Tippe of Berea, Kentucky-based Booneway Farms, which used the Ale-8-One syrup to make the jelly. The jelly enjoyed a measure of popularity but was never more than a novelty and the last jars were packed in 1988. Also in the late 1980s Ale-8-One teamed up with Ruth Hunt Candies of Mt. Sterling, Kentucky, to produce beverage-flavored Ale-8-One suckers, which were offered for a limited time. A more serious effort at expanding the company was the development of a diet version of Ale-8-One. Buddy Rogers began experimenting with the Ale-8-One formula in the mid-1980s and announced that Diet Ale-8-One would become available by the end of 1989. Many years would pass, however, before the company would be able to launch its first new soda since 1926.

Ale-8-One expanded its Carol Road facilities in 1989. The company spent $1.8 million to add a two-story office building and triple warehouse space. According to press reports Ale-8-One produced more than 140,000 bottles of Ale-8-One each day and posted revenues of $6.7 million in 1993, 80 percent of which came from sales to retail stores, gas stations, restaurants, and vending machines within a 50-mile radius of its plant. The 1990s was also marked by the death of Frank Rogers Jr., who passed away at the age of 77 in 1995. Buddy Rogers would serve as chairman as well as president of the company.

```
┌─────────────────────────────────────────────┐
│                                             │
│              KEY DATES                      │
│                  ■                          │
│ ─────────────────────────────────────────── │
│                                             │
│  1902:  George Lee Wainscott begins bottling flavored │
│         soft drinks.                        │
│  1926:  Wainscott introduces Ale-8-One.     │
│  1962:  Company is incorporated as Ale-8-One │
│         Company Bottling Company, Inc.      │
│  1968:  Roxa-Cola is discontinued.          │
│  2003:  Diet Ale-8-One is introduced.       │
│                                             │
└─────────────────────────────────────────────┘
```

The new century ushered in a host of milestones. Ale-8-One, the beverage, celebrated its 75th anniversary in 2001, while Ale-8-One, the company, celebrated its 100th anniversary a year later. Moreover, a fourth generation of the Rogers family, Buddy Rogers's oldest son Fielding, assumed a senior position in the company in 2003 when he was named vice president.

That year also saw the culmination of nearly 20 years of effort when Diet Ale-8-One was finally introduced in March 2003. Ale-8-One had always been known for leaving no aftertaste, and by employing sucralose and acesulfame potassium the company felt it was able to eliminate the aftertaste caused by aspartame, commonly used in diet drinks. The Diet Ale-8-One formula also contained no calories or sodium. It was originally available in 12-ounce bottles and later offered in 12-ounce cans and 20-ounce plastic bottles.

NEW DISTRIBUTION AGREEMENT: 2002

In the early 2000s Ale-8-One again made an attempt to expand beyond its core central Kentucky market and its 800,000 potential customers. A distribution agreement was reached with Coca-Cola Enterprises in 2002 to distribute Ale-8-One to the greater Louisville and Cincinnati area and additional counties in Indiana, adding another 3.9 million potential customers for Ale-8-One. Diet Ale-8-One was not part of the distribution agreement, however.

Ale-8-One pursued further diversification as the decade progressed. A recipe contest conducted at Sullivan University to help celebrate the 80th anniversary of the Ale-8-One drink elicited an entry for a salsa using the soda. The winning recipes were printed in a newspaper, where they were seen by John Morris of Allied Food Marketers, which was a marketing partner for the Kentucky Department of Agriculture's Kentucky Proud "buy local" program that sought to switch some farmland from tobacco to the planting of other crops.

Morris suggested to northern Kentucky food processor Millard Long that it should consider commercializing the Ale-8-One salsa. Ale-8-One was skeptical but eventually agreed to a licensing deal and began working with Long to perfect a salsa recipe that made use of Kentucky-grown tomatoes and peppers. Following some testing at Ale-8-One potluck gatherings, the salsa recipe was fine tuned, and the new product made its debut in October 2006.

Additional Ale-8-One products making use of Kentucky produce were to follow. In the fall of 2007 Ale-8-One Apple Butter was introduced. It combined Ale-8-One concentrate and flavorings with the pressed pulp left over from the production of cider made from the apples of ten Kentucky orchards. Next, Ale-8-One turned its attention to barbeque sauce. A Lexington radio host, Michael Bandy, known for the popular *Bandy and Bailey* morning show, approached the company to combine the taste of Ale-8-One with his favorite barbeque sauce. Another licensing deal resulted in the 2008 launch of Bandy and Bailey's Ale-8-One Barbeque Sauce, which made use of Kentucky honey and sorghum. With media clout behind the product, it became available in a number of area restaurants.

GEORGIA DISTRIBUTION DEAL STRUCK: 2010

In spite of efforts to diversify, sales of Ale-8-One soda remained the company's primary business. Whether it would ever break out beyond its local roots remained to be seen, but there was no doubt that the product had a passionate following and there appeared to be no shortage of people willing to champion the beverage. In 2010, for example, a Georgia resident, Duane Sudderth, who was familiar with Ale-8-One through family who lived in Winchester and brought home cases of the drink every time he paid a visit, secured a distribution deal in Georgia after several years of making his case to the company. The popularity of Ale-8-One was not likely to diminish in the years to come, nor would the devotion of the Rogers family, which expressed no interest in selling the company and had another generation in the wings ready to take charge.

Ed Dinger

PRINCIPAL COMPETITORS

The Coca-Cola Company; Dr. Pepper Snapple Group, Inc.; PepsiCo, Inc.

FURTHER READING

"Ale-8-One Board Chairman Frank Rogers Dies at 77," *Lexington Herald-Leader*, May 2, 1995, p. B2.

"Ale-8-One Ventures into Salsa Market," *Gray County (KY) News Gazette*, October 5, 2006, p. 19.

Baldwin, Amy, "Ginger Drink's Creator Sought Class Image," *Lexington Herald-Leader*, October 11, 1999, p. 11.

———, "Kentuckians Aplenty Pop the Top of Ale-8-One but Winchester Company Plans Slow Growth beyond Rural Roots," *Lexington Herald-Leader*, October 11, 1999, p. 10.

Fortune, Beverly, "Ale-8-One Is Working to Increase Distribution," *Lexington Herald-Leader*, March 21, 1993, p. 10.

Mead, Andy, "Ale-8-One Admirers Can Now Have Their Drink and Eat It, Too," *Lexington Herald-Leader*, December 30, 1985, p. A1.

Pack, Todd, "Answer to Pop Quiz: Diet Ale-8-One Is Firm's 1st New Soda since 1926," *Lexington Herald-Leader*, January 14, 1989, p. B1.

Swartz, Kristi E., "Ale-8-One Soft Drink Now in Georgia," *Atlanta Journal-Constitution*, May 19, 2010.

American Tire Distributors Holdings, Inc.

―――――――――■―――――――――

12200 Herbert Wayne Court, Suite 150
Huntersville, North Carolina 28078
U.S.A.
Telephone: (704) 992-2000
Toll Free: (800) 222-1167
Fax: (704) 992-1384
Web site: http://atd-us.com

Private Company
Founded: 1935 as City Service Station
Employees: 2,300
Sales: $2 billion (2009 est.)
NAICS: 423130 Tire and Tube Merchant Wholesalers

■ ■ ■

American Tire Distributors Holdings, Inc., (ATD) is a
leading independent wholesaler of tires, offering such
brands as Bridgestone, Continental, Goodyear, Pirelli,
Michelin, and Uniroyal as well as budget and private-
label brands. The private company based in Huntersville, North Carolina, also offers more than 30 brands of
wheels in over 250 styles and a complete range of
service shop tools and supplies. Customers are served
from 82 strategically located regional warehouses. Additionally, ATD offers a variety of marketing support
programs, sales training, and other dealer services,
including the ATDOnline system for checking product
availability, placing orders, and accessing account
information 24 hours a day, seven days a week. ATD is
owned by private-equity firm TPG Capital, which
bought the company in 2010.

COMPANY FOUNDED: 1935

ATD was established as in 1935 in Lincolnton, North
Carolina, by James Harlan Heafner, a high school
principal. Equipped with a mold for tire recapping, he
set up shop in the former City Service Station and
initially adopted that name for his tire distribution
business. He focused on used and recapped tires. For
eight years Heafner continued to serve as a principal,
tending to his outside business before school when he
lined up his work for later in the day. After school he
removed the seats from his 1933 Ford and was able to
stash 55 tires in the back and open trunk. He then
drove to area service stations and used-car lots to peddle
his wares. In 1943 the 39-year-old Heafner faced a
crossroads in his life. He had an opportunity to become
a professor at the University of North Carolina at
Chapel Hill, stay on as a public school administrator, or
devote all of his time to his tire business. He chose tires.

Heafner moved to a larger location in 1949 and for
a time would also operated a Nash Automobile dealership on the same property. He changed the name of his
company to Heafner Tire Company and continued to
focus on recaps and used tires, but he soon realized that
he needed to focus on new tire sales. A key to his success was his ability convince tire dealers that he could
provide them with more regular deliveries than the
regional warehouses of tire manufacturers. In this way
the dealers could keep smaller inventories and not have
their money tied up in excess stock. Heafner opened his
first branch warehouse in Charlotte, North Carolina, in
1954. Six more branches in surrounding cities in North
and South Carolina followed over the next several years,

COMPANY PERSPECTIVES

We believe excellent service and exceptional value distinguish a good company from a great one.

allowing Heafner to post his first $1 million sales year in 1967.

BFGOODRICH BEGINS PRODUCTION OF PRIVATE TIRE BRAND: 1976

In the 1960s the company ceased tire retreading. To spur further growth, Heafner recognized that he needed his own tire brand to serve as an alternative to the national brands, which were territorially restricted. As a result, in the late 1960s he formed the Global Tire and Rubber Company, a buying group that retained mold ownership over a proprietary tire. Heafner Tire enjoyed a growth spurt, opening 10 warehouses in surrounding states. In 1973 the company enjoyed its first $1 million sales month. In the meantime, Global Tire was dissolved in 1972, its molds purchased by Heafner Tire, which then commissioned McCreary Tire and Rubber Co. to produce the Regul tire for the company. In 1976 production of Regul tires was transferred to BFGoodrich Company. Two years later Heafner Tire began selling tires on a retail basis and began opening Retco Tire Stores that in addition to tires sold wheels and batteries and provided auto service.

Under the leadership of James Heafner, Heafner Tire continued to grow into the 1980s when nine more warehouses opened. The company expanded beyond tire sales in 1983 with the launch of Heafner Data Services, which took advantage of its computer infrastructure to offer dealers data services. Heafner Tire also pursued external growth. The company's first acquisition was completed in 1985 with the purchase of Gulfport, Mississippi-based Beech Tire Mart, a dealer that brought with it five warehouses in Mississippi, Arkansas, Florida, and Tennessee, and a wheel weight manufacturing plant. A year later, James Heafner turned over control of the business to his daughter, Ann Gaither. He passed away in 1988.

Gaither was more than ready to assume control of Heafner Tire, despite coming to the business later in life. After graduating from the University of North Carolina at Greensboro in 1953 she taught junior high school music and then spent 18 years raising four children and helping her husband with his hosiery

business. In 1974 her father fell ill and she joined Heafner Tire on a temporary basis to help out. She became interested in the business, took some classes at Catawba Community College, and went to work for the company on a permanent basis in 1974, joining the advertising and marketing department. It was little more than a place for her, rather than a career plan, because her father had a limited vision of a woman's place in business.

DAUGHTER NAMED CEO: 1984

Gaither soon made her mark with the company and earned the respect of James Heafner. She took notice of the Regul brand, which was not performing especially well, and developed a package of promotional materials and helped design dealer ads. Her success in this effort was not only appreciated by her colleagues but also gave her confidence that she had something to offer the company. Moreover, her father became an active supporter. Gaither was named vice president of marketing in 1977 and the following year became senior vice president. Although she was named chief executive officer and assumed day-to-day control in 1984 she continued to work under her father from a desk in his office until his retirement. During that period she was able to listen in on his calls and participate in meetings as she prepared to succeed him at the helm of what was now a $100 million a year company. He also lived long enough to see his grandsons become involved in the company.

Ann Gaither ran Heafner Tire until 1996 when she turned over operation control to her son, Bill Gaither. Under her leadership, the company added five more branch warehouses as well as a small retreading unit that along with the wheel weigh business was divested in 1996. By this stage, Heafner Tire was generating annual sales of $170 million from 31 wholesale stores in 11 southeastern states. Under Bill Gaither, Heafner Tire introduced a dealers marketing support package in 1997 in an attempt to help independent tire dealers at a time when they were threatened by a consolidating marketplace. Heafner Tire also looked to grow larger. In 1997 it acquired the Oliver & Winston, Inc., chain of 132 stores. To fund further acquisitions, the company also forged a relationship with mezzanine investors: Brown Brothers, Harriman & Company, and Commercial Bank.

Even more significant transactions were made in 1998 when Heafner Tire's parent company, J.M. Heafner Company, Inc., merged with ITCO Logistics Company and The Speed Merchant Inc., a California-

```
┌─────────────────────────────────────────┐
│                                          │
│            KEY DATES                     │
│               ■                          │
│  ─────────────────────────────────       │
│                                          │
│  1935:  High school principal James      │
│         Harlan Heafner launches          │
│         wholesale tire business.         │
│  1943:  Heafner pursues tire business    │
│         full time.                       │
│  1988:  Heafner dies.                    │
│  1998:  Company merges with ITCO         │
│         Logistics Company.               │
│  2002:  American Tire Distributors       │
│         name is adopted.                 │
│                                          │
└─────────────────────────────────────────┘
```

based chain known as Competition Parts Warehouse, was acquired to provide coverage in the western United States. The roots of ITCO dated to 1962 and the launch of Turnage Tire in Wilson, North Carolina, by Tom and Leonard Turnage. Four years later it became known as Interstate Tire Company and began distributing tires on a wholesale basis. It took the name Interstate Tire Company, ITCO, in 1974 and in the 1980s moved into the mid-Atlantic states. In the 1990s it moved into new markets in Georgia, Florida, and Virginia. The Speed Merchant, on the other hand, was established in Santa Clara, California, in 1971 by Art Soares. The company entered the wholesale market in 1979 under the name Competition Parts Warehouses, and over the next 15 years added locations in California as well as Arizona.

NAME CHANGE: 1999

Heafner added to its West Coast presence in 1999, acquiring California Tire Company, LLC, which added four distribution centers. Later in the year Boston-based Charlesbank Capital Partners, LLC, acquired majority control of J.H. Heafner, which was subsequently reincorporated in Delaware as Heafner Tire Group, Inc. As the new century began, Heafner was well represented on both coasts and looked to expand to other parts of the United States. In May 2000 it acquired Lincoln, Nebraska-based T.O, Hass Tire Co. A month later Heafner acquired the American Tire Distributors wholesale distribution business of Merchants, Inc., adding four distribution centers in the northeast.

At the start of the 21st century Heafner began a two-year reorganization effort in which the company shed its tire retailing assets, including Winston Tire, 28 T.O. Hass Tire Co. stores, and the retail stores of The Speed Merchant. It also built up it dealer support programs, introducing the AutoEdge program to provide marketing support, a dealer loyalty program called Heaf-Net Rewards, and the Xpress Performance program to provide speedy delivery of high-performance products at no extra charge.

In July 2002 Heafner adopted the American Tire Distributors name, which management believed offered greater brand potential for a national enterprise. With the focus squarely on distribution, the company consolidated its offices in Lincolnton and Charlotte, North Carolina, and opened a new corporate headquarters in Huntersville, North Carolina. Later in the year ATD rolled out a new national distribution network to serve independent tire and wheel retail dealers. The company expanded further in 2004 with the acquisition of Texas Market Tire, Inc., operator of Big State Tire Supply in Texas, New Mexico, and Oklahoma, followed by the addition of Target Tire, which bolstered ATD's presence in the Southeast. Sales for the year increased to $1.28 billion.

Expansion continued in the middle years of the decade. In 2005 the company entered new markets in Idaho, Utah, and Wyoming as well as in parts of Colorado and Nevada through the acquisition of Wholesale Tire Distributors, Inc., Wholesale Tire Distributors of Wyoming, Inc., and Wholesale Tire Distributors of Idaho, Inc. In 2006 ATD acquired Silver State Tire Company and Golden State Tire Distributors to add markets in Nevada and northern California, and expanded into Minnesota and western Wisconsin through the acquisition of Samaritan Wholesale Tire Company. A year later ATD filled out its footprint in Colorado with the addition of Jim Paris Tire City, and in Texas with the purchase of Homann Tire Wholesale, which also brought with it ATD's first distribution center in Louisiana. A pair of acquisitions followed in 2008: Gray's Wholesale Tire Distributors and Am-Pac Tire Dist. Inc. In the meantime ATD added to what it had to offer to dealers through the ServiceBay slate of programs and services introduced in 2006.

STOCK OFFERING ABANDONED: 2010

ATD increased revenues to about $2 billion in 2009, making it one of the fastest-growing private companies in the United States. To take advantage of its momentum, the company filed plans in February 2010 to raise $230 million in an initial public offering of stock. Instead, however, having received a great deal of interest from private-equity firms after the filing, ATD elected to sell the business to private-equity firm TPG Capital for $1.3 billion. TPG was best known for its takeover of Burger King, Petco, and J. Crew. How long TPG would hold ATD remained to be seen, but it was likely that the company would continue to grow in the near term.

Ed Dinger

PRINCIPAL SUBSIDIARIES

TireBuyer.com.

PRINCIPAL COMPETITORS

TBC Corporation; Tire Centers, LLC; Wal-Mart Stores, Inc.

FURTHER READING

Buggs, Shannon, "Businesswoman Likes to Shake Things Up," *Raleigh (NC) News & Observer*, May 5, 1996, p. B1.

"Heafner Data Services Enters Dealer Software Market," *Modern Tire Dealer*, March 1983, p. 51.

"Heafner Group: A Work in Progress," *Modern Tire Dealer*, February 1999, p. 26.

Soo, Ken, "Lincolnton Tire Store That, More," *Charlotte Observer*, November 25, 1985, p. 14D.

Warren, Wendy, "She Makes Tire Business' Wheel Turn," *Charlotte Observer*, July 9, 1990, p. 3D.

Wolf, Alan M., "American Tire Agrees to Buyout, Scraps IPO," *Raleigh (NC) News & Observer*, April 21, 2010.

Angang Steel Company Ltd.

---

396 Nan Zhonghua Road
Tiedong District
Anshan City, 114003
China
Telephone: (+86 412) 6734881
Fax: (86 412) 6722093
Web site: http://angang.wspr.com.hk

Public Company
Incorporated: 1933 as Showa Steel Works
Employees: 31,254
Sales: RMB 70.06 billion ($10.28 billion) (2009)
Stock Exchanges: Hong Kong Shenzhen
Ticker Symbol: 00347
NAICS: 331111 Iron and Steel Mills

■ ■ ■

Angang Steel Company Ltd. (Ansteel) is one of China's leading steel producers, and also one of the country's oldest steel manufacturers. Ansteel is based in Anshan City, in Liaoning Province in northeastern China. The company produces a wide range of steel products, including hot rolled sheets, cold rolled sheets, color coating plates, medium and thick plates, galvanized steel sheets, wire rods, and heavy section and seamless pipes. In 2009 the company produced more than 20.5 million metric tons of iron, and more than 20 million metric tons of steel. The company also produced and sold nearly 19 million metric tons of steel products.

Ansteel has been a prominent player in the ongoing consolidation of the Chinese steel industry. For example, in 2010 the company acquired Baogang Group, Pangang Group, and Panzhihua Iron and Steel. The company has also held an agreement to merge with Benxi Iron and Steel Group since 2005, although the actual merger has been postponed. The completion of the Benxi merger, expected to create a new company called Anben Iron and Steel, would allow Ansteel to claim the lead in the Chinese market, with more than 50 million tons of steel production per year.

Ansteel is the Hong Kong and Shenzhen-listed arm of parent company Anshan Holding, which maintains a 67.28 percent share of Ansteel, and is itself wholly controlled by the Chinese government's State-Owned Assets Supervision and Administration Commission of the State Council. Ansteel is led by Chairman Zhang Xiaogang and posted revenues of RMB 70 billion ($10.3 billion) in 2009.

MANCHURIAN ORIGINS IN 1918

Anshan's prominence as the center of China's iron and steel industry dated from the early years of the 20th century. Before this time, Anshan was a small, provincial town in Liaoning Province. The discovery of vast iron ore and other mineral deposits in the region, coupled with the construction of the South Manchurian Railway, brought new prominence to the city. Anshan had been struggling at the dawn of the 20th century. After being burned to the ground during the Boxer Rebellion, the city had been caught in the middle of the Russian-Japanese War of 1904–05. At the outcome of that war Anshan and the rest of the region, which became known as Manchuria, fell under Japanese control.

KEY DATES
■

1918: Anshan Zhenzing Iron Ore Company and Anshan Iron and Steel Works are founded in Anshan, China.

1931: The companies are merged as Showa Steel Works.

1948: Steel mill operations relaunched as Anshan Iron and Steel Company (Angang) by People's Republic of China (PRC) government.

1985: Angang purchases U.S. Steel's Fairless Hills, Pennsylvania-based rod mill for transfer to Anshan complex.

1992: Angang creates subsidiary Angang Steel Company Ltd.

1997: Ansteel is listed on the Hong Kong Stock Exchange as Angang's publicly listed arm.

2005: Angang and Benxi Iron and Steel agree to merge to form Anben Iron and Steel.

2010: Angang announces cooperation agreement with U.S. Steel Development to build a steel mill in the United States.

The Japanese set in motion a new era of industrialization for Anshan and Liaoning Province in general. This led to the creation in 1918 of a new company, Anshan Zhenzing Iron Ore Company Unlimited, as a mining and steel production joint venture between Japanese and Chinese interests. That same year saw the creation of a second company, Anshan Iron and Steel Works, in order to build a steel mill and begin producing steel as a subsidiary of the South Manchurian Railway Company.

These operations were reorganized following the Japanese occupation of Manchuria in 1931 into a single company controlled by the Japanese and holding a monopoly over the region's mining and steel industries. In 1933 the company was renamed Showa Steel Works. In 1937 a new *zaibatsu*, the Japanese form of diversified conglomerate, was established to take control of Showa Steel Works, including its iron ore mining operations and a nearby coal mining operation established in order to supply Showa Steel with fuel. Other operations included electric power plants, coal liquefaction, a cement works, and a brick factory.

Showa Steel's production reached approximately 500,000 metric tons at the beginning of the 1930s. Following its takeover by the *zaibatsu*, the company invested in new technology, known as the Krupp-Renn process, which had been developed in Germany. By 1939 Showa Steel had succeeded in installing the new equipment, and by 1941 had succeeded in raising its iron bar production to 1.75 million metric tons and its steel production to one million metric tons. Just one year later, Showa Steel had raised its total output to 3.6 million metric tons, making the complex one of the largest iron and steel producers in the world at that time.

WAR YEARS

Showa Steel enjoyed the position of being China's largest and most modern steel complex in the years leading up to World War II, and played a prominent role in equipping the Japanese war effort. The plant's scale also made it a highly prized target. Throughout the war, Anshan was subjected to heavy bombing from the U.S. Air Force's fleet of B-29 Superfortress bombers. The Japanese defense nevertheless managed to minimize the damage, and Showa Steel lost only approximately one-third of its output capacity.

Nevertheless, the Soviet army overran Manchuria, and then dismantled the iron and steel complex and transported it back to the Soviet Union. Although returned to China following the Japanese defeat, Anshan and the rest of the former Manchuria remained the center of fighting during the Chinese civil war. As a result, the city struggled to rebuild its steel mills. The Communist victory in 1948 and the creation of the People's Republic of China finally enabled the Anshan iron and steel complex to begin work on its full-scale reconstruction. At that time, the total output at China's remaining steel mills reached just 160,000 tons per year.

The new Chinese government set out its own industrialization policies, centered on the northeast in general and on Anshan in particular. In December 1948 the government created a new company, Anshan Iron and Steel Company, or Angang, merging the steel mills that had been part of the former Anshan iron and steel complex. The new company immediately launched the reconstruction of its steel mills and succeeded in restoring production by July 1949.

Anshan played a central role in the Mao government's Stalin-inspired First Five-Year Plan, which focused especially on expanding the country's steel industry. The government initially focused on developing a network of large-scale steel mills, including Anshan, which rapidly expanded its production to its prewar levels. Other major mills founded during this time were the Wuhan, Tangshan, and Hebei steel complexes. By the middle of the 1950s the country's total steel output neared three million tons.

GREAT LEAP FORWARD IN 1958

Mao veered away from Soviet influence during the second half of the 1950s. In 1958 the country replaced the Five-Year Plan model with what was called the Great Leap Forward. The massive expansion of the Chinese steel industry featured as the centerpiece of the country's new industrial policy. This took the form of the creation of a large number of large-scale steel complexes. The period was also marked by a high degree of decentralization, as local and regional governments were encouraged to develop their own steel industries. This resulted in the establishment of a myriad of small "backyard" steel mills. At the height of the Great Leap Forward, the country counted some 600,000 steel furnaces, raising China's total production to more than 18.5 million tons by 1960.

Despite its name, the Great Leap Forward resulted in what amounted to a big step backward for the country's industrial infrastructure. In order to sustain the huge volumes called for by the Mao government, the new mills relied on scrap metals, including the contribution of pots and pans, tools, fences, and other iron and steel utensils and equipment. The success in raising steel production volumes came at a high cost, as the quality of the country's steel plummeted.

This in turn had a huge impact on China's other industries, leading to a long series of industrial breakdowns and failures that severely hampered the country's economic growth. The steel industry itself was most prominently affected by the errors of the Great Leap Forward, and by 1962 total production had plummeted once again, to less than seven million tons.

The government took steps to restore centralized control to the country's steel industry in the middle of the 1960s. The country broke off relations with the Soviet Union, and turned to the West for its technology needs. In 1965 China installed its first steel mills using basic oxygen furnace technology, which not only raised production levels, but also offered a considerable drop in the dust and pollution caused by the traditional open-hearth methods. Angang fitted out its own foundries with the new technology, building two basic oxygen furnaces at the beginning of the 1980s.

CHINESE STEEL FLAGSHIP

The Chinese government succeeded in reining in the excesses of the steel industry, focusing its investment efforts on developing a smaller number of major steel producers. By 1980, although the company still boasted more than 800 largely local and regional steel companies, it also counted more than 10 companies capable of producing more than one million tons of steel per year.

Among these, Angang emerged as the steel industry's flagship. Major investments enabled Angang to grow into the country's largest iron and steel complex, adding two new basic oxygen furnaces in 1983. By then the company also operated 10 blast furnaces and 24 open-hearth furnaces. The Chinese government's new economic reform policies also played a role in the company's expansion, as contacts with the western world developed strongly during the decade. This enabled the company to make a major purchase, of U.S. Steel's Fairless Hills, Pennsylvania-based rod mill, in 1985. Angang then dismantled that factory and rebuilt it in its Anshan complex, adding nearly 500,000 tons of steel products to its capacity.

The completion of that transfer helped boost Angang's total production to 7.4 million tons by 1987. The Chinese government launched a new $850 million modernization program that year. This effort not only upgraded Angang's smelting, sintering, rolling, and casting technology, it also helped raise its total production past eight million tons by 1990. At the same time, the investment permitted Angang to increase its production of higher-grade steels.

This investment was followed by a still more ambitious expansion effort launched the following year. In 1988 Angang laid out plans for six new steel projects, including a converter steel mill, a seamless tubing mill, a continuous casting facility, and a rolling mill, among others. Scheduled for completion within eight years, the company's new investment plans raised its total steel output past 10 million tons. As part of this effort, Angang also moved beyond Liaoning Province for the first time, establishing two rolling mills in Hainan Province, in southern China.

LAUNCHING ANSTEEL IN 1997

Angang benefited from the Chinese government's new steel policies in the 1990s, which involved dramatically reducing the country's steel imports in favor of its domestic production. The new policies, which fit into the government's movement toward a free-market economic model, also granted Angang, as well as a number of the country's other major steel producers, far greater autonomy, including the right to develop its own sales and marketing operations, starting in 1993. The company quickly took advantage of this, forming an iron ore mining partnership with Portman Mining Ltd. in Australia that year.

Angang also began preparing for a public offering of part of its assets, creating a subsidiary in 1992 called Angang New Steel Company Ltd., as a producer of steel pipe sections. In 1997 this company was reincorporated as a joint stock company, with Angang as its sole shareholder. Angang New Steel, which later adopted the nickname Anstee, then took over three plants from Angang, including a cold rolling mill, a wire rod factory, and a thick plate factory. Following that transfer, Ansteel listed its shares on the Hong Kong Stock Exchange. Angang, itself wholly owned by the Chinese government, remained Ansteel's major shareholder, with more than 62 percent of its stock.

Ansteel helped drive Angang's growth in the new decade. For example, in 2000 the company spent $158 million building a galvanized steel plant, completed in 2002. In 2001 Ansteel invested $8.6 million to build a new tandem reversing rolling mill, producing primarily rails, as well as beams and special sections, adding another 750,000 metric tons per year of production capacity.

BENXI MERGER AGREEMENT IN 2005

Despite this growth, Ansteel and parent Angang found themselves outpaced by a number of rivals, including other state-owned companies such as Shanghai Baosteel and Wuhan Steel, but also by the privately controlled newcomer Jiangsu Shagang. In the meantime, China's dramatic economic growth had also stimulated a new boom in the steel industry. The country's steel industry soon counted more than 4,000 steel companies. Total production figures had grown from 100 million tons in 1998 to top 200 million tons by 2003.

Angang launched a new effort to regain its leadership position. For this, the company was aided in part by the Chinese government's new efforts to rein in what it considered to be an over-invested steel industry. The government then began encouraging the wholesale consolidation of the Chinese steel industry, sparking a new era of mergers and consolidations.

Angang joined the consolidation drive, and by 2005 once again claimed the second-place position in terms of total output. In that year, the company reached an agreement to merge with the industry's number five player, Benxi Iron and Steel Group, creating a new market heavyweight. As part of the merger plan, the two companies agreed to merge their publicly listed arms, Ansteel and Bengang. The merged company then proposed to take the name of Anben Iron and Steel Group.

However, the actual merger of the two companies' operations was put on hold, as both companies continued their independent development. In the meantime, Angang continued investing in boosting its capacity. For example, in 2006 the company opened a new integrated steel works with the capacity to produce 5.2 million metric tons of iron, and five million metric tons of steel, as well as 4.6 million metric tons of steel products per year. The new complex helped raise Angang's total crude steel capacity past 17 million metric tons by the end of that year.

NEW ACQUISITIONS IN 2010

While Angang and Ansteel awaited the completion of the Benxi steel merger, Angang began targeting new acquisitions in the south of China. This led the company to launch bids for Panzhihua Iron and Steel in Sichuan Province, and Fujian Sangang Co. in Fujian Province in 2008. The new acquisitions were expected to add another 10 million metric tons to Angang's total.

As part of this effort, Angang began acquiring stakes in Panzhihua's three publicly listed subsidiaries, starting in 2008. By February 2010 the two companies had completed their merger agreement. The slow pace of many of the Chinese steel industry's mergers reflected the mix of local, regional, and national interests present in the sector. Most of the local and regional governments were reluctant to relinquish control of their steel industries due to the loss of revenues on one hand and the potential loss of jobs on the other. As a result, merger negotiations often broke down over manpower deployment and tax allocations and related issues.

Angang's attempt to take over Fujian Sangang was helped by an agreement to invest in the further development of Fujian Province's steel industry. The company took a step closer to its goal in February 2010, when it announced plans to spend $557 million to build a new cold rolling and galvanizing mill in Fujian Province, with a projected capacity of more than one million tons.

The company's plans to merge with Benxi also appeared to be making progress. The merger had reached another stop after Benxi launched the takeover of Beitai Iron and Steel Group. The two companies succeeded in completing their own merger agreement in May 2010, paving the way for the Angang and Benxi merger to proceed. The completion of the merger was expected to catapult Angang back into the Chinese steel industry's leadership, with a total production capacity of 50 million tons.

In the meantime, Angang marked a new milestone for the Chinese steel industry. In May 2010 the company announced that it had signed a cooperation agreement with U.S. Steel Development Corp. to take an equity investment in four new U.S. Steel projects in the United States. The agreement included Angang's agreement to build a new deformed steel bar plant in Mississippi, marking the first investment by a Chinese steel company in the U.S. steel industry. The new plant was expected to be placed under the company's listed Ansteel arm. Angang Steel Company Ltd. had thus emerged in the new century as China's steel industry flagship.

M. L. Cohen

PRINCIPAL SUBSIDIARIES

Angang Steel Logistics (Wuhan) Company Limited; ANSC-TKS Galvanizing Co., Ltd. (50%); ANSC-Dachuan Heavy Industries Dalian Steel Product Processing and Distribution Co., Ltd. (50%); Changchun FAM Steel Processing and Distribution Company Limited (50%); TKAS (Changchun) Steel Service Center Ltd. (50%).

PRINCIPAL DIVISIONS

Northeast China; North China; East China; South China; Central South China; Northwest China; Southwest China; Export Sales.

PRINCIPAL OPERATING UNITS

Cold Rolled Sheets; Galvanized Steel Sheets and Color Coated Plates; Hot Rolled Sheets; Large Steel Products; Medium Plates; Seamless Steel Pipes; Silicon Steel; Thick Plates.

PRINCIPAL COMPETITORS

ArcelorMittal; Baosteel Group Corp.; Changcheng Special Steel Company Ltd.; Guangdong Shaoguan Iron and Steel Group Company Ltd.; Jiangsu Shagang Steel Co. Ltd.; Libyan Iron and Steel Co.; Nippon Steel Corp.; Qingdao Iron and Steel General Corp.; Thyssen-Krupp Steel AG; Wuhan Iron and Steel Co.

FURTHER READING

"Angang Group to Challenge ArcelorMittal," *SinoCast Daily Business*, May 20, 2010.

"Angang Steel: Injection of US Projects Is Pending," *SinoCast Daily Business*, May 20, 2010.

"Anshan Fuels Takeover Speculation," *American Metal Market*, September 11, 2008, p. 13.

"Anshan Merger Talks with Panzhihua Done," *American Metal Market*, February 9, 2010, p. 7.

"Anshan Turns Takeover Sights to Steelmakers in the South," *American Metal Market*, May 13, 2008, p. 15.

"Ansteel Expanding with $557m Mill," *American Metal Market*, February 3, 2010, p. 10.

"Ansteel Intends to Merger Baogang," *Business Daily Update*, June 2, 2010.

"Ansteel to Bring Pangang under Its Umbrella," *TendersInfo*, May 27, 2010.

Dyer, Geoff, "Chinese Steelmakers Set for Merger," *Financial Times*, August 16, 2005, p. 24.

Li, Hongmei, "Angang Steel Plans Share Issue to Raise $2.7b for Greenfield Mill," *American Metal Market*, October 3, 2007, p. 14.

Teo, Vivian, "Angang, Benxi Merge as China Pushes Revamp," *American Metal Market*, August 16, 2005, p. 1.

Anta Sports Products Ltd.

Unit 4408, 44th Floor
COSCO Tower
183 Queen's Road Central
Hong Kong
Telephone: (+852) 2116 1660
Fax: (+852) 2116 1590
Web site: http://www.anta.com.cn

Public Company
Incorporated: 1994
Employees: 10,435
Sales: RMB 5.87 billion ($1.1 billion) (2009)
Stock Exchanges: Hong Kong
Ticker Symbol: 02020
NAICS: 316219 Other Footwear Manufacturing

■ ■ ■

Anta Sports Products Ltd. is one of China's top two sporting goods companies, alongside rival Li Ning. The company, listed in Hong Kong but based in Jinjiang City, in Fujian Province, is also one of the country's fastest-growing and most integrated sporting goods retailers. Anta's operations span the full range from research and design to manufacturing, distribution, and retailing. Anta has pioneered sports branding in China, teaming up with a long list of notable athletes, including Olympic gold medalist Yang Yang; Chinese tennis star Zheng Jie; world-ranked tennis player Jelena Jankovic; and Luis Scola, of the Houston Rockets basketball team. Anta captured the plum position as official

sportswear partner for the Chinese Olympic Committee in 2009.

Anta has also built up one of China's largest sports retailing operations, with nearly 6,600 stores in operation at the beginning of 2010 and planned to open up to 900 more stores through that year. Anta's stores, which include 12 large-scale flagship stores, feature exclusively Anta-branded footwear, sports apparel, and accessories. The company has two additional Anta-branded retail formats, a chain of more than 340 Sports Lifestyle stores, and nearly 230 Kids Series stores. Anta's stores target the mid-level mass-market sportswear sector.

At the end of 2009 Anta also acquired the retail distribution rights for the high-end Fila brand, including 50 stores in mainland China, as well as stores in Hong Kong and Macau. Footwear remains the company's largest product segment, accounting for nearly 55 percent of its revenues of RMB 5.9 billion ($1.1 billion) in 2009. Nearly all of the company's sales are concentrated on the Chinese market, with international sales providing less than 1 percent of its total revenues.

Anta supports its retail operations with its own manufacturing division, which includes 24 footwear production lines in five factories, as well as two clothing factories, all in Fujian Province. The company's own production capacity tops 15 million pairs of shoes, and reaches nearly seven million items of clothing each year, and is supplemented by third-party manufacturers. Anta, which began as an original equipment manufacturer (OEM), continues to supply the overseas OEM markets. Anta went public on the Hong Kong

Stock Exchange in 2007, and is led by Ding Shizhong, son of the company's founder.

ORIGINS

Anta's origins can be traced to the small town of Chendai, part of Jinjiang City in China's Fujian Province, which emerged in the 1990s as the country's footwear capital. At the end of the 20th century, the town, with a population of just 80,000, boasted more than 3,000 shoe manufacturers, and accounted for 40 percent of China's total footwear production. Another interesting feature of Chendai was the prevalence of the Ding family name, introduced into the region by Arabian traders around the 10th century. By the dawn of the 21st century, approximately one-fourth of Chendai's residents bore the Ding family name.

Among them was the family of Ding Shizhong, which formed a sales partnership with a Chendai shoe factory in 1981. Ding Shizhong entered the footwear business in 1987 at the age of 18, when he traveled to Beijing, taking with him 600 pairs of shoes and 10,000 yuan in capital. Ding succeeded in selling out his initial stock and over the next four years built up a strong business in the capital city. Ding returned to Chendai in 1991 with more than 20 million yuan. By then, Ding's family had broken with their original partner, establishing their own factory in Chendai in 1990.

Ding's time in Beijing coincided with a major new trend in the global footwear industry. The rise of the Nike footwear brand represented something of a revolution in the sports shoe market. That company became one of the first in the industry to reject the traditional manufacturing-based business model of the footwear industry and instead focus its efforts wholly on product design and marketing. Instead, Nike turned to low-cost manufacturers in developing markets, especially in China. Nike's success forced other sports shoe manufacturers to follow suit. By the end of the 1980s, Chendai and the Fujian Province had quickly become the center of this new OEM market.

ANTA FOUNDED: 1994

The sporting goods market remained underdeveloped in China at that time. Sales of sports shoes and sports clothing were focused almost entirely on the practice of the sports themselves, in contrast to Western markets, where sportswear had become everyday apparel. However, as China's economic reforms, launched in the late 1970s, began to produce a growing middle class, more and more Chinese were attracted to the high-profile Western sports brands.

Ding had recognized the potential of this new market while still in Beijing. Returning to Chendai, Ding began developing the idea of launching his own sports shoe brand. Ding hoped to establish not merely a Chinese sports shoe brand, but one that could compete on a global scale. Ding was forced to put his plans on hold, however, since the family footwear company lacked the manufacturing technology needed to compete against the major international sports shoe brands.

The OEM market provided the means for the company to acquire both the technology and the scale it needed in order to launch its own sports shoe brand. The Ding family company began producing for the OEM market starting in 1993. The company differed significantly from most of its rivals, which focused their production on shoes for the export market. Instead, Ding's factory from the start also produced shoes for the new but growing Chinese sports shoe sector. This market was led by Li Ning, the Olympic gold medalist who had founded his own shoe company in 1992. By 1994, Ding had gained the scale needed to launch his own sports shoe company, called Anta, which means "safe step" in Chinese.

Anta's sports shoe sales grew slowly through the middle of the decade, before the company implemented its first full-fledged brand development strategy in 1997. During this time, the company focused especially on building its own retail distribution network. For this, the company adopted a policy of avoiding China's larger "Tier One" cities, such as Beijing, Guangdong, and Shanghai, which were already dominated by the major global sports shoe brands, and by the homegrown Li Ning brand.

Anta instead focused on building a presence in the smaller "Tier Two" and "Tier Three" cities, which nonetheless represented a population base of more than 150 million people. As part of this effort, Anta adopted a mid-market strategy, offering lower-priced shoes in order to avoid direct competition with high-end brands such as Nike and adidas. Anta's retail strategy further focused on selling its shoes only through its own store network, which exclusively featured the growing range of Anta products.

KEY DATES

1990: The Ding family establishes a footwear factory in Chendai, Jinjiang City, in Fujian Province, China.
1994: Ding Shizhong leads the family in establishing its own footwear brand, Anta.
1999: Anta launches its brand marketing strategy, starting with an endorsement contract with table tennis icon Kong Linghui.
2002: The company expands into sportswear.
2003: Anta begins international expansion strategy, setting up a store in Singapore.
2007: Anta goes public on the Hong Kong Stock Exchange.
2010: Anta announces plans to open 900 stores through the year.

BRANDING STRATEGY INTRODUCED IN 1999

Ding Shizhong took over as the company's managing director in 1999. One of Ding's first decisions as head of the company was to reorient its strategy to focus more strongly on its marketing effort. To this end, Anta became one of the first of the Chinese sports shoe manufacturers to begin signing on celebrity endorsers. This effort started off strongly, as the company signed on Chinese table tennis icon, and world champion, Kong Linghui. The company then adopted a new slogan, "I like what I choose," supporting the highly successful ad campaign featuring Kong.

Celebrity sponsorships fit into the company's larger strategy of developing its own sports marketing arm. Over the next several years, the company lined up a series of partnerships and endorsement contracts, both with athletes and with sports organizations. Sales of the company's shoes rose correspondingly, backed by the steady growth of the country's retail wing.

By 2001 Anta's marketing and retailing strategy had propelled the company to the lead of the Chinese sports shoe market. The company's growing strength also enabled it to move into the country's "Tier One" markets, starting with the opening of a first Beijing store that year. While the group remained committed to the midrange shoe market, it nonetheless focused its marketing strategy on building its reputation as a professional sports shoe manufacturer. This, in turn, supported the extension of Anta's product range beyond footwear into the clothing and accessories markets. The company's

clothing line debuted in 2002. In 2003 the group introduced its sports accessories line as well.

TARGETING THE INTERNATIONAL MARKET

While Anta continued building its position in China, Ding attempted to fulfill his early ambition of creating a global sports shoe brand capable of competing with the world's leading brands. In 2003 Anta launched its first international operation, opening its first foreign store in Singapore that year. The company also signed an endorsement contract with Mengke Bateer, the Mongolian-born basketball player then playing with the San Antonio Spurs.

Anta quickly expanded into other foreign markets, primarily targeting the Southeast Asian region. However, in 2004 the company attempted to extend its retail operations, and brand, further afield, adding operations in Greece, Hungary, the Czech Republic, and Ukraine. At the same time, Ding announced the company's future plans to acquire an established global brand.

China nonetheless remained Anta's core market, as the group extended its retail operations to a fully national scale by 2004. This set the stage for the company's dramatic expansion through the middle of the decade. In 2004 the company reported total revenues of RMB 311.5 million. Three years later Anta's total revenues neared RMB 3.2 billion. A large part of this growth came from the company's expanding clothing sales. In 2004 these represented just over 13 percent of the group's total sales. By 2007 apparel accounted for more than 43 percent of the company's revenues.

During this period Anta also instituted a new international branded products division, signing contracts to develop retail operations under the adidas, Reebok, and Kappa brand names. By 2007 the company had opened more than 170 stores under these brands. This division, however, remained quite modest in comparison with the development of the Anta retail chain, which topped 4,700 outlets by then. The company sold the international brand division, which failed to achieve profitability, in 2008.

CHINESE SPORTSWEAR LEADER IN 2010

Anta's own international expansion effort also flagged in the second half of the decade. By 2009 the company had refocused its attention almost entirely on the Chinese market, and had abandoned its quest to acquire an established global sports shoe brand. Instead, Anta continued to build up retail operations, which topped

5,000 stores in 2008. The company's sales also continued their strong growth, passing RMB 4.6 billion by the end of that year. Helping to drive the market was the growing interest in sportswear as everyday apparel, as more and more Chinese embraced this Western-inspired trend.

The growth of the middle class in China played a major factor in driving both Anta's expansion and interest in the sports and sportswear sectors in general. Anta gained additional momentum in the run-up to the Beijing Olympic Games in 2008, despite being unsuccessful in becoming an official sponsor of the games. This surge in interest in sports and sporting goods helped provide the foundation for Anta's highly successful initial public offering, with a listing on the Hong Kong Stock Exchange in 2007.

Anta made new progress in its marketing arm through the end of the decade. The company signed on two Houston Rockets players in 2008, Steve Francis and Luis Scola. (The owner of the Houston Rockets had also become a major Anta shareholder.) In 2009 the company signed up international tennis star Jelena Jankovic. Anta also became the official sportswear partner of the Chinese Olympic Committee that year.

By the beginning of 2010 Anta's retail operations had expanded to more than 6,600 stores, including nearly 1,000 stores added in 2009 alone. The company announced plans to open as many as 900 new stores through 2010. These were to include the company's newest retail formats, Sports Lifestyle, featuring sportswear clothing and footwear, and Kids Series, targeting the youth market. By 2010 the company had opened 340 Sports Lifestyle stores and 230 Kids Series stores. Also that year, Anta entered the high-end sportswear market, after acquiring the retailing rights to the Fila brand for the Chinese, Hong Kong, and Macau markets at the end of 2009. As the leading Chinese sportswear brand, Anta remained focused on its ambition of becoming one of the world's top 10 sportswear brands in the 21st century.

M. L. Cohen

PRINCIPAL SUBSIDIARIES

Anta International Investment Limited; Anta (Changting) Sports Products Co., Ltd.; Anta (China) Co., Ltd.; Anta (Quanzhou) Sports Products Limited; Anta (Xiamen) Sports Goods Co., Ltd.; Anta Enterprise Group Limited; Anta International Limited; Jinjiang Anta Trading Co., Ltd.; Motive Force Sports Products Limited; Xiamen Anta Investment Management Company Limited; Xiamen Anta Trading Co., Ltd.

PRINCIPAL DIVISIONS

Apparel Manufacturing; Footwear Manufacturing; Sales and Trading.

PRINCIPAL OPERATING UNITS

Accessories, Apparel, Footwear.

PRINCIPAL COMPETITORS

Nike Inc.

FURTHER READING

"Anta Playing Catch-up with Li Ning," *SinoCast Daily Business Beat*, May 15, 2009.

"Anta Popularizes Image via NBA Player," *Alestron*, October 22, 2007.

"Anta Sports Gets Listed in HK," *SinoCast, LLC China Financial Watch*, July 12, 2007.

"Anta Sports to Open 600 More Outlets This Year," *China Knowledge Newswires*, February 25, 2010.

"Anta Turns Focus to Domestic Market for Growth," *Business Daily Update*, February 13, 2009.

He, Sophie, "Anta Steps Up on Better Prices," *Standard*, February 25, 2010.

Kwong, Howard, "Interest in Sports Boosts Mainland Sector," *South China Morning Post*, September 1, 2008.

Lu Haoting, "In Chendai, the Name Ding Rings a Bell," *China Daily*, January 6, 2009.

Madden, Normandy, "Chinese Sportswear Brand Anta Aims to Become Next Nike," May 7, 2007, p. 34.

Wong, Torrance, "China Picks Anta as Sportswear Sponsor," *South China Morning Post*, June 24, 2009.

B2W Companhia Global do Varejo

Rua Coelho e Castro, 60
Rio de Janeiro 20081-902
Brazil
Telephone: (55 21) 3478-3100
Web site: http://www.b2winc.com

Public Company
Incorporated: 2006
Employees: 1,435
Sales: BRL 5.11 billion ($2.94 billion) (2009)
Stock Exchanges: São Paulo
Ticker Symbol: BTOW
NAICS: 454111 Electronic Shopping; 454113 Mail-Order Houses; 561510 Travel Agencies

■ ■ ■

B2W Companhia Global do Varejo is a Brazilian retail company whose brands, Americanas.com, Submarino, Shoptime, Ingresso.com, Submarino Finance, B2W Viagens, and Blockbuster, offer a wide assortment of products and services divided into over 30 categories. B2W (Business-to-Web) operates through various distribution channels, including the Internet, catalogs, television, and kiosks. Besides its business-to-consumer (B2C) products and services, the company provides e-commerce services (business-to-business, or B2B) to leading companies. The more than 700,000 product items offered include CDs, DVDs, electronics, computers, hardware, cameras, and cellular telephones. B2W also sells additional online services, including travel, ticketing, and photo processing.

As the Brazilian equivalent of Amazon.com, Inc., B2W dominates electronic commerce in that country but is facing competition from heretofore traditional retailers. The company is majority owned by Lojas Americanas S.A., one of Brazil's largest store retailers.

ORIGINS: 1995–2000

The origins of B2W lie in the establishment of GP Investimentos in 1993 by three investment bankers, Jorge Paulo Lemann, Marcel Hermann Telles, and Carlos Alberto Sicupira. One of their private equity funds was devoted to investing in Brazilian companies, with an emphasis on technology. One of this fund's investments was in Shoptime, established in 1995 as the first Brazilian home shopping television channel. It also operated through its catalog and in 1999 launched its own Web site on the Internet.

Inspired by the success of Amazon.com in the United States, Antonio Bonchristiano, a junior partner in GP, founded a virtual bookstore named Booknet in 1996. Like Amazon, it was soon selling music CDs as well as books. As Booknet entered other markets, it was renamed Submarino in 1999. GP became the major shareholder of Submarino S.A.

GP also invested heavily in Lojas Americanas S.A. (Lasa), a large but financially troubled discount retail chain. In 1999 Lasa launched Americanas.com S.A. Comércio Electrónico. Americanas.com was a virtual store that, like Submarino, was accessible on the Internet. The electronic site initially targeted the high-end customers who owned most of the computers in Brazil at the time. It then expanded to the middle class by means of kiosks placed in Lojas Americanas stores. Soon Americanas.com was making available big-ticket items generally not available in the stores, such as computer hardware and software and larger electronic equipment. Foreign private equity funds bought a one-third stake in the company in 2000 for $40 million.

THE RISE OF SUBMARINO

Submarino expanded rapidly, adding home products to its wares and briefly opening subsidiaries in Argentina, Mexico, Portugal, and Spain. This growth was to be financed by an initial public offering (IPO) of stock in the United States, but after the collapse of the technology stock market on Wall Street in 2000, the company had to retrench. However, it became profitable in 2002 and by the end of the year was the largest virtual store in Brazil.

A leader in e-commerce technology, Submarino implemented a tool to customize Web pages in accordance with client profiles. It offered itself as a platform for virtual store chains that did not have their own structures for packaging, storage, distribution, or service. Submarino was also noted for speed of delivery. Online purchases reached the customer in São Paulo, South America's largest city, in 24 hours and those in the other Brazilian state capitals in 36 hours. It also assumed responsibility for payment by credit or bank card. Submarino's roster of corporate clients came to include 15 of Brazil's largest companies, including Gradiente Eletrônica S.A. and Nokia do Brasil Tecnologia Ltda.

Nivea, the body care brand of Beisdorf AG, was one of the first businesses in Brazil to entrust to Submarino the execution of its sales, shipping, and delivery. One of the other services that Submarino performed for Nivea was to identify the last purchase made by a customer, which helped the company to reposition the product. Natura Cosméticos S.A., Brazil's largest

cosmetics company, also hired Submarino for the execution of all sales, shipment, and fulfillment of orders, both inside and outside the country. Submarino's revenues came chiefly from a 20 percent commission on sales, while competitors who offered only a platform charged about 5 percent. The company also began to sell products under its own name in 2004.

Submarino made its IPO of stock the following year, raising BRL 472 million ($196 million) for 48 percent of the shares. This enabled the company to acquire Ingresso.com, which offered ticket purchases and services over the Internet for movies, theater and other shows, soccer games, theme parks, and cultural events. In addition, it purchased Travelweb, an online travel agency. Travelweb became the nucleus of Submarino Viagens (Submarino Travel) the following year. Submarino Finance, founded in 2006, was a joint venture with French-based Cetelem S.A. that offered the Submarino credit card for the purchase of products on the company Web site.

BRAZIL'S LARGEST E-COMMERCE COMPANY: 2006

Americanas.com also struggled in its early years, but it became profitable by the end of 2001, and its revenues were estimated at nearly those of Submarino in 2002. It attracted customers by offering interest-free payment plans extending as long as 12 months. In addition to its business-to-consumer sales, the company entered the business-to-business market by operating a virtual store for the mobile phone company Oi and the pay television channel Cartoon Network.

In 2005 Americanas.com purchased TV Sky Shop S.A., owner of Shoptime, for BRL 126 million ($52 million). This acquisition extended its share of the Brazilian consumer e-commerce markets in which it was engaged to 40 percent. The company was also reaching more than 9,000 businesses. Submarino and Americanas.com merged in 2006 to form B2W. B2W immediately became Brazil's largest e-commerce company, with some 60 percent of the market.

In 2007 B2W acquired the rights to use the Blockbuster trademark on the Internet and established a service for online DVD rentals through the B2W subsidiary Blockbuster Online and its Web site, www.blockbuster.com.br. Blockbuster Online offered plans with unlimited return time. In early 2009 Blockbuster Online had the largest collection of DVD titles in Brazil, with more than 12,000 different movies and delivery in 55 cities located in five states. Rio de Janeiro and São Paulo enjoyed Sunday and same-day delivery service.

KEY DATES

1996: Antonio Bonchristiano founds a virtual bookstore named Booknet.

1999: Booknet is renamed Submarino; Americanas.com is launched by Lojas Americanas S.A.

2006: Submarino and Americanas.com merge to form B2W.

2007: A deal with Blockbuster enables B2W to begin offering online DVD rentals.

2009: B2W is named best Brazilian retailer by a business magazine.

Lojas Americanas's purchase of Blockbuster Brasil S.A. enabled the store chain to establish Americanas Express, a format that it initially introduced in 127 of its store units. The 20-year transaction with Blockbuster Inc. authorized Lojas Americanas to make any changes in the Blockbuster Brasil stores, including transforming them into Americanas Express units and renting films in street kiosks.

OPPORTUNITIES AND CHALLENGES: 2008–09

In 2008 B2W launched a new Web site for Submarino. It was designed to enhance navigation, promote broader interaction with customers, and simplify the purchasing process. An interactive menu allowed not only for more accurate searches for products but also permitted customization in accordance with each client's preferences.

Shoptime also launched a new Web site in 2008, with much more efficient navigation, organized design, and features that enhanced the view of the products. More space was made available to show television and catalog promotions.

B2W held 51 percent of the Brazilian e-commerce market sectors in which it was engaged in 2008 and 46 percent in 2009, according to analyst estimates. The company was beginning to feel the effects of greater competition. Nova PontoCom was created near the end of 2009 by the integration of the online operations of Ponte Frio, Casas Bahia, and Extra, three big retail chains. The new entity had an estimated 18 percent of the market in 2009.

Magazine Luiza S.A., another big retailer, held an estimated 8 percent from sales it made over the Internet. Walmart.com, launched in Brazil in October 2008, held about 4 percent of the market in 2009. The Brazilian subsidiary of Carrefour SA, one of the world's largest supermarket chains, initiated its own online operations in March 2009.

Business analysts speculated that competition would force B2W to seek better relations with its suppliers. The company had a reputation for taking a tough line, demanding lower prices and the right to stretch out payment. According to executives who had sources close to B2W, one alternative being considered was to negotiate exclusive supply contracts with companies, such as Sega Corporation for video-game components and Casio Computer Co., Ltd., for watches.

B2W was also considering acquiring online niche sites such as those marketing perfumes and shoes. Such specialized Web sites were believed to account for about 20 percent of the e-commerce market. Another proposal was expansion to other countries, a possibility previously almost unexplored by Brazilian electronics retailers. In November 2009 Ingresso.com initiated operations in Mexico.

It was also considered likely that B2W would have to work harder to fend off competition based on services as well as price. Carrefour, for example, offered on its Web site such extras as installation and maintenance of electronic products and support by telephone for computers. Casas Bahia had been producing over 400 videos on its Web site to demonstrate its LCD television sets and video cameras.

BEST RETAIL COMPANY IN BRAZIL: 2009

B2W was cited as best retail company in Brazil by the 2009 edition of *Exame Melhores e Maiores*, the annual review of Brazilian companies by its leading business publication. In 2008 the company ranked second in profitability among major companies in its sector, and it was first in profit per employee.

Americanas.com was offering over 36 product categories through its distribution channels, which included the Internet, telesales, and kiosks. Over 500,000 items were being offered in categories such as electronics, CDs, DVDs, computers and other information technology products, home appliances, books, games, stationery, toys, fragrances, and wines. Americanas.com also offered digital services such as photo printing, wedding lists, and prepaid mobile phone credit. In addition, it offered logistics expertise, as well as its technology platform, to major business groups in Brazil and abroad, in order to carry out the distribution of products on behalf of its clients.

Submarino was offering 28 product categories through its sales channels, which included Internet, telesales, and catalogs, with a strong emphasis on the sale of books, CDs, DVDs, electronics, computers and other information technology, video games, and online services. Besides business-to-customer services, Submarino was offering business-to-business e-commerce services for major business groups.

Shoptime was also operating through the Internet, telesales, and catalogs. Some 20 product categories were being offered to more than 3.5 million customers. The emphasis was on bed, bath, and dining items, information technology, and the exclusive "Fun Kitchen" and "La Cousine" lines of domestic utensils. Shoptime's television channel was reaching more than 20 million Brazilian households. Operating around the clock, it transmitted 11 hours a day of live, interactive programming. Some 400,000 copies of the catalog were being distributed throughout Brazil seven times a year.

The B2W subsidiary B2W Viagens, operating through Americanas Viagens, Submarino Viagens, and Shoptime Viagens, was created in 2008. It offered such travel services as tourism packages, air tickets, online hotel reservations, cruises, travel insurance, and car rentals in Brazil and abroad. The company was reaching its customers through the Internet, telesales, and kiosks. Gross revenue came to BRL 28.92 million ($15.8 million) in 2008.

Ingresso.com was offering ticket purchase technology and services over the Internet for movies, theaters, rock concerts, soccer games, theme parks, and cultural events. With more than one million registered customers, it was the largest online sales outlet for movie theater tickets in Brazil. This B2W subsidiary sold 1.77 million tickets in 2008, when it had gross revenue of BRL 9.58 million ($5.23 million).

Submarino Finance, a joint venture of B2W and Cetelem S.A., was offering the Submarino credit card for the purchase of products on the Submarino Web site. The card permitted interest-carrying installment payments of up to 24 months, an exclusive rewards program, special promotions such as product discounts, and a loyalty point redemption program. More than one-fifth of Submarino's sales were made through its own credit card in 2008. Gross revenue for Submarino Finance came to BRL 244.32 million ($133.51 million).

Robert Halasz

PRINCIPAL SUBSIDIARIES

Blockbuster Online; B2W Viagens; Ingresso.com.

PRINCIPAL COMPETITORS

Magazine Luiza S.A.; Nova PontoCom; Walmart.com.

FURTHER READING

Cesar, Ricardo, "Os reis do comércio eletrônico," *Exame*, October 26, 2006, pp. 102–04.

Correa, Cristiane, "Todas as faces da GP," *Exame*, January 9, 2002, pp. 50–54.

Filgueiras, Maria Luíza, "O outro grande negócio do Submarino," *Gazeta Mercantil*, July 25, 2007, p. C8.

Fusco, Camila, "Um líder sob ataque," *Exame*, March 10, 2010, pp. 52–54.

Gomes, João Paulo, "Á espera da Amazon," *Exame*, September 14, 2005, pp. 42–44.

Karp, Jonathan, "From Bricks to Clicks," *Wall Street Journal*, September 22, 2003, p. R7.

Lethbridge, Tiago, and Cristiane Correa, "Juntos contra a Wal-Mart," *Exame*, December 6, 2006, pp. 110–14.

Maranhão, Tiago, "A força do varejo.com," *Exame Melhores e Maiores 2009*, pp. 322–24.

Paduan, Roberta, "Vesti azul," *Exame*, February 12, 2003, pp. 66–69.

BASKETVILLE.
Since 1842

Basketville, Inc.

■

8 Bellows Falls Road
Putney, Vermont 05346
U.S.A.
Telephone: (802) 387-5509
Toll Free: (800) 258-4553
Fax: (802) 387-5235
Web site: http://www.basketville.com

Private Company
Founded: 1941 as West River Basket Company
Employees: 100
Sales: $94.9 million (2009 est.)
NAICS: 424990 Other Miscellaneous Nondurable
   Goods Merchant Wholesalers

■ ■ ■

A private company based in Putney, Vermont, Basketville, Inc., makes a wide variety of baskets and woven products for such uses as laundry, storage, harvesting, and picnicking. Products include totes and shoppers, backpacks, office supply baskets, serving trays, pie and cake baskets, bread and bun baskets, wall baskets, fruit bowl baskets, ice buckets, bathroom baskets, and utensil caddies. Materials used include willow, tropical beech, rush, sea grass, paper rope, and maize.

Basketville products are sold through major retailers and are also available online through the company's Web site and at a Basketville outlet store in Putney, Vermont. In addition to the Basketville brand and private labels, the company offers the Home Theory brand of mass-market storage baskets, sea grass trunks,

and desk accessory baskets. The Basketville outlet store and Web site also offer all-weather wicker furniture, kitchen gadgets, Vermont foodstuffs, area wines, and candles.

ORIGINS: 1842

The art of basket weaving was practiced by the Native Americans in New England using strips of swamp ash, and taught to the European settlers. The roots of Basketville date back to 1842 when Sidney Gage and Company, a sawmill and basket shop, was founded by William P. Gage in North Westminster, Vermont, a town north of Putney. The baskets produced were used in farm and household chores for such tasks as storage, harvesting, and hauling. Another component of what would become Basketville was established in the village of Williamsville, the West River Basket Corporation, named for the West River that provided power to the sawmill. A fire destroyed the operation in the 1930s and the company was relocated to Putney.

The man who would coin the Basketville name and serve as the driving force behind the company for half a century was Frank G. Wilson. Born in Connecticut in 1919, he was the son of an auto mechanic who brought his family to Vermont, where he bought Sidney Gage and Company in the 1930s. After graduating from high school in 1937, Wilson attempted to enlist in the Navy, but because of his age he needed his parents' consent. This was not forthcoming, in large part because his father was buying the basket company and needed the labor of Wilson and his 10 siblings. Wilson thus became an apprentice basket maker at his father's business,

COMPANY PERSPECTIVES

Basketville is a leading manufacturer of baskets and woven products for major retailers worldwide.

spending four years learning the craft of making fine baskets from a master craftsman, William LeClair, who at the time was over 80 years of age.

WILSON BUYS WEST RIVER BASKET

Wilson struck out on his own in 1941 when he bought West River Basket from a man named Dwight H. Smith with the understanding that Wilson would sell all of his baskets to Smith, who would then sell them in a basket shop he maintained in Putney or distribute them for sale at roadside stands in the region. It was a rocky relationship. The first day that Wilson went to work at West River Basket, he discovered the hardware and basket nails had been removed by Smith, who insisted that the deal was for the business, not the hardware. Subsequently, Smith would pay for Wilson's baskets by check on a Friday after the banks closed, and invariably on the following Monday the check would not be honored due to insufficient funds.

As a result, Wilson had to deal with several bad checks of his own. The banks were forgiving, however, because Wilson was providing much needed jobs in the community. The power company also helped out by waiting several months until Wilson was on his feet before turning on the meter. In addition to producing splint baskets from native ash and oak, West River Basket produced wooden white pine buckets, pails, and tubs, a business the company would pursue for many years.

Soon after Wilson went into business, the United States entered World War II. Wilson helped in the war effort by buying trees for logging and then delivering the wood to Connecticut, where it was used to make wire reels for military use. Nevertheless, Wilson's local draft board decided that his work was not important enough to keep him from serving in the military and in 1944 Wilson was drafted into the U.S. Navy. As a result, he was forced to shutter West River Basket. Although seven years earlier Wilson had been eager to join the Navy, at this time he found his service tedious. He was kept stateside doing office work in a personnel department before being sent to fire control school as the war came to an end.

FIRE DESTROYS BUCKET FACTORY: 1949

Wilson was eager to resume basket making after the war but expanded too quickly and was forced to file for Chapter 11 bankruptcy protection in order to stabilize the business. Additionally, a fire in March 1949 destroyed the company's bucket factory. West River Basket continued to be a wholesale operation in the postwar years, selling the bulk of its products to the New York City firm of Leipzig and Lippe, which provided baskets to such accounts as Sears, Roebuck; Montgomery Ward; and S&H Green Stamps. One of the principals, Bill Leipzig, was responsible for introducing the fitted picnic basket that became West River Basket's top selling item, followed by the pie and cake basket that had layered compartments for carrying baked goods with other items.

Terms with Leipzig and Lippe were not generous, however, and Wilson was barely able to turn a profit. He began to nurture other accounts and in 1956 launched a retail operation, eventually severing his ties to Leipzig and Lippe. The first retail store was established next door to the basket factory in Putney. Although Wilson's baskets were popular, customers began asking for baskets made from materials other than the native ash and oak used by West River Basket.

To meet that request Wilson began buying small quantities of product from Import Basket Jobbers. Because these foreign-made baskets and other items generated substantial sales, Wilson began looking to buy directly from foreign basket companies, which paid lower wages and could offer less-expensive items. Wilson wrote to the U.S. ambassadors to countries known to export baskets, asking for the names of exporting companies. He then began buying baskets overseas by mail. Later Wilson would travel the world looking for baskets to sell through his retail operations.

ADDITIONAL RETAIL STORES OPEN: 1957

Wilson opened a second retail store in Sunderland, Vermont, in 1957. Later in the year a third store was opened in Venice, Florida, to attract the business of people who went to Florida for the winter. This was an era when Vermont's ski industry was just taking shape and there were few visitors to the state who might buy baskets from the Vermont shops during the cold months.

In the ensuing years other retail stores were added in Manchester, Vermont; Franklin, North Carolina;

KEY DATES

1842: Sidney Gage and Company, a sawmill and basket shop, is founded in Putney, Vermont.
1941: Frank Wilson acquires West River Basket Company.
1956: Wilson opens first retail store and begins importing.
1996: The Putney factory closes and all manufacturing moves to China.
2006: Six retail stores are closed.

Northboro and Sturbridge, Massachusetts; Paradise, Pennsylvania; Myrtle Beach, South Carolina; Williamsburg, Virginia; and Lake George, New York. The imported baskets also helped Wilson land a notable contract in the 1950s when West River Basket filled 16,500 Madeira willow baskets with an assortment of Domino sugar packets that the American Sugar Company presented to stockholders and other important people associated with the company.

West River Basket ended the 1950s with a fire in July 1959 caused by defective wiring that destroyed its main building. The company quickly rebuilt, opening a "fireproof" factory in late 1959, setting the stage for strong growth in the 1960s. Employment increased from 60 to 140 by 1970, and sales increased by 50 percent during the decade. Most of the profits came from retailing and importation rather than the manufacture of baskets. To drive further sales and profits Wilson launched a national sales organization in 1961 and registered the Basketville name, which then replaced West River Basket as the name of the company.

CHINA TIES ESTABLISHED: 1971

One of the first foreign sources for baskets Wilson pursued was Hong Kong, where he often paid visits to his supplier, a Mr. Mock, who became a close friend. Wilson was in Hong Kong when President Richard Nixon lifted the embargo on Chinese imports in 1971, and he and Mock made a visit into Canton to purchase baskets and begin establishing relationships in the country. In the process, Wilson became one of the first U.S. businessmen to trade with the Communist country. Basketville later began producing specially designed baskets in China, assembled from materials prepared in Putney, shipped by water to Hong Kong, and then transported inland to China. The finished, labor-intensive baskets were then shipped back to the United States to Basketville's Brattleboro, Vermont, warehouse.

While running Basketville and globetrotting, Wilson also ran for office and served in the Vermont legislature from 1969 to 1972. In the 1980s Wilson began to turn over control of Basketville to his sons, Steven and Gregory, and in the 1990s he retired completely. He then devoted much of his time to travel in search of old baskets and Early American and old cast-iron farm equipment for a museum he established. He also maintained an extensive collection of pottery, and served as a consultant to companies in the former states of the Soviet Union that were adjusting to a capitalist system.

Conditions for the basket industry changed in the final years of the century. The cost of labor was too high in the United States to remain competitive and an increasing amount of Basketville's production was moved to China. The end of an era came in 1996 when the Putney factory was closed. Basketville, as a result, became more of a design and marketing operation. The retail stores also became less important as the new century dawned. Basketville instead began to focus its attention on serving the needs of its wholesale customers, including the development of private-label offerings and the Home Theory mass-market brand.

RETAIL STORES CLOSE: 2006

The Basketville stores struggled in the early years of the new century. In 2006 Basketville elected to close several of its remaining retail stores, located in Sunderland, Vermont; Paradise, Pennsylvania; Myrtle Beach, South Carolina; Williamsburg, Virginia; and Lake George, New York. All that remained were the locations in Venice, Florida, and Putney. The Venice store remained opened for another two years, but it too was closed in 2008. As a result, Basketville's retail operations were reduced to the Putney store and its Internet business, but product offerings were expanded beyond baskets to include wicker furniture, area wines, maple syrup, other Vermont foodstuffs, candles, seasonal decorations, kitchen gadgets, crafts, games, puzzles, and a variety of nostalgic items.

In July 2009, just days short of his 90th birthday, Frank Wilson died of complications from Alzheimer's disease. He left behind a well-established brand in Basketville, and a strong reputation for selling high-quality products and providing superior customer service. While there was no expectation that the company would enjoy substantial growth in the years to come, there was every reason to believe that it would remain a healthy concern.

Ed Dinger

PRINCIPAL COMPETITORS

Texas Basket Company; Suyuan International Limited; Yinshi Trade Co., Ltd.

FURTHER READING

Putney Historical Society, *Putney: World's Best Known Small Town*, Charleston, SC: Arcadia Publishing, 2003.

Weiss-Tisman, Howard, "Basketville to Close Six of Its Stores," *Brattleboro Reformer*, September 15, 2006.

————, "Basketville's Founder Frank Wilson Dies at 89," *Bennington Banner*, July 29, 2009.

Whitney, Bill, "Beauty by the Bushel in Basketville," *Sunday Republican*, April 11, 1999.

Wilson, Frank G., *Basketville*, New York: Vantage Press, Inc., 1990.

Bel-Art Products Inc.

6 Industrial Road
Pequannock, New Jersey 07440
U.S.A.
Telephone: (973) 694-0500
Web site: http://www.belart.com

Private Company
Incorporated: 1946
Employees: 1,295
Sales: $44.7 million (2009 est.)
NAICS: 339111 Laboratory Apparatus and Furniture
Manufacturing; 326122 Plastic Products and Pipe
Fitting Manufacturing

■ ■ ■

Privately held Bel-Art Products Inc. is a Pequannock, New Jersey-based manufacturer of Scienceware branded products used in laboratories and classrooms as well as industrial settings. Products include beakers, centrifugeware, clamps and holders, cylinders, desiccators, flasks, funnels, filters, jars, pipettes, pitchers, racks, stoppers, tubing, trays, and a variety of bags, cartons, and cans. Bel-Art offers eye and skin safety, aprons, and cleaning supplies, as well as labels and organizers. In addition, the company sells fume hoods, colorimeters, magnetic stirrers, and siphons and pumps. All told, the company offers 3,500 items.

Scienceware products are sold around the world through a network of dealers in the United States and about 50 other countries, as well as catalogs and online through the Bel-Art Web site. Other brands include Spinbar magnetic stirring bars, Sterileware sampling tools, Secador desiccator cabinets, KLETT colorimeters, and Poxygrid racks. The bulk of the products are manufactured in the United States in plants located in New Jersey, Maryland, and Missouri. Bel-Art also offers custom manufacturing services, including sterilization services, product packaging, inventory management, and the coordination of shipments on Bel-Art's fleet of trucks.

Further subsidiaries include Maddak Inc., maker of home health care and Aids for Daily Living (ADL) products; Ricca Chemical Company, a chemical testing solutions provider; and Applied Coatings, Inc., a manufacturer of release, corrosion-resistant, and decorative coatings. Bel-Art is led by President David Landsberger, whose parents founded the company. His father, Kurt Landsberger, remained chairman and chief executive officer in 2010.

ORIGINS

Bel-Art Products was founded in 1946 by husband-and-wife team Kurt and Anny (Terkel) Landsberger, both Jews who had fled Europe because of the rise of Nazi Germany in the 1930s. Kurt Landsberger was born in Prague, Czechoslovakia, in 1920, and grew up in Vienna, Austria, with his mother and stepfather. His father was a salesman in England working for the Parker Pen Company. In 1938, during the annexation of Austria by Germany, his father sent for Landsberger, who along with his mother and stepfather traveled to London while they had the chance.

As World War II began, they were able to make their way to New York City in December 1939, several months before London was bombed in what became known as the Battle of Britain. Anny Terkel, born in Vienna, also made her way to New York, where she met Kurt Landsberger. They were married in 1943. Upon his arrival in the United States, Landsberger took any job he could find, including as a pants presser. He was not especially happy with any of the jobs he held during this time, because as he recalled years later in the *Business Journal of New Jersey*, June 1990, "all of them created a big distinction between labor and management." It was a relationship he kept in mind when he and his wife started their own business.

In the meantime, Landsberger was willingly drafted into the military in 1942. He wanted to participate in the war effort but as an alien was not permitted to volunteer. Born with a clubfoot, he could have applied for a deferment, but instead accepted his induction into the U.S. Army, which made good use of his fluency in German. In the spring of 1943 he was sent to a new German prisoner of war camp in Trinidad, Colorado, where he served as an interpreter. He would later write a book about his experiences there.

After his discharge from the service, Kurt and Anny Landsberger moved to New Jersey. There in 1946 they invested their life savings of $400 to start a company that used plastic to make household items. For the name of their company they chose Bel-Art Products. "When we first started," Landsberger explained in a 1990 interview with *Journal of Commerce*, "we thought we were going to make fancy, little aprons for housewives."

MOVE INTO LABWARE

Bel-Art's move into labware was accidental, the result of Kurt Landsberger's realization that the plastic materials they used were chemical resistant. Bel-Art began selling aprons to laboratory and medical supply houses. Other products for these markets then followed and Bel-Art added the necessary molds and equipment to produce a wide variety of plastic laboratory ware. The Landsbergers also became involved in producing medical aids for the elderly and disabled. This business was conducted by a subsidiary, Maddak Inc. Another business, Applied

Coatings, would be established in Pequannock in 1982. The company would also launch its own in-house advertising agency, D&S Marketing Associates, to produce catalogs, corporate literature, and marketing fulfillment materials.

Bel-Art began exporting products in the early 1960s, due in large measure to Kurt Landsberger's love for travel. He became a frequent visitor to trade shows, such as the Achema chemical products fair held every three years in Frankfurt, Germany, where Bel-Art began displaying its products in the early 1960s. Landsberger was able to build a business in Europe and Scandinavia, as well as the Far East. Bel-Art enjoyed some success in Taiwan and Hong Kong despite the trade protections enjoyed by the plastic industry in those countries. Japan offered even greater opportunities and in time became a major market for Bel-Art.

FAMILY ATMOSPHERE EMPHASIZED

Sales reached the $1 million mark in 1963 and $5 million in 1978. The pace picked up in the 1980s as revenues doubled to $10 million in 1985 and by the end of the decade totaled $20 million. Another key to success was the company's family atmosphere, a reflection of Kurt Landsberger's early work experience in the United States and a conscious effort to break down barriers between labor and management. As a result, there were no reserved parking spaces for management.

Landsberger also made a wide variety of unusual benefits available to employees. They were allowed to make use of in-house operations, including a travel center, advertising agency, and notary public. A doctor was regularly brought in to provide free checkups. Moreover, employees were encouraged to supervise themselves and provided with ample opportunity for advancement. A telephone receptionist, for example, would one day become the company's office manager and personnel director. Kurt Landsberger also kept his door open to all employees, and was more than willing to provide advice on personal matters if asked.

The Bel-Art plant in Pequannock and the Maddak plant in Wayne, New Jersey, included volleyball courts, ping-pong tables, and a lending library. Coffee was free on Wednesdays, and several times a year the company provided employees with free lunches and dinners. The company culture led to a strong bond with employees that paid countless dividends to Bel-Art. The family atmosphere also extended to the two sons of Kurt and Anny Landsberger, who were cared for by company employees while their mother worked. David Landsberger would eventually join the company.

KEY DATES

1946: Kurt and Anny Landsberger launch Bel-Art Products.
1963: Sales reach $1 million.
1982: Applied Coatings established.
1989: Sales total $20 million.
2010: Anny Landsberger dies.

By 1989, David Landsberger, then 40 years old, was president of Bel-Art when he narrowly avoided tragedy. On a flight from Denver to Chicago he lost his seat reservation during a connection and was moved to another section of the plane. One of the engines failed, causing shrapnel to sever the plane's hydraulic systems. With limited control of the craft, the crew made an emergency landing in Sioux City, Iowa. The United Airlines Flight 232 broke apart upon impact, killing 111 of the 285 passengers and one crew member. David Landsberger had been assigned a seat in one of the sections that remained intact. It came to a stop, upside down in a cornfield. Landsberger was able to crawl out of the wreckage and walk away from the crash unharmed.

EXPANSION THROUGH ACQUISITIONS

It was David Landsberger who in the 1990s led Bel-Art through a period of expansion with a series of acquisitions, while his parents focused on other endeavors. In 1996 Bel-Art purchased the assets of Manostat Corporation, adding a pipetting line to round out Bel-Art's pipetting accessories. While another company would acquire Manostat's other core line, pump products, Bel-Art retained the services of Manostat's president, Amanda Bader.

Later in the 1990s Bel-Art acquired the Safe Lab Specialty Glassware and Stoppers product lines from BH Scientific Glass of Santee, California. The company also bought the Vectra Precisionware line from Zuckerman-Honickman, Inc., of King of Prussia, Pennsylvania. These plastic containers withstood excessive vibrations and stayed closed during shipment, making them ideal for a variety of packaging, laboratory, and sampling applications. Another acquisition during this time was the assets of Valencia, California-based DBM Scientific, resulting in the addition of several new products, including centrifuge tubes, disposable pipetting re-

servoirs, a deep well plate, and an eight-channel transfer pipette.

Also in the late 1990s Bel-Art bought the assets of Kezar Enterprises, broadening its slate of laboratory accessories. Kezar produced high-quality splash shields and phlebotomy transport trays. Bel-Art next acquired the assets of Maryland-based NuTech Molding Corporation, a custom injection molding company. Bel-Art then moved its injection molding assets from New Jersey to Maryland. The combined operation did business under the NuTech Manufacturing Corporation name. The Pocomoke, Maryland, plant was enlarged from 30,000 square feet to 60,000 square feet. Half of the plant housed the Bel-Art machines, while in the other half NuTech continued to pursue its wide-ranging injection molding business, while taking steps to expand into new medical and laboratory product lines.

EMPHASIS ON PRODUCT DEVELOPMENT

Bel-Art pursued further growth at home and abroad as the new century dawned. The company did not look to outsource manufacturing, however. More than 80 percent of Scienceware-branded products were produced in Bel-Art's three U.S. factories. Furthermore, each year the company introduced about 200 new products. Bel-Art cast a wide net in product development. It encouraged inventors to bring ideas and in many cases worked with inventors to bring new products to market. Bel-Art also reached out to lab personnel, asking them to consider turning makeshift laboratory solutions, or improvements on existing products, into new commercial products.

Additionally, Bel-Art continued to look for opportunities to add products through acquisitions. In late 2009, for example, Bel-Art fleshed out its slate of insulated ice buckets and pans by purchasing the assets of Magic Touch Icewares International Corporation. Magic Touch served many of the same customers as Bel-Art, offering an array of ice buckets, ice pans, and floating racks. Moreover, the Magic Touch products were capable of holding liquid nitrogen in addition to the ice, dry ice, and dry ice-alcohol slurries used in laboratories.

In March 2010 Anny Landsberger passed away at the age of 86. Kurt Landsberger, approaching 90 years of age, survived her and remained the chairman of the board and CEO. David Landsberger had for some time been the driving force behind Bel-Art's continued growth, while preserving the company's core values that had been instilled by his parents. There was every reason to expect the family owned and operated company to maintain those values and enjoy continued success serving the scientific community for years to come.

Ed Dinger

PRINCIPAL SUBSIDIARIES
Applied Coatings, Inc.; Maddak Inc.

PRINCIPAL COMPETITORS
Becton Dickinson and Company; Sigma-Aldrich, Inc.; Thermo Fisher Scientific Inc.

FURTHER READING
"Anny Landsberger," *Newark (NJ) Star-Ledger*, March 5, 2010.

"Bel-Art Products," *Journal of Commerce*, December 28, 1990, p. 8A.

Gill, David, "Fostering a Family Atmosphere," *Business Journal of New Jersey*, June 1990, p. 50.

Mendoza, Manuel, "Seat Change Probably Saved His Life," *Record* (New Jersey), July 21, 1989, p. A1.

O'Crowley, Peggy, "Kurt Landsberger," *I Am NJ—NJ.Com*, November 11, 2007.

Bell's Brewery, Inc.

—■—

8938 Krum Avenue
Galesburg, Michigan 49053-9558
U.S.A.
Telephone: (269) 382-2338
Web site: http://www.bellsbeer.com

Private Company
Incorporated: 1983 as Kalamazoo Home Brewery Supply
    Co.
Employees: 84
Sales: $12 million (2005)
NAICS: 312120 Breweries

■ ■ ■

Maintaining its headquarters in the western Michigan town of Galesburg, Bell's Brewery, Inc., is a microbrewery producing a wide variety of highly regarded craft beers, including ales, porters, lagers, and stouts. Bell's beers are available in about 18 states in the Midwest, Mid-Atlantic, and southeastern United States as well as in Washington, D.C., and Arizona. In addition, the company operates the Eccentric Café in Kalamazoo, Michigan, and sells non-beer merchandise online. Another venture, Bell's Brewery Farms, grows barley in Michigan for the company's two breweries, located in Kalamazoo and Comstock, Michigan. The Kalamazoo facility also includes a general store that sells Bell's branded apparel, totes, and posters, as well as bar gear, home brewing supplies, and miscellaneous items. The company is headed by its founder and majority shareholder, Larry Bell.

FOUNDER, ILLINOIS TRANSPLANT

Larry Bell was raised in Illinois and moved to Kalamazoo, Michigan, in the late 1970s to attend college. Early on Bell developed a passion for beer. During a trip to Washington, D.C., to visit his brother, Bell was introduced to several new beers and began a beer can collection. Upon moving to Kalamazoo he discovered new regional brands that furthered his interest.

Perhaps of more importance, he had three roommates who liked to drink beer, and the idea of home brewing as a way to save money appealed to him. Moreover, Bell worked at Sarkozy Bakery in Kalamazoo where a coworker was a homebrewer. His interest piqued, Bell bought a book about beer making and the equipment to brew a five-gallon batch. Bell's initial attempt at making his own beer was less than successful. He called what he produced "rocket fuel," heavy on sugar and high in alcohol.

Bell's first beer had the saving grace of being inexpensive, costing about 12 cents a bottle to produce and providing him with enough incentive to buy better books and make further experiments. His ambitions also began to grow as friends clamored for more of his beer. In 1982 the Real Ale Company opened in Chelsea, Michigan, and Bell observed their operation.

Bell also paid attention to developments on the West Coast where the microbrewery movement had emerged back in the 1970s. Aware that Michigan embraced trends several years after the West Coast, Bell decided the time might be right to stake his claim in the microbrewery business. While the thought of starting a microbrewery began to take shape, Bell was also given an opportunity to further his skills. Paul Todd of Kalamazoo Spice Extraction Company hired him to do some experimental home brewing using the company's new hop extracts.

SUPPLY COMPANY LAUNCHED: 1983

In the summer of 1983 Bell launched his own company, a home brewing supply business, using $200 his mother had given him as a birthday present. He spent $35 to incorporate the Kalamazoo Home Brewery Supply Co. Inc. and the remaining $165 on inventory. To raise further funds he made a deal with a local attorney to set up a stock sale in exchange for a share of the proceeds. Bell also used six shares of stock to receive six months of free rent in a building, which he also agreed to clean up. Bell moved into the space and was open for business on a sporadic basis while he worked elsewhere. Not only did he sell supplies to home brewers, he sold them stock in his company. Kalamazoo Spice also said it would buy stock, matching the number of shares he sold to others.

With the proceeds from the stock sale and a loan co-signed by his wife, Bell was able to raise $39,000, far less than the $250,000 minimum a microbrewery was advised to have on hand to launch an operation. Nevertheless, Bell moved into a building on Kalamazoo Avenue in December 1984. He received his federal license in August 1985 for Kalamazoo Brewing Co. Inc., becoming the first microbrewery east of Boulder, Colorado.

Made in a 15-gallon soup pot, the first beer was sold on September 19, 1985. Initially Bell sold his brew in cube containers, essentially beer in a bag in a box, because he could not afford a minimum order of bottles. He did manage to bottle beer for the holiday season, but had to rely on used bottles, in particular those from Wisconsin's Huber Bock, whose label floated off easily in the hand-washing process. Bell and his employees also filled, capped, and labeled the bottles by hand.

The soup pot was soon replaced by a three-vessel, one barrel system, but the early years remained a

struggle. According to the *Kalamazoo Gazette*, the company was twice on the verge of bankruptcy: "Times were so hard during one early period that Bell and his staff kept the company's thermostat turned to 50 degree most days to save money. They would turn the temperature up to 60 degrees on weekends, when most people came to buy the beer."

ECCENTRIC CAFÉ OPENS: 1993

Self-distributing, Kalamazoo Brewing held on and by 1989 the brewery was shipping more than 500 barrels of beer a year when it secured its first wholesale arrangement to sell throughout the state of Michigan. In 1990 the company was able to graduate to a 2-barrel system and the following year added a 15-barrel system, which was soon followed by a 30-barrel system. In June 1993 Bell's became the first Michigan brewery permitted to serve beer by the glass to the public and the company opened a beer garden on the site of a former rail yard that took the name the Eccentric Café.

Sales reached $1.4 million in 1994 as Kalamazoo Brewing entered a period of steady growth and doubled in size every four years, gaining economies of scale in the process. A second brew house was added to keep up with demand, focusing on draft beer production, which accounted for about 60 percent of sales. The Eccentric Café also thrived and began serving foods as well as a selection of Bell's brews.

Kalamazoo Brewing continued to grow in the new century. The increase in volume led to some quality problems, however, which led to a restructuring of the operation. In addition to some staff changes, there was increased training and greater attention paid to detail. In 2002 the company opened a new 32,000-square-foot, 50-barrel brew house in Comstock, Michigan, about 12 miles from Kalamazoo. The choice of location was due in large measure to the efforts of the city of Comstock to attract the business, while Kalamazoo made little effort to keep the brewery within the city limits. The new facility also played a factor in improving the quality of the end product. The first beer brewed in the Comstock facility was shipped in December 2002.

BELL'S NAME ADOPTED: 2008

The Comstock brewery was soon expanded to add extra storage and refrigeration capacity. In addition, the company acquired warehouse space in Kalamazoo in 2005. By this stage the company was generating annual sales of about $12 million from distribution in ten states. Also in 2005 the company elected to change its name to Bell's Brewery Inc. For years, customers had referred to the brewery as Bell's, so that name change was more a reflection of this reality than a branding effort.

Bell pulled his business out of Chicago and Illinois in general in 2006, dissatisfied with his distribution channel. Indianapolis-based National Wine and Spirits Inc. had distributed the brewery's products in Illinois but then wanted also to sell the rights to Chicago Beverage Systems, which in the opinion of Larry Bell would have given short shrift to the brand. Because of Illinois laws, Bell had no choice in the matter. In November 2006 he elected to withdraw from the Illinois market, which accounted for about 11 percent of the company's business, and thwart the sale of the Kalamazoo brands to Chicago Beverage.

A year later he was able to create three new beers for the Chicago market that had not been assigned to National Wine and Spirits. That effort prompted National to threaten lengthy and expensive litigation. According to state law, however, the company could assign new brands to any distributor of its choosing. Bell's assigned the new products to Central Beverage Co. and Schamberger Brothers, Inc., and began shipping in early December 2007.

While sorting out the problems in Illinois, Bell's made improvements to its Kalamazoo operation, including the opening of a general store offering a variety of Bell's merchandise. The company also made plans in the fall of 2007 for a $5.2 million major upgrade and expansion in Comstock that would increase production capacity from 90,000 barrels of beer a year to 140,000 barrels a year. Included in the effort were six 200-barrel fermenters, a 400-barrel fermenter, a new keg line capable of filling 280 kegs per hour, and a 10,000-square-foot warehouse. The upgrades were completed in early 2008.

FARMING SUBSIDIARY FORMED: 2008

Larry Bell pursued a new, related venture in 2008, when he formed Bell's Brewery Farms LLC, purchasing an 80-

acre farm in Shepherd, Michigan. Initially the land grew soy beans, due to crop rotation, but the goal was to produce barley for the brewery as a way to control costs that had been adversely impacted by the high price of hops and barley. In the meantime, the new division reached an agreement with an area farmer to grow barley for the brewery, which could then be used to produce specialty brews using Michigan barley and partial Michigan hops.

Bell's looked to expand its headquarters in 2009. A new $5.2 million project launched in the spring of that year added 15,000 square feet of office space. In Kalamazoo, in the meantime, the company continued to maintain 40,000 square feet of space, but only 3,000 of that was employed for production. Most of the remainder was devoted to warehousing products but also included a workshop and the general store.

In March 2010 Bell's began work on a $2.5 million renovation project in Kalamazoo to expand the Eccentric Café. The Café had always offered live music and would be upgraded to provide a large performance venue capable of hosting more than 300 people and include a green room for performers. The café appropriated space behind its bar and planned to add an atrium entryway as well as a new parking lot and make improvements to the beer garden and patio.

The new music room was also designed to open onto the garden, which would allow the Café to accommodate upward of 1,000 customers and attract more prominent artists, who were attracted to college towns like Kalamazoo. The higher visibility of the café was expected to help promote the Bell's brand as well. There was no completion date set for the project, which was dependent on cash flow rather than bank loans. The brewery was steadily expanding its marketing reach, its products becoming available in many parts of the country, 28 states in all, and there was every reason to believe that growth would continue in the years to come.

Ed Dinger

PRINCIPAL SUBSIDIARIES

Kalamazoo Brewing Co., Inc.; Bell's Brewery Farms LLC.

PRINCIPAL COMPETITORS

Anheuser-Busch InBev SA/NV; The Boston Beer Company; Heineken USA Inc.

FURTHER READING

Liberty, John, "Bell's Expanding Downtown Café," *Kalamazoo Gazette*, March 18, 2010, p. A1.

————, "Bell's Farm Purchase May Lead to New Specialty Brew," *Kalamazoo Gazette*, May 3, 2008.

————, "Kalamazoo Beer to Make Return in Illinois Next Week," *Kalamazoo Gazette*, December 1, 2007.

Parikh, Jane C., "Kalamazoo Brewing Co. Plans Warehouse at Former Lumberyard Site," *Kalamazoo Gazette*, February 19, 2005, p. A5.

————, "Local Brewer Pulls Out of Illinois Market," *Kalamazoo Gazette*, November 12, 2006.

Reid, Peter V. K., "Kalamazoo-Brew: Larry Bell Has Built His Kalamazoo Brewing Co. on a Foundation of Good Beer and Loyal Customers," *Modern Brewery*, May 12, 1997.

Wood, William R., "Happy Birthday, Bell's," *Kalamazoo Gazette*, September 5, 2005, p. D1.

Woodruff, David, "Local Entrepreneur Hopes to Tap into Kalamazoo Beer Market," *Kalamazoo Gazette*, September 22, 1985.

BLRT Grupp A.S.

Kopli 103
Tallinn, 11712
Estonia
Telephone: (+372) 610 2408
Fax: (+372) 610 2999
Web site: http://www.bsr.ee

Joint-Stock Company
Founded: 1912
Employees: 3,233
Sales: EEK 4.8 billion ($377.15 million) (2009)
NAICS: 336611 Ship Building and Repairing; 325120 Industrial Gas Manufacturing; 332313 Plate Work Manufacturing; 423930 Recyclable Material Merchant Wholesalers; 551112 Offices of Other Holding Companies

■ ■ ■

BLRT Grupp A.S. is a diversified company focused around a core of shipbuilding and ship repair. The Tallinn, Estonia-based company also owns subsidiaries involved in metal construction manufacturing, machine building, metal trading and scrap metal processing, and port services and road transport services. BLRT Grupp, the successor of Baltic Ship Repairers, operates three shipyards, including the former Russian-Baltic Shipyard and the former Noblessner Shipyard in Tallinn; the Klaipėda shipyard, through subsidiary Vakarų Laivų Gamykla, in Lithuania; and the Turku Repair Yard in Finland.

The company also operates a shipbuilding joint venture with Fiskerstrand in Norway and a ship repair and marine services joint venture with Wärtsilä in Estonia and Lithuania. BLRT also includes metal construction manufacturer BLRT Marketex; steel construction and machine manufacturer BLRT Masinaehitus; ELME, a supplier of metals and industrial products; ELME Messer Gas, an industrial gas supply joint venture with Germany's Messer Group; and Vakaru Refonda Ltd., a leading scrap metal processor in Estonia. Altogether, BLRT operates more than 65 subsidiaries in Estonia, Lithuania, Latvia, Finland, Norway, Russia, and Ukraine. The company is a joint-stock company led by CEO and Chairman Fjodor Berman. In 2009, BLRT reported revenues of EEK 4.8 billion ($377.15 million).

BUILDING THE RUSSIAN NAVY IN 1912

BLRT's history reaches back to the beginnings of Estonia's shipbuilding and ship repair industry. As part of Russia, Estonia represented an important strategic location on the Baltic Sea. During the late 19th century, as the Industrial Revolution reached the region, the city of Tallinn grew in importance. The nearby Kopli Peninsula became the focus of much of the city's industrial development, and ultimately became part of Tallinn itself. The rise of industrial manufacturing concerns, including a mechanical engineering company and a electro-technical factory, also helped build a skilled labor force in the area.

These features led to the choice of Tallinn as the location for a new shipyard complex as the Russian navy

rushed to replace the Imperial Baltic Fleet. That fleet
had traveled 18,000 miles to reinforce Russia's far-
eastern navy during the Russian-Japanese War of 1904–
1905, only to be destroyed in 1905. Soon after, the Russian imperial government launched plans to rebuild the
fleet. In 1911, the government settled on Tallinn as its
main military shipyard and naval port.

This led to the creation of the Russian-Baltic
Shipyard in Kopli in 1912. The new state-owned
company began building what was to become one of the
largest industrial complexes in the region, with full-scale
metallurgical, machine building and engineering
capabilities. The first phase of the complex reached
completion in 1913, permitting the company to launch
production that year. The entire complex became
operational by 1915. By 1916, the shipyard had
completed its first three destroyers.

SOVIET ERA SHIPBUILDER

The Russian-Baltic Shipyard, like the area's other
industrial operations, was forced to cut back on its
production amid a shortage of raw materials. The region
also found itself increasingly vulnerable to attack during
World War I. As a result, by 1917, much of the region's
industry, including Russian-Baltic, was transferred to
safer quarters in St. Petersburg. The company's fortunes
continued to be compromised as World War I ended
and Estonia gained its independence from the newly
established Soviet Union.

The former Russian-Baltic Shipyard struggled
through the years of Estonia's independence, particularly
into the 1930s amid the Depression era and the
country's fragile political stability. During this period,
the company absorbed the operations of rival Bekker
Shipyard, which had also started operations in 1913.

Founded as part of France's Augustin Normand, the
Bekker shipyard had also abandoned Tallinn for St.
Petersburg. Returning to Estonia, the company struggled
to resume operations, in part because of the plundering
of its factory following its evacuation. Bekker remained
more or less solvent through the early 1920s, and
continued to struggle into the 1930. In 1934, the
Estonian government, which had acquired a growing
share of the Bekker Shipyard, decided to dissolve the
company and merge its operations into the Russian-
Baltic Shipyard.

SHIP REPAIR AFTER WORLD WAR II

Estonia lost its independence at the beginning of World
War II, when the country was overrun first by Germany,
and then by the Soviet Union. Following the war, the
country was officially absorbed into the Soviet Union,
becoming Estonia SSR. The country's shipyards came
under control of the Soviet authorities. As a result, the
former Russian-Baltic Shipyard found itself converted
from shipbuilding to ship repair. The company later
became known as Baltic Ship Repairers (BSR), and
became responsible for repairing Soviet military vessels.

Into the 1970s and 1980s, the company's focus
shifting more and more to repairing fishing boats. BSR
also developed expertise in the railway sector, providing
repair and maintenance services for the Oslo-Tallinn-
Moscow railroad and the Stockholm-Tallinn-Moscow
railroad. Joining BSR during this period was Fjodor
Berman. Born in 1951, Berman had earned a degree in
mechanical engineering from Kaliningrad Technical
University. In 1975, Berman joined BSR as an engineer.
By the end of the 1980s Berman had risen through the
ranks to be named the company's chief executive officer
in 1990.

Berman immediately expanded BSR's sphere of
operations to include repairs on tanker and cargo ships,
as well as ferries and small cruise ships. The company
also began planning a return to shipbuilding, as Estonia
regained its independence amid the breakup of the
Soviet Union. In 1993, the company established its own
engineering subsidiary, later known as BLRT IK. This
enhanced the company's ship repair capabilities and
enabled it to provide ship conversion and modernization
services. The engineering subsidiary also became an
important part of the group later reentry into shipbuilding.

At the same time, Berman recognized the importance of expanding the company beyond its main
ship repair business. By building up a diversified range
of operations, the company hoped to achieve a degree of
financial stability amid the upheavals caused by Estonia's

KEY DATES

1912: The company is founded as the Russian-Baltic Shipyard to rebuild the Russian Baltic Fleet.
1940s: Under Soviet control the company focuses on ship repair, and becomes Baltic Ship Repair (BSR).
1996: BSR is privatized by the Estonian government, then reenters shipbuilding the following year.
2001: BSR acquires Western Shipyard (later VLG) in Lithuania and changes its name to BLRT.
2007: BLRT acquires Turku Ship Repair Ltd. in Finland.
2010: BLRT announces it might seek to acquire Finnish shipbuilder Uudenkaupungin Työvene.

transition to a market-based economy. One of the company's first diversification efforts was the creation of a trade subsidiary ELME. The new company originally focused on ensuring BSR's supply of raw materials, as well as its power supply and the repair and maintenance of its industrial equipment. ELME quickly branched out into production, taking over machinery producer Taglas in 1994. The company began distributing technical and medical gases, including oxygen, nitrogen, and hydrogen, in 1994, then entered the metals trade in 1996. That operation later led to the establishment of a dedicated subsidiary, ELME Metall, in 2001. Another subsidiary, ELME Trans, was created out of BSR's former railroad repair unit.

PRIVATIZED IN 1996

BSR continued to target expansion into a number of related areas where it could put its industrial and mechanical expertise to use. In 1995, for example, the company launched a new production center for the manufacturing of large-scale metal constructions. The company quickly scored a number of important contracts, particularly in the Scandinavian market. By 1997, the company had completed its return to shipbuilding, launching a vessel built for the Estonian Border Guard that year.

BSR remained owned by the Estonian government through the first half of the 1990s. In the second half of the decade, the government put into place a privatization program, completing the country's relatively smooth transition to a market-based economy. BSR's turn came in 1996, when the government agreed to sell the company to a group of shareholders led by Berman. At that time the company took the form of a joint-stock company. Berman emerged as the group's controlling shareholder.

BSR's shipbuilding operations grew strongly at the turn of the century. The company received its first major order, for a series of fish farming barges for a group of Norwegian companies in 1999. In that year, also, BSR's operations were granted ISO 9001quality standards certification by Lloyd's Register Quality Assurance. The following year, the company took over the struggling Tallinn Sea Factory. In this way, BSR added a new slipway, expanding its access to the Baltic Sea. The company's ELME group also expanded in 1999, creating a gas distribution joint venture with Germany's Messer Group for the Baltic region.

ACQUIRING VLG IN 2001

In the new decade, BSR set out to establish itself as a major presence in the Baltic shipbuilding and ship repair sector. Toward this end the company acquired a 92.8 percent stake in Lithuanian rival Vakarų Laivų Remontas, based in Klaipėda. Also known as Western Shipyard, the company had been founded in 1966 as a ship repair dock, becoming operational in 1969. In that year, the company completed its first major repair, of the *Sovetskaja Arktika*. The company completed a major expansion in 1975, raising its total workforce to 2,600. Western Shipyard specialized in repairing fishing trawlers and fish processing vessels.

In the early 1990s, following Lithuania's independence, the Lithuanian government began disposing of its large fishing fleet. The drop-off in repair work led Western Shipyard to begin competing for repair orders on Western vessels. The first of these came in 1993, when the company carried out the repair work on the *Marika*, a bulk carrier from Greece. In 1998, Western Shipyard expanded into shipbuilding proper, completing its first vessel, a fishing boat that same year. This year also market the company's privatization, when the Lithuanian government agreed to sell the company to Vestern Invest AS in Norway.

This deal soon unraveled, however, giving BSR the opportunity to acquire the shipyard in 2001. With three major shipyards in the Baltic region, and more than 20 diversified subsidiaries, the company changed its name that year, becoming BLRT Grupp. Two years later, BLRT restructured its Lithuanian operations, which took on the new name of Vakarų Laivų Gamykla, or VLG. This subsidiary mirrored BLRT's Estonian business, with diversified operations including shipbuilding and ship repair, and machine and metal construction manufacturing. In 2003, for example, VLG founded JSC Western Stevedoring, providing cargo handling services to the port of Klaipėda. BLRT also created a new subsidiary for VLG's existing transport repair business, JSC ELME Transportas that year.

ENTERING FINLAND IN 2007

BLRT build up a strong order book through the middle of the decade. During the second half of the decade, the company's Tallinn shipyard routinely repaired more than 165 ships per year, while its counterpart in Klaipėda added another 130 vessels per year. BLRT had also expanded its shipbuilding business, founding BLRT Laevaehitus, which took over the former Noblessner Shipyard in Tallinn in 2003. The company then invested some EEK 150 million (approximately $12 million) in restoring and modernizing the shipyard, including its 11 slipways. The new company quickly filled its order book, completing several boats for the Estonian Coast Guard, as well as for Estonia's Maritime Administration and a work vessel for the Kaliningrad Port Authority. The company also developed its multipurpose seagoing escort tug boat.

BLRT also expanded its repair business in the second half of the decade. In 2005, the company joined with ship engine giant Wärtsilä Corporation to develop a ship maintenance and repair joint venture at BLRT's Tallinn yard. The following year, the two companies extended their partnership, forming a new joint venture at BLRT's Klaipėda facilities.

The company nonetheless faced a major restriction as it continued to expand its ship repair and shipbuilding operations. Ferries and small cruise liners represented a major segment of the ship repair market. The rising economies of the Baltic and Scandinavian region, however, had led to steady increases in vessel size at the turn of the century. As a result, BLRT found itself unable to accommodate the larger vessels.

In 2007, the company solved this problem by acquiring Turku Repair Yard Ltd., based in Nantali, Finland. This company, founded in 1989, had originally operated in the Permo shipyard, then transferred its operations to Nantali in 2004. The addition of Turku Repair Yard, with a dry dock 265 meters in length and 70 meters in width, allowed BLRT to offer full repair services on both sides of the Baltic Sea, as well as accommodate the region's larger vessels.

FACING THE ECONOMIC DOWNTURN IN 2009

BLRT reached a new partnership in 2007 as well, when it formed a shipbuilding joint venture in Klaipėda with Norway's Fiskerstrand Verft. BLRT Fiskerstrand proved successful from the start, and by 2009 had gained orders for eight vessels, including a 112-meter ferry worth a total of EUR 160 million ($224 million). Also in 2007, BLRT's Lithuanian subsidiary established a new shipbuilding record, when it was awarded a $45 million contract to build an offshore wind farm support ship. BLRT also celebrated that year with the order to build three new ferryboats for the Saaremaa Shipping Company.

The company's celebratory mood faded into the end of the decade, as it felt the brunt of the global economic collapse. In to 2009, the company's revenues dropped by some 30 percent from the previous year's EUR 295 million ($413 million). The company's sales continued to drop through 2009, falling back to $377 million. The company faced a new hit early in 2010, when it lost in its bid to build a new ship for the Estonian Coast Guard to Finnish rival Uudenkaupungin Työvene. In response, BLRT announced that it might seek to acquire the Finnish firm instead, in order to establish a presence in the Finnish shipbuilding market as well. Despite the difficult economic period, BLRT had succeeded in establishing itself as a major force in the region's shipping industry and one of Estonia's leading industrial companies.

M. L. Cohen

PRINCIPAL SUBSIDIARIES

Arefonte Chemicals Grupp; BLRT EKO; BLRT Era; BLRT IK; BLRT Invest; BLRT Kinnisvara; BLRT Laevaehitus; BLRT Marketex; BLRT Masinaehitus; BLRT McGregor; BLRT Rekato; BLRT RPK; BLRT Toorik; BLRT Transiit; Elme; Elme Messer Gaas; Elme Metall; Elme TKS; Fiskerstrand BLRT (50%); Refonda; Tallinn Shipyard; Turku Repair Yard (Finland); Vakarų Laivų Gamykla (Lithuania); Wärtsilä BLRT Estonia (50%).

PRINCIPAL DIVISIONS

Machine Building; Manufacture of Metal Constructions; Metal Trading; Port Services and Stevedoring; Road Transport Services; Scrap Metal Processing; Ship Repair and Conversion; Shipbuilding.

PRINCIPAL OPERATING UNITS

Elme; Marketex; Tallinn Shipyard; Turku Repair Yard; Vakarų Laivų Gamykla (VLG); Vakaru Refonda Ltd.

PRINCIPAL COMPETITORS

A.P. Møller Maersk Group; Aker ASA; Alstom S.A.; MAN SE; MTU Friedrichshafen GmbH; STX Europe A.S.; VT Group plc.

FURTHER READING

"After Losing the Contracting Work Commission for a New Border Guard Ship for Estonia to the Finnish Company Uudenkaupungin Tyovene, BLRT Is Considering Buying the Finnish Shipyard," *Baltic Times*, March 17, 2010.

Niitra, Sirje, "Estonian Company to Assist in Building Stockholm Subway Tunnel," *Postimees*, January 23, 2009.

Tere, Julian, "BLRT Invested 156 Mln Kroons in Factory in Vilnius," *Baltic Course*, October 17, 2008.

————, "BLRT Is Considering Buying a Shipyard in Finland," *Baltic Course*, March 13, 2010.

————, "BLRT Slashes Salaries by 10–15% in Estonia," *Baltic Course*, May 12, 2009.

Vitismann, Madli, "The BLRT Grupp Expands around the Baltic," *Scandinavian Shipping Gazette*, March 25, 2008.

"Wartsila Gives Boost to Baltic," *Lloyds List*, March 3, 2006.

Britannia Industries Ltd.

———— ■ ————

5/1A Hungerford Street
Kolkata, 700 017
India
Telephone: (91 033) 2287 2439
Fax: (91 033) 2287 2501
Web site: http://www.britannia.co.in

Public Company
Incorporated: 1918 as Britannia Biscuit Company Ltd.
Employees: 1,982
Sales: INR 31,122 million ($746.70 million) (2009)
Stock Exchanges: Bombay
Ticker Symbol: 500825
NAICS: 311812 Commercial Bakeries; 311513 Cheese Manufacturing; 311514 Dry, Condensed, and Evaporated Dairy Product Manufacturing; 311821 Cookie and Cracker Manufacturing

■ ■ ■

Britannia Industries Ltd. is one of India's leading food companies, producing and distributing a variety of biscuits (cookies), cakes, breads, and dairy products. Britannia also controls two of the country's most popular brands, Britannia and Tiger. Combined, these brands command more than one-third of the total British market for biscuits. The company also places consistently among India's Top 10 Trusted Brands. Other brands in the company's stable include Nutri-Choice, Good Morning, Vita Marie, and 50-50.

In addition to its operations in India, Britannia has expanded to a number of international markets, includ-

ing Sri Lanka and the Middle East. The company also operates a dairy joint venture in New Zealand. Britannia is listed on the Bombay Stock Exchange. The Bombay Burmah Trading Corporation, controlled by the Wadia family, is its largest shareholder, with a nearly 51 percent stake. Britannia is led by Managing Director and CEO Vinita Bali. In 2009 the company's sales reached INR 31.12 billion ($746.7 million).

BISCUIT BAKERY ORIGINS: 1892

Britannia traces its origins to a small biscuit bakery based in a house in Calcutta (Kolkata), set up in 1892 with less than 300 rupees. Biscuits were a British specialty, closely related to the American-style cookie. That bakery was taken over by the Gupta brothers at the dawn of the 20th century, and renamed V.S. Brothers. By 1910, with the availability of electrical power, the company had installed its first production machinery.

In 1918 the Gupta brothers brought in a new partner, C. H. Holmes, a British entrepreneur living in Calcutta, and the company incorporated as Britannia Biscuit Company Ltd. Backed by Holmes, the company began a new expansion effort, importing machinery from overseas in order to increase its production capacity. By 1921 Britannia had become the first biscuit manufacturer in India to introduce the use of gas ovens.

Britannia began its development into a national company in 1924, when it opened a new factory in Bombay. During this time, Peek, Frean and Co., a leading biscuit maker in the United Kingdom, Canada, and Australia, acquired a majority stake in the company.

Peak, Frean was part of the larger Associated Biscuits Manufacturing Ltd. Other subsidiaries in that company included Huntley and Palmers, Meltis Limited, and Suchard Chocolate. Associated Biscuits later evolved into Associated Biscuits International Ltd. (ABIL), becoming part of the RJ Reynolds snack foods empire during the 1980s. At the dawn of the 21st century, ABIL had become part of United Biscuits.

Britannia itself registered strong growth through the 1930s, as sales rose past 16 million rupees. The years of World War II provided new opportunities for the company, as it turned 95 percent of its production capacity to supplying the British war effort with service biscuits.

EXPLORING NEW PRODUCTS

Britannia began exploring new product areas in the years following World War II and India's independence. The company launched its own line of sliced and packaged bread, Delbis, starting in 1954. In 1958 the company built a dedicated production facility in Delhi. The consumption of white bread until then had remained largely confined to the country's British population. Britannia helped pioneer the marketing of white bread for the larger Indian market. In 1963 the company established a second bread production facility in Bombay. Britannia then began to expand its bread range, introducing a variety of bread types and packaging sizes.

The company also explored the snack food market beyond biscuits during that decade. Britannia launched its first line of packaged cakes in 1963, and rapidly claimed a leading share of that category. The company expanded its range over the next decades to include a variety of bar cakes in an assortment of flavors. The company also introduced chunk cakes, and in the 21st century cupcakes and a line of vegetarian cakes called Veg Cakes were added.

Britannia remained a pure manufacturing company until the 1970s, with its distribution handled by another company, Parry's. However, in 1975 Britannia moved to establish its own distribution operations. The company went public in 1978, listing its shares on the Bombay Stock Exchange. As a result, Associated Biscuits reduced its stake in the company to 38 percent. The listing marked the first time since its founding that the company's shareholding was majority controlled by Indians. In 1979 the company adopted a new name, Britannia Industries Ltd.

THE REIGN OF THE BISCUIT KING

Britannia's independence proved short-lived, however. In 1982 a majority stake in the company was acquired by Nabisco Brands Inc., part of Standard Brands (later RJR Nabisco) in the United States. That company also acquired control of Associated Biscuits. Through Nabisco, Britannia came under the control of Rajan Pillai, who became known as the Biscuit King in the 1980s.

Born in Kerala in 1948, Pillai had achieved his first business success by investing in a hotel development in Goa. Pillai moved to Singapore in the mid-1970s, where he established 20th Century Foods, a packager of peanuts and potato chips. While unprofitable, the company provided Pillai with an introduction to Ross Johnson, then head of Standard Brands. Pillai persuaded Johnson to acquire his company, and Johnson, impressed by Pillai, appointed him to take over as head of Nabisco's Asian-based operations, including Britannia. Pillai also structured a partnership deal with BSN (later known as Danone) during this time.

RJR Nabisco launched a major streamlining, following its $25 billion leveraged buyout of Kohlberg Kravis Roberts & Company in the late 1980s. As part of this effort, Johnson lent Pillai $30 million to back Pillai's buyout of Associated Biscuits International Ltd. in 1989. Pillai created a new company for this purpose, called Britannia Industries Pte. Ltd., based in Singapore, which paid $44 million to RJR Nabisco. The buyout gave Pillai control of six major Asian-region food companies with total sales of $400 million and earned Pillai the title of Biscuit King. Britannia India remained the largest part of Pillai's empire, with 6,000 employees and revenues of $170 million in the late 1980s.

NEW OWNERS IN 1993

Pillai's empire, built entirely on debt, quickly came crashing down around him when Johnson and other creditors became suspicious of the financial underpin-

KEY DATES

1892: Britannia originates as a small bakery in Calcutta (Kolkata).
1918: The company incorporates as the Britannia Biscuit Company.
1924: Britannia is acquired by Peek, Frean, and becomes part of Associated Biscuits Manufacturing.
1954: Britannia launches production of sliced and packaged bread.
1978: Britannia is listed on the Bombay Stock Exchange.
1993: A partnership between Wadia Group and Danone acquires control of Britannia.
1997: Britannia launches the highly successful Tiger brand.
2002: Britannia begins its international expansion with a joint venture in New Zealand.
2009: Wadia buys out Danone's share of Britannia.

nings of his empire. In 1993, when creditors demanded that Pillai pay up, Pillai was forced to sell pieces of his biscuit empire. Among these sales was one to Britannia India of a company called Ole, which Pillai sold to Britannia for $7.24 million. The transaction caught the attention of Singapore's Commercial Affairs Department, which launched an investigation into Pillai's financial dealings. In 1993 the Singapore court charged, and ultimately convicted, Pillai on several counts of fraud. Pillai escaped sentencing, however, fleeing to India.

The affair sparked a battle for control of the remains of Associated Biscuits International. By the end of 1993 Pillai had lost control of the company, which became jointly owned by Groupe Danone and India's Wadia Group. By 1995 the Associated Biscuits partnership had succeed in wresting control of Britannia Industries in India from Pillai as well. In July of that year Pillai was arrested and placed in jail, where he died under mysterious circumstances.

While the partnership between Wadia and Danone remained an uneasy one, Britannia Industries continued its record of steady growth through the 1990s. The company expanded its production capacity, entering the next decade with a network of nearly 50 factories. The company also rejuvenated its marketing effort, launching the successful "Eat Healthy, Think Better" slogan in 1997. Also that year, Britannia's operations expanded to include fresh milk and dairy products. The company

also launched a number of new brands, including 50-50 crackers in 1993, Milk Bikis in 1996, and NutriChoice, a healthful products brand, in 1998.

The launch of the Tiger brand in 1997 gave Britannia its greatest success to date. Tiger, which developed a line of glucose biscuits, quickly captured a leading share of that market segment in India. By the end of its first year, Tiger had also become Britannia's largest-selling brand, posting sales of more than INR 1 billion. Tiger also helped fuel the growing conflict between Britannia and Wadia on one side and Danone on the other, as Britannia accused Danone of secretly launching the Tiger brand in Indonesia and other markets in breach of their agreement.

INTERNATIONAL EXPANSION STARTS IN 2002

Britannia meanwhile had built up a portfolio of 24 brands. In 2001 the company decided to streamline its brand focus, however, reducing its major brands to just nine, led by its Britannia and Tiger flagships. Britannia by this time had been recognized as the leading food brand in India, with a recognition rate of nearly 100 percent. The company was also ranked on the *Forbes* list of the world's top 200 small companies, and had been awarded the second-place ranking in the Most Trusted Brands list of the *Economic Times*.

With its market penetration in India approaching 40 percent, Britannia launched an international expansion strategy. This began in 2002 when the company reached a partnership agreement with New Zealand's dairy giant Fonterra. The company also established its own subsidiary there, called Britannia New Zealand Foods Pvt. Ltd., which then formed the joint venture Fonterra BNZF that year. The company's next move overseas came in 2007, when the company created a joint venture with Dubai's Khimji Ramdas Group. The partnership then acquired a 70 percent stake in Strategic Foods International Co., based in Dubai, and a 65.4 percent stake in Al Sallan Food Industries, in Oman.

Britannia entered the Sri Lanka market in 2008, forming a wholly owned subsidiary, Britannia Lanka. That company then began manufacturing and distributing Britannia's brand family, including Milk Bikis and Vita Marie Gold. The following year Britannia bought out Fonterra's part of a New Zealand joint venture, which was renamed Britannia Dairy Pvt. Ltd.

In the meantime, the dispute between Britannia's major shareholders over the Tiger brand had come to a head. In 2007 Wadia threatened to take Danone to court over its use of the Tiger brand outside of India in violation of Britannia's intellectual property rights.

Danone, which had been refocusing its operations around its core dairy products business, ultimately agreed to sell its stake in the company to the Wadia Group in 2009.

HEALTHY FOODS IN 2010

Britannia's growth remained strong throughout this period. In 2006 the company acquired a 51 percent stake in Daily Bread, a baked goods retail group in Bangalore. After exiting the milk sector in 2005, Britannia returned to this market with the 2009 launch of a new line of ultrahigh temperature (UHT) long shelf-life milk products, including Slimz, a cholesterol-free milk product. For the launch, Britannia acquired the license to use the Fonterra brand in India. The company also announced plans to expand its Persian Gulf-based operations into the wider Middle East and North African regions in the next decade.

Back at home, Britannia was faced with the soaring costs of basic commodities, global grain shortages, rising fuel transport costs, and a deepening global economic crisis. The company's profits suffered as a result, slipping by 37 percent at the end of 2009.

Under the leadership of CEO Vinita Bali, Britannia began targeting higher value-added products in order to shore up its shrinking margins in 2010. The company announced plans to roll out additional products to take advantage of the fast-rising demand for healthy and functional food products. At the beginning of 2010 the company also targeted the higher-end "adult" biscuit market, with the launch of Pure Magic, a chocolate and vanilla flavored biscuit. Britannia hoped to continue its long-established tradition as one of India's leading foods companies in the years to come.

M. L. Cohen

PRINCIPAL SUBSIDIARIES

Al Sallan Food Industries Company SAOG (Oman); Britannia and Associates (Dubai) Private Co. Limited; Britannia and Associates (Mauritius) Private Limited; Britannia Lanka Pvt. Ltd. (Sri Lanka); Britannia New Zealand Foods Private Limited (51%); Daily Bread Gourmet Foods (India) Private Limited (75%); Ganges Valley Foods Private Limited; International Bakery Products Limited; J B Mangharam Foods Private Limited; Manna Foods Private Limited; Strategic Brands Holding Company Limited (United Arab Emirates; 70%); Strategic Food International Co. LLC (United Arab Emirates; 70%); Sunrise Biscuit Company Private Limited.

PRINCIPAL DIVISIONS

Biscuits; Dairy Products; International.

PRINCIPAL OPERATING UNITS

50-50; Britannia; Britannia Milk; Britannia Good Day; Britannia Marie Gold; Britannia Nice Time; Britannia Treat; Britannia Veg Cakes; NutriChoice; Tiger.

PRINCIPAL COMPETITORS

Associated British Foods plc; Federal Foods LLC; Hari Nagar Sugar Mills Ltd.; IFFCO Group; Kuwait Flour Mills and Bakeries Company; Sara Lee Corp.; Strauss Ltd.; Unilever N.V.; United Biscuits Holdings plc; Wittington Investments Ltd.

FURTHER READING

"Bali Eyes Expansion Plans for Britannia," *Mail Today*, November 10, 2009.

"BIL's Pure Magic," *DNA*, February 24, 2010.

"Biscuit Majors Slug It out for Bigger Chunk of Mkt Bite," *Financial Express*, January 21, 2010.

"Competition Brings in New Investments," *Mint*, April 12, 2010.

"How the Cookie Crumbled," *Financial Express*, April 10, 2009.

Jacobs, Kevin, "Wadia Looks to Buy Danone's Britannia Stake," *just-food.com*, October 9, 2008.

"Ness Wadia Joins Jeh on Britannia Board," *Economic Times*, May 1, 2010.

Pravag, Anjali, "Britannia Looks at More Chocolate Offerings," *Business Line*, April 6, 2010.

Sharma, Praveena, "Britannia May Go for Another Price Revision," *DNA*, December 30, 2009.

Vats, Rachit, "Britannia Eyes Health Dairy Biz," *Hindustan Times*, April 24, 2010.

Compagnie Générale des Établissements Michelin

—■—

23, place des Carmes-Déchaux
Clermont-Ferrand, 63040
France
Telephone: (+33 4) 73-32-20-00
Fax: (+33 1) 45-66-15-53
Web site: http://www.michelin.com

Public Company
Incorporated: 1889 as Michelin et Compagnie
Employees: 109,193
Sales: EUR 14.8 billion ($21.21 billion) (2009)
Stock Exchanges: Euronext Paris
Ticker Symbol: ML
NAICS: 326211 Tire Manufacturing (Except Retreading)

■ ■ ■

Compagnie Générale des Établissements Michelin (Michelin) is the world's largest tire company with outlets in 170 countries. It owns about 70 manufacturing plants located in 19 countries across four continents. Rubber plantations in Brazil provide part of the company's raw materials requirements. The company produces tires and other products under the Michelin, BF Goodrich, Kleber, Taurus, Uniroyal, and other brand names, and also operates tire service centers under the TCi Tire Centers and Euromaster brand names.

Michelin is also a notable publisher of maps and guides, of which it sells 800,000 per year. Although accounting for only a small portion of its revenue, these items have immense promotional value. The stars awarded to restaurants by Michelin Guide Rouge inspectors are among the most coveted accolades of European haute cuisine. Edouard Michelin took over leadership of the company in 1999. However, the fourth-generation Michelin family member died in a boating accident on May 26, 2006. Michel Rollier was named his successor.

19TH-CENTURY ORIGINS

As a tire company, Michelin dates back to the 1880s, when the original Michelin brothers, André and Edouard, took over a rubber products business created by their grandfather, Aristide Barbier, and his cousin, Edouard Daubrée. This firm's premises were in Clermont-Ferrand, in the Auvergne. Set up in 1830 to manufacture sugar, the Daubrée-Barbier enterprise had diversified into rubber several years later at the instigation of Daubrée's Scottish wife, Elizabeth. As a child Elizabeth had played with rubber balls made by her uncle, Charles Macintosh, an inventor who pioneered the use of rubber in waterproofing clothes and gave his name to rubberized raincoats. A rubber workshop was opened at Clermont-Ferrand and was soon making not only rubber balls but also other rubber products, including hoses and drive belts.

A manager ran the firm, at that time also manufacturing agricultural equipment, for a few years after the death of the original partners. Business had declined by 1886, when 33-year-old André Michelin stepped in. He was an entrepreneur in his own right, making picture frames and locks in Paris, and under his management the Clermont-Ferrand enterprise took a turn for

COMPANY PERSPECTIVES

Michelin's corporate mission is to enhance the mobility of people and goods, which is a key factor in economic and social development. Our product and service offering is deeply rooted in a commitment to continuously improving our tires, to make them safer, more durable and more fuel efficient while using fewer raw materials. For the past 120 years, Michelin teams have leveraged their creativity, skills and dedication to bring to market new, improved, longer lasting solutions aligned with customer needs, year after year.

the better. However, André sometimes had to attend to his Paris shops at the expense of Clermont-Ferrand. In 1888 the family prevailed upon Andre's brother Edouard, six years his junior, to abandon his fine arts studies and come to Clermont-Ferrand. The firm, whose most successful line was then rubber brake pads for horse-drawn vehicles, was incorporated as Michelin et Compagnie the following year.

FIRST DETACHABLE TIRE
PATENTED: 1891

In 1889 a cyclist arrived at the workshop asking to have a punctured Dunlop tire repaired. Pneumatic tires, first patented in 1845 but not commercially exploited at the time, had been reintroduced in 1888 by Scotsman John Boyd Dunlop, but were still rare enough to be a curiosity, as solid tires were the norm. Edouard Michelin found the repair a major undertaking, involving three hours of work followed by an all-night drying session. The repair did not hold, but Edouard, struck by the comfortable ride that the troublesome tires gave, set to work on a design that would retain the comfort without the trouble. In 1891 the workshop patented a detachable tire, repairable in minutes rather than hours. That fall the brothers persuaded a cyclist to demonstrate their tires in a 1,200-kilometer race.

Michelin's rider sustained five punctures on the first day. Even so, he won the race, with an eight-hour lead over the favorite. The earliest Michelin tire took 15 minutes to change, but by June 1892 the time was down to two minutes. Michelin organized another race. Nails surreptitiously planted in the road caused 244 punctures, affording ample opportunity to prove how easy repairs were. By 1893, 10,000 cyclists had fitted their vehicles with Michelin tires.

Michelin launched a pneumatic tire for horse-drawn hackney carriages the following year. The fleet of five Paris cabs that test drove the tires gained such an advantage in terms of quietness and comfort that the other cabbies were driven to sabotage. However, soon even the saboteurs were converted, and 600 Paris cabs were running on Michelin tires by 1903. In 1895 Michelin introduced the world's first pneumatic tire for automobiles. Three cars, specially built to test the tire, were entered in a race in June 1895. The Michelin brothers themselves drove one, the Éclair, meaning "forked lightning." Despite frequent punctures, engine fires, and gearbox failures, the Éclair was a success. Only 9 out of 19 competitors finished within the time allowed of 100 hours for 1,209 kilometers. The Éclair was the ninth. This was the first of many races in which Michelin tires distinguished themselves.

THE MICHELIN MAN GREETS
THE 20TH CENTURY

By the dawn of the 20th century pneumatic tires were becoming the norm for the automobile industry, as well as for bicycles, carriages, and cabs. Competition was intense, with 150 tire companies in France alone by 1903. Elsewhere, Pirelli, Dunlop, Goodyear, Goodrich, and Firestone were all entering the field as well. A strong brand image was crucial in this climate, and Michelin came up with a brilliant one. The Michelin man, a rotund figure composed of tires, was born around 1898. His nickname of Monsieur Bibendum came from the caption of an early poster that read *Nunc est bibendum*, a phrase from Horace meaning "Time for a drink." The glass flourished by the convivial Michelin man contained not alcohol but nails and sharp pebbles. Michelin tires, it was implied, would gobble up such objects with no lasting ill effects.

Monsieur Bibendum became one of the most widely recognized logos in the world. Apart from promoting tires, Monsieur Bibendum embellished Michelin guides and maps. The first such publication, the Guide Rouge to France, appeared in 1900. Initially distributed free, it contained tire information along with journey planning advice, including hotel listings. Guides to Europe, North Africa, and Egypt followed, as did an English-language edition of the guide to France in 1909. Michelin also furnished motorists with itineraries via an information bureau.

The company was opening its first foreign subsidiaries about the same time that its foreign guides appeared. A subsidiary was launched in the United Kingdom in 1905, and another in Italy the following year. The acquisition of rubber plantations in Indochina also came in 1905. Meanwhile, tire technology was

KEY DATES

■

1888: Edouard Michelin joins the family rubber manufacturing business.

1891: Company launches its first detachable tire design.

1895: Company launches first pneumatic automobile tire.

1898: The Michelin man, or Monsieur Bibendum, logo debuts.

1910: Company begins publishing road maps.

1946: Company launches its radial tire.

1975: Company opens a manufacturing plant in South Carolina.

1990: Michelin acquires Uniroyal Goodrich and becomes the market leader in the tire industry.

1999: Company acquires Tire Centers LLC in the United States.

2006: Cofounder's great-grandson, Edouard Michelin, dies in a boating accident; Michel Rollier is named his successor.

advancing rapidly. In 1903 Michelin introduced a tire with a sole of leather and studs of steel. The detachable wheel rim came three years later, allowing a car to carry spare Michelin tires, as did the victor of the first ever Grand Prix, at the La Sarthe circuit. By 1913 Michelin had simplified the way wheels were attached to the vehicle, giving a neater solution to the problem of punctures. Motorists could then carry a spare wheel.

A PERIOD OF EXPANSION

Michelin was on the lookout for new applications for its tires. Around 1908 they were starting to be fitted to trucks, using twin wheels to take the heavy weight, a system tested on Clermont-Ferrand buses. Michelin linked its name to the aeronautical industry by instituting a flying competition, offering FRF 100,000 for the first pilot to complete a difficult course culminating in a landing on the peak of the Puy de Dôme mountain, near Clermont-Ferrand. Cynics said the brothers were getting free publicity by setting an impossible task, but in fact the prize was won in 1911, on the third anniversary of its creation.

When World War I came in 1914, Michelin adapted its workshops to the production of bombers for the French air force. It supplied 100 bombers free and the remaining 1,800 at cost. After the war Michelin's

technological developments continued. In 1917 Michelin introduced the Roulement Universel, or all-purpose, tire with molded treads. Two years later the woven canvas infrastructure of previous tires was replaced by parallel cord plies.

Advances in low-pressure tires dramatically extended tire life expectancy during this time. The first hackney carriage tire had been capable of about 129 kilometers, with pressure of 4.3 kilograms per square centimeter. By 1923 there was a car tire with pressure of 2.5 kilograms per square centimeter, able to cover 15,000 kilometers. The 1932 figures were 1.5 kilograms and 24,195 kilometers or more. Improvements to durability and road holding continued throughout the 1930s.

THE INTERWAR YEARS

By 1930 Michelin was the 17th-largest tire vendor in the world. Throughout the 1920s and 1930s the company continued to expand overseas, with tire plants at Karlsruhe, Germany, and in Belgium, Spain, and Holland. The opening of a wire factory in Trento, Italy, illustrated that Michelin was aware of the advantages of controlling the manufacture of components of the tire making process as well as that process itself.

The interwar years brought a surge in the amount of motorized traffic to all parts of the developed world. Michelin produced not only reliable tires but also guides and maps. The company had started to publish road maps as early as 1910, the first maps of France especially designed for motorists. Michelin then extended coverage to more European countries, and to Africa and the United States. It published a series of detailed regional guides, the forerunners of the Guides Verts. Michelin's Information Bureau continued to offer free advice and itineraries, and Michelin campaigned for road numbering and signposting.

The technical advances of the 1930s included the Pilote, a car tire that provided superior road holding by increasing the ratio of width to depth. In 1937 the Metallic, an innovative design reinforcing rubber with steel cords to support heavier truckloads, appeared. U.S. competitors were experimenting with synthetic rubber. Michelin was also researching this technology in the late 1930s, although it was not until after the war that the company began to manufacture butyl for making inner tubes.

In 1935 Michelin, initially in the person of Edouard's son Pierre, went to the rescue of automobile manufacturer Citroën, then bankrupt. Michelin effectively ran Citroën for almost 40 years, until Peugeot took it over in 1974, and together the two companies made up the largest industrial group in France. Assisted by other family members, André and Edouard Michelin remained at Michelin's helm until they died, André in 1931 and Edouard in 1940. On Edouard's death his son-in-law Robert Puiseux took charge.

THE WAR EFFORT

Puiseux led the company through World War II and on to a fertile period of expansion and innovation. The family was closely involved with the resistance movement during World War II, and several Michelins were interned in concentration camps. André's son Marcel died in Buchenwald, and Marcel's son Jean-Pierre was shot in action in Corsica.

Michelin kept going despite these losses, although its German, Italian, and Czech plants were confiscated, and the factory at Cataroux, France, was crippled by Allied bombardments in 1944. Michelin had a long established policy of admitting only employees to its factories. Remarkably, although its French factories were obliged to produce tires for the Nazis, it managed to keep even the Germans off the premises. Inside, the patriotic Michelin workers were "customizing" their products for the occupying forces. Encountering the subzero temperatures of the Russian front, Michelin tires mysteriously disintegrated, but only the ones that were fitted to German vehicles.

Michelin maps were an invaluable weapon in the Allied armory. Michelin provided official maps for the French army at the outbreak of the war, and more than two million were distributed to the liberating forces in 1944. The U.S. War Department reprinted the Guide Rouge for use during the Normandy landings. After the war Michelin, unlike some French companies, was free of any suggestion of Nazi collaboration. It swiftly regained its Italian and German property and reconstructed its bombed-out Cataroux plant.

Michelin then declared a policy of expansion in both the industrialized and the developing world, which would be energetically pursued in the following decades. Many new factories would open in France, producing not only tires but also wire, wheels, and tooling. In Italy, Germany, the United Kingdom, and other parts of Europe, existing plants would be modernized and new ones added.

REVOLUTIONIZING DRIVING: 1946

The year 1946 saw what was arguably Michelin's most important single contribution to tire technology, the radial tire. Instead of a crisscross or cross-ply casing of fabric or steel cords, the radial tire casing was a single

ply of cords placed across the tire, perpendicular to the direction of travel. This technology vastly improved road holding, flexibility, and durability. The radial tire, developed in secret during the German occupation, was commercially launched in 1949 as the X-tire, and Michelin had to expand its capacity rapidly to keep pace with the public demand for these tires.

By 1969, 30 million X-tires per year were rolling off the production lines. Michelin built on its early lead by quickly making radial tires available for more and more vehicle types. During the 1950s X-tires for trucks and earthmovers were launched. Along with other manufacturers, Michelin also began to make tubeless tires. It had patented such a tire in 1930, but had encountered some practical problems. However, during the middle to late 1950s tubeless tires caught on, and by the early 1960s there were tubeless X-tires.

Meanwhile, there were changes at the top of the company. In 1955 François Michelin, the 29-year-old grandson of cofounder Edouard, became *gérant*, or joint managing partner, alongside head partner Robert Puiseux. On Puiseux's retirement in 1960, François became head partner, and over the next 30 years led Michelin to the number one position in the world tire market. Unlike many of its European competitors, which set up agreements with U.S. manufacturers, Michelin had continued to undertake the vast majority of its research and development activities itself. François maintained this policy, and 1963 marked the opening of a new Michelin test center at Ladoux, not far from Clermont-Ferrand.

INTERNATIONAL EXPANSION

The company had been expanding steadily in Europe, and then began to look further afield. During the 1960s factories opened in Nigeria, Algeria, and Vietnam. Michelin also had an eye on the United States, where it had started a sales office in 1948, targeting owners of foreign cars. In 1965 Michelin entered into a contract with Sears, Roebuck to supply replacement tires for U.S. cars. This venture proved so successful that by 1970 Michelin was selling 2.5 million tires per year through its own U.S. outlets.

Overcapacity was felt in the European tire market during the 1970s, but Michelin pursued its expansion elsewhere. In the United States it constructed its first manufacturing plants in South Carolina in 1975 and also built plants in Canada and Brazil. Much research continued to go toward perfecting radial technology. During the mid-1960s the XAS tire made the radial concept available to the fastest cars. In 1979 radial tires would help Jody Scheckter drive his Ferrari to victory as the Formula 1 World Champion.

In the 1970s Michelin developed several new product lines for the long-distance road haulage market. With the introduction of radial tires for aircraft in 1981, and motorcycles in 1987, Michelin could offer radial technology for virtually all types of vehicles. The basic technology continued to improve, with new ranges being launched almost every year. The M series, which appeared in 1985, offered a completely new range of state-of-the-art radial tires. Among these, the MXL became Europe's best-selling tire by 1990, when its replacement, the MXT, was introduced.

THE UNIROYAL DEAL: 1990

In 1960 Michelin had been the 10th-largest tire manufacturer in the world, but by 1980 it was second only to Goodyear. The acquisition of of the U.S. tire company Uniroyal Goodrich in 1990 made Michelin indisputably the market leader. However, the Uniroyal deal was concluded just as a major recession hit the automobile and tire market. Faced with a loss of FRF 5.27 billion for 1990, Michelin in April 1991 had to cut costs by laying off 15 percent of its workforce. Not the first but the largest round of job cuts during that period, this was an especially painful step for an employer that had encouraged its workers to see themselves as participants in the enterprise.

François Michelin told the press that the main problem was not the acquisition of Uniroyal, but pressure from the automobile industry, which in the prior decade had forced tire prices down by 50 percent in real terms. In 1991, despite the pessimism expressed by some analysts about Michelin's prospects, the company itself was looking forward to reaping the benefits of the Uniroyal acquisition when the economy emerged from recession. The strengths of the two companies in the U.S. replacement tire market were complementary, and North America represented more than one-third of the total tire market. Michelin also expanded its footholds in Japan, Thailand, and South America.

Michelin continued to innovate and expand during the 1990s. The company targeted the booming Asian markets for expansion and went head-to-head with Japan's Bridgestone and other major tire makers. After the opening of its first joint venture factory with Thailand's Siam Cement in 1988, Michelin's presence in that country increased, with new factories added in 1992 and 1993. The two companies opened a fourth factory in the Philippines in 1995. Michelin entered China a year later with a joint venture with Shen Yang Tire Factory, opening a new plant in Shen Yang.

CONTINUED GROWTH: 1991–99

Michelin established its Euromaster service center chain in Europe, acquiring a number of existing chains across Europe and converting them to the Euromaster format, launched in 1991. Michelin moved deeper into Eastern Europe, buying the largest tire manufacturer in Poland, Stomil-Olsztyn, in 1995, followed by leading Hungarian rubber producer Taurus in 1996. One year later Michelin enhanced its wheel production with the acquisition of Germany's Kronprinz GA. Meanwhile, in the United States Michelin recovered from the recession and with its Michelin, Goodrich, and Uniroyal brands, captured a leading share of the U.S. tire market.

On the consumer front, Michelin introduced the "green tire" in 1992, capable of reducing pollution and increasing fuel efficiency. Later in the decade, the company unveiled its revolutionary new PAX tire and wheel "run-flat" system, capable of rolling for as much as 80 miles after a puncture. In 1999 the company debuted a tubeless tire for mountain bicycles. The company boosted not only its automobile tires, but also its heavy vehicle tires. In 1998 Michelin opened a new facility in South Carolina to produce "Earthmover" tires, such as the 3.92-meter-tall low-pressure tire capable of supporting loads up to 600 tons.

Michelin boosted its U.S. presence and extended its service operations with the 1999 acquisition of Tire Centers LLC, the leading independent tire distributor in the United States. In 2001 Michelin unveiled a new tire design for the Concorde jet, which had been grounded after an accident two years earlier. Concorde operations ceased in 2003.

François Michelin formally appointed youngest son Edouard to take over leadership of the company in 1999. The elder Michelin, who had by then reached the retirement age of 72, nonetheless extended his own contract to remain with the company for another three years. The following year, the massive recall of more than 4.5 million Firestone tires in the United States opened a new opportunity for the French company. Michelin ramped up production to help fill the gap left by its U.S. rival, and along the way managed to win contracts to outfit a number of new car designs. The boost proved short-lived, however. By the middle of 2001 the dip in the U.S. economy, responsible for a dramatic drop-off in new car purchases, sent Michelin's U.S. revenues plunging.

MICHELIN IN THE 21ST CENTURY

Nevertheless, revenues grew dramatically during 2001 due in part to the company's establishment of Michelin

Shanghai Warrior Tire Co. Ltd. in China and the acquisition of two Romanian tire plants from Tofan Grup SA. With 2001 tire sales of $13.4 billion, Michelin stood as the largest tire manufacturer in the world at that time.

Growth over the next several years stemmed from international expansion and new product development. During 2002 the company broke ground on its factory in Davydovo, Russia. The facility produced its first tire in July 2003 and officially opened the following year. Michelin also partnered with Apollo Tyres Ltd. to produce radial truck tires in India. In 2005 Michelin tires were on the maiden flight of the Airbus A380, the world's largest passenger aircraft at the time. The company launched its first New York City Michelin Red Guide that year. During 2006 the company debuted the Michelin Tweel, a non-pneumatic wheel concept that did not contain pressurized air and was puncture-proof.

On May 26, 2006, Edouard Michelin was killed in boating accident while bass fishing off the coast of Brittany. While the investigation proved inconclusive, experts believed his ship was hit by a freak wave known to happen on what was considered to be a dangerous stretch of French coastline. Co-managing partner Michel Rollier quickly took the helm and was faced with managing the company through this crisis while battling rising raw material costs. Amid fierce competition and climbing prices for steel, rubber, and oil the company worked to cut production costs in Europe and North America by as much as 20 percent.

BATTLING THE TOUGH ECONOMY: 2007 AND BEYOND

By trimming expenses and focusing on growth in China, Brazil, Russia, India, and Vietnam, Michelin resumed sales growth in 2007. The company launched its Energy Saver tire that year, which had nearly 20 percent lower rolling resistance than the typical passenger car tire. During 2008 the company introduced its first Hong Kong and Macau Michelin Guides.

By 2008 high raw material costs, an oversupply of product, and a drop in demand took their toll on Michelin's bottom line. Due to these factors, Michelin was forced to lay off nearly 7 percent of its employees while shuttering plants in Alabama and Ota, Japan, in 2009. The company's sales fell by nearly 10 percent in 2009 while net income fell to EUR 104 million.

Despite the drop in sales and profits, Michelin fared better than many of its competitors and was positioned to take advantage of growth, especially in what were called the BRIC countries, which included Brazil, Russia, India, and China. It produced 150 million tires in 2009 and remained in a close race for the top position in the industry with competitor Bridgestone.

The company launched its first global advertising campaign in 2009. The ads were rolled out in North America and were expected to be seen in more than 55 countries by 2011. Based on the tagline "The Right Tire Changes Everything," Michelin claimed the company's tires would save money, would last longer than the competition's products, and would enable drivers to make quick stops in wet or challenging driving conditions. While Michelin had a long history of success behind it, the company would need to stay one step ahead of its competitors in order to remain an industry leader in the years ahead.

Alison Classe
Updated, M. L. Cohen; Christina M. Stansell

PRINCIPAL SUBSIDIARIES

Compagnie Financière Michelin (Switzerland); Manufacture Française des Pneumatiques Michelin (40%).

PRINCIPAL COMPETITORS

Bridgestone Corporation; Continental AG; The Goodyear Tire & Rubber Company.

FURTHER READING

Betts, Paul, "Michelin Races to Re-engineer Itself for 21st Century," *Financial Times*, June 4, 2010.

Davis, Bruce, "Michelin Going Forward after Leader's Death," *Rubber & Plastics News*, June 19, 2006.

Hollinger, Peggy, "Tyre Company Treads Prudently through the Downturn," *Financial Times*, January 6, 2010.

Kanter, James, "Michelin Acts to Stabilize Leadership," *International Herald Tribune*, May 30, 2006.

"Michelin Regains Traction," *Automotive News Europe*, June 25, 2007.

"Michelin Restructuring Brings to Profit in 2009," *Les Echos*, February 15, 2010.

"Michelin Teams Up with Apollo Tyres," *Rubber & Plastics News*, December 8, 2003.

Morais, Richard C., "The Old Lady Is Burning Rubber," *Forbes*, November 26, 2007.

Revill, John, "Punctureless 'Tweels' among Tyre Company's Innovations," *Birmingham Post*, February 15, 2006.

Compal Electronics Inc.

---

581 Jui-Kuang Road
Neihu
Taipei, 114
Taiwan
Telephone: (+886 2) 8797-8588
Fax: (+886 2) 2659-1566
Web site: http://www.compal.com

Public Company
Incorporated: 1984
Employees: 3,345
Sales: TWD 626.2 billion ($19.42 billion) (2009)
Stock Exchanges: Taiwan
Ticker Symbol: 2324
NAICS: 334119 Other Computer Peripheral Equipment
    Manufacturing

■ ■ ■

Headquartered in Taiwan, Compal Electronics Inc. is a leading manufacturer of notebook computers, display products, automotive electronics, and other digital consumer electronics. Beyond Taiwan, the company has operations in the People's Republic of China (where it manufactures products at its Kunshan factory), Vietnam, Poland, Brazil, and the United States. In 2010 Compal employed a workforce of approximately 3,345 people. On numerous occasions the company has been recognized by *Business Week* as one of the world's leading 100 information technologies companies.

FORMATIVE YEARS

Compal traces its roots back to 1984, when the company was established with $2 million in capital. CRT monitor production commenced in 1985, and the company began making laptop personal computers in 1989. A major setback took place in 1988, however, when the company suffered a factory fire that nearly resulted in its demise. It was also in 1988 that Compal President Barry Lam left the company to start Quanta Computer, which would become a major rival.

Several key milestones were reached during the first half of the 1990s. In addition to bringing its Pin-cheng factory online in Taoyuan, the company unveiled the world's first 386SX notebook computer in 1990. Compal began trading on the Taiwan Stock Exchange two years later, and received ISO 9001 certification in 1994.

The production of 10.4-inch LCD monitors began in 1995. Compal received Taiwan's Symbol of Excellence award in 1997 for a space-saving LCD monitor that included features such as low power consumption. That year, Compal transferred its CRT monitor production to China and achieved ISO 14001 certification. In 1998 the company achieved a $250 million deal to supply LG Semicon Co. with dynamic random access memory chips and thin-film transistor LCDs. For the year, sales surpassed $1.1 billion.

EARLY GROWTH

A number of key developments took place in 1999. That year, notebook computer shipments totaled 700,000 units, and were projected to reach 1.2 million units in 2000. It was also in 1999 that Compal revealed plans to begin selling the True 500, a personal computer kit for do-it-yourself assembly. Priced at $500, the True 500 would be sold online, with first-year sales projected to reach 12,000 units.

In May 1999 Compal completed construction of a second monitor facility in China. Physical growth that year also included the establishment of a new headquarters facility in the Neihu District in Taipei. During the second half of the year Compal revealed plans to enter the handheld computer and server markets. Via a tie-up with Qualcomm, the company also indicated it would enter the communication and network sectors and begin manufacturing code-division multiple access (CDMA) phones.

Compal's notebook computer production levels reached 1.15 million units in 1999. During the latter part of the year, Toshiba Corp. began outsourcing the production of its PX100 notebook computer to Compal, as part of an effort to reduce costs. One final achievement in 1999 was the company's receipt of China's Silver National Award of Excellence.

ENTERING THE 21ST CENTURY

Compal ushered in the new millennium with sales of $2.38 billion. In 2000 production of 15-inch CRT monitors began in China. Midway through 2001 Compal revealed that it would provide approximately two million monitors to NEC, which had plans to purchase $10 billion worth of computer parts from Taiwan over the course of five years.

For the year, Compal's capital increased to $621.7 million, up from $498.5 million in 2000. By this time the company had established operations in Taiwan, China, England, the Netherlands, the United States, and South Korea. In recognition of its performance, *Money Magazine* named Compal as one of Asia's best-managed companies.

By 2002 Compal was under the leadership of President Ray Chen. At that time the company completed construction of a 30,000-square-meter notebook computer plant in China's Jiangsu Province. Initially, the facility would produce approximately 100,000 notebook computers per month. For the year, notebook shipments from mainland China were expected to reach two million units, representing about half of the company's total notebook production.

In October 2002 Salomon Smith Barney completed a $345 million convertible bond issue for Compal. By this time the company was focused on bolstering its mobile handset business. Manufacturing was under way for leading companies such as Motorola Inc., as well as emerging companies like China's Haier Corp. and East-com Corp. Compal indicated that phones would account for 25 percent of sales in 2003, compared to 10 percent in 2002.

Compal ended 2002 by receiving approval from the Federal Communications Commission (FCC) for the sale of a new smart phone using Microsoft Windows software. The company also partnered with United Microelectronics Corp. to invest in the U.S.-based tablet computer developer Motion Computing Co. Annual sales totaled $3.63 billion. In addition, Compal was named to *Business Week*'s Info Tech 100 ranking.

MAJOR MANUFACTURING INROADS

Compal began 2003 by announcing that it had received an order to produce tablet personal computers for Gateway. A second notebook computer factory was brought online in mainland China at this time. According to reports from industry analysts, Compal was the only company in Taiwan producing laptops for companies such as Toshiba, Dell Computer, and Hewlett-Packard. In addition, the company also received orders from Apple Computer.

On the product front, Compal introduced a new camera handset in 2003, as well as the first 15.4-inch Intel Centrino CPU notebook computer. In December 2003 Compal began producing plasma display television panels. Revenues increased to $4.71 billion, and the company once again was named to *Business Week*'s Info Tech 100 listing.

Compal kicked off 2004 by acquiring a 40 percent, $9.8 million ownership interest in the DVD player manufacturer Accesstek Inc. The deal with Micro Star International Co. Ltd. was made to facilitate the company's expansion into the home media center market. In addition to DVD players, Compal was concentrating on the production of LCD TVs, server-computers, and wireless local area network equipment. In addition, the company began producing LCD projectors for Hitachi Corp.

KEY DATES

1984: The company is established with $2 million in capital.
1992: Compal begins trading on the Taiwan Stock Exchange.
1999: A new headquarters facility is established in Neihu, Taipei.
2005: The company moves all of its notebook computer production to mainland China.
2010: Motorola's European cable modem business is acquired.

Notebook computer production continued to remain a focus during the middle of the decade. By 2003, Compal and competitor Quanta Computer Inc. had cornered 41 percent of the global production market. As part of its expansion strategy, Compal announced it would establish a third notebook computer factory in China, with a monthly production capacity of 2.1 million notebook computers. In November the company indicated that its annual notebook production would grow from 7.5 million units in 2004 to approximately 10 million units in 2005.

MANUFACTURING RELOCATES TO CHINA

Compal ended 2004 by announcing plans to move all of its notebook computer production to mainland China in 2005. At that time, the company's facility in northern Taiwan was slated to be repurposed as a research and development center. Compal ended the year with sales of $6.32 billion. In recognition of the company's achievements, President Ray Chen was named Taiwan's best CEO by *Institutional Investor*.

Compal started 2005 with high hopes for its cell phone operations. Specifically, the company projected substantial growth in its Compal Electronics Inc. and Compal Communications Inc. subsidiaries. With handset shipments expected to reach 16 million units in 2005, the company was poised to become Taiwan's leading handset manufacturer.

Midway through the year Compal received orders to produce 100 models of third-generation mobile handsets for Motorola Inc. The company ended the year on a high note. In December subsidiary Compal Communications became Taiwan's leading cell phone handset manufacturer when its shipments exceeded five

million units, setting a national sales record. Overall, the company generated sales of $7.03 billion.

In August 2006 Compal invested in Arcadyan Technology Corp., a supplier of devices such as home gateways and access points. Two months later the company suffered a setback when Toshiba revealed plans to begin sourcing notebook computers from competitor Asustek in May 2008. Difficulties continued in November, when Compal appealed a California court's ruling that it had infringed upon patents held by Korea-based Samsung Electronics Co. Ltd.

PRODUCT EXPANSION

It was around this time that President Ray Chen announced that the company had earmarked between TWD 3 billion and TWD 4 billion to begin acquiring notebook computer components and parts manufacturers, especially makers of computer cases and cell phone handset cases. The company finished 2006 on a strong note, shipping 1.78 million notebook computers in December alone. For the year, Compal's capital increased to TWD 38.1 billion, and revenues reached $9.49 billion.

Heading into 2007, Compal put a strong emphasis on the production of LCD TVs, shipments of which were expected to more than double by the year's end, reaching 500,000 units. That year the company rolled out a new series of digital high-definition (HD) TVs. Additionally, Compal introduced its mobile Internet device (MID) product. Notebook computer sales remained strong. During the first quarter alone the company shipped 4.9 million units, an increase of 80 percent from the same period in 2006.

Physical growth also continued. A second overseas manufacturing location was planned in Vietnam. In addition to expanding production at its existing plant in Kunshan, China, Compal constructed a second plant in Kunshan. The new facility focused on the manufacturing and sale of molds, molding devices, and mold parts.

Compal continued to receive industry recognition during 2007. In addition to being included in *Business Week*'s Info Tech 100 for the seventh consecutive time, the company was named one of Asia's Top 50 Enterprises by *Forbes*. Compal ended the year with sales of $13.02 billion and capital of TWD 38.6 billion.

CONTINUED GROWTH AND EXPANSION

During the latter years of the decade Compal was ranked as the second-largest original device manufacturer in the world, with a global workforce of

20,000 people. The company began 2008 by securing new business from Chinese computer manufacturer Lenovo Group Ltd. Compal was among three Taiwanese manufacturers (including Quanta Computer and Wistron Corp.) chosen to produce Lenovo's IdeaPad. In addition, Compal also secured a manufacturing contract with Syntax-Brillian Corp. to produce 300,000 LCD HDTVs.

Product innovation continued to be an important theme at Compal in 2008. The company benefited from a new laptop production contract from Dell Computer, which chose it to produce a competitor to Apple Inc.'s MacBook Air. In addition, Compal begin producing netbook computers. These small, low-cost laptops were aimed at consumers who mainly wanted to access the Internet and stay connected to social network sites like Facebook.

Geographic expansion continued in 2008 as the company established new notebook computer service factories in Brazil and Poland. In addition, production at the company's new factory in Vietnam's northern province of Vinh Phuc was slated to begin in 2009. By 2013 Compal planned to shift 50 percent of its computer production to the $500 million plant. Compal ended 2009 with revenues of $12.83 billion, and capital of TWD 38.8 billion.

INDUSTRY LEADER

In mid-2009 Compal chose Teradyne, Inc.'s, TestStation LH in-circuit test systems to provide testing for the high-volume production of both netbook and notebook computers. In August of that year the company appointed the Bank of New York Mellon as the depositary bank for its sponsored Global Depositary Receipt program. Compal was hopeful that the bank could help it attract additional global investors.

In late 2009 Compal revealed plans to invest $180 million to construct additional facilities in China's Kunshan City. In addition to four plants, plans for a new headquarters facility, as well as a research and development center, were announced. By this time Compal held an estimated 23 percent of the global notebook computer market.

Compal began 2010 by acquiring Motorola's European cable modem business. Following delays that were attributed to the global economic recession, construction of the company's $500 million plant in Vietnam continued, and the facility was slated to open during the second half of the year. In addition, Compal announced that it would increase the salaries of its workers in mainland China as part of a retention effort.

During its first quarter-century of operations, Compal had firmly established itself as a leading technology manufacturer. In addition to an expanding global footprint and relationships with many of the world's technology companies, the company continued to broaden its horizons by branching out into new product areas. With this in mind, Compal appeared to have excellent prospects for continued success in 2011 and beyond.

Paul R. Greenland

PRINCIPAL SUBSIDIARIES

Bizcom Electronics, Inc. (USA); CEB Eletronica Do Brasil Industria E Comercio Ltda (Brazil); Łódź (Poland).

PRINCIPAL COMPETITORS

Inventec Corporation; Quanta Computer Inc.; Wistron Corporation.

FURTHER READING

"Compal Ventures into Multimedia Business by Acquiring Accesstek," *Asia Africa Intelligence Wire*, January 2, 2004.

Einhorn, Bruce, and Susan Zegel, "The Underdog Nipping at Quanta's Heels; Notebook Maker Compal Is Closing the Sales Gap with Its Archrival," *Business Week*, October 21, 2002, p. 26.

"Quanta, Compal Shift Notebook PC Production to Mainland China," *Asia Africa Intelligence Wire*, December 30, 2004.

"Taiwan Compal's Laptop Plant Back on Track in Vietnam," *AsiaPulse News*, March 8, 2010.

"US-Based Motorola Sells European Cable Modem Business to Compal," *Broadband Monthly*, February 2010, p. 8.

Craftmatic Organization Inc.

3050 Tillman Drive, Suite 200
Bensalem, Pennsylvania 19020
U.S.A.
Telephone: (215) 639-1310
Fax: (215) 639-9744
Web site: http://www.craftmatic.com

Private Company
Founded: 1966
Employees: 150
Sales: $48.6 million (2008 est.)
NAICS: 337910 Mattress Manufacturing; 442110
    Furniture Stores

■ ■ ■

Craftmatic Organization Inc. is a Bensalem, Pennsylvania-based manufacturer and direct marketer of Craftmatic Adjustable Beds, which are also sold through independent distributors and licensees in the United States and Australia. The high-end beds, similar to hospital beds in that they can be adjusted mechanically, offer such amenities as variable speed massage options, personal temperature control, and wireless remote controls. They are available in single, double, queen, and king sizes, as well as dual configurations. In addition to the standard 80-inch length, all beds are available in 74-inch and 84-inch lengths.

The company claims that more than one million of its adjustable beds are in use. Over the years, Craftmatic commercials have become well-known late night television fare. The company has also acquired unwanted notoriety for questionable sales practices, mostly targeting the elderly, which have led to regulatory fines and admonitions. Craftmatic is led by its longtime president, Stanley A. Kraftsow.

KRAFTSOW TURNS TO SELLS: 1966

Although Stanley Kraftsow began his business career as an accountant, he was no stranger to sales. His father, Edward Kraftsow, oversaw a stable of door-to-door salesmen who from the 1930s to the 1950s sold household goods on an installment plan in Philadelphia, Pennsylvania. Later he owned a small store in the city, the Contour Chair Lounge Co., which sold lounge chairs produced by a St. Louis chair manufacturer. Born in 1939, the younger Kraftsow graduated from Temple University in Philadelphia in 1961 with a degree in accounting. He then went to work for a large area accounting firm but eventually grew discontented. "It was a long drawn-out process to move up the ladder," he told the *Philadelphia Inquirer* in 1986. "You were considered a dummy. I just didn't see any immediate payback." In 1966 he quit and went to work for his father selling contour chairs, giving up a $165 weekly salary as an accountant for the $25 his father paid him to start out.

Kraftsow proved to be an energetic salesman. He quickly learned about a California contour-chair distributor that was doing well with direct sales to homes. He followed suit and enjoyed success. Just three months after launching his new career Kraftsow took charge of the store following the death of his father. He

COMPANY PERSPECTIVES

You'll never understand how much a Craftmatic Electric bed may change your life, until you get one. There's no other adjustable bed in the world like it. With superior construction, comfort, and adjustability!

was then able to gradually exit retail selling and devote all of his attention to direct selling in homes. He also acquired territorial distributorships from the chair manufacturer as they became available, adding Maryland and later Ohio.

COMPANY BEGINS SELLING ADJUSTABLE BEDS: 1974

Kraftsow supported his sales efforts with an increasing amount of advertising, resulting in a growth in sales from $160,000 in 1966, the last year before direct selling, to $4 million in 1974. It was also in 1974 that Kraftsow began selling adjustable beds in the Greater Philadelphia area. Three years later he stopped selling chairs and organized a wholesale network to distribute the beds, supported by local and cable television advertising that mostly ran late at night. Kraftsow also stretched his advertising dollars by making use of discounted rates, willing to be preempted by other advertisers who would pay the full rate. Paying just 20 percent of that amount made it worthwhile to Kraftsow to be flexible.

The televisions ads, as well as the brochures that were sent after viewers called a toll-free telephone number, were just the first step in selling adjustable beds. Follow-up calls sought to arrange an in-home appointment during which Craftmatic used a variety of aggressive techniques to close a sale, as revealed by an examination of the methods conducted by *Forbes* in 1990.

After completing a weeklong training session, Craftmatic salesmen followed a tight script, which in the 1980s would include a 15-minute videotape. The salesmen were trained to ask about medical conditions and encourage potential customers to end their suffering by purchasing an adjustable bed. Only then was the list price revealed. That number could then be whittled down. If necessary the salesman, who had already triggered his beeper, could ask to call his office as he packed his materials. He would then have a phone conversation

with a "Mr. Cohen," portrayed as the "big boss" who was in reality anyone available in the "Cohen room" set up to handle these next-level situations.

Customers were allowed to listen to the conversation that revealed a testimonial had fallen through. They were then given an opportunity to receive a discount if they stepped in to write a testimonial letter and allowed their picture to be taken. "Mr. Cohen" would also speak with them if further pressure was needed to close the sale. "The whole thing is like a bad play," one former salesman told *Forbes*. "But if the salesmen don't call the Cohen room, if you don't do it the way they want it, they fire you. Or they don't give you leads for a few days."

BUSINESS PRACTICES QUESTIONED

Many of the sales leads were developed through direct-mail pieces touting a $400 Craftmatic bed, which only a handful of people actually bought. They were steered instead to the far more expensive premium product. What critics would call bait-and-switch, Kraftsow and his attorney insisted was merely "upselling," because the inexpensive product was actually kept in stock. Nevertheless, in the late 1980s the company signed several consent decrees and assurance of voluntary compliance agreements with both state and federal agencies, including a May 1989 consent decree with the Pennsylvania Bureau of Consumer Protection connected to bait-and-switch charges.

Two years earlier the company was fined by the state for misleading customers with discounts based on such factors as age and health, as well as for offering "free" prizes for the purchase of a bed that were converted into a discount if the customer agreed to forfeit the prize. Consent decrees were also signed with the states of Washington and Oregon. In 1985 Craftmatic signed a consent agreement with the Federal Trade Commission to answer a claim that it did not adequately respond to warranties on beds sold through distributors, failing to notify customers that they would be responsible for shipping costs on beds returned for repair. Twice in the 1980s Craftmatic established $300,000 restitution funds.

CONTOUR CHAIR LOUNGE, INC., ACQUIRED: 1983

Kraftsow first became involved in manufacturing in 1980 but fared poorly, losing money for the next two years. The plant and assets were then sold to Missouri's Leggett & Platt Inc., which became Craftmatic's exclusive supplier of adjustable beds. In 1983 Craftmatic

KEY DATES

1966: Stanley Kraftsow begins selling contour chairs in his father's store.
1974: Kraftsow begins selling adjustable beds.
1986: The company is taken public as Craftmatic/Contour Industries Inc.
1992: Contour Chair unit is dissolved and the company name is changed to Craftmatic Organization Inc.
2010: U.K. subsidiary closes.

also acquired Contour Chair Lounge, Inc., which had struggled in recent years, and resumed selling adjustable chairs. Sales increased from $14.1 million in fiscal 1983 to $34 million in fiscal 1985. A year later Kraftsow took the company public as Craftmatic/Contour Industries Inc. The March 1986 stock offering raised about $8.5 million for the company, and Kraftsow pocketed another $5 million but retained control of the corporation, whose shares traded on an over-the-counter basis. The company closed the 1980s by recording sales of $51 million.

Notoriety continued to dog Craftmatic in the 1990s. Kraftsow also faced a class-action lawsuit related to the accuracy of the documents used in Craftmatic's initial public stock offering. The matter was settled in 1991. In the meantime, the New York State attorney general sued Craftmatic in 1991 for false advertising and deceptive sales practices that included claims the adjustable beds could cure arthritis and heart disease, and curb snoring and wrinkles. A settlement was reached two years later.

In 1992 the company ran afoul of authorities in Massachusetts over what was considered deceptive advertising for its Contour Chair line and entered into a consent agreement. The company also settled complaints in Indiana, Texas, and Iowa in 1992. More damaging was the investigative television program *Inside Edition*, which ran an exposé on Craftmatic's lounge chair business. The report challenged the company's claim that the chairs were custom made. Sales plummeted and in 1992 Craftmatic disbanded the Contour Chair Lounge Company. Craftmatic/Contour subsequently changed its name to Craftmatic Organization Inc.

SALES DIP: 1992

Craftmatic's sales fell to $12 million in 1992 and the company posted a $3.4 million loss. The price of its

stock also declined to a low of 63 cents, and Craftmatic was subsequently taken private. The company attempted to diversify, establishing a subsidiary called Chicken Wizard of Media Inc., which owned and operated franchised chicken restaurants, but it made no material impact on the balance sheet, and adjustable beds remained Craftmatic's core business. Kraftsow looked overseas for new sales opportunities. In 1993 he established an operation in the United Kingdom, which was followed by a branch in the Republic of Ireland and a subsidiary in Australia.

As Craftmatic entered the new century it appeared to be well positioned to take advantage of a graying baby boom generation that as it grew older would enter the company's primary customer demographic. However, the company continued to court controversy, both in the United States and the United Kingdom. Craftmatic ran into trouble in Florida, leading to a three-year investigation by the state attorney general's office in response to customer complaints, mostly from retirees who said they were pressured into buying beds they did not want or could not afford. The matter was settled in 2007 when an agreement was reached that included $130,000 in consumer restitution. The company also had to pay the attorney general's office $53,540 for costs and contribute $20,000 to the Seniors vs. Crime program, a nonprofit organization devoted to curbing the victimization of the elderly.

Craftmatic also ran into trouble with new federal do-not-call regulations. The company and three subsidiaries were accused of running a sweepstakes in which consumers filled out entry forms in hopes of winning a free Craftmatic bed. They were told that their phone numbers would serve as the entry number. They were then subjected to sales calls without granting permission or having been notified. In 2007 Craftmatic agreed to pay a $4.4 million penalty to the Federal Trade Commission.

INVESTIGATIVE TELEVISION PROGRAM EXPOSE: 2008

Craftmatic also had to contend in 2008 with another *Inside Edition* exposé, which used hidden cameras and a 71-year-old actress to record some of the company's sales practices, reminiscent of the Cohen room, including a call to the "home office," where someone on the other end offered further discounts to close a sale. The salesperson claimed that the bed had cured his acid reflux disease and told the actress it could do the same for her.

In addition, the program sent a producer posing as a trainee to record a sales training session. The independent contractor leading the session urged the salespeople to put on a show. "The bigger the show, the more the dough," she told them, and also emphasized the need to close the sale that very day. "Not tomorrow, not after they talk to their doctor, their daughter, their son … send their granddaughter through college, help out their, you know, blood-sucking leechy kids." *Inside Edition* shared the footage with Missouri's U.S. Senator Claire McCaskill, a member of the Senate Committee on Aging, who then sent a letter to the Federal Trade Commission requesting an investigation.

Craftmatic also encountered problems in Australia and the United Kingdom where sales practices also came into question. In 2010 Kraftsow decided to close the doors of Craftmatic UK Ltd., which went into voluntary liquidation in May of that year. Although the parent company's reputation was sullied in many quarters, the Craftmatic brand was still well known and the company continued to find buyers for its adjustable bed. However, Craftmatic's longtime president was by then in his 80s, leaving the long-term prospects for the company very much in doubt.

Ed Dinger

PRINCIPAL SUBSIDIARIES

Craftmatic Industries; Craftmatic Pty Ltd.

PRINCIPAL COMPETITORS

Sealy Corporation; Simmons Company; Temper-Pedic Inc.

FURTHER READING

Binzen, Peter, "For Him, Success Is a Custom Fit, and He's Adjusted Well," *Philadelphia Inquirer*, July 7, 1986, p. C3.

Burstein, Jon, "Bed Maker Craftmatic Settles Attorney General's Complaint," *South Florida Sun-Sentinel*, August 21, 2007.

Davidson, Paul, "Do-Not-Call Violators Get Zinged $7.7M in Fines; Bedmaker Craftmatic Agrees to Pay $4.4 Million," *USA Today*, November 8, 2007, p. B1.

"Firm to Stop Selling Lounge Chairs, Blames TV Program," *Tulsa World*, May 23, 1972, p. C8.

Meeks, Fleming, "'Upselling,'" *Forbes*, January 8, 1990, p. 70.

Moriarty, Rick, "Craftmatic Settles N.Y. Lawsuit," *Post-Standard* (Syracuse, N.Y.), August 13, 1993, p. A1.

Wallace, David, "For Most, Things Are Looking Up," *Philadelphia Business*, January 4, 1993, p. 8.

Dead River Company

———■———

55 Broadway
Bangor, Maine 04401-5201
U.S.A.
Telephone: (207) 947-8641
Fax: (207) 990-0828
Web site: http://www.deadriver.com

Private Company
Incorporated: 1907 as Dead River Timberland Company
Employees: 1,000
Sales: $75 million (2009 est.)
NAICS: 424720 Petroleum and Petroleum Products
  Merchant Wholesalers (Except Bulk Stations and
  Terminals)

■ ■ ■

Dead River Company is a family-owned, private company based in Bangor, Maine, that is involved in a variety of businesses. It is one of northern New England's largest distributors of petroleum products, providing both homes and businesses in Maine, New Hampshire, and Vermont with heating oil, kerosene, propane, diesel fuel, and gasoline. Dead River offers service plans, including 24-hour burner service, and sells and installs a variety of propane stoves, fireplace, and space heaters.

It also sells and installs boilers, furnaces, and water heaters. The company's TankSure program monitors and tests above-ground fuel oil storage tanks. In addition, Dead River operates a regional chain of about 20 convenience stores, all located in Maine, that sell gasoline on a retail basis. The company is also involved outside of northern New England in it real estate investments. Dead River maintains offices in Maine, New Hampshire, and Vermont. Dead River continues to be owned by the founding Hutchins family.

COMPANY INCORPORATED 1909

Charles P. Hutchins cofounded Dead River Company in 1909, but the roots of the enterprise were actually planted two years earlier when he and partner William C. Atwater brought some timberland in Maine. Hutchins had been born into modest circumstances near Rutland, Vermont, in 1865. After graduating from high school, he moved to Boston and found work as a coal salesman with a Boston coal wholesaler, Haddock & Company. It was here that he met Atwater, a New Yorker.

At the turn of the new century the ambitious young men left Haddock to start their own coal wholesaling business, which because it was about 90 percent owned by Atwater took the named William C. Atwater & Co. The company maintained its headquarters in the Wall Street district of New York City, but Hutchins, who was also secretary of the corporation, remained in Boston to serve as the New England sales representative.

One of Hutchins's accounts was the Great Northern Paper Company, whose need for coal to keep its boilers stoked was as great as its need for capital. Often Great Northern paid Hutchins in notes. The company was interested in opening a new mill but stretched for funds it was not able to purchase the timberland to feed the grinders and chippers. Great

Northern's energetic owner, Garrett Schenk, persuaded Hutchins and Atwater to purchase the township he had in mind. In exchange, Great Northern would contract for the land's timber. More importantly, Great Northern would be in the market for more coal. Hutchins and Atwater formed Carrabassett Timberland Company to make the acquisition in 1907, and were so pleased with the venture that in 1909 they again followed Schenk's recommendation and bought another timber township on a remote stretch of the Dead River in western Maine. To make that purchase, Hutchins and Atwater formed the Dead River Timberland Company in October 1909.

Hutchins and Atwater would purchase additional timber lands, some of which was not contracted by Great Northern. As a result, the coal men became directly involved in cutting and processing. Hutchins's son, Curtis Marshall Hutchins, began working for Dead River during the summers, starting in 1923. After graduating from Williams College in 1928, he spent a year at the University of Maine School of Forestry and then joined the family business. By this time the stock market had crashed and the United States was plunged into the Great Depression, so that by 1932 there was virtually no demand for Dead River's timber. It was also in 1932 that 67-year-old Charles Hutchins suffered a stroke and his son took charge of Dead River. Atwater also had sons, but they were older, already well involved in the coal business and lacked the forestry training of the younger Hutchins.

OIL BUSINESS ACQUIRED: 1936

Hutchins knowledge of forestry would be less important than finding creative ways to make money to pay the taxes on Dead River's timberlands. The company became involved in pulp production and in this pursuit acquired a pulpwood broker, Webber & Tupper, in 1936. Its operating partner was William Tupper and its financial partner was Alburnie E. Webber, a Bangor, Maine, Ford automobile dealer and a franchised distributor of Esso Petroleum products.

Upon Tupper's unexpected death, Webber offered to sell Webber & Tupper to Dead River, a deal that would include four gas stations and a small petroleum bulk storage plant with two 30,000 gallon split tanks that held kerosene, heating oil, and two grades of gasoline. Hutchins initially planned to divest these assets but his most talented employee, Clyde Jacobs, needed something to do after the liquidation of a plywood company that failed to work out for Dead River. Moreover, many people at the time were making the switch from coal to oil to heat their homes.

Dead River benefited from a sharp increase in gasoline sales in 1938 and the company soon decided to expand its oil business as well. In 1940 it bought a small water terminal in Calais, Maine, to cut transportation costs. To run this enterprise, the Dead River Oil Co. was formed and established its headquarters in Portland, Maine. Hutchins's presidency at Dead River was interrupted by World War II when he served as an officer in the U.S. Navy. Because of his unique qualifications, however, he was dispatched by the navy in 1943 to Washington when he was put in charge of the paper division of the War Production Board.

Following his discharge from the service, Hutchins resumed his duties at Dead River. In 1947 he became chairman of the board as well as president. The postwar years were also a time of expansion for Dead River on a number of fronts. In 1946 the Oil Division began distributing bottled gas as well as heating oils. To support this business, Dead River acquired Citizens Gas Company in 1951. Two years later a separate bottled gas division, L.P. Gas, was formed. Dead River's gasoline sales also skyrocketed during the postwar years. The home heating oil business enjoyed its own growth spurt, due in large measure to the adoption of a partnership arrangement with local dealers, the first of which was forged with Eastern Oil and Supply in Eastport, Maine, in 1948. In essence, Dead River bought 50 percent interests in established dealerships and the selling dealer served as the working partner. Dead River provided the necessary financing and shared the profits. It was an equitable arrangement that resulted in a series of partnerships over the next dozen years. The largest deal of this type came in 1952 when Dead River bought a stake in Webber Tanks, a major tank farm owned by Alburnie Webber.

FAMILIES SPLIT ASSETS: 1950

Over the years, the business interests of the Hutchins and Atwater families diverged. Curtis Hutchins held a 13 percent interest in the coal business, while the Atwaters owned a sizable stake in Dead River's common and preferred stock. A trade of interests was arranged in 1950. The split became final in 1963 when Dead River acquired the last of the Atwaters' preferred stock.

```
┌─────────────────────────────────────────────┐
│                                             │
│              KEY DATES                      │
│                  ■                          │
│  ─────────────────────────────────────────  │
│  1907:  Charles Hutchins starts a forest    │
│         products company.                   │
│  1936:  Dead River acquires gas stations.   │
│  1981:  Real estate division is formed.     │
│  2003:  Maine home heating oil business of  │
│         Irving Oil is acquired.             │
│  2009:  Dead River convenience stores       │
│         switch to Shell branded gasoline.   │
│                                             │
└─────────────────────────────────────────────┘
```

Hutchins remained president until 1957, but continued to serve as chairman while pursuing a variety of business ventures and other interests.

Dead River became involved in a variety of businesses in the 1960s, including wholesale drugs, potato farming quick photo processing shops, the lobster business, and modular housing. Dead River was more successful in taking advantage of its vast land holdings. Because of the skiing boom that took place after World War II, the company had received numerous requests for campsites on its land in the Sugarloaf Mountain region. In 1967 Dead River formed a Recreation Division to develop its property. In the late 1960s the company opened a shopping center in the Sugarloaf region. More than 200 A-frames houses and chalets were also built along the Carrabassett River and about 50 luxury homes were added in the area. In the early 1970s, Dead River acquired Spring Hill Development Corp. of South Berwick, Maine, to further pursue its interest in the housing market.

The man who would lead Dead River through the final decades of the 20th century and into the next, P. Andrews Nixon, joined the company in 1970. During his tenure Dead River gas stations made the transition to convenience stores. The company also formed a real estate division, Dead River Properties, in 1981. The unit essentially served as an investment vehicle for the Hutchins family, but it would also lease and manage properties. In the late 1990s Dead River expanded its reach by becoming the primary investor in the Windalier Fund, established by Boston-based Great Island Co., a firm that specialized in the development and management of shopping centers and focused its activities on the Northeast.

CURTIS HUTCHINS DIES: 1978

Nixon also became Dead River's chairman of the board following the death of 78-year-old Curtis Hutchins in

1985. He led the company into the new century, overcoming such problems as an ice storm in 1998 that made the vital delivery of home heating oil highly dangerous. Dead River also had to contend with increased competition from Portsmouth, New Hampshire-based Irving Oil Corporation, which made inroads in southern Maine in both home oil and retail gasoline sales in the 1990s.

Dead River became especially aggressive in the new century in expanding its home heating oil business through the acquisition of smaller independents. In 2001 Dead River acquired Winslow, Maine-based Chase Fuel Co., picking up 1,600 customers, mostly residential. Later in the year the heating oil and propane delivery business of J.D. Thomas Inc. was added in eastern Washington County in Maine. Also in 2001 Dead River acquired Hamels Fuels of Brewer, Maine, a small distributor in business since 1932.

Further acquisitions were completed later in the early 2000s, the most significant of which came in February 2003. Irving Oil elected to sell its home heating business in northern and Down East Maine to Dead River. Later in the year, Dead River resumed its acquisition of smaller players, buying Scottway-Lucas Oil Co. of Robbinston, Maine. The heating oil and propane business of North Haverhill, New Hampshire-based Bradford Pratts Petroleum was acquired in September 2005. A year later Dead River acquired the heating oil and propane service business of Tibbetts Building & Fuels in Lincoln, Maine.

Dead River entered a period of transition in leadership as well. In late 2006 Nixon announced that he planned to retire in April 2008, allowing ample time for his successor, Robert A. Moore, to prepare to take the reins. A graduate of the University of Maine School of Law, Moore had joined Dead River in 1995 as vice president and general counsel and three years became a senior vice president responsible for managing Dead River's petroleum operations. Starting in January 2007 he took over the newly created position of president and chief operating officer as he was groomed for the next 15 months to replace Nixon.

SWITCH TO SHELL BRAND: 2009

In the meantime, Dead River opened a convenience store in Bangor in the spring of 2007. It was also significant because it included a Shell gas station. Since the mid-1930s Dead River had been a distributor of Exxon, then Esso, motor fuels. Exxon was in the process of discontinuing its indirect and direct retail gasoline sales in the northeastern states. In need of a new partner, Dead River in June 2009 reached an agreement to convert its locations to the Shell brand. While the switch marked the passing of an era, Dead River remained healthy and well placed to compete successively in northern New England for many years to come.

Ed Dinger

PRINCIPAL SUBSIDIARIES

Dead River Oil Company; Dead River Properties.

PRINCIPAL COMPETITORS

Citgo Petroleum Corporation; Cumberland Farms, Inc.; Irving Oil Company.

FURTHER READING

"Curtis Hutchins, 78; Industrialist," *Boston Globe*, September 17, 1985, p. 79.

"Dead River Buys Northern Petroleum," *Caledonian-Record*, September 17, 2005.

"For Dead River, It's More than Oil," *Portland Press Herald*, December 6, 2005, p. C2.

Hutchins, Curtis Marshall, and Russell H. Peters, *Dead River Company: A History 1907, 1972*, Farmington, ME: Knowlton & McLeary, 1972, 74 p.

"New England Petroleum Distributor Upgrades Operating Technology," *Bulk Transporter*, January 1, 2010.

"Oil Firm Names CEO's Successor," *Bangor Daily News*, December 5, 2006, p. 5.

Sambides, Nick, Jr., "Dead River Setting Up Branch Office," *Bangor Daily News*, September 26, 2006, p. 4.

Derma Sciences Inc.

214 Carnegie Center, Suite 300
Princeton, New Jersey 08540
U.S.A.
Telephone: (609) 514-4744
Toll Free: (800) 825-4325
Fax: (609) 514-0502
Web site: http://www.dermasciences.com

Public Company
Incorporated: 1984
Employees: 174
Sales: $48.5 million (2009)
Stock Exchanges: OTC
Ticker Symbol: DSCI
NAICS: 339112 Surgical and Medical Instrument Manufacturing; 325412 Pharmaceutical Preparation Manufacturing; 541710 Research and Development in the Physical Sciences and Engineering Sciences

■ ■ ■

Princeton, New Jersey-based Derma Sciences Inc. is a leading manufacturer of skin and wound care products. The company's offerings fall within five specific categories, including: specialty securement and closure devices (wound closure strips and catheter and tubing fasteners), traditional wound care, advanced wound care, burn care, and skin care/bathing. Derma Sciences maintains manufacturing operations in both Nantong, China, and Toronto, Ontario, Canada, and has U.S. distribution facilities in St. Louis, Missouri, and Houston, Texas. The company sells the majority of its products to health-care distributors that serve four main market segments, including: primary care physicians, acute care hospitals and subacute wound clinics, home care providers, and long-term care and rehabilitation operations. In addition to manufacturing and marketing its own products, Derma Sciences also serves as a contract manufacturer for other firms.

FORMATION

Derma Sciences traces its roots back to the 1980s when Mary G. Clark, a nurse from Old Forge, Pennsylvania, produced a homemade ointment that was successful in healing chronic wounds. After securing a patent, she established Derma Sciences to market the treatment. With assistance from friends and her sons, the company was incorporated in Colorado on September 10, 1984. Derma Sciences proceeded to make a name for itself in the advanced wound care market with its topical treatment, which was given the name Dermagran.

Growth continued at a measured pace during the company's formative years. Finally, on May 13, 1994, Derma Sciences went public, raising more than $4 million. Developments continued in early 1995 when Atlanta, Georgia-based Scherer Healthcare agreed to acquire Derma Sciences in a $20.27 million stock swap. By this time the company had annual sales of approximately $4.7 million. Scherer and Derma Sciences also attempted a joint hostile takeover of Procyte Corporation, which was ultimately abandoned.

In 1996 Derma Sciences' sales grew to about $6 million annually. Developments at this time included U.S. Food and Drug Administration (FDA) approval of

COMPANY PERSPECTIVES

The markets we serve are large and growing. Our mission is to enhance shareholder value by servicing a significant portion of these markets as a fully integrated wound care product provider.

a new zinc-saline liquid bandage named Dermagran Hydrogel Wound Dressing. In addition to use as a topical skin protectant, the new product was approved for use on both burns and dermal wounds. In the absence of a direct sales force, Derma Sciences focused heavily on tradeshow advertising and direct-mail promotion, as well as advertisements in health-care industry journals and trade magazines.

RELOCATION TO PENNSYLVANIA

During the mid-1990s Derma Sciences faced off against several noteworthy competitors. These include the likes of Johnson & Johnson, Carrington Laboratories Inc., Calgon-Vestal/Convatec, and Coloplast Sween. On the international front, in 1996 the company established a contract with South Africa-based Manta Medical Systems Ltd. for the distribution of its wound care product line throughout Zimbabwe, Mozambique, South Africa, Namibia, and Malawi. Midway through that year the company relocated to Pennsylvania, where it constructed a new headquarters facility. Derma Sciences ended the year with a net loss of $1.4 million on sales of $4.46 million.

In January 1998 cofounder and President John T. Borthwick, son of cofounder Mary Clark, stepped down as company president. However, he remained with the organization as a director. Specifically, Borthwick worked to develop a new division focused on managed care customers. At this time Richard S. Mink also was promoted from vice president of marketing to chief operating officer. In addition, Derma Sciences' shareholders approved the creation of 1.75 million shares of preferred stock.

During the late 1990s Derma Sciences furthered its growth by forming strategic joint ventures with other companies, including United Kingdom-based Innovative Technologies Group plc. In addition, the company grew its private-label distribution business. In this area, the company allowed other suppliers to market the Derma Sciences line of alginate wound care products under different brand names.

ACQUISITION STRATEGY

In 1998 Derma Sciences began pursuing an acquisition strategy. Several important deals took place during the latter part of that year. In September Genetic Laboratories Wound Care Inc. was acquired and became a wholly owned subsidiary. This deal allowed the company to offer wound closure products and specialty fasteners used for securing tubes and catheters. Two months later the company acquired the skin care product company Sunshine Products Inc., which also became a wholly owned subsidiary. Derma Sciences ended 1998 with a net loss of $1.8 million on sales of $9.2 million.

By 1999 Derma Sciences was led by Chairman and CEO Edward J. Quilty. The company moved forward with a focus on increasing its market share. Derma Sciences' strategy benefited from the fact that it had a 35-member direct-selling organization.

In April Derma Sciences established a distribution partnership agreement, valued at approximately $1 million annually, with Covington, Kentucky-based Omnicare Inc. The deal was significant because Omnicare was the nation's largest provider of pharmacy services to long-term care institutions. Two months later Derma Sciences' board of directors approved a one-to-five reverse stock split, which increased the number of the company's outstanding common shares from approximately 1.33 million to 6.63 million. In late 1999 Derma Sciences merged its Genetic Laboratories business into the larger organization. The company ended the year with a net loss of $2.4 million on sales of $10.1 million.

A NEW MILLENNIUM

By 2000 founder Mary Clark had officially retired, but she remained affiliated with the company as a research consultant and director. Clark's son, John Borthwick, served as vice president of sales. Many of the patients who had started using the company's Dermagran product during the mid-1980s remained customers, speaking to the product's effectiveness. Revenues reached an estimated $9.5 million, and the company employed approximately 50 people.

A significant development took place in mid-2000 when Derma Sciences restructured its sales force in a move expected to save $1.2 million annually. Specifically, a vice president of sales and marketing was put in charge of field sales. Reporting to that position were and three regional sales managers, four direct-selling specialists, a product marketing manager, two nurse clinicians, and three internal sales support staff members, as well as independent distributors and manufacturers' representatives.

KEY DATES

∎

1984: The company incorporates in Colorado.
1994: Derma Sciences goes public, raising more than $4 million.
1995: Georgia-based Scherer Healthcare agrees to acquire Derma Sciences in a $20.27 million stock swap.
1996: The company relocates to Pennsylvania.
2007: Derma Sciences introduces its MEDIHONEY line of wound dressings that contain Active Manuka (Leptospermum) Honey from New Zealand.

In August founder Mary Clark and Vice President for Scientific Affairs Robert P. DiGiovine received the company's third patent for an ointment called Nutra Shield, which protected patients' skin from friction and moisture. An important leadership change took place that month when Chief Financial Officer Stephen Wills left the company. He was succeeded by Bristol-Myers Squibb executive John E. Yetter. Finally, in October Derma Sciences' common stock was removed from the NASDAQ SmallCap Market after failing to maintain a minimum closing price of $1 and began trading on the OTC Bulletin Board.

CONTINUED ACQUISITIONS

In September 2001 Derma Sciences received exclusive sales and distribution rights in the Americas and Japan for Soft Wash, a line of disposable body cleansing sponges that were used in nursing homes, home health settings, and hospitals. One year later the company acquired the assets of the Toronto, Ontario, Canada-based wound care and medical device manufacturer Dumex Medical Inc. for $3.76 million. Derma Sciences ended 2002 with net income of $61,368 on net sales of $11.75 million.

Midway through 2003 Derma Sciences' Dumex Medical subsidiary received ISO 9001:2000, ISO 13485:1996, and EN46001:1996 certifications. The certifications affirmed Dumex Medical's quality standards, and gave it additional credibility as Derma Sciences sought to expand the operation. Finally, in November the company signed a multiyear product supplier agreement with the national distributor McKesson Medical-Surgical, which called for the production of a new line of McKesson-branded products. Derma Sci-

ences ended 2003 with net income of $22,241 on net sales of $17.94 million.

Derma Sciences began 2004 by acquiring Kimberly-Clark Corporation's wound care assets. The $2.6 million deal involved a manufacturing operation that was relocated from Kimberly-Clark's Texas facility to Derma Sciences' facility in Toronto, Ontario. In addition, the company integrated Kimberly-Clark's wound care and wound closure products into its own product line.

On the financial front Derma Sciences continued to see its net sales climb during the middle of the decade. Net sales totaled $19.88 million in 2004. However, the company recorded a net loss of $2.34 million that year. On a similar note, sales reached $23.5 million in 2005, but the company lost $909,104.

PRODUCT EVOLUTION

In early 2006 Derma Sciences established a multiyear agreement to produce a branded line of wound dressings for Smith and Nephew plc. In April the company bolstered its lineup of wound care products by acquiring Tenafly, New Jersey-based Western Medical Inc., which manufactured specialty medical textile compression, support, and protective dressing products, for $6.5 million. At the same time the company raised $6.5 million via the sale of 10.9 million shares of its common stock.

One final development in 2006 occurred when the FDA approved Derma Sciences' new antimicrobial silver alginate dressing, which was named ALGICELL Ag. The product was billed as a cost-effective alternative to other silver antimicrobial dressings. In addition to delivering similar benefits, ALGICELL was more absorbent than competing products. Sales continued climbing in 2006, reaching $27.9 million. Best of all, the company turned a profit with net income of $668,739.

A major breakthrough took place in 2007 when Derma Sciences announced plans to introduce a new line of wound dressings that contained Active Manuka (Leptospermum) Honey from New Zealand. The dressings, which were given the brand name MEDIHONEY, were the first such products to receive approval from both Health Canada and the FDA. The FDA approved the use of the new product for the treatment of both burns and wounds in July 2007.

Moving forward, the company planned to market the dressings to those using silver-based dressings. That market was then valued at roughly $100 million. Subsequently, Derma Sciences began putting more muscle behind its operations. In addition to hiring a director of clinical affairs, the company hired a national sales director, as well as additional sales representatives. Leading up to the launch of MEDIHONEY, which took place in October, the product received positive media coverage, including a full-length article in the *Washington Post*.

One final development in 2007 was the acquisition of certain assets of Nutra Max Products Inc.'s first-aid division. Specifically, the division served retail, medical, and industrial markets with branded and private-label adhesive strips and other first-aid products. Following the deal, Nutra Max's offerings were integrated into Derma Sciences' existing product line. The company ended the year with a net loss of $2.3 million on sales of $34.1 million.

FOCUS ON MEDIHONEY

Derma Sciences began 2008 with nine direct sales representatives, up from two only a year before. The company announced plans to expand its sales force to 12 people by the end of the year, and 21 by 2009. The additional salespeople were needed to support new products such as MEDIHONEY. In April Derma Sciences signed a three-year supply agreement for MEDI-HONEY with MedAssets Supply Chain Systems, one of the largest group purchasing organizations in the United States.

In 2008 MEDIHONEY was featured in a full-page story in the June issue of *National Geographic*, serving to strengthen awareness of the product. A major milestone was reached in July when reimbursement codes were secured for MEDIHONEY, allowing customers to bill Medicare Part B, Medicaid, and private insurance for the dressings. More recognition came in August when MEDIHONEY was featured on the *CBS Evening News*.

In early 2008 Derma Sciences entered Phase II clinical trials for a new rapid wound-healing and scar-reduction product called DSC127. Applications for the new product included both scar reduction and very large diabetic foot ulcers. In the United States alone, the market for such a product was estimated at approximately $4 billion per year. The company entered its first patient in the trial in November. For the year, Derma Sciences recorded a net loss of $4 million on sales of $50.2 million.

ACCELERATED PRODUCT DEVELOPMENT

Derma Sciences began 2009 on a high note when the FDA approved its new BIOGUARD Barrier Dressings for marketing and distribution. The new dressings gave health-care providers an additional means of preventing the spread of deadly bacteria such as Methicillin-resistant Staphylococcus aureus (MRSA). Following the approval, sales were slated to begin midway through the year. In late 2009 Derma Sciences' shareholders approved a reverse stock split, allowing the company to meet minimum share-price requirements needed for listing on the NASDAQ Global Market or NASDAQ Capital Market.

Progress continued in early 2010 when Derma Sciences secured perpetual and exclusive worldwide licensing rights for MEDIHONEY via licensing deals with New Zealand-based Comvita New Zealand Ltd. In addition, the two companies also entered into a medical honey supply agreement, a manufacturing agreement calling for Derma Sciences to produce MEDIHONEY brand over-the-counter products, and a collaborative research and development agreement.

It also was in early 2010 that Derma Sciences expanded a licensing agreement with Boca Raton, Florida-based Quick-Med Technologies Inc. The deal allowed Derma Sciences to expand its lineup of BIO-GUARD wound dressings, which incorporated Quick-Med's Nimbus antimicrobial technology. Additionally, Derma Sciences also established an exclusive distribution agreement with Medline Industries for its BIOGARD products.

Midway through 2010 Derma Sciences announced another new product. Its XTRASORB dressing was the company's first foam wound dressing. The market for such products was estimated to be $300 million. Based on its history of product innovation, Derma Sciences appeared to have good chances for continued success during the 21st century's second decade.

Paul R. Greenland

PRINCIPAL SUBSIDIARIES

Derma First Aid Products, Inc.; Derma Sciences Canada Inc.; Sunshine Products, Inc.

PRINCIPAL COMPETITORS

ConvaTec; Covidien plc; Johnson & Johnson.

FURTHER READING

"Company News; Scherer and Derma Sciences Drop Bid for Procyte," *New York Times*, March 2, 1995.

"Derma Sciences Announces Launch of MEDIHONEY Wound Care Dressing," *Business Wire*, October 17, 2007.

"Derma Sciences Finalizes Licensing Agreement for Worldwide Rights to MEDIHONEY," *Chemical Business Newsbase*, February 25, 2010.

"Derma Sciences Launches XTRASORB Foam Wound Dressing," *PR Newswire*, May 4, 2010.

"Derma Sciences Receives FDA Approval for Its Next-Generation Antimicrobial Silver Alginate Wound Dressing," *Business Wire*, September 19, 2006.

"Derma Sciences Receives FDA Clearance for Its Active Manuka Honey Product," *Business Wire*, July 23, 2007.

Johnson, Christopher, "New Jersey-Based Wound-Care Firm Derma Sciences Works to Cure Financial Ills," *Times Leader*, November 6, 2000.

DZ Bank AG

Platz der Republik
Frankfurt am Main, D-60265
Germany
Telephone: (49 69) 7447-01
Fax: (49 69) 7447-1685
Web site: http://www.dzbank.de

Private Company
Founded: 1883
Incorporated: 1883 as Landwirtschaftliche Genossen-
   schaftsbank AG Darmstadt
Employees: 24,642
Total Assets: EUR 388.52 billion ($556.83 billion)
   (2009)
NAICS: 522110 Commercial Banking; 522130 Credit
   Unions; 522298 All Other Nondepository Credit;
   522310 Mortgage and Nonmortgage Loan; 522390
   Other Activities Related to Credit Intermediation;
   523920 Portfolio Management; 524113 Insurance
   Carriers

■ ■ ■

DZ Bank AG, Germany's fifth-largest financial institution, is a group of banks and other financial services
institutions that serves some 30 million clients in
Germany and elsewhere in the world. The central
company in this group, the DZ Bank, is a network of
approximately 1,000 cooperative banks (*Volksbanken*,
which are similar to U.S. credit unions) with more than
12,000 branches. They provide a variety of banking
services including personal banking, retail, and corporate
banking.

DZ Bank's offerings are strengthened by a roster of
other financial service firms it owns. These include the
Deutsche Genossenschafts-Hypothekenbank AG, which
is active in the commercial real estate sector; Bausparkasse Schwäbisch Hall, active in the home mortgage
market and whose primary product is the *Bausparver-
trag*, or mortgage savings plan; R+V Versicherung,
which provides a broad palette of insurance services to
individuals and corporate clients; VR Leasing,
Germany's volume leader in the leasing sector, which
deals in contracts for, among others, vehicles, information technology and communication equipment, and
real estate; Union Investment Group, which offers
investment management services to private and
corporate clients; and TeamBank AG, which provides
various consumer credit products.

DZ Bank is based in Frankfurt am Main, Germany.
The home offices of its numerous subsidiaries are
located throughout the Federal Republic and Europe.
DZ Bank has branch offices in Europe, North America,
and Asia. Cooperative banks and associations own more
than 90 percent of DZ Bank's share capital.

COOPERATIVE BANKS
ESTABLISHED IN LATE 19TH
CENTURY

Rapid industrialization in the mid-19th century and
increasing competition due to freedom of trade put
higher demands on German farmers and craftspeople,
who often lacked the resources to invest in machinery or

better-quality raw materials. The formation of raw materials purchasing associations and credit cooperatives in the mid-1800s offered a solution to small businesses in rural areas.

In 1864 Friedrich Wilhelm Raiffeisen, a mayor, founded the first rural credit cooperative in Heddesdorf near Neuwied, about 60 miles northwest of Frankfurt, and was the driving force behind the establishment of similar institutions in other counties. The credit cooperatives or *Kreditgenossenschaften* enabled farmers and craftspeople to jointly purchase raw materials or machinery at lower prices and to receive loans at reasonable interest rates. In 1876 Raiffeisen established Landwirtschaftliche Zentral-Darlehenskasse in Neuwied, a central cooperative bank for the region's farmer's cooperatives, followed by the foundation of Anwaltschaftsverband ländlicher Genossenschaften, a national association of cooperatives, in Neuwied in 1877.

A second leading figure in the early German cooperative movement was Wilhelm Haas, an attorney and civil servant who later became a member of the state parliament and a member of the German House of Representatives, the Reichstag. In 1872 Haas cofounded a farmers' joint purchasing association in Friedberg, 30 miles north of Frankfurt. In the same year Haas initiated the foundation of a regional umbrella organization for several farmers' purchasing associations, which was joined by 15 members that year. Haas's organization quickly attracted additional members, including purchasing, credit, and savings cooperatives.

In 1883 Haas cofounded Vereinigung deutscher landwirtschaftlicher Genossenschaften, a second national association of farmer's cooperatives besides Raiffeisen's. In the same year a number of savings and credit cooperatives in Hesse, supported by Haas, set up the regional cooperative bank Landwirtschaftliche Genossenschaftsbank AG Darmstadt. The new bank balanced the liquidity of its members and handled the payment transactions for the joint purchasing of raw materials. Finally, Haas founded Landwirtschaftliche Reichsgenossenschaftsbank eGmbH, a national cooperative bank based in Darmstadt.

MASSIVE GROWTH AND CONSOLIDATION AFTER 1900

Around the turn of the 20th century the cooperative movement in Germany reached new highs. After the *Genossenschaftsgesetz*, a new law that regulated cooperatives, had been passed in 1889 which allowed the establishment of limited liability cooperatives, new credit and purchasing cooperatives sprang up everywhere. By 1903 the number of credit cooperatives had grown to over 12,000 with a combined membership of roughly three million. About 4,000 rural cooperatives were members of Raiffeisen's general association while Haas's Vereinigung, which was renamed Reichsverband der deutschen landwirtschaftlichen Genossenschaften in 1903, had attracted 7,000 rural member cooperatives. The remaining roughly 1,250 cooperatives were based mostly in cities and organized in two main associations.

Raiffeisen's members received financial services from Landwirtschaftliche Zentral-Darlehenskasse in Neuwied, which became Deutsche Raiffeisenbank AG in 1923. Haas's members cooperated with regional cooperative banks, the number of which had roughly doubled to approximately 50 between 1895 and 1900. A third central cooperative bank, Preussische Zentralgenossenschaftskasse, which had been founded by the Prussian government in Berlin in 1895, provided subsidized loans to rural cooperatives through the regional cooperative banks.

In 1910 Raiffeisen's association moved to Berlin and was renamed Generalverband der deutschen Raiffeisengenossenschaften, the general association of German Raiffeisen cooperatives, in 1917. Haas's Reichsverband moved to Berlin in 1913. However, his central bank, the Reichsgenossenschaftsbank, was heavily indebted and consequently liquidated in 1912. The regional Landwirtschaftliche Genossenschaftsbank in Darmstadt was liquidated as well, but was replaced by the newly established Zentralkasse der hessischen landwirtschaftlichen Genossenschaften.

After World War I the German farming sector entered a period of severe crisis. As many farmers were not able to repay their loans, cooperative banks had to write off large sums. The galloping inflation of the early 1920s further exacerbated the situation. In 1928 the German government launched an emergency plan to overcome the crisis that provided large funds for the recovery of the rural cooperative system. To make the

KEY DATES

1883: Regional cooperative bank Landwirtschaftliche Genossenschaftsbank AG Darmstadt is established in Hesse.

1895: The Prussian central cooperative bank Preussische Zentralgenossenschaftskasse is founded in Berlin.

1929: The Frankfurt Cooperative Pact creates a united association of cooperative banks and credit unions.

1949: The new central cooperative bank Deutsche Genossenschaftskasse is founded in West Germany.

1975: A new law allows the bank, which is renamed DG Bank, to expand its activities.

2001: Southwestern German cooperative bank GZ-Bank merges with DG Bank to form DZ Bank.

system more efficient, the German government favored the creation of a single central association for the whole country. After lengthy negotiations, an agreement was finally reached between representatives of the Raiffeisen and Haas organizations.

The so-called Frankfurt Cooperative Pact of 1929 created a united association of rural credit cooperatives in Germany. In 1930 Raiffeisen's Generalverband and Haas's Reichsverband merged to form Reichsverband der deutschen landwirtschaftlichen Genossenschaften-Raiffeisen-e.V. headquartered in Berlin. With a membership of 36,000 cooperatives and four million individual members united under its organizational roof, it was the world's largest association of its kind. The heavily indebted Deutsche Raiffeisenbank was liquidated and its business was taken over by several regional cooperative banks.

UNDER NAZI CONTROL AFTER 1930

After Adolf Hitler's National Socialists (Nazis) took over political power in 1933, they placed the cooperative system under their leadership. While leading positions in the cooperative banking sector were filled with Nazi conformists, Andreas Hermes, the president of the Reichsverband, stepped back from his position in protest of the Nazi's political course. In 1932 the government-controlled Preussische Zentralgenossenschaftskasse was renamed Deutsche Zentralgenossen-

schaftskasse and became Germany's only remaining central cooperative bank in 1939.

The central farmers' cooperatives association, the Reichsverband, was integrated into the Reichsnährstand, an organization that controlled the production and distribution of agricultural products. Democratically elected bodies were abolished and the liberal cooperative movement was stigmatized as a capitalist institution. As the Nazis prepared the country for war, they used credit cooperatives to collect funds for armament.

As most resources were used in the war effort, there were fewer and fewer consumer goods available for the German population, who ended up putting their disposable income into their savings accounts. With lending activities almost down to zero during the war, cooperative banks invested the deposits of their members in government bonds. As the war progressed, many regional cooperative banks were damaged or destroyed during bomb attacks.

NEW START AFTER WORLD WAR II

After the end of World War II the German cooperative system had to be rebuilt from scratch. Deutsche Zentralgenossenschaftskasse had lost its headquarters in the Soviet-occupied Eastern part of Berlin, and its assets (mostly government bonds of the German Reich) had become worthless. After a new national association for rural cooperatives, the Deutscher Raiffeisenverband, had been established in Bonn in 1948, the new central cooperative bank Deutsche Genossenschaftskasse (DGK) was founded in Frankfurt am Main in 1949. The driving force behind the establishment of the new organizations was former Reichsverband president Andreas Hermes, who, after being arrested and put under death sentence by the Nazis, managed to escape in the last days of the war, and became the new president of Deutscher Raiffeisenverband.

The reestablishment of a free market economy in the newly founded Federal Republic of Germany was the basis of the revival of democratically governed cooperatives. By 1950 there were about 12,000 credit cooperatives in West Germany. During the postwar "economic miracle" years of the 1950s their membership rose sharply, which resulted in healthy growth of the cooperative banks. The 1950s and 1960s, however, saw many credit cooperatives merge to form larger entities.

By 1970 their number had dropped by about 40 percent. Consequently, the number of credit cooperatives serviced by a regional cooperative bank decreased dramatically, while their growing financial assets diminished the importance of the regional banks' traditional main task, the balancing of the liquidity of their members. On the other hand, a new banking law abolished the regulation of interest rates in 1967, resulting in increasing competition between cooperative and commercial banks.

CENTRAL BANK ESTABLISHED BY LAW IN 1975

In 1971 the central farmer's cooperative association Deutscher Raiffeisenverband merged with the central urban cooperative association Deutscher Genossenschaftsverband to form a new umbrella organization, which was named Deutscher Genossenschafts- und Raiffeisenverband. One year later the new Bundesverband der Deutschen Volksbanken und Raiffeisenbanken became the new central association of cooperative banks in West Germany. Following the merger, many regional cooperative banks of the two formerly separate organizations merged as well.

In 1975 a new law was passed that enabled the central cooperative bank Deutsche Genossenschaftskasse, which was renamed Deutsche Genossenschaftsbank, DG Bank for short, to expand its business activities. The bank was allowed to take over the business of regional cooperative banks and to establish subsidiaries in Germany and abroad. In the following years DG Bank evolved as a national central bank based on cooperative principles. In 1976 the bank opened its first subsidiaries abroad in the United States and Hong Kong.

DZ BANK FORMED BY MERGER IN 2001

The consolidation of the German cooperative banking system continued in the 1980s. When the Bavarian central cooperative bank Raiffeisen-Zentralbank struggled financially in 1985 its banking activities were transferred to DG Bank. One year later another regional cooperative bank in Bavaria, Bayerischen Volksbanken AG, merged with DG Bank. In 1989 a new agreement regulated the cooperation between the regional cooperative banks and DG Bank, leaving them the option to remain independent. In the same year DG Bank merged with the Northern German Norddeutsche Genossenschaftsbank and with Raiffeisen-Zentralbank in Hesse.

After the reunification of Germany in 1990 the West German cooperative banks helped set up similar institutions in Eastern Germany and provided the necessary financial backing. In July 1990 DG Bank became the central bank for the Eastern German cooperative

banks. By that time, the consolidation of the Western German cooperative banking system had progressed. The number of credit cooperatives had further decreased to about 3,000, 60 percent of which received financial services from DG Bank. However, when the bank got into financial difficulties due to losses incurred through securities trading activities in 1991, the consolidation process was halted until the end of the decade.

In 1998 DG Bank was transformed into a stock corporation that was owned by a number of cooperative banks. Two years later two large cooperative banks in southwestern Germany, SGZ-Bank and GZB-Bank, merged to form Genossenschafts Zentralbank, or GZ-Bank. Finally, 2001 saw the merger of GZ-Bank and DG Bank, after the latter was struggling with huge losses from bad loans, a shrinking corporate client roster, and unsuccessful flotations of stocks at Frankfurt's New Market, according to the *Banker* on September 1, 2006. The merger created Germany's fifth-largest financial institution which was named DZ Bank AG.

As *Handelsblatt* reported on June 10, 2002, the bank introduced highly restrictive guidelines for giving out new loans to minimize future risk after DZ Bank had to write off EUR 2 billion in losses on loans. The new policy caused protests from large cooperative banks, which started looking elsewhere for credit. *Agrarzeitung Ernaehrungsdienst*, reported on March 24, 2004, that DZ Bank eliminated roughly 2,000 jobs over three years to cut costs. In 2003 DZ Bank acquired the German private bank Norisbank, which specialized in retail loans, and sold it at a healthy profit to Deutsche Bank three years later, according to the *Banker* in 2006.

DZ Bank's plans in 2006 to go public to finance further international expansion, as well as the merger with WGZ-Bank, another large central cooperative bank in Western German North Rhine Westphalia, were put on hold. In the second half of the decade the bank strengthened its investment banking arm and expanded its activities in Asia. On February 21, 2008, *Börsen-Zeitung* reported that, due to the financial crisis in the later years of the decade, DZ Bank had to adjust its security paper portfolio by EUR 1.4 billion in 2007, mainly due to bad bank bonds and asset-backed securities, and the losses incurred by its mortgage banking subsidiary DG Hyp.

In 2009 DZ Bank strengthened its capital base by raising EUR 900 million in fresh capital within the cooperative financial services network. In 2010 the bank announced that it was out of the red, with earnings before taxes of EUR 836 million in 2009, after producing losses of EUR 1.5 billion caused mostly by trading activities in 2008. With an economic recovery not expected before 2011, DZ Bank was planning to focus on its main role as the central institution for Germany's cooperative financial services network.

Evelyn Hauser

PRINCIPAL SUBSIDIARIES

DZ Bank SE (95.4%); VR-Leasing AG(83.5%); DZ Equity Partner GmbH (100%); Union Asset Management Holding AG (73.4%); DZ Private Wealth Managementgesellschaft S.A.; DZ Bank International S.A. (89.7%); DZ Bank Ireland (100%); VR Kreditwerk AG (100%); ReiseBank AG; DZ Privatbank (Schweiz) AG (80%); Bausparkasse Schwäbisch Hall AG (81.8%); Deutsche Genossenschafts-Hypothekenbank AG (100%); TeamBank AG Nürnberg (91.1%); R+V Versicherung (74%).

PRINCIPAL COMPETITORS

Commerzbank AG; Deutsche Bank AG; Sparkassen-Finanzgruppe; WestLB AG; WGZ Bank.

FURTHER READING

"DG Bank Looks toward Growth Despite Crises," *Frankfurter Allgemeine Zeitung*, October 6, 1998, p. 23.

"DZ Bank Causes Storm among Credit Cooperatives," *Handelsblatt*, June 10, 2002.

"DZ Bank muss Milliardenbetrag abschreiben—Gewinnprognose wird aber beibehalten," *Börsen-Zeitung*, February 21, 2008, p. 1.

"DZ Strives to Push Home Advantage after Exploiting Banking Crisis," *EuroWeek*, September 25, 2009.

"Germany: A Merger of Equals?" *Banker*, March 1, 2002.

"Making That Tractor Roar," *Banker*, September 1, 2006.

"Umstrukturierung zeigt Erfolge," *Agrarzeitung Ernaehrungsdienst*, March 24, 2004, p. 4.

Was dem Einzelnen nich möglich ist, das vermögen viele, Frankfurt am Main, Germany: DZ Bank AG, 2008.

Eiffage S.A.

———■———

163, quai du Docteur Dervaux
Asnieres-sur-Seine, 92600
France
Telephone: (+33 01) 41 32 80 00
Fax: (+33 01) 41 32 81 10
Web site: http://www.eiffage.com

Public Company
Incorporated: 1844 as Fougerolle
Employees: 70,958
Sales: EUR 13.6 billion ($19.57 billion) (2009)
Stock Exchanges: Euronext Paris
Ticker Symbols: FGR FP; FOUG.PA
NAICS: 236220 Commercial and Institutional Building Construction; 237310 Highway, Street, and Bridge Construction; 237990 Other Heavy and Civil Engineering Construction; 238210 Electrical Contractors and Other Wiring Installation Contractors; 541330 Engineering Services; 551112 Offices of Other Holding Companies; 561210 Facilities Support Services

■ ■ ■

Based in France, Eiffage S.A. is one of Europe's leading construction and public works companies. Eiffage has over 500 subsidiaries, which operate in five fields. Construction (Eiffage Construction) provides construction, property development and civil engineering services. Public Works (Eiffage Travaux Publics) handles public works projects including road and railway construction and maintenance. Energy (Eiffage Energie) handles electrical contracting ranging from lighting systems and communication networks to overhead power lines. Metal (Eiffel) works in metallic construction, including glass facades works. Concessions and PPPs (Eiffage Concessions) finances, manages, and operates toll roads and carparks, data networks, and structures such as prisons and hospitals built by the company. Over 80 percent of its work is in France, with the rest primarily in other European countries.

A publicly held company traded on the Paris stock exchange, 24 percent of Eiffage is owned by Eiffage employees. The founding company, Fougerolle, which celebrated its 160th anniversary in 2004, is France's oldest continuously operating construction and engineering firm.

19TH-CENTURY FOUNDATION

The Fougerolle name entered French history in the 1840s, with the completion of the Nivernaise canal, a structure totaling 174 kilometers and joining the Loire and Yonne Rivers in the Burgundy region. Philippe Fougerolle, a mason from the central Creuse River region of France, later joined by Jacques Fougerolle, founded the family construction firm in 1844.

Jacques Fougerolle lost his life in the construction of the Saint Gothard tunnel in the Swiss Alps on the Swiss-Italian border. At 15 kilometers in length and carved through the 3,200-meter-tall Saint Gothard mountain, it remains one of the region's most important railroad and highway structures. Fougerolle's death did not, however, spell the end of the family's company, which completed the Saint Gothard tunnel in 1882.

Before the end of the century Fougerolle's activity had spread through much of France and included for the first time projects in Paris. An early Parisian project was the digging of the Metro line connecting the Porte de Clichy with the Place de la Trinité. While Fougerolle expanded its operations in France, it also was participating in international projects, including the construction of the Namur fortifications in Belgium by 1890. In 1903 the company put into place the Adolphe bridge for Luxembourg.

By the turn of the century Fougerolle was receiving projects from farther abroad. In 1908 Fougerolle received the contract for the construction of the Rio Grando del Sul port in Brazil. At the same time, the company was completing some 2,500 kilometers of roads for the soon-to-disappear Ottoman Empire. The outbreak of World War I, while restricting the company to its French operations, nevertheless called Fougerolle into service. One project, carried out in 1915, was the addition of a second passage to the railroad between Paris and Amiens. This was to ensure the supply chain to the French army in its effort to halt the advancing German army.

CONTINUED GROWTH: 1920–50

After World War I, Fougerolle, organized under the company name Le Soliditit Français, returned to both its domestic and international activities. A chief French project of the period was achieved in 1921, when Fougerolle constructed a series of large-scale dirigible hangars at Orly, later the site of the country's domestic airport. During this same period, Fougerolle was contracted to build the refitting supports in the shipbuilding port of Toulon. The resulting structure set scale records for the time.

The 1920s saw the company extend its business into the French-controlled colonial regions. Projects included the construction of the port of Dakar, Senegal, in 1927 and the building of the Deir Ez Zor bridge over the Euphrates on the border between Iraq and Syria. In the next decade Fougerolle received the contract to build

a road from Mogadishu, Somalia, to the Ethiopian border.

As Fougerolle was growing, the de Marchena brothers, Albert and Ernest, along with Gino Valatelli, founded a company in 1924. Called Auxiliare d'Entreprises Electriques et de Travaux Publics, it would become better known as SAE.

In the climate of approaching war in the 1930s, Fougerolle participated in the building of the Maginot line, a series of fortifications designed to protect France against German invasion. Just prior to the outbreak of hostilities, the company finished constructing an arm of the Parisian Metro, leading to the Porte de Montreuil.

In the postwar period Fougerolle played a central role in the French reconstruction, while also fulfilling major projects in the soon-to-be-former French colonies of Africa. Fougerolle continued to expand its operations, chiefly through adding subsidiaries, while remaining largely decentralized. Its subsidiaries, which tended to range in size from 80 to 200 employees, kept their own names and continued their operations on an essentially local scale. Fougerolle itself remained a relatively small operation, clinging to its independence as the construction industry in France gravitated to a small circle of large, government-influenced or publicly held conglomerates.

Among the company's major projects of the postwar period were the digging of a hydroelectric tunnel in Tanzania; a role in the construction of the 1,420-meter suspension bridge at Tancarville, near the city of Le Havre; the construction of the Bin el Ouidane dam in Morocco in 1954; followed by the Serre-Ponçon dam in the French Alps in 1960; and construction of the Sydney Opera House from 1963 to 1973.

GROWING PAINS: 1970–88

In 1970 the company reorganized under the name Société des Entreprises Fougerolle Limousin, but remained primarily a family-led entity. Buoyed after nearly two decades of French economic growth, the company prepared to expand its activities. In 1973 it bought out the Société Nouvelle de Constructions et de Travaux, a building construction specialist, and, a year later, took over the company Gifor, which specialized in laying foundations. The Arab oil embargo of 1973, and the resulting economic crisis, cut deeply into Fougerolle's growth plans.

The French banking leader Paribas made a friendly attempt to merge Fougerolle into the larger Spie-Batignolles in 1980. Fougerolle's insistence on independence, however, blocked that move. Then the

```
┌─────────────────────────────────────────────┐
│                                               │
│              KEY DATES                        │
│                   ■                           │
│  ─────────────────────────────────────        │
│  1844:  Phillipe Fougerolle establishes family │
│         construction company.                  │
│  1924:  Auxiliare d'Enterprises Electriques et de │
│         Traveaux Publics (SAE) is founded.     │
│  1992:  Fougerolle and SAE merge, creating Eiffage. │
│  2001:  Eiffage wins its first major concessions │
│         contract.                              │
│  2004:  Millau viaduct opens.                  │
│  2007:  Eiffage beats back takeover attempt by Span- │
│         ish contractor Sacyr Vallehermoso.     │
│                                               │
└─────────────────────────────────────────────┘
```

company ran into trouble on a number of its international construction sites, most notably in Iraq and Nigeria. Taking losses on these projects, Fougerolle was lashed by a new recession and a collapse of the French construction market. By 1982 Fougerolle was near the edge of bankruptcy.

Several important shareholders and financial backers rescued Fougerolle. These included Paribas, the French oil giant Total, and the French conglomerate Générale des Eaux. The latter, taking some 30 percent of Fougerolle, began making plans to merge Fougerolle into its own construction and civil engineering subsidiaries.

Placed in charge of rebuilding Fougerolle was Jean-François Roverato, heir-apparent to then CEO Louis Lesne. Roverato, who had entered the company in 1975 at the age of 30, had served as the company's head of French development and later served as head of its international division. Roverato quickly succeeded in restoring Fougerolle to health. This made it possible for Lesne to refuse Générale des Eaux's efforts to take control of the smaller company.

Roverato was named the company's managing director (CEO) in 1987. By then, he had initiated an expansion drive, leading Fougerolle into a number of acquisitions of smaller construction, road-building, and engineering firms. Fougerolle's acquisitions included IGB, Fontaine, Gallego, and Clement in 1990. In 1991 the company added Batiment et Genie Civil Thélu, Rosina, GCI, Cattirolo Lepage, as well as 40 percent of Germany's Walter Bau, and a share in Paris-based maintenance services firm Avenir Entretien.

Each of Eiffage's member companies operated independently of the others, with its own equipment, resources, networks, employees, and corporate cultures, while providing opportunities for synergy and cooperation among member companies. Member companies reflected a similar federation structure, operating more or less as holding vehicles for their own subsidiaries. This structure provided the flexibility of localized and specialized services, while offering the backing of a national operation.

When he assumed command of Fougerolle, Roverato received from the company's major investors the right to open the company to new capital at will. This flexibility served Fougerolle well in its struggle to maintain its independence. By the late 1980s Générale des Eaux was pushing harder for a merger of the mid-sized Fougerolle with CGE's construction division. Paribas, ally and owner of 40 percent of Fougerolle, refused to sell its shares to CGE, thwarting the conglomerate's aims.

EMPLOYEE OWNERSHIP AND A MERGER: 1989–92

In 1989 Roverato performed a coup that prevented CGE from proceeding with a hostile takeover. With the participation of Paribas, Roverato announced an employee buyout of Fougerolle's operations. More than 10,000 Fougerolle employees participated in the operation, which created the employee shareholding group Financiére Fougerolle and gave Fougerolle majority control of 56 percent of its operations.

CGE, which saw its dream of taking over Fougerolle thwarted, increased its own position in the company to 34 percent, giving it a minority position. This provided the ability to block further moves by the company, particularly should Fougerolle seek a fresh expansion of capital. However, this block would become effective only after June 1992.

In April 1992 Fougerolle announced that it was taking over the Société Auxiliaire d'Entreprise (SAE), France's second-largest building construction firm. With nearly FRF 30 billion in annual revenues, SAE was close to three times Fougerolle's size. Yet SAE had been facing difficulties, with the collapse of the worldwide construction market in the late 1980s, followed by the Persian Gulf War and economic recession of the early 1990s.

With its share price weakened, SAE was threatened with a hostile takeover. In 1990 the company weathered a raid on its stock by the Belgian promoter Michel Pelége. SAE was rescued at the time by Fougerolle and Paribas. Each company took some 10 percent of SAE's shares. Two years later, Roverato, who was eager to shed CGE's influence on Fougerolle before the June 1992 deadline, approached SAE with a proposition: in exchange for shares in Financiére Fougerolle, the smaller Fougerolle would take over SAE's operations.

The operation, worth some FRF 5 billion, was a success, bringing SAE and Fougerolle together, while following the company's long-held federation concept. The united companies became France's fourth-largest construction and engineering firm, with nearly FRF 38 billion ($7.158 billion) in annual sales and profits of $77 million. Following the takeover, CGE's part in the group was reduced to less than 33 percent, depriving the conglomerate of its minority block. By 1997 CGE began looking to sell off its holdings in the merged company.

A NEW COMPANY: 1993–99

Taking the name Eiffage, the company continued the expansion course that had been begun by Fougerolle at the start of the decade. Despite the ongoing economic crisis, the company hardly rested, adding more than 10 new subsidiaries in 1992 alone, including the Dutch Fraanje and the Belgian Delens. Eiffage also absorbed a number of existing SAE subsidiaries, including Quillery and Norelec. One subsidiary, Eiffel Construction Metallique, constructed the Eiffel Tower in 1889 and the Louvre Pyramid 100 years later. Several Fougerolle subsidiaries specializing in building construction were regrouped under Eiffage as well.

After taking control of Walter Bau, with 74 percent of the German company's shares, in 1994, Eiffage enhanced its French road construction capacity with the 1995 acquisition of Beugnet. In response to the depressed construction and public works market, Eiffage began extending its services capacity, including augmenting its share of Avenir Entretien and acquiring 100 percent of SíES, Paris-based specialist in cleaning services worth some FRF 400 million in annual sales. By the mid-1990s the company counted more than 50 subsidiary companies, operating throughout France and on the international front.

Eiffage had managed to resist the collapsing construction market into the mid-1990s. Nonetheless, in 1996, with its revenues slipping back to FRF 32.7 billion, the company posted a loss of nearly FRF 890 million. The company was forced to make cuts, notably in its real estate and services subsidiaries, without renouncing its interest in building a stronger position in these sectors. At the same time, Eiffage continued to insist on its federation model of construction and public works subsidiaries, despite the inevitable competition that existed among some of its subsidiaries.

France's return to economic growth would come none too soon for Eiffage. By the end of 1997 the company reported profits for the year of FRF 605 million, despite the continued decline of its revenues. Eiffage was criticized as too heavily reliant on the French market, which continued to account for more than 80 percent of the company's sales in 1998. However, Eiffage continued its extension into the real estate and services market. Its purchases included 17.1 percent position of the highly profitable Autoroute services company, Cofiroute.

A BRIDGE THAT FLOATS IN CLOUDS: 2000–04

As economic growth picked up in Europe, governments faced significant public debt along with a severe need for investment in public infrastructure. Transportation projects, notably highways and high-speed railroads, were in particular demand.

As with the rest of Europe, the French legal framework allowed public entities, such as cities, provinces, and the national government, to award contracts to private companies to build and operate stand-alone projects that generated their own income. These included toll roads, parking garages, and railroads. The public entity conceded to the contractor the fees from the users of the project (tolls, for example) for a negotiated period of years. At that time the project would transfer to the original public entity.

These concession contracts were known as BOT agreements, for "build, operate, and transfer." The private company financed (or arranged financing for) the construction and operation and repaid its investors from the fees it collected over the years. This structure was growing in popularity throughout Europe. The public entities were able to upgrade or expand public infrastructures without going into debt and the private companies earned a more consistent and higher margin than on traditional construction projects.

In 2001 Eiffage won the concession BOT contract for a motorway in Portugal with a virtual toll system. It also won the bid to build a bridge (along with toll booths) over the Tarn River at Millau in southern France. It beat out bigger competitors by conducting extensive research into just about every aspect of the project and by pledging to finance the project through its own balance sheet. Eiffage would collect tolls for 75 years before turning the bridge over to the government.

Thirty-four months after work began and ahead of schedule, the 1.52 mile-long Millau Viaduct opened to traffic in December 2004. The London architectural firm Foster & Partners created the original design to have a minimal effect, both visually and environmentally, on the countryside along the Tarn valley. The result was the longest and highest cable-stayed structure in the world. The roadbed deck sat 804 feet in the air. The bridge consisted of six spans each

1,122 feet long plus an anchor span at each end. The seven concrete piers that supported the spans were 230 to 803 feet high and met with the legs of the steelwork pylons, which soared to 1,132 feet above the valley floor, holding the cables. Drivers headed to Spain and the Mediterranean for summer vacation no longer experienced 30-mile backups.

Eiffage was also building and managing car parks. In 2002 it financed construction of six underground and one above-ground parking lots in Kraków, Poland. The company would operate the lots for 30 to 37 years, collecting fees for the 1,600 car spaces and 150 bus spaces. Two years later it bought the Epolis Group, the second-largest parking lot operator in France and Belgium. The acquisition brought to Eiffage some 1.5 million parking spaces.

PUBLIC-PRIVATE PARTNERSHIPS AND A TAKEOVER BID: 2005 AND BEYOND

In 2005 Eiffage won a BOT contract for a prison. It thus became the first private company to be totally responsible for the construction and operation of such a structure in France. This was a result of France's new laws in 2004 supporting public-private partnerships (PPPs). The new legal structure allowed public owners to generate private financing and operations as they did under concession systems but to pay contractors over time rather than tying payment to fees from the users of the project.

Later in 2005, Eiffage moved to its new headquarters in Asnieres-sur-Seine and reorganized its operations. Civil engineering and road building were combined in Eiffage Travaux Publics; infrastructure operation and management in Eiffage Concessions; electrical engineering and Forclum combined; metallic construction activities joined with Eiffel; and all building was now under Eiffage Construction. The company ended the year with revenues of EUR 8.5 billion ($11.8 billion).

Eiffage and Australia's Macquarie Infrastructure Group formed Eiffarie, to bid on toll-road operators being sold by the French government. Its first acquisition was the government's holding in Autoroutes Paris Rhin Rhône (APRR). In October 2006 APRR announced it would increase toll rates on the 2,600 kilometers of roads. By 2007 APRR was the fourth-largest motorway operator in Europe.

Eiffage continued to move aggressively into public partnerships and concessions, winning a BOT contract for the A65, a toll road in southwestern France. As this was happening, Spain's second-largest construction company was making a move into France. Rich with real estate profits from Spain's property boom, Sacyr Vallehermoso began buying Eiffage shares. Within six months, it controlled 32.1 percent of the company.

At Eiffage's 2007 annual shareholders' meeting Sacyr demanded four board seats as it was now 33 percent of the company. Eiffage blocked the request, which led Sacyr to make a takeover bid of EUR 9.75 billion ($13.6 billion). That fall, a French stock exchange regulator found Sacyr guilty of conspiring with other Spanish groups to try to take over Eiffage. As a result, Sacyr would be required to make a full takeover bid of up to EUR 11.8 billion ($18.5 billion) for the company. In March 2008, a French court overturned the full bid requirement and Sacyr sold its shares to French institutional investors.

Despite the pressure and distraction of the Sacyr activities, Eiffage continued to grow. It created a joint venture with another Spanish company to carry out a BOT for a high-speed railroad project between Spain and France. This was the first cross-border project in Europe since the Channel Tunnel, which opened in 1994. Although this one also included tunnels, they were beneath the Pyrenees mountains. Eiffage also continued to invest in other companies, acquiring a majority stake in Czech construction firm, Tchas. Revenues for 2007 totaled EUR 12.6 billion ($17.5 billion).

The year 2008 saw a new PPPs law allowing broader types of projects on an experimental basis through 2012. Among the contracts Eiffage won were partnerships for building and operating hospitals, police stations and a sports stadium. By 2010 it was building and would be managing a new national police headquarters in France and a huge shopping mall and retail park in Portugal and had moved significantly into broadband networking activities.

During the global recession, Eiffage and other French construction companies benefited from the French government's stimulus package of building projects. The company also continued to make acquisitions, including Clemessy, a French electrical installations unit, Dutch rail contractors Heitkamp Rail GmbH and Heijmans Rail BV, and some 15 companies for its Metal division. Revenues for 2009 rose slightly, although income was down 2.3 percent from 2008.

The year 2010 began with a jolt as a court ruled that Eiffage could no longer use the Eiffel name for its metal-work subsidiary. Both the company and the descendants of Eiffel indicated they might reach an agreement allowing Eiffage to continue using the name. Roverato, who had reached the company's retirement age of 65, had his contract as CEO extended for one year. The time was to be used to look for a successor. Eiffage appeared to have a strong base to meet the change coming from new leadership and uncertain economic times.

M. L. Cohen
Updated, Ellen D. Wernick

PRINCIPAL SUBSIDIARIES

Eiffage Construction; Eiffage Travaux Publics; Forclum; Clemessy (99.86%); Eiffel Participations; Financière Eiffarie and Eiffarie (50%); A'Liénor (65%); Crystal; Verdun Participations (51%).

PRINCIPAL OPERATING UNITS

concessions and public-private partnerships; construction; public works; energy; metal.

PRINCIPAL COMPETITORS

VINCI; Bouygues SA; Hochtief; ACS; Skanska AB.

FURTHER READING

Barjonet, Claude, "Eiffage entend consolider son redressement en 98," *Les Echoes*, March 19, 1998, p. 10.

———, "La reprise du batiment donne du tonus a Eiffage," *Les Echoes*, September 15, 1998, p.14.

Chevlolot, Pascal, "Bonne surprise sur Eiffage," *Option Finance*, March 23, 1998, p. 25.

"Eiffage to Search for New Head, Roverato Extended," *Reuters*, April 21, 2010.

Hollinger, Peggy, "Landmark Ruling Robs French Group of Eiffel Name Rights," *Financial Times*, January 13, 2010, p. 18.

Kren, Lawrence, "Bridge on the River Tarn," *Machine Design*, April 18, 2002, p. 48.

Lignieres, Paul, and Simon Ratledge, "PPP a la francaise," *Public Private Finance*, December 2003, p. 21.

Reina, Peter, "Multispan, Cable-Stayed Crossing Is High-Level Landmark," *ENR: Engineering News-Record*, March 15, 2004, pp. 24–29.

Studeman, Frederick, et al., "Profits from Adversity," *International Management*, January–February 1994, p. 36.

"SWOT Analysis," *France Infrastructure Report*, Q2 2010, pp. 6–8.

EMBLAZE™

Emblaze Ltd.

———◆———

Emblaze House
1 Emblaze Square, Industrial Area
P.O. Box 2220
Ra'anana, 43662
Israel
Telephone: (+972 09) 769 9333
Fax: (+972 09) 769 9800
Web site: http://www.emblaze.com

Public Company
Incorporated: 1996 as GEO Interactive Media Group
    Ltd.
Employees: 663
Sales: $473.8 million (2009)
Stock Exchanges: London
Ticker Symbol: BLZ
NAICS: 511210 Software Publishers; 541511 Custom
    Computer Programming Services; 541512
    Computer Systems Design Services

■ ■ ■

Former Israeli high-technology star Emblaze Ltd. has
been reinventing itself as a technology holding company
with investments in two broad technology areas: Growth
Activities and Innovation Activities. The Growth Activities division is grouped around Emblaze's ownership of
51 percent of Formula Systems, the leading publicly
listed Israeli software company and information technology (IT) services company. Formula controls 50 percent
of Matrix IT Ltd., and is Israel's largest provider of IT
integration services, including proprietary software

development services. Formula also holds a 58 percent
stake in Magic Software, a software developer, and 70
percent of Sapiens International NV, an international IT
services provider. Formula Systems accounted for nearly
99 percent of Emblaze's total revenues of $474 million
in 2009.

Emblaze's Innovation Activities division provides a
link to the company's background as a high technology
start-up. This division is focused around three primary
holdings, including a 65 percent stake in Zone-IP Ltd.,
which developed Internet protocol (IP)-based communication equipment and systems; a 95 percent stake
in Emoze Ltd., which has developed a BlackBerry-like
push e-mail system for a wide range of portable wireless
devices; and full control of Else Ltd., formerly Emblaze
Mobile, which has been one of Israel's leading mobile
technology companies.

In 2009 Else introduced its own mobile multimedia
and communications platform, Else Intuition, which
provides the basis for the company's first mobile
handset, the First Else. Emblaze hoped to bring the
handset to market in 2010. Emblaze is led by cofounder
and Chairman Naftali Shani, and CEO Guy Bernstein.
The company is listed on the London Stock Exchange
but is headquartered in Ra'anana, Israel.

BACKGROUND IN THE ISRAEL
DEFENSE FORCES

For much of its history, Emblaze was closely associated
with Eli Reifman. Born in Russia in 1971, Reifman immigrated to Israel in 1975, when he was just four years
old. Reifman's upbringing helped prepare him for a

COMPANY PERSPECTIVES

Our strategy is focused on improving our business performance through constant examination of our businesses in order to achieve long-term sustainable growth in the economic value of the Group. We are targeting growth in revenue and profits through a combination of organic growth, strategic mergers & acquisitions as well as active involvement in portfolio companies.

career in business, as he described to *Ha'aretz*: "It's an extremely militant household. Their expectations were overwhelming. A 90 was a failing grade. I grew up on aspects of my parents' Russian character, of shooting first and asking questions later."

Reifman was still in high school when he launched his first business, a small company involved in international trade based out of his parents' home. Following high school, Reifman completed his service requirement in the Israeli armed forces. Reifman was soon assigned to the Israel Defense Forces' Training Development Center (TDC), where he was placed in charge of the Technical Development Department. During this time Reifman also served as the TDC's acting chief, where he oversaw the production of a number of multimedia-based military simulators.

While at the TDC, Reifman became friends with Sharon Carmel, also born in 1971, who led the Technical Development Department's research and development effort, focusing on Internet applications. Carmel also spent time as the TDC's head of production. Joined by another friend at the TDC, Tzuri Dabosh, Reifman and Carmel recognized the potential for combining and developing the TDC's multimedia and Internet technologies for civilian applications.

MULTIMEDIA FOCUS IN 1994

The three partners sought out a more experienced partner to help them establish their business. This led them to Naftali Shani, then in his early 40s, who had previously served as general manager of Bank Leumi subsidiary Bartrade Ltd. Shani had also served as a treasurer and comptroller for the office of Israel's prime minister. In 1994 the four partners incorporated a new company, called GEO International Computer Based Training Ltd., with Shani as chief executive officer. As its name implied, the company initially sought to apply

Reifman's and Carmel's simulator experience to the training and education sector.

GEO quickly changed focus, however. At the time, the home computer market was experiencing two significant trends. The first accompanied the arrival of affordable CD-ROMs, the progress that had been made in computer graphics and sound systems, and ultimately, the release of Windows 95. These elements combined to establish multimedia applications as the true driving force of the personal computing market. The rise of the Internet represented the second major trend in home computing, as new and more sophisticated graphical interfaces provided greater accessibility to the Internet and a new range of content.

GEO's background in both Internet and multimedia applications placed the company in a strong position where these two trends converged. The company changed its name, becoming GEO Interactive Media Group Ltd., and set out developing its first major project. By 1996 the company had succeeded in introducing Emblaze, one of the first technologies capable of compressing and delivering multimedia content over the Internet. A key feature of Emblaze was that it enabled content providers to stream media without requiring users to install additional software (i. e., plug-ins).

DOT-COM ERA DARLING

GEO quickly capitalized on the success of Emblaze and in October 1996 the company went public, becoming the first Internet stock to list on the London Stock Exchange's Alternative Investment Market (AIM). The offering, for 12 percent of the group's shares, raised $19 million for the company, and valued the company at $160 million. GEO then prepared to launch the first commercial application of the Emblaze technology, called Emblaze Creator. The company also announced plans to extend its technology with an e-mail application.

Reifman took charge of GEO's international marketing effort, which included the opening of an office in Palo Alto, California, in order to be closer to Silicon Valley. The charismatic Reifman quickly emerged as the most visible face of the young company. He also displayed a remarkable talent for marketing, especially to the investment community. In 2000 Reifman took over the company's CEO position. Shani remained as the group's chairman.

By 1998 GEO had moved its listing to the London Stock Exchange's main board. The company then found itself riding the crest of the dot-com wave, as investors poured billions of dollars into the new army of technol-

KEY DATES

■

1994: Eli Reifman and three others found GEO Interactive Media Group in Israel.

1996: GEO lists on London's Alternative Investment Market (AIM) exchange following the launch of its Emblaze multimedia streaming technology.

1998: GEO moves its listing to the London main board.

2001: The company changes its name to Emblaze Ltd.

2007: Emblaze acquires 50.1 percent of Formula Systems Group, a leading Israeli software and information technology services company.

2009: Reifman is indicted for shareholder fraud and forced to step down from Emblaze's board of directors.

ogy start-ups. GEO itself became one of the most notable success stories during this period. In 1999 the company announced a new extension of its Emblaze technology, capable of delivering video to mobile telephones. The announcement helped drive the company's share price still higher. At its peak between 1999 and 2000 GEO had become one of the dot-com sector's market darlings, valued at more than $4.5 billion.

Indicative of the times, GEO's success was all the more remarkable in that the company, despite its strong technology, had yet to develop a truly commercially viable business model. In 1999, for example, the company launched a new generation of its media delivery platform, called Emblaze OnDemand. By then, however, the company had been outpaced by its rivals, and in particular Real Networks. The company beat a retreat from the Internet market and changed its business model, defining itself as a "wireless streaming solutions provider."

CHANGING MODELS IN 2000

Reifman and the other GEO founders continued to profit strongly from the investor demand for the group's stock. For example, in January 2000 the company completed a private placement of 10 million shares, generating nearly $300 million. Toward the end of that year, the company appeared ready to deliver on its promise. In September 2000 the company opened its U.S. headquarters, in New York, in support of the

launch of the wireless iteration of Emblaze. The technology promised the capability of delivering MPEG-4 compliant video and audio content to cellular telephones. The company pinned its hopes on the launch. As one GEO executive explained to *RCR Wireless News*: "The U.S. market growth and potential is enormous, and we have the full intention to be a leading provider of audio and video solutions to the millions of wireless subscribers here."

While the Emblaze platform continued to inspire investor interest, GEO had taken steps to hedge its bet, as it were, by developing a more diversified base of operations. To this end the company developed its own semiconductor division, buying Zapex Research Ltd. This company, which became known as Emblaze Semiconductor, brought the company the technology to develop multimedia-capable chips for mobile telephones. Soon after, Emblaze Semiconducator succeeded in winning a contract to equip a new mobile telephone from Samsung for the Korean market.

In 2000 GEO paid $33 million to acquire Orca Interactive Ltd. This purchase extended the group's multimedia delivery operations to interactive television applications. In June 2001 the company joined in the creation of Alphacell, a joint venture with Poalim Investment and Leader Holding and Investment, which sought to develop Java-based mobile telephones featuring touch screen technology, MP3 playback, and video streaming capacity. By then GEO had also changed its name, becoming Emblaze Ltd. in February 2001. The acquisitions helped the company achieve modest revenues of $30 million in 2000 and $23 million in 2001.

DOT-COM BUST IN 2002

While these investments helped diversify the group's business, they also helped position the company to take advantage of the forthcoming rollout of the new "3G" (third generation) high-speed cellular networks. As Reifman told *New Media Age*: "We don't know which is the most promising. … To go forward, this market is going to require new breeds of terminal, handset, set-top box, network and infrastructure—all the things Emblaze does. These aren't four separate businesses. We're selling all of our solutions to the same customers. Carriers need all the solutions we offer."

However, Emblaze was also reliant on the telecommunications carriers to implement the high-speed networks. When these failed to materialize, shares in the telecommunications and high-technology sector plummeted. Emblaze then found itself with cutting-edge technology with little hope of commercializing it in the near term. The group's hopes, and share price, suffered even more following disappointment over the world's first 3G network, launched by SK Telecom in South Korea. This network debuted in 2001, using the Samsung handset developed in partnership with Emblaze. However, the system barely reached 80 kilobits per second, falling just within the minimum standards established by the International Telecommunications Union for 3G networks.

Emblaze's revenues had dropped by more than 70 percent by the end of 2002, to less than $7 million. The company, which had posted a net loss of $29 million in 2001, then saw its losses deepen, past $91 million. The company's share price also fell, to just $1.10 per share.

SPIN-OFF STRATEGY IN 2004

Emblaze, which continued pouring money into the research and development effort, once again changed its business model in response to the new market conditions. The company bought out its partners in Alphacell Wireless in 2002, forming the basis for a new subsidiary, Emblaze Mobile. This company then began developing its own multimedia-capable mobile telephone handset.

Emblaze completed another acquisition that year, buying UCnGo, a developer of multimedia-messaging (MMS) technologies, which became Emblaze Transcoding. The company also announced its intention to buy its own mobile telephone factory. This led the company to South Korea, where it purchased a 60 percent stake in Innostream Inc. and its factory in 2004.

At the same time, Emblaze launched a streamlining effort. The company sold Emblaze Semiconductor in 2004, raising $54 million in cash. Emblaze also spun off Orca Interactive that year, listing that company on the London AIM, raising an additional $22 million.

Emblaze continued to struggle to raise its revenues, which barely topped $6 million in 2004. Instead, the company launched a series of technology spin-offs. In November 2004 the company merged Emblaze Transcoding into a joint venture with the transcoding business of Philips, forming Adamind Ltd. That company was then floated on the London AIM, raising $26 million for the company. Emblaze, which completed several similar deals through the middle of the decade, sold off its stake in Adamind in 2006, netting an additional $17 million in the process.

FORMULA ACQUISITION IN 2006

Emblaze succeeded in bringing a mobile telephone handset to the market in 2005. For this, the company avoided taking on directly the major handset producers, including Nokia, Siemens, and LG. Instead, the company targeted the "bespoke" market, that is, developing handsets for third parties according to their specifications. The company succeeded in signing up Orange Israel, among others, and by the end of 2005 the company posted its highest-ever revenues, of $120 million. Next, Emblaze targeted a wider rollout of the handset, entering the U.K. market. By the end of 2006, Emblaze's total sales had topped $350 million. The company continued to operate at a loss, however, posting a net loss of more than $9.8 million.

In the meantime, Reifman once again began steering the company in a new direction. In November 2006 Emblaze agreed to pay $70 million to acquire a 33.4 percent stake in Formula Systems, the leading Israeli software group, founded in 1985. Over the next several months, Emblaze continue to acquire shares in Formula Systems, taking control of the company with a 50.1 percent stake in March 2007.

The deal raised eyebrows, notably because of Reifman's willingness to acquire Formula at a premium price. As *Ha'aretz* described the purchase: "For the last 12 years [Reifman]'s been running a financial bubble called Emblaze, a company that managed to raise a humongous $700 million from English investors thanks to his extraordinary marketing skills. It has changed its business model three, four, or five times, lost a combined, oh, about $200 million and has yet to generate material operating income. Reifman is probably sick of being called a bubble boy, and he's probably been looking for a profitable business to meld into Emblaze. Buying a giant like Formula could fill the void inside Emblaze with real business, and grant Reifman some legitimacy."

FOUNDER OUSTED: 2009

As it turned out, the Formula acquisition set in motion Reifman's ouster from the company he had founded 12 years earlier. In December 2006 Reifman turned over the CEO position to Guy Bernstein, taking instead a position as Emblaze's vice-chairman. Emblaze, in the meantime, had been hard hit by a freeze on value-added tax payments in the United Kingdom, which plunged Emblaze Mobile into losses. Emblaze Mobile was shut down in May 2007, and then resurrected as Else Ltd.

A number of Reifman's personal investments failed, leaving him deeply in debt. In an effort to pay off part of his debt, Reifman in November 2008 attempted to sell his stake in Emblaze. Instead, Reifman found himself indicted for committing shareholder fraud. When he refused a court order to turn over his 39 million shares in Emblaze to the company, Reifman was given a 45-day jail sentence for contempt of court, and then placed under house arrest. During 2009, Reifman, who reportedly survived an assassination attempt that year, was forced to step down from Emblaze's board of directors as well.

In the meantime, CEO Bernstein set out to restructure Emblaze's remaining operations. The company took on more of the structure of an investment holding company, regrouping its operations into two main divisions, Growth Activities and Innovation Activities. The former division included Formula Systems, and its three main holdings, Matrix IT, Magic Software, and Sapiens International.

The latter division regrouped Emblaze's historic operations in the mobile communications sector. These included the group's shareholdings in Emoze, a company developing a push e-mail delivery system, similar to that used for Research in Motion's Black-Berry, for other mobile and wireless handset systems; and Zone-IP, which developed IP-based wireless video communications and video conferencing applications.

ANOTHER REDEFINITION

Emblaze continued to seek commercial outlets for its technologies. Toward the end of the decade the company launched its Monolith device, described as an all-in-one communication device, combining a telephone, a camera, an MP3 player, GPS, and other features. While that project struggled to get off of the ground, and appeared doomed in the face of the success of the Apple iPhone and similar devices, Emblaze returned to the handset market in November 2009 with the introduction of a new mobile handset, the First Else, based on Else's Intuition software platform.

Formula continued to represent nearly 99 percent of Emblaze's total revenues, which neared $474 million for 2009. Emblaze, which had pioneered the live streaming market only to be beaten to the market by Apple and other competitors, struck back in 2010, announcing that it had notified both Apple and Microsoft that these companies had infringed on Emblaze's streaming media patents. Founder Reifman also returned to the headlines, claiming to have been the target of a new assassination attempt in April 2010. In the meantime, Emblaze, having survived the dot-com fallout at the dawn of the 21st century, hoped to redefine itself as a technology-focused investment holding company.

M. L. Cohen

PRINCIPAL SUBSIDIARIES

Else Ltd.; Emoze Ltd.; Formula Systems (1985) Ltd. (51.67%); Magic Software Enterprises Ltd. (58.19%); Matrix IT Ltd. (50.2%); NextSource Inc.; Sapiens International Corporation N.V. (70.4%); Zone-IP Ltd.

PRINCIPAL DIVISIONS

Growth Activities; Innovation Activities.

PRINCIPAL OPERATING UNITS

The Formula Group; Emoze; Zone-IP; Else; Emblaze Vcon; Matrix; Magic; Sapiens.

PRINCIPAL COMPETITORS

Aladdin Knowledge Systems Ltd.; AudioCodes Ltd.; BluePhoenix Solutions Ltd.; Clal Industries and Investments Ltd.; EduSoft Ltd.; Freescale Semiconductor Israel Ltd.; Magic Software Enterprises Ltd.; Microsoft Israel Ltd.; Radvision Ltd.; Taldor Group.

FURTHER READING

"Emblaze," *Computer Weekly*, February 16, 2010.

"Emblaze Appoints New CEO," *Total Telecom Online*, December 11, 2006.

"Emblaze's Confusing Evolution," *Investors Chronicle*, September 6, 2007.

"GEO Interactive Changes Name to Emblaze," *RCR Wireless News*, February 19, 2001, p. 54.

Green, Saguy, "Cut a Deal, Catch a Plane," *Ha'aretz*, September 29, 1998.

Hoffman, Tzachi, "Eli Reifman's Emblaze Mobile Launches Touch-screen Phone," *Globes*, November 26, 2009.

King, Ian, "Emblaze Fights Break-up Bid from Corporate Raiders," *Times*, February 23, 2009.

Mitnick, Joshua, "Israeli Company Proudly Enters the Handset Market, but It Starts Small," *New York Times*, March 22, 2004, p. C4.

Morrison, Diane See, "Emblaze (Strategic Play)," *New Media Age*, May 23, 2002, p. 28.

Neate, Rupert, "Bankrupt Dotcom Guru Escapes Another Assassination Attempt," *Daily Telegraph*, April 10, 2010, p. 27.

Sharvit, Noam, "Reifman Back to Jail," *Globes*, December 22, 2009.

Shauli, Avi, "Debts Force Eli Reifman to Sell Emblaze Shares," *Israel Business Arena*, November 26, 2008.

Shoval, Ofri, "Stand-up Guru," *Ha'aretz*, July 10, 2008.

Engelberth Construction, Inc.

463 Mountain View Drive
Colchester, Vermont 05446-5966
U.S.A.
Telephone: (802) 655-0100
Toll Free: (800) 639-9011
Fax: (802) 655-4882
Web site: http://www.engelberth.com

Private Company
Incorporated: 1972
Employees: 260
Sales: $87 million (2009 est.)
NAICS: 236220 Commercial and Institutional Building
Construction; 236210 Industrial Building
Construction

■ ■ ■

Engelberth Construction, Inc., is a privately held general construction firm that focuses on commercial projects in Vermont, New Hampshire, northeastern New York, and Massachusetts. It is one of the largest construction companies in Vermont. In addition to its headquarters in Colchester, Vermont, Engelberth maintains a branch office in Keene, New Hampshire. Industries served include colleges and universities, including work for such major area schools as Dartmouth College and the University of Vermont; public schools; health care and laboratories; industrial; assisted and independent living; office, including both public and private projects; hospitality, in particular resort projects; recreation, including athletic facilities, ranging from football fields

to the International Luge Training Complex in Lake Placid, New York; and retail, featuring supermarkets, malls, and other retail facilities.

Engelberth also offers preconstruction planning services such as estimating, feasibility studies, value analysis/engineering, logistics planning, bid package assembly, and procurement. Founder Otto Engelberth serves as chairman and chief executive officer, but most of the day-to-day decisions are made by longtime lieutenant and company President Pierre LeBlanc and Executive Vice President and Chief Financial Officer Tom Clavelle.

INDIANA ORIGINS

Otto Engelberth was born in Hammond, Indiana, in 1939, and raised on a hog and dairy farm near Warsaw in northern Indiana. He was the youngest child of a large family, the son of immigrants who came to the United States from Germany in the 1920s. His father was a trained bricklayer who in the 1920s and 1930s owned masonry and ceramic tile businesses. He learned construction from his father and put those skills to use on the farm, where his family took care of all of its construction needs. He had no intention, however, of farming or pursuing construction. Rather, he grew up dreaming of becoming a baseball player, and later, as was typical growing up in Indiana, home of the Indianapolis 500, he longed to become a race car driver. He enrolled at Purdue University to study mechanical engineering, but dropped out after a difficult first semester and moved to California to study at a race car mechanic school as a way to pursue his interest in

```
┌─────────────────────────────────────┐
│  COMPANY PERSPECTIVES               │
│              ■                      │
│  We build relationships for life.   │
└─────────────────────────────────────┘
```

racing. However, he thought better of that career choice a few months later, and returned home to resume his studies at Purdue.

After graduating from Purdue, Engelberth went to work on an interstate highway project for the Illinois State Highway Department. He was soon drafted into the U.S. Army and assigned to the Corps of Engineers. He became familiar with New England when he was assigned to the Cold Regions Laboratory in Hanover, New Hampshire. After his discharge he moved to Vermont in 1963 and went to work for a number of construction companies over the next several years, including Pizzagalli Construction Company in South Burlington, Vermont. He spent four years at Pizzagalli before striking out on his own, a step he had been planning to take since his marriage at the age of 26.

COMPANY LAUNCHED: 1972

In 1972 Engelberth and his wife started Engelberth Construction out of their home in Essex Junction, Vermont, with $20,000. Half of the money came from a second mortgage on their house and the balance from a loan provided by Engelberth's mother. "We got a couple of file drawers and used a door as a desktop, and away we went," he recalled in an interview with *Vermont Business Magazine.*

The firm's first project in 1972 was the Chittenden Bank branch in Westfield, Vermont. Overall, the early years were a struggle for Engelberth Construction. Although the company completed almost $1 million worth of work in its first year, it lost money. However, Engelberth Construction gradually turned a profit and expanded beyond a home-based company. An important early customer was IBM, for which the first work was completed in 1973. It was the start of a long-term relationship with IBM. Repeat business with IBM and other clients would be a key to the development of Engelberth Construction.

Annual sales were in the $3 million range in 1982 when Engelberth decided measures had to be taken to enable the 50-person company to enjoy stronger growth. He focused on building a flexible and productive workforce, achieved by eliminating underperforming people, offering higher pay and better benefits, and providing

training to assemble a strong roster of employees. "If we had the chance to get a good carpenter we'd hire them," Engelberth stated in a 1998 profile of the firm in *Vermont Business Magazine.* He did not, however, expand too far from home base, limiting bidding to projects that offered a commute that could allow his employees to be home with their families at night. "When you start growing and start to dislocate people they get disoriented," he explained. "In the long term it's not in the best interest of the company."

SKILLED EMPLOYEES BECOME SCARCE

Later in the 1980s Engelberth Construction opened an office in Lebanon, New Hampshire, that allowed it to bid on projects along the Interstate 89 corridor that ran from Hanover, New Hampshire, to New London. The company also took on projects in nearby New York markets. Annual revenues reached the $30 million level in 1988 and the firm ranked in the top 50 of Vermont's largest companies according to *Vermont Business Magazine.* Due to the ready availability of bank credit at the time, Vermont enjoyed a development boom, but a real estate crash in 1989 brought this to an abrupt end. Engelberth Construction was able to weather the tough times, but during the recession that followed the crash many tradespeople exited the construction field, never to return.

In 1989 there had been 17,850 construction workers in Vermont. Ten years later that number had dipped to 13,200. Moreover, young people were less interested in pursuing trade occupations, leading to a lack of replacements for a graying pool of labor that was beginning to retire. As a result, as the economy picked up in the 1990s and construction projects became more plentiful, one of the largest concerns of Engelberth Construction and other contractors was finding enough skilled employees.

ORGANIZATIONAL CHANGES

Because the company had made an effort to develop a skilled and loyal workforce, Engelberth Construction fared better than most construction firms during the labor crunch of the 1990s. It was also in the late 1980s and early 1990s that Engelberth Construction changed its organizational structure, abandoning a traditional command-and-control approach in favor of a team-oriented organization. Rather than employees hoarding information as a way to maintain power, they were given a common set of information and encouraged to work together to achieve a mutually beneficial result. The advent of the Internet also helped the company to

KEY DATES

1972: Engelberth Construction is founded in Essex Junction, Vermont Company.
1973: First contract with IBM is awarded.
1994: Bedford, New Hampshire, office opens.
1997: Pierre LeBlanc is named Vermont division president.
2008: Revenues reach $124 million.

extend its team structure to designers, subcontractors, and clients, who were also provided with information and integrated into the process for the betterment of the project.

In addition, Engelberth Construction made changes to its compensation structure to improve the company culture. It added what it called "variable pay," to supplement regular pay and the company's benefits package. Based on the result of what employees directly controlled, it was issued on a quarterly basis. The higher an employee was in the organization, the greater percentage of base pay came from variable pay.

Revenues totaled $40.3 million in 1992, a strong performance at a time when the construction industry was struggling. A year later revenues increased to $69 million, but that amount was somewhat misleading, given that $11 million of the total was a residence project in Shelburne, Vermont, that had been delayed and shifted into 1993. Engelberth Construction opened a full-service office in Bedford, New Hampshire, in 1994 to grow the business further in New Hampshire.

LEBLANC NAMED PRESIDENT: 1997

Business was stagnant for a period in the mid-1990s but rebounded well as the economy roared back to life. By 1998 the company, enjoying the benefits of another boom period, posted annual revenues of $95 million. Business began to drop off and revenues dipped to $85 million as the decade came to a close. A major project in the late 1990s was the $20 million contract to construct the Grand Summit Hotel at Mount Snow in West Dover, Vermont. It was a massive endeavor completed in 11 months, requiring the company to work seven days a week to keep pace.

In 1997 Pierre LeBlanc was named president of the Vermont division of the company. He began to take over much of the day-to-day responsibilities from Otto

Engelberth, eventually becoming president of the entire firm. LeBlanc, with strengths in estimating and project management, had been with the company since 1979 and had served as vice president of operations.

Vermont enjoyed record economic expansion in the late 1990s and into the new century. Engelberth Construction's revenues remained flat at $85 million. The company could have taken on more projects but the shortage of skilled workers did not allow it to expand beyond 270 employees. Other area construction firms became overly ambitious but took on more work than they could handle, resulting in a failure to meet timetables. Rather than tarnish its reputation, which for decades had generated repeat business and remained the key to sustained growth, Engelberth Construction elected to take on only the work it could reasonably handle. It did, however, secure one of Vermont's most attractive contracts at the dawn of the new century, the Maple Tree Place retail, office, and residential complex in Williston, Vermont. In addition, the firm landed a contract for a set of luxury resident duplexes at the Stratton Mountain resort.

SIGNIFICANT CONTRACTS

Engelberth Construction continued to win its share of significant contracts. It completed the Mascoma Savings Bank operations center in Vermont in 2004. In that same year it broke ground on the Sudikoff Laboratory project at Dartmouth College. A year later the firm began work on another university project, a history museum at Norwich University in Northfield, Vermont. In 2007 Engelberth Construction won a $27.2 million contract to build the Tuck School Living and Learning Complex at Dartmouth College. It was a 65,000-square-foot mixed-use facility that included classrooms, dormitory residences, study areas, and kitchens.

Notable projects for Engelberth Construction continued in 2008. The company began work on a $12 million two-pool swim center in Hartford, Vermont. The firm was also selected as the manager of a $21 million building and renovation project for New London Hospital. These contracts helped Engelberth Construction to boost revenues to $124 million in 2008. Like the rest of the country, however, Vermont was feeling the pinch caused by a downturn in the housing market and a credit crunch that led to difficult years in the local construction industry.

Although Engelberth Construction experienced a slip in revenues to $87 million in 2009, it performed better than most, due in no small measure to its long-term relations and sterling reputation. The company won one of the few large new available contracts in the

$25.7 million Castleton Student Initiative at Vermont's Castleton State College, for building a stadium and athletic fields. Engelberth Construction was poised to secure its share of important contracts in the New England market when the economy improved.

Ed Dinger

PRINCIPAL DIVISIONS

New Hampshire; Vermont.

PRINCIPAL COMPETITORS

Bread Loaf Corporation; John A. Russell Corporation; Pizzagalli Construction.

FURTHER READING

"Construction Companies: There's a Lot of Work, but Trouble Finding Workers," *Vermont Business Magazine*, January 1, 1999.

Edelstein, Art, "Engelberth Grows Despite Building Slowdown," *Vermont Business Magazine*, January 1994, p. 27.

————, "Engelberth Stays Close to Home," *Vermont Business Magazine*, April 1998, p. 56.

Edwards, Bruce, "Local Construction Follows Nation down Rabbit Hole," *Rutland Herald*, March 30, 2009.

Kelley, Kevin, "Construction Boom Affected by Labor Crunch," *Vermont Business Magazine*, January 2001.

"Q&A: Engelberth Sets Sights on Building New Career in Montpelier," *Vermont Business Magazine*, September 2000.

Entergy Corp.

639 Loyola Avenue
New Orleans, Louisiana 70113
U.S.A.
Telephone: (504) 576-4000
Fax: (504) 576-4428
Web site: http://www.entergy.com

Public Company
Incorporated: 1949 as Middle South Utilities
Employees: 15,000
Sales: $10.75 billion (2009)
Stock Exchanges: New York
Ticker Symbol: ETR
NAICS: 221122 Electric Power Distribution; 22121 Natural Gas Distribution; 221112 Fossil Fuel Electric Power Generation; 221113 Nuclear Electric Power Generation; 551112 Offices of Other Holding Companies

■ ■ ■

Entergy Corp. is a holding company for utilities that supply electrical energy to more than 2.7 million customers in the middle south of the United States, including Arkansas, Louisiana, Mississippi, and Texas. The company is the nation's second-largest owner of nuclear power plants with 11 units in its holdings. Its subsidiaries also provide natural gas service to 189,000 customers in Baton Rouge and New Orleans. Entergy operates over 15,500 miles of high-voltage transmission lines and 1,550 transmission substations. The company planned to spin off its nuclear holdings as Enexus

Energy Corp. but dropped the strategy in 2010 after the New York State Public Service Commission rejected the plan.

ORIGINS AND EARLY HISTORY

Although Entergy was incorporated as a public company called Middle South Utilities (MSU) in 1949, its four constituent power companies had operated as an interdependent system for 25 years. These companies were Arkansas Power & Light, Louisiana Power & Light, Mississippi Power & Light, and New Orleans Public Service, Inc. In 1981 Arkansas-Missouri Power was merged into Arkansas Power & Light after having been owned by MSU since the early 1970s.

During the 1950s, the company was one of the fastest-growing utility systems in the United States, largely because of the industrialization of its territory and the ensuing rise in the standard of living. Much of this expansion sprung from industrial development programs initiated by MSU-supplied companies. Among the more significant and economically resilient industries founded were oil, natural gas, and chemicals. Large manufacturers, including General Motors, built plants in the region. Reynolds Metals brought the area the electricity-intensive aluminum industry. In addition, from 1945 to 1955, use of electricity per residential customer in the middle South rose faster than the national average. Three of the four constituent companies did not have a rate increase from the end of World War II until the early 1960s. From 1947 through 1951, MSU and its predecessor companies spent $236 million on plant expansions, financed by common stock sales in 1950, 1951, and 1952.

In 1953 MSU became involved in a dispute with the U.S. government. Edgar H. Dixon, head of MSU, and Eugene A. Yates, head of the Southern Company, proposed a plant to supply power to the Tennessee Valley Authority (TVA), which would make this power available to the Atomic Energy Commission. The plan stirred up a battle in Congress between those favoring government ownership of utilities and those favoring investor ownership, eventually causing U.S. President Dwight Eisenhower to void the contract. Although the government claimed that the contract's cancellation was based on a conflict of interest by an investment banker, Adolphe Wenzell, who was advising both the utilities and the government, the utilities sued the government in 1955. The U.S. Court of Claims found no conflict of interest and granted the utilities $1.8 million in damages in 1959.

NUCLEAR ENERGY AND OTHER DEVELOPMENTS: 1960–69

Despite the legal battle, the 1950s were prosperous for Middle South, as the next decade would also prove to be. In 1961 MSU was one of 11 private power firms, headed by Robert Welch of Southwestern Electric Power Company, to offer to exchange energy with the TVA, whose surplus summer power would be exchanged for the companies' surplus power in the winter, effecting considerable savings for both parties.

In a similar agreement in October 1967, Middle South united with Southern Company to coordinate planning and operation of their facilities for 10 years. Such partnerships were part of a general trend among utilities to foster joint ventures and cooperation. The plan included mutual assistance in case of emergencies that would reduce probability of large-scale power failures. The firms also planned to coordinate building of plants and long-distance power lines. The two systems were directly connected with each other through transmission facilities in Mississippi and Louisiana and indirectly connected through neighboring systems.

The increasing need for electricity in MSU's region called for $1.12 billion worth of construction during the 1960s, or about $118 million per year during the decade. During the 1960s, total electric energy sales almost tripled, going from 10.4 billion kilowatt-hours in 1959 to 31 billion kilowatt-hours in 1969. Although annual electricity use per household increased more than two and a half times, and revenue per customer nearly doubled, increased efficiency meant that the average cost to the customer per kilowatt-hour decreased 28.6 percent during the decade.

When founded, MSU assumed unlimited availability of natural gas as its major fuel source. During the 1960s, however, gas became increasingly scarce, and MSU had to consider other fuel options. In 1967 the company began construction of its first nuclear plant, built by its Arkansas Power & Light subsidiary. The $140 million plant was erected in Russellville, Arkansas, at the Dardanelle Reservoir on a 1,110-acre parcel of land. It began producing energy in 1974.

Beginning in 1969, due to the Federal Power Commission's heightened restriction of interstate natural gas delivery, MSU founded its System Fuels, Inc., subsidiary to provide fuel for utility operations. By 1974 the subsidiary had located six natural gas wells. It also purchased fuel oil. By 1974 MSU was building four 700-megawatt coal-fired units, the first to go into operation in 1978. MSU bought the coal for these units from Kerr-McGee Oil Company and Peabody Coal Company.

CONTINUED NUCLEAR FOCUS AND NEW PLANT CONSTRUCTION: 1970–85

MSU was a leader in the trend toward nuclear energy. In the 1970s it planned to derive 43 percent of its new capacity, which was 2,965 megawatts, from nuclear power plants. Among the company's most significant research projects were those underway at the Southwest Nuclear Research Center near Fayetteville, Arkansas. Installed there was the Southwest Experimental Fast Oxide Reactor, which at the time was the only reactor in the United States fueled with plutonium oxide. Its purpose was to verify the safety and desirability of breeder reactors. To back the project MSU joined with

KEY DATES

1949: Middle South Utilities (MSU) is incorporated.

1961: MSU begins a power exchanging contract with the Tennessee Valley Authority.

1967: MSU begins a cooperative agreement with Southern Company; construction begins on Russellville, Arkansas, nuclear plant.

1981: MSU's Arkansas-Missouri Power is merged into Arkansas Power & Light.

1989: Middle South Utilities is renamed Entergy Corporation.

2000: Entergy acquires TLG Services and Indian Point 3 nuclear plant and signs agreements with The Shaw Group, Koch Industries, and Framatome Technologies.

2002: The Vermont Yankee nuclear power plant is acquired.

2005: Hurricanes Katrina and Rita knock out power to 1.8 million customers combined.

2010: The New York State Public Service Commission rejects Entergy's plans to spin off its nuclear holdings as Enexus Energy Corporation.

13 other investor-owned companies, called Southwest Atomic Energy Associates, as well as General Electric, the U.S. Atomic Energy Commission, and the Karlsruhe Nuclear Research Center of Germany.

In 1974, with the company's Arkansas nuclear plant in operation, two MSU subsidiaries, Mississippi Power & Light and Middle South Energy, Inc., began construction of two more nuclear plants at the Grand Gulf station in Mississippi. During the early 1970s, however, the system continued to rely on natural gas. In 1974 oil provided 27 percent of total fuel requirements, gas 68 percent, and nuclear and hydroelectric production about 5 percent.

In 1975, to secure a steady fuel supply until its nuclear and coal-based facilities would be in full operation in the 1980s, MSU entered a joint project with Northeast Petroleum and Ingram Corp. The companies founded Energy Corporation of Louisiana to build a $300 million refinery in Garyville, Louisiana, producing low-sulfur fuel oil. Floyd Lewis, who began as a lawyer with New Orleans Public Service, became president of MSU in 1970. He led the company through a decade of growth despite mounting economic stress. Debilitating

outside factors included the Middle East oil embargo and the attendant rise in fuel costs; environmental and other controls on construction; inflation and interest rates that increased building costs; and the nuclear accident at Three Mile Island that strengthened the resolve of the U.S. antinuclear movement. In 1977 sales topped $1 billion, a 23 percent increase from 1976.

By 1977 MSU was involved in its most ambitious construction program ever. From 1970 through 1976, it had spent $2.67 billion on plant expansion. Expenditures of $2.37 billion were anticipated for 1977 through 1979. However, while new production sites formerly lowered utility rates, the opposite became true: new plants, whether coal or nuclear, were time-consuming and expensive to build. It took 6 to 8 years for a coal-run facility and 10 to 14 years for a nuclear plant, with a cost of $1,000 to $2,000 per kilowatt. MSU sought numerous rate increases to cover its costs, but regulators would not allow the construction costs to be reflected in rates until the plants were operational.

MSU continued to build, tying up capital in plants under construction that it was unable to invest to generate income for most of the decade. From 1974 through 1985, MSU sank $6.1 billion into construction of its Grand Gulf and Waterford nuclear plants. During construction, MSU was able to disguise its financial weakness through the allowance for funds used during construction, which allowed it to register the profits it would make on its construction assets if the plants were in fact producing. In 1985 such noncash credit constituted 91 percent of MSU's earnings.

OVERCOMING HARDSHIPS: 1985–89

Reality set in, however, after production began at Grand Gulf in mid-1985. The facility, owned by MSU subsidiary System Energy Resources, Inc., sold power wholesale to MSU's four operating companies according to an allocation established by the Federal Energy Regulatory Commission. The commission also set the wholesale cost of Grand Gulf's power. The rate increases needed to cover these costs were so high, up to 20 percent, that state regulatory commissions initially refused any increase at all.

The company absorbed more than $330 million in Grand Gulf construction costs, planning to recover the rest through gradual rate increases over the next decade. It also took a substantial loss on its $950 million investment in the rudiments of the second Grand Gulf plant, whose construction was halted by the Mississippi Public Service Commission (MPSC). MSU stopped paying its common stock dividends in order to save money. Mississippi regulators finally granted a $326 million interstate wholesale rate increase to Mississippi Power & Light in September 1985.

In 1986 President and Chairman Floyd Lewis was hospitalized, and Edwin Lupberger assumed Lewis's duties as MSU's difficulties continued. The interest rate the company had to pay on its debt rose, and common stock sold for 50 percent to 75 percent of book value, as contrasted with the 110 percent to 120 percent typical of a healthy utility stock. Lupberger, in an interview with *Forbes*, July 28, 1986, characterized the company's situation as "more uncertain than it's been since the Depression."

In 1987 the Mississippi Supreme Court rescinded the MPSC's 1985 rate increase. Mississippi Power & Light appealed to the U.S. Supreme Court, saying that cancellation of the increase would bankrupt it. At the same time, Louisiana regulators reduced by $28 million a $76 million increase granted to another subsidiary. Standard & Poor's lowered its ratings on $7 billion worth of MSU debt and preferred stock. On June 28, 1988, the U.S. Supreme Court ruled that the 1985 Mississippi rate increase was valid, and as a result MSU's security ratings were upgraded. More than $200 million that had been collected, but held in escrow pending the court's decision, was released on August 11, 1988. Although earnings continued to be lower than the previous year, overall financial stability of the organization was on the upswing, as evidenced by the reinstatement on September 10 of its quarterly common stock dividend for the first time since its 1985 suspension.

By the end of 1988, the company's financial recovery was basically complete, although its stock continued to sell at 75 percent of book value, nearly 39 percent less than the industry average. In late 1988, MSU consolidated the management of all four of its nuclear plants at System Energy Resources, a move expected to lower costs by $23 million.

Lawsuits questioning other nuclear investments continued to plague MSU. Lupberger, fearing the uncertainty and strain of more drawn-out litigation, negotiated a compromise agreement called Project Olive Branch, settling the suits out of court. This hoisted the company's return on capital nearer to the industry average of 8.6 percent. Its stock price rebounded as well.

NAME CHANGE TO ENTERGY: 1989

At the annual meeting on May 19, 1989, shareholders approved changing MSU's name to Entergy Corporation. Heading into the 1990s, the company had largely regained financial stability. In 1991 its New

Orleans Public Service subsidiary reached an agreement with the New Orleans City Council that let the utility recover a portion of its investment in the Grand Gulf nuclear plant. Late in 1991 Entergy increased its common stock dividend.

One of the biggest changes in the nuclear power industry came with federal deregulation that began in the early 1990s. Public entities sold their nuclear plants for very low bids. Most private companies did not want such risky ventures, but Entergy decided to expand its nuclear power operations. In 1999 it purchased the Pilgrim Nuclear Power Station in Plymouth, Massachusetts. The following year it acquired two more facilities: the Indian Point 3 plant in Westchester County, New York, and the James A. Fitzpatrick plant in Oswego County, New York. In 2001 it closed its purchase from Con Edison of Indian Point 2 plant.

Thus Entergy played a key role in the resurgence of the nuclear power industry. Entergy and Exelon, the industry leader, spent almost $4 billion to buy 15 nuclear plants. The private owners of such plants by the late 1990s had "reversed years of mismanagement and cost overruns to turn the plants into the reliable, profitable atomic engines they were meant to be," said *Time*'s Daniel Eisenberg. Of course, the storage of radioactive waste remained a challenge for the nation's 103 operating nuclear plants that produced about 20 percent of the country's electricity.

Meanwhile, Entergy owned, managed, or invested in many fossil-fuel and hydroelectric generating plants that in 2001 generated over 30,000 megawatts of electricity in the United States and other nations. Only five of its generating units used hydroelectric power. Seven units used coal. According to its Web site, Entergy had 58 units that used oil, natural gas, or a combination of the two energy sources.

Entergy Corporation's operating revenues went from $7.16 billion in 1996 to $9.53 billion in 1997, $11.49 billion in 1998, and $8.77 billion in 1999. Its consolidated net income in 1996 was $490.6 million. That went to $300.9 million in 1997, $785.6 million in 1998, and then $595 million in 1999.

SUCCESS IN THE NEW MILLENNIUM

The firm's 2000 annual report described a good year for Entergy. It had four quarters of record earnings, and its stock price at the end of the year was at a record level. Entergy ranked first among surveyed American utilities for its one-year progress in customer satisfaction, according to a study published in April 2000. Other 2000 highlights included forming a joint venture called

Entergy-Koch, L.P. with Koch Industries, a major energy trading and marketing firm, and cooperating with The Shaw Group to create Entergy Shaw, L.L.C., a power plant construction firm. Entergy in 2000 also acquired TLG Services, a nuclear decommissioning company, and signed a contract with Framatome Technologies to help nuclear plants renew their licenses. Plans to merge with FPL Group, the parent of Florida Power & Light, were called off in 2001.

In 2001 Entergy and other power companies continued to deal with divisive issues such as global warming and climate change. Since some blamed carbon dioxide emissions from fossil fuel plants for the so-called greenhouse effect, Entergy and some other energy companies committed themselves to the reduction of such emissions.

Another power controversy in 2001 was electrical transmission. Entergy proposed a privately funded expansion of the grid system that was disputed by municipal power agencies and other critics. Such public policy disputes kept Entergy's leaders busy as they dealt with state regulatory bodies and the Federal Energy Regulatory Commission. The good news for the power industry was the growing population's increased demand for electrical energy. That helped fuel Entergy's rising stock prices. Its shares increased 63 percent over one year to about $41 per share at the end of April 2001.

The company continued with its growth plans in 2002, adding the Vermont Yankee nuclear power plant to its holdings. The company's success at this time was noted throughout the industry. Entergy was awarded the prestigious Edison Award that year, which was considered one of the industry's highest honors. It was also ranked fifth on the Dow Jones Sustainability Index in 2002.

In order to focus on its core power and nuclear operations, the company sold several foreign interests in Argentina, Chile, Peru, Spain, and the United Kingdom during 2002. In 2004 the company sold Gulf South Pipeline Company to TGT Pipeline LLC for approximately $1.14 billion. Merrill Lynch & Co. acquired the company's Entergy-Koch Trading unit that year.

OVERCOMING HURRICANES IN 2005

Disaster struck in 2005 when Hurricanes Katrina and Rita hit the Gulf states in August and September, respectively. The two storms knocked out power to 1.8 million customers combined. Entergy was forced to temporarily relocate its headquarters and its assets were considerably damaged by the worst storms in its history.

Entergy's New Orleans subsidiary, which was hit the hardest by the disaster, filed for Chapter 11 bankruptcy protection in September of that year. Entergy New Orleans emerged from bankruptcy protection in 2007.

While the company worked to shore up the electrical system in New Orleans, it sought to recover costs related to the damage. By early 2006, the costs were estimated at $705 million in Louisiana Public Service Commission territories. Entergy came under fire during this period when it attempted to pass along higher rates to its customers. Critics opposed the rate hikes and claimed consumers should not have to pay higher fees while company executives continued to received large bonuses, fly on corporate jets, and receive perks that critics deemed frivolous.

Meanwhile, Entergy continued to bolster is nuclear holdings. During 2007 the company purchased the Palisades nuclear plant located near South Haven, Michigan, from Consumers Energy Company. By that time, the company owned 11 reactors and managed a 12th facility. It also acquired the Calcasieu Generating Facility in southwestern Louisiana during 2008 and the Ouachita Plant, which was located near Monroe, Louisiana.

ATTEMPTING TO RESTRUCTURE: 2007–10

During 2007 the company set plans in motion to restructure its business operations. In order to comply with varying state regulations, the company opted to separate its Louisiana and Texas operations. The move created Entergy Gulf States Louisiana LLC and Entergy Texas Inc. It also announced its intention to spin off its nonutility nuclear business. By 2008 it had created Enexus Energy Corporation to operate as its nuclear power spin-off. Equagen L.L.C. was also established as the joint venture that would be owned by Entergy and Enexus and operate the nuclear facilities. The company dropped its plans in early 2010, however, when the New York State Public Service Commission rejected the spin-off proposal due to concerns about increasing debt levels.

The company's nuclear business hit another roadblock in early 2010 when the Vermont Senate voted not to extend the operating license for the Vermont Yankee nuclear plant. Radioactive leaks had been discovered in 2009 and were partially responsible for the Senate's decision, which would force the plant to close by 2012 when its license expired. The company continued to promote nuclear power as a clean and reliable energy source but the debate on its merits continued throughout the industry and development of nuclear reactors remained a political hot topic. The debate surrounding the United States' future energy sources was also fueled by the massive oil spill in the Gulf of Mexico that was caused by an explosion on the BP plc Deepwater Horizon oil rig in April 2010. The spill was considered to be the largest environmental disaster in U.S. history.

The first decade of the 21st century had proved challenging for Entergy with devastating hurricanes and storms, a global economic downturn, fluctuating energy markets, and the growing need to reduce greenhouse gas emissions while finding environmentally friendly and safe energy alternatives. Despite these challenges, the company had won numerous industry awards and secured record-setting earnings. While future U.S. energy policies remained uncertain, Entergy appeared poised for growth as the second-largest nuclear power producer in the country with revenues surpassing $10 billion.

Elaine Belsito
Updated, David M. Walden; Christina M. Stansell

PRINCIPAL SUBSIDIARIES

Entergy Arkansas, Inc.; Entergy Gulf States Louisiana, L.L.C.; Entergy Louisiana LLC; Entergy Mississippi, Inc.; Entergy New Orleans, Inc.; Entergy Texas, Inc.; Entergy Nuclear Entergy Solutions LLC; Entergy Solutions District Cooling, LP; Entergy Thermal, LLC.

PRINCIPAL COMPETITORS

AEP Texas Central Company; CenterPoint Energy, Inc.; Southern Company.

FURTHER READING

Blankinship, Steve, "Mergers and Acquisitions," *Power Engineering*, May 2001, p. 21.

Brull, Steven, "Mushrooming Profits," *Institutional Investor*, May 2001, pp. 38–45.

Chesto, Jon, "Entergy Drops Spin-Off Plans," *Patriot Ledger*, April 6, 2010.

"CMS Unit to Sell Michigan Nuclear Power Plant to Entergy for $380M," *Power Market Today*, July 13, 2006.

Cook, James, "A Nuclear Survivor," *Forbes*, July 28, 1986.

Eisenberg, Daniel, "Nuclear Summer," *Time*, May 28, 2001, pp. 58–60.

Gray, Robert T., "The Timeless Skills of a Modern Manager," *Nation's Business*, December 1983.

"La.-Based Entergy Corp. Splits Louisiana, Texas Operations," *New Orleans City Business*, July 30, 2007.

Lorenzetti, Maureen, "CO(2) Battles Just Beginning," *Oil & Gas Journal*, March 26, 2001, p. 25.

"Louisiana PSC Puts Entergy Chief on Rack," *Electric Utility Week*, January 23, 2006.

Radford, Bruce W., "Entergy's Grid Grab," *Public Utilities Fortnightly*, March 1, 2001, p. 4.

Rago, Joseph, "The Weekend Interview with J. Wayne Leonard: The Carbon Cap Dilemma," *Wall Street Journal*, March 28, 2009.

Sidel, Robin, "FPL, Entergy Blame Each Other as They Call Off $8 Billion Merger," *Wall Street Journal*, April 3, 2001, p. A4.

Slawsky, Richard, "Katrina Zaps Power, Threatens Move from N.O. for Fortune 500 Entergy," *New Orleans City Business*, December 26, 2005.

Wald, Matthew L., "Countdown at Indian Point 3: An Early Test of Nuclear Plant's New Private Ownership," *New York Times*, May 13, 2001, p. 13.

———, "Vermont Senate Votes to Close Nuclear Plant," *New York Times*, February 24, 2010.

Farm Family Holdings, Inc.

344 Route 9W
Glenmont, New York 12077
U.S.A.
Telephone: (518) 431-5000
Fax: (518) 431-5975
Web site: http://www.farmfamily.com

Wholly Owned Subsidiary of American National Insurance Company
Incorporated: 1996
Employees: 600
Total Assets: $1.3 billion (2000)
NAICS: 524126 Direct Property and Casualty Insurance Carriers

■ ■ ■

Through its subsidiaries, Farm Family Holdings, Inc., provides life and property and casualty insurance products in 12 northeastern states. Headquartered in Glenmont, New York, the principal subsidiaries of Farm Family have exclusive endorsements to market insurance products to Farm Bureau members in five states. The company became part of American National Insurance Company in 2001.

FARM BUREAU MOVEMENT ORIGINS

The history of Farm Family Holdings is very much a part of the Farm Bureau movement and the dozens of insurance companies created by state organizations. The first county farm bureau was established in 1911 in the Binghamton, New York, Chamber of Commerce to sponsor an extension agent from the U.S. Department of Agriculture. The tag "bureau" soon was applied to state farming organizations. By 1919, 500 members representing state farm bureaus (or representing states that were in the process of organizing) gathered in Chicago to form a national organization that would become the American Farm Bureau Federation (AFBF). More commonly, the organization became known as the Farm Bureau.

From its inception, the Farm Bureau faced the question of what was to be its focus: education or commerce. According to Orville Menton Kile in his book *The Farm Bureau through Three Decades*, "Those who favored active business operations wanted heavy fees and a big budget; the advocates of the purely educational type of organization not only felt that a big fund was not needed, but that its existence would be a constant temptation to embark upon commercial pursuits."

One of the earliest commercial ventures pursued by individual state farm bureaus was auto insurance, as a "service to member" operation. The pioneer in this field was the founder of State Farm Insurance, George Mecherle of Bloomington, Illinois. He created a mutual insurance company for rural and small-town drivers who in the early 1920s were paying higher premiums even though they had fewer accidents than drivers in more urban areas. By linking insurance rates to risk levels, Mecherle was able to offer significantly lower premiums than his competitors. He also signed agreements with state farm bureaus, which would receive a fee for each of

COMPANY PERSPECTIVES

Family is proud of its long-standing role of service to the agribusiness community in the Northeastern United States. Over the years, Farm Family has earned a solid reputation, with an established tradition of trust. Farm Family agents are insurance professionals who recognize that personal service is the key to meeting individual and business concerns.

their members who purchased policies. Some state farm bureaus took Mercherle's lead and formed their own mutual auto insurance companies: Ohio in 1926, Illinois in 1927, and New Hampshire in 1928. Not only did insurance generate revenue for the farm bureaus, it acted as an inducement for membership.

EARLY GROWTH

In the words of an early Farm Bureau insurance executive, Murray Lincoln, quoted in *Dollar Harvest*, "When we first started our insurance company, it never dawned on me that we would ever insure anyone but farmers. But once we started insuring farmers other than Farm Bureau members, we found that we simply could not keep out the barber in the small town, the grocer, the gas station attendant, the shopkeeper, or any other type of small businessman. Finally, as our company grew, we had to throw out the window the concept of restricting our insurance only to farmers." Expanding in a similar manner, state Farm Bureaus began sponsoring insurance companies that also sold fire, casualty, and life insurance policies.

Affiliation with the Farm Bureau proved to be a powerful selling tool. According to *Dollar Harvest*, "When a Farm Bureau insurance agent knocks on the door in many areas of the country, he immediately has the respectability of the organization working for him. If the man or woman who answers the door is not a member himself, perhaps his father was, or maybe his son is active in a 4-H club which meets in the Farm Bureau building. In any case, the image is not the same as that presented by other insurance companies, and image is all-important in the sale of insurance."

Because so many county agricultural agents also sold Farm Bureau memberships and Farm Bureau products, the private state Farm Bureau organizations gained quasi-governmental status. Many people even assumed that the Farm Bureau was in fact a government

agency. Across the country, Farm Bureau insurance companies flourished. The Ohio Farm Bureau Mutual Automobile Insurance Company founded in 1926 would, 30 years later, elect to drop "Farm Bureau" and coin a new corporate name to expand into states that already had Farm Bureau insurance companies. The name chosen was Nationwide Insurance.

LAUNCHING THE FARM FAMILY INSURANCE COMPANIES IN 1953

In 1953 the Farm Bureaus of seven northeastern states sponsored the creation of the Farm Family Life Insurance Company. Then on April 21, 1955, with the help of AFBF, the Farm Bureaus of New York, New Jersey, Delaware, West Virginia, Connecticut, Rhode Island, Vermont, New Hampshire, Massachusetts, and Maine sponsored what would become the lead entity of the Farm Family Insurance Companies: Farm Family Mutual Insurance Company, incorporated under the laws of the state of New York. On November 16, 1956, Farm Family Mutual began business, working together with Farm Family Life and sharing office facilities with the New York Farm Bureau in Glenmont, New York. In 1988 Farm Family Life created a subsidiary, United Farm Family Insurance Company, to serve as a reinsurer for Farm Family Mutual.

The reputation of the Farm Bureau and its network of businesses was tarnished in 1967 when ranking New York Congressman Joe Resnick, chairman of a subcommittee of the House Agriculture Committee, began to question the practices of the Farm Bureau. After his House colleagues refused to look further into the Farm Bureau, Resnick held his own public hearings across the country.

After his death, his aide Samuel R. Berger, who would become national security adviser to President Bill Clinton, compiled the information for publication in *Dollar Harvest*. Berger charged, "The Farm Bureau is far more than simply an organization of farmers, as it so often claims. The nation's largest farm organization has been quietly but systematically amassing one of the largest business networks in America. ... The Farm Bureau empire now spans the economy: from insurance to oil, from fertilizer to finance companies, from mutual funds to shopping centers. ... The Farm Bureau claims it is in business simply to provide 'services to its members.' But the Farm Bureau business activities now clearly dominate the organization. ... Over the years the farmer has increasingly become customer, not constituent to the Farm Bureau." In short, Berger claimed, "The Farm Bureau has become a giant, self-serving bureaucracy," and "Membership has become little more than a device through which Farm Bureau products are sold."

KEY DATES

1919: Farm Bureau is established as a national organization.

1926: Ohio State Farm Bureau begins selling insurance.

1953: Northeastern Farm Bureaus establish Farm Family Life Insurance.

1955: Farm Family Mutual Insurance Company is established.

1988: United Farm Family is created as a subsidiary of Farm Family Life.

1996: Farm Family Mutual converts to stock ownership and becomes a subsidiary under newly created Farm Family Holdings, Inc.

1999: Farm Family Life and United Farm Family are purchased by Farm Family Holdings.

2001: Farm Family Holdings is sold to American National Insurance Company.

2003: Timothy A. Walsh is named president and CEO of Farm Family.

2007: The company is rated the top seller of agribusiness lines in nine states.

Despite the unwelcome notoriety, the Farm Bureau and its affiliated businesses, such as the Farm Family insurance companies, continued to prosper. The largest line of business for Farm Family was auto insurance, comprising about 40 percent of the group's total. The company's "flagship product," and second-largest line, would become its "Special Farm Package '10,'" which combined personal, farm, and business property and liability insurance for farm owners and other agricultural related businesses. In 1983 Farm Family Life entered the flexible premium/benefit market with its Family Universal Life Policy. United Farm Family expanded beyond reinsurance to engage in limited, direct underwriting operations in 1993.

RESTRUCTURING PROCESS BEGINS IN 1995

In November 1995, the Farm Family Insurance Companies reached a turning point when the chief executive officer of the group, Philip P. Weber, announced that Farm Family Mutual would convert from a mutual property and casualty insurer into a stockholder-owned company. Although the company had been growing, to reach the next level Farm Family Mutual contended that it needed access to additional

capital that was difficult for a mutual to raise. To accomplish the demutualization plan, a holding company was formed, Farm Family Holdings, Inc.

Policyholders, who legally were the owners of Farm Family Mutual, then would receive shares of common stock in the holding company, pending a review by the New York State Insurance Department and approval from policyholders. Farm Family Holdings then planned to make a public offering of its stock. What would happen to Farm Family Life and United Farm Family was not addressed at the time, but at a later date Weber indicated that he hoped to eventually bring the sister companies into the fold.

Farm Family faced some opposition to its conversion plans during the only public hearing held in April 1996. Whereas Weber testified that the conversion would provide immediate benefits to policyholders, those opposed to the plan complained that the policyholders' meeting was scheduled during planting season and also expressed concerns that the best interests of policyholders might conflict with the best interests of stock owners. The Center for Insurance Research, a consumer watch-dog group, sent a letter to state regulators claiming that Farm Family's management would profit personally from the conversion. Nevertheless, on May 1, New York State Superintendent of Insurance Edward J. Muhl approved the demutualization plan, stating that it was fair and equitable and in the best interests of policyholders.

DEMUTUALIZATION AND 1996 CREATION OF FARM FAMILY HOLDINGS

A special meeting for policyholders of Farm Family Mutual was scheduled for June 17, 1996, to vote on the plan. It passed with 93 percent of the policyholders approving demutualization, with some 22,000 policyholders voting either in person or by proxy. Farm Family officials characterized the support as "overwhelming," and critics maintained that "7 percent against indicates a degree of policyholder cynicism." As part of the conversion, Farm Family Mutual changed its name to Farm Family Casualty Insurance Company and became a subsidiary of Farm Family Holdings.

In the midst of turbulent stock market conditions, Farm Family Holdings made a public offering of its stock in July 1996 and fell short of the expectations it expressed in papers filed with the Securities and Exchange Commission (SEC). Hoping to raise $54.3 million at $22 per share, the company actually raised $39.4 million at $16 per share. Trading on the New York Stock Exchange, however, Farm Family stock began to rise steadily in price.

In December 1996 Farm Family initiated moves to reduce expenses and make the company more competitive in the insurance marketplace. It offered early retirement to more than 60 employees, a plan that after an outlay of $600,000 would save the company as much as $225,000 a year. The company also changed retirement benefits to tie them closer to the company's profitability. Furthermore, Farm Family announced that it was looking into offering mutual funds and related financial products.

Almost 15 percent of Farm Family shares were sold in February 1997 to two of the country's largest investment companies: Franklin Resources of San Mateo, California (8 percent), and Fidelity Management and Research Co. of Boston (6.36 percent). A spokesman with the Center for Insurance Research was quick to suggest that, as predicted, policyholders were losing control of their company. By the time Farm Family held its first annual meeting since converting from mutual to stock ownership, another large block of shares, 6.67 percent of the total, was sold to Gotham Partners L.P. and an affiliate. Other large holders of Farm Family stock included Crabbe Huson Small Cap Fund and the Crabbe Huson Group Inc. of Portland, Oregon, with 7.4 percent, and W.R. Berkley Corp. of Connecticut, with 5.18 percent. During this time, the price of Farm Family stock climbed from its initial $16 per share to almost $23 per share.

At the annual meeting a stock option plan for employees was approved, with executives allowed to buy 215,000 shares at no less than 85 percent of the stock's fair market price, in order to create financial incentives for management (officers and directors held less than 12,000 shares in the company). Weber alone would receive an option on 75,000 shares. The stock option plan for other employees did not include discounts. In addition, papers filed in connection with the meeting indicated that Weber's base salary increased by 18.75 percent over the previous year and that the directors awarded him a $114,000 bonus in connection with the initial public stock offering.

GROWTH AS A PUBLIC COMPANY: 1997–99

By October 1997 the price of Farm Family stock had risen to a 52-week high of $30.75. In December the company announced a tentative agreement to purchase Farm Family Life and its subsidiary United Farm Family for $37.5 million, pending approval from stockholders and members of several Farm Bureaus that were stockholders of Farm Family Life. It would be another 18 months before the transaction was finalized and all

the Farm Family insurance companies could be brought together under the publicly traded holding company.

Farm Family reported 1997 profits of $18.9 million on revenues of $173.7 million, a significant improvement over 1996 when the company reported a $6.9 million profit on $146.9 million. In the proxy statement released before its April 1998 annual meeting, it was revealed that four investors owned 28 percent of the company's stock, with the largest block, nearly 10 percent, held by the FMR Corp. of Boston. The filing also indicated that Weber's total compensation was up 28 percent over the previous year, increasing from $403,090 in 1996 to $518,815 in 1997.

On January 1, 1998, the reinsurance agreement between Farm Family Casualty and United Farm Family was terminated. United Farm Family then expanded its direct underwriting operations, selling the product portfolio of Farm Family Casualty in Maryland and Pennsylvania, increasing Farm Family's reach from 10 states to 12. It was not until April 1999 that the acquisition of Farm Family Life and United Farm Family was finalized.

In February 1999, Farm Family reported that 1998 earnings were up 6.7 percent over the previous year. It also continued cost-cutting measures, including the reduction of its extended earnings program for sales agents. Although the price of its stock dropped almost 4 percent during the first few months of 1999, it made a dramatic gain, almost 11 percent, when in July it was announced that Farm Family would be added to the Russell 2000 Index of small capitalization of stocks.

Profits declined slightly in 1999 compared with 1998, due to a one-time accounting change. Excluding that increase, Farm Family's operating income increased by 34 percent over the previous year. In April 2000, Farm Family held its annual meeting, and shareholders elected a new director to the company's board: Edward J. Muhl, the former New York State superintendent of insurance, who four years earlier had approved Farm Family's plan to demutualize.

OVERCOMING BAD PRESS: 2000

In April 2000, charges against the Farm Bureau resurfaced on the CBS television show *60 Minutes*. The implication of the story was that Farm Bureau-affiliated insurance companies conflicted with the Farm Bureau's tax-exempt status and that the group was more concerned about the plight of large agribusinesses than with family farms.

In addition, Defenders of Wildlife, an environmental group founded in 1947 that was bitterly opposed to some of the policy positions of the Farm Bureau, issued a white paper called "Amber Waves of Gain," intended to be an update of *Dollar Harvest*. The report was especially critical of Farm Bureau-affiliated insurance companies such as Farm Family: "In many states, the nonprofit farm bureaus also own all or most of the stock of the insurance companies. And those stocks pay dividends to the state organizations. The farm bureaus also benefit from using insurance customers to inflate their membership members, since everyone who buys a policy must join the bureau. The insurance companies also benefit from the alliances. ... state farm bureaus have lobbied hard for limits on medical malpractice damage awards. And AFBF is pushing for privatization of Social Security, which could bring a profit windfall to insurance company and financial investment firm ventures. Relating any of those issues to agriculture is a far stretch, but they certainly affect the Farm Bureau's bottom line."

BECOMING PART OF AMERICAN NATIONAL: 2000–01

In November 2000, Farm Family and American National Insurance Co. announced a merger, pending approval from the state Insurance Department and Farm Family shareholders. The $280 million transaction would make Farm Family a subsidiary of the larger Texas-based American National, allowing it to offer its agricultural insurance products in 46 states.

Weber assured Farm Family customers that they would continue to work with the same agents and, as a result of the merger, also could expect a wider variety of products. Also as a result of the merger, according to SEC filings, Weber would received a $2.8 million cash payment for unexercised Farm Family stock options and, 18 months after the merger, would be in line to receive a $1.8 million retention payment. The merger was finalized in April 2001 and Farm Family became a subsidiary of American National.

FARM FAMILY: 2002 AND BEYOND

Operating as a subsidiary of American National, the Farm Family group of companies continued to grow during the early years of the new millennium. Timothy A. Walsh was named president and CEO in early 2003 and under his leadership, the company continued to position itself as a specialized provider of property and casualty insurance to farms, small businesses, and individuals in 12 states in the Northeast.

Farm Family expanded its offerings under American National and during 2007, the company was rated the

top seller of agribusiness lines in nine states. By that time, Farm Family and its subsidiaries were fully integrated as part of American National's Multiple Lines business, which included life, annuity, accident and health, property and casualty insurance lines. Overall, this division had 2007 revenues of $1.4 billion.

By 2008, the Farm Family group of companies found itself operating in a volatile economy. Financial markets in the United States were faltering, due in part to a rapid rise in home values and poor credit and investment policies. According to the First American Loan Performance Index, the average U.S. home price almost doubled from 2000 to 2006. During what analysts called the housing bubble, mortgage requirements were less stringent and homebuyers were offered subprime mortgage loans and adjustable rate mortgages with low introductory interest rates. This practice led to a bursting of the bubble and the housing market found itself in crisis with the number of home foreclosures skyrocketing.

The financial woes of U.S. banking, credit, and mortgage companies led to an economic recession that was felt across the globe. Insurance companies also felt the pinch and were forced to control costs and revamp business operations. Farm Family and its parent remained somewhat shielded from the downturn, thanks in part to American National's cautious investment policy. The company assured policyholders and shareholders it remained in sound financial condition in a company press release published in September 2008.

Despite its prudent investment practices, American National's property and casualty arm suffered losses during 2008 and 2009, due mainly to catastrophic losses related to weather including Hurricanes Ike and Gustav. The company continued to see losses related to Hurricane Katrina as well. American National posted a loss of $154 million in 2008. With its business in the Northeast, the Farm Family companies remained fairly untouched by these extreme weather conditions.

Despite these losses, Farm Family was well positioned for future growth. The company's parent had over $20 billion in assets during 2009 and had returned to profitability. Farm Family continued to offer its clients a variety of insurance products including farmowners, homeowners, personal and business auto, pollution liability, whole life, term life, and annuities. While the U.S. economy was slow to recover and Farm Family and its parent remained subject to unpredictable weather, the rise in revenues and profits bode well for the company. As American National CEO Robert Moody told the *Houston Chronicle* in May 2010, "We've been in business a long time, and we see it getting brighter rather than dimmer."

Ed Dinger
Updated, Christina M. Stansell

PRINCIPAL SUBSIDIARIES

Farm Family Life Insurance Company; Farm Family Casualty Insurance Company; United Farm Family Insurance Company.

PRINCIPAL COMPETITORS

AgFirst Farm Credit Bank; Nationwide Agribusiness Insurance Company; State Farm Mutual Automobile Insurance Company.

FURTHER READING

Aaron, Kenneth, "Merger Extends Insurer's Reach," *Albany (NY) Times Union*, November 2, 2000, p. E1.

"American National Completes Acquisition of Farm Family Holdings," *PR Newswire*, April 10, 2001.

"American National Updates Hurricane Katrina Loss Estimate," *PR Newswire*, December 13, 2005.

Berger, Samuel R., *Dollar Harvest*, Lexington, MA: Heath Lexington Books, 1971.

"Consumer Watchdog Attacks Farm Family Plan to Go Public," *Albany (NY) Times Union*, April 24, 1996.

Defenders of Wildlife, "Amber Waves of Gain," white paper, April 2000.

"Defenders of Wildlife Report: Farm Bureau Hurts Those It Claims to Help," *U.S. Newswire*, April 10, 2000.

"Farm Family CEO Defends Plan to Shift to Stock Company," *Albany (NY) Times Union*, April 3, 1996, p. B9.

"Farm Family Sale Done," *Albany (NY) Times Union*, April 11, 2001.

"An Open Letter from American National," *PR Newswire*, September 19, 2008.

Patel, Purva, "Chronicle 100 The Other Nine at the Top-Public Companies American National Insurance Co.," *Houston Chronicle*, May 23, 2010.

G-III Apparel Group, Ltd.

512 Seventh Avenue
New York, New York 10018
U.S.A.
Telephone: (212) 403-0500
Fax: (212) 403-0551
Web site: http://www.g-iii.com

Public Company
Incorporated: 1974 as G-III Leather Fashions, Inc.
Employees: 1,880
Sales: $800.86 million (2010)
Stock Exchanges: NASDAQ
Ticker Symbol: GIII
NAICS: 315220 Men's and Boys' Cut and Sew Apparel Manufacturing; 315222 Men's and Boys' Cut and Sew Suit, Coat, and Overcoat Manufacturing; 315224 Men's and Boys' Cut and Sew Trouser, Slack, and Jean Manufacturing; 315230 Women's and Girls' Cut and Sew Apparel Manufacturing; 315233 Women's and Girls' Cut and Sew Dress Manufacturing; 315234 Women's and Girls' Cut and Sew Suit, Coat, Tailored Jacket, and Skirt Manufacturing; 315239 Women's and Girls' Cut and Sew Other Outerwear Manufacturing; 315292 Fur and Leather Apparel Manufacturing; 315299 Other Cut and Sew Apparel Manufacturing; 448140 Family Clothing Stores; 533110 Brand Name Licensing

∎ ∎ ∎

G-III Apparel Group, Ltd., is a designer and manufacturer of quality jackets and coats for men and women, sportswear, dresses, and women's suits. It produces and distributes its clothing under licensed brands, its own brands, and private-label brands. Licensed fashion brands include Calvin Klein, Cole Haan, Dockers, Ellen Tracy, Guess?, Jones New York, Kenneth Cole, Levi's, Nine West, Sean John, and Tommy Hilfiger. G-III has sports licenses with the National Football League, National Basketball Association, Major League Baseball, National Hockey League, Touch by Alyssa Milano, and more than 100 colleges and universities in the United States.

The company sells dresses and outerwear under its own Andrew Marc and Marc New York brands and has licensed the brands for women's shoes, men's accessories, women's handbags, and men's cold weather accessories. It owns several other brands, including Marvin Richards, G-III, Jessica Howard, Eliza J, Black Rivet, G-III by Carl Banks, and Winlit. At the beginning of 2010 G-III also operated 121 retail outlet stores in 35 states, the majority of which were Wilsons Leather Outlet stores. Although a public company, it was still run by the founding family.

FROM PRIVATE TO PUBLIC COMPANY: 1956–89

Aron Goldfarb opened his leather coat company, G&N Sportswear, in 1956 in New York City's garment district. It was specializing in women's coats when his 22-year-old son Morris joined the company in 1972. Morris Goldfarb augmented the business, which was reorganized in 1974 as G-III Leather Fashions, Inc.,

COMPANY PERSPECTIVES

Our goal is to build an all-season diversified apparel company with a broad portfolio of brands that we offer in multiple channels of retail distribution.

with overseas production facilities. The company began selling moderately priced women's leather coats and jackets under the G-III label.

The company expanded its product lines in 1981 and began selling higher priced, more fashion-oriented women's leather apparel under the Siena label. In 1985 Morris Goldfarb succeeded his father as CEO. The following year the company had sales of $20 million and made a small profit. By 1988 G-III was among the largest, if not the largest, independent importer and wholesaler of leather apparel in the United States. The company had net income of $727,000 on net sales of $30.3 million in fiscal 1987 (the year ended July 31, 1987) and net income of $2.7 million on net sales of $50 million in fiscal 1988.

Even as it moved more upscale with its women's leather apparel, G-III introduced a line of men's leather apparel. The big seller was its brown leather bomber jacket. The popularity of the movie *Top Gun* led to a fashion fad for the jackets and G-III sold over one million of them in 1989. That represented 80 percent of its volume.

G-III grew rapidly, but it was undercapitalized. The firm attracted the interest of Lyle Berman, a Minnesota-based entrepreneur who had organized Ante Corp. as a venture capital firm and knew the Goldfarbs personally. Like them, Berman had operated a family-owned leather apparel business, although on a retail level. An agreement was reached in August 1989 by which Ante acquired G-III in an exchange of stock. Ante shareholders received 15 percent of the outstanding common stock in the merged entity, which took the name G-III Apparel Group, Ltd. The Goldfarbs remained in charge of management, and Berman became a director.

G-III earned an impressive $9.5 million on net sales of $98.8 million in fiscal 1989. In December 1989 G-III, then publicly held because of the merger, had a secondary offering that marketed nearly one-third of the outstanding common stock at $13 a share. Following the offering, Morris Goldfarb owned some 39 percent of the stock. Aron Goldfarb owned another 18 percent.

BEYOND LEATHER: 1990–92

Leather, and the bomber jacket, continued to carry the company. However, Morris Goldfarb began exploring ways to diversify. In 1990 G-III formed a textile division to design, import, and market a moderately priced line of women's textile outerwear and sportswear. In 1992 it introduced a men's textile outerwear line.

G-III's moderately priced apparel for women typically retailed at from $40 for sportswear items to $300 for coats. The men's wear line consisted of coats and jackets in the $150 to $500 range. Moderately priced apparel for women accounted for more than 85 percent of net sales in fiscal 1989, while men's wear accounted for only 5 percent. G-III's goods were being sold mainly to department and specialty stores in the United States. Sales also were being made to cable television shopping networks and direct-mail catalog companies.

The number of customers to whom goods were shipped increased from about 1,000 in fiscal 1989 to about 2,000 in fiscal 1990. That year revenues reached $161.9 million and net income was $9.6 million. Units of The Limited accounted for 32 percent of G-III's sales in 1990. G-III opened a 13-person branch office in Seoul, South Korea, at that time to act as an intermediary between the company and various Korean and Hong Kong manufacturers.

The leather products G-III was designing and manufacturing were marketed as sexy status symbols. In the 1970s the industry had been turning out unwieldy, boxlike coats and jackets in dull colors, but the product offered in 1990 was being made from animal skins that had been treated to be more supple and colorful. It could be embossed and silk-screened to achieve many looks.

Of $175.5 million in sales during fiscal 1992, leather accounted for 90 percent. Analysts said the company controlled about 12 percent of the women's leather market and 3 percent of the men's market. The G-III label accounted for 70 percent of sales in that year, private-label merchandise for 20 percent, and the fast-growing Colebrook textile division, which featured coats and jackets in a variety of fabrics that included wools, cottons, and synthetic blends, for 10 percent.

In 1992 G-III established Global Apparel Sourcing Ltd. to act as the sourcing arm for retailers who wanted production of any type of apparel merchandising. G-III had expanded its own sourcing efforts. When the company went public in 1989, almost all of its merchandise was being produced in South Korea, but by early 1993 Korea was accounting for only half, with the balance spread to other areas, including Hong Kong

KEY DATES

1956: Aron Goldfarb opens G&N Sportswear, selling women's leather coats.
1974: Company incorporates as G-III Leather Fashions.
1988: G-III Leather Fashions enters men's leather apparel market.
1989: Company changes its name to G-III Apparel Group, Ltd., following initial public offering.
1990: Company introduces women's textile outerwear and sportswear under its own labels.
1993: Company begins producing and distributing team logo outerwear for National Football League.
2001: Company enters into licensing agreement to sell women's textile coats.
2007: G-III starts buying companies and brands.
2008: G-III acquires Andrew Marc and Wilsons Leather Experts.

A 1995 licensing agreement with Kenneth Cole Production called for G-III to produce and market three outerwear labels bearing the Kenneth Cole name. This line debuted in 1996, with coats in leather, high-tech nylons, rubberized fabrics, and microfiber. That same year G-III entered into an agreement with the National Hockey League (NHL) to market a line of outerwear apparel with the NHL team logos.

G-III formed a joint venture in 1997 with BET Holdings to produce a BET line of outerwear, sportswear, and accessories aimed at African American and urban shoppers. Also in 1997, Goldfarb rewarded Jeanette Nostra-Katz, a veteran company executive, by vacating the presidency and promoting her to the office. Goldfarb remained chief executive officer.

Over the next several years G-III developed partnerships with such brands as Jones New York, Timberland, and Sean John, rapper Sean "Diddy" Combs's brand. It also produced outerwear for companies as diverse as Caterpillar, Nike, and Nine West. However, as it moved to diversify its outlets, G-III faced a financial roller coaster. During fiscal 1994 (the year ended January 31, 1994) G-III had net income of $1.3 million on peak sales of $208.9 million. The following year the company lost $11.7 million on net sales of $171.4 million. Sales fell still further in fiscal 1996, to $121.7 million, but the company lost only $397,000 by reducing costs through tighter control of inventory levels and improved product sourcing.

The causes for the decline were primarily the bankruptcy of several major customers, heavy competition from big fashion designers, and the end of the bomber jacket fad. G-III was suffering from a lack of both a brand identity and the resources to establish one. Revenues fell still further, to $117.7 million in fiscal 1997, but the company had net income of $3.1 million, mainly because of further economy measures. These included consolidating merchandise divisions, reducing inventory, decreasing borrowing levels, and subleasing one of its warehouses. By 2000 the company was turning a profit again.

and Indonesia. Independent contractors in the United States produced about 20 percent of the company's goods.

OUTERWEAR FASHION LICENSING: 1993–2000

G-III pioneered fashion licensing in the sports field in 1993. It signed a licensing agreement with NFL Properties, Inc., the licensing arm of the National Football League (NFL), for a line of leather outerwear developed as a joint venture between G-III and former New York Giants linebacker Carl Banks. The agreement formed G-III/Carl Banks and provided for producing jackets and coats for men, women, and children. All jackets carried NFL team logos and colors.

By early 1994 G-III had opened six retail factory outlet stores to sell in-season merchandise and overstock. It opened a new 30,000-square-foot corporate showroom on Seventh Avenue in Manhattan's garment district. Leather was accounting for about two-thirds of overall company sales volume. Also in 1994, G-III signed an agreement with the Chinese government to jointly own a leather apparel factory in northern China and market the products in that country. G-III would own 39 percent of the factory, with the Chinese government holding the remainder.

DRESSES AND SPORTSWEAR ADDED: 2001–06

G-III worked closely with its licensors. Once an agreement was reached, the company assigned a top-level manager to the brand. That manager linked the licensor and a brand-specific design and marketing team. Each brand's design and merchandising was shaped specifically for that brand. Cost savings overall resulted from each of the brands/divisions with G-III using the same information technology and financial systems and sharing the same quality control and sourcing offices in China.

This close relationship was the foundation for the company's initial strategy for diversification. Its efforts focused on persuading its license partners to expand licenses in order to add new product categories. During the first half of the new decade, G-III launched a line of women's wool outerwear for Jones New York, leather outerwear for men under the Timberland label, as well as outerwear for Sean John, Kenneth Cole New York, and Kenneth Cole Reaction. This was followed by a new line of adult outerwear under an expanded license with the NFL.

In 2005 G-III initiated a new strategy, one of acquisitions. It bought rival coat companies J. Percy for Marvin Richards for $19.2 million and stock, and Winlit Group Ltd. for about $7.3 million. Among the assets it acquired were the licenses to make coats and jackets for Calvin Klein, Guess?, Ellen Tracy, and Tommy Hilfiger. Meanwhile, G-III took major steps to diversify beyond seasonal outerwear.

In 2006 G-III shipped its first women's suits and dresses, each under the Calvin Klein label. Customers for these products included Macy's, Dillard's, and Lord and Taylor. It also diversified into sportswear, signing an agreement to make junior women's sportswear for the Sean John label. Later that year the company produced sportswear for young men and boys for a Wal-Mart label.

These moves expanded the collection of brand names G-III offered, the types of products, the variety of retailers within its distribution system, and the range of price points. All this was occurring as retail chains consolidated and customers shifted from department stores to specialty stores. G-III marketed its efforts as providing retailers opportunities to reduce their suppliers for nationally recognized brands and private labels. For brand owners G-III's expansion strategies offered a means to consolidate the number of licensees they worked with.

G-III celebrated its 50th anniversary in 2006 with the strongest year in its history to that time. Sales reached $427 million, an increase of 31.8 percent over the previous year. Income jumped 86 percent to $13.2 million. These results occurred during one of the warmest fall and winter seasons in U.S. history.

2007 AND BEYOND

In 2007 the company began acquiring the actual brands. It bought Jessica Howard Ltd., which designed and marketed moderate and better dresses under the Jessica

Howard and Eliza J brands. G-III also purchased Industrial Cotton, which provided denim products for the junior market to stores including Sears, JCPenney, Kohl's, and Belk.

The company added dresses and women's suits to its license for the Ellen Tracy label. These purchases helped counter the seasonality of outerwear. They also contributed to the bottom line with higher margins than coats and jackets. During the year it also expanded its sports-related offerings with Touch by Alyssa Milano, aimed at young women.

In 2008 G-III added better women's sportswear to its Calvin Klein license and launched a line of performance wear for that label. This consisted of clothing for women to wear for yoga, running, tennis, and biking. It also signed an agreement for a line of contemporary dresses for the Jessica Simpson label. At the same time, the license with Sean John for junior women's sportswear was terminated.

G-III then bought Andrew Marc for $42 million. This brought to G-III the Andrew Marc and Marc New York brands for women's and men's luxury outerwear, to which the company added a line of dresses for each brand. Assets also included licenses for men's and women's outerwear under the Levi's and Dockers brands. The purchase caused G-III to move in a new direction as it began licensing the Andrew Marc brand for items outside G-III's established areas of expertise. The initial licenses were for women's shoes and men's accessories, followed later with women's handbags, men's cold weather accessories, and men's jeans and denim sportswear.

Later in 2008 G-III expanded into retail operations when it bought the assets of Wilsons Leather Experts for $22.3 million. These included 116 retail stores, an e-commerce operation, and a distribution center. Wilsons Leather was the result of a merger in 1988 between 99-year-old Bermans Leather and Wilsons House of Suede and Leather. G-III named the new division Wilsons Leather Outlet and made its own outlet stores a part of it.

A recession and reduced consumer spending challenged G-III and the entire fashion industry as sales dropped, especially for higher priced items. The company experienced a loss in income for 2008. Its responses ranged from cutting executive pay to streamlining its infrastructure. These actions, combined with its greater diversity of offerings and distribution channels, led G-III to record revenues in 2009. The company that once depended on a single style of leather bomber jacket had built a portfolio of 32 clothing brands, a retail operation, and its own licensing operation. Although still primarily an outerwear designer and manufacturer, G-III was becoming an all-season diversified apparel company.

Robert Halasz
Updated, Ellen D. Wernick

PRINCIPAL SUBSIDIARIES

AM Apparel Holdings, Inc.; AM Retail Group, Inc.; Andrew & Suzanne Company Inc.; Ash Retail Corp.; CK Outerwear, LLC; G-III Hong Kong Ltd.; G-III Leather Fashions, Inc.; G-III Retail Outlets, Inc.; J. Percy for Marvin Richards, Ltd.; Kostroma Ltd. (Hong Kong); Wee Beez International Ltd. (Hong Kong).

PRINCIPAL COMPETITORS

Amerex Group Inc.; Columbia Sportswear Company; Reebok.

FURTHER READING

Curan, Catherine, "G-III Apparel, Once Cold, Is Now Hot Winter Item," *Crain's New York Business*, October 23, 2000, p. 4.

Feitelberg, Rosemary, "G-III Reaches Far and Wide," *WWD: Women's Wear Daily*, August 2, 2005, p. 8.

Fiedler, Terry, "Blind Faith: Investors Who Anted Up for Leather Expert Lyle Berman's Blind Pool Won Big," *Corporate Report Minnesota*, March 1990.

Poggi, Jeanine, "G-III's Expanded Offerings Seen as Key to Longevity," *WWD: Women's Wear Daily*, November 19, 2007, p. 9.

Swibel, Matthew, "Skinned," *Forbes*, January 22, 2001, pp. 122–23.

Zager, Masha, "Fashion 'Melting Pot' G-III Diversifies Its Business," *Apparel Magazine*, November 2009, pp. 10–14.

Gap Inc.

The Gap, Inc.

---

2 Folsom Street
San Francisco, California 94105-1205
U.S.A.
Telephone: (650) 952-4400
Toll Free: (800) 427-7895
Web site: http://www.gap.com

Public Company
Incorporated: 1969 as The Gap Stores, Inc.
Employees: 135,000
Sales: $14.2 billion (2010)
Stock Exchanges: New York
Ticker Symbol: GPS
NAICS: 448140 Family Clothing Stores; 448210 Shoe
(Except Bowling, Golf, Spiked) Stores

∎∎∎

Founded as a single store by Donald G. Fisher and his wife Doris, The Gap, Inc., has evolved into a major retail company with well-known brands including Gap, Banana Republic, Old Navy, Piperlime, and Athleta. The firm sells a variety of casual-style and urban chic clothing to men, women, and children in more than 3,100 stores in the United States, France, Japan, Ireland, and the United Kingdom. There are also franchised locations in 100 other foreign countries. An online division sells the various brands via Web sites and a toll-free number. Company founder Donald Fisher died in 2009, leaving an enormous and enduring influence on American casual style.

CAPITALIZING ON THE GENERATION GAP: 1969–75

Donald Fisher, a member of a family that made its home in California for generations, was 40 years old and a successful real estate developer in 1969 when he took note of a new trend among the increasingly disaffected youth of the times. Blue jeans, for years made chiefly by Levi Strauss & Co. for laborers and outdoorsmen, were suddenly becoming a part of the counterculture's standard costume. Durable, inexpensive, comfortable, and sufficiently offbeat, jeans were the perfect uniform for a generation of young people anxious to demonstrate antipathy to corporate America.

Fisher was said to have conceived of The Gap when he was unable to find the right size of Levi's jeans in a department store in Sacramento, California. He realized that jeans had become more popular than existing merchandising outlets could accommodate, and like hamburgers, stereo equipment, and gasoline, they could be sold through a chain of small stores devoted solely to that product. With the help of his wife, Doris, Fisher opened a shop near San Francisco State University in one of his own buildings, offering a combination of records and jeans.

Their intention was to attract jeans customers by means of the records, but at first no one noticed the jeans, and Fisher was driven close to bankruptcy. In desperation, he placed ads in local newspapers announcing the sale of "four tons" of jeans at rock-bottom prices, and the clothes were soon gone. To emphasize the youthful ambiance of his new store, Fisher named it

The Gap, an allusion to a then hot topic, the Generation Gap.

IMMEDIATE SUCCESS

When Fisher incorporated his business as The Gap Stores, Inc., it was an immediate success. Although the Fishers had no experience in retailing, the combination of jeans, low prices, and wide selection proved irresistible to the huge market of 14- to 25-year-olds. Fisher added new outlets in San Francisco and was soon enjoying the benefits of chain store merchandising: centralized buying and advertising, excellent name recognition, and uniform pricing.

Initially, the company's buying program was singularly uncomplicated, as the stores carried only one product, jeans by Levi Strauss & Co. The stores were brightly painted, often orange, filled with circular metal display racks known as "rounders," and usually enlivened by rock and roll music. To hold down rental costs, the Fishers kept stores small, about 3,000 to 4,000 square feet. They located most of their stores in shopping centers, many of them enclosed in malls.

Two years after opening its first stores, Gap's sales were running at $2.5 million annually, and the Fishers converted the company into a public corporation, although they retained the great majority of stock. They very quickly opened stores across the United States, while maintaining tight control over the critical accounting, purchasing, and marketing functions of what was soon a sizable corporation. In five years sales had increased almost 50-fold, to $97 million, and the number of stores had grown to 186, spread over 21 states.

Analysts credited the company's success to the Fishers' observance of a few cardinal rules of retailing: Gap stores replaced stock with maximum speed; prices were low and stayed that way; big sellers were kept on the rack until they stopped moving, rather than being retired in favor of new styles simply for the sake of novelty; and only a few types of items were stocked (jeans, shirts, light jackets), each offered in its complete range of colors and sizes, ensuring a minimum of disappointed customers.

The company's growth was also made possible by the extensive national advertising of Levi Strauss, which provided 100 percent of Gap's merchandise during its early years. Such dependence on a single supplier had obvious dangers, however, and around 1973 Gap began marketing several labels of its own, as well as national brands other than Levi's. These proved crucial to the company's short- and long-term health. By 1975 Gap stores generated $100 million in net sales.

UPS AND DOWNS: 1976–80

By 1976 the Fishers were ready to make their first substantial public stock offering. The company's spectacular growth had attracted widespread interest, and its May offering of 1.2 million shares sold quickly at $18 per share. Coincidentally, however, the retail industry went into a steep slide, which, when combined with Gap's large expenditures for new stores, pushed the company into the red for the final quarter of its fiscal year, ending July 31.

The value of the newly issued stock fell to $7.25, prompting nine separate class-action suits from outraged stock purchasers who alleged that the Fishers had tried to dump their holdings before Gap announced its bad news. These charges came despite the fact that the Fishers sold only about 10 percent of their holdings during the period in question. Rather than wage endless litigation, Gap settled the suits in 1979 for a total of $5.8 million, or 40 cents per share, and did its best to mend its frayed relations with Wall Street.

Adding between 50 and 80 stores annually, Gap pushed its sales to $307 million in 1980 and was close to achieving nationwide representation. However, members of the great wave of youngsters who had come of age wearing blue jeans in the 1970s were older, wealthier, and more conservative by this time, and the Fishers were attempting to break out of the jeans niche by expanding Gap's selection of clothing. Several experimental chains featuring upscale fashions were tried and brought together under the Taggs name but later liquidated because they were unprofitable. Gap stores were enlarged to handle increasing amounts of what became known as casual wear and were frequently moved outside of shopping centers to freestanding locations, where space was plentiful and rent lower per square foot.

Along with the search for a line of clothes to appeal to an older clientele, the Fishers also faced Levi Strauss & Co.'s decision to supply big mass marketers such as

KEY DATES

■

1969: Don and Doris Fisher open their first store in San Francisco, California.
1976: The company offers 1.2 million shares to the public.
1983: Millard Drexler is named president; the firm acquires Banana Republic.
1986: The first GapKids store is opened.
1990: BabyGap is launched.
1994: The Old Navy brand is established.
1997: Gap Web site debuts.
2002: Drexler retires; Paul Pressler is named CEO.
2004: Robert Fisher succeeds his father, company founder Don Fisher, as chairman.
2006: Online-only Piperlime brand launched.
2007: Glenn Murphy leads company as chairman and CEO after departure of Pressler.
2008: Comprehensive revamp of Web sites allows users to shop multiple brands with one cart.

Sears and J.C. Penney with its jeans. Levi's were then widely available, underscoring Gap's need to develop a label and look of its own. The company's own brands, created during the 1970s, generated about 45 percent of Gap sales in 1980, with Levi's adding an equal amount and other national brands making up the balance. In order to avoid inundation by the rising tide of jeans discounters, the company would have to fashion a new, exclusively Gap image.

NEW LEADERSHIP

To accomplish this task, Donald Fisher hired Millard "Mickey" Drexler as president. Drexler, then 40, had just solved a similar problem with Ann Taylor, creating a more chic image for the chain while also quadrupling sales. Drexler accepted the job as president at the end of 1983 and was given a block of stock that would make him one of the country's wealthiest retail executives at that time.

Drexler immediately began Gap's comprehensive transformation, in spite of the company's then excellent financial status. The new president found little that he liked. Proliferating competition in jeans and Gap's youthful marketing image had forced the company into a price-driven volume business. Its orange-painted stores were cluttered with rounders displaying merchandise of many labels that Drexler later described to the *New York Times* as "trendy but not tasteful ... well, just plain

ugly." Furthermore, most consumers perceived Gap as strictly for teenagers at a time when people who grew up in the 1960s were developing more up-market tastes.

Drexler began by eliminating all private-label brands but one: Gap. Henceforth, Gap would be known not only as a store, but as a line of clothes as well. Drexler created a large in-house design staff to develop clothes that would be casual, simple, made of natural fibers, and more clearly differentiated by gender than were jeans. The look was informal but classic: still denim-based but including a variety of shirts, skirts, blouses, and sweaters in assorted colors and weaves. It was clothing for people who wanted to look and feel young without appearing slovenly or rebellious, a description that fit a vast number of U.S. consumers in the 1980s.

A NEW IMAGE

Gap stores were substantially revamped. Neutral grays and white replaced the garish orange, and the ubiquitous rounders gave way to shelves of neatly folded clothing under soft lighting. The company's advertising, as devised by Drexler's longtime colleague, Magdalena (Maggie) Gross, shifted from radio and television to upscale magazines and newspapers and featured older models engaged in familiar, outdoor activities that were not necessarily connected with youth culture.

The advertising campaign was enormously successful in helping to change the public's perception of the company. Gap came to signify good taste of an informal variety, and the Gap brand name soon acquired the necessary cachet for the company to compete with other retailers of casual wear such as Benetton and The Limited. In addition, the word "stores" was dropped from the company's name.

Drexler's revolution at Gap cost a good deal of money, and financial results for 1984 were poor, with profits down 43 percent to $12.2 million. By the middle of the following year, however, gross revenue, profits, and same-store sales were all up. Furthermore, the company had fresh energy and a merchandising focus that could carry it for years to come. In the meantime, Gap had acquired a number of other retail chains. Foremost among these was Banana Republic, founded in 1979 by another California husband and wife team, Melvyn and Patricia Ziegler.

The two-store chain of safari and travel clothing outfits, bought by Gap in 1983, had a well-established catalog business. After its acquisition and the introduction of private-label clothing lines, Banana Republic's sales doubled each year through the mid-1980s but slowed quickly thereafter. Despite the mixed results of the Banana Republic acquisition, the company continued to seek out other chain stores. Pottery Barn, acquired in 1984, was a housewares chain of about 30 stores in New York and California. After several problematic years, it was divested in 1986.

That same year, Drexler sought to fill another clothing need of the baby boomer generation with the debut of GapKids, featuring comfortable, durable clothes for the children of parents who shopped at Gap stores. The concept was a huge success, and along with Banana Republic (which peaked in the late 1980s with revenue of more than $250 million a year) figured prominently in Gap's long-range planning.

GAP CONTINUES ITS CLIMB

Gap's first international store was opened in London in 1987. Additional stores soon sprang up throughout the United Kingdom, Canada, and France. Stateside, however, Banana Republic's safari gear bubble burst, and it became a money-losing liability. Gap also tested the higher end of the clothing market with Hemisphere, a nine-store chain of upscale sportswear with European styling. Created in 1987, the same year the company broke $1 billion in sales, Hemisphere offered elegant fashions. The concept could not weather a severe recession, however, and was disposed of only two years later.

In 1990, as Banana Republic searched for secure footing, GapKids prospered and led to a new venture, babyGap. Like GapKids, babyGap was a huge success and became a popular attraction in GapKids stores. Gap was looking very good at the start of the decade. A stock split occurred in September, and at year-end the company's 1,092 stores generated $1.9 billion in sales with net earnings of $144.5 million. In the early 1990s Banana Republic was refocusing its image while GapKids and babyGap flourished. Overall, revenue, net income, and return-on-equity were all outstanding ($2.5 billion, $229.8 million, and 40.2 percent respectively due to another stock split in June) in 1991, and virtually every year since Drexler's program had taken effect in 1985.

In 1991 the Fisher family still held more than 40 percent of the company, which then operated more than 1,216 stores in the United States, Canada, and the United Kingdom, with plans to expand total sales area by 15 percent annually. Not only had Gap followed its baby boomer clientele as they grew older and wealthier, it provided for their children, too. GapKids was the fastest-growing segment of the company as a whole, with most of the more than 223 GapKids stores housing a babyGap department for infants and toddlers.

OLD NAVY INTRODUCED

Although 1992 marked a dip in profits and sales growth due to slower returns and increased competition, the company addressed these problems by turning away from unisex clothing to more gender-specific items. Along with refurbishing stores and placing more emphasis on women, Gap came back with record numbers in 1993 and a new franchise, originally called Gap Warehouse. Lacking the trademark flair associated with the company, Drexler hired an outside firm to come up with a new name, to no avail. Then when strolling in Paris with colleagues, Drexler saw the perfect name for the down-market stores painted on a building: Old Navy. Launched in 1994, Old Navy Clothing Company, with stores nearly twice as big as other Gap stores, filled with sturdy, value-priced (20 to 30 percent lower) clothing for the entire family, became another Gap sensation.

Banana Republic, meanwhile, was gaining ground with urbane elegance as a hip alternative to Gap's casualness. To shore up its product line, the upscale clothier initiated a shop-within-a-shop concept, featuring different collections, jewelry, and leather accessories. By 1994 there were 1,507 Gap-owned stores (188 were Banana Republic) contributing to the company's $3.72 billion in sales. Within a year, there were 1,680 stores. International stores had surged as well, from 124 in 1994 to 164 in 1995. Gap's corporate statistics were equally robust. A two-for-one stock split paid out dividends in March, sales grew 18 percent to nearly $4.4 billion, and net earnings rose 11 percent to $354 million over the previous year's $320 million.

In 1995 Donald Fisher decided to relinquish his duties as CEO of Gap, Inc. His successor was Mickey Drexler, who added the responsibilities of CEO to those of president. Fisher remained chairman, however, and still kept a hand in running the company he founded nearly 30 years before. By 1996 Gap's dominance of the fashion scene was fixed, and consumers of all ages could find something in one of its stores.

RETOOLED IMAGE IN 1997

By the late 1990s, however, Drexler felt that Gap had strayed too far into the trendy genre and was losing customers as a result. He retooled Gap's image in 1997, emphasizing a return to simplicity and the company's most basic offerings: pocket tees, jeans, and khakis. Longtime advertising director Maggie Gross left the firm after Drexler pulled the plug on a print campaign that did not gel with Gap's new basic image. That year, the firm went back to television advertising with commercials that highlighted Gap Easy Fit jeans featuring celebrities that included Lena Horne, LL Cool J, and Luscious Jackson. In 1998 the firm launched another round of highly successful television commercials, featuring its line of khaki pants. The company also entered the online market during this time, introducing gap.com, along with gapkids.com and babygap.com. Banana Republic and Old Navy began catering to on-line shoppers shortly thereafter.

Gap grew at a rapid rate during the latter half of the 1990s, securing record sales and earnings. In 1997 sales at Old Navy surpassed $1 billion while overall company sales grew to $6.5 billion. Sales climbed to $9 billion the following year, bolstered by the opening of 356 new stores. The company could then claim that one new store opened each day. In 1999, 570 new stores were added to the company's arsenal as net earnings exceeded $1.1 billion. According to the *National Post*, the company had grown by 24,000 percent from 1984 to 1999.

The new century, however, brought with it rocky times for the 30-year-old retailer. During 2000 the company opened 731 new units and sales grew to $13.6 billion, but net income fell to $877 million while comparable store sales fell by 5 percent. In April 2000 sales began declining. In 2001 the company posted a $7.7 million loss. "Simply put," wrote Anne Kingston in the *National Post*, "The Gap has lost its groove. Its merchandising is unfocused and it has lost ground to competitors. The formula that made it great no longer has the same currency. More damningly, Gap Inc. has alienated shoppers."

NEW LEADERSHIP AGAIN BRINGS CHANGES

The company was losing market share in the over-30 category and was having difficulty appealing to a younger audience. Gap had also come under fire for its labor practices in third-world countries. Various labor groups claimed Gap advocated sweatshop labor overseas. In response, the company created a global monitoring program to supervise factory conditions where its clothes were manufactured.

Drexler announced his retirement during 2002 and later took a job to head rival J. Crew Group Inc. After Drexler's departure, Fisher began his search for a new leader, one whose management style could catapult Gap back into the upper echelon of retail fashion. Paul Pressler, an executive from Walt Disney Co., was tapped to revive the company just as Drexler had been called upon to do in the 1980s. Pressler began to implement a series of sweeping corporate changes focused on customer research, strategic planning, new advertising,

and store closures. Net income for fiscal 2002 bounced back to $477 million.

Gap Inc. earned $1 billion on record revenues of nearly $16 billion in 2003. Sales peaked at $16.3 billion the next year as earnings grew more than 15 percent. There were nearly 3,000 stores at that time. A number of initiatives were under way. The company introduced maternity clothes in 2003 at gapbody and Old Navy stores after trying them out as online exclusives for three years. Old Navy began offering plus sizes the following year. Banana Republic had broadened its offerings with jewelry, swimwear, and sunglasses. Robert Fisher succeeded his father Don Fisher as chairman of the board in 2004.

Not all the experiments panned out, however. Ill-fated attempts to woo teen buyers with disposable fashions fared poorly as Old Navy could not match swifter rivals in bringing designer knock-offs to market. Forth & Towne, a new chain aimed at baby boomer women, lasted only a couple of years before being closed in June 2007.

Gap Inc.'s online efforts met with more enduring success. The Web sites underwent an extensive overhaul in 2005. The next year, the company added a new, online-only brand called Piperlime. It specialized in shoes at first, adding handbags after several years. In 2008 another comprehensive revamp of the Web sites allowed users to shop multiple online brands with one cart and one shipping fee.

FIRST INTERNATIONAL FRANCHISES IN 2005

Gap left Germany after eight years in 2004, selling 10 stores there to Hennes & Mauritz AB. Sales continued to slide in Britain and France. The parent company continued to invest in Europe, introducing its first Banana Republic store in March 2008 on London's Regent Street.

The company also began to use franchising arrangements to extend the Gap and Banana Republic brands into new areas overseas, beginning in January 2006 with an agreement with FJ Benjamin to bring 30 Gap and Banana Republic stores to Singapore and Malaysia. The next year, it signed the Al Tayer Group, a Dubai-based luxury retail specialist, to bring the brands to the Middle East. By 2008 the company had 100 franchised locations. The company was entering the vast, untapped Chinese market in fall 2010 with corporate owned stores.

In 2006 Gap introduced a collection to raise money for (PRODUCT) RED, a program to help African women and children with AIDS. Around the same time,

Banana Republic was fielding a Green Collection of eco-conscious apparel. In 2007 Gap began working with the Council of Fashion Designers of America/Vogue Fashion Fund to have new talents create updates on its signature pieces.

None of this helped sales, however. In 2007 the company hired Goldman Sachs to help it explore strategic alternatives, including a possible sale of all or part of itself. Gap Inc. made an acquisition of its own in 2008, buying Athleta Inc. for $150 million. The Petaluma, California-based marketer of yoga and running clothes for women had been launched 10 years earlier.

SIGNS OF RECOVERY

Pressler, known for his emphasis on consumer research, was credited with restoring Gap Inc.'s financial footing. He also better differentiated the company's brands from each other, although not always to great success. Banana Republic's rush to the extremes of fashion alienated shoppers looking for career basics and Old Navy's reach into the disposable fashions favored by teens had its T-shirts slipping into commodity status. The Gap brand suspended its television advertising through most of 2007 and 2008 while it struggled to resolve its merchandising issues.

As same-sales slogged through an extended slump the company felt that someone more in tune with fashion trends was needed at the top. Glenn Murphy took over the company as chairman and CEO after Pressler's departure in 2007. A veteran of supermarket and drugstore retailing, Murphy had led Canada's Shoppers Drug Mart through a turnaround.

Old Navy, the brand that had been most affected during years of decline, was also quickest to recover. It overhauled stores and returned to its value-oriented strengths as the withering economy drove shoppers down-market. The namesake Gap stores continued to struggle, in spite of the successful launch of its "1969" line of premium jeans.

Donald Fisher died in September 2009 at the age of 81, having left an incalculable influence on the world of American retail fashion. Known for support of arts and education, he and his wife had assembled a collection of 1,100 pieces of contemporary American art and donated millions of dollars to charter schools.

Jonathan Martin
Updated, Taryn Benbow-Pfalzgraf;
Christina M. Stansell; Frederick C. Ingram

PRINCIPAL SUBSIDIARIES

Athleta, Inc.; Banana Republic (Japan) Y.K.; Banana Republic, LLC; Gap (Canada) Inc.; Gap (France) S.A.S.; Gap (Japan) K.K.; Gap (UK) Limited; Gap Europe Limited (UK); Gap International B.V. (Netherlands); Gap Stores (Ireland) Limited; Old Navy, LLC.

PRINCIPAL DIVISIONS

Gap North America; Banana Republic North America; Old Navy; International; Gap Inc. Direct.

PRINCIPAL COMPETITORS

Abercrombie & Fitch Stores Inc.; American Eagle Outfitters Inc.; Hennes & Mauritz AB; J. Crew Group Inc.; J.C. Penney Company, Inc.; Kohl's Corporation; Sears Brands, LLC; Target Corporation.

FURTHER READING

Barmash, Isidore, "Gap Finds Middle Road to Success," *New York Times*, June 24, 1991.

Boorstin, Julia, "Fashion Victim," *Fortune*, April 17, 2006, p. 160.

Dell, Kristina, "Why the Gap Keeps Getting Crushed," *Time*, February 5, 2007, p. 50.

Fisher, Donald, and Art Twain, *Falling into the Gap: The Story of Donald Fisher and the Apparel Icon He Created*, Berkeley, CA: Creative Arts Book Co., 2002.

Foley, Bridget, and Kristin Young, "Gap, Banana: The Big Makeover," *WWD*, April 20, 2004, p. 6.

Kingston, Anne, "Bridging the Gap," *National Post* (Canada), May 4, 2002.

Lee, Louise, "Gap Goes Global; The Retailer Hopes a Middle East Franchise Deal Will Be a First Step toward Revving Up Its Lackluster International Business," *Business Week Online*, April 18, 2006.

Moin, David, "Gap Eyes Growth Online, Overseas," *WWD*, October 16, 2009, p. 2.

———, "Gap Inc. Enters Middle East," *WWD*, April 18, 2006, p. 2.

Reingold, Jennifer, "Gap: Decline of a Denim Dynasty," *Fortune*, April 30, 2007, p. 96.

Smith, Stephanie D., "Changing of the Guard," *Money*, April 1, 2003, p. 61.

Tedeschi, Bob, "Putting It Together on Just One Page at Gap," *New York Times*, September 12, 2005, p. C2.

Golden Star Resources
Ltd.

■

10901 West Toller Drive, Suite 300
Littleton, Colorado 80127-6312
U.S.A.
Telephone: (303) 830-9000
Toll Free: (800) 553-8436
Fax: (303) 830-9094
Web site: http://www.gsr.com

Public Company
Incorporated: 1992
Employees: 2,200
Sales: $400.7 million (2009)
Stock Exchanges: American
Ticker Symbol: GSS
NAICS: 212221 Gold Ore Mining

■ ■ ■

Littleton, Colorado-based Golden Star Resources Ltd., which also maintains offices in the Canadian city of Toronto, is an international gold mining company. It has two operating mines (Bogoso/Prestea and Wassa/HBB) in Ghana, in West Africa's Ashanti Gold Belt. By 2009 the company had produced more than two million ounces of gold since its inception. Each year, Golden Star Resources devotes between $10 million and $20 million to exploration activities. Although most of the company's exploration occurs near its existing operations in Ghana, it also has other West African properties in Sierra Leone, Niger, Côte d'Ivoire, and Burkina Faso. In addition, Golden Star Resources also has properties in Brazil.

ORIGINS AND EARLY GROWTH

Golden Star Resources originated on May 15, 1992, via the amalgamation of South American Goldfields Inc. and predecessor Golden Star Resources Ltd., which had originally incorporated in 1984 as Southern Star Resources Ltd. As part of the deal, one Golden Star share was exchanged for every 3.25 shares of South American Goldfields. David K. Fagin was named chairman and CEO of the merged companies.

By December 1992 Golden Star Resources was a stakeholder in one of the largest gold mines in the Caribbees (West Indies), along with the Canadian company Cambior and the Guyanan government. The companies had invested approximately $152 million in the mine, located in Guyana's Omai District, which was slated to begin producing gold in 1993.

Growth continued in late 1994 when Golden Star Resources and its Pan African Resources Corp. subsidiary cemented an agreement, worth approximately $1 million, with Lafayette Mining Corp. for an 80 percent stake in its Gabon, West Africa-based Eteke Gold Prospect. Around the same time, the company announced that it would return mineral rights associated with the Guyana-based Mahdia Prospect to the government of Guyana and write off its investment in the project. This occurred when a potential partner decided not to pursue development activities.

In early 1995 Golden Star Resources received authorization from Côte d'Ivoire's Mines and Energy Ministry to conduct gold reconnaissance work across a 15,000-square-kilometer area. As part of the arrangement, the ministry agreed to grant the company seven-

COMPANY PERSPECTIVES

Golden Star's goal is to grow its business in Ghana, other selected countries in West Africa, through organic growth and accretive acquisitions. The Company is well financed and has a strong, experienced and operationally focused management team.

year exploration permits. In addition, Golden Star Resources received authorization to explore and mine gold deposits in a 1,800-square-kilometer area of west central Ethiopia known as Dul.

It also was in 1995 that Golden Star Resources and its Southern Golden Star subsidiary established a 50-50 joint venture with the largest gold producer in Brazil, the Cia Vale do Rio Doce mining company, in order to mine gold in the eastern Amazon state of Para. The joint venture involved a $4 million investment from Golden Star Resources, which would be used to fund exploration activities for 30 months. Another development in 1995 was the amalgamation of the company's Pan African Resources Corp. subsidiary with Ontario, Canada-based Humlin Red Lakes Mine Ltd., in a deal intended to facilitate access to capital markets. Finally, in mid-1996 Golden Star Resources President David A. Fennell assumed the additional role of CEO.

ACQUISITION OF BOGOSO

In mid-1999 Golden Star Resources struck a deal with a consortium of banks to acquire a 70 percent stake in Bogoso Gold Ltd., which operated the Bogoso Gold Mine in Ghana, in West Africa's Ashanti Gold Belt. A 20 percent equity interest in Bogoso was acquired by Australia-based Anvil Mining NL, with the government of Ghana holding the remaining 10 percent. By this time Jim Askew was serving as president and CEO of Golden Star Resources, overseeing a company that had significant diamond and gold exploration interests in both Africa and South America.

In August 1999 Golden Star Resources agreed to acquire Birim Goldfields Inc. The $5.7 million deal was part of a strategy to bolster the company's production efforts in Ghana, where Birim had complementary capabilities. However, when Birim sold the Mampon deposit on its Ghana-based Dunkwa concession (the only defined resource in its portfolio) to Ashanti Goldfields, Golden Star Resources withdrew its offer in

September. That same month the company, along with Anvil Mining, completed the purchase of the Bogoso mine.

The company ended the 1990s by naming Peter Bradford, Anvil Mining's managing director, as its president and CEO. Bradford also had served as managing director of the Bogoso mine. His appointment came at a pivotal time in the company's history, as Golden Star Resources began its evolution from a fledgling exploration company to a successful gold producer and developer.

PRESTEA DEAL

In mid-2000 the company increased its ownership stake in the French exploration company Guyanor Resources SA from 71 percent to 72.6 percent. In August Golden Star Resources revealed that it had signed a letter of intent to acquire a 90 percent stake in the Prestea property, located to the south of its Bogoso mine, by securing 90 percent of the company Barnex (Prestea) Limited from Barnato Exploration and Western Areas.

The Prestea deal was important to Golden Star Resources because it would add oxide ore reserves to its Bogoso mine, thereby extending its life by several years. The purchase was complex and encountered a number of delays. However, the acquisition was completed in 2001, allowing the company to mine surface deposits there for about five years.

Also in 2001, Golden Star Resources reached an agreement to acquire Anvil Mining's 20 percent equity interest in the Bogoso mine. This was accomplished when the company secured three million shares of Anvil in exchange for its stake in Bogoso Gold Ltd. The deal was completed in September, at which time Golden Star Resources increased its interest in the mine from 70 percent to 90 percent.

WASSA MINE ACQUIRED

Golden Star Resources acquired the Wassa mine in late 2002. Midway through the following year, the company agreed to spend $5.5 million to acquire the Ghana-based Obotan plant from Australia's Resolute Mining, along with a 4.5 percent interest in Australia's Red Back Mining. In 2004 Golden Star Resources produced about 148,000 ounces of unhedged gold at Bogoso/Prestea. The company ended the year by completing construction activities at the new Wassa mine, which was expected to produce about 120,000 ounces of gold in 2005.

Exploration continued at an aggressive pace in 2005. That year the company earmarked $15 million

```
┌─────────────────────────────────────────────┐
│                                             │
│              KEY DATES                      │
│                  ■                          │
│  ─────────────────────────────────────────  │
│  1992:  Golden Star Resources is formed.    │
│  1999:  The company acquires a 70 percent   │
│         stake in Bogoso Gold Ltd., which    │
│         operates the Bogoso Gold Mine in    │
│         Ghana, West Africa.                 │
│  2001:  Golden Star Resources acquires      │
│         Anvil Mining's 20 percent equity    │
│         interest in the Bogoso mine.        │
│  2002:  The Wassa mine is acquired.         │
│  2007:  Gold is produced at the company's   │
│         Bogoso Sulfide Processing Plant     │
│         using bio-oxidation technology.     │
│                                             │
└─────────────────────────────────────────────┘
```

for its exploration program. In April commercial operations began at the new Wassa carbon-in-leach (ore processing using cyanide) processing facility. Four months later Golden Star Resources offered to acquire competitor IAMGOLD Corp. However, IAMGOLD encouraged its shareholders to vote against the tie-up, because the company was interested in pursuing a $2.1 billion merger with South Africa-based Gold Fields Ltd.

In September 2005 Golden Star Resources suspended work at its Plant-North pit at the Bogoso/Prestea mine in order to perform mitigation work required by the Ghana Environmental Protection Agency. These mitigation measures included the construction of a new police station and the relocation of an existing one, the erection of a fence around its Phase 3 pit development, and the construction of a bypass road. These projects were completed in mid-October.

LEADERSHIP CHANGES

By mid-2006 Golden Star Resources was in the process of carrying out a sulfide expansion project at its Bogoso/Prestea mine that would significantly increase processing capacity. In October of that year an important leadership change took place. Chief Financial Officer Allan Marter retired and was succeeded on an interim basis by Vice President of Finance and Controller Roger Palmer.

In February 2007 Golden Star Resources named Newmont Mining Corp. executive Tom Mair as senior vice president and chief financial officer. The following month the company announced that it had begun producing gold from the Bogoso Sulfide Processing Plant, which used bio-oxidation technology (a means of processing involving bacteria to oxidize refractory sulfide ore). Within the context of the company's goal of

becoming a mid-tier gold producer, President and CEO Peter Bradford indicated that this represented a significant milestone for the organization.

The Bogoso Sulfide Processing Plant encountered a number of design and mechanical-related problems during its commissioning phase. However, construction of the facility, which had an annual capacity of 3.5 million meteric tons, was completed in July 2007. Commercial production commenced at that time, and the company was working with equipment manufacturers to address the problems it had experienced during the commissioning phase.

It also was in 2007 that President and CEO Peter Bradford announced plans to relinquish his position at the end of the year. In addition, the company's Wassa mine received a "most improved mine" award from the Ghana Environmental Protection Agency. Late in the year, the company commenced development of its Benso mine on property it had acquired in late 2005.

In December 2007 Golden Star Resources named Chief Financial Officer Tom Mair as interim president and CEO. Vice President of Finance and Controller Roger Palmer was temporarily named chief financial officer and corporate compliance officer. Tom Mair was formally named president and CEO in March 2008. Another leadership change occurred when Newmont Mining Corp. executive Scott D. Barr was named chief operating officer. An experienced metallurgical and chemical engineer, Barr had served as Newmont's chief technical officer.

FOCUS ON GROWTH AND PRODUCTION

During the third quarter of 2008 Golden Star Resources began transporting ore from its Benso mine to the Wassa plant for processing. Development of the company's Hwini-Butre mine, which it had acquired in late 2005, began in the fourth quarter. In addition, the company completed critical repairs at its Wassa mine, following mechanical failures that took place in August. During 2008 Golden Star Resources devoted approximately $15.8 million to exploration efforts in both South America and West Africa.

In 2009 the exploration investments of Golden Star Resources totaled about $9 million. Midway through the year, the company began transporting ore from Hwini-Butre to its Wassa plant for processing. In addition, the company revealed that, following negotiations with the Volta River Authority, its power costs in Ghana would be significantly reduced, thanks to lower power utility rates.

By this time Golden Star Resources was evaluating gold properties in Brazil, and was in the process of carrying out regional reconnaissance projects in Ghana, Côte d'Ivoire, and Sierra Leone. Additionally, the company reported that more advanced drilling was under way in Niger, Ghana, and Burkina Faso. In December 2009 Golden Star Resources completed an offering of 20 million shares of its common stock, generating net proceeds of $71.6 million.

For the year, the mineral reserves of Golden Star Resources reached 48.3 million metric tons. This marked an increase of 14 percent, or 450,000 ounces, over 2008. The improvement was attributed to a number of factors, including engineering changes, gold price increases, successful exploration initiatives, and cost reductions. In early 2010 the company indicated that it would significantly increase its annual exploration budget.

Moving ahead into the second decade of the 21st century, Golden Star Resources was focused on transforming itself into a mid-tier gold producer. In support of this objective, the company remained committed to evaluating opportunities to increase its annual gold production, including possible mergers and acquisitions. Based upon its success during the 1990s and the first decade of the new century, the company appeared to have good prospects for continued success.

Paul R. Greenland

PRINCIPAL SUBSIDIARIES

Caystar Holdings (Cayman Islands); Bogoso Holdings (Cayman Islands); Wasford Holdings (Cayman Islands); Golden Star Exploration Holdings (Cayman Islands); Golden Star (Bogoso/Prestea) Ltd. (Ghana; 90%); Golden Star (Wassa) Ltd.

PRINCIPAL COMPETITORS

AngloGold Ashanti Ltd.; Gold Fields Ltd.; IAMGOLD Corporation.

FURTHER READING

"Golden Star and Anvil Complete the Purchase of the Bogoso Gold Mine in Ghana," *PR Newswire*, September 30, 1999.

"Golden Star Announces Successful Completion of US$75.0 Million Common Share Offering," *Internet Wire*, December 17, 2009.

"Golden Star Increases Mineral Reserves 14% in 2009," *Internet Wire*, February 18, 2010.

"Golden Star Reports First Gold Production from Bogoso Sulfide (BIOX(R)) Processing Plant," *Business Wire*, March 28, 2007.

"Golden Star Resources Ltd. Acquisition of 90% of Bogoso Completed," *PR Newswire*, September 6, 2001.

"Golden Star Resources Names New CEO," *Africa News Service*, March 10, 2008.

Dairy Products, Inc.

Grassland Dairy Products, Inc.

N8790 Fairground Avenue
Greenwood, Wisconsin 54437
U.S.A.
Telephone: (715) 267-6182
Fax: (715) 267-6044
Web site: http://www.grassland.com

Private Company
Incorporated: 1904 as Farmers Progressive Creamery
　　Company
Employees: 224
Sales: $1.12 billion (2008 est.)
NAICS: 311512 Creamery Butter Manufacturing

■ ■ ■

Based in Greenwood, Wisconsin, Grassland Dairy Products, Inc., is a family-owned-and-operated dairy products company serving the retail, foodservice, private label, and industrial sectors. The company is best known for its butter products, which are sold in all 50 states and several foreign countries. Grassland is the largest privately owned butter manufacturing company in the United States, generating well over $1 billion in annual sales. It is also regarded as the oldest independent butter maker.

Retail products include salted and unsalted solid and stick butter, whipped butter, and spreadable butter. The company's ultrapremium butter is sold under the Wuethrich label, the Grassland and Fall Creek names are applied to the premium product, and Country Cream is the company's value brand. Grassland sells a trans fat

free butter blend under the Golden Goodness label. These products are also sold under private labels. In addition, Grassland butter products, including bulk sizes, patties, chips, and cups, are produced for foodservice customers. Grassland offers industrial customers butter in larger quantities as well as cream, buttermilk, skim milk, cheeses, milk protein concentrate, sour cream, and cultured products.

The company also produces skim milk, whole milk, cheddar cheese, and cream cheese replacers, and supplies custom products and blends. These industrial products, sold to the world market, are used to manufacture cheese powders and products, seasonings, soups, sauces, dressings, confections, frozen foods, cookies and crackers, snacks, and prepared frozen mixes. Grassland operates plants in Greenwood, Wisconsin; West Point, Nebraska; and Hyrum, Utah. The Greenwood plant is supplied by about 850 producers within a 200-mile radius who each day deliver more than three million pounds of milk. Grassland is owned and managed by third- and fourth-generation Wuethrich family members.

SWISS ORIGINS

The man behind the birth and growth of Grassland Dairy was John Samuel Wuethrich. He was born in 1883 in Switzerland, where he learned the art of cheese making from his father, Samuel Wuethrich. In 1892 the family immigrated to the United States, settling in Woodland, Wisconsin, to continue making cheese. John Wuethrich furthered his dairy education by enrolling at the Dairy School in Madison, Wisconsin, graduating in

COMPANY PERSPECTIVES

At Grassland, everything we do is dedicated to providing exceptional quality, service and value, while leading the industry with customer-focused innovation.

1902. He went to work as a butter maker in the town of Greenwood for Karl Grashorn, who then dispatched him to Clark County, which would one day emerge as the state's largest dairy county, to manage the Greenwood Creamery.

Wuethrich soon left Grashorn's employ to start a creamery in Doylestown with his two brothers, Alfred and Fred. In 1904 Wuethrich returned to Clark County to help organize the Farmers Progressive Creamery Company, the forerunner of Grassland Dairy, in the town of Eaton. Area farmers had raised $1,000 to start the business and persuaded the 22-year-old Wuethrich to join them as a butter maker. He was said to have arrived with just 50 cents in his pockets.

Wuethrich was responsible for constructing the plant and installing the machinery, and once it was operational, he soon became general manager. He was also a stockholder in the company. The Farmers Progressive Creamery operation was similar to the two-dozen other creameries that had developed in Clark County since the late 1890s when butter was no longer churned by farm wives and bartered at the local general store. Farmers had begun to band together to build dairy processing plants, a movement that gained momentum after the dawn of the 20th century. At that time the ready availability of an inexpensive hand-cranked cream separator allowed farmers to store the less abundant cream until there was enough to make it worthwhile to ship to the processing plant, while keeping the much higher volume of skimmed milk for calves and pigs.

PARTNERS BOUGHT OUT: 1914

Wuethrich produced both cheese and butter, sold in 60-pound wooden tubs. He made do with very little equipment, housed in a small frame building. A short time after becoming the general manager, he became ill and was sent to the hospital. Upon his return, he found that the creamery was $4,000 in debt. Eventually he paid off the debt and was left with $38 for himself. He used that money and sold a horse to buy 40 acres of wild land on which to start his own dairy farm, raising a herd of Holstein cattle to supply the new creamery.

Wuethrich married in 1909 and settled in Clark County. His wife gave birth to two sons, John D. and Lee Allen, and Wuethrich wanted to leave a business for them. In 1914 he bought out his partners and became the sole owner of Farmers Progressive Creamery. Two years later he also acquired an idle cheese factory in the township of Weston.

Wuethrich renamed Farmers Progressive Creamery as John Wuethrich & Sons. The company was later renamed the John Wuethrich Creamery Co. His farm took the name Grass Land Dairy Farm. In time, he coined the "Grassland" brand for the sweet cream butter he sold in Wisconsin. A press profile of him in 1925 revealed a well-to-do dairyman whose gross annual income was $25,000. He owned three large farms and 100 head of Holstein cattle. Moreover, the creamery was reported to have paid farmers $3 million in the previous 17 years.

Wuethrich's son, John Drummond Wuethrich, eventually took over the management of the creamery. Upon the death of his father in October 1948, following two years of deteriorating health, he shared ownership of the business with his brother, Lee Allen Wuethrich, and together they ran the business while their mother served as president.

Significant changes were made to the creamery operation under the leadership of the second generation. Farm milk cans gave way to large stainless steel storage tanks, which were in turn replaced by three churns that operated continuously. By the late 1950s the creamery was turning out nine million pounds of butter a year, sold in Wisconsin under the Grassland name and delivered under 53 other brands by a fleet of 23 refrigerated trucks to such markets as Cleveland, Pittsburgh, Detroit, northern Illinois, and Toledo, Ohio.

BROTHER RETIRES: 1972

Lee Wuethrich retired in 1972, prompting John D. Wuethrich to consider selling the creamery. However, his son Dallas expressed a strong desire to become involved in the company. As a result, the father and son assumed complete ownership and the creamery business was renamed Grassland Dairy Products, Inc. The operation was upgraded to keep pace with demand. For example, in 1987 a new evaporator system was installed, allowing Grassland to turn its buttermilk into a premium product. A butter oil system was installed in 1993 to permit the production of butter oil and anhydrous milk fat.

In addition to organic growth, Grassland also expanded through external means. In 1993 Grassland acquired North Salt Lake, Utah-based Dave Mortensen

KEY DATES

1904: John S. Wuethrich helps organize the Farmers Progressive Creamery Company.
1914: John S. Wuethrich acquires creamery from his partners.
1948: John S. Wuethrich dies.
1993: Dave Mortensen Inc. is acquired.
2005: Grassland acquires West Point Dairy Products Inc., adding two butter production plants.

Inc., which did business as Mortensen Food Products, buying it out of bankruptcy court for $1.15 million. Mortensen was a longtime producer of butter and other dairy products. The loss of several major customers had put a pinch on its finances, leading to insufficient funds to run the company and eventually to bankruptcy. The addition of Mortensen allowed Grassland to better serve its customers in the region. Previously it had to purchase milk in Idaho and ship it to the Wisconsin plant for processing.

With Dallas Wuethrich succeeding his father as president, Grassland remained in the vanguard of the butter industry by introducing new products. To satisfy the needs of industrial customers, Grassland in 1996 introduced milk fat fractions, branded Butter Crystals. The product was developed in conjunction with Systems Bio-Industries Inc. Butter Crystals were ideal for making ice cream, low-fat cheese, spreadable butter, baked goods, and confections.

BUTTER EARNS TOP INTERNATIONAL PRIZES: 2006

In the mid-1990s Grassland recognized an opportunity when New York chefs began looking for domestic sources of higher-fat butter, such as those made in Europe. These products were part of butter's renewed appeal after years during which margarine had cut into market share. To fill that need, Grassland began producing European-style butters, which contained 83 percent butterfat by weight instead of the 80 percent butterfat of traditional butter. The extra butterfat produced a creamier texture and the butter was easier to spread. European-style butter would account for only about 5 percent of Grassland's overall butter production, but it commanded a higher price and was more profitable than traditional butter. Moreover, the company gained prestige by entering its new butters in major competitions.

After winning a U.S. championship, Grassland swept the unsalted butter category in the 2006 World Championship Cheese and Butter contest, taking all three prizes for its European-style unsalted butter. Grassland then introduced a new line of unsalted butter inspired by the winning entry. The new line included Wuethrich Clarified Butter, intended for cooking, and Wuethrich 83% European Salted and Unsalted Butter. These were packaged in several sizes for both the retail and foodservice channels.

Grassland approached its 100th anniversary as the 21st century began. In anticipation of the event, the company redesigned its packaging, including a modernized, brighter logo. It was just the sixth time in its history that the company had changed its carton designs. The company made other changes to the business as well. In 2005 Grassland acquired West Point Dairy Products Inc., adding a pair of butter production plants that operated five churns between them. The plants were located in West Point, Nebraska, and Hyrum, Utah.

Additional churns helped to increase production, but a redesign of Grassland's warehouse was needed to make sure that stock did not sit too long. A lack of storage space had necessitated constant rotation of stock, as well as off-site storage, resulting in a costly and inefficient operation. To address the problem, Grassland in the early years of the decade redesigned its warehouse and installed a gravity flow pallet rack system that made use of all available overhead space. The new design ensured that the first items that entered the warehouse were the first ones shipped. As a result, stock rotation was no longer needed, nor was off-site storage.

COOPERATIVE PLANT ACQUIRED: 2008

In 2002 Grassland began accepting milk from farmers, instead of buying cream from various sources. A new facility to store and process that milk opened a year later, constructed to accommodate future expansion. Grassland added another production facility in May 2008 when it acquired the former Greenwood Milk Products Cooperative. A few months later the Greenwood-area facility began processing about 1.5 million pounds of milk each day to make cheese.

Then in the second century of operation, Grassland was being run by the third generation of the Wuethrich family, and members of the fourth generation, the two sons of Dallas Wuethrich, were playing key roles as well. The elder son, Tayt, was a buyer, while the younger son, Trevor, served as director of marketing. Having created a world-class operation, Dallas Wuethrich and his sons remained passionate about the business and were eager to keep Grassland prosperous and in family hands for many years to come.

Ed Dinger

PRINCIPAL SUBSIDIARIES

Greenwood Milk Products; Wuethrich Brothers-Nebraska, LLC.

PRINCIPAL COMPETITORS

Dean Foods Company; Kraft Foods Inc.; Land O'Lakes, Inc.

FURTHER READING

"Badger Farmer Got Started with $.50," *Ironwood Daily Globe*, May 23, 1925.

Bringard, Lara, "Wisconsin Firm Completes $1.15 Million Purchase of Mortensen Food Assets," *Enterprise*, June 28, 1993.

Curtiss-Wedge, Franklyn, *The Biographical History of Clark County, Wisconsin*, Chicago: H.C. Cooper, Jr., & Co., 1918.

Herzog, Karen, "Churning Out Quality: Wisconsin's European-Style Butters Makes Judges, Cooks and Diners Melt," *Milwaukee Journal Sentinel*, August 16, 2006.

Oncken, John F., "Clark County Is Heart of Wisconsin Dairy Land," *Madison (WI) Capital Times*, July 10, 2008.

"Sons Follow Father's Footsteps," *Milwaukee Sentinel*, April 14, 1957, p. 42.

Groupe Stalaven S.A.

BP 94, 13 rue de Brest
Yffiniac, F-22120
France
Telephone: (+33 02) 96 63 80 00
Fax: (+33 02) 96 63 80 24
Web site: http://www.stalaven.fr

Wholly Owned Subsidiary of Euralis
Incorporated: 1986
Employees: 1,400
Sales: EUR 212 million ($296.8 million) (2009 est.)
NAICS: 311612 Meat Processed from Carcasses; 311412 Frozen Specialty Food Manufacturing; 311812 Commercial Bakeries

■ ■ ■

Groupe Stalaven S.A. is one of France's fastest-growing food processors. The Brittany-region company is also one of its most diversified, with a range of foods spanning from delicatessen meats to salads and desserts. Stalaven has built up a network of six factories in France and also operates a noodle production subsidiary in Poland. Each year the company produces more than 50,000 metric tons of delicatessen meats, patés, savory pastries, chilled and frozen prepared ready-meals, and fruit-based desserts, for total sales of EUR 212 million ($297 million) in 2009.

Stalaven supplies the three major retail food channels in France, producing private-label foods for the large-scale distribution sector; supplying the institutional and restaurant sector; and serving local independent butchers, grocers, and similar retailers. This latter sector accounts for as much as 40 percent of the company's total sales each year. While most of the company's sales remain within France, Stalaven has built up an international sales network to 10 countries. Stalaven is still controlled by the founding family, led by President Thierry Meuriot and Franck Meuriot, grandsons of founder Jean Stalaven. The company's 1,400 employees own 4 percent of its shares. Cooperative group Euralis acquired a 65 percent stake in the company in 2009.

FAMILY DELI IN 1945

Jean Stalaven inherited his family's delicatessen in Bourbriac, in the Côtes d'Armor in the northern part of France's Brittany region, in 1945. The Stalaven family had operated the shop for several generations. France's postwar era offered a number of new opportunities for expanding the business. The development of new refrigeration technologies helped extend the shelf life of many of Stalaven's meats, patés, and other deli products. During the 1950s more and more households were equipped with refrigerators. At the same time, the Brittany region had led France in the development of a new retail format, the American-style self-service supermarket. These were quickly equipped with refrigerated delicatessen sections.

France's rising prosperity during the 1950s, and the development of a true leisure sector in the postwar era, also stimulated the demand for prepared foods. Stalaven was quick to adapt to this new demand and by 1955 had moved to a larger shop in nearby St. Brieuc. Stalaven's early success stemmed from a commitment to the high quality of his products. Stalaven also put into place a strong service policy. To this end, the company set up its own sales department in 1960, backed by a logistics and distribution platform. This extension enabled Stalaven to promise next-day delivery to his growing list of customers. These expanded operations also supported Stalaven's growth beyond the Brittany region onto a national level.

INDUSTRIAL OPERATIONS IN 1965

The rising popularity of Stalaven's products led the company to the next step in its evolution, as it moved to industrialize its production. This took place in 1965, when the company opened a 3,000-square-meter factory in St. Brieuc. Stalaven's workforce had grown to 34 people by then. The company modernized its production and logistics capacity two years later, adding its first computerized systems. Jean Stalaven also invested in training programs, notably supporting the creation of a technical school for delicatessen workers in Loudéac, which opened in 1968.

Stalaven's production reached a new level in 1970. The company expanded its factory that year to include more than 10,000 square meters of production space. The expansion also permitted the group to incorporate a new generation of modernized production lines, not only raising its quality levels, but also supporting its expanding product range.

In the mid-1970s Stalaven made its first moves beyond the Brittany region. In 1975 the company opened a new logistics platform in Thiais, near Rungis, site of France's largest wholesale foods market. In that same year Stalaven also acquired U.K.-based Charcuterie Ltd., which operated a factory in London. Stalaven's payroll also grew strongly during this period, increasing to 234 employees by 1975.

NEW ORGANIZATIONAL STRUCTURE IN 1986

Jean Stalaven's daughter, Jeanine Meuriot, joined the company in 1980 and eventually took over its leadership

from her father. Stalaven remained active in the company he had founded, and continued to visit its factories regularly even into his 90s. In the meantime, Stalaven, which posted sales of 97 million francs in 1980, prepared for even greater growth. Innovation provided an important key to unlocking Stalaven's potential. In 1980 the company laid claim to the introduction of a new grocery category, called "Traiteur" (Catering), and featuring ready-made salads and meals. The success of this new line helped raise Stalaven's revenues to FRF 215 million in 1984.

Stalaven had also completed a new acquisition by then, of a stake in a deli meats producer based in Nouméa, in New Caledonia, in 1983. Stalaven later acquired full control of that factory. In 1985 the company bought Salaisons Boutot, a prominent producer of cured sausages and hams based in the Corrèze region. Other investments during this time included a new expansion of the St. Brieuc factory, which reached a total production surface of 20,000 square meters.

Stalaven adapted its operational structure to its emerging position as one of France's leading food producers. In 1986 the company incorporated as a limited liability company, Groupe Stalaven S.A. The company also set up a new organizational structure, based around its three primary distribution channels: local commerce, supermarkets, and restaurants and catering. In 1988 the Stalaven family created a new holding company to take over their ownership of the group, in order to preserve their control. By then the company had begun its long-term relationship with French bank Credit Agricole, which gained a 12 percent stake in the company.

NEW HABITS

By the late 1980s France's retail food industry was deeply involved in a major transition. The rising dominance of the supermarket sector brought about a change in French shopping habits. Smaller groceries, butchers, and delicatessens found it increasingly difficult to compete against the product range, pricing, and convenience of the larger supermarkets and hypermarkets. At the same time, the massive entry of French women into the workforce meant that households had less time to devote to cooking meals. Food producers, including Jean Stalaven, rushed into the new and rapidly growing market for ready-made meals and other processed foods.

Stalaven responded to these new trends by opening four new factories in 1989, including two in Yffiniac, in the Côtes d'Armor, producing salads and savory pastries,

KEY DATES

■

1945: Jean Stalaven takes over his family's delicatessen in Bourbriac.
1965: Stalaven opens his first factory, in St. Brieuc.
1975: Stalaven acquires Charcuterie Ltd. in London, England.
1986: The company reincorporates as Groupe Stalaven S.A.
1989: Stalaven builds four new factories, including one in Australia.
2006: Euralis acquires a 20 percent stake in Stalaven.
2009: Euralis becomes Stalaven's majority shareholder with a 65 percent stake.

and a third in Dunkerque, producing cooked ready-made meals. The company also invested another FRF 20 million expanding its St. Brieuc factory. The company took steps to expand its overseas operations, setting up a factory in Brisbane, Australia, to supply salads and ready-made meals to that market.

The investments paid off strongly for the company, which saw its sales climb past FRF 380 million in 1989 and to more than FRF 500 million by 1991. The Yffiniac factories accounted for 50 percent of the group's total revenues by then. The company's prepared salad sales were especially strong, leading it to invest in the expansion of the Yffiniac facility. Yffiniac also became the site of the company's new headquarters. The company also launched plans to double its Boutot sausage and cured ham operation in 1992. Other investments that year included the completion of a new 5,000-square-meter logistics platform at Yffiniac, and the acquisition of Aux Jambon Français.

This acquisition was followed by the purchase of Tradicoupe and its Le Clos Gourmand brand in 1996. Also that year, the company announced a new investment of FRF 104 million in order to expand its production capacity. As Jean Stalaven told *Usine Nouvelle*: "After growing 22 percent in 1995, our production lines have reached the saturation point." The company's revenues had grown past FRF 830 million by then. Two years later Stalaven's sales topped FRF 930 million.

NEW BRAND IN 2001

Jeanine Meuriot retired in 1999, turning over the leadership of the company to her sons, Thierry and

Franck Meuriot. Among their first initiatives was to invest FRF 30 million in modernizing the company's information technology infrastructure. The new system, which became fully operational in 1999, helped the company achieve greater efficiency in its logistics platform, capable of processing more than 88,000 orders each day.

Stalaven began developing its own branded image, launching the first in a series of television advertisements in 1999. This led the company to the creation of its own branded line of ready-made meals, called "Jean Stalaven, Le Cuisinier Traiteur," for the self-service supermarket sector. The company also targeted an expansion of its foreign sales. Toward this end, the company acquired Rudix, a Polish deli meats producer, in 2001. That subsidiary later changed its name to Jean Stalaven Polska.

Stalaven's revenue growth had slowed somewhat in the new decade, just barely topping EUR 150 million (roughly FRF 1 billion) in 2000. The company also struggled with its profitability, losing money for the first time in 2000. Part of the reason for this was the ongoing consolidation of the French supermarket sector, especially the merger between Carrefour and Promodes. With fewer supermarket groups, the company found itself faced with stiffer competition from other processed foods suppliers, as well as increasing pressure to lower prices from the supermarket groups themselves.

PARTNERING WITH EURALIS IN 2006

Stalaven returned to profitability by 2003, in part by investing in a new sector, prepared fruit dishes, through the acquisition of I.D. Fruits. Also that year, Stalaven brought in three new financial partners, Unigrains, Agro, and Institut de Participations de l'Ouest, which took over the stake in the company previously held by Credit Agricole. Stalaven also opened up its shareholding to its employees, who acquired a 4 percent stake in the company at this time.

Stalaven focused on broadening its product range through the middle of the decade, targeting the creation of innovative product lines to stimulate its revenue growth. The company developed its own research and development kitchens, led by Chef Michel Daniélou. This permitted the company to introduce a new and highly successful range of fish pastry products. The company also developed a new range of fresh prepared salads, launching construction of a new EUR 9 million factory in Saint-Agathon in 2005. Featuring 7,000 square meters of production space, the plant became operational in 2007.

In the second half of the decade Stalaven sought out a larger partner to help back its further development. This led the group to establish in 2006 an alliance with French cooperative Euralis, which acquired an initial stake of 20 percent in Stalaven. Euralis, based in France's southwest, had traditionally focused on the production of grains and seeds. During the late 1990s Euralis entered the market for foie gras, rapidly becoming a leader in that market. In the early years of the new century Euralis, like many of France's agriculture cooperatives, sought to expand its operations into the higher-margin prepared foods sectors.

Backed by Euralis, Stalaven continued its own growth, seeing its sales jump from EUR 156 million in 2006 to EUR 219 million into 2009. Part of this growth came from the company's fresh salad division, reinforced in 2007 by the purchase of a 33 percent stake in another prepared salad specialist, 3 Gourmands. Toward the end of the decade the company acquired a stake in Gastronomes du Dauphine and took over Vendée-based SAG as well. The company also dropped development of its Jean Stalaven supermarket brand, having failed to build a significant share of that market.

Stalaven and Euralis continued to develop their relationship, as Euralis's share of the company rose to 50 percent toward the end of the decade. In October 2009 Euralis moved to take over majority control of Stalaven, raising its stake to 65 percent. The acquisition marked the beginning of a new era of growth for Stalaven, as the company set its sights on topping the EUR 350 million sales mark by 2015.

M. L. Cohen

PRINCIPAL SUBSIDIARIES

Argoat Salades; I.D. Fruits; Jean Stalaven Polska Sp. z o.o.; Salaisons Boutot; Société SAG.

PRINCIPAL DIVISIONS

Cooked Ham; Catering Salad; Savory Pastry; Catering Entrée; Prepared Meals; Dried Sausage; Dessert.

PRINCIPAL OPERATING UNITS

Catering; Delicatessen; Fruits and Vegetables; Local Commerce.

PRINCIPAL COMPETITORS

Bertin S.A.; Cooperl Arc Atlantique S.C.A.; Doux S.A.; Fleury Michon S.A.; Madrange S.A.; Myasomolprom Industrial Group; Nestlé France S.A.S.; Socopa S.A.; Terrena S.C.A.; Unilever N.V.; VION Holding N.V.

FURTHER READING

Alvarez, Bruno, "Le Traiture Stalaven Ne Connâit Pas la Crise," *Ouest France*, December 5, 2008.

"Chez Stalaven, Trois Nouveaux Concepts," *Points de Vente*, May 3, 2010.

Crosskey, Peter, "Chilled Foods Firm Stalaven in Strategic Deal," *just-food.com*, September 27, 2007.

Déniel, Patrick, "Stalaven, le Traiteur Éclectique," *Usine Nouvelle*, January 21, 2010.

————, "Stalaven Guetteur de Tendances," *Usine Nouvelle*, December 14, 2007.

Du Guerny, Stanislas, "Euralis Avale Stalaven," *Usine Nouvelle*, September 24, 2009.

————, "Stalaven Mise sur l'Innovation," *Usine Nouvelle*, March 4, 2004.

Riberolles, Vincent, "Stalaven Reprend en Main le Rayon Traiteur à la Coupe," *LSA*, November 12, 2009.

"Stalaven: Euralis Prend le Contrôle du Traiteur Breton," *Le Télégramme*, September 24, 2009.

Violette, Christophe, "Euralis Nourrit les Grands Appétits de Stalaven," *Ouest France*, November 6, 2009.

H.P. Hood L.L.C.

6 Kimball Lane
Lynnfield, Massachusetts 01940
U.S.A.
Telephone: (617) 887-3000
Toll Free: (800) 343-6592
Fax: (617) 887-8484
Web site: http://www.hood.com

Private Company
Founded: 1846
Employees: 4,500
Sales: $2.2 billion (2008)
NAICS: 311500 Dairy Product Manufacturing

■ ■ ■

H.P. Hood L.L.C. is a major dairy company based in Lynnfield, Massachusetts. The privately held company offers fluid milk, cream, egg nog, sour cream, cottage cheese, ice cream, frozen novelties, and juices and drink products. In addition to the Hood brand and private labels, regional brands include Simply Smart, Calorie Countdown, Heluva Good, Kemps, Crowley, Penn Maid, Axelrod, Rosenberger's, Maggio, Brigham's, and Lactaid. Products are mostly found in New England, sold in supermarkets, convenience stores, and distributed through foodservice channels, but in recent years the company's reach has spread across the United States. Hood also maintains a home delivery service that in addition to dairy products offers meats, produce, bread and other baked goods, beverages, specialty, seasonal, and foodservice items. Hood maintains 22 manufacturing plants in several states, including Mas-

sachusetts, Connecticut, Maine, New York, Vermont, and Virginia.

MID-19TH-CENTURY ROOTS

H.P. Hood was founded by Harvey Perley Hood. He was born in Chelsea, Vermont, in 1823, and worked on his father's farm until 1845 when he moved to Boston to become a baker's apprentice. He soon became interested in the dairy industry, however, and in 1846 struck out on his own, buying a small retail milk business that took his name. For health reasons he moved to Derry, New Hampshire, in 1856 and continued to supply Boston with milk, in the process becoming the first dairy to transport milk by rail. Two years later he acquired the large Redfield dairy farm in Derry and quickly expanded the operation as he grew his company into one of New England's largest dairy concerns, with offices in Boston, Lynn, and Salem, Massachusetts.

Two of Hood's three sons, Charles and Gilbert, joined the company, which was incorporated in 1890 as H.P. Hood and Sons. Two years later they moved the headquarters to Charlestown, Massachusetts, where in 1900 a new plant was open. It was also in the 1890s that Hood became the first Northeast dairy to pasteurize its milk and extend the shelf life of its products. The company also introduced sanitary glass bottles and invented a glass bottle washer, eliminating the traditional milk cans and dippers for dispensing milk.

FOUNDER DIES: 1900

In June 1900 Harvey Hood died at his Derry farm, according to news accounts, following an attack of

COMPANY PERSPECTIVES

For more than 150 years, the name Hood has been synonymous with fresh, quality dairy products that taste great.

apoplexy from which he did not regain consciousness. His sons carried on the business. The eldest, Charles, took over as president, a post he held until his retirement in 1925. The next eldest son, Gilbert, succeeded him, The third son, Edward, also served as a vice president. Gilbert Hood died in 1936, followed a year later by Charles, whose son Harvey P. Hood took the reins. Edward Hood passed away in 1943.

Under second-generation leadership, Hood expanded into ice cream, launching production in 1909. It was also during this period that the company opened its first ice cream stand on Beacon Street in Boston. The company's first dedicated ice cream plant opened in Lynn, Massachusetts, in 1918. By the early 1920s Hood was operating 60 ice cream retail stores.

Hood continued to grow in the New England market. In 1950 the company acquired five Vermont milk plants from Sheffield Farms Company. Hood also began to distribute orange juice through a joint venture established with a Florida company in late 1955. Hood became so dominant that in the 1950s and 1960s it had to contend with antitrust violations, accused of price-fixing schemes to drive out smaller competition as well as to increase profits from government sales. The U.S. Department of Justice filed an antitrust suit against Hood and another area dairy company, accusing them of attempting to monopolize milk distribution in parts of New England. The matter was settled in 1953 when Hood agreed to sell some of its assets in Vermont and Maine and abide by other stipulations.

In 1960 several smaller dairies filed suit against the company, alleging that Hood engaged in a price-cutting war as a way to force them out of business. The federal government also took issue with Hood and two other large milk distributors in 1962, charging they engaged in a conspiracy to fix milk prices and overcharge the state of Massachusetts and 34 eastern Massachusetts communities. Hood pleaded guilty to the charges in 1964. Hood along with the Great Atlantic & Pacific Tea Co. Inc (A&P) was also accused of violating antitrust regulations by conspiring to constrict the sale of milk in the Boston area, essentially through giving discriminatory discounts to area milk dealers.

COMPANY TAKEN PUBLIC: 1972

A nonfamily member took charge of Hood in 1970 when John M. Fox was named president and chief executive officer. Fox was best known as the founder of the Minute Maid Corporation. After the company was sold to Coca-Cola in 1960 he enjoyed a second career as president and chairman of United Fruit Company before joining Hood. Under his leadership, Hood was taken public and renamed H.P. Hood Inc. in 1972, its shares mostly held by the Hood family and only lightly traded on an over-the-counter basis. Under Fox, Hood implemented a $9 million expansion program that included a new Pennsylvania cheese processing plant and upgrades to a Florida citrus production plant.

In 1975 Fox succeeded 65-year-old Gilbert H. Hood, a grandson of the founder, as chairman. Fox also brought in a former lieutenant from United Brands, Edward Gelsthorpe, to become president and chief operating officer. Fox retired in 1978, the same year that Harvey P. Hood passed away. A year later the Hood family decided the time had come to sell the business. Hood posted sales of $493.9 million and net income of $1.2 million in fiscal 1979, but faced increasingly stiff competition in orange juice and yogurt, both of which were key growth areas. Over the years Hood had made attempts to diversify but enjoyed little success with ventures in eggs, jams and jellies, and frozen pizza. More recently, in 1972, Hood acquired Chicago-based Reed Candy, maker of hard candy rolls. It also looked far a field by acquiring Unfinished Furniture Inc. of East Bridgewater, Massachusetts.

FAMILY OWNERSHIP ENDS: 1980

When New England dairy farmers learned that the Hood family was looking to sell the business, they grew concerned because Hood was one of the largest buyers of milk in the region. As a result, Agway Inc., a farm cooperative that provided many of these farmers with supplies, took notice and decided it was in everyone's best interest for Agway to purchase Hood. Rather than assume all of the risk, it insisted that the New England dairymen form a cooperative and contribute an equal amount of money, $28 million, to recapitalize the new Hood company. The dairymen, organized as Agri-Mark Inc., took control of Hood's fixed assets to secure a guaranteed buyer of their milk, and receive half of Hood's profits. Thus, in 1980 family ownership of H.P. Hood came to an end after 134 years.

By this time area competitors had fled the cities for country locales, but Boston was eager to keep Hood and in the early 1980s made low-cost federally backed loans available to Hood to renovate its Rutherford Avenue plant. It was an effort that did not pay off in the long-run. The plant design was poor, putting Hood at a competitive disadvantage with rivals in the country with their streamlined plants.

Hood increased revenues to $600 million by 1990 but business began to decline, due in large measure to poor sales to the convenience store channel in Boston where most fluid milk sales were made. To make matters worse, Agri-Mark did not agree with the direction pursued by Hood, which was making investments in New York State the co-op thought ill advised. Agri-Mark sold its interest in Hood to Agway. In 1992 Agway then decided to exit the consumer products field. Again state and city officials made an effort to keep the business in Boston by attempting to broker a sale of Hood to its 1,750 employees in return for wage and benefits concessions. The deal fell through at the last minute, however.

NEW OWNER: 1995

Sales dipped to $550 million in 1994 but Hood was steadily losing market share to its chief competitors: Cumberland Farms, Garelick Farms, the Stop & Shop supermarket chain dairy division, and West Lynn Creamery. Hood elected to lay off employees at its Charlestown dairy plant and move fluid milk production to plants in Agawam and Portland, Maine. It was done in collaboration with potential buyers, and after two years on the block the company was finally sold in late 1995 when a partnership formed by John A. Kaneb, whose family was a major New England distributor of Gulf Oil products, agreed to buy Hood. An entity called Catamount Dairy Holdings Limited Partnership paid $100 million, including the assumption of debt, for the business.

The Charlestown plant continued to produce dairy products other than fluid milk as well as juices, but in 1996 the owners elected to cease operations entirely. The 23-acre property was then developed into a mixed-use business complex, and in 2000 Hood opened a

325,000-square-foot fluid milk facility in Winchester, Virginia. In the meantime, Hood redesigned many of its products, added new novelty products, and burnished its image through aggressive radio and television advertising. Moreover, the company was reorganized and a team-building program implemented.

Hood turned around its business by the start of the new century. It was a time of consolidation in the dairy industry, and in 2000 Hood looked to participate in the trend by merging with Dallas, Texas-based National Dairy Holdings, a move that would create the second largest dairy with annual sales of about $3 billion, trailing only Dean Foods and its $10 billion in sales. The merger did not pass regulatory muster with the Justice Department and was scrapped in the spring of 2003.

Hood enjoyed strong internal growth as sales improved to the $1 billion level in 2003. The company also pursued external growth. In April 2004 it acquired Binghamton, New York-based Crowley Foods LLC and Minneapolis, Minnesota-based Kemps LLC. Following the acquisitions H.P. Hood & Sons changed its name to H.P. Hood L.L.C. In 2007 Hood acquired Sacramento, California-based Crystal Cream & Butter Co., a company that was founded in 2001 and brought with it $182 million in sales. Further acquisitions followed. In 2007 Hood acquired the well-known Brigham's premium ice cream brand. Brigham's vanilla ice cream was the number one selling frozen food in New England. Established in 1914, the company also maintained 28 full-service restaurants in Massachusetts, offering sandwiches as well as ice cream, which were acquired by a Baltimore, Maryland, firm. These additions helped Hood to record $2.2 billion in revenues in 2008. Hood was also extending its reach well beyond New England, positioning the company for continued growth.

Ed Dinger

PRINCIPAL DIVISIONS

Hood Home Delivery.

PRINCIPAL COMPETITORS

Associated Milk Producers Inc.; Dean Foods Company; Dreyer's Grand Ice Cream Holdings, Inc.

FURTHER READING

Ackerman, Jerry, "Family Purchases H.P. Hood," *Boston Globe*, December 21, 1995, p. 50.

———, "Hood Calls It Quits in Charlestown," *Boston Globe*, March 1, 1996, p. 66.

———, "Hood Will Lay Off 157, Shift Work to Maine, Agawam," *Boston Globe*, May 4, 1995, p. 72.

———, "Plans Calls for Workers to Buy Hood," *Boston Globe*, January 26, 1994, p. 41.

"Harvey Perley Hood Dead," *Boston Daily Globe*, June 19, 1900, p. 24.

Mohl, Bruce A., "A Complex Farewell for H.P. Hood," *Boston Globe*, March 16, 1980, p. 1.

"State Sues Milk Firms," *Berkshire Eagle*, June 19, 1965, p. 17.

Van der Pool, Lisa, "Challenging Market Milks Profits from Iconic Dairy," *Boston Business Journal*, August 27, 2007.

Vennochi, Joan, "Hood's History," *Boston Globe*, June 7, 1996, p. 37.

HealthTronics, Inc.

———■———

9825 Spectrum Drive, Building 3
Austin, Texas 78717-4930
U.S.A.
Telephone: (512) 328-2892
Toll Free: (888) 252-6575
Fax: (512) 328-8510
Web site: http://www.healthtronics.com

Public Company
Incorporated: 1995 as HealthTronics Surgical Services,
Inc.
Employees: 658
Sales: $185.3 million (2009)
Stock Exchanges: NASDAQ
Ticker Symbol: HTRN
NAICS: 334510 Electromedical and Electrotherapeutic
Apparatus Manufacturing; 561110 Office
Administrative Services; 621498 All Other
Outpatient Care Facilities

■ ■ ■

Headquartered in Austin, Texas, HealthTronics, Inc.,
provides both urological products (including surgical
lasers and lithotripters) and services (including lithotripsy and prostate therapy) to physicians, hospitals,
surgery centers, and clinics. HealthTronics also operates
its ClariPath Laboratories anatomical pathology laboratory in Augusta, Georgia, which helps physicians detect,
diagnose, evaluate, and treat medical conditions such as
cancer. The company claims to operate the nation's largest fleet of lithotripsy systems. The company's service

solutions team provides around-the-clock, nationwide
urology equipment maintenance to health-care
providers.

FORMATION

HealthTronics traces its roots to December 1995, when
the company was incorporated in Georgia as Health-
Tronics Surgical Services, Inc. Focused on opportunities
in both orthopedics and urology, HealthTronics began
operations in May 1996. Midway through the following
year the company received approval from the Food and
Drug Administration (FDA) to market a lithotripter
called the LithoTron. Lithotripters are devices that break
kidney stones into small pieces using high-energy shock
waves.

After securing approval from the FDA, HealthTronics began establishing partnerships with physicians and
selling LithoTron devices, which were sourced from
Switzerland-based HMT High Medical Technologies
AG. In 1996 HMT granted HealthTronics the right to
acquire manufacturing rights to the LithoTron, as well
as a shock wave surgery system called the OssaTron,
which was used to treat orthopedic conditions. The
company had already secured exclusive North American
distribution, marketing, and selling rights for the two
products.

HealthTronics went public in August 1999, secur-
ing about 400 shareholders via its initial public offering.
The company's stock began trading on the NASDAQ
Bulletin Board, under the symbol HTRO, in October
1999. That month the HealthTronics Technology
Services Division was established to provide warranty

COMPANY PERSPECTIVES

Our product portfolio includes a full line of urology equipment and products including lithotripters, surgical lasers for treatment of BPH, and anatomical pathology services. As a service provider, HealthTronics offers the latest technology in lithotripsy services and prostate therapy services including BPH treatments and prostate cancer treatments.

and post-warranty equipment maintenance. In November the company's stock became more easily accessible when it was moved to the National NASDAQ Market and began trading under the symbol HTRN. The company ended the year with net income of $1.6 million on net revenue of $24.4 million.

ENTERING THE 21ST CENTURY

The company rang in the new millennium under the leadership of Chairman and CEO Argil Wheelock. In January 2000 HealthTronics acquired New Brunswick, New Jersey-based New Jersey Kidney Stone Treatment Center, located within Robert Wood Johnson University Hospital. By this time the company had equipment and services located in 35 states and had installed its 75th lithotripsy system.

On October 12, 2000, HealthTronics secured FDA approval to market the OssaTron for the treatment of heel spurs. In addition, the company completed an FDA clinical trial of the OssaTron for use in treating tennis elbow. As it had done with lithotripsy, HealthTronics proceeded to establish partnerships with health-care providers for orthotripsy services. The company ended the year with net income of $2.6 million on net revenues of $34 million.

HealthTronics made significant headway with its OssaTron device in 2001. That year the company brought 45 of the devices to the marketplace, carried out significant physician training initiatives, and performed about 2,700 treatments. Midway through the year HealthTronics struck a deal with HealthSouth Corp. to acquire a general partner interest in Gulf Coast Lithotripsy Associates LP, which was the largest lithotripsy provider in the Houston, Texas, area.

NAME CHANGES

It was also in mid-2001 that HealthTronics changed its name. After achieving its initial objectives of securing

FDA approval for its lithotripter and orthopedic shock wave systems, the company had changed its focus to providing noninvasive surgical services to patients. Subsequently, it adapted the name HealthTronics Surgical Services, Inc. By this time the company's operations included some 500 physician partners and 53 lithotripsy operations.

Midway through 2002 the Litho Management, Inc., subsidiary of HealthTronics sold its interest in U.S. Lithotripsy, L.P., for $6.8 million. That year net income totaled $8.54 million on net revenue of $87.19 million. Growth continued in 2003, by which time HealthTronics had 90 lithotripsy devices, along with 20 prostate treatment devices, in place throughout North America. In addition, it had 57 OssaTron shock wave devices in operation. For the year, net income totaled $5.26 million on net revenue of $88.41 million.

In early 2004 HealthTronics Surgical Services acquired HMT Holding AG, which controlled the manufacturer MT High Medical Technologies AG. HMT High Medical manufactured both the OssaTron and LithoTron devices, along with several others. In February the lithotripter manufacturer Medstone International, Inc., was sold in a deal worth $19 million. In November of that year, HealthTronics Surgical Services merged with Austin, Texas-based Prime Medical Services, Inc., in a $145 million stock deal. Following the merger, the surviving corporation was named HealthTronics, Inc.

ORTHOPEDICS BUSINESS SOLD

Another pivotal development that occurred in 2004 was the sale of the company's orthopedics business unit. By this time the company was led by President and CEO Brad Hummel. The company operated a subsidiary named AK Specialty Vehicles, which focused on mobile medical vehicles used to provide services such as MRI, CAT scan, PET scan, and lithotripsy, as well as vehicles used as mobile command and control centers, and for satellite newsgathering purposes. For the year HealthTronics saw its revenues increase 20 percent, reaching $193.1 million.

By early 2005 HealthTronics had established 105 lithotripsy partnerships in 47 states nationwide. These involved approximately 3,000 urologists. Early that year the company completed a $175 million refinancing, which would result in annual savings of about $3 million. In May HealthTronics introduced a new intraoperative urological imaging system called UroVantage. Two months later the company acquired a 33 percent stake in Mount Vernon, Washington-based Cascade Urological Services LLC and Cascade Laser Services LLC.

```
┌─────────────────────────────────────────┐
│                                         │
│            KEY DATES                    │
│                                         │
│              ─ ■ ─                       │
│                                         │
│  1999:  HealthTronics goes public.      │
│  2001:  The company changes its name    │
│         to Health-Tronics Surgical      │
│         Services, Inc.                  │
│  2004:  HealthTronics Surgical Services │
│         merges with Austin, Texas-      │
│         based Prime Medical Services,   │
│         Inc., and the surviving         │
│         organization is named           │
│         HealthTronics, Inc.             │
│  2006:  HealthTronics sells its AK      │
│         Specialty Vehicles business     │
│         to Wisconsin-based Oshkosh      │
│         Truck Corp. for $140 million.   │
│  2010:  Pennsylvania-based Endo         │
│         Pharmaceuticals Inc. agrees     │
│         to acquire HealthTronics for    │
│         $223 million.                   │
│                                         │
└─────────────────────────────────────────┘
```

HealthTronics sold its Orthopedic Electrocorporeal Shockwave Lithotripsy operations in a $10.4 million deal with SanuWave, Inc. According to CEO Brad Hummel, the deal would allow HealthTronics to focus its efforts on the company's urology business. The company rounded out the year on a high note when it was included in *Forbes* magazine's 200 Best Small Companies list.

SALE OF SPECIALTY VEHICLES DIVISION

HealthTronics began 2006 by retaining the investment banking firm Robert W. Baird & Co. to manage the sale of its AK Specialty Vehicles division. In February the company's new anatomical pathology laboratory opened its doors on the campus of the Medical College of Georgia. The following month, HealthTronics secured exclusive distribution rights for a new FDA-approved surgical laser device named Revolix, which was used to treat a medical condition called benign prostatic hyperplasia. In June HealthTronics finalized the sale of its AK Specialty Vehicles business to Wisconsin-based Oshkosh Truck Corp. in a $140 million deal.

A number of leadership changes also took place in 2006. The company began the year with Chief Financial Officer John Q. Barnidge serving as interim president and CEO. In March HealthTronics named R. Steven Hicks as chairman. Argil Wheelock, M.D., remained with the company as a board member and chief medical adviser. The following month Sam B. Humphries was named president and CEO. Midway through the year the company named James S. B. Whittenburg as president of its Urology Services division. Finally, Ross A. Goolsby was named chief financial officer in December, succeeding Barnidge.

In 2006 the company's revenue from continuing operations reached $142.9 million, down from $152.3 million in 2005. Net income totaled $8.7 million, down from $9.2 million the previous year. The company began 2007 by announcing plans to acquire a 35 percent stake in Willow Grove, Pennsylvania-based Keystone Mobile Partners LP, which provided lithotripsy services in the areas of eastern Pennsylvania and Greater Philadelphia. HealthTronics finalized its acquisition of Keystone Mobile Partners in June 2007.

DEATH OF CEO

In May 2007 President and CEO Sam Humphries took a medical leave of absence after suffering a severe heart attack. He was succeeded on an interim basis by Urology Services Division President James Whittenburg. In May the FDA approved the company's new LithoDiamond ULTRA lithotripter. The company also unveiled its TotalRad Radiation Therapy Solutions initiative, which provided urologists with new image-guided radiation therapy technology for use in the treatment and management of prostate cancer.

CEO Humphries passed away in August 2007 at the age of 65. In addition to his accomplishments with HealthTronics, Humphries had enjoyed a medical industry career that spanned more than 25 years. Following the death of Humphries, Whittenburg was officially named president and CEO.

HealthTronics began 2008 by agreeing to acquire the urological cryosurgery services provider Advanced Medical Partners, Inc. The company had ownership stakes in some 30 different entities and operations in 46 states. It had performed more than 7,000 procedures, and had relationships with some 500 physicians. The deal, which was completed in April, helped HealthTronics to further diversify its business operations.

Another acquisition followed in mid-2008. At that time HealthTronics acquired the anatomical pathology laboratory services provider UroPath LLC in a $7.5 million deal. The company, which had processed more than 400,000 specimens, served approximately 450 physicians and 50 urology practices in 17 states nationwide. Around the same time HealthTronics sold its office building and announced it would relocate to a new facility under construction in North Austin, Texas.

PURSUIT OF ENDOCARE

It was also in 2008 that HealthTronics made an unsolicited bid for the Irvine, California-based tumor technology firm Endocare, Inc. The company's initial offer was rejected in August. HealthTronics made a second attempt in September, offering to acquire the firm for $26.9 million. However, the offer was withdrawn that same month when no dialogue occurred between the two companies. One final development in 2008 was the resignation of Chief Financial Officer Ross Goolsby. Richard A. Rusk was appointed chief financial officer on an interim basis.

The company's plans to merge with Endocare resurfaced in mid-2009. After Endocare terminated an agreement to merge with Galil Medical Ltd., the companies moved forward with a deal that stood to bolster the cryosurgery business of HealthTronics. Galil Medical challenged the merger by filing a suit in Delaware court. In addition, Galil pursued the enforcement of its merger agreement with Endocare.

Nevertheless, HealthTronics completed its acquisition of Endocare in July, and the latter company became a wholly owned subsidiary of HealthTronics. In August Endocare announced that it would eliminate 98 of its approximately 120 employees. One final development in 2009 was the official appointment of Richard Rusk as chief financial officer.

PROPOSED ACQUISITION BY ENDO PHARMACEUTICALS

HealthTronics began 2010 by announcing that it would open a new 15,000-square-foot manufacturing facility in central Texas on March 1. Constructed as a result of the Endocare acquisition, the new plant resulted in the creation of 45 new jobs in the fields of customer service, manufacturing, and engineering. In all, the company's global workforce grew to include approximately 650 people.

A major development took place in May 2010 when the Pennsylvania-based specialty pharmaceutical company Endo Pharmaceuticals Inc. agreed to acquire HealthTronics for $223 million. The deal called for HealthTronics to become a wholly owned unit of Endo Pharmaceuticals. Shareholders quickly challenged the deal, resulting in investigations by several law firms to determine whether or not the company's board violated its fiduciary duty or state law by agreeing to the merger without pursuing and considering other potentially higher offers. One analyst indicated that the company's share price was worth $2 more than the offer of $4.85 per share made by Endo Pharmaceuticals.

The status of the proposed acquisition of Health-Tronics by Endo Pharmaceuticals remained unclear in June 2010. Regardless of the outcome, however, the company had achieved remarkable growth since its establishment during the mid-1990s. The company's prospects for continued success seemed strong in the years ahead.

Paul R. Greenland

PRINCIPAL SUBSIDIARIES

HealthTronics Service Center, LLC; Lithotripters, Inc.; Medstone International, Inc.; Prime Kidney Stone Treatment, Inc.; Prime Lithotripter Operations, Inc.; Prime Lithotripsy Services, Inc.; Prime Medical Operating, Inc.; Sun Medical Technologies, Inc.; HealthTronics Group, L.P.; Surgicenter Management, Inc.; HT Lithotripsy Management Company, LLC; HT Prostate Therapy Management Company, LLC; Litho Group, Inc.; Florida Lithology No. 2, Inc.; HT Prostate Services, LLC; West Coast Cambridge, Inc.; Integrated Lithotripsy of Georgia, Inc.; Midwest Cambridge Inc.; T2 Lithotripter Investment, Inc.; AmCare Health Services, Inc.; AmCare, Inc.; NGST, Inc.; Dallas Lithotripsy L.P.; Southern California Stone Center, LLC; Mobile Kidney Stone Centers, Ltd.; Advanced Urology Services, LLC; Prostate Therapy Associates; Cryopartners; HealthTronics Urology Services, LLC; Advanced Medical Partners in Radiation, LLC; Mid-Atlantic Mobile Lithotripsy, LLC; Gold Coast Urology Services, LLC; Blue Ridge Urology Services, LLC; Advanced Medical Partners, Inc.; Advanced Litho Associates, LLC; SEFL Cryo Associates, LLC; Southeast Cryotherapy, LP; Southern States Cryotherapy, LP; Tri-States Cryosurgical Partnership, LP; West Coast Cryotherapy, LP; Endocare, Inc.; Litho Management, Inc.; Metro Atlanta Cryo Associates, LLC; Midwest Urologic Laser Services, LLC; Muncie Laser Services, LP; Orange Acquisitions Ltd. (Israel); P1 Mobile Solutions, LLC; Prostate Laser Technologies, LLC; Surgical Services, LLC; U.S. Surgical Services, LLC; Urohealth, B.V. (Netherlands).

PRINCIPAL COMPETITORS

Boston Scientific Corporation; C. R. Bard, Inc.; Siemens AG.

FURTHER READING

"HealthTronics Agrees to Be Sold," *Austin American-Statesman*, May 6, 2010, p. B7.

"HealthTronics Named to *Forbes* List of the 200 Best Small Companies," *Business Wire*, October 17, 2005.

"HealthTronics Sells Building, to Lease One Being Built," *Austin American-Statesman*, June 26, 2008, p. B8.

"HealthTronics Sells Its Orthopedic ESWL Business for $10.4 Million," *Business Wire*, August 2, 2005.

"HealthTronics to Change Its Name to HealthTronics Surgical Services, Inc.," *Business Wire*, May 22, 2001.

Rockwell, Lilly, "HealthTronics CEO Was Longtime Leader in Medical Devices Industry," *Austin American-Statesman*, August 10, 2007.

Romell, Rick, "Oshkosh Truck Makes Deal: It Will Buy Maker of Specialty Vehicles for Medicine, Media," *Milwaukee Journal Sentinel*, June 24, 2006.

Hon Hai Precision
Industry Company, Ltd.

2 Zihyou Street
Tucheng City, Taipei 236
Taiwan
Telephone: (886 2) 2268 3466
Fax: (886 2) 2268 6204
Web site: http://www.foxconn.com

Public Company
Incorporated: 1974 as Hon Hai Plastics Corporation
Employees: 5,200
Sales: TWD 1.42 trillion ($44.65 billion) (2009)
Stock Exchanges: Taiwan
Ticker Symbol: 2317
NAICS: 334110 Computer and Peripheral Equipment Manufacturing; 334119 Other Computer Peripheral Equipment Manufacturing

■ ■ ■

Hon Hai Precision Industry Company, Ltd., operates as the largest contract manufacturer in the world. The company manufactures a wide variety of electronics products including computers, consumer electronics, connectors, flat-panel displays, gaming devices, motherboards, and televisions. Its customers include Apple Inc., Dell Inc., Hewlett-Packard Co., Microsoft Corp., and Nokia Corp. Operating internationally under the Foxconn name, Hon Hai has grown dramatically through a combination capital investment, an early entry into the Chinese market, new product development, and through key acquisitions. Listed on the Taiwan stock exchange, Hon Hai has long distinguished itself by its discretion. Despite its desire to remain out of the public spotlight, the company's labor practices came under fire in 2010 after a series of suicides took place at its facilities in China. The company remains led by founder and Chairman Terry Guo.

FROM PLASTICS TO CONNECTORS: 1980–89

Kuo Tai-ming (also known by the Westernized name Terry Guo) had initially trained as a sailor, but decided instead to enter manufacturing in the early 1970s. In 1974, Kuo and brother Kuo Tai-chiang founded a small plastics company in Taipei's Tucheng industrial zone. The company, originally called Hon Hai Plastics Corporation, started out making plastic parts for black-and-white televisions. The company quickly added its own mold-making equipment, and in 1975 changed its name, to Hon Hai Industrial Corporation. Sales that year were just TWD $16 million (less than $500,000 at 2003 exchange rates).

Kuo Tai-ming was committed to leading his company into Taiwan's major leagues. Kuo would later claim not to have taken more than three days off at a time over the next nearly 30 years, working 15 hours per day, six days per week. As the famously reclusive Kuo told *Business Week* in a rare interview: "You need real discipline. A leader shouldn't sleep more than his people; you should be the first one in, the last one out."

By the late 1970s, Kuo had begun to develop an interest in the new market of the computer and electronics industries. Although the basis of these industries remained in the United States and Europe for

COMPANY PERSPECTIVES

Since 1974, Foxconn had always been guided by three Foxconnian visions: Through the most efficient "Total Cost Advantages" to make comfort of electronic products usage an attainable reality for all mankind; Through the proprietary one-stop shopping vertical integrated eCMMS model to revolutionize the conventional inefficient electronics outsourcing model; Through the devotion to greater social harmony and higher ethical standards to achieve a win-win model for all stakeholders including shareholders, employees, community and management.

the time being, manufacturers had begun to look to the Far East for the production of certain components. This was a trend that ultimately led to the rise of a number of Asian countries, especially Taiwan, as manufacturing centers for the computer industry.

Kuo quickly recognized the potential for producing computer components and led the company into developing its own range of products. At first, Kuo targeted the connectors market, and by 1981 Hon Hai, which adopted the name Foxconn for its international sales, had converted itself to a specialist subcontractor of connectors for the computer industry. Where other manufacturers focused on producing more high-profile components, Hon Hai concentrated its efforts on developing and producing the parts to connect the components together. In 1982, the company added a new product line, electric wire assembly. This was not the most exciting segment of the computer sector, yet it was perhaps the most universal, meeting the needs of the variety of computer formats and systems in existence at the time. Hon Hai's commitment to such low-profile segments enabled the company to grow strongly through the 1980s.

Kuo backed up his capacity to adapt to new markets with a willingness to invest in infrastructure. In 1983, for example, the company opened a new factory, also in Tucheng. The new facility enabled the company to step up both production and quality levels. Hon Hai began targeting the world's emerging computer industry giants as customers. By the end of the decade, the company had achieved a prominent place in the order books of many of the world's largest computer companies. The company's growth enabled it to adopt a policy of working closely with and exclusively for top tier companies. Unlike its competitors, however, Hon

Hai made no effort to enter the branded market, contenting itself with an original equipment manufacturer role.

CHINESE PRODUCTION BEGINS: 1988

Like many of the other rising Taiwanese computer manufacturers, Hon Hai at first gained an edge through its ability to churn out products at low prices compared to its Western competitors. Kuo recognized early on, however, that the strong growth in Taiwan's economy and the resulting rise in wages would cut into the company's ability to compete on price. In response, Kuo led Hon Hai to the Chinese mainland, becoming the first Taiwanese manufacturer to launch production on the continent in 1988.

Hon Hai went public in 1991, listing on the Taiwan stock exchange. Despite the public offering, the company, and Kuo, maintained their publicity-shy, almost secretive nature. While market observers complained about the group's lack of financial transparency, particularly for leaving unclear the source of the group's profits, shareholders had little to complain about. Within 10 years the group had become Taiwan's leading private-sector computer company with a market capitalization worth $8 billion. Kuo's more than 25 percent stake in the company placed him among the world's 500 richest people.

EXPANSION AND NEW PRODUCT DEVELOPMENT: 1993–2000

The public offering enabled Hon Hai to begin a new era of expansion, with a focus particularly on the international manufacturing scene. The company moved to expand its fledgling mainland China operation with the construction of two new factories, in Shenzhen and Kunshan. Both factories launched production in 1993.

In 1994, Hon Hai added research and development sites in the United States and Japan. The move brought the company not only closer to these two primary computer markets, it also brought it closer to its main customers. Hon Hai, which traded as Foxconn overseas, showed itself a ready partner for the industry's major players, especially in its willingness to adapt to its customers' requirements by developing new products and entire product lines. For this effort, Hon Hai built up a strong team of more than 3,000 engineers and 100 Ph.D. holders.

Hon Hai's team of developers became one of the most dynamic in the Taiwanese high-tech sector, registering nearly 300 new patents in 1995 alone. By the

KEY DATES

■

1974: Kuo Tai-ming and his brother set up Hon Hai Plastics Corporation in Tucheng, Taiwan, to produce plastic components for black-and-white televisions.

1975: Company changes name to Hon Hai Industrial Corporation and begins development and production of molded parts.

1988: Company launches first manufacturing operations in mainland China.

1991: Hon Hai goes public on Taiwan stock exchange.

1996: Hon Hai begins production of PC cases, becoming world leader within one year.

2000: Hon Hai opens factory in Czech Republic to produce iMac computers for Apple; takes over Intel's motherboard production facility in Puerto Rico.

2001: Hon Hai enters production of mobile telephone components.

2002: Hon Hai begins construction of new $1 billion facility in mainland China.

2003: Construction of new $1 billion LCD factory in Taiwan is undertaken; Motorola cell phone factory in Mexico is acquired.

2009: Hon Hai posts the first drop in annual revenues in company history.

beginning of the 21st century, the company had received more than 2,000 patents, many of which were developed in response to specific customer requests. Following its customers led the company into a variety of new markets, such as the launch of personal computer (PC) cases and enclosures production in 1996. By investing massively, the company entered its new area with a bang. Within a year, Hon Hai counted among the world's largest PC case and enclosure groups, building "barebones" units for IBM, Dell, Apple, and Compaq, among others. Hon Hai had also by then become the world's leading maker of connectors for the computer industry.

As part of its new business, Hon Hai began preparing to move closer to its customers. In 1998, the company opened production facilities in England and Scotland. The following year, Hon Hai added manufacturing capacity in the United States, including an SMT production site in Houston, and in Ireland, where the group built a facility in direct support of the company's contract to supply enclosures for Dell's European PC operation. The group also joined in on the fast-rising notebook computer sector, launching a new subsidiary, Omni Switch Inc., in partnership with Quanta Computer Inc. and Inventec Corp. By the end of that year, the group's sales had topped TWD 52 billion ($1.5 billion).

Hon Hai's long-standing relationship with Apple brought it to the European continent in 2000, when the group constructed a factory in the Czech Republic in order to supply the bare-bones PCs for Apple's newest generation of iMac computers. Meanwhile, the company continued to expand its product range, adding motherboards for Intel. This move included Hon Hai's takeover of Intel's manufacturing site in Puerto Rico. The company signed on another important client that year as well, when it agreed to produce components for Sony Corporation's PlayStation 2 console.

DIVERSIFIED TECHNOLOGY GROUP IN THE NEW CENTURY

By the end of 2001, Hon Hai had claimed the lead as the world's number one motherboard manufacturer. The company's revenues reflected the group's growth, soaring past $4.5 billion and winning the group the position as Taiwan's leading private-sector computer component manufacturer. By then, however, Hon Hai had already begun to take steps to ensure its growth streak would continue into the new century. As computer sales slowed at the beginning of decade, Hon Hai sought new areas for expansion, developing a "3C" strategy of developing computer, communications, and consumer electronics components.

The company launched the communications branch of its new strategy in 2001 by entering the mobile telephone market. By the beginning of 2002, the company had succeeded in winning a contract to supply components to cell phone leader Nokia. In that year, Hon Hai found its first target for the consumer electronics sector, launching a new $1 billion facility in Taiwan to produce liquid-crystal-display (LCD) screens in August 2002. At the same time, Hon Hai announced construction of an industrial complex in China as well.

As group sales rocketed past TWD 245 billion ($7.3 billion) in 2002, Hon Hai showed no signs of slowing down. In that year, the company received new orders from both Gateway and Apple that were expected to boost it to the top of the world's computer component suppliers. Hon Hai's mobile telephone operation also picked up steam, as the company announced its acquisition of Finland's Eimo Oy in September 2003. One month later, Hon Hai followed up that acquisition with an agreement to acquire Motorola's Mexico-based cellular phone manufacturing plant for $18 million. The company also announced its plans to develop component manufacturing operations for the increasingly computer-laden automobile market. Former sailing student Kuo Tai-ming continued to lead his multinational components empire with a steady hand.

A GLOBAL LEADER: 2004 AND BEYOND

By 2004, Hon Hai stood as the world's largest manufacturing services provider for computer, communications, and consumer electronics components. Part of its growth stemmed from acquisitions. During 2005 it purchased Chi Mei Communication Systems and Antec Electronics. It acquired digital camera manufacturer Premier Image Technology Corp. in 2006. Hon Hai also expanded quickly by developing new products and entering new markets including LCD manufacturing. Innolux Display Corp. was founded by Kuo in 2003 to manufacture LCDs. Innolux acquired Chi Mei Optoelectronics in early 2010 to create Chi Mei Innolux Corporation, one of the largest LCD manufacturers in the world.

From 1996 through 2006, Hon Hai's revenues had grown by nearly 50 percent per year. Revenues for 2006 reached $40.6 billion. Known for his desire to remain out of the public eye, founder Kuo, who by that time was one of the richest men in Asia, admitted to the *Wall Street Journal* in 2007, "We are so big we cannot hide anymore." The company came under fire in 2006 when British newspapers began reporting Hon Hai employees worked long hours and received low wages while making Apple Inc.'s popular iPod product. Apple launched an investigation but found few violations. Hon Hai began manufacturing the iPhone during 2007. Along with Apple's popular products, Hon Hai was manufacturing Sony's PlayStation 3 gaming console, the Nintendo Wii, and the Microsoft Xbox 360 console by 2009.

The company found itself in the spotlight once again in 2010 when its labor practices came under fire after a series of suicides at its Shenzhen factories in China. By May of that year, ten employees had committed suicide and two additional workers had attempted to take their own lives. At the time, workers were paid approximately $32 for a 40-hour workweek, which was reported to be above the minimum wage in the region. Critics however, claimed employees were forced to work long hours, meet strict production quotas, and that overall conditions were harsh. In response to the public outcry, Hon Hai raised wages at its facilities in Shenzhen.

Meanwhile, Hon Hai had been battling a global economic downturn that began to affect its business. For the first time in its history, the company posted a drop in annual sales during 2009. Revenues were $44.65 billion for the year, down nearly 4 percent from 2008 figures. Demand for mobile handsets and desktop computers was falling, which contributed to the drop in sales.

Nevertheless, Hon Hai was optimistic growth would return in 2010. The company had more than 25,000 patents under its belt and was focused on developing new applications in nanotechnology, heat transfer, and wireless connectivity. The company was the largest exporter in China, the second-largest exporter in Czech Republic, and ranked 294 on the *Fortune* Global 500 listing. While the staggering growth of the past decade would be difficult to replicate, Hon Hai would no doubt remain a leader in the electronics world for years to come.

M. L. Cohen
Updated, Christina M. Stansell

PRINCIPAL SUBSIDIARIES

Foxconn International, Inc.; Fox Semicon Integrated Tech Inc.; Foxteq Engineering; Chi Mei InnoLux Corporation; Omni Switch Inc.

PRINCIPAL COMPETITORS

ASUSTeK Computer, Inc.; Flextronics International Ltd.; Jabil Circuit, Inc.

FURTHER READING

Barboza, David, "Deaths Shake a Titan in China," *New York Times*, May 27, 2010.

Chin, Spencer, "Hon Hai Follows the Leaders," *EBN*, December 15, 2002, p. 16.

Dean, Jason, "The Forbidden City of Terry Guo," *Wall Street Journal*, August 11, 2007.

Flannery, Russell, "Out of the Limelight," *Forbes*, April 14, 2003, p. 44.

Hille, Kathrin, "Further Growth for Hon Hai Precision," *Financial Times*, September 1, 2003, p. 16.

"Hon Hai Encounters First-Time Sales Decline in 2009," *Taiwan Economic News*, January 14, 2010.

"Hon Hai Lands NT$16 Bil Orders," *China Post*, September 7, 2003.

"Hon Hai Precision Remains Largest Private Maker in Taiwan in 2002," *Taiwan Economic News*, April 28, 2003.

"Hon Hai to Supply Xbox 360 Console," *China Knowledge Press*, October 15, 2009.

"The King of Outsourcing," *Business Week*, July 8, 2002, p. 62.

Kok, Charmian, and Perris Lee Choon Siong, "New LCD Giant Created," *Wall Street Journal*, November 16, 2009.

Sanders, Sol, "In China, a Model under Threat," *Washington Times*, June 14, 2010.

Wang, Lisa, "Hon Hai to Enter LCD-TV Business," *Taipei Times*, June 26, 2006.

———, "Premier Deal Focuses Eye on Hon Hai," *Taipei Times*, June 26, 2006.

———, "Taiwan's Technology Leader Kuo Tai-ming," *Taiwan News*, June 2, 2001.

Houchens Industries, Inc.

700 Church Street
Bowling Green, Kentucky 42102
U.S.A.
Telephone: (270) 843-3252
Fax: (270) 780-2877
Web site: http://www.houchensindustries.com

Private Company
Founded: 1917
Employees: 16,826
Sales: $2.5 billion (2010 est.)
NAICS: 445110 Supermarkets and Other Grocery
    (Except Convenience) Stores; 236115 New Single-
    Family Housing Construction (Except Operative
    Builders); 312221 Cigarette Manufacturing;
    423930 Recyclable Material Merchant Wholesalers;
    453991 Tobacco Stores; 524210 Insurance Agencies
    and Brokerages; 531120 Lessors of Nonresidential
    Buildings (Except Miniwarehouses)

■ ■ ■

Headquartered in Bowling Green, Kentucky, Houchens Industries, Inc., has roots in the grocery business. However, the company's operations are very diverse. In addition to grocery and convenience stores, the company's operations include insurance, construction, crushed stone aggregates and asphalt paving, fence materials manufacturing and distribution, optical store franchising, juice concentrate manufacturing and distribution, manufacturing, property management, quick-service restaurants, recycling, software and Web

site development, stock brokerage and financial services, and tanning supply distribution. In 2010 the employee-owned company's workforce included approximately 16,000 people.

FORMATION

One of ten children, company founder Ervin G. Houchens grew up in a three-room log cabin. In 1917, at the age of 19, he opened his first grocery store in rural Barren County, Kentucky, where he grew up. It was a modest enterprise, housed in a 12-foot-by-20-foot shed. Less than three years later he was able to relocate his business to Cross Roads, Kentucky, growing it into a general merchandise store.

The rise of the Houchens grocery chain began in 1931 when the then seasoned businessman opened three stores in Glasgow, Kentucky. Despite operating during the lean years of the Great Depression, Houchens was able to significantly expand his operations during the 1930s, branching out to other Kentucky communities. After opening stores in Munfordville and Scottsville, he entered Horse Cave, Cave City, Elizabethtown, and Vine Grove in 1937, followed by Bowling Green and Franklin in 1939.

Until the early decades of the 20th century, grocery stores were full-service operations, primarily offering dry goods, with clerks filling customers' orders one by one. Even early chains such as the A&P stores followed this model. In 1916 Clarence Saunders introduced self-service grocery stores when he opened his first Piggly Wiggly in Memphis, Tennessee. The concept proved popular, and by the 1930s grocery chains and

COMPANY PERSPECTIVES

What's important to us? Our Values. Listening and reacting to customers. Fair and honest dealings with all. Operating profitably to enhance our future. Innovation and action without a fear of failure. Open communication with all employee-owners.

independents alike began switching over to self-service, which led to the rise of modern supermarkets offering a wide range of products.

The first Houchens store to follow the new model was one of the Bowling Green outlets in 1939. This store was progressive in other ways as well. It was the first grocery store in the city to host a live radio broadcast, and it also offered frozen food lockers for rent, a concept that proved successful until the introduction of affordable home freezers.

EARLY GROWTH

Houchens moved into six new Kentucky communities after World War II: Russellville, Auburn, Fountain Run, Gamaliel, Tompkinsville, and Hodgenville. Following a fire in November 1945 that destroyed the company's Glasgow warehouse and a nearby store, the company relocated its headquarters to Bowling Green. There it took over the wholesale grocery warehouse business of J.D. Reynolds Company, and Houchens reorganized the business as Bowling Green Wholesale, Inc. He later added a slaughterhouse and meat-processing plant to his growing enterprises. To give back to the community, Houchens also established the Houchens Foundation, a nonprofit corporation that since 1945 contributed millions of dollars to civic and religious organizations.

In the 1950s Houchens further expanded his operations in Kentucky, and in 1952 ventured beyond the state for the first time when he opened a store in Lafayette, Tennessee. Altogether, the company added stores in eight new communities during the decade and another seven in the 10 years that followed.

In 1960 the company was active on a number of fronts. It became involved in investing in real estate used for strip shopping centers. The company also attempted to diversify by moving into the variety store industry. It created a number of Houchens Family Centers and Ben Franklin Family Variety Stores, but this venture never proved entirely successful, and 20 years later the company began to close down these operations.

Of more long-term importance was the debut in 1960 of the company's first full-service supermarket, located in Bowling Green. All of the company's stores would soon adopt the larger format. Moreover, in 1960 Houchens created an employee profit sharing plan, which began the process of employees taking a vested interest in the business.

NAME CHANGE: 1972

In 1972 the growing company changed its name to Houchens Industries, Inc. The 1970s brought even greater growth for the company and represented a high-water mark in terms of profitability for Houchens supermarkets. Eight new communities were entered during the decade, five in Kentucky and three in Tennessee. At its peak, Houchens had 55 supermarkets in operation.

In the following decade, the company adjusted the mix and engaged in remodeling efforts to meet the challenge of a changing environment in the grocery business. In addition to building larger new stores, some older units were sold in the early 1980s, while others were remodeled and expanded. Of significance during this period was the Schnucks Company's introduction of a super warehouse-style store to the region, prompting a price war with major rival Kroger and adversely affecting about half of the Houchens stores as well. The war led to the practice of honoring manufacturers' coupons at twice their stated value.

Then over 80 years old and nearing retirement, Ervin Houchens looked to secure the future of the company and its employees. In 1981 he signed a letter of intent to sell Houchens Industries to the Memphis food distribution company of Malone & Hyde Inc. for $58 million. In addition to 10 food distribution centers serving a wide swath of the Southeast, Malone & Hyde also owned 45 supermarkets and 165 drugstores, as well as a number of sporting goods and auto parts stores. In the end, however, both parties backed away from the deal.

COMPANY SOLD TO RED FOOD

Houchens retired in September 1983 at the age of 85, remaining as chairman emeritus but devoting the bulk of his time to the activities of his foundation. Before turning over control of the business, he completed the sale of Houchens Industries to Red Food of Chattanooga, Tennessee. His nephew, Ruel Houchens, became president of the subsidiary, having worked for the company since 1942 when he was employed at age 13 by a Houchens store in Glasgow. Under new

KEY DATES

1917: Ervin G. Houchens opens his first grocery store.
1931: The grocery chain begins with the opening of three stores in Glasgow, Kentucky.
1945: Bowling Green Wholesale, Inc., is formed as a parent corporation.
1960: The first Houchens supermarket opens.
1972: The company's name is changed to Houchens Industries.
1983: Founder Ervin Houchens retires at age 85.
1988: The business becomes employee owned.
1990: Houchens opens its first Save-A-Lot store.
1992: Ervin Houchens dies.
2004: Sales surpass $2 billion.

corporate ownership and the leadership of Ruel Houchens, the company continued to remodel and expand its stores in the mid-1980s. Volume grew so high for the chain that the company's warehouse was no longer able to adequately supply its stores and an outside supplier had to be contracted.

After five years of operating under Red Food and its French parent company, food wholesaler-retailer Promodes, the employees of Houchens Industries reached a deal to buy the company. The proceeds would allow Promodes to invest in Red Food and other operations in Chicago. However, according to *Supermarket News*, the corporate parent saw little prospect for growing Houchens, noting that "an industry observer in the region said, 'The speculation is that Houchens turned out to be impervious to being converted to Red Food's methods of operation'"

There were few changes in the way Houchens operated, and its many stores continued to project a family-owned business atmosphere. Ruel Houchens lined up investors to finance the employee buyout and subsequently became the company's CEO and chairman when the transaction was completed in November 1988. In October 1996 the company made the final payment on the bank note that made an employee buyout possible.

Independent once more, Houchens Industries again began to grow its business. In 1989, after it acquired the Dave and Steve Super-Key stores in the Bowling Green area, the total number of stores in the chain returned to 47. As the economy slowed in the early 1990s Houchens turned to a discount, limited-selection format

to fuel further expansion. In January 1990 the company opened its first Save-A-Lot store in Hardinsburg, Kentucky.

Houchens quickly rolled out other stores, and picked up 30 Save-A-Lot stores in a 1994 acquisition of outlets located in Alabama and Kentucky. Total outlets numbered 86 by the middle of the decade and nearly 140 by 2000, spread across 11 states. In the early 1990s Save-A-Lot became Mor-For-Less, but less than a year later it returned to its original name.

FOUNDER DIES: 1992

Ervin Houchens died on August 17, 1992. The top leadership position then passed out of the hands of the Houchens family in February 1993 when Jimmie Gipson, who had been with the company since 1965, was elected to the posts of president and chief executive officer. A few months later he succeeded Ruel Houchens as chairman of the board. During this transition period, the board toyed with the idea of taking the company public, going so far as to draw up a prospectus, but in the end elected to shelve the idea.

Under new management, Houchens then made a concerted effort to expand its private-label line, an industry growth area in which the company lagged behind its competition. Immediate plans were launched to double the number of items it offered to 300, with a further goal of increasing to 800 products in five years. Moreover, Houchens initiated plans to offer 300 to 400 health and beauty care products under the Home Best label.

In the late 1990s Houchens faced a challenge from well-financed grocery chains that began to open megastores in excess of 200,000 square feet in size. In order to compete, Houchens began to pursue a counterstrategy of opening smaller Save-A-Lot stores, in the 10,000-square-foot range, many of which were located in the shadow of the retail giants. Other Houchens stores, because of their smaller size, were able to open inside neighborhoods rather than in the fringe areas that megastores targeted because of real estate limitations. The company found that no matter where their units were located, they were able to find a niche with customers who felt that the megastores were simply too big and preferred shopping at a smaller supermarket for certain everyday products.

As a result, Houchens saved money on a number of levels. Fewer employees were needed to run the stores, and real estate costs were lower because the company was often able to take advantage of abandoned retail centers. Houchens also began to diversify beyond its core holdings of Houchens Markets and Save-A-Lot outlets. The Tobacco Shoppe discount cigarette venture, operating out of Save-A-Lot stores, was launched in 1997. In May 1998 Houchens acquired the 42-unit convenience store chain Jr. Food Stores, Inc.

Less than a year later Houchens acquired Southern Recycling, Inc., a Bowling Green company that had a long history with Houchens. Its founder, David Bradford, originally operated a parking lot sweeping business, and one of his major customers was Houchens. Bradford realized he could make extra money from the discarded corrugated boxes he found in the parking lots by baling them and selling them to a local paper mill. In 1981 he started Southern Recycling, and over the years expanded his operation to the recycling of iron products and other metals, as well as a curbside recycling operation.

ENTERING THE 21ST CENTURY

In 2000 Houchens became involved in the construction industry when it acquired Stewart and Richey Construction Company, a 200-employee, 14-division, full-service business operating in Kentucky and Tennessee. Like Southern Recycling, it too became a wholly owned subsidiary of Houchens, as did Center of Insurance, acquired in September 2000. Center of Insurance, in operation since 1948, was a full-service insurer, offering business, personal, life, and health insurance, as well as surety bonds to customers in central Kentucky and Tennessee. Furthermore, in 2000 Houchens remained active in growing its main business, acquiring two Foodland Stores in Kentucky, as well as opening two new Save-A-Lot stores in New York and Virginia and acquiring nine other Save-A-Lot stores in Alabama and Georgia.

Houchens continued to add to its supermarket chains in 2001 when it opened a new Save-A-Lot store in Niagara Falls, New York, and acquired seven existing operations in West Virginia and Georgia. The company also took over a Piggly Wiggly Store in Tompkinsville, Kentucky, and subsequently converted it to the IGA brand. Several months later the company's IGA operation expanded to four other Kentucky communities, and additional IGA stores were purchased in 2002. In the meantime, the company acquired another 35 Save-A-Lot stores, adding two new states, Texas and Illinois, to its area of operation.

The company's efforts at diversification also took a major step forward with the August 2001 acquisition of Commonwealth Brands, the fifth-largest American cigarette manufacturer in terms of sales volume. It produced cigarettes under such brand names as USA Gold, Montclair, Malibu, Natural Blend, Riviera, and

Sonoma. For Houchens, Commonwealth Brands served as an ideal complement to its Tobacco Shoppe operations. A year later, in August 2002, Houchens entered into a partnership agreement with Remington Capital LLC, a boutique investment banking firm. The two parties agreed to jointly acquire manufacturing businesses that would then be managed by the principals of Remington Capital.

FURTHER DIVERSIFICATION AND EXPANSION

In April 2004 Houchens announced plans to diversify its operations by acquiring Sikeston, Missouri-based Food Giant Supermarkets. The deal resulted in the addition of 90 supermarkets in eight states. Houchens Industries saw its annual sales surpass the $2 billion mark in 2004.

During the middle of the decade Houchens experimented with new store formats. In Warren County, Kentucky, the company revealed that it was about to begin testing a new rural store format called Crossroads, which spanned 10,000 square feet. Additionally, the company began converting several stores to its IGA and IGA Express models.

In early 2005 a $10 million partnership was established with Chicago-based Metal Management Inc. Via a joint venture arrangement, plans were made to construct a large, 6,000-horsepower scrap metal processing operation in Nashville, Tennessee, as well as a feeder yard in Bowling Green, Kentucky. Houchens contributed 26 acres of land for the facility in Nashville, which was located along the Cumberland River.

By 2005 Houchens operated more than 320 stores in 13 states. In addition, the company ranked as the largest Save-A-Lot licensee nationwide, with some 200 stores in 11 states. Growth was furthered that year by the acquisition of eight Arkansas-based Mad Butcher stores.

FOCUS ON IGA BRAND

Houchens next announced plans to put more of an emphasis on its IGA-branded stores. In addition to ramping up the introduction of its Crossroads IGA format, the company moved to convert Houchens stores to Hometown IGA locations throughout Kentucky and Tennessee. Work also began on the conversion of 40 Jr. Foods convenience stores in Tennessee and Kentucky to the IGA Express format. In 2006 the company saw its sales reach approximately $2.5 million, some 60 percent of which was attributed to food and convenience store sales.

In late 2006 Houchens remained under the leadership of Jimmie Gipson, who was then 65 years of age. Although he had no plans to retire, a succession plan called for Spencer Coates to assume leadership of the company. Coates came from the company's cigarette operation, which then generated some 20 percent of annual sales. By 2007 he had become company president, with Gipson continuing as chairman and CEO.

In early 2007 Houchens sold its CBHC/Commonwealth Brands cigarette operation to London-based Imperial Tobacco Group plc in a deal worth $1.9 billion. Moving forward, the company planned to use proceeds from the sale for acquisition and expansion purposes. In November Houchens struck a deal with Pittsburgh-based PNC Financial Services for the acquisition of J.J.B. Hilliard, W.L. Lyons, Inc. The Louisville, Kentucky-based financial brokerage firm had 76 locations throughout West Virginia, Tennessee, South Carolina, Ohio, North Carolina, Mississippi, Michigan, Kentucky, Indiana, Illinois, Georgia, and Arkansas.

More acquisitions occurred in mid-2008. At that time Houchens agreed to acquire Jasper, Indiana-based Buehler Foods, which had annual sales of approximately $281.8 million. The deal added 22 grocery stores to the company's lineup, including 1 Kentucky store, 5 Illinois locations, and 16 sites in Indiana. Houchens indicated it would continue operating the stores under the Buehler name.

Plans changed in late 2009, however, when Houchens decided to change the name of its Buehler Foods stores in Kentucky, Indiana, and Illinois to the Everyday IGA brand. A similar name change was planned for Houchens Markets stores in Kentucky, and White's Fresh Foods stores in Virginia and Tennessee. In all, plans were made to change approximately 43 stores to the IGA name over the course of three years. By this time Houchens had changed 45 of its stores to the Everyday IGA brand.

Houchens began the next decade with sales of more than $2.5 billion. The company operated roughly 230 Save-A-Lot stores in 15 states and 85 convenience stores. In addition to its strong lineup of IGA-branded sites, Houchens also owned some 90 conventional stores in eight states operating under the Mad Butcher, Food Giant, and Piggly Wiggly names. Additionally, its IGA Crossroads rural concept continued to be well received.

With its success in the grocery trade, and diversification into other industries, Houchens appeared to have excellent prospects for continued success during the second decade of the 21st century.

Ed Dinger
Updated, Paul R. Greenland

PRINCIPAL SUBSIDIARIES

Blake, Hart, Taylor & Wiseman Insurance Agency, Inc.; American Sun Systems; Cohen Fashion Optical; Buehler's Buy Low; Center of Insurance; TS Trucking LLC; Van Meter Insurance Group; White's Fresh Foods; Tampico Beverages, Inc.; Stewart-Richey Construction, Inc.; Stephen's Pipe & Steel LLC; Southern Recycling Inc.; Browning Oil Company; Scotty's Contracting & Stone; Retail Electronics; Pan-Osten Co.; Sims Metal Management Limited; Insurance Specialists; Hitcents Inc.; J.J.B. Hilliard, W.L. Lyons, LLC; Food Giant Supermarkets; Four Seasons Sales & Service, Inc.

PRINCIPAL COMPETITORS

The Kroger Co.; Wal-Mart Stores, Inc.; Winn-Dixie Stores, Inc.

FURTHER READING

Dowdell, Stephen, "Red Food to Sell Houchens to Employees," *Supermarket News*, August 1, 1988, p. 1.

Hamstra, Mark, "Houchens Set to Acquire Food Giant," *Supermarket News*, April 26, 2004, p. 8.

"Houchens Industries Buys Financial Brokerage," *Progressive Grocer*, November 19, 2007.

"Houchens Sells Cigarette Unit to Imperial Tobacco," *Progressive Grocer*, February 12, 2007.

McCann, Joseph, "MMI Makes Inroads into Southeast Market via Houchens Joint Venture," *American Metal Market*, February 1, 2005.

Zwiebach, Elliott, "Houchens Converts More Stores to IGA," *Supermarket News*, October 19, 2009.

——, "Houchens to Acquire Buehler Foods," *Supermarket News*, May 5, 2008.

——, "IGA Okay for Houchens; Diversified Retailer Plans to Expand Presence of IGA Banner," *Supermarket News*, September 25, 2006, p. 23.

Hunter Roberts
Construction Group LLC

2 World Financial Center
New York, New York 10281-2602
U.S.A.
Telephone: (212) 321-6800
Fax: (212) 321-6990
Web site: http://www.hunterrobertscg.com

Private Company
Founded: 2004
Employees: 264
Sales: $949.7 million (2008 est.)
NAICS: 236220 Commercial and Institutional Building
Construction; 541420 Interior Design Services

■ ■ ■

Hunter Roberts Construction Group LLC, a 21st-century creation, has grown to become one of the largest companies in its field in the New York City metropolitan area. It also has offices in other cities in the northeastern United States. Hunter Roberts is engaged in construction and project management, general contracting, and consulting. Based in Lower Manhattan's World Financial Center, the company belongs to the management team for the World Trade Center complex as owner representative for the Port Authority of New York and New Jersey.

THE FOUNDING OF HUNTER
ROBERTS

Hunter Roberts was founded in 2004 by Robert Fee, who had been chief executive officer of Turner

Construction Company before retiring in 2003. Fee recruited a dozen executives from Turner Construction, one of the giants in the construction field and the second-largest such company in the New York City metropolitan area in terms of annual revenue. Among the executives Fee recruited were James C. McKenna, who became president (and subsequently chief executive officer), and John Fumosa, executive vice president. McKenna had been head of Turner's New York City unit, and Fumosa had been in charge of Turner's New Jersey office.

Anticipating a building boom in the metropolitan area not seen since the destruction of the Twin Towers in 2001, Fee received the initial $50 million for Hunter Roberts as an investment from MidFirst Bank, based in Oklahoma City. Hunter Roberts had about 100 employees by the end of 2005.

In its first three years the company opened offices in Philadelphia; Charlotte, North Carolina; and Bedminster, New Jersey. It also opened a Boston office in 2006 but found the New England market hard to penetrate and closed this office in 2008. Hunter Roberts opened a new regional office in Stamford, Connecticut, in 2009. The Bedminster office was ultimately moved to Newark.

SIGNIFICANT EARLY
UNDERTAKINGS

Hunter Roberts was cited in the July 2008 issue of *New York Construction* as Contractor of the Year for 2007–08. Interviewed for the cover story in that issue, Fee pointed to two projects as advancing the company in its

COMPANY PERSPECTIVES

Mission. For Hunter Roberts, it is about our understanding of the expectations of our clients, partners and the communities we work in. From pre-construction to completion, we bring financial resources, depth of expertise, accountability and recognized leadership. The result is a common understanding which enables success and the ability to assemble the right team to build enduring relationships.

initial years. One was a 24-story residential tower at 188 Ludlow Street on Manhattan's Lower East Side, which had to be built over a subway line. "That was like our first really big deal," Fee told the magazine. "Definitely the most complicated. We took it through preconstruction, we gave them a completion guarantee, which put us at a risk that a contractor normally does not take." He also cited the Village in downtown Newark, a University Center Student Housing project being developed privately for multiple colleges. Completed in 2007, it consisted of two buildings plus a parking garage.

In the article Fee also mentioned 77 Hudson in Jersey City. One of the largest mixed-use developments in New Jersey, this project, also called Hudson Greene, consisted of two 50-story residential towers on the Hudson River waterfront, a 10-story garage, and a ground-floor area for high-end retail space. The concrete cast-in-place structure was supported by massive beams and pile caps at grade and thousands of deep piles. Since a different developer owned each tower, Hunter Roberts needed meticulous communication strategies in order to keep all parties up to date with information and to fulfill the goals of two separate clients. Fee told *New York Construction* that the $390 million job "was a leap of faith on both of our parts both with the ownership and the contractor to do a job of that size."

Fumosa, who had been put in charge of the company's Pennsylvania division, pointed to a "watershed" job in Philadelphia, saying, "There were three large projects at Temple [University] and there were four contractors chasing them, and we ended up getting the Tyler School of Art, a $55 million job, and we were in business when we got that for maybe a year-and-a-half and a lot of people were surprised." The new building was a three-story steel structure with masonry walls and featured energy efficient construction techniques.

OTHER PHILADELPHIA PROJECTS

Another Hunter Roberts project in Philadelphia was its construction management of an apartment building called The Residences at 1401 Walnut Street in Center City. Completed in 2007, this renovation transformed a historic office building into 36 luxury apartments. At 1352 South Street, Hunter Roberts provided design and building services for a new parking, retail, and residential complex. The seven-story concrete structure, completed in 2006, accommodated 72 condominium units. Another condominium project involved the conversion of the former Keystone Automobile Club parking garage at 23 South 23rd Street into 84 units ranging from lofts to bi-level penthouses. Hunter Roberts provided construction management services for this undertaking, also completed in 2006.

In 2007 Hunter Roberts won a five-year construction management agreement with the Philadelphia Housing Authority as part of an ongoing revitalization of its properties. About midway through this agreement the firm had been awarded 13 projects worth around $20 million in total. These projects included demolition of abandoned homes and rehabilitation of multiple properties at various locations, including roofing and related work. Also in Philadelphia, Hunter Roberts was general contractor for the Annenberg Public Policy Center for the University of Pennsylvania. The building, which included broadcast studios and conference and office space, was completed in 2009.

CONTRIBUTIONS TO THE SPORTING LIFE

By the fall of 2007 Hunter Roberts had expanded into the health care, retail, and commercial markets, in addition to residential and education. The company entered a new field about this time when it received the contract to provide preconstruction services for a new training facility for professional football's New York Jets on a 26-acre site in Florham Park, New Jersey. The company then provided construction management services for a complex that included five football fields and a two-story campus building for administration and training facilities.

In January 2008 work began on another sports project, the Red Bull Arena in Harrison, New Jersey, for Major League Soccer's New York Red Bulls. Hunter Roberts was the general contractor for the 25,000-seat arena, which featured a state-of-the-art cantilevered roofing system that sheltered the seats while leaving the grass field open to the sun and other elements. Other features included three television and three radio broadcast areas, and a 360-degree wraparound message board. The arena

KEY DATES

2004: Robert Fee founds Hunter Roberts Construction Group.
2006: Hunter Roberts completes Temple University art school building in Philadelphia.
2008: Hunter Roberts completes a 24-story residential tower in Manhattan.
2010: Red Bull Arena soccer stadium opens in Harrison, New Jersey.

opened on time for the 2010 season.

Hunter Roberts added to its roster of sports-related clients in 2009, when it provided preconstruction services to World Wrestling Entertainment during a headquarters expansion program for a new $55 million operations facility. Another sports project consisted of construction management services at Franklin Field, long the site of University of Pennsylvania football games. Construction of the George Weiss Pavilion, due for completion in 2010, featured an intercollegiate strength and conditioning center for the university's 33 athletic teams, a fitness center for student and staff recreational use, and retail tenant space.

OTHER TRISTATE AREA PROJECTS

In New Jersey, Hunter Roberts was also providing construction management and general contracting services for the exterior skin replacement of Kennedy Memorial Hospital in Stratford; preconstruction services for Georgian Court University's Wellness Center at its Lakewood campus; and contracting services for Lincoln Park Municipal Facilities, which involved erecting four separate buildings.

In November 2007 Hunter Roberts began pouring the concrete foundation for an 18-story residential condominium in downtown Stamford, Connecticut, with completion scheduled for the summer of 2009. In Manhattan in 2008, construction was begun on the Gouverneur Healthcare Services's $180 million, four-year modernization and expansion project to serve the Lower East Side and Chinatown community. Gouverneur consisted of a long-term nursing facility and the largest city-run community center.

Among the residential buildings in Manhattan for which Hunter Roberts provided construction management services was 122 Greenwich Avenue in Greenwich

Village. The 11-story glass curtain wall structure contained 36 condominium units. Like 188 Ludlow Street, this building, completed in 2009, was erected over an active subway line.

In downtown Brooklyn, Hunter Roberts presided over the gut renovation of the landmarked Williamsburgh Bank building between 2006 and 2008. The upper floors, mostly medical and dental offices, remained operational during the entire construction process. Once these tenants had moved into their new suites, Hunter Roberts began the gut renovation of floors eight through 29 to house 179 residential condominium units.

Hunter Roberts received a $6 million contract from one of the federal government's first economic stimulus projects in 2009. The project, which had been in the works but never funded, was to add restaurants and shops to the new Manhattan terminal for the ferry linking the borough to Staten Island. It was also to feature a glassed-in area with sweeping views of New York Harbor.

HUNTER ROBERTS INTERIORS

An interiors unit soon became an important part of the Hunter Roberts group. This unit furnished five floors for Goldman Sachs Group, Inc., in Jersey City. Another high-profile interior client was AON Services Corporation, which was expanding throughout the metropolitan area. Other office interior clients included Citibank and the law firm Reed Smith, LLP. Its work for the latter earned Hunter Roberts the Best Interiors Project award in 2008 from *New York Construction*. During the year the interiors group was awarded more than 40 new projects, of which over 26 were for repeat clients.

Also in 2008, Hunter Roberts Interiors entered the broadcast/media market sector by completing a new office and studio space installation for MTV Networks in Manhattan. The following year it was renovating a series of floors for the Manhattan offices of The Nielsen Company. It was also renovating the Surrey Hotel on the Upper East Side and had been selected to construct the new office headquarters in Lower Manhattan of the city government's Department of Transportation.

Another field for the interiors group was construction for the lobby and infrastructure market. During 2008 and 2009 it completed newly designed lobbies for the midtown Manhattan office buildings at 1330 Avenue of the Americas, 444 Madison Avenue, and 575 Lexington Avenue. Hunter Roberts at that time was in the process of renovating the observation deck and the landmarked lobby, as well as performing infrastructure upgrades throughout the building, for the renovation of the Empire State Building.

Not all interiors clients were commercial companies. For historic Trinity Church, near Wall Street in Lower Manhattan, Hunter Roberts was general contractor for the restoration of the bell tower in the steeple. The 300-year-old bells were removed and reinstalled in 2006. The business recession that began in 2008 cast a pall on many ambitious construction plans involving Hunter Roberts, including two high-rise buildings planned in Philadelphia. Also scrapped was the proposed Soleil Center in Raleigh, North Carolina. This 46-story building would have been the city's tallest. Hunter Roberts closed its Charlotte office and the satellite office in Raleigh at the end of 2009.

Robert Halasz

PRINCIPAL DIVISIONS

Core Shell Group; Hunter Roberts Interiors.

PRINCIPAL COMPETITORS

Bovis Lend Lease, Inc.; Skanska USA Building Inc.; Structure Tone, Inc.; Tishman Construction Corporation; Turner Construction Company.

FURTHER READING

Agababian, Ron, "Project Diversity Playing Key Role in Firm's Expansion," *Real Estate Weekly*, March 25, 2009, p. 5B.

"Contractor of the Year Hunter Roberts," *New York Construction*, July 2008.

Haughney, Christine, "Pickup in Building Activity Brings Industry Shake-ups," *Crain's New York Business*, March 7, 2005, pp. 27–28.

Hoyle, Amanda Jones, "Hunter Roberts' Dilemma: Exit Carolinas Market or Sell the Division," *Triangle Business Journal*, January 23, 2009.

McCabe, Kelly, "Hunter Roberts Construction Group—Red Bull Arena," *Building and Construction Northeast*, February 9, 2010.

Miller, Joanna, "Low Overhead, Fast Growth," *Construction Today*, October 2007, pp. 189–90.

Prior, Jim, "NJ's Top Construction Firms Flush with New Work," *New Jersey Business*, October 2007, pp. 58–60.

Rubin, Debra, and Richard Korman, "Entry of New York Competitors Signals Building Market Shift," *ENR/ Engineering News Record*, February 21, 2005, p. 13.

Saltonstall, David, "14.9 M Ferry Terminal Job among First Funded by Stimulus Money," *New York Daily News*, May 10, 2009, p. 7.

Yanover, Yori, "The Project," *Grand Street News*, November 2008.

Hypermarcas S.A.

Av. Juscalino Kubitschek 1830
São Paulo 04530-900
Brazil
Telephone: (55 11) 4166-1000
Fax: (55 11) 4191-4875
Web site: http://www.hypermarcas.com.br

Public Company
Incorporated: 2002 as Assolan Industrial Ltda.
Employees: 2,524
Sales: BRL 2.63 billion ($1.51 billion) (2009)
Stock Exchanges: São Paulo
Ticker Symbol: HYPE
NAICS: 311421 Fruit and Vegetable Canning; 311930 Flavoring Syrup and Concentrate Manufacturing; 325412 Pharmaceutical Preparation Manufacturing; 325611 Soap and Other Detergent Manufacturing; 325612 Polish and Other Sanitation Good Manufacturing; 325620 Toilet Preparation Manufacturing

∎ ∎ ∎

Hypermarcas S.A. has the most complete portfolio of brands in Brazil of any Brazilian-owned company in the market segments in which it is engaged: cleaning products, health and beauty products, food products, and nonprescription medications. It markets and retails these products and manufactures many of them. This company has made a billionaire of its flamboyant majority owner within the first decade after its founding.

ORIGINS

João Alves de Queiroz Filho, known throughout the Brazilian business community as Júnior, founded Hypermarcas. His father formed the basis of the family fortune in 1969, when he started a company named Arisco that produced and sold a seasoning for meat. After the senior Alves de Queiroz suffered a stroke in the early 1990s, leadership passed to Júnior, who was already closely involved in the business.

Arisco eventually became the third- or fourth-largest Brazilian-owned enterprise in the food sector. It also entered the household cleaning market in 1993. Liquid detergent was added later, and a steel wool scouring pad named Assolan was introduced in 1996. By this time the Wall Street investment firm Goldman Sachs & Co. had taken a one-fifth share in the company.

Arisco was producing and marketing 470 products when Júnior sold the company to the U.S. company Bestfoods in 2000 for $490 million, plus the assumption by Bestfoods of more than $260 million in debt. Bestfoods was purchased a few months later by the giant multinational food and household products company Unilever.

The sale was made in the wake of a recession that resulted in the devaluation of Brazil's currency, the real. This event greatly increased Arisco's debt, since 90 percent of what it owed was denominated in dollars. Júnior denied that he had sold the company for that reason, however. He said that he had done so because Arisco needed to double in size to compete successfully against its rivals and he lacked enough capital to make new acquisitions.

KEY DATES

2001: João Alves de Queiroz Filho buys cleaning product maker Assolan Industrial Ltda.
2006: Assolan adds food products and personal care and beauty products; Hypermarcas Industrial Ltda. is established.
2007: Hypermarcas adds over-the-counter medications.
2008: Hypermarcas makes its initial public offering of stock.
2009: Hypermarcas spends over $1 billion to make five new acquisitions.

RE-CREATING THE BUSINESS

Júnior was frustrated when Unilever allowed some of Arisco's products, such as its seasonings, to fall into obscurity for lack of investment in marketing. He was determined to reconstruct Arisco, beginning with cleaning products. The first step, taken in 2001, was the purchase of Assolan Industrial Ltda. from Prátika Industrial Ltda., which had once been an Arisco division. This acquisition was made through Monte Cristalina, S.A., the family holding company. He acquired Help Industrial, a firm that also made scouring pads, at the same time.

Productive capacity was doubled at the Prátika plant, located in Júnior's home base of Goiás, which also began turning out synthetic sponges and steel straws. At this time Assolan held only about 5 percent of the steel wool scouring pad market, which was practically a monopoly for Bombril S.A. and its eponymous product. By 2006 Assolan's share had reached about 30 percent. Help, in addition to making steel wool scouring pads under its own name and as proprietary brands for two supermarket chains, produced Scotch-Brite for 3M Company. Monte Cristalina next purchased a number of poorly performing local steel wool companies in several parts of Brazil.

In 2003 Assolan expanded into other surface cleaning products, concentrating production at the Goiás plant. Later in the year the company secured the rights to the brand name Fisibra from Fisibra Fibras Sintéticas do Brasil Ltda., a company owned by Unilever Brasil Ltda. Fisibra was a manufacturer of detergents, multiuse cleaning products, sponges, and cleaning cloths.

In early 2004 Unilever Brasil sold to Júnior Castro Verde Participações Ltda., a company that owned a property adjacent to the Goiás plant. At the same time

Júnior also purchased from Unilever the machinery and equipment needed to produce liquid detergents and multiuse cleaning products. In 2005 his enterprise returned to powdered detergents by acquiring Quimivale Industrial Ltda. and Distribuidora Clean Ltda. The company began marketing their products under the brand name Assim.

A NEW HOUSEHOLD PRODUCTS EMPIRE: 2006–07

Júnior's intent was to make Assolan the Brazilian version of Procter & Gamble Co. Such a consumer products empire would be based on the same pillars that had made Arisco a success: experience in manufacturing and distributing products, and emphasis on mass marketing. The acquisition program was not restricted to cleaning products. In 2006 Assolan initiated its food division by purchasing Bessan Indústria e Comércio de Alimentos S.A., whose brands included Etti, Salsaretti, and PuroPuré. Bessan, which specialized in tomato sauces and canned vegetables, was renamed Etti Produtos Alimentícios Ltda.

Assolan also entered the field of personal care and beauty products in 2006, by means of the purchase of a half-share of Bisa Participações Ltda., the holding company for Éh Cosméticos S.A., which had been recently created by Cristiana Arcangeli to offer hair products to the public, including shampoos, conditioners, and finishers, under the brand name Éh!. The rest of the shares were acquired in 2008. Hypermarcas Industrial Ltda. was established in 2006. Assolan was incorporated into this entity in 2007. The company's name subsequently became Hypermarcas S.A.

In acquiring his growing roster of companies, Júnior concentrated on ones that were producing everyday consumer goods for Brazil's mass market of almost 200 million but were facing issues of one kind or other. Some were making good products but not marketing them successfully. Others were family companies facing succession difficulties. Júnior convinced the owners that he was offering fair value and would not allow the work of a lifetime to be wasted and the brands they had created to disappear.

According to a cover story in the business magazine *Exame*, Júnior personified a style of management typically Brazilian: He combined technical sophistication and a concern for cost control with intuition, aggressiveness, and the capacity to make quick decisions with an ability to engage personally with the other party and the willingness to make concessions when necessary. These qualities enabled him at times to outbid multinational companies with more money in hand but tied to a more rigid business model.

Júnior was assisted in his ambitions by veteran Arisco executives such as Nelson Mello, president of Hypermarcas, and Claudio Bergamo, the company's chief executive officer, whose job was to absorb and integrate the acquired companies. In addition, Júnior had close ties dating from the 1990s with bankers working for big Wall Street investment firms who could provide needed capital.

FURTHER ACQUISITIONS IN 2007

Júnior also relied on his own intuition to make deals not anticipated by his advisers. In 2007, while preparations were being made to take Hypermarcas public, he decided to interrupt the process in order to purchase DM Farmacêutica Ltda., the national leader in over-the-counter drugs. With the support of four Mexican bankers, Júnior was able to assemble the BRL 1.1 billion ($570 million) needed to buy DM for BRL 1.2 billion ($622 million). By taking Hypermarcas into a new market segment, he hoped to make the company less vulnerable to competition from Unilever and Procter & Gamble.

The acquisition immediately tripled Hypermarcas's annual revenues. It also underlined Júnior's strategy of buying strong brands and sustaining them by heavy investments in marketing. DM's brands were located in two consumer markets that were among the fastest growing, particularly among the average Brazilian: over-the-counter medications and personal care items.

Hypermarcas made other acquisitions in 2007. With the objective of consolidating its participation in all segments of cleaning and hygiene, it purchased Sul Química Ltda. and its subsidiary Fluss Indústria e Comércio Ltda. These companies were leaders in pest control products in southern Brazil. Hypermarcas also bought Finn Administradora de Marcas Ltda. and certain assets of Boehringer Ingelheim do Brasil Química e Farmacêutica Ltda., thereby expanding its interests in the part of the food market related to well-being and health.

GOING PUBLIC IN 2008

In May 2008 Hypermarcas made its initial public offering (IPO) of stock, selling more than 36 million shares at BRL 17 ($9.24) per share on the São Paulo exchange. The BRL 612 million ($333 million) raised exceeded by more than 10-fold Júnior's original investment of about $30 million in the enterprise.

During the next few months, the company used some of the funds collected for further acquisitions. Ceil Comércio e Distribuidora Ltda., a Brazilian holding of

Revlon Consumer Products Corporation, became the initial entry of Hypermarcas into hairstyling products. The company also bought Niasi Indústria e Cosméticos Ltda. and Aprov Comércio de Cosméticos Ltda., thereby strengthening its line of cosmetics and entering the nail polish and hair dye markets. It also purchased the hair care brands of Brasil Global Cosméticos Ltda. and NY Looks Indústria e Comércio Ltda., and acquired by stock swap Laboratório Americano de Farmacoterapia S.A. This brought the number of companies acquired by Hypermarcas and its predecessor and related companies to 22 in six years.

Hypermarcas's IPO of stock proved well timed, for the world financial crisis of late 2008 cast a pall on the Brazilian stock market. The resulting fall in business activity led to reduced consumer spending, and as a result the company lost money during the third quarter of the year.

MORE ACQUISITIONS: 2009–10

By the end of 2009 economic conditions had improved markedly in Brazil. Hypermarcas ended the year with gross revenues up 48 percent over 2008. Net profit was up by 51 percent. Hypermarcas spent about BRL 2 billion (about $1.15 billion) in making five acquisitions during the year. The largest was the purchase of Laboratório Neo Química Comércio e Indústria S.A. for BRL 1.3 billion ($750 million), half of it in the form of Hypermarcas stock to the selling Gonçalves family, which also secured two seats on the nine-member board. The Neo Química acquisition marked the entry of Hypermarcas into generic prescription drugs and also into the prescription drugs called "similars" in Brazil because they differed little in composition from drugs patented by foreign companies although not produced under license.

According to Bergamo, Hypermarcas still had BRL 500 million (about $290 million) for new acquisitions. Before the year was out, the company had also acquired Pom Pom Produtos Higênicos Ltda., a producer of sanitary products for babies; Indústria Nacional de Artefatos de Látex Ltda., a condom maker; and Hypernova Medicamentos Participações S.A. Versoix Participações Ltda., manufacturers of Jontex condoms, was purchased for BRL 101 million ($58 million).

The Hypermarcas juggernaut continued into 2010, supported by about $1.1 billion raised in two share offerings on the São Paulo stock market. In March the company announced the purchase of Sapeka Indústria e Comércio de Fraldas Descartáveis Ltda., proprietor of several brands of disposable diapers. This was followed by the acquisition of Facilit Odontológica e Perfumaria

Ltda., manufacturer of oral hygiene items, and York S.A. Indústria e Comércio, producer of feminine pads, bandages, and other sanitary products. In April Hypermarcas purchased Luper Indústria Farmacêutica Ltda., a producer of medications, for BRL 52 million. Neo Química was reported to be considering developing and marketing a drug for erectile dysfunction.

Hypermarcas had nine factories at the end of 2009. Eight of them were functioning around the clock and close to installed capacity. The Neo Química plant had idle capacity and was operating two shifts a day. Hypermarcas was planning in 2011 to add a cosmetics factory and one that combined cosmetics, personal hygiene, and cleaning products in 2011. A new distribution center was scheduled to go into operation in 2010.

PORTFOLIO OF PRODUCTS

By this time, Hypermarcas ranked as the fifth major laboratory in Brazil in pharmaceutical products. It was first in over-the-counter drugs. Its medications included Benegrip, the leader for flu symptoms; Engov, the leader for hangovers; Rinosoro, the leader in nonprescription nasal decongestants; Tamarine, the leader in laxatives; and Doril, second for analgesics.

Hypermarcas was first in the self-service field for beauty and personal hygiene. Its brands included Monange, the leader in moisturizers; Paixão, the leader in body oils; Risqué, the leader in nail varnishes; Bozzano, the leader in hair gels, shaving cream, and aftershave lotion; and Jontex and Olla, first and second, respectively, in condoms.

With regard to food products, Hypermarcas was first in sweeteners and second in tomato sauce. Its brands included Finn, leader in powdered sweeteners; Zero Cal, leader in liquid sweeteners; and Salsaretti, second in tomato sauces. Hypermarcas had one of the widest portfolios of brands in the cleaning and hygiene sector. Its products in this category included Assolan, in second place in steel wool, and Mat Inset, the leader in electric insecticides.

Hypermarcas was spending one-fifth of its revenues on marketing. It was among the largest advertisers in Brazil, with print advertisements appearing in newspapers and magazines, and commercials on television. The company's ad campaigns were directly tied to celebrities, with endorsements of products by big names such as the actress Xuxa, the actress Mariana Ximenes, and the soccer star Ronaldo. Hypermarcas was said to rank second among Brazilian enterprises in the hiring of artists and other celebrities for this purpose.

In early 2010 the company became the largest sponsor in the history of Brazilian soccer to date by signing on the Corinthians club as it entered its centennial year. In return for BRL 38 million, players would wear jerseys bearing the logos of some of the company's leading brands.

Júnior and his executives saw as their major challenge the need to maintain the velocity of Hypermarcas's growth. The immediate goal was to buy a new business on an average of one every two months in 2010 and to reach annual revenue of BRL 10 billion in five years. By then, company executives foresaw fewer acquisition opportunities available and hence future growth within the enterprise itself.

Hypermarcas was not ruling out expansion abroad, however. Júnior pointed out that due to the world economic crisis many companies were available inexpensively in the United States and Europe. He was said to be eyeing a small American pharmaceutical laboratory and a European cosmetics maker. However, Hypermarcas did not see much synergy with its existing businesses in Brazil.

Júnior held just over half of Hypermarcas's shares of common stock in early 2010 through two companies that he controlled. He had already made clear that none of his three children would assume a role in managing the business. At age 57, he continued his lifelong habit of working about 10 hours a day, maintaining his energy through daily exercise, preferably swimming in his own pool. Intensely competitive, he was a passionate driver of such sports cars as a classic red Ferrari and the only Aston Martin DB9 in Brazil, and counted as one of his best friends the Brazilian former Formula One champion Nelson Piquet. His fortune was estimated at $2.5 billion by *Exame*.

Robert Halasz

PRINCIPAL OPERATING UNITS

Beauty and Personal Hygiene; Cleaning and Hygiene; Food Products; Pharmaceutical Products.

PRINCIPAL COMPETITORS

Aché Laboratórios Farmacêuticas S.A.; Bombril S.A.; Procter & Gamble do Brasil S.A.; Unilever do Brasil Ltda.

FURTHER READING

Blecher, Nelson, "Por dentro da Arisco," *Exame*, April 7, 1999, pp. 105–13.

———, "O sono acabou," *Exame*, February 23, 2000, pp. 16–18.

Guimarães, Camila, "Arisco II, o retorno," *Exame*, February 15, 2006, pp. 56–57.

Madureira, Daniele, "Hypermarcas começa a produzir na região Nordeste," *Notícias Financieras*, December 8, 2009.

Onaga, Marcelo, "O império das marcas," *Exame*, January 27, 2010, pp. 20–29.

———, "Uma Unilever em miniature," *Exame*, February 27, 2008, pp. 48–51.

Rebouças, Lidia, "Começar de novo," *Exame*, February 6, 2002, pp. 56–58.

Wheatley, Jonathan, "Assolan's Babies Battle for Market Share," *Financial Times*, March 16, 2005, p. 9.

IAMGOLD Corp.

———— ■ ————

401 Bay Street, Suite 3200
Toronto, Ontario M5H 2Y4
Canada
Telephone: (416) 360-4710
Toll Free: (888) 464-9999
Fax: (416) 360-4750
Web site: http://www.iamgold.com

Public Company
Incorporated: 1991
Employees: 6,482
Sales: $914.3 million (2009)
Stock Exchanges: Toronto New York
Ticker Symbols: IMG (Toronto); IAG (New York)
NAICS: 212221 Gold Ore Mining

■ ■ ■

Headquartered in the Canadian city of Toronto, Ontario, the International African Mining Gold Corporation (IAMGOLD) is involved in the business of gold mining and production. Each year, the company produces about one million ounces of gold. During the early 2010s IAMGOLD's operations included seven mines on three continents. At that time the company concentrated its efforts in several geographic areas, including West Africa, Québec, and the Guiana Shield of South America.

ORIGINS AND EARLY GROWTH

Mark Nathanson and William Pugliese established IAMGOLD in 1991. However, the efforts of its

cofounders can be traced back to the late 1980s. In 1988 Nathanson began negotiating with the government of Mali in West Africa for the right to explore for gold in Western Mali's Kayes region. The Sadiola exploration concession, which spanned 13,000 square kilometers, was acquired by Nathanson and Pugliese two years later, and the privately held International African Mining Gold Corporation (IAMGOLD) was established in 1991.

In 1991 IAMGOLD identified the Sadiola Hill gold deposit, which contained 7.1 million ounces of gold reserves and resources. Via a joint venture with Anglo American (later AngloGold Ashanti) called SEMOS, plans were made to construct the Sadiola Hill mine. The two companies continued to work together into the mid-1990s, forming a regional exploration venture in six West African countries in 1994.

In 1996 the company poured its first gold bar at Sadiola in West Africa. Exploration commenced in Argentina, Ecuador, and Brazil that year. IAMGOLD went public in 1996, and it shares began trading on the Toronto Stock Exchange. The company continued working with AngloGold Ashanti at this time. In 1997, IAMGOLD's first year of production, the two companies acquired the Yatela gold deposit via a joint venture arrangement.

During the late 1990s IAMGOLD operated in a market characterized by low gold prices. Despite this, the company managed to turn a consolidated net profit of $2.5 million in 1997. IAMGOLD ended the year with a cash position of $41.9 million, up from $35.9 million the previous year. At this time IAMGOLD was led by President and Chief Operating Officer Todd Bruce.

EXPLORATION FOCUS

By early 1998 IAMGOLD was exploring 10,000 square kilometers in five West African countries. In addition to Argentina, Ecuador, and Brazil, exploration work was also under way in Peru and Bolivia. Early the following year the company announced that, according to the results of a feasibility study, its 50-50 Yatela joint venture with AngloGold Ashanti contained an estimated 1.92 million ounces of gold.

IAMGOLD and AngloGold continued their partnership by announcing an exploration joint venture in Ecuador in September 1999. In exchange for a 50 percent stake in the deal, AngloGold agreed to invest $5.5 million for exploration efforts in a project area spanning approximately 3,400 square kilometers. In turn, IAMGOLD agreed to initially operate the exploration programs.

In 1999 the company reported record production at its Sadiola Gold Mine in West Africa, which produced 542,955 ounces of gold. This increased production led to record profits and cash flow for the year. Specifically, gold sales reached $63.46 million, up from $60.34 million the previous year. In addition, net income surged to $13.19 million, up from $8.77 million in 1998.

PRODUCTION BEGINS AT YATELA

In January 2000 IAMGOLD named John Ross as its chief financial officer. Ross, who succeeded Mahendra Naik, previously served as the company's controller, and had served as an officer since 1996. IAMGOLD reached several important milestones in 2001. After construction work was completed at the Yatela Gold Mine in Mali, West Africa, at a cost of $73 million, the company poured its first gold there on May 9, 2001.

It was also in 2001 that cofounders William Pugliese and Mark Nathanson sold a collective 4.4 million shares of IAMGOLD, in order to raise money for

other business interests. Following the sale Pugliese continued to hold 22 percent of the outstanding shares, while Nathanson controlled 14 percent. The company ended the year on a high note when its Sadiola Gold Mine produced a record 536,047 ounces of gold.

In January 2002 IAMGOLD announced that, moving forward, the company would pay dividends to its shareholders in either Canadian dollars or gold (gold bullion depository certificates). In addition, IAMGOLD implemented a Gold Money Policy. This involved the conversion of a substantial share of its discretionary cash into gold.

ACQUISITION OF REPADRE

In October 2002 IAMGOLD announced plans to acquire the Toronto, Ontario, Canada-based mining company Repadre Capital Corp. The deal, a $213.9 million stock swap, resulted in a debt-free, midsize gold producer with four mining operations and annual gold production levels of 450,000 ounces. It was also in 2002 that IAMGOLD began trading on the American Stock Exchange.

IAMGOLD's acquisition of Repadre Capital was completed in 2003. Repadre executive Joseph F. Conway was chosen as the company's new president and CEO. In addition, Todd Bruce was named chief operating officer. William Pugliese and Mark Nathanson continued as co-chairmen.

As part of the Repadre deal, IAMGOLD secured a number of different operations. These included joint venture interests in the Ghana, Africa-based Tarkwa and Damang mines. During the summer of 2003 a $159 million expansion of the Tarkwa Mine was announced in conjunction with fellow stakeholders Gold Fields Ltd. and the government of Ghana.

PURSUIT OF WHEATON RIVER

In March 2004 IAMGOLD announced an agreement to acquire the Vancouver, Canada-based gold mining company Wheaton River Minerals Ltd. for $2.2 billion in stock. The proposed deal stood to create North America's fifth-largest gold mining company (the third-largest in Canada). It also would significantly expand the company's operations, which would grow to include seven mines in West Africa, Australia, and the Americas, with an annual production of approximately one million ounces.

The proposed acquisition was immediately threatened by several takeover offers. Golden Star Resources offered to acquire IAMGOLD for $920 million, while Coeur d'Alene Mines Corp. offered to

KEY DATES

1991: Mark Nathanson and William Pugliese establish International African Mining Gold Corporation (IAMGOLD).

1996: The company pours its first gold bar at Sadiola, West Africa; IAMGOLD goes public on the Toronto Stock Exchange.

2002: IAMGOLD begins trading on the American Stock Exchange.

2003: IAMGOLD acquires Repadre Capital Corp.

2005: The company lists on the New York Stock Exchange.

2006: IAMGOLD acquires the Canadian gold producer Cambior Inc., via a stock swap worth approximately $3 billion.

2009: IAMGOLD acquires Orezone Resources Inc. and its Essakane Gold Project in Burkina Faso, West Africa.

acquire Wheaton River Minerals for $1.8 billion. Initially, both companies emphasized their commitment to continue with their merger plans. Ultimately, however, IAMGOLD's shareholders voted against the deal in July.

Golden Star Resources continued to pursue IAMGOLD following the collapse of its proposed merger with Wheaton River Minerals. In order to prevent a hostile takeover by Golden Star, IAMGOLD implemented a "poison pill" plan. Specifically, the plan allowed existing shareholders to acquire new half-price shares in the event that a prospective bidder's ownership interest exceeded more than 20 percent of all shares.

GOLD FIELDS MERGER ATTEMPT FAILS

In August 2004 a merger agreement was made with Gold Fields Ltd. The $2.1 billion stock swap stood to create the world's seventh-largest gold producer, and the fourth-largest in North America. Specifically, it called for the development of a new publicly traded Gold Fields unit named Gold Fields International Ltd., led by Gold Fields Chairman Chris Thompson as president and CEO. The unit would include all of the mining interests of Gold Fields beyond South Africa, in which Gold Fields would have a 70 percent ownership interest.

Further complicating the situation, in October 2004 South Africa-based Harmony Gold Mining Co.,

that country's largest gold producer, attempted a hostile takeover of Gold Fields. The proposed tie-up would create the largest gold producer in the world, with an annual production of 7.5 million ounces. Harmony argued that its deal would have more of an immediate benefit to the Gold Fields shareholders than the IAMGOLD merger.

By late 2004 IAMGOLD and Gold Fields were still moving ahead with their merger plans. However, in December the companies announced that they were changing the merger terms. In order to sweeten the deal, IAMGOLD agreed to a $200 million reduction in the amount of cash contributed by Gold Fields.

Despite the intentions of both organizations, opposition to the merger remained. Russia's MMC Norilsk Nickel, which had a 20 percent ownership stake in Gold Fields, did not support the company's planned merger with IAMGOLD, and instead supported the Harmony deal. On December 7, 2004, Gold Fields announced that it was unable to receive the majority approval of its shareholders, bringing an end to the proposed merger.

ACQUISITION OF CAMBIOR

In 2004 IAMGOLD saw its gold production reach 432,000 ounces for the year. However, net income plummeted approximately 50 percent. Earnings, which totaled $20 million in 2003, fell to $11.2 million. Much of the decrease was attributed to transaction-related costs associated with unfruitful mergers.

Following the disappointments of 2004, IAMGOLD experienced several positive developments. In 2005 the company listed on the New York Stock Exchange. In September 2006 IAMGOLD agreed to acquire the Canadian gold producer Cambior Inc., via a stock swap worth approximately $3 billion. By creating a company able to produce some 1.1 million ounces of gold annually, the deal stood to catapult IAMGOLD to the upper echelon of mid-tiered gold producers.

Cambior's shareholders approved the merger with IAMGOLD in November 2006. After the Superior Court of Québec granted its approval that same month, the deal was finalized. IAMGOLD then became the 10th-largest publicly traded gold company in the world. As part of the merger, IAMGOLD also secured ownership of Suriname, South America-based Rosebel Gold Mines, as well as the Québec, Canada-based Doyon Division Gold Mine and the Botswana, Africa-based Mupane Gold Mine.

SALE OF SLEEPING GIANT

During 2006 IAMGOLD focused on integrating its newly acquired operations. This task was completed by the year's end. In October 2007 IAMGOLD agreed to sell its Sleeping Giant Mine near Amos, Québec, to Cadiscor Resources Inc. In December IAMGOLD announced that, for the seventh consecutive year, it would pay an annual dividend to its shareholders.

In mid-2008 IAMGOLD revealed that an internal study of a deposit, referred to as Warrenmac, which was part of its Westwood exploration project in Québec (near the company's Doyon Mine), contained significant gold and other base metals. IAMGOLD anticipated that production could begin in 2010. A related development followed this discovery when the company revealed plans to acquire the participation royalty on its Doyon/Westwood property from Barrick Gold Corporation for $13 million.

A similar strategy unfolded in France, where IAMGOLD filed to acquire Euro Resources S.A.'s participation royalty associated with its Rosebel Gold Mine. In November IAMGOLD struck a deal with Cadiscor Resources Inc. for the sale of its Dormex property, located around the Sleeping Giant Mine, in exchange for a 1 percent royalty on gold and silver production, as well as a 1.5 percent royalty on base metal deposits.

IAMGOLD paid an annual dividend to its shareholders for the eighth consecutive year in 2008. By this time the company's operations had grown to include eight mines on three continents. Production totaled 997,000 ounces, up 3 percent from 2007. The company's top-producing mine was Suriname-Rosebel (315,000 ounces), followed by Mali-Sadiola (172,000 ounces).

ACQUISITION OF OREZONE RESOURCES

One other significant development in 2008 occurred when IAMGOLD announced plans to acquire Orezone Resources Inc. and its Essakane Gold Project in Burkina Faso, West Africa. The deal was completed in 2009. That year IAMGOLD earmarked a $219 million investment for the Essakane Gold Project, which would cover the construction of water management structures, pre-stripping, mining equipment, and mill equipment and construction.

IAMGOLD ended 2009 by paying a dividend to its shareholders for the ninth consecutive year. Moving forward the company established a goal to increase annual production to 1.8 million ounces by 2012. A

major leadership change took place in January 2010 when Joseph Conway, longtime president and then CEO, announced his resignation. During his tenure, the company had achieved significant growth and evolved into one of Canada's top intermediate gold producers. Until a replacement could be found, Peter C. Jones was named acting CEO.

In May 2010 IAMGOLD announced that the company's new Essakane Gold Mine in Burkina Faso was expected to begin production in June. This was much earlier than expected. Initial plans had projected that production would begin toward the end of 2010. Looking ahead to 2011, IAMGOLD's efforts were especially targeted toward the areas of West Africa, Québec, and the Guiana Shield of South America. Based upon its strong performance over several decades, the company appeared to have excellent prospects for continued success in these regions and elsewhere.

Paul R. Greenland

PRINCIPAL SUBSIDIARIES

IAMGOLD-South America Corporation (Barbados); Repadre Capital (BVI) Inc. (British Virgin Islands); Repadre International Corporation (Barbados); IAMGOLD-Québec Management Inc. (Canada); IAMGOLD Burkina Faso Inc. (Canada).

PRINCIPAL COMPETITORS

Barrick Gold Corporation; Newmont Mining Corporation; Randgold Resources Ltd.

FURTHER READING

Bresnick, Julie, "Shareholders of Iamgold Nix Wheaton Tie-up," *American Metal Market*, July 8, 2004, p. 1.

"Co-Chairmen of IAMGOLD Corporation Complete Sale of 4.4 Million Shares," *PR Newswire*, May 25, 2001.

"Gold Fields Shareholders Do Not Approve IAMGOLD Transaction," *PR Newswire*, December 7, 2004.

"Iamgold to Acquire Orezone's Essakane Gold Project," *E&MJ—Engineering & Mining Journal*, January–February 2009, p. 14.

King, Laura, "Canadian Gold Miners Join Forces," *Daily Deal*, October 29, 2002.

Lerner, Matthew, "Barrick Extends NovaGold Offer; Iamgold, Cambior Complete Deal," *American Metal Market*, November 9, 2006, p. 7.

ICO, Inc.

———————————————— ∎

1811 Bering Drive, Suite 200
Houston, Texas 77057
U.S.A.
Telephone: (713) 351-4100
Fax: (713) 335-2201
Web site: http://www.icopolymers.com

Wholly Owned Subsidiary of A. Schulman, Inc.
Incorporated: 1978
Employees: 805
Sales: $300 million (2009)
NAICS: 326122 Plastics Pipe and Pipe Fitting
Manufacturing

∎ ∎ ∎

Houston, Texas-based ICO, Inc., is a manufacturer of specialty resin concentrates and provider of specialized polymer services. Powders produced by ICO are used to produce such items as toys, household furniture, automobile parts, fertilizer, paint, and metal and fabric coatings. ICO also offers toll process services for the size reduction and compounding of both plastic and non-plastic materials.

The company's Wedco Technology, Inc., unit provides blending, packaging, distribution, warehousing, and procurement services. The Bayshore Industrial, L.P. unit mostly serves the film industry by producing specialty compounds, concentrates, and additives. All told, ICO maintains 20 facilities in nine countries, including plants in California, Indiana, Pennsylvania, Tennessee, and Texas. Since 2009, ICO has been a

subsidiary of A. Schulman, Inc.

COMPANY INCORPORATED: 1978

ICO was incorporated in Texas in 1978. Based in Fort Worth, Texas, the company served the oil-field sector, testing, inspecting, and servicing piping and other equipment. By 1984 ICO was generating sales of $67 million and net income of $2.8 million. In 1985 the company was on the verge of being sold to Brunswick Corp., but the deal was called off at the 11th hour when Brunswick became concerned about pretax losses incurred by ICO in the second quarter of 1985. Matters would only grow worse for ICO and other companies involved in the oil and gas industry, as oversupplies led to a collapse in petroleum prices that devastated many companies in the sector. ICO restructured its debt and managed to stave off bankruptcy in 1988.

ICO limped into the 1990s, continuing to serve the petroleum industry by testing, inspecting, reconditioning and coating sucker rods and tubular goods. In December 1990 James Shanahan, Jr., took over as interim chairman and chief executive officer, posts he assumed on a permanent basis the following year. He ran the company from Cincinnati where he was executive vice president and general counsel of Pacholder Associates, an investment firm that held a 34 percent interest in ICO. To be closer to the bulk of its customers, the company also moved its headquarters to Houston, where it maintained a testing facility, in 1991, a fiscal year in which it posted revenues of $37.5 million and a net loss of $3.5 million. A year later sales fell to $34.6 million, but so too did costs, narrowing the net loss to less than $400,000.

In the mid-1990s ICO completed a series of acquisitions that mostly expanded its oil-field services business. In 1993 it acquired Tubular Ultrasound Corporation, a Texas tubular inspection company. A year later ICO added Shearer Supply Ltd., a Canadian provider of sucker rod inspection and reclamation services; Permian, a provider of cement lining for tubing and casing; Frontiers Inspections Services, Inc., a New Mexico provider of tubular inspection services; and B&W Equipment Sales and Mfg., Inc., maker of parts and components for tubular testing and inspection. The following year, ICO added Kebco Pipe Services, Inc., a provider of tubular testing, inspection, and reconditioning services in West Texas; and R.J. Dixon, Inc., providing similar services in the Gulf Coast area.

CHANGE IN DIRECTION: 1996

In 1996 the seeds were planted that would ultimately transform ICO into a specialty polymers company. In August of that year ICO acquired Wedco Technology, Inc., of West Portal, New Jersey, for $55 million in cash and stock. Wedco served the petrochemical industry by grinding plastic pellets into powder, which petrochemical companies then sold for use in the manufacture of toys, paints, and automotive parts. Wedco had enjoyed strong growth in the past four years, having increased revenues from $29.1 million in 1991 to $43.6 million in 1995. The addition of Wedco provided ICO with much needed diversity, important given the cyclical nature of the oil-field services industry.

In the second half of the 1990s ICO continued to build its petrochemical processing business. In July 1996 it acquired a pair of sister companies for $5.8 million: Beaumont, Texas-based Polymer Service, Inc., and East Chicago, Indiana-based Polymer Service of Indiana, Inc. Both companies provided size reduction, compounding, and other processing services to the petrochemical industry. Late in 1996 ICO paid $18.5 million in cash and stock for Bayshore Industrial, Inc., a provider of concentrates and compounds to resin producers in the United States.

Further acquisitions followed in 1997 and 1998. Two deals were completed in April of that year, the micropowders business of Exxon Chemical Belgium and the $7.8 million purchase of Rotec Chemicals, a European manufacturer of concentrates used in a variety of plastics processes. In July 1997 ICO acquired Verplast S.p.A. for about $35 million. Located in northern Italy, Verplast provided petrochemical processing services and supplied value-added plastics materials for rotational molding, the manufacture of containers and other hollow plastics, and other plastics powder applications.

Auckland, New Zealand-based J.R. Courtenay (N. S.) Ltd. and its Australian subsidiary, Courtenay Polymers Pty. Ltd., were acquired in March 1998. Using proprietary formulations, they offered a wide range of size reduction and compounding services and sold polymer powders to rotational molding and metal coating customers in New Zealand and Australia. Also in 1998, ICO acquired a French company, Soreco S.A., which provided color matching and color compounding services for engineered plastics used by manufacturers of appliances, electronics, cosmetics, and other consumer products.

OIL-FIELD SERVICES DEMAND FALLS: 1999

In fiscal 1997 ICO posted sales of $198 million, $100 million of which was generated by its petrochemical processing assets. Petrochemical processing would grow even more important in fiscal 1998 when total sales grew to $281.3 million and net income to $3.8 million, the increase due almost entirely to petrochemical processing, which contributed $177.2 million in revenues. A year later, demand for oil-field services fell, resulting in a drop in revenue from $104.1 million to $74.9 million for ICO's oil-field services unit. The company's petrochemical processing business, on the other hand, continued to grow, increasing sales by another $10.2 million.

As ICO entered the new century, it was clear that petrochemical processing had become the company's core business. ICO added to the operation in September 2000 by acquiring Sanko Manufacturer, a Malaysian provider of specialty powders and size reduction and compounding services to its home country's rotational molding, metal, coating, textile, and injection molding industries.

ICO then hired Wall Street's Bear, Stearns & Co. Inc. to help it consider strategic alternatives regarding the oil-field services business. Out of this process emerged a deal in April 2001 to sell the oil-field services assets to Varco International, Inc., for $165 million in

KEY DATES

■

1978: ICO is founded as oil-field services company.
1996: Wedco Technology and Bayshore Industrial is acquired.
1998: Courtenay Polymers is acquired.
2002: Oil-field services assets are sold.
2010: ICO is sold to A. Schulman, Inc.

cash. The final price tag would be $137.4 million plus the assumption of $3.6 million in debt when a sale for most of the assets was finally completed in September 2002. The proceeds were used to retire debt and invest further in ICO's polymers processing business. What remained of ICO's oil-field services unit was then sold to Permian Enterprises, Ltd., in July 2003 for $4 million.

ICO's reorganized business generated revenues of $206.6 million in fiscal 2003. Due to changes in accounting the company posted a net loss of $50.6 million for the year. In fiscal 2004 ICO reorganized its business into four geographical areas: ICO Americas, Bayshore Industrial, ICO Europe, and ICO Australasia. Revenues improved to $257.5 million in fiscal 2004, when the company returned to profitability, albeit modestly, recording net sales of $257,000.

NEW CEO HIRED: 2005

As fiscal 2005 came to a close in September 2005, ICO named A. John Knapp, Jr., as its new president and chief executive officer. The former president of Andover Group Inc., a Houston real estate investment and development company, took the reins of a company that increased revenues to $296.6 million and net income to $2.3 million in fiscal 2005. Under Knapp's leadership, ICO continued to grow in fiscal 2006 when the company netted $9.8 million on sales of $324.3 million.

Demand for ICO's products and services increased sharply in fiscal 2007, leading to an increase in revenues to $417.9 million and net income of $26.6 million. To take full advantage of this spike in demand, ICO expanded capacity in its Malaysia and Australia operations during fiscal 2007, and in the fourth quarter of the year it opened a new location in the United Arab Emirates. These additions helped ICO to grow revenues to $446.7 million in fiscal 2008. Due to higher operating production costs and other factors, however, net income fell to $15.3 million.

Also of concern in fiscal 2008 was a slow down at the Bayshore Industrial segment and ICO's Australian business. Growth in Brazil helped to offset this drop-off but in fiscal 2009 a global economic downturn led to a sharp decrease in demand. Sales dipped below $300 million for the year. To make matters worse, a collapse in resin prices reduced margins so that ICO recorded a net loss of $1.24 million in fiscal 2009.

COMPANY SOLD: 2009

In December 2009, two months after it completed fiscal 2009, ICO agreed to be acquired by Akron, Ohio-based A. Schulman, Inc., for $191 million in cash and stock. Schulman had first made overtures in the spring of 2009, prompting ICO's board to consider selling the company. Founded in 1928 in Akron by Alex Schulman, the company had its roots in rubber. Schulman bought and sold wholesale and scrap rubber, but was forced because of shortages during World War II to become involved in the scrap plastic business. Following the war Schulman left the scrap markets in favor of producing plastic compounds. The company then developed a niche in the 1960s by engineering plastics to meet customers' specific needs, allow Schulman to grow on the basis of quality rather than price. As a result, the focus was on organic growth rather than acquisitions.

It was not until the 1990s that Schulman began to aggressively pursue external growth. A French company, Diffusion Plastique, was acquired in 1991. In the mid-1990s Schulman completed a series of acquisitions to grow its domestic business. Overseas, the company opened plants in Mexico and Indonesia, and in 2000 acquired a plant in Italy. After a downturn in the economy at the start of the new century, Schulman resumed growth, opening plants in Poland and China as well as Akron. In 2009 the company announced plans to build a plant in India.

What made the acquisition of ICO an attractive acquisition to Schulman was that there was little overlap and that in a single stroke it could expand both its domestic and international operations. The Bayshore unit was especially attractive, because it built up Schulman's U.S. assets in the masterbatch market, producing a mix of additives used in coloring raw plastic. In Europe, ICO helped Schulman increase its ability to serve the rotational molding industry. The deal also increased Schulman's revenues by about 25 percent.

The sale of ICO to Schulman was delayed because ICO's board of directors insisted on a stock transaction, thus permitting its shareholders to benefit from the combined company. Schulman, on the other hand, was reluctant to dilute the stock of its shareholders. Eventually a compromise was found and payment was made with a mix of cash and stock. When the acquisition was completed in 2010 it marked the end of one chapter in ICO's history and the beginning of a new one that offered a good deal of hope for the future.

Ed Dinger

PRINCIPAL SUBSIDIARIES

Bayshore Industrial, L.P.; Courtenay Polymers Pty. Ltd.; ICO Europe B.V.; Soreco S.A.S.; Wedco Technology, Inc.

PRINCIPAL COMPETITORS

Kraton Polymers LLC; PolyOne Corporation; Total Petrochemical.

FURTHER READING

Durgin, Hillary, "ICO to Diversify with Wedco Purchase for $55 Million," *Houston Chronicle*, August 1, 1995.

Feger, Helene, "Acquisition Halted by Losses, ICO Says," *Dallas Morning News*, June 22, 1985, p. 2G.

"ICO Proposes Plan to Avoid Bankruptcy," *Dallas Morning News*, March 23, 1988, p. 2D.

Mella, "ICO Agrees to Sell Its Oilfield Services to Varco," *Midland Reporter-Telegram*, April 3, 2001.

Pearson, Anne, "ICO Cuts Costs to Ride Out Tough Times," *Houston Chronicle*, April 27, 1992, p. 6.

Smith, Jack Z., "ICO Leaving Fort Worth for Houston," *Fort Worth Star-Telegram*, February 12, 1991, p. 1.

Wooten, Casey, "Plastics Purchase Folds ICO into A. Schulman," *Houston Business Journal*, December 11, 2009.

Ingles Markets, Inc.

———————■———————

2913 U.S. Highway 70 West
Black Mountain, North Carolina 28711-9103
U.S.A.
Telephone: (828) 669-2941
Fax: (828) 669-3678
Web site: http://www.ingles-markets.com

Public Company
Incorporated: 1963
Employees: 18,600
Sales: $3.25 billion (2009)
Stock Exchanges: NASDAQ
Ticker Symbol: IMKTA
NAICS: 445110 Supermarkets and Other Grocery
    (Except Convenience) Stores; 311511 Fluid Milk
    Manufacturing

■ ■ ■

Ingles Markets, Inc., is a regional supermarket chain with nearly 200 stores in North Carolina, South Carolina, Georgia, Virginia, Tennessee, and Alabama. In addition to its Ingles banner, the company also operates several stores under the Sav-Mor name. Most Ingles stores are located in rural areas, small towns, or suburban communities within 280 miles of the firm's headquarters/distribution center in Asheville, North Carolina. Ingles Markets also owns a milk processing plant that supplies dairy products for sale in Ingles stores and other outlets. In addition, the firm owns 76 shopping centers, almost all of which contain an Ingles supermarket.

To provide one-stop convenience for busy consumers, Ingles also sells numerous nonfood items, from office supplies to health and beauty care items, and provides other services such as in-store pharmacies, gas stations, sit-down cafés, check cashing, takeout meals and deli items, floral shops, and video rentals. Ingles Markets sells national brands as well as private-label items. All stores are open seven days a week and many operate 24 hours a day.

ORIGINS

After working in the grocery business with his parents in Asheville, North Carolina, Robert P. Ingle started his first store in 1963 in his hometown. In that same year, the company began buying a significant part of its merchandise from Merchant Distributors, Inc. (MDI), a wholesale grocery distributor based in Hickory, North Carolina. MDI continued to provide mainly frozen foods, produce, and slow selling items not stockpiled by Ingles well into the new millennium.

Gradually Ingles opened new stores in the 1960s and 1970s. To support its expanded operations, Ingles Markets in 1978 built a new warehouse/distribution center in Asheville. From this 450,000-square-foot facility, the company shipped various items to its retail stores in North Carolina and neighboring states.

EXPANSION AND A PUBLIC OFFERING: 1980–89

In September 1982 Ingles Markets acquired its own milk plant. Purchased from Sealtest, the plant operated as a wholly owned Ingles subsidiary called Milkco, Inc. By 1996 it was North Carolina's second-largest milk processing and packaging plant. Milkco supplied 90 percent of the fluid milk for Ingles supermarkets. It also sold citrus, dairy, and bottled water items to various customers such as other grocery stores and food distributors. These non-Ingles buyers represented about 58 percent of Milkco's business by 1996.

Milkco's corrugated boxes for shipping milk and other products were another important aspect of its business. They protected the bottled goods from damage and kept them cold. According to Ingles's 1996 annual report, Milkco was "the only dairy processing plant in the Southeast with this capability." Milkco also was committed to using packaging that could be completely recycled.

In 1982 Ingles gained a new president and chief operating officer. Landy B. Laney had been an executive officer and director of Ingles since 1972. He would serve in his new capacity until 1996.

In the late 1980s Ingles Markets took some important steps to expand its operations. In December 1986 it sold 23 shopping centers to Atlanta's IRT Property Company for $50 million, although the book value on those properties was only $33 million. In turn, Ingles leased the same centers from IRT and continued to operate them. At the same time, Ingles maintained ownership of 38 other shopping centers, a result of Robert Ingle's personal involvement in choosing properties.

The following year Ingles used another method to raise money for its expansion. In September 1987 Ingles became a public corporation by selling its stock under the symbol IMKTA on the NASDAQ for $13 per share. Only Class A stock was offered to the public. Robert Ingle maintained control over the company by holding almost 75 percent of its Class B stock, which controlled company voting rights.

Using funds from the sale of its shopping centers and its stock offering, Ingles Markets opened new stores in the late 1980s. In 1989, for example, it opened 17 new stores to reach a total of 156 in North and South Carolina, Georgia, Tennessee, and Virginia.

OVERCOMING THE COMPETITION

According to *Food People* magazine, by 1990 Ingles enjoyed 45 percent of the grocery market in its Asheville base but had only 8 percent of the market in the state. All Ingles stores were west of Greensboro, leaving the eastern part of the state for other chains.

Food Lion, one of Ingles's main rivals, was a larger chain. For example, it planned to open about 100 new stores in 1990, several times the number planned by Ingles. Jack Ferguson, Ingles's chief financial officer, said in the March 1990 *Business North Carolina*, "We try to find our niche in the market. We don't go head to head with Food Lion or Bi-Lo or Winn-Dixie or Kroger where they've got the market share. We say we're price competitive, but we don't say we're a price leader."

To avoid directly confronting such larger chains, Ingles Markets concentrated on rural areas or small towns and suburbia, where there were fewer stores and thus less competition. In the late 1980s the company built its first stores in Atlanta's remote suburbs. Analysts pointed out that this strategy resulted in modest but consistent growth.

To differentiate itself from some of its competitors, Ingles used ads to remind consumers that it was owned entirely by Americans. Two competitors based in North Carolina, Food King and Bi-Lo, were owned largely by Europeans. Those ads probably were ineffective, since Food King and Bi-Lo gained more of the state's market share than did Ingles.

In any case, Ingles stock performance in the late 1980s reflected its relatively slow growth compared to its competitors. Its stock reached a high of $13.38 by the end of 1987 but then declined to about $9 per share by the end of the decade.

TAKEOVER RUMORS: 1990

In early 1990 a persistent rumor concerning Ingles Markets surfaced again. Wall Street speculation that Ingles would be acquired by Publix Super Markets of Lakeland, Florida, resulted in Ingles's stock increasing to its highest point in 52 weeks. However, both Publix and Ingles representatives and analysts familiar with those firms discounted the rumor.

By the end of fiscal 1990, at the end of September, Ingles reached a new landmark in its history. For the first time in its 27-year history, the company had over $1 billion in annual sales. An increase of 11.4 percent from 1989 sales of $903.8 million resulted in 1990 sales of $1.007 billion. However, net income declined 37 percent from $15.9 million to $10 million due mainly

KEY DATES

1963: Robert Ingle opens his first store in Asheville, North Carolina.

1978: Ingles Markets builds a new warehouse/distribution center in Asheville.

1982: The company acquires its own milk plant.

1987: Ingles Markets goes public.

1989: Seventeen new stores open during the year.

1994: Ingles Markets opens its first store in Alabama.

1995: A new produce warehouse is opened.

1996: Company opens its first MegaStore.

2000: Ingles Markets opens its first in-store pharmacy.

2008: Sales exceed $3 billion.

to the firm's sale of marketable equity securities.

Corporate sales continued to increase in fiscal year 1991, reaching a company record of $1.044 billion; net income was $10.7 million. Based on that performance, one of Ingles's stock holders demonstrated its confidence in the grocery chain by buying more stock. Merchant Distributors, Inc., in November and December 1991 purchased 122,500 shares of Ingles Class A shares, giving it a total of 270,000 shares, 6.3 percent of all Class A stock. In addition, Merchants owned 150,150 shares of Ingles Class B stock.

In January 1992 Lloyd Kanev, the author of Smith Barney's Inefficient Market Series, raised his rating of Ingles's stock from "Hold" to "Buy." Kanev stated in the *Insiders' Chronicle* of January 27, 1992, "As a potential strategic acquisition by another supermarket chain, the company … would be worth a fair premium to book value."

APPEALING TO CUSTOMERS: 1992

Ingles Markets in 1992 took several steps to improve its competitiveness and appeal to its customers. It tried a new ad campaign pushing what it called the "Ingles Challenge," which encouraged customers to do their own price comparisons, instead of the company printing comparative price lists in the newspaper. The chain also added in 1992 the increasingly popular 12-pack option to its private-label sodas previously available only in six-pack, two-liter, and three-liter sizes. Available by the Fourth of July weekend, the 12-pack was introduced to compete with discount and club stores.

By August 1992, 75 percent of the company's 160 in-store bakeries had changed their methods of preparing and presenting their baked goods. Instead of using premade frozen goods, it began using scratch/mix formulas for several items, including cookies and cakes. The frozen items were easy to order and then thaw at the store, but the quality improved when the store's own personnel prepared those items. To emphasize customers' desire to serve themselves, Ingles took its baked items from behind glass displays and placed them on flat tables.

Jim Owens, Ingles's new vice president over bakery-deli operations, began special cake promotions in 1992, which he had learned at his previous position at Safeway. By cutting prices during these sales, Ingles was able to increase its cake sales by as much as 30 percent.

In October 1992 Ingles announced it would reverse its 1986 deal with IRT by buying back the 23 shopping center properties it sold and then leased in 1986. It paid IRT $55.6 million for the 22 centers in North Carolina and one in Georgia.

In fiscal year 1992 Ingles's sales increased to $1.06 billion, but its net income dropped to $5.5 million, the lowest in several years. The chain reduced the number of its stores to 170. After a successful test in two stores, Ingles Markets in March 1993 announced it would introduce new drinkware sections in all of its 170 stores. It featured plastic glasses, tumblers, and bowls from April through September and then glass items from October through March. Prices on this merchandise were low enough to compete with the discount chains, particularly Kmart and Wal-Mart.

Also in March the company was fined $10,000 by the Georgia Department of Agriculture for repeated violations at 13 stores, including the presence of rodents and insects, outdated goods, and unsanitary equipment. State officials placed the 13 stores on probation for six months and said they would work with the firm to overcome those defects.

EXPANDING INTO ALABAMA: 1994

In fiscal year 1994 Ingles opened its first store in the state of Alabama. The Jackson, Georgia, store, one of the chain's first to feature new video releases, began operations in October 1994. The following month the firm added a new store in Black Mountain, North Carolina, just a few miles east of the corporate headquarters in Asheville.

The opening of the Morristown, Tennessee, store in summer 1995 illustrated an interesting trait of Ingles corporate culture. To gain firsthand knowledge of customers' opinions, Laney was there posing as a bagger. "The customer doesn't know me from you or anybody else," said Laney in the July 1995 *Progressive Grocer*. "So I know they're not trying to butter me up. ... The customers like the wide aisles in that store. I heard that more than anything." Chairman Robert Ingle also liked to participate in such store openings, a custom that employees liked because it gave them a sense of closeness to their leaders.

To deal with the challenge of growth, in 1995 Ingles created two new positions. Ed Kolodzieski, formerly with Tampa, Florida's Kash n' Karry for 18 years, became Ingles's first vice president of strategic planning. The company also created the new title of director of frozen foods.

NEW PRODUCE WAREHOUSE
OPENS IN 1995

The company took a major step forward in October 1995 when it opened its new produce warehouse in Asheville. In the December 11, 1995, *Supermarket News*, Robert Ingle stated, "We need this kind of facility to handle the needs imposed by our substantial and continuing growth." Vice president Ed Kolodzieski added, "We now have 100% control of the buying, warehousing and distributing process." Previously Ingles had purchased its fresh produce from Merchants Distributors. The new facility increased the company's ability to upgrade its quality control.

The new produce warehouse was part of an overall expansion of Ingles's warehouse/distribution center. The new 310,000-square-foot addition also contained sections for dry goods, meat, poultry, deli, and dairy products. The new warehouse sections brought the total size of the Asheville facility up to 760,000 square feet.

The Asheville warehouse/distribution center was managed and run by the Asheville firm of Thomas & Howard Company. Ingles used its fleet of 103 tractors and 438 trailers to ship merchandise to its retail stores, using truck drivers employed by Thomas & Howard.

In the 1990s many Americans emphasized eating more nutritious foods. Ingles Markets responded in several ways, including 1996 ads and special sales to encourage customers to eat frozen fruits and vegetables five times a day. In 1991 the Produce for Better Health Foundation, the National Cancer Institute, and the National Institutes of Health had started the Five-a-Day program. Following the suggestions of the American Frozen Food Institute, Ingles decided to stress the value of frozen foods that retain most of their vitamins and other nutrients. Ingles used quotes from the sponsors and the Five-a-Day logo in its promotionals.

The grocery chain in 1996 also used the National Frozen Foods Month of March to promote the consumption of all kinds of frozen foods. Ingles continued its past practice of running TV ads in the six states with at least one of its stores and also radio ads in North and South Carolina. The company also tried innovations such as a school sampling program and a kitchen-appliance sweepstakes to increase sales of frozen foods. The frozen food hoopla even included inflated penguins floating in the air and little airplanes pulling balloons reminding consumers of Frozen Foods Month.

THE LAUNCH OF THE
MEGASTORE: 1996

To provide more space for its goods and services, Ingles Markets on June 30, 1996, opened its first MegaStore, a 59,000-square-foot facility in the Atlanta suburb of Dacula. Soon other MegaStores were opened, including ones in Forsyth, Griffin, and Cleveland, Georgia; Hendersonville and Waynesville, North Carolina; Kingsport and Knoxville, Tennessee; and Boiling Springs, South Carolina.

Unlike the 42,000- and 52,000-square-foot stores opened several years earlier with two entrances, the new 54,000- and 59,000-square-foot MegaStores featured one major entrance to lead customers into a preferred shopping route. The first section they came to was a fresh foods section with three new Ingles offerings: freshly made pizzas, self-service rotisserie chicken, and chilled ready-to-eat prepackaged meals. Each new MegaStore also included a two-story sit-down café, a full-size bakery, a video section, a floral division, and various customer services such as check cashing, photocopying, gift certificates, and UPS and fax assistance.

The difference between these new stores and the older smaller format was "like night and day," said Neal Polaske, Ingles labor director in the September 2, 1996, *Supermarket News*. Robert Ingle added: "We are confident that our new look and schedule fits our program of continued growth and progressive changes to our stores. The go-ahead for any program is the response of our customers, and based on continuing sales increases, it is evident that our stores are being very well-received." The company's financial record for fiscal year 1996 confirmed Ingles's comment. Annual sales and income reached record highs of $1.473 billion and $20.7 million. On December 28, 1996, president and COO Landy Laney voluntarily retired at age 65. He was replaced by Vaughn C. Fisher, the company's former vice president for sales and marketing who had worked for Ingles for 24 years.

In 1997 Robert P. Ingle remained board chairman and CEO. His son Robert P. Ingle II served as vice president of operations. As the chain approached the new millennium, it continued to focus on serving its customers in the Southeast. As Ingle stated in the July 1995 *Progressive Grocer*, "We're going to enhance our concentration where we already are," instead of moving into new areas.

Ingles Market's prospects in the late 1990s were positive. With modern stores featuring computerized inventory, checkout, and even computerized work scheduling, the firm had made the necessary investments to remain on the cutting edge of the grocery business. In April 1997 the chain received the Retailer of the Year award from McNeil Consumer Products. Comparable store sales increased by 7.1 percent in 1999, which was the largest increase the company had seen over the past five years.

INGLES IN THE 21ST CENTURY

Ingles Markets entered the new millennium on solid ground despite fierce competition in the supermarket industry. In order to provide more services to its customers, the company opened its first in-store pharmacy at its location in Fletcher, North Carolina, in 2000 and also began offering fuel stations at this same location. A company executive explained the strategy to *Supermarket News* in 2000, "The better experience you provide to the customer, the more loyalty you can build."

During fiscal 2000, the company opened four new stores, remodeled a total of 11 stores, and closed two locations. Net income for the year grew by 12.5 percent over the previous year to $21.1 million, the largest net income in company history to that time.

The company focused on revamping nine of its stores while closing seven older locations during 2001. Five additional stores were shuttered in 2002. Ingles Markets focused on slow and steady growth during this period as larger competitors began eating into its market share. Instead of rapid expansion into new markets, the company opted to strengthen its existing stores while closing older and unprofitable locations. Four stores were closed in 2003 while four new stores opened their doors.

Ingles Markets secured its 40th consecutive year of net sales growth in fiscal 2004 and sales surpassed $2 billion for the first time that year. Robert Ingle II was named chairman that year while founder Ingle remained CEO.

At the same time, the company became the target of a Securities and Exchange Commission (SEC) investigation related to its accounting procedures for vendor allowances. As a result of the investigation, the company was forced to restate its earnings for fiscal 2002, 2003, and 2004 but the restatements had little impact on the company's bottom line. The company's chief financial officer resigned in 2005.

CONSISTENT SALES GROWTH: 2006 AND BEYOND

The company's strategy during this period appeared to be paying off. By focusing on controlling costs while expanding product offerings in its stores, Ingles Markets was securing impressive financial results. Net income rose by 60.3 percent over the previous year in fiscal 2006 to $42.6 million. Company sales grew by 14.9 percent over the previous year to $2.61 billion.

Net income continued its rise in 2007. The company opened a total of seven new and remodeled stores that year. According to the company, customers made over one million visits to its stores throughout the year. Sales exceeded $3 billion in 2008.

The company opened a store under the Sav-Mor banner in Greeneville, Tennessee, during 2009. The discount format was smaller than a traditional Ingles store and carried a limited selection of groceries, fresh meat, and produce. The company operated seven Sav-Mor stores in 2009.

Between 2008 and 2009, the company opened and remodeled a total of 22 stores. This growth took its toll on the company's profits but store sales continued their upward climb. Ingles Markets secured its 45th consecutive year of sales growth in 2009 when revenues reached $3.25 billion. Net income fell from $52.1 million in 2008 to $28.8 million for the year.

At this time competition was fierce and the faltering economy in the United States put pressure on Ingles Markets to keep prices low while offering its customers a better shopping experience than its competitors. While market conditions forced the company to slow its expansion efforts, it continued to eye new store development and existing store expansion and remodeling as necessary for its future growth. With 45 years of sales increases under its belt, Ingles Markets appeared to be on track for success in the years to come with founder Ingle at the helm as CEO and son Robert P. Ingle II as chairman.

David M. Walden
Updated, Christina M. Stansell

PRINCIPAL SUBSIDIARIES

Milkco, Inc.; Sky King, Inc.; Ingles Markets Investments, Inc.; Shopping Center Financing, LLC; Shopping Center Financing II, LLC.

PRINCIPAL COMPETITORS

Food Lion, LLC; Publix Super Markets, Inc.; Wal-Mart Stores, Inc.

FURTHER READING

Bennett, Stephen, "The Sweet Sound of the Big Ring," *Progressive Grocer*, July 1995, p. 88.

Boehning, Julie C., "Ingles Encourages Customers to Get 5 a Day from Frozens," *Supermarket News*, June 10, 1996, p. 31.

"Fisher Moves Up at Ingles Markets," *Supermarket News*, January 6, 1997, p. 6.

Hamstra, Mark, "Ingles Sees Profits Fall, Then Rise, after Accounting Changes," *Supermarket News*, February 7, 2005.

Harper, Roseanne, "Ingles' New Prototype Touts Deli, Food Service," *Supermarket News*, September 9, 1996, p. 23.

———, "Ingles Raises Size, Sales, Self-Service," *Supermarket News*, September 9, 1996, p. 56.

———, "'Meals to Go' Gets 'Go' Sign from Ingles Chainwide," *Supermarket News*, November 11, 1996, p. 29.

"Ingles Multifaceted Strategist," *Progressive Grocer*, November 1995, p. 12.

"Jingo Jingles for Ingles," *Business North Carolina*, March 1990, p. 68.

Moore, Amity, "Ingles Generates Sales with New Program Emphasis," *Supermarket News*, March 25, 1996, p. 39.

Redman, Russell, "Ingles Ice Cream Ads Heat Frozens Volume," *Supermarket News*, August 21, 1995, p. 25.

"SEC Probes Ingles Markets," *Drug Stores News*, December 13, 2004.

Springer, Jon, "Expenses for New Stores Sink Ingles' Q4 Profits," *Supermarket News*, December 14, 2009.

———, "Ingles Expands Discount Concept," *Supermarket News*, November 30, 2009.

Stickel, Amy I., "Ingles Opens Produce Warehouse," *Supermarket News*, December 11, 1995, p. 32.

"Store Development Costs Hit Ingles Markets Profits," *JustFood*, April 30, 2010.

Tibbits, Lisa A., "Ingles Extends Streak of Consecutive Gains," *Supermarket News*, January 2, 1995, p. 8.

Zimmerman, Susan, "Breakfast Is Cooking; Low-Fat Entries and General Convenience Are Keeping Sales of Frozen Breakfasts Hot," *Supermarket News*, June 21, 1993, p. 8A.

Zweibach, Elliot, "Sales Up, Profits Down at Ingles Markets," *Supermarket News*, August 15, 2005.

Ixia

———————— ■ ————————

26601 West Agoura Road
Calabasas, California 91302
U.S.A.
Telephone: (818) 871-1800
Fax: (818) 871-1806
Web site: http://www.ixiacom.com

Public Company
Incorporated: 1997 as Ixia Communications, Inc.
Employees: 1,073
Sales: $178 million (2009)
Stock Exchanges: NASDAQ
Ticker Symbol: XXIA
NAICS: 334515 Instrument Manufacturing for Measuring and Testing Electricity and Electrical Signals

■ ■ ■

A NASDAQ-listed company based in Calabasas, California, Ixia develops test systems that allow service providers, network managers, network equipment manufacturers, governments, and enterprises to validate the functionality, conformance, performance, and reliability of complex networks, devices, and applications. Ixia's highly scalable solutions generate, capture, characterize, and emulate network and application traffic, establishing definitive performance and conformance metrics. Ixia's test systems specialize in cutting-edge technology such as 4G-LTE, 10/40/100 Gigabit Ethernet, and use a wide range of industry-standard interfaces, including Ethernet, SONET, ATM, and wireless connectivity.

Ixia equipment can be purchased, leased, or rented for short-term projects. Ixia Education Services offers courses around the world, on-site and online, to teach customers how to make the best use of Ixia products. To keep pace with changes in the marketplace and pursue innovations in Internet protocol (IP), the company maintains Ixia Labs, headed by Errol Ginsberg, chief innovation officer, company founder, and chairman of the board.

ORIGINS

Errol Ginsberg was born and raised in South Africa, where he displayed a gift for electronics. Nevertheless, he initially studied to be a dentist after enrolling at the University of Witwatersrand in Johannesburg. He soon grew disenchanted with that choice and tried different engineering disciplines before electing to pursue a degree in electrical engineering to become involved in electronics and computers. After graduation he decided to move to California's Silicon Valley where there were more opportunities in high technology than in South Africa. Moreover, his home country was still saddled with a policy of apartheid that Ginsberg found untenable. He arrived in the United States at the age of 25 in 1981 with $4,000 in savings.

Ginsberg found work as an engineer with Imperial Technology. After three years he went to work for a young company, Tekelec, Inc., that produced telecommunications test equipment. In February 1996 he joined NetVantage Inc., a network equipment manufacturer, as vice president of engineering. Little more than a year later he decided to strike out on his own to take advantage of the growth in the Internet and to fill a perceived need for equipment to test network performance.

IXIA INCORPORATED: 1997

In May 1997 Ginsberg incorporated Ixia Communications, Inc., named for a flower native to South Africa. With $1.6 million in seed money from Jean-Claude Asscher, his former boss and chairman at Tekelec, and a short-term loan of $500,000, Ginsberg set up shop above a Mexican restaurant. The next several months were devoted to research and development as well as establishing ties to potential customers.

The company's first product, which began shipping in April 1998, was the Ixia 1600 chassis, featuring 4-port 10/100 Ethernet load modules and 2-port gigabit Ethernet load modules. Ixia became profitable within the first quarter of selling the product. Later in 1998 the company began shipping the Ixia 200 chassis and the Tcl/TK ScriptMate. Manufacturing was outsourced to third-party contract manufacturers and assembly companies, an approach that freed up capital for research and development.

More advances followed in 1999. Multiuser and real-time latency features were introduced, as was round-trip flow emulation and measurement. New products included Packet Over SONET OC12c/3c, the QoS Test Suite, the IP MultiCast Test Suite, and the gigabit over copper load module. During its first full year of product shipments, mostly to Cisco Systems, Ixia recorded sales of $24.5 million and net earnings of $4.8 million in 1999. Investments of $2.8 million in research and development in 1999 also led to further product introduction in 2000, including the Ixia 100 Qos Performance Tester with integrated GPS, the packet over SONET OC-48c, Ixia terabit router tester, and the cable modem automated test suite.

INITIAL PUBLIC STOCK OFFERING: 2000

The fast-growing Ixia moved to larger accommodations in April 2000, launched Ixia Europe Limited in the United Kingdom in July, and opened offices in Santa Clara, California, in September of that year. The company also filed to make an initial public offering of stock despite a severe downturn in the high-technology sector. The offering was completed in October 2000, netting Ixia $72 million. The opening share price of $13 quickly increased to $20 and continued to grow, eventually peaking at $36 in 2001.

Ixia expanded further in 2001, introducing a number of new products, including new routing protocol emulations, the 10GbE family of products, and Net Ops, the first comprehensive suite of hardware-software solutions for network monitoring, optimization, traffic engineering profiling, and security. Ixia also opened an office in Shanghai, China, in February of that year.

In November 2001 Ixia acquired Caimis Inc., a nearby company that developed network monitoring products. Its technology was then incorporated into Ixia's traffic engineering products to flag inefficient routes or data flows. Additionally, Caimis's geographic tools that translated IP addresses to graphical maps enhanced Ixia software used to detect denial-of-service attacks by allowing it to show service providers the parts of a network adversely impacted.

Sales increased to $77.2 million and net income improved to $9.75 million in 2001. A year later a slowdown in the economy and a decrease in telecommunications spending led to a decline in sales to $67.6 million and a dip in net income to $3.4 million. Nevertheless, the company did not cut back on its investment in research and development, spending $13.3 million in 2001 and $17.5 million in 2002. Also of note in 2002, Ixia acquired the ANVL product line from Empirix to add protocol conformance testing.

Ixia sought to become even more competitive in 2003 by adding software testing components. It acted as a distributor for Radview Software Ltd., whose products allowed Web sites to test their ability to handle strenuous network conditions. In July 2003 Ixia acquired its own network testing software, paying $17.5 million to NetQ Corp. for a perpetual license to its Chariot product line. The move broadened Ixia's customer base and pleased investors who had been punishing the price of Ixia stock but then bid up the price.

REACHING MORE CUSTOMERS

The addition of software products helped Ixia to increase revenues to $83.5 million in 2003 and net income to $8.7 million. Network equipment makers such as Cisco remained Ixia's core customers, but the company then made an effort to broaden its customer

KEY DATES

1997: Company is incorporated as Ixia Communications, Inc.
1998: First products ship.
2000: Company is taken public.
2008: Atul Bhatnagar is named CEO.
2009: Ixia acquires Catapult Communications and Agilent Technologies N2X product line.

base to financial services firms that could not afford to have their networks go down. Merrill Lynch became a customer, as did a number of corporations, including Northrop Grumman, Lockheed Martin, and Microsoft.

To secure business with government agencies that had their own mission-critical concerns, Ixia lured several sales engineers away from a competitor, Spirent Communications, and they led the charge in landing federal contracts. Government clients would include MIT Lincoln Laboratory, the Defense Information System Agency, the Joint Interoperability Test Command, and the U.S. Navy. As a result of these efforts, revenues continued to climb in 2004, approaching $117 million, while net income surged to $18.9 million. To maintain its technological edge, Ixia spent $25 million on research and development.

Revenues increased to $150.9 million and net income to $28.5 million in 2005. A year later sales increased to $180.1 million, but that was due to $25.9 million in deferred revenue that was reversed and recognized during the year. Net income fell to $13.5 million in 2006, partially the result of changes in the way stock options were accounted.

IXIA 3.0: 2007

Ixia entered a new stage in its development in late 2007, what the company called Ixia 3.0. On the one hand, it meant the transformation from a company that initially depended on basic traffic generation and analysis tools for 10 and 100 megabit speeds to the advanced test tools required by converged communications that delivered voice, video, and data over IP at speeds as fast as 10 gigabits per second. On the other hand, it meant a reorganization at the top ranks of management.

In September 2007 Atul Bhatnagar was named president and chief operating officer. He became chief executive officer in March 2008, succeeding Ginsberg who then became chairman of the board and served as

chief innovation officer for the newly formed Ixia Labs, created to drive further product development to keep the company on the cutting edge and competitive in a fast-changing marketplace.

Bhatnagar brought with him more than 20 years of experience. Born in India, he earned a degree in electrical and electronics engineering from the Birla Institute of Technology and Science in 1978. He went to work for Hewlett-Packard, holding a number of assignments in both Asia and North America, and led the development of the OpenView Wireless Network Management business. He then became vice president of Advance WebSwitching Products at Alteon Web Services, later acquired by Nortel. He was subsequently named general manager of Nortel's Enterprise Data Networks Division, which produced a full range of Secure Ethernet Switches, Enterprise Routers, Secure WLAN Solutions, and innovative IPSEC/SSL VPN offerings.

Bhatnagar took over a company that recorded $174.1 million in sales and net income of $7 million in 2007, but he had to contend with a softening economy that kept sales to a modest increase to $175.9 million in 2008. Ixia also recorded a net loss of $15.9 million. Nevertheless, Ixia continued to introduce innovative new products, such as 40 and 100 gigabit test solutions, developed in the Ixia Labs under the aegis of the company's founder.

To support growth Ixia also added new iSimCity executive briefing centers and customer proof-of-concept labs to its sales offices in Santa Clara and in Bangalore, India, where an office was opened a year earlier to expand Ixia's presence in the Asia Pacific region. Other centers were to follow elsewhere around the globe, allowing Ixia customers to use the company's professional services as well as to schedule third-party tests in the laboratory.

PAIR OF ACQUISITIONS COMPLETED: 2009

Ixia's balance sheet showed little growth in 2009, when revenues fell short of the $178 million mark while the company lost $44.2 million, but the company took steps to position itself for future growth. Ixia completed a pair of significant acquisitions. In June it paid $105 million for Catapult Communications, a maker of 3G and 4G wireless network test solutions that provided an excellent complement to Ixia's products that served wired networks. In October 2009 Ixia paid $44 million for Agilent Technologies' N2X Data Network Testing Product Line, a deal that included customers as well as research and development teams. Ixia and Agilent then joined forces to introduce the industry's first High-Definition Multimedia Interface (HDMI) 1.4 protocol test solution in early 2010.

The addition of Catapult and Agilent's N2X product line helped Ixia to post strong results in the first quarter of 2010. Revenues increased 67.1 percent over the same period the previous year to $62 million. Ixia appeared to be enjoying a resurgence in sales. With a broader slate of equipment and services, and a market that showed no signs of slowing down, Ixia was well situated for strong growth in the years to come.

Ed Dinger

PRINCIPAL SUBSIDIARIES

Ixia Europe Limited; Ixia Technologies Private Limited; Ixia (Beijing) Trading Company Limited.

PRINCIPAL COMPETITORS

Agilent Technologies, Inc.; Anritsu Corporation; Spirent Communications plc.

FURTHER READING

Berry, Kate, "Ixia's Diversification Results in Sales Growth for Its Test Tools," *Los Angeles Business Journal,* November 8, 2004, p. 30.

"Errol Ginsberg," *Telecommunications Americas,* December 2002.

"Ixia Names Atul Bhatnagar as New CEO," *Wireless News,* March 12, 2008.

Monroe, Robert, "Ixia IPO Off to Big Start in Trading," *Daily News of Los Angeles,* October 19, 2000, p. B2.

Rash, Wayne, "Ixia Launches True 10 Gigabit Ethernet Test Device," *eWeek,* May 24, 2007, p. 1.

Sturdevant, Cameron, "Deal Could Strengthen Traffic Tests," *eWeek,* August 25, 2003, p. 51.

Thuresson, Michael, "Ixia Reaches Yearly High Point with Acquisition of Software," *Los Angeles Business Journal,* July 14, 2003, p. 26.

J.D. Heiskell & Company

116 West Cedar Street
Tulare, California 93274
U.S.A.
Telephone: (559) 685-6100
Toll Free: (800) 366-1886
Fax: (559) 686-8697
Web site: http://www.heiskell.com

Private Company
Incorporated: 1906
Employees: 280
Sales: $3.1 billion (2008 est.)
NAICS: 311119 Other Animal Food Manufacturing

■ ■ ■

J.D. Heiskell & Company is a privately held grain and commodity trading firm based in Tulare, California. Trading offices are maintained in Elkhorn, Nebraska; Amarillo, Texas; and Minneapolis, Minnesota. Additional sales offices are located in Tulare and Ontario, California; Wiggins, Colorado; Wendell, Idaho; Portales, New Mexico; and Friona, Texas. Heiskell also operates feed mills in Tulare, Pixley, and Ontario, California; and Gooding, Twin Falls, and Wendell, Idaho. A corn flaking and rolling facility is operated in Mountain Home, Idaho.

The company focuses on the production of high value, best cost feed rations, and custom vitamin and mineral packages, and provides customers with nutrition consultation services. Transloading facilities in seven western states are used to export grains and other com-

modities to Mexico and markets in the Far East and Pacific Rim. In addition, the company operates the Heiskell's Feed Depot Retail Store in Visalia, California. In business since 1886, Heiskell is professionally managed but remains family owned.

ORIGINS

The founder of J.D. Heiskell & Company was Jefferson Davis Heiskell. He was born in August 1861 several months after the Civil War broke out and named for the president of the Confederacy. His father, a native of Virginia, had come to California in 1849 with a group of men from Tennessee to participate in the gold rush of northern California. He was one of the many who did not strike it rich but stayed in the state to farm and dabble in politics. After marriage, he settled in the town of Indian Diggins, California. As an adult, the younger Heiskell became a grain dealer in Stockton, California, employed by the Farmers Union Grain and Milling Co.

According to company sources Jefferson Heiskell was dispatched in 1886 to Tulare, California, to oversee the construction of a grain storage warehouse. Two years later he moved his family to Tulare to run the warehouse, which was well situated in the San Joaquin Valley along the Southern Pacific Railroad. He also bought grain from area farmers to be shipped north by rail to Stockton and San Francisco, and ran a mill operation.

When Farmers Union elected to exit the grain storage business, Heiskell bought the warehouse in 1906. He launched J.D. Heiskell & Company, setting up his office next to Tulare's telephone company. In 1912 he

COMPANY PERSPECTIVES

At heart, J.D. Heiskell & Co. is a family business, built on generations of dedication to the principles of excellence, innovation, accountability, professionalism and integrity.

took on a partner, Arthur Bulock, forming Heiskell and Bulock, to open a grain warehouse in Delano, California.

JOHN HEISKELL JOINS FIRM: 1919

Heiskell had two daughters, Elizabeth and Eleanor, and a son named John. Elizabeth was the first of the children to join the family business. After teaching school for a year in northern California, she returned to Tulare during World War I to help run the company. She would become office manager and secretary of the company, while her sister Lucy would eventually become a vice president. Their brother served in the U.S. Army in France during World War I, and after his discharge in 1919 he joined Heiskell & Bulock in Delano, where he worked for the next five years.

In 1926 Jefferson Heiskell opened a cotton mill next to the grain warehouse. A year later he died, and his son became president and owner of J.D. Heiskell & Company. John Heiskell then added to the cotton business by acquiring the Tulare Oil Milling Company, which extracted cottonseed oil. A warehouse was also added in the transaction and converted into a mechanized bulk feed plant.

Most of Heiskell's grain had been used by poultry operations. However, the dairy industry enjoyed rapid growth in Central California and after World War II the area dairies became the largest grain consumers. To better serve this important customer base, Heiskell added to its feed milling capabilities in the 1950s. In the following decade the company was one of the first in the feed industry to hire nutritional specialists to develop new dairy feeds. Along the way, Heiskell became involved in other ventures as well. The company owned Heiskell Farms and acquired the Tulare Hardware Company, which in 1966 was renamed Heiskell Hardware.

The 1950s also brought involvement in the family business from a third generation. In 1955 John Heiskell's son-in-law Dale W. Hillman joined the company at the behest of his father-in-law, who had no sons to

take charge of the company. In 1970 John Heiskell retired and Hillman assumed control. Two years later John Heiskell died at the age of 82, both of his sisters having passed away several years earlier. Under Hillman's direction Heiskell continued to grow as well as modernize. In 1972 a new computerized mill was constructed, one of the first of its kind in California.

THIRD GENERATION ASSUMES CONTROL: 1991

The extra production capacity of the renovated mill would be greatly needed in the 1980s when demand for feed increased significantly in the area. Because of a development boom in Southern California, many dairy farmers elected to sell their valuable real estate and move their dairy operations to the San Joaquin Valley, especially in Tulare County, which by the end of the 1980s boasted the largest concentration of dairy animals in the United States.

To meet an increasing demand for feed, Heiskell laid two miles of railroad tracks in 1989 and added six 100-foot concrete silos to its Tulare location to create a unit train operation that allowed the company to become a major buyer and shipper of midwest grains. In the meantime, another generation of the Hillman family became involved in the company. Scot Hillman, son of Dale Hillman and great-grandson of the founder, joined the family business in 1980 after earning degrees in history and communications from Stanford University. Over the next decade he worked in all facets of the operation, including several years as a commodities trader. In 1991 his father turned over day-to-day control, naming Scot Hillman president. Dale Hillman remained chief executive officer and chairman of the board, however.

Under Scot Hillman, the company increased its production capacity by 30 percent in 1992 with the acquisition of DeRaad Milling in Lemoore, California. Heiskell then grew sales by 40 percent in one stroke in 1995 when it reached a long-term agreement to manufacture feed for the members of Tulare-based Dairyman's Cooperative Creamery Association, which subsequently closed its own feed mill in town. By the end of the decade Heiskell's Tulare mill was the highest-volume single feed production facility in the United States, processing in excess of 500,000 tons of grain each year, 95 percent of which was dairy feed.

PM AG PRODUCTS DIVISIONS ACQUIRED: 2000

With the start of the new century, Heiskell reached a crossroads in its history. The time had come to either

```
┌─────────────────────────────────────────────┐
│                                               │
│              KEY DATES                        │
│                  ▪                            │
│  ─────────────────────────────────────────    │
│  1886:  Jefferson Davis Heiskell opens grain  │
│         warehouse in Tulare, California, for  │
│         employer.                             │
│  1906:  Heiskell acquires warehouse to form   │
│         J.D. Heiskell & Company.              │
│  1927:  Founder dies.                         │
│  1970:  John Heiskell retires and Dale        │
│         Hillman assumes control.              │
│  2000:  Grain division of PM Ag Products is   │
│         acquired.                             │
│  2008:  Revenues top $3 billion.              │
│                                               │
└─────────────────────────────────────────────┘
```

grow much larger in order to remain competitive or sell out. The company chose the former course and in April 2000 Heiskell acquired the grain division of PM Ag Products Inc., adding feed and grain milling operations in Ontario and Pixley, California; Ferndale and Granger, Washington; and Wendell, Idaho. Heiskell's production capacity then topped 1.5 million tons of feed per year, propelling Heiskell to the top ranks of the country's feed manufacturing companies. As a result, Heiskell bolstered its position in the dairy feed business in the San Joaquin Valley while gaining some geographic diversity. Revenues grew to more than $1 billion, earning Heiskell a place on the *Forbes* magazine list of America's largest privately held companies in 2002.

The new century also brought changes to the top ranks of management. Scot Hillman was named CEO in 2001, and he turned over the presidency to Duane A. Fischer, the first nonfamily member to hold the post. Fischer was well seasoned in the grain industry, having spent nearly three decades at Omaha, Nebraska-based Scoular Grain Co., where he served as CEO before his departure in 2000 at the age of 50. In search of a new challenge, he elected to move to California to work for Heiskell.

To spur further growth in the early years of the new century, Heiskell invested in a major upgrade at its Pixley site, replacing front-end loaders with equipment to allow for the mechanical mixing of ingredients. The facility became the highest producing feed mill in the United States. The Washington State mills in Granger and Ferndale were sold to Cargill, Inc., in 2003 as Heiskell looked to focus on new markets. In keeping with this strategy, the company formed a joint venture with J.R. Simply Land & Livestock in 2004 to build the world's largest grain rolling facility at that time in Mountain Home, Idaho.

EXPANDING PRESENCE

To gain a greater presence in the important Midwest market, Heiskell moved its commodity merchandising and accounting operation to a modern new facility in Elkhorn, Nebraska, in 2005. The company also expanded in the Southwest. Later in 2005 it acquired a feed manufacturing plant and grain elevator in Portales, New Mexico, followed a year later by the purchase of a storage and transloading facility located about 50 miles away in Friona, Texas. These operations laid the foundation for Heiskell's new Southwest Business Group.

Heiskell also continued to grow its business in other key regions. In 2006 it added a new 10,000-ton capacity storage barn in Bliss, Idaho, which allowed Heiskell to begin shipping unit trains of distillers dried grains and other products to Idaho customers. A similar commodity barn, albeit twice the size, was erected a year later near the Friona, Texas, operation. Later in 2007, in a move to strengthen its position in the Midwest, Heiskell opened a trading office in Minneapolis, Minnesota. Two of the new traders hired by the branch possessed international experience, which Heiskell leveraged to begin shipping feed commodities into Mexico as well as the Pacific Rim.

REVENUES TOP $3 BILLION: 2008

As a result of its expansion on a number of fronts, Heiskell increased annual sales to $1.92 billion in fiscal 2007, according to *Forbes*. A year later that amount increased more than 60 percent to $3.1 billion, resulting in a jump to number 139 on the *Forbes* list of top private companies in the United States. Although a downturn in the economy hampered business in 2009, Heiskell continued to pursue an expansion program. It added to its Southwest Business Group with the opening of a new regional office in Amarillo, Texas. Early in 2010 Heiskell acquired the Land O'Lakes Purina Feed blending facilities in Twin Falls and Gooding, Idaho, to grow its direct dairy-producer business in Idaho and northern Utah. Heiskell also received a license to continue to blend proprietary Land O'Lakes Purina Feed products for its customers in the area.

As the decade progressed there were further management changes. In 2007 Scot Hillman succeeded his father as chairman of the board, while turning over the CEO post to Fischer. There was no doubt, however, that the Hillmans planned to keep ownership in the family. Scot Hillman's son, named Jefferson Davis, was in his early 20s and being groomed to one day take charge of the company. The company had enjoyed exceptional growth in the past decade and there was every reason to believe that the future held further promise.

Ed Dinger

PRINCIPAL SUBSIDIARIES

J.D. Heiskell Holdings LLC; Heiskell's Feed Depot Retail Store.

PRINCIPAL COMPETITORS

Ag Processing Inc., A Cooperative; Archer Daniels Midland Company; Cargill, Incorporated.

FURTHER READING

Howie, Michael, "Heiskell to Buy PM Ag's Feed, Grain Milling Business," *Feedstuffs*, April 24, 2000, p. 1.

"J.D. Heiskell: We Sell Feed," *Valley Voice*, May 17, 2006.

Jordon, Steve, "Family-Owned California Grain Firm Taps Nebraska Expertise," *Omaha World-Herald*, August 25, 2005.

Mitchell, Annie R., *A Modern History of Tulare County*, Visalia, CA: Ltd. Eds. of Visalia, 1974, 203 p.

Palmer, Joshua, "J.D. Heiskell and Co. Acquires Area Feed Facilities," *Twin Falls (ID) Times-News*, January 5, 2010.

Pollock, Dennis, "Celebrating 120 Years," *Fresno Bee*, February 17, 2006, p. 1.

———, "J.D. Heiskell Spans 116 Years," *Fresno Bee*, April 6, 2002, p. 7.

Jiangsu Shagang Group Company Ltd.

Jin Feng Zhang
Jiagang, 215625
China
Telephone: (+86 0512) 5856 8872
Fax: (+86 0512) 5855 1627
Web site: http://www.sha-steel.com

Private Company
Incorporated: 1995 as Jiangsu Shagang
Employees: 26,700
Sales: CNY 146.3 billion ($21.42 billion) (2009)
NAICS: 331111 Iron and Steel Mills

■ ■ ■

Jiangsu Shagang Group Company Ltd. is China's leading privately held steel producer, with a total production capacity of more than 34 million tons per year at the beginning of 2010. This ranks Shagang among China's top four steel producers, and, with revenues of CNY 146 billion ($21.4 billion) in 2009, as the 35th-largest company overall. Founded in 1975, Shagang has grown especially since launching an acquisition strategy in 2006. As a result, the company had acquired a number of other, largely Jiangsu Province-based steel producers, including Anyang Yongxing, Huigang Special Steel, Jiangsu Xixing, and, in early 2010, Xing Rui Special Steel. The company is also the largest shareholder in Yonggang Group, and controls Australian iron ore mining group Grange Resources. Jiangsu Shagang is led by Chairman Shen Wenrong, a cofounder of the company and its controlling shareholder.

CHINESE STEEL INDUSTRY BACKGROUND

China's steel industry long struggled to keep up with the steadily rising demand spurred by the Communist government's ambitious industrial policies in the 1960s and 1970s. While this era saw the rise of a number of national, and even global champions, their output remained insufficient to cover the country's needs. In order to fill the gap, large numbers of small-scale "backyard" steel companies were created, generally by local and regional governments. These companies, however, tended to produce low-quality pig iron.

The Chinese government made several attempts to shutdown these producers and centralize control of the steel industry. Into the 1970s, the government also began importing more modern steel production technology from Western and Japanese producers, helping to raise both output levels and quality. The government's steel industry policies, however, remained subject to the country's political situation as a whole. During times of political instability, such as the struggle for power following the death of Chairman Mao, steel production suffered.

As a result, China's total steel output barely topped 30 million tons by the middle of the 1970s. During the decade, the growing pressure toward economic reform culminated in the new Open Door policies inaugurated by the Deng Xiaoping government. The promise of a new boom in the country's industrial development further heightened the need for dramatic increases in steel output. The government responded, calling for the

KEY DATES

1975: The predecessor to Jiangsu Shagang is established by a group of Zhangjiagang entrepreneurs in Jiangsu Province.

1995: The company changes its name to Jiangsu Shagang.

2001: Jiangsu Shagang goes private; purchases and transfers the Hoesch steel mill from Germany to Zhangjiagang.

2006: The company completes its first major acquisition, of Huigang Special Steel.

2010: Jiangsu Shagang acquires Jiangsu Xixing and announces plans to raise its total production to 30 million tons per year.

country's production to rise to 80 million tons into the 1980s.

STEEL START-UP IN 1975

Many of China's economic reform policies hinged on the decentralization of the country's economy. While Beijing continued to set the tone for the country's economic growth, much of the actual implementation of these policies fell to the country's local and regional governments. Many of these governments encouraged the development of their own steel industries, backing the creation of a new generation of primarily small-scale steel producers. Into the end of the 1970s, China counted more than 800 steel companies.

Jiangsu Province became one of the first and largest beneficiaries of the new economic reforms. This province ultimately emerged as China's second-richest province, after Guangdong, near Hong Kong. The Jiangsu government had already funded the launch of a number of steel producers, such as Qinjiang Iron and Steel Works (later Jiangsu Huaigang), founded in 1970.

Much of the growth of the province's steel industry occurred at the local level, however. In 1975, for example, a group of local entrepreneurs joined together to found their own steel company in Zhangjiagang, in the south of Jiangsu Province. The company's beginnings were extremely modest, based on an initial capital base of just 450,000 yuan (roughly $54,000). Among the company's founders was Shen Wenrong, then 29 years old, who later emerged as the group's leader.

Shagang (the company officially changed its name to Jiangsu Shagang only in 1995) succeeded in building

its first electric-arc furnace into the early 1980s. By 1984, Shagang had joined the legions of small-scale steel producers that appeared in China during this decade. Led by Shen, however, Shagang put into place its own ambitious growth plan. The group's willingness to turn to the West for technology formed a major part of Shagang's strategy from the late 1980s. This strategy resulted in the company completing a number of purchases of cutting-edge equipment and technologies from the United States, the United Kingdom, Switzerland, and Germany.

CHANGING OWNERS IN 2001

Shagang also sought out partnerships with foreign steel producers. This led the company to team up with South Korea's Pohang Iron and Steel (also known as POSCO), in 1996. The two companies formed Zhangjiagang Pohang Stainless Steel in 1996, building a factory capable of producing 400,000 tons of stainless steel per year. Further investments at the factory raised its total capacity to 600,000 tons by the middle of the next decade. The joint venture also expanded to include a galvanizing plant, with a yearly output of 150,000 tons.

Shagang's own production increased steadily through the 1990s and by the turn of the century had topped 4.5 million tons of rolled steel by 2001. Shagang set its sights on joining the ranks of China's major steel producers, with plans to raise its production past 20 million tons per year.

In the meantime, China's total steel output was in the midst of a major growth phase. Into the late 1990s, the country's total steel output had risen to 100 million tons. By 2003, steel production in China had doubled, topping 200 million tons, more than the total output of the United States and Japan combined. Another 50 million tons of steel production capacity were expected to come online by 2005. This dramatic growth had a number of consequences, including driving up the prices of iron ore, as well as global shipping rates. These factors led the Chinese government to attempt to rein in further expansion of the country's steel industry.

The government began putting pressure on regional and local governments to reduce their investments in expanding their steel capacity. A number of provinces, including Jiangsu, began selling their steel assets to a series of management buyouts. Jiangsu Shagang itself changed its ownership status in 2001, when Shen Wenrong led the company's buyout. Shen himself gained a 17 percent stake in the company directly, while the Shagang's employees acquired 35 percent. The company claimed to be the largest privately held steel company in China. Nonetheless, parts of the Chinese government retained an interest in the company, including 25 percent held by Jiangsu SASAC, and another 23 percent held by the Shagang's own labor union, itself controlled by the Communist Party. The company's hopes to go public were dashed, however, when the Jiangsu government decided to give the province's stock listing quota to rival Nanjing Steel Co. instead of to Shagang.

DOUBLING CAPACITY IN 2002

As a more-or-less private company, Shagang was better able to resist the central government's attempts to slow down the steel industry's growth. The company continued to benefit from the Jiangsu government's willingness to approve new expansion, despite the concern by the State Development and Planning Commission (SDPC) that the sector approached what it considered a level of 'overinvestment.' More importantly, Shagang could rely on the region's banks, as these began seeking new investment opportunities, especially among nongovernmental enterprises into the new decade.

Shagang's own investment interest turned toward establishing itself as a major player in the higher-end and higher-quality specialty steel categories. Among the most important of these was the high-end steel slab segment, used in the manufacture of automobiles. The company was unable to rely on its own technology for this, however. At the time, very few Chinese steelmakers were capable of producing high-quality automotive steel. Shagang took a first step in this new direction in 2001, when it added a new one-million-ton per year special steel production line based in technology and equipment brought in from Switzerland and Germany. This project, completed in 2002, cost the company $42 million.

Shagang by then had spotted a new opportunity both to boost its specialty steel technology sector and to double its own steel capacity. In 2001, ThyssenKrupp, in Germany, announced its plans to sell its Dortmund-based Hoesch steel mill. That mill was a major supplier to Mercedes Benz and Volkswagen, among other automakers. The company also had launched an automobile production joint venture in Shanghai, near Shagang's Zhangjiagang base.

Shen flew to Germany, where he successfully negotiated not only the purchase of the Hoesch mill, but also a continued supply contract for the Shanghai automotive plant. The company then raised eyebrows when it announced that it intended to dismantle the Hoesch mill and rebuild it in Zhangjiagang. The cost of the mill was just $49 million, while the rebuilding process, which included a substantial redesign and upgrade, cost $2.6 billion. Nonetheless, Shagang easily

beat original forecasts that the process would required eight years and more than $4 billion before the start of production. Instead, Shagang's new plant was fully operational in just four years.

ACQUISITION DRIVEN FROM 2006

The middle of the decade brought new challenges for the company. The company found itself affected by the scandal involving another privately held Jiangsu company, Tieben Cast Iron Steel Co. Tieben, founded in 2000, had launched construction of a new 8.4-million ton steel mill. This project came to halt, however, when investigators charged the company with the illegal takeover of nearly 1,700 hectares of farmland. The resulting scandal cast a pall over the entire privately held steel sector. Over the next two years, large numbers of the country's small and midsized companies went bankrupt.

Shagang fared better than others, but remained restricted by the SDPC's new directives, which emphasized the growth of the companies large-scale, state-owned steel companies. As part of the new directives, privately held companies were forced to place new expansion projects on hold. Companies were also barred from allowing foreign companies to acquire a majority of their shares, scuttling a planned linkup between Shagang and POSCO.

Instead, Shagang instituted a new acquisition-based strategy in order to gain scale. The company began acquiring stakes in a number of other steel companies in Jiangsu Province, a strategy encouraged by the Jiangsu government. The company's first major acquisition came in 2006, when it acquired more than 90 percent of Jiangsu Huaigang Iron and Steel Co. Ltd, the largest steel producer in northern Jiangsu. The addition of Huaigang boosted Shagang's production by another three million tons. Following the merger, the company launched a major expansion of Huaigang, converting its production to specialty steels.

Shagang looked beyond Jiangsu for its next purchase. In September 2007 the company paid CNY 2 billion to acquire an 80 percent stake in Yongxing Steel Co., the largest privately held steel producer in Henan Province. This purchase, along with a new 2.5-million-ton expansion in development by Yongxing, boosted Shagang's annual production by another one million tons. By the end of that year, Shagang had completed another major acquisition of 25 percent of Yonggang Group, also in Jiangsu and located just 10 kilometers from Shagang. This purchase raised the company's total yearly production by another five million tons.

CHINA'S LARGEST PRIVATE COMPANY IN 2010

Shagang continued its buying spree into 2008, acquiring a 51 percent stake in Jiangsu Xinrui Special Steel Co. Ltd. With an annual production of just 300,000 tons per year, that company remained a minor player in the steel industry. On the other hand, Xinrui, which had been founded in 2003, had been appointed to take over the operations at the Tieben mill. In this way, Shagang gained access to Tieben's own production, which had topped 1.2 million tons per year. Shagang promised to invest in the Tieben mill in order to expand it to its originally planned capacity. These additions helped boost Shagang's total production past 25 million tons by the end of 2008, placing the company firmly among the ranks of China's largest steel producers.

Into the end of the decade, Shagang focused on solidifying its integrated operations. The company launched an effort to reduce its reliance on foreign iron ore suppliers, setting up a mining subsidiary in Australia. In 2008, that company merged with Australia's Grange Resources, giving Shagang control of the Savage River mine in Tasmania, with iron reserves of 131 million tons, and the Southdown Mine, in Western Australia, with reserves of 388 million tons. By 2010, Shagang's mining operations already produced three million tons of iron ore, and the company planned to raise its production to 10 million tons by 2013.

Shagang also boosted its technology base, spending $66 million to build the Shagang Iron and Steel Research Institute. As Shen told *China Daily*: "Without its own core technologies, Shagang cannot become one of the best steelmakers in the world. Though our production capacity is now approaching that of South Korea, our research and development capabilities still lag far behind our Korean counterparts."

Shagang in the meantime continued seeking new steel expansion opportunities as well. This led the company to acquire Jiangsu Xixing Group Co., Ltd., adding another one million tons to its total production. At the same time, Shagang continued to expand its production elsewhere, promising to top 30 million tons by the end of the year. Shagang also formed two strategic partnerships in 2010. The first took the form of a strategic synergy and cooperation agreement with Baosteel Group. The second, with China National Coal Group, helped ensure the company's fuel supply. In just a decade, Jiangsu Shagang had risen from a minor regional player to become one of the largest steel producers in China, and in the world.

M. L. Cohen

PRINCIPAL SUBSIDIARIES

Anyang Yongxing Co. Ltd.; Grange Resources Ltd. (Australia); Huaigang Special Steel Co. Ltd.; Jiangsu Xixing Group Co., Ltd.; Xing Rui Special Steel Co. Ltd.; Yonggang Group (25%).

PRINCIPAL DIVISIONS

Steel Production; Scrap Metal Recycling; Iron Ore Mining.

PRINCIPAL COMPETITORS

Apeejay Surrendra Group; ArcelorMittal; Baoshan Iron and Steel Company Ltd.; BHP Billiton Ltd.; Cargill Inc.; JFE Holdings Inc.; Jiangsu Huaiyin Steel Group Company Ltd.; Kosaya Gora Iron Works Joint Stock Co.; Libyan Iron and Steel Co.; Nippon Steel Corp.; Xingtai Iron and Steel Corporation Ltd.

FURTHER READING

Chan, Carol, "Overseas Listing Still an Option for Shagang," *South China Morning Post*, January 5, 2009.

"China's Baosteel, Shagang Strike Cooperation Deal," *ADP News China*, February 24, 2010.

"China's Shagang Group to Buy Stake in Australian Miner Grange," *AsiaPulse News*, August 20, 2009.

Gong Jing, "Shagang the Integrator," *Caijing Magazine*, February 25, 2008.

———, "Shagang's Rise," *Caijing Magazine*, February 25, 2008.

Jones, Bob, "Shagang Aims to Grow through Acquisitions," *American Metal Market*, October 11, 2007, p. 12.

"Shagang 2010 Steel Output Targets to 30 Million Tonnes," *TendersInfo*, February 4, 2010.

"Shagang Building 3.5M-Tonne Hot-Rolling Mill," *American Metal Market*, January 24, 2008, p. 13.

"Shagang Eyes Henan Steel and Coke Industries for Investment," *Russia & CIS General Newswire*, January 29, 2010.

"Shagang Hoping for Overseas Sales," *Business Daily Update*, January 7, 2009.

"Shagang to Focus on Innovation and Mergers Rather than Expanding Production," *China Business News*, September 4, 2006.

"Shagang to Raise Steel Product Quality to Replace Imports," *China Business News*, October 14, 2009.

"Shen Wenrong on Course to Become China's Mittal?" *China Stakes*, July 13, 2009.

"Shen Wenrong: The Steel Industry Giant," *China Daily*, October 19, 2007.

John Keells Holdings plc

PO Box 76, 130 Glennie Street
Colombo, 2
Sri Lanka
Telephone: (+94 011) 230 6000
Fax: (+94 011) 230 7087
Web site: http://www.keells.com

Public Company
Incorporated: 1901 as E. John & Company
Employees: 10,501
Sales: LKR 41.02 billion ($359 million) (2009)
Stock Exchanges: Colombo
Ticker Symbol: JKH
NAICS: 551112 Offices of Other Holding Companies;
    721110 Hotels (Except Casino Hotels) and Motels

∎ ∎ ∎

John Keells Holdings plc (JKH) is Sri Lanka's largest publicly listed company, and one of the country's oldest, tracing its history back to the 1870s. JKH operates as a holding company with diverse interests both in Sri Lanka and abroad. The company operates through six primary divisions: Transportation, Leisure, Property, Consumer Foods and Retail, Information Technology, and Financial Services.

The Transportation division includes port operations, including a major stake in the South Asia Gateways Terminal, as well as marine bunkering, shipping, logistics, and airport and airline services operations. Companies in this division include Lanka Marine Services, John Keells Logistics, and Mack Air.

This division, which accounted for 30 percent of the group's revenues in 2009, operates in Sri Lanka, the Maldives, and India. Through its Leisure division, JKH is the leading hotel operator in Sri Lanka and the Maldives, where it owns seven hotels and four hotels, respectively, operating under the Cinnamon and Chaaya brands. The company claims to operate 40 percent of all luxury-class hotels in Sri Lanka. The Leisure division, which includes subsidiaries such as Walker Tours and Serene Holidays, contributed 19 percent to the company's sales in 2009.

JKH's Consumer Foods and Retail (CF&R) division operates the Keells Super supermarket network, and is also a major Sri Lankan producer of beverages, meat products, ice cream and frozen confectionery, and convenience foods both for the domestic and export markets. This division includes Keells Food Products and Ceylon Cold Stores. CF&R added 27 percent to group sales in 2009. Financial services, including stakes in Union Assurance and National Trust Bank, added 11 percent to sales, while Information Technology and Property accounted for 5 percent and 3 percent, respectively. JKH also remains connected to its historic operations in tea brokering and trade. The company is listed on the Colombo Stock Exchange, and is led by CEO and Chairman Susantha C. Ratnayake. JKH's revenues reached LKR 41.02 billion ($359 million) in 2009.

BRITISH TRADE OUTPOST ORIGINS

John Keells Holdings (JKH) began with the arrival in the second half of the 19th century of two English

COMPANY PERSPECTIVES

Our Corporate Vision: Building businesses that are leaders in the region. Our Values: We are passionate about changing constantly, reinventing and evolving, striving to get things right the first time, doing the right things always, constantly raising the bar, fostering a great place to work, building strong relationships based on openness and trust.

brothers, George and Edwin John, to what was then the British colony of Ceylon. By that time, Ceylon had developed into a major center of British trade, giving rise to a community of produce brokers shipping crops, including coffee, fruits, spices, and other goods back to England. George John came to Ceylon first, setting up the family's first business there. His brother Edwin arrived sometime later, in 1870, and joined his brother's business.

At that time, the Johns established an office in Kandy, in the Central Province, then the main plantation and trade center in Ceylon. Shortly thereafter, the brothers brought a nephew, W. G. John, into the business, and opened an office in Colombo. That partnership soon dissolved, however. Instead, in 1878 Edwin John went into business for himself, establishing E. John on Colombo's Upper Chatham Street.

John struggled through his first decade in business, in part because he operated independently of Mincing Lane in London. Mincing Lane had long served as the hub of much of British colonial trade, particularly in tea and spices. Ceylon's plantation and trade sectors had largely focused on coffee through much of the 19th century. By the 1880s, however, demand for coffee had waned as tea consumption in the British Empire soared.

In 1890 John brought in a new partner, Herbert Tarrant, who had established a successful career as a tea taster for a prominent Mincing Lane tea buyer. With Tarrant on board, E. John began to grow quickly, adding several more partners by 1895. These included A.C. Rogers, who joined in 1892, Reginald John in 1895, Lionel Ottley Leefe, who joined the company in 1895 and became a partner in 1901, and C. E. Haslop, also in 1901. In that year, the company became known as E. John & Company. By then E. John had established itself as a major trader in tea, as well as rubber and other commodities.

POST-INDEPENDENCE MERGERS

Ceylon's independence in 1948 prompted a restructuring of the country's trade sector. E. John joined in this restructuring, merging its operations with two other prominent tea brokers, Geo. White & Company, and Wm. Jas. and Hy Thompson & Company, both based in London. E. John then expanded its own name to become E. John, Thompson, White & Company. At the same time, E. John hired on two Ceylonese for the first time, starting as assistants, beginning the company's transition from a British-led company to a fully Sri Lankan company. (Ceylon became known as Sri Lanka after 1972.)

E. John's transition toward the modern-day John Keells Holdings gained momentum at the end of the 1950s, when the company merged with two other prominent brokers, Keell & Waldock Ltd., and E. John Thompson, founded at the dawn of the 20th century. The merger, launched in 1959 and completed by 1960, represented the largest merger in the country's trading industry to date. The new company became known as John, Keell, Thompson White Ltd.

In the next decade the future JKH began laying the foundation for its growth into Sri Lanka's largest diversified conglomerate. Sri Lanka's popularity as a tourism destination led the company to enter that industry, with the purchase of Walkers Tours and Travels (Ceylon) Ltd. in 1973. That company was one of the leaders in the domestic tourism market. The following year, the company reincorporated as a rupee-quoted public company and changed its name to John Keells Ltd.

Soon after, John Keells acquired a majority stake in the Mackinnons Mackenzie Group of Companies, completing the purchase in 1974. The origins of Mackinnons Mackenzie dated to the colonial era, when the group acted as a shipping agent for both the P&O and British Steam Navigation companies. Mackinnons Mackenzie had later expanded into the cargo forwarding and travel and tourism industries as well. John Keells also began investing in Sri Lanka's hotel sector toward the end of the 1970s, forming the basis for its future Leisure division.

DIVERSIFICATION STRATEGY DEVELOPED

As the company developed its diversification strategy, it also reorganized its structure. This process started in 1978, when the company created a new company, John Keells Holdings Ltd. (JKH), as the holding company for all of its operations. In 1986 JKH went public, listing its shares on the Colombo Stock Exchange. This offer-

KEY DATES

■

1870: Edwin John joins his brother's trading company in Ceylon (Sri Lanka).

1878: Edwin John establishes his own trading house in Colombo, called E. John.

1901: The company incorporates as E. John & Company.

1948: E. John merges with Geo. White & Company, and Wm. Jas. and Hy Thompson & Company, forming E. John, Thompson, White & Company.

1960: Three-way merger creates John, Keell, Thompson White Ltd.

1974: The company changes its name to John Keells Ltd.

1991: John Keells Holdings (JKH) acquires Whittalls group.

1996: The company makes its first international expansion, acquiring a hotel in the Maldives.

2003: JKH acquires Asian Hotels; the South Asia Gateway Terminal (SAGT) is completed.

2009: JKH raises its stake in SAGT to 42 percent; the company rebrands its logistics operations as John Keells Logistics.

ing was the exchange's largest to date. In 1994 JKH became the first Sri Lanka company to achieve a listing on a foreign exchange, when it began selling global depositary receipts on the Luxembourg Stock Exchange.

By then, JKH had begun a new period of transition, displaying the willingness to explore new high-growth sectors that would allow it to maintain its position as Sri Lanka's largest publicly held conglomerate. A major milestone for the company came in 1991, when it bought the Whittalls Group of Companies. This deal, the largest ever in Sri Lanka at the time, brought three major companies into the JKH fold. The first of these was Ceylon Cold Stores, one of Sri Lanka's largest food companies, with leading positions in the production of carbonated soft drinks and ice cream. Whittalls also controlled Ceylon Holiday Resorts, which included the Bentota Beach and Coral Gardens hotels. Lastly, JKH also entered the insurance market through a major stake in Union Assurance, launching the company's financial services division.

JKH quickly followed the Whittalls deal with a number of new investments. The company formed a joint venture with DHL International, forming DHL

Keells, Sri Lanka's first express parcel delivery operator, in 1992. The group also added a restaurant division, which succeeded in winning the Pizza Hut franchise for Sri Lanka in 1993. In the middle of the decade the company took steps to expand its transportation and logistics businesses, setting up a joint venture with P&O Nedlloyd to act as that company's shipping agent in Sri Lanka. By 1995 JKH had added Trans-Ware Logistics to operate a container depot in partnership with Singapore's Keppel Group and the Malaysian International Shipping Corporation.

FOREIGN MOVES

JKH launched its first investment in the plantation sector in 1995, forming a joint venture to acquire stakes in Kegalie and Maskeliya plantations, representing 42 estates with a combined total surface of more than 20,000 hectares of tea and rubber plantation. The company then formed its own company, Keells Plantation Management Services, which complemented these holdings with a controlling stake in the 12,000-hectare Namunukula Plantations in 1997.

JKH had completed its first foreign acquisition by then, buying the 80-room Velidhu Resort Hotel in the Maldives in 1996. JKH expanded its presence in the Maldives market at the end of the decade, buying up the luxury bungalow complex, Hakura Island Resort. The company extended its shipping agent operations in India in the next decade, setting up the Matheson Keells Enterprises (Pvt) Ltd. joint venture in 2000. The company then established Mack Air Services in the Maldives, providing ground services to such airlines as American Airlines, Jet Airways, and Gulf Air.

In 1998 the company formed a partnership creating Nations Trust Bank (NTB), which then took over the Colombo branch of Hong Kong-based Overseas Trust Bank. The company also became the leader of the consortium developing the $1 billion South Asia Gateway Terminal (SAGT) at the Colombo Port's Queen Elizabeth Quay. JKH became SAGT's lead shareholder, with a 26.5 percent stake.

HOTEL LEADER IN 2004

By the end of the 20th century, the company's plantation operations had become its largest, generating 38 percent of total group revenues. The food and beverage market came next, accounting for 20 percent, while the company's leisure holdings and transportation operations represented 14 percent, and 8 percent, respectively. The company's total revenues had also grown strongly during the decade, more than doubling from LKR 4.5 billion in 1995 to nearly LKR 10.5 billion by the end of 2000.

JKH continued to seek new expansion opportunities. This led the company to the purchase of a 60.5 percent stake in Asian Hotels Corporation in September 2003. The LKR 4 billion ($40 million) deal represented the largest carried out through the Colombo Stock Exchange to date. By October of that year, JKH had raised its holding in Asian Hotels Corporation to 84 percent. That company, renamed Asian Hotels & Properties, added two five-star hotels, the Colombo Plaza and the Trans Asia, to the group's existing portfolio. As a result, JKH claimed a 40 percent share of Sri Lanka's luxury hotel market, and also became the country's leading hotel group in the three- to five-star hotel classes.

In 2004 the company restructured its hotel and leisure holdings into a new subsidiary, John Keells Hotels Ltd. The company then completed several new hotel and resorts deals through the rest of the decade. These included the acquisition of an 80 percent stake in Yala Village Hotel in 2005, and the leases on two Maldives resorts, the Dhonveli Beach and Spa and the Ellaidhoo Tourist Resort, in 2006. The company also launched its own hotel brands in that year, Cinnamon Hotels & Resorts and Chaaya Hotels & Resorts. The first Cinnamon resorts opened in Alidhoo Island in the Maldives in 2007. By the end of the decade, the company had completed a public offering of John Keells Hotels, selling an initial 7 percent. In March 2010, as the company announced plans to develop hotel properties on Sri Lanka's east coast, the company launched a new share offering in the company, raising LKR 3.6 billion.

EMPHASIS ON TRANSPORTATION AND LOGISTICS

By the end of 2009, JKH's Leisure division, which included its hotels and related operations, accounted for 19 percent of the group's total revenues. The company had exited a number of other businesses by then, including fast-food restaurants and, by 2006, plantation ownership. The company had focused instead on building up its Transportation division, which received a major boost with the completion of SAGT in 2004. JKH continued to raise its stake in SAGT, to 42 percent by 2009. Other additions to the group's Transportation division included Lanka Marine Services, the country's only marine bunkering (ship-based) fuel supplier, acquired from the Sri Lanka government in 2003.

JKH also grouped its growing logistics operations under the Transportation division. These included a shipping and logistics joint venture established in 2000 in India. In 2008 JKH bought out its partner in that venture, which by then had opened offices in eight major cities in India. Following this takeover, JKH in 2009 restructured its logistics businesses, including Mack International, under a new brand, John Keells Logistics. By the end of that year, the Transportation division had become the company's largest, at 30 percent of its total revenues.

JKH had in the meantime also continued to build up its food business, including supermarket operations, regrouped under a new Consumer Foods and Retail (CF&R) division. This division had grown strongly through the decade, in part through a move into foreign markets. For example, in 2000 the company launched sales of its Elephant House ice cream brand in the Maldives, and by the end of the decade claimed to have captured 48 percent of that market. In 2008 JKH's Keells Food Products subsidiary moved into India, setting up as John Keells Foods India (Pvt). At the same time, the company also developed its own supermarket operation, under the Keells Super banner, becoming a major force in the Sri Lanka retail sector.

The CF&R division thus became the company's second-largest, generating 27 percent of its total revenues in 2009. Revenues had maintained their steady growth, topping LKR 20 billion by the middle of the decade, and passing LKR 40 billion ($350 million) in 2010. The company's success was all the more remarkable given that it had been achieved despite Sri Lanka's long-running civil war. The end of that conflict in 2009 and the beginning of a peaceful era promised to bring new growth opportunities for John Keells Holdings plc in the future.

M. L. Cohen

PRINCIPAL SUBSIDIARIES

Ceylon Cold Stores plc (80.47%); JK Properties (Pvt) Ltd.; JayKay Marketing Services (Pvt) Ltd. (80.47%); John Keells Foods India (Pvt) Ltd. (83.18%); John Keells Hotels plc (92.69%); John Keells Logistics (Pvt) Ltd.; John Keells Logistics India (Pvt) Ltd.; John Keells Stock Brokers (Pvt) Ltd. (90.04%); Keells Food Products Mauritius (Pvt) Ltd. (83.18%); Keells Food Products plc (83.18%); Keells Hotel Management Services Ltd.; Keells Shipping (Pvt) Ltd.; Lanka Marine Services (Pvt) Ltd. (99.44%); Mack Air (Pvt) Ltd.; Mackinnon Mackenzie & Co (Shipping) Ltd. (99.69%); Nations Trust Bank plc (29.9%); Trans Asia Hotels plc (85.02%); Union Assurance plc (80.6%).

PRINCIPAL DIVISIONS

Consumer Foods and Retail; Financial Services; Information Technology; Leisure; Property; Transportation.

PRINCIPAL OPERATING UNITS

Chaaya Hotels and Resorts; Cinnamon Hotels and Resorts; Elephant; John Keells Computer Services; John Keells Logistics; Keells; Keells Super; Lanka Marine Services; Mack Air; Union Assurance.

PRINCIPAL COMPETITORS

Aitken Spence plc; Ceylon Trading Company Ltd.; Hayleys plc; Kuruwita Textile Mills plc.

FURTHER READING

"Cash Call: Sri Lanka JKH Hotel Unit to Raise Rs3.6 Billion to Expand," *Lanka Business Online*, January 21, 2010.

"Chaaya Blu: JK Hotels Answer to the Burgeoning of East Coast Tourism," *Sri Lanka Daily Mirror*, March 11, 2010.

"Health Step: Sri Lanka John Keells Enters Health Business," *Lanka Business Online*, December 16, 2009.

"Hotel Unit of Sri Lanka's JKH to Raise US$31.4 Mln to Expand," *AsiaPulse News*, January 26, 2010.

"JKH Launches New John Keells," *Daily News*, May 1, 2009.

"John Keells to Lead Huge Land Reclamation Project to Expand Colombo Harbour," *AFX Asia*, March 15, 2007.

"Keells to Invest $100 Million in Sri Lanka Hotels amid Recovery," *TendersInfo*, November 26, 2009.

"Slow Growth: Sri Lanka Keells Food Invests in India Despite Losses," *Lanka Business Online*, February 2, 2010.

"Sri Lanka Firm Claims 48-Pct Share of Maldives Ice Cream Market," *AsiaPulse News*, July 9, 2009.

K-VA-T Food Stores, Inc.

201 Trigg Street
Abingdon, Virginia 24210
U.S.A.
Telephone: (276) 628-5503
Toll Free: (800) 826-8451
Fax: (276) 623-5440
Web site: http://www.foodcity.com

Private Company
Founded: 1955
Employees: 12,000
Sales: $1.8 billion (2008 est.)
NAICS: 445110 Supermarkets and Other Grocery
(Except Convenience Stores)

■ ■ ■

K-VA-T Foods Stores, Inc., is an Abingdon, Virginia-based independent regional supermarket chain doing business as Food City. In addition to 95 supermarkets operating under the Food City name, the chain also includes 10 Super Discount Foods stores. As the corporate name suggests, Food City does business in Kentucky, Virginia, and Tennessee. About 75 of the stores include pharmacies, and 56 offer Gas'N Go fuel stations in the parking lots. Many units also offer banking services. Distribution for the chain is handled by a company-owned 1.1 million-square-foot distribution center located in Abingdon.

In addition to major brands, Food City offers such private labels as Food City, Food Club, Valu Time, Full Circle, and Top Care. The chain also offers legacy brands, bringing back a number of popular regional labels, including Kay's Ice Cream, Terry's Snack Foods, Lay's Meat, and Kern's Bread. Additionally, Food City owns Misty Mountain Spring Water, LLC, which supplies the chain with bottled water and offers private-label water to outside customers. Members of the founding Smith family are the primary owners of Food City, with employees controlling about 14 percent of the company through a profit sharing plan.

COMPANY FOUNDED: 1955

K-VA-T started out as a Piggly Wiggly franchisee when the company's first store was opened in Grundy, Virginia, in 1955 by longtime CEO Jack C. Smith, his father Curtis, his uncle Earl, and his cousin Ernest. After graduating from high school Jack Smith gained an appointment to the U.S. Naval Academy in 1944. His studies were accelerated due to World War II and he earned a degree in electrical engineering in three years, although the war was over by that time. Smith then spent the next seven years in active duty.

When Smith was discharged from the Navy in 1954 he had a wife and two daughters to support. He returned home to Grundy, hoping to become involved in a business with his father and cousin, who were partners in a Ben Franklin store. Smith had hoped to acquire some of the chain's variety stores that had become available. However, upon his arrival Smith learned that the deal had not materialized. He was therefore forced to move in with his parents and look for a way to make a living.

Grundy in the early 1950s had a population of less than 2,000, served by a 3,000-square-foot A&P grocery store. Smith was dispatched to this store one day by his mother and soon learned that only one of the two checkout stands was ever used. In his efforts to find employment, he had been wondering what a small town like Grundy needed, and by the time he had finished waiting 45 minutes in line he had his answer: a new grocery store.

Smith teamed up with his cousin and father, along with an uncle who owned a piece of land in town, to build a supermarket that was 8,800 square feet in size. He also contacted the Piggly Wiggly supermarket chain and received approval to become a franchisee. Piggly Wiggly did not offer any support, however. Smith turned instead to Johnson City, Tennessee-based Giant Wholesale for help in properly setting up a supermarket.

Grundy's new Piggly Wiggly store opened on November 17, 1955. It did not meet with much initial success, however. Grundy was a hardscrabble community dominated by coal miners and their families who were not attracted to the colorful Piggly Wiggly look, preferring instead to wait in line at the old A&P. Smith and his partners barely hung on, generating just $600,000 in 1956, the store's first full year in business, barely enough to keep the doors open.

A chance occurrence in the form of a flood proved to be the store's deliverance in its second full year in business. While the A&P was forced to shut its doors during the flood, the Piggly Wiggly, located on higher ground, remained open and took advantage of its competitor's difficulties. Sales in 1957 increased to $1.7 million. Furthermore, customers grew accustomed to the Piggly Wiggly store and continued to shop there even after the A&P resumed operations. Sales approached $3 million in 1958.

SECOND STORE OPENS: 1963

With one successful store under his belt, Smith was ready to expand by 1963, when he acquired a second Piggly Wiggly store in South Williamson, Kentucky. Two years later he added a newly constructed store in Prestonsburg, Kentucky, followed by another acquisition

in Pikeville, Tennessee. All of the stores were conveniently located along U.S. Route 460. Smith accelerated his expansion in 1974 with the acquisition of six Piggly Wiggly stores in Virginia. A year later he acquired five more Piggly Wiggly stores in Virginia.

After doing business with Giant Wholesale for 20 years, Smith grew frustrated with his longtime supplier, which refused to carry Piggly Wiggly's high-margin private-label products. As a result, Smith joined with three other Piggly Wiggly franchisees, altogether operating 24 stores, to form their own wholesale operation in 1975 called Mid-Mountain Foods. Operating out of three small warehouses, Mid-Mountain began to supply the partners' stores with Piggly Wiggly private-label products as well as some commodity items to make the deliveries economical. The rest of Smith's supplies were still purchased from Giant. Gradually Mid-Mountain expanded and eventually it was able to meet all of Smith's needs, allowing him to sever ties with Giant.

Smith's son, Steven C. Smith, joined his father in 1979 at the age of 22. He was assigned to oversee a new store format the company was testing in three locations called Sav-U Discount Foods, which offered a limited assortment of items. The stores performed poorly and closed within a year. "That was my humble start in the grocery business," the future K-VA-T chief executive told *Supermarket News* in a 2005 profile.

PIGGLY WIGGLY SOLD: 1984

The Smith family had always maintained a good relationship with Piggly Wiggly, but it began to fray after Memphis, Tennessee-based wholesaler Malone & Hyde acquired the chain in 1984. The new owners told Jack Smith that they would provide him with new store locations only if he signed an agreement stating he would only operate Piggly Wiggly stores. As long as he could decide whether a location was worthwhile or not, Smith was willing to serve as an exclusive Piggly Wiggly franchisee. He soon changed his mind, however, when he learned that Greenville, Tennessee-based Quality Foods and its Food City chain of 19 stores was for sale.

At the time, Smith's 11 Piggly Wiggly stores were generating $95 million in business a year while the Food City stores were doing $175 million. Smith, eager to essentially triple his business in a single stroke, met with Quality's owners and struck a deal to purchase the Food City stores. He also negotiated a buyout from his Piggly Wiggly contract. He then applied the Food City name to his Piggly Wiggly stores. Smith was also in need of a new corporate name. "We wanted a neutral name, and we wanted an acronym you could pronounce," he told *Supermarket News*. "So I came up with K-VA-T, which

KEY DATES

1955: Jack Smith and partners open Piggly Wiggly store in Grundy, Virginia.
1975: Mid-Mountain Foods opens as wholesale distribution center.
1984: Food City acquired and name adopted.
1998: Food City opens its first fuel center.
2002: Chain tops $1 billion in sales.
2007: Jack Smith dies.

stands for Kentucky, Virginia and Tennessee—the three states in which we operate." For the most part, the company operated as Food City.

Converting the Piggly Wiggly stores led to a break-even year in 1985, but Smith and Food City soon resumed expansion. In 1989 Smith saw another opportunity, the chance to acquire the 47-unit White Food Stores chain. These stores made up in location what they lacked in performance. However, because several of the locations overlapped with Food City stores, the Federal Trade Commission (FTC) insisted that Smith would have to close some stores.

Unhappy with the terms, Smith withdrew his petition but soon learned that one of his Mid-Mountain partners was interested in acquiring the stores Smith had been asked to divest. The stores were sold and Food City was able to file a new petition to acquire White Food. The deal was completed in late 1989. The company devoted 1990 to converting the White Food stores to the Food City banner. After some closures and a $1 million loss for the year, the company emerged with about 30 new stores, bringing the total number of units to 60.

FIRST FUEL CENTER OPENS: 1998

The 1990s brought other changes as well to Food City. Early in the decade the chain became involved in NASCAR racing and began sponsoring a pair of races, the Food City 500 in the spring and the Food City 250 in the fall at the Bristol International Raceway in Tennessee. In 1993 Steve Smith was named president and chief operating officer after previously serving as vice president of store operations. Two years later Food City undertook a restructuring of its nonfood sections, enlarging the health and beauty care departments in a bid to become more competitive against mass retailers such as Wal-Mart.

The stores were also planogrammed for the first time, resulting in a greater consistency between stores. In 1996 Food City began considering the addition of fuel centers after the subject was discussed at a National Grocers Association attended by Steve Smith, who championed the idea. After two years of study, Food City opened its first fuel center at a Food City store in Lebanon, Virginia. It proved successful, and the concept was rolled out to about 20 additional stores over the next four years.

The late 1990s also brought new stores to the Food City chain. In 1998 the company acquired Coeburn, Virginia-based Kennedy's Piggly Wiggly Stores, adding 11 stores, including eight in southwest Virginia, two in southeast Kentucky, and one in east Tennessee. Together they combined for about $70 million in annual sales. Moreover, Kennedy's Piggly Wiggly was the remaining partner in Mid-Mountain Foods, giving Food City complete ownership of the company. The name of the business was subsequently changed to the Food City Distribution Center. The chain closed the decade with another acquisition purchasing seven Winn-Dixie stores in the Knoxville, Tennessee, market. Three smaller Food City stores in the area were closed in favor of the larger Winn-Dixie units. Food City also increased its efforts to grow internally, opening four new stores in 1999.

STEVE SMITH NAMED CEO: 2001

Several new stores opened in the new century and others were remodeled. There was also a changing of the guard during this period. In 2001 Steve Smith replaced his father as CEO. The elder Smith retained the chairmanship, a post he held until his death at the age of 81 in 2007, when his son assumed that title as well. In the meantime, Food City continued to add fuel centers as well as pharmacies and in-store banks to keep pace in the highly competitive supermarket business.

Food City recorded its first $1 billion sales year in 2002 and continued to look for opportunities to grow. In 2006 it acquired eight Bi-Lo supermarkets in Tennessee as sales volume climbed to $1.6 billion. By 2010 Food City was operating more than 100 supermarkets. Rumors had been circulating on the Internet that Food City was for sale. Steve Smith quashed those rumors, however. He issued a statement indicating that Food city "is not for sale and probably won't be in my lifetime."

Ed Dinger

PRINCIPAL SUBSIDIARIES

Food City Distribution Center; Misty Mountain Spring Water, LLC.

PRINCIPAL COMPETITORS

Food Lion, LLC; The Kroger Co.; Wal-Mart Stores, Inc.

FURTHER READING

"Food City Mourns Loss of Founder," *Progressive Grocer*, March 16, 2007.

George, Richard, "Staying Focused; K-VA-T Has Been Delighting Consumers for More than 50 Years," *Grocery Headquarters*, June 2008, p. 24.

Ghitelman, David, "K-VA-T Food Stores: On Being the Local Hero," *Supermarket News*, September 25, 2003, p. 22.

Hamstra, Mark, "K-VA-T Boosts Presence in Tennessee," *Supermarket News*, May 7, 2007.

Simpson, Barbara, "Food City Buys White Stores," *Supermarket News*, September 4, 1989, p. 2.

Zweibach, Elliot, "A Guiding Force for Half a Century," *Supermarket News*, April 4, 2005, p. 16.

————, "K-VA-T Sets Buy of Seven Stores from Winn-Dixie," *Supermarket News*, July 19, 1999, p.1.

————, "K-VA-T's New Focus," *Supermarket News*, August 23, 1999, p. 1.

KAJIMA
CORPORATION

Kajima Corporation

3-1 Motoakasaka
1-chome Minato-ku
Tokyo, 107-8388
Japan
Telephone: (81 3) 5544 1111
Fax: (81 3) 3470 1444
Web site: http://www.kajima.co.jp

Public Company
Incorporated: 1930 as the Kajima Construction
    Company
Employees: 15,608
Sales: ¥1.64 trillion ($17.47 billion) (2010)
Stock Exchanges: Tokyo
Ticker Symbol: 1812
NAICS: 234120 Bridge and Tunnel Construction;
    234930 Industrial Nonbuilding Structure Construc-
    tion; 234990 All Other Heavy Construction;
    236220 Commercial and Institutional Building
    Construction; 2373210 Land Subdivision; 237310
    Highway, Street, and Bridge Construction; 237990
    Other Heavy and Civil Engineering Construction;
    238210 Electrical Contractors; 238910 Other
    Specialty Trade Contractors; 541310 Architectural
    Services; 541330 Engineering Services

∎∎∎

The Kajima Corporation is one of the oldest and largest
construction companies in Japan and a global leader.
The firm's services include design, engineering,
construction, and real estate development. Kajima builds

high-rise structures, railways, power plants, dams, and
bridges.

Although the company is known internationally for
its expertise in civil engineering and design, most of its
revenues come from domestic construction work. The
company also acts as a real-estate developer, typically
owning a completed project for two or three years
before selling it. A downturn in the construction
industry during the 1990s prompted Kajima to expand
its operations to the environmental sector, specifically
waste treatment, water treatment, soil rehabilitation, and
environmental consulting.

Kajima has 13 branch offices in Japan, where it
obtains the bulk of its revenues. Its international
subsidiaries are located in more than 20 countries
throughout Asia, Europe, and North America. Kajima is
active in Southeast Asia and the United Kingdom, and
the United States, where it owns regional firms such as
Batson-Cook and Hawaiian Dredging and Construction
Company.

EARLY HISTORY

Kajima was founded in 1840 by Iwakichi Kajima, an innovative carpenter and designer. Construction remained
the family trade of Kajima's sons, who witnessed the
transformation of Japan from an isolated nation into a
developing regional power after the Meiji Restoration in
1868.

The industrial modernization policies of the Meiji
government created a demand for newer and larger
factories and buildings as well as railroad lines and

COMPANY PERSPECTIVES

Our extensive experience and expertise in the development, design, and construction of all types of structures, from dams, bridges and tunnels to skyscrapers and resorts, combined with our innovative construction technologies, has led to the Kajima name being well recognized worldwide. These prominent capabilities and a successful track record have also garnered us the respect, trust and confidence of our clientele and that of society. It is this in which we take pride and find the drive for Kajima's sustainable growth in the years to come.

tunnels. Kajima built the first European-style commercial building in Japan, an office structure for the Hong Kong-based Jardine Matheson & Company, and entered the field of railroad construction in 1880 under the name Kajima Gumi. The company quickly established a reputation for excellence in railroad bed construction and tunneling. As Japanese industry continued to grow, Kajima Gumi completed a greater number of industrial and infrastructure projects.

Kajima Gumi began construction of hydroelectric dams during the 1920s. Relatively unaffected by the worldwide economic depression, Kajima Gumi became a public company on February 22, 1930, capitalized at ¥3 million. With the involvement of private stockholders, the company was able to devote more capital to larger projects. With a larger scale of operations, Kajima Gumi became active as an industrial contractor.

Extreme right-wing elements of the Japanese military rose to power during the 1930s, advocating a neo-mercantilist economy and Japanese colonial domination of East Asia and the western Pacific. As part of their "quasi-war economy," large industrial projects were undertaken which were intended to augment Japan's war-making capabilities. Like many other Japanese companies, Kajima Gumi attempted to remain divorced from politics. However, because of the nature of its business, and the overwhelming coercive power of the militarists, the company became an active participant in the Japanese war effort.

POSTWAR OPPORTUNITIES

Japan was so completely devastated by World War II that it was largely unable to feed or rebuild itself. This created great opportunities for construction companies such as Kajima Gumi, who were needed to build new structures and repair others that had been damaged.

Kajima Gumi was reorganized under the commercial laws imposed by the Allied occupation commander and reestablished in 1947 as the Kajima Construction Company. Two years later, the company established the Kajima Institute of Construction Technology (KICT), where new construction materials and engineering technologies could be developed. The Institute, located in Tokyo's Chuo ward, employed 233 specialists and was the first private research institution of its kind in Japan.

In the early 1950s, Kajima began to design nuclear reactor complexes, which necessitated the expansion of the research institute. In 1956, the institute was relocated to the Tokyo suburb of Chobu. The following year Kajima built the Number 1 reactor, Japan's first nuclear reactor, at the Japan Atomic Energy Research Institute's Ibarakiken complex. Kajima completed Japan's first skyscraper, the 36-story Kasumigaseki Mitsui Building in 1968.

INTERNATIONAL EXPANSION: 1960–92

During the 1960s, the company undertook an increasing number of projects outside Japan, constructing buildings and dams in Burma, Vietnam, and Indonesia. After establishing its reputation of excellence overseas, Kajima was chosen to complete a variety of projects in Taiwan, South Korea, the Philippines, Malaysia, Thailand, and Hong Kong. By the time Kajima set up a Los Angeles-based subsidiary in 1964, it was ranked the largest construction company in the world by contract volume.

The company's name was changed to the Kajima Corporation in 1970 to better reflect its international character and wide range of engineering services. New technologies developed by KICT were continually applied, particularly in the area of aseismic structures. The institute built an "earthquake simulator" in 1974. A year later, a hydraulics laboratory was established which placed Kajima in a leading position among Japanese companies in dam, breakwater, and ocean platform construction.

Kajima was given full responsibility by the East German government to build the International Trade Center Building in East Berlin, free of government restrictions or demands that local companies be involved in the project. This project marked Kajima's emergence from East Asia. Projects in the United States, Turkey, Algeria, and Zaire followed.

As early as the 1960s, Kajima used shield tunnel borers, but KICT introduced new processes which

KEY DATES

1840: Iwakichi Kajima establishes a construction company.
1930: Kajima Gumi goes public.
1947: The firm is reestablished as the Kajima Construction Company.
1957: Kajima builds Japan's first nuclear reactor.
1970: The firm changes its name to Kajima Corporation.
1985: The firm completes tunneling work for the Seikan Tunnel.
1999: The company reports a loss of approximately $2.6 billion due to debt disposal.
2000: Kajima establishes an environmental division.
2003: State-of-the-art Shiodome Tower built in Tokyo for Kyodo News.
2007: Kajima builds new headquarters in Tokyo.

improved the safety and efficiency of established tunneling methods, using water jets and concrete-spraying robots. Kajima also developed a shield tunnel borer capable of making sharp turns, and it was one of several companies involved in the construction of the 54-kilometer Seikan Tunnel, linking the Japanese islands of Honshu and Hokkaido. Tunneling work was completed in 1985 and the Seikan Tunnel project was finished three years later.

In 1982, the Kajima Corporation was awarded the Deming Prize for engineering excellence. During the 1980s, it continually received recognition for its achievements. By this time, Kajima held almost 1,100 Japanese patents, 72 of which were registered in foreign countries.

In addition to its other major construction activities in the 1980s, Kajima worked on building a floating oil storage facility near Nagasaki capable of holding six million kiloliters (32.4 million barrels) of oil. The company was also working on an integrated method for decommissioning aging nuclear power plants, a service that would become increasingly important as nuclear power plants neared the end of their 40-year life spans.

During the 1980s, Kajima remained under family management. However, when Seiichi Kajima's marriage produced no sons, his daughter Ume married Morino Suke, a career diplomat and scholar who was adopted into the family and given the name Kajima. His first son, Shoichi Kajima, was the company's president until 1990, and a brother-in-law of both the chairman and

honorary chairman. Akira Miyazaki was named president in 1990.

By the early 1990s, the Kajima Corporation was extremely competitive in railroad, dam, and other civil engineering projects. It also remained one of the strongest Japanese companies in the overseas markets. Kajima maintained an excellent financial situation with few liabilities and high earnings. The company's research institute and continued strength in the construction of nuclear power plants and earthquake-resistant skyscrapers were indispensable assets that secured the company's place in the Japanese industry.

It was at this time that the Japanese economy as a whole was experiencing strong growth. Kajima made key investments and demand in the construction industry was strong. In 1991, the firm's net income increased by more than 50 percent over the previous year. The positive financial results continued in 1992 as the firm completed construction on Tokyo East 21, a state-of-the-art office tower, hotel, and commercial complex.

BATTLING ECONOMIC CHALLENGES: 1993–2003

Japan's economy soon began deteriorating, which led to a drop in demand for Kajima's services. Overall, the Asian economy was weakening and personal consumption was falling. The Great Hanshin Earthquake prompted an increase in reconstruction services in 1995; however, Kajima's fortunes, along with many large Japanese companies, faltered during the latter half of the 1990s. During this period, the company focused on increasing the number of new contracts, promoting efficiency, and bolstering profitability. During 1998, revenues and gross profit fell.

The financial hardships continued and in 1999, Kajima was forced to post a $2.6 billion pretax loss due in part to the write-off of bad loans and assets that the company had taken on during the early 1990s. That year the firm launched its "New Three Year Plan" that included strategies centered on enhancing marketing efforts, cost cutting, streamlining corporate operations, and improving research and development, along with improving the overall financial position of the company.

In response to the downturn in the construction industry, Kajima set its sights on diversification in the new century. In October 2000, the firm created an environmental division focused on waste and water treatment, soil rehabilitation, and environmental consulting. Kajima eyed the waste-to-resource industry as key to its future growth. Japan's Ministry of Economy, Trade, and Industry believed that the market for waste treatment and recycling in Japan would grow to ¥22 trillion by 2010.

During fiscal 2002, the company launched another management plan, titled the "Next Three Year Plan." Japan's economy and financial condition continued to be problematic and while new government programs and reform promised relief, steady recovery had yet to be seen. As such, Kajima focused on improving its competitiveness by targeting the renovation, housing, and environmental industries. The company also began to develop new business ventures and continued with aggressive research and development activities. Bolstering profits from real estate and international operations and restructuring organizational operations to improve overall profits were also key parts of the firm's strategy. While Kajima faced a challenging future, Kajima management remained confident that the company would remain a leading contractor for years to come.

In 2003 the company completed Tokyo's Kajima Tower, later renamed Shiodome Tower. Kyodo News used the state-of-the-art building as a headquarters. It was located on the site of the Shimbashi Railway Station, the birthplace of Japanese railroads. Kajima built a replica of the station had burnt down in 1923. The group lost ¥4.5 billion in fiscal 2003 partly due to the cost of shutting down a pension fund. Revenues slipped 14 percent to ¥1.62 trillion for the year.

INTERNATIONAL DEVELOPMENTS: 2003–08

Kajima had begun to participate in many private finance initiatives (PFIs), an alternative means of financing social infrastructure projects such as hospitals, apartments, schools, and fire stations. PFIs originated in the United Kingdom in 1992. By the end of the decade, their use had spread to Japan as well.

Kajima remained committed to the U.K. PFI business for the long term, although it proved to be risky. Kajima's U.K. construction unit (it also had development and design subsidiaries) lost £2 million in fiscal 2003 and another £73 million the next year. It lost another £84 million in 2005 after pulling out from a housing project in Cambridge.

Kajima bought Hawaii's largest construction company in 2002. Hawaiian Dredging and Construction Company had been formed in 1902 by Walter Dillingham, and participated in much of Hawaii's development throughout the 20th century, reclaiming nearly 5,000 acres of swampland from downtown Honolulu to Waikiki and building many of Hawaii's large structures. Kajima had been working with it since the early 1980s, building branch offices for Central Pacific Bank.

Kajima strengthened its involvement in the southern United States with the January 2008 purchase of Batson-Cook Company. Based in West Point, Georgia, with offices in Atlanta, Tampa, and Jacksonville, Batson-Cook had annual sales of $480 million focusing on private-sector projects. It had been established in 1915.

Another area of interest was Southeast Asia, particularly Singapore, where Kajima was active in commercial real-estate development projects. Even with this reach, the bulk of the group's revenues came from Japan.

Competition for public-sector civil engineering work was as fierce as ever at home as well as abroad. Kajima was part of a group that landed a ¥540 billion expressway contract in Algeria in September 2006. The project illustrated the increased risks involved with international contracts due to currency fluctuations, larger scale, and slimmer margins.

Problems on such large projects resulted in serious impact to the company's bottom line. Pretax profits fell 50 percent in fiscal 2007 to ¥29.6 billion. Kajima was carrying a debt load of around ¥500 million, much more than that of its rivals. The company completed its first ever stock-buyback at the end of calendar 2007.

NEW RULES AFTER 2006

Domestic construction remained the largest contributor to Kajima's profits, followed by domestic real-estate development. Civil engineering work became scarcer, and less lucrative, after a new antimonopoly law went into effect at the beginning of 2006. Kajima was one of several dozen Japanese construction companies involved in a bid-rigging scandal that preceded it.

Kajima was developing two expensive projects of its own: building a new headquarters and renovating the research center. For its own headquarters in Tokyo, Kajima built a pair of buildings totaling 524,300 square feet (48,680 square meters). They were finished in August 2007. Each featured the latest in environmental technology, predicted to reduce building energy costs by 30 percent, as well as an earthquake warning system. A new laboratory for the research institute was completed in April 2009, with the remainder of the institute to be finished in three years.

The old head office building was demolished in September 2008 using the first ever application of Kajima's new Cut and Take Down Method. This involved building internal core walls in the building center, gutting one floor at a time from the bottom, and lowering the building on jacks. The method was thought to be more efficient, safe, quiet, and environmentally friendly.

Revenues approached ¥2 trillion ($20 billion) in the fiscal year ended March 31, 2009; 88 percent of this came from Japan. The group posted a net loss after five years of profits. While government civil engineering contracts were up, the global economic slowdown was having a negative effect on private-sector orders as clients canceled or deferred projects. Hundreds of smaller Japanese construction companies collapsed in 2008 as government infrastructure investment continued its several-year decline and housing starts began to slide.

Revenues slipped 16 percent in fiscal 2009 (the year ended March 2010) to ¥1.64 trillion ($17.47 billion). Kajima posted a rare ¥7 billion operating loss, although it was able to post net income of ¥13.2 billion after losing ¥6.3 billion the previous year.

Updated, Christina M. Stansell; Frederick C. Ingram

PRINCIPAL SUBSIDIARIES

Kajima U.S.A. Inc.; Kajima Associates, Inc. (USA); Kajima Building and Design, Inc. (USA); KBD Construction Services, Inc. (USA); Batson-Cook Company (USA); Batson-Cook Development Company (USA); Chung-Lu Construction Co., Ltd. (Taiwan); KCS West, Inc. (USA); Hawaiian Dredging and Construction Company, Inc. (USA); Industrial Developments International, Inc. (USA); Commercial Developments International, Inc. (USA); Kajima Development Corporation (USA); KUD International LLC (USA); The Austin Company (USA); Ilya Corporation; Trading Co., Ltd.; Kajima Europe Ltd. (UK); Kajima Partnerships Ltd. (UK); Kajima Properties (Europe) Ltd. (UK); Kajima Europe B.V. (Netherlands); Kajima Overseas Asia Pte. Ltd. (Singapore); Kajima Design Asia Pte. Ltd. (Singapore); Kajima France Development S.A.R.L.; Kajima Czech Design and Construction s.r.o. (Czech Republic); P.T. Kajima Indonesia; P.T. Senayan Trikarya Sempana (Indonesia); Thai Kajima Co., Ltd. (Thailand); Ramaland Development Co., Ltd. (Thailand); Kajima (Malaysia) Sdn. Bhd.; Kajima (Shanghai) Construction Co., Ltd. (China).

PRINCIPAL DIVISIONS

Civil Engineering Management; Business Development; Civil Engineering Design; Building Construction Management; Architectural Design; Nuclear Power Department; Real Estate Development; Engineering; Environmental Engineering; Machinery and Electrical Engineering; Overseas Operations.

PRINCIPAL OPERATING UNITS

Hokkaido Branch; Tohoku Branch; Kanto Branch; Tokyo Civil Engineering Branch; Tokyo Architectural Construction Branch; Yokohama Branch; Hokuriku Branch; Chubu Branch; Kansai Branch; Shikoku Branch; Chugoku Branch; Kyushu Branch; International Division.

PRINCIPAL COMPETITORS

Obayashi Corporation; Shimizu Corporation; Taisei Corporation.

FURTHER READING

Conner, Elizabeth, "Batson-Cook Gets New Owner," *Columbus (GA) Ledger Enquirer*, December 27, 2007.

"Japan's Kajima Books 337 Bln Yen Extra Loss in FY98," *AsiaPulse News*, March 31, 1999.

"Japan's Kajima Develops Continuous-Feed Soil Cleaning System," *AsiaPulse News*, September, 17, 2002.

"Japan's Kajima Develops Technology to Recycle Waste Concrete," *AsiaPulse News*, December 4, 2001.

"Japan's Kajima Yr to March Group Pretax Loss $2.6 Bln," *AsiaPulse News*, June 9, 1999.

Kikuchi, Takeshi, "Towering Project Costs Take Wrecking Ball to Kajima Profits," *Nikkei Weekly* (Japan), January 28, 2008.

Kinoshita, Hirohide, "Builder Hobbled by Downturn, Heavy Debt Load," *Nikkei Weekly*, April 27, 2009.

———, "Financial Picture Dims for Kajima," *Nikkei Weekly* (Japan), February 25, 2008.

Leitch, John, "PFIs Boost Kajima Presence in UK," *Contract Journal*, June 11, 2003, p. 7.

Reina, Peter, and Gary Tulacz, "No Keeping Contractors Home after They've Seen the World," *ENR*, August 25, 1997, p. 67.

KAR Auction Services, Inc.

13085 Hamilton Crossing Boulevard
Carmel, Indiana 46032-1412
U.S.A.
Telephone: (317) 815-1100
Toll Free: (800) 923-3725
Fax: (317) 843-4898
Web site: http://www.karholdingsinc.com

Public Company
Incorporated: 2006 as KAR Holdings Inc.
Employees: 12,648
Sales: $1.73 billion (2009)
Stock Exchanges: New York
Ticker Symbol: KAR
NAICS: 423110 Automobile and Other Motor Vehicle
    Merchant Wholesalers

■ ■ ■

Listed on the New York Stock Exchange, Carmel,
Indiana-based KAR Auction Services, Inc., and its
subsidiaries operate used-vehicle auctions and provide
related services. The company's flagship unit is ADESA,
the second-largest wholesale used-vehicle operation in
North America, which includes about 60 wholesale car
sites. Mostly sold to used-car dealers, the vehicles are
provided by rental car companies, commercial fleet
operators, financial institutions, and vehicle manufacturers, as well as other used-vehicle dealers.

Another unit, Insurance Auto Auctions, operates
another 150 salvage auction sites, which sell vehicles
that can be repaired for resale. All told, KAR Auction is

involved in the sale of more than three million used and
salvage vehicles each year. In addition to auction fees,
KAR Auction generates revenues from related value-
added services, such as inspections, storage, transportation, reconditioning, and titling. Subsidiary Automotive
Finance Corporation provides financing to the used-car
industry.

ADESA FOUNDED: 1989

The roots of KAR Auction date to 1989 when Mike
Hockett launched a used-vehicle auction business, Auto
Dealers Exchange Management, Inc., in Birmingham,
Alabama. Hockett was very familiar with the selling of
new and used cars, as well as the wholesale auction
business. His father had been involved in all three
aspects of the industry in Indianapolis, Indiana. Hockett
had begun his career in 1966 by managing an auto auction his father had acquired two years earlier. In 1979
he took on a partner to strike out on his own, opening
an auction in Indianapolis and buying other sites in Illinois and Birmingham, Alabama. After a decade of doing business together, Hockett and his partner split in
1989 and Hockett was left with the Birmingham auction to run. It was a time of consolidation in the
wholesale vehicle auction business, and Hockett formed
Auto Dealers Exchange Management to participate in
the acquisition of auction sites.

Hockett focused his initial efforts on a narrow
region of the country, buying auctions in Ohio,
Kentucky, and Tennessee. In 1992 he joined forces with
the president and co-owner of Indianapolis Auto Auction, Gary Pedigo, resulting in Auto Dealers Exchange

Services of America Corporation, or ADESA. Hockett served as chief executive officer of the Indianapolis-based company and quickly moved to take ADESA public to fund further expansion. The initial stock offering was completed in April 1992, with Hockett retaining majority control of the company.

AUTOMOTIVE FINANCE CORPORATION ACQUIRED: 1994

ADESA entered the Canadian market in 1993 with the acquisition of Montreal Auto Auction. Other auctions in Canada soon followed. A year later an agreement was reached with General Motors Canada to sell rental repurchase vehicles. Early in 1994 ADESA added to its capabilities by acquiring Automotive Finance Corporation to provide on-site financing to customers. Later in the year, ADESA acquired auctions in Miami and Austin, Texas. Pedigo also left the company at this time, selling his interest to purchase a Chevrolet dealership in Indianapolis.

ADESA was taken private in January 1995 when Minnesota Power & Light (MP&L) acquired an 80 percent stake at a cost of $162 million. Hockett retained a sizable interest and remained in charge, but a year later MP&L exercised an option to buy out Hockett and his management team. MP&L installed the head of ADESA's Canadian branch, James P. Hallett, as the new president and chief executive officer. Hallett would eventually become the CEO of KAR Auction. A Canadian who graduated from Algonquin College, Hallett became involved in the retail automotive business in 1975. After managing new car franchises, he opened a pair of car auctions in 1990: Ottawa Dealers Exchange and The Greater Halifax Dealer Exchange. He sold the sites to ADESA in 1993 and took over as the head of ADESA's Canadian operations.

Hallett took over a company in ADESA that operated 16 wholesale car auctions. He grew the business at a measured pace, acquiring auctions and building new ones while expanding Automotive Finance Corporation. The rate of growth picked up in 2000 when ADESA added auctions in San Diego and Los Angeles, and acquired Canadian Auction Group and its 13 auctions and dealer financing sites located across Canada. A short

time later ADESA benefited from the growth of its chief rival Manheim Auctions, which had to shed some auctions to skirt federal antitrust laws and complete an acquisition of ADT Automotive. As a result, ADESA added one auction from Manheim Auctions and eight auctions from ADT Automotive, extending the company's reach to Atlanta, Colorado Springs, Kansas City, Phoenix, San Francisco, and Seattle, as well as Clearwater, Orlando, and Tampa, Florida.

Hallett expanded ADESA further as the new century unfolded. Early in 2001 the company acquired ComSearch, Inc., an online parts location and insurance adjustment audit services provider, and Auto Placement Center, Inc., a Rhode Island operator of eight New England salvage auction sites. Later in the year a site was added in Tulsa, Oklahoma, and in 2002 a new salvage auction was opened in Orlando. These operations helped to spur revenue growth to $844 million in 2002 and net earnings to $93 million.

HEADQUARTERS MOVED: 2004

MP&L, then known as ALLETE, decided in 2003 to spin off ADESA, which accounted for nearly two-thirds of the parent company's revenues. As a separate company, ADESA was expected to increase shareholder value. While preparations were made for a public stock offering as well as a distribution of ADESA shares to ALLETE shareholders, ADESA continued to expand its offerings. It then included LiveBlock, an Internet service that allowed customers to remotely bid on cars and was being rolled out to ADESA's auction sites. Moreover, in the spring of 2004 ADESA moved its headquarters to a new facility located in Carmel, Indiana, an Indianapolis suburb.

In June 2004 ALLETE shareholders received 93 percent of ADESA, and the balance, 6.25 million shares, were sold in a public stock offering. ALLETE's CEO, David Gartzke, then took over as president, CEO, and chairman of ADESA and Hallett was relegated to the vice president's post. When the year came to a close, revenues improved to $931 million and net income totaled $105.3 million. ADESA had performed well under Hallett's leadership, the number of auction sites having increased threefold to 56. Nevertheless, in May 2005 Hallett left the company.

Although he refused to elaborate, Hallett made it clear to the press that he had been fired. At the same time, his son, Sean Hallett, was embroiled in his own problems with ADESA. The company had sued him in November 2004. He owned a vehicle auction company that owed Automotive Finance Corp. and a related company $1.7 million. ADESA insisted, however, that

KEY DATES

∎

1989: Mike Hockett launches Auto Dealer Exchange Management, Inc., to participate in acquisition of auction sites.
1992: Auto Dealers Exchange Services of America (ADESA) created through merger.
1995: Company is taken private.
2007: ADESA is sold to KAR Holdings Inc.
2009: KAR Holdings is taken public as KAR Auction Services, Inc.

there was no connection between that matter and the departure of Hallett.

KAR HOLDINGS PURCHASES ADESA: 2007

Hallett became president of Columbus Fair Auto Auction in Columbus, Ohio, but he would return to ADESA two years after his departure. ADESA did not fare particularly well during his absence, due primarily to difficult business conditions. The number of vehicles coming off lease had declined, especially in 2006, and retail sales of used cars and trucks had also softened. ADESA considered major significant capital investments but was afraid such actions would depress the company's already weakened stock price.

In July 2006 ADESA contacted 17 possible buyers, 10 of which showed enough interest to submit a preliminary bid. However, none of them met the November 8 deadline to submit a final bid. Two days later a group of four private-equity firms offered $27 a share for ADESA. They included two New York firms, Kelso & Co. and GS Capital Partners, San Francisco's ValueAct Capital, and Boston's Parthenon Capital. ADESA was especially attractive to Kelso and Parthenon because they owned an asset that could be combined with ADESA: Insurance Auto Auctions Inc. (IAAI), an Illinois-based salvage auction company that operated 95 auction sites.

Over the next several weeks, ADESA and the equity firms' newly created entity, KAR Holdings Inc., negotiated the final price. ADESA was able to persuade KAR Holdings to improve its offer to $27.85 a share, but with no competing interest, KAR Holdings decided to rescind the offer and return to its original $27 bid. Discussions came to an end, but were revived a few days later when KAR Holdings agreed to the higher price and a sales agreement was reached. The deal was valued

at $3.7 billion, which included $2.5 billion in cash, the assumption of $700 million in debt, and the contribution of IAAI.

ONLINE CAPABILITIES EXPANDED

The sale of the company was approved by ADESA shareholders in April 2007. At that time Hallett returned, hired by the new owners as the company's CEO. He immediately took steps to create more of an entrepreneurial spirit in the company, paying visits to customers and listening to their concerns and advice. Many of them urged him to expand the business and, in particular, to upgrade its Internet technology in order to build ADESA into a national chain.

In short order, improvements were made to ADESA's Internet capabilities, which were integrated into a single operating system. The company also introduced to its auctions the V-TRACE system, or Vehicle Tracking Repair and Condition Enhancement, which electronically recorded charges for repairs, bodywork, and other services performed on a vehicle. V-TRACE was incorporated into the auction management system to reduce errors and increase efficiency. ADESA also expanded its repair capabilities in December 2007 with the acquisition of a paintless dent repair provider called Dent Demon.

ADESA continued to make improvements to its online capabilities in 2008 when it began rolling out its LiveBlock technology to all of the lanes of its auction sites. In this way dealers from around the world who were trained by the company on the system could participate in ADESA auctions. In 2009 ADESA looked to stimulate business with former Chrysler, Dodge, and Jeep dealers by helping them to liquidate inventory or buy and sell used vehicles online as they made the transition to used-vehicle dealers.

KAR AUCTION SERVICES NAME ADOPTED: 2009

KAR Holdings generated revenues of $1.8 billion in 2008 and posted a net loss of $216.2 million. Sales dipped the following year but the company returned to profitability. In November 2009 KAR Holdings changed its name to KAR Auction Services, Inc., a preliminary step to once again taking the business public. In December 2009 an initial public offering of stock was completed, followed by the underwriters exercising an over-allotment option, netting KAR Auction $310.3 million. The company had hoped to raise as much as $391 million by pricing its shares from $15 to $17. It had to settle instead for $12 per share, due in large measure to its hefty $2.5 billion debt load.

KAR Auction began focusing on the reduction of its debt while continuing to bolster its online capabilities. In 2010 it joined forces with online auto auction company Auction Pipeline Inc. to create a service called Plus, which in essence brought the vehicles listed for sale by both companies together into a single database. In addition, ADESA retooled its Web site to make it easier for dealers to buy and sell cars. KAR Auction was a distant second to Manheim, the world's largest wholesale automobile auction business, but there was ample opportunity for the company to increase market share in the years to come.

Ed Dinger

PRINCIPAL SUBSIDIARIES

ADESA; Automotive Finance Corporation; Insurance Auto Auctions, Inc.

PRINCIPAL COMPETITORS

Comerica Incorporated; Dealer Services Corporation; Manheim Auctions.

FURTHER READING

Andrews, Greg, "Awkward Auction of ADESA Leaves Investors Miffed," *Indianapolis Business Journal*, February 5, 2007, p. 4A.

Cowan, Lynn, "KAR Faces Bumpy Road to Its IPO," *Wall Street Journal*, December 10, 2009.

O'Malley, Chris, "Car Auction Executive Driven Out," *Indianapolis Business Journal*, May 16, 2005, p. 1.

Sawyers, Arlena, "ADESA Seeks to Take 3rd Turn as Public Company," *Automotive News*, September 28, 2009, p. 6.

———, "ADESA Ties Growth Goals to Dealer Services," *Automotive News*, February 8, 2010, p. 38.

———, "Auction Companies Combine Online," *Automotive News*, January 11, 2010, p. 21.

———, "Hallett 'Excited' about ADESA Return," *Automotive News*, March 26, 2007, p. 36.

Kaydon Corporation

315 East Eisenhower Parkway, Suite 300
Ann Arbor, Michigan 48108-3330
U.S.A.
Telephone: (734) 747-7025
Fax: (734) 747-6565
Web site: http://www.kaydon.com

Public Company
Incorporated: 1941 as The Kaydon Engineering
    Company
Employees: 2,084
Sales: $441.1 million (2009)
Stock Exchanges: New York
Ticker Symbol: KDN
NAICS: 332991 Ball and Roller Bearing Manufacturing;
    333999 All Other General Purpose Machinery
    Manufacturing

■ ■ ■

Ann Arbor, Michigan-based Kaydon Corporation produces custom, performance-critical products for a wide range of customers. Specifically, the company makes bearings and components, custom rings, filters and filter housings, fuel cleansing systems, gas-phase air filtration systems and replacement media, industrial presses, linear deceleration products, metal alloy products, shaft seals, and specialty balls. These products are used in applications that include everything from aerospace, defense, and alternative energy to robotics, security, and medicine. Kaydon's business is organized into four main segments: Friction Control Products; Velocity Control Products; Sealing Products; and Other.

WORLD WAR II ORIGINS

The Kaydon Engineering Company was founded in 1941 in Muskegon, Michigan, in order to support the United States' entry into World War II. Kaydon originally provided a specially designed thin-section bearing for the gun mounts on the U.S. Navy's ships. By the end of the war, Kaydon had expanded its bearings line beyond military applications. A hallmark of the company's products, however, was that they were custom-designed, specially engineered, and difficult to manufacture solutions for customer equipment problems. The company's dedication to such specialty products would continue to guide Kaydon throughout its history.

Kaydon clung to its bearings, growing to three manufacturing plants through the 1960s. That was when the company attracted the attention of Glen Bailey. Bailey had spent much of the decade working as a midlevel manager for ITT Corp. under Harold Geneen; Bailey's job was to take Geneen's acquisitions in the wire and cable industry and turn them around to profitability.

In 1967 Bailey decided to go into the turnaround business for himself, acquiring New Jersey-based Keene Packaging Associates for $1.7 million. With $65 million in loans, Bailey set out to build his own $1 billion conglomerate. Through the 1970s Bailey acquired some 20 small companies, which together neared $300 million in revenues by the beginning of the 1980s.

COMPANY PERSPECTIVES

We perform as an extension of our customers' engineering and manufacturing functions, with a commitment to identify and provide engineered solutions to design problems through technical innovation, cost-effective manufacturing and outstanding value-added service.

Bailey's second acquisition was Kaydon, which he bought in 1969. Over the next decade, Bailey pumped some $50 million into Kaydon, upgrading its plants to state-of-the-art equipment, adding specialty filtration products to its line, and expanding Kaydon's facilities to seven plants for a total of 900,000 square feet of manufacturing space. At the same time Bailey guided Kaydon toward new customers in its core markets and brought the company into new markets, including the robotics industry and the developing market for CAT scanners. Bailey's strategy for Kaydon was working: by 1975 the company was posting nearly $36 million in revenues, and four years later the company topped $65.5 million in sales. By 1981 Kaydon's sales had risen to $85 million. The company's operating profits also saw steady growth, from $3.8 million in 1975 to $22.4 million in 1981.

REBIRTH

By then, however, Bailey had soured on the conglomerate concept. Instead, Bailey sought to build a different type of corporate empire. He restructured his collection of companies, combining them into separate divisions, and renamed the parent corporation as Bairnco (*bairn* was a Scottish word for "child"). Bailey's idea was to nurture the separate divisions until they could be spun off as independent companies.

Bailey would appoint himself chairman of each new spin-off. As he told *Business Week*, "Big companies kill the entrepreneurial spirit. I'd much rather have five $200 million companies with highly motivated management than a single, institutionalized $1 billion one."

Bailey sought to nurture the entrepreneurial spirit in his management as well. Managers of the Bairnco divisions were given ample incentive to build the division by being offered the opportunity to take over the leadership of a newly spun off company. Further incentive was added in the form of performance bonuses: all employees could double the salaries with bonuses linked

to the division's net income. Lastly, while Bailey would himself take a share of stock in a new spin-off, management of the newly independent company would also receive a large share of the company's stock.

Despite the recession of the early 1980s, which saw Kaydon's sales drop to $80 million in 1982 and then to $72 million in 1983, Bailey was ready to give birth to Bairnco's first "child" by 1984. In April of that year Bairnco spun off Kaydon Corporation to stockholders. Bailey was named chairman of the new public entity, and received 9 percent of the company's stock, while Kaydon's management, including President Richard Shantz, received a total of 20 percent of the stock, at $2 per share.

The new Kaydon debuted at $3.50 per share, and within five years its stock price would climb to $30 per share. Kaydon also began its return to independence with a heavy debt load: some $60 million in cash debt against $10 million in equity. Yet, as the market for the company's bearings and filtration products began to recover, Kaydon's revenues rebounded, climbing to a new high of $86 million, for net earnings of $5.7 million.

DIVERSIFICATION AND EXPANSION

Under Shantz, Kaydon adopted the growth strategies of its former parent, and began extending into new product areas. Kaydon sought to redefine itself from a producer of specialty bearings to a manufacturer of custom-designed and engineered product solutions. By 1984 the company had added bearings for jet engine components and an antifriction roller lift valve assembly for the automotive market. The latter product, which helped to reduce engine exhaust emissions, quickly proved successful among automobile makers rushing to meet new federal emissions restrictions.

Kaydon looked beyond internal expansion to fuel the company's growth. Taking another lesson from its former parent, the company set out on the acquisition trail. Its first acquisition came in 1986, with the $29.6 million cash purchase of Koppers Company's Ring and Seal division. Ring and Seal, located in Baltimore, Maryland, had originally produced cast-iron stoves as far back as 1832, then made cannon balls during the Civil War, but by the 1980s had matured into a specialized producer of sealing rings and shaft seals for a customer base similar to Kaydon's bearings and other products.

The acquisition quickly lifted Kaydon's revenues, to $112.5 million in 1986 and to $133.5 million the following year. Earnings were also strong, reaching $17 million for 1987. By then, Kaydon had made its second

KEY DATES

■

1941: The Kaydon Engineering Company is founded in Muskegon, Michigan, to support the United States' entry into World War II.

1969: Glen Bailey acquires Kaydon.

1984: Parent company Bairnco spins off Kaydon Corporation to stockholders.

1988: Kaydon makes its first international move by constructing a plant for its newly formed maquiladora subsidiary in Mexico.

1996: Glen Bailey steps down from Kaydon's board of directors.

2009: Kaydon completes an $80 million wind energy capacity expansion program.

acquisition, a $5.1 million cash purchase of the Spirolox specialty retaining ring division of TRW Inc. In 1987 Shantz took over the chairmanship of the company from Bailey, who remained on the board of directors. In November of that year Lawrence Cawley, who had joined the company in 1985, was named president and chief executive officer.

The company's market focus was also undergoing a shift. While aerospace and military continued as the company's primary market segment, replacement parts and export had grown to nearly one-third of company sales. At the same time, the company was rolling back sales to the automotive and agricultural markets, in the face of shrinking profit margins, to represent only 6 percent of sales.

GOING INTERNATIONAL

In 1988 Kaydon made its first international move. The company constructed a plant for its newly formed maquiladora subsidiary in Mexico, in order to produce large bearings (up to 120 inches in diameter) for the construction industry. The following year Kaydon went international again with the acquisition of IDM of Reading, England. At the same time Kaydon acquired Electro-Tec Corp. of Blacksburg, Virginia. The two acquisitions, made for $22 million in cash, brought the company into the slip ring business.

Used for transmitting electrical signals or power between rotating and stationary members of electromechanical devices, slip rings fit well into Kaydon's portfolio of highly engineered, customized specialty products. The IDM acquisition also gave Kay-

don an important foothold for expanding into the European market. Together the acquisitions helped boost the company's revenues to $151 million. Inside Kaydon management, Cawley succeeded Shantz as company chairman, while Stephen Clough, who had been serving as vice president, was named the company's president.

As Kaydon entered the new decade, it continued on its expansion through acquisition strategy. Next up was the $40 million cash purchase of Cooper Bearings, based in King's Lynn in the United Kingdom, and its Cooper U.S.A. subsidiary. The Cooper acquisition further enhanced Kaydon's status in the specialty bearing market, adding Cooper's line of highly specialized split roller bearings, further strengthening Kaydon's European position and placing the company among the world leaders of the specialty bearing market.

CHALLENGING TIMES

Meanwhile, the company had been working to refocus the company's market emphasis, boosting the revenue share of replacement parts and exports to nearly 40 percent of sales, while lessening its reliance on the weakening military and aerospace markets, and phasing out of the automotive market (which the company left in 1995). Despite an upsurge in military orders surrounding the Persian Gulf War, the company's growth was hampered by the recession of the early 1990s. In 1991 Kaydon posted its first and only revenue decline since its spin-off in 1984. In that year, Kaydon also moved its corporate headquarters from Muskegon to Clearwater, Florida.

By 1992, however, the Cooper acquisition allowed Kaydon to post a rebound, gaining some $23 million in sales to end the year with $183 million. Over the next three years, Kaydon continued to add to its stable of subsidiaries, and its revenues, with four acquisitions. These included Kenyon Corp., Industrial Tectonics Corp., DJ Moldings Corp., and in 1995, the $22 million cash purchase of Seabee Corp., a privately held designer and producer of custom-engineered machinery components.

Kaydon's strong record of successful acquisitions was helping the company build its revenues to nearly $300 million, with net earnings of more than $50 million, by year-end 1996. At this time Bailey stepped down from Kaydon's board of directors to concentrate on his own corporate empire. The company moved forward under the continued leadership of Chairman Cawley.

CHALLENGES CONTINUE

In early 1997 Kaydon acquired the Kansas-based manufacturer Great Bend Industries Corp. The $22 million cash deal was the company's fifth acquisition since September 1995. Great Bend became part of Kaydon's newly formed Fluid Power Group. In all, Kaydon employed roughly 2,300 workers in the United States, Mexico, Germany, and England.

Brian Campbell served as Kaydon's president and CEO during the late 1990s. The company ended the decade on a sour note, due in part to sluggish conditions within the industrial sector. Its stock, which sold for $41.05 a share in early 1999, plummeted to $23 per share by October.

These difficult conditions prompted Kaydon to lay off approximately 200 workers. The company's shareholders gave the green light for an equity incentive program that called for the distribution of approximately $50 million worth of stock (2 million shares) to certain employees over a six-year period. Despite these difficulties, Kaydon ended the decade with cash reserves of $100 million, as well as $300 million in credit for acquisition purposes.

A NEW MILLENNIUM

Acquisitions continued during the new millennium. In early 2001 Kaydon spent $70 million to acquire Farmington Hills, Michigan-based ACE Controls Inc. and ACE Controls International Inc. The two companies, which manufactured industrial valves and shock absorbers, helped Kaydon further diversify its business.

Toward the end of the year Kaydon was evaluating plans to potentially sell its struggling Fluid Power Products Group. The operation was incurring operating and cash flow losses as the result of slack demand for hydraulic fluid power products. For the year, Kaydon recorded a net loss of $4 million on sales of $285.6 million.

Kaydon continued to deal with difficult economic conditions in 2002. During the first half of the year the company generated net income of $8.4 million, down from $16.9 million during the first half of 2001. In 2002 Kaydon's board of directors approved a plan to buy back up to 3.4 million shares of the company's stock. At this time the company was engaged in two lawsuits, resulting in legal costs of $2.8 million during the first half of the year alone.

In 2003 Kaydon generated net income of $33.8 million on revenues of $294.1 million. Following a brief pause, the company made plans to shift back into acquisition mode. Specifically, Chairman and CEO

Brian Campbell indicated that the company would spend as much as $250 million on acquisitions in 2004 alone. Among Kaydon's acquisitions during the middle of the decade was Purafil Inc., a manufacturer of gas-phase air-purification systems. That year, Kaydon also sold its Power and Data Transmission Products unit to Moog Inc. in a $72.4 million deal.

CAPITAL EXPANSION

As Kaydon headed into the end of the first decade of the 21st century, the company began putting more of a focus on the wind energy sector. Specifically, more than $30 million was earmarked to increase production capacity for large-diameter bearings used in wind turbines. By increasing capacity at the company's plants in Monterrey, Mexico, and Sumter, South Carolina, Kaydon positioned itself for success in a market that was expected to grow from $11.4 billion in 2005 to $44 billion in 2010.

Important leadership changes took place at Kaydon in early 2007. At that time Campbell announced plans to retire as the company's chairman, president, and CEO in May. He was succeeded in all three positions by James O'Leary. In addition, John R. Emling was promoted from senior vice president of operations to senior vice president and chief operating officer.

In mid-2007 Kaydon's board of directors approved a 25 percent increase in the company's regular quarterly dividend. In addition, the board okayed additional expansion of Kaydon's wind energy initiative. Specifically, an additional $25 million in capital expenditures was approved over the course of 18 months. For the year capital expenditures totaled $56 million, compared to $26.3 million in 2006. Expansion continued during the latter part of the year when Kaydon acquired Ann Arbor, Michigan-based Avon Bearings Corp. in a $55 million cash deal.

CONTINUED WIND ENERGY FOCUS

The wind energy market continued to be of great importance to Kaydon in 2008. Several management changes took place in October of that year as part of an internal restructuring effort that was meant to ramp up growth within the company's turntable bearing business, which served the wind energy market. Specifically, L. Jeffrey Manzagol was named president of the company's Industrial Bearings division, including the turntable business. In addition, Emling was named group president of three businesses: Kaydon Custom Bearings, Filtration, and Sealing Products.

In early 2009 Chief Financial Officer Kenneth Crawford announced he would step down on June 30 to accept a position with another company. Peter DeChants, senior vice president of corporate development and strategy and company treasurer, was named his successor. Despite difficult economic conditions, Kaydon continued paying dividends to shareholders in 2009. Better still, in the third quarter the company actually increased its regular quarterly dividend from $0.17 per share to $0.18 per share.

During the first half of 2009 Kaydon completed its wind energy capacity expansion program. In all, the company had invested about $80 million since 2006. Subsequently, sales within Kaydon's Friction Control Products business segment, which included wind energy customers, had increased steadily during the second half of the decade. From $32.9 million in 2007, sales reached $80.5 million in 2008 and $103.0 million in 2009.

Expansion continued at Kaydon in 2010. Midway through the year the company announced plans to expand its Sumter, South Carolina, facility, which had recently received AS9100B aerospace industry certification, in order to accommodate increased demand for custom bearings. At the same time plans were made to cease operations at Kaydon's Mocksville, North Carolina, facility. Moving forward, Kaydon appeared to be positioned for continued success during the 2010s.

M. L. Cohen
Updated, Paul R. Greenland

PRINCIPAL SUBSIDIARIES

Kaydon Ring and Seal, Inc.; Kaydon S. de R.L. de C.V. (Mexico); Cooper Roller Bearings Company Limited (UK); The Cooper Split Roller Bearing Corp.; Cooper Geteilte Rollenlager GmbH (Germany); Cooper Roller Bearings (Hong Kong) Company Limited; Industrial Tectonics Inc.; ITI Japan Trading Company; Kaydon Custom Filtration Corporation; Kaydon Acquisition XI, Inc. (d/b/a Canfield Technologies, Inc.); Kaydon Acquisition XII, Inc. (d/b/a Tridan International, Inc.); Indiana Precision, Inc.; ACE Controls, Inc.; ACE Controls International, Inc.; ACE Japan, L.L.C.; ACE Stossdaempfer, GmbH; ACE Automation Control Equipment Private Limited (India); Purafil, Inc.; Purafil Europa B.V. (Netherlands); Avon Bearings Corporation; Cooper Roller Bearings Do Brasil Assesoria Empresarial Sociedade Ltda. (Brazil); Ace Controls (Suzhou) Co., Ltd. (China).

PRINCIPAL OPERATING UNITS

Friction Control Products; Velocity Control Products; Sealing Products.

PRINCIPAL COMPETITORS

Aktiebolaget SKF; Kaman Corporation; The Timken Company.

FURTHER READING

"Bairnco: An Empire that Spins Off Companies to Grow," *Business Week*, April 30, 1984, p. 68.

Bodipo-Memba, Alejandro, "Brief: Ann Arbor-Based Kaydon Buys Ohio Bearings Maker," *Detroit Free Press*, October 29, 2007.

"Kaydon Corp. Announces Plans to Expand Its Custom Bearings Operations in Sumter, S.C.," *Business Wire*, May 18, 2010.

"Kaydon Corporation Announces New Leadership Structure and Management Appointments," *Business Wire*, October 24, 2008.

"Kaydon Corporation Announces Plan for Leadership Transition," *Business Wire*, February 27, 2007.

Kingman, Nancy, "Bairnco Spins Off Kaydon, Plans More Similar Ventures," *American Metal Market*, April 30, 1984, p. 15.

Strong, Michael, "Spending Spree; Kaydon Corp. Wants to Strengthen Business Mix with Select Acquisitions," *Crain's Detroit Business*, May 17, 2004, p. 3.

Keystone Foods LLC

300 Barr Harbor Drive, Suite 600
West Conshohocken, Pennsylvania 19428
U.S.A.
Telephone: (610) 667-6700
Fax: (610) 667-1460
Web site: http://www.keystonefoods.com

Wholly Owned Subsidiary of Marfrig Alimentos S.A.
Incorporated: 1973
Employees: 13,700
Sales: $6.54 billion (2008 est.)
NAICS: 311612 Meat Processed from Carcasses; 311615
    Poultry Processing

■ ■ ■

Keystone Foods LLC is a Philadelphia, Pennsylvania-
area based company that manufacturers and distributes
beef, pork, fish, and poultry products to McDonald's
restaurants as well as other restaurants, grocery stores,
and butcher shops in the United States and other
countries. Product offerings include frozen hamburger
patties, fish patties, beef and chicken fajita strips,
chicken nuggets, chicken breast filets, chicken wings,
and breaded chicken patties. Each year Keystone delivers
260 million pounds of beef, 400 million pounds of
chicken, and 25 million pounds of fish to McDonald's
alone.

Processing facilities and about 30 distribution
centers are maintained in North America, Europe, the
Middle East, Australia, New Zealand, and the Asia
Pacific region. In addition, Keystone operates M&M

Restaurant Supply, providing a full range of foods and
dry goods and logistical services to its restaurant
customers. It also maintains a research and development
unit to create new products as well as prototypes for
market research. In June 2010 Brazilian meat processor
Marfrig Alimentos S.A. announced that it would acquire
Keystone for $1.26 billion.

ORIGINAL TIES TO MCDONALD'S

Keystone Foods was established to supply frozen
hamburger patties to the McDonald's restaurant chain.
Credited with the idea was S. Jackson Catt, a New York
food broker. He was about 50 years old in the early
1960s when he was working on behalf of a frozen meat
products company, signing up distributors across the
country. In his travels he came across numerous Mc-
Donald's restaurants and recognized that there might be
an opportunity to supply frozen ground beef patties to
the growing hamburger chain. McDonald's at that time
was also troubled by the inconsistent product they were
receiving from 180 individual suppliers around the
country. The weight and shape was not consistent and
the ground beef spoiled too quickly.

Catt took his idea to a South Philadelphia
company, S. Lotman & Son, a meat rendering business.
That company was run by Samuel Lotman, who had
begun his career as a wholesale meat jobber, and his son
Herbert, who was in his early 30s at the time. The
younger Lotman led the development of a process to
quick-freeze beef patties at their optimal level of taste
and texture, thus pioneering cryogenic freezing
technology. Around 1963 Catt and Herbert Lotman

persuaded McDonald's to introduce the patties on a trial basis at 10 McDonald's restaurants in Washington, D.C., and the Lotmans began producing quick-freeze burger patties at their south Philadelphia plant. They were a success, and on the strength of a handshake deal a long-term relationship with McDonald's was established.

KEYSTONE TAKEN PUBLIC: 1975

Catt served as a senior executive for the company, which initially did business as S. Lotman & Son. To exclusively serve the needs of McDonald's, a subsidiary was formed in the early 1970s under the name Equity Meat Corp., owned by Herbert Lotman, his brother-in-law Jeffrey Weinberg, and Catt. In 1972 Equity opened a plant in Folcraft, Pennsylvania, and the South Philadelphia operation closed in September 1974. The new plant allowed Equity to increase beef patty production from 1.5 million pounds in 1970 to 50 million pounds in 1972. A second Equity plant was opened in North Baltimore, Ohio. By 1975 Equity was producing about 28 million frozen patties a week, supplying 1,200 McDonald's restaurants on the East Coast. Also in 1975 the business was taken public as Keystone Foods and its stock was eventually listed on the New York Stock Exchange.

In the meantime, Keystone deepened its ties to McDonald's. The two companies joined together to develop a total distribution operation, so that individual restaurants in the chain could receive everything they needed in a single delivery, from frozen products and buns to dry goods and paper products. To achieve this end, Keystone acquired M&M Restaurant Supply in 1974. In addition to consolidated deliveries that improved efficiencies, the new concept also created economies of scale, allowing for volume purchasing and the reduction of cost to customers. Single deliveries also allowed store managers to spend more time on their core responsibilities.

The relationship between McDonald's and Keystone was strengthened further in the mid-1970s when the restaurant chain had to contend with a beef shortage. Keystone was able to secure domestic supplies and then developed a cattle-management program in

1976 to provide McDonald's with a reliable supply of beef.

CHICKEN PRODUCT DEVELOPED

Keystone also helped McDonald's in the development of Chicken McNuggets in the late 1970s. Chicken McNuggets, or McChicken as it was known at the time, was the brainchild of Fred L. Turner, McDonald's chairman and CEO. He telephoned Herbert Lotman, and according to Lotman, he said, "I have an idea. I want a chicken finger-food without bones, about the size of your thumb. Can you do it?" Although Keystone had never worked with chicken products, Lotman, rather than letting this opportunity slip by, agreed to lead a development team that would include three employees from Keystone and three from McDonald's. Work on the project was conducted at a new plant in Tennessee acquired by Equity to sell frozen steaks and other portion-controlled beef products to restaurants and hotels.

Six months later the group unveiled a new product that took the McChicken name. Initially introduced in test markets in 1980, the product enjoyed so much success that Keystone dedicated the Tennessee plant to its production. The company had invested $500,000 in the late 1970s to produce beef, and the plant was just beginning to turn a profit when the conversion was made. It was not a difficult decision. The plant would have been fortunate to grow sales to the $25 million range after five years, while the chicken business was likely to grow as high as $200 million in just two to three years.

CHICKEN MCNUGGETS
INTRODUCED WORLDWIDE: 1983

Keystone also spent $9.2 million to open a second chicken production plant in Reidsville, North Carolina, constructed in less than four months. That extra capacity would be needed when Chicken McNuggets were introduced worldwide in 1983. Within a few weeks McDonald's was the second-largest chicken retailer worldwide, trailing only Kentucky Fried Chicken in market share. Moreover, the effort launched Keystone's new research and development group.

Samuel Lotman served as chairman of the board of Keystone until his retirement in the late 1970s. Catt was also at retirement age. He died in 1982, followed a year later by the death of Lotman. Herbert Lotman was left as chairman and CEO. He inherited a company that posted revenues of $420 million in fiscal 1981. In addition to its core food processing business, Keystone also

KEY DATES

1963: Keystone's predecessor begins producing frozen beef patties for McDonald's.

1972: Processing plant opens in Folcraft, Pennsylvania.

1975: The business is taken public as Keystone Foods.

1980: Production of McChicken (later known as McNuggets) begins.

1995: Keystone establishes a new division, Key-Farms Foodservice, to produce chicken products for quick-serve restaurants.

2008: Keystone ends sponsorship of McDonald's LPGA Championship tournament.

2010: Marfrig Alimentos S.A., a meat processing company based in Brazil, acquires Keystone.

owned RGM Services Inc., a provider of carpet and upholstery cleaning services through a license with Sears, Roebuck & Co. Acquired in 1980, RGM was a bid to diversify into consumer services that failed to take hold. The future growth of Keystone would continue to be linked to McDonald's.

Although Keystone never formalized its relationship with McDonald's, investors did not appear worried because it was clear that Keystone's contribution to the giant restaurant chain was important and not easily duplicated. Nor did the handshake deal dissuade possible suitors. In 1982 majority control of Keystone was acquired by a British food processor, Northern Foods plc, for $69.1 million. Northern had been expanding and investing its money outside of the United Kingdom. It was no stranger to the Philadelphia area, having acquired a pork-products company, Bluebird Inc., three years earlier. However, Bluebird lost money and Keystone did not meet expectations. As a result, Northern divested the U.S. companies in 1986, and Herbert Lotman became Keystone's owner.

Despite its problems with Northern, Keystone was able to expand overseas in the 1980s. McKey Food Services was established in France to produce frozen beef patties for restaurants in France, Belgium, and Morocco. In Malaysia, MacFood Services was formed to produce beef, chicken, and fish products for quick-serve restaurants in Malaysia, Hong Kong, and Singapore. Also in the 1980s Keystone grew its domestic business. Its KeyFresh Foods unit began working with Wawa Foods Markets of Wawa, Pennsylvania, in 1989 to create

the Fresh Buffet line of refrigerated entrées for sale in Philadelphia-area Wawa convenience stores.

CHARITY GOLF TOURNAMENT ESTABLISHED: 1981

Despite his responsibilities in running Keystone Foods, Lotman found time in the early 1980s to help found a charity golf tournament that would become a matter of pride for both Keystone and McDonald's. The seeds were planted while Lotman was playing golf with Frank Quinn, a McDonald's restaurant owner and operator in central New Jersey. The two men discovered they both harbored a dream about starting a charity golf tournament with McDonald's and decided to work together to make it a reality. Rather than working with the men's PGA Tour, they decided to team up with the women's LPGA tour.

The first professional-amateur tournament, called the McDonald's Kids Classic, was held in Malvern, Pennsylvania, in 1981. Expected to lose money, it raised $200,000 for charity. The event proved highly popular and successful, and in the early 1990s the McDonald's LPGA Championship became one of the four major women's golf tournaments. Lotman and Quinn continued to run the event and Keystone cosponsored it with McDonald's until 2008. Due to the poor economy at that time, the event was no longer able to turn a profit for charity. The LPGA then took over the tournament. In all, the event raised more than $33 million for Ronald McDonald Houses and Ronald McDonald House Charities worldwide.

Keystone continued to expand at home and abroad in the 1990s, as annual sales topped the $1 billion mark by mid-decade. Manufacturing plants were added in Australia, China, and Thailand. The company also opened distribution centers in Europe and Korea. At home, Keystone established LD Foods in Wisconsin in 1995 to produce fish portioned for sale to quick-serve restaurants located in the eastern United States. Also in 1995 Keystone established a new division, KeyFarms Foodservice. Based in Gadsden, Alabama, it produced chicken products for quick-serve restaurants. Later in the decade Keystone expanded its domestic poultry operations by constructing new plants in Georgia and Kentucky.

PLANT OF THE YEAR: 2010

By the end of the 1990s Keystone was posting annual revenues of about $3 billion. Growth continued in the new century on a number of fronts. The McKey Foods plant in Thailand was expanded to supply McDonald's restaurants in Japan and Korea. Keystone expanded its Alabama operation with the addition of an 185,000-

square-foot facility, allowing the company to better serve the growing U.S. poultry business. The state-of-the-art plant was named 2010 Plant of the Year by *Food Engineering Magazine*, due primarily to its focus on food safety and quality control.

Keystone also extended its international reach. In 2005 the company acquired three distribution centers in Australia and six distribution centers in the United Kingdom. Another distribution center was added in New Zealand in 2008. Keystone's annual revenues were then in the $6 billion range. The company's relationship with McDonald's remained strong, and there was every likelihood that Keystone would continue to enjoy success for many years to come. In June 2010, the company announced that it had reached an agreement to be acquired by one of Brazil's largest processors and exporters of meat, Marfrig Alimentos S.A. The deal, worth $1.26 billion in cash and debt, was the last in a string of acquisitions for the Brazilian company. Management at Keystone, according to a June 2010 article in the *Philadelphia Inquirer*, believed that Marfrig's "business in Latin America and Europe complements Keystone's units in Asia and the English-speaking world."

Ed Dinger

PRINCIPAL SUBSIDIARIES

Keystone Distribution UK Ltd.; Keystone Foods (AP) Ltd.; Keystone Foods Pty Ltd.

PRINCIPAL COMPETITORS

JBS S.A.; OSI Industries, LLC; SYSCO Corporation.

FURTHER READING

DiStefano, Joseph N., "PhillyDeals: Keystone Foods Sold to Brazil's Marfrig Alimentos," *Philadelphia Inquirer*, June 16, 2010.

"11 Million Hamburgers a Week," *Delaware County Times*, February 24, 1976, p. 24.

"Keystone Forms Foodservice Division," *Nation's Restaurant News*, August 7, 1995.

"Phila. Meat Firm Prepares Hamburgers for McDonalds," *Hanover (PA) Evening Sun*, May 1, 1975, p. 3.

Rouse, Ewart, "Keystone Basks in Glitter of Golden Arches," *Philadelphia Inquirer*, May 15, 1981, p. C12.

"Samuel Lotman, Businessman," *Philadelphia Inquirer*, August 22, 1983, p. B4.

Stock, Craig, "British Firm to Buy Keystone Foods," *Philadelphia Inquirer*, January 14, 1982, p. B7.

Korea Electric Power Corporation

411 Yeongdong-Daero
Gangnam-gu
Seoul, 135-791
South Korea
Telephone: (+82 2) 3456-4264
Fax: (+82 2) 556-3694
Web site: http://www.kepco.co.kr

Public Company
Incorporated: 1898 as Hansung Electric Company
Employees: 20,177
Sales: KRW 31.5 trillion ($25.03 billion) (2008)
Stock Exchanges: Korea New York
Ticker Symbol: KEP
NAICS: 221122 Electric Power Distribution

■ ■ ■

Korea Electric Power Corporation, also known as KEPCO, is one of the world's largest power generation companies with a capacity of 64,583 megawatts (MW) in 2008. The company began to dismantle its more than 40-year monopoly of South Korea's electric power industry in early 2001. Since that time, KEPCO has been restructuring its operations, splitting up its non-nuclear power generation operations into five separate regional businesses including Korea South-East Power Co. (KOSEPCO), Korea Southern Power Co. (KO-SPO), Korea Midland Power Co. (KOMIPO), Korea Western Power Co. (KOWEPO), and Korea East-West Power Co. (KEWESPO).

The restructuring included plans to privatize these subsidiaries, but plans were shelved in 2004 and again in 2008 due to weak market conditions. As part of its restructuring, KEPCO also created a sixth business, Korea Hydro & Nuclear Power Co. (KHNP), which took over all of the company's nuclear power and hydroelectric power generating facilities, accounting for just over 35 percent of the group's total power generation capacity. Listed on both the Korean and New York stock exchanges, KEPCO remains 51 percent controlled by the Korean government.

ROYAL ORIGINS

Soon after Thomas Edison connected the first electric lightbulb, the Korean government, then in the waning decades of the final Han dynasty under King Kojong, sent a delegation to visit Edison and view his invention. Edison convinced the delegation of the need for electric lighting in King Kojong's Kyongbok palace. Orders for a generator were placed in 1884. However, political unrest, including an attempted coup, pushed back completion of the first generator, and the palace lights were not switched on until early 1887.

Initial reception of the new technology was limited, with many fearful of electricity as a supernatural force. The technology suffered a new setback when the original engineer assigned by Edison to install the generator died in an accidental shooting. Nevertheless, King Kojong remained supportive of the technology and ordered a new generator for Changdok Palace, which at the time of its completion in 1897 was the largest power generator in the region. By 1891 the original Kyongbok power plant was replaced with a new and larger facility, which was completed in 1894.

By the end of the decade, the royal government had recognized the potential of electrical power and was determined to extend it to the public sector. In 1898 King Kojong granted authorization for the creation of a joint venture with two American businessmen, Henry Collbran and Harry Rice Bostwick, called the Hansung (or Seoul) Electric Company. The new company, 50 percent owned by the king himself, was charged with establishing a public electrical lighting network in Seoul, and contracted with Collbran and Bostwick Company to build an electric streetcar system as well.

Hansung Electric completed its first power plant in 1899 at Tongdaemun. By the end of that year the company had succeeded in launching its streetcar service, and soon after had turned on its first electric lights in Seoul's Chongno Street. With a monopoly on Seoul's electricity and streetcar systems, Hansung Electric continued to build up its public lighting network at the beginning of the 20th century, and began offering electrical service to private homes as well.

JAPANESE COMPETITION

The occupation of Korea by Japan following 1905 brought new competition to Hansung Electric. A group of Japanese businessmen set up a rival gas-lighting system, which proved highly competitive for some time. Meanwhile, Hansung Electric's American owners were under increasing pressure to sell out to its Japanese rivals, in a deal that cut out the country's former ruler. Korea's electrical power system continued to develop under Japanese occupation, and a number of new companies were established, including Kyungsung Electric Company in 1915, the Chosun Electric Company in 1943, and the Namsun Electric Company in 1946. The bulk of Japanese investments in power generation went to the northern half of the country. Since Korea itself had virtually no natural fuel deposits, the country's power plants were established closer to Chinese coal supplies.

Japan's capitulation at the end of World War II led to the division of Korea into the Allied-dominated south and the Soviet-dominated north in 1945. In the initial postwar years, the northern half of the country continued to supply the southern half with electrical power. However, the outbreak of the Korean War in 1950 caused the power grid between the two halves to be cut overnight, leaving South Korea, with its undeveloped power generation capacity, in economic chaos. Power shortages became commonplace, especially as the war destroyed much of South Korea's existing electrical power infrastructure. In the years following the war, the Korean government initiated a number of power-saving measures, such as not allowing elevators to stop at the first three floors of buildings, and barring escalators from early subway stations.

GOVERNMENT-LED ELECTRICAL POWER COMPANY: 1961–89

The military-backed coup of 1961 and the installation of a military government introduced a new period not only to Korea's economy but to its electrical power sector as well. In 1961 the government grouped together the three existing regional companies, Kyungsung, Namsun, and Chosun, to form a single, nationally operating electric power entity, Korea Electric Company, which became known as KECO.

While austerity measures continued through the 1970s, the government began ambitious investment and development programs that were ultimately successful in transforming South Korea into one of the region's financial and industrial heavyweights. Part of that development program included massive investments in boosting the country's power-generation capacity.

Furthermore, the government recognized early on that South Korea's lack of natural resources made it too dependent on foreign resources for its power supply. As early as 1962, the country initiated plans to develop its own nuclear power industry with the aim of reducing its reliance on fossil fuels. Backed by the United States, Korea launched its nuclear development program. In the meantime, the country was hard hit by the Arab oil embargo and the resulting worldwide recession in the early 1970s, further stimulating its drive toward nuclear power capacity.

Korea brought its first nuclear-based power generation facility online in 1978. That plant, the Kori-1, was built by Westinghouse, a U.S. company, and boasted a capacity of nearly 600 MW. The country also began awarding contracts for new nuclear plants, with eight new plants to open by the end of the 1980s. In the meantime, the Korean government moved in 1982 to take complete control of KECO, which was then renamed Korean Electric Power Corporation, or KEPCO.

KEY DATES

1887: The first electric lights are turned on in Korea's Kyongbok palace.

1898: Americans are contracted to build an electric network in Seoul, forming the Hansung (Seoul) Electric Company (50 percent owned by the king).

1915: Kyungsung Electric Company is founded.

1943: Chosun Electric Company is founded.

1946: Namsun Electric Company is founded.

1961: South Korean government leads the merger of Kyungsung, Chosun, and Namsun into the new Korea Electric Company, or KECO.

1982: Korea Electric is taken over by the government and renamed Korea Electric Power Corporation (KEPCO).

1989: KEPCO goes public with 21 percent of shares.

2001: KEPCO restructures by separating its power generation operations into six independently operating subsidiaries.

2008: Kim Ssang-su is elected CEO; privatization plans are put on hold.

KEPCO continued adding nuclear power facilities to its grid throughout the 1980s, bringing the country's total to nine by the end of the decade. The company also began planning its next phase of reactors, meant to bring the country's total to some 17 by the beginning of the 21st century. KEPCO sought to develop its own reactor designs in the late 1980s. In the meantime, the company's total nuclear output topped 4.75 million kilowatts by 1986, representing 26 percent of its total power-generation capacity.

PREPARING FOR DEREGULATION: 1989–99

KEPCO went public in 1989 as part of the Korean government's larger privatization program. In that year the company, then one of Korea's largest nonfinancial corporations, listed some 21 percent of its stock on the Korean stock exchange. The government remained in control of the decision making, however, particularly its policy of charging low rates to industrial and other customers, including farmers, in order to stimulate the economy. While this policy achieved its goal, it hampered KEPCO's ability to invest in new power-generation capacity. Nevertheless, the company re-

mained profitable, posting earnings of $557 million on 1993 revenues of $9.3 billion.

KEPCO continued to target growth in its domestic market in the mid-1990s, announcing a five-year, $40 billion investment program to boost its generating capacity by more than 60 percent. The company, which listed its shares (as American Depositary Receipts, or ADRs) on the New York Stock Exchange in 1994, had also adopted a new strategic direction: that of international expansion. This new strategy came in part because of increasing signs of the Korean government's interest in opening up the domestic power market to competition, originally expected to occur as early as 1997.

KEPCO's first step onto the international front came in 1993, when it was awarded a contract to upgrade and operate a power-generating facility in Manila, Philippines. In 1995 KEPCO increased its presence in that country when it received a contract to relocate two of its existing Korean power plants to Cebu, which boosted the group's total generating capacity in the Philippines to more than 1,000 MW (as compared with its total Korean capacity of 28,000 MW).

KEPCO began a new restructuring drive in preparation for the coming deregulation. Part of the company's preparation involved the hiring of a new chief executive, the first to be chosen through an open recruitment process. The new CEO, Chang Young-sik, launched the company on a restructuring drive, shedding a number of businesses, including its telecommunications investments, some of which were spun off into a new company, Powercomm, in 2000. KEPCO also cut back its workforce by more than 3,700.

OVERCOMING OPPOSITION IN THE 21ST CENTURY

KEPCO remained hampered by a spiraling debt, which in the last half of the 1990s had more than doubled, topping KRW 33 trillion by 2000, including some $10 billion in foreign debt. By then the broad outline of the government's plans for the company were in place, involving the breakup of KEPCO into a number of independently operating power generating subsidiaries. However, these plans met with growing resistance from the country's unions, forcing the company to make a number of concessions, including a pledge to retain majority control of the companies to be spun off. At the same time, analysts warned that KEPCO would have to raise its rates, especially its artificially low industrial rates, if the privatization effort was to succeed.

Massive strikes across the country forced the government to place KEPCO's restructuring and the deregulation of the Korean market on hold until 2001. The company created six new subsidiaries that year. Five of them—Korea South-East Power Co. (KOSEPCO), Korea Southern Power Co. (KOSPO), Korea Midland Power Co. (KOMIPO), Korea Western Power Co. (KOWEPO), and Korea East-West Power Co. (KEWESPO)—represented the company's regionally operating fossil fuel generating facilities and were slated to be sold as privatized companies to foreign and domestic investors. The sixth company, Korea Hydro & Nuclear Power Co. (KHNP), which grouped the company's nuclear and hydroelectric facilities, was to remain under KEPCO's control.

The first of the companies slated for privatization was KOSEPCO, which was also the smallest. Initially slated for 2001, the sale, which faced continued resistance, finally appeared to be under way at the beginning of 2003, when the government promised to select its preferred bidder. At the same time, the government reiterated its determination to privatize all five of KEPCO's power-generating subsidiaries, with an eye toward full deregulation, including distribution to private homes, by 2009.

KEPCO expected to become one of the region's powerhouses before then, announcing plans to expand throughout the region. As part of that strategy, the company created a new subsidiary in November 2002, KEPCO International, which took over the operations of its former overseas division. At the same time, the company debuted its latest foreign venture, a 1.2 MW natural gas power plant in Ilijan, Philippines, that country's largest.

KEPCO continued to seek new international projects in 2003, with bids on 10 different projects in markets including Saudi Arabia, the United Arab Emirates, and Myanmar. In February 2003 the company announced plans to build a new 500 MW power plant in Indonesia. At the same time, KEPCO was finalizing contracts to begin construction of two coal-fired power plants in China.

DEREGULATION ON HOLD: 2003–10

A sluggish global economy and lack of investor interest forced the Korean government to delay its offering of KOSEPCO and the other power generating subsidiaries in late 2003. The sale was called off again in 2004, after the government concluded a sale would lead to supply and pricing issues in the region's energy market.

President Lee Myung-bak, who favored deregulation, began working on plans to merge several government-owned corporations into a single holding

company entity after taking office in February 2008. While KEPCO was originally included in the plans, the government announced later that year that it was shelving its plans to privatize KEPCO's subsidiaries. Also that year, Kim Ssang-su was elected CEO of the company.

Kim, the former head of LG Electronics Inc. and the first executive of a private company to be named to KEPCO's top position, was tapped to overhaul KEPCO. The company faced huge losses due to rising fuel costs and a freeze on electricity rate increases. Overall, the company posted a net loss of $2.35 billion in 2008, which was the first loss in its history.

Despite the rough economic and market conditions, KEPCO forged ahead with its growth plans. During 2008 the company won a $500 million power project in Jordan to build, own, and operate the Al Qatrana Combined Cycle Gas Turbine Power Station. The company also won the bid to construct Kazakhstan's Balkhash Thermal Power facility.

Later that year KEPCO acquired a 17.07 percent interest in Canada-based Denison Mines Inc. As part of the deal, the company secured rights to uranium produced by Denison, which would supply nearly 8 percent of Korea's annual consumption. KEPCO also secured a $2.5 billion contract to build and operate the Rabigh Heavy Oil Power Plant in Saudi Arabia.

LOOKING TOWARD THE FUTURE

With little growth available in its domestic market, KEPCO focused on international expansion to fuel its bottom line. Under Kim's leadership, the company set the goal to become "A Global Top 5 Utility for Green Energy" as part of its 2020 New Vision. To reach this goal, the company worked to convert its conventional power network to the Smart Grid, which was an emerging technology that allowed real-time monitoring of electricity output and demand. It also focused on green technologies, which included carbon capture and storage facilities, new green power plants, and creating infrastructure necessary for charging electric vehicles.

The company also aimed to invest heavily in nuclear power projects. It won a bid to build four reactors in the United Arab Emirates and expected other projects to follow. It eyed Turkey, Russia, and Jordan as future growth areas. With projections of sales reaching $76 billion by 2020, KEPCO was optimistic about its future. While the Korean government's privatization plans remained in question, the company forged ahead with its expansion plans. With its 2020 New Vision strategy in place, KEPCO believed it was on track for success in the years to come.

M. L. Cohen
Updated, Christina M. Stansell

PRINCIPAL SUBSIDIARIES

Korea Hydro & Nuclear Power Co. Ltd.; Korea South-East Power Co. Ltd.; Korea Midland Power Co. Ltd.; Korea Western Power Co. Ltd.; Korea Southern Power Co. Ltd.; Korea East-West Power Co. Ltd.; Korea Power Engineering Co. Ltd.; Korea Plant Service & Engineering Co. Ltd.; Korea Nuclear Fuel Co. Ltd.; Korea Electric Power Data Network Ltd.

PRINCIPAL COMPETITORS

AES Corporation; CLP Holdings Limited; Huaneng Power International Inc.; Suez-Tractebel S.A.

FURTHER READING

"KEPCO CEO Stresses Overseas Expansion," *Euclid Infotech–Procurement News*, February 10, 2010.

"KEPCO Feels the Crunch of Koreans Using Less Power," *Joins.com*, April 16, 2009.

"KEPCO Unit's IPO Is Delayed," *Asian Wall Street Journal*, December 16, 2003.

Kim, Mi-hui, "All Five Power Companies to Be Privatized," *Korea Herald*, January 28, 2003.

————, "KEPCO to Expand Overseas Business," *Korea Herald*, November 15, 2002.

Kirk, Don, "South Korea: Utility to Start Privatization," *New York Times*, October 10, 2002.

"Korea's KEPCO to Decide on Prime Bidder for KOSEP Next Month," *Asia Pulse News*, February 7, 2003.

"New CEO Determined to Reform KEPCO," *Korea Herald*, September 11, 2008.

Ramstad, Evan, "South Korea Puts Merger of State Firms on Table," *Wall Street Journal*, March 13, 2008, p. A12.

Kramer Beverage
Company

———■———

161 South 2nd Road
Hammonton, New Jersey 08037-1427
U.S.A.
Telephone: (609) 704-7000
Fax: (609) 704-7100
Web site: http://www.kramerbev.com

Private Company
Incorporated: 1924
Employees: 125
Sales: $40 million (2007 est.)
NAICS: 424810 Beer and Ale Merchant Wholesalers

■ ■ ■

Kramer Beverage Company is a Hammonton, New Jersey-based beer distributor serving six southern New Jersey counties: Atlantic, Camden, Cape May, Cumberland, Gloucester, and Salem. Domestic brands include Coors and Yuengling. Kramer also offers such imported brands as Corona, Guinness, Modelo, Molson, Rodenbach, Moosehead, Red Stripe, and Grolsch. Kramer's Specialty Products Division offers a wide variety of craft beer brands, including Blue Moon, Brooklyn Lager, Erie Brewing Co., Great Lakes, Magic Hat, Ommegang, and Samuel Adams.

In addition, Kramer carries flavored malt beverages, such as Smirnoff Ice products, Captain Morgan beverages, Twisted Tea drinks, Mike's Hard Lemonade, and other Mike's drinks. Kramer also sells Coors and Kalber nonalcoholic beer. The company operates out of a 168,000-square-foot warehouse facility in Hammonton,

near the Atlantic City Expressway. Kramer is family owned with a fourth generation of the Kramer family, Mark Kramer, serving as president. His father, Charles W. Kramer, is chief executive officer and chairman of the board.

COMPANY FOUNDED: 1924

Kramer Beverage Company was founded in Atlantic City, New Jersey, in 1924 by Benjamin Kramer. Born in Poland, Kramer immigrated to the United States in 1912. He was one of many businessmen attracted to the opportunities presented by Atlantic City, a resort town established in 1854. The only compelling reason for developing a community on the insect-infested spit of land then known as Absecon Island was that it was the closest point to the Atlantic Ocean from Philadelphia. The businessmen who sponsored the creation of the Camden and Atlantic Railroad and built Atlantic City were interested in offering an alternative to Cape May, America's first seaside resort.

The railroad made it possible for Philadelphians to visit Atlantic City on day trips. Nevertheless, several decades passed before Atlantic City became the tourist destination its founders envisioned. Playing a key role was the introduction of a boardwalk that became the central attraction. In addition to wholesome family attractions, Atlantic City also became known for gambling long before legal casinos were introduced.

When Benjamin Kramer began his business in Atlantic City in 1924, Prohibition was well under way in the United States, and because of its coastal location, Atlantic City had become a major East Coast hub for rumrunners and bootleggers. Kramer bottled and distributed Olympic brand soft drinks as well as mixers that, despite Prohibition, did not lack for alcoholic fortification, especially in Kramer's territory, Atlantic and Cape May counties in New Jersey. He expanded his business in 1927 with the acquisition of the rights to Cliquot Club, a popular national soda brand at the time.

As sales increased, Kramer moved the company to a larger location in Atlantic City in 1929. The business, despite being seasonal for the most part, was also large enough then to allow him to employ his brothers, Harry and Paul. Extending the season was always a concern for Atlantic City, which would build a massive convention center to bring off-season business. City leaders would also create the Miss America beauty pageant, held at the convention center, to serve the same purpose.

BEER DISTRIBUTION RIGHTS ACQUIRED: 1934

By the start of the 1930s Prohibition was widely regarded as a failure. People drank more than ever, and much of what they imbibed included dangerous concoctions resulting in numerous deaths and cases of blindness. To override the 18th Amendment to the Constitution that made alcoholic beverages illegal, Congress passed the 21st Amendment in 1933. Conventions were then held in each of the 48 states, with approval by two-thirds of the states required for passage of the amendment and the repeal of Prohibition. Even before Utah became the 36th state to ratify the amendment in December 1933, laws regulating beer were loosened. As the breweries ramped up production, Kramer quickly secured licenses to distribute Ballantine and Piel's branded beer in 1934.

Once beer sales were introduced, Kramer made another move in 1935, setting up a warehouse in a former parking garage on Virginia Avenue in Atlantic City. It would become the company's home for nearly half a century. It was also in 1935 that Kramer's son, Arnold, joined the company to begin the second generation of family involvement. In 1948 another son, Daniel, went to work for Kramer Beverage as well. By this time, Atlantic City was showing signs of decay due

to a decline in rail travel. A postwar crackdown on organized crime brought an end to backroom casinos, and it was only the annual engagement of New Jersey native Frank Sinatra at the famed 500 Club in Atlantic City that kept the resort afloat in the 1950s. By the early 1960s, however, the town had become so seedy that even Sinatra shied away.

The third generation of the Kramer family became involved in Kramer Beverage in 1964 when Charles Kramer went to work for the company after graduating from Rutgers University. His arrival coincided with the demise of Atlantic City as well as the declining popularity in the company's soft drink brands. Conditions were so dire by the early 1970s that Arnold Kramer's accountant urged him to liquidate the company. However, because his son remained interested in the business, he held on.

Other family members joined the business as well, Arnold Kramer's son Stephen in the early 1970s and daughter Lynn in 1975. It was also in the mid-1970s that the company decided to leave the soft-drink business to focus its attention on beer. Atlantic City in the meantime made gaming legal to revive the local economy, and casinos began bringing in much-needed new customers for Kramer Beverage. The Kramer family was also willing to invest in the business, in the 1970s becoming one of the first beer distributors to computerize its operations.

MOVE TO EGG HARBOR: 1981

Kramer Beverage left Atlantic City for a new facility in Egg Harbor Township in 1981, a move that set the stage for the company to expand its territory and product offerings. A major turning point occurred in the early 1980s when Charles Kramer recognized an opportunity with the emerging popularity of California Coolers. They were not distributed on the East Coast, prompting Kramer to fly to California to meet with the founders of California Coolers and persuade them to leap over multiple states in the rollout of the product to allow Kramer Beverage in 1983 to begin selling their products in southern New Jersey. In addition to Atlantic and Cape May counties, he secured the rights to Cumberland, Camden, Salem, and Gloucester counties to make full use of the new Egg Harbor warehouse. While California Coolers would not have staying power, Kramer Beverage had expanded its footprint and was prepared to move forward.

The next pivotal event in the development of Kramer Beverage, and the most significant in its history, took place later in the 1980s and was another example of Charles Kramer's assertiveness. This time he flew to

```
┌─────────────────────────────────────────────┐
│                                               │
│              KEY DATES                        │
│                   ■                           │
│  ─────────────────────────────────────────    │
│  1924:  Company is founded to distribute soft drinks. │
│  1934:  Company begins distributing beer.     │
│  1983:  California Coolers opens new markets.  │
│  1987:  Kramer begins distributing Coors products. │
│  2002:  Company moves to new facility.         │
│                                               │
└─────────────────────────────────────────────┘
```

Colorado to make a cold call on Coors Brewing Co., which at the time was expanding its distribution east of the Mississippi River. Kramer arranged to meet with the executive responsible for selecting distributors who, as it turned out, was looking at the New Jersey market. Kramer impressed him with his knowledge of the beer business, and in 1986 Kramer Beverage secured the distribution rights for Coors beer in its six-county market. The official introduction occurred in February 1987, when Kramer Beverage began distributing Coors to 1,340 locations in southern New Jersey.

FOURTH GENERATION JOINS COMPANY: 1992

Coors became the most important brand for Kramer Beverage and the key to the company's subsequent growth. In the 1990s Coors Light was the best-selling product Kramer Beverage had to offer. The distributor did so well that Coors presented Kramer Beverage with its highest honor in 1992, the Coors Founder's Award, created to recognize excellent sales performance and other special achievements. The year 1992 was also noteworthy because Charles Kramer's son, Mark D. Kramer, became the fourth generation of the family to join the family business. A Rutgers graduate like his father, Mark Kramer earned an MBA degree at Drexel University in Philadelphia, Pennsylvania, and gained some experience in the beverage industry by going to work at Coca-Cola Bottling Company of Philadelphia before joining his father.

Kramer Beverage enjoyed a steady increase in sales during the 1990s. While Atlantic City and its casinos provided a good deal of business, it was the densely populated western counties outside of Philadelphia, particularly Camden and Gloucester, that provided most of the revenue. Other brands distributed by Kramer Beverage at the end of the 1990s were Corona, Guinness, Yuengling, Harp, Bass, Samuel Adams, Colt 45, St. Ides, Beck's, and Moosehead. In addition to Coors Light, the company's other leading brands were an import, Corona, and a regional Pennsylvania brand, Yuengling.

Kramer Beverage was cramped for space as the decade came to a close. In addition to its longtime facility in Egg Harbor, the company maintained another warehouse in Camden County, and to meet summer demand it rented additional warehouse space. In November 1999 the company acquired 20 acres in the Second Road Industrial Park in Hammonton, New Jersey. It was an ideal place to construct a new warehouse and corporate offices. Located in the middle of the company's distribution area, it also had better access to major highways. Moreover, by moving outside of Atlantic County, Kramer Beverage did not have to compete with casinos for employees and had a larger labor pool from which to draw. The new 168,000-square-foot state-of-the-art facility, completed in 2002, included a 40,000-square-foot cooler with an advanced energy management system and a 20,000-square-foot drive-through for loading trucks.

SPECIALTY PRODUCTS DIVISION: 2009

In 2008 Mark Kramer succeeded his father as president of Kramer Beverage. Charles Kramer remained chairman of the board. Conditions had changed considerably since Charles Kramer had taken the reins from his own father. In recent years, due in large part to a recession, consumers were drinking less beer in bars and restaurants, but they were drinking more at home, and what they did drink was of higher quality and often the product of one of the many craft breweries that had been cropping up in the final two decades of the 20th century. Kramer Beverage carried its share of craft beers and ales, but to better serve this increasingly important sector the company formed a Specialty Products Division in 2009.

The company developed a channel-specific sales team to sell craft beers as well as imported and specialty brands. Its buyers would also look to bring new brands to the craft lineup that already included Samuel Adams, Ommegang, and Magic Hat. With a young family member in charge of the company, there was every reason to believe that, given its ability to adapt to the times, Kramer Beverage would remain a thriving concern for years to come.

Ed Dinger

PRINCIPAL DIVISIONS

Specialty Products Division.

PRINCIPAL COMPETITORS

Harrison Beverage Co.; Ritchie & Page Distributing Co., Inc.; Warren Distributing Company South.

FURTHER READING

Arney, Pat, "Beer Distributor Chooses Hammonton Park," *Press of Atlantic City*, November 25, 1999, p. A1.

Bezanis, Penny, "The Family Business: Entrepreneurs Sold Their Dreams in the Press," *Press of Atlantic City*, July 16, 1995, p. 20.

Fink, Julie, "Kramer Beverage Is Celebrating 85 Years," *Hammonton Gazette*, September 16, 2009, p. 1.

Karolefski, John, "A Time for Celebration: Kramer Beverage Co. Reaches Some Major Milestones," *Beverage World*, August 15, 2009, p. 88.

Post, Kevin, "Prohibition to Recession, Family Manages to Stay in Business," *Press of Atlantic City*, January 3, 2010.

Swavy, Joseph, "Kramer Finds New Facility Central to Success," *Press of Atlantic City*, January 23, 2002, p. A11.

Kumpulan Fima Bhd.

Suite 4.1, Level 4, Block C
Plaza Damansara
45 Jalan Medan Setia 1
Bukit Damansara
Kuala Lumpur, 50490
Malaysia
Telephone: (+60 03) 2092 1211
Fax: (+60 03) 2092 5923
Web site: http://www.fima.com.my

Public Company
Incorporated: 1988
Employees: 1,300
Sales: MYR 369.07 million ($107 million) (2009)
Stock Exchanges: Kuala Lumpur
Ticker Symbol: KFIMA
NAICS: 551112 Offices of Other Holding Companies

■ ■ ■

Kumpulan Fima Bhd. is a Malaysian holding company for a diversified range of industrial and property investments. Kumpulan Fima is organized into seven divisions: Manufacturing, Food, Plantation, Biodiesel, Bulking, Trading, and Property Investment. With the exception of the Property Investment division, most of the company's holdings are grouped under its primary subsidiary, Fima Corporation. The group's Manufacturing division is chiefly involved in the security printing sector, supplying the Malaysian government with passports and other security documents.

Kumpulan Fima's Food division produces fruit juices, especially pineapple juice for both the Malaysian and export markets. This division also operates a fish cannery in Papua New Guinea. The company's Plantation division controls nearly 52,500 hectares of oil palm and pineapple plantations, and also operates a palm oil processing facility. The Bulking division provides bulk storage facilities for edible and petroleum-based oils and other liquids. Through Fima Biodiesel Sdn. Bhd., Kumpulan Fima has also entered the production of biodiesel fuels.

The group's Trading division operates largely through Malaysian Transnational Trading Corporation (MATTRA), which markets and distributes military products, ranging from paints and other aircraft chemicals and sealants to sophisticated components and equipment for the aerospace industry. The company's Property Investment division is focused primarily on the company's ownership of the Plaza Damansara in Kuala Lumpur. Kumpulan Fima is led by Managing Director Encik Roslan bin Hamir, who also serves as chairman of Fima. Both Kumpulan Fima and Fima Corporation are listed on the Kuala Lumpur Stock Exchange. The bin Hamir family controls nearly 55.5 percent of Kumpulan Fima. In 2009 Kumpulan Fima recorded total revenues of MYR 369 million.

GOVERNMENT INVESTMENT COMPANY: 1972

Kumpulan Fima was founded as a government investment company in 1972 under the auspices of Ministry of Finance Incorporated, the holding company for

COMPANY PERSPECTIVES

The Group recognizes the need to strike a harmonious balance between its business pursuits and its corporate social responsibility. The Group strives to maintain the best values and practices in the Group's relationships with employees, shareholders, regulators and business associates.

Malaysia's Finance Ministry. Kumpulan Fima owed its creation to the Malaysian government's launch of its New Economic Policy (NEP) in 1971. The NEP sought to redress Malaysia's historic economic imbalance, in which the ethnic Malaysian majority (known as the Bumiputra) controlled only a tiny portion of the country's economy.

The vast majority of Malaysia's industrial, financial, and economic wealth was controlled at that time by foreign enterprises or the country's ethnic Chinese population. In 1970 the Bumiputra's share of the country's wealth amounted to less than 2.5 percent. This situation had led to a great deal of civil unrest, which resulted in the outbreak of rioting against the country's Chinese population in 1969. A new government then came into power, promising to develop a more equitable balance among the country's ethnic groups.

Kumpulan Fima initially invested in the food sector, developing a range of holdings involved in packaged foods. The company's food business focused especially on pineapples, both for the Malaysia and export markets. The company developed its own brands, Malapine and Besta, which became popular throughout Western Asia and into the Middle East region as well. Kumpulan Fima itself built up a pineapple plantation business, controlling more than 1,200 hectares in the country's Johor region. Kumpulan Fima's food sector interests later broadened to include livestock feed and cattle breeding. The company also developed a small fish canning business based in Papua New Guinea.

METAL BOX ACQUISITION: 1981

Kumpulan Fima enjoyed strong links to the Malaysian government. Among the company's early directors was Mahathir Mohamad, who left the company when he became Malaysia's prime minister in 1981. The company began branching out from its initial foods focus in the late 1970s. For example, in 1979 the

company established a new subsidiary, Fima Bulking Services, which began operating a liquid bulking terminal in Northport, Port Klang.

Another of Kumpulan Fima's areas of interest developed in May 1982 with the creation of Malaysian Transnational Trading Corporation (MATTRA), which sought to develop a Japanese-style business as a general trading company. MATTRA was formally launched in 1983 by Mahathir himself. Initially focused on importing and distributing military-grade paints, sealants, and other chemicals, MATTRA expanded its operations to include a variety of parts and equipment for the aerospace industry.

In the meantime, Kumpulan Fima completed the takeover of what was to become its most important asset, Metal Box Holdings Malaysia. Metal Box originated from a British company established in 1921 in order to produce metal tins and cans. After securing a near-monopoly of the can market in the United Kingdom, Metal Box had expanded internationally, including into the former British colonies of Malaysia and Singapore. Metal Box undertook a diversification strategy in the 1970s, leading the company to restructure and divest parts of its overseas holdings. Metal Box Holdings Malaysia was founded in 1974 in order to acquire the operations of Metal Box Company of Malaysia Ltd. The company then went public in 1976, but remained controlled by its British parent through the end of the decade.

The public offering provided Metal Box Holdings with the capital to launch its own diversification effort. In 1977 the company completed the acquisition of Security Printers Sdn. Bhd., which enabled it to become a major security printing company in Malaysia. In 1981, as Mahathir left Kumpulan Fima to take up the prime minister's office, Kumpulan Fima moved to take control of Metal Box Holdings and its security printing and other operations. Kumpulan Fima initially acquired a 33 percent stake in the company, which subsequently took the name of Fima Metal Box.

MANAGEMENT BUYOUT IN 1990

Kumpulan Fima continued to build up its range of assets through the 1980s. In 1981 the company acquired a controlling stake in United Plantations Bhd., one of Malaysia's largest plantation holders, founded in the 19th century by Danish interests. Kumpulan Fima's acquisition of United Plantations came as part of the country's NEP and the government's ongoing efforts to shift the country's assets to Malaysian ownership. Kumpulan Fima continued to invest in Malaysia's foods sector throughout the 1980s, notably through the purchase

KEY DATES

1972: Malaysian government establishes Kumpulan Fima.

1974: Metal Box Holdings Malaysia acquires the operations of Metal Box Company of Malaysia Ltd.

1981: Kumpulan Fima acquires control of Metal Box Holdings, which becomes Fima Metal Box.

1990: Kumpulan Fima is privatized through a management buyout.

1993: Kumpulan Fima sells the metal and packaging operations of Fima Metal Box, which becomes Fima Corporation.

1996: Kumpulan Fima goes public on the Kuala Lumpur exchange.

2007: Fima Corporations enters oil palm plantations sector through the purchase of PT Nunukan Jaya Lestari.

2010: Fima Corporation is reclassified as an industrial company.

of a 3.4 percent stake in Nestlé (M) Bhd., the publicly listed Malaysian arm of the Swiss Nestlé group.

Support for the Mahathir government had begun to slip toward the end of the 1980s, prompting the government to begin privatizing a number of state-controlled companies. This process was carried out in part through a series of management buyouts (MBOs), effectively transferring these companies to political allies of the Mahathir government. Kumpulan Fima's own privatization was slated for September 1990, just prior to the general election of that year.

In preparation for Kumpulan Fima's MBO, the government carried out another privatization, of the Government Printing Department, which was then acquired by Fima's Security Printers Sdn. in December 1989. That company then gained the virtual monopoly over all government security printing contracts, excluding banknotes.

Kumpulan Fima then completed its own MBO, led by Ismail Basir, who had taken over as the company's head in 1981 from Mahathir, and then became the group's chairman in 1986. In 1990, Basir, together with Kumpulan Fima Managing Director Ismail Mohamed Noor, through their own holding company, Kegiatan Makmur, paid the government MYR 190 million.

Shortly after, Kumpulan Fima sold off its stake in United Plantations, raising MYR 125 million.

NEW DIRECTIONS

At the time of the MBO, Kumpulan Fima's revenues neared MYR 252 million, rising to MYR 281.5 million in 1991. The majority of these came through the company's manufacturing and trading divisions, including its security printing and food packaging operations, which combined to generate 89 percent of group sales. However, in the 1990s Kumpulan Fima began exploring a wider diversification, notably in the area of securities brokering. For this the company set up a new business, Fima Securities Sdn. Bhd.

The growth of this business led Kumpulan Fima to exit the packaging sector. In 1993 the company agreed to sell its metal and packaging operations to CarnaudMetalbox. That company, created in France as a licensee of Metal Box, had acquired control of the former Metal Box operations in England and elsewhere. Following the sale of the Metal Box business, Fima Metal Box became Fima Corporation, and refocused its own business around a core of security printing and property management. This latter division expanded in 1995 with the acquisition of Plaza Damansara, a five-story building located in Kuala Lumpur's Damansara Heights area. Kumpulan Fima listed its shares on the Kuala Lumpur Stock Exchange the following year.

In the next decade, Malaysia's Securities Commission created new guidelines designed to force the consolidation of the country's brokerage sector. The guidelines called for the reduction of the number of brokerages from 64 to a narrower pool of 15 large-scale universal brokerages. As a result, Kumpulan Fima sought out a merger partner for its own securities operations. In August 2000 the company announced an agreement to merge Fima Securities with Peninsula Securities. The two companies also announced their intention to complete several more acquisitions in order to secure universal brokerage status. However, in 2003 Kumpulan Fima decided to exit the sector altogether, selling its brokerage division to Rational Victory Sdn. Bhd.

DIVERSIFIED HOLDINGS IN THE 21ST CENTURY

Kumpulan Fima, which had maintained a small oil palm plantation business, decided to focus on building up this area of business instead. The dawn of the 21st century had marked a crisis period in the oil palm sector, in part because of the dramatic growth in the number of plantations in Malaysia and elsewhere during the 1990s. The resulting slump in palm oil prices had caused a drop in land prices. Kumpulan Fima was thus able to buy up new plantations inexpensively, and by the end of the decade the company boasted a total plantation size of more than 50,000 hectares.

This total included nearly 20,000 hectares of plantations held through Fima Corporation, which had itself launched an investment in oil palm plantations in 2007. In that year, Fima Corporation acquired an 80 percent stake in PT Nunukan Jaya Lestari, which in turn held a 35-year lease on more than 19,793 hectares, as well as its own oil mill complex. By this time Fima Corporation had also expanded its security printing business through the creation of a joint venture with Giesecke & Devrient GmbH of Germany. Fima, which acquired 30 percent of the joint venture, was thus able to add the printing of banknotes to its other security documents printing operations.

These acquisitions led Fima Corporation, which had originally been classified as a property group, to change its classification to that of industrial products group in May 2010. This subsidiary, by then led by Basir's son Ahmad Riza bin Basir, remained Kumpalan Fima's largest asset, accounting for most of the company's MYR 369 million in revenues in 2009. Kumpulan Fima had evolved from a government-owned investment vehicle to become a diversified holding company at the beginning of the 21st century.

M. L. Cohen

PRINCIPAL SUBSIDIARIES

Boustead Oil Bulking; FCB Plantation Holdings Sdn. Bhd.; Fima Biodiesel Sdn. Bhd.; Fima Bulking Services Berhad; Fima Corporation Berhad; Fima Metal Box Holdings Sdn. Bhd.; Fimachem Sdn. Bhd.; Fima-Mr. Juicy Sdn. Bhd.; International Food Corporation Limited (Papua New Guinea; 95.6%); Ladang Fima Sdn. Bhd.; Malaysian Transnational Trading (MATTRA) Corporation Berhad; Pineapple Cannery of Malaysia Sdn. Bhd.; PT Nunukan Jaya Lestari (Indonesia).

PRINCIPAL DIVISIONS

Manufacturing; Property Investment; Food; Plantation; Bulking; Trading; Biodiesel.

PRINCIPAL OPERATING UNITS

FIMA.

PRINCIPAL COMPETITORS

Boh Plantations Sdn. Bhd.; Boustead Holdings Bhd.; DRB-HICOM Bhd.; Kim Loong Resources Bhd.; Kuala Lumpur Kepong Bhd.; PPB Group Bhd.

FURTHER READING

Chong, James, "Fima Corp. Reclassified into Industrial Products Sector," *TheEdgeProperty.com*, May 10, 2010.

Dupont, Kevin Paul, "Kumpulan Fima Sells Stake in Unit," *Worldsources*, January 14, 2003.

"Fima Plans to Buy More Local Palm Oil Estates," *Bernama*, August 8, 2000.

"Fima Unit Set to Take Over Peninsula Securities," *Business Times*, August 9, 2000.

Ismail, Zaidi Isham, "Fima Set to Pay Dividends Again," *Business Times*, January 31, 2006.

———, "Kfima Aims for Better Dividends," *Business Times*, August 27, 2008.

"Kumpulan Fima Eyes New Sector," *New Straits Times*, August 9, 2000.

Lock, S. N., "K. Fima Near-Term Price Trend to Re-challenge Overhead Resistance," *Business Times*, December 7, 2004.

"Malaysia's Kumpulan Fima to Buy More Oil Palm Estates," *AsiaPulse News*, August 9, 2000.

Landauer, Inc.

———————■———————

2 Science Road
Glenwood, Illinois 60425-1586
U.S.A.
Telephone: (708) 755-7000
Toll Free: (800) 323-8830
Fax: (708) 755-7016
Web site: http://www.landauerinc.com

Public Company
Incorporated: 1956 as R.S. Landauer, Jr. and Company
Employees: 430
Sales: $93.8 million (2009)
Stock Exchanges: New York
Ticker Symbol: LDR
NAICS: 541380 Testing Laboratories; 334513 Instruments and Related Product Manufacturing for Measuring, Displaying, and Controlling Industrial Process Variables

■ ■ ■

Since 1954, Landauer, Inc., has provided radiation dosimetry (dosage measurement) services to hospitals, medical and dental offices, university and national laboratories, nuclear power plants, and other industries. The company manufactures various types of radiation detection monitors for measuring dosages of x-ray, gamma radiation, and other penetrating ion radiations by means of optically stimulated luminescent, film, and thermoluminescent badges worn by its clients' personnel. The company also distributes and collects these monitors and provides analysis, reporting, and record keeping of exposure findings. Landauer's subsidiary, HomeBuyers Preferred, Inc., provides a radon monitoring service and radon remediation. Landauer also provides the medical physics industry with therapeutic and diagnostic physics services and educational services.

GETTING STARTED AS A ONE-MAN LAB: 1954–68

In 1954, Robert Landauer began to provide radiation monitoring, or dosimetry, services. Landauer's interest in dosimetry began as a child in the 1930s, when he had on occasion accompanied his father as Landauer, Sr., made his rounds calibrating radiology equipment used in medical x-ray therapy. After serving in World War II, the younger Landauer worked part time with his father while earning a degree at the University of Chicago. He then worked for two and a half years in the commercial radiation instrumentation field before starting his own dosimetry company out of his home in Park Forest, Illinois, in 1954. According to company literature, he began "with a few borrowed dollars and a prayer." Landauer formally incorporated R.S. Landauer, Jr. and Company in 1956.

At first, Landauer did most of the work himself, which included marking film, processing badges, and preparing reports for clients. Purdue University, General Electric, and Michael Reese Hospital were his early customers, lending credibility to his business, and Landauer's venture expanded steadily. In 1959, the company introduced the practice of cumulative total reporting to the marketplace. By 1965, the company processed more than a million dosimeters. It permanently archived the results of its monitoring.

In 1968, Landauer and Company merged with Tech/Ops, Inc., becoming the R.S. Landauer division of Tech/Ops. The combined company pioneered a number of innovations that made their services more user-oriented: an eight-millimeter film system; a smaller, more convenient badge for clients' employees to wear to monitor radiation exposure; and an automated film reading system. Badges used film emulsion, which darkened with exposure, to record the wearer's exposure to radiation. In 1973, Tech/Ops expanded its offerings to provide Landauer's Thermo Luminescent Dosimetry (TLD) service as a means of improving its finger badges. In 1978, it introduced neutron track etch technology, which it called Neutrak, and, in 1982, nitrous oxide dosimetry, called Nitrox. The company leased rather than sold its detection badges to customers, who returned the badges to Tech/Ops for processing. The company also took its first major step toward doing business internationally with the Nagase-Landauer Ltd. joint venture, an undertaking that provided dosimetry service in Japan in 1973.

CAPITALIZING ON HOME RADON MONITORING: 1987–90

In 1987, Landauer and Tech/Ops incorporated as Tech/Ops Landauer, Inc., to carry on the radiation business previously handled by Tech/Ops. This business included the activities of Terradex Corporation, a pioneer in the field of radon gas detection and measurement that had been purchased by Tech/Ops in 1986. It also included Landauer-Nagase Ltd. and Tech/Ops Sevcon Inc., Tech/Ops's solid-state electronic speed controller business. The move to incorporate followed Tech/Ops decision to divest itself of its businesses, a decision it implemented in 1988 when it transferred its radiation monitoring

business to Tech Ops/Landauer, Inc., in exchange for shares of common stock. After it began to operate independently in 1988, Tech/Ops Landauer purchased Terradex Corp. Tech/Ops Landauer began trading on the American Stock Exchange under the symbol TOV.

Tech/Ops Landauer received a boost in 1988 when the U.S. Environmental Protection Agency and the U.S. surgeon general issued a public health advisory concerning radon gas. The gas, a naturally occurring radioactive element found as a result of uranium decay in soil and rock formations, can infiltrate into basements of homes. It was presumed that exposure to radon gas could cause significant health risks.

The ensuing radon scare created business opportunities for Tech/Ops, the industry leader in radon detection. With more than 50 percent of the $12 to $15 billion market nationwide, its share price shot upward in anticipation of further growth. Thomas M. Fulton, Tech/Ops Landauer's president and CEO, speaking of the $20 million company's opportunity for expansion, was quoted in a 1988 article in *Crain's Chicago Business* as saying, "We're ready to ride it as far as it's gonna take us."

Detecting radon gas in homes was simple. Most detection services at the time sold inexpensive canisters containing charcoal to absorb the gas. These were placed in homes through one heating season, which was a time when most households were closed tight, cutting off natural escape routes for the gas. At the end of the season, the canisters were removed and sent off for processing to assess radon level of a particular house. Tech/Ops offered somewhat more sophisticated measuring devices in home testing kits, which it also had the capability of monitoring.

Tech/Ops Landauer's revenues for fiscal 1989 reflected growth directly attributable to its radon test kits: a 31 percent increase to $25.9 million overall, of which approximately 25 percent was brought in by its radon detection business. By 1990, however, public concern about household radon had abated and demand for radon detectors had slowed. The downturn in the first quarter of fiscal 1990 for the company was sudden and steep. By the end of the year, the company's sales had fallen 5 percent to $24.7 million.

Fortunately for Tech/Ops Landauer, the demand for dosimeters remained strong. The basic dosimetry business continued to post unit growth of 4 to 5 percent a year. In addition, while retail demand for radon testing kits fell, institutional demand remained strong. Tech/Ops Landauer had contracts to provide kits for the U.S. Department of Agriculture, the U.S. Army, and school districts in Wisconsin, Virginia, and Minnesota. In addition, other industries were facing the need for

KEY DATES

1956: R.S. Landauer, Jr. and Company is incorporated.
1968: Landauer merges with Tech/Ops, Inc.
1987: Company is reincorporated as Tech/Ops Landauer, Inc.
1991: Company's name is shortened to Landauer, Inc.
1992: An office in the United Kingdom opens.
1995: Landauer becomes the first U.S. company certified by Canada's Atomic Energy Commission.
2002: The company's common stock begins trading on the New York Stock Exchange.

dosimeters, among them airports, whose baggage handlers were exposed to x-rays, and airlines, whose pilots were exposed to cosmic radiation at high altitudes. Between 1990 and 1995, the company grew at a steady 15 percent rate per year. In 1993, it renovated and expanded its facilities at a cost of $2.2 million.

NEW DOSIMETRY
TECHNOLOGIES: 1990–2002

In 1991, the company changed its name to Landauer, Inc., and formulated plans for expanding its services into Europe. In 1992, Landauer, Inc., took a major step toward overseas expansion when it opened an office in the United Kingdom. It also began collaborating with Pacific Northwest Laboratory to develop new dosimetry technology, which it called optically stimulated luminescence (OSL) technology. This technology used materials that luminesced when stimulated with beams of light to determine levels of radiation exposure. Until that time, traditional dosimetry methods relied upon heat exposure and were less precise. In 1994, Landauer acquired the exclusive worldwide license for use of the new technology, which it introduced shortly thereafter. That year radon gas detector kits sales were down to less than $1 million from more than $6 million in 1989. Nonetheless, overall sales for fiscal 1994 at Landauer rose 8 percent to $31.7 million.

In 1995, Landauer became the first U.S. company whose products were certified by Canada's Atomic Energy Commission. It was also the leading company in its market niche in the United States, providing radiation monitoring for corporate clients such as the Fermi National Laboratory, the Mayo Clinic, and Columbia/

HCA Healthcare Corp. It controlled nearly half of the domestic $75-million market for radiation monitoring and was the number two company in its market niche in Japan. In fiscal 1995, revenues were up 8 percent to $34 million.

In 1998, Brent A. Latta replaced Fulton upon the latter's retirement after 21 years as president and chief executive officer of Landauer. Latta had joined Landauer in 1987 and had been vice president of marketing and executive vice president. Also in 1998, Landauer acquired a 75 percent interest in the radiation dosimetry business of Servico de Assessoria e Rotecao Radiologica S/C Ltda. (SAPRA) of Brazil.

By mid-1999, about 40 percent of Landauer's customers in the United States had been converted to OSL, which it called Luxel; the rest were converted by the end of 1999. The company began to introduce film strips, which had to be replaced monthly, to crystals, which lasted a year or longer, toward the end of 1998. This change drove income down temporarily due to a $3 million write-off of film-based radiation measurement technology. However, 1998 revenues were still up 7 percent to $42.7 million.

With Landauer's cutting-edge technology, the company experienced steady growth in the early years of the 21st century. It also used its new technology to expand in Europe and other markets. Nevertheless, only a small percentage of Landauer's sales came from overseas. Landauer entered into a collaborative agreement with Matsushita Industrial Electric Company to develop a series of instruments and radiation detectors based on OSL technology in 2001. It also began offering service to customers in China that year. In 2002, the company's common stock began trading on the New York Stock Exchange; Latta and Landauer's chairman of the board were there for the ringing of the opening bell on the day the company made the switch from the American Stock Exchange.

GROWTH THROUGH
ACQUISITION: 2003–09

During 2003 the company launched its InLight dosimetry system, which allowed its clients the ability to monitor radiation levels in-house using the company's OSL technology. By this time, Landauer controlled over 50 percent of the U.S. market and had a client base of nearly 60,000. With revenues and profits on the rise, the company continued to steadily expand its business over the next several years. It acquired full ownership of LCIE-Landauer Ltd., a joint venture it had created in 2002 in Europe with Laboratoire Central Industries des Electriques.

Brent Latta retired in 2005 and was succeeded by William E. Saxelby, a longtime executive in the medical and health-care industries. Under his leadership, the company reorganized several departments, made key changes in its executive team, and cut nearly $1.3 million in costs during 2006. That year revenue reached a record $79 million while net income rose by 11 percent over the previous year. The company's InLight business experienced significant growth that year, especially in overseas markets.

Saxelby's strategy at this time was to expand its international business, which proved successful. In late 2007, Landauer established a joint venture in Australia and also made inroads in Mexico in 2008. The company experienced another record-setting year when revenues climbed to $90 million in 2008. Global revenues increased by 24 percent that year.

During 2009 Landauer acquired the personal dosimetry services business of Sweden-based Studsvik AB. It also purchased Gammadata Mattenknik AB, a radon measurement services provider in the Scandinavian region of Europe. Its most significant purchase of 2009 was the $22 million buyout of Global Physics Solutions Inc. (GPS). The deal gave Landauer a foothold in the medical physics services industry, which was estimated to be a $1 billion market in the United States. According to a November 2009 *Biotech Week* article, this market provided clinical physics support, equipment commissioning, accreditation support, imaging equipment testing, and educational services.

Saxelby explained the company's interest in GPS in the aforementioned article. "As we look to expand the scope of our core occupational health monitoring business, the Medical Physics Services sector is attractive to us because it is a service model that complements our core business focus of radiation safety and exhibits attractive growth characteristics."

Saxelby's instincts proved correct. Despite challenging economic conditions, Landauer managed to secure a 4 percent increase in revenues during 2009 while net income rose by 2 percent. Landauer's InLight products continued to experience solid demand while its international business continued to grow at a steady pace.

Saxelby and his executive team expected the company's revenue and net profit growth to continue into 2010 and beyond. By that time, the company provided dosimetry services to more than 1.6 million

people primarily in the United States, Japan, France, the United Kingdom, Brazil, Canada, China, Australia, and Mexico. It had also broadened its product and services arsenal through the GPS purchase, which left it well positioned for growth in the lucrative medical physics services industry. While only time would tell if Saxelby's expansion strategy would continue to pay off, the CEO was confident the company was on track for success in the years to come.

Carrie Rothburd
Updated, Christina M. Stansell

PRINCIPAL SUBSIDIARIES

HomeBuyer's Preferred, Inc.; Global Physics Solutions, Inc.; Landauer-Europe, Ltd.; SAPRA-Landauer, Ltda. (South America; 75%); Beijing-Landauer Inc. (70%); Landauer Australia Pty. Ltd. (51%); ALSA Dosimetria, S. de R.L. de C.V. (Central America; 56.25%); Nagase-Landauer, Ltd. (Japan; 50%).

PRINCIPAL COMPETITORS

Abatix Corp.; Mirion Technologies Dosimetry Services Division; Nagase & Co., Ltd.; Compagnie de Saint-Gobain.

FURTHER READING

Bailey, Jeff, "Fat Margins: Market Share, Penetration Score," *Wall Street Journal*, May 13, 2003.

"Landauer Acquires Global Physics Solutions, Inc. as Platform to Expand into Medical Physics Services Market," *Biotech Week*, November 25, 2009.

"Landauer Inc. Reports Fiscal 2008 Fourth Quarter and Full Year Results," *PR Newswire*, December 2, 2008.

McKeough, Kevin, "Landauer: Radiating Revenue," *Crain's Chicago Business*, May 21, 2007.

Murphy, Lee, "New Radiation Meter Fuels Landauer Gain," *Crain's Chicago Business*, February, 19, 2001, p. 45.

Stazewski, Len, "Firm's Fortunes Ride Radon Scare," *Crain's Chicago Business*, February 26, 1990, p. 11.

Strahler, Steven R., "Profits Detected in Radon Gas Scare," *Crain's Chicago Business*, September 26, 1988, p. 1.

"Studsvik Disposes of Dosimetry Ops," *M&A Navigator*, October 5, 2009.

"William E. Saxelby Elected President, CEO of Radiation Detection Service Company," *Life Science Weekly*, October 18, 2005.

Larsen and Toubro Ltd.

L&T House, Ballard Estate
PO Box 278
Mumbai, 400 001
India
Telephone: (+91 022) 6752 5656
Fax: (+91 022) 6752 5858
Web site: http://www.larsentoubro.com

Public Company
Incorporated: 1946 as Larsen & Toubro Private Ltd.
Employees: 37,357
Sales: INR 336 billion ($7.31 billion) (2009)
Stock Exchanges: Bombay
Ticker Symbol: 500510
NAICS: 236220 Commercial and Institutional Building
    Construction; 237210 Land Subdivision; 237990
    Other Heavy and Civil Engineering Construction;
    333120 Construction Machinery Manufacturing

■ ■ ■

Larsen & Toubro Ltd. (L&T) is one of India's leading
engineering, construction, and manufacturing
companies. The Mumbai-based company is a major
player in India's public works and infrastructure sectors,
and also competes on an international scale designing
and building projects for the energy, shipbuilding, heavy
industry, and other industries. L&T is organized into six
primary divisions: Engineering and Construction
Projects; Heavy Engineering; Construction; Electrical
and Electronics; Machinery and Industrial Products; and
Information Technology (IT) and Technology Services.

The Engineering and Construction division remains
the group's largest area of business, representing 82
percent of its total revenues of $7.31 billion in 2009.
This division provides turnkey design, engineering, and
construction services across a wide range of industries,
including commercial and residential construction; roads
and bridges; ports and harbors; airports; steel factories
and other industrial projects; and installations for the oil
and gas and energy sectors. This division also includes
the group's Heavy Engineering operations, based at the
company's large-scale Hazeri plant, where it produces
components for nuclear power plants and coal and
thermal power plants; shipbuilding and marine
components; and other components for weapon systems,
the chemical and refinery industries, and the aerospace
and aviation industry.

Long active in the Middle East and other regions,
L&T has launched a drive to expand its operations to a
truly multinational level, adding new sales and marketing subsidiaries throughout the Asia Pacific region,
Africa, and North, South, and Central America. The
company expected to raise the share of international
operations, which reached 15 percent of total group
revenues in 2009, to as much as 25 percent by the
middle of the next decade. L&T is listed on the Bombay Stock Exchange and is led by Chairman and
Managing Director Anilkumar Manibhai Naik.

DANISH PARTNERSHIP IN 1938

Two Danish engineers, Henning Holck-Larsen and
Soren Kristian Toubro, who had come to India in the
early 1930s, founded Larsen & Toubro Ltd. Former

COMPANY PERSPECTIVES

Vision. L&T shall be a professionally-managed Indian multinational, committed to total customer satisfaction and enhancing shareholder value. L&T-ites shall be an innovative, entrepreneurial and empowered team constantly creating value and attaining global benchmarks. L&T shall foster a culture of caring, trust and continuous learning while meeting expectations of employees, stakeholders and society.

schoolmates, Larsen and Toubro had both joined F.L. Smidth & Co., the Copenhagen-based manufacturer of cement-making machinery. Smidth's operations also included civil engineering, together with the construction of cement factories and the company's machinery.

In 1934 Smidth sent Toubro, then 28 years old and a year older than Larsen, to oversee the construction of the Madukkarai Cement Works in Coimbatore, India. In the meantime, Larsen had been gaining his own experience in international markets, with assignments in Poland, Iran, Iraq, Lebanon, and Syria.

Larsen joined Toubro in India in 1935, helping him establish the Rohri Cement Factory in Hyderabad, near the Sukkur dam. Soon after, the Indian government commissioned three new cement factories, and Larsen and Toubro stayed on in India to oversee their construction as well. These factories later formed the network of factories that gave rise to Associated Cement Companies, the largest producer of cement in India.

Larsen and Toubro began developing plans to go into business for themselves. At first, the partners discussed the idea of entering the cement sector in other markets, including China and Madagascar. In the end, however, Larsen and Toubro decided to remain in India, recognizing that country's industrial potential as the independence movement gained momentum. While vacationing in Matheran in 1938, Larsen and Toubro laid out plans for their own company.

With help from the local Danish consul, who owned a business called Wimco, Larsen and Toubro opened their own office in Bombay (Mumbai). The office, as Larsen recalled to the *Financial Express*: "was too small for the two of us, so when one of us sat, the other went out looking for business—that helped."

Larsen and Toubro initially targeted the import market, selling dairy machinery from a Danish manufacturer. However, the outbreak of World War II

in 1939 brought about sharp restrictions in imports to India. In response, Larsen and Toubro opened their own shop, from which they provided repair services. When Denmark was overrun by Germany in 1940, imports of dairy equipment ceased altogether. By then, however, Larsen and Toubro had gained enough expertise servicing the imported machinery to begin producing their own dairy equipment.

CONSTRUCTION AND ENGINEERING IN 1944

Despite heavy taxes imposed by the British authority, with excess profit taxes reaching 97.5 percent, Larsen and Toubro's business prospered. The partners began expanding their operations during the war years. The British navy's difficulties keeping up with its ship repairs provided the partners with their next opportunity. Because of the growing threat of Japanese naval operations in the region, ships could not always be brought into port in India.

Instead, Larsen and Toubro acquired the Italian vessel *Hilda* and refitted it as a repairs facility. Anchored outside Bombay Harbor, the *Hilda* served as a base for Larsen and Toubro's repair crews. As Larsen described it: "[S]hips would line up on either side and we had fitted *Hilda* out completely as a workshop. We would clamber on to their vessels and work fast; often, there would be prisoners-of-war on board—some Italians, some Chinese. Those were incredible days."

Meanwhile, the company set up additional repair and fabrication facilities onshore. The company thus began developing the heavy engineering expertise that would become an important part of its future success. Wartime brought other opportunities as well. The Tata family, which was building one of India's leading industrial conglomerates, had commissioned a soda ash factory, the construction of which was overseen by a team of German engineers. However, the outbreak of war led to the internment of German civilians in India. Tata turned instead to Larsen and Toubro to complete the factory. This provided the partners with invaluable experience in the engineering market, notably in the field of factory installations.

Engineering and construction soon grew into one of Larsen and Toubro's major businesses. In 1944 the partners established a new company, called ECC (for Engineering and Construction Contracts), in order to provide full-scale engineering and construction services, both for India's public works and infrastructure projects and for its growing industrial sector.

KEY DATES

■

1938: Henning Holck-Larsen and Soren Kristian Toubro found a company initially importing dairy equipment into India.

1944: Larsen and Toubro enter the engineering and construction market, forming ECC.

1950: Larsen & Toubro Ltd (L&T) goes public.

1979: L&T secures first foreign contract, to build the Abu Dhabi International Airport.

1987: L&T launches production at its main Hazira Works heavy engineering facility.

1999: A. M. Naik becomes CEO and refocuses L&T on large-scale contracts.

2009: L&T wins a $750 million contract to build a shipyard in Tamil Nadu.

L&T FROM 1946

Larsen and Toubro had not abandoned the original trade operations, however. With the end of World War II, the partners established new trade relationships with a range of British companies, becoming the sales agents for a variety of production equipment and machinery used in the bakery, soap, and glass industries.

A new opportunity came when Larsen and Toubro spotted the resale potential of the construction equipment left behind in India at the end of the war. In 1945 Larsen and Toubro approached Caterpillar Tractor Company in the United States, proposing to buy and then resell that company's equipment, which otherwise would have been abandoned. Caterpillar agreed, and Larsen and Toubro brought in new investors in order to raise the cash needed to buy the equipment. The partners then incorporated their company as Larsen & Toubro Private Limited (L&T) at the beginning of 1946. The company went public four years later.

The Caterpillar deal helped raise L&T's profile as the company entered a new period of expansion. L&T's Danish background enabled the company to continue to prosper, even after India's independence from Great Britain in 1947. As Larsen told the *Financial Express*, "Nothing major changed after the British left, the Indian government treated us in much the same way as their predecessors did."

Nevertheless, L&T cooperated with the Indian government's aims to develop its domestic talent pool. As Larsen recalled in the *Rediff Business Interview*: "Once, right in the beginning, we were told that our company had too many foreigners and that we should

Indianise the management. The government was right in saying so."

STEADY POSTWAR GROWTH

L&T grew steadily through the 1950s, adding new operations such as cable laying and ship demagnetization in the postwar period. The growth of ECC led the company into the production of building materials, notably cement. The company's cement production quickly reached 300 metric tons per year, and ultimately grew to more than 5,000 metric tons per year by the dawn of the 21st century.

L&T also expanded beyond its Bombay base, adding operations in New Delhi and Calcutta before expanding to a national scale. By 1961 the company had established a new regional headquarters in Manapakkam, in the Madras region. This expansion enabled L&T to contribute to many of India's high-profile public works and infrastructure projects, growing into one of the leading players in that sector. By 1966 L&T had broken into the ranks of India's top 75 companies. Less than a decade later, L&T ranked as the 25th-largest Indian company.

By then, Toubro had retired from active management of the company, followed shortly by Larsen. L&T brought in Indian managers to lead the company in their place. Both Toubro, who died in 1982, and Larsen, who died in 2003, maintained positions on the company's board of directors.

L&T's growth continued during the 1970s and 1980s. Much of the group's development involved building up highly integrated operations. These included an extension into the manufacture of construction machinery and equipment. For example, in 1975 the company built a new factory in Bangalore in order to produce hydraulic excavators. The company later regrouped this business into a joint venture with Singapore-based Komatsu Asia Pacific.

FIRST INTERNATIONAL
CONTRACT IN 1979

By the middle of the 1970s, L&T's portfolio included a large number of India's largest infrastructure contracts, ranging from building the nation's freeway system to its dockyards, airports, and other public works projects. L&T had also gained particular expertise in the energy sector, with a range of projects building oil refineries, power generation plants, and the country's first nuclear power facilities. The company had also boosted its heavy engineering operations, particularly as applied to the power generation sector, with a diversified manufacturing capacity including such critical components as motor control centers and low-tension gear systems.

This range of expertise provided L&T with the leverage to move into the international engineering and construction market at the end of the 1970s. For this, L&T targeted the Middle East market. This region remained largely underdeveloped at that time, and, given the prevailing political and economic turmoil surrounding the Arab oil embargo, provided the Indian company with an easier entry than other developing markets. L&T scored its first success in the region in 1979, when it won a subcontracting order to build the Abu Dhabi International Airport. The company quickly followed this up with an oil field development subcontract in Abu Dhabi and the subcontract to build a processing plant in Qatar.

With India's own rapid growth during the 1980s, however, L&T returned its attention to its domestic operations for much of that decade. One of the company's most significant milestones at that time came with the construction of its heavy engineering facility, the Hazira Works, in south Gujarat. Construction of the site began in 1985, with initial production launched two years later. Through the 1990s, L&T continued to expand the site. As a result, L&T expanded its range of heavy engineering operations to include large-scale machinery and plant equipment for a variety of industries, including the steel and nuclear power industries, as well as the aerospace, petrochemical, oil and gas, and fertilizer industries.

L&T launched a new expansion of the Hazira Works in 2009, scheduled for completion in 2011. In the meantime, the company continued to build up its manufacturing network, boasting 22 factories throughout India by the start of that decade.

FOCUSING ON LARGE-SCALE PROJECTS FROM 1999

India's growing economic clout during the 1980s and 1990s had attracted a new range of international competitors, squeezing L&T's profit margins. However, the Middle Eastern market, especially the Persian Gulf region, had begun its own boom at the same time. Faced with growing competition at home, L&T decided to relaunch its international expansion.

The company focused on the region's energy sector, competing for contracts as a primary contractor. L&T won its first bid in the region in 1993, securing the $48 million contract to build an electrical power substation in Ras al-Khaimah. L&T's operations in the region grew strongly, culminating with the $125 million contract to build a 200 MW power plant in Dhofar, Oman, in 2001. This marked the largest power generation contract to be awarded in the region to date.

Leading L&T by then was Anilkumar Manibhai Naik, who had started with the company in the 1960s as a junior engineer and had led the development of the Hazira Works before becoming CEO in 1999. Naik instituted a major cultural change in the company, particularly by refocusing the company as a profit-driven enterprise.

Under Naik, L&T stepped up its efforts to expand its range of international operations. The company also developed a new strategy focusing its operations on large-scale projects, targeting a narrower spectrum of sectors, including the oil and nuclear energy industries, and road, railway, and airport construction. As Naik announced to *India Today* in 2009: "Smaller, simpler projects will be scrapped and over time, what is now our core will no longer be our core. We also want diversity of geography. We'll be firing from many cylinders."

TARGETING $12 BILLION IN SALES BY 2015

By then, L&T had gained a number of new high-profile contracts. For example, in 2008 the company added a contract to build 22 critical reactors for Kuwait National Petroleum Company, in a deal worth more than $420 million. Also that year, the company signed a $240 million contract to build a steel plant in Bihar for Indian Railways. Other projects at the end of the decade included a $247 dam in Bhutan, and a mosque, hotel, and apartment complex in Oman for $245 million. By 2010 the company had also launched construction on two major new projects in India, a $750 million shipyard in Tamil Nadu, and a $520 million monorail in Mumbai.

While the group's ECC business continued to be the main driver of the company's growth, L&T's heavy engineering operations made steady gains as well, successfully adding contracts through the Persian Gulf region, as well as in Algeria, Brazil, China, Malaysia, Sri Lanka, Tanzania, and Vietnam. This success led the company to launch a still more ambitious international expansion strategy, with plans to raise its revenues, from $7.3 billion in 2009, to $12 billion or more by 2015. As part of this effort, L&T expanded its international sales and marketing network, launching new subsidiaries in Brazil, Germany, Nigeria, and South Africa. From its one-room office origins in 1938, L&T had grown into a major player in the global market in the 21st century.

M. L. Cohen

PRINCIPAL SUBSIDIARIES

L&T Finance Limited; L&T Infrastructure Development Projects Limited; L&T Infrastructure Finance

Limited; L&T International FZE; L&T Tech Park Limited; L&T Transportation Infrastructure Limited; L&T Urban Infrastructure Limited; L&T-Case Equipment Private Limited; L&T-ECC Construction (M) SND. BHD (Malaysia); Larsen & Toubro Infotech Limited (L&T Infotech); Tractor Engineers Limited (TENGL).

PRINCIPAL DIVISIONS

Construction; Electrical and Electronics (EBG); Engineering and Construction Projects (E&C); Heavy Engineering (HED); IT and Technology Services; Machinery and Industrial Products (MIPD).

PRINCIPAL COMPETITORS

Atlos India Ltd.; Bridge and Roof Company Ltd.; East Coast Constructions and Industries Ltd.; Jaiprakash Associates Ltd.; Navayuga Engineering Company Ltd.; NTPC Ltd.; Punj Lloyd Ltd.; Tata Sons Ltd.

FURTHER READING

Arora, Simran, "We Will Invest Heavily in High Technology Areas," *Financial Express*, October 2, 2009.

Ashiwal, Shashi, "A Giant in Engineering," *Frontline*, April 5, 2005.

Bhattacharjee, Dwijottam, and Murali Gopalan, "Ninety Summers Later, Holck-Larsen Looks Back in Wonder," *Financial Express*, July 4, 1997.

"Creating Advantages out of Adversity," *Indian Express*, February 26, 2010.

Diwanji, A. K., "Henning Holck-Larsen: The Great Dane," *Rediff Business Interview*, March 14, 1998.

Dutta, Ashok, "To Dream and Dare," *MEED Middle East Economic Digest*, April 1, 2005, p. 6.

"Engineering Marvel," *Forbes Global*, June 22, 2009, p. 22.

"L&T to Bid for Airport Projects in West Asia," *Business Line*, April 20, 2010.

"Larsen and Toubro on Aggressive Expansion Abroad," *Steel Guru*, May 8, 2010.

Patel, Nishika, "Larsen & Toubro: Going All the Way," *India Today*, October 15, 2009.

Verma, Virendra, "L&T's Shopping Spree," *Business Today*, September 6, 2009.

"We'll Be $12 Billion Big by 2015," *India Business Insight*, December 26, 2006.

Latham & Watkins L.L.P.

---

885 3rd Avenue
New York, New York 10022-4834
U.S.A.
Telephone: (212) 906-1200
Fax: (212) 751-4864
Web site: http://www.lw.com

Private Company
Founded: 1934
Employees: 2,000
Sales: $1.92 billion (2008)
NAICS: 54111 Offices of Lawyers

∎∎∎

Latham & Watkins L.L.P. is one of the world's largest law firms, with about 2,000 attorneys practicing in nearly 30 offices across the globe. It represents business clients in many industries, including energy, health care and life sciences, media and entertainment, real estate, and technology. From its historic foundation of tax and labor law, Latham & Watkins has diversified to provide counsel on virtually all aspects of modern business practice, including financing, bankruptcy, regulatory compliance, environment, litigation, and intellectual property issues. Because of the firm's emphasis on teamwork and cooperation, it has often been cited as one of the nation's best-managed law firms. Industry trade publication *Legal Business* named Latham & Watkins Law Firm of the Decade in 2007.

THE DEPRESSION AND WORLD WAR II

Dana Latham and Paul R. Watkins were both born in Illinois in the late 1890s. Latham graduated from Harvard Law School in 1922, and Watkins studied law at Illinois Wesleyan University. In January 1934 the partners founded a law firm in Los Angeles. Latham's expertise was in state and federal tax law, while Watkins, formerly the general counsel for Pacific Finance Corporation, built a strong practice in labor law.

In spite of the Great Depression, the new law firm prospered. Its first significant client was Consolidated Rock Products Company, which was still a client 50 years later. Within a year the partnership had gained clients including Pacific Finance Corporation; the Crushed Stone, Sand & Gravel Association, which was the predecessor of the Southern California Rock Products Association; West Shore Company; the Rule Company; Western Geophysical Company; and the London retailer Fortnum & Mason.

Soon after the United Geophysical Company was founded in 1937, it began using the services of Latham & Watkins. As United Geophysical was exploring for oil overseas, especially in Central and South America, the law firm gained its first experience in international law. When Consolidated Engineering Corporation was spun off from United Geophysical and became a public corporation, Latham & Watkins began its initial venture into securities law. Herbert Hoover Jr., the son of President Herbert Hoover, played an important role in helping Latham & Watkins gain several early clients, including United Geophysical.

The partnership developed an emphasis on labor law after the passage of the National Labor Relations Act in 1935, which guaranteed collective bargaining. The firm represented employers in many union disputes, and major unions opposed the firm. By the time World War II began in 1939, Latham & Watkins had four attorneys. During the war, the company continued to prosper, in part because many new laws and regulations were enacted as part of the war effort.

In the early years of World War II, Latham began representing Major Corliss Champion Moseley, who ran aviation companies based in Southern California. During the war Moseley trained some 26,000 pilots and 13,000 mechanics at the Glendale, California, airport under a federal contract and was a key player in building up civilian and military aviation capabilities during the war and into the early 1950s.

POST-WORLD WAR II PRACTICE

In the early postwar period the firm grew as it recruited young attorneys and some of its veterans returned, and in 1949 Latham & Watkins established its first written partnership agreement. By 1954 the firm employed 14 attorneys and had begun to develop a litigation practice. In 1967 Latham & Watkins remained modest in size with just 30 attorneys, but rapid growth in the years ahead made it one of the nation's largest firms, surpassing many law firms that were much older.

Clinton R. Stevenson was chosen managing partner in 1967. Three years later Latham & Watkins installed a new computer system, "the first installation of its size and nature in a law firm west of the Mississippi," according to its corporate history, *Bold Beginnings*. In 1972 two partners opened an office in Santa Ana, Orange County, in a building owned by one of the firm's clients, C.J. Segerstrom & Sons. By 1983 the Orange County office had moved to Newport Beach and employed 21 attorneys.

In 1978 the firm recruited its first experienced attorneys in order to open a branch office in Washington,

D.C. Carla Hills, secretary of the U.S. Department of Housing and Urban Development under President Gerald Ford, was hired to head the new office. This office developed new clients, such as Synfuels and Continental Wingate, and the location allowed the firm to better serve other clients, including Sears, Roebuck; The Signal Companies; Hughes Aircraft; and Mars, Inc.

From 1978 to 1981 the firm devoted many of its resources to representing Gulf Oil Corporation in the so-called uranium cases, wherein Westinghouse Electric Company sued Gulf for alleged price fixing of uranium. Westinghouse had sold nuclear power plants to several electrical utilities and agreed to provide them with uranium fuel. This was a particularly important case, since in the mid-1960s the United States had placed an embargo on imported uranium as a way to aid domestic suppliers. In 1981 Gulf and Westinghouse settled a major part of their dispute out of court.

Latham & Watkins established a San Diego office in 1980. In its early years this office handled real estate development for Torrey Enterprises and Mobil Land Development Company, conducted litigation in the AFTRA antitrust case, and represented National Semiconductor, Intermark, Oak Industries, Nucorp Energy, and other clients. In early 1982 extended negotiations resulted in a merger between Latham & Watkins and the Chicago firm Hedlund, Hunter, & Lynch, which employed 20 lawyers and specialized in litigation. This was the firm's first merger, a difficult but productive turning point in its history. By 1983 the firm had grown to 237 attorneys and added new specialties such as bankruptcy, commercial, and international law.

The growth of Latham & Watkins in the late 1970s and 1980s was part of a national trend as many law firms expanded rapidly, often by hiring experienced attorneys from rival law firms. In the late 1970s the nature of the law profession changed to become more competitive, especially after the U.S. Supreme Court ruled that professional restrictions against advertising were unconstitutional, and the *American Lawyer* and the *National Law Journal* were founded to provide information on law firm management and finances.

LOYALTY LEADS TO SUCCESS: 1985–89

In 1985 David H. Maister, president of the Boston consulting firm Maister Associates, described Latham & Watkins in a *Sloan Management Review* article, as a prime example of a well-managed "one-firm firm" that emphasized institutional loyalty. He noted: "In contrast to many of their (often successful) competitors who emphasize individual entrepreneurialism, autonomous

KEY DATES

1934: Dana Latham and Paul Watkins found the law firm in Los Angeles.

1978: Firm starts an office in Washington, D.C.

1985: A New York City office is opened.

1990: Offices in San Francisco and London are established.

1992: A Moscow office opens.

2002: Offices open in Brussels and Milan; company operates seven European offices.

2005: Company's New York office becomes the firm's largest branch.

2007: Gross revenues surpass $2 billion.

profit centers, internal competition and/or highly decentralized, independent activities, one-firm firms place great emphasis on firmwide coordination of decision making, group identity, cooperative teamwork, and institutional commitment."

To promote that kind of corporate culture, Latham & Watkins discouraged individual stardom by having few status symbols for prominent partners, relied on training its own lawyers while recruiting few experienced lawyers from the outside, and seldom acquired other law firms. It also used its institutional history as a way of promoting long-term thinking and loyalty to the firm. Although many Latham & Watkins attorneys were specialists, Maister wrote, "What strikes any visitor to a one-firm firm is the deeply held mutual respect across departmental, geographic, and functional boundaries." While the law firm had a strong leader in Clinton Stevenson, it emphasized open communication and the participation of other partners and even junior associates in recruiting, selecting new partners, and compensation issues.

OVERCOMING CHALLENGES: 1990–93

In 1990 the law firm founded a San Francisco branch in temporary offices at 580 California Street, and later that year signed a lease for up to 60,000 square feet at 505 Montgomery Street. The office's managing partner, Robert Dell, stated in the *San Francisco Business Times*: "We want to make it a full-service firm, so we'll start with a core group of finance and corporate attorneys and a litigation group with emphasis on securities litigation." Responding to an economic downturn, in 1991 Latham & Watkins assigned 20 attorneys to its

Insolvency Project, which advised clients on how to handle bankruptcy and restructuring. In some cases, the law firm advised companies that it had helped expand through leveraged buy-outs and high-yield bonds. Other firms such as San Francisco's Brobeck, Phleger & Harrison also shifted some of their resources to meet the new demands.

In 1991 Latham & Watkins also released 43 junior associates, a drastic move in light of its commitment to retain attorneys from the time they were hired to the time they retired. This decision came as the firm's profits plummeted in the early 1990s, partly as a result of the bankruptcy of Drexel Burnham Lambert, the law firm's major investment banking client in the booming 1980s.

In 1993 the firm made a major change that rewarded individual efforts of those "rainmakers" who brought in more business, thus ending the seniority system that was part of the firm's team approach. Nevertheless, in a 1997 article in the *American Lawyer*, firm partners insisted that the Latham & Watkins emphasis on collegiality remained intact, although some outside observers had their doubts.

RETURN TO PROFITABILITY: 1996–99

In any case, Latham & Watkins rebounded as the economy improved and its rainmakers brought in more business. In 1997 at least 100 partners brought in a minimum of $1 million each in billings. Profitable clients also improved the bottom line. For example, Latham & Watkins defended Navistar International Transportation Corporation, the owner of Denny's restaurants, when it was charged with racial discrimination lawsuits settled in 1996. It also represented Minnesota Mining and Manufacturing Company (3M) when it was sued for injuries caused by its breast implants.

Latham & Watkins and other firms like Netscape, Pacific Bell, Sun Microsystems, and Goldman Sachs backed the work of the Electronic Frontier Foundation to protect individual liberties in cyberspace while also promoting responsible use and regulation of such resources. "We need an appropriate balance," said EFF's Executive Director Lori Fena in an interview in the March/April 1998 *Online* to maximize First Amendment rights while also protecting minors from pornography. The foundation dealt with such issues as government regulation of electronic commerce, restrictions on encryption, and the growing volume of unwanted e-mail.

In late 1997 Latham & Watkins helped America Online (AOL) in its opposition to junk e-mail, also known as spam. AOL gained a court injunction that barred Over the Air Equipment Inc., an advertiser of pornographic Web sites, from sending its unrequested messages to AOL subscribers. "The notion is to pursue them vigorously until the overall effect of deterring spam has been achieved. If you can do it with five suits, that's a good number. If it takes more than that, we'll file more," said Latham & Watkins partner Everett Johnson in the *Washington Post*.

In the late 1990s Latham & Watkins continued to be a leader for corporate financial transactions. In 1998 it participated in mergers and acquisitions worth almost $60 billion, over $36 billion in private and public financings, and over $30 billion in a private 144A placement. Its corporate clients included Amgen; Bear, Stearns & Company; Cedars-Sinai Medical Center; DreamWorks SKG; Harrah's Entertainment; Hilton Hotels; Hughes Communications; Kohlberg Kravis Roberts & Company; Nestlé U.S.A.; Nintendo of America; Smith Barney; and Safeway.

To keep its clients informed using the Internet, Latham & Watkins created the International Environmental Network as a full-text database with the latest government laws and regulations. The firm also established the Regulatory Flexibility Group, an extranet-based "advocacy consortium of Southern California companies working with regulators to find new ways to reduce emissions from manufacturing plants," according to the firm's Web site.

In July 1999 the *American Lawyer* ranked Latham & Watkins as the nation's fourth-largest law firm, with gross revenues of $502 million. The firm also ranked 17th in revenues per lawyer ($605,000) and 14th in average compensation for all partners ($870,000). Despite the firm's prosperity, it also confronted challenges from other large firms, some with as many as 2,000 lawyers, and big accounting firms that also employed hundreds or even thousands of lawyers.

MOVING INTO THE NEW MILLENNIUM

Latham & Watkins focused on growth in both domestic and international markets during the early years of the new millennium. In order to be closer to its high-tech customers including AOL, Gemini Networks, and Cogent Communications, the firm opened an office in northern Virginia in 2000. Its European business was bolstered the following year when offices were established in Hamburg and Frankfurt. The company gained strong presence in Paris as well through its merger with Stibbe Paris, the French arm of Dutch law firm Stibbe N.V. Latham & Watkins European offices

grew to seven in 2002, with new branches opened in Brussels and Milan.

The company experienced success during this time period. During 2003 it was named to the *American Lawyer*'s first "A List," which ranked the top U.S. law firms based on revenue per lawyer, pro bono participation, associate satisfaction, and workplace diversity. That same year the company was awarded the American Bar Association's Pro Bono Publico Award due to its increasing commitment to pro bono work. From 1998 to 2002, the company almost tripled the average number of pro-bono hours logged by its attorneys. From 2000 through 2008, the company provided over one million pro bono service hours.

During 2005, the company's New York office became the firm's largest location with nearly 270 lawyers. Its multimillion dollar client list included The Goldman Sachs Group Inc., Credit Suisse Group, Deutsche Bank AG, and Bear Stearns Companies Inc. Additional offices were established in Munich and Shanghai that year. By 2007, the company had 14 international offices with the opening of new locations in Madrid, Barcelona, and Rome. Latham & Watkins eyed the Middle East market as its next growth area and opened three offices in the region in 2008 including Dubai and Abu Dhabi in the United Arab Emirates and one in Doha, Qatar.

CONTINUED SUCCESS: 2005 AND BEYOND

Under the leadership of chairman and managing partner Robert Dell, Latham & Watkins focused on strengthening its litigation department while growing its business abroad. The firm experienced a number of high-profile wins including the 2004 antitrust case against Oracle Corporation that attempted to block its $10 billion purchase of PeopleSoft Inc. It also secured major wins for clients Ernst & Young L.L.P. and Philip Morris.

The company's revenues grew significantly under Dell's tenure, increasing 430 percent from 1994 through 2005. The company's gross revenues surpassed the $2 billion mark for the first time in 2007. That year Latham's domestic operations included its representation of Oracle Corp., Advanced Micro Devices Inc., and Kyphon during multibillion dollar acquisition deals. The company's lawyers also advised on $182.6 billion in debt offerings and $72.7 billion in public-equity offerings, including $32 billion of initial public offerings. During 2007, the company was named "Law Firm of the Decade" by U.K.-based *Legal Business*.

Profits and gross revenues fell in 2008 as the company's exposure to financial markets, and the collapse of client Bear Stearns, took a toll on its bottom line. With global economies faltering, Latham & Watkins was forced to control costs and froze associate salaries in 2009. Nevertheless, Dell and his partners were convinced that the company was on track for success in the years to come. Through its focus on international expansion and its strong litigation record, Latham & Watkins did indeed appear to be well positioned for any future challenges that may come its way.

David M. Walden
Updated, Christina M. Stansell

PRINCIPAL COMPETITORS

Baker & McKenzie, L.L.P.; Dewey & LeBoeuf, L.L.P.; Simpson Thacher & Bartlett, L.L.P.; Weil, Gotshal & Manges, L.L.P.

FURTHER READING

Dewey, Katrina M., "How an Upstart L.A. Firm Made It to the Top," *California Law Business*, October 8, 1990, pp. 28–30.

Eaglesham, Jean, "Lathams Unveils Merger with Paris Law Firm," *Financial Times*, September 7, 2001.

Frankel, Alison, "Intelligent Design; With Clever Hires and Global Ambition, Latham Built a Global Powerhouse," *American Lawyer*, January 1, 2006.

Galanter, Marc, and Thomas Palay, *Tournament of Lawyers: The Transformation of the Big Law Firm*, Chicago: University of Chicago Press, 1991.

Hidula, Scott, and Lisa Davis, "Major Law Firm Notes Intent on Large Lease Here," *San Francisco Business Times*, May 28, 1990, p. 3.

Hock, Sandy, "What Goes Up and Comes Down May Be Restructured," *San Diego Business Journal*, August 12, 1991, p. 17.

Kizilos, Peter, "Interviews with Infopros: Lori Fena," *Online*, March/April 1998, pp. 35–38.

"Lathams Opens in Virginia as Part of High-Tech Boom," *Lawyer*, June 26, 2000.

Leibowitz, Wendy R., "Lawyers Find Niches on the 'Net,'" *National Law Journal*, November 23, 1998, pp. A1, 7.

Lloyd, Richard, "Profits Drop 21 Percent at Latham & Watkins," *New York Law Journal*, February 11, 2009.

Longstreth, Andrew, "How Latham Took Manhattan," *American Lawyer*, June 1, 2005.

Maister, David H., "The One-Firm Firm: What Makes It Successful," *Sloan Management Review*, Fall 1985, pp. 3–13.

Osborne, D. M., "Latham's Leap Forward," *American Lawyer*, April 1997, pp. 47+.

Peck, Austin H., Jr., *Bold Beginnings: A Story about the First 50 Years of Latham & Watkins*, Los Angeles: Latham & Watkins, 1984.

Pollock, Ellen Joan, "Singing the Latham Song," *American Lawyer*, October 1986, pp. 125–31.

Todd, Ross, "Peer Approval; How Did Latham & Watkins Become the AM Law 200's Most Admired Firm?" *American Lawyer*, December 1, 2006.

"Washington Hearsay," *Washington Post*, December 22, 1997.

Les Schwab Tire Centers

20900 Cooley Road
Bend, Oregon 97701
U.S.A.
Telephone: (541) 447-4136
Web site: http://www.lesschwab.com

Private Company
Founded: 1952
Employees: 7,000
Sales: $1.6 billion (2010 est.)
NAICS: 441320 Tire Dealers; 421130 Tire and Tube
    Wholesalers; 441310 Automotive Parts and Acces-
    sories Stores

∎ ∎ ∎

Les Schwab's first attempt at selling tires in Prineville, Oregon, blossomed into one of America's largest and most successful independent tire chains: Les Schwab Tire Centers (Les Schwab Tires). Les Schwab Tires includes over 420 locations throughout Oregon, Washington, Idaho, Montana, California, Nevada, Alaska, and Utah. Les Schwab Tires prides itself on continued customer service. The practice of greeting customers as they drive into the shop's parking lot has long been a company trademark. In addition to selling tires and batteries and doing alignment, brake, and shock work, Les Schwab Tires also provides retread services and produces custom wheels. Founder Les Schwab died in 2007, leaving CEO Dick Borgman at the helm.

HUMBLE BEGINNINGS

Les Schwab tried his hand at many trades before settling on the franchised tire business. Orphaned at a young age, Schwab was left to fend for himself when he was just 15 years old. He proved that he was capable of taking care of himself and his brother when he persuaded the principal of his school to let him out early to deliver newspapers. This job allowed him to earn the $8.00 a month he needed to pay the rent for himself and his brother. By the time he was 16, Schwab had become circulation manager of one of the newspapers he had been delivering.

After serving in World War II and working once again as the circulation manager upon his return to Oregon, Schwab was eager to open a business of his own. In 1952 he and his wife Dorothy sold their house, borrowed $1,100 from Dorothy's brother, and purchased OK Rubber Welders, a franchised tire shop in Prineville, Oregon. Although Schwab barely knew anything about tires, he was able to make a success of his store, grossing approximately $10,000 in sales a month, and $150,000 in the first year. Schwab expanded his business to include two more stores in the next two years.

By 1955, when Schwab acquired his third OK Rubber Welders store in Redmond, Oregon, he knew that operating as a franchise was not going to work for him. The business was not his own creation and he had too many ideas and theories that he wanted to try. Soon after he acquired the third store, Schwab changed the name of his shops to Les Schwab Tire Centers. He then

COMPANY PERSPECTIVES

Our success has been made possible by our wonderful customers, and by valuing the unique contributions and hard work of our employees. We are proud to feature Neat Clean Stores, Supermarket Selection, Sudden Service, Convenient Credit and Warranties in Writing. Pride in Performance is the value that drives us at Les Schwab. We take pride in our customer service and pride in our employees. As a company we try to incorporate this belief into everything we do. Our company goals are to continue to provide the legendary Les Schwab level of customer service, to be original and innovative, and to stay independent.

developed and began implementing an idea that became known as the "supermarket tire concept."

The supermarket tire concept turned his tire warehouse into a showroom that customers could walk through in order to select the exact tires that they would like to purchase. Schwab also aimed to stock multiple brands of tires in each size to give customers more options. Schwab's idea was not popular with the major tire distributors but proved to be an incredibly successful business strategy for Les Schwab Tires.

INDEPENDENT THINKING

As Schwab opened more stores, he became increasingly independent in his strategic business plans. In 1966 Schwab decided to take down all of the rubber companies' signs that advertised particular brands of tires and replace them with his own Les Schwab Tires signs. Many of the rubber companies were disgruntled at this change. One supplier who objected adamantly to Schwab's new practice found his brand dropped from Schwab's offerings altogether.

Schwab added six stores and a retread shop in Idaho in 1966, bringing to 18 the count of stores he owned. Retreading was a significant addition to the Les Schwab Tires business plan. Les Schwab Tires would retread worn tires and sell them with the same warranty that came with a new tire. By 1972 Schwab had increased his number of stores to 35, and he was still opening new stores. Les Schwab Tires was able to grow at such a fast rate partly due to the company's sales success. Les Schwab Tires was doubling its sales volume every five years at this time.

INTRODUCING COMPUTERS IN 1982

The Les Schwab Tire Centers Prineville headquarters had been computerized since 1972, but it was not until 1982 that the company began considering the possibility of computerizing individual retail stores in order to speed up the invoice process. The company updated its computer system to IBM System/38 and dial-up modem technology and began the process of outfitting its stores with a computer network. Once 80 stores were computerized, a measurable difference from the previous system was seen.

The computerized stores sent out invoice statements 10 days earlier than before, and received payments earlier as a result. The system that Les Schwab Tires had chosen to use had many advantages. It was relatively inexpensive, it used a programming language in which the Les Schwab Tires programming staff was already fluent, and the system was programmed so that if a store had serious computer troubles, they could be dealt with remotely from headquarters.

In 1994 when Les Schwab Tires found that the point-of-sale terminals in their retail stores were not operating as well as they needed them to be, the company opted to look for a new solution. "The problem," explained Les Schwab Tires Telecommunications Manager Pam Ontko, "boiled down to transaction speed and memory capacity. During regular business times, transactions took about 30 seconds to process, but during our peak times the old terminals we had been using could take as long as three minutes to obtain a transaction authorization. This caused extensive queuing at checkout counters and caused anxiety for the customer waiting for their credit card to process."

Les Schwab Tires opted to install the T7E terminals from Hypercom, Inc., in Phoenix, Arizona. The new terminals were significantly quicker than the previous ones, and featured considerably more memory capability. Ontko noted, "The T7E has separate, single, labeled keys to press to perform the most common functions, and so requires minimal training. In fact, after installing the initial 12 stores, we fine-tuned the instructions that include some special procedures for our stores. From this, our stores were able to install the equipment." The process for generating reports and other daily transactions was simplified with the new system, due to its user-friendly layout. The new computers also gave Les Schwab Tires some of the tools it needed to stay competitive, like the capability to support debit/ATM cards, check scanners, and other necessary business components.

KEY DATES

1952: Les Schwab purchases franchised OK Rubber Welders tire store in Prineville, Oregon.

1966: Les Schwab abandons OK Rubber Welders franchise concept; changes business name to Les Schwab Tire Centers.

1972: Les Schwab opens his 35th Les Schwab Tire Centers store.

1982: Company begins computerizing individual retail stores.

2000: *Modern Tire Dealers* magazine recognizes Les Schwab as Tire Dealer of the Year.

2006: Dick Borgman is named CEO.

2007: Founder Les Schwab dies at the age of 89.

2008: Company headquarters move to Bend, Oregon.

COMPASSIONATE COMPANY

Les Schwab Tires took advantage of many opportunities to raise and donate money to charity. Some of the community service activities that Les Schwab Tires was involved in were uniquely suited to the company. The company donated tires/wheels to the Cottage Grove, Oregon, Police Department's D.A.R.E. (Drug Abuse Resistance Education) program. A police officer who was part of the D.A.R.E. program drove an elaborately decorated and stereo-sound enhanced Geo Tracker, a car that was recovered from a drug dealer, when making rounds to the local elementary schools to teach the seven-part D.A.R.E. program.

Les Schwab Tires also contributed to the community through the company's participation in the Society of Vintage Racing Enthusiasts Group's Northwest Vintage Races. In addition, Les Schwab Tires became well known for its practice of sponsoring sports teams (usually basketball teams) in towns where the company had shops.

TIRE DISPOSAL ISSUES

A general concern about the growing piles of old vehicle tires grew into legislation in the early 1990s. Many of the states in which Les Schwab Tires operated passed their own laws, and in 1991 an Idaho law went into effect that prohibited the disposal of tires in landfills. In 1994 Idaho's Board of Health and Welfare voted to require a tracking system for used tires.

These types of laws were passed because it was found that tire piles posed major fire risks. Les Schwab

Tires noted that their company had a built-in $1.00 fee on all new tire sales that was designated to pay for tire cleanup. The company piled its tires and waited patiently for an economical solution to the problem of disposing of old tires. However, by 1996 Les Schwab Tires headquarters had more than four million tires stacked a few miles west of it, and still no economical and environmentally sound solution regarding the old tires was in sight.

The company eventually found ways to dispose of the tires. Les Schwab launched several tire recycling and reuse programs. The company also began to work with vendors that were involved in scrap recovery. Some of its partners worked on the development of tire-derived fuel as an alternative energy source. Old tires were also converted into materials used in civil engineering projects such as backfill for retaining walls and drainage material used in land applications. Other Les Schwab vendors transformed rubber from waste tires into flooring for gyms, workout studios, and playgrounds.

SEIZING OPPORTUNITIES

When the Asian currency markets fell in 1998 and the Asian automobile market plummeted, Les Schwab Tires wasted no time taking advantage of the strong value of the dollar in Korea. Les Schwab Tires quickly entered the Korean rubber market and scooped up the deals left behind when tire suppliers' customers began to bow out of orders.

Another example of the ability of Les Schwab Tires to quickly turn a potentially harmful situation into a success for the company occurred in 2000, when Firestone tires, in a highly publicized tire recall, recalled tires that had been standard on the Ford Explorer. While Ford dealerships and Firestone tire stores were having trouble servicing all of the people who were flooding their shops, Les Schwab Tires was ready and waiting. Schwab's history of stocking Firestone-brand tires made them uniquely prepared to deal with the influx of people seeking tire replacements. Furthermore, when the tire recall went into effect, Schwab had begun to stock thousands of extra tires in its Prineville tire warehouse and hired additional truck drivers to distribute them. Les Schwab Tires replaced the tires for free as long as the $100-a-tire reimbursement Firestone was willing to pay was not exceeded.

TIRE DEALER OF THE YEAR

In 2000 Les Schwab, at the age of 83, received recognition as *Modern Tire Dealers* (*MTD*) magazine's Tire Dealer of the Year. Les Schwab was the eighth person to be chosen as the recipient of this award. During the ceremony that took place at the Les Schwab headquarters in Prineville, Les Schwab Tires was awarded an etched-glass plaque, a portrait of Les Schwab, and a $1,000 donation in his name to the Prineville Community Hospital. During a speech given by an old friend and former editor, Lloyd Stoyer of *MTD*, Les Schwab was honored for his business and personal successes. Stoyer spoke of Schwab's policy of sharing 51 percent of the company's profits with employees, stating that, "Never in the history of the tire industry has one person been so generous to so many." Les Schwab's wife, Dorothy, was also honored for her role in the company's success. She was presented with a dozen roses while the crowd applauded her with a standing ovation.

Les Schwab Tires was repeatedly selected in polls as one of the public's favorite businesses. In 1990 the company was awarded one of Oregon State University's Family Business Awards. In 2002 the *Wenatchee Business Journal*'s Readers' Choice Awards announced Les Schwab the winner in their "Best Customer Service" category.

CHANGES IN THE 21ST CENTURY

Les Schwab Tires entered the new millennium on solid ground. Sales surpassed the $1 billion mark for the first time in 2000. At the same time, the company was ranked the best national passenger vehicle and light truck tire retailer in customer satisfaction by J.D. Powers for the fourth consecutive year. While the company continued to rely on the core fundamentals set in place by founder Les Schwab, it began to undergo a series of strategic changes that included growth into new markets, as well as a new leadership team. Dick Borgman was named CEO in 2006 and eventually became chairman upon Phil Wick's retirement in 2008.

Founder Les Schwab died in 2007 at the age of 89. Both of his children preceded him in death. His son Harlan was killed in an automobile accident in 1971. Daughter Margie Denton, slated to eventually take over the company, died of cancer in 2005. After Les Schwab's death, his widow Dorothy and his four grandchildren remained on the company's board of directors but were not active in day-to-day operations. Upon Schwab's death, Borgman pledged to lead the company with the founder's vision in mind.

HEADQUARTERS RELOCATED TO BEND, OREGON

Les Schwab's headquarters remained in Prineville until 2008, when operations moved to Bend, Oregon. By

then, the Prineville location had grown from the 1,400-square-foot shed with no running water that Schwab purchased in 1952 to a large cluster of buildings including a three-story administrative building with offices for 150 staffers, a large training-and-meeting facility, a computer center that kept Les Schwab Tire Centers computers running in five states, and the largest retread shop in America. Within eyesight of the administrative headquarters, Schwab had created a storage area for four million scrap tires that would be chopped up and buried. The Prineville compound also included a 450,000-square-foot warehouse that stored hundreds of thousands of new tires.

Although Prineville was significantly off the beaten track, Schwab had opted to keep Les Schwab Tire Centers headquartered there for much of its history. In 1995 when word leaked out that Les Schwab Tires was considering moving its headquarters to be closer to the regions where the company was expanding, Prineville's community rallied to keep Les Schwab Tires where it was. Phone calls streamed into Les Schwab Tire Centers headquarters, and a plan was concocted to help the company build the new warehouse it needed at the site of the Prineville Airport Industrial Park. Prineville was delighted when Les Schwab Tires decided to stay and the town credited the company with its burgeoning growth.

The company eventually set plans in motion in 2006 to move out of Prineville in favor of Bend, Oregon, a larger city with amenities that appealed to many of Les Schwab's executives. Prineville had seen significant growth since 1995 and unemployment rates were at their lowest levels since the 1960s. While residents were sad to see the company leave in 2008, the move did not devastate the local economy.

A December 2008 *Oregonian* article explained the move, claiming, "The transition is emblematic of broader changes at Schwab, which is breaking with a number of traditions as it seeks to expand from its folksy roots as a regional company rooted firmly in the Northwest into a multibillion-dollar enterprise that spans the entire West." By the time the new $33 million headquarters opened, there were over 410 Les Schwab Tire Centers in operation across eight states and the company was securing approximately $1.6 billion in annual sales.

As the company entered a new era in its history, it faced many challenges brought on by a faltering economy, problems in the U.S. auto industry, and high raw material costs. Industry shipments were down by 6 percent in 2008, to the lowest levels since 1997, and Les Schwab was forced to undergo a round of layoffs. The company also pared back its expansion plans but continued to eye California and other western states as crucial markets for growth in the years to come. While a recovery in the tire industry as well as the U.S. economy was expected to be slow, Les Schwab Tire Centers appeared to be well positioned to handle future challenges.

Tammy Weisberger
Updated, Christina M. Stansell

PRINCIPAL COMPETITORS

Discount Tire Co.; Sears, Roebuck & Co.; TBC Corporation; Wal-Mart Stores, Inc.

FURTHER READING

"Les Schwab Tire Picks Up Property on Bangerter for Sixth Utah Store," *Enterprise*, June 23, 2003.

Linsalata, Vera, "His 'Vision' to Continue," *Tire Business*, June 4, 2007.

Marshall, John, "Northwest Chain Store Enhances Customer Service and Lowers Operational Costs by Replacing Outdated POS Terminals," *Chain Store Age Executive and Shopping Center Age*, June 1994, p. 92.

Maynard, Micheline, "Firestone's Crisis Is Other Dealers' Opportunity," *New York Times*, September 17, 2000.

"*MTD*'s Tire Dealer of the Year: Family, Friends Honor Les Schwab," *Modern Tire Dealer*, December 2000, p. 10.

Rogoway, Mike, "Schwab Handoff Planned in Detail," *Oregonian*, May 23, 2007.

———, "Tire Giant Rolls Hub out of Town," *Oregonian*, December 13, 2006.

———, "Tire King Treading Carefully into Future," *Oregonian*, December 17, 2008.

Schwab, Les, *Les Schwab Pride in Performance: Keep It Going*, Bend, OR: Maverick Publications, 1986.

Line 6, Inc.

26580 Agoura Road
Calabasas, California 91302-1921
U.S.A.
Telephone: (818) 575-3600
Fax: (818) 575-3601
Web site: http://line6.com

Private Company
Founded: 1985 as Fast Forward Designs, Inc.
Employees: 250
Sales: $100.6 million (2008 est.)
NAICS: 334310 Amplifiers (Auto, Home, Musical Instrument, Public Address) Manufacturing; 339992 Electric Musical Instruments Manufacturing; 423490 Other Professional Equipment and Supplies Merchant Wholesalers

∎∎∎

Line 6, Inc., applies advanced digital technology to meet the needs of musicians. The company's founders Michel Doidic and Marcus Ryle developed some of the most successful musical electronics for other companies in the 10 years preceding their launch of Line 6 as a manufacturing spin-off of their consulting business. They applied digital signal processing (DSP) technology to develop new tools for guitarists. The company's original product, the AxSys 212, was a digital modeling amplifier capable of replicating the classic sounds of dozens of vintage tube amplifiers. The POD incorporated the same modeling technology in a desktop device. Other spin-offs incorporating Line 6's DSP technology followed, including Variax digital guitars, which emulated the sounds of dozens of instruments.

Line 6 was soon changing the way music was made. Their products replaced bulky, expensive, and temperamental equipment and created new sonic possibilities through the ability to edit tone signatures with software. The products appeal to working musicians who have adopted the new equipment for live performances as well as studio recordings, while remaining attainable for serious amateurs. The digital amps created the fastest-growing segment of the $400 million U.S. guitar-amp industry, attracting competition from established manufacturers.

Line 6 has continued to develop innovations. In 2008 the company acquired a manufacturer of digital wireless systems for instruments and microphones, adding another state-of-the-art product line. Line 6 announced another cutting-edge niche product in April 2010, a connector and software to link Apple iPhones to MIDI devices. Based in Southern California, Line 6 contracts its manufacturing to suppliers in China. The company markets its products in more than 60 countries and has a sales office in the United Kingdom.

ORIGINS

Line 6, Inc., cofounders Marcus Ryle and Michel Doidic, a native of France, met while working as designers at Oberheim Electronics, Inc., an early synthesizer manufacturer based in California. Like most of the employees at Oberheim, Ryle had a background in musical performance, having classical piano training and

COMPANY PERSPECTIVES

Line 6's passion for excellence and commitment to the development of new technologies has attracted the industry's best engineers and designers, a formidable roster of artist endorsers, and an active, informed user base—a combination that leaves Line 6 well-equipped to take on the enviable challenges of continued growth.

experience in the Los Angeles music scene. In 1985, with a team of 10 engineers, they formed the consulting firm Fast Forward Designs, which helped manufacturers develop some of the most successful electronics products of the day. These included the Alesis Quadraverb, Quadrasynth, and ADAT, the latter a revolutionary product that made digital recording affordable for the home user. Other clients included DigiDesign, Fostex, and Tascam.

By about 1990 the price of digital signal processing (DSP) chips had fallen enough to make it feasible to apply the technology to the needs of electric guitarists. These processors had become ubiquitous, even appearing in cellular phones. Line 6 used Texas Instruments chips at first, and then switched to ones made by Austin, Texas-based Freescale Semiconductor, Inc.

After a decade in business, Ryle and Doidic began to develop a product of their own, establishing a manufacturing division called Line 6. The name came from an announcement the receptionist would give to warn of visitors while the engineers were conducting secret research. Guitarists were a ripe market. Most of the electronic innovations that had revolutionized music in the previous two decades (primarily synthesizers) had been geared toward keyboard players. Very little had been developed for guitarists outside of a few digital effects, although guitars were among the most played instruments in the world.

The distinctive fuzz guitar sound so central to rock music was originally created by playing too loud, overdriving the speakers, and forcing harmonic overtones into prominence. The resulting tone was influenced by many factors. Line 6 set out to measure all the attributes and develop ways to reproduce them digitally. The company assembled a collection of vintage amplifiers, choosing the most representative examples of classic models manufactured by Fender, Vox, Mesa Boogie, Soldano, Matchless, and others. The company used a similar process to model effects such as reverb and distortion.

FIRST PRODUCT IN 1996

Line 6 brought out its first product, the AxSys 212, in 1996. It was described as the first digital modeling guitar amplifier. A 100-watt stereo amp, it provided access to dozens of amps and effects at the flick of a switch. The technology was awarded a U.S. patent in 1998. By this time the company had an update of its original, called the Flextone, which retailed for $799.

The technology lent itself to other new products, including software for Pro Tools called Amp Farm. In 1997 Line 6 brought amp modeling to the desktop with a compact unit called the POD, considered Line 6's breakthrough product. The POD enabled recording and practice at lower sound levels than the ear-splitting volumes electric guitarists required to produce the best tone. It also spared musicians from having to select and place microphones to capture the sound, which was an art in itself. In addition to a selection of vintage amp sounds, the POD included a range of digital effects.

A dozen guitarists were dispatched to several hundred stores for demonstrations. Device controls were deliberately kept simple, with knobs rather than LCD screens for quick changes between presets. Such products could save professional musicians hours of expensive setup time and simplify work in the studio and life on the road. With amps price at around $1,000 and effects units at $250, they remained attainable for serious amateurs. Early users among top-selling musical artists included the Dixie Chicks, Clint Black, Todd Rundgren, and the Wallflowers. Within a decade that list included U2, Duran Duran, Metallica, and No Doubt.

VENTURE CAPITAL IN 1997

Revenues were $2.3 million in 1996, Line 6's first year in business, and grew to $3.5 million in 1997. In that year the company attracted $3.1 million in venture capital from Palo Alto's Sutter Hill Ventures, which had been an early backer of DigiDesign Inc., a pioneering musical electronics company that had unsuccessfully tried to develop its own digital amp. Redpoint invested another $10 million in May 2000.

Peter Gotcher, founder of DigiDesign Inc. (which merged with Avid Technology in 1995) joined Line 6's board of directors in 1997. The founders handed off the CEO position to Mike Muench, a Harvard MBA and veteran of IBM and Apple Computer (as well as a keyboard player in local rock bands). Doidic became chief technology officer while Ryle served as senior vice president of new business development. The next year the company moved to new headquarters in Thousand Oaks and a 38,000-square-foot manufacturing facility. One of the fastest-growing companies in the country,

KEY DATES

1985: Former Oberheim Electronics engineers Michel Doidic and Marcus Ryle found Fast Forward Designs, Inc., as a consulting business.
1995: Doidic and Ryle start Line 6, Inc., to make their own products.
1996: The first digital modeling guitar amplifier, Line 6's AxSys 212, debuts.
1997: The POD brings digital amp and effect modeling to the desktop.
2000: Line 6 introduces its own line of guitar effects pedals, as well as POD units for bass guitar and rack mount use.
2001: Vetta stereo amp is introduced.
2002: Variax offers digital modeling capabilities in a guitar.
2007: Spider Valve amplifier is introduced.
2008: X2 Digital Wireless Systems is acquired.

Line 6 reached $23 million in revenues in 1999 and was reportedly making a profit.

By 2000 the company had about 200 employees and was a regular on the *Inc.* list of the 500 fastest-growing small companies in the United States. It was one of the top five amplifier manufacturers in the United States by this time, and the segment it created and led was the fastest growing in the $400 million U.S. guitar-amp industry. The company's success had attracted competition from established amp manufacturers, who introduced their own digital modeling amplifiers. Yamaha Corp. USA was reportedly second in digital amps at this time.

In 2000 Line 6 introduced its own line of guitar effects pedals, as well as POD versions for bass guitar and rack mount use. The next year it rolled out its top-of-the-line Vetta amp, which featured studio-quality effects. Line 6 was also developing tools to exploit the possibilities of the Internet, which was showing the potential to be a transformative force in music making. Users would eventually be able to download new tones for their PODs via Line 6's ToneTransfer library and save or e-mail their own settings or transfer them to other Line 6 products.

VARIAX LAUNCHED IN 2002

In late 2002 Line 6 introduced another groundbreaking product, the Variax guitar, which listed for $1,400, with an average street price around $1,000. It used noise-free piezo pickups rather than traditional magnetic pickups, which were prone to interference (hum). Line 6's digital modeling techniques allowed it to replicate the sounds of various types of electric and acoustic guitars, and even a banjo and sitar.

Line 6 followed the original solid-body electric Variax with a similar concept built around an acoustic guitar body. Geared toward the needs of country and folk musicians, the Variax Acoustic could alter the pitch of individual strings, providing virtual capoing and instant alternative tunings. A Variax bass followed.

Revenues were $38 million in 2002. The company continued to develop a constant stream of innovative products. GuitarPort software and peripherals, introduced in 2002, allowed guitarists to play along with remixed legendary rock songs. Revenues were $44.2 million in 2003 and still increasing every year, reaching $58.5 million in 2004 and $69 million in 2005.

The LowDown series of bass amplifiers appeared in 2006. They were followed the next year by Spider Valve guitar amplifiers, which combined digital modeling capabilities with the responsiveness of a real tube. Another new development in 2007 was a battery-powered version of the POD. Line 6 made its POD modeling technology available to players of the Guitar Hero World Tour game in 2008.

Revenues reached $100 million in 2008. By this time Line 6 had approximately 250 employees. The company had distribution in more than 60 countries. In early 2008 Line 6 acquired X2 Digital Wireless Systems, Inc. Formerly known as Xwire, it had been founded by industry pioneer Guy Coker. Digital wireless systems offered many advantages over traditional analog wireless, such as better sound quality and more flexibility and ease of use. In 2009 Line 6 introduced its XDR95 handheld wireless microphone and Relay G30 Digital Wireless System for guitars.

Line 6 remained true to its mission of developing useful innovations for musicians. It announced another cutting-edge niche product in April 2010, a connector and software to link Apple iPhones to MIDI devices for performance, editing, or data backup purposes.

Frederick C. Ingram

PRINCIPAL SUBSIDIARIES

Line 6 Digital Wireless, Inc.

PRINCIPAL COMPETITORS

Behringer GmbH; Fender Musical Instruments Corporation; Gibson Guitar Corp.; LOUD Technologies Inc.; Marshall Amplification plc; Nady Systems, Inc.; Peavey Electronics Corporation; Vox Amplification Ltd.; Yamaha Corp.

FURTHER READING

Brinsley, John, "Fast-Growing Amp Firm Is Hitting Web," *Los Angeles Business Journal*, October 2, 2000, pp. 3, 14.

Fox, Jacqueline, "Playing by the Numbers: Agoura Hills Company Leads Industry in Manufacturing of Digital Guitars, Amplifiers as It Helps Musicians Cut Costs, Set-Up Time," *San Fernando Valley Business Journal*, March 31, 2003.

"The Lineage of Line 6," *Pro Sound News Europe*, May 11, 2010.

Lucas, Michael P., "Digital Amps Making Some Noise: The High-Tech Devices Let Guitar Players Choose Their Sound; Thousand Oaks-Based Line 6, Which Introduced Them, Has a Hit on Its Hands," *Los Angeles Times*, February 17, 2000, p. C1.

Nank, John, "Tune In, Turn On; How Mike Muench Gives His Staff the Freedom to Succeed at Line 6 Inc.," *Smart Business*, March 2007.

Weiss, Jeff, "Guitar, Amp Manufacturer Plugs In to Artists' Desire for Innovation," *San Fernando Valley Business Journal*, October 24, 2005, p. 14.

White, Paul, "Line 6: Inside the Modelling Factory," *Sound on Sound*, March 2006.

**Mansfield
Fuels. Simplified.**

Mansfield Oil Company

1025 Airport Parkway S.W.
Gainesville, Georgia 30501-6813
U.S.A.
Telephone: (770) 532-6266
Toll Free: (800) 695-6626
Fax: (770) 718-3053
Web site: http://www.mansfieldoil.com

Private Company
Incorporated: 1957
Employees: 265
Sales: $4.4 billion (2008)
NAICS: 424720 Petroleum and Petroleum Products
Merchant Wholesalers (Except Bulk Stations and
Terminals)

■ ■ ■

Mansfield Oil Company is an independent distributor
of petroleum products, including biofuels, and a
provider of related services to a wide variety of
industries. Each year the privately held company delivers
more two billion gallons of petroleum products,
procured from independent and major suppliers, to
customers across the United States. They include truck
fleets; rental car companies; grocery stores; convenience
stores and gas stations; marinas; universities; utilities and
power generation plants; airports; forestry agencies;
waste management facilities; and federal, state, and local
government agencies, including about 700 school
districts.

For independent retailers looking for a branded
gasoline without its own name attached, Mansfield offers the Solo brand. The company also maintains branding relationships with a large number of major fuel
brands, including BP, Citgo, Chevron, Crown,
Marathon, Texaco, and Conoco-Phillips. Retail customers make up 20 percent of the company's business,
government clients contribute another 30 percent, and
the balance of Mansfield's revenues come from its commercial accounts. Mansfield also offers fuel supply and
logistics management services, allowing customers to
outsource all or part of their fuel distribution needs.
Strategic fuel supply services help customers to control
fuel costs.

Mansfield also offers a retail fuel program to help
retailers sell gasoline under their own name or through a
private label. For fleets, Mansfield provides reporting
and tracking services as well as fleet cards. Another
service, consigned fuel and third party billing, allows
customers to maintain a supply of fuel that is owned by
Mansfield until it is pumped from the ground, thus
limiting capital expenditures. Because of the volatility of
fuel prices, Mansfield also provides customers with a
variety of hedging and price risk services.

To help customers deal with natural disasters, such
as hurricanes, floods, earthquakes, tornadoes, and
wildfires, as well as power outages and even terrorist attacks, Mansfield offers emergency response and planning
services. Subsidiary C&N Companies serves the marketing needs of independent, farmer-owned cooperative
ethanol refiners. Mansfield maintains its corporate
headquarters in Gainesville, Georgia, and regional offices
in Chicago, Denver, Detroit, and Houston. The

COMPANY PERSPECTIVES

Our success is the result of a thorough understanding of the industry, a commitment to improvement, and an adaptation to market changes. We have a history of establishing and maintaining long-term, mutually profitable client relationships.

company is owned and managed by the Mansfield family.

COMPANY FOUNDED: 1957

Mansfield oil was founded in Gainesville, Georgia, in 1957 when John E. Mansfield, Sr., and his wife bought a small oil distributorship. Focusing on North Georgia, the company expanded over the years and by 1980 the company was a major distributor of gasoline in the area. At this point it began to expand in a number of directions. The military became a major customer, as Mansfield landed a number of significant contracts. For example, in 1984 the company won a $10.2 million gasoline, diesel fuel, and fuel oil contract from the Defense Logistics Agency.

Mansfield Oil became involved in the retail sale of gasoline in 1980 when John Mansfield opened a convenience store under the Kangaroo name on Sycamore Street in Gainesville. The store proved successful and a year later he launched Kangaroo Inc. to operate the Kangaroo convenience store chain. By this time his son, John E. Mansfield, Jr., was also involved in the business. He had become a vice president of Mansfield Oil in his early 20s in 1978. Another son, Michael F. Mansfield, joined the company in 1981. It was in that year that John E. Mansfield, Jr., was made president of the new Kangaroo convenience store chain.

John Mansfield, Jr., headed Kangaroo until 1985, during which time the chain expanded in the Gainesville area. In 1986 he founded Onyx Petroleum and served as president of the petroleum marketing concern. Michael Mansfield took over the Kangaroo stores and began to grow that concern into a regional chain. In March 1986 Kangaroo Inc. acquired 22 Jiffy convenience stores from North Carolina's Food Lion Inc. The Kangaroo chain would spread throughout the Southeast, at one point topping 100 units in size. It was an innovative operator, embracing new ideas, such as offering premium coffee, well before other convenience store chains.

KANGAROO STORES DIVESTED: 1999

Splitting its attention between a wholesale business and the retail Kangaroo chain proved unwieldy for the Mansfield family as the 1990s came to a close. The decision was made to focus on the wholesale business, and Mansfield Oil began to shed the Kangaroo stores. In 1998, 10 of the stores were sold to Conoco Inc. and converted to the Conoco banner. The last of the stores, 49 units in all, as well as the Kangaroo name, were sold to North Carolina-based The Pantry Inc. in November 1999 for $46.5 million according to Securities and Exchange Commission documents. The Pantry was a fast-growing chain in a time of consolidation and earlier in the summer had made its entry into Georgia with the acquisition of a dozen stores in the Augusta area. The Pantry then embraced Kangaroo as its core brand, a testament to what Mansfield Oil had accomplished with the convenience store chain.

With the divestiture of the Kangaroo chain, Mansfield Oil focused on expanding its wholesale business across the country under the leadership of Michael Mansfield. Over the next decade the company increased sales volumes 10 to 20 percent each year. A key to that success was the growth in value-added services Mansfield Oil made available to its customers, many of whom were small independent retailers, convenience store as well as grocery retailers, who were struggling to survive in a market that would see record-high gasoline prices. They also had to contend with the increasing use of credit cards by their customers, the fees of which cut into profits.

VALUE-ADDED SERVICES OFFERED

Mansfield's outsourcing options helped retailers in a number of ways. The company was capable of offering a turnkey retail fueling solution, including initial permitting and construction. Mansfield also offered its own Solo brand of gasoline to retailers who wanted a branded product but did not want to attach the store name. Moreover, Mansfield offered partnership relationships with retailers in which it owned the tanks and dispensers and supplied and managed the fuel. Should the retailer decide to take on the responsibility of managing the fuel product, Mansfield was willing to sell its investment to the retailer. Mansfield also helped to find buyers if necessary, having learned from experience that it cost more to remove the tanks and equipment than to just leave them.

Mansfield's flexibility helped greatly to grow the retail side of the business, but it was also aided in the

1957: John E. Mansfield, Sr., and his wife found Mansfield Oil Company.

1980: First Kangaroo convenience store opens for retail sale of gasoline.

1999: Mansfield divests Kangaroo to focus on its wholesale business.

2008: Company offices open in Denver and Chicago.

2009: C&N Companies is acquired.

early years of the 21st century as major oil companies began to withdraw direct service to convenience stores and small retailers, including grocery stores and marinas. Mansfield was more than willing to help fill that gap. In February 2008 the company hired three executives to its Retail Sales and Operations unit. All of them had experience, and success, in running convenience store operations.

MILITARY CONTRACTS CONTINUE

Mansfield Oil also continued to serve the U.S. Department of Defense in the new century. In the summer of 2002 the company won a $10.25 million contract to supply gasoline, diesel fuel, and heating oil to the U.S. Army, U.S. Navy, and U.S. Air Force, as well as some federal civilian agencies at sites in Washington, D.C., Indiana, Kentucky, Maryland, Tennessee, and Virginia. In 2005 Mansfield Oil received a five-year contract worth as much as $5.4 million to supply gasoline, fuel oil, and low-sulfur diesel to the U.S. Army and federal civilian agencies. In May 2009 Mansfield won one of its largest contracts, nearly $57 million, to supply fuel to the Defense Energy Support Center in Fort Belvoir, Virginia.

In addition to organic growth, Mansfield looked to expand through acquisitions. In April 2008 it acquired the commercial and industrial business unit of Denver, Colorado-based TransMontaigne Product Services Inc., which provided supply chain management services for gasoline and diesel fuel delivery to gas stations, convenience stores, and government agencies. The deal allowed Mansfield to open a Denver office, staffed by the TransMontaigne personnel it inherited, and expand its involvement in western markets.

A few weeks later, Mansfield opened a regional marketing office in Chicago to better serve the Midwest.

Mansfield looked for other ways to support its retail customers as well. In 2009 it struck a deal with Hot Stuff Foods to make food options available to its convenience store operators, another part of Mansfield's effort to become a one-stop resource for retail fuel providers.

C&N COMPANIES ACQUIRED: 2009

In a time of soaring fuel prices and a call for the development of alternative fuels, Mansfield was committed to positioning itself for future developments. The company's biofuel sales grew 44 percent in 2008. Sales increased at an even more rapid rate in 2009. In June of that year it hired a director of biofuels and business development. One month later, Mansfield acquired Bloomington, Indiana-based C&N Companies, a major ethanol marketer as well as biodiesel producer.

Established in 2000, C&N served the marketing needs of independent, farmer-owned co-op ethanol refiners. All told, it represented 500 million gallons of ethanol and 150 million gallons of biodiesel production from 11 plants from Indiana to Mexico. Later in 2009 Mansfield's ethanol marketing division signed a three-year agreement with Minnesota's Heron Lake BioEnergy, which each year processed 18 million bushels of corn at its dry grind plant to produce 50 million gallons of ethanol.

Mansfield added to its alternative fuels portfolio in June 2010, acquiring most of the assets of Orange, California-based Western Ethanol. The company supplied and distributed ethanol in California, as well as Arizona, Idaho, Nevada, Oregon, and Washington. Also in 2010, C&N entered into marketing agreements with a pair of Iowa companies that produced biofuels, Permeate Refining and East Fork Biodiesel LLC.

FOCUS ON GROWTH: 2010

To grow its alternative fuels and other businesses, Mansfield continued to open regional offices. A Detroit office was followed in March 2010 with a new marketing office in Houston, Texas, the fourth of what was planned to be six regional offices to create a national network of marketing and operations centers. In addition, C&N opened an office in Minneapolis, and another subsidiary, Mansfield Renewable Energy, opened an office in Charlottesville, Virginia.

Moreover, Mansfield pursued a new fuel additive, Diesel Exhaust Fluid (DEF), which was gaining strength in Europe, where it was being dispensed at fuel islands.

A urea-based chemical, DEF was used as a catalyst in the emissions-reduction process, and was poised to play a key role in diesel engine powered vehicles meeting new stricter emissions standards. Mansfield forged a manufacturing partnership with Yara International ASA, which produced the Air1 brand of DEF, and made plans to distribute the product through its national network.

Whether it was DEF, alternative fuels, or offering new services to retail customers, Mansfield was a company determined to remain relevant in a changing market place. The company also continued to grow at a steady pace. In 2005 it posted revenues of $2.1 billion, placing it 165th on the *Forbes* list of the largest private companies in the United States. Three years later that amount more than doubled to $4.4 billion, earning the company the 83rd slot on the list. There was every reason to believed that Mansfield was poised to move further up in those rankings in the years ahead.

Ed Dinger

PRINCIPAL SUBSIDIARIES

C&N Companies; Mansfield Fuel Systems; Mansfield Fuel Logistics; Mansfield Fleet.

PRINCIPAL COMPETITORS

Global Partners LP; Gulf Oil Limited Partnership; World Fuel Services Corporation.

FURTHER READING

Donohue, Bill, "The World According to Mansfield," *CSP Independent*, September 2008, p. 46.

Gilbert, Debbie, "North Carolina Company May Buy Kangaroo," *Gainesville (GA) Times*, October 8, 1999, p. 1A.

Gunter, Ford, "Mansfield Oil Officially Arrives with Houston Office," *Houston Business Journal*, April 2, 2010.

King, W. B., "Mansfield Oil Acquires TransMontaigne," *Convenience Store News*, April 30, 2008.

Peabody, Alvin, "Some Still Celebrate the Family Business," *Gainesville (GA) Times*, November 5, 2000, p. 4B.

Reid, Keith, "Mansfield Oil: A Clear Focus, but a Company that Defies Conventional Definitions," *National Petroleum News*, February 2010, p. 14.

Marc Glassman, Inc.

5841 West 130th Street
Cleveland, Ohio 44130
U.S.A.
Telephone: (216) 265-7700
Fax: (216) 265-7737
Web site: http://www.marcs.com

Private Company
Incorporated: 1979
Employees: 6,850
Sales: $1.23 billion (2009 est.)
NAICS: 446110 Pharmacies and Drug Stores

■ ■ ■

Privately held Marc Glassman, Inc., is the operator of about 61 Marc's Deeper Discount Drug Stores in central and northeast Ohio, concentrating on the Akron, Canton, Cleveland, Columbus, and Youngstown markets. In addition, Marc's operates several stores in Connecticut under the Xpect Discounts Drugs banner. While most of the stores include pharmacies and carry typical drugstore health and beauty product lines, Marc's is best known for its closeout section, offering a wide variety of merchandise sourced from around the world by the chain's team of buyers. Because these attractively priced products turn over quickly, regular customers tend to make frequent visits, prompting them to do other shopping at Marc's for the sake of convenience.

Marc's has adjusted this successful formula by also adding produce, meat, dairy, frozen foods, and groceries

at discount prices, providing customers with another reason to shop at the chain. Marc's also offers discount fuel cards, money grams, money orders, and prepaid phone cards. The only credit card the company accepts is Discover, preferring instead to provide approved customers with check-cashing privileges. Marc's seeks to appeal to a wide range of shoppers, as demonstrated by its longtime sponsorship of a classical music program on a Cleveland radio station along with its willingness to hire a professional wrestler to make store visits. The company's founder and owner, Marc Glassman, serves as chairman. He rarely gives interviews and his employees are forbidden to speak to the press.

ORIGINS

Marc Glassman was raised in Cleveland, Ohio, where his father owned an auto wrecking company. He received his undergraduate degree from Cornell University, followed by a master's degree from Yale University and a master of business administration from Harvard Business School. On a postgraduate trip to Hong Kong he became attracted to discount retailing, but launched his business career by cofounding a fast-food restaurant chain in Vermont that he eventually sold to Burger King. Flush with cash, he spent the next year traveling around the world. In 1975 he returned to Cleveland and his interest in discount retailing was rekindled when he discovered a 20,000-square-foot Bernie Shulman's variety store doing a brisk business.

Bernie Shulman's was established by Cleveland retail legend Bernie Shulman, who had made his mark by launching the Revco discount drugstore chain in

1956. He sold the business in 1965 and after a decade in retirement returned to Cleveland to open a variety store in Cleveland's Mayfield Heights district. It was this store that would catch Glassman's attention. Glassman went to work at the store as a manager to learn the business from Shulman.

In 1979, three years after Shulman died, Glassman planned to strike out on his own and open a deep discount drugstore in Las Vegas, but soon realized that the demographics were wrong in that market. There were too few families, and people who came to gamble in town were not in the mood to search out bargains. "People in Las Vegas wouldn't go across the street to save a few dollars," Glassman told the *Akron Beacon Journal* in 1991. "It's just not their nature." Instead, Glassman decided to return to Cleveland. In 1979 he opened his first Marc's in Middleburg Heights with $750,000 furnished by a pair of major investors.

IMMEDIATE SUCCESS

Marc's enjoyed immediate success, due in large part to Glassman's energy, which allowed him to work 16-hour days, and his ability to buy merchandise with good discounts. In addition to bankruptcy sales, odd lots, overruns, and auctions, Glassman made periodic buying trips to the Far East. He essentially relied on instinct in determining what his customers would buy, but avoided apparel and televisions because it took too long to turn over such merchandise.

The keys to Marc's success were low prices, volume sales, and rapid turnover. Niceties were ignored. Merchandise was piled high in bulk bins and cut cases, labeled with hand printed signs; credit cards were not accepted; checkout lines were long and tedious; and promotional sales events were eschewed. All of this reinforced the idea that everyday prices were low and bargains were to be had. The quick turnover of merchandise kept Marc's customers coming back sooner rather than later to see what might be new.

Glassman opened additional Marc's stores and bought the original Shulman's store in 1983 from the widow of Bernie Shulman. By the fall of 1986 he was operating four Marc's stores and a pair of Bernie Shulman's stores. He also owned Marc's Rock Bottom Closeouts, two Bernie Shulman's Delis, and Marcs No Name Restaurant in Cleveland, as well as a 433,000-square-foot distribution center on 43 acres of land located near the Cleveland Hopkins International Airport. Each store also maintained its own warehouse. Outside of Ohio, Glassman franchised his closeout concept as the Texas Drug Warehouse and Drug Warehouse. For fiscal 1986 the company posted sales in excess of $100 million.

Glassman ran a lean operation. In addition to several buyers, Glassman employed just one vice president, a district manager, and individual store managers. In 1991 he turned over day-to-day control to a new president and chief operating officer but remained actively involved and continued to buy closeout merchandise. By this time the company was operating 12 Marc's stores in northeast Ohio as well as six Bernie Shulman's stores, and four Xpect Discounts stores in Connecticut. Annual sales reached $310 million and Marc's controlled 20.5 percent of the Cleveland-Akron drugstore market. In 1991 *Drug Store News* ranked the chain number 24 on its list of the top 50 drugstore chains.

FLAGSHIP STORE OPENS: 1992

Marc's opened a flagship store under the Bernie Shulman's banner in 1992, taking over a 68,000-square-foot former Ames department store in Garfield Heights, Ohio, that provided 41,000 square feet of selling space. It featured wider aisles and larger departments but would be just as crowded as the smaller Marc's stores. Combined, the stores generated $412.3 million in sales in 1993, a 26 percent increase over the previous year. During 1993 Glassman also decided to convert his eight Bernie Shulman's stores to the Marc's name. The four stores in Connecticut and Massachusetts continued to operate as Xpect Discounts.

Marc's faced increasing competition from Wal-Mart, price clubs, and other discounters, but continued to grow in the mid-1990s. The opening of new stores brought the total number of Marc's to 38 in Ohio, plus four Xpect Discounts stores in Connecticut and one in Massachusetts. Sales improved to $531 million in 1996. Four new stores opened in the late 1990s and sales increased to $595 million as the decade came to a close, earning Marc's a spot on the *Forbes* magazine list of the 500 largest privately held companies.

Sales improved at a steady rate in the early years of the new century. Six new stores were opened in 2001, when the company recorded sales of $740 million, an mix was then rolled out to the other stores over the next year.

KEY DATES

1979: Marc Glassman opens first discount drugstore.
1983: Glassman acquires original Bernie Shulman's store.
1993: Bernie Shulman's stores adopt the Marc's name.
2002: Marc's enters central Ohio market.
2006: Sales top $1 billion mark.

amount that placed Marc's at number 410 on the *Forbes* 500 largest private companies list in 2001. To maintain growth Glassman began to adjust an already successful formula. In March 2002 he opened a new store in Brook Park, Ohio, that devoted a large portion of its 40,000 square feet to discounted produce, dairy, case-ready meat products, and groceries.

Glassman had no interest in turning Marc's into a hybrid grocery store, but the additional product lines offered obvious advantages. According to the April 2002 *Supermarket News* each household averaged 15 trips a year to a drugstore but 75 trips to supermarkets. Marc's customers thus had an additional reason to visit, providing additional opportunities to purchase the stores' high-volume, quick-turn merchandise.

MOVE INTO CENTRAL OHIO: 2002

Marc's closed its Massachusetts store and moved into new markets in June 2002, opening its first store in central Ohio in the highly competitive Columbus area. All told, three stores were opened in 2003 and sales increased to $844 million from 53 Marc's stores and four Xpect Discounts drugstores. Sales grew to $954 million two years later. To maintain momentum, Marc's continued to make changes to its business model and store format.

In March 2006 the company revamped its store in the Solon area of Cleveland to include wider aisles and less clutter. It was also better organized, brighter, and offered more food items, including a gourmet cheese island and an expanded produce section that included organics, as well as larger dairy and frozen food sections. While management insisted that customers could do most, if not all, of their grocery shopping at Marc's, the store did not dispense with its closeout merchandise. The treasure hunt aspect of shopping at Marc's remained a key attraction. The new layout and product

An online digital photo service was introduced in 2005, and customers were given the option of refilling prescriptions online in 2006. The chain also increased its courtesy offerings. In addition to postage stamps, prepaid phone cards, and money orders, Marc's in 2007 began offering prepaid gas cards in conjunction with Speedway SuperAmerica LLC, a Marathon Oil Co. gas station and convenience store chain. The cards, available in $25, $50, and $100 denominations but sold only on a cash basis, could be used at the pump at Speedway stations, where users received a discount of 10 cents a gallon. The cards thus offered an incentive for drivers to purchase them and helped bring further business to Marc's while serving as a marketing tool.

While some aspects of Marc's changed, others remained the same. The chain continued to rely on cash registers rather than point-of-sale terminals and chose to save money by using closeout plastic bags that were either blank or bore the logo of other stores. The chain began to accept Discover credit cards, but continued to ignore the major credit cards and their steep charges in favor of checks and cash. However, Marc's did invest in technology when it offered clear-cut cost savings. In 2007 the company entered into contracts to implement handheld terminals and wearable computers to improve warehouse efficiency.

SALES TOP $1 BILLION: 2006

Two new Marc's stores were opened in 2006 and another unit opened in 2007. As a result, sales topped the $1 billion mark in 2006. To maintain growth, the chain continued to tweak its winning formula by adding such ethnic products as Wanchai Ferry Chinese dinner kits, Old El Paso taco dinner kits, and Taco Bell flavored taco shells and salsa with cheese. Marc's was also willing to try more unusual ideas. In 2008 it added Marc's Carpet for Less kiosks at 25 of its stores. The service, developed with Carpet Warehouse Inc. of Ohio, allowed customers to select carpet at an in-store kiosk and schedule in-home visits to have measurements taken and quotes provided by Carpet Warehouse representatives. The kiosks could also be used to schedule installation.

Marc's faced increased competition from the Walgreen and CVS drugstore chains as well as mass merchandisers, but had clearly carved out a strong regional position, where it continued to increase its share of its home market. With revenues of $1.23 billion in 2009, the chain ranked at number 13 on *Chain Drug Review*'s top 50 drug chains by dollar volume. Because Marc's mix of health and beauty products, supermarket fare, and closeout bargains had stood the test of time, and management had shown a willingness to adjust with changing conditions, there was every reason to expect further success in the years to come.

Ed Dinger

PRINCIPAL COMPETITORS

CVS Caremark Corporation; Walgreen Co.; Wal-Mart Stores, Inc.

FURTHER READING

Alaimo, Dan, "Leading Ohio Drug Chain Increasingly Stocking Grocery Items," *Supermarket News*, April 22, 2002, p. 75.

Cho, Janet, "Closeout King Marc's Beefs Up Groceries," *Cleveland Plain Dealer*, March 3, 2006, p. C1.

"Marc's Changes with the Times," *Chain Drug Review*, April 23, 2007, p. 175.

"Marc's Makes Discount Drug Retailing Work," *Chain Drug Review*, April 29, 2002, p. 192.

"Marc's Succeeds on Its Own Terms," *Chain Drug Review*, May 2, 2005, p. 160.

"Marc's Tinkers with Formula in Its New-Concept Store," *Chain Drug Review*, May 1, 2006, p. 175.

Rhoden, Yalinda, "Strategy for Success," *Akron Beacon Journal*, August 19, 1991, p. C1.

McKee Foods Corporation

10260 McKee Road
Collegedale, Tennessee 37315-0750
U.S.A.
Telephone: (423) 238-7111
Fax: (423) 238-7101
Web site: http://www.mckeefoods.com

Private Company
Incorporated: 1957 as McKee Baking Company
Employees: 6,000
Sales: $1.20 billion (2010 est.)
NAICS: 311810 Bread and Bakery Product Manufacturing; 311821 Cookie and Cracker Manufacturing; 311230 Breakfast Cereal Manufacturing

■ ■ ■

Family-owned and operated since its inception in 1934, McKee Foods Corporation is most famous for its Little Debbie snack cake line, which is the leading snack cake brand in the United States based on sales. The company sells over 160 varieties of Little Debbie multipack and single-serve snacks that can be found across the United States, Canada, Puerto Rico, Mexico, and on U.S. overseas military bases. McKee Foods also sells approximately 30 snacks and granola cereals under the Sunbelt brand. The company provides cookies, breakfast pastries, and various snacks to the foodservice industry through its Fieldstone brand.

Subsidiary Blue Planet Foods Inc. produces and supplies granola, grain-based cereals and cereal inclusions, toasted oats and grains, cereal and granola bar bases, pie shells, and doughnut and dessert toppings to the industrial food market. Little Debbie, named after the granddaughter of the company's founders, celebrated its 50th anniversary in 2010.

COMPANY ORIGINS

The company was born during the heart of the 1930s Depression. A young North Carolina couple, O. D. and Ruth McKee, lost their savings after a bank failure and moved from their home in Hendersonville to Chattanooga, Tennessee, in 1933. O. D. found work as a bakery salesman, selling Virginia Dare Cakes from Becker's Bakery, a local establishment, for five cents each. By 1934 O. D. had purchased his own delivery truck. He then found out that Jack's Cookie Company, another Chattanooga bakery, was up for sale. O. D. cashed in his truck and he and Ruth became owners and operators of their first business. According to the company publication *The Story Behind Little Debbie Snack Cakes*, the two "were ideal business partners because her cautious, conservative nature was the perfect complement to his risk-taking, adventuresome spirit."

In 1935 the couple moved the business to a new location and began making soft cookies and cakes. A year later they handed the business over to Ruth's father, Symon D. King, and returned to North Carolina to launch a new bakery. Located in Charlotte and named Jack's Cookie Company like its predecessor, the business was highly successful. In 1946, O. D., who "always had a gift for innovation and automation," built a new, state-of-the-art plant. During this period he also invented a soft oatmeal crème pie, "the company's oldest continuous product," according to *Milling & Baking News*.

The McKees sold their Charlotte business in the early 1950s and considered retiring. They decided instead to return to Chattanooga to manage the original Jack's, then called King's Bakery and owned by Ruth's brother, Cecil King. In 1954 O. D. and Ruth McKee purchased the company stock, and the foundation for the McKee Baking Company was born. As he had previously, O. D. served as salesman, inventor, and production manager, while Ruth operated as purchaser, personnel manager, and office manager.

In 1957, when they outgrew the Chattanooga bakery, the operation moved to nearby Collegedale, Tennessee. It was at this location that the company established its headquarters and grew into a major private corporation. The original Collegedale plant was expanded more than a dozen times before a sister plant was added. In 1982 the McKee family launched a third plant in Gentry, Arkansas, and a fourth followed eight years later in Stuarts Draft, Virginia. By this time Ruth had passed away and O. D. had transferred management to his sons, Ellsworth and Jack, while retaining his chairmanship.

INTRODUCTION OF LITTLE DEBBIE IN 1960

In 1960 the company made history in two ways. First, after leading the industry in mass production of small snack cakes, it conceived the "family" pack of 12 individually wrapped cakes sold as one multipack unit. Second, it began affixing the Little Debbie brand, named after Ellsworth's daughter Debra, to its products.

Both Little Debbie and the family pack remained the company's most significant generators of sales. The momentum of these two landmark events fueled a proliferation of snack cake varieties since that time, including the introduction of the Sunbelt line in 1981.

By 1982 McKee Baking, with $130 million in sales, ranked 22nd in the industry, behind such billion-dollar giants as Continental Baking and Interstate Bakeries Corporation. (Interstate purchased Continental in 1995 and changed its name to Hostess Brands Inc. in 2009.) Sales at the time were concentrated principally in the Midwest, Southwest, and West. By 1987 the company was able to boast annual sales growth of 10 to 15 percent since the advent of Little Debbie, a product line that had then expanded to 32 varieties available in 41 states. McKee succeeded in surpassing Continental's Hostess, Interstate's Dolly Madison, and other major national brands through its low pricing.

According to *Forbes* writer William Stern, the feisty competitor sold its products through supermarkets for 50 percent to 70 percent less than other comparable items. Nevertheless, the company's net margins after such heavy undercutting were approximately 6 percent, while the average for the industry was 5.5 percent. "What's to stop McKee's giant competitors from matching its low prices?" queried Stern. "Common sense. … They are giant corporations with giant overhead, while McKee is a family business. And, even with lower prices, it would take them years to get the economies of scale McKee gets from its overwhelming market share."

COMPETITIVE EDGE

McKee maintained its low overhead by employing an independent distribution system and by expanding production only to keep pace with demand. Another advantage it had over the competition was the long shelf life of its naturally preserved products, which was three to four times as long as that of Hostess Twinkies.

After 1980 McKee enhanced its market share by selling to convenience stores as well as supermarkets and by periodically rolling out national television campaigns, such as a memorable one launched in 1985 featuring impersonator Rich Little. New products, including Little Debbie Fancy Cakes and the Little Debbie Snack Favorite line, also served as powerful inducements to buyers, at least half of them age 15 and under.

The company changed its name in 1991 to McKee Foods Corporation. Under CEO Ellsworth McKee, the Tennessee bakery preserved its highly private identity and strong family management, with many third-generation McKees holding high positions within the company. Although investment houses and bakery

KEY DATES

1934: O. D. and Ruth McKee start their first business in Chattanooga, Tennessee.

1935: The couple moves the business to a new location and begins making soft cookies and cakes.

1936: The McKees hand the business over to Ruth's father, Symon D. King; Jack's Cookie Company opens in Charlotte, North Carolina.

1954: O. D. and Ruth McKee purchase the company stock of King's Bakery in Chattanooga.

1957: Bakery operations move to Collegedale, Tennessee.

1960: The Little Debbie brand makes its debut.

1981: The Sunbelt line is launched.

1991: Company changes its name to McKee Foods Corporation.

2009: The Little Debbie Chocolate Cupcake product is launched.

2010: Little Debbie celebrates its 50th anniversary.

competitors, especially Continental, hoped for the family to sell, with its highly profitable status as the largest independently owned company of its kind in the country, and with consumer demand and snack cake share still rising, there was little incentive to do so.

CONTINUED MARKET LEADER: 1990–99

The recession in the early 1990s provided fuel for the company's growth. With their lower prices, the Little Debbie and Sunbelt brands attracted new consumers looking to shave expenses. To keep up with the company's steady growth, McKee Foods opened two new bakeries, one in Arkansas and the other in Virginia. In keeping with the company's conservative approach to expansion, the new plants provided just enough capacity to keep up with existing demand. McKee produced baked goods only to fill orders. By 1999 the bakery in Gentry, Arkansas, was employing 1,265 people, and the one in Stuarts Draft, Virginia, employed 925 people.

In the mid-1990s Ellsworth McKee handed the reins to his brother Jack, who took over as president and chief executive officer. Ellsworth continued to provide input into running the business from his position as

chair of the board. McKee Foods continued to rely on brand recognition and customer loyalty to generate sales, rather than national advertising campaigns and a national sales force dedicated to drumming up orders and garnering shelf space in grocery and convenience stores. Sales rose from $525 million in 1991 to approximately $825 million in 1997. Although sales were up only a modest 0.7 percent in 1998, to $831 million, the company still dominated the snack cake market segment.

The company's Sunbelt brand benefited from the tremendous growth in the granola bar market in the 1990s. By 1998 the Sunbelt Granola Bar line accounted for $33.5 million in annual revenues. However, Americans were spending nearly a billion dollars a year on bars, and Sunbelt held only a fraction of that market, behind Kellogg's Nutri-Grain brand, the clear leader; the Quaker Oats Chewy granola bar line; and Kellogg's Rice Krispies Treats. McKee was used to battling the big-name brands, and the company moved to capture a greater piece of the granola bar category in the late 1990s.

McKee began a national marketing campaign in 1998 to promote its granola bar line in general and its new S'mores variety in particular. With print advertising in *People* magazine and television ads on game shows, talk shows, and home shows, the company hoped to reach its target audience of 25- to 49-year-old female heads of households with children aged 6 to 17. Employing a strategy that worked well with its Little Debbie brand, the company also challenged its competitors with lower prices, suggesting retail prices ranging from $1.49 to $2.49 per carton.

Despite competition from the Nabisco brand and baking giant Interstate Bakeries, McKee maintained its lead in its chosen snack cake niche and pursued modest expansion in the granola segment. Still family-owned and family-operated as of the late 1990s, McKee had reached number 247 on the *Forbes* list of the 500 largest private companies, and family members showed no sign of letting the company slip from their hands.

40TH ANNIVERSARY IN 2000

The company celebrated the 40th anniversary of its Little Debbie brand in 2000. It sold its 12 billionth multipack carton of Little Debbie snacks that year and the company's position as the largest independent bakery in the United States was solid. The Little Debbie Nutty Bar, which was the company's most popular product and the country's leading snack cake, was far ahead of Hostess's Twinkie product in terms of market share.

While most of its competitors looked to acquire other companies as a means of growth, McKee opted to expand its business from within by launching new products. During 2002 the company spent approximately $45 million to expand its Arkansas facility. It also spent $15 million that year on two national advertising campaigns featuring its Little Debbie snack cakes and its Sunbelt granola bars. During 2006 the company set plans in motion to upgrade its Collegedale facility. The $50 million revamp included the addition of nearly 175 jobs and increased the size of the plant by 50 percent.

OVERCOMING CHALLENGES TO REMAIN A MARKET LEADER

Michael McKee, Jack's son, was named president of the company in 2002. He eventually took over as CEO upon his father's retirement, while Ellsworth remained chairman. With family members remaining at the helm, McKee Foods faced challenges in the next few years that plagued both the company and its competitors. The high costs of packaging, fuel, and corn used to make sweeteners forced the company to revamp its strategy. During 2006 the company raised the price of its individual Little Debbie fudge brownie for the first time in approximately 10 years, from 25 cents to 35 cents.

At the same time, the company voluntarily recalled its Little Debbie Nutty Bars in Chicago and Ohio after internal quality control checks determined there could be small metal particles in the product. McKee was part of a much larger recall in 2009 when it removed its Little Debbie Peanut Butter Toasty and Little Debbie Peanut Butter Cheese sandwich crackers from store shelves due to potential salmonella risks. The products were manufactured by Kellogg Company, which received its peanut paste from Peanut Corporation of America (PCA). PCA was the source of a large salmonella outbreak during 2008 and 2009.

During 2009 the company shuttered its bakery in Chattanooga and moved production to its locations in Collegedale and Arkansas. It launched its new Little Debbie Chocolate Cupcake product that year, hoping to cash in on the growing popularity of cupcakes. It marked the debut of the product with a television advertising campaign and a "One Million Little Debbie Cupcakes Giveaway" promotion where consumers could register to win a carton of the cupcakes. Winners were announced on October 18, 2009, which was recognized as National Chocolate Cupcake Day.

The company celebrated the 50th anniversary of the Little Debbie brand in 2010. The occasion was marked with a 75-pound oatmeal crème pie, along with a vacation giveaway sweepstakes that included the introduction of a Boeing 717 aircraft named Little Debbie 1. AirTran Holding Inc., the company's partner in the promotion, oversaw the inaugural flight of the co-branded plane on February 12, 2010.

By this time, more than 150 billion Little Debbie snack cakes had been consumed since their launch in 1960. The company, which remained on the *Forbes* list of the 500 largest private companies, was determined to retain its status as a family-run independent business. With approximately $1.2 billion in sales and a solid market position, McKee Foods appeared to be on track for continued success in the years to come.

Jay P. Pederson
Updated, Susan Windisch Brown; Christina M. Stansell

PRINCIPAL SUBSIDIARIES

Blue Planet Foods Inc.

PRINCIPAL COMPETITORS

Hostess Brands Inc.; Lance Inc.; Tasty Baking Company.

FURTHER READING

"Family Clout Backs Philosophy of Independence in Era of Mergers," *Milling & Baking News*, November 11, 1988.

Flessner, Dave, "Little Debbie Snack Cake Brand Celebrates 40th Anniversary," *Knight-Ridder/Tribune Business News*, August 12, 2000.

"McKee Baking Sets July Start for Production at New Virginia Plant," *Milling & Baking News*, May 8, 1990.

"McKee Foods Announces Voluntary Nationwide Recall of Little Debbie Peanut Butter Toasty, Peanut Butter Cheese Sandwich Crackers Because of Possible Health Risk," *US Fed News*, March 28, 2009.

"McKee Plans 'Little Debbie' Plant in Virginia," *Bakery Production*, May 1987.

"McKee's New Snack Plant Begins Production," *Bakery Production*, August 1990.

Pare, Mike, "McKee Grows," *Chattanooga Times/Free Press*, June 28, 2006.

———, "McKee Marks Little Debbie's 50th," *Chattanooga Times/Free Press*, May 16, 2010.

"Some May Find Iconic Brownie's Price Increase Hard to Swallow," *Capital*, October 7, 2007.

Stern, William, "Mom and Dad Knew Every Name," *Forbes*, December 7, 1992.

The Story Behind Little Debbie Snack Cakes, Collegedale, TN: McKee Foods Corporation.

Thompson, Stephanie, "McKee Eyes S'More Media for Sunbelt," *Brandweek*, October 19, 1998, p. 10.

Wong, Elaine, "Little Debbie Takes Chocolate Cupcakes on Tour," *Progressive Grocer*, September 24, 2009.

MegaChips Corporation

4-1-6 Miyahara
Yodogawa-ku
Osaka, 532-0003
Japan
Telephone: (+81 06) 6399 2884
Fax: (+81 06) 6399 2886
Web site: http://www.megachips.co.jp

Public Company
Incorporated: 1990
Employees: 253
Sales: ¥52.77 billion ($537.23 million) (2009)
Stock Exchanges: Tokyo
Ticker Symbol: 6875
NAICS: 541512 Computer Systems Design Services

■ ■ ■

MegaChips Corporation is Japan's only fabless developer of large-scale integration (LSI) chips and systems for electronic devices ranging from game consoles to cellular telephones and home energy systems. A fabless chip maker designs and develops integrated systems, and then outsources their production to contract manufacturers. Much of the company's growth has come through its long-standing association with Nintendo Entertainment Corporation, and the company continues to supply the console giant with LSIs and LSI-based systems. Also known as "system-on-a-chip," this latter product line incorporates several functions normally accomplished by individual LSIs onto a single chip. Nintendo accounts

for approximately 87 percent of the company's annual sales, which neared ¥53 billion ($540 million) in 2009.

The company also produces LSIs for digital camera image processing, integrated voice processing and image transmission for cellular telephones, security cameras and related systems, and many other products. In 2010 the company announced plans to launch a new range of chips for use in new-generation home energy smart grids, as well as a focus on providing chips for Japan's pachinko machine industry. The company expected these and other new product categories to help it reduce its dependence on Nintendo to 50 percent of sales by 2015 or sooner. MegaChips is listed on the Tokyo Stock Exchange and is led by President Yukihiro Ukai.

FABLESS PIONEER IN 1990

MegaChips was the brainchild of Masahiro Shindo, who had worked as an engineer leading the development of semiconductors and memory chips for Mitsubishi Electric, and then for Ricoh Company Ltd. During the 1980s Shindo recognized the potential for the new large-scale integration (LSI) chips beginning to emerge at that time. LSI represented a major advance in integrated circuit technology, vastly multiplying the number of integrated circuits that could fit onto a single chip. The new chip designs, which packed far more processing power and information into smaller chip sizes, would quickly revolutionize the electronics products market.

Shindo attempted to interest Ricoh in developing its own LSI production. When his suggestion was refused, Shindo decided to go into business for himself, setting up MegaChips Corp. in 1990. "Megachips" was a word often used to describe the new LSI chips. Shindo lacked the capital needed to found a full-scale semiconductor company, however. At first Shindo even found it difficult to find a bank to provide him with start-up capital. Instead of renting an office, Shindo could work only in space provided by various community centers in Suita, in Osaka Prefecture.

Another emerging trend in the semiconductor industry enabled Shindo to overcome these obstacles. Starting in the United States in the 1990s a new type of semiconductor company had begun to appear that avoided the massive investment needed to build manufacturing facilities, known as "fabs." The "fabless" companies, as they were known, instead focused their operations entirely on designing and developing semiconductor and chip designs. The fabless company then contracted with a third-party manufacturer for its actual production.

The fabless model enabled Shindo to launch his own company despite his lack of funds. As a result MegaChips became Japan's first, and only, fabless semiconductor company, a distinction it maintained into the next century. Shindo gathered a team of engineers, and before the end of its first year the company had succeeded in developing and marketing its first LSI chips.

TEAMING WITH NINTENDO

MegaChips initially started out working as a contract chip developer. The company soon found its first success when it produced its first chip for fast-growing Nintendo Entertainment Corporation. The company's first product for Nintendo was a chip controlling the flash memory-based cartridges for the company's Super NES, which remained in production from 1990 to 1993.

The success of this first chip led MegaChips to refocus its business in 1991 from contract manufacturing to the growing market for application specific integrated circuits (ASICs). Standard integrated circuits could be used for a variety of applications. ASICs, on the other hand, were designed to perform a specific function and were developed according to the customer's specifications.

MegaChips continued to expand its technological base during the middle years of the decade. A major new milestone for the company came in 1995, when the company received the contract to develop chips for the hugely successful Nintendo 64 gaming console. MegaChips also extended its operations during this time with the launch of its new Systems Division, focused on the application specific standard products (ASSP) market. ASSP represented a further step in integrated circuit design. Instead of individual circuits, the company then began developing products encompassing a variety of tasks (such as video, audio, processing, and memory functions) integrated into a single chip. ASSPs were also known as "system on a chip" designs.

MegaChips extended its range of operations to include systems driving such applications as picture-in-picture and digital image conversion for televisions, home local access networking (LAN) functionality, and commercial video delivery services. The group's customer-specific ASICs division, largely grouped around its work for Nintendo, remained the company's core business. The relationship between the two companies deepened in the second half of the 1990s with the launch of Nintendo's Game Boy. Once again, MegaChips Corp.'s chip design powered the new system's cartridges. The worldwide success of the Game Boy provided a new boost to the company's revenues, which neared ¥31 billion by 1999.

PUBLIC OFFERING IN 1998

MegaChips had completed a number of expansion moves by this time. The company moved to new headquarters in Osaka's Yodogawa-ku district in 1996. MegaChips added an office in Taipei the following year, bringing it closer to its main manufacturing partners. The company stepped up its sales operations as well, opening an office in Tokyo in 1998. This helped raised the group's profile, particularly in the industrially advanced eastern region of the country.

At the end of the year the company's sales operations expanded again, as it joined with Mitsui & Co. to form a sales joint venture, Visual Communications Inc. This company then merged with another sales company, Cameo Interactive Ltd., becoming Megafusion Corporation in 2000. Through Megafusion, the company diversified into software, focusing on importing audio recording, sequencing, and processing software for the Japanese consumer and professional markets.

MegaChips by then had turned to outside capital to support its expansion. The company launched its first

KEY DATES

1990: Masahiro Shindo founds MegaChips as Japan's first fabless semiconductor company.
1998: MegaChips goes public on Japan's over-the-counter (OTC) market.
2000: MegaChips lists its shares on the Tokyo Stock Exchange's main board.
2004: MegaChips restructures as a holding company.
2007: The company restructures again, adopting a two-division structure.
2010: MegaChips announces plans to target the pachinko and smart grid sectors.

stock offering in 1998, listing its shares on Japan's over-the-counter (OTC) market. By the end of 2000 the company had shifted its listing to the Tokyo Exchange's main board. Soon after, all of the company's employees received shares in the company.

The public offering helped fuel a further expansion of the company's operations as it extended its design expertise in the new century. Digital imaging became an increasingly important focus of the group's development arm, and in 2000 MegaChips teamed up with Display-tech Inc. to develop an LSI imaging chip to power that company's digital camera displays. The new chip enabled image capture resolution of up to 16 megapixels, far surpassing the top of the range for the time, six megapixels.

MegaChips Corp.'s technology boosted the company's profile again the following year, as it became the first to develop an integrated LSI system capable of simultaneously processing both voice and video. The chip specifically targeted the mobile telephone market and the forthcoming high-speed networks. The breakthrough added to the company's portfolio of 50 patents, with another 150 patents pending.

HOLDING COMPANY STRUCTURE IN 2004

In the meantime, the company continued to power Nintendo's successes. The year 2001 represented a particular highlight for the company, with the launch of two new Nintendo gaming systems, the Game Boy Advance and the Nintendo Cube. As a result, Mega-Chips Corp.'s sales soared, nearing ¥54 billion ($450 million) by the end of that year.

The company was soon hit by the crash of the global high technology market, however. The company's revenues dropped sharply as a result, down to ¥38 billion in 2002, and then to ¥29 billion ($240 million) by the end of 2003. MegaChips Corp.'s troubles had also exposed it to a hostile takeover attempt by one of Shindo's former employers. The takeover offer introduced a new crisis in the company, as its employee-shareholders split between a group that wanted to accept the offer and a group that refused to sell.

Shindo led a meeting with all of the company's employees in order to find a resolution for this crisis. In the end, the company's employees agreed to maintain MegaChips Corp.'s independence, establishing a new set of management principles. As part of the agreement, MegaChips restructured into a holding company overseeing two main subsidiaries, MegaChips LSI Solutions, for its largely Nintendo-oriented operations, and MegaChips Systems Solutions. The company also took full control of Megafusion, buying out its partners in 2003.

MegaChips Corp.'s restructuring continued into the next year, as its sales dipped again, below ¥26 billion. The company's audio software operations were transferred to a newly created subsidiary, which took on the Cameo Interactive name, and subsequently sold off in October 2004 to eFrontier Inc. During the restructuring Shindo stepped down as the company's chairman and relinquished his majority control of the company, becoming a simple shareholder. Taking his place was Shigeki Matsuoka, who had been the company's chief executive prior to the restructuring. The company then named Yukihiro Ukai to head its LSI Solutions subsidiary and Tetsuo Hikawa to head its Systems Solutions subsidiary.

LOOKING BEYOND NINTENDO

In the second half of the decade MegaChips launched a new attempt to reduce its reliance on Nintendo. The company targeted a diversified array of technologies, including the 3G mobile handset market, set to take off as telecommunications operators finally began implementing their high-speed networks. MegaChips also developed systems for a variety of other products, including digital cameras, video cameras, including real-time webcams, and commercial grade digital video recorders. The company, which had largely focused its product development on high-end consumer markets, also sought an entry into the larger mid-priced markets.

MegaChips Corp.'s sales regained their momentum, hovering around the ¥30 billion market through 2006. Nintendo once again provided the key for the group's revenue growth, with the launch of two new blockbuster gaming devices, the Wii and the Nintendo DS. The global popularity of both products helped drive the company's sales to nearly ¥45 billion in 2007, and past ¥50 billion by 2008. By then, MegaChips had once again restructured, merging subsidiaries MegaChips LSI Solutions and MegaChips Systems Solutions back into the company. Instead, the company established two divisions, LSI Business and Systems Business. Yukihiro Ukai became the company's chief executive at that time.

Despite the success of both the Wii and the DS, MegaChips, which relied on Nintendo for some 87 percent of its revenues, continued to look beyond Nintendo. Part of the company's motivation was the growing popularity of rival gaming systems, such as the Sony PSP Go, which loaded new games via download. While Nintendo continued to employ the use of memory-based cartridge systems, driven by MegaChips Corp.'s chips, the console company's adoption of a new technology remained a major threat to Megachips Corp.'s future sales.

In response, MegaChips launched a new diversification strategy in 2010. The company then targeted two distinct markets. The first of these was the development of LSI chips and systems for the pachinko machine sector, which remained one of most popular entertainment markets in Japan. The company hoped to generate as much as ¥5 billion from this market by 2012.

MegaChips Corp.'s other new market focus involved developing smart grid technologies. The company expected to roll out its first device, which could be used by consumers to measure their home electricity usage, in 2011. The company targeted revenues of as much as ¥10 billion per year from this and future smart grid products. In this way, MegaChips hoped to reduce Nintendo's share of its total revenues to just 50 percent by the middle of the decade.

M. L. Cohen

PRINCIPAL SUBSIDIARIES

MegaChips (Hong Kong) Ltd.; Shun Yin Investment Ltd. (Taiwan).

PRINCIPAL DIVISIONS

LSI Business; Systems Business.

PRINCIPAL COMPETITORS

China Electronics Corp.; Fujitsu Ltd.; Huawei Technologies Company Ltd.; KDDI Corp.; NEC Corp.; Seven Techno Company Ltd.; Sumitomo Corp.

FURTHER READING

"Acrodea, Megachips Jointly Develop Vivid Communicator," *Telecompaper Africa/Asia*, December 3, 2007.

Adkoli, Jayashree, "MegaChips, Silicon Motion Team to Develop TV Tuner Chip," *TMCnet*, October 21, 2008.

Harding, Robin, "The Right Customer Is Vital," *Financial Times*, July 20, 2009, p. 17.

Hatekeyama, Mitsuo, and Juichi Koyama, "An Entrepreneur Is Sort of an Artist: Evolution of MegaChips Corporation and Its Management Principles," in *Graduate School for Creative Cities, Osaka City University, Lecture No. 11*, June 23, 2005.

"Japan's Megachips to Shift System Chip Focus to Phones, Cameras," *AsiaPulse News*, October 13, 2004.

"MegaChips, Nintendo, Taiwan Firm Agree to Tie Up on LSI Supply," *Japan Semiconductor Scan*, March 26, 2001.

Onomitsu, Go, and Hiroshi Matsui, "Megachips Wants Smart Grid, Pachinko to Cut Nintendo Reliance," *Bloomberg*, February 3, 2010.

Mitsubishi Electric Corporation

2-7-3, Marunouchi 2-Chome
Chiyoda-ku
Tokyo, 100-8310
Japan
Telephone: (81 3) 3218-2111
Fax: (81 3) 3218-2185
Web site: http://www.mitsubishielectric.com

Public Company
Incorporated: 1921
Employees: 106,931
Sales: ¥3.66 trillion ($37.4 billion) (2009)
Stock Exchanges: Tokyo Osaka London Euronext Frankfurt
Ticker Symbol: MIELY
NAICS: 333921 Elevator and Moving Stairway Manufacturing; 334111 Electronic Computer Manufacturing; 335999 All Other Miscellaneous Electrical Equipment and Component Manufacturing; 33429 Other Communications Equipment Manufacturing; 334413 Semiconductor and Related Device Manufacturing; 334419 Other Electronic Component Manufacturing; 51334 Satellite Telecommunications

∎ ∎ ∎

Even though it shares a name and common heritage with nearly 40 different companies, Mitsubishi Electric Corporation is an independent company with operations that span the globe. The firm is involved in the manufacture, marketing, and sales of electrical and electronic equipment used in information processing and wireless communications, space development and satellite communications, consumer electronics, industrial technology, energy, transportation, and construction. The global economic downturn has forced Mitsubishi to restructure operations and focus on its most profitable businesses. During this process the company stopped manufacturing mobile handsets. Mitsubishi was the only major Japanese electronics manufacturer to report a profit in fiscal 2009.

The original Mitsubishi company (the name means "three diamonds" in Japanese) was originally founded shortly after the Meiji Restoration in 1868 by Yataro Iwasaki, an enterprising samurai who gained control of shipping in Tosa prefecture in the first years of Japan's industrial expansion. Japan grew into a major economic and military power in the western Pacific, in many ways as a result of Mitsubishi's ambitious maritime activity. The company connected Japan with foreign markets and succeeded in establishing a shipping monopoly, despite a powerful challenge from rival Mitsui.

EARLY HISTORY

By the mid-1910s Mitsubishi was one of the largest companies in Japan, with diversified interests in heavy manufacturing, mining, real estate, banking, and trading. In order to attract investor capital, the Iwasaki family created several independent companies out of Mitsubishi's subsidiaries. Mitsubishi Electric was one of them and was created in 1921.

Mitsubishi Electric originated in 1905 in the parent company's Kobe shipyard as a manufacturer of electrical

COMPANY PERSPECTIVES

The Mitsubishi Electric Group's corporate statement, "Changes for the Better," represents our goal and attitude to always strive to achieve "something better," as we continue to change and grow. It is a statement that promises "to create an ever better tomorrow" to our customers by the initiative of each and every one of our employees, who seek to improve themselves by aiming for "the better," and daily aim to "improve technologies, services, and creativity," as stated in our corporate philosophy.

equipment for ships and mining. Five years later, the division constructed a large-capacity induction motor (the first in Japan) and a turbine generator.

As a victor in World War I, Japan gained recognition as a legitimate naval power in the Pacific. In order to preserve and enhance its position, Japan expanded its navy and merchant marine, creating even greater demand for new ships equipped with generators and other electric devices. As the major shipbuilder in Japan, Mitsubishi engineered a merger between the electric machinery departments of Kobe Shipbuilding & Engine Works and its own Mitsubishi Shipbuilding company. Shares in the new company, Mitsubishi Electric, were sold to investors, and the capital raised was used to acquire new manufacturing space and equipment.

Mitsubishi Electric, however, was unable to develop devices technologically competitive with those manufactured by foreign companies. Like NEC, which had negotiated an extensive cooperative agreement with Western Electric, Mitsubishi-Electric became closely associated with another U.S. electronics manufacturer, Westinghouse Electric. Their agreement, concluded in 1923, provided Mitsubishi Electric with Japanese marketing and licensing rights for a number of Westinghouse products and designs. As a result, Mitsubishi Electric successfully built a large 2,300-kVA vertical-axis-type hydraulic generator.

Mitsubishi Electric remained the favored supplier of large and small electrical devices to all the various Mitsubishi companies while maintaining its expertise in maritime electronics and gaining new strengths in other fields such as communication, power transmission, lighting, and consumer appliances. In 1931 Mitsubishi Electric began commercial production of passenger elevators and started exporting fans to China and Hong Kong. Two years later, reacting to greater domestic demand for home appliances, the company began marketing refrigerators.

WARTIME TROUBLES

The 1930s were a difficult period for Japan's *zaibatsu* (conglomerates) like Mitsubishi. The 12 major Japanese companies had become inextricably linked to the government through a 50-year industrial modernization program. However, the government had recently been taken over by a quasi-fascist element in the military whose aim was to establish absolute Japanese supremacy in eastern Asia. In their effort to modernize and arm Japan for war, the militarists called upon industrial concerns such as Mitsubishi Electric to provide a vast array of equipment.

While Mitsubishi Heavy Industries eventually became the principal manufacturer of warplanes, particularly the notorious Zero, Mitsubishi Electric developed radio sets for the Zero and other aircraft, and later became deeply involved in additional military projects.

With World War II well under way, Mitsubishi Electric came under increasingly strict control by the government. The company was compelled to follow all military directives and, as a result, in 1944 established a research laboratory whose goal was to develop new instruments for naval and aerial battle management. By August 1945, however, the war was lost, and Japan's battered industries came under the control of government agencies directed by the occupation authority.

Mitsubishi Electric began the enormous task of rebuilding its business after the war. Helped by reconstruction loans but impeded by difficult labor regulations, supply shortages, weak domestic demand, and the dissolution of the *zaibatsu*, Mitsubishi Electric struggled to survive. By 1948, the company had resumed production of consumer and some industrial items, including straight-tube fluorescent lamps. Military production, once the primary source of Mitsubishi's profits, had been banned by the occupation authority.

FOREIGN EXPANSION RESUMES: 1954

Having reestablished marketing agreements with foreign manufacturers, Mitsubishi Electric began selling televisions in Japan in 1953. After completing several successful industrial projects, Mitsubishi resumed foreign operations in 1954 with the completion of a power substation in India.

KEY DATES

1921: Mitsubishi Electric Manufacturing is formed.

1945: The firm comes under control of government agencies directed by the occupation authority.

1948: Production of consumer and industrial items resumes.

1963: Company name changes to Mitsubishi Electric Corp.

1973: Sales offices are established in Great Britain, the United States, Brazil, and Argentina.

1993: The company installs the world's fastest elevator in the Landmark Tower in Yokohama.

1995: The firm begins construction on one of the largest color liquid-crystal-display manufacturing plants in Japan.

2000: Company forms alliances with both Boeing Company and Toshiba Corp.

2003: Renesas Technology Corp. is formed as a joint venture with Hitachi Ltd.

2008: The company exits the mobile handset business.

As a result of the Korean War, the U.S. government decided to end its extractive, punitive policies toward Japan. Instead, it encouraged the Japanese to build a large and modern industrial infrastructure that would allow Japan to serve as a bulwark against the expansion of communism in the East. Increasingly, in the name of efficient industrial organization, the Japanese government permitted the former *zaibatsu* companies to reestablish ties. The Mitsubishi logo, banned by the occupation authority, was readopted by all the Mitsubishi companies, including Mitsubishi Electric. With the benefit of freer association among the engineering, manufacturing, marketing, and financing wings of the Mitsubishi group, Mitsubishi Electric gained an increased ability to compete in the largely unregulated foreign markets.

The rich U.S. and European markets were already dominated by large electrical-equipment manufacturers like Westinghouse, General Electric, Philips, and GEC, and the Japanese government had passed legislation to protect domestic manufacturers against these companies. Mitsubishi Electric recognized that it could not compete against the large manufacturers until it had first established a stronger base in consumer sales and industrial projects. The increased incomes of Japanese consumers and the ability of Japanese companies to

compete on price in middle-technology projects provided Mitsubishi Electric with two important ways to achieve that goal.

CONTINUED INTERNATIONAL EXPANSION AND PRODUCT INNOVATION: 1960–69

In 1960 the company became one of the first in Japan to begin production of color televisions, marking a commitment to maintaining market share in the emerging high end of the market. After production of several electric locomotives for the Japanese railway system, Mitsubishi Electric exported its first one, to the government of India, also in 1960.

During the 1960s, Japanese products gained a reputation for poor quality and simple technology. In electronics, however, the Japanese Ministry of International Trade and Industry assisted companies by coordinating technological developments and protecting certain key markets. One of the earliest to show leadership in technological pursuits, Mitsubishi Electric unveiled a computer prototype in 1960, and the following year began production of its Molectron integrated circuit.

In order to reflect both a corporate reorganization and a more international view, the company's name was changed in 1963 from Mitsubishi Electric Manufacturing to Mitsubishi Electric Corporation, or Melco. The company made its first overseas investment in Thailand in 1964, and two years later concluded a sale of electric locomotives to Spain. In communications, Melco completed the first of several antenna designs for satellite earth stations and placed a remote weather station on the summit of Mount Fuji. Mitsubishi's development of communications technologies later led to its selection for government projects and electronics work with the U.S. Department of Defense.

Melco funded much of its industrial and high-technology research by cross-subsidizing: taking profits from the consumer and business markets and applying them to government and industrial projects with long lead times but large rewards. Among Melco's successes in the low-ticket markets were air conditioners, color televisions, and small office computers. In order to reduce costs in certain areas of research, Melco revived its technical-exchange agreement with Westinghouse in 1966. In later years, Melco began to sell technology to Westinghouse, marking a significant appreciation in Mitsubishi's status.

GROWTH CONTINUES: 1970–85

The increased quality of Japanese products and the continued production-cost advantages enjoyed by

Japanese companies led to tremendous demand overseas. It was at this point, around 1970, that Japan's export-led expansion moved into a new phase of feverish growth. In 1972 and 1973 alone, Melco established sales companies in Great Britain, the United States, Brazil, and Argentina, and another was opened in Australia in 1975.

Predicting a gradual deterioration in production-cost advantages in Japan relative to other developing Asian nations, Melco began making substantial overseas investments, building a television plant in Singapore in 1974 and another in Thailand three years later.

Until then, Mitsubishi Electric had been primarily a manufacturer of industrial equipment. The oil crisis of 1973–74, however, critically damaged the company's business in that field and, perhaps more than any other event, convinced Mitsubishi's president, Sadakazu Shindo, that the only way to maintain growth was through expanded consumer sales. One product, aimed directly at the domestic household market, was the futon dryer; 600,000 were sold in 1977 alone.

Melco was one of several companies that elected to develop a home video-recording system based on Matsushita's VHS design. The VHS, although it entered the market a full year after Sony's rival Betamax system, became established as the industry standard. Companies that developed the Beta system, particularly Sony, lost not only a great deal of money in sales but, more important over the longer term, market share. Melco's rising acceptance in the home video market was complemented by the introduction of such other new products as large-screen projection TVs.

Mitsubishi Electric added sales organizations in West Germany and Spain in 1978, and in Canada in 1980. In order to reduce transportation costs and hedge against rising protectionist sentiment in foreign markets, Melco established television-production facilities in the United States and Britain in 1980, and in Australia in 1982. The following year, Melco opened an integrated-circuit plant in the United States, a cathode-ray-tube plant in Canada, and a VCR plant in Britain. The new plants created thousands of jobs in these countries and revitalized several local economies. By 1985, Mitsubishi Electric's sales had reached ¥2 trillion, double the amount just five years earlier.

Mitsubishi Electric's unusual corporate personality was largely derived from the years Sadakazu Shindo presided over the company. During his presidency, Shindo remained the guiding force at Mitsubishi Electric. Among his strongest legacies were a commitment to frank discussion, honest criticism, and individualism. He was known to have favored the hiring of high school graduates over college graduates,

contending that they were only slightly less knowledgeable, but much more willing to ask questions and work in teams.

DIVERSIFICATION AND EXPANSION: 1988–95

During the late 1980s, Mitsubishi Electric was well diversified within the electronics industry, deriving approximately equal amounts of profit from communications, consumer products, heavy machinery, and industrial products. In its effort to overtake competitors such as Hitachi and Toshiba, the company concentrated its resources on new-product development. The task of selling the products was handled through Mitsubishi Shoji, its former parent trading company, and much of that sales effort was concentrated in the Middle East in an attempt to retrieve what were called oil yen.

By maintaining close relations with both Westinghouse and General Electric, Mitsubishi Electric bet much of its future success on the integrated microcircuitry that made possible everything from simple industrial robots to artificial intelligence. During the late 1980s, Mitsubishi continued to become more firmly established as an industry leader as it found new applications for these technologies in its existing product lines.

Mitsubishi continued new product development and expansion into the 1990s. The firm purchased the hardware division of Apricot Computers and developed both a 4-megabit static random access memory and a 64-megabit dynamic random access memory (DRAM) chip in order to broaden its reach into the U.S. semiconductor market. In 1992 the firm announced plans to join a U.S. and Canadian telecom project in which it would provide telephones for a new satellite system. The following year, Mitsubishi secured a contract from the Japanese Defense Agency to develop surface-to-air missiles. The company's heavy machinery segment also installed the world's fastest passenger elevator in the Landmark Tower in Yokohama. In 1995, Mitsubishi began production on a color liquid-crystal-display (LCD) manufacturing plant, which was one of Japan's largest, in order to take advantage of the growing demand for LCDs.

A major portion of Mitsubishi growth efforts during the mid-1990s was focused towards the American market. In an effort to boost profitability and competitiveness, the company restructured its U.S. subsidiaries, Mitsubishi Electronics America and Mitsubishi Consumer Electronics America, creating a new company consisting of the audiovideo and cellular mobile telephone businesses of both subsidiaries in

1995. The firm also joined the General Magic Alliance, dedicated to developing communication products and services whose membership included Apple, AT&T, France-Telecom, Fujitsu, Matsushita, Motorola, Northern Telecom, Philips, Sony, Sanyo, and Toshiba.

OVERCOMING HARDSHIPS: 1995–2000

While continuing its focus on growth, Mitsubishi was forced to overcome hardships during the latter half of the 1990s. In 1995 a devastating earthquake rocked through Kobe and Osaka, Japan. While there were no company fatalities, seven production facilities and four research laboratories were damaged. At the same time, the company began buying finished goods overseas to use in its electric power equipment division in order to combat a strong yen that was wreaking havoc on domestic profits. However, while many Japanese-based firms began moving production overseas, Mitsubishi was able to maintain most of its domestic manufacturing.

In 1997 the firm became part of a public payoff scandal in which *sokaiya*, or corporate racketeers, were paid for their silence during shareholder meetings. In November of that year, Mitsubishi executive Yoshiki Sugiura was arrested for allegedly paying off a *sokaiya*. According to Tokyo police, the firm had been involved in the payoffs since 1985. Its shareholder meetings had lasted an average of 30 minutes with only two questions brought to the table over a 10-year period.

During that same year, the Japanese economy began faltering, and personal consumption declined due in part to the April 1997 rise in Japan's national consumption tax. Semiconductor prices also fell, forcing the firm to report consolidated losses for the first half of 1997. This was the first consolidated loss ever reported by the firm.

Losses continued into 1998 as many of the firm's product segments fell victim to falling prices, including the audiovisual equipment and air conditioning product lines. Sales fell in the company's industrial machinery and automation equipment division, as well as in the home electronics division. During that year, Ichiro Taniguchi, a longtime Mitsubishi employee, replaced Takashi Kitaoka as president.

Mitsubishi reported losses in 1999 while Japan's economy continued to remain unstable. Focusing on short-term recovery plans, the company restructured its foreign subsidiaries involved in the semiconductor, audiovisual, and personal computer industries, while at the same time focusing on securing increased sales and developing new products. Eyeing both the computer and communications industry as growth areas, the firm

put plans in motion to divest unprofitable businesses as well as cut nearly 10 percent of its workforce.

FACING CHALLENGES IN THE NEW MILLENNIUM

While unfavorable economic conditions continued into the new millennium, Mitsubishi management set forth a strategic plan that consisted of the following goals: to become a prime global manufacturer of satellites and onboard equipment; secure a leading position as a telecommunications infrastructure manufacturer; and to use the firm's mobile phone business as a core for future expansion into the multimedia terminal equipment. The company also focused on its basic operations in electric power equipment, public infrastructure, transportation equipment, building systems, housing equipment, electrical appliances, factory automation, and automotive equipment while divesting businesses deemed unprofitable.

As part of its strategic plan, Mitsubishi was awarded a contract from the Japanese government to supply the Multipurpose Transport Satellite-2 in July 2000. The contract, along with others, secured the firm's position as the leading satellite manufacturer in Japan. The company also formed a partnership with Boeing Co. to develop a high-speed communications network that would enable aircraft to receive online video and two-way Internet communications. An alliance was also formed with Toshiba Corp. that enhanced Mitsubishi's international power transmission and distribution business. In fiscal 2001, Mitsubishi reported an increase of net income to ¥124.8 billion ($1.01 billion).

During 2003 the company worked to control costs and reevaluated several of its business operations. That year the company formed a joint venture with Hitachi Ltd. that joined the two company's semiconductor businesses. The venture, named Renesas Technology Corp., focused on large-scale integrated circuits and was 55 percent owned by Hitachi while Mitsubishi controlled the other 45 percent. Mitsubishi also partnered with Toshiba Corp. that year to create Toshiba Mitsubishi-Electric Industrial Systems Corp., an electric equipment manufacturer. During 2008 the company exited the mobile handset business due to falling demand and heightened competition.

At the same time, the company faced a public crisis when it admitted its guilt in participating in a price-fixing cartel from 1998 to 2002. Mitsubishi and other large memory-chip manufacturers shared information that allowed them to "fix" the price of DRAM sold to computer manufacturers. The European Commission fined seven companies $404.2 million in 2010.

NEW PRODUCT DEVELOPMENT AND CONTRACTS: 2003 AND BEYOND

Along with realigning its businesses, Mitsubishi focused on new product development and securing lucrative contracts. During 2003 the New York City Transit Authority tapped the company to provide air conditioning unit for 660 subway cars. That same year it launched OPTUS-1, its first overseas satellite. Hinode, a solar observatory satellite, was launched in 2006. During 2009 the company received a $66 million contract from Orbital Sciences Corp. to provide proximity link system components to the Cygnus spacecraft that would be used for nine National Aeronautics and Space Administration (NASA) space missions to the International Space Station. At the time, it was the largest contract secured by a Japanese firm for work on a NASA program.

Known throughout its history for its innovation, the company continued to develop and launch cutting-edge products. These items did not gain immediate acceptance on a global level, however, demonstrated the company's focus on research and development. In 2003 the company developed an optical noncontact fingerprint sensor. The following year it released a refrigerator designed to increase vitamin C content, as well as an LCD module that could be viewed from both sides.

As part of the company's "Environmental Vision 2021" program, Mitsubishi worked to reduce its carbon footprint as well as produce environmentally friendly products. During 2008 it introduced an air conditioner that detected a person's motion and location. The company claimed it could save up to 50 percent in energy use. The company also stepped up product of solar panels and other renewable energy products.

At the same time, the company's large-scale video display units, known as Diamond Vision, were breaking records in sporting arenas across the globe. First installed in Dodger Stadium in 1980, Diamond Vision took advantage of high-definition technology to provide sport fans a larger-than-life experience. During 2009 the company installed its Diamond Vision screen at the National Football League's Dallas Cowboys Stadium in Texas. The screen, which measured approximately 11,200 square feet, was recognized that year by the Guinness Book of World Records as the largest high-definition screen in the world. That standing was slated to be overtaken in 2010 when Mitsubishi and partner Sojitz Corp. installed a larger Diamond Vision screen at Dubai's Meydan Racecourse.

While Mitsubishi's financial performance faltered in 2009 due to the severe economic downturn plaguing global markets, it managed to secure a profit of approximately $124 million. As most of its peers in the Japanese electronics sector suffered losses, the company pulled ahead by controlling costs and restructuring operations. Conditions remained harsh in 2010 but Mitsubishi appeared to be well positioned to overcome future challenges.

Updated, Christina M. Stansell

PRINCIPAL SUBSIDIARIES

Tada Electric Co., Ltd.; Toyo Electric Corporation; Mitsubishi Electric Power Products, Inc.; Mitsubishi Elevator Asia Co., Ltd.; Toshiba Mitsubishi-Electric Industrial Systems Corporation; Mitsubishi Hitachi Home Elevator Corporation; Shanghai Mitsubishi Elevator Co., Ltd.; Meiryo Technica Co. Ltd.; DB Seiko Co., Ltd.; Mitsubishi Electric Automotive America, Inc.; Mitsubishi Electric Thai Auto-Parts Co., Ltd.; Electric Power-steering Components Europe s.r.o.; Mitsubishi Electric Automation, Inc.; Mitsubishi Electric Automotive Czech s.r.o.; Shizuki Electric Co., Inc.; Nippon Injector Corp.; Shihlin Electric & Engineering Corp.; Mitsubishi Electric TOKKI Systems Corporation; Mitsubishi Precision Co., Ltd.; SPC Electronics Corp.; Seiryo Electric Co., Ltd.; Miyoshi Electronics Corp., Oi Electric Co., Ltd.; Melco Display Technology Inc.; Mitsubishi Electric Metecs Co., Ltd.; Renesas Technology Corp.; Powerex, Inc.; Mitsubishi Home Appliance Co., Ltd.; Mitsubishi Electric Lighting Corp.; Mitsubishi Digital Electronics America Inc.; Mitsubishi Electric Consumer Products (Thailand) Co., Ltd.; Shanghai Mitsubishi Electric & Shangling Air-Conditioner and Electric Appliance Co., Ltd.; Mitsubishi Electric (Guangzhou) Compressor Co., Ltd.; Siam Compressor Industry Co., Ltd.; Osram Melco Ltd.; Kang Yong Electric Public Co., Ltd.

PRINCIPAL DIVISIONS

Energy and Electric Systems; Industrial Automation Systems; Information and Communication Systems; Electronic Devices; Home Appliances.

PRINCIPAL COMPETITORS

Hitachi Ltd.; NEC Corporation; Toshiba Corporation.

FURTHER READING

DeTar, Jim, "While Others Cut Back, Mitsubishi Renews Commitment to the DRAM Market," *Electronic News*, May 25, 1998.

"Guinness World Records to Recognize Dallas Cowboys and Mitsubishi Electric Diamond Vision for World's Largest

Video Display," *China Weekly News*, October 13, 2009.

Kawa, Toshinari, "Mitsubishi Elec Needs New Core Ops as Machinery Struggles," *Nikkei Weekly*, June 1, 2009.

Kiviniemi, Peppi, "EU Fines Chip Firms for Cartel's Price Fixing," *Wall Street Journal*, May 20, 2010.

Mitsubishi Electric Corp., "History," Tokyo, Japan: Mitsubishi Electric Corp., 2001.

"Mitsubishi Electric Names Yamanishi as Next President," *Daily Yomiuri*, February 20, 2010.

"Mitsubishi Electric Posts 1st-Ever Group Loss," *Jiji Press Ticker Service*, November 27, 1997.

"Mitsubishi Electronic Outlines Consumer Electronics Strategy," *AsiaPulse News*, September 14, 2000.

"Mitsubishi Feels Chill," *Control and Instrumentation*, January 1999, p. 16.

"Mitsubishi Plans Restructuring," *Appliance*, June 1999, p. 16.

"Mitsubishi Says Sayonara to Handset Business," *CMP TechWeb*, March 3, 2008.

"Mitsubishi Wins Contract to Supply Orbital with Cygnus Guidance Systems," *Satellite Today*, October 23, 2009.

Morishita, Kaoru, "Electronics Makers Entangled in Scandal," *Nikkei Weekly*, November 17, 1997, p. 6.

Takenaka, Kiyoshi, and Reiji Murai, "Mitsubishi Elec to Treble Solar Panel Sales," *Reuters News*, March 31, 2010.

Muralo Company Inc.

148 East 5th Street
Bayonne, New Jersey 07002-4252
U.S.A.
Telephone: (201) 437-0770
Toll Free: (800) 364-8969
Fax: (201) 437-0664
Web site: http://www.muralo.com

Private Company
Incorporated: 1894
Employees: 250
Sales: $29 million (2009)
NAICS: 325510 Paint and Coating Manufacturing

■ ■ ■

The Muralo Company Inc. and its subsidiaries produce high-quality paints, brushes, and rollers for both professional painting contractors and do-it-yourself customers. Products of the privately held, Bayonne, New Jersey-based midsized manufacturer include interior and exterior paints, waterproofing paint, masonry shield, interior and exterior primers, enamels and floor coatings, faux finishes, high-gloss paints, mold and mildew-resistant paint, fire-retardant paint, spackle for filling and repairing surface imperfections, and pastes for wall coverings.

Subsidiary Elder & Jenks, Inc., the oldest brush maker in the United States, offers a wide variety of brushes, rollers, and trays, as well as telescopic arms and bucket grids. Muralo is known for its innovation. It was the first independent paint manufacturer to offer latex

paint, latex house paint, and latex waterproof masonry paint. Unlike many other paint manufacturers, Muralo does not maintain any retail stores, nor are Muralo and Elder & Jenks products sold through home centers or big-box retailers.

Rather, the company prefers to rely on its reputation for high-quality products and innovation to attract the attention of independent paint and decorating products dealers, who it believes are better able to sell Muralo's high-quality wares. The company is owned and managed by the second and third generations of the Norton family. Much of the manufacturing is done by subsidiary Norton & Son Inc. The company operates plants in the United States, Australia, and South Africa.

MURALO FOUNDED: 1894

The Muralo Company was founded on Staten Island, New York, in 1894 by Jose Berre King, a prominent merchant and capitalist who was involved in a wide variety of enterprises. The involvement of the Norton family with the business began 11 years later when Staten Island-born Edward Norton, Sr., joined Muralo. He stayed until 1921, when he set out to start his own paint manufacturing company, U.S. Kalsomine Company, specializing in whitewash. He ran that business until he started another paint company, Norton & Son, in 1944. His son, Edward Norton, Jr., was serving in the U.S. Marines in the Pacific during World War II at the time, and would not join his father until his discharge in late 1945.

To start Norton & Son, Ed Norton, Sr., invested his family's savings to acquire a two-story building in

Jersey City, New Jersey, and set up a paint manufacturing operation. The business began as a four-person operation and struggled to establish itself. Norton received a major break when giant retailer Sears, Roebuck was in immediate need of a new paint supplier and turned to Norton & Son, which worked nonstop to meet the need. This was the foundation for a fruitful, long-term relationship. With Sears as its largest customer, Norton & Son was soon able to open a new plant in Bayonne, New Jersey.

While Ed Norton, Sr., was enjoying success, his old employer, the Muralo Company, had fallen on hard times. In the early 1940s it ranked as the world's largest water-based paint company, operating plants in Chicago, Los Angeles, Australia, and South Africa, in addition to its Staten Island operation. The company suffered a steep decline following World War II, however, and in the early 1950s it lapsed into bankruptcy despite becoming the first independent paint manufacturer to make latex emulsion paint in 1953.

Ed Norton, Sr., was able to acquire Muralo out of bankruptcy in 1953. The company was reduced to just 24 employees and a single dealer when its operation was moved to Bayonne. Ed Norton, Jr., served as vice president of Muralo and played a key role in the 1956 development of a new interior/exterior latex waterproofing paint that was ideal for waterproofing basements and exterior masonry surfaces. In 1959 Ed Norton, Jr., was named Muralo's president. His father remained involved in the business until his death in 1974.

ELDER & JENKS ACQUIRED: 1960

Muralo completed a major acquisition in 1960 and achieved some diversity when it bought Elder & Jenks of Chicago, Illinois, the country's oldest continuously operating brush and roller manufacturer. That company was founded in Philadelphia, Pennsylvania, in 1793 by George W. Bocklous. Jonathan Jenks became owner in 1884 of what was then known as Elder & Jenks. The company was later bought from the Jenks family by the Maxwell family, who sold it to the Nortons. In 1961 Muralo added to Elder & Jenks by acquiring Elgin

Brush Company of New York City, and Keansburg, New Jersey-based Modern Accessories, maker of paint rollers. Elder & Jenks had been relocated to Bayonne by 1962, and a year later was bolstered by another acquisition, Caldwell, New Jersey-based Jacobus Brush Company. By the end of the 1960s roller manufacturing was also moved to Bayonne.

In addition to the Muralo Company, the Norton family completed a number of other acquisitions to build up the paint side of the business from World War II until the early 1980s. Three Jersey City, New Jersey, companies were acquired, including Prescott Paint and Hotopp Paint and Varnish Company, and Degen Oil Company in 1973. The Ultra Gloss Wax division of Witco Chemical in Paterson, New Jersey, was also purchased, as was Carlstadt, New Jersey-based Adhesium Company in 1975.

Muralo also looked to other parts of the country. In 1965 Olympic Paint & Chemical, with operations in Los Angeles and Phoenix, was acquired. Certain assets of Northbrook, Illinois-based Synkoloid Company were purchased in 1981. Synkoloid, a division of the Artra Group, manufactured a number of products that used asbestos, including paint and patching and insulation products. Muralo made sure that as part of the purchase agreement it was indemnified by Artra for any claims, liabilities, or lawsuits that might develop from products manufactured by Synkoloid. Artra would soon find itself defending claims related to asbestos. The asbestos claims were to become a problem for Muralo two decades later.

In the meantime, Muralo made advances on a number of fronts in its research and development efforts. Playing a key role in this regard was that department's head, Shashi Patel. In 1983 Muralo discovered that hollow glass bubbles could be used to fill and resurface without shrinkage or cracks, leading to the development of the Spackle Lite product. The development of an acrylic resin emulsion led to the creation of the company's Ultimate Mid Gloss Exterior House Paint in 1988. The durable new paint offered a fade-resistant finish and resisted flaking and peeling.

ULTRA WATERBORNE LINE
UNVEILED: 1992

Patel invented Muralo's next key product, the Ultra Waterborne line of matte, eggshell, satin, semigloss and gloss finishes, introduced in 1992. It was based on the company's fine particle waterborne styrene-acrylic resin and ceramic microspheres technology. A return to waterborne paints had become necessary due to new environmental regulations that sought to reduce the use of hazardous and ozone-depleting solvents that over the

KEY DATES

■

1894: Jose Berre King founds Muralo Company on Staten Island, New York.
1944: Norton & Son is founded by former Muralo employee Edward Norton Sr.
1953: Norton acquires Muralo.
1960: Muralo acquires brush and roller manufacturer Elder & Jenks.
2002: Graham Paint and Varnish Company is acquired.

years had become prevalent in the manufacture of paints.

Muralo added to its waterborne offerings in 1995 with the introduction of Ultra Tred, an epoxy coating product designed for use on floors and walls that had to withstand chemical damage and severe abrasion, such as car washes, garages, industrial settings, and school cafeterias and lockers. In addition to its own proprietary brands, Muralo in 1998 began producing the Waverly Waterborne Interior Paint line for Waverly, a New York home furnishings company. The 220 colors of the line were selected to complement Waverly's products.

Although Ed Norton, Jr., formally retired from the company in 1989, he remained actively involved and retained the chairmanship. In the summer of 2007, *New Jersey Business* reported that the 89-year-old Norton was still coming to work every day. There was no shortage of relatives on the payroll, including three sons, three nephews, a cousin, and a daughter-in-law. His son, James S. Norton, served as president, Ed Norton III was vice president of paint manufacturing, and the other family members also held important positions in the company.

GRAHAM PAINT ACQUIRED: 2002

Muralo remained a strong competitor as the new century began. In 2000 it leveraged its Mid Gloss technology to develop a new line it called Ultimate Low Lustre. The exterior coating product was designed to produce a lower gloss and sheen on siding. Muralo also added to its waterborne architectural coatings business in 2002 with the acquisition of Chicago's Graham Paint and Varnish Company, which brought $6 million in annual sales in addition to its line of waterborne paints. A year later Muralo and Graham introduced Aqua Borne Ceramithane, a waterborne acrylic-urethane clear coating suitable for all surfaces.

The early years of the new century also brought an unwanted distraction related to the Synkoloid acquisition of the early 1980s. In June 2002 Artra filed for bankruptcy. As a result, Muralo found itself the new target of asbestos claims. To deal with these successor liability claims in a court-approved process, Muralo filed for Chapter 11 bankruptcy protection in June 2003 until the matter could be sorted out. The move was not a reflection of the company's financial state and did not have any impact on Muralo's day-to-day business.

As the new century progressed, Muralo unveiled additional new products. It added to its spackle business in 2005 with the introduction of Professional Grade Spackle. It was geared toward contractors who needed a quick-drying product suitable for both interior and exterior use that was easy to sand. The product was also long lasting, resistant to drying up in the can.

CONTINUED INNOVATION

A year later Muralo introduced Decorative Floor Flecks. Available in emerald, ruby, and aqua, they not only added a decorative touch to painted garage and basement floors, but also provided slip resistance. In 2007 Muralo added Endure 100% Acrylic House paint to its slate of exteriors products, the culmination of the company's research and development efforts in recent years. Making use of advanced technology, Endure produced a thick yet flexible film in a single coat. It resisted peeling, cracking, blistering, and the buildup of mildew and algae. Moreover, it could be applied in cool temperatures, as low as 35 degrees Fahrenheit.

Muralo also kept abreast of consumers' growing preference for environmentally responsible products. In 2009 the company introduced its Breathe Safe line of eco-friendly products. The high-performance waterborne latex paints were virtually odorless, contained no harmful solvents, and met or exceeded Green Seal and LEED (Leadership in Energy & Environmental Design) green building requirements.

Muralo proved innovative in other ways as well. In 2007 the company launched it new Color Fashions program, which changed the way its colors were displayed by retailers. Rather than inundating potential customers with the 1,000 to 1,500 multicolor sample chips typically provided by a paint company, Muralo cut the number of samples to 304, made the chips larger, and limited them to a single color to prevent perception problems. Large sheets, $7^1/_2$ by 11 inches, were also made available to customers to take home and perhaps affix to a wall to get a better feel for the color in the proper context. Muralo was clearly a viable competitor in the paint industry, and with solid management provided by the Norton family, there was every reason to expect continued success in the years to come.

Ed Dinger

PRINCIPAL SUBSIDIARIES

Elder & Jenks, Inc.; Graham Paint; Norton & Son, Inc.

PRINCIPAL COMPETITORS

PPG Industries, Inc.; Sherwin Williams Co.; DuPont Coatings & Color Technologies Group.

FURTHER READING

"Asbestos Liabilities Force Muralo Co. to File Chapter 11 Petition," *Paint & Coatings Industry*, July 2003, p. 16.

Esposito, Christine, "Norton & Son: A Family-Run Success Story," *Nutraceuticals World*, August 9, 2005.

Hughes, Jennifer V., "Moore Hopes to Coat Nation with Trendy Paint Kiosks," *Record* (Bergen County, NJ), February 11, 2007.

"Muralo Acquires Graham Paint," *European Paint and Resin News*, March 31, 2002.

"Muralo and Norton: An Unbeatable Combination," *News 'N Views*, June 2008, p. 8.

Venturella, Krysta, "Paint Is More than Just a Label," *New Jersey Business*, July 2007, p. 57.

Myllykoski Oyj

———————■———————

Etelaeesplanadi 20
Helsinki, FI-00130
Finland
Telephone: (+358 09) 34 89 640
Fax: (+358 09) 34 89 650
Web site: http://www.myllykoski.com

Private Company
Incorporated: 1952
Employees: 2,989
Sales: EUR 1.21 billion ($1.68 billion) (2009 est.)
NAICS: 322121 Paper (Except Newsprint) Mills;
   322122 Newsprint Paper Manufacturing

■■■

Myllykoski Oyj is one of the world's leading paper producers. The family-owned Finnish company operates seven paper mills in Finland, Germany, and the United States, which produced nearly two million metric tons in 2010. The company is also allied with two German paper producers, Rhein Papier and Plattling Papier, helping to boost its total paper sales to nearly three million tons. Myllykoski specializes in the production of supercalendered and coated (SC) paper and lightweight coated (LWC) paper for the magazine publishing market, and also produces newsprint for the newspaper industry.

Myllykoski operates through two primary divisions, Myllykoski Europe and Myllykoski North America. The group's European division includes the company's 65 percent stake in Myllykoski Paper, based in Helsinki and

owned in partnership with M-Real. In Germany the company owns paper mills MD Albbruck, MD Plattling, and Lang Papier. This division produced 1.5 million metric tons in 2009, down from nearly two million the year before. Myllykoski Europe accounted for more than 80 percent of group revenues in 2009. In North America Myllykoski's operations focus on its 60 percent stake in Madison Paper Industries, owned in partnership with the New York Times Company.

The company produced nearly 300,000 metric tons of paper in 2009. Altogether, Myllykoski's operations generated revenues of EUR 1.2 billion ($1.7 billion) in 2009. This represented a drop of nearly 18 percent from the previous year, primarily as the result of decreased advertising spending amid the global economic recession. Myllykoski reported a loss, including nonrecurring items, of EUR 68 million for the 2009 year. The company remains controlled by the founding Björnberg family, with Carl Björnberg serving as chairman. Other members of the family serve on the company's board and are active in its management.

ORIGINS

Myllykoski Corporation originated as a small pulp mill situated on the Kymmene River near what was known as Myllykoski Station. A number of factors had contributed to the rapid growth of the pulp and paper industry in Finland. The country's vast forests represented a nearly inexhaustible supply of raw material. As lumber prices in Europe rose sharply during the second half of the 19th century, the exploitation of Finland's forests provided a new economic resource for

COMPANY PERSPECTIVES

Our mission. We excel in the production and marketing of innovative publication papers and provide customer focused solutions. Our vision. To be the premier publication paper brand, recognized for creativity and positive business solutions. Our values. Flexibility: We like new challenges and look for new opportunities. If our standard solutions are not sufficient, then we create a new one. Win-win situations are always expected.

the small country. The development of hydroelectric power technology also played a role in the timber industry's rise, as industrialists began harnessing the country's many rivers. This power source was also put to work in the production of wood pulp, the technology for which had been invented in 1846. Wood pulp helped revolutionize the paper industry, providing a more plentiful and renewable raw material supply.

In 1892 two brothers, Fredrik and Claes Björnberg, members of Finland's tiny Swedish minority, bought the Myllykoski mill and founded a new company called Myllykoski Trasliperi Aktiebolag (Myllykoski Mechanical Pulp Mill Company Ltd.). As demand for wood pulp developed at the beginning of the 20th century, the company grew strongly, and the Björnbergs soon decided to launch paper production as well. The company carried out a modernization and expansion of its original mill. Myllykoski then built a second mill in 1905 and a third mill in 1909. Both of the new mills were fitted out with machinery from the Finnish manufacturer Viborg Engineering Works. By 1918 the company's paper output had risen to 1,300 tons per year, while its pulp production reached 638 tons.

The Björnberg brothers began preparing for the company's succession in the years leading up to World War I. The brothers initially looked to one of Claes's sons to take over as head of the company. However, he was killed during the Finnish civil war (also known as the War of Liberation) in 1918. Claes himself retired soon after. Since Fredik's son, C. G., was only 17 at the time, the company, faced with this management crisis, decided to bring in an outside manager.

JOINING UPM IN 1920

This led the company to Rudolf Walden, who emerged as another important figure in Finland's pulp and paper

industry. Walden, a general in the Finnish army, had acquired majority control of the Simpele paper mill in 1916. In 1918 the Björnbergs agreed to sell Walden a one-third stake in Myllykoski. Neither Simple nor Myllykoski produced enough pulp to ensure their supply. In order to fill the gap, the companies joined together to acquire majority control of a nearby pulp producer, Jämsänkovski, in 1920. Walden took over as head of the concern. In keeping with his business philosophy, which called for reducing costs while building volume, Walden led the merger of the three companies into a single business, called Yhtyneet Paperitehtaat Osakeyhtio. This company became more commonly known as United Paper Mills, or UPM.

Fredrik Björnberg died in 1924, and son C. G., by then 23 years old, joined the company's management alongside Walden. UPM launched a major expansion drive during the 1920s, expanding both the Jamsan and Simpele mills. The major thrust of the group's expansion effort focused on expanding and modernizing Myllykoski's operations, however. As a result, Myllykoski achieved major production gains, even before UPM's official creation. By 1920 the company's paper output had soared past 9,500 tons, while its pulp production had also climbed to more than 4,300 tons.

UPM continued to invest strongly in Myllykoski's expansion during the 1930s. This period saw Myllykoski emerge as a major Finnish newsprint producer, backed by the construction of a major new paper mill. The company also developed a strong export operation to the Soviet Union and elsewhere, facilitated by the construction of a private railway linking the Myllykoski site to the Finnish railway network. UPM itself expanded in the 1930s with the addition of another mill, Walkiakoski, also controlled by Walden.

However, with the outbreak of World War II Walden was called up for duty, as a general and then as Finland's minister of defense. Walden's son Juuso then took up the position as UPM's chief executive. After Rudolf Walden's death in 1946 the relationship between the younger Walden and C. G. Björnberg quickly soured. Through the end of the decade, Walden and Björnberg developed markedly different opinions on the direction UPM should take for its further expansion. This conflict extended to a personal level before long.

BREAKING UP IN 1952

By 1951 the two families decided on the unusual, and radical, solution of splitting UPM into two companies. For this they turned to an impartial mediator, who proposed allowing Björnberg to decide how the company should be divided. Walden, in turn, was given the right

KEY DATES

◼

1892: Fredrik and Claes Björnberg acquire a pulp mill in Myllykoski, Finland.

1905: Myllykoski enters paper production, building its first paper mill.

1920: Myllykoski merges into United Paper Mills (UPM), led by Rudolf Walden.

1952: UPM breaks up and the Björnberg family regains control of Myllykoski.

1981: Myllykoski acquires 60 percent stake in Madison Paper Industries in the United States in partnership with the New York Times Company.

1987: Myllykoski enters Germany with the acquisition of Gebrüder Lang (later Lang Papier).

1990: The company acquires the Mochenwangen and Albbruck paper mills in Germany.

1996: The company acquires Utzenstorf in Switzerland and forms an alliance with Metsä-Serla.

2009: The company sells the Utzenstorf mill and Madison's Alsip mill in the United States.

to choose which part his family would keep. Björnberg's real interest was in regaining control of Myllykoski. Toward this end, his division of the company was hardly equal. One part consisted almost solely of Myllykoski, while the other contained nearly everything else.

Walden took the bait, choosing the larger part, despite the fact that much of UPM's expansion and modernization efforts had primarily benefited Myllykoski. The division of the company was completed in 1952. As a result, the Björnberg family regained control not only of Myllykoski, but also of one of the most modern and efficient newsprint mills in the industry.

Myllykoski then began concentrating its operations on developing expertise in the production of more specialized papers for the publishing industry. The company especially targeted the expansion into supercalendered and coated (SC) papers, used primarily for magazines.

Myllykoski launched a diversification effort in the late 1960s. This led the company to enter the mining industry in 1968, and the development of the Luikonlahti Copper Mine. Over the next 15 years the company extracted some 10 million tons of copper ore. In 1979 the company also launched talc mining and production

at the site. However, the company exited this activity in 1983, selling the mine to Finnminerals Oy.

INTERNATIONAL EXPANSION

While copper mining represented a departure from Myllykoski's core business, the company also expanded its range of paper operations during the 1970s. In 1972 the company began acquiring stakes in Colombier, a young paper converting company based in the Netherlands. Paper converting involved processing paper stock into paper-based products, including envelopes, packaging, folders, and other similar items, and included such processes as splitting, folding, laminating, and stapling. Backed by Myllykoski, Colombier expanded its operations to the United Kingdom, Spain, and Finland. Myllykoski acquired full control of Colombier by 1975, but ultimately sold the business by 2000. Myllykoski also began developing a recycled paper business during the 1970s.

Myllykoski underwent a change in leadership in the second half of the decade. C. G. Björnberg retired in 1978 (and died in 1995). The Björnberg family remained at the head of the company, however, as brothers Fredrik and Carl then took up the chairman and CEO positions, respectively. Under this new generation Myllykoski laid plans for expanding its paper mill operations into the international market.

This effort began in 1981, when the company acquired a 60 percent stake in Madison Paper Industries in the United States. Myllykoski's partner in the purchase was the New York Times Company, which held the remaining 40 percent. The United States represented the world's largest paper market. Over the next two decades Myllykoski's U.S.-based subsidiary expanded its production capacity to nearly 300,000 metric tons per year.

Closer to home, Myllykoski also targeted the German market, another of the world's largest paper markets. The company took its first step there with the purchase of Gebrüder Lang (later Lang Papier) in 1987. That company had been founded in Ettringen, in Bavaria, as a groundwood pulp producer in 1897. Lang entered paper production with the construction of its own paper mill in 1910. The company later emerged as a leader in the development of recycled fiber technologies, starting in 1963. As part of Myllykoski, Lang undertook a major expansion program, backed by the construction of two new paper mills for a total investment of nearly EUR 500 million. Lang thus emerged as a major European paper producer with a total capacity of 600,000 metric tons per year.

ALLIANCES

Myllykoski remained on the lookout for new expansion opportunities in Germany. In 1990 the company expanded its presence there again with two significant new acquisitions, of Mochenwangen, in Baden-Württemberg, and Albbruck, in the heart of the Black Forest region. Albbruck was one of the oldest of Myllykoski's growing range of businesses, having begun as a pulp mill in 1870 before adding paper production in 1882. Following this acquisition Myllykoski spun off its Finnish paper operations into a new subsidiary, Myllykoski Paper, a process completed in 1995.

Myllykoski then completed two more new acquisitions, adding Switzerland's Utzenstorf Papier in 1996, and expanding its Madison Paper Industries subsidiary with the purchase of the Alsip paper mill in 2000. The Utzenstorf mill, launched in 1892, brought its own century-old experience in paper production. Utzenstorf had added recycled fiber-based production in 1968, and with the construction of a recycled fiber processing plant in 1995 claimed to handle 25 percent of all of Switzerland's recovered paper.

Myllykoski had in the meantime adopted a new, alliance-based strategy during the 1990s. This led the company to form a partnership in 1996 with Metsä-Serla (later M-Real), the Finnish paper giant, which had acquired MD Papier in Germany in 1996. As part of the partnership agreement Metsä-Serla acquired 35 percent of Myllykoski Paper in Finland and 50 percent of Albbruck in Germany. Myllykoski in turn gained a 50 percent stake in Metsä-Serla's MD Papier, which included two German paper mills, in Plattling and Dachau.

Myllykoski found three more partners during the 1990s. The company joined with Stora Enso Oyj, acquiring a 47.5 percent stake in Sunila Oy, a major pulp producer with a yearly capacity of 360,000 metric tons. In 1996 the company teamed up with Ikea to develop a new paper grade for the furniture giant, called M-plus. Myllykoski next formed a power generation alliance with Finland's Vattenfall Oy in 1999. This alliance resulted in the construction of a new steam power plant by Vattenfall at Myllykoski's site, commissioned in 2001.

STREAMLINING IN 2009

M-Real and Myllykoski began untangling their partnership at the beginning of the twenty-first century. Myllykoski acquired full control of MD Papier, including both the Plattling and Dachau paper mills, in 2001. The company then took back full control of MD Albbruck in 2002. The two companies nevertheless maintained their joint shareholding of Myllykoski Paper into the next decade.

Myllykoski focused on expanding and upgrading its existing operations in the first decade of the new century. The company also eyed the possibility of entering new European markets. These objectives appeared to come together in 2005, when Myllykoski announced plans to spend EUR 272 million building a new 380,000-metric-ton paper mill in Opatovice, in the Czech Republic. However, Myllykoski ultimately opted to build the plant next to its existing mill in Plattling, Germany. The launch of production of that mill in 2007 led to the closure of the group's Dachau mill that same year. The company had also completed a second investment in the meantime, of EUR 150 million, boosting its production of magazine papers at its Plattling, Lang, Myllykoski Paper, and Madison mills.

Myllykoski found itself hard hit by the global economic recession at the end of the decade. The financial crisis had led to a major drop-off in advertising spending, which in turn created a sharp decline in demand for magazine paper. By the end of 2009 Myllykoski's revenues had dropped by more than 18 percent, to EUR 1.2 billion ($1.7 billion). The company, which had slipped into the red in 2008, saw its losses deepen that year, to EUR 68 million.

In response, Myllykoski undertook a streamlining effort during 2009. As part of this process the group sold its Utzenstorf mill in Switzerland, as well as the Alsip mill in the United States. Myllykoski also exited the Sunila Oyj partnership, selling its stake to Stora Enso. Despite the streamlining, Myllykoski remained among the world's top producers of magazine grade papers, and the last of the family-owned paper groups that once dominated the world paper industry.

M. L. Cohen

PRINCIPAL SUBSIDIARIES

Lang Papier (Germany); Madison Paper Industries Inc. (USA; 60%); MD Albbruck (Germany); MD Plattling (Germany); Myllykoski North America Inc. (USA); Myllykoski Paper (65%).

PRINCIPAL DIVISIONS

Myllykoski Europe; Myllykoski North America.

PRINCIPAL OPERATING UNITS

Madison Paper Industries; MD Albbruck; MD Plattling; Myllykoski Paper; Lang Papier; Myllykoski Sales Network.

PRINCIPAL COMPETITORS

Anglo American PLC; Baykalsk Pulp and Paper Mill Joint Stock Co.; International Paper Co.; Nippon Paper Group Inc.; Oji Paper Company Ltd.; RGM International Private Ltd.; Stora Enso Oyj; Svenska Cellulosa AB; UPM-Kymmene Corp.

FURTHER READING

Anderson, Steven, "Myllykoski Introduces High Bulk Paper," *Pulp & Paper News*, March 9, 2010.

"Myllykoski Adopts Consistent Strategy to Maintain Closeness to Customer," *Pulp & Paper News*, April 2, 2010.

"Myllykoski Expands Its Product Range with High-Volume Paper," *Pulp & Paper News*, March 8, 2010.

"Myllykoski Gets All of MD Papier," *PIMA's North American Papermaker*, July 2001, p. 17.

"Myllykoski in Magazine Drive," *Print Week*, June 30, 2005, p. 19.

"Myllykoski Moves to Construct Czech Mill," *Print Week*, October 20, 2005, p. 20.

"Myllykoski Reported Operating Loss of Euro 18 Million in 2009," *Lesprom Network*, April 1, 2010.

Nippon Telegraph and Telephone Corporation

———————— ▪ ————————

3-1 Otemachi 2-chrome
Chiyoda-ku
Tokyo, 100-8116
Japan
Telephone: (81 03) 5205-5581
Fax: (81 03) 5205-5589
Web site: http://www.ntt.co.jp

Public Company
Incorporated: 1985
Employees: 196,300
Sales: $107.1 billion (2009)
Stock Exchanges: Tokyo Osaka Nagoya Fukuoka Sapporo
    New York London
Ticker Symbols: NTT; 9432
NAICS: 513322 Cellular and Other Wireless Telecom-
    munications; 513310 Wired Telecommunications
    Carriers

■ ■ ■

Nippon Telegraph and Telephone Corporation (NTT) is one of the largest telecommunications firms in the world. In 1999 NTT was reorganized as part of Japan's telecommunications reform and became a holding company for regional phone companies, NTT East and NTT West, and long-distance carrier NTT Communications. Along with traditional telephone services, NTT offers Internet access, broadband services, and mobile communication services. The company owns approximately 62 percent of Japan's leading cellular provider, NTT DoCoMo Inc. Japan's telecommunica-

tions sector continues to face increased competition from foreign entrants, leaving NTT heavily focused on developing its fiber-optic broadband services and next generation network. In 2010 the Japanese government owned 34 percent of NTT.

ORIGINS

In 1877, one year after its invention by Alexander Graham Bell, the telephone became available in Japan. At first its use was reserved for the government, public affairs organizations such as the police, and a few businesses. It was not until 1890 that telephone services became available to the general public. Lines were laid between Tokyo and Yokohama, connecting 155 Tokyo subscribers to 42 in Yokohama. The first long-distance service became available in 1899 between Tokyo and Osaka, and discussions began as to how the telephone industry could best be developed. In 1889 the government approved a state-run telephone system. Although there were calls for a privately run company to be established, the Sino-Japanese War of 1894–95 and the Great Depression of the 1930s meant that calls for privatization went unheeded.

In the 1930s the Ministry of Communications created a special telegraph and telephone system research committee, which discussed the establishment of a half-government, half-private company. Initial plans were made for the formation of Nippon Telegraph and Telephone Corporation but were abandoned again due to an economic downturn and a sudden decline in the number of telephone subscribers. The outbreak of World War II led to another drop in telephone subscrib-

COMPANY PERSPECTIVES

The NTT Group's Corporate Social Responsibility (CSR) refers to offering the highest quality and most reliable services as a responsible information and telecommunications carrier, thereby contributing to the creation of a safe, secure and prosperous society through communications that serve people, communities and the global environment. To this end, we conduct sound corporate activities as a fundamental basis and contribute to society through environmental protection and other activities to live up to stakeholders' expectations.

ers, to 468,000. Finally in 1952, after a bill for a public telephone company was passed, the Nippon Telegraph and Telephone Public Corporation (NTTPC) was formed, based on recommendations issued in a report by the government-run Telegraph and Telephone Restoration Council. In 1953 KDD Ltd. was established to facilitate international telecommunications, and international telegraph and telephone business was transferred to this company.

POSTWAR DEMAND FOR TELECOMMUNICATION SERVICES

The demand for telecommunication services increased as Japan began to recover after World War II. In 1953 NTTPC's first five-year expansion project for telegraph and telephone services started, leading to an increase in the number of subscribers from 1.55 million to 2.64 million. Fueled by consumers' needs and advances in telecommunications technology, by 1963 the number of subscribers had increased to 9.89 million. As NTTPC's domestic market grew rapidly, NTTPC began to expand into the international market, although at this time technical cooperation was the extent of NTTPC's international involvement.

The demand for telecommunication services continued to grow within Japan. By 1972 the number of telephone subscribers had reached 20 million. Despite the demand caused by such enormous growth, NTTPC saw two of its goals realized in 1977, when telephone services became available nationwide and the company was able to install services as soon as they were required. Automatic dialing also became nationally available, and with the goal of international involvement, an international office was opened in 1979.

NTT IS PARTIALLY PRIVATIZED: 1985

Moves toward privatization came slowly. Meanwhile, NTTPC began to examine its infrastructure. The second ad hoc commission on privatization in 1981 examined the "public" corporate side of NTTPC and saw privatization as a way of improving efficiency. A third report detailed plans for privatization, reorganizing the company's structure and making the data communications systems sector independent. In 1988 the latter was established as NTT Data Communication Systems Corporation (NTT Data), a wholly owned NTT subsidiary. NTT's corporation law went into effect on December 20, 1984. Nippon Telegraph and Telephone Corporation was newly launched as a privatized joint stock corporation on April 1, 1985, with the provision that the Nippon Telegraph and Telephone Law be subject to revision within five years.

On an international level, similar events were taking place in the United States and the United Kingdom. In 1984 the British Telecommunications Bill came into force, allowing the privatization of British Telecom and liberalizing the British telecommunications industry, as competitors such as Mercury were issued licenses to operate. The United States followed a similar pattern in 1984, when American Telephone & Telegraph Company's (AT&T) Bell System was broken up and restructured into seven regional holding companies.

After privatization, the market opened to new carriers to start operations in competition with NTT. In April 1985 three carriers, Daini-Denden, Nippon Telecom, and Teleway Japan, applied for approval to operate as telecommunications companies. One effect of direct competition was that NTT was obliged to make a reduction in long-distance rates and upgrade its services. In July 1985 several new services were launched. To further enhance performance NTT's business was restructured into divisional organizations and the research and development center was reorganized from four to nine laboratories. NTT's first subsidiary company was launched in April 1985 and marked the opening of a chapter in NTT's history that would lead to the establishment of over 80 subsidiaries. The first was NTT Lease Co. Ltd. Its activities included the leasing and installment sales of terminal equipment.

PRIVATIZATION LEADS TO CHANGES IN INTERNATIONAL GROWTH

In terms of international activities, privatization allowed NTT slightly more room to maneuver through the creation of subsidiaries that had greater powers abroad.

KEY DATES

■

1952: Nippon Telegraph and Telephone Public Corporation is formed.

1977: Telephone services become available nationwide in Japan.

1985: Nippon Telegraph and Telephone Corporation (NTT) is launched as a privatized joint stock corporation.

1987: NTT lists on First Section of the Tokyo Stock Exchange.

1988: NTT Data is established as a wholly owned subsidiary.

1992: Foreign investors are allowed to purchase shares of NTT for the first time.

1999: NTT is reorganized into a holding company with three major business units, NTT East, NTT West, and NTT Communications.

2000: Verio Inc. is acquired.

2002: The company posts a $6.35 billion loss, the largest ever recorded by a nonfinancial firm in Japan to that time.

2008: NTT launches a new strategy titled "Road to Service Creation Business Group."

Prior to privatization, NTTPC's overseas operations on the whole had been restricted to participating in international exchanges, sending experts abroad, and forming agreements with a number of countries. As early as 1954, NTTPC had accepted trainees from Taiwan, and up to the early 1990s accepted approximately 160 trainees from 60 countries a year. The expert dispatch scheme that started in 1960 resulted in more than 500 specialists being sent to 54 countries. During the 1960s and 1970s a whole series of technical assistance programs were arranged between participating countries and NTTPC.

NTTPC also extended its operations overseas by setting up representative offices. NTTPC's first overseas office opened in Bangkok in 1958, offering technical assistance, and a European base was established in 1965 with the opening of the Geneva representative office. This was followed in 1973 with the opening of NTTPC's London representative office. NTT Europe Ltd. was formally incorporated in the United Kingdom in 1989 to encourage cooperation with that country's own telecommunications industry and to help extend global networks for Japanese business users. In similar fashion, the representative office in Brasilia, Brazil, became an of-

ficially registered overseas subsidiary company in November 1987. Representative offices also opened in Jakarta, Indonesia, in 1972; in Kuala Lumpur, the Malaysian capital, in 1986; and in Singapore in 1990. After the restoration of diplomatic relations between China and Japan in 1972, NTTPC made a technical exchange agreement with China in 1980, leading to the opening of an office in Beijing in 1985.

U.S. PRESENCE

NTT had a presence in the United States as early as 1966, when NTTPC employees were sent to New York. In 1970 a branch office was established with the primary objective of forming connections with U.S. carriers, and that went on to play an important role in international procurement. Because of an increase in business, NTT's California representative office was established, and after privatization NTT expanded its U.S. operations, incorporating the two U.S. offices into NTT America Inc. NTT also established exchange programs with several U.S. companies, including NYNEX and Pacific Bell, and a number of equipment purchase agreements were made. In May 1986 a purchase agreement was set up with Northern Telecom in a $250 million deal.

NTT International Corporation (NTTI) was established in the year of NTT's privatization. Starting with ¥3 billion and 150 employees, it had become one of NTT's largest subsidiaries by the late 1980s. Originally established with the aim of providing consulting services related to the telecommunications industry and providing products to overseas buyers, NTTI was able to carry out a number of functions overseas that the NTT Corporation was unable to do because of Japanese regulations.

Marketing NTT's products overseas and carrying out market research to see which products would be profitable were two important functions of NTTI. A third was to provide services related to the establishment of telecommunications infrastructures. An example of such work was a development project funded through NTTI by the World Bank in Indonesia. Australia was another country in which NTTI was active, helping to develop a facsimile mail service in 1987. In Finland NTTI sold large numbers of handheld computer terminals to a Finnish bank.

THE RECRUIT SCANDAL: 1988

NTT's fluctuating fortunes following privatization tended to be reflected in the company's share price. In October 1986 the minister of finance invited tender for the initial price of NTT stock before flotation. The initial price decided on was ¥1.97 million. By February 9, 1987, NTT was listed on the Tokyo, Nagoya, and Osaka stock exchanges, and was soon extended to other Japanese stock exchanges as well. After shares were floated, they reached a high of ¥3.18 million in 1987 but then collapsed to ¥1 million by the end of 1990.

Another contributing factor to NTT's struggles during this time was the infamous "recruit scandal" that hit Japan in 1988, when a number of senior officials were accused of accepting bribes. Scandal hit NTT when its former chairman, Hisashi Shinto, received a heavy fine and a suspended jail sentence for his part in the illegal activities. The post of NTT chairman was left open until Haruo Yamaguchi was appointed to the post in the middle of 1990.

Although NTT corporation law originally obliged the government to hold one-third or more of the total number of outstanding shares at all times and stated that "no foreign nationals or foreign judicial persons" were allowed to possess NTT shares, after some deliberation in October 1990 NTT announced a plan overturning this law. In December 1990 the Japanese government declared that it would start selling 500,000 shares a year beginning in April 1991. In 1992 foreign investors were allowed to purchase NTT stock for the first time.

LAUNCHING NEW SERVICES: 1988–89

Privatization also forced NTT to examine its operational efficiency and to provide better customer services. On May 23, 1988, NTT Data Communications Systems Corporations was established as a wholly owned subsidiary. Aimed at designing data communications that linked hardware with software for financial institutions, private companies, and government organizations, NTT Data also provided training seminars and consultation facilities.

NTT Data proved to be a profitable part of the NTT group. In 1990 operating revenues from NTT Data increased to ¥306.1 billion. One of NTT Data's major achievements was helping to set up the Tokyo International Financial Futures Exchange System in June 1989. Further recognition came to NTT Data when it developed a special card that allowed Nissan car owners to store car history information. The new product won the 1989 Nikkei Annual Products Award.

Another significant move was the introduction in April 1988 of INS-NET 64, described as the world's first wide-area commercial integrated services digital network (ISDN). NTT, KDDI, and AT&T put together a three-day presentation simultaneously at sites in Japan and New York. Following this, NTT sponsored a global ISDN exhibition, NTT Collection '90. Approximately 40,000 visitors attended this exhibition that demonstrated the capability of ISDN and featured an actual ISDN linkup between NTT, AT&T, British Telecom, France Telecom, and Singapore Telecom.

NTT began to play a greater role in the area of international equipment procurement. In accordance with the General Agreement on Tariffs and Trade (GATT), by 1990 orders had grown by 9 percent to $352 million and included purchases as diverse as digital transmission equipment from AT&T, digital switching systems from Northern Telecom, and pocket bell pagers and cellular telephone equipment from Motorola. Procurement seminars were held at various European sites to encourage European suppliers, as well as in various cities in the United States.

FACING INCREASED COMPETITION

By March 1989 NTT's performance was suffering because of increased competition from other common carriers, the cost of launching NTT Data, and the enforced reduction in long-distance telephone rates. In order to bring about recovery, NTT reexamined its administrative structure and in April 1989 reduced its four-tiered administrative structure to three levels. Another cost-cutting reform was the reduction in staff numbers. At its peak in 1979, NTT had 330,000 staff, but by 1989 the company had reduced this number to 276,000. Not satisfied with this, however, the company had further plans for greater reductions in staff.

Among the problems faced by NTT was increased competition from other carriers and a plan whereby competitors were connected to the network at a rate that reduced NTT's profitability, led to some resentment. President Kojima favored the introduction of a new kind of access charge or fee system to create a fairer market.

In terms of long-term international strategy, Kojima did not have ambitious plans for NTT to play a full international role but favored a specific international strategy that meant installing a network in a country with less-developed telecommunication systems. In March 1991, however, discussions were under way for a joint venture between three of the most powerful telephone companies, NTT, the British telecommunications group, and the German telecommunications group Deutsche Bundespost Telecom.

This joint venture, called Pathfinder, offered a telecommunications network to large international companies. NTT was thus faced with the problem of operating internationally while still abiding with NTT corporation law. In an effort to exploit the potential of the European market as it moved toward greater unity, as well as the markets of Eastern Europe and the countries of the former Soviet Union as they became more accessible, NTT announced in June 1991 the establishment of a new subsidiary in Düsseldorf, Germany, NTT Deutschland GmbH.

In the early 1990s NTT's plans centered on streamlining its operations in a cost-effective fashion and offering high-quality service to its customers. In an attempt to promote a fair and open market, NTT opened the Fair Competition Promotion Office in 1990. In the long term, NTT stressed the need to develop ISDN technology and to realize the importance of the cellular mobile market.

The focus on ISDN and new broadband technologies, as well as mobile phone services, would prove to be cornerstones for NTT's growth strategy. Throughout the 1990s NTT increased its research and development efforts related to cutting-edge technologies. In 1992 it created subsidiary NTT Mobile Communications Network Inc., which eventually became NTT DoCoMo, to oversee the sales of its mobile phones. By 1997 NTT controlled nearly half of Japan's cellular market, which was deregulated in 1994.

DEREGULATION LEADS TO REORGANIZATION: 1996–99

Japan's telecommunications sector was changing rapidly during the late 1990s. Foreign companies were allowed into the Asian market, which brought on a wave of increased competition. In December 1996 NTT lost its monopoly on local service. In return, however, the firm received approval to offer international services for the first time. By 1997 it had operating licenses in the United Kingdom, France, Germany, Hong Kong, and Singapore.

As deregulation approached, company management struck a deal with the Japanese government to reorganize the company while at the same time keeping it largely intact. Reorganization plans were set in motion in 1997 and finalized two years later. NTT became a holding company for three major subsidiaries, NTT East Corp., NTT West Corp., and NTT Communications Corp. Its local phone operations were divided into NTT East and NTT West, while its long distance and international telecommunications operations became part of NTT Communications.

NTT management eyed the reorganization as a rebirth of sorts and an opportunity to make key strategic changes, cut costs, and revamp corporate culture. NTT's competitors, however, viewed the new company just as it had the old one. A 1999 *Economist* article claimed that, "as rivals see it, NTT continues to dominate local calls, long-distance, leased lines, cellular and data communications, just as it did before the break-up." The same article pointed out that NTT's reorganization in Japan was "nothing like the break-up of AT&T in America during the 1980s, nor the busting of most national telephone monopolies in the 1990s."

Even after its restructuring, NTT held on to nearly a 90 percent share of Japan's telecommunications market. By this time, its cellular subsidiary, NTT DoCoMo, also controlled a 57 percent share of Japan's cellular market. Because of NTT's longstanding control over Japan's infrastructure, Internet users in Japan paid an estimated five times more than Americans or Europeans for access. A July 1999 *Forbes* article claimed that a telephone line installation cost nearly 11 times more in Japan than in New York.

The Japanese government slowly put pressure on NTT to lower its prices. In late 1999 both NTT East and NTT West began offering flat-rate Internet service with an approximate monthly fee of $75. As Japan's Ministry of Public Management, Home Affairs, Posts, and Telecommunications became even more focused on increasing competition in Japan's information technology sector, NTT's close relationship with the government, which brought it many benefits, appeared to be diminishing.

NEW STRATEGIES FOR THE 21ST CENTURY

NTT entered the new century intent on maintaining its market share. In 2000 it made a $5.1 billion purchase of Verio Inc., a U.S.-based Internet solutions provider. Meanwhile, NTT DoCoMo had invested nearly $16 billion in global cellular companies that included AT&T Wireless and KPN Mobile in Europe. That plan backfired, however, when shares of many wireless firms in the United States and around the world began falling off. By October 2002 DoCoMo was forced to write off over $13 billion of its investments.

Overall, NTT was suffering due to Japanese deflation, increased competition, and a general slump in the information technology sector. During 2001 the company launched a three-year business plan aimed at restructuring its regional phone companies and shifting focus to integrated cellular and Internet services along with various broadband offerings. NTT West and NTT East launched B-FLET'S, a high-speed communications service that used optical fiber, that year. The company also eliminated much of its spending related to its fixed lines and planned to cut back on capital spending by 15 percent through 2003.

In 2002 Norio Wada was named president of NTT. During that fiscal year the company posted a $6.35 billion loss, the largest ever reported by a nonfinancial firm in Japan to that time. The company claimed restructuring charges and investment losses were to blame, in addition to continued deterioration of the economy and falling personal consumption. NTT's new leader pledged to position the company favorably in order to benefit from changing demand and new technologies. As competition in the global telecommunications industry continued to heighten, NTT faced many challenges.

The company made several moves to shore up its bottom line, including cutting costs and selling various assets. DoCoMo sold its 16 percent stake in AT&T Wireless Services Inc. in 2004. At the same time, NTT spun off real estate subsidiary NTT Urban Development Corp. These actions led to a 10 percent increase in net profits that year.

FOCUS ON NEW TECHNOLOGIES

With demand for fixed-line phone services falling, the company continued to focus on new broadband technologies. During 2004 the company announced a business strategy focused on expanding its fiber-optic broadband network to 30 million homes and offices by 2010. The expansion program was estimated to cost nearly $47 billion and included replacing existing copper lines that provided telephone services with new fiber-optic cables.

As part of the strategy, NTT reorganized its fixed-line companies, including NTT East, NTT West, and NTT Communications, in order to consolidate services under each company. For example, NTT Communications oversaw the company's Internet businesses while NTT East and NTT West would each operate Internet protocol (IP) phone services.

Increased competition forced the company to cut rates for both its fixed-line and cellular services during this period. While the company worked to revamp its operating structure, its financial performance was faltering. During fiscal 2005 the company reported a decline in both operating profit and revenues for the first time since its public offering in 1987.

Satoshi Miura was named president of NTT in 2007, while Norio Wada remained chairman. Under the guidance of this executive team, NTT launched a new strategy titled "Road to Service Creation Business Group" in 2008 that focused on completion of its IP structure for both its fixed-line and mobile communications network. The company launched its Next-Generation Network that year, which enabled its fixed-line customers to have access to fiber-optic broadband services.

EXPANDING MOBILE NETWORK

At the same time, subsidiary DoCoMo was looking to expand on its 3G mobile network and was developing its Long Term Evolution (LTE) standard, which would enable mobile users access to greater download speeds and greater capacity while using content such as video. By 2009 it offered its customers seven smartphones (mobile phones offering enhanced Web-based services), but was facing increasing competition from Apple Inc.'s iPhone product. The iPhone, sold through competitor Softbank Mobile Corp., was Japan's best-selling smartphone by 2010. DoCoMo released the Sony Ericsson Xperia, a smartphone that ran on Google Inc.'s Android operating system, that year.

Even with global economies in a state of flux during this time, NTT continued to forge ahead with its expansion plans. Subscriptions for its fiber-optic access services surpassed 11 million by March 2009. The company's growth in this area was partially attributable to the Japanese government's mandate that broadband services be made available to all Japanese households by 2015.

This mandate left the future of NTT in question, however. The company controlled nearly 70 percent of the country's fiber-optic network, which was capable of providing phone, Internet, and video services. Industry experts began to speculate that the government would either force NTT to spin off its fiber-optic infrastructure business or undergo a complete reorganization whereby NTT would assume full ownership of subsidiary DoCoMo. The latter would give NTT access to DoCoMo's cash flow, which could then be used to fund future fiber-optic expansion. While the government's plans for NTT remained up in the air, the company would no doubt face changes in the years to come.

Clare Doran
Updated, Christina M. Stansell

PRINCIPAL SUBSIDIARIES

Nippon Telegraph and Telephone East Corporation; Nippon Telegraph and Telephone West Corporation; NTT Communications Corporation; NTT DoCoMo Inc. (66.2%); NTT Data Corporation (54.2%).

PRINCIPAL COMPETITORS

KDDI Corporation; Softbank Mobile Corp.; Tokyo Electric Power Company.

FURTHER READING

"Foreign Adventures; Japanese Telecoms," *Economist U.S.*, May 11, 2002.

Fulford, Benjamin, "The Last Empire," *Forbes*, July 26, 1999, p. 51.

Guth, Robert A., "NTT Posts Loss of $6.35 Billion for Fiscal Year," *Wall Street Journal*, May 15, 2002, p. B6.

Ishibashi, Kanji, "NTT's Net Rises on Sale of Stake in AT&T Wireless," *Wall Street Journal*, May 13, 2005.

"Japanese Telecoms: Who Needs NTT?" *Economist U.S.*, December 18, 1999, p. 115.

"Nippon Telegraph and Telephone," *Economist U.S.*, July 3, 1999, p. 55.

"NTT Facing Harsh Reality," *Nikkei Weekly*, April 12, 2010.

"NTT Must Change in Accordance with Market," *AsiaPulse News*, June 28, 2002.

"NTT Operating Profit Dives 22% amid Discount War," *Nikkei Weekly*, May 16, 2005.

"There's No End to DoCoMo's Wireless Hangover," *Business Week*, October 14, 2002.

Wakabayashi, Daisuke, "iPhone Is Big in Japan," *Wall Street Journal*, May 19, 2010.

———, "KDDI Deal Sets Up Telecom Skirmish in Japan," *Wall Street Journal*, January 26, 2010.

Williams, Martyn, "U.S. Group Criticizes Japan's Telecom Deregulation Plans," *InfoWorld*, April 23, 2001, p. 75.

Nordea Bank AB

Smålandsgatan 17
Stockholm, SE-105 71
Sweden
Telephone: (+46 8) 614 7000
Fax: (+46 8) 105 069
Web site: http://www.nordea.com

Public Company
Incorporated: 1997 as Nordic Baltic Holding
Employees: 33,347
Total Assets: EUR 507. 54 billion ($727.42 billion)
(2009)
Stock Exchanges: NASDAQ OMX Nordic
Ticker Symbol: NDA
NAICS: 522320 Financial Transactions Processing,
Reserve, and Clearinghouse Activities; 551111 Offices of Bank Holding Companies; 523110 Investment Banking and Securities Dealing; 522110 Commercial Banking; 522120 Savings Institutions

∎∎∎

Nordea Bank AB operates as the largest financial services group in the Nordic and Baltic Sea region with 1,400 locations serving nearly 10 million customers. Its primary operations are in Sweden, Denmark, Finland, and Norway, as well as in emerging markets in Russia, Estonia, Latvia, Lithuania, and Poland. The company provides corporate banking services as well as retail and private banking services. Nordea also offers life insurance and pension products. Nordea is traded on the Copenhagen, Helsinki, and Stockholm stock exchanges and is one of the top 10 banking institutions in Europe.

19TH-CENTURY ORIGINS

The formation of Nordea at the beginning of the 21st century was the result of a long series of mergers through more than 150 years of Scandinavian banking history. Each of the major banks that made up the first pan-Scandinavian and one of the first pan-European banks traced its history to the 19th century and the beginnings of the modern Scandinavian banking industry. Many of the components that created the future Nordea group had also been operated as government-owned banking institutions.

Sweden's Nordbanken alone represented more than 170 years of banking history and the mergers of some 80 separate banks. The oldest of the Nordbanken banks was Wermlandsbanken, founded in 1832. Another early Swedish bank was Smålands Bank, founded in 1837. In 1848 a group of merchants in Göteborg founded their own bank, Göteborgs Privat Bank. Like Wermlandsbanken and Smålands Bank, this young bank operated primarily on local and regional levels.

The mid-19th century saw the formation of a number of other banks. In 1864 the Sundsvallsbanken was created and quickly became the primary financial institution for Sweden's forestry industry. Skaragborgsbanken, founded in 1865, captured that local market; the same year saw the formation of Uplandsbanken.

The first mergers among Sweden's banking industries began to appear toward the end of the 19th century. Among these were the mergers of Göteborgs Privat Bank with Stockholm's Enskilda Bank, which in 1898 merged with another Stockholm-based bank, Diskontobank. This step also marked an increasing tendency of the country's largely locally and regionally based banks to begin consolidating toward a more nationally focused market.

Another piece of the puzzle that was to become Nordbanken was the creation of Lantmannabanken in 1917. This bank was formed specifically to focus on Sweden's agricultural market. After a financial collapse in 1923, Lantmannabanken was restructured as Jordbrukarbanken and placed under the Swedish government's control, becoming the country's first state-owned bank. This bank was subsequently renamed Sveriges Kreditbank, indicating its national character.

The formation of the predecessor to Sveriges Kreditbank was accompanied in the private sector by a series of mergers that transformed Uplandsbanken into a major nationally operating bank. That bank merged with Sundsvall Handelsbank in 1917, then with both Gefleborgs Folkbank and Hudiksvails Kredibank in 1920. The newly enlarged bank became known as Uplandsbanken. Meanwhile, the Göteborgs bank was also growing, acquiring Kopparsbergs Enskilda Bank in 1922.

BANKING SECTORS IN FINLAND, NORWAY, AND DENMARK

This same period saw similar activity in Finland, leading toward the creation of Merita Bank in the mid-1990s. Finland's first commercial bank was formed in 1862, operating under the name of Suomen Yhdyspankki. While Sweden's banks remained largely local and regional, the new Finnish bank established national operations from the outset. The bank gained new competition in 1889, when Kansallis-Osake-Pankki was founded. The two banks remained limited to commercial and corporate banking until after World War II, when both banks established private customer services. In the meantime, the Suomen Yhdyspankki bank, renamed Pihjoismaiden Yhdyspankki after a merger in

1919, had become one of the country's leading commercial banks.

Meanwhile, in Norway Christiania Bank had followed a steadier course than its Scandinavian neighbors. Formed in 1848 in what was then known as Christiania (before the Norwegian capital city's name was changed to Oslo), the bank was originally known as Christiania Kredietklasses before changing its name to Christiania Bank og Kredietklasse in 1851.

Privatbanken had been founded in Denmark in 1857 and grew to become that country's largest bank. Led by Danish financial baron C. F. Tietgen, who had been behind such large-scale Danish companies as Tuborg, DFDS, the Great Northern Telegraph Company, and De Danske Spritfabrikker, Privatbanken faced competition from other nationally operating rivals. These included Andelsbanken, which was founded in 1925 and had its origins among the country's agricultural community before investing in Denmark's manufacturing industry. Another large-scale Danish bank was SDS Bank, which represented the grouping of many of the country's local and regional banks.

NATIONAL MERGERS IN THE 1970S

The formation of the European Community led to increasing consolidation among Scandinavia's banking communities in the 1970s. Each national market saw the mergers of many of its major players to create more powerful nationally operating banks with more capacity to compete on an international level, as well as to compete against other international banks, which were by then making strong inroads in their domestic markets. The process of consolidation created a small number of dominant players in each of the Scandinavian markets, including Nordbanken, Unidanmark, Merita, and Christiania Bank og Kredietklasse, which were the major components of the future Nordea.

Consolidation in Sweden began in earnest in 1972 with the merger of Göteborgs Bank with Smalandsbanken, forming Göteborgs Bank. Two years later Sveriges Kreditbank merged with another state-owned bank, Postbanken, operated by the country's postal system. That merger created Post-och Krediet-banken, or PK-Banken, then the largest bank in Sweden. That bank was to sink to third place, behind SE Banken and Svenska Handelsbanken, after the recession of the early 1980s.

Teaming up with Oslo's Christiania Bank og Kredietklasse, PKBanken began its first international operations, opening joint venture locations in Asia, the

KEY DATES

1972: Merger of Göteborgs Bank with Smalands-banken forms Götabanken.

1974: Sveriges Kreditbank merges with Postbanken to form PKBanken.

1975: Phjoismaiden Yhydspankki changes name to Union Bank of Finland.

1984: PKBanken is listed on Stockholm stock exchange.

1986: Union Bank of Finland merges with Bank of Helsinki; Sundsvallsbanken and Uplandsban-ken merger forms Nordbanken.

1990: Unibank is formed; PKBanken acquires Nordbanken, adopts Nordbanken name; Gota Bank is created.

1993: Nordbanken acquires Gota Bank.

1995: Union Bank of Finland merges with Kansallis-Osake-Pankki to form Merita Bank.

1997: Nordbanken and Merita merge and later take the name Nordic Baltic Holding.

2001: The Nordea Bank AB name is adopted.

United States, the United Kingdom, and Brazil. After the Swedish government placed PKBanken on the Stockholm stock exchange, the bank ended its association with Christiania Bank to focus again on the national market. PKBanken made two major acquisitions at the end of the 1980s, Sveriges Investeringsbank, founded by the Swedish government in 1967, and the Carnegie Fondkommision brokerage house, acquired in 1988.

The Nordbanken name first appeared in the mid-1980s, with the merger of Sundsvallsbanken and Up-landsbanken in 1986. When PKBanken acquired regionally focused Nordbanken in 1990, the latter name was maintained for the whole of the newly merged bank. That same year saw the creation of Gota Bank, formed through the combination of Göteborgs Bank, Werm-landsbanken, and Skaraborgsbanken. Nordbanken then acquired Gota Bank in 1993.

By this time, Nordbanken had once again come under full control of the Swedish government, which had been forced to rescue the bank from its financial collapse in 1992. Crippled by the global recession and the bottoming out of the country's real estate market, Nordbanken underwent replacement of its management, the sale of its bad debt portfolio to the Swedish government, and a reduction of its staff by some 20 percent.

By 1995 Nordbanken once again took a public listing on the Stockholm exchange as the government reduced its ownership position.

CONSOLIDATION AND GROWTH

Meanwhile, Nordbanken's Finnish neighbors were also undergoing a consolidation process. Phjoismaiden Yhyd-spankki, which had begun expanding internationally, anglicized its name to Union Bank of Finland in 1975. The bank had also begun to pioneer the use of electronic banking systems during that decade. In 1986 Union Bank of Finland was boosted by the merger with the Bank of Helsinki, then the country's third-largest bank. The recession of the early 1990s forced the breakup of another leading Finnish bank, Suomen Säästöpannki (Savings Bank of Finland), in 1993, with Union Bank and Kansallis-Osake-Pankki each taking a share of that bank's operations. By then, Kansallis-Osake-Pankki had grown through the 1992 merger with Suomen Työväen Säästöpannki, the savings bank operated by the Finnish labor movement. Three years later Union Bank of Finland, through its holding company Unitas Ltd., was merged with Kansallis-Osake-Pankki, creating Merita Bank.

In Norway, Christiania Bank had grown through mergers with Andresens Bank in 1980 and Fiskernes Bank in 1983. Hit hard by the recession of the early 1990s, Christiania was rescued by the Norwegian government, which became the bank's sole shareholder. However, by the late 1990 the Norwegian government had placed the bank back on the public market, reducing its holdings to just 35 percent by the end of the decade.

The recession also brought losses to Denmark's Unibank. That bank had been formed in 1990, merging the operations of Andelbanken, SDS Bank, and Privatbanken. Recovering from the crisis, Unibank strengthened its investment banking wing in 1996, when it established Aros Securities in a merger between its own equity business and the international investment operations of the ABB Group. That company became Fleming Aros in 1998 in another joint venture, which was ended after Unibank's entry into Nordea.

Unidanmark, parent company of Unibank, merged with the largest Danish insurance company, Tryg-Baltica, to create an enlarged financial services company. Unibank next looked toward Sweden, where it bought a controlling share of Trevise AB, an asset management business. Unibank then converted Trevise into a full-fledged private bank operation with offices in Sweden and Finland. Unibank also moved into Norway, acquiring that country's Vesta, making Unibank one of Scandinavia's leading insurance companies.

CROSS-BORDER MERGERS FOR THE 21ST CENTURY

Unibank's moves across Scandinavia represented the first of several sudden consolidations within the Scandinavian banking industry. Sharing similar and often intertwined histories, the Scandinavian countries were seen as good matches for partnerships. The coming of the single European currency spelled the dawn of a new era for the European banking industry as a whole, which had remained largely centered on domestic markets. While the banking industries in most of the European Community countries concentrated on consolidating their domestic markets, the Scandinavian markets, which had already undergone national consolidation efforts, were able to look beyond their borders for future growth.

Nordbanken and Merita were among the first and largest to join the new wave of cross-border mergers. The two banks merged in 1997, forming MeritaNordbanken. An important product brought to the new bank was its Solo Internet-based banking operation, which was on its way toward becoming one of the world's leading online banking services. The newly enlarged banking group then looked across Scandinavia for other potential partners. The next member joined in March 2000, when Unidanmark agreed to merge with MeritaNordbanken in a deal valued at $4 billion.

The new company, which took on the larger name of Nordic Baltic Holding in order to contain its continuing Nordbanken, Merita, and Unibank banking and financial services brands, soon added to its scope. At the end of December 2000, Christiania Bank og Kredietklasse became part of the leading financial services company in Scandinavia, a process begun in September 1999. By the time Christiania was added, Nordic Baltic Holding had chosen a new name for itself. The bank was then to be known as Nordea, a name built from the words "Nordic" and "Idea," suggesting the bank's willingness to extend its success beyond its Scandinavian base to the global scale.

While Nordea pledged to continue operating under its national brands, the company nonetheless moved toward the integration of its operations to create a single, pan-Scandinavian brand. One such move in this direction was the renaming of the former Unibank's Aros investment banking unit as Nordea Securities in April 2001. By December of that year, all business operations were consolidated under the Nordea name.

EXPANSION CONTINUES: 2002 AND BEYOND

With the Nordea brand firmly in place, the company spent the next several years divesting noncore and unprofitable assets while acquiring businesses that fit within its growth strategy. During 2002 it sold Europay Norge AS as well as its majority interest in Contant Oy and various general insurance holdings. That same year it set plans in motion to buy Poland's LG Petro Bank, the financing operations of Sonera Gateway Ltd., and a significant portion of Zurich Financial Services Group's non-life insurance businesses in Denmark and Norway.

During 2003 the company made several substantial divestments, including real estate holdings, and Tunturi Oy Ltd., a fitness equipment manufacturer based in Finland. Nordea continued to unload businesses the following year, including a hotel company based in Finland, the Finnish real estate investment firm Dividum Oy, and several real estate holdings based in Finland.

The company had turned its attention to growth in emerging markets in Poland and the Baltic region by this time. During 2004 Nordea acquired the Lithuanian portion of Poland-based Kredyt Bank SA. At the same time, it increased its share holding in International Moscow Bank (IMB) to 26.44 percent from 21.7 percent. Nordea purchased Sampo Group's Polish life insurance and pension business the following year.

In November 2006 Nordea announced its intention to acquire a majority stake in JSB Orgresbank, which would give it a strong foothold in the Russian market. The company had sold its interest in IMB earlier that year, paving the way for the deal that was finalized in March 2007. The company planned for slow but steady growth in Russia, and during 2009 Nordea ranked 18th in terms of corporate lending and 46th in retail lending in the Russian market. While Russia accounted for just 2 percent of its overall business, Nordea believed Russia would remain part of its long-term growth strategy.

While the company continued to sell various businesses, it bolstered its holdings by making small-scale acquisitions. During 2007 Nordea purchased a majority stake in Norway's Privatmegleren, a real estate broker with offices in Oslo, Kristiansand, Stockholm, and Tromsø. It bought nine branches of Roskilde Bank from the Danish government in 2008. Nordea expanded its Danish business in 2009 with the purchase of Fionia Bank. The acquisition doubled its market share in the Funen region of the country.

During this period, financial companies worldwide faced challenges amid what many analysts were calling the worst global recession since World War II. Banks across the globe either were shuttered or, receiving government funds to stay afloat, were forced to merge with larger, more financially viable institutions. Nordea survived the downturn by controlling costs, limiting its exposure to risky investments, pursuing growth internally, and avoiding costly large-scale acquisitions.

The uncertainty in financial markets continued into 2010. Although Nordea was well positioned among its peers, it remained cautiously optimistic about future growth. While it did not rule out a large merger in the coming years when markets recovered, it remained focused on maintaining its profitability. With its sights set on eventually expanding into new markets, Nordea appeared to be on track for success in the years to come.

M. L. Cohen
Updated, Christina M. Stansell

PRINCIPAL DIVISIONS

Account Products; Transaction and Finance Products; Capital Markets Products; Savings Products and Asset Management; Life and Pensions.

PRINCIPAL COMPETITORS

Danske Bank A/S; SEB AB; Svenska Handelsbanken AB.

FURTHER READING

Brown-Humes, "Nordea Plans Online Boost," *Financial Times*, February 22, 2001.

"E*Europe: Bank Leads by a Click over Mortar," *Time International*, May 1, 2000, p. 54.

Levring, Peter, "Nordea Aims to Diversify beyond Current Markets," *Reuters News*, July 23, 2009.

"Merita, Nordbanken Merge, Want Others to Join," *Reuters Business Report*, October 13, 1997.

"Nordea Bank Mulls Acquisitions in Poland, Baltics," *Dow Jones International News*, November 30, 2004.

"Nordea Buys 67 Pct of Privatmegleren," *Turkish Daily News*, November 28, 2007.

"Nordea Finalized Deal to Buy 75% Stake in JSB Orgresbank," *Dow Jones International News*, March 29, 2007.

"Scandinavian Models," *Economist*, May 20, 2000.

"Sweden: CEO Says Nordea Eyes M&As after Crisis," *Euclid Infotech*, March 24, 2010.

"Sweden's Nordea to Buy Assets of Denmark's Fionia," *Wall Street Journal Europe*, September 1, 2009.

Wallace, Charles P., "Admire Our Busy Signal," *Time*, June 19, 2000, p. B22.

Olympic Entertainment Group A.S.

Pronksi 19
Tallinn, 10124
Estonia
Telephone: (+372) 667 1250
Fax: (+372) 667 1270
Web site: http://www.olympic-casino.com

Public Company
Incorporated: 1999
Employees: 2,348
Sales: EEK 1.7 billion ($148.10 million) (2009)
Stock Exchanges: Tallinn Warsaw
Ticker Symbol: OEG IT
NAICS: 721110 Hotels (Except Casino Hotels) and Motels; 551112 Offices of Other Holding Companies

■ ■ ■

Olympic Entertainment Group A.S. is the leading casino operator in the Baltic market, with a strong presence in the Central and Eastern European markets as well. Olympic operated 66 casinos at the beginning of 2010, including 18 in Estonia, 21 in Latvia, and 10 in Lithuania. Other company markets include Belarus, with five casinos; Poland, with eight casinos; and Romania and Slovakia with two casinos each. All of Olympic Entertainment's casinos operate under the Olympic Casino brand and feature both slot machines and table gaming. The casinos also feature their own bars and entertainment venues.

Since February 2010 Olympic has also operated its own online casino gaming Web site. Olympic Entertainment is listed on the Tallinn and Warsaw stock exchanges. The company is led by founder and Chairman Armin Karu and CEO Indrek Jurgenson. Karu is also Olympic Entertainment's largest shareholder, through his Hansa Assets investment holding, with a share of 47.9 percent. In 2009 Olympic Entertainment generated total revenues of EEK 1.7 billion ($148 million).

POST-SOVIET CASINO GAMING COMPANY IN 1993

Born in 1965, Armin Karu recognized the opportunities for developing Estonia's leisure and entertainment sector in the post-Soviet era. The passage of the first laws permitting casino gaming in 1993 stimulated Karu to found his own company, called AS Benetreks. The company acquired its first concession at the Pirita Hotel, located next to the Tallinn Olympic Yachting Centre, site of the yachting and regatta competitions of the 1980 Summer Olympic Games.

The location provided Benetreks with the brand name for its casino, Olympic, later incorporated into the company's own name. The first Olympic casino featured nearly 40 slot machines, as well as various arcade games, including two pinball machines. While the company claimed this to be Estonia's first casino, its second property, opened at the Hotel Kungla (later renamed the Park Hotel) in July 1994, became the first to feature full-scale casino gaming, including table gaming. Following the Park Hotel's renovation in 1997, the Olympic casino there became Estonia's largest at that

COMPANY PERSPECTIVES

Our Vision. To be a global casino and resort operator with a passion for service excellence.

time. By the end of its first full year of operation, Benetreks had opened a third casino, the Mustakivi, featuring 42 slot machines.

Estonia's swift and relatively smooth transition to a free market economy by the middle of the decade provided the foundation for the growth of Benetreks through the 1990s. The company added six more casinos through 1997, including the Olympic Casino Nurmenuku in 1995, and the Olympic Casino Balti Jaam, in the passenger terminal of the Baltic Railway Station, in 1997. Not all of the company's casinos performed as well as the company hoped, however. The company opened a casino in Parnu, at the Sunset club, which closed in 1999. Another casino, in the Decolté club in Tallinn, opened in 1996 but was shut down after two years.

LOOKING ABROAD IN 2001

Olympic had nevertheless succeeded in claiming the lead in the small Estonian casino market by the end of the decade. The company continued adding new properties, including a casino in Narva in 1998, and new casinos in Tallinn in 1999 and 2001, as well as in Tartu and Maardu in 2001. By the end of that year, the company, which had adopted a holding company structure in 1999, operated 13 casinos. The company also changed its name in 2001, becoming Olympic Casino Group.

The tiny Estonian market had become crowded at the dawn of the 21st century. By the middle of the first decade of the new century, the gaming market had begun to approach saturation, with 15 companies operating more than 140 gaming establishments for a total population of just 1.35 million. As a result, Olympic began putting into place a Baltic region expansion strategy.

Olympic targeted the neighboring Lithuanian market for its first foreign expansion. Unlike other Baltic and Central and Eastern European markets, where casino legislation had been put in place in the early 1990s, Lithuania had remained closed to gaming, in large part due to the heavy influence of the Catholic church there. However, in 2001 the Lithuanian government drafted new legislation legalizing gambling.

Olympic set up a subsidiary in Vilnius and succeeded in gaining a casino license that same year. The company opened its first two slot machine "saloons" in Vilnius in February 2002. By the end of the year the company had also received authorization to add tables for games, as well as a roulette table.

Olympic took a different approach to the Latvian market, where casino gaming had been authorized since 1994. In August 2002 Olympic entered Latvia through the acquisition of an existing casino, the Casino Daugava in Riga. The company then refurbished the site, which reopened in April 2003 as part of the Radisson SAS Daugava hotel complex. The year 2003 also marked the opening of a new Lithuanian casino, in the Reval Hotel Lietuva, which became the largest casino in Vilnius at that time, with nearly 120 slot machines and 20 tables.

BEYOND THE BALTICS IN 2004

Olympic's Lithuanian operations remained primarily focused on the Vilnius market, but also expanded into the city of Kaunus with the opening of a casino there in 2004. The company operated eight casinos in Lithuania by the following year. Despite this smaller scale, Olympic's Lithuanian subsidiary contributed 30 percent to the group's total revenues, which reached EUR 56 million in 2005.

Olympic had established itself in the meantime as the second-largest casino player in Latvia. This was accomplished through the acquisition in December 2005 of Baltic Gaming, raising the group's total number of Latvian casinos to 38. The acquisition helped Olympic nearly double its revenues through 2006. It also raised the group's total number of Baltic casinos to 70, making it the clear leader in that region's casino market.

In light of this success, Olympic, which had changed its name in 2004 to Olympic Entertainment Group, once again revised its strategy. The company began targeting growth in the Central and Eastern European market, with a new goal of establishing itself as a leading casino player in this wider region. The company announced plans to expand its operations to 10 countries by 2010.

Olympic had taken a strong step into the region in 2004, when it added its first slot machine casino in Kiev, Ukraine. With a population of more than 47 million, Ukraine represented one of the largest markets in Eastern Europe. Olympic set its sights on building its presence there, expanding to four casinos in 2005, and nearing 20 casinos there by 2007.

In September 2007 Olympic expanded its Ukrainian business again, acquiring the five-casino Eldo-

KEY DATES

1993: Armin Karu founds AS Benetreks to operate casinos in Estonia under the Olympic brand name.

2001: The company changes its name to Olympic Casino and opens its first international casino in Vilnius, Lithuania, the following year.

2005: Olympic acquires Baltic Gaming.

2006: Olympic goes public on the Tallinn Stock Exchange as Olympic Entertainment Group.

2010: Olympic launches an online gaming site, Olympic-online.

rado group for EUR 9.2 million. This acquisition also gave the company its first table gaming operations in Ukraine. Olympic then launched a renovation and re-branding program for the Eldorado casinos, reopening its first two in 2008. By the end of that year, the company's Ukrainian subsidiary had expanded to 24 casinos, representing more than 12 percent of Olympic's revenues.

PUBLIC OFFERING IN 2006

Olympic Entertainment Group went public in 2006, listing its shares first on the Tallinn Stock Exchange and then in 2007 on the Warsaw Exchange. The public offering enabled founder Karu to reduce his stake in the company to just over 51 percent in 2007, and to just under 48 percent by 2010.

Olympic's Ukrainian operations encountered an impasse in July 2009. In May 2009, after a fire broke out in a competing casino, the Ukrainian government suspended all gaming licenses in the country, effectively shutting down the casino market there. Shortly after, the government passed new legislation withdrawing all licenses and extending the gaming suspension in order to draw up a new Law on Gaming. The new law was also expected to require the transfer of all of the country's casinos into specially designated areas. As a result of the suspension, Olympic was forced to shut down its casinos in Ukraine. By July 2009 the company's Ukrainian subsidiary had gone bankrupt, and Olympic exited Ukraine altogether.

Although Olympic suffered a setback in Ukraine, its international strategy remained successful elsewhere. The company entered Poland in 2005, acquiring Casino Polonia Wrocław Sp. Z.o.o. for EUR 9 million. Polonia provided Olympic with a gaming license in Poland, and

an agreement to develop a casino in the Warsaw Hilton Hotel. This casino, called the Olympic Casino Sunrise, opened in 2007. Through the end of that year, Olympic opened two more hotel-based casinos, at the Metropol and the Lysigoóry. By the end of 2009 the group's Polish operations boasted eight casinos. The entry into Poland, with a population of more than 38 million, also provided a major boost to group revenues, accounting for 26 percent of its total that year.

The Estonian market nevertheless remained the company's largest single revenue generator, with 30 percent of its total revenues at the end of the decade. The company's Olympic Casino Estonia subsidiary added an acquisition there, Nordic and its subsidiary Vikings, which had been acquired along with Baltic Gaming in 2005, bringing two more casinos into its fold. By the end of 2008 Olympic's Estonian operations had risen to 36 casinos. However, during 2009 the company launched a streamlining of its portfolio, leading to the closure of half of its casinos in Estonia.

EXPLORING NEW MARKETS

Olympic continued exploring new territories. The group entered the Belarus market in 2006, opening the Olympic Casino Eldorado, featuring 36 slot machines and a bar, in Minsk that year. This was followed in 2007 by three more casinos, the Olympic Casino Sparts, featuring 64 slot machines in the Expobel Trade Center; the Olympic Casino Neptune in the Manezh Trade Center; and the Olympic Casino Troy, with 44 slot machines. In 2008 the company added a casino in the town of Passazh as well.

Following its Belarus entrance, Olympic targeted another fast-growing market, Romania. The company entered that market through the acquisition in April 2007 of Empire International Game World and its three casinos, including the Napoleon, located in Bucharest's World Trade Center.

The group added four more casinos in Romania during 2008. By the beginning of 2009 the group's Romanian presence included nine casinos, with a total of 344 slot machines. In July 2009 the company celebrated the opening of what it called its flagship casino, the two-story Bora Bora, located in the Pull-mann Hotel in Bucharest. The new casino cost the company EUR 6.4 million to build, and featured 17 tables, 3 electronic roulette tables, and 72 slot machines, as well as a restaurant and VIP room.

By this time Olympic oversaw an empire of 133 casinos, spanning a total surface area of 38,877 square meters and generating revenues of more than $241 million. Despite posting a net loss of approximately $40 million for the 2008 year, the company remained optimistic in 2009. Olympic again revised its strategy, seeking to expand beyond its core casino operations into resort operations as well. The company also announced its interest in expanding into other markets, potentially including the United States in the future.

ONLINE GAMING IN 2010

For the time being, however, Olympic's focus remained on the Central and Eastern European region. The group added a new country to its list in 2008, opening its first casino in Slovakia, at the Radisson Blu Carlton Hotel in Bratislava. The largest casino in Slovakia at the time, the new casino featured 13 tables, as well as an electromechanical roulette table, and 62 slot machines. At the beginning of 2009 the company added a second casino in Slovakia, in Trnava, featuring 10 tables and 34 slot machines.

Olympic's optimism was put to the test in 2009. Already hit by its difficulties in Ukraine, Olympic then faced the deepening global economic crisis. As attendance rates dropped sharply, Olympic was forced to shutter a significant number of its casinos. The restructuring of the group's portfolio included the closing of 18 of its 36 casinos in Estonia, 12 casinos in Lativa, 6 in Lithuania, and 7 in Romania. Including the loss of the Ukraine casinos, the company's total dropped to 66 casinos. Its revenues shrank accordingly, falling back to EEK 1.7 billion ($148.10 million) for the year.

The worst of the recession appeared to be over by the beginning of 2010. Olympic then began targeting a new horizon, as the Estonian government moved toward implementing a legislative framework for the country's online gaming sector. Following the passage of the new law, which blocked nonregistered companies from operating in Estonia, Olympic launched its own gaming Web site in 2010, Olympic-online.com, featuring casino and poker games. Olympic Entertainment Group remained committed to its strategy of becoming a leading player in the Baltic and Central and Eastern European regions in the years to come.

M. L. Cohen

PRINCIPAL SUBSIDIARIES

Ahti SIA; Casino Polonia Wrocław Sp. Z.o.o. (Poland); Mecom Grupp UAB (Lithuania); Nordic Gaming AS; Olympic Casino Bel IP (Belarus); Olympic Casino Bucharest S.r.l. (Romania); Olympic Casino Eesti AS; Olympic Casino Group Baltija UAB (Lithuania); Olympic Casino Latvia SIA; Olympic Casino Slovakia S.r.o. (Slovakia); Olympic Casino Ukraine ToV.

PRINCIPAL DIVISIONS

Casinos; Casino Bars; Hotels.

PRINCIPAL OPERATING UNITS

Belarusian Segment; Estonian Segment; Latvian Segment; Lithuanian Segment; Polish Segment; Romanian Segment; Slovakian Segment.

PRINCIPAL COMPETITORS

Casinos Austria AG; Casinos Poland Sp. z.o.o.; Czech Casinos A.S.; Escor Casinos and Entertainment S.A.; Estoril-Sol SGPS S.A.; Raha-automaatiyhdistys; SAB-Miller plc; Société Française de Casinos S.A.

FURTHER READING

Angioni, Giovanni, "Olympic Online—The First Estonian Online Casino and Poker Room," *Estonia Free Press*, February 10, 2010.

Brettell, Ashley, "Olympic Cashes in Ukrainian Chips," *Baltic Times*, July 15, 2009.

"Bucharest Hotel Hosts New Olympic Casino," *Casino Journal*, June 2009, p. 19.

"Estonian Olympic Entertainment Group Debuts on Warsaw Stock Exchange," *Poland Business News*, September 26, 2007.

"Estonia to Start Blocking Foreign Gambling Sites," *Gambling Domains News*, March 13, 2010.

"Olympic Expands in Ukraine with Five-Casino Buy," *IGWB*, September 2007, p. 10.

"Olympic Reopens Second Casino in Ukrainian Capital," *IGWB*, May 2008, p. 9.

ONVEST

Onvest Oy

Mittalinja 1
Vantaa, FI-01260
Finland
Telephone: (+358 020) 48 55 111
Fax: (+358 020) 48 55 464
Web site: http://www.onvest.fi

Private Company
Incorporated: 1997
Employees: 4,951
Sales: EUR 1.53 billion ($2.1 billion) (2009 est.)
NAICS: 423610 Electrical Apparatus and Equipment, Wiring Supplies, and Related Equipment Merchant Wholesalers; 423740 Refrigeration Equipment and Supplies Merchant Wholesalers

■ ■ ■

Onvest Oy is a Finland-based, family-owned holding company focused around two main businesses. The larger of these is Onninen Oy, a leading wholesaler and supplier of technical wholesale materials and services, especially HEPAC (heating, plumbing, and air conditioning) components, systems, and equipment. Onninen is a leader in its market in Finland, and among the leading companies in the Baltic Rim, with subsidiaries in Norway, Sweden, Estonia, Latvia, Lithuania, and Poland. The company also operates subsidiaries in Russia, and in Kazakhstan since 2009. The company operates nearly 150 wholesale outlets primarily under the Onninen and Onninen Express names, including 42 sites in Finland. In 2009 international operations ac-

counted for 50.6 percent of Onninen's revenues, which in turn generated 87 percent of Onvest's total revenues of EUR 1.5 billion ($2.1 billion).

Onvest's other main business area focuses on providing construction, renovation, and property maintenance services through subsidiary Are Group. This company operates mainly in Finland but also has a subsidiary in St. Petersburg, Russia. Are Group added 12 percent to Onvest's total sales. Onvest also includes two investment subsidiaries, which operate in the long-term investments and security trading; and a property development division, with holdings in Finland, Sweden, Poland, and Russia. Leading Onvest since 2000 is Maarit Toivanen-Koivisto, a member of the founding Onninen family.

PLUMBING BUSINESS ORIGINS IN 1913

Onvest's growth into one of Finland's leading family-owned holding companies, and a leading player in the wholesale HEPAC (heating, plumbing, and air conditioning) materials sector in the Baltic Rim stemmed from a small plumbing business founded by Alfred Onninen in Turku, Finland, in 1913. Onninen called his company Wesi- ja lämpöjohtoliike O/Y and initially focused on providing plumbing installation services.

Onninen's company grew quickly and launched its first operations in the wholesale sector in the 1920s, supplying plumbers and building professionals in the area. This business grew even more rapidly than Onnin-

COMPANY PERSPECTIVES

Principles. Long-termism. The principle behind Onvest's business is steady growth and high solvency. The company is developed in the long perspective, factoring in the economic realities. Retaining ownership within the family is a choice that communicates long-term commitment. Responsibility. Responsibility makes itself apparent in the strong ethical principles which guide the Group's operations. Responsibility is emphasised in the company's human resource policy, in its long-term relationships with the surrounding society, and in the goal of responding to the customers' changing needs. Development. To stay a reliable and valued partner, constant improvement of operations are required. Retaining competitiveness demands the ability to innovate as well as the ability to adopt new things rapidly.

en's installation activities. Onninen recognized the potential for further growth beyond the Turku area. This led him to Helsinki, where he set up a new company for his wholesale business, called Vesijohtoliike Onninen Oy, in 1927.

Onninen continued to operate his plumbing contracting business during this period. The move to Helsinki enabled his wholesale business to grow still more quickly, however. By the end of the 1930s wholesale had become Onninen's primary business. The reconstruction of Finland following World War II presented new growth opportunities for the company, prompting Onninen to begin extending its operations on a national scale. Onninen began opening offices in many of Finland's major cities and towns through the end of the 1940s and into the 1950s.

Following Alfred Onninen's death in 1950 the company remained in family hands, with son-in-law Martti Auriala taking over as the group's managing director. The increasing sophistication of building heating and plumbing systems, along with the introduction of new air conditioning systems, led the company to develop its wholesale business into a full-fledged materials services group. The company not only supplied plumbers, but also building contractors and industrial installations. Onninen also became a major provider of materials for municipal engineering and other public works projects.

FIRST EXPORTS

A new generation took over the leadership of the company when Erkki J. Toivanen replaced his father-in-law as managing director in 1956. Toivanen became responsible for the company's growth into a truly national business, expanding its network throughout Finland during the 1960s. The company also changed its name during this time, becoming Vesionninen. The company extended its warehousing capacity during the decade, opening a new site in Hyvankiää. Beginning in 1969 Vesionninen then extended its operations into the newly emerging ventilation market.

In 1972 the company changed its name again, to Onninen. By then the company had grown to more than 2,000 employees and had become a leading player in Finland's wholesale HVAC (heating, ventilation, and air conditioning) and plumbing sectors. The company extended its range again, incorporating electrical wholesale and contracting services starting in 1972. During the 1970s Onninen also took advantage of Finland's proximity to the Soviet Union and the long-standing trade relationship between the two countries, launching its first exports to Russia. By the end of the decade Onninen's export operations had extended to a number of Middle East markets as well.

NEW FORMAT AND NEW MARKETS

Back in Finland, Onninen explored new market opportunities. In 1983 the company opened its first cash-and-carry outlet, called Pikaonninen, in Hämeenlinna. The success of this new wholesale format, which provided a one-stop shopping point for a range of technical products for the professional sector, encouraged Onninen to expand the concept into other Finnish markets.

By the beginning of the 21st century Onninen boasted more than 40 centers throughout the country. The cash-and-carry format later also supported the successful extension of the company's operations into the Swedish and Norwegian markets. In the meantime, Onninen claimed the leading position in the Finnish HEPAC sector during the 1980s.

Onninen continued to build up its own infrastructure at this time. The company launched construction of a new district warehouse and headquarters complex in Vantaa during the 1980s. This extension enabled Onninen to begin preparations for its wider expansion in the 1990s.

The late 1980s were marked by the collapse of the Soviet Union and the emergence of new market-based

KEY DATES

1913: Alfred Onninen founds a plumbing contracting business in Turku, Finland.

1927: Onninen adds a wholesale business, Vesijohtoliike Onninen Oy, in Helsinki.

1960s: The company changes its name to Vesionninen Oy.

1972: The company adds electrical contracting and wholesale, begins exports to Russia and other markets, and later changes its name to Onninen Oy.

1983: Onninen opens its first cash-and-carry center.

1992: Onninen establishes its first foreign business, in Tallinn, Estonia.

1993: Onninen acquires its main rival, OY Huber AB.

1997: The company restructures under a holding company, Onvest Oy.

2000: Onvest enters the Polish market with several acquisitions.

2009: Onvest enters the Kazakhstan market.

economies in the so-called Baltic Rim, comprising Estonia, Latvia, and Lithuania, but also including Poland and Russia. Finland's proximity to these markets made them a natural target for Onninen's expansion of international sales beyond exports. In the 1990s Estonia emerged as the most economically and politically stable market in the region. As a result, Onninen opened its first Baltic-region sales office in that country in 1992, in the city of Tallinn. In 1994 Onninen expanded its Estonian presence with the opening of a 4,200-square-meter warehouse in Tallinn. Two years later the group opened its first cash-and-carry outlet in Estonia, in Tartu.

By then Onninen had also entered Latvia, opening an office and an Onninen Express center in Riga in 1994. By 1995 the group's operations there had expanded to include its own dedicated 1,500-square-meter warehouse facility. Onninen also added its first Russian locations in 1994, and a site in Vilna, Lithuania, in 1995.

In the 1990s Erkki Toivanen turned over leadership of the company to Timo Peltola, who became president and CEO, while Toivanen remained as chairman of the company. Under Peltola, Onninen launched a new and highly significant expansion effort. Acquisitions then played a major role in the group's growth strategy,

including the group's successful expansion into the Swedish and Norwegian markets.

BECOMING ONVEST IN 1997

Onninen, like the rest of the HEPAC sector, struggled through Finland's deep economic recession at the beginning of the 1990s. The period also brought its share of opportunity for the company, however, as it completed a number of early acquisitions, including Ilmaexpertit Oy in 1992. By 1993 Finland's wholesale HEPAC sector was dominated by four large-scale companies, led by Onninen, which controlled a 39 percent share of the market. However, it had become clear by this time that the country's small size was inadequate to support the operations of four major wholesale groups. As a result, the sector began a consolidation drive. In October 1993 Onninen reached an agreement to acquire its main rival, Oy Huber AB. The merger created a true national heavyweight, with a market share of nearly 70 percent.

Another significant acquisition came early in that decade, when Onninen acquired a controlling stake in Are Group, a leading Finnish construction, renovation, and property services provider. Are had been part of Hantec, itself part of Novera Yhtyma. However, both Hantec and Novera Yhtyma had been forced to declare bankruptcy amid the recession. Are had been founded in 1924 as an electrical supplier in Jyväskylä, changing its name to Are Oy in 1938. The company extended its operations into contracting, launching an international division in 1969, and then offering its own exports to the Russian and Middle Eastern markets.

By 1995 Onninen had completed its acquisition of Are. The company restructured its own operations at that time, transferring its contracting operations, including Are, into a new company, also called Are Oy. This restructuring soon led to a wider reorganization of Onninen's operations, which by then had expanded to include 10 subsidiaries. In 1997 the company created a new holding company, Onvest Oy.

The group's subsidiary operations were then placed under two primary subsidiaries, the larger Onninen, for the company's technical materials division, and Are, which oversaw its Finnish construction and contracting business. Onninen also maintained two smaller divisions for its investment operations, including a securities trading arm and a property development business. Erkki Toivanen took the position as Onvest's first chairman and CEO.

ACQUISITION DRIVEN IN THE
21ST CENTURY

Onvest oversaw a growing number of acquisitions, primarily carried out through Onninen. The group's purchases included the steel division of Teraskonttori Oy in 1997, and Electrian, Danfoss Prokyl, and Hydronkon Winkiel in 1998. Are Oy also grew during this period, buying Ensto Oy's Trace Heating unit in March 2000. Also that year, the company launched a new cash-and-carry store format, Onninen Express, which the company rolled out to its smaller centers in Finland and abroad.

The company's acquisitions strategy targeted the group's international operations in the first decade of the new century. Poland received much of the company's international expansion energy, as a series of acquisitions were completed there. The company acquired seven Polish companies between 2000 and 2001, starting with two Wrocław-based companies, Felis SA and Elektrohurt, and Warsaw's Alinex Sp zoo, in September 2000. Other acquisitions included Elmetal Sp zoo, and ABC sp zoo, in Warsaw. Onninen also reinforced its Swedish operations, buying Elef AB's Electrical division in 2000.

That year marked a change in management for the family-owned company following the death of Erkki Toivanen. His place was taken by his daughter, Maarit Toivanen-Koivisto, who became the first woman to head the family group since its founding. Toivanen-Koivisto had not been groomed for the position, however. As she told *FBNeNews*, "My father allowed me to work in the business but never encouraged me to think of myself as the potential leader. He was of the generation that went through World War II and had quite traditional views on the place of women. He never told me very much about the business that he led for over 40 years."

NEW MARKETS IN 2009

Onvest renewed the expansion of its Finnish operations under Toivanen-Koivisto. The company entered the manufacturing sector in 2001, buying Belos AB Oy, a family-owned producer of materials handling systems. Are also expanded, buying building contractor Sensum Oy, and Kanberg Oy, a sprinkler and fire control systems wholesaler, in 2002. Are expanded into Jyvaskyla in 2008 with the purchase of the construction division of Rakennusliike Pelkonen Oy.

In the meantime, Onninen itself had been growing strongly. In 2002 the company added Eilag Teknikk, part of Expert Eilag ASA, establishing an electronic equipment wholesale operation in Norway. The following year, Onninen added the Finnish steel wholesale division of Algol Pharma Oy, based in Espoo. The company later followed this purchase with the acquisition in 2007 of Telekno Oy, based in Helsinki, which focused on the precision equipment wholesale market.

Onvest's operations soared throughout the decade, rising from EUR 951 million in 2001 to nearly EUR 2 billion by the end of 2008. Toivanen-Koivisto won recognition for this achievement, and in 2006 was named one of the most influential women in Finland. However, Onvest found itself hard hit by the growing global economic crisis at the end of the decade. By the end of 2009, both of the group's core businesses had seen a sharp drop in revenues, causing the group's total sales to drop back to EUR 1.5 billion for the year. The company managed to contain its losses, posting a net loss of EUR 300,000.

Onvest forged ahead with its growth despite the difficult economic climate. The group's international operations had by then grown to account for nearly 51 percent of its total. The company continued to target further growth abroad, launching operations in Kazakhstan in 2009. The company also expanded its manufacturing capacity, building a plastic pipe production unit at an existing factory in Moscow. This unit launched production in 2009, and expected to boost its capacity to 1.5 million meters during 2010. Onvest, led by the Onninen family, had grown from a small plumbing business to become the Baltic Rim region's technical materials leader in the second decade of the 21st century.

M. L. Cohen

PRINCIPAL SUBSIDIARIES

Onninen Oy; Are Oy; AS Onninen (Estonia); Onninen AB (Sweden); Onninen Polska Sp. z o.o. (Poland); SIA Onninen LAT (Latvia); UAB Onninen LIT (Lithuania); ZAO Onninen SPb (Russia); ZAO Tec Optom Onninen (Russia); Onninen-sijoitus Oy; Onnivaatio Oy.

PRINCIPAL DIVISIONS

Technical Wholesale Services; Services for Contracting, Maintenance, and Renovation of Properties; Investment Activities; Property Activities.

PRINCIPAL OPERATING UNITS

Onninen Oy; Are Oy.

PRINCIPAL COMPETITORS

ElektroSkandia Oy; Hedengren Oy Ab; Helvar Merca Oy Ab; Kauko-Telko Oy; Kontino Oy Ab; Machinery Ltd.; Philips Ab.; Siemens Osakeyhtioe; SLO Oy.

FURTHER READING

"Estonian Fiberoptical Cable Maker Baltronic OU Buys Teletekno Balti from Finns," *Estonian Trade and Investment Agency,* April 14, 2010.

"Onninen Oy Enters Exclusive Contract Negotiations with EDB," *Europe Intelligence Wire*, July 6, 2004.

"Onninen Oy Launches Plastic Pipes Plant in Russia," *Chemical Business Newsbase*, September 28, 2009.

"Onvest Oy and Maarit Toivanen-Koivisto," *FBNeNews*, February 11, 2010.

Quinn, John Paul, "Promise in the Baltic Rim," *Industrial Distribution*, May 1999.

Orchard Supply Hardware Stores Corporation

6450 Via Del Oro
San Jose, California 95119
U.S.A.
Telephone: (408) 281-3500
Fax: (408) 629-7174
Web site: http://www.osh.com

Wholly Owned Subsidiary of Sears Holdings Corporation
Incorporated: 1986
Employees: 7,000
Sales: $551.2 million (2008 est.)
NAICS: 444110 Home Centers; 444130 Hardware Stores

■ ■ ■

Orchard Supply Hardware Stores Corporation is one of the largest hardware and garden retail chains operating in California. During 2010 the Orchard Supply chain consisted of 85 stores that averaged 40,000 square feet. Featuring over 45,000 home, garden, and nursery products, Orchard Supply Hardware's stores are designed to attract customers seeking to complete the small tasks associated with repairing and maintaining a home. The company's stores, known for providing high levels of customer service, occupy a niche in the highly competitive California home improvement market that positions the stores as an alternative to the larger, warehouse-style retail home centers. Sears, Roebuck and Co. purchased the company in 1996. In April 2010 Sears Holdings Corp. held an 80.1 percent stake in Orchard Supply Hardware.

EARLY HISTORY

The company was established in 1931 as a supply cooperative for farmers residing in the Santa Clara, California, area, its formation occurring as the cooperative movement in the United States was in full swing. The company remained a farmers cooperative for the next two decades, and then began selling general hardware merchandise during the 1950s, a retail category that would be the foundation for the company's business for the next half century and beyond.

Throughout much of its early history, Orchard Supply operated as a modestly sized enterprise, a hardware store indistinguishable from the thousands of other hardware stores scattered throughout the country. For decades the company confined its operating territory to the northern California area, restricting itself to its home territory and operating as the quintessential "mom-and-pop" business. In comparison with the frenetic growth that would characterize the company during the 1990s, Orchard Supply pursued a serene and staid approach to business during its formative decades.

OWNERSHIP CHANGES: 1979–89

By the late 1970s, after shedding the cooperative vestiges of its past and moving into the retail sale of general hardware goods, Orchard Supply comprised seven stores, all located in northern California. W.R. Grace & Co. purchased Orchard Supply from its original owners in 1979. The size of the retail chain more than doubled during the next seven years, as expansion picked up pace under the aegis of an owner with deeper financial pockets. Orchard Supply was a 19-store company by July 1986, when Santa Monica-based Wickes Companies, Inc., acquired the retailer from W.R. Grace & Co.

The transaction was completed before the arrival of the individual who would lead Orchard Supply toward accelerated growth and prominence in the home improvement industry. Under the guiding hand of Maynard Jenkins, Orchard Supply ended a half-century of measured growth to embark on a future that would position the company as an industry leader a decade later.

Born in Orange, California, during the early years of World War II, Jenkins grew up in nearby Huntington Beach and attended Orange Coast College. The Southern California native spent his early professional career as a J.C. Penney management trainee. Jenkins later jumped ship to a competitor, spending time working for Sears, Roebuck and Co. before settling down at the Gemco division of Lucky Stores.

Jenkins spent 15 years at Gemco learning the retail trade and then was hired as president and chief operating officer of a 107-unit chain of drugstores operated by Seattle-based Pay 'N Save Stores in 1985. After a year at the dominant Pacific Northwest retail chain, Jenkins switched employers once again, joining Orchard Supply shortly after Wickes Companies acquired the 19-unit hardware retailer from W.R. Grace & Co.

By the time Jenkins joined Orchard Supply, the chain had added two stores to become a 21-store company. This was the starting point of the Jenkins era, a 10-year term that would witness the expansion of the Orchard Supply chain to 60 stores. Before this expansion occurred, however, Orchard Supply underwent several more ownership changes as the company was passed from parent company to parent company, led to private ownership, and then toward public ownership.

JENKINS SPURS GROWTH

Exactly two years after the arrival of Jenkins, Wickes Companies was purchased by Blackstone Capital Partners and Wasserstein Perella Partners, a transaction that also gave Orchard Supply new owners. As far as

Orchard Supply was concerned, the relationship lasted less than a year. In June 1989 Jenkins and other Orchard Supply management sought to restore the retailer's independence, enlisting the help of a limited partnership organized by the Los Angeles-based investment firm of Freeman, Spogli & Co. The result was a $134 million leveraged buyout that returned Orchard Supply to private ownership.

Coming off of $255 million in sales in 1988, Orchard Supply generated $280 million in sales during the year of the leveraged buyout. The financial increase was not an anomaly during the first years of Jenkins's influence over the fortunes of Orchard Supply. Between 1987 and the beginning of the 1990s Orchard Supply had added 10 stores and had posted consecutive record sales and earnings levels. By the beginning of the 1990s, Jenkins was heading a 33-unit chain as president and chief executive officer, ready to lead the company toward further expansion.

Although Orchard Supply was a nearly 60-year-old business as it entered the 1990s, longevity would give no retail competitor an edge during the decade ahead. In addition to the sweeping changes that had revolutionized the home improvement retail industry and dramatically altered the formula for success, the industry had become one of the most hotly contested businesses in the country. Led by Atlanta-based Home Depot, Inc., and Fullerton, California-based HomeClub, Inc., the retail home improvement industry was dominated by massive warehouse stores and discount pricing, two of the determinative characteristics of success that prevailed as the 1990s began.

TARGETING THE "FIX-IT" SHOPPER

Despite its promise as a rising contender, Orchard Supply adopted neither of these characteristics. The retail chain emphasized merchandise selection and customer service over pricing. It eschewed the vast floor spaces used by its most intimidating rivals, opting instead to stock twice the number of products in half the square footage typical of industry stalwarts Home Depot and HomeClub. Instead of attempting to attract the classic "do-it-yourself" customers who remodeled their own kitchens and bathrooms, Orchard Supply targeted the "fix-it" shopper, or those customers concerned with completing the smaller tasks associated with repairing and maintaining a home.

Orchard Supply thus distinguished itself from its larger competition as well as its scores of smaller competitors. Occupying the middle tier of home improvement retailing, Orchard Supply was positioned

KEY DATES

■

1931: The company is established as a supply cooperative for farmers.

1979: W.R. Grace & Co. purchases Orchard Supply from its original owners.

1986: Santa Monica-based Wickes Companies, Inc., acquires Orchard Supply; Maynard Jenkins is named CEO.

1989: A $134 million leveraged buyout returns Orchard Supply to private ownership.

1993: Orchard Supply goes public; seven former Builders Emporium stores are acquired.

1995: Five new stores open.

1996: Sears, Roebuck and Co. purchases the company.

1997: Jenkins leaves the company.

2005: Sears sells a 19.9 percent stake in Orchard Supply to Ares Management LLC.

2006: Orchard Supply celebrates its 75th anniversary.

midway between independent hardware stores and the much larger warehouse home centers, giving the company a viable market niche that would serve as its foundation in the future. The company at this time generated roughly half of its sales from female customers, a rare phenomenon in the home improvement industry. This exception from the norm was attributed to the differences between Orchard Supply Stores and the larger, more impersonal warehouse stores. Typically, home center stores derived their greatest percentage of sales from lumber and building materials, whereas Orchard Supply relied on plumbing products, housewares, and the 10,000-square-foot nursery that adjoined each unit to generate the bulk of its sales.

EXPANSION CONTINUES

It was this successful and unique retailing formula that Jenkins sought to expand throughout California during the 1990s. At the beginning of the decade, all Orchard Supply stores, which were typically 40,000-square-foot locations with 10,000-square-foot nurseries, were located within 300 miles of the company's 282,000-square-foot distribution center in San Jose, a territory that embraced northern and central California. As Jenkins charted the company's expansion in 1990, he intended to restrict expansion to California, and to open between two and five stores per year during the ensuing five years. Jenkins

was envisioning a 50-unit Orchard Supply chain by 1995.

The expansion projections announced by Jenkins in 1990 were met nearly precisely. By 1992 Orchard Supply's distribution center in San Jose had become too small to service the company's pressing need to keep its stores' shelves fully stocked. A new, 350,000-square-foot warehouse was established in Tracey, California, giving the company a massive warehouse that was situated equidistant from its expanding chain of stores in central and northern California. By 1993 the company operated more than 40 stores. Nevertheless, the need to expand further continued to prod Jenkins and the rest of Orchard Supply management. The company needed cash to fund this expansion, so in April 1993 Orchard Supply became a publicly traded company, completing an initial public offering of 3.8 million shares of common stock at $14 per share.

The cash raised from the conversion to public ownership would be needed as Orchard Supply picked up the pace of its expansion and came head-to-head with the industry's largest and most successful home improvement chains. Sales for fiscal 1993 climbed to $365 million, continuing the company's impressive string of annual revenue gains, and net income rose to $33,000 after being in the red for two years. However, before the year's financial results were announced in January 1994, Jenkins completed a deal that greatly overshadowed the importance of the encouraging financial figures. The contracts signed at the end of 1993 paved the way for Orchard Supply's entry into the most lucrative home improvement market in the United States.

ENTRANCE INTO SOUTHERN CALIFORNIA: 1993

In December 1993 Orchard Supply acquired seven former Builders Emporium stores, paying $20 million for the properties. For Jenkins, the price was worth it because six of the stores were located in the Los Angeles area and another near Santa Barbara, giving the company entry into the Southern California market for the first time. As Builders Emporium stores, each unit had generated $10 million in sales annually, a volume the stores were expected to maintain once they were converted to the Orchard Supply format. The acquisition provided the momentum to propel the company toward accelerated growth.

Ranging between 29,000 square feet and 71,000 square feet, the former Builders Emporium locations were converted into Orchard Supply stores during the first few months of 1994. Meanwhile, Jenkins began laying out ambitious expansion plans for the coming years. Looking ahead, he anticipated opening either 14 or 15 stores in 1994 and then 10 stores per year from 1995 forward, as he sought to turn what industry observers were hailing as the high-service alternative to warehouse stores into one of the massive chains vying for supremacy in the fiercely competitive market. By the end of 1994, 14 new stores had been added to the Orchard Supply chain, lifting sales for the year to $441.6 million and net income to more than $1 million.

POSITIONED FOR FURTHER GROWTH

The pace of expansion ebbed considerably in 1995, when five Orchard Supply stores were added to the chain, but the company's financial growth picked up the slack, rising robustly as stores were added to the lucrative Southern California market. Net income in 1995 (the company's 1996 fiscal year) rose from $1.1 million to $10.4 million, and sales increased 21 percent, reaching $532.4 million. Further expansion was needed to maintain this rate of growth, as was the money required to fund the establishment of new stores. In March 1996 the company sold $11 million shares of stock, providing it with the resources to continue dotting the California map with Orchard Supply stores.

With the money raised through the March 1996 stock offering, Orchard Supply planned to open between five and 10 new stores in 1996 and another five to 10 stores annually for the next several years, nearly all of which were expected to be located in Southern California. To support this growth, plans for the establishment in 1997 of a second distribution facility, also in Southern California, were under way as the company headed toward the late 1990s. By April 1996 Orchard Supply was a 60-unit chain, nearly three times the size of the company Jenkins joined a decade earlier. As Jenkins surveyed the road ahead from this point in the company's history, his confidence was high, although not overly optimistic.

THE SEARS PURCHASE: 1996

By this time, Orchard Supply was known as the most successful regional chain of midsized home centers in the United States and its history of financial success left it well positioned among its peers. It was at this time that the company caught the eye of retailer Sears, Roebuck and Co. Sears was looking to expand its hardware offerings and selected Orchard Supply as its growth vehicle. Sears offered $415 million for the company in a deal that would double its hardware revenues and give it

a substantial presence in California. For Orchard Supply, ownership by a national retailer promised faster growth.

Orchard Supply Hardware entered the next chapter of its history without Jenkins at the helm. The executive who had led the company through its successful growth period left in 1997 and was replaced by Gary Crittenden, a Sears executive who was put in charge of the Sears Hardware chain as well as Orchard Supply. Sears attempted to take the Orchard Supply name national in February 1997 when it rebranded and converted several of its Sears Hardware stores in Ohio to the Orchard Supply format. The tests proved unsuccessful and Sears opted to focus on growth of the Orchard Supply chain in its home market of California.

MOVING INTO THE 21ST CENTURY

Orchard Supply Hardware entered the new millennium with approximately 80 stores spread throughout California. During 2000 the company launched the largest remodel in its history to date at its Alum Rock location in San Jose. The store, which then stood at 62,000 square feet, opened in May of that year.

During 2004 company management announced plans to double the size of the then 84-store Orchard Supply chain and expand outside of California. Shortly after the growth plans were made public, Sears and retailer Kmart Holding Corp. announced a merger that would create one of the largest retailers in the country. Completed in 2005, the union created Sears Holdings Corp. and was structured to boost the sales of the Sears and Kmart chains. When the dust settled on the deal, Sears began to consider options for its Orchard Supply chain that included a possible public offering or a sale.

Sears opted for the latter and in 2005 sold a 19.9 percent stake in Orchard Supply to Ares Management LLC, a Los Angeles-based private-equity firm. Despite Orchard Supply's expansion plans, only two Orchard Supply Hardware stores were opened that year while five locations were remodeled. The company celebrated its 75th anniversary in 2006. Orchard Supply marked the occasion by partnering with the California Department of Education to build gardens at schools near Orchard Supply stores.

By this time the company was headed by CEO Rob Lynch. The faltering U.S. economy and weak sales in the retail sector forced the company to put its aggressive expansion plans on hold during this period. It instead refocused efforts on maintaining its reputation for customer service and wide selection, and slowly began testing new products such as home appliances and earth-friendly and energy efficient products. The company opened its 86th location in Vacaville, California, in 2006.

The company's store count increased to 88 in 2009 with the opening of its first store in Santa Rosa in Sonoma County. While retail conditions remained harsh at that time, Orchard Supply was determined to succeed. As CEO Lynch told *Do-It-Yourself Retailing* magazine in 2006, "Our original founder said, 'Take good care of your customers and they will take good care of you.' We continue to live by that motto today." Orchard Supply Hardware's commitment to its customers would no doubt continue to be the driving force behind the company for years to come.

Jeffrey L. Covell
Updated, Christina M. Stansell

PRINCIPAL COMPETITORS

The Home Depot, Inc.; Lowe's Companies, Inc.; Wal-Mart Stores, Inc.

FURTHER READING

Altman, Brad, "Orchard Blooms in California Sun," *Chain Store Age Executive with Shopping Center Age,* May 1990, p. 30.

Canlen, Brae, "The OSH Alternative," *Home Channel News,* July 17, 2006.

———, "OSH Sells Stake to Equity Firm," *Home Channel News,* October 17, 2005.

Davey, Tom, "Orchard Supply Wants Four Hardware Stores in This Area," *Business Journal Serving Greater Sacramento,* December 10, 1990, p. 2.

Desjardins, Doug, "Calling All Eco-Friendly Products," *DSN Retailing Today,* March 19, 2007.

Hart, Steve, "Gradual Rebound for Retail," *Press Democrat,* September 18, 2009.

Kauffman-Peters, Heather, "Growing in New Areas: Orchard Supply Hardware Celebrates 75 Years of Serving Customers," *Do-It-Yourself Retailing,* May 1, 2006.

"OSH's Handyman in Chief," *Chain Store Age,* May 1, 2006.

Shuster, Laurie, "Getting Serious about Casual Furniture," *Home Improvement Market,* June 1996, p. G6.

———, "Orchard Raises Cash to Expand in So. California," *Home Improvement Market,* April 1996, p. 10.

———, "Orchard Supply Hardware: Sears Eyes California Prize," *Home Improvement Market,* September 1, 1996.

Petroliam Nasional Bhd (PETRONAS)

Tower 1, PETRONAS Twin Towers
Kuala Lumpur City Centre
Kuala Lumpur, 50088
Malaysia
Telephone: (603) 2051-5000
Fax: (603) 2026-5050
Web site: http://www.petronas.com

State-Owned Company
Incorporated: 1974
Employees: 16,000
Sales: MYR 264.2 billion ($77 billion) (2009)
NAICS: 211111 Crude Petroleum and Natural Gas
    Extraction; 324110 Petroleum Refineries

■ ■ ■

Petroliam Nasional Bhd, or PETRONAS, operates as a state-owned entity controlling Malaysia's oil and gas resources. The company and its subsidiaries are involved in nearly every aspect of the industry, including upstream exploration, oil and gas production, downstream oil refining, marketing and distributing petroleum products, gas processing, gas transmission pipeline network operations, liquefied natural gas (LNG) marketing, and petrochemical manufacturing and marketing.

As a member of the *Fortune* Global 500, PETRO-NAS has operations in over 30 countries around the world and is involved in approximately 70 international exploration and production upstream ventures. Nearly 40 percent of its revenues stem from its overseas operations. During 2009 Malaysia's hydrocarbon reserves were 20.18 billion barrels of oil equivalent (boe) while the company's international reserves in Africa, Southeast Asia, the Middle East, and Central Asia were 6.84 billion boe. PETRONAS produced a total of 9.2 million tons of petrochemical products during fiscal 2009.

ORIGINS

PETRONAS was not the first company to extract oil or gas in Malaysia. Oil was first found in what was to be Malaysia at the end of the 19th century, and in 1910 Royal Dutch/Shell first drilled for oil in Sarawak, then a British colony. It was still the only oil company in the area in 1963, when the Federation of Malaya, having achieved independence from Britain six years before, absorbed Sarawak and Sabah, both on the island of Borneo, and became Malaysia. The authorities in the two new states retained their links with Royal Dutch/Shell, which brought Malaysia's first offshore oil field onstream in 1968.

Meanwhile, the federal government turned to Esso, Continental Oil, and Mobil, licensing exploration off the state of Trengganu, in the Malay Peninsula, the most populous region and the focus of federal power. However, by 1974 only Esso was still in the area. It made its first discoveries of natural gas in that year and then rapidly made Trengganu a bigger producer of oil than either Sarawak or Sabah. By 1974 Malaysia's output of crude oil stood at about 81,000 barrels per day.

COMPANY PERSPECTIVES

■

Our mission is to be a Leading Oil and Gas Multinational of Choice.

GOVERNMENT CONCERNS

Several factors converged in the early 1970s to prompt the Malaysian government to set up a state oil and gas company, as first proposed in its Five-Year Plan published in 1971. Power in the world oil industry had begun to shift away from the majors, a small group of private oil concerns which then controlled more than 90 percent of the oil trade, toward the Organization of Petroleum Exporting Countries (OPEC), as well as a proliferation of new private and state companies joining in the search for reserves. By 1985 the majors, reduced in number from seven to five, would be producing less than 20 percent of the world total. It seemed that Malaysia would either have to join the trend or continue to leave its oil and gas entirely to Royal Dutch/Shell and Esso, multinational corporations necessarily attuned to the requirements of their directors and shareholders, rather than to the priorities of the government of a developing country.

An agreement between Malaysia and Indonesia, signed in 1969, had settled doubts and disputes about each country's claims over territorial waters and offshore resources at a time when both were heavily indebted to Organization for Economic Cooperation and Development governments and banks as well as to the International Monetary Fund and the World Bank. Setting up a state oil and gas company, through which the government could get international capital but avoid tangling with foreign oil companies or governments, had worked for Indonesia, and thus was deemed appropriate for Malaysia as well. The oil crisis of 1973–74 made the government even more aware of Malaysia's dependence on foreign oil and foreign capital in general.

A WORKABLE COMPROMISE

Another factor in the decision was that the technology had recently been developed for extensive exploration and drilling offshore. The local geography included a combination of broad basins of sedimentary rock with calm and shallow waters around the Sunda Shelf, making exploration for gas and oil relatively easier and more successful than in most other areas of the world. Malaysian crude turned out to be mostly high quality with low sulfur content.

A final and crucial factor in the creation of PETRONAS, and its continuation in much the same form since, was the political stability of Malaysia. Since the restoration of parliament in 1971, the country was ruled by the National Front (Barisan Nasional), the heirs to the Alliance Party which had been dominant from 1957 to 1969 and the originators in 1971 of the New Economic Policy, which was designed to improve the economic position of Bumiputras (native Malays) relative to Chinese and Indian Malaysians and to foreign corporations. The difficulties this policy caused for foreign companies and investors were outweighed by the benefits they believed they gained from Malaysia's political stability.

The Malaysian government chose to create a state company, rather than using taxes, production limits, leasing, or other familiar instruments of supervision. The government wanted, and needed, the cooperation of the majors but also sought to assert national rights over the use of the country's resources. A state company, having both supervisory powers over the majors and production activities of its own, was a workable compromise between allowing the majors full rein and excluding them, along with their capital and expertise, altogether.

PETRONAS TAKES SHAPE: 1974

PETRONAS was established in August 1974 and operates under the terms of the Petroleum Development Act passed in October 1974. It was modeled on PERT AMINA, the Indonesian state oil and gas company founded in 1971 in succession to PERMINA, which had been set up in 1958. According to the 1971 plan, PETRONAS's goals would be to safeguard national sovereignty over oil and gas reserves, to plan for both present and future national need for oil and gas, to take part in distributing and marketing petroleum and petrochemical products at reasonable prices, to encourage provision of plants, equipment, and services by Malaysian companies, to produce nitrogenous fertilizers, and to spread the benefits of the petroleum industry throughout the nation.

Having created PETRONAS, the government then had to choose what forms its dealings with private oil companies would take. PETRONAS's first move was to negotiate the replacement of the leases granted to Royal Dutch/Shell on Borneo and to Esso in the peninsula with production-sharing contracts (PSCs), which remained the favored instrument, alongside joint ventures, ever since. These first contracts came into effect in 1976. Allowing for royalties to both federal and state governments, and for cost recovery arrangements, they stipulated that the remainder would go 70 percent

KEY DATES

1974: The Malaysian government creates PETRONAS.

1983: PETRONAS enters the refining and distribution market.

1985: The first stage of the Peninsular Gas Utilization Project is completed.

1990: PETRONAS begins oil exploration outside of Malaysia in Myanmar.

1994: Subsidiary PETRONAS Dagangan Bhd lists on the Kuala Lumpur Stock Exchange.

1997: Company headquarters are moved to the 88-story PETRONAS Twin Towers.

2003: The Malaysia liquefied natural gas (LNG) Tiga Plant opens.

2005: The company and its partners deliver first LNG cargo to Asean LNG Trading Co.

2007: Malaysia's first deepwater field, Kikeh, goes onstream.

2008: Company purchases Star Energy plc and a 40 percent stake in the Gladstone LNG project.

to PETRONAS and 30 percent to the foreign company. Esso began oil production in two offshore fields in 1978, exporting its share of the supply, unlike PETRONAS, whose share was consumed within the country.

PETRONAS went downstream for the first time in 1976, when it was chosen by the Association of South East Asian Nations (ASEAN) to begin construction on the second ASEAN joint industrial project, a urea plant. The subsidiary, Asean Bintulu Fertilizer, was based in Sarawak and exported ammonia and urea all over the world. Also in 1976, Malaysia became a net exporter of oil, but exports were at such a low level that the country was ineligible to join OPEC. This situation benefited Malaysia and PETRONAS by allowing the company a degree of commercial and political flexibility and reinforcing PETRONAS's chief purpose, developing Malaysian self-reliance.

PETRONAS supervised its foreign partners' oil activities, taking no direct role in production until 1978, when the government saw to the creation of a subsidiary for oil exploration and production, PETRONAS Carigali. It began its work in an oil field off the peninsula. PETRONAS retained its supervisory powers over all oil and gas ventures, particularly on issues of health and safety and environmental control.

DEVELOPING NATURAL GAS

The government was determined to develop Malaysia's natural gas as well as its oil. In 1974 five tankers for LNG were ordered by the Malaysia International Shipping Corporation (MISC), of which the government owned 61 percent. These were to take LNG exports out of Malaysia, save the cost of hiring foreign tankers, and expand the country's fleet under its own control, in contrast to cargo shipping, which was controlled by international conferences.

Shell BV, the Royal Dutch/Shell subsidiary that was building the LNG plant off Sarawak with Japanese and Asian Development Bank aid, accepted production sharing with PETRONAS but balked at sharing equity, transport management, or refining. Negotiations went on, pushing commencement further and further back, until 1977, when PETRONAS and the government, faced with the costs of maintaining the tankers between delivery and first use, surrendered management rights, which led to a repeal of part of the Petroleum Development Act. PETRONAS took 60 percent of equity in the new company Malaysia LNG. The Sarawak state government took 5 percent, and the other 35 percent was divided equally between Shell BV and the Mitsubishi Corporation. Production of LNG in Sarawak began in 1983.

When PETRONAS Carigali formed an exploration and production company with Société National Elf Aquitaine of France in 1982, it allowed Elf better terms for recovering costs than it had offered in earlier ventures. This development came against the background of the government's imposition of a depletion policy on PETRONAS, Royal Dutch/Shell, and Esso in an attempt to postpone the exhaustion of oil reserves. These were then estimated to be about 2.84 billion barrels, and it was officially predicted that by the late 1980s Malaysia would be a net oil importer once again.

By 1980 oil and gas represented 24 percent of Malaysian exports, and the government decided to impose a tax on these exports at a 25 percent rate. The new policy and the new tax combined to cause Malaysia's output and exports of crude oil to fall in 1981 for the first time since PETRONAS had been established. Output rose again, beyond its 1980 level, in the following year, but exports took until 1984 to surpass their 1980 level.

The depletion policy was being undermined by external circumstances, however. Through the early 1980s, a worldwide oil glut, which OPEC proved unable to control, forced the Malaysian government to increase production to offset deterioration in its balance of increased payments to a deficit of $1 billion. It became clear that this could only be sustained by relaxing the conditions for joint ventures between PETRONAS and the major oil companies. In 1982 the PETRONAS-government share, which had risen to 80 percent, was cut to 70 percent, and taxes on company income were also cut.

MOVING INTO REFINING AND DISTRIBUTION: 1983

PETRONAS went into refining and distribution in 1983. It initiated the construction of refineries at Malacca and at Kertih in order to reduce its dependence on Royal Dutch/Shell's two refineries at Port Dickson and Esso's refinery in Sarawak. These two majors, and other foreign companies, already covered much of the domestic retail market, but the new subsidiary PETRONAS Dagangan was given the initial advantage of preference in the location of its stations. By 1990, 252 service stations carried the PETRONAS brand, all but 20 on a franchise basis, and another 50 were planned. Some were set up on grounds of social benefit rather than of strict commercial calculation.

As production from Royal Dutch/Shell and Esso's existing fields moved nearer depletion, the companies sought new fields and new contracts. In 1985 the government and PETRONAS revised the standard PSC, increasing the rate of recovery of capital costs from 30 percent to 50 percent of gross production in the case of oil and from 35 percent to 60 percent in the case of natural gas, abolishing signature, discovery, and production bonus payments, and increasing the foreign partners' share of the profits.

At first the drastic fall in oil prices during 1986, which cut Malaysia's income from exported oil by more than a third even though the volume of exports rose by 16 percent, discouraged interest in the new arrangements, but by 1989 PETRONAS had signed 22 new contracts with 31 companies from 11 countries. However, the contract period was still restricted to five years, as compared, for example, with the 35-year contracts available in neighboring Singapore. In addition, there was still a 25 percent levy on exported crude oil, a measure that was intended to promote the domestic refining industry. These conditions, cited as disincentives to foreign investment, were eventually relaxed over the next several years.

The government and PETRONAS aimed to encourage the replacement of fast-depleting oil within Malaysia itself and simultaneously to foster heavy industries that could help reduce the country's overwhelming dependence on exporting its natural resources. In 1980 petroleum products accounted for 88 percent of the country's commercial consumption of energy, the rest being provided from hydroelectric plants in Sarawak, too far away from the main population centers to become a major alternative. Five years later, gas accounted for 17 percent, hydroelectricity for 19 percent, coal for 2 percent, and petroleum products for 62 percent of such consumption, and about half of each year's gas output was being consumed in Malaysia.

BECOMING A MAJOR LNG PLAYER: 1985

The PETRONAS venture responsible for this shift in fuel use, and along with Malaysia LNG for Malaysia's becoming the third-largest producer of LNG in the world, was the Peninsular Gas Utilization Project (Projek Penngegunaan Gas Semenanjung), which aimed to supply gas to every part of the peninsula. Its first stage was completed in 1985, following the success of smaller gasification projects in the states of Sarawak and Sabah, and involved the extraction of gas from three fields in the Natuna Sea, between the peninsula and the island of Borneo; its processing in a plant at Kertih on the peninsula's east coast; and its distribution to the state of Trengganu by pipeline and abroad via an export terminal.

PETRONAS's least successful venture was its ownership of the Bank Bumiputra, the second-largest, but least profitable, of the commercial banks incorporated in Malaysia. PETRONAS spent more than MYR 3.5 billion over five years trying to rescue the bank from the impact of the bad loans it had made, starting with its support of the Carrian property group of Hong Kong, which collapsed in 1985, taking the bank's share capital down with it. In 1991 PETRONAS sold the bank back to another state company, Minister of Finance Inc., and announced its intention to concentrate on oil, gas, and associated activities in the future.

Just as PETRONAS was disposing of this liability, the crisis caused by the Iraqi regime's invasion of Kuwait culminated in military action against Iraq by the United States. PETRONAS had already raised Malaysia's oil production rate from 605,000 to 650,000 barrels per day in late 1990 as the crisis unfolded. This move only reinforced the company's awareness of the need to vary its policies, since, with known reserves of 2.94 billion barrels, and assuming no new major finds of oil, Malaysia risked seeing output decline to 350,000 barrels per day in 2000 and running down to depletion within another five years.

This was exacerbated by the possibility that Southeast Asia in general would enjoy rapid economic growth in the 1990s, so that demand for oil there would rise twice as fast as demand in the relatively more sluggish, more mature economies of North America and Europe. The Malaysian government, and its state oil and gas company, was forced to decide what mixture of policies to adopt in response.

BATTLING OIL DEPLETION

Exploration was by no means at an end and could yet produce more reserves. The Seligi field, which came onstream at the end of 1988 and was developed by Esso Production Malaysia, was one of the richest oil fields so far found in Malaysian waters, and further concessions to the majors would encourage exploration of the deeper waters around Malaysia, where unknown reserves could be discovered. Meanwhile, computerized seismography made it both feasible and commercially justifiable to re-explore fields that had been abandoned, or were assumed to be unproductive, over the past century. In 1990 PETRONAS invited foreign companies to re-explore parts of the sea off Sabah and Sarawak on the basis of new surveys using up-to-date techniques.

Another way to postpone depletion was to develop sources of oil, and of its substitute, natural gas, outside Malaysia. Late in 1989 the governments of Vietnam and Myanmar (Burma) invited PETRONAS Caligali to take part in joint ventures to explore for oil in their coastal waters. In 1990 a new unit, PETRONAS Caligali Overseas Sdn Bhd, was created to take up a 15 percent interest in a field in Myanmarese waters being explored by Idemitsu Myanmar Oil Exploration Co. Ltd., a subsidiary of the Japanese firm Idemitsu Oil Development Co. Ltd., in a production-sharing arrangement with Myanmar Oil and Gas Enterprise. Thus began PETRONAS's first oil exploration outside Malaysia.

In May 1990 the governments of Malaysia and Thailand settled a long-running dispute over their respective rights to an area of 7,300 square kilometers in the Gulf of Thailand by setting up a joint administrative authority for the area and encouraging a joint oil exploration project by PETRONAS, the Petroleum Authority of Thailand, and the U.S. company Triton Oil. In a separate deal in October 1990 the Petroleum Authority of Thailand arranged with PETRONAS to study the feasibility of transferring natural gas from this jointly administered area, through Malaysia to Thailand, by way of an extension of the pipelines laid for the third stage of the Peninsular Gas Utilization Project.

That project was on course to becoming a major element in the postponement of oil depletion. Contracts for line pipes for the second stage of the project were signed in 1989 with two consortia of Malaysian, Japanese, and Brazilian companies. This stage, completed in 1991, included the laying of 730 kilometers of pipeline through to the tip of the peninsula, from where gas could be sold to Singapore and Thailand; the conversion of two power stations, Port Dickson and Pasir Gudang, from oil to gas; and the expansion of PETRONAS's output of methyl tertiary butyl ether (MTBE), propylene, and polypropylene, which were already being produced in joint ventures with Idemitsu Petrochemical Co. of Japan and Neste Oy of Finland. The third and final stage of the project was to lay pipelines along the northwest and northeast coastlines of the peninsula and was completed in 1997.

SHIP-OWNING VENTURE: 1990

Another new venture in 1990 was in ship owning, since PETRONAS's existing arrangements with MISC and with Nigeria's state oil company would be inadequate to transport the additional exports of LNG due to start in 1994 under the contract with Saibu Gas. PETRONAS did not lose sight of the government's commitment to Malaysian self-reliance, and the company's second refinery at Malacca, completed in 1994, with a capacity of 100,000 barrels per day, promoted the same policy.

The fact that the Malacca refinery was built in a joint venture with Samsung of Korea, the Chinese Petroleum Corporation of Taiwan, and Caltex of the United States did not negate the policy, since the subsidiary company PETRONAS Penapisan (Melaka) had a decisive 45 percent of equity while sharing the enormous costs of, and gaining advanced technology for, the project. Furthermore, the refinery's completion enabled PETRONAS to refine all of the crude oil it produced, instead of being partially dependent on refining facilities in Singapore.

PETRONAS, with its policies of promoting self-reliance, helping to develop associated industries, and varying the sources and uses of oil and gas, played an important role in the Malaysian economy as a whole. The contribution of oil taxes to the federal government's revenue hovered at around 12 percent to 16 percent until 1980, when it showed a marked increase to 23 percent, followed by another leap to 32 percent in 1981. From then until 1988 the proportion fluctuated between 29 percent and 36 percent. PETRONAS was not just another big oil company. It controlled a crucial sector of the economy and remained an indispensable instrument of the state.

EXPANDING GLOBALLY: 1995–2003

During the mid- to late 1990s, international exploration, development, and production remained key components in PETRONAS's strategy, along with diversification. A key discovery was made in the Ruby field in Vietnam in 1994. That year, the firm also saw its first overseas production from the Dai Hung field in Vietnam and established its first retail station outside of Malaysia in Cambodia. In 1995 a subsidiary was created to import, store, and distribute liquefied petroleum gas (LPG). In addition, the company's polyethylene plant in Kertih began operations. PETRONAS marked a significant milestone during this time, when two of its subsidiaries, PETRONAS Dagangan Bhd and PETRONAS Gas Bhd, went public on the Kuala Lumpur Stock Exchange.

In 1996 PETRONAS entered the aromatics market by way of a joint venture that created Aromatics Malaysia Sdn Bhd. It also signed a contract with China National Offshore Oil Corporation and Chevron Overseas Petroleum Ltd. to begin exploration of block 02/31 of the Liaodong Bay area in China. While the Asian economy as a whole suffered from an economic crisis during 1997 and 1998, Malaysia was quick to bounce back due to successful government reforms. From its new headquarters in the PETRONAS Twin Towers, established in 1997, the state-owned concern continued its development in the oil and gas industry.

During 1997 PETRONAS heightened its diversification efforts. The firm set plans in motion to build three petrochemical plants in Kuantan as well as an acetic facility in Kertih. Its first LPG joint venture in China was launched that year, and the company acquired a 29.3 percent interest in MISC. In 1998 PETRONAS's tanker-related subsidiary merged with MISC, increasing PETRONAS's stake in MISC to 62 percent. That year, PETRONAS introduced the PETRONAS E01, the country's first commercial prototype engine. The company also signed a total of five new PSCs in 1998 and 1999, and began oil production in the Sim field in Iran.

PETRONAS entered the new century determined to expand its international efforts. The company forged deals for two new exploration plots in Pakistan and began construction on the Chad-Cameroon Integrated Oil Development and Pipeline Project. By 2002 PETRONAS had signed seven new PSCs and secured stakes in eight exploration blocks in Gabon, Cameroon, Niger, Egypt, Yemen, Indonesia, and Vietnam. The firm also made considerable progress in its petrochemicals strategy, opening new gas-based petrochemical facilities in Kertih and Gebeng.

By 2003 Malaysia was set to usurp Algeria as the world's second-largest producer of LNG with the completion of the Malaysia LNG Tiga Plant. PETRONAS had transformed itself into a global oil company

over the previous decade, becoming a national symbol for success. The company realized, however, that it would have to continue its aggressive growth strategy in order to ensure its survival in the years to come.

CONTINUED GROWTH

Over the next several years, PETRONAS continued its steady growth in order to maintain its position as a leading international oil and gas concern. During 2004 the company signed several PSCs, including one with the Malaysia-Thailand Joint Development Authority for an offshore overlapping area between the two regions. In addition, the company established a marketing company in China and formed Pars LNG Co. with partners Total and the National Iranian Oil Company. PETRONAS also set plans in motion that year to purchase Kuwait Petroleum (Thailand) Ltd. from Kuwait Petroleum International Ltd., which would give it a stronger foothold in Thailand's oil and gas industry.

One of the company's major accomplishments in 2005 was the delivery of its first LNG cargo to Asean LNG Trading Co. The delivery, made with partners BG International Ltd. and Egyptian General Petroleum Corp., marked PETRONAS's first export of LNG cargo from Egypt. During 2006 the company signed a 20-year agreement to supply LNG to Japan's Chubu Electric and Power Co. It also inked a deal to supply LNG to China's Shanghai LNG Company Ltd. for the next 25 years. PETRONAS broke ground on its base oil plant, the first of its kind in Southeast Asia, that year.

During 2007 the company's first deepwater project, named Kikeh, went onstream and began producing oil. The well was discovered in 2002 by Murphy Sabah Oil Co. Ltd. and was brought online using the first Truss Spar floating production unit outside of the Gulf of Mexico. The Kikeh field was thought to have a recoverable reserve of 400 million to 700 million barrels of oil.

PETRONAS signed several contracts in 2008 worth approximately $793 million. The upstream projects would enhance Malaysia's gas production and allow it to continue to supply both its domestic and foreign markets. The company also made several acquisitions that year, including U.K. energy company Star Energy plc, and a 40 percent stake in the Gladstone LNG project. Gladstone was a joint venture with Santos Ltd. created to develop and operate a gas liquefaction plant in Queensland, Australia.

PETRONAS stood on solid ground by 2009. It remained focused on bolstering Malaysia's crude oil and gas reserves and its LNG complex in Bintulu, Sarawak, was one of the largest LNG production facilities in the world. The company's revenue grew each year from

2005 through 2009. Net income followed the same path until 2009, when the global economic crisis hit the oil and gas industry. Falling demand led to an oversupply and crude oil prices fluctuated dramatically during 2009. Malaysian crude oil went from $125.45 per barrel to $50.69 per barrel by the end of the fiscal year.

Despite the adverse operating conditions, there were six new PSCs awarded during the year while seven new oil fields and nine gas fields were brought onstream. In addition, subsidiary PETRONAS Carigali discovered gas reserves in Malaysia's first high-pressure, high-temperature well in the Kinabalu field. Late in the year PETRONAS and Royal Dutch Shell won the development rights for Majnoon, a large field in southern Iraq. During 2010 PETRONAS set plans to motion to offer its petrochemicals and its heavy engineering subsidiaries to the public. While the oil and gas industry continued to face uncertainty as it relied on the health of global economies, PETRONAS appeared poised for success as a fully integrated oil and gas company in the years to come.

Patrick Heenan
Updated, Christina M. Stansell

PRINCIPAL SUBSIDIARIES

PETRONAS Carigali Sdn Bhd; PETRONAS eLearning Solutions Sdn Bhd; KLCC Holdings Sdn Bhd; Polypropylene Malaysia Sdn Bhd; PETRONAS Assets Sdn Bhd; MTBE Malaysia Sdn Bhd; Gas District Cooling Holdings Sdn Bhd; PETRONAS Hartabina Sdn Bhd; PETRONAS Penapisan Sdn Bhd; Bekalan Air KIPC Sdn Bhd; PETRONAS Research Sdn Bhd; PETRONAS Maritime Services Sdn Bhd; PETRONAS Fertilizer Sdn Bhd; PETRONAS Management Training Sdn Bhd; PETRONAS Methanol Sdn Bhd; PETRONAS Trading Corp. Sdn Bhd; Malaysian International Trading Corporation Sdn Bhd; SPE Engine Solutions Sdn Bhd; PETRONAS Chemical Group Sdn Bhd; PETRONAS Technical Services Sdn Bhd; Petrosains Sdn Bhd; Vinyl Chloride Malaysia Sdn Bhd; Styrene Monomer Sdn Bhd; PETRONAS Cambodia Co. Ltd.; PETRONAS NGV Sdn Bhd; Sanzbury Stead Sdn Bhd; PETRONAS International Corp. Ltd.; PETRONAS South Africa Pty Ltd.; PETRONAS India Holdings Company Pte Ltd.; PETRONAS Ammonia; Institute of Technology PETRONAS Sdn Bhd; PETRONAS Lubricants International Sdn Bhd; PETRONAS Capital Ltd.; Energas Insurance Ltd.; PETRONAS Base Oil Sdn Bhd; PETRONAS Aviation Sdn Bhd.

PRINCIPAL COMPETITORS

Chevron Corp.; Exxon Mobil Corp.; Royal Dutch Shell plc.

FURTHER READING

Akanni, Fred, "PETRONAS Charges into Africa," *Offshore*, February 1999, p. 18.

Creffield, David, *Malaysia*, London: Euromoney Publications, 1989.

"Discovery of Kikeh," *Oil and Gas Journal*, December 10, 2007.

Hamid, Hamisah, "Asia Needs to Set Up Energy Stockpile," *Business Times Malaysia*, October 5, 2002, p. 1.

Klapp, Merrie Gilbert, *Sovereign Entrepreneur*, Ithaca, NY: Cornell University Press, 1987.

"Malaysia Ships First LNG Cargo to Shanghai Terminal," *Platts Oilgram News*, October 30, 2009.

"Malaysia's Petronas Exports First LNG Cargo from Egypt," *Dow Jones Energy Service*, March 7, 2005.

Mehta, Harish, "Foreign Firms Happy with KL-Viet Offshore Oil Accord," *Business Times Singapore*, June 30, 1992, p. 9.

"Oil MNCs Happy with PETRONAS' New Contracts," *Business Times Singapore*, August 7, 1992, p. 8.

"PETRONAS Inks $793 Million in Upstream Deals," *Platts Oilgram News*, November 3, 2008.

"PETRONAS Makes Further Inroads into Sudan's Oil Industry," *Business Times Malaysia*, April 29, 2003, p. 4.

Tibin, Newmond, "PM Says M'sia Must Improve Competitiveness in Oil and Gas Industry," *Bernama: The Malaysian National News Agency*, May 8, 2003.

Toh, Eddie, "M'sia Resilient in Absorbing Shocks," *Business Times Singapore*, April 14, 2003.

Williams, Timothy, "Under Tight Security, Iraq Sells Rights to Develop 2 Oil Fields," *New York Times*, December 12, 2009.

Piedmont Natural Gas
Company, Inc.

—————— ■ ——————

4720 Piedmont Row Drive
Charlotte, North Carolina 28210
U.S.A.
Telephone: (704) 364-3120
Fax: (704) 365-8515
Web site: http://www.piedmontng.com

Public Company
Incorporated: 1950
Employees: 1,821
Sales: $1.64 billion (2009)
Stock Exchanges: New York
Ticker Symbol: PNY
NAICS: 221210 Natural Gas Distribution

■ ■ ■

Piedmont Natural Gas Company, Inc., operates as an energy services firm that distributes natural gas to over one million residential, commercial, and industrial customers in North and South Carolina as well as Tennessee. Through its subsidiaries, the company is also involved in various energy-related businesses including unregulated natural gas marketing, interstate natural gas storage, and intrastate natural gas transportation. During 2010 the company sold half of its stake in its unregulated energy supply venture SouthStar Energy Services LLC.

A DIFFICULT BEGINNING

The years after World War II witnessed a natural gas pipeline "boom" in the United States, and in 1950

Henry Blackford, Sr., Priestly Conyers, Jr., and Donald S. Russell, Sr., sought to construct a pipeline from Texas to the as-yet unserved Piedmont region of the Carolinas. When the Federal Power Commission instead granted Transcontinental Pipeline Company (Transco) permission to construct a pipeline to the area, rather than giving up on the gas business entirely, the three South Carolinians purchased from Duke Power Company the right to distribute manufactured gas to a number of North Carolina cities. The sale was finalized on May 1, 1951.

Piedmont's first year was a difficult one. The company inherited 34,000 customers and 300 former Duke employees, but reportedly had no offices, minimal and aging cast-iron pipe, and a collection of rusty automobiles. An old Studebaker dealership was eventually pressed into service as Piedmont's first corporate office, but the conditions inside were far from comfortable. Crates served as chairs and desks, the roof leaked and sometimes flooded the office, and employees labored without benefit of air conditioning. Moreover, plans to convert the business to natural gas by tapping into Transco's pipeline were impeded by the lack of steel pipe, a shortage caused by the Korean War. Losses during the first year totaled $1 million.

A SERIES OF FIRSTS

The end of 1952 brought two significant events for the company: steel pipe became available from Great Britain, and Buell Duncan was hired as president. Duncan came to Piedmont with experience in the gas business, having served as director of Florida's Southern

Atlantic Gas Company. He also possessed a background as a civic leader and the desire to increase the company's community exposure. His efforts helped initiate what John Maxheim, a later Piedmont executive, would call the company's corporate culture.

In subsequent years, Piedmont experienced significant growth and an important sequence of firsts. The company made its first profit of $373,000 in 1953, more than doubling this figure the next year by earning $760,000. Its first dividend of 20 cents per share was issued in 1956, and the first annual report to stockholders appeared in 1957. In that same year, revenue surpassed $10 million and net income soared to $1 million. The first shareholders' meeting took place in Charlotte, North Carolina, in 1958.

Piedmont continued to expand its customer base and develop its internal resources throughout the 1950s and 1960s. Between 1951 and 1957, 16,000 new customers signed on with the company, bringing the total number served to 50,000. By 1960 that number was 75,000, and in 1964 the company reached the 100,000 mark. An engineering staff was organized in 1953, and the company moved into new headquarters, complete with a gas-powered clock, in 1962. Piedmont acquired Carolina Natural Gas Company in 1968, thereby gaining 9,000 new natural gas customers and 1,000 new propane customers in Hickory and the surrounding areas.

THE GAS CRISIS

Beginning in the 1970s, however, increasingly severe gas shortages gripped the United States, and Piedmont's period of untroubled growth was stalled. Gas suppliers nationwide, but predominantly in Texas, curtailed deliveries when regulation of the wellhead price of natural gas by the Federal Power Commission (FPC) set prices at levels that did not enable them to make a profit for some wells. In response, regulatory agencies such as the FPC, the North Carolina Utilities Commission (NCUC), and the South Carolina Public Services Commission (SCPSC) set in place gas rationing plans in 1971.

Since industrial customers received lower rationing priority than residential and small commercial custom-

ers, curtailments had a noticeable impact on Piedmont's earnings. Piedmont faced gas volume curtailments of 4.3 percent in 1971, 11 percent in 1972, and 24 percent in 1973. By 1974 Piedmont's curtailments had reached 40 percent, and then edged up to 56 percent the next year. In 1974 the state regulatory commissions in both Carolinas ordered Piedmont to refrain from adding customers until the shortage had abated. A mild winter in 1975 helped avert a gas crisis in North Carolina, but 1976 ushered in bitterly cold weather during which interstate pipelines could fulfill only a quarter of demand.

Nevertheless, while the situation was a difficult one for the company, it still managed to turn a profit. In the mid-1970s the company was able to secure both NCUC and SCPSC approval for a curtailment tracking adjustment formula that was intended to stabilize earnings by adjusting customers' rates in response to curtailments. Piedmont also sought rate increases in 1974 and 1977. By 1978, with stock prices plummeting, Piedmont still claimed a net income of $5 million and 185,000 customers.

In 1978 Congress passed the Natural Gas Policy Act (NGPA), which took the first steps toward deregulating the gas industry and created a new agency, the Federal Energy Regulatory Commission, to replace the FPC. John Maxheim, head of Piedmont Natural Gas, was critical of portions of the act that he feared would increase gas prices. Signs of deregulation were welcome, however, and the company routinely began to voice its pro-deregulation stance. Curtailments essentially ended in 1979. In 1982 Piedmont joined with three other utilities to call for a nationwide conference to discuss the challenges emerging in the new marketplace.

A DEREGULATED MARKET: 1980–84

Piedmont experienced strong growth during the next several years. In 1979 alone, the company provided fuel to 6,500 new customers, an increase greater than any throughout the previous six years. A total of 9,000 customers joined Piedmont's rolls in 1980. The company recorded $9.3 million in net income during the same year, a 60 percent increase over 1979, and embarked on a $16.3 million program of system expansion. By 1981, when demand for natural gas was at an all-time high, the company gained 11,000 customers and finished a new corporate headquarters building in Charlotte. Although the following recession year witnessed a 16 percent decline in earnings, cold temperatures in 1983 reversed the downward trend as Piedmont benefited from record-breaking consumption.

Nevertheless, there were rough times ahead. Inflation was an ongoing problem, and gas prices rose as predicted in the wake of the NGPA, with consumers paying 80 percent more for natural gas in 1983 than in 1978. As a result, much new residential construction had turned to electricity to meet home heating needs during the early 1980s. Piedmont and other gas utilities thus had to build non-revenue producing pipeline through the electrical "doughnuts" these subdivisions had created. The state of the wholesale natural gas market was somewhat unpredictable, and Piedmont had to contend with widely fluctuating gas prices from its suppliers.

In 1981 and again in 1982 Piedmont sought rate increases, citing fluctuating oil prices and low consumption of natural gas as damaging to its competitiveness. It dropped its request, instead offering a decrease, when Transco dropped the wholesale price of natural gas.

To shield itself from this uncertain situation, the company and its subsidiaries moved to diversify. Piedmont had sold propane fuel and marketed natural gas- and propane-powered appliances since the 1950s. In the 1980s it moved into a number of additional new areas. In 1981 PNG Energy Company purchased Gilley and Tolley Fuel Company and began to operate its coal

business under the name of PNG Coal and Oil Company. Also during that year, PNG Communications Company entered the cable television market, and PNG Conservation Company began selling solar water heaters, branching out into electricity-producing solar voltaic cells in 1983. By 1984 nonutility endeavors represented 4.4 percent of business.

SIGNIFICANT GROWTH: 1984–95

By the late 1980s the gas market was functioning more predictably, and Piedmont was providing fuel to a total of 300,000 customers, a number that represented a rate of increase that was three times the national average. In 1985 the company acquired Tennessee Natural Resources, the parent of Nashville Gas Company, which at the time served 61,000 customers, and, between 1986 and 1995, signed on 20,000 new customers each year.

In 1984 Piedmont opened a Houston office and formed a joint venture with natural gas marketers in Texas that allowed it to market wholesale gas to other utilities and large-volume customers beyond its three-state area. By 1990 Piedmont was serving 415,000 customers, and its continued success was attracting notice. Duke Power, provider of electrical service in the Piedmont region and longtime Piedmont competitor, began to seek ways to counteract the company's aggressive marketing and growth in the residential and small commercial markets.

Piedmont continued to grow at a remarkable rate throughout the early 1990s. The company continued to add customers, including a record 28,100 customers in 1993, and common stock dividends grew at a rate above the industry average between 1991 and 1996. In 1995 Piedmont recorded a net income of $38 million and was honored by the Newcomen Society of the United States, an organization founded in 1923 to promote and recognize important contributions to free enterprise. John Maxheim was selected by *Financial World Magazine* as CEO of the Year that same year in the gas utility category.

NEW CHALLENGES AND JOINT VENTURES

The gas business continued to change, and Piedmont had to diversify to adapt to new circumstances. As deregulation progressed during the middle and late 1990s, the company formed an increasing number of joint ventures with other utilities and natural gas suppliers. In 1994 Piedmont's subsidiary, Piedmont Energy Company, became a 51 percent partner in Resource Energy Services Company, LLC, which focused on providing gas acquisition, transportation, and storage services to industrial and large commercial customers in the Southeast.

In 1995 Piedmont Intrastate Pipeline Company, a division of one of the Piedmont subsidiaries, Piedmont Energy, joined with several other utilities to extend the Cardinal Pipeline of North Carolina 65 miles to a point in the vicinity of Raleigh. That same year, Intrastate announced plans with Transco and two other North Carolina utilities to build a liquefied natural gas terminal near Transco's main line in North Carolina under a joint venture called Pine Needle LNG Company.

Among Piedmont's most important joint ventures was the formation of SouthStar Energy Services, LLC, with AGL Resources of Atlanta and Dynergy, Inc., of Houston, the holding company for Atlanta Gaslight, the Southeast's largest natural gas distributor. In addition to selling natural gas to industry and large commercial customers in the eight-state southeast region, SouthStar was formed to provide electricity and natural gas to residential and small business customers. In the fall of 1998, when Georgia became the first state in the region to open its utility market to competition, SouthStar, doing business as Georgia Natural Gas Services, began marketing unregulated natural gas services to its customers.

OVERCOMING COMPETITION: 1995–99

Competition also increased with deregulation. In 1995 the NCUC awarded natural gas service in four North Carolina counties to newcomer Frontier Utilities over Piedmont's competing bid. Two years later Piedmont protested plans by BASF, a chemical company and manufacturer of plastics, pharmaceuticals, and crop protection products, to buy its natural gas directly from Transco, Piedmont's supplier.

In order to meet the challenges of future deregulated competition, Piedmont began a process of cost cutting. In 1994 the company sold properties acquired during the early 1970s on which it had sought natural gas deposits, since the production from its finds no longer justified administrative costs. Piedmont also ended its natural gas appliance sales and installation business in 1996 after 45 years of involvement when revenues no longer justified expenses. In 1997 the company eliminated 126 positions from its workforce to help ensure that Piedmont would remain competitive.

Piedmont continued to prepare to meet the challenges of the increasingly competitive gas market. Natural gas doubled its share of the home heating market between 1992 and 1998, during which time

Piedmont expanded both its customer base and earnings. In 1997 the company enjoyed a net income of $54.1 million, an 11.4 percent increase over the previous year. The mild winter of 1997–98 made a dent in sales, but Piedmont continued to add new customers at a much faster rate than most utilities across the nation. In 1998 the NCUC granted Piedmont permission to use $26.2 million from specially designated and regulated expansion funds to expand its service into three more North Carolina counties. Piedmont was providing services to 673,000 customers in that year and had grown into the second-largest gas utility in the southeastern United States.

MOVING INTO THE 21ST CENTURY

While the early years of the new millennium proved challenging, Piedmont was successful in increasing its business as an independent entity. After 22 years of service, Maxheim retired in 2000, leaving Ware F. Schiefer at the helm as CEO. Under Maxheim's leadership, Piedmont had increased dividends every year and its customer count increased from 185,000 in 1978 to over 710,000 by February 2000.

Maxheim retired as chairman in 2003. Schiefer announced his retirement that same year. Thomas E. Skains, who had been elected president of the company in February 2002, was tapped to lead the company as chairman, president, and CEO. Piedmont made several key acquisitions during this management transition, including the 2001 purchase of the natural gas distribution system of Atmos Energy Corp. The deal added the Gaffney region of Cherokee County, South Carolina, to Piedmont's service area. Piedmont purchased North Carolina Gas Service, an NUI Corp. subsidiary responsible for natural gas distribution in Rockingham and Stokes counties, the following year.

Piedmont continued to expand its natural gas distribution business in 2003 when it acquired North Carolina Natural Gas (NCNG) for $425 million. The purchase added 176,000 customers in eastern and southern North Carolina. The purchase also included a stake in Eastern NC, a joint venture with Albemarle Pamlico Economic Development Corp., which provided natural gas services to 14 counties in eastern North Carolina. NCNG and Eastern NC adopted the Piedmont Natural Gas name in 2005. Piedmont sold its interest in Heritage Propane Partners, L.P., in 2004.

CONTINUED SUCCESS IN TRYING TIMES

While Piedmont remained on solid financial footing, it experienced problems in 2005 when Hurricane Katrina interrupted Gulf Coast gas production. Consumer bills increased by nearly 50 percent, prompting numerous customer complaints. The steep rate increases and poor customer service led to an investigation by the NCUC. The company appeared to be back on track, however, when it initiated a series of rate cuts in 2006. During 2007 and 2008 the company was ranked highest in the southern region in business customer satisfaction by a J.D. Power and Associates study.

The next few years were marked by increasing energy commodity prices and faltering global economies. Nevertheless, Piedmont delivered record results in 2008. It added 20,500 new customers that year, making it one of the fastest-growing natural gas utilities in the United States. Net income was $110 million and the company increased its dividend for the 30th consecutive year.

Skains was named chairman of the American Gas Association (AGA) in 2009. His strategy was to promote natural gas as a responsible energy choice. He maintained that increased direct use of natural gas would reduce greenhouse gas emissions, energy consumption, and energy costs. He also believed it was necessary to gain access to domestic natural gas supplies that had yet to be tapped. The company claimed that industry studies proved there was at least a 100-year supply of natural gas under U.S. soil. Overall, Skains and the AGA worked to convince the Obama administration and Congress that domestic natural gas consumption needed to be a crucial component of the country's future energy and environmental policies.

At the same time, Skains continued to focus on strengthening Piedmont's natural gas distribution business in North Carolina, South Carolina, and Tennessee. In early 2010 the company completed the sale of a 15 percent interest in its unregulated business, SouthStar Energy Services, to AGL Resources Inc. Piedmont retained a 15 percent earnings and ownership stake in the company. The trend of record financial results continued in fiscal 2009 when net income grew to $122.8 million. With over one million customers including 61,000 wholesale clients, Piedmont appeared to be well positioned as one of the fastest-growing natural gas companies in the United States.

Carrie Rothburd
Updated, Christina M. Stansell

PRINCIPAL SUBSIDIARIES

Piedmont Energy Partners, Inc.; Piedmont Hardy Storage Company, LLC; Piedmont ENCNG Company, LLC; Piedmont Interstate Pipeline Company; Piedmont Intrastate Pipeline Company; Piedmont Energy Company.

PRINCIPAL COMPETITORS

Dominion Resources Inc.; Duke Energy Corp.; SCANA Corp.

FURTHER READING

"Buyout Could Put Other Gas Companies on the Market," *Asheville Citizen Times*, November 17, 1998, p. B8.

"Georgia Natural Gas Takes Greater Share of SouthStar Energy Services from Piedmont," *Foster Natural Gas Report*, August 21, 2009.

Jarboe, Michelle, "Piedmont Asks for Natural Gas Rate Reduction," *Greensboro News & Record*, February 18, 2006.

Johnson, Leslie Williams, "Piedmont Natural Gas Enters New Territory as Georgia, Others Deregulate," *Charlotte Observer*, July 16, 1998, p. B5.

"NUI Sheds Another LDC," *Platts Retail Energy*, May 17, 2002.

"Piedmont, a Partner with Dominion on the Greenbrier Pipeline Project, Continues to Develop and Expand Its Distribution Network in the Southeast," *Foster Natural Gas Report*, October 31, 2002.

"Piedmont to Increase Footprint with $425 Million Purchase of NCNG," *Inside F.E.R.C.'s Gas Market Report*, October 25, 2002.

Share, Jeff, "New AGA Chairman Not Lacking for Issues," *Pipeline & Gas Journal*, April 1, 2009.

Plaza Construction
Corporation

■

260 Madison Avenue
New York, New York 10016
U.S.A.
Telephone: (212) 849-4800
Fax: (212) 849-4855 and 849-4874
Web site: http://www.plazaconstruction.com

Wholly Owned Subsidiary of Fisher Brothers
Incorporated: 1986
Employees: 450
Sales: $984 million (2008 est.)
NAICS: 236220 Commercial and Institutional Building
    Construction; 541420 Interior Design Services

■ ■ ■

Plaza Construction Corporation is one of the largest
construction companies in the tristate metropolitan New
York City area and is also active in Florida and
Washington, D.C. The company offers a variety of
construction services, including construction management, general contracting, and project management in
the building and rehabilitation of residential and office
high-rise buildings. It is also engaged in a variety of
retail and institutional projects. Privately owned, the
company is a subsidiary of Fisher Brothers, a family-
owned real estate and financial management business.

FISHER BROTHERS: 1938–62

Carl Fisher started the family business in the early 20th
century as a general contractor who built apartment

houses in New York City. His son Martin started a
construction business in 1915. Martin and his younger
brothers Larry and Zachary founded Fisher Brothers in
1938 as a family-owned private partnership. Its office
was in the city's borough of Queens.

Following the Great Depression and World War II,
there was a pent-up demand for new housing that Fisher
Brothers, like many developers, sought to satisfy. The
firm constructed residential properties in all of the city's
boroughs except Staten Island, and also on Long Island
and in suburban Mount Vernon, New York. The Park
Briar Apartments in Forest Hills received the 1953
Queens Chamber of Commerce award for excellence of
design, construction, and civic value. Fisher Brothers
also built the Sherry Frontenac hotel in Miami Beach
and the Seville, also in southern Florida, in 1947.

Fisher Brothers moved its headquarters to Manhattan in 1955. A clear indication that it was going upscale
in real estate development was the apartment house it
erected that year on Sutton Place, one of the borough's
most exclusive neighborhoods. The firm followed this
up with Imperial House, a 30-story apartment building
with terraces on East 69th Street. Designed by the
eminent firm of Emery Roth & Sons and completed in
1960, Imperial House was at that time the tallest
residential structure built in New York since World War
II. It offered views of Central Park and the East River
and featured central air conditioning.

Completed in 1962 on the southeast corner of Fifth
Avenue and East 60th Street, Parc V, a residential
cooperative, was across the street from one of New

York's swankiest hotels, the Pierre. It was also close to the renowned Plaza and faced Central Park.

BUILDING THE FISHER OFFICE TOWERS: 1955–82

By this time Fisher Brothers had entered the big-time Manhattan commercial development market, in 1955 erecting a 21-story office building at 400 Park Avenue, just north of Lever House, one of the classics of the International style of architecture (which Fisher Brothers later tried to purchase and demolish). This was the first of several such buildings that Fisher Brothers developed and constructed. Eventually the firm came to build and own more than eight million square feet of high-grade office space in midtown Manhattan alone.

The 1960s were a boom decade for the national economy and for blue-chip corporations seeking office space in midtown Manhattan. Fisher Brothers erected several high-rise office towers and retained ownership. The first was a 44-story building at 605 Third Avenue, completed in 1963 and named the Burroughs Building for its anchor tenant, the Burroughs Corporation.

Many of these towers, such as 299 Park Avenue, were designed by Emery Roth & Sons. This 44-story structure, across the street from the famed Waldorf Astoria Hotel, required building a platform over railroad tracks leading to and from Grand Central Station. Completed in 1967, the new building required more massive trusses and girders than any other structure along Park Avenue to date. It became headquarters for Fisher Brothers.

In 1968 Fisher Brothers constructed a 27-story office building designed by Emery Roth & Sons on 42nd Street just east of Fifth Avenue. The Emigrant Savings Bank occupied the ground floor. In 1969 the firm completed Burlington House, a 50-story office tower at

1345 Avenue of the Americas. This 600-foot-high structure occupied the entire block between West 54th and West 55th streets and exceeded one million square feet of office space. A garage in the building could accommodate several hundred cars. One year later Fisher Brothers completed the 42-story Stevens Tower, which was named for J.P. Stevens & Co., the anchor tenant.

A PERIOD OF DIVERSIFICATION

In 1971 Bankers Trust Company agreed to pay a record $266 million over a 30-year period to lease space in a proposed office building that was to be named for the company. Located in the financial district opposite the World Trade Center and completed in 1974, this two-square-block, 40-story structure was the last major high-rise to be built in New York City for five years.

These projects were carried out by the firm's own in-house general contractor, Fisher Brothers Construction Company. During the planning stages members of the company's construction team worked in concert with project architects and engineers to establish structural, mechanical, and electrical systems. Then it managed all subcontractors and monitored the quality and efficiency of construction work through daily on-site direction.

With the national economy in recession and New York City in even worse financial shape, Fisher Brothers decided in the mid-1970s to sell its residential properties and, while continuing to develop and manage commercial real estate investments, to diversify its investment portfolio into sectors other than real estate. With little demand for office space, the partners decided to concentrate on building management and other services, including cleaning, which became a highly profitable line of work for the company, rather than putting up more office buildings. At the same time, Fisher Brothers began investing in areas totally outside of real estate.

One more big office building went up before the Fisher Brothers abandoned the field: Park Avenue Plaza. With the backing of Prudential Insurance Company of America, the firm spent over $22 million on acquisitions for the site. Despite its name, this glass-sheathed 44-story structure, designed by the firm of Skidmore, Owings & Merrill (SOM) and completed in 1982, was erected mid-block between East 52nd and East 53rd streets and did not abut the avenue. To earn a zoning variance, the firm created a public pedestrian galleria with waterfalls, shrubbery, and skylights. Writing in *New York* about the project, which in the end required an additional substantial payment to the neighboring Racquet and Tennis Club, C. Ray Smith called SOM's design "its best architecture ever."

KEY DATES

1938: Fisher Brothers is founded as a family-owned private partnership.

1986: The in-house Fisher construction arm becomes the Plaza Construction Corporation.

1996: Plaza is chosen to modernize 55 Water Street in Manhattan's financial district.

2002: Plaza wins several awards for its work on a 50-story tower at 1745 Broadway.

2009: The firm is construction manager for 11 Times Square, a 40-story office tower.

PLAZA CONSTRUCTION'S EARLY YEARS: 1986–99

Fisher Brothers Construction Company had fewer than 50 employees and annual revenue of only $40 million before it ceased to be in-house in 1986, when it became Plaza Construction Corporation, a wholly owned subsidiary of Fisher Brothers. It was expected not to depend on its parent's construction needs for business but rather to aggressively seek other clients.

By this time Fisher Brothers was largely operated by the grandsons and great-grandsons of Carl Fisher. One of the latter was Steven Fisher, who left college after one year to work at Plaza Construction. He advanced to president and chief executive officer while trying to improve the company's prospects in a crowded and competitive field. Beginning in 1991, Plaza steadily increased its business volume. During 1994 and 1995 the firm was awarded assignments for more than $200 million for interior installations, as well as comprehensive infrastructure upgrades of several signature properties.

Writing in *Real Estate Weekly* in early 1996, the company's CEO maintained, "Plaza is selective in the projects that we accept. We do not operate as a high volume producer who is likely to ignore quality control requirements. Our focus on delivering select projects permits us to involve our Executive Committee, composed of senior Fisher Brothers and Plaza Construction professionals, in every phase of the construction process."

In 1996 Plaza Construction was chosen to modernize 3.5 million square feet of space at 55 Water Street, a big office building in the financial district of Lower Manhattan. The company was cited by *New York Construction News* for its infrastructure and interior work on this project. Plaza received awards in 1997

from the Queens County Chamber of Commerce and the Queens County Builders and Construction Association for its work on the Flushing Manor Geriatric Center.

Plaza billed its clients for an estimated $300 million in 1998. Fisher, then 38, became the firm's chairman the following year. In 2004 the firm partnered with KM Construction Co. to form a Florida affiliate, KM/Plaza Construction.

21ST-CENTURY AWARDS AND ACCOLADES

Plaza made many improvements for Fisher Brothers, still located at 299 Park Avenue, including four diesel generators and a new roof. The company also rehabilitated Burlington House (which had been renamed the Alliance Capital Building), including a generator installation, lobby renovation, and a new cooling tower and riser system.

Plaza was construction manager for a 50-story tower at 1745 Broadway in midtown Manhattan. Half was commercial space, including the headquarters of Random House, Inc. Most of the rest consisted of condominium apartments. This project combined a steel commercial structure with a cast-in-place residential tower. Due to the building's close proximity to subway tunnels, extensive shoring and bracing was needed for the excavation and foundation work. The building received several awards, most notably the 2002 Award of Merit for Best Mixed-Use Building of the Year, awarded by *New York Construction News*.

A 20-story dormitory for New York University, completed in 2000 on East 14th Street, was one of the first buildings constructed in Manhattan under the newly enacted seismic requirements of the city building code. Plaza was the general contractor for the project, which featured a sloped tensile-structure skylight over its cafeteria and the use of durable materials in the interior, including terrazzo for the floors and jura stone and maple for the walls, as well as stainless steel and glass. *Interiors* magazine cited this building as the best educational facility of the year.

Another educational project for Plaza was the New York University School of Law, a structure consisting of two cellar levels and 10 floors of offices, meeting/seminar areas, faculty housing, and classrooms. The new building's proximity to existing historic landmarks required the delicate underpinning of the structures during the excavation and foundation phase. In addition, the project site had to be dewatered first because of the high groundwater table, only about 22 feet below grade.

WORKING THROUGH RECESSION

Zachary Fisher had helped to save the mothballed aircraft carrier U.S.S. *Intrepid* and place it on the Hudson River shore of midtown Manhattan in 1982. It became the world's largest privately owned maritime museum. Plaza was the construction manager for the demolition of the Visitor's Center and erection of a new one next to the ship's bow. The museum's exhibits remained totally accessible to visitors during the entire project, completed in 2000. Plaza was also construction manager for the renovation of the New York City Police Museum on lower Broadway.

Among the new residential buildings for which Plaza was the construction manager in this period was Chartwell House, a residential condominium on Manhattan's Upper East Side completed in 2001. Plaza was also the co-developer. The Sierra, erected in 2002, was a 13-story rental building on West 15th Street for which the company was construction manager.

KM/Plaza Construction was the general contractor for the Marquis, the second-tallest building in Miami. The 67-story structure, completed in 2009, housed a boutique hotel and residential condominium units on Biscayne Boulevard, offering sweeping views of Biscayne Bay and the downtown Miami skyline.

Plaza was construction manager for Gateway Center, a shopping center near Yankee Stadium in New York City's borough of the Bronx. Completed in 2009, Gateway Center housed such big-box retailers as Target and Best Buy.

Another important project completed in New York in the midst of recession was 11 Times Square, a 40-story glass office tower that was completed in 2009 and opened to its tenants in 2010. Plaza was the construction manager for the building, erected at the southwest corner of West 41st Street and Eighth Avenue.

Robert Halasz

PRINCIPAL COMPETITORS

Bovis Lend Lease, Inc.; Skanska USA Building Inc.; Structure Tone, Inc.; Tishman Construction Corporation; Turner Construction Company.

FURTHER READING

"Company Bases Growth on an Informed Bidding Process," *Real Estate Weekly,* May 20, 1998.

Croghan, Lore, "Steven Fisher, 38," *Crain's New York Business,* January 25, 1999, p. 16.

Diesing, Genevieve, "A Blossoming Commitment: Through Meetings, a Gritty Work Ethic and Strong Leadership, KM/Plaza Keeps the Focus It Needs to Construct Miami's Marquis on Time," *Construction Today,* February 2008, pp. 118–19.

Fisher, Steven, "New Construction and Development Industry Emerges," *Real Estate Weekly,* January 31, 1996, p. C9.

Huxtable, Ada Louise, "This Is the Bank That Zoning Built," *New York Times,* January 11, 1976, Section 2, p. 32.

"Integrity in Structures," *Construction Today,* September 2005.

Smith, C. Ray, "Squaring Off on Park Avenue," *New York,* November 27, 1978, pp. 47–52.

The PNC Financial Services Group Inc.

One PNC Plaza
249 Fifth Avenue
Pittsburgh, Pennsylvania 15222-2707
U.S.A.
Telephone: (412) 762-2000
Fax: (412) 762-2265
Web site: http://www.pnc.com

Public Company
Incorporated: 1983 as PNC Financial Corporation
Employees: 55,820
Sales: $16.2 billion (2009)
Stock Exchanges: New York
Ticker Symbol: PNC
NAICS: 551111 Offices of Bank Holding Companies; 52211 Commercial Banking; 523991 Trust, Fiduciary, and Custody Activities

∎ ∎ ∎

The PNC Financial Services Group Inc. is one of the largest diversified financial services companies in the United States, reporting total assets of $265.4 billion in 2010. PNC's growth in the late 1990s and early years of the new millennium came mainly from acquisitions, the most significant being the 2008 purchase of National City Corp. The $6.1 billion deal secured PNC's position as the fifth-largest U.S. bank, based on deposits. PNC's main businesses include consumer and small business banking, corporate and institutional banking, wealth and asset management, and residential mortgage banking. PNC also owns a 24.6 percent stake in Black-Rock Inc., one of the largest publicly traded asset management companies in the world.

ORIGINS

PNC Bank's immediate forerunner was PNC Financial Corporation, formed in 1983 from the merger of two Pennsylvania banking concerns, the Pittsburgh National Corporation and the Provident National Corporation. The Pittsburgh National Bank was incorporated in 1959, but its roots can be traced back to 1852, when steel magnates James Laughlin and B. F. Jones opened the Pittsburgh Trust and Savings in downtown Pittsburgh.

PNC Financial's other predecessor, the Provident National Bank, headquartered in Philadelphia, can also be traced to the mid-1800s. In 1847 the Tradesmens National Bank of Philadelphia opened its doors. After more than a century of banking and a series of name changes and acquisitions, it became the Provident National Bank in 1964. The Pittsburgh National Bank and the Provident National Bank combined their extensive banking experience in 1983. At that time, the newly formed bank holding company was no more than a medium-sized regional concern, but it rapidly developed into one of the nation's most powerful super-regional banks.

PNC's first chief executive, Merle E. Gilliand, had served as CEO at Pittsburgh National Bank for 11 years by the time PNC Financial was formed. Gilliand set the tone of PNC's management style, which has been described as "bottom-up management." He surrounded himself with competent senior executives and allowed

COMPANY PERSPECTIVES

For more than 150 years, PNC has been committed to providing our clients with great service and powerful financial expertise to help them meet their financial goals. We are also proud of our longstanding history of supporting the communities we serve—in education and the arts, and in many other ways. Here are the values developed by our employees that have guided us in the past—and continue to guide us today: Performance; Customer Focus; Respect; Integrity; Diversity; Teamwork; and Quality of Life.

them to make decisions on their own. This grassroots approach was rare in banking. Gilliand, however, contended that this method provided better service and, over the long run, a better bank. Under Gilliand's leadership, PNC emphasized quality, not size. Nonetheless, the strategy also proved very conducive to growth in the changing markets of the 1980s.

PNC's chief rival in the 1980s was the Mellon Bank. For years, Mellon controlled the large corporate accounts of Pittsburgh's many companies (the city ranked third in the nation in number of corporate headquarters). As a result, PNC was forced to cater to midsized companies and to businesses outside of Pittsburgh. However, when Pittsburgh's big companies experienced difficulties in the late 1970s and 1980s, PNC was not as exposed to the "rust belt" problems as the Mellon Bank. PNC, under Gilliand, was content to operate on a smaller scale than its rival, striving to provide all the same services with greater quality.

DEREGULATION PROMPTS GROWTH: 1980–89

Banking deregulation allowed, and to some extent encouraged, mergers between banks. As the 1980s wore on, a number of well-run banks found it in their interest to join forces with the PNC group. PNC's acquisition strategy focused on purchasing healthy banks, which would add to the corporation's overall strength. In 1984, PNC acquired the Marine Bank of Erie, Pennsylvania. A year later, it acquired the Northeastern Bancorp of Scranton, Pennsylvania. PNC's criteria for acquisitions were strict by industry standards. Acceptable banks were midsized, with assets of between $2 and $6 billion, had a solid market share in their operating regions, earned excellent return on equity and on assets, and ideally had expertise in a specific area of financial

services which would benefit the entire group. Close attention was also paid to whether or not the bank's management philosophy was compatible with PNC's.

In 1985, Thomas H. O'Brien replaced the retiring Merle Gilliand as CEO at PNC. At 48, O'Brien was the youngest CEO of any major U.S. bank. Ironically, he had started his banking career at PNC's archrival, the Mellon Bank, before earning his MBA at Harvard. O'Brien had risen quickly through the ranks of the Pittsburgh National Bank, eventually heading PNC's merchant banking activities, and finally becoming chairman and chief executive. As the top executive at PNC he continued Gilliand's bottom-up management style. O'Brien would let executives at affiliates implement their own ideas at their own bank without a great deal of interference from the top. As a result of the autonomy PNC gave its affiliated banks, the banking group was an attractive merger partner for exactly the healthy regional banks it wished to acquire. PNC could grow, and the new affiliates could take advantage of the extended services offered by the group. PNC became known for its friendly takeovers of successful banks.

Under O'Brien's conservative yet aggressive leadership, PNC grew at a tremendous rate. In 1986, the Hershey Bank joined the group. The following year, with the acquisition of Citizen's Fidelity Corporation of Louisville, PNC grew larger than its rival, the Mellon Bank. In 1988 PNC acquired the Central Bancorp of Cincinnati and the First Bank and Trust of Mechanicsburg. While acquisitions normally diluted the value of a corporation's stock for some time, PNC's careful planning allowed it to quickly make up for the dilution. By the late 1980s, Wall Street analysts were so confident in PNC's management that acquisition announcements did not seriously reduce the stock's price.

The relaxation of interstate banking regulations in the United States during this time created a new kind of bank: the super-regional. Super-regionals operated in a number of states, and began in the late 1980s to compete with the money center banks for a greater share of large corporate business. As midsized companies needed more services in the international trade arena, the super-regionals became more and more involved there as well. With its network spread throughout Pennsylvania, Kentucky, Ohio, and Delaware, PNC was the premier super-regional in the United States by 1987 and had become the nation's twelfth largest banking group. Its assets had more than doubled since 1983, and its earnings were among the highest in the industry.

Like many banks throughout the world, PNC was forced to set aside huge sums as a provision against bad debt in Third World countries in 1987. Unlike many banks, however, the PNC group still earned a substantial

KEY DATES

1847: The Tradesman National Bank of Philadelphia is established.

1852: Steel magnates James Laughlin and B.F. Jones open the Pittsburgh Trust and Savings.

1959: Pittsburgh Trust and Savings incorporates as Pittsburgh National Bank.

1964: After years of acquisitions and name changes, the Tradesman National Bank officially adopts the name Provident National Corp.

1983: PNC Financial Corp. is formed from the merger of Pittsburgh National Corp. and Provident National Corp.

1999: Company buys First Data Investment Services Group.

2000: The firm adopts a new brand strategy and changes its name to The PNC Financial Services Group.

2008: National City Corp. is acquired.

profit that year, despite its $200 million increase in loan loss reserves. While two-thirds of U.S. banks actually showed losses, PNC netted more than $255 million for its shareholders that year.

The banking group was very conservative in its lending throughout the 1980s. It set limits for the number of loans allowed to any particular industry and enforced stringent credit criteria. At the same time, PNC was energetic in its marketing. The corporation went after trust and money management business as well as corporate lending. PNC affiliates also showed higher than average earnings from fee income.

DIVERSIFICATION THROUGH ACQUISITION: 1990–93

PNC suffered a slight setback in 1989 and 1990 when it was caught with millions in nonperforming commercial real estate loans. Part of them were inherited through its late 1980s acquisitions and resulted in reduced earnings. The company responded by tightening its loan policies and beginning an effort to reduce its dependence on riskier commercial loans in favor of the more dependable consumer sector.

A restructuring in 1991 further reflected PNC's desire to diversify its holdings by focusing company operations on four core businesses: corporate banking, retail banking, investment and trust management, and

investment banking. The following year, with assets reaching $45.5 billion, PNC began a program of consolidation in which all its banks and most of its affiliated companies would take on the name PNC Bank. PNC Financial Corporation itself changed its name to PNC Bank Corp. in early 1993.

PNC's desire to diversify was evident in its non-bank acquisitions of the early 1990s. In 1993, PNC acquired the Massachusetts Company to boost its financial services offerings. That year it also acquired the Sears Mortgage Banking Group, a major home mortgage lender, from Sears Roebuck & Co. for $328 million in cash. The move immediately quadrupled PNC's mortgage business, pushing it into the top 10 nationwide. In 1994, a third major nonbank acquisition bolstered the bank's asset management area. The purchase of BlackRock Financial Management for $240 million in cash and notes increased PNC's amount of assets under management to $75 billion, the sixth-largest amount among bank asset managers.

These acquisitions, however, would pale in comparison to those overseen by chairman and CEO O'Brien in the mid-1990s. As a prelude, in 1993 PNC purchased First Eastern Corp. of Wilkes-Barre, Pennsylvania, for $330 million, solidifying its holdings in northeastern Pennsylvania. In keeping with his strategy of expanding only within or adjacent to PNC's existing retail banking territory, O'Brien then shifted his attention to the Philadelphia area and New Jersey, long a target for PNC growth. Early in 1995, PNC purchased 84 branches in southern and central New Jersey from Chemical Banking Corp. for $504 million. Then in July of that year, the bank announced it would acquire Midlantic Corp. of Edison, New Jersey, through a $2.84 billion stock swap. Midlantic's $13.7 billion in assets would give PNC a total of $75.8 billion in assets, making it the eleventh largest bank in the country. More importantly, PNC had purchased the third-largest bank in New Jersey and had achieved a significant presence there.

GROWTH AND EXPANSION LEADS TO RESTRUCTURING: 1997–99

Through its acquisitions in the early and mid-1990s, PNC Bank Corp. had in many ways created a unique type of bank that could provide a model for others to emulate. It was considered one of the top super-regionals in the country with more than 800 branches in the contiguous area of Indiana, Kentucky, New Jersey, Pennsylvania, and Ohio. At the same time, it was building a national and in some cases international presence in the areas of asset management services and investment banking. Its strong regional retail banking operations coupled with its diversified financial services businesses were designed to help it weather banking downturns that inevitably beset PNC's and other banks' earnings in the past. As barriers to interstate banking continued to fall and bank consolidation continued, PNC was forced to look for ways to remain competitive among its peers.

As such, PNC eyed the expansion of its consumer mortgage business as a potentially lucrative avenue. Through this unit, PNC put plans in motion in 1997 to expand its product offerings. During 1996 its customers had purchased $5.6 billion in mortgages. By cross-selling home equity loans, credit cards, and investment services to these customers, PNC hoped to tap into a niche market where most banks had failed. A 1997 *American Banker* article reported that "banks have failed at cross-selling in the past because they embraced mass marketing, instead of a targeted approach, and did not follow up." PNC however, felt that its mortgage business was well positioned to excel at this new approach. Its efforts proved fruitless, however, and PNC sold its consumer mortgage business in 2000 to Washington Mutual Home Loans Inc.

The company also began a restructuring effort during the late 1990s in order to pare back less profitable operations. In 1997 it closed nine branches and the following year sold 16 Western Pennsylvania-based branches to First Western Bancorp Inc. It also announced that it would sell its credit card business, which included 3.3 million accounts, to MBNA Corp. in order to focus on its investment services and other product lines. The company then made a $1.1 billion purchase of First Data Investor Services Group, a mutual funds and retirement plans services provider. The deal strengthened PNC's investment services subsidiary PFPC Worldwide, making it the leading full-service mutual fund transfer agent and the second-largest full-service mutual fund accounting services provider. PNC also spun off 30 percent of its BlackRock subsidiary in 1999 at $14 per share. Its restructuring efforts appeared to pay off, and in 1999 the company secured $1.3 billion in profits, a 13 percent increase over the previous year. Revenue also increased by 6 percent to $52 billion.

ADOPTING A NEW IMAGE FOR THE NEW MILLENNIUM

Signaling the firm's commitment to its diversified services, PNC adopted a new brand image and changed its name to The PNC Financial Services Group in 2000. That year, O'Brien retired, leaving James E. Rohr at the helm. While under new leadership, the company forged ahead with its plans to invest in high-growth business ventures as it maintained a strong hold on its consumer banking activities. Automated Business Development Corp. was acquired and became part of PFPC's operations. The company also teamed up with Perot Systems to create BillingZone, an electronic bill payment platform. This venture was sold in 2002.

By this time however, PNC not only faced increased competition as the industry continued to consolidate but rough economic times as well. A January 2002 *Institutional Investor* article claimed that both Rohr and PNC were "suffering in a generally difficult climate for banks; the recession has crimped loan growth, pushed credit losses higher and hurt the valuations in securities and venture capital portfolios." As PNC continually restructured and streamlined operations to battle the challenging economic climate, it was forced to post a $615 million fourth-quarter charge in 2001 in order to write down loans, restructure its venture capital business, and exit the auto leasing market.

PNC also came under fire during 2002 and 2003 as the Federal Reserve Board, the Securities and Exchange Commission, and the U.S. Department of Justice announced that they were investigating PNC's accounting practices. To top it off, the company was named in a shareholder class-action lawsuit that claimed that PNC and its auditor Ernst & Young LLP had violated the Securities Exchange Act of 1934 by misrepresenting PNC's financial results from July 19, 2001 to January 29, 2002. The claim also stated that both parties had not used proper accounting standards and therefore had misled investors about the financial condition of the firm. The class-action suit was settled in 2006.

As PNC battled litigation and turbulent economic times, management remained confident that the restructuring of its banking operations would lead to future earnings and profit growth. With a new corporate tagline, "The Thinking behind the Money," PNC was focused on remaining a leader among its peers.

EXPANDING THE BUSINESS: 2003–07

Under the leadership of Rohr, PNC opted to grow its business by way of acquisition. During 2003 the company purchased United National Bancorp. The deal gave PNC inroads in the central New Jersey and Eastern Pennsylvania markets. During 2005, PNC added Harris Williams & Co., a mergers and acquisitions advising firm, to its arsenal. The company's BlackRock venture also expanded its business, acquiring SSRM Holdings Inc. BlackRock then purchased the investment management business of Merrill Lynch & Co. Inc., which secured its position as one of the largest asset management companies in the world with over $1 trillion in assets under management.

One of PNC's more controversial acquisitions of this period came in 2005 when it bought Riggs National Corp. in a $645 million deal. The negotiations were highly contentious as Washington-based Riggs came under fire for violations of the Bank Secrecy Act. PNC attempted to lower its offer after the company pleaded guilty to criminal charges and Riggs subsequently filed suit for breach of contract. The two companies eventually came to an agreement and Riggs accepted PNC's lower offer. Upon completion of the purchase, PNC worked quickly to convert Riggs branches under the PNC name.

PNC continued to expand its business 2007 with the acquisition of Mercantile Bankshares Corporation, which bolstered its presence in the mid-Atlantic region of the United States. ARCS Commercial Mortgage, Yardville National Bancorp, and Sterling Financial Corporation were also acquired that year.

By this time, many financial companies in the United States were struggling due to their exposure to bad loans. With enormous losses stemming from poor investment strategies, many banks found themselves facing potential failure. The financial woes of U.S. banking, credit, and mortgage companies during this period led to an economic recession that was felt across the globe. PNC remained somewhat shielded from these problems, thanks in part to its solid risk management strategy and avoidance of certain leveraged buyout financing and subprime mortgage loans. Many of its peers however, were not as fortunate.

THE NATIONAL CITY DEAL: 2008–09

In October 2008, PNC announced that it planned to purchase National City Corporation, a bank based in Cleveland, Ohio. National City had been established in 1845, shortly after the Ohio Bank Act of that year brought a measure of stability to the state's banking system. Cleveland had endured three years without a bank of any kind and the City Bank of Cleveland, as National City Bank was initially known, was the first to be chartered under the new law.

The company grew steadily throughout its history. National City began to move decisively into full-service retail banking in the post-World War II era, adding a trust department, personalized checks and check sorting, home service representatives, and 24-hour depository services at each branch. The company also began investing in automation, purchasing its first computer in 1959. By the 1960s, National City had 24 branch of-

fices and had crossed the $1 billion asset mark. The bank took its first step toward becoming a major regional player in 1973, when it created National City Corp. as a holding company and made National City Bank its primary subsidiary.

National City experienced growth in the 1980s and 1990s by making key acquisitions. In 1984, it made a $315 million purchase of Columbus's BancOhio Corp. This union of Ohio's second- and third-largest banks created a $12.5 billion asset powerhouse that was 30 percent larger than its next largest rival, BancOne. In 1988 National City beat out four other bidders to win the hand of $6 billion (asset) First Kentucky National Corp. of Louisville. Merchants National Corp. of Indianapolis was purchased in 1991. The company then paid $2.1 billion to add Pittsburgh's Integra Financial Corp. to its holdings in 1995. Other significant purchases included First of America Bank Corporation in 1997, Provident Financial Group in 2004, as well as financial institutions in the Chicago, Florida, Milwaukee, and St. Louis markets.

During the financial crisis of 2007 and 2008 National City was hit hard, due in part to huge losses in its mortgage business. It was left with few options when PNC announced it would acquire the firm. A 2008 *Cleveland Plain Dealer* article explained the bank's predicament. "National City had been crippled after years of rapid expansion of its mortgage business, losses on high-risk loans and costly purchases of other banks and its own stock." The article went on to claim, "The bank's board decided to sell after regulators told National City it very likely would not receive money through the Treasury's $700 billion effort to bolster the financial industry, according to regulatory filings."

PNC, on the other hand, received $7.7 billion as part of the government's Troubled Asset Relief Program (TARP) with the condition that it would buy National City. The acquisition closed on December 31, 2008, and secured PNC's position as the fifth-largest bank in the United States based on deposits. National City branches were converted to PNC locations during 2009 and 2010. PNC repaid its TARP loan in February 2010. That same month, the company announced plans to sell PNC Global Investment Servicing Inc.

Under Rohr's leadership, PNC appeared to have weathered the economic crisis better than most of its competitors. With the exception of the fourth quarter of 2008, the company had posted profits in every quarter since the recession began in 2007. Overall, net income was $2.4 billion in fiscal 2009. With nearly 2,500 branches in approximately 15 states throughout the mid-Atlantic and midwestern regions of the United

States, PNC believed it was well positioned for growth in the years to come.

Updated, April Dougal Gasbarre; David E. Salamie;
Christina M. Stansell

PRINCIPAL SUBSIDIARIES

PNC Bancorp, Inc.; PNC Bank, National Association; PNC Bank Capital Securities, LLC; PNC Capital Leasing, LLC; PNC Preferred Funding LLC; PNC REIT Corp.; PNC Holding, LLC; PNC Funding Corp.; PNC Investment Corp.; PNC Venture, LLC.

PRINCIPAL COMPETITORS

Bank of America Corp.; Citizens Financial Group; JP-Morgan Chase & Co.

FURTHER READING

Chase, Brett, "Protégé Succeeds Mentor at PNC's Flagship Bank," *American Banker*, June 2, 1997, p. 5.

Fitzpatrick, Dan, David Enrich, and Damian Paletta, "PNC Buys National City in Bank Shakeout," *Wall Street Journal*, October 25, 2008.

Garver, Rob, "Jim Rohr Makes Right Choices in Trying Times for PNC, Industry," *American Banker*, November 30, 2007.

Gold, Jacqueline S., "Bank to Basics," *Institutional Investor*, January 2002, p. 91.

"Hail to the Chief," *US Banker*, March 2000, p. 14.

"In Brief: PNC Bank Selling Card Business to MBNA," *American Banker*, December 28, 1998.

Jarboe, Michelle, "Investors OK National City Sale," *Cleveland Plain Dealer*, December 24, 2008.

Lombaerde, Geert De, "PNC Bank Beat Goals to Boost 1999 Profits," *Business Courier Serving Cincinnati*, February 11, 2000, p. 4.

Pacelle, Mitchell, "PNC to Buy Riggs for $645 Million in New Agreement," *Wall Street Journal*, February 11, 2005.

"PNC Chairman: We Won't Be Forced to Merge," *American Banker*, August 7, 1998, p. 24.

Rieker, Matthais, "PNC 'Repositions' Itself, Taking $615M Charge," *American Banker*, January 4, 2002, p. 20.

Sabatini, Patricia, "PNC to Repay Bailout Money," *Pittsburgh Post-Gazette*, February 3, 2010.

Talley, Karen, "PNC Unit's Expansion Plan Includes Cross-Selling Push," *American Banker*, January 30, 1997, p. 81.

Tascarella, Patty, "PNC Trims Branches and Workers as Part of Major Restructuring Plan," *Pittsburgh Business Times*, February 27, 1998, p. 4.

Winokur, Cheryl, "PNC Unveils $1.1B Deal for First Data Subsidiary," *American Banker*, July 21, 1999, p. 1.

Ports Design Ltd.

Suite 3310-11, Tower One
Times Square, 1 Matheson Street
Causeway Bay
Hong Kong
Telephone: (+852) 25060 138
Fax: (+852) 25060 908
Web site: http://www.portsdesign.com

Public Company
Founded: 1961 as Newport Canada
Employees: 5,220
Sales: RMB 1.54 billion ($192 million) (2009)
Stock Exchanges: Hong Kong
Ticker Symbol: 00589
NAICS: 315232 Women's and Girls' Cut and Sew Blouse and Shirt Manufacturing; 315233 Women's and Girls' Cut and Sew Dress Manufacturing; 315234 Women's and Girls' Cut and Sew Suit, Coat, Tailored Jacket, and Skirt Manufacturing; 315999 Other Apparel Accessories and Other Apparel Manufacturing

∎∎∎

Ports Design Ltd. is the holding company for the Ports International and Ports 1961 luxury clothing and accessories brands. Ports is a highly integrated company, with its own manufacturing facilities, including its main facility in Xiamen, China, and a smaller factory in Toronto, Canada, and a design team led by Creative Director Tia Cibani. Ports Design's retail division accounted for nearly 93 percent of the group's sales of RMB 1.54 billion ($192 million) in 2009. This division oversees more than 300 stores in China, as well as shops in the United States, Canada, Europe, and elsewhere.

The company's small original equipment manufacture (OEM) division produces garments for third parties, primarily for the North American and European markets. This division accounted for less than 5 percent of the group's sales in 2009. In that year Ports Design created a new Licensed Brands Division, in order to include the BMW Lifestyle line of clothing, accessories, and more than 30 shops. Other brands in this division include Vivienne Tam, Armani, Max Mara, Ferrari, and, since 2010, Versace. Ports Design expected this division to account for 20 percent of group sales by 2015. Ports Design is listed on the Hong Kong Stock Exchange. The company is led by brothers Alfred and Edward Chan. The Chans also control the fast-growing Chinese high-end department store group PCD Stores (Group) Limited.

CANADIAN ROOTS IN 1961

Ports Design traces its origins to two families, both of whom immigrated to Canada from the Far East. Luke Tanabe was born in Vancouver in 1920. His parents had traveled to Canada from Japan and had set up a successful watch repair and jewelry store. Tanabe attended the University of British Columbia, where he studied business and finance. His career ambitions were cut short, however, with the outbreak of World War II and his internment in a Japanese detention camp. Tanabe was put to work by the Ontario Farm Service Force during this period.

Tanabe worked for a time as a glove salesman after the war. His success in this field led to an offer to establish a Canadian branch for a rival glove maker based in New York. In 1961 Tanabe moved into business for himself, forming a partnership with a Japanese company to establish a new company, Newport Canada. That company then began importing clothing from Japan and other Asian markets for the Canadian market.

By the middle of the decade Tanabe had decided to establish his own clothing company. Called Ports International, the new company at first focused on Japanese imports, including blouses featuring the new imitation silk fabrics being produced by Japan at the time. Tanabe soon began developing his own clothing designs. This effort led to his first true success, the No. 10 Blouse. This classically tailored blouse, made from Egyptian cotton, quickly propelled Tanabe to the forefront of Canadian fashion.

INTERNATIONAL GROWTH

Before long, Ports International outgrew its original storefront offices and established new headquarters in Vancouver's Royal Bank Tower. The company also opened a showroom on the Queen's Quay Terminal. Based on the success of the No. 10 Blouse, Ports International developed a full line of women's clothing, expanding its sales to a wide range of high-end department stores and other retailers. Ports International began its international expansion in the 1970s, adding its first store in the United States, on New York's Fifth Avenue. Other U.S. locations soon followed, including in Chicago; Washington, D.C.; and Boston.

Ports International made its first move into the European market in 1983, opening a store on New Bond Street in London, and shops in Bath and Cambridge. In the middle of the decade Ports International began targeting the Asian market, launching a new brand, Tabi International, and opening a store in Tokyo.

By the end of the decade Ports International had achieved sales of more than CAD 70 million, and oper-ated 50 stores, primarily in the United States and Canada. Under Tanabe, Ports International also received credit for launching the careers of a number of Canadian designers, including Dean and Dan Caten (of Dsquared2 fame). Tanabe himself retired in 1989.

NEW OWNERS IN 1989

Tanabe sold the company that year to Etac Sales Ltd., which had been established as a contract manufacturing company by another Canadian immigrant family in the 1970s. The Chan family had been prosperous in pre-Communist China, with interests in mining and textiles. Following the Communist Revolution, the family fled to Hong Kong, where they launched a small textiles manufacturing and export business. From Hong Kong the family, seeking new entrepreneurial opportunities, moved to Canada in order to expand into the textile market there. Elder son Edward Chan joined the family business, while his younger brother Alfred earned a degree in physics at McGill University.

Following his graduation, however, Alfred Chan decided to enter the textiles trade as well, setting up Etac Sales with his brother in 1975. The company at first focused on supplying North American retailers, including Kmart and Bargain Harold's, with clothing and home furnishings imported from Hong Kong and China, including from the family's own factory in Xiamen.

Through the 1980s, however, the Chans found themselves vulnerable to developing trends in the global retail market. Increasingly, manufacturers had begun to shut down their factories, instead turning to third-party producers in low-wage markets, including China and other Asian markets. At the same time, retailers also started to purchase directly from these manufacturers, eliminating middlemen like Etac.

The Chans recognized the need to evolve with the new market environment. As Alfred Chan told the *Wall Street Journal*, "As a contract manufacturer you're vulnerable, dependent on orders. I didn't want to be that way." Instead, Chan decided to develop his own portfolio of high-end clothing brands. The purchase of Ports International helped to jump-start the company's new strategy, bringing it a well-respected international brand name, and its own retail operations, including its prestigious Fifth Avenue location.

REBIRTH

Etac, which went public during this time, launched an expansion drive, doubling the number of stores in its retail network and boosting sales to more than CAD

KEY DATES

1961: Luke Tanabe founds Newport Canada as a clothing import business.

1966: Tanabe founds Ports International and begins designing his own clothing range, including the No. 10 Blouse.

1975: Alfred and Edward Chan found Etac Sales in Canada.

1989: Etac acquires Ports International after Tanabe retires.

1994: The Chans acquire the Chinese rights to the Ports International brand, as Etac declares bankruptcy.

2003: The company goes public as Ports Design Ltd. and launches the Ports 1961 luxury clothing brand.

2010: Ports Design opens a Ports 1961 store in London.

200 million ($165 million) by 1992. Etac then launched an acquisition drive, acquiring the Bretton department store group, boosting its retail operations to more than 150 stores. Another acquisition came in 1991, when the company acquired the rights to the well-known Canadian brand, Alfred Sung, for a 50-year period. That company had been owned by the Monaco Group, which had slipped into losses amid the economic recession of the time.

The poor economic climate, which caused the collapse of a number of Canadian retail and fashion groups, soon caught up with Etac as well. To make matters more difficult for the company, the Canadian government had eliminated the system of import tariffs that had kept many of Etac's larger U.S. competitors from entering the Canadian market. Already overextended from its expansion drive, Etac's retail operations suffered in the new competitive climate. The Chans were forced to exit the company, turning it over to its creditors. By 1994 Etac had been forced to declare bankruptcy. The company's shareholders bore the brunt of the loss, while the Chans found their reputation heavily tarnished.

FOCUS ON THE CHINESE MARKET

The Chans had not completely abandoned Ports International, however. In 1993 Alfred Chan reached an agreement with Etac's receivers to acquire the Asian

rights to Ports International, as well as its Xiamen factory, for CAD 6 million. As Chan explained to the *Wall Street Journal*: "We left open the door." Returning to China, which he had left when he was just two months old, Chan quickly recognized the potential for establishing a high-end clothing brand there.

At that time, the economic reforms launched by the Chinese government in the late 1970s were just beginning to transform the country. Nevertheless, by the early 1990s, the country was witnessing the growth of an upwardly mobile middle class. Moreover, the absence of other luxury brands in the market provided strong opportunities for the Ports International brand. As Alfred Chan added: "Every consumer was a blank piece of paper."

Ports International focused its growth on the Chinese market, establishing a retail network in the country's larger cities. By 1995 Ports International's clothing designs were featured in more than 200 retail locations, including a growing number of the company's own stores. Ports had also brought in a new creative team, led by Tia Cibani, a South African native and graduate of the Parsons School of Design. Cibani, who was also Alfred Chan's sister-in-law, had at first worked for Ports under the Caten brothers. When they left to found their Dsquared2 line, Cibani took over as creative director of Ports.

LUXURY BRAND IN 2003

The Chans brought in new institutional investors, including Suez Asia, in order to fuel the company's expansion in the rapidly growing Chinese market. Ports International enjoyed a number of advantages in the Chinese market, not the least of which was its early entry into the market. This enabled the company to secure its reputation as a top luxury brand before facing competition from its global rivals later in the decade.

To reinforce its image, the company began working early on with a number of the world's supermodels, including Claudia Schiffer and Kate Moss. The company's integrated operations also set it apart from competitors. By manufacturing its own clothing in China, the company remained a lower-priced alternative to other luxury brands. This too allowed the company to maintain its position at the top of the market.

Ports began to develop its own brand line at the dawn of the new century. In 2000 the company negotiated an exclusive license to develop and market a line of clothing and accessories under the BMW brand. The company launched the BMW Lifestyle line that year, opening the first retail locations under the new brand as well. The company expanded the BMW range through the decade to include men's and women's clothing and accessories, as well as other items, including a line of bicycles.

INTRODUCING PORTS 1961

Creative Director Cibani, in the meantime, had begun developing the concept for a new and higher-end clothing label, designed not only for the Chinese market, but also to reintroduce the Ports brand to the international fashion markets. In 2002 the company began testing the new brand, called Ports 1961 in honor of the year of the company's founding, with the opening of three flagship stores in Canada. The success of the launch encouraged the company to roll out a wider expansion, earmarking up to $80 million to support the brand. This included the opening of a 10,000-square-foot showroom in New York City in 2003. Ports went public in 2003, listing its shares under the Ports Design Ltd. name on the Hong Kong Stock Exchange.

The New York store in turn enabled the company to attract a number of celebrity clients, including Nicole Kidman, Portia de Rossi, and Sandra Bullock. The company's designs were also featured in two high-profile movies, *The Devil Wears Prada* and *Sex in the City*, further enhancing its reputation. As part of the effort to develop a celebrity client list, the company added the "Par Mains" ("By Hand") evening wear collection, which debuted in 2007. As a result, the Ports 1961 brand became a fixture in a number of high-end department stores, including Saks Fifth Avenue. In support of the company's growing North American sales, Cibani moved its design offices to New York City in 2007.

LICENSED BRANDS DIVISION IN 2009

Ports Design continued to seek out new additions to its branded lines. The company lost in its bid for the license for the Jil Sander brand in China. The company proved more successful in its bids for the licenses for Armani, Vivienne Tam, Max Mara, and Ferrari. This success led Ports to develop a new Licensed Brands Division in 2009. The company then forecast that the division would come to represent 20 percent of its total revenues by 2015. Ports Design took a large step in that direction in 2010, when it acquired the rights to famed Italian label Versace.

At the same time, the company began reshuffling its retail operations in China, shutting down a number of its older stores in favor of more high-profile locations, which opened under the Ports 1961 brand. This brand also spearheaded the expansion of the company's retail

operations to include a growing number of in-store boutiques, tapping into the rapid development of the department store sector in China since the beginning of the 21st century.

The growing success of the Ports 1961 label also encouraged Ports Design to expand its international operations in the next decade. This effort began with a return to the United Kingdom and the opening of a Ports 1961 store in Knightsbridge, London, in February 2010. At the same time, Ports Design celebrated its success in China, as *GQ China* placed the company among the top 10 luxury brands in the country. The Ports brand had weathered the often-stormy seas of fashion to become one of China's, and the world's, most prominent clothing brands.

M. L. Cohen

PRINCIPAL SUBSIDIARIES

Etac Fashion (Xiamen) Ltd. (PRC); Ports Asia Holdings Limited (British Virgin Islands); Ports International (Beijing) Co., Ltd. (PRC); Ports International Marketing (Xiamen) Ltd. (PRC); Ports International Marketing Ltd. (British Virgin Islands); Ports Retail (H.K.) Limited Hong Kong; Smythe Trading Company Limited (Samoa Islands); Xiamen Brimeland Garments Ltd. (PRC); Xiamen Xiangyu Ports Trading Co., Ltd. (PRC).

PRINCIPAL DIVISIONS

OEM; Retail; Licensed Brands; Other.

PRINCIPAL OPERATING UNITS

Ports 1961.

PRINCIPAL COMPETITORS

Beijing Guanghua Times Textile Import and Export Company Ltd.; Esquel Enterprises Ltd.; Garment Company No. 20; General Import-Export and Investment Corp.; Hongdou Group Company Ltd.; Zhejiang 3colour Costume Company Ltd.

FURTHER READING

Cheng, Andy, "Ports Sews Up Leather Venture with European Partner," *South China Morning Post*, March 29, 2006.

Dodes, Rachel, and Mei Fong, "Upstart Seeks to Create a Chinese Fashion Power," *Wall Street Journal*, March 10, 2007.

Flannery, Russell, "Tailored for China," *Forbes Global*, October 30, 2006, p. 58.

Pitts, Gordon, "Ports Finds Redemption in Shanghai," *Globe and Mail*, October 23, 2004.

"Ports Design Eyes Faster Store Chain Growth," *just-style.com*, April 6, 2006.

Pugh, Clifford, "Ethnic Dresses," *Houston Chronicle*, March 22, 2009, p. 3.

Shih, Toh Han, "Fashion Firm Seeks Liquidity in Listing," *South China Morning Post*, October 13, 2003.

Smith, Susan, "Luke Tanabe, 89, Entrepreneur," *Globe and Mail*, January 8, 2010.

Quiznos Corporation

1001 17th Street, Suite 200
Denver, Colorado 80202-2035
U.S.A.
Telephone: (720) 359-3300
Fax: (720) 291-0909
Web site: http://www.quiznos.com

Private Company
Incorporated: 1981 as Quizno's America Inc.
Employees: 200 (est.)
Sales: $200 million (2009 est.)
NAICS: 722211 Limited-Service Restaurants

■ ■ ■

Quiznos Corporation operates the number two submarine sandwich chain in the United States with more than 4,500 franchised quick-service restaurants producing made-to-order, oven-toasted sandwiches. Classic Italian submarines form the cornerstone of the Quiznos concept. Quiznos also serves salads, soups, and desserts. It has locations in more than 20 countries, including the United States, Canada, Puerto Rico, the United Kingdom, Australia, and Japan. Founder Rick Schaden and his family control the company with backing from investment firms CCMP Capital and Cervantes Capital. Franchise operators pay royalties and fees in return for the right to use properties and must agree to meet certain standards for food quality and customer service.

AN ITALIAN-STYLE DELI NAMED QUIZNO'S: 1981

Todd Disner and Boyd Bartlett formulated the brand concept and menu for The Quiznos Master LLC (originally Quizno's America) while operating a popular Italian restaurant, Footer's, in the Capital Hill neighborhood of Denver, Colorado. Using their knowledge of Italian foods, they developed an Italian-style deli, serving submarine sandwiches, soups, salads, and a few pasta dishes. In Footer's kitchen, Disner and Bartlett created recipes for red wine vinegar dressing and a proprietary soft baguette, essential ingredients in the classic Italian submarine that became the cornerstone of the Quizno's concept. They used quality meats, such as honey-cured ham and whole muscle meats, rather than chopped and formed meats. Before adding lettuce, tomatoes, and red onions, they oven-toasted the sandwich to melt the cheese and to bring out the flavor of the meat and bread.

Disner and Bartlett sought to attract an upmarket customer with a taste for a healthy alternative to fast-food hamburgers. In contrast to full-service restaurants, Quizno's offered a less-expensive option, with an atmosphere more pleasant than typical fast-food restaurants. They invented the faux-Italian name Quizno's, using some of the most remembered letters of the alphabet.

The first Quizno's opened in 1981, a few blocks from Footer's and near city and state offices, attracting a white-collar lunch crowd. During the next decade, 16 more Quizno's franchises opened in the Denver area and along the front range of the Rocky Mountains, and one franchise in Los Angeles. In 1990 each restaurant's sales averaged $27,000 per month.

The franchise grew without improvements to individual restaurants, however, and the quality of the product deteriorated at some locations. Disner and Bartlett did not have the capital to continue expanding the chain or to provide managerial or advertising support to existing franchises. They sold the company in 1991 to franchisee Rick Schaden, who owned and operated three units with his father, Dick Schaden, an aviation attorney. Disner maintained an 8 percent interest in the company and acted as consultant, while Bartlett became vice president of purchasing.

Rick Schaden's desire to own and operate a chain of restaurants began with employment at fast-food chains and a business plan he wrote for a university business class. Schaden was prompted to open a Quizno's franchise while patronizing one of the restaurants when he overheard a customer say, "This is the best sandwich I ever ate." With his father, Schaden opened his first Quizno's franchise in Boulder, Colorado, in 1987.

NEW OWNERS STRUCTURE FOR GROWTH

After purchasing the entire company in January 1991, the Schadens began to develop the infrastructure for future growth. Rick Schaden, as president, organized volume purchasing and standardized procedures for unit operations and new franchisee training. The Schadens planned for growth, seeking to expand into Florida, California, Kansas City, Chicago, and Detroit. New franchise agreements involved Schaden & Schaden, a franchisee separate from the corporation, for rights to two stores in the Detroit area. Four franchises were sold for the California market. In July Disner agreed to open 10 stores in Florida.

To open a franchise required initial capital of approximately $100,000, including the Quizno's franchise fee of $15,000. The franchise company charged an an-

nual royalty of 5 percent of sales as well. The Schadens asserted substantial control over the franchises, influencing choice of location and ingredient vendors and determining training procedures. At 1,800 to 2,000 square feet, each store offered approximately 60 seats. The decor conveyed the look of an Italian deli, with artificial salamis, cheeses, and strings of garlic hung around an open kitchen and with shelves holding olive oil and canned tomatoes. Italian poster art, black-and-white tile floors, pine wainscoting with oak trim, and carpeting in the dining area completed the atmosphere.

Under the leadership of the Schadens, Quizno's assisted its franchisees with new marketing initiatives. With a budget of $50,000, Quizno's launched an advertising campaign in June 1991, using the tagline "Good food. Good prices." Three television commercials promoted Quizno's as an alternative to fast food, emphasizing the lightness, taste, and healthfulness of a Quizno's meal. Radio advertising supplemented the television ads. In 1992 Quizno's increased the advertising budget to $250,000, raising $100,000 from franchise owners for cooperative advertising.

GOING PUBLIC: 1994

Rick Schaden attributed much of the success of the company's low-budget advertising to direct contact with customers as a supplement to commercial advertising. Unit managers distributed menus to businesses in their neighborhood, promoting office catering with box lunches and offering frequent-buyer discounts. The business lunch crowd, patrons from 25 to 45 years of age, accounted for approximately 80 percent of store revenues with sales occurring between 11:30 a.m. and 1:30 p.m.

To attract families in the evenings and on weekends, Quizno's offered free children's meals. The children's menu included pizza, spaghetti, and mini-subs, regularly priced at $1.99, including chocolate pudding and fruit punch. The company coordinated a 1992 promotion with the launch of the Colorado Rockies National League baseball team, during which Denver-area Quizno's restaurants sold baseballs for 99 cents with the purchase of a meal.

By the end of 1992 system-wide store sales increased from $7 million in 1991 to $8.5 million. With average per person sales at $5, average per unit sales reached $338,000 in 1992. By the end of 1993 Quizno's company-owned or franchised restaurants operated in Michigan, Illinois, Kansas, Iowa, Missouri, Georgia, Florida, Oregon, California, and Colorado. Average per unit sales increased to $360,000.

In February 1994 the Schadens took Quizno's public with an offering of one million shares of stock at

KEY DATES

1981: Todd Disner and Boyd Bartlett open the first Quizno's.
1991: Rick Schaden buys the company.
1994: Schaden takes Quizno's public; Quizno's Franchise Corporation purchases Schaden & Schaden, the company's separate franchise company.
1999: The first Quizno's opens in Tokyo.
2006: J.P. Morgan buys an undisclosed stake in the company.
2007: Turnaround expert Gregory Brenneman becomes CEO of the company.
2009: Rick Schaden resumes his former role of CEO.

$5 per share. The initial public offering yielded $4.4 million, which the company used to open new stores and pursue franchise sales, particularly through area directors.

AGGRESSIVE EXPANSION PROGRAM

The Quizno's program for expansion involved the recruitment of area directors. Quizno's sold the rights to certain market territories to area directors who agreed to sell and open a specific number of franchises within a predetermined amount of time. The usual schedule involved four new units the first year, six new units the second year, and an additional eight units the third year. Franchise territories followed the location of television markets, and general locations were planned ahead to avoid oversaturating a market area, a problem with other chain restaurants. Area directors paid fees to sell franchises, but earned commissions and royalties from franchise sales and revenues. In 1994 Quizno's found area directors for five territories: Dallas-Fort Worth; Seattle; Tucson, Arizona; Omaha and Lincoln, Nebraska; and Montana, northern Wyoming, and western South Dakota.

In November 1994 Quizno's Franchise Corporation purchased Schaden & Schaden, the then separate franchise company of the Schadens, for $2 million. The largest franchisee, Schaden & Schaden owned and operated six restaurants in Denver, three in Chicago, and two in Michigan, and held management contracts for five additional franchisees. The acquisition provided revenue and cash flow for training new franchisees and

managers. In order to improve cash flow, Quizno's also increased the initial franchise fee to $20,000 for full-size units and $10,000 for new, kiosk-type Express Quizno's units. Additional units that were opened required lower franchise fees.

Quizno's enhanced its area director program to promote more rapid development, waiving, for example, the requirement to open a flagship unit. In 1995 the company signed area directors for El Paso and Austin, eastern North Dakota, Minneapolis/St. Paul, western Nebraska, Cleveland, and Spokane. BBD Management of Vancouver signed a master franchise agreement, the term for international licensing of franchise rights, to open 30 Quizno's units in Canada during the next six years.

NUMBER THREE IN 1997

Prompted by higher construction and real estate costs, Quizno's in 1995 changed the store design to reduce start-up costs by 25 percent, from approximately $60,000 to $40,000. The 1,800-square-foot requirement was modified to 1,200 square feet. To accommodate the change, the company altered the kitchen layout from a double production line to a single line. Open counter service allowed for greater customer contact and, hence, fewer mistakes on customer orders. The smaller size of each store was conducive to greater flexibility in finding good store locations.

New store openings in 1995 included Boise; Phoenix; Denver; Raleigh; Indianapolis; Kenosha, Wisconsin; and Loveland, Colorado. In December 1995 the 100th Quizno's restaurant opened and, by the end of 1995, 112 Quizno's restaurants were in operation in 19 states with system-wide sales of $26 million.

In 1996 and 1997 the company's expansion efforts led to the sale of franchise territories and new restaurant openings. In 1996 the company opened 51 restaurants, including eight company-owned units. Over a dozen area directors agreed to sell franchises in Palm Beach County, Florida; Shreveport, Louisiana; Contra Costa County, California; Hartford and New Haven, Connecticut; Philadelphia; Knoxville; Richmond, Virginia; Huntsville, Alabama; and other areas across the United States. In 1997, 140 new restaurants opened. Quizno's also acquired Bain's Deli, a chain of 63 restaurants located primarily in shopping malls along the East Coast, for $1.2 million. Quizno's began to convert several of these stores to the Quizno's brand, and later converted units at shopping mall food courts and airports.

By the end of 1997 Quizno's had become the country's number three submarine sandwich franchiser, with 278 locations in the United States, Puerto Rico, and Canada. Subway held the number one position with 12,000 units, and Blimpie was number two with 1,500 units.

FORGING A NATIONAL AND INTERNATIONAL IDENTITY

The company launched its first national advertising campaign in 1998 with television spots on cable stations, including CNN, ESPN, and Discovery. The three television commercials focused on the fact that Quizno's submarine sandwiches were toasted, using the terms *toast* and *toasted* as puns. In the Denver area, where the advertisements aired on local stations during news shows, the commercials included a local promotion with the Colorado Lottery.

With eight units opened and 50 units planned for 1998, Quizno's Canada obtained master franchise rights to franchise up to 650 restaurants in Canada over the next 5 to 10 years, paying Quizno's $573,000 in fees. In March 1999 Quizno's Canada paid $510,000 for the rights to franchise 100 units in the United Kingdom over 10 years. Glenvista Enterprises paid $221,069 for the same number of franchises in the Australian states of Queensland, New South Wales, and Victoria.

Quizno's had been looking for someone to open franchises in Japan when Nick Nishigane of KMN USA LLC approached Quizno's to purchase the franchising rights. Nishigane thought that the food fit with Japanese tastes, finding the honey bacon club to be quite popular among KMN employees. He planned to hire a Japanese chef to adjust some of the sauce recipes and to supplement the menu with local dishes. In September 1998 KMN USA signed a master franchise agreement to develop up to 300 Quizno's in Japan during a period of 10 years. The agreement involved a percentage of territory and franchise sales as well as royalties on store revenues. The first unit opened in Tokyo in early 1999.

EXPANDING REACH

Quizno's did not rely solely on new franchise openings to expand the company's reach. In August 1998 a new subsidiary, Quizno's Kansas LLC, purchased the Stoic Restaurant Group. The 21-year-old company owned and operated 12 Sub & Stuff units, but had filed for bankruptcy. Quizno's Kansas, 70 percent owned by Quizno's Corporation and 30 percent owned by two area directors, purchased the company for $500,000. Quizno's planned to convert eight stores in prime locations to Quizno's stores, and either sell or close the remaining four units, bringing to 11 the total number

of Quizno's units in Wichita. Quizno's also sold rights to 49 of the 63 Bain's franchises, converted six of the shops to Quizno's, and retained eight Bain's franchises, hoping that the franchisees might convert to Quizno's.

With adjustments to its fees, Quizno's experienced a rise in first-time franchisees. The company lowered royalty fees a full percentage point to 7 percent of store revenues and lowered training fees from $15,000 to $10,000. Major areas of new store development included Toronto; Milwaukee; Jacksonville; Detroit; Sacramento; Baltimore; Washington, D.C.; Houston; and Columbus, Ohio. With 167 new restaurant openings in 1998 and 258 openings in 1999, at the end of fiscal 1999 there were 634 Quizno's sub shops in operation, including 25 company-owned units and 72 international locations.

With about one unit per day scheduled to open in 2000, Quizno's doubled its advertising budget to $10 million. The company hired a new marketing director, Rob Elliott, formerly with Little Caesar's Pizza. Under Elliott's leadership Quizno's retained a new advertising agency, Cliff Freeman & Partners. Freeman's credits included the Wendy's Hamburgers tagline "Where's the Beef?" and Little Caesar's, "Pizza! Pizza!" For Quizno's Freeman developed commercials based on the tagline "It's that good."

TAKING THE COMPANY PRIVATE IN 2001

At the end of fiscal 2000, Quizno's recorded corporate revenues of $41.4 million and garnered a net income of $1.1 million. Same-store sales for units open one year rose 7.9 percent. Of the 380 new sub shops opened in 2000, 52 units were located in foreign markets. In November 2000, after the stock's price had languished for several years, the Schadens restated a proposal to take the company private with a tender offer of $8 per share. The privatization deal finally closed in June 2001, with shareholders receiving $8.50 per share. However, 95 percent of non-Schaden shares voted against the move and three large shareholders sued, eventually winning four times the tender offer's payment in 2004.

By 2002 the growth of submarine sandwich chains, as well as sandwich restaurant chains, reflected the changing tastes of consumers. Those who had grown up on fast food were searching for a healthy alternative to burgers and pizza, leading to the development of a new category of food establishment positioned between fast-food and sit-down restaurants. According to *Nation's Restaurant News*, Quizno's was the fastest-growing chain in the "adult quick-service" or "fast casual" restaurant category with 1,200 units. It remained so throughout the next two years.

EXPANDING MARKET SHARE

To gain more market share, the company targeted its marketing efforts to attract younger customers. It dropped its old red-and-green Italian deli décor in favor of a purple, blue, and red scheme; expanded its condiment bar to include banana, jalapeno, and pepperoncini peppers and gourmet sauces and pickles; and installed a beverage station. Newer stores had a large viewing window in their ovens. Quizno's also discovered a growing crowd of family patrons, and expanded the evening menu for children accordingly.

The effort worked and by 2003 Quizno's had 2,000 restaurants (up from 1,000 in the year 2000). *Entrepreneur Magazine* listed Quizno's as number seven in its Top 10 Franchises of 2003. In 2005 Quizno's was number two on *Entrepreneur Magazine's* Top 10 Franchises list and third on *QSR Magazine's* Top 50 Chains list for its increase in sales in 2004.

By 2007 Quiznos restaurants numbered 5,000. However, Quiznos (which had dropped the apostrophe in its name in 2004) was the defendant in several lawsuits filed by potential franchisees who claimed that the company had pocketed their $25,000 licensing fee without finding them a store location within the promised 12-month time frame. In 2006 Quiznos disclosed that as of December 31, 2005, close to 3,000 franchisees, or 67 percent of those waiting to open a store, had not opened stores within the allotted 12-month period.

Other lawsuits from franchisees contended that the company forced them to buy everything, including cleaning supplies, music, and payroll and accounting systems, as well as food, at top dollar from Quiznos-owned suppliers and distributors.

CHANGES IN OWNERSHIP AND LEADERSHIP

Schaden put Quiznos on the market in 2006, and J.P. Morgan bought an undisclosed stake in the company. The company brought turnaround specialist Gregory Brenneman on board as chief executive in January 2007 to address franchisees' concerns. His company, Turnworks, took an equity position in Quiznos.

Brenneman noted that "food costs, as a percentage of revenue, were clearly out of line," in a 2007 *New York Times* article, and his goal became to reduce food costs enough that profits at an average Quiznos would climb by at least $10,000 a year. He also promised to cut back on company-issued coupons and lowered prices on some supplies.

Brenneman stepped down in 2008, and Dave Deno, formerly of rival YUM! Brands, replaced him as chief executive. Five months later, in 2009, Deno resigned and was succeeded by Rick Schaden. The Toasted Subs Franchisee Association, representing Quiznos franchisees, which still had four class-action suits with Quiznos pending, described Schaden's return in a 2009 *Denver Westward* article as a "slap in the face."

Meanwhile, Quiznos continued its battle to wrest the number one domestic sub slot from chief rival Subway with the launch of its Torpedo sandwiches in 2009. In addition, Quiznos aimed to win customers from the dominant burger chains and to increase its dinner traffic with new menu items, such as its prime rib sandwiches.

Mary Tradii
Updated, Carrie Rothburd

PRINCIPAL SUBSIDIARIES

QUIZ-DIA, Inc.; Quizno's Kansas LLC; The Quizno's Licensing Company; The Quizno's Operating Company; The Quizno's Realty Company; S&S, Inc.

PRINCIPAL DIVISIONS

Franchise Development; Franchise Support Services.

PRINCIPAL COMPETITORS

Burger King Holdings, Inc.; Chipotle Mexican Grill, Inc.; Decatur Subway Inc.; Domino's Pizza, Inc.; Doctor's Associates Inc. (Subway); Einstein Noah Restaurant Group, Inc.; International Dairy Queen, Inc.; Jack in the Box Inc.; McDonald's Corporation; Panera Bread Company; Sonic Corp.; Wendy's/Arby's Group, Inc., YUM! Brands, Inc.

FURTHER READING

Ahrens, Frank, "For Quizno's, Call It 'Super Sub-Day'; Sandwich Chain Making Encore Ad Appearance in Super Bowl," *Washington Post*, January 18, 2003, p. E1.

Bunn, Dina, "Quizno's Bags Juicy Japanese Deal," *Rocky Mountain News*, September 30, 1998, p. 2B.

Cebrzynski, Gregg, "Man Wrestles Dog, Woman Picks Trash in 'Bold' Ads for Quizno's Subs," *Nation's Restaurant News*, June 12, 2000, p. 16.

Centers, Jessica, "Rick Schaden, Accused of Ripping Off Franchisees, Is Back at the Helm of Quiznos," *Denver Westward*, March 5, 2009.

———, "You're Toast!: Franchise Owners Thought They'd Make a Fortune Serving the Toasted Sandwiches Created by Quiznos. Instead They Got Burned," *Denver Westward*, May

3, 2007.

Creswell, Julie, "Some Quiznos Franchisees Take Chain to Court," *New York Times*, February 24, 2007, p. 1.

Draper, Heather, "Quizno's Becomes Private with Shareholder Buyout," *Rocky Mountain News*, June 23, 2001, p. 3C.

"Judge Rules for Dissident Quizno's Shareholders," *AP State & Local Wire*, January 11, 2004.

Leib, Jeffrey, "Two Quizno's Execs Offer to Buy Company,"

Denver Post, December 30, 1998, p. C1.

Raabe, Steve, "Quizno's Management Launches a $23 Million Stock Buyback," *Denver Post*, November 14, 2000, p. C5.

Rubinstein, Ed, "Quizno's Sub Chain: On a Roll and in the Black," *Nation's Restaurant News*, July 27, 1998, p. 11.

Sweeney, Patrick, "Quiznos Sub Changing Look to Appeal to Younger Diners," *Denver Business Journal*, December 6, 2002, p. A6.

R.H. Kuhn Company, Inc.

2250 Roswell Drive
Pittsburgh, Pennsylvania 15205-1800
U.S.A.
Telephone: (412) 444-2300
Toll Free: (888) 696-7378
Fax: (412) 444-2330
Web site: http://www.roomfullexpress.com

Private Company
Incorporated: 1958
Employees: 360
Sales: $78.8 million (2006 est.)
NAICS: 442110 Furniture Stores

■ ■ ■

R.H. Kuhn Company, Inc., is a Pittsburgh, Pennsylvania-based retail furniture chain doing business under the name Roomful Express Furniture. The company operates 11 stores in western Pennsylvania, mostly in the greater Pittsburgh market, and one store in the Wheeling, West Virginia, area. A onetime freight liquidator, Kuhn shifted its focus to offer midpriced furniture package combinations, providing customers with entire rooms of furniture, in effect adding interior decoration to the value proposition.

Items are also for sale on an individual basis and available online through the Roomful Express Web site, which includes an interior design center and room planner tools. The company offers delivery, service plans, financing, and furniture repair. In addition to living room, dining room, and bedroom furniture, Roomful

Express stores sell mattresses, lighting products, entertainment centers, home office furniture, area rugs, and accent furniture. One of the chain's best selling brands is Ashley furniture. Since 2007 Kuhn has also operated licensed Ashley Furniture HomeStores in western Pennsylvania. R.H. Kuhn is owned and operated by the second generation of the Kuhn family.

COMPANY FOUNDED: 1958

The man behind the company name was Robert Hunter Kuhn. Born in West Virginia in the late 1920s and raised during the Great Depression, Kuhn went to work in the railroad yards of Charleston, West Virginia, before becoming a highly successful sewing machine salesman at Sears, Roebuck and Co. In 1958, at the age of 30, he struck out on his own, forming R.H. Kuhn Company. Cashing in his pension, he set up shop in Pittsburgh's Northside neighborhood and began importing Necchi sewing machines, a well-respected Italian brand that he began distributing throughout the northeastern United States. Kuhn added electronic home entertainment products and enjoyed excellent growth in the 1960s. He then added home furnishings to the mix in 1970, and three years later Kuhn's wholesale warehouse began distributing Bassett furniture.

The early 1970s also brought John F. "Jack" McGowan, a key employee and future chief executive, to the company. After graduating from high school in 1960, McGowan, like many Pittsburgh-area sons, joined his father in the steel mill rather than attend college. It was a grueling job and he soon opted for a salesman's life, going door to door to sell fire alarms and other

COMPANY PERSPECTIVES

We at Roomful Express Furniture are committed to helping our customers make a buying decision which best fits their personal lifestyle. We offer the best selection and immediate availability of name brand furniture at guaranteed lowest prices. We feel that going the extra mile for our customers is not just an obligation but a privilege. Our goal is to make our customers comfortable with every phase of their shopping experience from first visit through delivery and beyond.

products. He joined Kuhn in 1970 to sell sewing machines, stereos, and other electronics products door to door. Two years later he was in the office, promoted to vice president. In that capacity he helped Robert Kuhn transform the company from a wholesaler of sewing machines and electronics to a furniture retailer.

FREIGHT LIQUIDATORS NAME ADOPTED

In the 1970s Kuhn began acquiring failed furniture stores and inventory from struggling furniture retailers or shuttered stores. The company then began selling the merchandise in Freight Liquidators Furniture stores, employing the slogan, "More Than You Expect!" Kuhn carved out a niche in the value-priced furniture market in the Pittsburgh area and soon the wholesale division was phased out.

In the 1980s Robert Kuhn was joined by his son Michael, who had helped out at the warehouse since an early age, making deliveries and performing odd jobs. He did not plan on making furniture a career, however. "It took a lot of determination and persistence on my father's part to keep my interest in it," he told the *Pittsburgh Tribune-Review* in 2002. "I was working at restaurants, bussing tables and stuff, but I gravitated back to the business."

By 1990 there were 14 Freight Liquidators Furniture factory showrooms in western Pennsylvania, southeastern Ohio, and West Virginia. The chain generated $22 million in sales in 1990. Despite the recession, revenues improved to $24 million a year later. The company also began upgrading its outlets. For example, in 1991 Kuhn closed two area stores and bought a 63,000-square-foot former Ames Department Store site out of bankruptcy in Pittsburgh's Ross Township. In a

better location across the street from a major shopping mall, the new superstore was also able to add carpet, floor covering, and window covering departments.

Robert Kuhn's health began to fail, and in 1995 McGowan took over as chief executive officer while Michael Kuhn served as president. A year later Robert Kuhn died of pancreatic cancer at the age of 68. He left behind a company that ranked as one of the top 100 furniture retailers in the country, but the Freight Liquidators concept had reached a plateau at around $26 million.

As the 1990s came to a close Freight Liquidators began losing market share and the number of stores was trimmed to 10. A consultant was hired to analyze the business and the company was advised to upgrade the look of the stores. The chain had always taken a bare bones approach but then began to remodel the facades. Additionally, the interiors were reorganized to better show off the merchandise.

ROOMFUL EXPRESS CONCEPT DEVELOPED

The late 1990s also brought a new marketing concept to Freight Liquidators in the Roomful Express program. In short, the stores advertised and sold prepackaged designer-assembled combinations of furniture, most of which were ready for immediate delivery. It was not a new concept, having already proven successful for a Florida chain, Rooms-To-Go. The concept was designed to make shopping easier, especially for women, who accounted for 85 percent of all furniture sales but often had limited time available for furniture shopping. The concept was also advantageous to value retailers who did not provide interior decorating training to their sales people. Furthermore, by selling packages, the retailers were less likely to have their warehouses cluttered with odd lamps, tables, and other unsold items.

At the behest of McGowan, merchandise was upgraded, as were the chain's color circulars and television advertising. The Roomful Express program proved so successful that in 2000 the Freight Liquidators name was dropped in favor of Roomful Express. In that same year McGowan stepped down as CEO, turning over the reins to Michael Kuhn. McGowan would then fight an extended battle with lung cancer, eventually succumbing in 2007 at the age of 64.

NEW STORE FORMAT: 2002

By pursuing the Roomful Express concept, sales for the chain doubled to around $53 million in 2002. To maintain growth Kuhn hired retail space designer Connie Post to help develop a new design strategy as part of

```
╔══════════════════════════════════════════╗
║                                          ║
║             KEY DATES                    ║
║              ────■────                   ║
║                                          ║
║   1958:  R.H. Kuhn Company is formed to  ║
║          wholesale sewing machines.      ║
║   1970:  Company adds furniture to its   ║
║          offerings.                      ║
║   1995:  Robert Kuhn retires.            ║
║   2000:  Freight Liquidators name is     ║
║          dropped in favor of Roomful     ║
║          Express.                        ║
║   2005:  New headquarters opens.         ║
║                                          ║
╚══════════════════════════════════════════╝
```

an effort to redesign many of the stores. The plan was to create environments that were more style conscious while emphasizing comfort and convenience. The first renovation redesigned by Post and Pittsburgh architect Ralph Marovitch was completed in 2002 at a store in North Fayette, Pittsburgh.

Aimed at women ages 30 to 55, the new layout featured individual room settings, called "lifestyle pods," created by Post. One grouping, for instance, offered a West Indies look that included a ribbed sofa and loveseat accented by matching throw pillows, wrought-iron lamps, and other coordinated accessories. Next to implement the new store design was a former Ames site in Monroeville, Pennsylvania. This 80,000-square-foot store, renovated a year later using the same design, replaced a smaller location in Monroeville, allowing for a broader selection of merchandise.

STAYING PUT IN PENNSYLVANIA IN 2004

Due to the company's strong performance, Kuhn soon outgrew its 270,000-square-foot headquarters and distribution facility. In 2004 it received enticing offers to move outside the state, with Ohio presenting a $2.5 million package of financial incentives and West Virginia a $3.5 million package. Pennsylvania weighed in as well but offered just $2.7 million to Kuhn to stay. The company approached the state with the West Virginia offer and was finally persuaded to stay put in Pittsburgh in exchange for a $4.5 million package of financial incentives provided by the Commonwealth of Pennsylvania and local government, including a $1.25 million Pennsylvania Industrial Development Authority loan, a separate $500,000 loan for machinery and equipment, a $175,000 Opportunity Grant, job assistance training funds, and about $100,000 in Job Creation Tax Credits and other tax credits.

Later in the year Kuhn acquired a 597,000-square-foot facility, a former Horne's/Lazarus warehouse on a 24-acre site in the Chartiers Industrial Park in Pittsburgh's West End section, which was large enough to accommodate future expansion. The company began moving into the new facility in July 2005 and completed the transition two months later.

After settling into its new home, Kuhn continued to upgrade store locations. A larger footprint was not always pursued, however. In November 2007 the Roomful Express chain opened a custom-built store on the site of a former store as part of a new strip mall that would be anchored by a Wal-Mart Supercenter. The new structure included a 25,000-square-foot showroom and a 1,000-square-foot warehouse. Although smaller than the previous store by 8 percent, the new store employed a new layout that improved inventory display and generated greater sales per square foot.

ASHLEY STORES OPEN: 2007

Also of note in 2007, Kuhn opened a pair of Ashley Furniture HomeStores in Altoona and Johnstown, Pennsylvania. Ashley-branded furniture had always been a top seller for Roomful Express, prompting Kuhn to secure a licensing agreement to operate Ashley stores. In addition to the popularity of the merchandise, Ashley was a desirable partner because it provided licensees with direct ordering capabilities and frequent deliveries, which eliminated the high cost of maintaining inventory. Ashley's name recognition allowed Kuhn to expand eastward into desirable new markets. Kuhn had long since saturated the Pittsburgh market, where the company focused on building internal sales, and had been looking for new opportunities elsewhere in Pennsylvania. There was no interest in opening Ashley stores in Kuhn's home territory.

When La-Z-Boy closed its area stores in 2007, Roomful Express was quick to expand its La-Z-Boy selection. The chain also expanded its television advertising as part of an effort to polish its brand identity. The spots featured talking furniture, albeit without animated mouths, in familiar outdoor locales. The trick was reinforced by outfitting furniture in Roomful Express stores with motion-activated sensors so that furniture items spoke to customers as they passed by. The unstated message of the new ads, which did not mention prices or brands, was revealed by the ads' visuals. The furniture displayed was stylish and implied that Roomful Express was upgrading its image as well.

Kuhn pursued other ways to drive business. To bring more families into its stores, the company ran a promotion that offered tickets to a popular Hannah Montana concert. Additionally, Roomful Express redesigned its Web site and made a greater effort to generate online sales. To boost the number of shoppers providing contact information at store kiosks, which could be used to apply for financing, the company launched a sweepstakes card promotion that resulted in a 10-fold increase in registration.

Kuhn had proven to be a nimble operation from its inception, transforming itself from a sewing machine wholesaler to a retailer of distressed furniture to a purveyor of furniture ensembles. Under the leadership of the second generation of the Kuhn family, the future direction of the company remained to be seen but was likely to prove successful.

Ed Dinger

PRINCIPAL SUBSIDIARIES

Roomful Express Furniture.

PRINCIPAL COMPETITORS

Levin Furniture Company; Room Concepts; Value City Furniture.

FURTHER READING

Dyer, Ervin, "John 'Jack' McGowan," *Pittsburgh Post-Gazette*, August 27, 2007, p. B3.

Heuck, Douglas, "Robert Hunter Kuhn Founded Firm Selling Furniture from Failed Stores," *Pittsburgh Post-Gazette*, September 3, 1996, p. B4.

Kirkland, Kevin, "Roomful Express Gives New Store a Special Touch," *Pittsburgh Post-Gazette*, February 22, 2003.

Lindeman, Teresa S., "Burnishing Furnishing," *Pittsburgh Post-Gazette*, August 29, 1999, p. F1.

———, "Furniture Chain's Ads Seeks to Create a Brand Personality," *Pittsburgh Post-Gazette*, February 4, 2008.

Ransom, Lou, "Local Furniture Chain Evolves from Its Much Smaller Start," *Pittsburgh Tribune-Review*, September 12, 2002.

Schooley, Tim, "Roomful Sets Popular Ashley Brand for Standalone Stores," *Pittsburgh Business Times*, September 3, 2007.

Theodore, Larissa, "From Steel Mill to Career to Furniture," *Beaver County Times*, August 27, 2007.

R.T. Vanderbilt Company, Inc.

---■---

30 Winfield Street
Norwalk, Connecticut 06855-1329
U.S.A.
Telephone: (203) 853-1400
Toll Free: (800) 243-6064
Fax: (203) 853-1452
Web site: http://www.rtvanderbilt.com

Private Company
Incorporated: 1916
Employees: 620
Sales: $240 million (2008 est.)
NAICS: 212325 Clay and Ceramic and Refractory
   Minerals Mining

■ ■ ■

Maintaining its headquarters in Norwalk, Connecticut, R.T. Vanderbilt Company, Inc., is a privately held industrial minerals and chemicals company. Vanderbilt offers more than 800 products in 60 categories of minerals and chemicals, including clays, talcs, magnesium aluminum silicate, wollastonite, and a variety of waterborne chemicals. They are sold in about 80 countries. Industries served include adhesives, agriculture, ceramics, cosmetics, household products, paint, paper, petroleum, pharmaceutical, plastics, rubber, and wire and cable. Through subsidiaries Vanderbilt maintains a pair of chemical manufacturing facilities in Bethel, Connecticut, and Murray, Kentucky, and four mining operations. Chairman and Chief Executive Of-

ficer Hugh B. Vanderbilt, Jr., is the grandson of the company's founder.

COMPANY ESTABLISHED: 1916

R.T. Vanderbilt Company was founded in 1916 by Robert Thurlow Vanderbilt, a distant cousin of U.S. entrepreneur, Cornelius Vanderbilt. Born in 1885, he was raised in Brooklyn, New York. After becoming involved in the chemical drug manufacturing business, he obtained a contract to sell kaolin, a soft white clay produced by the Peerless Clay Company of Langley, South Carolina. He started R.T. Vanderbilt Company at a 42nd Street location in Manhattan in 1916, using $1,000 of his own money and a $24,000 family loan. The paper industry became an important market for Vanderbilt, and in 1916 he bought Peerless, renaming it Continental Clay. A year later he purchased additional reserves.

Aiken County, South Carolina, was the heart of the U.S. kaolin industry, pioneered by a New York wallpaper manufacturer, Richard McNamee, who established the Dixie Clay Company before the Civil War and began to discover reserves. Following the war he began to acquire clay-bearing property in the area and Dixie Clay became the first company to ship kaolin out of the state. The business remained in the McNamee family until 1923 when it merged with Continental Clay. Vanderbilt also acquired McNamee Lumber Co. of Bath, South Carolina.

Robert Vanderbilt was also a director of the North American Clay Company. Along with Continental Clay this company mined hard clays, which he began to sell to the rubber industry. In 1925 Vanderbilt signed a distribution deal with B.F. Goodrich and other rubber companies. Also in the early 1920s Vanderbilt began serving the ceramic industries, which had long been dependent on imported clays in the production of dinnerware and sanitary ware. Vanderbilt was a pioneer in providing the industry with a source of domestic clay under the Peerless brand name. In time, Peerless would find a wide variety of uses in pottery, industrial porcelains, and refractories, and as a raw material for fiberglass.

NEW MARKETS AND PRODUCTS

Vanderbilt continued to expand into new markets in the 1930s. Vanderbilt Minerals Corporation was also launched during the decade. The company made valuable contributions in smectite clays, which found uses in the foundry, oil well drilling, iron ore, and agriculture industries, and in the manufacture of industrial, chemical, and consumer products. Later in the decade Vanderbilt introduced its Veegum magnesium aluminum silicate product to the textile industry, but the main customer for it soon became a major manufacturer of men's toiletries. Veegum became too costly to ship as an aqueous dispersion, however, and following World War II was sold in a dry flake form, available in drums and sold to the personal care market. Over the years, new grades of Veegum were added to serve specific needs and broaden the demand for the product.

Continental Clay adopted the Dixie Clay Company name in 1946. Also during the postwar era, in the late 1940s, Vanderbilt began offering Nytal talc to the ceramics industry. A subsidiary, the Gouverneur Talc Company, opened a talc mine in upstate New York in 1948.

Vanderbilt entered another new market, petroleum, in the early 1950s, when some of the products sold to the rubber industry were chemically modified to make them useful as additives in lubricants and greases. Other petroleum products followed and in time petroleum would emerge as Vanderbilt's second-largest market. The early 1950s also saw a changing of the guard at the company. In August 1954 Robert Vanderbilt was struck and killed by a truck while he attempted to cross a

Midtown Manhattan street. His youngest son, Hugh Bedford Vanderbilt, took charge of the company, having joined his father after serving as a Marine from 1942 to 1946.

HEADQUARTERS MOVED TO CONNECTICUT: 1974

Under Hugh Vanderbilt's watch the company continued to prosper and grow into new markets. He made his home in Connecticut and in 1974 he moved the business to larger accommodations in Norwalk, Connecticut, located across the street from the company's research and development center. Four years later his son, Hugh Bedford Vanderbilt, Jr., joined him in the business. After graduating from Rollins College with a degree in chemistry and business, the younger Vanderbilt went to work as the company's advertising manager and director. He was well prepared for his responsibilities, having been groomed to learn the business since the age of 15, when he started in the mail room. He then served stints in the analytical laboratory, and in the advertising and purchasing departments.

In the early 1970s Vanderbilt had to contend with problems related to its tremolite talc operation. For years, mine and mill operators, as well as workers, had ignored the irreversible health hazards of talc, which caused "white lung" disease, talcosis. It was similar to black lung disease suffered by coal miners. In both cases lungs gradually hardened so that it became increasing difficult for oxygen to be transferred to the blood. In effect, the victims of the condition slowly suffocated to death. While the talc mines were bad, the mills where grinding occurred emitted an even greater amount of fine dust into the air.

In 1972 the Occupational Safety and Health Administration (OSHA) determined tremolite talc to be "asbestos-like." As a result, Vanderbilt and other companies involved in talc production, as well as their customers, had to treat tremolite talc as if it were asbestos and possibly carcinogenic. This marked the beginning of a fight between Vanderbilt and the government that would continue for three decades.

In 1974 Vanderbilt acquired the assets of another area talc company, International Talc, which had a poor safety record. Gouverneur, on the other hand, was regarded as a responsible operator, the first area company to spray water in the mine to keep down the talc dust. A number of International Talc's workers were found to be suffering from talcosis and brought compensation suits against Gouverneur Talc. A settlement was not reached until 1979.

Moreover, workers in other industries, such as tire manufacturing, were impacted by using talc that

KEY DATES

1916: R.T. Vanderbilt Company, Inc., is founded in New York City.

1954: Founder Robert Vanderbilt dies; his youngest son, Hugh Bedford Vanderbilt, takes charge of the company.

1974: Headquarters are moved to Norwalk, Connecticut.

2000: Third-generation Vanderbilt family member is named chairman.

2009: Talc production ends.

Vanderbilt produced. In the meantime, Vanderbilt lobbied against government efforts to study talcosis. Nevertheless, talc miners and their union were able to arrange for a study to be conducted by the National Institute for Occupational Safety and Health, which studied 710 men who worked with talc between 1947 and 1978.

TALC STUDY QUESTIONED: 1986

In 1980 the federal agency issued a report that showed a significant increase in asbestos-related diseases. According to the *Seattle Post-Intelligencer* in a 2000 report, "An unauthorized collaboration between Vanderbilt and two government scientists tried to discredit the study, and influenced a federal agency to abandon efforts to regulate the asbestos fibers found in the talc." The scientists were eventually disciplined but "the renegade report they produced is still hindering efforts to protect workers and consumers, health officials say."

In 1986 those scientists had questioned the study's conclusion that the talc mined by Vanderbilt contained asbestos-like fibers and disputed any connection between the talc and any lung disease workers may have contracted. These concerns with the study led to OSHA's 1992 decision to eliminate standards that would have regulated the asbestos-like talc in the Vanderbilt mines.

In 2000 the asbestos controversy returned to the spotlight when three crayon manufacturers decided to cease using talc as an ingredient after the *Seattle Post-Intelligencer* had two government-certified labs analyze crayons and found asbestos in 32 of 40 crayons. Crayons accounted for only 1.3 percent of the talc produced by Vanderbilt, but the symbolism had a far greater impact. In 2006 the first court award in the United States related to asbestos in industrial talc, concerning the death of a potter, was made against

Vanderbilt and another company. Vanderbilt elected to cease talc production at its New York mine and discontinue its industrial talc product line a few years later, citing a steady decline in the market for the product as the reason.

In the final years of the 20th century Hugh Vanderbilt, Jr., worked his way up through the organization. In 1991 he was named executive vice president and ran the Mining and Manufacturing unit. He then became Vanderbilt's president and chief operating officer in 1995, and a year later succeeded his father as chief executive officer. In June 2000 his father passed away, succumbing to cancer at the age of 70. At a meeting of the board of directors three months later, Hugh Vanderbilt, Jr., was elected chairman at the age of 44.

REORGANIZATION: 2002

In 2002 Vanderbilt reorganized its sales and marketing operations to better serve customers, both domestic and overseas. Three new market-driven global units were formed: Rubber and Plastics, Minerals, and Petroleum. The company then added to its business through distribution deals. In 2005 Vanderbilt became the North American distributor of ExxonMobil Chemical Company's Vistalon ethylene propylene diene (EPDM) rubber products. Two years later Vanderbilt became the U.S. and Canadian distributor of the polymer additives used in the plastic and elastomeric compounds produced by Songwon International Americas Inc., an affiliate of South Korea's Songwon Industrial. In 2008 Vanderbilt became the exclusive U.S. distributor of the sulfurized extreme pressure (EP) lubricant additive product lines manufactured by Arkema Inc., a French global chemical company.

By 2008 Vanderbilt was posting annual revenues of $240 million, 30 percent of which came from outside the United States, a strong performance despite a downturn in the economy. To grow its overseas business further Vanderbilt opened an office in Beijing, China. Moreover, Vanderbilt made plans to expand its Norwalk headquarters where, because of strong growth, employees had to share office space. A new two-story, 5,600-square-foot addition was built to provide more space for the company's researchers and administrative staff.

As the decade came to a close, Vanderbilt wound down talc production in New York, but it remained in operation longer than expected in order to meet the needs of customers who were unable to use formulations without talc. Because they were also customers of other Vanderbilt products, the company sought to maintain relationships by extending production of talc. By the fall of 2009, however, Vanderbilt terminated most of the employees and the operation was recast as the Gouverneur Mineral Division, which continued to mine and process wollastonite for use in plastics and ceramics, and in foundries. These and the other specialty products offered by Vanderbilt, as well as the diversity of industries it served, ensured that the company would remain a healthy concern in the years to come.

Ed Dinger

PRINCIPAL SUBSIDIARIES

Dixie Clay Company; Standard Mineral Company, Inc.; Vanderbilt Minerals Corporation; Vanderbilt Chemical Corporation.

PRINCIPAL COMPETITORS

ICC Industries Inc.; Imerys SA; Lubrizol Corporation.

FURTHER READING

Ellen, Martha, "Changes Made at Vanderbilt Mining Paying Off in Increased Production," *Watertown Daily Times*, December 18, 2009, p. B2.

————, "Vanderbilt Unsure about Repercussions of Decision to Make Crayons Talc-Free," *Watertown Daily Times*, June 14, 2000, p. 32.

Lloyd, Barbara, "Making Waves in a Flat Market," *Lubes-n-Greases*, November 1999.

Milner, Vivian G., "The Kaolin Industry Is King in Aiken County," *Aiken Standard*, June 5, 1988, p. 3.

"R.T. Vanderbilt Co., Inc.," *Ceramic Industry*, November 1992, p. 104.

"R.T. Vanderbilt Co., Inc.," *Drug & Cosmetic Industry*, June 1996, p. 94.

Schneider, Andrew, and Carol Smith, "Old Dispute Rekindled over Content of Mine's Talc," *Seattle Post-Intelligencer*, May 30, 2000.

Rent-A-Center, Inc.

———————————■———————————

5501 Headquarters Drive
Plano, Texas 75024-3556
U.S.A.
Telephone: (972) 801-1100
Toll Free: (800) 422-8186
Fax: (866) 260-1424
Web site: http://www.rentacenter.com

Public Company
Incorporated: 1986 as Vista of Puerto Rico, Inc.
Employees: 18,000
Sales: $2.75 billion (2009)
Stock Exchanges: NASDAQ
Ticker Symbol: RCII
NAICS: 532210 Consumer Electronics and Appliances
    Rental

■ ■ ■

Rent-A-Center, Inc., of Plano, Texas, is the largest chain of rent-to-own stores in the United States. The company owns and operates nearly 3,000 stores in 48 states, plus Washington, D.C., Puerto Rico, and Canada. In addition, a wholly owned subsidiary, ColorTyme Inc., serves as a national franchiser of rent-to-own stores, with 207 units in 33 states. All showrooms of both brands offer furniture, appliances, home electronics, and other accessories that can be rented by customers, who may terminate the contract on short notice or gain ownership of the merchandise after completing a stipulated rental period. Payments are made to the stores on a weekly, biweekly, or monthly basis. Rent-A-Center has been involved in considerable litigation over the years related to its pricing policies and various other business practices. Nevertheless, Rent-A-Center remains financially sound.

ORIGINS

The roots of the rent-to-own business reach back to the 1950s when a number of people pioneered the concept. For instance, Charles Loudermilk, Sr., founder of Atlanta-based Aaron Rents, started out in 1955 by renting Army surplus chairs for 10 cents a day. The founder of Rent-A-Center was J. Ernest Talley, widely acknowledged as the most influential figure in the development of the industry. In the 1950s he ran a retail appliance store with a cousin in Kansas. Because tightening bank credit prevented a number of customers from buying his merchandise, he hit on the idea of renting the items. If customers failed to meet the payments, he could always repossess the merchandise. However, if they reached the end of the rental agreement, they would own the merchandise and Talley would have made some extra cash in addition to increasing the sales volume of his appliance store.

In 1963 Talley developed a rent-to-own chain called Mr. T's, which by 1974 had grown to 14 stores. He sold the business, which became part of the Remco chain, and turned his attention to commercial real estate in the Dallas area. When the Texas real estate market suffered a crash he returned to the rent-to-own concept in 1987, establishing Talley Leasing with his son Michael. The new company rented appliances to apartment complex owners.

Talley returned to the consumer rent-to-own business in 1989 when he acquired a 22-store chain, Vista of Puerto Rico, which operated in both New Jersey and Puerto Rico. Talley changed the name to Vista Rent to Own. Drawing on his years of experience, he upgraded the chain, improving the selection of merchandise and customer approval procedures, as well as instituting inventory systems and a management training program. In April 1993 he greatly expanded his business by acquiring the 84-store Renters Choice Inc. and merging it with Vista.

The combined company then assumed the Renters Choice name, and again Talley upgraded the operations of the new units. Although the purchase would result in a $600,000 loss for 1993, revenues that stood at $15.8 million in 1991 would soar to $74.4 million in 1994. Profits of $1.8 million would increase to $5.5 million over the same period. Moreover, the operating margins for Renters Choice were much healthier than its rivals.

WINNING CUSTOMER APPROVAL

Talley's edge was in his stores' success in winning customer approval. While the industry average for delinquent accounts was 10 percent, the average at Renters Choice was just 6.5 percent of revenues. A main reason for this success was that Talley paid higher wages than his competitors, both for store clerks and managers. The company also attempted to weed out management trainees who harbored repressed hostilities or forced their personal philosophy on others. (The battery of psychological tests the company relied on, however, would become a source of conflict later in the 1990s.)

Behind this effort was an understanding that many customers turned to rent-to-own stores because they could not afford the outright purchase of a luxury item, such as a big-screen TV, or had poor credit because of frequent job changes, and would not respond well to employees who appeared to be judgmental. Because customers came into the store on a weekly basis to make their payments, it was inevitable that managers would develop some personal relationships with them. Talley preferred that those relationships be positive, especially since this would lead to repeat business.

Managers were granted considerable latitude on deciding if a customer was worth the risk, but at the same time, computer programming allowed the main office to monitor rental payments on a nightly basis. Accounts even a day late would be questioned. In short, Renters Choice developed a tightly run organization that gave it an edge in a highly fragmented industry. Of the approximately 8,000 competing establishments, many were small, poorly run operations ripe for acquisition and the Talley turnaround procedure.

GOING PUBLIC: 1995

In January 1995 Talley took Renters Choice public in order to fund further growth, raising nearly $26 million. Despite a general aversion for what was often considered an unsavory business, investors were attracted to Renters Choice from the start, and the stock, trading on the NASDAQ, made a steady climb in price.

In the spring of 1995 Renters Choice paid $20 million for Crown Leasing Corp. of Texarkana, which had recently filed for Chapter 11 protection. The deal added 72 stores in 18 states and expanded the presence of Renters Choice to the southern part of the United States. In the fall of 1995 the chain added 135 stores by acquiring Pro Rental Inc. of Dallas for $38.5 million in cash and notes. Pro Rental operated under two brands, Magic Rent-to-Own and Kelway Rent-to-Own. By the end of 1995, with its acquisitions only partially digested, Renters Choice boosted revenues to $133.3 million and net income to $10.7 million.

The chain had grown to nearly 320 stores by this time. Another 320 stores were added in 1996 when the company acquired ColorTyme of Dallas, which was a franchise operation rather than a company-owned chain like Renters Choice. The majority shareholder and chairman of ColorTyme was Talley's brother, Willie. Ever since his brother had suffered a stroke in the early 1990s, Talley had acted as his legal guardian, a situation that previously required notation in Securities and Exchange Commission filings because of possible conflicts of interest between ColorTyme and Renters Choice.

Because of the lack of large rent-to-own chains available for purchase in 1996, by the middle of the year Renters Choice hired a director of acquisitions in order

KEY DATES

■

1963: Ernest Talley establishes Mr. T's rent-to-own chain.
1974: Talley sells Mr. T's.
1987: Talley and son start Talley Leasing.
1989: Talley acquires Vista of Puerto Rico.
1993: Vista acquires Renters Choice and assumes name.
1995: Renters Choice goes public.
1998: Renters Choice acquires Rent-A-Center chain and assumes name.
2001: Talley retires.
2004: Rent Rite Inc. is purchased.
2006: Rent-Way Inc. is acquired.

to focus on identifying smaller chains and individual operations that were deemed to be underperforming. Between May and the end of the year, the company acquired 88 stores in 20 separate transactions at a cost of $25.3 million. In the process, Renters Choice added five new states to its operations and the company opened 13 new stores.

RENT-A-CENTER ACQUIRED: 1998

As a result of its aggressive expansion, Renters Choice more than doubled its revenues in 1996 over the previous year to $238 million, while posting a net income of $18 million. The company continued to grow in 1997, adding 71 stores in 18 separate transactions at a cost of $30.5 million. Another 10 new stores were also opened, bringing the total number of company-owned units by the end of 1997 to 504. Also in 1997, Renters Choice agreed to a $2.9 million settlement of a Wisconsin class-action lawsuit it inherited from Crown Leasing, which had been accused of charging usurious interest rates. In addition, in late 1997 Renters Choice was sued in a New Jersey court over a failure to provide certain disclosures in its contracts with customers. Despite these legal costs, Renters Choice remained extremely profitable. Revenues for 1997 grew to $327.5 million and net income to $25.9 million.

In 1998 Renters Choice had a dramatic surge in growth when it made two major acquisitions. First it paid $103 million to acquire the 176 stores of Central Rents, Inc. Located in the Los Angeles, California, suburb of Commerce, Central Rents provided Renters Choice with a substantial platform in the western United States, an area where it previously had very few

locations. The company added 43 stores in California alone. Although a substantial acquisition, it would soon be dwarfed by the $900 million purchase of the 1,400-store Rent-A-Center chain. Renters Choice would then assume the Rent-A-Center name and become the largest rent-to-own chain in the industry.

BRITISH CONGLOMERATE OPTS OUT

Rent-A-Center had been founded by Tom Devlin in Wichita, Kansas, in 1973. While attending college at Wichita State University in the mid-1960s, Devlin worked at an appliance store and was frustrated with the high rejection rate of his blue-collar customers. He and his boss developed a payment plan that allowed customers to rent an appliance until they had paid enough installments in order to gain ownership. Devlin went into business for himself in 1973 with a single rent-to-own store. He developed the Rent-A-Center chain with both company-owned stores and franchisees.

In 1987 he sold the business for $594 million to British conglomerate Thorn EMI, which had been involved in the long established English rent-to-own industry. In 1996 Thorn split from the EMI music business, but did not fare well on its own, hurt in large part by a strong economy that made rent-to-own a less attractive option.

Thorn also faced litigation over misleading interest rates in the United States, an ongoing problem that concerned U.K. investors, especially after a New Jersey judge ruled against the company in 1997, leaving it open to damages that had the potential of reaching $1 billion. As a consequence, Thorn was eager to unload Rent-A-Center and devote its resources to restructuring its British interests.

MERGER OF RENTERS CHOICE AND RENT-A-CENTER

Although Thorn sold Rent-A-Center to Renters Choice, it retained partial responsibility for pending damages in earlier lawsuits. In order to finance the acquisition, Renters Choice issued $235 million of convertible preferred stock to the New York investment firm of Apollo Management, which gained almost a 30 percent stake in the company. Renters Choice closed down the longtime Wichita headquarters of Rent-A-Center, consolidated operations in Plano, and then on December 31, 1998, changed its name to Rent-A-Center, Inc. For the year, with only a partial contribution from its new acquisitions, the company's revenues soared to $809.7 million, while income held steady at $24.8 million.

Investors showed some concern over Talley's ability to make the stiff debt payments taken on in 1998, and as a result the price of Rent-A-Center stock dropped. When the company continued to post strong results, investors expressed their relief by again bidding up the company's shares. The process of absorbing 1,400 new stores was not without incident, however, as a number of inherited managers objected to the company's personality testing, and initiated litigation.

Plaintiffs maintained that many of the 502 true-false statements of a psychological test were invasive, including: "I am very strongly attracted to members of my own sex;" "I have never indulged in any unusual sex practices;" "Evil spirits possess me at times;" and "I am a special agent from God." The company maintained that these were standard questions of the well-known Minnesota Multiphasic Personality Inventory exam, that computers scored the tests, and that the tests were not used against employees. Nevertheless, the company eventually reached a settlement on the case, agreeing to drop the test and pay $2 million in damages.

MARKETING CAMPAIGN LAUNCHED

Rent-A-Center did not acquire new stores in 1999 and focused on converting its recent additions to its way of doing business. It also launched a marketing campaign designed to improve the public impression of the rent-to-own industry. Television commercials, in both English and Spanish, were crafted to alleviate the uneasiness that many lower-income customers felt about doing business at a rent-to-own store. The emphasis was on consumers being empowered to enjoy upscale items that they would not otherwise be able to afford.

Rent-A-Center received a major boost in its marketing efforts when it signed well-known football analyst and television pitchman John Madden to serve as the public face of its advertising campaign, including in-store signage as well as television commercials. The company could afford Madden's hefty fee and the requisite advertising budget because of a major jump in revenues ($1.4 billion) and net income ($59.4 million) in 1999.

That trend would continue in 2000, as revenues rose to $1.6 billion and net income soared to $103 million. Furthermore, brand awareness improved significantly, much of which could be attributed to Madden. The company was also successful in better targeting its direct mail, and was able to free up dollars for even more broadcast advertising as a result.

EXPANSION IN THE 21ST CENTURY

Rent-A-Center renewed its plans for growth in 2000. As the undisputed leader in the rent-to-own industry, which remained very much fragmented, the company was well positioned to take advantage of its size to open new stores, as well as to acquire underperforming operations that could be converted to the Rent-A-Center format. The company also branched into offering "pay as you go" Internet-access service.

In October 2001 Talley announced his retirement. Talley was replaced as chairman and CEO by Mark E. Speese, who at the age of 44 had more than 22 years of experience in the rent-to-own industry. Speese had joined Talley in 1986 and had been instrumental in the company's growth. Rent-A-Center was set to benefit from a troubled economy, which would undoubtedly result in more business from lower-income customers, and was also well managed and set to improve its dominant position in the rent-to-own industry.

Rent-A-Center continued to grow its business by making strategic acquisitions. During 2003 the company added 295 stores operated by Rent-Way Inc. to its holdings in a deal worth approximately $100 million. The company posted record revenues and earnings that year. It purchased Rent Rite Inc., a private owner of 90 stores in 11 states, the following year. The company also gained a foothold in the Canadian market in 2004 by purchasing five rent-to-own stores in Edmonton and Calgary. The company's next big move came in 2006 with the purchase of Rent-Way Inc. for approximately $280 million. Rent-Way operated 800 stores in 30 states and was the third-largest rent-to-own retail chain in the country.

While revenues rose slightly to $2.31 billion in 2004, net earnings fell by 10.1 percent to $182.7 million. The company attributed its financial performance to a child-care tax payment made by the federal government, which customers then used to pay off their rental agreements early. In addition, rising fuel costs ate into customers' discretionary income during 2004. At the same time, the company took a $47 million pretax charge to settle a lawsuit brought about in 2002 by Benjamin Griego in California that claimed the company's pricing policies violated that state's laws. Nevertheless, Rent-A-Center opened 94 new locations during the year while acquiring a total of 302 stores.

OVERCOMING CHALLENGES

While Rent-A-Center had significantly increased its market share, it faced challenges related to continuing litigation and an economic downturn that negatively affected consumer spending. During 2007 the company settled a class-action lawsuit brought by New Jersey customers that claimed the company charged excessive interest rates. Rent-A-Center paid out nearly $109 million into a settlement fund as a result of the litigation.

In July 2009 the attorney general of the state of Washington filed a suit against the company for illegal collection practices. The company denied the allegations but agreed to abide by a list of restrictions on its collection practices as a result of the settlement. Some of the restrictions included limiting contacts with a customer to six times a week to discuss an overdue account, not engaging in violence, not trespassing in a customer's home or yard except to reach the main entrance, not discussing the account with anyone other than the debtor's spouse, and not obtaining payment through a customer's bank or credit card without authorization. In addition, Rent-A-Center agreed to pay the state $243,000 in attorneys' fees and legal costs, plus $100,000 to monitor and enforce the restrictions.

While the company battled legal problems as well as a faltering economy during the early years of the new millennium, it nevertheless maintained its growth strategy. From March 1993 through December 2008, its store count increased from 27 to over 3,000 locations. Overall, the company made 240 acquisitions during that period. The slowdown in consumer spending, however, forced the company to implement a strict cost-cutting strategy and a restructuring that included the closure of nearly 300 stores in late 2007 and 2008. The company's financial performance improved in 2009, leaving Rent-A-Center management confident that the company was on track for success in the years to come.

Ed Dinger
Updated, Christina M. Stansell

PRINCIPAL SUBSIDIARIES

ColorTyme, Inc.; ColorTyme Finance, Inc.; Get It Now, LLC; Rainbow Rentals, Inc.; RAC Canada Finance LP; RAC Canada Holdings; RAC National Product Service, LLC; Remco America, Inc.; Rent-A-Center Addison, LLC; Rent-A-Center East, Inc.; Rent-A-Center International, Inc.; Rent-A-Center Texas, LP; Rent-A-Center Texas, LLC; Rent-A-Center West, Inc.; Rent-A-Centre Canada, Ltd.

PRINCIPAL COMPETITORS

Aaron's, Inc.; Best Buy Co., Inc.; Wal-Mart Stores Inc.

FURTHER READING

Basas, Susan M., "Rent-A-Center Inc.," *Investor's Business Daily*, March 5, 2002.

Bodipo-Memba, Alejandro, and Matthew Rose, "Renters Choice to Acquire Thorn's U.S. Business," *Wall Street Journal*, June 18, 1998, p. A4.

Finz, Stacy, "Texas Company Settles over Nosy Questions to Employees," *San Francisco Chronicle*, July 8, 2000, p. A3.

Francis, Theo, "Rent-A-Center Grabs the Stage as Expansion Drive Pares Debt," *Wall Street Journal*, September 27, 2000, p. T2.

Kinney, Monica Yant, "$109 Million Cure for Rental Anguish," *Philadelphia Inquirer*, May 2, 2007.

Kraemer, Kristin M., "Company Says It Won't Harass Customers," *Tri-City Herald*, March 2, 2010.

"Rent-A-Center Announces Agreement to Acquire Rent Rite," *Business Wire*, April 24, 2004.

"Rent-A-Center Enters Canada with Purchase of 5 Stores," *Warren's Consumer Electronics Daily*, March 17, 2004.

"Rent-A-Center to Acquire Rent-Way Inc. for 0.54 Times Revenue," *Weekly Corporate Growth Report*, August 14, 2006.

Weil, Jonathan, "Renters Choice's Price May Finally Catch Up with Its Fundamentals," *Wall Street Journal*, April 8, 1998, p. T2.

RM plc

New Mill House, 183 Milton Park
Abingdon, OX14 4SE
United Kingdom
Telephone: (+44 0870) 700 300
Fax: (+44 08450) 700 400
Web site: http://www.rm.com

Public Company
Incorporated: 1994
Employees: 2,711
Sales: £346.9 million ($543.6 million) (2009)
Stock Exchanges: London
Ticker Symbol: RM
NAICS: 511210 Software Publishers; 541512 Computer
Systems Design Services

■ ■ ■

RM plc supplies computer-based systems, products, and services for the education and learning markets, primarily in the United Kingdom, but also in the United States, Australia, and India. RM focuses primarily on the Information Communications and Technology (ICT) services market to the national government and local school authorities, qualification providers, and individual schools in the United Kingdom, and to local school districts in the United States. RM is also a leading supplier to the Building Schools for the Future (BSF) initiative in the United Kingdom, and by the beginning of 2010 was providing the technological infrastructure for nearly 30 new BSF schools.

RM operates through three primary divisions. The largest is RM Learning Technologies, which incorporates the group's ICT and BSF business in the United Kingdom and the United States. This division contributed 76 percent of RM's total revenues of £347 million ($544 million) in 2009. The RM Education Resources division provides curriculum software and other resources for U.K. schools, adding nearly 18.5 percent to the company's sales. The RM Assessment and Data division, which supplies data outsourcing and assessment services, adds nearly 5.5 percent.

In addition to its operations in the United Kingdom, the company has offices in Massachusetts in the United States; Perth, Australia; and Kerala, India. RM plc is listed on the London Stock Exchange. The company is led by CEO Terry Sweeney and Chairman John P. Leighfield.

BRITISH MICROCOMPUTER PIONEER

RM plc was the brainchild of Mike Fischer and Mike O'Regan, who founded the company as Research Machines in the early 1970s. Fischer had originally studied physics at Oxford University. However, his real interest lay in electronics, and following graduation Fischer began working for Roussel Laboratories. During this time Fischer met O'Regan, who had graduated from Cambridge University with a degree in economics. When Roussel Laboratories began seeking a contractor to build a new type of electronic instrument, Fischer and O'Regan submitted a bid and won the contract.

In 1973 Fischer and O'Regan launched their own company, initially called Sintel, which focused on supplying mail-order electronic components and kits for the U.K. hobbyist market. The partners' objective from the outset was to raise capital in order to enter the business of producing scientific instruments. The company's beginnings were less than auspicious, backed by just £100 per month from Fischer's father, as well as their earnings working part time for a local telephone exchange. The mail-order business began to grow before long, however.

By the mid-1970s the partners had begun to refine their focus, targeting the nascent microcomputer market. Fischer, judging existing microcomputers of the time to be "amateurish," led the development of the company's own microcomputer, based on the then-standard x80Z format. In order to develop the computer Fischer and O'Regan brought in a third partner, David Small, who had previously worked for the National Hospital for Nervous Diseases. Small took charge of developing the firmware for the new computer, including its software-based front end.

Sintel's budget allowed it to buy only enough parts to build 250 computers. Sales of its first computer were launched in 1977, offered initially both as a kit and as a fully assembled unit, under the name Research Machines Computer Systems. By the end of the year Sintel had succeeded in selling all 250 of the computers, with a profit margin of 50 percent.

The company then set to work developing the next generation of its computers, and by 1979 had grown to more than 50 employees. In that year the company debuted its highly popular 380Z, equipped with dual floppy drives. The company ended sales of computer kits, focusing instead on fully assembled systems. Also that year, the company changed its name to Research Machines (RM).

TARGETING THE EDUCATIONAL MARKET

RM targeted the educational market almost from the start. The company's first computer was sold to a person

working for the local authority in Reading, where several educators had built a computer based on parts bought from Sintel. RM then approached the local authority and proposed that the company design and build a new computer for the city's school system. The move into the educational market enabled the company to avoid competing with larger companies, including IBM in the early 1980s, then focused on the business computing market.

RM soon established itself as a heavyweight in the educational computer sector, claiming a 40 percent market share by 1980. The company's major competitor at the time, BBC Microcomputer, claimed a higher sales volume. Nevertheless, RM's higher-priced machines enabled the company to claim a larger share of actual educational spending.

A large part of RM's success during the 1980s was due to its innovative technology. The company was one of the first to incorporate color graphics, as well as animation, into computers. RM, seeking to develop a multiuser computer system for use in the classroom, also laid claim to pioneering LAN (local access network) technology. This came about in 1983 when the company introduced its first network system, featuring keyboard-mounted processors linked to the 380Z as a central file storage and server system.

Other technology advances came during the middle of the decade. The group's next computer system, launched as the Nimbus in 1985, featured Piconet, an early serial bus system and precursor to the much later universal serial bus (USB) standard. By then Fischer and O'Regan had undergone a falling out with Small. In 1984 the partners turned to venture capitalists for funding in order to buy out Small's one-third stake, which had been given to him when he joined the company, for £1.5 million.

PC COMPATIBLE IN 1989

Despite RM's successes, the company struggled off and on with profitability, even coming close to bankruptcy during the mid-1980s. In the second half of the decade the computer market began a significant transition toward a unified standard based on the IBM computing platform and the newly emerging MS-DOS/Windows operating system under development by Microsoft. RM, one of the first in the United Kingdom to recognize the potential of the Microsoft system, began incorporating the MS-DOS/Windows system into its computers as early as 1985. The company was also an early entrant into the commercial computer-aided design (CAD) market, launching its first CAD systems in 1987.

RM began its shift toward the IBM-compatible market in 1989, launching its first personal computer

KEY DATES

1973: Mike Fischer and Mike O'Regan found Sintel as a mail-order supplier of electronics components and kits.

1977: The company builds its first microcomputer under the Research Machines name.

1979: The company changes its name to Research Machines.

1994: Research Machines goes public as RM plc.

1999: RM enters the Australian market.

2003: RM sets up an office in India.

2005: RM wins contract to build Scotland's Glow network.

2008: RM acquires Computrac in the United States.

2010: RM wins Building Schools for the Future contract in Essex in partnership with Skanska.

(PC) "clone," as these became known, that year. In the early 1990s the PC clone market shifted toward a modular concept, entirely based on standardized components. Amid the recession that buffeted the U.K.'s computer market, RM, which had continued to design and develop many of its own components, decided to convert its computer systems entirely to the IBM-compatible model by 1992. The company carried out a series of layoffs as a result. During this time, Mike O'Regan retired from the company, taking up a position as a nonexecutive director.

The change in strategy not only enabled RM to generate a stronger cash flow, but it also allowed the company to post stronger and more consistent profits. This in turn laid the foundation for the company's public offering and a listing on the London Stock Exchange in 1994 as RM plc. Fischer, who had previously been the company's managing director, took up the position as chief executive officer.

SERVICES MODEL

The move toward modular systems laid the groundwork for RM's next major development, which was a new focus on providing a full-fledged educational resources and services offering. This effort debuted in the early 1990s with the company's Windows Box, introduced in 1992 and expanded in 1994 as the Window Box Partnership. That year the company also introduced SuccessMaker, the first of its Integrated Learning Systems.

In 1993 the company expanded its range of networking services with RM Connect, based on the newly released Windows NT operating system. RM also introduced Internet for Learning (IFL) that year, providing an Internet access backbone developed specifically for the educational sector. The IFL system was a major success and within a year boasted more than one million hits each week. These successes helped propel RM to the top of the education market, as it became the ICT leader in the United Kingdom through the 1990s.

A major boost to the U.K. educational market came in 1997, when the new Labour government launched the National Grid for Learning as the first of a series of programs designed to modernize and enhance the technological offering of British schools. The new program included increased spending measures, directly benefiting RM and other players in the ICT market in the United Kingdom. Also in 1997, Mike Fischer decided to retire from active management of the company, taking up a seat on its board of directors. By this time RM had grown to more than 1,000 employees with annual revenues of £110 million ($170 million).

MOVE INTO OUTSOURCING

RM then began developing a new extension of its operations into providing full-scale managed services on an outsourcing basis to local authorities and other educational bodies. The company secured its first outsourcing contract in 1998. In 1999 RM became one of only 12 companies in the United Kingdom to receive certification as a managed services supplier.

This placed the company in a strong position to win a number of other highly lucrative outsourcing contracts. For example, in 1999 the company gained a 10-year, £43 million contract to provide ICT services for the Dudley educational system. The company gained another contract worth £5 million in South Lanarkshire to equip and manage that region's 21-strong secondary school network. The move into outsourcing also backed RM's first overseas expansion. This came with the contract to supply managed services to nearly 770 schools in Western Australia. As a result RM established a subsidiary called RM Australasia in Perth in 1999.

RM's range of operations continued to expand, and included a wider array of resources offerings. For example, in 2001 the company acquired Softease, a Derby-based educational publisher. This was followed in 2002 by the purchase of Helicon Publishing, which focused on electronic reference database and related products, from W.H. Smith. The company also developed a partnership with Harcourt Education that year to develop materials for online curricula. Another company success was its selection to provide online teacher training courses for the Department for Education and Skills (DfES), established by the British government in 2001.

STEADY GROWTH

By 2003 RM had gained another £4.7 million in DfES contracts. Also in 2003, RM added to its range of operations with the purchases of Forvus, a company specialized in providing data management and statistical analysis services to the public sector, and Peakschoolhaus Ltd., a provider of inspection services. By this time the company had a new series of high-profile contracts, including one worth £34.4 million with South Yorkshire's eLearning Partnership, and a £30 million contract to provide managed services to South Lanarkshire. These and other contracts allowed RM to achieve steady revenue growth, and by 2005 the company's total sales had topped £260 million per year.

RM continued to seek new growth opportunities through the end of the decade. The company completed a new series of acquisitions, including Sentinel Products in 2004, and Music Education Supplies in 2006. In 2007 RM added three more acquisitions: educational resource provider SpaceKraft; Asset, a provider of assessment and data services; and DACTA Ltd., a major distributor of Lego-branded educational products in Europe. Among the high-profile projects carried out by the company during this period was the 2005 rollout of Glow, the £37.5 million Scottish national digital intranet, connecting more than 3,000 schools and over 800,000 students in Scotland's school system.

INTERNATIONAL OBJECTIVES

RM's success in Australia led the company to explore a wider expansion of its international operations. As part of this effort the company changed the name of its Australian subsidiary to RM Asia-Pacific Pty Ltd. RM also took its first step into the Indian market, establishing offices in Kerala in 2003. The move, initially to provide support services for its U.K. operations, also provided the company with a foothold for a future entry into the Indian ICT market.

RM had in the meantime also established operations in the United States, opening an office in Massachusetts. The U.S. business quickly rose to become the company's largest foreign operation, outpacing its Australian subsidiary. In 2008 RM reinforced its presence in the United States through the acquisition of Computrac. The purchase boosted the company's U.S. revenues to 7 percent of its total, which topped £347 million for the year.

By then RM had begun to benefit from a new U.K. government education initiative, Building Schools for the Future (BSF). RM emerged as a leading provider of technological services for this project, which called for the construction of new schools throughout the country. RM had secured 28 BSF contracts by the beginning of 2010. This total rose in February of that year when RM teamed up with building group Skanska to win the BSF contract from Essex County Council, one of the largest BSF projects in the country.

At the same time, RM had continued to enhance its international scope, winning a contract to supply software and support services for the International Baccalaureate program, reaching more than 2,000 schools in nearly 140 countries. RM had grown from its origins as a mail-order electronics supplier to become one of the world's fastest-growing ICT and educational resources specialists.

M. L. Cohen

PRINCIPAL SUBSIDIARIES

AMI Education Solutions Ltd.; Caz Software Pty Ltd. (Australia); Computrac LLC (USA); Dacta Ltd.; Isis Concepts Limited; RM Asia-Pacific Pty Ltd. (Australia); RM Data Solutions Ltd.; RM Education plc; RM Education Solutions India Pvt. Ltd.; RM Educational Software Inc. (USA); SpaceKraft Ltd.; TTS Group Ltd.

PRINCIPAL DIVISIONS

RM Assessment and Data; RM Learning Technologies; RM Education Resources.

PRINCIPAL COMPETITORS

3M United Kingdom plc; Autonomy Corporation plc; Avid Technology Europe Ltd.; LogicaCMG plc; Pearson plc; Next plc; Northgate Information Solutions Ltd.; Reed Elsevier Group plc; Sage Group plc; Steria UK Corporate Ltd.

FURTHER READING

Crosland, Jonas, "Strong Growth at RM Group," *Investors Chronicle*, November 23, 2009.

Hague, Douglas, "Mike Fischer, Serial Entrepreneur," *Oxford Centre for Entrepreneurship and Innovation*, June 2005.

Murray-West, Rosie, "Wait for Project Work before Giving RM Its Final Grade," *Daily Telegraph*, November 25, 2003.

"RM Group All Tooled Up to Expand," *Birmingham Post*, March 12, 2008, p. 24.

"RM Group Gets Top Marks for Homework as Revenues Surge," *Independent*, November 26, 2006, p. 10.

Velaigam, Malar, "RM Goes International," *Investors Chronicle*, January 5, 2010.

———, "RM Proves Its Resilience," *Investors Chronicle*, November 24, 2008.

———, "Schools Bonanza for RM," *Investors Chronicle*, June 16, 2009.

Rockwood Holdings, Inc.

———————————— ■ ————————————

100 Overlook Center
Princeton, New Jersey 08540
U.S.A.
Telephone: (609) 514-0300
Fax: (609) 514-8720
Web site: http://www.rockwoodspecialties.com

Public Company
Incorporated: 2000 as K-L Holdings Inc.
Employees: 9,500
Sales: $2.96 billion (2009)
Stock Exchanges: New York
Ticker Symbol: ROC
NAICS: 325998 All Other Miscellaneous Chemical
Product Manufacturing

■ ■ ■

Rockwood Holdings, Inc., is a specialty chemicals and advanced materials company. Products include lithium compounds used to make batteries; surface treatment products for automotive and aircraft applications; wood treatment products for decks, fences, garden furniture, utility poles, and other items subjected to weather; iron oxide pigments for construction materials as well as pharmaceuticals, food, and cosmetics; clay-based additives used in personal care and household products, ink, paper manufacturing, and other applications; and titanium dioxide pigments, zinc sulfide, and barium sulfate additives used to produce synthetic fibers, paper, plastic, foils and films, cosmetics, and pharmaceuticals.

Rockwood also offers advanced ceramics used in hip joint components, cutting tools, dental structures, armor, and other applications; and specialty low smoke, low flame compounds used in wire and cable applications as well as medical devices, footwear, consumer products, automotive applications, and food and beverage packaging. Rockwood is based in Princeton, New Jersey, and maintains about 87 manufacturing facilities in 24 countries. The company is one-third owned by the investment firm Kohlberg Kravis Roberts (KKR).

COMPANY FORMED: 2000

Rockwood Holdings was cobbled together by KKR in 2000 from assets owned by a British chemicals company, Laporte plc, named after German-born chemist Bernard Laporte. In 1888 he established the firm in England to produce hydrogen peroxide for bleaching straw boaters that were popular at the time. Over the years Laporte plc diversified into other bleaching and laundry chemicals as well as specialty organic chemicals.

The seeds for the creation of Rockwood were planted in 1995 when Jim Leng was named chief executive officer at Laporte. He took over a company that was highly reliant on commodity products, which he began to sell off while beefing up the company's specialty chemicals group. Economic crises in Asia and Latin America, exacerbated by the effects of a strong British pound and consolidation in the chemicals industry in the late 1990s, hurt Laporte. The company's stock price dipped, making it difficult to fund acquisitions to maintain growth.

After an attempt to sell the company outright failed, Leng elected to divest its pigments and additives, compounds and electronic materials, and formulation products division to KKR in September 2000 for about $1.2 billion. Having sold units that generated 55 percent of its revenues, Laporte was left with its core specialty organics business, but was also vulnerable to takeover. Later in 2000 the remaining assets were sold to a German chemicals group, bringing an end to Laporte's corporate existence.

The assets acquired by KKK included AlfaGary Corp., Southern Clay Products Inc., and CSI Chemical Specialties, which together were involved in pigments, timber treatment, additives, compounds, and water technology. Together they generated annual sales of more than $700 million. The new company assumed the provisional name K-L Holdings Inc., and established its headquarters in Princeton, New Jersey, where Laporte Inc., the U.S. arm of Laporte plc, was located. Laporte Inc.'s president, Michael J. Kenny, became president of the new concern to bring continuity to the operations, which were spread around the world. About 60 percent of business came from North America, about 35 percent from Europe, and 5 percent from Asia.

ROCKWOOD NAME ADOPTED

A new name was sought for the Laporte castoffs, and in November 2000 Rockwood Specialties Group, Inc., was adopted. The new company did not, however, have a chief executive or chairman, and Kenny headed the company for the next year. Finally in November 2001 Seifi Ghasemi was named chief executive officer and chairman of Rockwood. The 56-year-old Ghasemi was born in Iran and came to the United States to study at Stanford University, where he earned a master's degree in mechanical engineering. He was the former CEO of GKN plc, a powder metallurgy company whose annual sales he increased from $300 million in 1997 to more than $1 billion in 2000.

Rockwood enjoyed meager success in its first three full years in operation, a time when the specialty chemi-

cal industry struggled in general. Annual revenues increased to about $800 million in 2003, $475 million of which was contributed by the performance additives segment. The company also posted net losses each year, due to interest payments on the company's high debt. In 2003 Rockwood lost $108 million but incurred $112.3 million in interest payments and another $38.3 million in refinancing expenses.

Despite its debt load, Rockwood looked to expand after a period of focusing on cost reduction. In 2003 it began a $7 million expansion and upgrade project at its French wafer reclaim facility to boost production, and a year later opened a plant in Suzhou, China, to produce PWB (printed wiring board) chemicals. Rockwood also sought to take advantage of low corporate prices caused by poor economic conditions to expand through acquisitions. The company's inorganic pigments division in February 2003 acquired Southern Color, a Georgia supplier of pigments, mortar products, and masonry coloring services to the construction industry. In the fall of that year the division bought the assets of a Canadian company, Smart Landscape Colors, the acquisition of which also brought to an end a patent infringement lawsuit involving granular color technology. Next, in early 2004, Rockwood acquired Silicon Technologies, a German wafer reclaim firm.

DYNAMIT NOBEL ACQUIRED: 2004

A far more significant acquisition was soon to follow. With financing arranged by KKR, Rockwood in April 2004 paid $2.7 million, including the assumption of debt, to acquire Dynamit Nobel's four specialty chemical businesses from Frankfurt, Germany-based MG Technologies AG. The four companies included Sachtleben Chemie GmbH, a white pigment manufacturer; CeremTec AG, a ceramics manufacturer; Chemeall GmbH, a surface treatment and lithium chemical manufacturer; and DNES Custom Synthesis, a pharmaceutical products maker.

Based in Troisdorf, Germany, Dynamit Nobel was founded by famed dynamite manufacturer Alfred Nobel, for whom the Nobel Prize was named. The four businesses, which would retain their separate identities, brought about $1.6 billion in annual sales to Rockwood. It also created, in the words of its CEO, a "unique global specialty chemicals and advanced materials company with a good geographic spread." There was little product overlap, resulting in a broader product portfolio and customer base as well as providing geographic diversi-fication.

Rockwood completed two other significant acquisitions later in 2004. In September one of its subsidiaries

```
┌─────────────────────────────────────────┐
│                                           │
│            KEY DATES                      │
│              ─────◆─────                   │
│                                           │
│   2000:  Rockwood Specialties is formed.  │
│   2003:  Expansion program begins.        │
│   2004:  Dynamit Nobel companies acquired.│
│   2005:  Company is taken public.         │
│   2007:  A secondary stock offering is    │
│          completed.                       │
│                                           │
└─────────────────────────────────────────┘
```

acquired the pigments and dispersions business of Johnson Matthey Plc, for $50.5 million, gaining plants in Kidsgrove and Sudbury in the United Kingdom, and Braeside, Australia, and sales offices around the world. This deal was followed in December 2004 with the merger of its Custom Synthesis segment with Groupe Novasel SAS to create a larger synthesis and separations company. The resulting company, called Groupe Novasep, was majority owned by Rockwood and generated $36 million in annual revenues.

PUBLIC OFFERING: 2005

With partial contributions from its new assets, Rockwood generated sales of $1.64 billion in 2004. Part of the plan from the beginning was to grow the company large enough to take it public. It August 2005 Rockwood achieved that goal by completing an initial public offering of stock for Rockwood Holdings, Inc., that netted about $435.7 million, money that was then used to pay down corporate debt. About 30 percent of the company was sold. Shares of Rockwood then began trading on the New York Stock Exchange.

Although the company's focus was on organic growth, Rockwood pursued acquisitions as opportunities arose. In October 2005 it purchased the performance additives business of Sud-Chemie AG, which were then folded into Rockwood's Clay Additives business unit led by Southern Clay Products. The unit added $50 million in annual sales and new customized products. Rockwood comprised 17 business units, organized into seven reporting units. Ghasemi also made it clear that the company was content to grow its individual businesses and felt no need to promote the Rockwood name or hire a consultant to coin a global brand.

GROUPE NOVASEP DIVESTED: 2007

For 2005, the company recorded revenues of $2.74 billion and turned its first annual profit, netting $95.8 million. A year later revenues approached $3 billion and

Rockwood improved its earnings to $103 million. Investors were not especially pleased with Rockwood's diverse portfolio and debt level. To help address these concerns, the company divested Groupe Novasep in January 2007. Rockwood was now reduced to six reportable segments: Specialty Chemicals, Performance Additives, Titanium Dioxide Pigments, Advanced Ceramics, Specialty Compounds, and Electronics.

Rockwood divested another unit in 2007, selling its electronics business for $265 million. Rockwood also added to its pigments business during the year. It paid $140 million for the global pigments business of Elementis plc, adding about $170 million in annual sales and production facilities in the United States, the United Kingdom, and China that provided global sourcing for customers. Moreover, the acquisition filled out Rockwood's range of pigment products and services and made it more cost effective. Also in 2007 Rockwood expanded it wood treatment business through the creation of a joint venture, Viance LLC Timber Treatment.

During 2007 a secondary offering of stock was conducted. None of the proceeds went to Rockwood. Rather, they were earmarked for investors taking out profits. As a result, KKR was no longer majority-owner, its stake reduced to about 40 percent, but it continued to maintain a strong influence on the direction of the company through its seats on the board of directors. Rockwood closed the year by increasing revenues to $3.14 billion in 2007 while net income grew to $317.1 million.

Further changes to Rockwood's business mix were made in 2008. The pool and spa chemicals business was divested, fetching $124 million, while both the surface treatment and color pigments and services segments expanded through bolt-on acquisitions. In addition, the Sachtleben Chemie TiO2 joint venture was formed, strengthening Rockwood's specialty titanium dioxide pigments business.

The last few months of 2008 brought a severe downturn in the economy. Nevertheless, Rockwood was able to generate record revenues of nearly $3.4 billion. The full impact of the recession was felt in 2009, yet Rockwood continued to perform well. Although revenues dipped below $3 billion, the company was still able to post a modest $21.1 million profit. More importantly, Rockwood enjoyed a strong fourth quarter, outperforming the economic recovery, and increasing margins in most of its business segments.

The company also made strides with its lithium compounds business, which held great promise because of transportation batteries that were likely to gain in importance in the years to come. The company's Chemetall operation received a $28.4 million grant from the U.S. Department of Energy to expand production of high purity compounds to support battery production. The German government also provided it with money to develop a pilot plant for recycling lithium-ion batteries. Sales of lithium for car batteries were limited, but in the near future its use was expected to increase dramatically in batteries as well as in pharmaceutical applications. As a result, Rockwood appeared to have a bright future ahead of it.

Ed Dinger

PRINCIPAL SUBSIDIARIES

Chemetall GmbH; Dynamit Nobel GmbH; Southern Clay Products, Inc.

PRINCIPAL COMPETITORS

Arch Chemicals, Inc.; Elementis plc; PolyOne Corporation.

FURTHER READING

Hagen, Tony, "Rockwood Finds Right Chemistry," *Trenton (NJ) Times*, November 29, 2000, p. C1.

Levi, Erica, "Rockwood Chemical Group Gets Long-Sought CEO," *Trenton (NJ) Times*, November 6, 2001, p. C1.

Milmo, Sean, "Laporte Sells Stake to KKR for $1.2 Billion," *Chemical Market Reporter*, October 2, 2000, p. 8.

Whalen, Laurie, "Industry Remixes Formula," *Trenton (NJ) Times*, April 20, 2004, p. D1.

Wood, Andrew, "Rockwood Specialties Achieving Critical Mass," *Chemical Week*, April 12, 2006, p. 19.

Wood, Andrew, and David Hunter, "Improving Rockwood's Top Line," *Chemical Week*, March 27, 2002, p. 41.

Young, Ian, "Rockwood to Acquire Four Dynamit Nobel Businesses," *Chemical Week*, April 28, 2004, p. 8.

Rose Hills Company

———■———

3888 Workman Mill Road
Whittier, California 90601
U.S.A.
Telephone: (562) 699-0921
Toll Free: (800) 327-8791
Fax: (562) 699-6372
Web site: http://www.rosehills.com

Wholly Owned Subsidiary of Service Corporation International
Incorporated: 1914 as Whittier Heights Memorial Park
Employees: 600
Sales: $135.6 million (2009 est.)
NAICS: 812210 Funeral Homes; 812220 Cemeteries and Crematories

■ ■ ■

A subsidiary of major death care company Service Corporation International (SCI), Rose Hills Company is the world's largest individually operated cemetery, each year performing more than 5,000 funeral services and 8,500 internments. The Whittier, California-based business includes a memorial park more than 1,500 acres in size, five chapels, three mausoleums, a mortuary, and a crematory. All told, the company's land holdings total about 2,500 acres. As a nondenominational cemetery, Rose Hills includes religion-specific sites, such as Covenant Lawn for Jews, Lutheran Lawn for Lutherans, Trinity Lawn for Catholics, Deseret Lawn for Mormons, and Cedarcrest Lawn for Muslims. Rose Hills also reaches out to the large Asian and Hispanic populations that live close to the cemetery. The Chinese, who pay

particular reverence to the dead, are especially accommodated.

The spring holiday Ching Ming, or "tomb-sweeping day," is the cemetery's busiest day of the year, a time when families feast, clean tombstones, and burn ceremonial paper goods, available for purchase at the cemetery, to help the departed negotiate the afterlife. Because many Asians consider the number eight lucky, the cemetery changed its street address from 3900 Workman Mill Road to 3888 Workman Mill Road. Rose Hills offers inclusive funeral plans as well as itemized products and services. Rose Hills also sells "pre-need" funeral and cremation packages, allowing people to make monthly payments toward future services at prevailing prices.

ORIGINS

The man regarded as the founder of Rose Hills was Augustus H. "Gus" Gregg. He was just a year old in 1870 when his family came to the Whittier area from Texas in a wagon train. As an adult he enjoyed success in real estate. He also planted some orange trees on a 14-acre plot of land three miles northwest of Whittier that had once been part of the famous 10,000-acre Rancho Paso de Bartolo Spanish land grant in what would come to be Los Angeles County. In 1914 a pair of men paid a visit to Gregg at his real estate office and asked him to sell them the 14-acre grove in order to create a much needed cemetery for Whittier. A price of $36,900 was agreed upon, the money to be raised through the sale of stock in a new company. However, a few months later the partners had managed to raise only $10,000 of the

$50,000 they had hoped to raise.

Gregg had no particular desire to own a cemetery, but he was well aware that the community needed one. Moreover, many of the stock purchasers who were in danger of losing their investment were friends of his. As a result, Gregg accepted the unsold stock in lieu of the money owed to him, and he subsequently established Whittier Heights Memorial Park. The first burial, costing $30, was conducted in 1915. To meet future needs an additional 100 acres of land was soon acquired. A public mausoleum, only the second to be built in California, opened in 1917.

JOHN GREGG ACQUIRES CEMETERY: 1929

It was Gregg's son, John D. Gregg, who was responsible for transforming tiny Whittier Heights into the vast Rose Hills operation. He was a high school student when his father opened the cemetery. He attended Whittier College and Oregon State University, studying engineering and mathematics but failing to earn a degree. He served in the military during World War I and afterward went into the sand and gravel business with his father and three partners, Aubrey Wardman, W. A. Johnson, and W. E. Hall. After selling the company in 1929, John Gregg was inactive for nine months, until his father suggested that he and his partners take over Whittier Heights. In 1929 he finally agreed and they bought the cemetery, which was 123 acres in size at the time. An entity called Bartolo Company was responsible for operating the cemetery.

John Gregg quickly moved to expand the cemetery. He recognized that the advent of the automobile made the cemetery ideally located to serve the needs of not only tiny Whittier but also Los Angeles. Ground was broken on a new large indoor mausoleum, El Portal de la Paz, in 1929. With a California mission design, it opened to the public a year later and over the years would be expanded five more times. It was also in 1930 that Whittier Heights changed its name to Rose Hills

Memorial Park, the result of a contest. The Rose Hills name would be displayed on a hillside in block letters in the style of the famous Hollywood sign, albeit half the height.

EXPANSION PROJECT

Gregg initiated a series of acquisitions of adjoining land, each time receiving the begrudging approval of his board of directors. Only when Gregg had acquired all available land did he finally stop making requests of his board, at least until a new opportunity arose following World War II. In the meantime, four garden mausoleums were added to the grounds, and in 1942 a crematorium was constructed.

Adjacent to Rose Hills was a large tract of land, 1,800 acres in size, but it was laced with steep canyons and gullies that created rainy season floodways, making it appear essentially worthless. Gregg thought otherwise, however, and at his behest Rose Hills acquired the property, whose untapped worth was considerable given its proximity to the 6.5 million people living in the Los Angeles metropolitan area. After aerial photographs were taken, a topographical map was constructed and plans were made to convert 750 adjacent acres into useable land, one of the largest private land projects of its kind ever attempted. Engineers estimated that 33 million cubic yards of earth would have to be moved to create the desired slopes of a cemetery. It was a massive undertaking, and all of the bids on the projects were far too expensive, prompting Rose Hills to do the work itself.

A soil analysis revealed a material that flowed freely with water. Rather than using bulldozers to topple ridges and fill in canyons, Rose Hills engineers decided to use water to accomplish the job. Bulldozers were used to expose the tops of ridges and high-pressure jets of water were then employed to create a freely moving mixture of soil to lower heights and fill in valleys. All told, 25 million cubic yards of earth were moved in the project, accomplished with just five bulldozers, a work crew of six, and a five-person engineering and survey team.

NONPROFIT CORPORATION FORMED: 1950

In 1950 Gregg formed a nonprofit corporation to run the cemetery, Rose Hills Memorial Park Association, for which he served as president. Two years later Rose Hills acquired all of the shares of Bartolo Company stock,

KEY DATES

1914: Gus Gregg founds Whittier Heights Memorial Park.

1929: Gus Gregg's son, John D. Gregg, acquires cemetery.

1930: Name is changed to Rose Hills Memorial Park.

1959: John D. Gregg dies.

1996: Loewen Group acquires Rose Hills.

2006: Parent company is acquired by Service Corporation International.

and Bartolo shareholders were to be paid according to a formula based on the gross selling price of all grave spaces, crypts, and other items. The mortuary was also spun off as a separate for-profit company. The Rose Hills structure did not pass regulatory muster, however, and its tax-exempt status was eventually revoked.

Rose Hills continued to expand in the 1950s. With the addition of the Rose Hills Mortuary and Flower Shop in 1956, Rose Hills became one of the country's first full-service cemeteries. Following John Gregg's death in September 1959, Rose Hills had to carry on without its dynamic, longtime leader, but by this time it was well established in the Los Angeles area. Although the primary elements of Rose Hills were already in place, further efforts were made to improve the property. For example, in 1986 Rose Hills opened the Gardens, a 3.4-acre section that offered private and semiprivate garden sites and other memorialization options. In addition, to accommodate an increased interest in cremation, the Gardens included a scattering lawn, urn gardens, and a 10-foot-high, 200-foot-long black granite wall on which names could be inscribed.

Rose Hills was an unusually large participant in the funeral home business, most of which were generally small, local, and family owned. That would begin to change in the 1980s as the "death care" industry took shape and efforts were made to bring consolidation to the business. Given that the baby boom generation was beginning to age and as a consequence the number of deaths and funerals would be increasing at a rapid pace in the years to come, there was growing interest in taking advantage of what was expected to be a "golden era" for death. One of the consolidators was the Loewen Group of Vancouver, Canada, which made its first acquisition in the United States in 1987. Its chief rival was Houston-based Service Corp. International (SCI).

CHANGES IN OWNERSHIP

By the fall of 1996 Loewen was North America's second-largest funeral and cemetery service company, operating more than 900 funeral homes and 271 cemeteries in the United States and Canada, trailing only SCI. In September 1996, Loewen, with the financial backing of Blackstone Capital Partners II Merchant Banking Fund L.P., acquired Rose Hills Memorial Park Association and The Rose Hills Company, Inc., for $241.3 million.

At the same time Loewen was acquiring Rose Hills, SCI was making a $3.1 billion offer to buy Loewen, claiming that Loewen was overpaying for properties such as Rose Hills and needed new ownership. Loewen dismissed the action as resentment over SCI's failure to acquire Rose Hills for itself, and what began as a friendly takeover turned decidedly hostile. Loewen fended off the attempt but it became clear that there was some truth to SCI's assertion that Loewen was not on a sound financial footing, due in no small measure to the acquisition war in which it was engaged with SCI. In June 1999 Loewen filed for Chapter 11 bankruptcy protection.

Although its parent company filed for protection from its creditors, Rose Hills, because it maintained its own cash flow and lines of credit, carried on its business with little or no impact. After selling off most of its holdings, Loewen emerged from bankruptcy in January 2002 as Alderwoods Group Inc., based in Cincinnati. With the business stabilized, Alderwoods was generating annual revenues of $700 million in 2005, making it the second-largest publicly traded North American funeral operator. In 2006 it was acquired by the number one operator, SCI, which was forced to shed some assets in order to satisfy antitrust concerns. Rose Hills was retained, however.

Although then part of SCI, little changed for Rose Hills. It maintained its unique place in the Los Angeles area and continued to upgrade its operations. A new lawn, SkyRidge, was unveiled in 2007. It was located on the highest elevation on the property and framed the western horizon toward the ocean, especially important to customers of Chinese descent. Rose Hills paid particular attention to maintaining a green operation. By 2010 the entire park was being irrigated with reclaimed water. Also in 2010 a new president, Patrick Monroe, was installed after the previous president, Kenton Woods, left to take a senior position at SCI. With 19 years of experience at various positions at the company, Monroe was well prepared to carry on the Rose Hills tradition as it approached its centennial.

Ed Dinger

PRINCIPAL SUBSIDIARIES

Rose Hills Mortuary Inc.

PRINCIPAL COMPETITORS

Carriage Services, Inc.; High Sierra Gardens; Stewart Enterprises, Inc.

FURTHER READING

Ferrell, Dave, "Life & Death: Inside America's Biggest, Busiest Cemetery," *Los Angeles Magazine*, July 2006, p. 78.

Garcia, Tracy, "Longtime Rose Hills Administrator Monroe Promoted to President," *Whittier Daily News*, February 21, 2010.

Larson, Erik, "Fight to the Death," *Time*, December 9, 1996, p. 62.

Myerson, Allen R., "Loewen Buys Big Cemetery," *New York Times*, September 21, 1996.

Richardson, James H., "The Story of Rose Hills," *Pasadena Independent*, May 1, 1959, p. 2.

Royal Gold, Inc.

———— ■ ————

1660 Wynkoop Street, Suite 1000
Denver, Colorado 80202
U.S.A.
Telephone: (303) 573-1660
Fax: (303) 595-9385
Web site: http://www.royalgold.com

Public Company
Incorporated: 1966 as Royal Resources Explorations, Inc.
Employees: 17
Sales: $73.8 million (2009)
Stock Exchanges: NASDAQ Toronto
Ticker Symbol: FGLD
NAICS: 523999 Miscellaneous Financial Investment
   Activities

■ ■ ■

Royal Gold, Inc., is a Denver, Colorado-based precious metals company that has enjoyed excellent results by managing royalty positions for its investors. The NASDAQ and Toronto Stock Exchange-listed company avoids the costs and risks of mining operations by acquiring percentages of a property's production for an upfront payment, and then receives royalties on a sliding scale. In some cases the company discovers deposits that it sells to operators in exchange for royalties. The more a property produces, the higher the royalty rate. If the economics dictate a lower level of production, Royal Gold takes a lower royalty.

Although Royal Gold focuses on gold it also receives royalties on silver, copper, and other precious metals. Its portfolio includes some 30 producing royalties, 20 development-stage royalties, and about 140 evaluation and exploration-stage royalties, primarily located in the United States, but also in Mexico, Africa, Canada, Chile, and other countries to a lesser extent. Royal Gold's most lucrative property is Nevada's Cortez Pipeline Mining Complex, which accounts for more than a third of the company's revenues. The low-cost structure, high-reward model has made it a favorite with institutional investors, who also trust the seasoned judgment of Royal Gold's executive team, led by Stanley Dempsey, longtime chairman and a trained geologist.

OIL AND GAS HERITAGE

Royal Gold's lineage can be traced to oilman John McCandish King, who stood six feet four and weighed 230 pounds. Born in Illinois in 1927, he was often ill as a youth and never completed college, despite attending three universities. He pursued politics and was elected to the Illinois House of Representatives at the age of 23. At the end of his two-year turn he parlayed $1,500 in leftover pay to drill a "wildcat," or speculative, oil well on a friend's Oklahoma farm. King struck it rich and turned his focus to the oil business.

King cofounded a company, King-Stevenson Oil & Gas Co., in Chicago in 1955. He was more interested in selling stakes in oil drilling partnerships than actually pursuing exploration and drilling activities. Because of loopholes at the time, oil exploration offered significant tax shelters to wealthy individuals, providing King with plenty of investors who benefited whether a well struck oil or not. These loopholes began to close in the late

COMPANY PERSPECTIVES

COMPANY PERSPECTIVES

Royal Gold, Inc., a leading precious metals royalty company, owns and manages royalties primarily on precious metals mines, with a focus on gold.

1950s, around the same time King moved to Denver. After his partnership broke up, he launched King Resources in 1961 to take over its oil and gas properties. He enjoyed little success until he decided to tap into a larger financial market.

King formed Colorado Corporation, which in 1966 introduced a pair of new funds that he marketed in much the same way as mutual funds. One was called Imperial-American Resources Fund, Inc., which focused on drilling in proven properties, while the other, a "wildcat" fund, was named Royal Resources Explorations, Inc. He enjoyed spectacular success in attracting small investors, whom he allowed to participate on an installment plan. King hired a pair of astronauts as executives to burnish the image of Colorado Corporation and its funds. Rather than keeping partnership funds separate, however, he commingled the money so that people exiting a fund had their interest sold to a new partnership, resulting in a scheme in which money from new investors paid off old investors.

DEMPSEY NAMED TO ROYAL RESOURCES BOARD: 1983

King enjoyed the life of a celebrated oilman for several years before his empire began to crumble. In 1976 he was sentenced to one year in prison after being convicted of fraud and conspiracy charges related to one of his ventures. A year later the stock of Royal Resources Exploration, Inc., was issued to Royal Resources Company, a corporation owned by King and his wife. The new Royal Resources continued to focus on oil and gas exploration. In 1981 it became known as Royal Resources Corporation. It became involved in securities fraud, which led to a court assigning an executive to take charge of the company. King was a trout-fishing friend of Stanley Dempsey, who in 1983 was asked to join the Royal Resources board of directors.

Dempsey came to Royal Resources with a mining background. Born in Indiana in 1939, he worked summers as a boy lighting fuses in his uncle's coal mine, all the while dreaming of one day traveling west to discover a gold mine. He came to Colorado in 1956 to enroll in the Colorado School of Mines to study geology, and

later transferred to the University of Colorado, where he completed his degree in geology and later earned a law degree in 1964. To pay for his education Dempsey leased and operated small tungsten and uranium mines in Colorado and Wyoming. After law school he went to work in the legal department at Amax, Inc., a major mining company. He would eventually run Amax's Australian operations.

After the mining industry suffered a collapse in the early 1980s, Dempsey left Amax and returned to Denver in 1983 to practice law. He became a partner at Arnold & Porter, where he handled mining transactions and public lands work. There he received a chance to join the board of directors for Royal Resources. With Ed Peiker he also cofounded Denver Mining Finance Corporation (DMFC), a merchant bank that provided funding as well as merger and acquisition services to mining companies.

Royal Resources enjoyed some success until crude oil prices collapsed in 1986. Royal Resources turned to Dempsey and DMFC for advice, and Dempsey developed a strategy to convert Royal Resources into a gold mining company. Dempsey was asked to take over the company to pursue this strategy, and in 1986 he became chief executive officer. He sold off the company's oil interests, and changed the name of Royal Resources to Royal Gold, Inc., in May 1987. DMFC also became a Royal Gold subsidiary and Peiker served as Royal Gold's president.

BUSINESS MODEL BEGINS TO CHANGE: 1987

Royal Gold started out operating gold mines in California and Colorado. However, with inadequate equipment it did not fare well as a gold exploration and production company, and its share traded at penny stock levels. When the stock market crashed in October 1987, Royal Gold began to transition away from production in favor of taking minority positions in gold properties that were being operated by major mining companies. With his knowledge and background, Dempsey also proved adept at buying and selling properties to keep the company solvent. A key deal was his $5 million acquisition of a 10 percent interest in the Hog Ranch gold mine in Nevada, which he then sold for $11 million in 1988.

Dempsey's investment acumen kept Royal Gold in business and allowed it to invest $1 million in a northern Nevada property, the Cortez Pipeline Mining Complex, which it explored with two other companies. Because money was running short, Dempsey sold Royal Gold's 20 percent profit share for $1 million to one of its partners, Place Dome, which subsequently announced that three million ounces of gold had been discovered at Pipeline.

Dempsey, far from pleased with this sudden revelation, sued and won back Royal Gold's stake, which was later converted into royalties. According to a 2005 *Forbes* profile on Dempsey, "Pipeline's success—8 million ounces of poured gold and counting—persuaded Dempsey to change his business model. Because he couldn't afford to operate even small mines, he closed them all, shrank his Denver office to 14 people and decided to emulate a couple of larger, royalty-based rivals." Dempsey continued to make sporadic attempts at exploration but would fare better with his royalty arrangements.

Royal Gold's stock was trading for just three cents a share in 1992 when the company began to enjoy a steady climb. It finally achieved profitability in fiscal 1997 after posting revenues of $3.7 million and net income of $589,000. The company closed the 1990s with two more losing years as revenues dipped, but rebounded in 2000 when Royal Gold netted nearly $4 million on revenues of $9.4 million, an especially impressive performance given the poor conditions of the gold industry at the time. It also set the stage for a decade of strong growth.

Low gold prices through much of 2001 resulted in revenues slipping below $6 million in fiscal 2001, and net income fell to $1.1 million. The terrorist attacks against the United States on September 11, 2001, however, led to a spike in gold prices and a surge in revenues for Royal Gold in fiscal 2002, when royalties increased to $12.3 million and net income totaled $10.7 million. The company also pursued new gold exploration opportunities in Greece and Bulgaria during the year.

HIGH DESERT MINERAL RESOURCES ACQUIRED: 2003

Royal Gold continued to add to its portfolio of gold-producing properties in fiscal 2003 by acquiring a one-third stake in another gold royalty company, High Desert Mineral Resources, a deal completed in December 2002. The addition of High Desert's interests, and continued strong performance from Pipeline, helped drive revenues to $21.3 million in fiscal 2004, which resulted in net earnings of $8.9 million. The price of gold continued to rise, from $410 per ounce in fiscal 2004 to $428 the following year.

Royal Gold was able to take advantage of this increase by financing the recommissioning of the Troy Mine in Montana, which in January 2005 began paying royalties. Because Pipeline's production began to decline, new revenue sources became increasingly important to Royal Gold's ability to maintain growth. In fiscal 2006 the company raised funds through a secondary stock offering and used the proceeds to acquire royalty interests in properties located in Nevada, Mexico, and Finland.

Revenues for fiscal 2006 reached $23.4 million and net income totaled $11.35 million. More acquisition followed in fiscal 2007, including the purchase of a royalty on Goldcorp's Penasquito deposit in Mexico, and a royalty on Barrick Gold's Pascua-Lama project in Chile. Royal Gold also acquired Battle Mountain Gold Exploration Corp., which held royalty positions on properties in North and South America. As a result, revenues jumped to $48.4 million in fiscal 2007 and net income to $19.7 million.

Royal Gold also benefited from deteriorating global economic conditions, as well as concerns about world stability, which led to record gold prices. In March 2008 the price of gold reached $1,011 per ounce. Royal Gold used its expertise to continue to add attractive properties. Early in 2008 it acquired three royalties from AngloGold Ashanti, and in July of that year the company acquired Barrick's portfolio of 77 royalties. Royal Gold's revenues increased to $66.3 million and net income grew to more than $24 million in fiscal 2008.

Royal Gold continued its strong performance in fiscal 2009 when the company also took steps to diversify its portfolio to include some of the world's most successful gold producing regions of the world. Revenues improved to $73.8 million and net income to $38.3 million in fiscal 2009. Given the breadth of its portfolio, the proven ability of its management team, and conditions that favored high gold prices, Royal

Gold appeared to be well positioned to maintain its strong growth pattern for at least the short term.

Ed Dinger

PRINCIPAL SUBSIDIARIES

Battle Mountain Gold Exploration Corp.; Denver Mining Finance Company, Inc.; High Desert Mineral Resources, Inc.

PRINCIPAL COMPETITORS

Anglo American plc; BHP Billiton Limited; Rio Tinto Limited.

FURTHER READING

Bradley, Hassell, "Royal Gold Climbs into Black," *American Metal Market*, May 15, 1990, p. 7.

"From Visiting a Coal Mine to Leading a Virtual Gold Company," *Amicas* (University of Colorado Law School), Fall 2008, p. 8.

Olien, Roger M., and Diana Davids Hinton, *Wildcatters: Texas Independent Oilmen*, College Station, TX: TAMU Press, 2007.

"Personalities: Big John," *Times*, May 25, 1970.

Raw, Charles, Bruce Page, and Godfrey Hodgson, *"Do You Seriously Want to Be Rich?"* New York: Viking Press, 1971.

Smith, Eric, "CEOs: Are They Worth What They're Paid?" *Colorado Business Magazine*, July 1988, p. 13.

Whelan, David, "Virtual Gold," *Forbes*, May 9, 2005, p. 71.

Saarioinen Oy

Pl. 108, Jaervensivuntie 1
Tampere, FIN-33101
Finland
Telephone: (+358 03) 244 7111
Fax: (+358 03) 244 7261
Web site: http://www.saarioinen.fi

Private Company
Incorporated: 1955
Employees: 2,229
Sales: EUR 330 million ($444.9 million) (2009 est.)
NAICS: 311612 Meat Processed from Carcasses; 311412 Frozen Specialty Food Manufacturing; 311421 Fruit and Vegetable Canning; 311520 Ice Cream and Frozen Dessert Manufacturing; 311615 Poultry Processing; 311812 Commercial Bakeries; 311919 Other Snack Food Manufacturing; 311930 Flavoring Syrup and Concentrate Manufacturing

■ ■ ■

Saarioinen Oy is the leading privately held food manufacturer in Finland. The Tampere-based company produces more than 600 products across a variety of categories from six factories. The company's Saarioisten Säilyke subsidiary produces nearly 30 million tons per year of jams, desserts, and fresh salads, as well as mayonnaise and other sauces and condiments. Another subsidiary, Liha-Saarioinen, produces sausages and other ready-made meat products, as well as pizzas, pies, crepes, and other baked goods.

Ruoka-Saarioinen is one of Finland's largest chicken processors and chicken-based ready-made meal producers. The company's Saarioisten Lihanjalostus subsidiary in Jyväskylä is a leading Finnish beef and pork processor, with production levels of 20 million kilos per year. Saarioinen also owns Meleco, the leading chilled ready-made meals producer in Estonia, and operates two subsidiaries in Sweden.

The retail sector accounts for 70 percent of the company's total production volumes of 60 million kilos per year. The company is also a major supplier to the HoReCa (hotel, restaurant, catering) sector as well as to schools, hospitals, and other institutional outlets. While Finland remains the company's largest market, Saarioinen has developed exports to the Baltic countries, Germany, and Russia. Saarioinen remained a privately held company, with sales of EUR 330 million ($445 million), in 2009.

FOUNDED IN 1941

Long before becoming one of Finland's most well-known food brands, Saarioinen had its roots in Finland's farming tradition. The presence of a farm at Saarioinen dated back to at least the end of the 15th century. In the 20th century the Saarioinen mansion remained a prominent local landmark. In 1941 the mansion was purchased by three members of the Avotie (or Avonius) family, Aukusti Asko Avonius and his nephews, Pentti Avotie, born in 1924, and Pentti's younger brother, Reino. The family initially focused on producing furniture, and then in 1946 began processing tobacco.

The transformation of the Saarioinen mansion into a food processing company started in the early 1950s. The family first developed a poultry business. The growth of this business inspired the introduction of a rooster as part of the company's logo in 1954. By then, the company had begun its expansion into other food categories as well. For example, in 1953 the farm opened its own cannery in Sahalahti, initially starting with beets grown on the Saarioinen estate.

The success of these early efforts encouraged the company to expand its food processing interests. The company formally incorporated this business as Saarioinen Oy in 1955. By 1957 the group had opened its first dedicated food processing factory, also in Sahalahti. Saarioinen focused from the start on developing a range of Finnish specialties, including a liver casserole, cabbage rolls, and meatballs. Originally the company had focused on producing foods grown on its own farms.

As sales grew in the 1960s, the company established a sales and purchasing office in Helsinki, led by Pentti Avotie, extending its raw materials purchases. The company's roots in farming nevertheless continued to influence its ingredients purchasing policies, with a focus on local sources. Finland remained the primary source of the company's ingredients into the 21st century.

STATE-OF-THE-ART EXPANSION

The company's poultry production, later regrouped under subsidiary Ruoko-Saarioinen, continued to expand strongly through the end of the 1950s and into the 1960s. Among Saarioinen's innovations during this period was the creation of a new hatchery in 1959. This hatchery introduced into Finland "broiler" chickens, which could be slaughtered at just five weeks old (as compared to 10 weeks or more for free-range chicken varieties). Poultry sales continued to drive the company's growth, a fact recognized by the updating of its logo to feature a new "golden rooster," Kulta-Kukko.

The construction of a new state-of-the-art food processing facility in Sahalahti helped propel Saarioinen to the top of the rapidly growing ready-to-eat food industry in Finland. The growth of the supermarket sector, especially during the 1960s and 1970s, and the development of self-service retailing, played a large role in the growing importance of ready-meals, as the new food types were called. The new larger supermarkets provided an expanded selling space over traditional groceries, and food processors were swift to fill the shelves of the new stores.

Other factors also played a part in the transformation of Finnish eating habits. The introduction of television broadcasting in Finland created new mealtime rituals. As more and more families began to eat their meals gathered around the television set, food companies rushed to provide new prepared foods and meals in formats designed to accommodate this trend. The changing demographics of the workplace also had an influence on eating habits. As more women joined the workforce, the time available for cooking fell sharply in many households.

Saarioinen's new factory, completed in 1969, was Finland's largest food processing facility at the time. Pentti Avotie became the company's managing director that year, a position he held for over two decades. Saarioinen also invested in new technology at the plant, including adding a range of freezing and chilling machinery and equipment from FrigoScandia in 1973. The new equipment enabled the company to expand its range of products to include a variety of chilled and frozen foods, and formed the foundation for the company's extension into the convenience food sector.

PIZZA SUCCESS IN 1981

Saarioinen responded to the rising demand for prepared foods by opening a new cannery in Huittis in 1972. The company added its own poultry slaughtering facility in Sahalahti in 1976. At the same time, Saarioinen worked on developing its range of recipes, moving beyond traditional Finnish foods to develop an increasingly large variety of foods. This effort led to one of the company's biggest successes, the introduction of its

KEY DATES

1941: Aukusti Asko Avonius and his nephews, Pentti and Reino Avotie, acquire the Saarioinen property.

1955: The family incorporates Saarioinen as a joint stock company to expand its food processing interests.

1969: Saarioinen opens a state-of-the-art factory in Sahalahti.

1981: The company introduces its best-selling ready-made pizza.

1991: Saarioinen reincorporates as a holding company.

2002: The company acquires a stake in AS Meleco in Estonia.

2009: Saarioinen completes construction of a second factory in Estonia.

ready-to-serve Pizza Bolognese in 1981. This product became the best-selling ready-made pizza in Finland.

Backed by this success, the company continued to invest in its expansion through the 1980s. In 1982 the company converged its poultry and food processing operations, launching a line of prepackaged sliced chicken. Two years later Saarioinen entered the meat processing sector, acquiring the Hameenlinna-based Mestari sausage factory. By 1987 Saarioinen had moved to integrate its meat processing business, launching a beef and pork slaughtering and processing facility in Jyväskylä. This facility was followed by the construction of a new food processing plant in Valkeakoski in 1988. The expanded capacity enabled Saarioinen to extend its range with a broader line of pizzas, meat pies, including the traditional Finnish favorite Karelian pie, crepes, Italian-style breads, and other baked goods.

In 1989 founder Pentti Avotie stepped down as the group's managing director. Avotie remained on as the company's chairman, serving until 2000. Avotie died four years later, at the age of 80. Saarioinen moved its headquarters to Tampere in 1991. The move precipitated a wider reorganization of the group's growing network of production facilities. In 1992 Saarioinen reincorporated as a holding company, while its factory and logistics operations were incorporated as fully owned subsidiaries. Ruoka-Saarioinen Oy became the subsidiary for the group's Sahalahti-based food and poultry operations, while Liha-Saarioinen Oy took over

the operation of the Valkeakoski factory. The Huittis factory was placed under Saarioisten Säilyke Oy.

INTERNATIONAL OPERATIONS IN 2002

Saarioinen's sales topped one billion Finnish marks in 1994 for the first time. The group continued to raise its production volumes in the second half of the decade, topping 60 million kilos per year by 1998. Part of this growth came through the expansion of the Valkeakoski factory, which took over as the group's primary slaughtering facility in 1995.

The company also sought new product lines at this time. In 1997 Saarioinen acquired the Sun Ice Cream brand, including a factory in Jakobstad. Sun played a role in Saarioinen's entry into the fast-growing functional foods category. Functional foods were products that included ingredients and additives providing purported health benefits. In Sun Ice Cream's case, this led to the launch of a line of "health fiber" ice creams in 2000. However, the Sun Ice Cream operation remained a small one, and in 2002 Saarioinen decided to exit the sector, selling the Sun Ice Cream brand to Ingman Foods.

Saarioinen's growth remained strong in other areas. The company opened a new state-of-the-art chicken processing facility at Sahalahti in 1998. This was followed by a major expansion of the Jyväskylä plant, which then took over all of the company's fresh meat processing operations in 2001. In 2003 the company centralized its warehousing and logistics operations in a new purpose-built facility at Valkeakoski. The company then placed this business into a dedicated subsidiary, Saarioisten Keskuslähettämö Oy.

Saarioinen's sales neared EUR 270 million in the new decade. The company had developed a small export business, developing markets in Sweden, the Baltic region, and in Russia and Germany. As part of this effort, the company created dedicated sales subsidiaries in Sweden and Estonia. In 2002 the company made its first foreign acquisition, buying a majority stake in AS Meleco in Estonia. This business, based in Tallinn, added the production of a range of pizza, salads, and other ready-to-eat food products. Saarioinen acquired full control of Meleco in 2006.

NEW FACTORY IN 2009

Saarioinen's international operations remained quite small, accounting for just 3 percent of its total at the middle of the decade. Meanwhile, the company continued to enjoy strong success in Finland through the decade, raising its total revenues to EUR 330 million ($445 million) by the end of 2009. Saarioinen had completed a new reorganization by then, spinning off subsidiary Liha-Saarioinen's Jyväskylä factory as a separate subsidiary, Saarioisten Lihanjalostus, in 2006. The company also sold its vegetable canning business to Felix Abba Oy in 2007. By this time, Saarioinen had named Ilkka Mäkelä as its new managing director.

Saarioinen remained on the lookout for new expansion opportunities. For example, in 2008 the company acquired the Dronningholm brand of jams and marmalades. The company also launched construction of a second factory in Estonia that year, in Rapla. That factory, which cost the company EUR 14 million ($20 million) to build, was completed in November 2009, and added more than 6,000 square meters of production space. Saarioinen looked forward to building on its position as one of Finland's leading food brands in the years ahead.

M. L. Cohen

PRINCIPAL SUBSIDIARIES

Arsaar Oy; AS Meleco (Estonia); Finnsaar AB (Sweden); Liha-Saarioinen Oy; Ruoka-Saarioinen Oy; Saarioinen Eesti Ou (Estonia); Saarioisten Keskuslähettämö Oy; Saarioisten Lihanjalostus Oy; Saarioisten Säilyke Oy; Sponsab AB (Sweden).

PRINCIPAL DIVISIONS

Fresh Convenience Foods; Snack Food; Meat and Meat Products.

PRINCIPAL COMPETITORS

B and C Toennies Fleischwerk GmbH and Company KG; Brake Brothers Ltd.; Danish Crown AmbA; HK-Scan Oyj; Nestlé Suisse S.A.; Nortura B.A.; Orkla ASA; Unilever; VION Holding N.V.

FURTHER READING

"HK Ruokatalo and Ruoka-Saarioinen Oy Sign Agreement on Raw Material Sourcing," *TendersInfo*, June 8, 2008.

"HK Ruokatalo, Saarioinen in Poultry Deal," *just-food.com*, February 28, 2008.

"Ice Cream Era to End for Small Finnish Town," *Nordic Business Report*, January 24, 2002.

"It's 'Safety from Start to Finnish' at Saarioinen Plants in Finland," *Quick Frozen Foods International*, January 1998, p. 116.

"Ruoka-Saarioinen Oy, Finland: Comprehensive Approach," *Eurofound*, October 29, 2009.

"Saarioinen to Cut 43 Jobs in Finland," *Nordic Business Report*, March 9, 2006.

"Saarioinen Acquires AS Meleco," *Nordic Business Report*, September 23, 2002.

Tere, Juhan, "Finnish Saarioinen Opens New Plant in Estonia," *Baltic Course*, October 23, 2009.

Saudi Basic Industries Corporation (SABIC)

———————— ■ ————————

PO Box 5101
Riyadh, 11422
Saudi Arabia
Telephone: (966 1) 225 8000
Fax: (966 1) 225 9000
Web site: http://www.sabic.com

■ ■ ■

Public Company
Incorporated: 1976
Employees: 33,000
Sales: SAR 103 billion ($27.47 billion) (2009)
Stock Exchanges: Saudi
Ticker Symbol: SABIC
NAICS: 325211 Plastics Material and Resin Manufacturing; 324110 Petroleum Refineries; 325120 Industrial Gas Manufacturing; 325181 Alkalies and Chlorine Manufacturing; 325188 All Other Inorganic Chemical Manufacturing; 325212 Synthetic Rubber Manufacturing; 325222 Noncellulosic Organic Fiber Manufacturing; 325312 Phosphatic Fertilizer Manufacturing; 325320 Pesticide and Other Agricultural Chemical Manufacturing; 331221 Cold-Rolled Steel Shape Manufacturing; 331319 Other Aluminum Rolling and Drawing; 551112 Offices of Other Holding Companies

■ ■ ■

Saudi Basic Industries Corporation (SABIC), is one of the world's leading petrochemicals companies and one of the lowest-cost producers, with access to the natural gas by-product of Saudi Arabia's vast petroleum reserves. SABIC operates in seven core business sectors: Chemicals, Metals, Fertilizers, Polymers, Performance Chemicals, Innovative Plastics, and Manufacturing. The company's Chemical operations account for approximately 60 percent of total output and include olefins, oxygenates, and aromatics. Olefins are used primarily to make plastics such as PVC, oxygenates are used in fuels and solvents, and aromatics are used mainly in the manufacture of packaging, fabrics, and bottles.

SABIC and its affiliated companies operate in 21 countries and serve customers across the globe. The company's domestic operations are located in Jubail Industrial City, which was custom-built for the company in the mid-1970s; Dammam; and Yanbu. SABIC remains controlled by the Saudi government at approximately 70 percent while the remaining 30 percent of the company's stock has long been reserved for citizens of Saudi Arabia and other Gulf Cooperation Council countries. The company has grown significantly via its acquisition strategy which included the $11.6 billion purchase of GE Plastics in 2007. SABIC is the largest public company in the Middle East.

CREATING SAUDI ARABIA'S PETROCHEMICALS INDUSTRY: 1976–77

Until the mid-1970s, Saudi Arabia remained relatively unindustrialized. The country's vast crude oil reserves were used almost exclusively for oil production and by-product hydrocarbon gases were simply flared off at the well-head. The sudden rise in oil prices in the 1970s, when the price of oil shoot up from just $2 per barrel to more than $30 per barrel, opened the potential for profitable investment in gas recovery and processing for the Saudi government.

The Saudi government decided to construct a Master Gas System to capture by-product gases for use not only as an energy source (the country converted much of its electrical power fuel infrastructure to natural gas at this time) but also to establish its own petrochemicals industry. To this end, the government set aside the small fishing village of Jubail, on the country's Gulf coast, as the site of a new "industrial city." A similar city was to be constructed in Yanbu, on the country's Red Sea coast. In order to populate that city with industries, and specifically petrochemical firms, the government created Saudi Basic Industries Corporation (SABIC) in 1976.

Work began on Jubail and Yanbu in 1977. In the meantime, SABIC prepared to launch its operations. As part of that effort, the company began sending staff to the United States for training. At the same time, the company began signing a variety of joint venture partners, which agreed to help the company establish its industrial operations, providing technology, training, and marketing support, in exchange for access to the company's plentiful and low-cost feedstock. By the end of that year, the company had signed agreements with Dow Chemical, Exxon, Mitsubishi, and Korf-Stahl.

By 1979, the company had created its first manufacturing affiliates: AR-RAZI, also known as the Saudi Methanol Company, in partnership with Mitsubishi Gas Chemical Company, formed for the production of methanol, SAMAD, or the Al-Jubail Fertilizer Company, a 50/50 partnership with the Taiwan Fertilizer Company for the production of urea, ammonia, and other products, and SAFCO, the Saudi Arabian Fertilizer Company, which was formed to produce ammonia, urea, sulfuric acid, and melamine. While many of the company's partnerships were formed with the giants of the global petrochemicals market, it also entered

partnerships with three Bahrainian groups, creating ALBA, GARMCO, and GPIC. At the same time, the company formed HADEED, the Saudi Iron and Steel Company. Construction on that company, as well as the SADAF site, began in 1980.

CREATING PARTNERSHIPS, GROUP COMPANIES: 1980–82

New partnerships were created that year, including Saudi Petrochemical Company (SADAF), in partnership with Pecten Arabian, a subsidiary of Shell; and, with Exxon, Saudi Yanbu Petrochemical Company (YANPET). Both of these ventures became diversified petrochemicals producers, with SADAF's range including ethylene, crude industrial ethanol, and styrene, while YANPET began operating further downstream, producing polyethylene and ethylene glycol. Another partnership formed that year, KEMYA, or the Al-Jubail Petrochemical Company, in partnership with Exxon Mobil, brought the company polyethylene and ethylene capacity.

These companies were followed with the creation of SHARQ and IBN SINA in 1981. The first, Eastern Petrochemical Company, of these was created in conjunction with a consortium led by Mitsubishi, and was formed to produce ethylene glycol. The second, National Methanol Company, added partners Hoechst-Celanese and Poan Energy-USA, as well as the production of chemical-grade methanol.

By 1982, most of SABIC's group of companies had been formed and were under construction, as the cities themselves, as well as their ports and airports, neared completion. That year marked another important moment in Saudi industrial history, when the country's ambitious Master Gas System was brought online.

PRODUCTIONS BEGINS: 1982

The first of SABIC's businesses to begin actual production was HADEED, which began producing steel products in 1982. By 1983, SAMAD and AR-RAZI had launched production as well. In that year, SABIC opened its new headquarters in Riyadh, and also launched two new subsidiaries, SABIC Marketing and SABIC Services. The company booked its first export shipment that year, sending 33,000 metric tons of chemical-grade methanol from its AR-RAZI affiliate to Japan.

Work continued on the company's growing list of affiliates, which was boosted by the addition of the National Chemical Fertilizer Company (IBN AL-BAYTAR) and GAS, formed to produce oxygen,

KEY DATES
◼

1976: Saudi Basic Industries Corporation (SABIC) is created as Saudi Arabia launches into petrochemical production in order to process petroleum gas by-products.

1982: The first of SABIC affiliate companies, HADEED (steel), begins production.

1984: SABIC is listed on the Saudi stock exchange, although the government maintains a 70 percent stake.

1988: The company opens international marketing offices in New York, London, Tokyo, and Hong Kong.

1997: The company opens its first foreign research and technology center in Houston, Texas.

2001: Production capacity tops 35 million metric tons.

2002: The company acquires the petrochemicals business of DSM, based in the Netherlands, as its first overseas expansion.

2007: GE Plastics is purchased in an $11.6 billion deal.

2008: Company signs partnerships with China Petrochemical Corp. and Saudi Aramco to expand its business in China.

worldwide market. The company's arrival during a global slump in the petrochemicals market proved an advantage. With access to Saudi Arabia's huge gas reserves, SABIC was able to enter the market with some of the lowest feedstock costs in the industry. SABIC's arrival forced a shift among the industry's previous major players, many of which moved further downstream in petrochemicals production, while others exited a number of markets entirely. At the same time, the company's Gulf region location placed it close to both the European and, especially, the fast-growing Asian markets.

In just 10 years, SABIC built a diversified base of some 21 separate affiliate companies, 13 of which were already operational. The companies manufactured some 20 different product groups, with export operations reaching more than 60 countries. The company also had a strong and growing brand name, Ladene, which was extended to all of the group's plastics products in 1986. By the end of that year, the company's total production had topped nine million metric tons. It also had become one of the country's major employers, with more than 8,000 people on payroll.

Two more SABIC companies came onstream before the end of the 1980s, boosting total production past 10 million metric tons. SABIC also began asserting itself on the worldwide market, opening offices in London, New York, Tokyo, and Hong Kong by 1988. The company also began construction on its Industrial Research and Technology complex, which opened in 1991, underscoring SABIC's commitment to developing its own technological expertise as it matured into a full-fledged global petrochemicals player.

EXPANDING PRODUCTION CAPACITY: 1990–95

In the early 1990s, SABIC began expanding production capacity at its existing operations, while at the same time broadening its product range. Among the company's new projects was a doubling of the HADEED steel plant's capacity, which reached two million tons per year at the start of the new decade. At the same time, production output doubled at the AR-RAZI site, which became the world's largest producer of chemical-grade methanol in 1992. A new 1.3-million-ton phosphate fertilizer plant at IBN AL-BAYTAR came online in 1991 and the company doubled urea production at SAFCO. The company also built two feedstock crackers for the production of propylene, a forerunner product for polypropylene.

By 1994, SABIC's production had jumped to more than 20 million metric tons. The company's sales were

nitrogen, argon, and krypton-xenon. IBN ZAHR, the Saudi European Petrochemical Company, was also formed with Neste Oy of Finland and Enichem of Italy for production of MTBE (methyl tertiary butyl ether, a key lead-free gasoline additive) and polypropylene. By 1984, production had started at IBN SINA, SADAF, KEMYA, YANPET, and GAS. The company also built its SABIC Technical Services Laboratory in Riyadh that year.

SABIC GOES PUBLIC: 1984

SABIC went public in 1984, although the Saudi government maintained a 70 percent stake in the company, and its shareholder base was restricted to Saudi and other citizens in the Gulf Cooperation Council countries. The newly public company began its first marketing efforts, launching the Ladene brand of linear low-density polyethylene products. When its first shipments began, in 1985, the company already boasted some 5 percent of total world production.

That year marked the end of SABIC's first-generation, ramp-up phase and its launch onto the more than $2.8 billion and it enjoyed strong profit growth. The Saudi government, which announced its intention to privatize many of the country's state-owned operations, also began plans to reduce its stake in SABIC, with an ultimate goal of trimming its shareholding to just 25 percent. These plans, however, were put on hold.

INTERNATIONAL HEAVYWEIGHT FOR THE NEW MILLENNIUM

In the meantime, SABIC's growth continued strongly into the 1990s with the creation of a number of new affiliate operations, including IBN RUSHD, the Arabian Industrial Fiberts Company, in conjunction with a consortium of Saudi fiber producers. Construction on the IBN RUSHD site at Yanbu began in 1993 and production came on stream in 1995. The following year, SABIC's Ibn Hayyan subsidiary created TAYF, the Ibn Hayyan Plastic Products Company, producing such products as wall coverings, artificial leather, and bookbinding products. That company launched production in 1999.

SABIC had continued to build up its international presence during the 1990s, opening a marketing subsidiary in India in 1993, and an office in France in 1994. Houston, Texas, became the site of its first international technology center in 1997, followed by New Delhi, India, in 1998. By then, the company had restructured its operations into five primary Strategic Business Units: Basic Chemicals, Intermediates, Fertilizers, Polymers, and Metals. The company also adopted the "wordmark" SABIC across all of its diversified operations, which were all accorded ISO 9002 quality certification that year as well.

SABIC stepped up its production at the beginning of the 21st century, boosting total capacity from 25 million metric tons in 1999 to more than 35 million in 2001. As it entered the new century, SABIC began eyeing further expansion, in particular by developing an international production base. In the meantime, the company had come into its own among the world's international petrochemicals heavyweights, joining the global top five in a number of key product categories. SABIC's technological development enabled it to launch its own, independent projects, such as the new $2 billion Jubail United Petrochemicals, which was started in 2001 and went onstream in 2004.

SABIC had not turned its back on future joint ventures, yet the company expected to participate in future ventures as an equal partner. As managing director Mohamed Al-Mady told *Chemical Week*: "We welcome joint venture partners, but we want more in exchange. Now that we have the market and training expertise, we must get something else in return, such as the right to use technology in other plants, or entry into a new market."

CONTINUED GROWTH: 2002–07

SABIC found a new market of a different sort in 2002, however. In that year, the company announced an agreement to buy the petrochemicals business of the Netherlands' DSM for EUR 2.25 billion. The move not only gave SABIC its first production operations outside of the Middle East, it also propelled the company into the number 11 spot (from number 22) in the ranks of the world's largest petrochemicals producers. The company also gained the number three and four positions in the worldwide polyethylene and polypropylene markets.

The addition of the DSM businesses, renamed SABIC Europe, boosted SABIC's total production past 40 million metric tons. By 2003, however, the company had laid plans to add an additional two million metric tons of capacity through the addition of a new monoethylene glycol plant in Al Jubail, as well as a new 800,000-metric-ton polyethylene plant. By the beginning of 2003, SABIC had grown into a diversified international operation with revenues of more than $9 billion. Already Saudi Arabia's largest industrial company, SABIC prepared to continue its expansion, including additional international acquisitions, in its bid to become a truly global petrochemicals player in the new century.

Sure enough, by 2005 the company was securing record revenues and profits and had moved up the 10th-largest petrochemical producer in the world while Bloomberg ranked SABIC as the 13th-largest company in the world based on market capitalization. The groundwork was laid that year for Yanbu-2, a large project that would expand SABIC's domestic manufacturing capacity.

CEO Mohamed Al-Mady told the *Middle East Economic Digest* in 2006, "According to our strategic plan, we intend to keep growing over the next 15 years. This won't be possible to do organically, so it will require the combination of acquisitions and grassroots capacity, not just in Saudi Arabia, but in India, Europe and all over the world." True to form, the company's next big move came in 2006 when it acquired the European chemicals and polymers division of Huntsman Corporation in a $700 million deal.

SABIC then set its sights on GE Plastics, which was owned by U.S.-based General Electric Co. Completed in 2007, the $11.6 billion acquisition was the largest in

SABIC history to date and gave the company a significant foothold in the North American plastics sector. The operations of GE Plastics, which manufactured a diverse array of products used such industries as automotive, electronics, and appliances were folded into the newly created subsidiary SABIC Innovative Plastics later that year.

OVERCOMING CHALLENGES: 2008 AND BEYOND

During 2007 SABIC supplied 55 million tons of product to customers in more than 100 countries. With production and net income reaching record levels that year, SABIC was well positioned to handle the challenges that it faced in 2008 when global economies began to falter as a result of the financial, credit, and housing crises in the United States. With demand for its products falling, SABIC's net income declined by 19 percent over the previous year in 2008.

In response to deteriorating market conditions, SABIC cut costs and launched a major restructuring effort that realigned the company into seven strategic business units including Chemicals, Metals, Fertilizers, Polymers, Performance Chemicals, Innovative Plastics, and Manufacturing. The company continued to focus on growth in emerging markets including Brazil, Russia, India, and China. During 2008 the company and China Petrochemical Corp. revamped their partnership of the $2.5 billion Tianjin Industrial Complex, leaving SABIC with 50 percent ownership of the petrochemical facility. In addition, subsidiary SABIC Shenzhen Trading Company Ltd. and Saudi Aramco formed a partnership to market polyolefin products made in China.

The SABIC2020 project, a strategy launched in 2006, was centered on the company's goal of achieving nearly 135 million metric tons in production by 2020. The company had increased its production levels dramatically throughout its history by forming key partnerships, alliances, and more recently by making large acquisitions. It had grown from production levels of 6.3 million metric tons in 1985 to 56 million metric tons by the end of 2008. While the global economy was slow to recover, SABIC believed its future success would come from increased demand in emerging markets. By that time, the company was clear about its ambitions. It planned to become the world's largest and most preferred chemicals company.

M. L. Cohen
Updated, Christina M. Stansell

PRINCIPAL SUBSIDIARIES

SABIC Innovative Plastics; Saudi Iron and Steel Co.; Petrokeyma; SABIC Acetylene B.V. (Netherlands); SABIC Petrochemicals B.V. (Netherlands); SABIC UK Petrochemicals Ltd.; SABIC Europe (Netherlands).

PRINCIPAL OPERATING UNITS

Chemicals; Metals; Fertilizers; Polymers; Performance Chemicals; Innovative Plastics; Manufacturing.

PRINCIPAL COMPETITORS

ExxonMobil Chemical; LyondellBasell Industries; Shell Chemicals Limited.

FURTHER READING

Alperowicz, Natasha, "Sabic Reaches Maturity," *Chemical Week*, January 10, 2001, p. 21.

"An Appetite for Acquisition," *Middle East Economic Digest*, December 22, 2006.

Clanton, Brett, "Mohamed Al-Mady, An Industry Leader, Says High Oil Prices May Slow Mergers but His Company Is a Long-Term Player," *Houston Chronicle*, November 6, 2007.

Deutsch, Claudia H., "Saudi Company Buying G.E. Plastics," *New York Times*, May 22, 2007.

Esposito, Frank, "GE Plastics Becomes Part of Sabic Stable," *Plastics News*, November 26, 2007.

"GE Nears Deal in Plastics Auction," *Wall Street Journal*, May 18, 2007.

Holloway, Robert, "Saudis Ready for Petrochemical Marketing Challenge," *Oil Daily*, January 29, 1985, p. 4.

Kapur, Mansi, "Saudi Chemical Major Eyes India," *Times of India*, December 28, 2006.

"Sabic and Aramco Strengthen Ties," *Middle East Economic Digest*, August 15, 2008.

"Sabic Completes Purchase of Huntsman's UK Base Chemicals and Polymers Business," *Al-Bawaba News*, December 31, 2006.

"Sabic Developing Key Role in Petrochemical Markets," *Oil and Gas Journal*, January 7, 1991, p. 19.

"Sabic Eyes the Future," *Middle East*, October 1994, p. 22.

"Sabic Looks to the Future," *Chemical Market Reporter*, March 24, 2003, p. 3.

"Sabic to Purchase DSM Petrochemicals Business," *Chemical Market Reporter*, April 8, 2002, p. 1.

Smith, Pamela Ann, "Saudi May Sell Control of Giant SABIC," *Privatisation International*, October 1994, p. 13.

"Unstoppable Sabic," *Fertilizer International*, November–December 1997, p. 47.

Schottenstein Stores
Corporation

■

1800 Molar Road
Columbus, Ohio 43207
U.S.A.
Telephone: (614) 221-9200
Fax: (614) 449-0403

Private Company
Founded: 1917
Employees: 30,050
Sales: $1.3 billion (2008 est.)
NAICS: 452110 Department Stores; 442110 Furniture
Stores; 448210 Shoe Stores

■ ■ ■

Schottenstein Stores Corporation (SSC) operates as a private investment firm with holdings in the retail industry. The company has a majority interest in Retail Ventures Inc., which operates the DSW chain of footwear and accessories stores. SSC also owns American Signature Inc., a furniture chain with approximately 130 stores operating under the American Signature and Value City Furniture names. The company has a stake in American Eagle Outfitters Inc. and operates SB Capital Group LLC, a professional services company specializing in retail liquidation. SSC is led by Chairman and CEO Jay L. Schottenstein, who in 2010 was also chairman of DSW Inc., Retail Ventures Inc., and American Eagle Outfitters.

EARLY HISTORY

The Schottenstein family's knack for spotting and taking advantage of retail liquidations was a key to their business success. Ephraim L. Schottenstein, a Lithuanian immigrant, settled in Columbus, Ohio, and established this family tradition in the late 19th century. The patriarch got a modest start, buying overstocked and outdated goods from local retailers and selling them out of a horse and buggy. Within a few years, Schottenstein was able open his first shop. He launched his namesake department store in 1917.

The business was nurtured by a second generation of Schottensteins, brothers Jerome, Saul, Alvin, and Leon. They joined the business just as the discount retail industry began gaining steam in the late 1940s. Jerome established a reputation as a hard worker while still in his teens. A 1992 retrospective in *Discount Store News* noted that he started "making buying decisions for the chain at an age when most of his peers would be going out on their first date." Known throughout the industry as "Jerry," he joined the executive ranks of the four-store Schottenstein chain in 1946 at the age of 20 and advanced to chairman and CEO in 1972.

Led by Jerry, the Schottensteins earned a nationwide reputation by engineering buyouts of infamous failures. Perhaps the best-known example of the Schottenstein technique was the 1980 acquisition of the entire 31-store inventory of E.J. Korvettes. Once a mighty budget retailer, Korvettes had suffered years of mismanagement before going bankrupt. Through an affiliate, M.H. Fishman & Co., Jerry Schottenstein purchased merchandise with a retail value of $58 mil-

KEY DATES
∎

1917: Ephraim L. Schottenstein opens his first store.

1946: Jerry Schottenstein joins the executive ranks of the four-store chain.

1962: The Value City chain is acquired.

1991: Retail Ventures Inc. is acquired; Value City goes public.

1992: Jerry Schottenstein dies; third-generation Jay L. Schottenstein leads the family business.

1994: American Eagle Outfitters goes public.

2000: Filene's Basement Corp. is purchased.

2005: DSW Inc. (Value City) is spun off.

2008: Retail Ventures sells the Value City Department Store chain; Schottenstein Stores Corporation acquires majority stake in crystal manufacturer Steuben Glass from Corning Inc.

2009: Filene's Basement is sold.

lion for $25 million and managed the Korvettes going-out-of-business sales. Known for his intuitive deal making, Schottenstein also participated in the much-publicized liquidation of 2,500 cars from the ill-fated DeLorean Motors enterprise.

VALUE CITY ACQUISITION

Jerry Schottenstein had also directed the pivotal 1962 acquisition of Value City Stores, which had been established in 1909. According to a 1992 article in *Forbes*, Ephraim forbid the application of the family name to any store open on Saturday, the Jewish Sabbath. As a result, the Value City chain kept its name. The corporate culture of opportunism was then reflected in Value City's purchasing department. The chain's three-dozen buyers averaged over a decade of experience each, a quality that helped earn them the personal connections vital to off-price and closeout buying. Vendors trusted the chain not to abuse their invaluable brand names.

The Value City stores, which at 80,000 square feet were two to three times larger than other off-price merchandisers, allowed for bulk purchasing and a wider variety of merchandise. Selection was so vast that Tony Lisanti, editor of *Discount Store News*, in 1992 characterized Value City as "an off-price, value-driven mall, a collection of specialty stores under one roof." This deal making allowed Value City to sell national

branded merchandise at substantial discounts (40 percent to 70 percent) from department store prices.

SUCCESS AT VALUE CITY: 1970–89

The chain's influence in the off-price and closeout segment of retailing expanded quickly in the 1970s and 1980s. Value City set itself apart from competitors such as TJX Companies' TJ Maxx, Mellville Corporation's Marshall's, Filene's Basement, and MacFrugals by offering both off-price and closeout merchandise lines under one roof. These two classes of discount merchandise could be differentiated both by the types of goods and by the manner in which they were procured. The off-price category referred to soft goods, generally apparel items that were acquired at a discount by the retailer after the beginning of a fashion season. The term *closeout* generally applied to discontinued hard goods that were discounted by the manufacturer for quick sale.

About 60 percent of Value City's merchandise was apparel, 25 percent of the offerings were hard lines (including housewares, toys, and jewelry), and the remaining sales were generated through leased departments selling shoes and health and beauty aids. The chain was also distinguished from some of its competitors by its emphasis on high-quality brands, which constituted about one-fourth of Value City's merchandise. Only one-fourth of the chain's offerings were described as "budget quality."

Another, less obvious contributor to Value City's success at the time was technology. Computerized inventory controls, including electronic registers, bar-coding systems, and point-of-sale scanning, helped this and other chains achieve peak efficiency by shrinking inventories, accelerating turnover, and reducing lead times. Automated distribution centers incorporated high-speed sorters and radio communications to enhance efficiency. Value City's internal computer network permitted "micro-marketing," the tailoring of merchandise offerings for each individual store.

Schottenstein Stores Corp. grew along with the off-price discount segment throughout the late 1980s. According to a report prepared by the NPD Consumer Purchase Panel and cited in *Women's Wear Daily* in 1992, "off-price discounters gained about 56 percent of the total apparel market from 1985 to 1991, which translated into sales of about $7 billion." By 1989 SSC's 47 stores generated an estimated $771 million in annual sales.

VALUE CITY GOES PUBLIC: 1991

In the spring of 1991 SSC offered a 25 percent stake in the Value City chain to the public. The stock sale, which forced the Schottensteins to publicize the financial records of their largest retail interest, raised $72.7 million for debt reduction and allowed the family to maintain its control of the board of directors and its executive positions. Before the year's end, a second stock flotation raised another $21.4 million for debt reduction. The shares, which initially sold for $19 each, rose to $50 before a 2-for-1 split in 1992.

However, a third stock flotation in April 1992 was less successful because of investor concerns over conflicts of interest between SSC and Value City. The most obvious of these was that the proceeds of the $50 million stock offering were intended to finance Value City's acquisition of GB Stores, Inc., a 13-store chain purchased by SSC in 1990 from the founding Glosser brothers. Moreover, SSC's 50 percent-owned Shonac Corp., which operated licensed shoe departments in Value City stores and was eventually renamed DSW Inc., generated another source of conflict. In the face of the failed stock offering, Value City took on new debt to retire $25 million in GB Stores debt and reimburse SSC for $23 million in assets. The GB units were slated for conversion to the more successful Value City format.

RETAIL VENTURES ACQUISITION

In 1991 SSC completed the acquisition of Retail Ventures Inc., the Pennsylvania-based operator of the 150-store American Eagle Outfitters chain. The concept featured private-label outdoor wear, footwear, and accessories. Founded in 1977, Retail Ventures had over $100 million in annual sales by the time SSC assumed full ownership. SSC had taken a 50 percent stake in the chain as early as 1980, when the founding Silverman family encountered fiscal difficulties. Jay Schottenstein assumed the presidency of the division. Although most of the chain's units were located in the East and Midwest, Retail Ventures also had a nationally distributed mail-order catalog.

Jerry Schottenstein succumbed to cancer March 10, 1992, at the age of 66. According to a March 16, 1992, story in *Business First-Columbus*, the hard-driving executive was "working in his office on the morning of the day he died." The family business mantle fell to son Jay L. Schottenstein, who had worked at the company since 1976 and eventually advanced to the board of directors in 1982 and a vice chairmanship in 1986. Saul Schottenstein, the only surviving member of the second generation, stayed on as SSC president. George Iacono, who had come to SSC from Marshall's in 1984, advanced to the posts of president and general merchandise manager of Value City.

In the years following its partial spin-off, Value City and its executives generally garnered high praise. Even in

a difficult retail climate Value City moved forward strongly, reporting same-store sales increases of 10 percent. Under the slogan "Better Living for Less," the chain's sales doubled from 1987 to 1992, when they topped $600 million.

The chain also bucked a mid-1990s "retrenchment" in the off-price segment. Although such stalwarts as Filene's Basement and TJ Maxx faltered when traditional department stores began to meet the off-price challenge, Value City's sales and operating profits continued their climb. In anticipation of expanding the chain to 100 stores, the company built new distribution centers for its hard and soft lines in the early 1990s. Executives set their sights on surpassing the $1 billion mark by the dawn of the 21st century.

AMERICAN EAGLE GOES PUBLIC: 1994

SSC revisited the public financial markets in 1994 with the sale of about 40 percent of American Eagle Outfitters Inc. to the public. The chain had suffered back-to-back losses totaling over $14 million in 1991 and 1992 but made operating income of $7.5 million on revenues of $168 million in 1993. Late in 1994 an SSC affiliate bought the 26-store Steinbach Inc. chain of department stores. Although terms of the acquisition were not publicized, it was known that Steinbach had revenues of approximately $225 million in 1993.

As SSC headed into the late 1990s, company management was optimistic about its future. The firm's heritage of market savvy, both in terms of merchandising and corporate acquisitions, continued under the direction of the newest generation of leadership. The company's commitment to discounting also seemed well placed in a consumer culture intent on quality and value. Furthermore, SSC's strategy of selling minority interests in its affiliates allowed the company to raise money for debt reduction and future acquisitions without relinquishing Schottenstein family control.

MOVING INTO THE 21ST CENTURY

SSC spent the early years of the new millennium increasing its holdings. The company and its investors acquired stores and property from bankrupt retailers and by 2003 owned nearly 50 shopping centers. According to a November 2003 *Forbes* article, SSC earned $72 million on sales of $650 million during 2002.

Meanwhile, Retail Ventures and its stores, which by this time included Value City Department Stores, Filene's Basement Corp., and DSW Shoe Warehouse, was struggling. Same-store sales were dropping and high expenses were hurting the company's bottom line. DSW pulled ahead, and by 2004 was securing annual sales of $915 million. Retail Ventures spun off DSW, its most profitable holding, in 2005. The company used the funds from the public offering to bolster its faltering Value City chain. By then, it was evident that Value City's success in the early 1990s was well in its past.

Conditions in the retail sector were challenging as the U.S. economy began faltering during this period. Consumer spending slowed and retailers found themselves in a precarious situation. The attempts of Retail Ventures to breathe life back into Value City failed and the company put it up for sale in 2006. Value City Department Stores was eventually sold in 2008 to VCHI Acquisition Co. The chain announced it was filing for bankruptcy later that year and opted to close all of its stores.

Filene's Basement, which Retail Ventures purchased in 2000, sold designer men's and women's apparel, jewelry, shoes, and home goods at discounted prices. It had approximately 36 locations in major metropolitan areas including Boston, Chicago, New York, and Washington, D.C. It too faced challenges during the economic downturn and announced in early 2009 that it would shutter 11 of its stores. Shortly thereafter, Retail Ventures sold the company to an affiliate of retail liquidator Buxbaum Group. Filene's declared Chapter 11 bankruptcy protection and was purchased by Syms Corp. later in the year. During 2010 there were approximately 25 Filene's Basement stores in 10 states.

GOING UPSCALE

When the dust settled, Retail Ventures was left with its DSW holdings. SSC's Value City Furniture chain, which had been separated from the Value City Department Stores business, had weathered the economic downturn thanks in part to its American Signature line of furniture. American Signature stores began opening and by 2002 there were five locations that offered high-end furniture and accessories. By 2010 American Signature operated nearly 130 stores in 20 states under the American Signature and Value City Furniture names.

At the same time, SSC began bolstering its luxury holdings. In 2006 the Adrienne Vittadini brand of women's apparel and accessories was purchased. During 2007 the company acquired the Judith Leiber brand, which designed upscale handbags. It purchased the Italian brand Shirò, another high-fashion handbag and clothing designer, in 2008. The company also acquired a majority stake in crystal manufacturer Steuben Glass

from Corning Inc. that same year. Taryn Rose, a shoe brand that offered footwear ranging in price from $150 to $450, was added to SSC's luxury holdings in 2010.

While SSC's portfolio had changed, its focus on retail investments remained strong. With retail mogul and third-generation family member Jay Schottenstein at the helm, SSC was poised to remain among the top 500 privately run firms in the United States in the years to come.

April Dougal Gasbarre
Updated, Christina M. Stansell

PRINCIPAL SUBSIDIARIES

Retail Ventures Inc.; Value City Furniture Inc; American Signature Inc.

PRINCIPAL COMPETITORS

Collective Brands Inc.; J. C. Penney Company Inc.; The TJX Companies Inc.

FURTHER READING

Barmash, Isadore, *More Than They Bargained For: The Rise and Fall of Korvettes*, New York: Lebhar-Friedman Books, 1981.

Koselka, Rita, "The Schottenstein Factor," *Forbes*, September 28, 1992, p. 104.

Lisanti, Tony, "Value City a Sign of Retail Vitality," *Discount Store News*, October 5, 1992, p. 8.

"Off-Price Apparel Chains Pressed to Differentiate," *Discount Store News*, March 20, 1995, p. 6.

Phillips, Jeff, and William Jackson, "Schottenstein Passes Empire to Son, Jay," *Business First-Columbus*, March 16, 1992, p. 1.

Reynolds, David J., "Retail Veteran Rings Up an Employee Discount," *Wall Street Journal*, January 14, 2009, p. C6.

Rose, Marla Matzer, "Schottenstein; Retailer Buys Up Luxury Brands," *Columbus Dispatch*, July 25, 2008.

Schneiderman, Ira P., "Off-Price Discounters Double Dollar Volume from 1985 to 1991," *Women's Wear Daily*, November 4, 1992, p. 42.

Tatge, Mark, and Evan Hessel, "The Wasteland; The Schottenstein Company Retail Ventures Seems to Be Making Good Money," *Forbes*, November 24, 2003.

Tell, Caroline, "Schottenstein Buys Taryn Rose," *Women's Wear Daily*, March 3, 2010.

Tosh, Mark, "Off-Price: A Change in Store," *Women's Wear Daily*, March 29, 1995, p. 14.

Walters, Rebecca, "American Eagle Going Public," *Business First-Columbus*, March 21, 1994, p. 1.

Zargani, Luisa, "Schottenstein Buys 50% of Shirò," *Women's Wear Daily*, July 16, 2008.

Sebastiani Vineyards, Inc.

389 Fourth Street East
Sonoma, California 95476
U.S.A.
Telephone: (707) 933-3200
Toll Free: (800) 888-5532
Fax: (707) 933-3370
Web site: http://www.sebastiani.com

Wholly Owned Subsidiary of Foley Family Wines, Inc.
Founded: 1904
Employees: 100
Sales: $7.5 million (2007)
NAICS: 31213 Wineries

■ ■ ■

Sebastiani Vineyards, Inc., produces premium California table wines under the Cherryblock and Sebastiani labels. With roots dating back to 1904, Sebastiani Vineyards developed into a major wine producer under the control of the founder's son, August Sebastiani, who focused on marketing inexpensive, jug wines. August Sebastiani's son Sam assumed the reins of control in 1980 but was fired six years later after attempting to transform the winery into a more upscale wine producer.

Sam Sebastiani's younger brother Don, a former California legislator, took command in 1986 and during the course of the next decade tripled the winery's production volume. By the end of the 1990s, Sebastiani Vineyards was producing more than seven million cases of wine each year. The company sold its Turner Road Vintners division in 2001 in order to refocus on

premium wines from Sonoma County. Mary Ann Cuneo, the granddaughter of founder Samuele Sebastiani, took over that year when Don left to pursue other business ventures. Sebastiani Vineyards was a family-owned and -operated business until 2008, when it was purchased by Foley Family Wines, Inc.

1895: SAMUELE SEBASTIANI ARRIVES IN AMERICA

Sebastiani Vineyards began producing wine in 1904, when the patriarch of the family, Samuele Sebastiani, started a modest wine-producing business in Sonoma, California. A native of the Tuscany region in northern Italy, Sebastiani immigrated to the United States in 1895, arriving with the clothes on his back, a thorough understanding of how to produce wine, and little else. Young and poor, Sebastiani did what he could to provide food and shelter for himself in his new surroundings. He worked in gardens and performed other odd jobs until he saved enough money to buy a horse and a wagon. With the horse and wagon, Sebastiani hauled cobblestones from a quarry in Sonoma, cobblestones that were used to pave the streets of San Francisco, 40 miles to the south, and to lay the tracks for the city's famed cable cars. After nearly a decade of such work, Sebastiani had saved enough money to start a business truer to his heart. In 1904 he purchased a Sonoma vineyard and began producing his own wine, practicing a craft whose intricacies had been handed down through generations of Tuscans.

The land Sebastiani purchased had been operating as a vineyard for nearly 80 years before he purchased it

COMPANY PERSPECTIVES

■

As part of Foley Family Wines, Sebastiani will maintain its commitment to producing singular wines from the appellations of Sonoma County.

in 1904. The vineyard's first owners were disciples of a sect whose origins were not far from Sebastiani's birthplace. In 1825 Franciscan monks residing at San Francisco Solano, a mission near Sonoma, enlisted the help of local Native Americans to clear the land for the vineyard. When Sebastiani began working the old Franciscan vineyard, he concentrated on producing Zinfandel, which he sold to familiar clientele. Sebastiani, using his horse-drawn wagon, delivered his Zinfandel to workers toiling at the Sonoma quarry, selling it by the cup and by the jug. Sebastiani worked at the vineyard until his death, establishing a legacy as one of the pioneers of northern California's wine country, destined to be the epicenter of wine production in the United States.

SECOND GENERATION TAKES OVER IN 1952

Sebastiani's son, August, purchased the winery from his father's estate in 1952, and with his wife, Sylvia, developed the family business into one of the largest wineries in the United States. As a vintner, August Sebastiani displayed a talent for marketing his wines to a broad customer base, selling Sebastiani wines, as his father had, by the jug. He increased the winery's production volume 100-fold during his nearly 30-year reign by tapping into the demand for table wines, relying almost exclusively on inexpensive wines marketed to the masses.

August Sebastiani was the first vintner to market premium varietal wines in a magnum size. He introduced "Nouveau" Gamay Beaujolais to U.S. consumers and he created a blush wine known as Pinot Noir Blanc, two examples of Sebastiani labels that fueled the winery's rise during the latter half of the 20th century. By the end of his tenure in 1980, Sebastiani Vineyards ranked as the sixth-largest table wine producer in the United States, controlling 3.9 percent of the market. His death in 1980 devolved stewardship of the winery to the third generation of Sebastianis and marked the beginning of a tumultuous, divisive decade for the Sonoma-based company.

August Sebastiani's eldest son, Sam J. Sebastiani, took control of the winery in 1980, assuming leadership

at the age of 39. Under Sam Sebastiani's control, radical, sweeping changes were implemented that reflected a wholesale change in the winery's strategy. Sebastiani immediately led the winery away from its dependence on inexpensively priced jug wines and toward a new existence as a trendy upscale winery, capable of producing award-winning, high-quality wines. His objective for Sebastiani Vineyards, as he once wrote in an industry newsletter, was "to fall out of the top 10 from quantity, to the top 10 in quality," a dramatic shift in stance engendered by his vision that premium wines would be the choice of consumers in the years ahead. Sebastiani's prognosticative skills were laudable, prompting the publisher of the *Grape Intelligence Report* to remark, "[Sebastiani] saw that the days of jug wines were numbered in a worldwide shift toward premium wines," but Sebastiani's execution and timing led to difficult years for the winery.

TROUBLES LEAD TO NEW MANAGEMENT: 1986

A number of factors conspired against Sebastiani's ambitious plan to upgrade the winery's image, particularly a worldwide grape glut that delivered a pernicious blow to the California wine industry. Also hampering Sebastiani's progress were increased competition from foreign wines, the growing popularity of California wine coolers, and a decrease in worldwide wine consumption. Furthermore, Sebastiani Vineyards' mainstay business, which was the production of inexpensive table wines, was plagued by escalating production costs during the early 1980s. The winery's financial troubles began to mount.

Undaunted by declining sales, Sebastiani pushed ahead with his plans, systematically changing everything from labels to promotional techniques in effort to recast Sebastiani Vineyards as a premium wine producer. At one point, he offered to recall more than $2 million worth of lower-priced wine to blend it with private reserves. "If it's a choice of dumping the advertising and dumping the wine, you dump the wine," Sebastiani remarked, revealing his priorities for Sebastiani Vineyards' future. He continued to direct capital toward an aggressive and expensive marketing campaign, despite declining sales, persisting with a program that struggled to identify the proper direction to pursue.

Several marketing directors endeavored to find the appropriate image for the winery and failed, prompting Sebastiani and his wife, Vickie, to lead the marketing of Sebastiani Vineyards themselves. The couple traveled across the country, staging flamboyant wine tastings that proved highly successful. The peripatetic Sebastianis gained worldwide recognition for their winery, but back

KEY DATES

1904: Samuele Sebastiani begins to produce wine.

1952: Sebastiani's son, August, purchases the winery from his father's estate.

1986: Mary Ann Cuneo, Richard A. Cuneo, and Don Sebastiani take over leadership of the company.

1987: The Vendange brand is introduced.

1994: Sebastiani Vineyards eclipses Sutter Home Winery Inc. to rank as the largest winery in the Bay Area.

1997: Annual sales surpass the $200 million mark for the first time.

2001: Turner Road Vintners is sold to Constellation Brands Inc.; Don Sebastiani leaves the company.

2004: The company celebrates its centennial.

2009: Foley Family Wines, Inc., completes its acquisition of Sebastiani Vineyards.

in Sonoma concerns were heightening as sales sagged. By 1985 Sebastiani Vineyards had slipped from being the sixth-largest producer in the country to the eighth-largest producer, while its market share had fallen from the nearly 4 percent earned by August Sebastiani to 2.3 percent. The stage was set for a family feud, a public rift between Sebastiani family members that centered on the prudence of Sam Sebastiani's vision.

On January 2, 1986, Sam Sebastiani received a letter from his mother, Sylvia, long a powerful figure at Sebastiani Vineyards and holder of 92 percent of the company's stock. While her husband developed the winery into one of the largest in the country, Sylvia Sebastiani exerted her own considerable influence over the company, regularly appearing at the winery to greet visitors and entertain guests. After August Sebastiani's death, Sylvia Sebastiani presided as the winery's board chairwoman, from which position she watched her son's dealings with the family business and grew increasingly displeased.

In her letter, Sylvia Sebastiani noted that "the winery was being run very, very poorly" amid concerns about "incredibly high expenditures of money." The letter informed Sam Sebastiani that he and his wife, who served as the winery's director of food and wine, had been fired, a decision Sylvia Sebastiani said she reached in agreement with her daughter and fellow board member, Mary Ann Cuneo, and her other son, Don Se-

bastiani, a Sebastiani Vineyard board member and a representative of the Eighth District in California's state assembly. Concurrent with the ouster of her son and daughter-in-law, Sylvia Sebastiani announced she was stepping down as chairwoman to be replaced by her son Don. Mary Ann Cuneo's husband, Richard A. Cuneo, the winery's senior vice president and secretary-treasurer, was named to replace Sam Sebastiani as president and chief executive officer on an interim basis.

NEW LEADERSHIP LEADS TO RENEWAL: 1986–99

Before the end of 1986, Don Sebastiani assumed full control over the winery, serving as both chairman and chief executive officer, with Cuneo serving under him as president. Under Don Sebastiani's control, the winery arrested its financial slide, bolstered by the strength of its largest brand, August Sebastiani Country Wines. The brand paid homage to the individual responsible for developing the winery into a major producer, a tribute Don Sebastiani sought to extend through his managerial approach by emulating his father's hallmark achievement: dramatically increasing production volume.

During his first decade in command, Don Sebastiani increased the winery's production volume threefold, expanding at a pace that vaulted Sebastiani Vineyards past its competitors to reign as the quantitative champion of Bay Area wine producers. The company's growth was driven by the success of a full range of brands that positioned the winery in the most lucrative retail price categories. Sebastiani Vineyards' notable success was its Vendange brand, introduced in 1987. Marketed at the lower end of the price scale, the Vendange brand developed into the fastest-growing brand in the country by the early 1990s, helping Sebastiani Vineyards eclipse Sutter Home Winery Inc. in 1994 to rank as the largest winery in the Bay Area.

The company, by this point, was registering an annual growth rate of approximately 15 percent, thanks to the growing demand for its Vendange brand and its superpremium Sonoma Series brand. August Sebastiani Country Wines, holding sway as the company mainstay brand, was experiencing slower growth as the winery entered the mid-1990s, but a national promotional campaign, which was the largest in Sebastiani Vineyards' history, was launched in late 1994 to spur sales of the midpriced, popular premium brand.

By the late 1990s, there were seven brands composing Sebastiani Vineyards' product line, each catering to mainstream consumer tastes and competing in different price categories. Annual sales in 1997 surpassed the $200 million mark for the first time, increasing more than 13 percent from the previous year's total. The $200.9 million in sales generated in 1997, drawn from the production of more than seven million cases of wine, was more than three times the total registered when Don Sebastiani first assumed leadership of the winery in 1986.

CHANGES IN THE NEW MILLENNIUM

Increased competition from large wine and beverage companies forced the company to revamp its strategy during the early years of the new millennium. As a relatively small and private entity, Sebastiani Vineyards found itself unable to compete against the larger firms that had cash on hand and the means for rapid expansion. As such, Sebastiani Vineyards underwent several changes that vastly restructured its organization. The company's first move came in 2001 when it sold the Turner Road Vintners division to Constellations Brands Inc. The $295million deal marked Sebastiani Vineyards departure from the value-price wine market. Turner Road, which produced more than seven million cases of wine in fiscal 2001 and secured $204 million in revenues, was the company's largest division by far. Its brands included Vendange, Talus, Nathanson Creek, Heritage, Farallon, and La Terre.

At the time of the deal, Don Sebastiani left the company to pursue other business ventures and left Mary Ann Cuneo and Richard Cuneo at the helm as CEO and chairman, respectively. Under new leadership and with the sale of Turner Road behind it, Sebastiani Vineyards was positioned to focus on its fine wine division, which produced 150,000 cases per year and generated approximately $20 million in sales. This segment of the market was generally considered to be the fastest growing and most profitable in the wine industry.

The company used the proceeds from the sale to reduce debt and expand its Sonoma facilities, which included 300 acres of vineyards. The company reopened its refurbished Winery & Hospitality Center, which provided wine tasting, tours, an art gallery, and wine education, in late 2001. Sebastiani Vineyards celebrated its 100th anniversary in 2004. The company offered its Secolo label to mark the occasion. Secolo, which was the Italian word for century, was a blend of cabernet sauvignon, malbec, merlot, petit verdot, and petite sirah.

NEW OWNERSHIP: 2008 AND BEYOND

The company experienced slow and steady growth over the next several years and by 2007 was producing

250,000 cases of chardonnay, cabernet, merlot, and other varietals. Sebastiani Vineyards continued to face stiff competition from larger entities including Constellation Wines, which was part of Constellation Brands Inc., and E. & J. Gallo Winery. These companies, with revenues in the billions of dollars, had lower costs of distribution and larger resources for sales and marketing expenses. Sebastiani Vineyards once again found itself in a position where it needed to make a significant change in order to remain afloat.

After 104 years of family ownership, the company announced in 2008 that it had agreed to a sale to Foley Family Wines Inc. Headed by William P. Foley II, Foley Family Wines had been established in 1996 and had grown through a series of acquisitions based in Santa Barbara County including Lincourt Vineyards, Las Hermanas Vineyard, and Firestone Vineyard. Merus, based in Napa Valley, and Three Rivers Winery, which was located in Walla Walla, Washington, were also purchased. The addition of Sebastiani Vineyards to Foley Family's holdings gave it access to premium assets in Sonoma County.

While it was rumored that all of the Sebastiani family members did not agree to the sale, CEO Cuneo believed it was in the best interest of the company to sell to Foley Family Wines rather than be taken over by a large wine and spirits conglomerate. The sale, completed in early 2009, left Sebastiani Vineyards positioned as a subsidiary in Foley Family's growing arsenal. No longer a family-owned entity, Sebastiani Vineyards embarked on a new chapter in its history as crafter of premium wines in Sonoma County.

Jeffrey L. Covell
Updated, Christina M. Stansell

PRINCIPAL COMPETITORS

Constellation Wines U.S. Inc.; E. & J. Gallo Winery; Jackson Family Wines.

FURTHER READING

Appel, Ted, "Sebastiani CEO to Exit," *Santa Rosa (CA) Press Democrat*, February 6, 2001.

Carlsen, Clifford, "Sebastiani Vineyards Unseats Sutter Home for No. 1," *San Francisco Business Times*, March 25, 1994, p. 21.

"Executive Profile: Don Sebastiani," *San Francisco Business Times*, December 4, 1998, p. 10.

Finz, Stacy, "Turning the Wine Industry on Its Head," *San Francisco Chronicle*, October 13, 2006.

Firstenfeld, Jane, "Foley Scoops Up Sebastiani," *Wines & Vines*, February 1, 2009.

Hinkle, Richard Paul, "After 100 Years, Sebastiani Endures and Thrives," *Wines & Vines*, March 1, 2004.

Lonsford, Michael, "Sonoma's Sebastiani: An Old Reliable," *Houston Chronicle*, June 6, 2007.

Rose, Bleys W., and Guy Kovner, "Vintage Ending: Sale of Pioneering Sebastiani Vineyards Caps Legacy Rooted in Family Differences," *Santa Rosa (CA) Press Democrat*, December 21, 2008.

Shandrick, Michael, "Wine Family Feud Erupts; President Fired by Mom," *San Francisco Business Journal*, January 13, 1986, p. 1.

"What Holidays Mean to Them," *Beverage World*, October 1994, p. 22.

Winchester, Jay, "Ripe for a Change," *Sales & Marketing Management*, August 1998, p. 81.

Sepracor Inc.

---

84 Waterford Drive
Marlborough, Massachusetts 01752
U.S.A.
Telephone: (508) 481-6700
Fax: (508) 357-7499
Web site: http://www.sepracor.com

Wholly Owned Subsidiary of Dainippon Sumitomo Pharma Co., Ltd.
Incorporated: 1984
Employees: 2,400
Sales: $1.29 billion (2008 est.)
NAICS: 325412 Pharmaceutical Preparation Manufacturing

■ ■ ■

A subsidiary of Japan's Dainippon Sumitomo Pharma Co., Ltd., Sepracor Inc. is a specialty pharmaceutical company. Its efforts are focused on the discovery, development, and commercialization of new pharmaceutical products, especially in the areas of respiratory and central nervous system disorders. In addition to Sepracor's Marlborough, Massachusetts, headquarters, the company has domestic operations in Fort Lee, New Jersey. Internationally, Sepracor maintains Canadian facilities in Mississauga and Windsor, Ontario, as well as in the province of Nova Scotia.

ORIGINS

Timothy J. Barberich cofounded Sepracor in 1984 and became its president and chief executive officer. After earning a college degree in chemistry, Barberich went to work in 1971 as a junior chemist for American Cyanamid Co., where he gained firsthand knowledge about the vagaries of synthetic drugs. In Brazil he participated in the demonstration of a deworming medicine, in which a prized bull was injected with a new wonder drug, only to watch, along with a square filled with farmers, as the animal dropped dead, the victim of an unintended side effect.

The underlying chemical problem had been known for well over 100 years, uncovered in the mid-1800s by famed scientist Louis Pasteur, who discovered that some organic molecules, called chiral chemicals, feature mirror images, or left-handed and right-handed versions called optical isomers. ("Chiral" is derived from the Greek word for hands, *kheir*.) In short, while a medicine can provide beneficial traits on the one hand, it may also cause devastating side effects on the other.

A famous and tragic example of this phenomenon was the drug thalidomide in the 1950s. One of its isomers relieved pregnant women of morning sickness, while its mirror image produced horrifying birth defects. Despite their knowledge of optical isomers, researchers until recently simply did not have the expertise to separate the left-handed and right-handed versions, resulting in medicines that contained mixtures of both, with side effects tolerated as long as they were not too harmful.

Barberich began to work on separation techniques when he joined Millipore Corporation, a Bedford, Massachusetts, firm that developed separation products for

COMPANY PERSPECTIVES

Sepracor is dedicated to discovering, developing and commercializing innovative pharmaceutical products and services that improve health and quality of life. We understand our responsibility to ensure that decisions are guided first and foremost by what is in the best interests of patients. We are committed to the welfare of the patients we serve, the success of our employees and to increasing shareholder value.

high-tech companies. By the time he left to form Sepracor he was the general manager of the company's medical products division. Striking out on his own, Barberich was interested in using the new separation technology to purify chemicals for sale to pharmaceutical companies.

EARLY CHANGE IN STRATEGY

A friend introduced Barberich to venture capitalist Robert Johnson, who several years earlier had been instrumental in funding Genex, one of the first biotech start-ups. With Johnson providing $500,000 in seed money, Barberich teamed with James Mrazek, president of Carnegie Venture Resources, and Dr. Robert Bratzler to create Sepracor. Soon after the new company began its operations, however, it became apparent that the demand for pure chemicals from biotech companies, Sepracor's target customers, would not materialize.

Biotechs, after several years of buildup and investor enthusiasm, were facing the stark reality of needing to back up their expansive claims with profits. However, product development was slow and venture capital dried up, which in turn had an adverse effect on Sepracor's business plan. As a result, Sepracor would change its strategy, and its history would begin to mirror the other biotech start-ups.

In 1985 Sepracor created a subsidiary, BioSepra, devoted to its original chemical purification business, while it began to focus on developing purified versions of well-known drugs, in effect eliminating sinister (left-handed) side effects to create an improved strain. Barberich hoped to sell the company's expertise to the large pharmaceuticals, only to find no interest. He then decided to commit $10 million to the development of purified drugs without outside help, compounds that by law the company would be able to patent.

A LUCRATIVE NICHE

It appeared to be a potentially lucrative niche, especially in light of pharmaceutical companies' disdain for pursuing the work. The culture of research departments was one that placed a high emphasis on original work. Moreover, to eliminate side effects by using separation techniques was a tacit admission that something might be wrong with a pharmaceutical firm's product.

Sepracor, therefore, found itself in a strong position in the late 1980s. It could develop what amounted to new drugs with far less developmental resources. It concentrated on the most profitable medicines that were nearing the end of their 14-year patent terms, at which point generic-drug makers would be able to manufacture less expensive versions.

Sepracor's strategy was to present pharmaceutical companies with a patented, purified version of their compound, then strike a deal. The pharmaceutical would be able to pump new life into an old brand, since the new form of the drug would overshadow the generic knockoff with the old side effects, while essentially gaining a new patent term. The pharmaceutical would bear the manufacturing and marketing costs, and Sepracor would pocket a royalty as well as make money by selling the purified active ingredients to their partners.

Moreover, Sepracor was well aware that the pharmaceutical could better fund legal teams. By working with the pharmaceutical Sepracor could avoid costly and potentially devastating patent litigation. In many ways it was an elegant plan that would one day capture the imagination of many investors, while at the same time causing pharmaceuticals to label Sepracor as little more than a pirate operation. By 1990 Sepracor had applied for patents on purified forms of 40 major drugs.

COMPLETION OF INITIAL PUBLIC OFFERING

Sepracor's plan to make an initial public offering (IPO) of stock was postponed by the Gulf War but eventually took place in September 1991, when the company worked with Lehman Brothers to sell 4.6 million shares at $10 per share. Despite losing almost $15 million in 1991 and no immediate prospects for gaining profitability, Sepracor had a market capitalization of $160 million. Also in 1991, Sepracor acquired IBF Biotechnics, a French firm, in order to become involved in the chromatography-based and membrane-based separation techniques used in the manufacture of peptides and proteins.

A ruling by the U.S. Food and Drug Administration (FDA) in early 1992 would then provide a boost to

KEY DATES

1984: Timothy J. Barberich cofounds Sepracor to purify chemicals for sale to pharmaceutical companies.

1991: Initial public offering of stock is made.

1994: Company spins off BioSepra and HemaSure.

2001: Sepracor initiates direct-to-consumer marketing efforts to sell its products.

2009: Sepracor is acquired by Japan's Dainippon Sumitomo Pharma Co., Ltd., for $2.6 billion.

2010: Sepracor is merged with Dainippon Sumitomo Pharma America, Inc.

the company, as well as signal a long-term change in the pharmaceutical landscape. The FDA ruling required that all new chiral drugs be tested to determine if a pure isomer form would eliminate unwanted side effects. While Sepracor's scientific principles may have been vindicated by this ruling, it also meant that the major pharmaceutical companies would be forced to engage in similar research and that the number of future candidates for purification would eventually dry up. Nevertheless, Sepracor still held a large number of promising patents to exploit.

The first of these patents that forced a major pharmaceutical to deviate from the usual posture of disdain for Sepracor involved the antihistamine Seldane, produced by Marion Merrell Dow. An FDA ruling that required Seldane to carry a warning about potentially fatal cardiac arrhythmia had crippled sales, which dropped by some 30 percent, from $900 million in sales posted in 1992. Sepracor, looking for more cash, and Marion, saddled with declining sales, needed one another. In June 1993 they struck a deal that called for Marion to invest $10 million in Sepracor, thus gaining a 6 percent stake, as well as paying another $7.5 million in a licensing agreement, plus 8 percent in royalties.

The new drug, Allegra, would not only be free of the FDA warning and regain lost sales, but would provide Marion with an extended life on its antihistamine product. For Sepracor, Allegra provided a welcome revenue stream. However, the terms were not as advantageous as the company could have commanded if it had been better positioned financially and did not need help in getting Allegra through clinical trials.

Nevertheless, the Marion agreement lent much needed credibility to Sepracor with investors as well as other pharmaceutical companies, which would then be more willing to do business with Sepracor. It was imperative, however, for Sepracor to have enough ready cash to fund development in order to hold out for the best possible licensing deals in the future.

BIOSEPRA AND HEMASURE SPUN OFF

In 1994 Sepracor engineered two simultaneous public spin-offs of divisions to improve its finances, while retaining a controlling interest in both. Underwritten by David Blech, who had gained a reputation for biotech IPOs, BioSepra netted $18.3 million, and two weeks later HemaSure, devoted to the purification of donated blood products, netted $13.1 million. By providing separate funding for these businesses, which were draining cash and required some time before they would become profitable, Sepracor was better positioned to finance its core business of purifying blockbuster drugs.

Soon after, however, Blech's firm was forced to suspend operations because of its own financial woes, and any company associated with it was punished by investors. Sepracor's stock price fell from a high of $14 to just $4, while the recent spin-offs also suffered significant erosion. Believing that the company needed someone with credibility in the financial community to present Sepracor's case, Barberich hired a new chief financial officer. David Southwell was hired away from Lehman.

The British Southwell had known Barberich since his involvement with Lehman's underwriting of Sepracor's IPO. His immediate priority as the new CFO was to raise at least $5 million cash before the end of 1994 in order to stave off failure. After considerable effort he lined up $10 million in financing from the Oscar Frank Delano Partners Fund. Conditions improved even more in January 1995 when news that the patent for Allegra had finally been issued bumped Sepracor's stock price by 50 percent. The stock would receive a further boost later in the year when the company reported encouraging news on two other potential products. There was talk on the street that Sepracor would be generating $3 billion in sales in three years.

RAISING CASH FOR DEVELOPMENT

In order to continue development of these drugs and realize that promise, however, Southwell estimated that the company's burn rate of cash would have to increase from $30 million a year to $45 million. Over the next several months he engineered a variety of financial deals to meet the challenge. Taking advantage of a rebound in the stock market for biotech stocks, he raised $67 million on a secondary offering of Sepracor stock. He also raised an additional $47 million to fund HemaSure, which reduced Sepracor's stake to 37 percent and allowed the company to remove the spin-off from its books.

Southwell then raised $81 million in a convertible bond offer through Lehman. Finally, in March 1996 Southwell oversaw the IPO of a complicated spin-off and merger: the Sepracor SepraChem division, which created chemical synthesis products, merged with an Eastman Kodak spin-off, chemicals manufacturer Sterling Organics, to create ChiRex Inc. The $87 million raised in the offering funded the acquisition, while again taking the business off Sepracor's books to allow it to focus on its central work. By the middle of 1996, when all the transactions were complete, Southwell had garnered over $120 million for Sepracor, which provided the company with a two-year financial cushion and, as a result, greater control over the rights of some potentially lucrative drugs it had in the pipeline.

FAVORABLE FDA RULING IN 1997

Early in 1997 the price of Sepracor stock rose significantly following an FDA ruling that forced the removal of Seldane from the shelves and paved the way for Allegra to replace it. Moreover, the company was nearing completion of a purified form of Albuterol, an asthma medication that generated $1.4 billion in sales each year, as well as a key ingredient used in the antihistamine Claritin. By the end of 1997 Sepracor would sign an agreement with Schering-Plough Corporation to develop a purer form of Claritin, which generated $1.3 billion in annual sales and was less than five years away from patent expiration. The price of Sepracor stock rose above $40.

A few months later the prospects appeared even brighter when Sepracor received a patent for a purified form of fluoxetine, marketed as Prozac by Eli Lilly & Co., with sales approaching $3 billion a year. Then in July 1998 Sepracor licensed a new form of Propulsid, a popular heartburn medication with over $1 billion in annual sales, to Johnson & Johnson. Earlier in the year the companies had also agreed to work together on an improved version of Johnson & Johnson's Hismanal antihistamine.

It appeared that Sepracor had finally gained acceptance with the major pharmaceutical firms and that it would soon begin to realize robust profits after years of loss, with some analysts predicting it would be a $10 billion company in a matter of years. Nevertheless, in 1997 the company generated just $15.3 million in

revenues and posted net losses of $26.1 million. In 1998 revenues would increase modestly, coming in at $17.4 million, while the loss ballooned to $93.3 million.

Sepracor's prospects were buoyed when it sold the rights for the purified form of Prozac to Lilly for $90 million. The price of the company's stock soared to $140 per share by March 1999, giving it a market capitalization well over $3 billion. Not all investors were convinced, however, as an unusually high number of the company's outstanding shares were controlled by short sellers anticipating that the price would tumble.

When Johnson & Johnson backed out of the Hismanal deal, investors began to question whether Sepracor's other agreements were as solid as first believed, and the price of the company's stock plummeted to $55 by May 1999. Sepracor received some good news, however, when the FDA granted approval for the company to market Xopenex, a purified version of an asthma medication, the first product that it would market on its own.

SETBACKS

Sepracor's hopes for a future lucrative revenue stream derived from Prozac were dashed in 2000. The company suffered damage through its association with the drug, the integrity of which came into question when it was revealed that over the years Lilly had suppressed evidence that Prozac contributed to suicidal tendencies in a small percentage of patients. Even worse news came in October 2000 when Lilly terminated its agreement with Sepracor after patients in clinical trials for the new version developed abnormal heart rhythms. The stock immediately lost almost one-third of its value. Over the next several months the price of Sepracor stock plunged to less than $24 per share.

Sepracor retained a number of other potentially moneymaking refined versions of blockbuster drugs in the pipeline, but the company clearly had to use its purification techniques in the development of entirely new drugs. As part of its transition to becoming a more traditional pharmaceutical business, it initiated direct-to-consumer marketing efforts to sell its products in 2001. Although revenues in 2000 increased to $85.2 million, Sepracor lost $204 million after having lost $183 million in 1999.

In mid-2001 BioSphere Medical Inc. completed a public offering of four million shares of its common stock. Two million of the shares were held by Sepracor. The company planned to use proceeds from the offering, priced at $11 per share, to strengthen its capabilities in the areas of manufacturing, sales, and marketing, and for the development and commercialization of new products.

In November Sepracor established a five-year research and development agreement with France-based Cerep. The arrangement provided Sepracor with access to Cerep's BioPrint database, which contained information about the in vitro and in vivo properties of approximately 2,000 existing pharmaceuticals. By working together, the companies hoped to identify potential new drugs more quickly.

Sepracor suffered another setback in early 2002 when the FDA rejected its Soltara allergy drug. In an effort to reduce costs, the company repurchased $131.1 million in 7 percent convertible bonds, which were due in 2005, at a price of $84.8 million. The move saved Sepracor $29.7 million. In 2003 the company saw its sales increase 37 percent, reaching $260 million.

INSOMNIA DRUG SUCCESS

The market for insomnia drugs was achieving considerable growth during the middle of the decade. By early 2004 more than 82 million Americans over the age of 15 were suffering from the condition. Sepracor's new insomnia drug, Estorra (later named Lunesta), was one of several new pharmaceuticals coming on the market that stood to wrest market share away from Sanofi-Sythelabo's popular Ambien. The FDA approved Lunesta on February 27, 2004, and by April 26 the company saw its stock increase from $28 to $53.

In addition to Lunesta, Sepracor continued focusing on the development of new drugs. In early 2004 the company announced plans to conduct a Phase 2 proof-of-concept study of SEP 0226330, a new adrenaline and dopamine reuptake inhibitor. In September Sepracor agreed to repurchase $99.9 million worth of its common stock, and priced $500 million in convertible notes for private sale.

Sepracor began 2005 by announcing a three-year research and development collaboration with Acadia Pharmaceuticals Inc. The deal involved Sepracor's initial purchase of $10 million of Acadia's common stock, followed by an additional $10 million purchase upon the one-year anniversary of the collaboration. Long-term, the drug development tie-up was potentially worth as much as $75 million.

In 2005 Lunesta generated sales of $329.2 million for Sepracor. By mid-2006 the drug's success had created speculation that the company eventually would be acquired by a leading pharmaceutical firm. Several key management changes were announced at Sepracor in March 2007. At that time Adrian Adams was named president and chief operating officer. In addition, W. James O'Shea was chosen to fill a newly created vice-chairman position. Timothy Barberich continued to serve as chairman and CEO, but indicated that Adams would be elevated to the CEO position within six months.

In September 2007 Sepracor announced the establishment of an international alliance with Glaxo-SmithKline plc pertaining to its insomnia drug. Specifically, the arrangement allowed GlaxoSmithKline to market the drug under the name Lunivia in all global markets beyond the United States, Canada, Mexico, and Japan, where Sepracor continued to market it under the Lunesta brand name. In all, the deal was worth up to $155 million for Sepracor.

LEADERSHIP CHANGES

More leadership changes took place in October 2007. At that time Mark Iwicki was chosen to fill the company's new chief commercial officer position. In addition, Thomas Hoover was named vice-president of new products planning, Dean Giovanniello was named vice-president of marketing, and Jay Smith was named senior vice-president of sales.

In early 2008 Sepracor established an exclusive licensing agreement with Bial to develop and market the latter company's antiepileptic drug, BIA 2-093, in the United States and Canada. The agreement called for Sepracor to pay Bial $75 million up front, plus additional milestone-based payments. The deal strengthened Sepracor's central nervous system drug lineup and allowed the company to secure a stake in the antiepileptic drug market, which was estimated to be worth roughly $4 billion in the United States alone.

Additional leadership changes also took place in 2008. In January Timothy Barberich announced plans to retire as an executive of the company. However, he continued to serve Sepracor as chairman of the board. Midway through the year Chief Financial Officer David P. Southwell announced his retirement, ending a 14-year career with the company. He was succeeded by Executive Vice-President of Corporate Finance, Administration, and Technical Operations Robert F. Scumaci.

In June 2008 Sepracor acquired the specialty pharmaceutical company Oryx Pharmaceuticals Inc., which marketed branded drugs to hospitals and specialists throughout Canada. Specifically, Oryx concentrated on therapeutic treatments for central nervous system disorders, pain, infectious disease, and cardiovascular problems. The deal involved an initial payment of $50 million to Oryx's shareholders, plus additional milestone-based payments worth as much as $20 million.

Like other industries, the pharmaceutical sector was contending with difficult economic conditions by early 2009. At that time Sepracor announced a corporate restructuring and workforce reduction plan. The initiative called for the elimination of 530 jobs, or 20 percent of its workforce, along with operating expense reductions totaling about $210 million. In addition, plans were made to eliminate 410 contract sales positions.

ACQUIRED BY DSP

In September 2009 Sepracor announced an agreement to be acquired by Japan's Dainippon Sumitomo Pharma Co., Ltd. (DSP), in a $2.6 billion deal. The acquisition was completed in October, with Sepracor becoming an indirect, wholly owned subsidiary of DSP. Several key developments followed in early 2010. At that time President and CEO Adrian Adams tendered his resignation. Saburo Hamanaka was named the company's new chairman, and Mark Iwicki was promoted to the role of president and chief operating officer.

DSP announced plans to merge Sepracor with Dainippon Sumitomo Pharma America, Inc. Sepracor would continue as the surviving organization. The merger was completed on April 1, 2010, providing parent company DSP with a single North American operation. Sepracor had a strong pipeline of potential respiratory and central nervous system drugs in development. In addition to making its own discoveries, the company planned to continue pursuing other strategic growth opportunities, including collaboration and licensing arrangements, as well as potential mergers and acquisitions. As part of DSP, Sepracor's prospects for continued success during the second decade of the 21st century seemed excellent.

Ed Dinger
Updated, Paul R. Greenland

PRINCIPAL SUBSIDIARIES

Sepracor Canada (Nova Scotia) Limited (Canada); Sepracor N.V. (Netherlands Antilles); Sepracor Research and Development Trust; Sepracor Pharmaceuticals (Ireland) Ltd.; Sepracor Canada, Inc.; Sepracor RM, Inc.; Sepracor Pharmaceuticals, Inc. (Canada).

PRINCIPAL COMPETITORS

Cephalon, Inc.; GlaxoSmithKline plc; Sanofi-Aventis.

FURTHER READING

"Dainippon Sumitomo Pharma Co., Ltd., Completes Acquisition of Sepracor Inc.," *Business Wire*, October 20, 2009.

Johannes, Laura, and Thomas M. Burton, "Son of Prozac," *Wall Street Journal*, December 7, 1998, p. A1.

Marcial, Gene G., "Seeking Sepracor?" *Business Week*, May 31, 2004, p. 104.

Petersen, Melody, "As Lilly Ends Prozac Pact, Sepracor Stock Falls Nearly 30%," *New York Times*, October 20, 2000, p. C6.

"Sepracor Announces New Management Changes and Plans for Merger with Dainippon Sumitomo Pharma America," *Business Wire*, February 19, 2010.

"Sepracor Completes Acquisition of Oryx Pharmaceuticals and Expands Operations in Canada," *Business Wire*, June 3, 2008.

"Timothy J. Barberich to Resign as Executive Chairman of Sepracor and Will Continue to Serve as Chairman of the Board," *Business Wire*, January 3, 2008.

Sirona Dental Systems, Inc.

30 30 47th Avenue, Suite 500
Long Island City, New York 11101
U.S.A.
Telephone: (718) 482-2011
Fax: (718) 482-2011
Web site: http://www.sirona.com

Private Company
Founded: 1877
Incorporated: 1886 as Vereinigte Physikalisch-Mechanische Werkstätten Reiniger, Gebbert & Schall
Employees: 2,298
Sales: $713 million (2009)
Stock Exchanges: NASDAQ
Ticker Symbol: SIRO
NAICS: 339114 Dental Equipment and Supplies Manufacturing; 334517 Irradiation Apparatus Manufacturing; 339112 Surgical and Medical Instrument Manufacturing

■ ■ ■

Sirona Dental Systems, Inc., is a leading international manufacturer of equipment for dental practices, clinics, and laboratories. With a focus on high-technology solutions, Sirona provides dental chairs for treatment centers, traditional and digital X-ray and imaging systems and software, and computer-aided-design/computer-aided-manufacturing (CAD/CAM) systems for the manufacturing of ceramic restorations in dental laboratories as well as dental instruments and hygiene

systems. The company's main technology subsidiaries include Schick Technologies in Long Island City, New Jersey, specializing in intraoral radiographic imaging systems; BlueX Imaging, a manufacturer of dental radiographic systems in Assago, Italy; and siCAT in Bonn, Germany, which develops three-dimensional imaging software for dental implant planning and diagnosis.

Headquartered in Long Island City in the United States, the company's executive management is based in Salzburg, Austria, while Sirona's main manufacturing plant is located in Bensheim near Frankfurt am Main in Germany. In addition, Sirona has subsidiaries in Denmark, the United Kingdom and France, Japan and China, South Korea and Australia, and sales offices in Egypt, Saudi Arabia, the United Arab Emirates, and Russia. The company is listed on the NASDAQ.

EARLY FOCUS ON CUTTING-EDGE TECHNOLOGIES

Sirona's history goes back to the year 1877 when the mechanical engineer Erwin Moritz Reiniger started his own business in Erlangen, a German city 10 miles north of Nuremberg, where he worked at the local university. He rented a studio, set up his own workshop, and started building electrotechnical devices for medical use as well as other physical and optical instruments which he displayed and sold in his showroom. Seven years later Reiniger employed a staff of 15, including mechanics, carpenters, screw makers, apprentices, a shop assistant, and a bookkeeper.

In 1885 Reiniger visited an exhibition in Strasbourg where he met with precision mechanics Karl Schall and Max Gebbert who together ran a small company in Stuttgart that produced lamps for medical use, including forehead, oral and laryngeal lamps. A few months later, on January 1, 1886, the three entrepreneurs merged their businesses and founded Vereinigte Physikalisch-Mechanische Werkstätten Reiniger, Gebbert & Schall, Erlangen-New York-Stuttgart oHG, the United Physical-Mechanical Workshops of Reiniger, Gebbert & Schall (RGS), a general partnership headquartered in Erlangen.

Right from the beginning, RGS employed cutting-edge technologies in its products. Only one year after its foundation, the company presented the world's first electric dental drill built by RGS engineer William Niendorff, which was soon being mass produced. The company's lamps were equipped with small electric lightbulbs, a novelty at the time.

The company's network of affiliates in Germany and other countries was quickly expanded, counting more than 140 sales agents by 1888. However, in the beginning the business failed to generate enough profits. In 1888 Karl Schall left the company and moved to London where he set up his own firm and represented RGS in the United Kingdom. In the following years Schall built a growing roster of customers for RGS in the United Kingdom and its colonies, resulting in increasing sales for the company.

In the late 1880s and early 1890s RGS's range of products was expanded as well. In addition to incandescent lamps, lamp fittings, and dental drills, the company manufactured equipment and electrodes for galvanization, faradizations, endoscopies, and induction apparatus. In 1893 RGS moved to a newly built factory in Erlangen. By then, the company's workforce had grown to roughly 100. Two years later Reiniger left the company, with Gebbert remaining as its sole owner.

Only a few days after the news of Wilhelm Conrad Röntgen's spectacular discovery of X-rays had made the headlines, Gebbert contacted the German physics professor in Wurzburg to explore the business opportunities of the new technology. A few months later RGS presented another world-first—the first commercial X-ray unit. Realizing the enormous market potential of the new technology, particularly in the medical field, Gebbert decided to focus his business activities on manufacturing X-ray apparatus. In 1905 the company launched "Record," the world's first dental X-ray unit.

FORMING PARTNERSHIPS AFTER DAWN OF 20TH CENTURY

At 51 Max Gebbert suffered a stroke and had to refrain from managing the business. He passed away in 1907, and the company was transformed into a corporation in which his wife held a majority stake. In the following years, a time of political and economic crises, RGS began to cooperate with other players in the market to survive a world war, the Great Depression, and hyperinflation.

Two years into World War I, in 1916, RGS started cooperating with Vereinigte Elektrotechnische Institute Frankfurt-Aschaffenburg (Veifa), another manufacturer of X-ray machines and other electrotechnical apparatus used in medicine. In the same year the two companies entered a cooperation agreement with Hamburg-based C.H.F. Müller, which later became known as Philips, on the delivery of X-ray tubes. Later in the decade RGS joined two newly founded trade associations of X-ray equipment manufacturers. In 1920 RGS and Veifa founded Phönix, a manufacturer of glass tubes based in Rudolstadt.

Under increasing pressure by the postwar economic recession and beginning inflation, RGS together with 17 other companies formed Industrieunternehmen Berlin, or INAG Industrial Enterprises, the holding company of a conglomerate of manufacturers of medical and dental products, in 1921. The new organization opened up new markets in Germany as well as abroad for RGS. However, the acquisition and incorporation of unprofitable firms into INAG by one of the top managers after World War I turned into a financial disaster for the company.

After the introduction of the new rentenmark, which put an end to hyperinflation in November 1923, it became obvious that INAG, and therefore RGS, were both deeply in debt. The only way out was to look for a financially strong partner with similar interests, which was found in Berlin-based Siemens & Halske AG, one of RGS's main competitors. In 1925 Siemens & Halske

---

KEY DATES
■

1877: Erwin Moritz Reiniger starts building medical electrotechnical devices in his workshop.

1886: Vereinigte Physikalisch-Mechanische Werkstätten Reiniger, Gebbert & Schall (RGS) is founded.

1887: RGS engineer William Niendorff builds the first electric dental drill.

1905: The company manufactures the world's first dental X-ray unit.

1925: RGS is taken over by Siemens & Halske and becomes Siemens & Reiniger AG.

1956: A new dental treatment unit carries the name Sirona.

1966: The company becomes part of Siemens AG.

1997: Sirona Dental Systems is established after the sale of Siemens' dental division to institutional investors.

2006: The company merges with U.S.-based Schick Technologies and is listed on the NASDAQ.

---

acquired INAG, Veifa, and RGB, which were merged with the company's own electromedical division. A new company, Siemens-Reiniger-Veifa GmbH (SRV), was created as a joint marketing organization.

The 1925 merger of the four companies into one created a leading player in the field of electromedical equipment. While Siemens & Halske was technologically more advanced, RGB and INAG had built a better developed marketing organization. Therefore, SRV marketed the products of all these firms, including the Berlin-based INAG firms Adam Schneider AG, a manufacturer of dental chairs, E.F.G. Küster GmbH which made sterilizers and disinfectants, and Medicihaus AG, a producer of operating chairs and surgical instruments.

RAPID GROWTH BEFORE AND DURING WORLD WAR II

The onset of the Great Depression in the early 1930s made it necessary to raise productivity and to streamline the company's organization. In 1932 most of the company's production activities were moved to the RGS plant in Erlangen. RGS, SRV and Phönix were consolidated and united under the organizational umbrella of the new company Siemens-Reiniger-Werke AG (SRW) headquartered in Berlin.

In the following years the company enjoyed a period of rapid growth. In 1934 SRW introduced the world's smallest X-ray unit, called X-ray sphere. Five years later two new dental treatment units, Triumpf and Artifex, were launched. By 1937 there were 18 SRW sales offices and 8 branches specializing in dental products in Germany. In addition the company had established 25 sales offices in other European countries, 16 branches in the United States, and sales agencies in Egypt, South Africa, Australia, and Asia. With a workforce of roughly 5,000 worldwide just before the onset of World War II, SRW was Germany's largest manufacturer of electromedical equipment.

During World War II the company was increasingly involved in the production of armaments and war goods and employed an increasing number of women, foreign laborers, and prisoners of war. As the war progressed, it became more and more difficult to carry on the production of electromedical goods since it required skilled personnel, who were drawn into the military in growing numbers and could not be easily replaced. After SRW's site in Berlin had fallen victim to bombs, company headquarters were moved to Erlangen in 1943 and 1944. To prevent the production facilities for electromedical goods in Erlangen from suffering the same fate, the production of these goods was spread out to 15 different manufacturers, some of them abroad.

After the war had ended, Erlangen, which was home to a large military hospital complex that accommodated roughly 6,000 patients, was occupied by the U.S.-Allied forces. In April 1945, the SRW plant was closed down and most of the inventory destroyed. However, only a few weeks later the U.S.-military government gave SRW permission to resume production. In 1947 company headquarters were officially moved to Erlangen as was Siemens & Halske's medical engineering department. By 1949 SRW had rebuilt its worldwide sales network. Three years later, more than 3,000 employees worked at the company, which in 1952 celebrated its 75th anniversary.

SIRONA PRODUCT LINE STIRS GROWTH AT NEW LOCATION

It was in 1956 when Siemens-Reiniger Werke launched a new dental treatment unit that carried the brand name Sirona. In addition to featuring the latest dental technologies, it was stylish and modern in design. Within only eight months the company received orders for more than 1,000 units. Two years later the company put out the air-powered Sirona Turbine, a dental drill with an exceptionally high rotation speed.

In 1962 the world's first panorama image X-ray system, and the Sirona glare-free twin-panel surgical light were launched. Three years later the Sirona micro motor was introduced, the first mass produced motor that was inbuilt into the hand pieces of dental drills. In 1968 the company launched Sirolux, an innovative operating light equipped with halogen lamps and cold-light reflectors. In the same year a special Sirona unit was introduced that was designed and equipped according to the special needs of customers in the United States.

The constant stream of innovations put out by Siemens-Reiniger was the result of continued investment in research and development (R&D) and modern production facilities. In 1963 SRW built a brand-new production facility for medical-technical and dental products and equipment in Bensheim near Frankfurt am Main. The new factory's workforce grew quickly from about 240 in 1964 to 600 two years later, with part of the personnel being skilled workers from the Erlangen factory. In 1966, Siemens-Reiniger Werke was renamed Wernerwerk für Medizinische Technik and, as part of a major reorganization, became part of the medical technology and engineering division of the newly formed Siemens AG. In 1969 the company's R&D and sales organizations for dental products were relocated to Bensheim.

In the early 1970s the Sirona product line was so successful in the marketplace that customers hat to wait up to one year for their new dental units, due to the large backlog of orders. To keep up with this rapid growth, production capacity in Bensheim was roughly doubled. Later in the decade a state-of-the art education and training center, a spacious showroom, and a large cafeteria completed the new facility.

INNOVATION CONTINUED FROM 1980 ON

During the 1980s and 1990s Wernerwerk continued to develop a series of new high-tech products. In 1980 the company launched its dental treatment unit Sirona M1, more than 35,000 of which were sold in 13 years, making it one of the world's best-selling models. Five years later Wernerwerk launched CEREC, a highly innovative CAD/CAM system for the instant production of ceramic inlays by dentists, which, however, flopped commercially at the time.

In 1994 the company introduced a number of new products, including a digital X-ray system, the new C1 line of dental chairs, a high-speed hand piece, and the second generation of the CEREC system. The first digital panorama X-ray system was launched one year later.

REORGANIZATION AND GROWTH AFTER 1997 DEPARTURE FROM SIEMENS

The year 1997 marked a new era for the company when Siemens sold its dental products division to a group of private investors through the European investment firm Schroder Ventures. On October 1, 1997, a new company, Sirona Dental Systems GmbH, was established. By then, Sirona was the undisputed world market leader in its field with DEM 900 million in annual sales, about 2,700 employees, and a tightly knit network of sales offices around the world.

In the following years the company underwent a thorough cost-cutting and restructuring program, directed by former Xerox manager Franz Scherer. In 1998 the decision was made to focus solely on manufacturing, and the sales and distribution departments were transferred to the newly founded distributor Demedis. Furthermore, the company invested heavily in new product development in its chosen major areas of activity, including dental treatment units, handheld instruments, conventional and digital imaging systems, and dental CAD/CAM systems. Finally, a communication campaign was launched to publicize the new company name Sirona and what it stood for.

In 2003 the private-equity firm EQT together with Sirona's management bought the company. Two years later the company changed owners again when it was acquired by Chicago-based private-equity investment firm Madison Dearborn Partners. In 2006 Sirona acquired the U.S.-based Schick Technologies, a leading supplier of intra-oral radiographic imaging systems based in Long Island City, New Jersey, in a stock-for-stock reverse merger. Sirona's owners held about two-thirds in the new Sirona Dental Systems, Inc., while Schick's shareholders held one-third. In the same year the company was listed on the technology stock exchange, NASDAQ. The reverse merger created the world's leading manufacturers of dental equipment and products, with combined revenues of roughly $500 million.

In the first decade of the new millennium Sirona further expanded its product line and global presence. In 2004 the company acquired the Danish manufacturer of dental hygiene and sterilization equipment Nitram Dental, and the Chinese HTC Hipwo group, one of the largest manufacturers of treatment centers in China. In addition, the company established subsidiaries in France, Great Britain, Spain, and Japan. Three years later Sirona introduced a new generation of its CAD/CAM restoration equipment called CEREC Connect. It allowed the instant electronic transfer of digitally scanned data right from the dental chair to the laboratory where, with the help of virtual design software, restorations such as crowns and bridges could be modeled on the computer and then sent to Sirona's infiniDent outsource center to be "printed" as a three-dimensional model in resin.

In 2010 the company launched another groundbreaking innovation. The inEos Blue 3D scanner worked with short-wavelength visible blue light to produce highly precise three-dimensional scans of molds for the design of digital models. With a leading edge over its competitors, continued high investments in R&D, and a strong focus on cutting-edge technologies, Sirona saw itself well positioned for future growth in a globally thriving market.

Evelyn Hauser

PRINCIPAL SUBSIDIARIES

Sirona Dental Systems, Inc.; Sirona Dental Systems LLC; Schick Technologies, Inc.; Sirona Dental Systems GmbH (Germany); siCAT GmbH & Co. KG (Germany); Sirona Dental GmbH (Austria); Sirona Dental Systems Ltd. (UK); Sirona Dental Systems SAS (France); Sirona Dental Systems S.r.l. (Italy); BlueX Imaging (Italy); Nitram Dental a/s (Denmark); Sirona Dental Systems K. K. (Japan); FONA Dental Systems Co., Ltd. (China); Sirona Dental Systems Trading (Shanghai) Co., Ltd (China); Sirona Dental Systems Korea Limited (South Korea); Sirona Dental Systems Pty Ltd. (Australia).

PRINCIPAL COMPETITORS

Carestream Health, Inc.; Dentsply International Inc.; Hu-Friedy Manufacturing Company, Inc.; KaVo Dental; RitterConcept GmbH; Young Innovations, Inc.

FURTHER READING

"Henry Schein Adds Darby Units; Sirona/Schick Merger Complete," *Medical Device Week*, June 22, 2006.

Johnson, Holland, "Schick in $1.5 Billion Reverse Merger Deal to Acquire Sirona," *Medical Device Week*, September 27, 2005.

"Schroder European Fund Closes First Major Deal," *UK Venture Capital Journal*, November 1997, p. 29.

"Sirona inLab," *Dental Lab Products*, May 2008, p. 66.

"Sirona, the Dental Company," *Dental Lab Products*, May 2007, p. 61.

"Sirona to Ring NASDAQ Closing Bell," *Business Wire*, August 30, 2006.

"Speedy Scan," *Dental Lab Products*, February 2010, p. 4.

Wechsel, Wandel, Wachsen. Die ersten fünf Sirona Jahre, Bensheim, Germany: Sirona Gruppe, 2002.

Standard Chartered plc

■

1 Basinghall Avenue
London, EC2V 5DD
United Kingdom
Telephone: (+44 207) 885 8888
Fax: (+44 207) 885 9999
Web site: http://www.standardchartered.com

Public Company
Incorporated: 1969 as The Standard and Chartered
     Banking Group Ltd.
Employees: 73,800
Total Assets: $435 billion (2008)
Stock Exchanges: London
Ticker Symbol: STAB
NAICS: 522110 Commercial Banking; 522210 Credit
     Card Issuing; 522293 International Trade Financing

■ ■ ■

Standard Chartered plc is one of the world's leading
international banks. With operations in more than 70
countries, the bank had approximately 70,000
employees, 1,600 branches, and 5,500 ATMs at the end
of the first decade of the 21st century. Standard
Chartered generates a significant portion of its operating
income from Asia. In 2008 the Other Asia Pacific region
alone accounted for 17 percent, followed by India
(15%); Hong Kong (15%); Middle East and Other
South Asia (14%); Singapore (11%); Americas, United
Kingdom, and Europe (10%); Africa (8%); Korea (7%);
and Malaysia (3%).

ORIGINS

Standard Chartered was formed in 1969 as a merger
between the Standard Bank, which did business
throughout Africa, and the Chartered Bank, which operated branches throughout India, China, and
southeastern Asia. Lacking a truly strong domestic
network, the banking group's progress was largely
dependent upon Third World economic and political
conditions and emerging markets.

Both the Standard Bank and the Chartered Bank
had been in operation for more than a century when
they combined forces. The Chartered Bank, originally
incorporated in 1853 as the Chartered Bank of India,
Australia, and China under a charter from Queen Victoria, was influential in the development of British
colonial trade throughout Asia. Up until World War II,
British trade in Asia flourished, and the Chartered Bank
prospered.

The Standard Bank was established in 1862 as the
Standard Bank of British South Africa by a schoolmaster
named John Paterson. Paterson had eclectic interests,
including mining, railroad promotion, and real estate
development. He set out to make Standard a large bank,
and proceeded to acquire smaller banks throughout
southern Africa. For the next century, the bank played a
significant role in the banking of the region.

Since both banks were products of the colonial era,
with similar structures and experience, they made an
excellent match. Their complementary geographic coverage and similar historical backgrounds made for a
relatively smooth transition.

COMPANY PERSPECTIVES

Leading by example to be the right partner for its stakeholders, the Group is committed to building a sustainable business over the long term that is trusted worldwide for upholding high standards of corporate governance, social responsibility, environmental protection and employee diversity.

INTEGRATION AND EXPANSION INTO EUROCURRENCY MARKETS

The new Standard and Chartered Banking Group took its time integrating the management of the two banks. Throughout 1970 each former unit performed its operations more or less unchanged. Bank branches continued to operate under their old names for a number of years. Each was able to expand independently in its own markets, and there was no need to immediately restructure either of the bank's operations. However, the company slowly began to develop long-term plans for the entire bank.

Standard Chartered's first chairman, Sir Cyril Hawker, came to the group from the Bank of England, where he had served since 1920. His sensitivity to the needs of developing nations made him an excellent choice to guide Standard Chartered in its early years. In 1970 Hawker brought Standard Chartered deeper into the Eurocurrency markets. Both the Standard Bank and the Chartered Bank had entered these markets in the 1960s. By 1970, Standard Chartered was using funds generated in the Euro-markets to finance projects throughout the world.

Because of its Third World involvement Standard Chartered dealt with more problems than most banks. Unstable political and economic conditions posed a constant threat to the bank. During the 1960s, some branches were nationalized by the countries in which they operated. In the 1970s, although conditions were generally calmer, Standard Chartered had to be prepared to adapt to the sometimes-unpredictable whims of governments in Africa and Asia. Wars and rebellions were a constant threat.

When new regimes came to power, Standard Chartered's branches were at times subject to new regulations, nationalization, or a transfer of ownership to native financiers. In 1970, for example, the African nation of Zambia partially nationalized the Standard Bank operating there. Nationalization was the greatest fear of any overseas bank operating in politically

unstable countries. At the same time, however, these regions were often very profitable.

In 1971 the Eastern Bank, a Middle Eastern bank Chartered had acquired in 1957, became fully integrated with the Chartered Bank. The Standard Bank's Nigerian branches had a good first year in the reconstruction period after the civil war there ended in 1970. Operations in Hong Kong, Singapore, and Malaysia showed strong results in the early 1970s, although depressed economic conditions in South Africa resulted in a poor performance for the Standard Bank branches operating there.

Nevertheless, the bank's dependence on the unreliable conditions of Third World nations induced it to seek a stronger foothold in industrialized nations to add stability to its international network. Throughout the early 1970s, the bank increased operations in European and U.S. capital markets and began to cooperate with other international banks.

In 1973 the banking group diversified heavily. The acquisition of Mocatta and Goldsmid Ltd. brought Standard Chartered into the gold and precious metals markets. The group's computer leasing company, Standard and Chartered Leasing, expanded into European markets. The banking group also formed a partnership in a merchant bank.

FOCUS ON OVERSEAS COMMERCIAL BANKING

By 1974, Standard Chartered's gradual integration was complete and the managements of the Standard Bank and of the Chartered Bank came together under one roof. In August 1974 Sir Cyril Hawker retired and was replaced by Lord Barber. Barber oversaw the formulation of a long-term strategy for the bank. Standard Chartered would concentrate on what it did best: overseas commercial banking. Unlike a growing number of international banks during this period, Standard Chartered did not intend to branch into other areas of financial services.

The bank would continue to strengthen its European position to offset fluctuations in Third World economies, but would not attempt to enter retail banking in Britain. The 17 British branches Standard Chartered already operated focused on import-export financing and banking support services.

In 1974 Standard Chartered's diversity was key in insulating it from a worldwide recession. In October 1975 the group changed its name to the Standard Chartered Bank Ltd. However, subsidiaries throughout the world still operated under their old established names. The bank grew throughout the late 1970s.

KEY DATES

1853: The Chartered Bank incorporates as the Chartered Bank of India, Australia, and China under a charter from Queen Victoria.

1862: The Standard Bank is established as the Standard Bank of British South Africa in British South Africa.

1957: The Chartered Bank acquires the Eastern Bank of the Middle East region.

1969: The Chartered Bank and Standard Bank merge, forming The Standard and Chartered Banking Group Ltd.

1975: The company changes its name to Standard Chartered Bank Ltd.

1986: Company wards off a hostile takeover attempt by Lloyds Bank.

2002: Standard Chartered begins listing its shares on the Hong Kong Stock Exchange.

2003: Custodial bank status approval is received from the People's Bank of China, paving the way for future growth.

2007: Standard Chartered agrees to acquire American Express Bank Ltd. for $860 million.

2008: The company eliminates 572 jobs at its South Korea headquarters and implements a hiring freeze in Hong Kong.

2009: Standard Chartered Korea Ltd. President and CEO David Edwards retires and is succeeded by Richard Hill.

Profits improved consistently, and assets continued to grow. In 1979 Standard Chartered made a major acquisition in the United States by purchasing the Union Bancorp of California.

As international banking competition became more intense, Standard Chartered's management began to see weaknesses in the bank's lack of a domestic base. In 1981 the group bid on the Royal Bank of Scotland Group. This bank had the domestic branch network that Standard Chartered wanted and was amenable to a takeover by Standard Chartered. However, a rival bid by the Hongkong and Shanghai Bank sent the issue to the British Monopolies Commission, which ruled against both bids. The banking group entered the 1980s heavily reliant on the financial success of underdeveloped nations.

FINANCIAL WOES

The 1980s were difficult times for many of the countries where Standard Chartered operated. Singapore and Malaysia fell into a serious recession in the mid-1980s. As Hong Kong's shipping industry struggled to survive, a number of large loans went bad, putting Standard Chartered in serious financial straits. By 1986 the Standard Chartered Bank was in financial disarray. The bank's strategy of focusing on commercial banking proved to have been an error, as large customers were choosing international banks that could provide them with a complete line of financial services, including stockbroking and issuing commercial paper. Capital markets and money markets were deregulated in many countries in 1986, leading to increased competition for which Standard Chartered was unprepared.

Standard Chartered's affiliate in South Africa had performed inconsistently in the 1980s, but was for the most part a profitable venture. Growing political pressure to divest South African holdings caused the bank some unrest. Standard Chartered was reluctant to sell its 39 percent interest in the bank at the unfavorable exchange rate of the time and take a large loss. Finally, in 1987 the bank divested its South African holdings, ending its 125-year presence in that nation. It was the last foreign bank to leave South Africa.

In 1986 London saw an explosion of mergers and acquisitions among banks with the financial deregulation known as the "Big Bang." Standard Chartered became the target of a takeover by Lloyds Bank, which Standard Chartered's chief executive, Michael McWilliam, was determined to prevent. The purchase of 35 percent of Standard Chartered's shares by three businessmen helped to thwart the Lloyds bid. Standard Chartered received a thrashing in the British press when it became known that one of its "white knights," Tan Sri Khoo, had received a large loan from the bank just before he invested in its shares. The bank called for an investigation to clear its name and was vindicated by the Bank of England a year later.

TROUBLES CONTINUE

Although Standard Chartered was successful in warding off the hostile takeover by Lloyds, its troubles were not over. The banking community's dependence on the Third World caught up with it in 1987, when, due to larger loan-loss provisions, Standard Chartered showed a net loss of £274 million. McWilliam tried to restructure the bank's operations and replaced many high-ranking executives. Chairman Sir Peter Graham stated that the bank needed to inject new capital through a rights issue. In 1988 the bank reversed its position on divesting noncore assets to raise capital and sold the United Bank of Arizona to Citibank, and later sold its profitable Union Banking group to California First, a subsidiary of the Bank of Tokyo.

Standard Chartered's situation began to improve in 1988. A new rights issue in September 1988 helped repair the bank's capital balance. Profits for the first half of 1988 were £154 million compared to a loss of £222 million during the same period a year before. McWilliam, who had directed the bank's operations during its stormiest year, resigned in early 1988 and Sir Peter Graham, who had been chairman for only two years, retired. Rodney Galpin took over as both chairman and chief executive. Galpin had spent most of his career at the Bank of England and intended to be a "hands-on" chairman.

FOCUS ON EMERGING MARKETS

Standard Chartered continued to restructure in the 1990s. It divested holdings in Europe, the United States, and Africa and made a series of job cuts. Unprofitable businesses were shut down and internal operations were streamlined. Management began a new strategy of focusing on consumer banking, along with corporate and institutional banking in Asia, Africa, and the Middle East.

Even as Standard Chartered pared back certain operations, it continued to delve into emerging markets. In 1990 it reentered the Vietnamese market, and then two years later began operating in Cambodia and Iran. Tanzania followed, along with Myanmar in 1995. By the mid-1990s, the company had offices in every country in the Asia Pacific region except for North Korea. While both the Asian and African markets proved tumultuous, the company's financial performance remained strong. In 1997 the bank secured pretax profits of £870 million.

The bank then began a series of acquisitions that would strengthen its position in the emerging markets industry. In 1998 it acquired a majority interest in Banco Exterior de Los Andes, which enabled the firm to offer its banking services as well as trade finance services in Colombia, Peru, and Venezuela. The following year, the global trade finance business of Union Bank of Switzerland was purchased. The bank also acquired a 75 percent stake in Thailand's Nakornthon Bank PLC. In the fall of 1999 Standard Chartered increased its presence in China by opening a Beijing branch office.

In 2000 the company made two of its largest acquisitions to date. The first was the $1.34 billion cash purchase of ANZ Grindlays Bank's South Asian and Middle Eastern banking operations. The deal added 116

branches to Standard Chartered's growing arsenal. The next acquisition was that of Chase Manhattan Corp.'s Hong Kong consumer banking and credit card operations. The $1.32 billion purchase secured the bank's position as Hong Kong's largest credit card operator with a 25 percent market share. The company also sold its Chartered Trust unit to Lloyds TSB that year for £627 million.

Forbes magazine commented on the bank's commitment to its Asian markets in October 2000. The article claimed that while most financial institutions had been exiting the turbulent Asian scene, Standard Chartered "took a strikingly different road. Rather than hit the brakes, its chairman, Sir Patrick Gillam, and its CEO, Rana Talwar, accelerated their plans to become the international bank most focused on Asia, and to a lesser degree, the world's other emerging markets." While pretax earnings fell by 42 percent during 1997 and 1999, revenues continued to grow despite the Asian economic collapse.

LEADERSHIP CHANGES

By 2001 speculation arose that Standard Chartered might be courting takeover offers. Talwar agreed to consider these offers if the price was right. However, Gillam pushed to keep Standard Chartered intact. Shareholders agreed with Gillam's approach and in December of that year, Talwar, who had been named CEO in 1998, was ousted from the company. Mervyn Davies, whose focus proved to be on the company's independence, was chosen to assume Talwar's position.

Standard Chartered began listing its shares on the Hong Kong Stock Exchange in October 2002, offering 30 million shares for EUR 11.02 each. The company ended the year with 500 locations in 50 countries, and a workforce of approximately 28,000 people. Standard Chartered at this time was focused on doing more business in Asia, where it had roughly $100 million in assets under administration. In January 2003 the bank secured custodial bank status approval from the People's Bank of China, paving the way for future growth.

By early 2004 Standard Chartered ranked as one of Asia's largest credit card issuers. At that time the company had issued some six million credit cards in Taiwan, Thailand, India, Malaysia, Singapore, and Hong Kong. In Hong Kong alone, the organization cornered 20 percent of the local market. Looking ahead, Standard Chartered anticipated offering cards directly to Chinese consumers, following regulatory changes that would open up that country's retail banking market. It also was in 2004 that Standard Chartered acquired 19.9 percent of northern China-based Bohai Bank, secured a license to open a branch in Karachi, Pakistan, and received clearance to establish a stand-alone Islamic Banking Branch.

In January 2005 Standard Chartered agreed to part with $3.3 billion to acquire Korea First Bank. One year later the state-owned, Singapore-based investment firm Temasek Holdings agreed to spend $4 billion for a 12 percent ownership interest in Standard Chartered. After acquiring 152.4 million Standard Chartered shares, Temasek became the bank's largest shareholder. In September 2006 Standard Chartered's Pakistan subsidiary acquired a 95.37 percent stake in Union Bank Ltd. in a $431 million cash deal. That same month, Standard Chartered parted with $1.2 billion to acquire Taiwan-based Hsinchu International Bank.

Standard Chartered's growth and progress did not go unnoticed. In October the Dubai-based investment firm Istithmar spent $1 billion to secure a 2.7 percent interest in the bank. The company ended the year by partnering with First Data Corp. subsidiary First Data International to establish a merchant-acquiring services business named Merchant Solutions Pte Ltd. Finally, the departure of Chairman Bryan Sanderson allowed for the promotion of Mervyn Davies to nonexecutive chairman, and Finance Director Peter Sands to CEO.

ACQUISITION ACTIVITY INTENSIFIES

Acquisitions continued in 2007, beginning with a deal in India, where Standard Chartered had achieved profits of $403 million in 2006. In August 2007 the company partnered with the Securities Trading Corporation of India to acquire ownership of UTI Securities. The following month, the United Kingdom-based petroleum financing operation Harrison Lovegrove and Co. was acquired. Also in September, Standard Chartered agreed to acquire American Express Bank Ltd. The $860 million deal with American Express Company resulted in the addition of more branch licenses in India, where the company was the largest foreign bank.

Midway through 2008, Standard Chartered expanded an existing bancassurance partnership with Prudential plc. First established in 1998, the agreement initially applied to the markets of Malaysia, Singapore, and Hong Kong. The new agreement also included Thailand and Japan, and extended the tie-up between the two firms to 2016.

In 2008 Standard Chartered's operating income increased 26 percent, reaching $13.9 billion. Operating profits also climbed 13 percent, totaling $4.6 billion. As economic conditions became more difficult that year, the company revealed plans to trim 572 jobs at its South Korea headquarters and to implement a hiring freeze in Hong Kong.

By early 2009 Standard Chartered was pursuing measured growth in the United States, with plans to establish a mergers and acquisitions/financing team to assist companies interested in expanding their operations to the Middle East, Africa, and Asia. At this time Standard Chartered attributed approximately 90 percent of its business to these same areas. The bank ended the year with a major leadership change. In December, Standard Chartered Korea Ltd. President and CEO David Edwards retired, and was succeeded by Richard Hill, who had served as the Korea subsidiary's chief financial officer and head of strategy.

Updated, Christina M. Stansell;
Paul R. Greenland

PRINCIPAL SUBSIDIARIES

First Africa Group Holdings Limited; Standard Chartered Bank; Standard Chartered First Bank Korea Limited; Standard Chartered Bank Malaysia Berhad; Standard Chartered Bank (Pakistan) Limited (98.99%); Standard Chartered Bank (Taiwan) Limited; Standard Chartered Bank (Hong Kong) Limited; Standard Chartered Bank (China) Limited; Standard Chartered Bank (Thai) Public Company Limited (99.97%); Standard Chartered Receivables (UK) Limited; Standard Chartered Financial Investments Limited; Standard Chartered Debt Trading Limited; Standard Chartered Private Equity Limited (Hong Kong); Standard Chartered—STCI Capital Markets Limited (74.9%).

PRINCIPAL DIVISIONS

Consumer Banking; Wholesale Banking.

PRINCIPAL COMPETITORS

ABN AMRO Holding N.V.; Citigroup Inc.; HSBC Holdings plc.

FURTHER READING

Choi, Hae Won, and Mary Kissel, "Deal Marks a Big Bet on Banking in Korea," *Wall Street Journal Europe*, January 11, 2005, p. C4.

"Dubai's Istithmar Buys 1 BLN USD Stake in Standard Chartered," *Europe Intelligence Wire*, October 6, 2006.

Heller, Richard, "Damn the Torpedoes! Full Speed Ahead!" *Forbes*, October 2, 2000.

"Not One of Us; Standard Chartered Bank," *Economic Review*, December 8, 2001.

Robinson, Karina, "A Perfect Fit in an Exotic Bank," *Banker*, October 2001, p. 40.

Rozens, Aleksandrs, "Standard Chartered Eyes U.S. Growth; U.K. Giant to Bulk Up in M&A Forex," *Investment Dealers' Digest*, March 13, 2009, p. 1.

"StanChart to Buy American Express Bank; India Presence to Grow," *PTI—The Press Trust of India Ltd.*, September 18, 2007.

"Standard Chartered Digesting but Still Hungry," *Middle East Economic Digest*, March 9, 2001, p. 7.

"Standard Chartered Is Not in a Rush to Issue Cards in China," *Cardline*, February 13, 2004, p. 1.

"Standard Chartered Readies Operations for China Connection," *Operations Management*, January 27, 2003, p. 5.

"World Business Briefing Asia: Singapore: Buying a Stake in British Bank," *New York Times*, March 28, 2006, p. C6.

Thos. Moser
Cabinetmakers Inc.

■

72 Wright's Landing
Auburn, Maine 04211-1237
U.S.A.
Telephone: (207) 784-3332
Toll Free: (877) 708-1973
Fax: (207) 784-6973
Web site: http://www.thosmoser.com

Private Company
Incorporated: 1972
Employees: 100
Sales: $406.1 million (2009 est.)
NAICS: 337122 Nonupholstered Wood Household
Furniture Manufacturing

■ ■ ■

Thos. Moser Cabinetmakers Inc. (Thos. Moser) is a privately held, Auburn, Maine-based maker of hand-crafted, high-end, hardwood furniture. The company focuses on American Shaker and other classic designs, as well as contemporary designs developed by the company's craftsmen, including its founder, Thomas Moser. It also emphasizes black cherry wood as a primary material, sourced mostly from the Allegheny region of New York and Pennsylvania. Other hardwoods include maple, walnut, and oak.

The company's slate of some 200 products includes lounge and dining chairs, rockers, tables, bedroom and dining room cases, bookcases, and desks. The company also offers a wide range of library furniture. Thos. Moser furniture is available for purchase via the company's

Web site and catalog, and showrooms located in Boston, Los Angeles, New York, San Francisco, Washington, D.C., and Freeport, Maine. Although the company serves the residential market, the bulk of its sales come from institutional customers.

ORIGINS

Thomas Moser was born in Chicago in 1935, the son of an immigrant stereotyper who assembled the lead printing plates used at the time by the *Chicago Tribune*. Moser was about 13 when he lost both of his parents, and at 15 he dropped out of high school to join the Air Force during the Korean War. Upon his discharge he decided to continue his education, despite earlier lackluster classroom performances. It was only because he was a veteran that Moser was able in 1957 to gain entrance to the State University of New York at Geneseo. He studied speech education during the day and tuned pipe organs at night. After earning a bachelor's degree he went on to graduate school at the University of Michigan and Cornell University.

It was also at Geneseo that Moser built a small house for his family and developed an interested in working with his hands. While pursuing his postgraduate education Moser taught in high schools and state colleges, and during the summers he renovated houses that he and his wife then sold. He also did woodworking, refurbishing antique furniture, as well as crafting the occasional reproduction that his wife sold at a small antiques store she opened in their home. It was in the mid-1960s, during a yearlong contract teaching English at the College of Petroleum and Minerals in Dhahran,

COMPANY PERSPECTIVES

■

Thos. Moser Cabinetmakers is guided by our mission to build furniture that celebrates the natural beauty of wood; is of simple, unadorned, graceful line; and is crafted for a long, useful life.

Saudi Arabia, that Moser suffered from what he called "project-deficit syndrome." To assuage his need, he converted an old Volkswagen minibus into a camper.

After Saudi Arabia, Moser moved his family to Maine, where he taught at the University of Maine, Orino. He then relocated to Lewiston, where he taught at Bates College. However, by 1971 he had grown disenchanted with academia while developing a passion for craftwork that could not be satisfied by occasional house renovations. One summer evening while sitting at a table with his wife, Moser suggested that he could make a living making these tables. The idea took root and rather than seek a sabbatical, Moser requested a one-year leave of absence to see if he could make a living crafting wooden furniture.

COMPANY STARTED: 1972

As 1972 came to a close, Moser's leave of absence began and he launched his company. For a business name he considered such possibilities as The Dovetail Shop and Shaker Inspired, but instead took the advice of a friend who suggested "Thomas Moser, Furniture Maker." Moser tweaked the name, employing the 18th-century abbreviation "Thos." and substituting the more traditional "Cabinet Maker" for "Furniture Maker."

For a workshop Moser borrowed $8,000 and bought an abandoned Grange hall in New Gloucester, Maine, that in recent years had been used to store apple crates. It was no more than a rudimentary space, lacking windows, plumbing, and heat. After some remodeling it was ready by the spring of 1972, and Moser began producing kitchen cabinets for a house he was renovating. He had few tools at his disposal, just a small table saw, belt sander, saber saw, and an assortment of hand tools. Due to his lack of funds he primarily used pine as a material, produced from boards cut at a local sawmill from trees on his 52-acre woodlot.

After completing the kitchen cabinets, Moser turned out his first piece of furniture in his new shop, a Shaker round stand made out of walnut. He then received his first commission, building a kitchen cupboard for a neighbor, and other commissions soon followed on the strength of word-of-mouth recommendations. In April 1973 he placed his first advertisement in *Down East* magazine, which marked the formal launch of Thos. Moser.

FIRST EMPLOYEE HIRED: 1974

Moser's early designs drew heavily on such traditional forms as Shaker, Queen Anne, and Pennsylvania Dutch. He used some student help, including his four sons, but it was not until 1974 that he hired his first employee, a man named Ed Boyker, a self-taught carpenter who had spent many years building interiors for wealthy area mill owners. At this stage the company was not yet turning a profit. Moser and his wife would exhaust their savings and sell their house before achieving profitability in the fourth year of business.

Moser had initially considered limiting himself to the use of hand tools as part of his aesthetic, but quickly abandoned the idea. While he had a love for the craft of woodworking, he started Thos. Moser as a way to support his family and to maintain a middle-class lifestyle. "I never had any intention of being a craftsman selling products in a tent on the grass," he told *New England Business* in 1985. While he made sure that the pieces his shop turned out were predominantly handmade, he did not hesitate to use machinery to complete the more mundane tasks as a way to improve profitability.

Some of his workers took a more idealistic approach, however. A number were recent college graduates in search of an alternative lifestyle, while others had left Wall Street careers for a simpler life in the country. Moser thus had to contend with workers who objected to his replacing the workshop's incandescent bulbs with fluorescent lights, which he finally had to install in the dead of night. One worker threatened to quit if Moser allowed an air compressor in the shop.

PURSUING THE INSTITUTIONAL MARKET

An even more contentious issue arose around 1982. Moser had enjoyed success with catalog sales, but once these reached a plateau he looked to develop sales with contractors and architects who would order scores of items at one time. In the early 1980s the company received its first large commercial contract, supplying furniture to the Atlantic City Public Library for $300,000. To further pursue the institutional market, Moser would need volume production, a goal he planned to meet by purchasing new machines and hiring unskilled workers to turn out the company's standard pieces.

KEY DATES

■

1972: Thomas Moser establishes his woodworking shop in a former Grange hall in New Gloucester, Maine.
1974: Moser hires his first employee.
1987: New workshop opens in Auburn, Maine.
1993: New York City showroom opens.
2009: Recession leads to layoffs.

His regular workers were so upset that they held a meeting without his presence to express their displeasure. Moser eventually placated the complainers by building a separate facility where the new workers could produce the standard pieces. In a matter of three years, more than a third of Thos. Moser's sales were from contractors and architects, but he also lost some workers who opposed the direction the company was taking.

EMPHASIS ON DESIGN

To keep pace with strong demand, Thos. Moser built a new 40,000-square-foot workshop in an industrial park in Auburn, Maine, in 1987. By the end of the decade, in which sales increased 33 percent on average each year, the company was generating sales of $5.5 million. Sales were flat to start the 1990s due to a recession, but demand soon rebounded. In the meantime, Moser began looking for new sources of inspiration. He developed a New Century Series that drew on the Arts and Crafts movement of the late 1800s.

Much of Thos. Moser's sales were generated from showrooms that were opened in Portland, Maine; Alexandria, Virginia; Philadelphia; and San Francisco. In 1993 the company added a presence in New York City, opening a showroom on the Upper East Side of Manhattan. A showroom in Los Angeles then followed and the Auburn shop was expanded. By 1993 Moser was ready to devote much of the time spent managing the enterprise to designing furniture instead. To achieve that end, he formed five teams with about 10 employees in each and allowed them to make more production decisions. A former Digital Equipment Corporation executive, Harry Fraser, was brought in to serve as chief executive officer. In September 1995 Moser was able to turn all of his attention to design.

After pursuing other ventures, Moser's sons returned home to become more involved in the family business, and Moser wanted to grow the business to provide them with a future. Annual sales were in the $7 million range by 1995 when Fraser and the Moser family took steps that they hoped would increase sales to $30 million in seven to 10 years. The company hoped to increase the number of catalogs in circulation from 35,000 copies sold for $10 each to 135,000 catalogs distributed for free or at a nominal charge. The company's revamped Web site would also distribute catalogs, and merchandise would later become available for purchase online. Thos. Moser also sought to grow contract sales to libraries and other institutions.

SURVIVING TOUGH TIMES

The 21st century brought a number of other changes to Thos. Moser. Moser continued to travel around the world in search of inspiration, but increasingly his son David became the company's chief designer. None of the products was of his design at the start of the decade, but by 2006 about 40 percent of the pieces were designed by David Moser. Many of the items were developed in a prototype shop where David Moser and three employees tried out new materials and techniques, the best of which would make their way into the Thos. Moser catalog. Although then in his 70s, Thomas Moser also continued to pursue his craft and expressed no interest in retirement.

The American furniture industry in the meantime was hard hit by foreign competition, especially from China, and in the early years of the new century more than 120,000 furniture jobs, or about one-third of the total workforce, were lost. Because of the quality of its craftsmanship and the luxury market to which it catered, Thos. Moser was not impacted. However, the company was not able to withstand the economic problems caused by the collapse of the housing market and a credit crunch that accompanied a recession toward the end of the decade. Early in 2009, faced with low orders, Thos. Moser was forced to cut employment and restructure its management team. Nevertheless, the company remained well positioned to enjoy long-term success, and the Moser family appeared committed to running the business through at least the third generation.

Ed Dinger

PRINCIPAL COMPETITORS

Bernhardt Furniture Company; Drexel Heritage Furniture Industries; L. & J.G. Stickley, Inc.

FURTHER READING

Goad, Meredith, "A Style No Longer All His Own," *Maine Sunday Telegram*, March 25, 2007, p. A1.

Harkavy, Jerry, "Sitting Comfy on a Business," *Bangor Daily News*, November 27, 1993.

LaFlamme, Mark, "Recession Hurts Moser," *Lewiston (ME) Sun Journal*, January 9, 2009, p. A1.

Moser, Thomas, *Thos. Moser Artistry in Wood*, Portland, ME: Blue Design, 2002.

Simon, Jane, "Hands vs. Machines," *New England Business*, May 6, 1985, p. 77.

Tieto Oyj

PO Box 38, Aku Korhosen tie 2-6
Helsinki, FI-00441
Finland
Telephone: (+358 0207) 20 10
Fax: (+358 0207) 26 88 98
Web site: http://www.tieto.com

Public Company
Incorporated: 1999 as TietoEnator Oy
Employees: 16,880
Sales: EUR 1.71 billion ($2.31 billion) (2009)
Stock Exchanges: Helsinki Stockholm NASDAQ
Ticker Symbol: Tiei V
NAICS: 518210 Data Processing, Hosting, and Related
    Services; 541513 Computer Facilities Management
    Services

■ ■ ■

Tieto Oyj is a leading provider of information technology (IT) services to the Scandinavian and Northern European markets. Tieto focuses on three major areas of operations: IT Services, including project-specific services, application service management, infrastructure services, and industry-wide services and applications; Research and Development (R&D) Services; and Digital Transformation and Consulting Services. Application management accounts for more than 30 percent of group revenues. Project services, including R&D services, add another 30 percent to sales, and information and communication technology (ICT) infra-

structure accounts for approximately 20 percent of the group's revenues.

In 2009 Tieto's revenues topped EUR 1.7 billion ($2.3 billion). Finland remains Tieto's largest market, accounting for 48 percent of its revenues, followed by Sweden at 25 percent. The other Scandinavian markets, as well as the United Kingdom and Germany, are also major markets for the company. Tieto has also been expanding beyond Northern Europe, building up a strong presence in Russia and other European markets, as well as sales in North America and India, China, and other Asian markets. In 2010 the company counted nearly 17,000 employees worldwide. Tieto's shares are traded on the Helsinki, Stockholm, and NASDAQ stock exchanges. Hannu Syrjaelae is the company's CEO and president.

ORIGINS IN DATA PROCESSING: 1968

Tieto's origins can be traced to the very beginning of Finland's IT services market, with the creation by the Union Bank of Finland in 1968 of a subsidiary providing in-house data-processing services. Called Tietotehdas, the company originally operated from Union Bank's computer center, working with the bank's mainframe computer system. Tietotehdas quickly expanded to providing other information technology services for the bank, and then began supplying IT services to a number of Finnish forestry companies as well.

Tietotehdas soon became a public company, with headquarters in Espoo, and remained the only IT

COMPANY PERSPECTIVES

We specialize in areas where we have the deepest understanding of our customers' businesses and needs. Our superior customer centricity and expertise in digital services set us apart from our competitors. We focus on serving large and medium-sized organizations in our main markets—Northern Europe, Germany and Russia. In telecom, forest, oil and gas as well as digital services, we serve our customers globally. We work hand in hand with many of the world's leading companies and organizations and grow in step with them.

services company listed on the Helsinki stock exchange through most of the 1980s. The company continued to expand its range of customers and by the end of the 1970s encompassed a wide variety of industries. Acquisitions played an important role in the company's early growth, starting with the purchase in 1976 of Finnsystems Oy, a developer of software and systems for IBM mainframe computers. Another significant acquisition came in 1984 with the purchase of Tietojyvä Oy. This company focused on developing data-processing systems and software for public administrations, including the Finnish Parliament, as well as the print and publishing industry.

By the middle of the 1980s Tietotehdas had become Finland's leading IT services company. In 1985 the company adopted a new strategy calling for the group to expand into international markets before 1990. This goal was quickly accomplished with two new acquisitions in 1987. The first of these included the data processing and computer center operations of future cell phone giant Nokia, which had itself expanded strongly outside of Finland during the decade. Tietotehdas added its own international operations soon after when it acquired nearly 55 percent of leading Swedish IT services group Mods Datema. With this acquisition Tietotehdas not only nearly doubled its total sales, to FIM 450 million (approximately $210 million), but also established the company as the leading IT services company in Scandinavia, and one of the largest in all of Europe.

ACQUISITIONS TARGET EXPANSION IN FINLAND

Tietotehdas completed a string of acquisitions through the end of the 1980s and into the 1990s. These

purchases targeted the company's expansion in its core Finnish market and included ASW Systems in 1988, Tietoässä and Finnish Data Power in 1990, Carelcomp and Datacity Information Systems in 1993, and Financial Software Technology and Suunnittelu ja laskenta in 1994.

The company changed its name to TT Tieto in 1995. Also that year, the company launched the first of a number of partnerships, starting with government-owned VTKK Group. As a result, the Finnish government acquired a stake in Tieto. Other partners included PT Finland and Unic Oy, the latter helping the company build its range of financial sector and personnel management technologies and services. In 1996 the government sold its stake in TT Tieto to PT Finland. At the same time, Tieto acquired that company's Avancer Oy, adding expertise in both the telecommunications and logistics industries.

In 1998 TT Tieto changed its name again, to Tieto. The company had completed several new acquisitions by this time, once again targeting international growth. These included Axo Systems and Huld & Lillevik, both in Norway, in 1996 and 1997, respectively. Tieto also made its first move beyond the Scandinavian market, acquiring Latvia's Konts SIA in 1998. The company then turned to Sweden, where it acquired Entra Data AB in 1999.

ENATOR ACQUIRED: 1999

International expansion had become a company imperative in the late 1990s. This strategy was driven in large part by the rapid international growth of its core customers, including Nokia and other industrial, banking, and financial sector customers. As these companies expanded their own geographic bases, Tieto found itself in competition not only with its Scandinavian rivals but also with the rapidly growing IT services groups in Europe. Many of the largest U.S. groups, such as Andersen Consulting and Electronic Data Systems, had also made a strong entry into the new market at this time.

Tieto was forced to seek out a partner in order to expand the scale of its operations, as well as to strengthen its international presence. As the company's then CEO Matti Lehti told the *Financial Times*: "Our market place is integrating and customers are seeking pan-European suppliers on IT consulting, systems development, and maintenance."

This led Tieto to begin discussing a possible merger with its main Swedish rival, Enator, as early as 1997. Enator was the younger group, having been formed in 1995 through the merger of three IT services subsidiaries of Sweden's Celsius AB. The new company became known as Celsius Information Systems (CIS). Celsius had begun building up its IT services wing in the early 1990s, buying the FFV group, including its IT services subsidiary Telub, in 1991. Other acquisitions included Dotcom, Miltest, Försvarsmedia, Systecon, and Vexa.

After CIS merged with another Swedish IT services group, Adedata, in 1996, it changed its name to Enator. Enator was spun off from Celsius as a public company soon after, listing on the Stockholm stock exchange. The company then boosted its consulting services business, buying up majority control of Programmera in 1998. Enator then focused on building its international presence, buying Kvatro Telecom in Norway and SoftProjekt in Germany in 1998, and then NetDesign in Denmark in 1999.

OUTSOURCING TREND: 2001

Tieto's takeover of Enator cost the company EUR 920 million. The newly enlarged company took on a new name, TietoEnator, and became the leading IT services company in the Scandinavian region, with more than 10,000 employees. While the company remained small in comparison with its U.S. rivals, it had gained sufficient scale to compete against the European IT services groups, including Cap Gemini, Atos, and Sema.

TietoEnator's focus at the dawn of the 21st century involved consolidating its position as a regional leader, while also extending its reach beyond Scandinavia to include other Northern European markets. This strategy led to a new flurry of acquisitions, including MAS GmbH, a German provider of IT services largely for the forestry market, in 2000. The company added the health-care market to its range that year, buying European Medical Solutions, based in Norway.

TietoEnator added several new acquisitions in Finland, including Softema, Tietokesko, and Parcomp.

The company also benefited from a new trend toward outsourcing in the IT sector, as corporations that previously had maintained their own IT divisions began to turn to third parties. TietoEnator picked up several new operations as a result, including Rautaruukki's information systems unit, the product development division of Nokia Networks, and Sampo Group's processing and network business. Other outsourcing contracts followed, including with Ericsson in 2002 and TeliaSonera in 2003.

TietoEnator's regional expansion increasingly positioned the company as a growing presence in the Northern European market. In 2002 the company added operations in Lithuania, through Lietuvos Telekomas. The company reinforced its operations in Germany, buying Sykora there, which also added operations in the Czech Republic. In 2003 the company bought another German company, Inveos AG, which was focused on the banking and insurance markets. The group's revenues at the end of that year approached EUR 1.4 billion.

INTERNATIONAL EXPANSION

As TietoEnator's major customers moved beyond the European market, TietoEnator followed, adding small operations in the United States and China. The company also leveraged its long-standing expertise, notably in the forestry industry, to extend its operations into Russia and a number of Asian markets. While the company achieved strong organic growth through the middle of the decade, it also completed a number of acquisitions in order to build up selected areas of its operations.

For example, in 2004 the company completed seven smaller acquisitions, boosting its health-care component. These included an entry into the Netherlands through the purchase of Sweden's InformationsLogik. TietoEnator also added its first operations in India through the purchase of Germany's ITB AG, which operated a research and development division there.

The £46.6 million ($75 million) acquisition of AttentiV allowed TietoEnator to enter the banking sector in the United Kingdom in 2005. The company also strengthened its Baltic region presence that year through the purchase of Alise in Latvia. The company reinforced its presence in Germany in the second half of the decade, buying Waldbrenner, Topas Consulting, and Cymed, as well as taking over the communications research and development unit of Siemens, in 2006.

This last acquisition fit in with TietoEnator's increasing focus on a select number of IT services markets, including the booming telecommunications sector. This industry represented the company's single-largest business area, accounting for one-third of the group's revenues. In order to broaden its range of services to this sector, the company added several new acquisitions, including Sofnetix, a wireless and mobile systems software developer in Finland, and RTS Networks in Poland. Additionally, the outsourcing contracts for Ericsson's design center and parts of the Finnish research and development units for Nokia Siemens Networks were both added in 2007.

TietoEnator stepped up its Asian presence in 2007, paying $21 million to acquire Fortuna Technologies, a developer of mobile telephone "turnkey" software (software taking charge of all telephone functions) for the Asian and European markets. This and other acquisitions, including Abaris in Sweden, helped maintain the company's steady revenue growth, as sales neared EUR 1.8 billion for the year.

BECOMING TIETO IN 2009

The growth in revenues had for the most part been matched by strong profits. In 2006 the company posted a pretax profit of nearly EUR 125 million. However, by the end of 2007 the company's profits crashed, resulting in a year-end loss and a plunging share price. As a consequence, CEO Matti Lehti was replaced by Hannu Syrjaelae, who was appointed to take over the leadership of the company in December 2007.

The company's financial difficulties soon caught the eye of investment group Nordic Capital, however. In March 2008 Nordic, through its Cirdon Services unit, launched a takeover bid for TietoEnator. This bid, for EUR 1.1 billion, was promptly rejected by TietoEnator and its major shareholders as too low.

The takeover attempt nevertheless encouraged TietoEnator to draft a restructuring program designed to cut costs. The company adapted its operating strategy at the same time, setting into place a more global orientation. As part of this effort, the company expected to reduce its reliance on the Finnish and Scandinavian markets, which continued to represent nearly 75 percent of its total revenues. The company also sought to increase the numbers of its "offshore resources," that is, its employees and operations outside of Finland. By the end of 2009 the company's foreign workforce represented 30 percent of its total. Also that year, the company shortened its name to Tieto Oyj.

Despite Tieto's increasing emphasis on developing as a truly global business, the Northern European region remained its core market. In keeping with this, the company announced its intention to continue to expand its presence in this market, targeting the number one

position by 2011. This led the company to invest EUR 18 million to build the first phase of a projected 6,000-square-meter data center in its Espoo home in 2010.

Tieto saw its revenues slip back amid the global recession, to EUR 1.7 billion ($2.3 billion) in 2009. The company's cost-cutting effort had nevertheless proved successful, allowing the company to post pretax profits of EUR 70 million. The difficult economic climate provided new opportunities for expansion. The company acquired part of Affecto, based in Latvia, in 2009. At the beginning of 2010 the company announced plans to open two new offices, in Hangzhou, China, and in Bangalore, India. In March of that year the company expanded its operations in Russia as well, buying T&T Telecom. Tieto expected to remain among the leaders in the European and the global IT services market.

M. L. Cohen

PRINCIPAL SUBSIDIARIES

Abaris AB (Sweden); Banxolutions (UK) Ltd.; Baysoft Technologies s.r.l. (Italy); JLLC Tieto (Belarus); Teledynamics B.V. (Netherlands); Tieto Services Oy; Tieto Sweden AB; Tieto Sweden Health Care & Welfare AB; Tieto UK Ltd.; TietoEnator AttentiV Systems Ltd. (UK); TietoEnator Energy Inc. (USA); TietoEnator Finance Partner AB (Sweden); TietoEnator Financial Solutions B.V. (Netherlands); TietoEnator Software Technologies Pvt. Ltd. (India).

PRINCIPAL DIVISIONS

IT Services; Research and Development Services; Digital Transformation and Consulting Services.

PRINCIPAL OPERATING UNITS

Finland; Sweden; International.

PRINCIPAL COMPETITORS

Atos Origin SA; Cap Gemini SA; KPMG Deutsche Treuhand-Gesellschaft Aktiengesellschaft; PwC Deutsche Revision AG.

FURTHER READING

Burt, Tim, "Tieto to Take Over Enator in EUR 920m Deal," *Financial Times*, March 4, 1999, p. 33.

"Finnish Tieto Sells French Unit to Devoteam," *M&A Navigator*, April 26, 2010.

Morarjee, Rachel, "TietoEnator Surges after Cidron Bid," *Financial Times*, March 22, 2008, p. 33.

"Russia's T&T Telecom Acquired by Tieto," *Nordic Business Report*, March 1, 2010.

"Tieto Corporation Presents Its Renewed Business Strategy," *Nordic Business Report*, December 9, 2008.

"Tieto Powers Delovoy Peterburg's Internet Portal," *Telecompa-*

per Europe, April 29, 2010.

"Tieto to Expand in China, India," *Nordic Business Report*, February 3, 2010.

"Tieto to Spend EUR 18m on Building Data Centre in Finnish Espoo," *Nordic Business Report*, January 25, 2010.

"TietoEnator Corporation Launches New Corporate Brand," *Nordic Business Report*, December 1, 2008.

Trader Joe's Company

—————————■—————————

800 South Shamrock Avenue
Monrovia, California 91016
U.S.A.
Telephone: (626) 599-3700
Fax: (626) 301-4431
Web site: http://www.traderjoes.com

Private Company
Incorporated: 1967
Employees: 16,000
Sales: $8 billion (2009 est.)
NAICS: 445110 Supermarkets and Other Grocery
(Except Convenience) Stores; 445310 Beer, Wine,
and Liquor Stores

■■■

Trader Joe's Company operates a chain of unique grocery stores that have been described as equal parts discount warehouse club, natural foods store, specialty grocer, and neighborhood store. The company's resourceful buying practices allow the Trader Joe's stores to offer an ever-changing inventory of about 2,000 unusual food items, wine, and other products. About 98 percent of the product assortment is food, much of it natural, cruelty-free, and made without artificial ingredients.

The business has grown steadily since its inception, through innovation and sharp management techniques. The company was purchased in 1979 by the Theo Albrecht Trust, which also owns European supermarket discounter Aldi Nord. (Brother Karl Albrecht's Trust

owns Aldi Sud, whose subsidiaries include the Aldi stores in the United States.) In 2010 there were over 340 Trader Joe's stores operating in 28 states and Washington, D.C.

ORIGINS: 1958–67

Although Trader Joe's was not officially founded until 1967, its origins can be traced to the Pronto Markets. This chain of convenience stores was started by a subsidiary of the Rexall Drug Co. in 1958. The venture reflected the intent of Rexall, an operator of a chain of drugstores, to get in on the burgeoning convenience and corner food-stand market. Rexall appointed Joe Coulombe, age 26, to head the new division, and for tax purposes, put it in his name. During the late 1950s and early 1960s Coulombe built Pronto into a chain with a considerable presence in Orange County, California. He did this by focusing on specialty and closeout items, including health and beauty aids and ice cream.

In 1962 Rexall decided to get out of the convenience store industry. Coulombe bought Pronto and its four stores, selling part of the company to Pronto employees. In the mid-1960s Southland Corp.'s successful 7-Eleven chain was bearing down on smaller competitors such as Pronto and was planning an aggressive expansion in Pronto's region. One of Coulombe's largest suppliers then told Coulombe he was selling his company to 7-Eleven. Coulombe, who had become dissatisfied with the convenience-store format, started looking for something different.

Coulombe's research found two trends he developed into a new marketing scheme. First of all, consumers

COMPANY PERSPECTIVES

■

We buy direct from suppliers whenever possible, we bargain hard to get the best price, and then pass the savings on to you. If an item doesn't pull its weight in our stores, it goes away to gangway for something else. We buy in volume and contract early to get the best prices. Most grocers charge their suppliers fees for putting an item on the shelf. This results in higher prices … so we don't do it. We keep our costs low—because every penny we save is a penny you save. It's not complicated. We just focus on what matters—great food + great prices = Value.

were becoming increasingly educated and sophisticated, and were expecting more from their shopping experiences. Secondly, global air travel would become more affordable with the launch of the Boeing 747 jumbo jet. Coulombe decided to develop a food store at which well educated, but not necessarily well paid, people could buy foods that would impress themselves and their friends. Coulombe opened the first Trader Joe's tropical-themed outlet in South Pasadena in 1967.

At 7,500 square feet, it was three times the size of a Pronto store. Coulombe's initial concept was to reposition Pronto as an upscale food market/liquor store located near educational centers. That decision was influenced by the health of the liquor business at the time. The first store offered an extensive assortment of liquor, including 100 brands of Scotch whisky and all 17 types of California wine available at that time.

DEFINING THE TRADER JOE'S STORE: 1970–79

In 1971 the aerospace industry collapsed and the local Orange County economy plunged. The recession squarely hit Coulombe's targeted customers, who were no longer throwing many parties. To overcome the slowdown, Coulombe added cheese, nuts, and dried fruits, fashioning a sort of combination health food shop and liquor store. He ordered unique food items from different parts of the world to attract customers, and he labeled the foods with sprightly, entertaining labels such as "Kiwi from Paradise Juice," and "Look Ma! No Refined Sugar!" The stores experimented with all types of health foods and beverages, and generally avoided marketing mammoths such as Coca-Cola and Budweiser.

Among Coulombe's most successful tactics in the early 1970s was his journal *Fearless Flyer* (originally called *Trader Joe's Insider Report*), which aroused environmental awareness through stinging commentary on conservation issues. Distributed to the general public, the *Fearless Flyer* brought hordes of environmentally conscious customers into Trader Joe's, which began stocking increasing amounts of vitamins, biodegradable products, and health foods.

Focused on that key market, Trader Joe's boosted sales and profits steadily until 1976. In that year, California legislators deregulated the supermarket industry. The change boded poorly for Trader Joe's liquor segment. Since the Great Depression the state had effectively subsidized the sale of milk and liquor by markets. Many smaller convenience stores had come to rely on milk and liquor sales, even to the point of advertising other items below cost just to get customers into their shops. Deregulation quashed that practice, and many mom-and-pop stores failed.

As the giant supermarkets flexed their muscles in the newly deregulated grocery industry, Trader Joe's quickly adapted to the new environment. Coulombe dropped his grocery supplier, cut the number of products, and outsourced distribution. In 1979 Trader Joe's, and its 23 stores, was purchased by the family trust of German billionaire Theo Albrecht, who also owned part of the immensely successful Aldi discount stores in Europe. Albrecht retained Coulombe as CEO.

PERFECTING THE TRADER JOE'S STRATEGY: 1980–89

During the early and mid-1980s Coulombe continued to perfect Trader Joe's inventory and market position and to slowly grow the California chain. He gradually moved away from the intense environmental rhetoric in the *Fearless Flyer*, for example, and evolved with his core market. That meant positioning the Trader Joe's stores to appeal to the emerging upwardly mobile, or "yuppie" crowd, which was exhibiting increasingly sophisticated shopping patterns. Unique beers and wines remained a major attraction, but Coulombe also began bringing in more perishables and unique dry food items. The *Fearless Flyer* continued to be a primary marketing tool, but it was toned down and used to provide entertaining and useful information such as health tips and new store items.

Furthermore, Coulombe bolstered the attraction of his inventory by keeping a sharp focus on value and targeting the well educated but less-than-affluent consumer. Wines and other alcoholic beverages were often displayed in cases and most stores had only a few

```
┌─────────────────────────────────────────┐
│                                         │
│            KEY DATES                    │
│            ───────■───────              │
│                                         │
│  1958:  Joe Coulombe selected to manage the Pronto │
│         Market chain in Los Angeles, California.   │
│  1967:  First Trader Joe's store opens in South    │
│         Pasadena, California.                      │
│  1979:  The Theo Albrecht Trust buys the Trader    │
│         Joe's chain.                               │
│  1993:  The company expands outside California and │
│         opens stores in Phoenix, growing the Trader│
│         Joe's chain to 59 stores.                  │
│  1996:  East Coast expansion is launched; Trader Joe's│
│         Web site debuts.                           │
│  2000:  Trader Joe's headquarters moves to Monrovia,│
│         California.                                │
│  2006:  Company opens first stores in New York City│
│         and in the Southeast.                      │
│                                         │
└─────────────────────────────────────────┘
```

rows of shelving. While the average store size increased during the 1970s and 1980s, the average Trader Joe's store was still only about 6,000 square feet by the late 1980s, about half the size of the typical Los Angeles supermarket.

Although his strategy of maintaining a continually changing inventory may have seemed like an expensive and daunting proposition to larger markets and super-stores, Coulombe managed to keep prices low. Trader Joe's efficiency was partly the result of its cash policy. The company paid cash for all purchases and funded growth internally as well as through the deep-pocketed Albrecht family. Innovative, low-cost advertising was a major money saver as well. Trader Joe's cost-saving private label constituted about 80 percent of the company's product offering.

Also minimizing expenses was the company's unusual purchasing program. The company's own branded items, such as fresh salsa and unique pastas, for example, were supplied by a constantly changing set of small, independent contractors. The foods they supplied were often discontinued items that Trader Joe's bought at a discount. Those contractors and other suppliers were found by Trader Joe's own buying team, which traveled throughout America and Europe in search of interesting items and bargains.

The result of Coulombe's innovative inventory and pricing strategy was huge profit margins. In 1989 Trader Joe's chalked up an estimated $150 million in sales. That figure reflected gross sales of more than $800 per square foot, extremely high compared to grocery

industry norms. Furthermore, because its stores were usually located on non-prime real estate, the company's fixed overhead was relatively low.

By the late 1980s the nearly 60-year-old Coulombe had built Trader Joe's into a chain of 30 outlets, most of which were in the Los Angeles and San Diego regions. In 1988 Coulombe selected 55-year-old John V. Shields to succeed him at the helm. Shields, who had known Coulombe since Stanford University, had been a senior vice president at Macy's and then moved to Mervyn's. Following a short transition period, Coulombe stepped aside and Albrecht welcomed Shields as the new chief.

GROWING THE TRADER JOE'S BUSINESS: 1990–96

Shields maintained much of Trader Joe's unique product mix and marketing strategy, as evidenced by a transaction conducted shortly after he took control of the chain. In a rapid-fire deal, Trader Joe's wrote a check for $1 million worth of wine from the Napa Valley Mihaly winery. The winery had just been purchased by a group of Japanese investors who planned to make sake, or rice wine, at the winery. They did not need the inventory of wines that were popular in the United States, so Trader Joe's moved quickly in a deal that brought it 240,000 bottles of wine at a bargain price. A similar deal about the same time brought 3,000 cases of a mid-level char-donnay to Trader Joe's. Trader Joe's was selling the bottles for $2.99 while nearby liquor stores were charging $8.50.

Deals such as these kept the company's cash registers ringing into the early 1990s. Despite an economic downturn and another depression in the California defense industry, the Trader Joe's stores continued to perform. Inventory was broadened to include a variety of frozen foods, candies, bakery items, juices, and even dog food. Moreover, Trader Joe's was among the largest retailers of maple syrup and wild rice, among other distinctions. Meanwhile, Shields was working to expand the enterprise. By late 1991 there were 43 Trader Joe's operating in California, including several new stores in the San Francisco Bay Area. Total sales for the company were topping $250 million annually, and the average size of the outlets had grown to about 7,500 square feet.

Shields stepped up Trader Joe's expansion activity in 1992 and 1993, moving outside of California into Phoenix and growing the chain to 59 stores by late 1993. By that time, the chain was generating revenues of about $500 million annually (about 40 percent of which came from imported goods). Trader Joe's inventory had swelled to include about 1,500 items in each store, including many goods from former Soviet-bloc countries such as Hungary and the Czech Republic. The company was also boosting purchases from Caribbean nations as a result of new trade agreements signed by the United States in that region. Its major advertising tools continued to be its *Fearless Flyer* and word of mouth, but by the mid-1990s it was also promoting through radio spots and ads in local media.

Trader Joe's grew to about 65 outlets in 1994 and grossed about $600 million, representing average annual per-store sales growth of about 10 percent over the past five years. The company established stores in the Pacific Northwest late in 1994 and opened several more outlets throughout Oregon and Washington within a few years. By mid-1995 Trader Joe's was operating 72 outlets and was generating an estimated $1,000 per square foot.

EAST COAST EXPANSION: 1996–2000

In 1996 Trader Joe's began its aggressive East Coast expansion. Shields had identified the Northeast corridor, the 500 miles between Boston and Washington, D.C., as prime territory. With more colleges and universities than any other area in the country, its population perfectly matched Trader Joe's target shoppers. In order to maintain the company's culture in the jump across country, Shields sent 25 employees to the East Coast. The company eventually established Trader Joe's East, a subsidiary and eastern operations center in Boston. Heading those operations was Doug Rauch, who had joined Trader Joe's in 1977 and was named president in 1994. The first two stores opened in Boston in 1997 and within three years there were over 20 stores along the corridor.

Evidence of the growing popularity of Trader Joe's was the circulation of the *Fearless Flyer,* which had grown to 800,000 before rising delivery costs forced the company to begin distributing it in the stores rather than through the mail. Trader Joe's quickly moved to leap over the *Fearless Flyer* postage barrier, however. In 1996 the company went online, offering customers state-specific *Fearless Flyers* and other useful information via the Internet, including detailed product listings, special announcements, recipes, contact information, and directional maps to stores.

Trader Joe's made another savvy technology investment in 1997, which enabled it to quickly cut costs and position itself for improved communications and data sharing. The company invested in a satellite network that enabled the company to get a volume discount on credit transaction costs for all of its stores on the network, a huge savings overall. The network was also capable of carrying other kinds of data for the company, including sales data, product availability and spoilage information, delivery schedules, personnel and payroll data, and e-mail messages.

In 1998 Trader Joe's moved to expand its specialty food business and began going upscale by regularly stocking imported items at higher price points. New imported items include ceramic ware and crystal ware from Italy and Germany. Previously, the company had offered such items on a limited basis, as two-week specials. The specials proved to be so popular with customers (many of whom kept asking store employees about the next special) that it made sense to feature them as regular items. Overall, imported selections in the nonfood, general merchandise category at Trader Joe's doubled from the previous year.

NEW LEADERSHIP: 2001

In 2000 the company moved its headquarters to a much larger site in Monrovia, California. That same year, it opened its first stores in the Midwest, in the Chicago suburbs. John Shields retired in 2001. Under his watch the company had grown from about 30 stores to over 100 units, with sales increasing from $132 million to around $1 billion. His successor was Dan Bane, hired by Trader Joe's in 1998 to be president of the company's western operations. Bane was named chairman and CEO in July 2001. Among the first things Bane did was to introduce price scanners to the stores, followed by Charles Shaw wines. Trader Joe's sold the wine for $1.99 a bottle and it quickly became known as "Two Buck Chuck." It proved to be one of the company's best sellers ever.

Trader Joe's outlets were averaging 8,000 to 12,000 square feet, which was about double the size of some of the original Trader Joe's stores. Despite the still relatively small size of its stores, the company continued to have far higher sales per square foot than the average grocery store in the United States. By 2002 more than 160 stores in 15 states made up the Trader Joe's chain, with sales reaching $1.67 billion.

The company's popularity often reached cultlike proportions. Potential customers lobbied Trader Joe's executives as well as local politicians and developers to bring a store to a community. When a new store opened, the lines were often long and the shoppers always enthusiastic. Industry analysts pointed to several factors for this, including a carefully selected customer demographic; well-trained and well-compensated employees; low prices for unusual and tasty items; its small size; its apparent authenticity; and the quirky humor evident throughout the store.

A major factor in Trader Joe's ability to set itself apart from other grocery chains was its focus on private labels. Of the items it carried, 80 percent were private labels, compared to 16 to 20 percent for the industry as a whole. The company's humor was evident in many of the label names as well. In addition to Trader Joe items, shoppers looked for Trader Giotto for Italian items, Trader Ming for Asian items, and Trader Juan for Latin and Mexican food. There was also the Trader Darwin brand of vitamins and supplements, for "the survival of the fittest."

These labels helped Trader Joe's maintain high quality and offer premium ingredients from around the world. For example, in 2001 the company announced it would eliminate all genetically modified ingredients from its private-label items within a year. The label strategy was also a major contributor to the company's low prices. Although some private labels were low-cost versions of national brands, most were from small producers. Buying directly from these vendors enabled Trader Joe's to cut out the middleman.

By 2006 the company was operating over 255 stores. That year it opened its first store in New York City, and the Southeast saw its first Trader Joe's units, in Georgia and North Carolina. *Consumer Reports* ranked Trader Joe's the second-best supermarket in the country (behind Wegman's).

CONTINUED SUCCESS

Following Trader Joe's 40th anniversary, the economy contracted and consumers grew more frugal. By 2009 retailers of all types had slashed inventories. As a result, the number of product choices on grocery shelves grew smaller. Trader Joe's value-driven strategy still appeared to be on target. The company continued to carry from 2,000 to 3,000 items (compared to 20,000 to 40,000 in the typical supermarket). It got rid of its slowest selling items each week, replacing them with other products. It continued to open new stores. The size of some of the new stores, at 12,000 to 15,000 square feet, was larger than the company average. The tropical décor, hand-painted signs, Hawaiian shirts, and store lobster remained constant. Expansion continued to be self-financed without going into debt.

Staff turnover remained low, even as the number of stores grew to over 300. This loyalty was due in large measure to the company's tradition of hiring friendly people, training them well, and paying competitive wages. Both part-time and full-time workers received comprehensive health benefits. The company also provided a company-funded retirement plan.

According to a 2008 article in *Supermarket News* by Elliot Zwiebach, 60 percent of the company's growth came from new openings. Stores open more than one year were growing at about 10 percent annually and accounted for 40 percent of the chain's growth. That growth figure reflected the company's ongoing attentiveness to what its customers wanted.

For example, to help counter obesity and address other health concerns, the Trader Joe's label offered Low Calorie Lemonade, Reduced Guilt Pita Chips with Sea Salt, Multigrain Hamburger Buns, and Organic Ketchup, among other items. In 2010 the company discontinued its sale of farmed salmon and announced that within two years all its seafood purchases would be from sustainable sources.

Trader Joe's had little direct competition. Its business model of gourmet food, wine, and health supplements at value prices in an entertaining environment was unique and well integrated and thus difficult to duplicate. However, some supermarket chains introduced their own premium-quality/low-cost labels or formats. As a result, Trader Joe's increased spending on radio advertising in the first quarter of 2010 to $7.1 million, a jump of 29 percent from the previous year.

Industry analysts and consultants had suggestions for the company. These included supplying more fresh produce; offering Internet shopping and home delivery; expanding to more rural areas; and opening larger stores in more prime locations. It remained to be seen if any of these suggestions would be implemented, but it seemed likely that Trader Joe's would continue to make its decisions as it had been doing successfully for over 40 years, by anticipating where the customer was going and being there ahead of the crowd.

Dave Mote
Updated, Heidi Wrightsman; Ellen D. Wernick

PRINCIPAL COMPETITORS

Fresh & Easy (Tesco); Whole Foods Market.

FURTHER READING

Armstrong, Larry, "Trader Joe's: The Trendy American Cousin," *Businessweek*, April 26, 2004, p. 62.

Blair, Adam, "Trader Joe's Satellite Network Cuts Credit Transaction Costs," *Supermarket News,* September 8, 1997, p. 31.

Gustafson, Mary, "Trader Joe's Remarkable Journey," *Private Label Buyer*, November 1, 2008, pp. 42–46.

Lewis, Len, *The Trader Joe's Adventure: Turning a Unique Approach to Business into a Retail and Cultural Phenomenon,* Chicago: Dearborn Trade Publishing, 2005.

Mallinger, Mark, and Gerry Rossy, "The Trader Joe's Experience: The Impact of Corporate Culture on Business Strategy," *Graziadio Business Report* (Pepperdine University), Volume 10, Issue 2, 2007.

Speizer, Irwin, "Shopper's Special," *Workforce Management*, September 2004, pp. 51–54.

Thayer, Warren, "Trader Joe's Is Not Your 'Average Joe!,'" *Private Label Buyer*, June 1, 2002.

"Trader Joe's Case Study: Retaining a Niche Position in Low-Cost, High Quality Food Retail," *DataMonitor*, October 2008.

Zwiebach, Elliot, "Ship Shape," *Supermarket News*, June 30, 2008, pp. 16–23.

———, "Trader Joe's Sails through Shifting Fortunes," *Supermarket News*, June 30, 2008, pp. 20–21.

UAB Koncernas MG Baltic

J. Jasinksio str. 16b
Vilnius, LT-01112
Lithuania
Telephone: (+370 85) 2786 219
Fax: (+370 85) 2786 206
Web site: http://www.mgbaltic.lt

Private Company
Incorporated: 1992 as Investicinis Fondas
Employees: 1,000
Sales: LTL 1.61 billion ($636.10 million) (2008)
NAICS: 551112 Offices of Other Holding Companies

■ ■ ■

UAB Koncernas MG Baltic is a leading diversified holding company in Lithuania, with operations throughout the Baltic region. The Vilnius-based company is organized into three primary divisions: MG Baltic Trade; MG Baltic Investment; and MG Valda. The Trade division includes the company's controlling stakes in Stumbras, the leading producer of alcoholic beverages in Lithuania; wholesaler Mineraliniai vandenys, a leading Baltic-region distributor of alcoholic beverages and tobacco products; Tromina, a logistics company; and ethanol producer Biofuture. The Investment division focuses on three primary business areas: retail clothing, through Apranga; construction via Mitnija and SIA MTK; and media, with holdings including UPG Baltic, Alfa Media, Neo-Press, Mediafon, and commercial television broadcaster LNK.

The third division, MG Valda, oversees the group's real estate and property development operations. These include the "Business Triangle" development in downtown Vilnius. MG Baltic is a limited liability company founded in 1992 and controlled by founder and President Darius Mockus. The company reported revenues of LTL 1.6 billion ($636 million) in 2008.

FREEDOM FOR THE FREE MARKET IN 1992

Born in 1965, Darius Mockus received a degree in industrial planning at Vilnius University. Mockus quickly emerged as one of Lithuania's up-and-coming businessmen during the 1980s, leading a cooperative known as Litas. In 1990 Mockus became one of the six founders of the Lithuanian Free Market Institute (LFMI), created in the aftermath of the collapse of the Soviet Union in order to help guide Lithuania to a free market economy. As part of the LFMI, Mockus also helped oversee the founding of Lietuvos birza, the Lithuanian Stock Exchange.

Mockus then took the lead of one of the new exchange's first listed corporations, Investicinis Fondas (IF, for Investment Fund), in 1992. That company, which included more than 12,000 shareholders, took full control of 10 companies, and maintained shareholdings in another 30 companies. IF also owned a number of real estate interests in Vilnius and elsewhere in Lithuania. Among the earliest companies owned or controlled by IF were the former Ukmergë Sewing Factory, the Ðiauliai Furniture Factory, Prienai Aviation, and the Dvareiony ceramic factory.

The Lithuanian government's ongoing privatization program provided IF with much of its early momentum. In 1993 the company purchased a former state-run mineral water and juice shop on Vilnius's Gedimino Avenue, called UAB Mineraliniai vandenys. The company then acquired the Virsupis dairy store, and mineral water company Birstono. These operations were combined into Mineraliniai vandenys, which then began focusing on sales of alcoholic beverages. By 1997 Mineraliniai vandenys held the top spot in the Lithuanian alcoholic beverages retail sector. The company also expanded strongly into the wholesale trade. In the next decade, the company emerged as Lithuania's leading supplier of alcoholic and other beverages, as well as tobacco and other products, serving more than 6,000 customers.

ADDING APRANGA IN 1993

Another significant milestone in the future MG Baltic group's development came in 1993, when IF acquired a controlling stake in Apranga, the former state-owned national clothing trade center. That company had been founded as a clothing and footwear wholesaler in 1945. Apranga entered the retail market in 1992, opening its first store. As part of its privatization, Apranga went public in 1993, with IF emerging as its leading shareholder. Apranga then refocused its business entirely on retail operations.

Through the end of the decade, Apranga began developing a range of retail concepts, starting with the launch of the first Aprangos Salonas in 1994. This store format, later renamed City, catered especially to Lithuania's small but growing business clothing market. In 1997 the company added a second format, the youth-oriented Aprangos Galerija. By the end of that year, Apranga neared 10 stores.

IF continued to invest strongly in developing the retail company. A third format, a haute-couture boutique known as Mados Linija, opened in 1999, expanding the group's retail range into the high end of the market. The following year, Apranga succeeded in securing its first licensed retail brand, opening the first Mango women's clothing store in the Baltic region. In 2001 Apranga acquired the rights to the Hugo Boss brand in Lithuania as well.

IFANTA IN 1999

IF had in the meantime added a number of other businesses to its growing portfolio. In 1994 the company took over Mevasta, an import and retail group that focused on sporting goods, toys, and leisure items. IF's list of retail operations grew to include such names as Sigute, Gastronomija, 10000 smulkmenu, and Zydrasis Saltinelis. In 1995 IF created a new company, Troja, to take over these retail businesses. Also in 1995, IF placed Mineraliniai vandenys under a new holding company, called Minvista. Another extension of IF's operations came in 1998, with the creation of Tetraneta, focused on Lithuania's fast-growing information technology (IT) market.

IF's real estate and development operations took off from the mid-1990s. In 1995 the company placed its properties into a new holding company, called Valda. By 1997 Valda had completed its first major development project, the 4,000-square-meter IKI-Apranga trade center. Valda emerged as a leading property developer at the dawn of the 21st century, completing such projects as the MG Valda office building and the Shakespeare Too hotel in Vilnius.

Darius Mockus had begun taking steps to take full control of the company by this time. The economic crisis in Russia in the late 1990s disrupted the Lithuanian market as well. IF found itself hard hit by the difficult financial climate. Mockus seized the opportunity to buy out the company's shareholders, which numbered about 8,000 at the time. Mockus created a new holding vehicle for this, JSC Ifanta, gaining control of the former IF's operations in 1999.

MG BALTIC IN 2000

The restructuring of the former IF's holdings continued at the beginning of the next decade. Minvista was renamed MG Baltic in 2000. By 2003 MG Baltic had become the name of the group's holding company. Ifanta became MG Baltic Investment, and Valda became MG Valda. The company's other operations, including Mineraliniai vandenys and logistics company Tromina, founded in 2000, were placed under a third operating company, MG Trade.

KEY DATES

■

1992: Darius Mockus leads the creation of Investici-nis Fondas (IF), one of the first companies listed on the Lithuanian Stock Exchange.

1993: IF acquires UAB Mineraliniai vandenys and the Apranga national clothing trade center as part of Lithuania's privatization program.

1995: IF forms the Valda real estate and property development company.

1999: Mockus acquires sole control of the company, which is later restructured and renamed MG Baltic.

2003: Stumbras, the leading alcoholic beverages producer in Lithuania, is acquired.

2006: MG Baltic acquires construction company UAB Mitnija.

2010: Apranga retail store network tops 110 stores in Lithuania, Latvia, and Estonia.

MG Trade completed a major acquisition that same year, when it won its bid to buy a controlling stake in Stumbras AB from the Lithuanian government. Founded in 1906 in Kaunus, Stumbras had grown into Lithuania's largest distillery, producing vodka, brandy, herbal bitters, and liqueurs. In addition to being a major supplier in Lithuania, Stumbras had built up a large international sales operation, reaching the Baltic region, Scandinavia, the United Kingdom, Germany, and other European markets, as well as North America, and the Middle East, among other markets.

MG Baltic moved into the media sector in 2003, buying Lithuania's commercial television broadcaster, LNK TV, from Bonnier Entertainment of Sweden. The company acquired majority control of Lithuanian news agency ELTA that year. MG Baltic's Apranga retail business completed its first international expansion, opening a Hugo Boss store in Riga, Latvia. In 2004 Apranga gained two new Baltic-region retail franchises, Zara and Emporio Armani.

MG Baltic celebrated the completion of the Baltic Center business complex in 2003, and the 16-story Victoria office building in 2004. Both were part of MG Baltic's three-hectare "Verslo trikampio" ("Business Triangle") development at the heart of Vilnius. MG Valda moved into the Latvian property market the following year, launching the development of a residential complex as well as a logistics center in Riga.

ADDING CONSTRUCTION IN 2006

MG Baltic's growing property development arm stimulated the group's interest in the construction sector in the second half of the decade. This led the company to acquire UAB Mitnija in 2006. This company, based in Kaunas, had been founded under the Special Works Trust in 1962, originally supplying electrical and plumbing services to the region's agricultural concerns. By the end of the 1980s, this company had added renovation and small-scale public works projects, before launching a diversification drive at the start of the 1990s. The company was privatized in 1993 as AB Salvyda. In 1995 Salvyda was restructured, with its construction business spun off into a new company, Mitnija.

Mitnija grew rapidly, particularly by targeting projects in Russia, and by 1997 had grown to 2,000 employees. The collapse of the Russian market took Mitnija along, however, and by 1998 the company had shed more than 75 percent of its payroll. Mitnija adopted a new strategy at the dawn of the 21st century, targeting large-scale projects for major corporations. The company extended its operations in 2002 with the purchase of steel construction specialist Vilmeta, although selling its factory in 2005. Mitnija grew even more strongly as part of MG Baltic and by 2008 claimed a 9 percent share of the Lithuanian construction market.

By then, however, the construction industry had become the source of a rare setback for MG Baltic, which at that time claimed a spot among Lithuania's top 10 corporations. In 2007 MG Baltic attempted to enter the Latvian construction sector, buying up a 75 percent stake in Kalnozols Celtnieciba, which was then renamed MTK Construction. That company held the number six position in Latvia, and promised a strong entry into the market. However, the deal quickly turned sour when MG Baltic discovered that Kalnozols had been suffering heavy losses before the sale. By 2009 MTK had been forced into liquidation, while MG Baltic attempted to recover part of its losses from the firm's original owners.

MEDIA OPERATIONS EXPAND IN 2007

While MG Baltic's move into the Latvian construction industry proved a disappointment, the company's other operations continued to perform strongly in the second half of the decade. Mineraliniai vandenys, for example, remained a driving force behind the group's revenue growth, generating approximately one-third of the group's total of LTL 1.4 billion ($550 million) in 2007.

Mineraliniai vandenys launched its own international expansion that year, opening agencies in Estonia, Latvia, and Poland.

MG Baltic's media operations also grew in 2007, with the acquisition of the Lithuanian magazine publishing group, UAB UPG Baltic. That company's portfolio of titles included *Stuff*, *Autocar*, *PC Gamer*, and other computer titles, including *A-Zet*. The company then acquired Mediafon, a provider of call transit and technical support services for television voting and virtual mobile phone operators.

Apranga represented another major growth sector for MG Baltic, as that company expanded its retail operations from just 23 stores in 2003 to more than 100 by 2008. By that time, Apranga had extended its range of retail store brands with a number of new additions, including Max Mara, Bershka, Ermenegildo Zegna, and Pull and Bear. Apranga, which claimed a 35 percent share of the Lithuanian clothing market, had also successfully extended its operations into Latvia and Estonia.

In 2007 Apranga invested nearly $4 million in the opening of its first upscale department store, a 3,000-square-meter site to replace the Grand Duke Palace shopping mall in downtown Vilnius. The following year, Apranga added a new licensed brand, Stradivarius, to its Baltic region operations. The company opened the first of a projected 10 Stradivarius stores in Vilnius that year. By 2009 the company had opened its first Stradivarius store in Estonia.

WEATHERING THE ECONOMIC CRISIS

By this time, MG Baltic had carried out a new restructuring and streamlining of its operations. Under its new organization, MG Baltic targeted six primary markets: Clothing Retail; Trading and Fast Moving Consumer Goods; Media; Construction; Manufacturing; and Real Estate Management and Project Development. As part of this restructuring the company also created MG Baltic Media, which regrouped its various media businesses as a subsidiary of MG Baltic Investment. In 2008 MG Baltic launched preparations to list MG Baltic Media on the Lithuanian Stock Exchange as well.

MG Baltic had begun to feel the effects of the growing global economic crisis by this time. The group's retail operations were on the front line of the sudden drop in consumer spending. As a result, Apranga's revenues dropped by nearly 20 percent from the end of 2008 to the end of 2009. The company nevertheless remained committed to its future growth, carrying out a reshuffling of its locations that resulted in the closure of

13 stores and the opening of 21 new stores in 2009. In 2010, as the recession appeared to ease, Apranga opened a number of new stores, including under the Hugo Boss and Emporio Armani names in Estonia and Latvia.

MG Baltic remained confident despite the harsh economic climate. Founder and owner Darius Mockus also remained committed to the free market ideals upon which he had founded the company nearly 20 years before. As one of Lithuania's largest companies, MG Baltic expected both to survive and to continue to grow from strength to strength in the new decade.

M. L. Cohen

PRINCIPAL SUBSIDIARIES

AB Biofuture; AB Stumbras; APB Apranga; SIA MTK Construction; UAB Alfa Media; UAB Laisvas ir nepriklausomas kanalas; UAB Medianon; UAB MG Baltic Investment; UAB MG Baltic Trade; UAB MG Valda; UAB Mineraliniai vandenys; UAB Mitnija; UAB NeoPress; UAB UPG Baltic; UAB Tromina.

PRINCIPAL DIVISIONS

MG Baltic Trade; MG Baltic Investment; MG Valda.

PRINCIPAL OPERATING UNITS

Apranga; Stumbras; MTK Construction; Mitnija; Tromina.

PRINCIPAL COMPETITORS

AB Invalda; A.S. Ventspils nafta; BLRT Grupp A.S.; Kedainiai; Koncernas Vikonda UAB; LEO LT, AB; Maxima Grupe UAB; UAB Koncernas Achemos grupe; UAB Vakaru medienos grupe.

FURTHER READING

"Apranga Group Opens First 'Stradivarius' Store in Baltic States," *Baltic Course*, April 9, 2008.

"Lithuania's Apranga to Invest up to 4.3 Mln Eur in Vilnius Department Store," *AFX Europe*, March 16, 2007.

"Media Arm of MG Baltic to Hold IPO in Spring, List on Vilnius Stock Exchange," *AFX News*, October 1, 2008.

"MG Baltic Acquires Commercial TV Station LNK from Bonnier Entertainment," *Nordic Business Report*, December 17, 2003.

Pavilenene, Danuta, "Apranga Opened 21 Stores in 2009," *Baltic Course*, January 18, 2010.

————, "MG Baltic Earns Profit of 103 Million Litas in 2007," *Baltic Course*, May 9, 2008.

————, "MG Baltic's Investment into Latvia Was Unsuccess-ful," *Baltic Course*, September 28, 2009.

————, "Turnover of Apranga Decreased by 23% in 2009," *Baltic Course*, January 5, 2010.

Uncas Manufacturing Company

150 Niantic Avenue
Providence, Rhode Island 02907-3118
U.S.A.
Telephone: (401) 944-4700
Fax: (401) 943-2951

Private Company
Incorporated: 1911 as Sorrentino & Lanigan Company
Employees: 225
Sales: $465 million (2009 est.)
NAICS: 339914 Costume Jewelry and Novelty
Manufacturing; Jewelry (Including Precious Metal)
Manufacturing

■ ■ ■

Based in Providence, Rhode Island, Uncas Manufacturing Company is a privately held costume jewelry manufacturer, producing thousands of different items, including rings, earrings, bracelets, pins, charms, hair ornaments, and custom-made gifts. The company works with all metals, precious or not, allowing it to adapt to any trend in the marketplace. While the Uncas name is little known to consumers, the same cannot be said for the company's primary customers, among them the Walt Disney Company, Wal-Mart, J.C. Penney, Sears, and the Home Shopping Network. Uncas covers all channels of distribution, including retail chains, direct-mail catalogs, department stores, television networks, and other jewelry manufacturers. Uncas offers a complete service to its customers. It keeps track of

fashion trends and designs the jewelry, manufactures the items, and ships them to customers.

The company takes a cellular approach to manufacturing, relying on small groups of employees rather than an assembly line. In this way, Uncas is able to quickly complete smaller orders. Such nimbleness has allowed the company to successfully fend off Asian competition and continue to manufacture in the United States. The company's 100,000-square-foot plant in Providence includes a 5,000-square-foot plating area. Uncas also maintains a showroom on Fifth Avenue in New York City and a sales office in Hong Kong. The company is owned and managed by the Corsini family.

COMPANY FOUNDED: 1911

Uncas was founded as a ring manufacturer in 1911 as Sorrentino & Lanigan Company by Vincent Sorrentino and John E. Lanigan. Sorrentino was born in Italy in 1892 and immigrated to the United States at the age of 15 in 1906. He came to Providence in that year and began to learn the plumbing trade as an apprentice. Providence by this time had emerged as the largest jewelry manufacturing center in the United States, and Sorrentino quickly abandoned plumbing to become an apprentice in a jewelry factory.

The company Sorrentino started with Lanigan was a one-room operation that crafted rings on a contract basis. Sorrentino soon bought out his partner and renamed the business Sorrento Ring Company. In 1915 he changed the name again. A fan of James Fenimore Cooper's *The Last of the Mohicans*, Sorrentino drew on the book for inspiration. Uncas was the child of Chin-

KEY DATES

1911: Sorrentino & Lanigan Company is founded to manufacture rings.
1915: Vincent Sorrentino renames business Uncas Manufacturing.
1961: Stanley Sorrentino succeeds father as president.
1991: Longtime employee John M. Corsini buys Uncas.
1998: Uncas acquires Vargas Manufacturing Company.

gachgook, the last chief of the Native American Mohican tribe, and because he was the last pureblooded member, he was regarded as the last of the Mohicans and, thus, the novel's title character.

Uncas Manufacturing enjoyed steady growth under its sole owner. Manufacturing was moved to a larger facility in 1919. Uncas then acquired the former plant of the Rogers Screw Company in 1928. After the three-story facility was renovated, Uncas moved its operations there in March 1929 and then operated the largest ring plant in the United States at that time. It employed some 800 people, mostly producing marcasite rings. Despite the Great Depression that then gripped the nation, Sorrentino was able to keep his people employed. Most of Uncas's business came from F.W. Woolworth's, S.S. Kresge's, and other five-and-dime stores, which carried the company's inexpensive silver wedding bands. During this time Uncas also enjoyed success with rings featuring white stones in Tiffany-style settings.

Sorrentino provided much needed jobs during a time of want, making him especially popular within the Italian American community in Rhode Island. To curry favor with this constituency, newly elected Republican governor William H. Vanderbilt appointed Sorrentino as director of the Department of Social Welfare in 1936. Given that Sorrentino lacked any obvious qualifications for the post, the selection was met with harsh criticism from many Democratic officials. Italian Americans, Republicans and Democrats alike, did not share that view and overwhelmingly praised his selection.

ADAPTING TO THE TIMES

Sorrentino did not give up jewelry for politics, however. He continued to run Uncas and adapt to the times. As five-and-dime stores, which at one time accounted for as much as 60 percent of his business, introduced self

service, rings became a prime target of shoplifters. Uncas turned to other sales channels, a move that would play a key role in the company's longevity. Additionally, Uncas kept tabs on what consumers wanted. During World War II the company produced military rings.

During the postwar baby boom of the 1950s Uncas produced Kiddiegem sterling silver rings and also began offering pins. The company developed scatter pins with which girls adorned their sweaters, including its popular "Turtles on Parade" pins. The company also took advantage of the increasing popularity of television, becoming involved with the *This Is Your Life* program that began airing in 1952. Uncas worked with the show's sponsor, Hazel Bishop, producing "This Is Your Life" lockets that were sent to viewers who mailed in a proof of purchase of a Hazel Bishop product and a nominal shipping fee.

Uncas continued to adapt as the 1960s brought significant cultural changes. Vincent Sorrentino's son, Stanley Sorrentino, took over as president in 1961. His father would pass away in 1976. Instead of military rings, the company then offered peace rings. In the late 1960s Uncas enjoyed its greatest success with the introduction of the mood ring, the backing of which made use of a material that changed colors, ostensibly reflecting the wearer's changing mood. Whether accurate or not, the mood ring was a sensation and Uncas found it difficult to keep up with demand. Also of note during this period, Uncas became a pioneer in the jewelry industry in 1967 when it installed a computer to control inventory. In that same year, it also installed automated barrel plating machines, which increased production by 75 percent.

FOUR-DAY WORKWEEK INTRODUCED: 1982

During the 1970s Uncas began to shift its focus from rings to becoming a full-fledged jewelry manufacturer that was able to meet the complete needs of its customers. Nevertheless, rings remained an important category. In addition to making women's jewelry the company began to cater to men by producing money clips and tie tacks. Uncas would also become a major distributor of Cross pens in the United States.

Uncas switched to a four-day workweek in 1982. The idea first took root in 1978 when a blizzard prevented workers from reaching the plant. Backed up with orders following the storm, the company instituted flexible hours, so that many employees worked from 7:00 a.m. to 5:00 p.m. The hours proved so popular that in September 1982 the company made the longer workday permanent, and in this way the workweek could be shortened to four days. Friday hours were paid at an overtime rate.

Not only were workers happy to have three-day weekends, the company enjoyed ancillary benefits. At the time, the jewelry business was in a slump, and the shorter week allowed Uncas to save money on heating the plant on Fridays. Moreover, the extra time during each workday improved productivity because workers did not have to interrupt their work at the end of the day as often. The four-day workweek also became a recruiting tool in attracting new employees.

Uncas continued to develop its product offerings in the 1980s. In 1983 it acquired Curtman Co., another Providence manufacturer, and began offering cameo jewelry. Uncas forged a relationship with Walt Disney Productions to become the official jewelry maker for Disneyland and Disney World, producing items that featured Disney cartoon characters, in particular Mickey Mouse. Uncas would later become the jewelry supplier to Disney stores in the United States, Europe, and Japan. Uncas also took advantage of other media opportunities in the 1980s. Mid-decade it introduced a jewelry line called "The Colby Look," a tribute to *The Colbys* television program, a spin-off of the hit series *Dynasty*.

JOHN CORSINI BUYS UNCAS: 1991

In 1991 Stanley Sorrentino turned over the presidency to longtime employee John M. Corsini, who subsequently bought the company and became chief executive officer and chairman of the board. A 1965 graduate of the University of Rhode Island, Corsini joined Uncas a year later in the sales and marketing department, eventually become vice president of sales and marketing before becoming the first non-Sorrentino family member to lead the company. Uncas nevertheless remained a family business, as Corsini brought in his own children to continue the tradition established by his former employer.

Corsini's daughter Tisha proved to be a talented designer, especially in creating items for the amusement park channel. Another daughter, Daryl, was involved in international sales, overseeing business in Australia, Hong Kong, Japan, and Euro Disney in Paris. Corsini's son Christopher became an executive vice president and at the dawn of the new century was responsible for opening the Uncas office in Hong Kong.

Under John Corsini's leadership, Uncas instituted a cellular manufacturing system to remain competitive in an industry that had mostly shifted production to Asia. Instead of having a piece of jewelry travel an assembly line on which each worker completed a specific task, Uncas brought together cells, or small groups of employees, to work together in close quarters to produce a piece of jewelry. Long delays between stations were eliminated, resulting in quicker turnarounds and the ability to handle smaller orders.

VARGAS MANUFACTURING ACQUIRED: 1998

Uncas's 75,000-square-foot, four-story facility did not provide an ideal setup for cellular manufacturing, however. The setup constricted flow and hindered efficiency, leading the company to look for a new plant. In early 1998 Uncas acquired Vargas Manufacturing Company, which occupied an 84,000-square-foot, single-story building that was more modern and better suited for cellular production. A major addition to the facility had been completed in the 1970s. Vargas also had ties to Uncas. Over the years of ownership by the Sorrentino family, Uncas trained a number of employees who would go on to start their own jewelry companies, including Vargas, as well as Clarke & Coombs Company, Su-Ann Creation, and International Ring.

Vargas was an attractive acquisition for reasons other than the plant layout. It was more advanced in computer-aided design than was Uncas. Vargas also employed some highly talented people who became a valuable addition to Uncas. Moreover, Vargas was involved in some different markets than Uncas, requiring that it maintain a showroom on Fifth Avenue in New York City. Uncas inherited the showroom and those markets, which included the electronic media market and the selling of merchandise on television shopping channels.

As the economy softened at the start of the new century, Uncas remained an aggressive competitor. A director of new business development was hired and Uncas looked to become involved in more new markets and to cultivate additional accounts. The company's designers also continued to travel widely and remained in touch with changes in style and fashion, anticipating trends in order to present customers with new jewelry products. Under the ownership of the Corsini family, with a second generation well entrenched in the operation, Uncas appeared to be well positioned to enjoy continued success as a U.S. manufacturer embarking on its second century in business.

Ed Dinger

PRINCIPAL COMPETITORS

1928 Jewelry Company; K&M Associates L.P.

FURTHER READING

"John M. Corsini Promoted to President and Chief Operating Officer of Uncas Manufacturing Co.," *Jewelers Circular*

Keystone, October 1991, p. 158.

Joselow, Froma, "Jewelry Workers Make Every Weekend a Three-Day Vacation," *Providence Journal*, May 16, 1988, p. 1.

———, "Uncas Ringing Up Another Big Year," *Providence Journal*, July 20, 1986, p. F1.

"Uncas Mfg. Relies on Flexibility to Endure," *Providence Business News*, June 25, 2001, p. 4.

"Uncas Mfg. Set for 85th Anniversary," *Providence Journal*, May 25, 1996, p. B10.

Wyss, Bob, "Rhode Island's Uncas Manufacturing Co. Acquires Rival," *Providence Journal*, February 5, 1998.

United Plantations Bhd.

Jendarata Estate
Teluk Intan, 36009
Malaysia
Telephone: (+60 05) 641 1411
Fax: (+60 05) 641 1876
Web site: http://www.unitedplantations.com

Public Company
Incorporated: 1917 as United Plantations Ltd.
Employees: 7,029
Sales: MYR 816.67 million ($249.84 million) (2009)
Stock Exchanges: Malaysia NASDAQ OMX Copenhagen
Ticker Symbol: UTDPLT
NAICS: 111998 All Other Miscellaneous Crop Farming;
115112 Soil Preparation, Planting, and Cultivating

■ ■ ■

United Plantations Bhd. (UP) is one of Malaysia's most well-known oil palm plantation operators. The company controls nearly 41,000 hectares of oil palm plantation in Malaysia, and since 2006 also owns 40,000 hectares of development land in Indonesia. Of the group's plantations, 90 percent grow oil palms and the remainder is devoted to the production of coconuts. UP has long played a leading role in the drive to raise oil palm efficiency and output. The company boasts fruit yields of 29.05 metric tons per hectare. The company's crude palm oil (CPO) yields reached 6.31 metric tons per hectare in 2009, compared to the industry average of just 3.93 metric tons per hectare.

The company's total CPO production neared 200,000 metric tons in 2010. The company also produced more than 53,000 metric tons of palm kernel that year. UP expected to raise its CPO yield as high as 8.0 metric tons per hectare in the next decade. In addition to palm plantations, UP operates six palm oil mills. The company is a leading Malaysian producer of edible oils, specialty fats, and soap ingredients through its Unitata refinery subsidiary. UP also enjoys a long-standing and close relationship with Denmark's Aarhus United, one of the world's leading producers of specialty fats and edible and specialty oils. UP owns 43 percent of Aarhus, which in turn holds 23 percent of UP.

Ho Dua Tiam is the company's CEO. Brothers Carl Bek-Nielsen and Martin Bek-Nielsen serve as executive directors and through a family holding control more than 47 percent of UP's stock. UP is listed on the Malaysian stock exchange as well as on the NASDAQ OMX Copenhagen exchange. UP generated revenues of MYR 816.67 million ($249.84 million) in 2010.

DANISH ORIGINS

Malaysia's relationship with Denmark dates back to the late 19th century, when a number of Danish settlers in what was then the Kingdom of Siam helped defend Bangkok against an attack by the French navy in 1885. Among the settlers was Aage Westenholz, a civil engineer who had arrived in Bangkok that same year and who had previously served as an officer in the Danish army. In reward for his help in resisting the French assault, Westenholz and a number of other Danish settlers were granted the electricity supply concession for the city of Bangkok by the king of Siam.

At the beginning of the 20th century Westenholz became interested in the growing market for rubber and other plantation products developing in the region particularly on the Malay Peninsula. Rubber in particular had come into strong demand from the West, as the invention of the internal combustion and other engines had given rise to the growing automobile industry. In 1906 Westenholz acquired more than 800 hectares of rubber plantation in Jendarata, in Lower Perak, forming the Jendarata Rubber Company.

Westenholz quickly expanded his range of plantation holdings to include the Westenholz Brothers Coconut Estates, located along the Bernam River in Selangor. A younger cousin, Commander William Lennart Grut, joined Westenholz during this time. Other plantations that came under the control of the Westenholz family included the Corner and Raja Una estates, as well as the Kuala Bernam and Sungei Bernam coconut estates.

ADDING OIL PALMS

Grut took over the business after Westenholz retired in 1911. In 1917 Grut merged all of the family's plantation holdings under a single company, called United Plantations Limited (UP). By this time, UP's Danish roots had led Grut to become interested in another fast-growing plantation market, oil palms. Denmark's involvement in the palm oil market stemmed from the second half of the 19th century, when a number of Danish companies began developing cattle feed products from oil derived from palm kernels. Among these companies was Aarhus Palmekaernefabrik, founded in 1871, and later known as Aarhus Oliefabrik and then as Aarhus United. That company pioneered the refining of palm oil into food grade oils in the early 1880s, and by the dawn of the 20th century had become a leading international supplier of vegetable oils.

Demand for both coconut and palm oil soared in the 20th century as Aarhus pioneered a new refining method that led to the development of the first all-vegetable margarine. The rising demand for palm kernels encouraged UP to enter this area. In 1918 the company planted its first oil palm test site, a 16-hectare site at the Sungei plantation along the Bernam River.

Grut met with a Mr. Blumendall, a native of the Netherlands, which led to the company's deeper investment into oil palms. In the middle of the 1920s the company acquired nearly 2,500 hectares about 60 kilometers north of its existing plantations along the Bernam River. Blumendall took charge of the new estate, known as Bernam Berhad, and UP began planting some 2,000 hectares of oil palms, becoming one of the first large-scale oil palm plantations in Malaysia. UP created a separate company for its oil palm business, called Bernam Oil Palms, in 1926.

THE BEK-NIELSEN ERA BEGINS: 1951

Oil palms grew to become UP's major area of focus through the middle of the 20th century. In the early 1950s the company launched a research and development effort in order to develop new palm planting techniques and materials, particularly for the conversion of existing rubber plantations to oil palm growing. The company initially worked in cooperation with the Malay Department of Agriculture. UP then founded its own dedicated research department in 1962. Over the next decades, the company's research efforts focused more and more on raising oil palm yield rates, both in the number of fruit per hectare and in the amount of CPO extracted per hectare.

The 1950s also marked the beginning of a new era for UP. In 1951 a new arrival from Denmark, Borge Bek-Nielsen, took up a position as an assistant engineer at Bernam Oil Palms. Bek-Nielsen rapidly rose through the company's hierarchy. In 1966 UP and Bernam Oil Palms merged together, forming United Plantations Berhad. Bek-Nielsen quickly rose to the top of the combined company, becoming its executive director in 1971. Bek-Nielsen also began acquiring shares in the company, which was later brought under a holding vehicle, International Plantations and Finance (IPF). By the middle of the 1970s Bek-Nielsen had gained majority control of UP.

Bek-Nielsen had by then established himself as a central figure in Malaysia's oil palm industry, ultimately earning himself the nickname of Malaysia's "Palm Oil King." Under Bek-Nielsen, UP significantly expanded its plantation acreage, which topped 27,500 hectares in the early 1980s. The company also established a reputation for operating Malaysia's best-run oil palm plantations, consistently posting yields outpacing the national

KEY DATES

1906: Aage Westenholz of Denmark founds the Jendarata Rubber Company.

1917: Under William Lennart Grut, the Westenholz family plantations are merged to form United Plantations Limited (UP).

1926: UP founds an oil palm plantation, Bernam Berhad.

1951: Borge Bek-Nielsen begins working for Bernam Berhad.

1966: United Plantations and Bernam Berhad merge to form United Plantations Berhad (UP).

1981: Kumpulan Fima acquires control of UP.

1991: Control of UP is acquired by Aarhus Oliefabrik.

2006: UP acquires oil palm plantations in Indonesia.

2010: UP reports revenues of $250 million and total crude palm oil (CPO) production of 200,000 metric tons.

average. This in turn enabled the company to remain profitable even during slumps in palm oil demand.

THE NEW ECONOMIC POLICY: 1981

UP also launched an international expansion effort under Bek-Nielsen, adding operations in Norway, Australia, and Mexico. UP's international growth also led to the development of a long-standing relationship with Aarhus Oliefabrik. UP had moved into palm oil refining in the early 1970s, setting up subsidiary Unitata Berhad in 1971. Unitata succeeded in launching production by 1974, with Aarhus becoming an important customer. UP later became Aarhus's largest supplier of palm oil and palm kernels.

Aarhus and Unitata developed a joint venture partnership together toward the end of the decade. In 1978 Bek-Nielsen, through UP, began acquiring a stake in Aarhus itself. Bek-Nielsen continued to buy up blocks of Aarhus shares over the next year, allowing UP to gain control of the Danish oil and fats giant in 1979. The two companies remained linked together through the end of the century, with Aarhus acquiring a stake in IPF in 1981. In 1991 Aarhus bought 32 percent of UP directly, later reducing its shareholding to 20 percent. UP's own stake in Aarhus United later stabilized at 43 percent.

In the meantime, UP itself had undergone a series of ownership changes. The Malaysian government, led by Mohamed Mahathir, had instituted its New Economic Policy (NEP), which called for the "Malayanization" of the country's economy. As part of its effort to shift a greater share of economic wealth to the majority ethnic Malay population, the government imposed strict foreign ownership limits on a number of industries, including the plantation sector. As a result, UP's Danish owners sold UP to Kumpulan Fima in 1981, a state-held holding company closely associated with the Mahathir government. This left just 25 percent of UP's shares with Bek-Nielsen. Nevertheless, Bek-Nielsen remained at the head of the company throughout the decade.

UP continued to expand its acreage as part of Kumpulan Fima, adding another 4,000 hectares by 1983. Toward the end of that decade, the Malaysian government began reversing much of the NEP. This included the foreign ownership restrictions, and beginning in 1987 foreigners were again allowed to acquire land. The Bek-Nielsen family acted quickly, buying more than 10,000 hectares of palm oil plantation owned by Gula Perak Bhd. These were placed under a new company, United International Enterprises (UIE). UIE then began clearing and replanting the land with new higher-yield palm varieties. This in turn enabled UIE to become one of Malaysia's most efficient oil palm plantation operators in the 1990s.

The weakening of the Mahathir government's political base at the end of the 1980s led the government to launch a major privatization effort, spinning off much of the government's holdings, including Kumpulan Fima, in a series of management buyouts (MBOs). Kumpulan Fima completed its own MBO in 1990. Soon after, in 1991, Kumpulan Fima agreed to sell its controlling stake in UP to Aarhus Oliefabrik for MYR 125 million. Bek-Nielsen thus again gained ownership control of UP.

STEADY PROGRESS

Bek-Nielsen brought his sons into the business, starting with elder son Carl Bek-Nielsen, who joined the company at the age of 20 as a cadet planter, and then left Malaysia to study in Denmark. In 1998 Carl Bek-Nielsen returned to UP, taking up the position as corporate affairs officer before becoming an executive director in 2000. By then, his brother Martin Bek-Nielsen, who started with UP at age 19 as a cadet planter in 1994, had taken over as the group's corporate affairs officer, before becoming an executive director in 2001.

United Plantations and United International Enterprises operated as separate entities until 2003, when the latter became a full-fledged subsidiary of UP. The merger raised UP's total acreage past 38,000 hectares. At the same time, Aarhus Oliefabrik changed its name to Aarhus United in order to underscore the close relationship between itself and United Plantations.

UP increased its plantation size again in 2004, buying the more than 2,500-hectare Lima Blas Estate from rival group Socfin. This increased the company's total landholding past 40,000 hectares. At the same time, UP continued to raise its CPO yields. The company had made steady progress in this area, boosting its yields to nearly 5.5 metric tons per hectare by 2007, as compared with the national average of 3.83 metric tons. By the end of the decade UP's CPO yield topped 6.3 metric tons per hectare. Over the next 10 years, the company expected to raise its yields past 8.0 metric tons per hectare.

INVESTING IN INDONESIA: 2006

UP made a series of new investments through the decade, including the launch of a bio-energy facility in 2005. In 2006 the company turned its attention to the promising and lower-wage Indonesian oil palm market. UP reached an agreement to acquire two oil palm plantation companies there, Mirza Pratama Putra and Surya Sawit Sejati, representing a combined holding of more than 30,000 hectares. The following year the company completed a new acquisition, of Sawit Seberang Seberang, raising its total acreage in Indonesia to 40,000 hectares. The company then began replanting its Indonesian plantations, a process expected to be completed within 10 years.

UP marked a new milestone in 2008 when it became the first Malaysian oil palm company to achieve certification under the country's voluntary Roundtable on Sustainable Palm Oil guidelines. The company completed its first shipments of sustainable palm oil in October of that year. UP's efforts to increase its CPO yields played a role in the growing share of palm oil and palm kernel oil in the global edible oil market. These oils represented more than 38 percent of global edible oil consumption, while accounting for just 5 percent of agricultural land. In contrast, soybean oil, which claimed nearly 28 percent of the global market, accounted for 43 percent of the world's agricultural land. With the world's population expected to near 10 billion by the middle of the 21st century, UP's efforts to increase oil palm yields would be a crucial part of meeting the challenges of the future.

M. L. Cohen

PRINCIPAL SUBSIDIARIES

Bernam Advisory Services Sdn. Bhd.; Bernam Agencies Sdn. Bhd.; Berta Services Sdn. Bhd.; Butterworth Bulking Installation Sdn. Bhd.; PT Sawit Seberang Seberang (Indonesia; 95%); PT Surya Sawit Sejati (Indonesia; 95%); Unitata Berhad; United International Enterprises (M) Sdn. Bhd.

PRINCIPAL DIVISIONS

Plantations; Palm Oil Refining; Others.

PRINCIPAL OPERATING UNITS

United Plantations; Sawit Sebarang Sebarang; Unitata Berhad; United International Enterprises (M) Sdn. Bhd.; UP Research Department.

PRINCIPAL COMPETITORS

Boh Plantations Sdn. Bhd.; Chin Teck Plantations Bhd.; Hap Seng Plantations Holdings Bhd.; IOI Corporation; Kumpulan Fima Bhd.; MBf Holdings Bhd.; MHC Plantations Bhd.; PPB Group Bhd.; Sime Darby Corporation Bhd.; United Malacca Bhd.; YTL Corporation Bhd.

FURTHER READING

Damodaran, Rupa, "Milestone for United Plantations," *Business Times*, August 28, 2008.

Donvang Parks, Charlotte, "Tan Sri Dato' Seri Bek-Nielsen … a Great Man and Mentor Has Passed Away," *ScandAsia News*, April 10, 2005.

"Key Role in Sustainability to Continue," *Business Times*, March 10, 2010.

Martin, Susan M., *The Up Saga*, Copenhagen: NIAS Press, 2003.

"Nation's Palm Oil Masters," *Business Times*, July 21, 2000.

"Old Values Carried on by Bek-Nielsen Brothers," *Oil & Fats International*, September 1, 2004.

Singh, Jaspal, "United Plantations Focus on Research Bearing Fruit," *Business Times*, June 5, 2006.

"Utd Plantation Launches Bio-Energy Facilities," *Business Times*, September 15, 2006.

United Stationers Inc.

One Parkway North Boulevard, Suite 100
Deerfield, Illinois 60015-2559
U.S.A.
Telephone: (847) 627-7000
Fax: (847) 627-7001
Web site: http://www.unitedstationers.com

Public Company
Incorporated: 1981
Employees: 5,800
Sales: $4.71 billion (2009)
Stock Exchanges: NASDAQ
Ticker Symbol: USTR
NAICS: 421420 Office Equipment Wholesalers; 421430 Computer and Computer Peripheral Equipment and Software Wholesalers; 421490 Other Professional Equipment and Supplies Wholesalers; 422120 Stationery and Office Supplies Wholesalers; 422130 Industrial and Personal Service Paper Wholesalers

■ ■ ■

United Stationers Inc. is the holding company for United Stationers Supply Co., the largest wholesale distributor of business office products in the United States (it also has operations in major cities in Mexico). The company carries more than 100,000 items in several categories: technology products, office supplies, janitorial and break room supplies, office furniture, and industrial supplies.

United Stationers operates 67 distribution centers and sells to 30,000 customers including traditional office supply retailers, office furniture retailers, mail-order houses, computer resellers, mass merchandise outlets, and organizations of smaller retailers who band together to profit from volume-buying discounts. United has remained profitable in an increasingly difficult industry by focusing on customer service and expanding into new markets.

In April 1995 Wingate Partners, a Dallas-based private-equity fund, purchased United Stationers for approximately $258 million and merged it with rival office-products wholesaler Associated Stationers Inc. New growth platforms were added through the acquisitions of janitorial products supplier Lagasse, Inc., in 1996 and industrial supplies distributor ORS Nasco in 2007, each made through the United Stationers Supply Co. subsidiary. The company also added a line of consumable computer products in 1998.

ORIGINS

Until the 1990s, United Stationers was primarily a family-run business. Its roots date back to 1921, when a trio of businessmen, Morris Wolf, Harry Hecktman, and Israel Kriloff, purchased a 15-year-old office supply company in Chicago called Utility Supply Co. Operating as an "industrial loft stationer," Utility sold supplies such as paper, file folders, pens, and ink to businesses in Chicago's downtown Loop district by making sales calls to nearby offices. The sales representatives would fill the order at Utility's loft space on the top floor of an older building, then return the next day to deliver the order.

COMPANY PERSPECTIVES

Our vision is to become a high-performance organization, delivering exceptional value through superior execution of innovative marketing and logistics services. We value people, honesty and integrity, respect and dignity, customers and suppliers, quality and continuous improvement, teamwork, and accountability. This vision and these values are more than just words. They form the centerpiece for our growth, because they attract talented people who want to work in this kind of an environment, and the best manufacturers and resellers who share these beliefs.

This was the standard procedure for selling office supplies at that time.

Kriloff, a grocer, brought financial expertise to the business. Wolf and Hecktman brought considerable salesmanship as well as a customer base, having worked as salesmen for two of Chicago's top office supply companies. When the three men purchased the company, it was bringing in little more than $12,000 in annual sales. By the end of their first year in business together, the three partners had increased Utility's annual sales 10-fold to $120,000. The company grew steadily through the 1920s, profiting from the booming U.S. economy of that decade. Although growth slowed considerably after the stock market collapse of 1929, the company was able to survive the ensuing economic depression.

Following a trend started in 1892 by P. F. Pettibone & Co., and taken up by Utility's rival Horder's Associated Stationers Supply Co., Utility entered into another era of retailing in 1935 when it published its first catalog. "Acting as an ever-present representative of Utility Supply Co.," said company materials, "The catalog could be sent to thousands of customers anywhere in the country; successfully soliciting orders by mail or telephone." In 1937 Utility expanded again, opening its first retail store in the heart of Chicago's bustling Loop.

In 1939 Hecktman and Wolf bought Kriloff's share of the business, and Kriloff retired in Florida. By this time Utility operated five retail outlets and had expanded its loft to serve as a warehouse for its retail outlets, to house administrative offices, and also to continue to serve customers through direct industrial sales.

Utility's foundation was shaken, however, when the United States became involved in World War II, creating a dearth of office products because most raw materials were used in the war effort. To keep the business afloat, Utility began offering general merchandise in its catalogs, at one time offering more than 1,000 non-office products. The venture into non-office supplies was ultimately unsuccessful, and by the end of World War II the company was again concentrating solely on office products.

RAPID GROWTH FOLLOWING WORLD WAR II

The postwar era was a period of tremendous growth for Utility. The company mailed an extensive series of low-priced office supply catalogs to retailers across the nation, developing a reputation as "the people from Chicago with the low prices." By 1948 the company was mailing as many as two million catalogs per year and enjoying annual sales of $2 million. Mail order accounted for 40 percent of sales, another 40 percent were through the company's retail outlets, and the remaining 20 percent were through direct industrial sales.

In the early 1950s the company made several major changes in its sales operations. The most important was Morris Wolf's decision to operate a segment of Utility as an office-products wholesaler, selling directly to independent office-products retailers. There were two potential problems that Utility faced in this decision. The first was the potential for conflict with its existing retail and mail-order businesses. Wolf ultimately realized that the customers of Utility's wholesale business would enter into direct competition with Utility's own retail businesses.

The solution the company devised was to establish a chain of franchised office supply stores, thus creating a "natural outlet" for their wholesale goods, which they hoped would expand both retailing and wholesaling. Franchises were opened in Milwaukee, Wisconsin, and Kankakee, Illinois. However, due to the scarcity of foot-traffic in these towns (as opposed to the high-density, heavily traveled Chicago Loop), the stores were unsuccessful. Attempts to boost franchise sales by sending sales representatives directly to potential industrial customers were also fruitless. By the late 1950s, Utility decided to discontinue its franchise operations and concentrate on wholesale, Chicago retail, and national catalog sales.

The second obstacle was the need to convince office-products manufacturers that Utility was serious about wholesaling, and not simply looking for a means of purchasing products at lower prices. Wilson Jones

KEY DATES

1922: Precursor of United Stationers Supply Co. is incorporated in Illinois.

1981: United Stationers becomes a publicly traded company with a listing on the NASDAQ.

1984: United Stationers forms a computer-supplies division.

1992: Fort Worth-based Stationers Distributing Company is acquired; total revenues exceed $1 billion.

1995: Wingate Partners acquires United Stationers, combines it with Associated Stationers.

1996: Lagasse Brothers, Inc., a New Orleans-based distributor of janitorial products, is acquired.

1998: U.S. and Mexican office-supply operations of Abitibi Consolidated are acquired.

2003: War on Waste initiative seeks to remove $100 million in annual costs within five years.

2006: United Stationers acquires Sweet Paper Corp., a Florida-based supplier of paper products to the food service industry; Canadian operations are divested.

2007: Industrial supplies distributor ORS Nasco is acquired for $180 million.

Co. was the first manufacturer to take an interest in Utility as a wholesaler, which paved the way for other manufacturers to sell through the company.

Wholesaling became an even larger part of Utility's operations as office supply retailers began to appreciate the advantages of ordering from a wholesaler, as opposed to ordering directly from manufacturers, who frequently required dealers to buy large quantities of an item in order to receive a price discount. Many office supply businesses were family operations that catered to a limited customer base. Although Utility's prices were slightly higher than manufacturers' discount prices, often it was to a retailer's advantage to buy small quantities from a wholesaler on an as-needed basis, as opposed to buying large quantities of an item when only a few were needed. The fact that many retailers needed only small quantities of certain items on an irregular basis served Utility's wholesale business well.

EMPHASIS ON WHOLESALING

During the 1940s Howard Wolf, Morris Wolf's son, began working in the business. He assumed the position

of vice president in charge of wholesale operations in 1952. Utility's burgeoning wholesale business grew. By 1956 the company had expanded to larger quarters, purchasing a building at 641 West Lake Street in Chicago, a move that doubled its warehouse and administrative office space. By 1960 the company's business volume had grown so much that Utility expanded into neighboring buildings, doubling its warehouse space again to over 300,000 square feet. In March 1960 Utility adopted the name United Stationers Supply Co. for its wholesaling business. Its chain of retail stores retained the name Utility Stationery Stores.

Catalogs also served to boost sales of Utility's wholesale division. Early on, Utility realized that to generate its own sales, the independent retailers using Utility's business would need to generate sales. In 1959 Utility borrowed a concept from Horder's Associated Stationers Supply, its closest competitor, and began "syndicating" its office supply catalogs. For just under $2.50, retailers could buy 100 catalogs from Utility, with the store's name printed on the front cover. Utility took the concept a step further than its competitor, offering retailers a rebate on the price of catalogs based on a percentage of the products bought through the catalog from Utility Wholesale Supply Co. Benefits to retailers were twofold. The catalog served as a marketing tool for retailers, and the more the retailer purchased from Utility, the less the overall cost of catalogs.

Utility's wholesale division grew rapidly during its first decade of operation. By 1966 coordination of activities was becoming a difficult and time-consuming task. Howard Wolf addressed the problem by purchasing an IBM 360/30 to track and record invoices, accounts receivable, and item demand. When the company began planning construction of a new warehouse in Forest Park, Illinois, Utility once again hired IBM to install a computerized inventory management system. The system was the first in the office-products industry and represented a bit of a gamble for the company. It was so successful, however, that IBM published numerous articles on the project.

FOUNDERS RETIRE IN 1967

In 1967, having grown their company's sales from $12,000 to $10 million, Morris Wolf and Harry Hecktman retired, and Morris's son Howard assumed the position of president and chief executive officer. The company's wholesale business grew quickly under the younger Wolf. By 1970 two-thirds of United's $15 million in annual sales came from its wholesale division. In addition to its catalog subscription program, Utility instituted a number of programs such as pricing services and promotional specials aimed at providing value-added services to retailers. In addition, Utility began furnishing retailers with a computer system that provided a direct ordering link to its warehouses.

United also grew sales by expanding its catalog line. A promotional service launched in the early 1960s offered around 100 items at discount prices on colored flyers printed with the retailer's name. Later Utility began publishing abridged catalogs targeted to specific groups or market segments. An office furniture catalog was introduced in 1967, a data-processing catalog appeared in 1970, and in 1976 United's Basic Office Needs Directory debuted, offering a collection of frequently requested office supplies.

United continued to focus on its wholesale operations, expanding its business with the 1971 purchase of the wholesale division of Mutual Papers Co. of Detroit. United converted the newly acquired facilities into its first regional distribution center, directly linking operations at the Detroit warehouse with United's new computer system in Chicago. The venture was difficult and complex. However, after a year of operational difficulties that severely strained the company's financial resources, United's regional distribution center began to turn a profit. When United opened a second regional warehouse in Pennsauken, New Jersey, in 1973, the company experienced no start-up troubles.

The company then developed a number of local distribution centers (LDCs), low-cost redistribution points where shipment from its larger warehouses could be broken down for delivery to individual retailers nearby. This system assisted United in penetrating new markets and also offered lower costs to retailers as well as overnight delivery to most locations. In the mid-1970s, United established LDCs in St. Louis, Milwaukee, Kansas City, Minneapolis-St. Paul, Boston, and New York.

GOING PUBLIC IN 1981

In 1978 United sold its retail centers and began concentrating solely on expanding its wholesale business. Net sales that year were $106 million. Three years later, in August 1981, the company incorporated United Stationers Inc. (USI) to serve as a holding company for United Stationers Supply Co. USI went public on the NASDAQ later that year and proceeds from the offering were used to construct a third regional distribution center in the Los Angeles area. Earnings in USI's first year as a public company were $4.8 million on sales of $200 million.

Sales grew steadily in the early 1980s, fueled by an increase in the number of white-collar workers and demands for computer-related office supplies. With its network of local and regional distribution centers, United was poised to profit from the demand, growing at a faster rate than both the wholesale and retail segments of the office supply industry. The increased sophistication of computers greatly aided in inventory management, allowing retailers to order goods through a computerized system and have them delivered by the following day.

The boom in the office supply industry was short-lived, however. Around 1985, office supply superstores and warehouse clubs began to threaten the existence of independent office-products retailers, which made up United's traditional customer base. Independent retailers sold to two types of end markets. The first (and largest) was the corporate market, which was reached through outside sales representatives and catalogs, and remained unaffected by superstores. The second, smaller market comprised walk-in and small-purchase customers, whose business was more at risk of being attracted by the new superstores. United responded to the changing marketplace by developing marketing concepts to help independent retailers recapture some of the walk-in market segment. At the same time, the company sought to benefit from the changes by aggressively marketing to superstores and mail-order houses.

RESPONDING TO MARKET CHALLENGES

Sales in 1987 hit $720 million. However, the corporate market (which had remained unscathed by the growth of superstores) was beginning to shrink as many businesses began downsizing. United responded by lowering prices and instituting volume-buying incentive programs, as well as targeting the specific needs of regional and local markets. To do this, the company continued to fortify its warehouse operations. By 1987 United had built nine more LDCs, providing access to markets in California, Texas, and the eastern, midwestern, and southern regions of the United States. The following year, it opened a regional distribution center in southern Illinois, and another in upstate New York, bringing to 14 the total number of regional distribution centers.

Sales from 1989 to 1991 hovered just below, but never broke, the $1 billion mark. The slumping office supply market was taking its toll on United, and in 1990 the company instituted a decentralization plan, laying off 15 percent of its staff at its headquarters near Chicago. The following year United expanded into the Canadian market by purchasing certain assets of an office supply wholesaler with warehouses in Canada and establishing its first foreign subsidiary, United Stationers Canada, Ltd.

In 1992 sales broke the $1 billion level, fueled by the acquisition of Stationers Distributing Company, a Fort Worth, Texas-based general office-products wholesaler with $425 million in sales and distribution centers across the United States. While much of the company's growth in the early 1990s was fueled by acquisition, United constantly sought new ways to market its products, creating a furniture division and a custom source division to market personalized products, as well as establishing its own line of office supplies, marketed under the Universal brand name. Sales in 1994 were $1.47 billion, slightly higher than 1993 sales. Net income declined 26.3 percent, due to unexpected expenses arising from merging the operations of Stationers Distributing into its own.

NEW OWNERS IN 1995

In April 1995 Wingate Partners, a private-equity fund, purchased United Stationers for approximately $258 million and merged it with its own subsidiary, office-products wholesaler Associated Stationers Inc. The purchase placed 81 percent of United's outstanding stock under Wingate's control. The merged companies assumed the United Stationers name. By 2000 Wingate had reduced its holdings to 3.5 percent.

Jeffrey K. Hewson, president and CEO of United Stationers since 1990, resigned after the takeover. Former Associated Stationers chief Thomas W. Sturgess then led the company until stepping down in late 1996. Sturgess was replaced as chairman by Wingate Partners cofounder Frederick B. Hegi. Randall W. Larrimore succeeded him as CEO a few months later. Larrimore was formerly head of MasterBrand Industries, the hardware division of American Brands Inc. (later Fortune Brands, Inc.).

United Stationers formed a facilities supply division in 1994 and made one of its most important growth moves with the 1996 acquisition of Lagasse Brothers, Inc., a New Orleans-based distributor of janitorial products. From annual revenues of $80 million, it would become the basis of the company's fastest growing line, approaching $1 billion within 10 years. Lagasse acquired local supplier Peerless Paper Mills Inc. in 2001. By this time Lagasse had 600 employees and 25 distribution centers.

In 1998 United Stationers acquired the U.S. and Mexican office-products operations of Canadian newsprint and paper products group Abitibi-Consolidated Inc. for $110 million (CAD $157 million). This added revenues of $350 million, including the Azerty computer-consumables business, which was folded into the existing MicroUnited division,

established in 1984. In 2000 United Stationers bought the Canadian operations, adding another $115 million in annual sales.

In July 1999 United Stationers made a foray into online order fulfillment for independent office supply stores, signing up E-Commerce Industries Inc. to provide online storefronts to tap into its own warehouses. The next year it joined a plan to revive Winnipeg's venerable Willson Stationers Ltd. as an online store.

These efforts left the company exposed to the bursting of the technology bubble. In addition, there was a glut of furniture on the market from closed Internet start-ups, depressing sales in one of its newer business areas. Net profits slipped 38 percent to $57 million in 2001, while revenues remained just below the $4 billion mark. United Stationers continued to invest heavily in its own information technology operations, seeking a competitive advantage.

WAR ON WASTE LAUNCHED IN 2003

After years of growth orientation, the company placed new emphasis on efficiency in 2003 when it introduced its War on Waste program. This was an effort to make operations more efficient by focusing on such things as reducing the number of product returns. After serving as chief operating officer for a year and a half, Richard Gochnauer became company president and CEO following the retirement of Randall Larrimore in December 2003. Gochnauer had previously been president of Golden State Foods.

In 2004 revenues were about $4 billion and there were about 6,000 employees. The company carried 40,000 items from 400 manufacturers and had 15,000 resellers as customers. It had long been considered the largest wholesaler of office supplies in the United States, with only one comparable national rival, S. P. Richards Company.

In addition to independent retailers, United Stationers also supplied office superstores such as Staples, typically providing their low-volume items. Following their lead, the company began contracting for private-label manufacturing of its own product lines in China. Most of its products had previously been procured in the United States.

In early 2006 United Stationers acquired Sweet Paper Corp., a Hialeah, Florida-based supplier of janitorial supplies and products for the food service industry, for $124.5 million. Sweet Paper Corp. had annual sales of $250 million. In the same year United Stationers sold its Canadian operations, which had annual sales of $150 million, to Toronto's Synnex Canada Ltd.

Industrial supplies distributor ORS Nasco was acquired for $180 million in 2007. Based in Muskogee, Oklahoma, ORS Nasco had annual revenues of $285 million. United Stationers saw ORS Nasco as a platform for the same kind of growth it had achieved with its venture into janitorial supplies through the acquisition of Lagasse.

Revenues continued a steady climb in 2008, rising almost 7 percent to nearly $5 billion. Sales slipped to $4.7 billion in 2009 as the economy struggled to recover from the global credit crisis, but net income rose slightly to $101 million.

Maura Troester
Updated, Frederick C. Ingram

PRINCIPAL SUBSIDIARIES

United Stationers Supply Co.; ORS Nasco, Inc.; Lagasse, Inc.; Azerty de Mexico, S.A. de C.V.; United Stationers Hong Kong Limited.

PRINCIPAL COMPETITORS

S. P. Richards Company.

FURTHER READING

"Acquired United Stationers Accepts Sweeter Deal," *Chicago Tribune*, February 15, 1995.

Arndorfer, James B., "Online, Old-Line Don't Mix; Unhappy Internet Foray Burns United Stationers," *Crain's Chicago Business*, February 11, 2002, p. 4.

Burke, Erica, "The Paper Trail: United Stationers Inc.—the Largest Wholesaler of Office Supplies in the United States— Focuses on Creating a More Efficient Supply Chain and Robust Customer Service," *US Business Review*, January/ February 2005.

Ebeling, Ashlea, "Paper Tiger," *Forbes*, February 21, 2000, p. 71.

Gorman, John, "Profits Aren't Stationary at Office Supplier," *Chicago Tribune*, July 15, 1985.

Howes, Carol, "Willson Stationers to Get Relaunch as eSupplies.com: FutureLink Founder Cameron Chell behind New Venture," *National Post* (Canada), April 6, 2000, p. C4.

Murphy, H. Lee, "Paper Firm's Push: Diversify; United Stationers Touts Furniture, Janitorial Goods," *Crain's Chicago Business*, July 10, 2006, p. 13.

Pincus, Ted, "United Stationers Gets a Dose of Exhilaration," *Chicago Sun-Times*, Bus. Sec., October 14, 2003, p. 47.

Taylor, Marianne, "United Stationers Cuts Staff at Des Plaines Office," *Chicago Tribune*, March 22, 1991.

"United Cuts the Slack; Restructuring Plans Hit Jobs as United Stationers Seeks to Reduce Its Cost Structure," *Office Products International*, November 2006, p. 9.

Weber, Thomas E., "E-Commerce Industries to Ally with Wholesaler," *Wall Street Journal*, July 8, 1999, p. B6.

Young, David, "Firm Seeks United Stationers Merger," *Chicago Tribune*, January 10, 1995.

Vale S.A.

———— ■ ————

Avenida Graça Aranha 26
PO Box 2414
Rio de Janeiro, 20005
Brazil
Telephone: (+55 21) 3814 4477
Fax: (+55 21) 3814 4040
Web site: http://www.vale.com.br

Public Company
Incorporated: 1942 as Companhia Vale do Rio Doce
Employees: 57,043
Sales: $23.94 billion (2009)
Stock Exchanges: New York São Paulo
Ticker Symbol: VALE
NAICS: 212210 Iron Ore Mining; 212299 All Other Metal Ore Mining; 212221 Gold Ore Mining; 212222 Silver Ore Mining; 482111 Line-Haul Railroads; 483111 Deep-Sea Freight Transportation

■ ■ ■

Formerly known as Companhia Vale do Rio Doce (CVRD), Vale S.A. is the world's largest producer of iron ore and the largest diversified mining company in the Americas. The company is the world's second-largest producer of nickel and one of the largest producers of manganese ore, ferroalloys, bauxite, alumina, and kaolin. Vale is also involved in the production of aluminum, copper, coal, potash, cobalt, and platinum group metals. The company has exploration activities in 21 countries across the globe and operates railroads, maritime terminals, and a port in Brazil that support its mining

activities. The company adopted the Vale name in 2007 as part of new brand identity campaign. It officially changed its corporate name to Vale S.A. in 2009.

Starting from two integrated mine-railroad-port systems, Vale grew to become a symbol of Brazil's industrial prowess over the course of the second half of the 20th century. To fully understand the history behind Vale, one must look at the economic and geopolitical environment of Brazil during the 20th century. Beginning centuries before the founding of Vale, explorers had traveled Brazil's remote Doce River Valley in search of gold and other precious natural resources. In 1891, Brazil's first Republican Constitution dramatically altered the nation's mining regulations to allow landowners the rights to mineral reserves found on their property. However, the law allowed the underground mineral reserves to be worked by foreign-owned companies. At that time, geological explorations began to reveal abundant supplies of iron concentrated in the rich earth of the remote Minas Gerais state, where three billion tons of the ore lay buried. Huge mining companies in France, the United Kingdom, the United States, and Belgium swiftly purchased many of these iron-ore beds at well below market value. In 1919, U.S. entrepreneur Percival Farquhar purchased the Itabira Iron Ore Company from its British founders. With the help of his other company, the Vitoria-Minas Railroad, Farquhar planned to build a monopoly in Brazilian iron ore production and exports.

THE EARLY YEARS

In the 1930s, Brazil was facing a major economic and political crisis. The outcome of that year's presidential

COMPANY PERSPECTIVES

Our vision is to be the largest mining company in the world, and to surpass established standards of excellence in research, development, project implementation and business operations.

election was challenged by a political-military insurrection, with power ultimately handed to Getulio Vargas. The so-called 1930 Revolution and Brazil's newest leader championed a movement toward nationalism. The Vargas years (1930–45) in Brazil were characterized by the creation of a powerful interventionist federal government, and this sentiment applied to the nation's valuable supply of mineral reserves. Political concerns arose over the growing foreign ownership of mines at this time. In a conciliatory gesture, Farquhar and other mine owners "Brazilianized" the Itabira Iron Ore Company, splitting it into Companhia Brasileria de Mineracao and Itabira Mineracao.

As Vargas tightened his political control over Brazil, he began to focus on a pro-development philosophy. The Vargas regime pushed for a transition from an agricultural economy to an industrialist one in Brazil.

In 1940, Vargas sought to establish capital-intensive national industries, with emphasis on steel, electricity, transportation and weaponry. With World War II in full swing, Europe and its allies had a growing need for iron ore. Mineral-rich Brazil used this to its advantage, garnering favors from the Allied nations. The Washington Agreements were signed in March 1942 by Brazil, the United Kingdom and the United States, defining the bases for establishing iron ore production and export in Brazil.

Vargas obtained a $45 million EX-IMBANK loan from the United States to establish the first major steel-producing plant in Latin America, Companhia Siderugica Nacional (CSN). The Washington Agreements also called for the transfer of United Kingdom-owned Itabira Mines to the Brazilian government along with the Vitoria-Minas Railroad. In exchange, Brazil declared war against the Third Reich. Vargas also obtained another $14 million loan from the US EXIM-BANK to purchase machinery and equipment. On June 1, 1942, Vargas created the Companhia Vale do Rio Doce (CVRD), in accordance with the Washington Agreements, and began fulfilling his plan to modernize the Brazilian economy.

1950–69: REACHING CARAJAS

CVRD was originally designed to provide raw materials for CSN. In 1949, the company was supplying 80 percent of Brazil's iron ore exports. By this time Vargas had been out of power for four years, but he was elected to the presidency again in 1951. Vargas quickly resumed his industrialization plan for Brazil and in 1952 created the National Bank for Economic Development (BNDE) to finance industrial pursuits. It was also this year that the Brazilian government took over definitive control of CVRD operations.

By that time, an aging Vargas realized his political clout was waning and he began losing favor among the Brazilian industrial elite. Besides his creation in 1953 of Petrobas, a government-owned oil monopoly, the last years of Vargas's rule were lacking in industrial-based achievements. Political rivals and rumors of corruption began to plague Vargas, who committed suicide in the presidential palace in 1954. A new president, Juscelino Kubitschek, advocated many of the same modernization ideas of Vargas, but his equally ambitious plan involved a triangulated strategy between the Brazilian state-owned companies, private Brazilian firms, and European and American nationals. With the Kubitschek plan underway, the late 1950s proved to be the most productive in Brazil's history.

In 1959, CVRD inaugurated the Paul Wharf at the Port of Vitoria with the start-up of regular exports of fines and run-of-mine ores. Later, the company incorporated its own shipping arm, Vale do Rio Doce Navegacao SA (Docenave), which grew to become one of the top 10 shipping companies in the world. The company's first long-term iron ore supply contracts were also signed in 1962. Five years later, CVRD incorporated another important subsidiary, Florestas Rio Doce (FRDSA). CVRD reached another important milestone that year. By 1967, the company ranked among the six largest export companies in the world.

In 1968, CVRD employee Jose Eduardo Machado, a geologist with the Ore Prospecting Center, reached Carajas, or Amazonia, for the first time. Geological surveys would later prove that Carajas held the world's largest iron ore reserves, more than 18 billion tons. The next year, the first CVRD palletizing plant was inaugurated at Tubarão, Espírito Santo State.

1970–89: BUILDING A CONGLOMERATE

CVRD continued to incorporate numerous subsidiaries during the next two decades. The company, in association with US Steel, incorporated the Amazonia Mineracao SA mining company in 1970. The next year it

KEY DATES

1942: Companhia Vale do Rio Doce (CVRD) is incorporated as a federally owned company.

1952: Brazilian government takes control of CVRD operations.

1962: Company incorporates shipping arm as Vale do Rio Doce Navagacao (Docenave).

1968: A CVRD geologist reaches Carajas (Amazonia) for the first time, site of the world's largest iron ore reserves.

1975: CVRD becomes the world's largest iron ore exporter.

1977: CVRD is awarded exclusive mining rights to Carajas.

1997: CVRD is privatized.

2000: Company is listed on New York Stock Exchange.

2007: INCO Ltd. is acquired.

2009: Company officially changes its name to Vale S.A.

incorporated a prospecting subsidiary, Rio Doce Geologia e Mineracao (Decegeo). The company absorbed $82 million in investments over the next seven years as it completed the widest ranging geological survey ever carried out in Brazil. It was through this prospecting drive that CVRD discovered 35 new deposits of 11 different minerals in 13 Brazilian states. In 1973, CVRD incorporated the Celulose Nipo-Brasileria XACENIBRA pulp mill and Companhia Italo-Brasileria de Pelotizacao-Itabrasco palletizing plant (with CVRD owning 50.9 percent and with Italy's Finsider International owning the balance).

Four additional subsidiaries were incorporated in 1974. A pelletizing plant, Companhia Nipo-Brasileira de Pelotizacao-Nibrasco, was set up as a joint venture with a group of Japanese steel mills headed by Nippon Steel that year. Companhia Hispano-Brasileira de Pelotizacao, another pelletizing plant, was set up by CVRD with Spain's Ensidesa. Aluminio Brasileiro SA (Albras) was incorporated as a joint venture aluminum production company by CVRD and Nippon Amazon Aluminum to produce primary aluminum. Mineracao Rio do Norte (MRN), a multinational mining consortium set up to work bauxite deposits along the Trombetas River, Para State, was incorporated in 1974 as well.

In 1975, CVRD became the world's largest iron ore exporter, with 16 percent of the seaborne market for this product. By 1976, the company was bringing in export revenues of $717 million through its products and became Brazil's leading foreign exchange earnings generator. Two more mining subsidiaries were incorporated that year: Minas da Serra Geral (MSG) and Urucum Mineracao SA, a mining company set up to work the Urucum and Jacadigo manganese reserves near Corumba, Mato Grosso State. In 1977, CVRD was awarded exclusive mining rights for Carajas. Just as it had done with the Vitoria-Minas railroad, CVRD began constructing an integrated mine-railroad-port system to accommodate the ore mined from Carajas. In 1978, CVRD began work on the Carajas Railroad.

CVRD incorporated another aluminum subsidiary in 1978 called Alumina do Norte do Brasil. The early 1980s saw several more start-ups for CVRD. Valesul Aluminio SA and Minas Serra Geral, mining iron ore, began operating in 1982. The next year, CVRD started operations at the Coaling Terminal in Ponta de Tubarão and at the Timbopeba Iron Ore Mining Project. In 1984, CVRD started gold production at Fazenda Brasileiro in Bahia State. In 1987, CVRD incorporated Bahia Sul Celulose, in association with Companhia Suzano de Papel e Celulose, to produce bleached eucalyptus pulp.

1988–97: PRIVATIZATION ON THE HORIZON

By the late 1980s, political and economic turmoil in Brazil prompted constitutional reform efforts in the Congress. After decades of military rule, democracy came to the forefront with the drafting of the new constitution in October 1988. Among the elements of the so-called Citizenship Constitution were limits on presidential terms and enhanced voting rights for citizens. Some argued the document gave the government too many responsibilities, while imposing undesirable restrictions on foreign investors. However, Brazil was in the midst of an economic crisis during these years, and citizens were ready for new solutions that were not explored during the years of military rule. One effect of the constitutional changes was that a more negative attitude developed toward the state monopolies held in energy and mining, and it was this shift in attitude that paved the way toward the eventual privatization of these industries.

During the years that led to the privatization of CVRD, the company acquired stakes in a number of steel and pulp mills. In 1992, CVRD started operations at its Bahia Sul Celulose pulp mill, and it inaugurated the Capitao Eduardo-Costa Lacerda branch line in Minas Gerais State, linking the Vitoria-Minas Railroad to the Federal Railroad Network (RFFSA). The new 46-

kilometer stretch of track sped the outflow of products from the cerrado savannas while significantly reducing freight costs. On June 10, CVRD signed its first management contract with the Brazilian government, its majority stakeholder.

In 1993, CVRD purchased a stake in steelmaker Companhia Siderurgica Nacional (CSN), which likewise held a small share in CVRD. That year, CVRD became the leading gold producer in Latin America with 12 tons per year. In 1994, the company announced record iron ore sales of 101 million tons. The 1995 acquisition of stock control of SEAS, a manganese iron ore plant in France, opened up fresh prospects for CVRD products on the European market.

The Brazilian government's $45 billion plan for privatization soon extended to its prized industrial conglomerate. CVRD was included in Brazil's National Privatization Program by Decree No. 1,510 on June 1, 1995, but the road to privatization would not be a smooth one. For the last 50 years, the state had directly intervened in the Brazilian economy by running its largest industrial companies, including CVRD. Once the task of modernization was nearly complete, it was time for private enterprise to take over to improve the efficiency of the economy. With Brazil then accounting for 40 percent of Latin America's economy as a whole, this was a significant undertaking. Given Brazil's history, it looked as if attracting foreign investors would remain a challenge.

The sale of CVRD was considered controversial because, unlike other state-owned companies, it was profitable and well-managed. By early 1997, President Fernando Henrique Cardosa had planned to sell the government's 51 percent of CVRD for an estimated $5 billion. A year earlier, CVRD had signed its first private-sector partnership agreement with Southern Star Resources Ltd, a U.S. company, to work the gold deposits. However, progress toward privatization was slow in order to ensure public support.

1997: CVRD IS PRIVATIZED

After weeks of worker-led protests outside the Rio de Janeiro stock exchange and court-ordered delays, a Brazilian consortium led by CSN emerged as the winner of the privatization auction for CVRD in May 1997. CSN bid $3.4 billion for 41.73 percent of the common shares held by the Brazilian government, with a premium of 19.99 percent over the asking price. The consortium also included four Brazilian pension funds, Banco Opportunity and NationsBank of the United States. CSN, which was itself privatized in 1993, shocked investors by winning the CVRD prize. Although CSN was Brazil's

largest steelmaker, two more powerful Brazilian consortiums were considered the likely winners of the auction. CSN was under the direction of Benjamin Steinbruch, who was 43 and considered to be a relative upstart in the Brazilian business community, but CVRD's iron ore business, transportation network and other business assets made Steinbruch's company an overnight giant in the steel industry.

In 1998, CVRD reported its best-ever financial performance with profits of BRL 1,029 billion, a new record for private companies in Brazil. That same year, CVRD produced record iron ore output at Carajas of 45.8 million tons. CVRD remained under the leadership of Steinbruch as chairman and CEO until 1999, when former ambassador Jorio Dauster was appointed the new CEO of the company. Dauster took on a complex shareholder structure and a cumbersome group of noncore businesses when he inherited the helm. The company began divesting noncore assets in order to revive interest in CVRD stock, which had begun to lose value since privatization.

In 2000, CVRD began to focus on its core businesses of mining and logistics. The company looked to sell its pulp and paper assets along with noncore assets in its steel and transportation sectors. In early 2001, CVRD sold its interest in Bahia Sul as a first step toward withdrawing from the pulp and paper industry, and in March of that year the company sold its 10.3 percent stake in CSN. Expansion also remained an important goal that year, with CVRD setting plans in motion to develop five more copper mines in Carajas. The company also looked to diversify in order to decrease its reliance on iron ore revenues, which in 2001 comprised up to 60 percent of group sales. Dauster announced plans in 2001 to expand CVRD's low-level alumina, aluminum and bauxite base to build stronger alternate sources of revenue. The company also began forming Valepontocom and other Internet ventures to develop an e-commerce business. In 2001, CVRD began developing portals related to its mining and logistics businesses.

GROWTH IN THE 21ST CENTURY

Under the leadership of Roger Agnelli, CVRD experienced significant growth during the early years of the new millennium. With Agnelli at the helm, CVRD grew into the second-largest mining company in the world with an eye on becoming number one by focusing on acquisitions, key partnerships, developing new projects, and spending heavily on capital investments. During 2002, the company inaugurated the Sossego project. Sossego was the company's first commercially developed copper project that had the potential to catapult it into the upper echelon of copper mining. Sossego officially began production in 2004 and was a cornerstone in the company's diversification efforts and the country's strategy to convert itself from an importer to a major exporter of copper. By 2005 CVRD's total net exports were valued at approximately $6.3 billion, or 14.1 percent of Brazil's total for the year.

During this period CVRD made several acquisitions that bolstered its holdings. During 2003 CVRD acquired 50 percent of the shares of Brazilian iron mining company Caemi Mineração e Metalurgia S.A. (Caemi) in a $426.4 million deal. It also purchased Canico Resource Corp., a Canadian nickel mining firm, in 2005. Its largest deal however, came in 2006 when it made a $17.6 billion play for INCO Limited. The acquisition of the Canadian nickel mining company positioned CVRD as the one of the largest nickel producers in the world. CVRD finalized the purchase in January 2007. With nickel holdings part of its growing arsenal, CVRD found itself on solid financial ground with demand for commodities like iron ore and nickel increasing at a rapid rate.

In addition to its acquisition strategy, the company was spending billions on capital investments including the Brucutu Project, which was the world's largest mining and plant complex involved in the production of iron ore. The company was also forming key partnerships designed to diversify its holdings as well as boost its core iron ore business. During 2007, CVRD signed an agreement with the state of Espírito Santo and Baosteel Group Corporation, the largest steel producer in China. The project was created to build an integrated steel plant with an initial capacity of five million tons per year. The company also formed a natural gas exploration venture with Shell Brazil.

VALE MOVES FORWARD: 2007 AND BEYOND

By 2007, CVRD was the second-largest mining company in the world. The company had seen significant growth over the previous 10 years. Its market capitalization had grown from $10 billion in 1997 to $150 billion by 2007. The company launched a $50 million branding campaign that year that included the adoption of the Vale name. By using the Vale name, the company hoped to become well known throughout the world. A December 2007 *Wall Street Journal* article summed up the company's need to establish itself as a well-recognized global player. "Over the past few years, the iron-mining industry's profile has surged in importance as a ravenous appetite for metals to feed Asia's building boom has sent prices of commodities soaring. That's turned companies like Vale into huge

profit makers on whose products nations' economies rely." The company officially adopted the Vale S.A. corporate name in 2009.

With revenues and profits soaring, Vale set its sights on making its next big purchase and in late 2007 announced its offer for Switzerland's Xstrata Plc, the world's fifth-largest mining concern. The deal, estimated at $90 billion, would have placed Vale in the top spot in the mining industry. The two companies abandoned their plans in 2008 however, when they failed to reach a suitable agreement.

At the same time, economies around the world began to falter and demand in the Americas and Europe, responsible for nearly half of overall revenues, fell dramatically. During 2009 operating revenues fell to $23.94 billion, down from $38.51 billion in 2008. Operating profits also dropped sharply. Nevertheless, the company spent $12.7 billion in a capital investment program during the year to strengthen its business.

During 2010, Vale focused on bolstering its fertilizer holdings by acquiring Bunge Ltd.'s Brazilian fertilizer assets in a $3.8 billion deal. It also purchased a majority interest in BSG Resources Limited, an iron ore mining firm in Guinea. Despite the hardships of 2009, president and CEO Agnelli believed Vale was on track to prosper once again in the years to come. Demand in China, which was one the company's strongest markets, was climbing. Growth in emerging markets and the eventual recovery in the Americas and Europe positioned Vale for future growth.

Simon Katzenellenbogen
Updated, Rebecca Rayko Cason;
Christina M. Stansell

PRINCIPAL SUBSIDIARIES

CVRD Overseas Ltd. (Cayman Islands); Minerações Brasileiras Reunidas S.A.; Vale Inco Ltd. (Canada); Vale International S.A. (Switzerland).

PRINCIPAL COMPETITORS

BHP Billiton; Cliffs Natural Resources Inc.; Rio Tinto Ltd.

FURTHER READING

Barham, John, "Shaping Up for the Struggle of the Titans: Interview Jorio Dauster: Recasting the Mining Group Will Tax All the Ex-Diplomat's Skills," *Financial Times*, July 8, 1999, p. 12.

"Brazil Miner CVRD Closes in on No 2 Spot in Mining World," *Dow Jones Commodities Service*, October 23, 2006.

"Brazilian Copper Mine Inaugurated," *Lloyd's List*, July 6, 2004.

"Brazil's Iron Giant Reaches for the Top," *Business Week*, March 3, 2008.

Colitt, Raymond, "Vexed Question of Ownership," *Financial Times*, May 15, 2000.

De Lima, Paulo-Tarso Flecha, "Liberalism versus Nationalism: The Prodevelopment Ideology in Recent Brazilian Political History (1930–1997)," *Presidential Studies Quarterly*, June 1999 p. 370.

Dyer, Geoff, "CVRD Kicks Off Disposals with Bahia Sul Sale," *Financial Times*, February 23, 2001.

Fick, Jeff, "CVRD Gains on Iron Ore's Rise," *Wall Street Journal*, October 3, 2007.

———, "Vale Buys Iron-Ore Stake in Guinea," *Wall Street Journal*, May 1, 2010.

"The Iron Chancellor," *Economist*, January 17, 1998, p. 63.

Oppenheimer, Andres, and Katherine Ellison, "Latin America for Sale? Awaiting the Broader Shift to Private Enterprise, Latin America Frets over Pitfalls of the Past," *Miami Herald*, August 17, 1996, p. A1.

Osava, Mario, "Government Claims Victory in Battle over Privatization," *Interpress Service*, May 7, 1997.

Regalado, Antonio, "Vale Seeks to Expand Name Recognition," *Wall Street Journal*, December 26, 2007.

"A Sorry State," *Economist*, March 27, 1999, p. 9.

"Vale Announces Name Change to Vale SA," *Reuters Significant Developments*, May 25, 2009.

Wang, Michael, "CVRD Mulling Plans to Beat Brazil Energy Woes," *Dow Jones Newswires*, May 8, 2001.

Valio Oy

PO Box 10, Meijertie 6
Helsinki, FIN-00039
Finland
Telephone: (+358 010) 38 1121
Fax: (+358 09) 562 5068
Web site: http://www.valio.com

Cooperative
Founded: 1905 as Voinvienti-osuusliike Valio r.l.
Employees: 4,410
Sales: EUR 1.79 billion ($2.52 billion) (2009 est.)
NAICS: 311511 Fluid Milk Manufacturing; 311512 Creamery Butter Manufacturing; 311513 Cheese Manufacturing; 311520 Ice Cream and Frozen Dessert Manufacturing

■ ■ ■

Valio Oy is Finland's dominant milk and dairy products company. The company collects and processes approximately 86 percent of the country's total milk production. In 2009 Valio took in nearly 1.9 million liters of milk. Valio produces a wide range of products, including cheese, whey-based drinks, and other drinks, for the consumer and institutional markets, as well as ingredients for the global dairy and food processing industries. Valio is also one of the world's leading producers of functional dairy products, or products that claim health improvement benefits, including lactose-free milks, cheeses, and other products, and probiotic drinks and products containing the probiotic bacterium Lactobacillus GG (LGG).

Valio directly markets its products to a number of markets, including Sweden, Belgium, the Baltic States, Russia, China, and the United States, where the company operates its own sales and production subsidiaries. Valio sells its functional ingredients, especially LGG, on a licensed basis throughout the world. The company markets its products under such consumer brands as Valio, Valio Butter, Valio Gefilus, Viola, Valio Atleet, Valio Yoghurt, Vache Bleue, and Zero Lactose, as well as Finlandia and Real Goodness in the United States. The company's ingredients sales include whey and milk powders and LGG.

Finland remains the company's largest market, at 66 percent of sales, which neared EUR 1.8 billion ($2.5 billion) in 2009. Fresh dairy products account for 44 percent of company sales, cheese adds nearly 33 percent, and butter and spreads generate nearly 12 percent of sales. Valio is a limited company owned by 22 shareholder cooperatives, which in turn represent nearly all of Finland's dairy farmers. Pekka Laaksonen is the group's chief executive officer, while Antti Rauhamaa serves as Valio's chairman.

BUTTER COOPERATIVE IN 1905

Valio originated as a cooperative called Voinvienti-osuusliike Valio r.l, set up in 1905 in order to develop exports of Finnish butter. The company's membership initially counted 17 dairy cooperatives. Valio set up headquarters in the port town of Hanko, and at first focused on sales to England.

Valio quickly added to its product range, shipping a number of other dairy products starting in 1909. The

COMPANY PERSPECTIVES

Mission: To promote the business of Valio milk producers. Value: Responsibility for well-being. Operating principles: We create genuine innovative products. Customer and product profitability guide our operations. We take personal responsibility and learn from experts. We generate robust results and secure the future. Vision: Valio will be the leading brand in its field in Finland and the nearby countries, and pioneer health and well-being concepts worldwide.

company also broadened its membership base. By 1912 the company counted 172 dairy farmer-members, a number that nearly doubled before the end of World War I. A key factor behind this membership growth was a peculiarity of the Finnish dairy market, which was primarily made up of small farms. In the early 1970s, for example, the average Finnish herd size stood at just 6 cows. At the beginning of the 21st century average herd size still remained low, at just 12 cows.

A significant milestone for Valio came in 1916, when the company established Valio Laboratory, its own research facility. The addition of this facility marked a step in Valio's expansion beyond its role as a sales and marketing body, enabling the company to solidify its role as an important partner for Finland's diary industry. The addition of a research wing also played a role in Valio's emergence as a dairy foods processing company.

SILLAGE METHOD IN 1928

Valio's research and development effort itself received a major boost with the addition to the staff of future Nobel Prize-winner Artturi I. Virtanen in 1916. By 1921 Virtanen had been appointed laboratory manager. Much of his research then focused on the field of pH measurement and adjustment. Valio's butter exports had long been plagued by the difficulty of preserving the product during shipping to England. Because Finnish butter was produced using the fermentation method, it remained highly perishable during transport. In 1926 Valio Laboratory developed a means of buffering the butter's pH levels, helping to stabilize the butter for longer voyages. The company succeeded in patenting the method, called AIV Butter Salt, in 1929.

Valio Laboratory also turned its attention to problem solving at the other end of the production chain. Finland's harsh winters meant that the feed available to the country's dairy cattle became nutritionally poor. In 1928 Virtanen led Valio Laboratory in the development of AIV silage, a nutrient-rich feed produced using the fermentation method and pH adjustment in silos. The silage method remained in use into the next century, and helped Virtanen win the Nobel Prize in 1945.

Also during the 1920s, Valio launched the production of Emmental cheese (a variety of Swiss cheese), and began supplying its first starter cultures to its dairy farmer members. This provided the company with a second processed dairy products line in addition to butter. These two remained the company's sole products into the early 1960s.

ADDRESSING LACTOSE INTOLERANCE: 1974

The company changed its name to Valio Meijerien Keskusosuusliike in 1955. Valio began exporting its cheese to the United States in 1958. Closer to home, Valio built up a presence in the Swedish market, while also developing a strong business supplying the nearby Russian and Baltic markets.

Finland nevertheless remained the company's largest market in the postwar era. Valio had grown strongly over the decades, and by the end of the century collected nearly 90 percent of all milk produced in the country. Part of this growth came through the group's decision to begin developing a line of fresh dairy products, including milk, yogurt, ice cream, and *viili* (a traditional cultured dairy milk product) and other Finnish specialties, starting in 1962.

During the 1960s the company also launched the production of ultrahigh-temperature (UHT) milk products. The UHT process produced milk capable of being stored for several months. In 1973 Valio launched its first line of liquid baby formula using UHT milk, under the Tutteli brand. The company then extended the Tutteli brand to include a line of porridges and purees, as well as formula.

Valio also set its research sights on the growing problem of lactose intolerance in Finland, which affected nearly one-fifth of the population. Lactose intolerance resulted when a person's body stopped producing the enzyme necessary to break down lactose, the milk sugar present in milk. Valio achieved its first breakthrough in this area when it developed a hydrolyzing process to break down lactose in milk itself. The company first applied its new technology to whey in 1974. By 1980 Valio had extended the process to milk itself, launching the Hyla Energa milk powder brand in

1980, followed by UHT milk in 1982. Both products featured reduced, although not altogether eliminated, lactose content.

PROBIOTIC BREAKTHROUGH IN 1990

The company meanwhile continued to invest in expanding its research and development division. In 1978 Valio Laboratory moved to a new state-of-the-art facility in Pitäjänmäki. The company also entered a partnership with the Chemistry Research Foundation, which placed its staff under the auspices of Valio Laboratory in 1980. That foundation then became known as the Nutrition Research Foundation.

The expansion of its research and development operations permitted Valio to broaden its product range as well. In the 1980s Valio began introducing as many as 100 new products each year. The company also continued to develop its hydrolyzing technology, as well as its marketing program. By the end of the 1980s, the company had succeeded in sensitizing the Finnish population to the problems surrounding lactose intolerance, driving up sales of the Hyla line.

In the late 1980s Valio became aware of a new type of bacterium called Lactobacillus Goldin and Gorbach, or LGG. The bacteria had been named after its discoverers, Barry Goldin and Sherwood Gorbach, who had worked together to develop the bacterium at Tufts University School of Medicine. LGG presented a number of health benefits when incorporated into milk products, notably for intestinal health. LGG represented an important breakthrough for the young market for "probiotic" products (that is, foods and ingredients providing measurable health benefits). LGG was the first probiotic to provide clinically measured results, and soon became the world's most-studied probiotic bacterium, with more than 300 studies supporting its health claims.

Goldin and Gorbach, however, proved unsuccessful in convincing the American dairy industry to take up LGG. This provided Valio with an opening, and in 1987 the company acquired the worldwide marketing rights for LGG. The company introduced its first LGG-containing product, a whey-based drink, under the Gefilus brand in 1990. Response to the new product was slow, however, and by 1993, with sales barely climbing, Valio nearly dropped the brand.

The company instead adapted its marketing strategy, rolling out a wider range of Gefilus products, including buttermilk in 1992, yogurt in 1995, and finally milk in 1996. Valio also launched a highly successful advertising campaign that year, based on the tagline: "Bacteria to the Rescue." This was followed by another popular campaign, the so-called stomach halo campaign. In 1997 the company added a line of LGG-containing fruit drinks. These were followed by the launch of mini-bottles in 1999.

NEW STRUCTURE

Both Valio and the Finnish dairy market had undergone a significant transformation by the end of the 1990s. The dairy industry underwent a major consolidation during this period. In the 1980s the Finnish dairy sector, like many European markets, had been beset by a high degree of overproduction. The introduction of new production and preservation technologies, including UHT milk, were important factors behind the steady rise in milk production.

By the early 1980s Finland's total milk production neared 3.2 billion liters, far more than the country's own consumption. With other European markets facing similar oversupply, and thereby limiting export potential, the Finnish government took steps to impose new production limits.

Finland's application for entry into the European Union, which enforced its own quota policies, provided a major impetus toward the reduction of Finland's production totals. By the beginning of the 1990s the country's total production had dropped to below 2.4 billion liters, and then dropped again to 2.0 billion liters by the beginning of the new century.

The reduction in milk production in turn sparked the consolidation of the dairy sector, and its multiplicity of small dairy farms. This enabled average herd size to double between the end of the 1970s and the beginning of the 1990s. Further consolidation ultimately boosted the average herd size among Valio's suppliers to 21 cows. This in turn brought about the emergence of a smaller number of larger cooperatives. At the beginning of the 1980s Valio's membership numbered nearly 150 cooperatives. By the early 1990s this number had dropped to 54. Through a continued series of mergers, the company's member-shareholders roster fell to just 22 by 2010.

Valio itself had taken on a new structure during this period. In the early 1990s the company's network of more than 20 processing facilities were restructured into regional dairy companies. These were then brought under Valio's control in 1992, at which time Valio changed its status, become a limited company, Valio Oy. The following year, the company took over all marketing activities for its owners' dairy operations as well.

INTERNATIONAL EXPANSION

The success of LGG had permitted Valio to expand its ingredients business to a global level, as the company signed on a growing list of licensees. Valio's sales reached more than 30 markets worldwide at the dawn of the 21st century. At the same time, Valio had also taken steps to add its own international operations.

In 1991 Valio acquired McCadam Cheese Co., a leading producer of cheddar and other cheeses, from Dean Foods. The company also developed a marketing subsidiary, Finlandia, based in New Jersey, for its cheese imports. Valio thus became a major player in the U.S. cheese market, with a major presence in the cheddar market, while also becoming the leading Swiss-type cheese importer.

Valio targeted markets closer to home as well. The collapse of the Soviet Union brought new opportunities, particularly in the Baltic markets. Valio entered Estonia first, setting up a sales and marketing subsidiary there in 1992, and then later developing its own production subsidiaries in that market. The following year the group launched export operations to Lithuania, and in 2002 added sales to Latvia via a joint venture.

Valio had added several new markets by then, starting with the creation of subsidiaries in St. Petersburg, Russia, and in Sweden in 1994. In 1996 the company acquired Belgium's Vache Bleue, the largest cheese wholesaler in that market. Valio was one of the first foreign companies to achieve success in China, starting in 1987 when the Finnish and Chinese governments developed a cooperation agreement. The company began marketing its own Valio brand, focusing on the

institutional sector, in China in 1991. In 2001 the company opened a representative office in Shanghai. This business gained full subsidiary status in 2008. By 2005 the company had become one of the first to be granted "Green Food" status in China, an intermediate category between conventional foods and organic foods.

GROWING COMPETITION AT HOME

Valio's research and development program achieved several new successes in the new decade. The company launched its first lactose-free milk in 2001, and quickly expanded the line, known as Zero Lactose, into a range of dairy products. The company then acquired the license for Benecol, a cholesterol lowering ingredient, from Raisio, launching the Evolus line of milk beverages for controlling blood pressure in 2001. By 2008 the company had launched a new product, Evolus Double Effect, which provided both cholesterol lowering and blood pressure regulating effects. The company also expanded its Gefilus line that year, launching Gefilus Max, containing LGG and three other probiotic bacteria.

Valio also moved to take advantage of the growing demand for weight-control products as the obesity epidemic began to take hold in Finland in the new century. The group launched a new line of low-fat cheeses, which became highly successful in Finland. These included Polar, a cheese containing just 5 percent milk fat (as compared to full-fat cheeses with fat content of 40 percent and higher). In 2005 Valio also introduced ProFeel, which it claimed was the world's lightest milk. In addition to being fat-free, the new product was also lactose-free, further reducing its caloric value.

Valio's international operations continued to grow strongly through the decade. The company's operations in the Baltic countries grew particularly strongly as Valio developed its own dairy processing facilities in Estonia. By the end of the decade, the company claimed a market share as high as 30 percent for fresh dairy and 10 percent for cheese in Estonia. The company further boosted its position there in 2004, when it acquired Voru Juust, a leading Estonian cheese maker. In 2006 Valio regrouped all of its operations in the region under a new subsidiary, Valio Baltic Ltd. The following year, the group added a dairy facility in Gathina, near St. Petersburg, backed by an investment of EUR 20 million. That site became fully operational in 2008. The company then reinforced its Russian sales, adding a cheese distribution facility in Moscow in 2009.

This international expansion became especially important for Valio as it faced growing competition in its home market. This came in the most part in the form of lower-priced foreign imports, and the rising strength of the hard discount sector, as Finnish consumers struggled through the worst economic recession since the 1920s. As a result, Valio saw its revenues slip by 3 percent at the beginning of 2010. Despite these difficulties, Valio remained Finland's dominant dairy company, with a fast-growing international presence and a global reputation for its dairy technologies.

M. L. Cohen

PRINCIPAL SUBSIDIARIES

OOO Valio (Russia); SIA Valio International (Latvia); UAB Valio International (Lithuania); Valio Baltic Ltd.; Valio Eesti AS (Estonia); Valio Shanghai Ltd. (70%; China); Valio Sverige AB (Sweden); Valio USA Inc.; Valio Vache Bleue S.A. (Belgium).

PRINCIPAL DIVISIONS

Fresh Dairy Products; Butter and Spreads; Cheese; Powdered Ingredients; Others.

PRINCIPAL OPERATING UNITS

Domestic; International.

PRINCIPAL COMPETITORS

Compagnie Laitiere Europeenne S.A.; Dagrofa A/S; Dairy Crest Group plc; Edeka Zentrale AG and Company KG; Etn Franz Colruyt S.A./NV; Lactalis International S.N.C.; Suedzucker AG; Terrena S.C.A.; Tine B.A.; Unibel S.A.

FURTHER READING

"Evolus Comes to Portugal," *Dairy Industries International*, August 2005, p. 6.

"Finnish Milk Company Valio Is Working with Russian Company Galktika to Build a New Dairy Facility in Gathina, South of St. Petersburg," *Dairy Industries International*, March 2006, p. 6.

"Innovation for Sale," *Dairy Foods*, September 2005, p. 71.

Kjoeller, Katrine, "Finnish Functionality," *Dairy Industries International*, August 2007, p. 18.

"Valio in Talks to Cut 90 Jobs," *just-food.com*, April 30, 2009.

"Valio Launches Lactose Free in US," *Dairy Industries International*, October 2009, p. 12.

"Valio Receives Green Food Label in China," *just-food.com*, April 4, 2005.

"Valio Rolling into Estonia," *Dairy Industries International*, November 2004, p. 11.

"Vivacious Valio," *Dairy Industries International*, March 2002, p. 8.

Verband der Vereine
Creditreform e. V.

Hellersbergstrasse 12
Neuss, D-41460
Germany
Telephone: (49 2131) 109-0
Fax: (49 2131) 109-8000
Web site: http://www.creditreform.de

Nonprofit Association
Founded: 1879 as Verein Creditreform zum Schutze gegen schädliches Creditgeben e. V.
Employees: 4,500
Sales: EUR 533 million ($741 million) (2009)
NAICS: 561450 Credit Bureaus; 561440 Collection Agencies; 511140 Database and Directory Publishers

■ ■ ■

United under the organizational umbrella of Verband der Vereine Creditreform e. V. (VVC), a nonprofit association or *Verein*, Creditreform is Germany's largest provider of credit-related business information and debt collection services. It consists of roughly 165,000 members and 130 regional branches in Germany which are legally independent limited partnerships. The branch offices collect and provide information on businesses and consumers. Creditreform's business model is based on mutuality. Customers who receive information agree to become members, and to provide information to the association in return.

In addition to credit-related information on individual businesses, Creditreform provides economic research reports on the business climate, insolvencies and trends in certain industries or countries. Its mainly small to midsized member companies also receive the *Creditreform* monthly trade magazine. Creditreform's international network organization, Creditreform International, operates branch offices in 19 mostly Central and Eastern European countries and in China. Through additional subsidiaries that are united under the holding company Creditreform AG, Creditreform also offers factoring, company and consumer credit ratings, and direct-marketing data compilation services.

COOPERATIVE CREDIT INFORMATION AGENCY FOUNDED 1879

The rapid expansion of national and international trade in the 19th century had been made possible by new means of transportation such as the railway and steam-powered ocean shipping, as well as by new means of communication, the telephone and the telegraph. It not only held great promise for businesses, but also posed great financial risk. To make sure that customers paid for the goods they received, collecting and exchanging information about their financial resources and trustworthiness became a common business practice and led to the emergence of credit information agencies.

In Germany, where a stock market crash in 1873 had caused a severe economic crisis that left many businesses struggling financially, paying habits deteriorated. At the same time, the first organizations that provided financial information on businesses were established. One of them was Verein Barzahlung Mainz, an associa-

Since 1879, our business has been to make our members' business more secure, no matter whether their customers are companies or private consumers, whether they are located in Germany or abroad, or whether it is a matter of just individual assignments or volume business.

tion of 25 small businesses founded on March 9, 1879, in Mainz, southwest of Frankfurt am Main. The association's initial goal to abolish credit altogether by refusing to sell goods to members who owed money to other members soon proved to be impractical and was replaced by the concept of "credit reform." The renamed Verein Creditreform zum Schutze gegen schädliches Creditgeben aimed at protecting its members from credit fraud by providing reliable information about the payment behavior of businesses through information exchange with similar organizations elsewhere as well as an outstanding debt collection service.

Although the cooperative idea was ridiculed by the two major commercial credit-related information agencies, and looked at skeptically by German authorities and by some members of the business community, it was embraced by a rapidly growing number of small businesses. In the early 1880s additional Creditreform associations sprang up in large cities across Germany, including Cologne, Frankfurt am Main, Nuremberg, Hannover, Heidelberg, and Munich. By 1883 there were 15 Creditreform associations. Together they founded the Federation of Creditreform Associations, Verband der Vereine Creditreform (VVC) in that year which was based in Mainz until headquarters were moved to Leipzig in 1888. To better manage the growing number of Creditreform associations, regional offices were established in addition to the central administration. In 1885 VVC launched its own trade magazine.

While the number of Creditreform associations in Germany continued to climb, the cooperative model made its way into other European countries. The establishment of a new department that provided information on businesses abroad was followed by the foundation of affiliated associations in Switzerland, the Netherlands, Belgium, Austria-Hungary, Denmark, and the United Kingdom. At the dawn of the 20th century Creditreform had reached its goal of establishing itself as a major player in the German market for credit-related

business information. By 1914 the number of Creditreform associations had grown to 269 with a combined membership of roughly 82,660, mainly small businesses.

REVIVAL AFTER WORLD WAR I AND HYPERINFLATION

The onset of World War I in mid-1914 brought Creditreform's growth to a sudden halt. As the German government took over control of the country's economy and assigned the production of war goods to designated manufacturers, the demand for business information dwindled. The remaining limited amount of free trade was often based on cash transactions. Creditreform was cut off from most of its affiliates abroad while many of the association's staff was drawn into the military or had to be laid off. The defeat of Germany in 1918 resulted in major losses of territories, and the number of Creditreform associations shrank from 269 to 240.

As the on setting postwar inflation caused prices to rise, Creditreform followed suit. However, to prevent a ruinous price war with its competitors, VVC together with three other large German business information agencies formed a cartel in 1920 and agreed to not undercut a certain price level. Their business soared for a short time, until the accelerating speed of the inflation made it increasingly difficult to conduct any business at all. As the German currency's value depreciated weekly at first, then daily, and at the height of hyperinflation even hourly, businesses were reluctant to sell any product or service on credit. While the price for Creditreform's information services had to be raised frequently, the demand for them dropped significantly. The introduction of a new currency in October 1923, however, put an end to hyperinflation.

When the German economy entered a period of recovery in 1924, the interest in credit-related information services rose rapidly. At the same time, customers asked for more detailed information. To keep up with the growing demand, Creditreform started collecting information about annual sales, equity capital, and the number of employees of businesses and lobbied for a suitable legal framework from German authorities. Through the newly established International Committee Creditreform the company also revived its cooperation with similar associations in other European countries, including Austria, Switzerland, Sweden, the Netherlands, and Czechoslovakia. In the early 1930s Creditreform introduced a standardized format for the information it provided. Moreover, the company launched a telephone information service for customer inquiries on small credits of up to 200 reichsmark.

KEY DATES

1879: Verein Creditreform is established in Mainz.

1883: The federal association Verband der Vereine Creditreform (VVC) is founded.

1947: A new central administration is set up in Neuss.

1979: Creditreform enters a cooperation with Dun & Bradstreet International.

1986: The cooperation between Creditreform and Dun & Bradstreet ends.

1992: Marketing information provider microm Micromarketing-Systeme und Consult is founded.

1995: The international network association Creditreform International is formed.

1999: The association's central database is accessible via the Internet.

2002: Holding company Creditreform AG is established.

2008: The company's first subsidiary in Asia is set up in China.

REORGANIZATION AFTER WORLD WAR II

After Adolf Hitler and his National Socialist Party came to power in 1933, the democratic structure and decision-making process at the Creditreform associations was replaced by the *Führerprinzip* or the "leader's principle." Creditreform's Jewish directors and employees were replaced by "Aryans." Commercial business information service providers were put under government control. In 1936 Creditreform's president of 35 years, the liberal attorney Dr. Georg Zöphel, resigned from his post under Nazi pressure. He was succeeded by Ernst Wolfram, a former colonial officer and managing director of the Creditreform association in Duisburg.

Under Wolfram's leadership Creditreform continued its operations through the difficult period of the late 1930s and even throughout World War II. By 1939 the number of Creditreform associations in Germany had grown to 423. In that year, however, new legislation was passed that gave local police authorities the power to allow or forbid credit rating bureaus such as Creditreform the provision of information about certain businesses or persons. In addition, the law called for a more stringent investigation of "non-Aryans." After heavy bombings had destroyed Creditreform head-

quarters in Leipzig in 1943, offices and the rescued business archives were moved to the Creditreform association in nearby Halle.

While Creditreform's business in Western Germany soared during the postwar years, the work of the associations located in the Soviet-occupied Eastern part of the country was made more and more difficult by the governing authorities. A new central association for all of Germany, the Creditreform Zentralverwaltung e. V., based in Neuss, near Düsseldorf, was founded in August 1947. One year later the operations of Creditreform's central clearing office were moved from Leipzig to Neuss. VVC was removed from the official register of associations in Leipzig by the chief of police in 1949. Twenty years later the Neuss-based central Creditreform association was renamed Verband der Vereine Creditreform.

Demand for Creditreform's information services grew rapidly during the postwar reconstruction years. In 1948 Creditreform reported revenues of roughly DEM 4 million, with some 550 employees serving about 26,000 members. While investors, entrepreneurs, and municipalities were securing the financial resources to rebuild the country, Creditreform rebuilt its network of information providers in Germany and abroad, updated its databases, and trained new personnel. In 1950 the association resumed the publishing of its *Creditreform* trade magazine.

MODERNIZATION AND INTERNATIONAL COOPERATION AFTER 1973

The boom years of the "German Economic Miracle," the 1950s and 1960s, were followed by a severe economic crisis caused by the oil price shock of 1973. The number of bankruptcies in Germany climbed throughout the decade, and the interest in credit-related information was high. In order to process the increasing volume of inquiries, Creditreform invested heavily in the modernization of its operations and in improved service quality. As one of the first European business information agencies Creditreform had a comprehensive teletype/telex network in place by 1974.

Later in the decade the association introduced a new format for its services with more detailed information and in a more easily comprehensible structure and design. A major strategic decision was made in 1979 when Creditreform entered a cooperation with the American market leader Dun & Bradstreet International. After the newly elected Creditreform president Carl-Arthur Frormann had sent all of the association's directors to the United States for a hands-on inspection of the world's first electronic data-processing systems, Creditreform introduced electronic data processing to its operations, integrating all of its 108 locally maintained archives. It was also during the 1970s when Creditreform launched a long-term public relations program as a major marketing tool. By the end of the decade Creditreform had become Germany's leading provider of credit-related business information with about 1,900 employees serving roughly 72,000 members.

In the early 1980s Creditreform worked closely together with Dun & Bradstreet. The latter acquired its information on Germany businesses from Creditreform, and Creditreform bought its information on foreign businesses from the American agency. The two companies also cooperated in the area of debt-collection. However, when it became obvious that Dun & Bradstreet intended to acquire the German partner and Creditreform resisted such a takeover, the American company, in an unexpected move, acquired one of Creditreform's competitors instead in 1984. The cooperation between Creditreform and Dun & Bradstreet ended two years later.

In the mid-1980s Creditreform launched its own proprietary online database, containing information on roughly 800,000 businesses, which could be accessed by all of the association's 107 offices. In addition, the company introduced a so-called credit-standing index, a combination of credit-related parameters that resulted in a rating between 100 and 600 that allowed customers to get an instant impression on the creditworthiness of a business. Moreover, Creditreform launched an information-by-phone service for all of West Germany and intensified its cooperation with other independent business information providers in Europe. In 1987 six Austrian Creditreform associations joined the German Creditreform Federation.

INTERNATIONAL EXPANSION, ONLINE DELIVERY AFTER 1989

The fall of the Berlin Wall in November 1989 opened the door to Creditreform's expansion into Eastern Europe. The company immediately began to collect information on businesses in Eastern Germany and opened several branch offices there in 1990. In the following years Creditreform started cooperating with local partners in Poland, the Czech Republic, Slovakia, Slovenia, and Hungary. In 1995 the German and Eastern European Creditreform associations founded the umbrella organization for the international Creditreform network, Creditreform International e.V. In the decade that followed, Creditreform International set up

branches in 20 countries, mainly in Central and Eastern Europe.

While being as close as possible to the customer through its many regional offices remained a crucial element of Creditreform's business model, the world of business information became instantly available anywhere in the world via computer networks in the 1990s. In 1993 VVC in cooperation with the German chambers of industry and commerce established ECOFIS, a company that set up and operated an independent private online network for the two organizations. In 2001 the company also took over the operation of Creditreform's data-processing centers in Neuss and Dortmund. The percentage of information requests provided online rose from about 30 percent in 1992 to over 90 percent a decade later. In 1999 Creditreform made its central database available via the Internet.

One of Creditreform's most important strategic decisions was to expand the range of its information services to marketing-related data. Made possible by electronic data-processing technologies, the importance of marketing directly to customers via the mail, the telephone, telefax, and e-mail rose constantly. Creditreform realized the enormous potential of this important growth market and established microm Micromarketing-Systeme und Consult, a subsidiary that specialized in the provision of detailed consumer data to marketers, in 1992. Five years later Creditreform together with the international consumer information provider Experian set up the joint venture Creditreform Experian GmbH (CEG). As a result, Creditreform's sales more than doubled during the 1990s.

NEW VENTURES AND FURTHER GROWTH AFTER 2000

Around the turn of the 21st century Creditreform launched several new business ventures that contributed to the organization's continued growth. In 1999 Creditreform established Crefo Factoring, a network of 18 regionally active companies offering factoring services, the acquisition of accounts receivable in exchange for instant cash, to small and midsized companies with annual sales up to six million euros. In 2000 the new subsidiary Creditreform Rating AG was founded, a rating agency for the credit standing of small and midsized companies, as well as for loans and bonds. Nine years later Creditreform Rating became the first organization in Germany to be officially approved by the federal German agency overseeing the financial services sector as an independent provider of credit ratings on companies and their creditworthiness.

Another new subsidiary, CEG Creditreform Consumer GmbH, which was founded in 1997, offered information on individual consumers to corporate members. The number of information requests handled by CEG rose from four million in 2003 to over 21 million in 2009. The establishment of the new holding Creditreform AG in 2002 provided an organizational umbrella for the company's growing number of subsidiaries. In 2004 Creditreform together with German business news publisher Verlagsgruppe Handelsblatt launched a new Internet portal with information on 16 million small and midsized businesses. In the same year the company established Creditreform Portfolio Management (CPM), a subsidiary for the acquisition of outstanding debt portfolios from local savings banks, mail order companies and telecommunications service providers which, however, stagnated with the onset of the global financial crisis that began in the late 2007.

By that time, Creditreform's annual revenues had passed the EUR 500 million mark, and the company reported a 70 percent share in the German market for credit-related business information. Creditreform had established itself in the Baltic States, followed by the setting up of Creditreform's first Asian subsidiary in China five years later. In the second half of the first decade of the 2000s, Creditreform continued to expand and improve its range of services. The company launched a database with information on the corporate structures of companies, including subsidiaries, corporate and personal shareholdings, suppliers, and customers in 2007. In 2010 Creditreform began to introduce new formats of its information services, from a quick overview to more detailed company dossiers and balance sheet analyses. In the same year, new personal data protection legislation in Germany required credit rating agencies to disclose the data they collected about individual consumers annually upon request at no extra charge.

Evelyn Hauser

PRINCIPAL SUBSIDIARIES

Creditreform AG; Crefo Factoring; Creditreform International e.V.; acoreus Collection Services GmbH; CEG Creditreform Consumer GmbH; CPM Creditreform Portfolio Management GmbH; Creditreform Rating AG; bedirect GmbH & Co. KG; microm Micromarketing-Systeme und Consult GmbH; Immo-Check GmbH.

PRINCIPAL COMPETITORS

arvato infoscore GmbH; Bürgel Wirtschaftsinformationen GmbH & Co. KG; D&B Deutschland GmbH; Hoppenstedt Holding GmbH; SAF Forderungsmanagement GmbH; SCHUFA Holding AG.

FURTHER READING

"Creditreform Collection Co Enters Estonian Market," *Baltic News Service*, October 15, 2002.

"Creditreform erste staatlich anerkannte Rating-Agentur," *Welt*, August 7, 2009, p.15.

"Creditreform Forecasts Record Turnover of Nearly 505m Euros (Creditreform peilt in diesem Jahr Rekordumsatz an)," *Europe Intelligence Wire*, August 24, 2006.

Frühauf, Markus, "Creditreform kauft faule Kredite," *Börsen-Zeitung*, August 24, 2006, p. 5.

"Verband der Vereine Creditreform Buys Controlling Stake in Lithuanian Company," *Baltic News Service*, March 29, 2003.

"Verlagsgruppe Handelsblatt and Creditreform Launch New Internet Portal (Handelsblatt grundet Firmenportal)," *Europe Intelligence Wire*, April 8, 2004.

XOMA Ltd.

2910 7th Street
Berkeley, California 94710-2700
U.S.A.
Telephone: (510) 204-7200
Toll Free: (800) 246-9662
Fax: (510) 644-2011
Web site: http://www.xoma.com

Public Company
Incorporated: 1981
Employees: 195
Sales: $98.4 million (2009)
Stock Exchanges: NASDAQ
Ticker Symbol: XOMA
NAICS: 325412 Pharmaceutical Preparation Manufacturing

■ ■ ■

Berkeley, California-based XOMA Ltd. is a leading biotechnology firm that focuses on the discovery and development of antibodies (proteins in the body that are critical for immunity). Via licensing and development collaborations, the company partners with larger pharmaceutical firms to develop and market products, from which it receives royalties. In addition, XOMA also licenses its antibody libraries and technologies to other companies. During the early 2010s the company was working on XOMA 052, an anti-inflammatory antibody with applications for treating diseases such as diabetes.

FORMATIVE YEARS

XOMA was established in 1981 by Patrick Scannon, who oversaw the company's scientific efforts, and John Lucas, who served as its first CEO. In 1983 Lucas, whose focus was on starting up new companies as opposed to running them long-term, began searching for a good CEO. In January 1984 he hired Steven Mendell away from Franklin Lakes, New Jersey-based Becton Dickinson & Co., giving the company instant credibility. "He was so energetic that I ended up sitting around in my office reading the *Wall Street Journal* all day," Lucas recalled in the June 22, 1987, issue of the *San Francisco Business Times.*

By early 1984 XOMA had garnered approximately $33 million in funding from venture capitalists. With hopes of securing expedited U.S. Food and Drug Administration (FDA) approval, the company concentrated on searching for cures to fatal diseases. One example was a treatment for metastatic melanoma. The company's researchers developed a toxin that, in turn, was attached to the monoclonal antibodies that respond to melanoma cells.

Lucas, who had remained chairman after the addition of Mendell, parted ways with XOMA right before the company went public in 1986. At that time Mendell was commanding an annual salary of $185,000. For the fiscal year ending December 31, 1986, XOMA recorded a net loss of $46.6 million on revenue of $110,000.

EARLY DEVELOPMENTS

As president and director of science, Patrick Scannon continued to lead XOMA's scientific endeavors during

COMPANY PERSPECTIVES

XOMA is redefining antibody innovation to create life-changing therapeutic antibodies.

the late 1980s. He did so in partnership with former FDA official Samuel Ackerman, whom the company had hired as vice president for medical and regulatory affairs. By this time XOMA was working on genetically engineered treatments for conditions such as graft-versus-host disease (a complication suffered by bone marrow transplant patients), as well as colorectal cancer and a bacterial infection known as septic shock. XOMA's work attracted the attention of major news media, including the *CBS Morning News* and the *Today Show*.

XOMA ended the 1980s with several key developments. In December 1988 the company applied for FDA approval of Xomazyme 65, its graft-versus-host disease treatment, which also was intended to be its first commercial product. In addition, plans were made for a $50 million debt offering, the proceeds of which were designated for the construction of a large manufacturing facility and the establishment of a direct sales force. In 1989 XOMA recorded a loss of $18.9 million on revenues of $10.4 million.

In April 1990 XOMA received a U.S. patent for its antiseptic shock drug, E5. In the April 23, 1990, issue of the *San Francisco Business Times*, XOMA spokeswoman Carol DeGuzman claimed that the patent for the new drug, which originated at the University of California at San Francisco during the early 1980s, covered "all other patent applications for mammalian derived monoclonal antibodies to treat septic shock." XOMA quickly filed a patent infringement lawsuit against Malvern, Pennsylvania-based Centocor Inc., which had developed a competing drug called Centoxin.

In October 1990 Richard Juelis was named chief financial officer of XOMA. That year the company lost $23.7 million on revenues of $20.5 million. Early the following year XOMA filed with the Securities and Exchange Commission to offer three million shares of its common stock. Midway through the year an FDA committee recommended approval of XOMA's graft-versus-host rejection drug, then called CD5-Plus, which XOMA hoped to market and distribute in partnership with Johnson & Johnson's Ortho Biotech division.

CHALLENGING TIMES

XOMA suffered a significant setback in 1991. Although the company won its patent infringement lawsuit against Centocor, an advisory committee of the FDA failed to recommend the approval of its E5 drug. Making matters worse, the committee recommended approval of Centocor's competing drug, Centoxin.

On the leadership front, John Castello was named both president and CEO in early 1992. In October of that year the company announced plans to cut 85 jobs from its workforce. Perhaps the most disappointing news came when the FDA ultimately failed to approve both E5 and CD5 Plus. XOMA was hopeful as both drugs continued in Phase III clinical trials.

From early 1992 to the first quarter of 1994 XOMA racked up losses of $86.7 million. With its cash reserves quickly disappearing, the pressure was on for the company to develop a marketable product. In early 1995 XOMA discontinued development of CD5 Plus and shifted its resources to the development of Neuprex, part of a line of bactericidal and permeability-increasing (BPI) protein products, which made regular antibiotics work more effectively.

XOMA's market capitalization dipped below $50 million in 1995, down from nearly $500 million earlier in the decade. Midway through 1996 the company was awarded a patent for its BPI protein products. XOMA ended the year with a net loss of $29.1 million on revenues of $3.6 million, and capped off the decade by raising $17.4 million via a private placement of three million shares of its common stock to institutional investors.

ENTERING THE 21ST CENTURY

XOMA began the new millennium by striking a deal with Deerfield, Illinois-based Baxter Healthcare Corporation. Specifically, Baxter's Highland Immuno division acquired world rights to XOMA's Neuprex drug, which had been slated for the treatment of meningococcemia, a bacterial infection that can cause meningitis. The company stood to receive $35 million in payments from Baxter as part of the arrangement between the two firms.

It also was in early 2000 that XOMA generated $30.7 million from the sale of its common stock to institutional investors. The company suffered a setback in November when Irvine, California-based Allergan Inc. decided to relinquish its rights to ophthalmic anti-infective products containing XOMA's BPI. Around the same time, XOMA filed a registration to sell up to 10 million shares of its stock over the following two years, which at time were valued at $112.5 million.

KEY DATES

1981: XOMA is established by Patrick Scannon and John Lucas.
1984: Steven Mendell is named CEO.
1992: John Castello is named president and CEO.
2003: Raptiva is XOMA's first drug to receive Food and Drug Administration approval.
2006: Steven B. Engle is named president and CEO.

In December 2002 XOMA and Genentech Inc. submitted a biologics license application for a psoriasis drug called Raptiva. The two companies also pursued testing of this drug for patients with moderate to severe rheumatoid arthritis. However, Phase II rheumatoid arthritis trials were halted in mid-2003 when the drug was found to be ineffective for that condition. Around the same time XOMA's arrangement with Baxter Healthcare for Neuprex fell apart when Baxter decided to terminate its license. Following the termination, XOMA was entitled to receive a $10 million payment from Baxter.

FIRST FDA APPROVAL

In September 2003 the FDA's Dermatologic and Ophthalmic Drugs Advisory Committee unanimously voted in favor of approving Raptiva. Two days later the company revealed plans to offer nine million shares of its common stock to the public, worth approximately $85.3 million. In October the FDA formally approved Raptiva, which was the first drug in the company's history to receive federal approval.

Patrick Scannon remained with XOMA as chief scientific and medical officer at the time of the Raptiva approval. Moving forward, the company would then have a revenue-producing drug. In the United States it would receive 25 percent of revenues, with partner Genentech receiving the rest. In terms of market potential, an analyst indicated that the worldwide market for biologic psoriasis treatments was between $1 billion and $2 billion, and that XOMA's new drug had the potential of securing a market share worth between $400 million and $500 million.

In early 2004 XOMA partnered with Emeryville, California-based Chiron Corp. A worldwide exclusive agreement was established between the two companies focused on the development of vaccines, small-molecule drugs, and therapeutic antibodies used for treating cancer. A small setback occurred later that year when XMP.629, an acne treating gel developed by XOMA, produced inconclusive results during a Phase II clinical trial. Following the bad news, the company saw its stock price plummet 35.1 percent.

Following the setback related to its acne gel, in November 2004 XOMA announced a deal with New York-based Zephyr Sciences Inc. worth more than $73 million. Specifically, Zephyr obtained an exclusive worldwide license pertaining to XOMA's BPI products, including Neuprex. In early 2005 when XOMA received an 18-month, $15 million contract from the National Institutes of Health's National Institute of Allergy and Infectious Diseases to develop three monoclonal antibodies against botulinum neurotoxin. The antiterrorism contract helped increase XOMA's stock price by 26 percent.

XOMA encountered another roadblock in mid-2005 when the company terminated its $73 million BPI-related agreement with Zephyr, which it claimed had not met certain financial requirements. Moving forward, XOMA indicated that it would continue to seek new partners, as well as appropriate treatment applications, for its BPI product line. XOMA ended 2005 by establishing a collaboration and cross-licensing agreement for antibody-related technologies with Oslo, Norway-based Affitech AS.

LEADERSHIP CHANGES

In November 2006 XOMA successfully completed its initial $15 million contract with the National Institutes of Health's National Institute of Allergy and Infectious Diseases. Early the following year, President and CEO Jack Castello announced plans to retire following the selection of a qualified candidate. In August XOMA named Steven B. Engle as its new president and CEO. Castello remained with the company as nonexecutive chairman through October 2007, at which time Engle assumed the additional role of chairman.

Several leadership changes took place in 2008. Early in the year seasoned pharmaceutical executive Mary L. Anderson was named vice president of business development. Among her responsibilities was the oversight of licensing activities related to the company's therapeutic pipeline. In October XOMA named Stephen K. Doberstein, PhD, as vice president of research.

By late 2008 XOMA was involved in approximately 13 active development projects. At that time the company restructured a collaboration agreement with the pharmaceutical company Novartis Vaccines and Diagnostics Inc. (formerly Chiron Corp.). The agreement covered six development programs, including a cancer treatment drug called HCD122. Essentially, the restructured arrangement between the two companies allowed XOMA to focus on other projects, including an anti-inflammatory diabetes drug called XOMA 052. Novartis assumed development control of the other drugs while paying royalties to XOMA.

POTENTIAL DIABETES BREAKTHROUGH

In December 2008 accelerated plans were announced for XOMA 052, which was slated to begin a Phase II clinical trial. The drug's prospects seemed very good. In a December 10, 2008, *GlobeNewswire* release, XOMA Chairman and CEO Steven Engle explained: "In September, we presented encouraging results supporting one of the most significant medical advances in diabetes in decades—a move from insulin therapy to anti-inflammatory treatment."

Additional leadership changes took place in 2009. Early in the year XOMA named Fred Kurland as chief financial officer. In October Susan Kramer, DrPH, was named vice president of project and alliance management. Among her duties was strategic and operational responsibility for the development of XOMA 052. The following month James R. Neal was named vice president of business development.

It also during the latter part of 2009 that XOMA announced plans to repay a $44.2 million loan from Goldman Sachs Specialty Holdings Inc. As part of this repayment, $25 million of the proceeds came from Genentech, which bought out its royalty obligation to XOMA for the company's Lucentis wet age-related macular degeneration drug. Around this time XOMA also generated $13.9 million by selling 18 million shares of its common stock to Azimuth Opportunity Ltd.

Heading into 2010 XOMA had a workforce of approximately 200 people. In April the company received a $1 million milestone payment from Takeda Pharmaceutical Company Limited under a collaboration agreement established between the two companies in 2006. That same month XOMA was awarded two new patents pertaining to the use of interleukin-1 beta antibodies for the treatment of inflammatory diseases and type 2 diabetes. Looking beyond XOMA's 30th anniversary in 2011, the company's prospects for success during the second decade of the 21st century seemed strong.

Paul R. Greenland

PRINCIPAL SUBSIDIARIES

XOMA (Bermuda) Ltd.; XOMA Ireland Limited; XOMA Limited (UK); XOMA Technology Ltd. (Bermuda); XOMA (US) LLC; XOMA Development Corporation.

PRINCIPAL COMPETITORS

Abbott Laboratories; Amgen Inc.; Pfizer Inc.

FURTHER READING

Carlsen, Clifford, "Xoma's Patent Gives It an Edge over Centocor," *San Francisco Business Times*, April 23, 1990, p. 9.

"Genentech, Xoma's Raptiva Receives Psoriasis Approval," *BioWorld Today*, October 29, 2003.

Paton, Huntley, "Xoma's Chief Hates the 'Hype Monster;' Mendell Instead Hypes Patients," *San Francisco Business Times*, June 22, 1987, p. 16.

Rauber, Chris, "Cured? Xoma Back from Death's Door," *San Francisco Business Times*, August 23, 1996, p. 3.

"Steve Engle Appointed Chairman of XOMA," *PrimeZone Media Network*, October 8, 2007.

"XOMA Appoints Steven B. Engle President, Chief Executive Officer and Director," *PrimeZone Media Network*, August 6, 2007.

"XOMA Provides Clinical Plan Update on Diabetes Drug Candidate; New Preclinical Animal Data Provides Additional Support for XOMA 052 Phase 2 Study Design," *GlobeNewswire*, December 10, 2008.

"XOMA Successfully Completes Initial $15 M Biodefense Contract with NIAID," *Chemical Business Newsbase*, November 6, 2006.

Yildiz Holding A.S.

Davutpa Cad Number 10, Topkapi
Istanbul,
Turkey
Telephone: (+90 0216) 524 24 00
Fax: (+90 0216) 524 24 00
Web site: http://www.ulker.com.tr

Private Company
Incorporated: 1970 as Ülker Gida Sanayi ve Ticaret
    Anonim Sirketi
Employees: 29,500
Sales: $10.9 billion (2009 est.)
NAICS: 551112 Offices of Other Holding Companies;
    311320 Chocolate and Confectionery Manufactur-
    ing from Cacao Beans; 311330 Confectionery
    Manufacturing from Purchased Chocolate; 311340
    Non-Chocolate Confectionery Manufacturing

■ ■ ■

Yildiz Holding is one of Turkey's largest privately held holding companies, with sales of nearly $11 billion in 2009. The company, which operates across nearly 70 companies, is also one of the country's most focused conglomerates, operating primarily in the confectionery and food sector. Yildiz's flagship company is publicly listed Ülker Bisküvi, Turkey's leading producer of cookies, snack cakes, chocolate, and other confectionery items, including chewing gum and soft drinks. Ülker (also written as Uelker) itself serves as a vertically and horizontally integrated holding company for many of Yildiz's interests. As such the company's subsidiaries include flour production, starch and sugar production, oil and margarine production and packaging, and paper and cardboard production. Since 2007 Ülker has also controlled the Godiva chocolate brand.

Yildiz's operations are organized into the following divisions: Food, Beverage, Confectionery, and Chewing Gum Group; Food, Frozen Food, and Personal Care Group; Godiva; Packaging, Information Technologies, and Real Estate Investments Group; and Ülker (Biscuit, Chocolate) Group. The company remains controlled by the founding Ülker family, and led by Murat Ülker, chairman and son of the company's founder.

BAKING COOKIES IN 1944

The Ülker family originally operated a small grocery in Istanbul. In 1944 Sabri Ülker and his older brother Asim decided to set up a small bakery business making cookies. The company began with just three employees and a single oven, but quickly added several more ovens. The brothers set a modest production goal of 250 kilos per day, and by the end of its first year, Ülker's production topped 75 tons.

Ülker initially focused on a single type of cookie. The popularity of its recipe encouraged the company to expand its production and its product line. In 1948 Ülker decided to move from its bakery and built its first factory, in the Topkapi area of Istanbul. The new facility allowed the company to triple its production in the next decade.

In 1950 Ülker began developing its own distribution and logistics operations in order to expand its sales beyond Istanbul to the wider Turkish market. The company made a crucial decision at the time not to add transportation charges to the price of its cookies. This encouraged a growing number of vendors, including small shops and Turkey's many street vendors, to agree to sell the company's cookies.

FIRST EXPORTS

Ülker's success was all the more remarkable because of Turkey's economic and political instability in the company's early years. The company's early growth had been hampered by a shortage of machinery and equipment in Turkey. However, in 1960 the company began importing production equipment from Germany. As a result, the group expanded its production line, as well as its product range.

Ülker incorporated as a limited liability company, Ülker Gida Sanayi ve Ticaret Anonim Sirketi, in 1970. At the same time, Ülker launched a sister company, Anadolu Gida, based in Ankara, as part of the group's national expansion effort. Unlike Ülker, which remained fully controlled by the Ülker family, Anadolu Gida was established as a joint stock company, providing the family with access to outside capital. Anadolu Gida opened its own factory, doubling Ülker's total production capacity. This in turn supported Ülker's first international moves, as the company launched its first exports to the Middle East markets.

In 1974 Ülker extended beyond cookie manufacturing for the first time, launching its own chocolate and chocolate candies production. The company quickly captured a major share of the Turkish market. Part of this success came from Ülker's decision to invest in its own research and development market. In this way Ülker sought to compete with the major international brands by raising its quality levels and by developing new and innovative confectionery and candy products. The growing success of Ülker's chocolate production led

the company to establish a dedicated factory in Istanbul in 1979.

VERTICAL INTEGRATION

In the 1980s Ülker also began to put into place the vertical integration strategy that led to the creation of a new holding company during the decade, called Yildiz Holding. This process started with the launch of the group's own packaging unit, allowing Ülker to become the first in Turkey to introduce cellophane packaging in 1979. In 1983 the company expanded its packaging operations with the opening of new production lines producing cardboard boxes and polypropylene. In another extension to its operations, Yildiz began producing some of its own production machinery and equipment during the decade. By this time Sabri Ülker had taken sole control of the company, and had been joined by his son, Murat.

Ülker extended its range of food production through the end of the decade as well. By the early 1990s the company had successfully established subsidiaries producing flour, margarine, and oil, in this way helping to ensure its supply of ingredients for its confectionery production.

The early 1990s represented a new period of growth for Ülker, as Turkey solidified its position as a major supplier of goods to the European Union. Turkey's own strong economic expansion had made it an attractive market for a number of major international companies as well, leading Ülker to begin developing a series of production partnerships. The first of these was signed with Cerestar in 1993, setting up Pendik Nisasta, a producer of glucose and corn starch. In 1995 the company launched another partnership, with Dankek, developing a line of packaged cakes and snacks for the Turkish market.

Ülker had also continued to develop its own operations. The group set up a third food subsidiary, called Ulstan Food Industry, and expanded its range to include soft and hard candies, chewing gum, and other such items. In 1994 Yildiz listed its Anadolu Gida subsidiary on the Istanbul stock exchange, gaining access to fresh investment capital. By then the Ülker family oversaw a growing empire of more than 20 companies, generating revenues of more than $700 million per year. The company's exports reached 75 markets worldwide by this time.

INTERNATIONAL GROWTH

Yildiz and Ülker continued seeking new markets in the second half of the 1990s. The company launched its own milk and dairy products brand, King Top, in 1996.

KEY DATES

1944: Sabri Ülker and brother Asim found a small bakery producing cookies in Istanbul.

1948: The Ülkers open a factory in Topkapi to increase production.

1970: The company is incorporated as Ülker Gida Sanayi ve Ticaret Anonim Sirketi.

1980s: Yildiz Holding is founded as the company pursues a vertical integration strategy.

1994: Yildiz lists subsidiary Anadolu Gida on the Istanbul stock exchange.

2000: Sabri Ülker retires and son Murat becomes company chairman.

2003: Ülker Bisküvi and Anadolu Gida merge, forming Ülker Gidu, which takes over Anadolu Gida's stock exchange listing.

2010: Ülker enters partnership talks with McCormick & Company.

The company also teamed up with Baycan Chewing Gum and Food Corp., a leading producer of chewing gum, as well as a traditional gum called mastic, starting in 1996. This partnership, to develop joint chewing gum production facilities, led to Yildiz's acquisition of Baycan in 2001.

Founder Sabri Ülker stepped down as the company's head in 2000, turning over its leadership to his son Murat Ülker. Yildiz then began developing an international expansion strategy. The company targeted markets where it already enjoyed a strong presence. This led the company to establish or acquire subsidiaries in a number of countries, including Kazakhstan and Ukraine, as well as in Saudi Arabia. In 2004 the company added a former government-owned cookie and chocolate factory in Algiers, Algeria. Also that year, the company built its first foreign factory, in Romania, forming Eurex Alimentaire.

Meanwhile, Yildiz maintained its steady expansion at home. The company restructured its operations into five distinct business units, each with its own executive management, in 2001. In 2002 the company reached a partnership agreement with Switzerland's Hero to begin producing baby foods under that brand for the Turkish market. The company also entered the ice cream market, and began marketing its own brand of Turkish coffee. The launch of its own line of soft drinks brought Yildiz new success, especially with the launch of Cola Turka, which quickly became a major rival for the more entrenched Coca-Cola brand.

Yildiz continued restructuring its holdings, leading to the decision to merge Ülker Bisküvi with Anadolu Gida in 2003. The new company was initially called Ülker Gidu, and took over Anadolu Gida's stock exchange listing. In 2007 that company renamed itself again as Ülker Bisküvi.

ACQUIRING GODIVA IN 2007

The company continued to add new partnerships through Ülker during the second half of the decade. In 2005 the company teamed up with Kellogg's, launching production of a line of cereals featuring both the U.S. company and Ülker's brand names on the package. The following year Ülker gained the license for the cholesterol-lowering ingredient Benecol from Finland's Raisio, launching the functional foods line Kalbim Benecol in Turkey. The company also extended the Hero brand in Turkey to include other products, such as Akta Vitale, a yogurt with probiotic cultures.

By the middle of the decade, Ülker had grown into Turkey's largest confectionery and foods company, with annual sales of more than $6 billion. The company remained relatively unknown at an international level. This changed at the end of 2007, when the company emerged as the winner in the bid to acquire famed Belgian chocolate maker Godiva from the Campbell Soup Company. Yildiz paid $850 million for Godiva, which became an independently operated part of the Ülker group of companies. Soon after, Yildiz acquired several smaller Turkish confectionery companies, including Oba Cay, Uno, and Krevitas.

Yildiz developed several new partnerships toward the end of the decade. In 2008 the company reached an agreement with British chocolate group Lovells to launch its brand in the Turkish market. In 2009 the company teamed up with Gumlink to produce non-chocolate confectionery products. Also that year, the company established a new chewing gum joint venture with the Continental Confectionery Company, and a partnership with Laurens Spethmann Holding, the European tea leader. In 2010 the company launched negotiations with U.S.-based McCormick & Company to develop a spice production partnership for the Turkish market. By then, Yildiz's total revenues, driven in large part by the Ülker group of companies, neared $11 billion. The company founded as small bakery in 1944 had grown into Turkey's leading food group in the new century.

M. L. Cohen

PRINCIPAL SUBSIDIARIES

Birlik Pazarlama (99%); Biskot Gida; GF Lovell Deutschland GMBH; Godiva Belgium BVBA; Hamle Company Ltd. (Kazakhstan); Hero Gida Sanayi ve Ticaret A.Ş; İdeal Gida San. ve Tic. A.Ş.; Ülker Bisküvi Sanayi A.Ş.

PRINCIPAL DIVISIONS

Food, Beverage, Confectionery, and Chewing Gum Group; Food, Frozen Food, and Personal Care Group; Godiva; Packaging, Information Technologies, and Real Estate Investments Group; Ülker (Biscuit, Chocolate) Group.

PRINCIPAL COMPETITORS

Ender Cikolata Sekerleme Gida San Tic A.S.; Kent Gida Maddeleri San ve Tic A.S.; Nestlé Türkiye Gida Sanayi A.S.; Sagra Gida Ueretim, Pazarlama San ve Tic A.S.; Seckin Hediye Sepetleri Gida San Ltd.

FURTHER READING

Can, Faruk, "Credit Crunch, Weak Dollar Pave Way for Ulker to Godiva," *Today's Zaman*, December 29, 2007.

Castano, Ivan, "Ustungida Mulls IPO of Ulker Chocolate Division," *just-food.com*, January 9, 2007.

"A 'Glo-cal' Approach," *Candy Industry*, October 2004, p. 24.

Pacyniak, Bernie, "White Spots, Dark Chocolate," *Candy Industry*, January 2008, p. 6.

Tiffany, Susan, "Ulker: Turkey's Leading Confectioner," *Candy Industry*, March 1998, p. 39.

"Turkish Company Buys Godiva," *Candy & Snack Business*, January–February 2008, p. 6.

"Ulker Gets Funds for Kazkh and Romanian Business," *Trade Finance*, December 2004, p. 15.

"Ulker Group Picks Up UK Lovells Chocolate Brand," *Candy Industry*, September 2008, p. 9.

"Ulker Moves to European Dominance," *Candy Industry*, June 1995, p. 92.

"Ulker Plans Further Global Expansion," *EMGPlus*, January 31, 2010.

"Ulker Scores a Big Hit with Godiva Acquisition Deal," *Euroweek*, April 4, 2008.

"Ulker to Produce Infant Food," *AsiaPulse News*, January 13, 2009.

Yum! Brands, Inc.

———— ■ ————

1441 Gardiner Lane
Louisville, Kentucky 40213
U.S.A.
Telephone: (502) 874-8300
Fax: (502) 874-8790
Web site: http://www.yum.com

Public Company
Incorporated: 1997 as Tricon Global Restaurants Inc.
Employees: 350,000
Sales: $10.84 billion (2009)
Stock Exchanges: New York
Ticker Symbol: YUM
NAICS: 722110 Full-Service Restaurants; 722211
    Limited-Service Restaurants; 533110 Owners and
    Lessors of Other Non-Financial Assets; 551112 Of-
    fices of Other Holding Companies

■ ■ ■

Yum! Brands, Inc., operates the Taco Bell, Pizza Hut, KFC, Long John Silver's, and A&W chains. The company is the largest quick-service restaurant concern in the world with approximately 37,000 locations in more than 100 countries across the globe. Taco Bell, Pizza Hut, and KFC were part of PepsiCo Inc.'s restaurant group until 1997, when they were spun off as Tricon Global Restaurants, Inc. Tricon changed its name to Yum! Brands in 2002, the same year that Long John Silver's and A&W were added to its holdings. By 2007, 10 years after it was spun off from PepsiCo, the company was deriving half of its profits from international operations.

PIZZA HUT SUCCESS LEADS TO PEPSICO PURCHASE

Pizza Hut Inc. was established in 1958 by brothers Dan and Frank Carney in their hometown of Wichita, Kansas. A friend suggested opening a pizza parlor, then a rarity, and the brothers borrowed $600 from their mother to start a business with partner John Bender. Renting a small building at 503 South Bluff in downtown Wichita and purchasing secondhand equipment to make pizzas, the Carneys and Bender opened the first Pizza Hut restaurant. On opening night they gave pizza away to encourage community interest. A year later, in 1959, Pizza Hut was incorporated in Kansas, and Dick Hassur opened the first franchised unit in Topeka, Kansas.

By 1971 Pizza Hut had become the world's largest pizza chain according to sales and number of restaurants, then just over 1,000 in all. A year later, the chain was listed on the New York Stock Exchange. Pizza Hut also achieved, for the first time, a $1 million sales week in the U.S. market. At the end of 1972 Pizza Hut made its long anticipated offer of 410,000 shares of common stock to the public. The company expanded by purchasing three restaurant divisions: Taco Kid, Next Door, and the Flaming Steer.

In addition, Pizza Hut acquired Franchise Services, Inc., a restaurant supply company, and J & G Food Company, Inc., a food and supplies distributor. The company also added a second distribution center, in

Peoria, Illinois. In 1973 Pizza Hut expanded further by opening outlets in Japan and Great Britain. Three years later, the chain had more than 100 restaurants outside the United States and 2,000 units in its franchise network. The company's 2,000th restaurant was opened in Independence, Missouri. By this time, Pizza Hut had caught the eye of PepsiCo Inc., the global soft drink and food conglomerate. In 1977 Pizza Hut became a cornerstone in PepsiCo's restaurant division.

PEPSICO ADDS TACO BELL

The Taco Bell brand was launched in 1962 by Glen Bell, a World War II veteran who had worked in the restaurant industry since 1946, when he opened his first hot dog stand in San Bernardino, California. His idea for franchising a Mexican-themed restaurant proved successful, and by 1970 Taco Bell had become a $6 million operation, producing annual profits of approximately $150,000.

The fast-food chain's success eventually drew the attention of PepsiCo Inc. as it sought to expand further into the restaurant business. After its new Pizza Hut unit unsuccessfully tried to launch a Mexican food concept of its own, PepsiCo altered its strategy and began wooing Glen Bell in order to buy Taco Bell outright. In February 1978 a deal was struck in which the Mexican fast-food chain was purchased for just under $125 million in stock. PepsiCo's strategy in acquiring Taco Bell was simple: The fast-food chain dominated the Mexican food market, so PepsiCo was buying market share.

For PepsiCo the challenge was to make Taco Bell less a regional ethnic food phenomenon and more a national fast-food chain. Glen Bell had originally sought to set Taco Bell apart from other fast-food chains, McDonald's in particular, and its preeminent position among other Mexican food chains, almost all of them regional or local rivals, was already secure. PepsiCo's decision to reposition Taco Bell was a challenge to the fast-food giants on a national scale.

The PepsiCo strategy emphasized that Taco Bell outlets would sport spartan simplicity in decor and menu, with a concentration on predictable quality, affordable prices, and clean and convenient surroundings. Taco Bell also moved swiftly to redesign the company logo. The old logo, a Hispanic man dozing under a giant sombrero, was replaced by a sparkling bell atop the company name. As Larry Higby, senior vice president of marketing at Taco Bell, noted in *Advertising Age*, "Usually when you try to turn something around, you look to develop breakthrough advertising. But we came to exactly the opposite conclusion: we needed to look more mainstream."

The strategy worked. Taco Bell grew rapidly during the early 1980s. By 1983, when John E. Martin took over as president, the chain had 1,600 outlets in 47 U.S. states, producing a total of $918 million in sales. The average Taco Bell franchise claimed sales of $680,000 that year, a significant increase over the franchise average of $325,000 in sales only three years earlier. As a measure of market strength, Taco Bell's nearest rival in the Mexican fast-food segment was Naugles, a California-based chain with only 160 outlets and 1983 sales of $84 million.

STRATEGY FOR SUCCESS

The company's success continued throughout the 1980s and came even as a recession led to savage price-cutting and cutthroat competition in the fast-food industry. This fact impressed industry analysts. A 1991 article in the *Harvard Business Review* named Taco Bell as the best performer in the fast-food industry at the time, surpassing traditional market leader McDonald's. The authors wrote, "If McDonald's is the epitome of the old industrialized service model, Taco Bell represents the new, redesigned model in many important respects."

Kentucky Fried Chicken (the company's name was changed to KFC Corp. in 1991), founded in 1952 by Harland Sanders, was added to PepsiCo's holdings in 1986 in an $840 million deal. The company had spent much of the decade securing profits and expanding, and PepsiCo believed it would be a successful addition to its burgeoning restaurant portfolio.

While KFC's international division saw significant growth during the 1990s, domestic sales were sluggish due to intense competition and failed product launches. Furthermore, relationships between its parent company and franchisees had deteriorated, and PepsiCo was not seeing the return on assets that it saw with its beverages

KEY DATES

1952: Harland Sanders establishes his first Kentucky Fried Chicken (later KFC) franchise.

1958: Pizza Hut is founded by brothers Dan and Frank Carney.

1962: The first Taco Bell location opens.

1977: PepsiCo purchases Pizza Hut.

1978: PepsiCo acquires the Taco Bell chain.

1986: Kentucky Fried Chicken is added to PepsiCo's holdings.

1997: PepsiCo spins off its restaurant holdings as Tricon Global Restaurants, Inc.

2002: Tricon acquires Long John Silver's Restaurants Inc. and A&W Restaurants Inc.; the company changes its name to Yum! Brands Inc.

2007: Yum! has 35,000 locations worldwide and earns half its profits outside the United States.

and snack food divisions. Consequently, PepsiCo decided to exit the restaurant business altogether.

TRICON GLOBAL RESTAURANTS CREATED: 1997

In the late 1990s PepsiCo drew together its restaurant businesses, including Pizza Hut, Taco Bell, and KFC. All operations were then overseen by a single senior manager, and most back office operations, including payroll, data processing, and accounts payable, were combined. In January 1997 the company announced plans to spin off this restaurant division, creating an independent publicly traded company called Tricon Global Restaurants, Inc.

The formal plan, approved by the PepsiCo board of directors in August 1997, stipulated that each PepsiCo shareholder would receive one share of Tricon stock for every 10 shares of PepsiCo stock owned. The plan also required Tricon to pay a one-time distribution of $4.5 billion at the time of the spin-off. The deal was approved by the Securities and Exchange Commission and completed on October 6, 1997.

FACING CHALLENGES

Pizza Hut, Taco Bell, and KFC fared well after the spin-off. Tricon immediately began to implement new strategies intended to bolster revenues and profits. The company also looked to strengthen its relationships with its franchise locations. In the case of Taco Bell, the

company began selling company-owned stores to its franchisees. Pizza Hut also received a major facelift in the wake of the spin-off. Hundreds of locations were sold back to franchisees and more than 700 locations were shuttered. Company headquarters were moved to Dallas, Texas. The company also filed suit against competitor Papa John's International Inc., claiming that its marketing tagline ("Better Ingredients. Better Pizza.") was false and misleading. A court ruled in favor of Pizza Hut in 2000. Meanwhile, KFC opened its first outlets in Vietnam and Guadeloupe.

As Tricon management worked to position itself as the leading operator in the quick-service restaurant industry, it faced several challenges. Ameriserve Food Distribution Inc., its main supplier, declared bankruptcy in January 2000. The problem was soon resolved, however, when McLane Company Inc. agreed to buy the faltering company in November 2000. Tricon was also pushed to shelve its successful advertising campaign featuring a talking Chihuahua in 1999 after Taco Bell franchisees demanded that future commercials tout the company's fresh food.

Prompted by faltering sales, the firm launched its "Think Outside the Bun" slogan in an attempt to lure customers to its new, fresher products. At the same time, two men filed suit against the chain claiming the firm stole their advertising idea for the talking Chihuahua. In 2003 a federal jury awarded $30.1 million to the two men.

NEW BRANDS AND NEW NAME: 2002

During 2002 Tricon added Long John Silver's Restaurants Inc. and A&W Restaurants Inc. to its holdings in a $320 million deal with Yorkshire Global Restaurants Inc. The company changed its name to Yum! Brands, Inc., that year, reflecting the company's shift to a multi-branding strategy. Nearly 2,000 company restaurants were multi-branded units, offering customers a choice of either Taco Bell and KFC or Taco Bell and Pizza Hut at one location. With the purchase of Long John Silver's and A&W, Yum! planned to aggressively pursue additional multi-branding strategies. In 2003 the company acquired the rights to the Pasta Bravo brand and planned to pair it with Pizza Hut.

Yum! also focused on international expansion, eyeing China, the United Kingdom, Mexico, and Korea as key growth markets. KFC had become China's leading brand, opening the country's first drive-through in Beijing in 2002. Overall, there were 800 KFCs and 100 Pizza Huts in China at that time, and during 2003 Taco Bell made its debut there. A&W also experienced a first:

it went international with the establishment of a restaurant in Hannover, Germany.

While exposure in the international arena was crucial to the future growth of Yum!, its presence in certain areas left it subject to criticism and violence. A KFC in Pakistan was set on fire by an angry mob protesting the U.S. bombing of Afghanistan in 2001. In June 2003 Chairman and CEO David Novak became the target of a demonstration held by the People for the Ethical Treatment of Animals (PETA) in Germany. PETA had recently launched a campaign against KFC and Yum! claiming that the animals purchased for its restaurants were abused and treated in an inhumane fashion. A protestor at a KFC took PETA's actions a step further and soaked Novak with fake blood and feathers.

MULTI-BRANDING SUCCESS

Nevertheless, Yum! remained dedicated to international expansion as well as its multi-branding strategy and customer service goals. Under Novak's direction, the company planned to open 1,000 new international units per year and at least 400 multi-branded units in the United States each year.

The pairing of Long John Silver's (LJS) with A&W in multi-branded restaurants was proving successful. Yum! was planning to double the number of LJS locations within a few years as it expanded it into a truly national chain. LJS was already the U.S. leader in quick-service seafood, with more than 1,200 restaurants in 2004, but with operations in only 36 states, there was room to grow.

In 2004 Yum! put a temporary halt on new domestic multi-branded locations for KFC, however, after three years of slipping sales. Nevertheless, the multi-branding concept endured. By 2005 Yum! had more than 2,800 multi-branded outlets in the United States. In a rare international multi-branding deal, the company signed an agreement with Moscow's Rostik Restaurants to develop 300 joint locations in Russia over five years. After a successful trial, the company decided in 2007 to add the WingStreet chicken concept to all domestic Pizza Hut locations.

The China division, which included Thailand and Taiwan, remained the largest growth area. There were 1,400 KFC restaurants in Mainland China by 2005, and another 400 in Thailand and Taiwan. The division also had nearly 300 Pizza Huts, most of them in the People's Republic. Yum! was also involved in India, another large emerging market, with 100 Pizza Hut restaurants and a handful of KFC outlets. Western European countries remained important as well. France's

KFC restaurants were among Yum!'s busiest and the chain was strong in the United Kingdom.

TAKING STOCK

Ten years after its spin-off from PepsiCo, Yum! Brands had halved the $4.7 billion debt it had inherited and was opening three restaurants a day somewhere in the world. It even brought its Tex-Mex chain Taco Bell to Mexico for the first time in 2007. With 35,000 restaurants in all, Yum! was second only to McDonald's on the world stage. KFC was Yum!'s largest brand, accounting for 45 percent of total revenues. There were 16,500 KFC restaurants globally.

Yum!'s management admittedly emulated McDonald's in a review of best practices in 2007, seeking to learn from its recent success in the U.S. market. One result of the survey was more snack and beverage options at Taco Bell and KFC. One area where Yum! clearly eclipsed McDonald's was its penetration into international markets. By 2007 half of its profits were coming from overseas. Its international stores tended to be more localized than those of McDonald's, typically devoting a quarter of the menu to familiar regional dishes.

By the end of 2009 Yum! had 3,500 restaurants in China. It had developed a Chinese-cuisine restaurant of its own, Shanghai-based East Dawning, and bought a minority stake in local hot-pot chain Little Sheep. Nevertheless, same-store KFC sales in China were slipping. Western cuisine in clean, air-conditioned stores was no longer a novelty. Yum! continued to expand the brand into hundreds of smaller cities in the center of the country. In larger cities, Pizza Hut evolved to match the lifestyles of China's rising middle class, with the appearance of delivery-only locations.

FOCUS ON INTERNATIONAL GROWTH

About 80 percent of Yum!'s domestic restaurants were franchised. Most of the overseas locations were as well, although the company bought out its partners in two notable instances. In 2006 it bought out Whitbread, its U.K. Pizza Hut partner since 1982. There were 600 units in Great Britain, and the market was becoming increasingly competitive. A temporary rebranding as "Pasta Hut" did not help much. In April 2009 Yum! bought out Central Restaurant Group, one of its Thailand Pizza Hut franchisees, while keeping it as its KFC franchisee there.

KFC had entered India in 1995 but after 10 years had only 10 stores in the whole country. It reached 74 stores by early 2010, when it began a major push with the goal of having 500 restaurants there within five years. While a little more than a third of the total population were vegetarians, they were concentrated in the north and west of the country, a marketing official told India's *Economic Times*. India was also used as a relatively rare international launching pad for Taco Bell. The Pizza Hut chain had 158 units there, half as many as rival Domino's Pizza Inc. Yum! reportedly had yet to break even in India.

France remained another priority international market for Yum! Brands. The company continued to expand its KFC and Pizza Hut chains there, expecting the dismal economy to guide consumers' eating habits down-market. With just under 200 restaurants divided between KFC and Pizza Hut, the company trailed Mc-Donald's 1,200 units in France.

Christina M. Stansell
Updated, Frederick C. Ingram

PRINCIPAL SUBSIDIARIES

A&W Restaurants, Inc.; KFC Corporation; LJS Restaurants, Inc.; Long John Silver's, Inc.; Pizza Hut, Inc.; Pizza Hut (UK) Limited; Taco Bell Corp.

PRINCIPAL DIVISIONS

KFC-U.S.; Pizza Hut-U.S.; Taco Bell-U.S.; LJS/A&W-U.S.; YUM Restaurants International; YUM Restaurants China.

PRINCIPAL OPERATING UNITS

KFC; LJS; Pizza Hut; Taco Bell; A&W.

PRINCIPAL COMPETITORS

AFC Enterprises Inc.; Burger King Corporation; CKE Restaurants, Inc.; Doctor's Associates Inc. (Subway); Domino's Pizza, Inc.; McDonald's Corporation; Papa John's International, Inc.; Wendy's International, Inc.

FURTHER READING

Blanchard, Ken, Jim Ballard, and Fred Finch, *Customer Mania! It's Never Too Late to Build a Customer-Focused Company*, New York: Free Press, 2004.

Einhorn, Bruce, Wing-Gar Cheng, and Wendy Leung, "Is China Fed Up with the Colonel's Chicken?" *Business Week*, February 22, 2010, p. 30.

Enz, Cathy A., "Multibranding Strategy: The Case of Yum! Brands," *Cornell Hotel and Restaurant Administration Quarterly*, February 2005, pp. 85–91.

"Fast Food's Yummy Secret—Yum! Brands," *Economist*, August 27, 2005, p. 61.

Garber, Amy, "Yum's Got the Whole World in Its Brands," *Nation's Restaurant News*, August 15, 2005, pp. 40–44, 81.

Hedlund, Steven, "Yum! Has Big Plans for LJS Nationwide," *SeaFood Business*, January 2004, pp. 1, 10.

Horovitz, Bruce, "Taco Bell's New Menu Goes for a Cheap Fill; Fast-Food Value King Reclaims Its Crown with Items under a Buck," *USA Today*, May 14, 2008, p. B1.

Novak, David, and John Boswell, *The Education of an Accidental CEO: Lessons Learned from the Trailer Park to the Corner Office*, New York: Three Rivers, 2007.

Schlesinger, Leonard, and James Heskett, "The Service-Driven Service Company," *Harvard Business Review*, September–October 1991.

Schreiner, Bruce, "Fast-Food Giant Kentucky-Based Yum Marks Eventful Decade since Spinoff," *Cincinnati Post*, October 13, 2007, p. A13.

Sharma, Amit, "As a Brand, We Are Targeting Non-Sensitive Vegetarians: Unnat Varma, KFC," *Economic Times* (India), April 12, 2010.

"Taco Bell Hopes It Has a Menu to Go," *Business Week*, October 16, 2001.

"Taco Bell Secures Fast-Food Presence," *Advertising Age*, July 16, 1984.

Wells, Melanie, "Happier Meals," *Forbes*, January 20, 2003, p. 76.

Whalen, Jeanne, and Jeff Jensen, "Taco Bell Hearing Call of the Border," *Advertising Age*, July 10, 1995, p. 6.

"Yum! to You … David Novak on Yum! Brands' 10 Years of Global Growth," *Nation's Restaurant News*, October 15, 2007.

Zorlu Holding A.S.

Zorlu Plaza, Avcilar
Istanbul, 34310
Turkey
Telephone: (+90 0212) 456 23 00
Fax: (+90 0212) 422 00 99
Web site: http://www.zorlu.com.tr

Private Company
Founded: 1953 as Zorlu Tekstil Kolektif
Employees: 25,000
Sales: $5 billion (2009 est.)
NAICS: 551112 Offices of Other Holding Companies;
221122 Electric Power Distribution; 423620
Electrical and Electronic Appliance, Television, and
Radio Set Merchant Wholesalers

■ ■ ■

Zorlu Holding A.S. is one of Turkey's largest privately held conglomerates, overseeing more than 50 companies and 25,000 employees, with combined revenues of $5 billion in 2009. Zorlu operates in four main areas: textiles, electronics and home appliances, energy generation, and real estate. Zorlu originated as a textiles workshop and textiles remains one of the group's core businesses. Companies in this division include Kortex, the leading producer of polyester yarns in Europe and the Middle East; Zorluteks Textile, one of the world's largest producers of home textiles and curtain fabrics; and the international chain of Linens retail shops. Zorlu's textiles operations also produce clothing under its own TAC and Valeron brands, as well as for a number of international brands, including Benetton and Pierre Cardin.

Zorlu's electronics and home appliances division operates through its 51.6 percent controlling stake in the Vestel Group of Companies. This Turkey-based manufacturer, acquired by Zorlu in 1994, is one of the world's largest manufacturers of home appliances and electronics products. The company is the leading producer of LCD televisions in Europe, commanding a market share of 18 percent in 2010. Vestel produces appliances on an original equipment manufacturing (OEM) and original design manufacturing (ODM) basis for many of the world's leading appliance brand names, as well as under its own Vestel brand. The company operates two of Europe's largest production facilities, in Manisa, Turkey, and in Alexandrov, Russia. In Turkey, Vestel also operates more than 1,000 Vestel stores and 1,400 Regal dealerships. Vestel generated total revenues of $3.6 billion in 2009, of which the export market accounted for 78 percent.

Two other divisions round out Zorlu's holdings. The energy division includes 14 company-owned-and-built power plants in Turkey, with a total generation capacity of 603 megawatts. The company's oil and gas subsidiary also produces 320 million cubic meters of natural gas each year. Zorlu also operates its own power plant engineering and construction operations, which operates in Turkey, Israel, and elsewhere. Zorlu's real estate division, launched in 2006, is its youngest. This division focuses on large-scale, high-profile projects in Turkey, including the 61,500-square-meter Zorlu Center in Istanbul, still under construction in 2010.

KEY DATES

1953: Haci Mehmet Zorlu founds a small textiles workshop in Babadag, Turkey.

1960s: Sons Ahmet and Zeki expand the company into retail sales.

1970s: Ahmet Zorlu takes over as head of the company and invests in modernization and expansion.

1993: Zorlu launches power generation operations.

1994: Zorlu diversifies by acquiring home appliance group Vestel.

1997: Zorlu acquires Denizbank.

2006: Zorlu launches its real estate division and begins Zorlu Center development in Istanbul.

2010: Zorlu announces plans to launch Vestel brand in Western Europe.

Zorlu Holding remains privately owned by the founding Zorlu family. Ahmet Zorlu, son of the company's founder, and chief architect of its growth into one of Turkey's leading conglomerates, remains its chairman. Zorlu posted revenues of around $5 billion in 2009, and expected these to grow past $6 billion in 2010.

ORIGINS IN TEXTILES IN 1953

Zorlu Holding started out as a small textiles workshop in Babadag (or Babadaeth), Denizli, in Turkey's West Anatolian region in 1953. Founder Haci Mehmet Zorlu was then 34 years old and the father of three. He called the company Zorlu Tekstil Kolektif, and began producing textiles using simple handlooms. The company later became known as Zorlu Mensucat Industry and Trade, focused on the production of white cloth and coverings.

Zorlu's sons Zeki and Ahmet joined him in the business. Ahmet Zorlu, then just 15 years old, had dropped out of school to help out at his father's company, and rapidly emerged as the company's driving force. In particular, Zorlu recognized the need to embrace and invest in the new technologies then in the process of revolutionizing the textiles industry. As the company incorporated new industrial production techniques and explored new textile materials, including polyester, used to produce synthetic yarns, Zorlu outpaced its competitors.

By the 1960s Zorlu had begun its first diversification. The company entered the retail market during that decade, opening its first shop in Trabzon. The company also began developing its own textiles brand, TAC. During the 1970s, as Ahmet took over the leadership of the company, Zorlu began targeting the export market, leveraging Turkey's low wages to expand its sales throughout Europe, and later to much of the world.

Zorlu then began developing a number of specialty textile operations. Among these was its Korteks Curtain business, launched in 1982. Supplied by Zorlu's fabric production units, Korteks focused on manufacturing finished curtains. Through a number of investments Korteks's production facility grew to more than 60,000 square meters, with a capacity of 4.4 million meters of embroidered curtains, and 5.2 million meters of guipure curtains, as well as 840,000 meters of appliqué guipure curtains. Korteks in turn supplied Zorlu's other textile producers with lace used both for clothing and upholstered furniture.

INTERNATIONAL EXPANSION

Zorlu continued to expand its textiles operations through the 1980s and 1990s. The company's growing export business led it to found Zorluteks Tekstil in 1988. This company then took over the marketing and distribution functions for Zorlu's other textile businesses, especially their export markets. The company targeted growth in the Commonwealth of Independent States (CIS), following the breakup of the Soviet Union, as well as markets in the Black Sea region. The company developed a network of more than 100 distribution centers in support of its growing sales to these markets.

Zorlu also invested in building its production capacity. In 1989 the company created a new subsidiary, Korteks Yarn, which opened a state-of-the-art polyester yarn factory. Korteks Yarn grew into Turkey's leading supplier of synthetic yarn, developing expertise across a wide range of yarn types and technologies. In 1993 this subsidiary became the first in Turkey to begin producing pre-oriented yarn directly from the polymer raw material.

Zorlu's textiles operations expanded on a truly international level through the 1990s, with its exports reaching more than 60 markets worldwide. Zorlu also began developing its international presence. For example, in 1994 the company set up a marketing and distribution subsidiary in Germany. That country, with its large Turkish immigrant community, was a natural market for Zorlu's growth. The company also began developing a strong export business to South Africa during the decade. This led the company to set up its own production subsidiary there, Korteks Textile (Africa) Pty

Ltd., which began operating in 1997. This subsidiary then acquired several South African curtain manufacturers in 1999, becoming the leading curtain maker in the market.

Zorlu had added two new markets by then. The company entered the United States in 1998, launching a sales and marketing subsidiary in New York. The company then added a production subsidiary there, Zorlu Manufacturing Company, which set up a 10,000-square-meter cotton bed linen factory in Georgia. Zorlu had established its presence in the Western European market at the same time through the purchase of Bel-Air Industries in France. This company, the leading producer of voile curtain and other home textiles in France, operated three factories with a combined total of 34,000 square meters of production space and an annual capacity of 25 million meters.

VESTEL IN 1994

Zorlu's textiles added several new businesses through the end of the 1990s. These included the production of linen, starting in 1997, and the completion of a 108,000-square-meter factory. This established the group as the largest producer of cotton fabrics in Europe, with a capacity of more than 230 million square meters per year (raised to 300 million square meters in 2005). The company also built a new 20,000-square-meter factory for the production of bedding, including quilts and bed linens. These new operations then led Zorlu into a new retail area, with the founding of the home textiles chain Linens Pazarlama in 2000. The Linens chain quickly expanded to nearly all of Turkey's major markets, as well as eight countries internationally.

While textiles remained an important part of Zorlu's business, the company had in the meantime engaged in a highly ambitious diversification strategy. This led the company to make a bid to buy troubled Turkish appliance manufacturer Vestel Group in 1994. Zorlu's move to take over the company was a risky one. The company had no experience in the home appliances and electronics industry, and was taking over a company that had fallen into severe financial difficulties. Hit hard by the recession of the early 1990s, Vestel had approached the verge of bankruptcy.

One of Ahmet Zorlu's first actions after the Vestel takeover was to travel to Asia, where he spent several weeks studying the major appliance and electronics companies there. The trip helped highlight a number of Vestel's competitive advantages. Among these was the company's proximity to the large European market, helping to reduce the cost of transporting goods.

Turkey's status as a privileged trade partner with the European Union provided it with an exemption from import duties, a major advantage over Asian-produced goods. At the same time, Turkey's lower wages enabled the company to compete on that level as well.

Ahmet nevertheless recognized that Vestel needed to develop sufficient scale in order to compete on an international level. To this end, Zorlu backed a major expansion of Vestel's production capacity. Between 1994 and 1997 Zorlu spent over $40 million redeveloping Vestel's manufacturing base. Among other features, Vestel modernized its corporate infrastructure, streamlining its business practices. Ahmet, with no experience in the industry, chose to leave Vestel's operations to its own management, providing advice rather than directives.

As a result, by the late 1990s Vestel's sales had grown by nearly 150 percent, while its profits soared by 500 percent. The group's exports had also begun to gain momentum, as Vestel developed a strong business providing OEM and ODM services for major appliance and electronics companies such as Sanyo, Mitsubishi, and Sharp. This enabled group exports nearly to double before the end of the decade.

BRANDED STRATEGY

Vestel's growth remained solid through the dawn of the 21st century. Zorlu continued to provide capital for the company's expansion, spending another $70 million through 2004. A portion of these funds was used to expand Zorlu's capacity for the production of "white goods" (refrigerators, washers, dryers, and other large home appliances). As part of this effort, Zorlu built Europe's largest appliance production center to date, in Manisa.

Vestel initially limited its branded operations to Turkey. In the new decade the company began building the Vestel brand in a number of markets, including Russia and other CIS states, as well as the Middle East and North Africa. The company extended its brand family in 2006 to include popular northern European brands Finlux and Luxor. These were followed by the acquisition of Vestfrost in 2008.

By then, Zorlu had taken Vestel public, although retaining majority control with a 51.6 percent stake. Vestel's revenues had climbed to $3.6 billion, with exports accounting for nearly 80 percent, helping to drive Zorlu's own revenues beyond $5 billion by the end of 2009. Vestel had also made significant gains in market share. In the booming market for LCD televisions, for example, the company claimed nearly 20 percent of the total European market.

FINANCIAL AND ENERGY SECTORS ADDED

Zorlu continued its diversification strategy in the meantime. The company entered the financial sector, buying Denizbank in 1997. This bank grew quickly under Zorlu to become Turkey's sixth-largest bank. This access to the financial market provided the company with the resources for its growth elsewhere, including the power generation sector.

Zorlu's expansion in the early 1990s had been hampered somewhat by the unreliable nature of Turkey's power supply at the time. In 1993 Zorlu decided to ensure its own power generation capacity, and built two power plants, in Luleburgaz and Bursa. Zorlu's strong growth during the decade, coupled with requests for power from other companies, led the company to invest in the construction of several new plants, including in Ankara, Kayseri, and Yalova.

Along the way, Zorlu's energy division developed expertise in power plant engineering and construction, permitting it to compete for contracts on an international level at the beginning of the new century. As a result, Zorlu began developing projects in Russia, Israel, and elsewhere. In Turkey the group's energy division expanded to 14 power plants, including natural gas, hydroelectric, geothermal, and fuel-oil technologies, with a total capacity of 603 megawatts. The company also developed its own oil and gas production subsidiary, capable of supplying 320 million cubic meters of natural gas per year. At the end of the decade Zorlu Energy also launched an investment into renewable energy generation, building a 54-turbine wind farm in Gokceda, for a total investment of EUR 210 million.

REAL ESTATE IN 2006

The success of Zorlu's power plant construction unit provided a new platform for the group's diversification. In 2006 Zorlu launched a new real estate division and began developing several large-scale projects in Turkey. Among these was the Zorlu Center, a massive 61,595-square-meter mixed-used facility, featuring a five-star hotel, a cultural and arts center, a shopping center, and residential apartments. Construction of the site was launched in 2007.

Also that year, the company acquired the Orkide Shopping Mall, as well as a number of unused tobacco warehouses in İzmir, as part of a plan to develop a new shopping and residential complex there. Fueling the group's real estate investments—the company paid EUR 800 million to acquire the land for the Zorlu Center in Istanbul—was the sale of Denizbank for EUR 2.6 billion ($3.2 billion) to Dexia in 2006.

The success of Zorlu's diversified operations had not overshadowed the growth of its core textiles operations. These had grown strongly in the new century, completing a number of international expansions. For example, in 2003 the company formed a joint venture with Iran's Atlas Pood. The new company, Atlas Tac, opened a polyester textile factory in Tabriz, Iran, in 2004. Zorlu also established a subsidiary in Turkmenistan, investing $55 million to build a raw cotton cloth factory there. That facility was fully operational by 2005. At the same time, the company built a small factory in Skopje, Macedonia, producing quilt covers, bedspreads, and bed sets.

By the beginning of 2010 Zorlu had grown into Turkey's largest privately held conglomerate, with more than 50 companies and more than 25,000 employees. The company continued to target further expansion, promising to boost its revenues past $6 billion by the end of that year. Toward that end, the company continued to look for new expansion opportunities. For example, in April 2010 the company announced plans to extend its Vestel brand and retail network into Western Europe, targeting France, the Benelux countries, the United Kingdom, and Italy at first. Ahmet Zorlu had successfully built his family's empire into one of Turkey's largest diversified companies.

M. L. Cohen

PRINCIPAL SUBSIDIARIES

Bel Air Gardinen Gmbh (Germany); Bel Air Industries S.A./France; Cabot Communications Ltd. (UK); Korteks Mensucat Industry and Trade S.A.; Korteks Textile (Africa) (Pty) Ltd. (South Africa); Linens Marketing S.A.; Veseg GmbH (Germany); Vestel Electronics Industry and Trade S.A.; Vestel Benelux B.V.; Vestel France S.A.; Vestel Holland B.V.; Vestel Hong Kong; Vestel Iberia (Spain); Vestel Italy Srl.; Vestel Russia; Vestel UK; Vestel USA; Zorlu Aviation S.A.; Zorlu Enerji Electricity Generation Autoproducer Group Co. Inc.; Zorlu Gmbh (Germany); Zorlu Grand Hotel; Zorlu Haskova (Bulgaria); Zorlu Home Tekstiles Products & Trade S.A.; Zorlu Industrial and Powerplants Construction Co. Inc; Zorlu Insurance S.A; Zorlu Manufacturing Company LLC (USA); Zorlu Mensucat Industry and Trade S.A.; Zorlu Petrogas Oil & Gas Co. Inc.; Zorlu Textile Industry and Trade S.A.; Zorlu USA Inc.

PRINCIPAL DIVISIONS

Textiles; Electronics and Home Appliances; Energy Generation; Real Estate.

PRINCIPAL OPERATING UNITS

Vestel Group; Korteks Yarns; Zorlutek Textile; Linens.

PRINCIPAL COMPETITORS

AXA Oyak Holding A.S.; Bayindir Holding A.S.; Boydak Holding; Ciner Group A.S.; Dogan Sirketler Grubu Holding A.S.; Dogus Holding A.S.; Haci Oemer Sabanci Holding A.S.; Koc Holding A.S.; Yildiz Holding A.S.

FURTHER READING

"Ahmet Nazif Zorlu, Chairman, Zorlu Holdings, Turkey," *Business Week*, July 7, 2003, p. 58.

Ersoy, Ercan, "Verstel Will Grow Europe TV Share to 18% in 2010, Zorlu Says," *Bloomberg*, April 9, 2010.

Shikoh, Rafi-uddin, "Turkey's Zorlu Group: A Diversification Success Story," *Dinar Standard*, February 3, 2005.

"Turkish Electronics Co. to Buy Shares in UK Co's Turkey Venture," *AsiaPulse News*, March 10, 2010.

"Ukraine Leads Zorlu Expansion in Home Textiles," *Turkish Daily News*, September 26, 2006.

"Zorlu Center to Further Increase Istanbul's Rapidly Rising Value in the World," *InPR*, September 23, 2009.

"Zorlu Founder Passes Away at 86," *Turkish Daily News*, July 6, 2005.

"Zorlu Holding Aims at $1.5 Million Exports," *Turkish Daily News*, June 10, 2002.

"Zorlu Holding Supports Aegean Region," *Turkish Daily News*, April 12, 2007.

Cumulative Index to Companies

Amblin Entertainment, 21 23–27

AMC Entertainment Inc., 12 12–14; 35 27–29 (upd.); 114 17–21 (upd.)

AMCC see Applied Micro Circuits Corp.

AMCOL International Corporation, 59 29–33 (upd.)

AMCON Distributing Company, 99 27–30

Amcor Ltd., IV 248–50; 19 13–16 (upd.); 78 1–6 (upd.)

AMCORE Financial Inc., 44 22–26

AMD see Advanced Micro Devices, Inc.

Amdahl Corporation, III 109–11; 14 13–16 (upd.); 40 20–25 (upd.) see also Fujitsu Ltd.

Amdocs Ltd., 47 10–12

AMEC plc, 112 13–16

Amec Spie S.A., 57 28–31

Amedisys, Inc., 53 33–36; 106 34–37 (upd.)

Amer Group plc, 41 14–16

Amerada Hess Corporation, IV 365–67; 21 28–31 (upd.); 55 16–20 (upd.)

Amerchol Corporation see Union Carbide Corp.

AMERCO, 6 351–52; 67 11–14 (upd.)

Ameren Corporation, 60 23–27 (upd.)

Ameri-Kart Corp. see Myers Industries, Inc.

América Móvil, S.A. de C.V., 80 5–8

America Online, Inc., 10 56–58; 26 16–20 (upd.) see also CompuServe Interactive Services, Inc.; AOL Time Warner Inc.

America West Holdings Corporation, 6 72–74; 34 22–26 (upd.)

American & Efird, Inc., 82 5–9

American Airlines, I 89–91; 6 75–77 (upd.) see also AMR Corp.

American Apparel, Inc., 90 21–24

American Association of Retired Persons see AARP.

American Axle & Manufacturing Holdings, Inc., 67 15–17

American Banknote Corporation, 30 42–45

American Bar Association, 35 30–33

American Biltrite Inc., 16 16–18; 43 19–22 (upd.)

American Booksellers Association, Inc., 114 22–27

American Brands, Inc., V 395–97 see also Fortune Brands, Inc.

American Builders & Contractors Supply Co. see ABC Supply Co., Inc.

American Building Maintenance Industries, Inc., 6 17–19 see also ABM Industries Inc.

American Business Information, Inc., 18 21–25

American Business Interiors see American Furniture Company, Inc.

American Business Products, Inc., 20 15–17

American Campus Communities, Inc., 85 1–5

American Can Co. see Primerica Corp.

The American Cancer Society, 24 23–25

American Capital Strategies, Ltd., 91 21–24

American Cast Iron Pipe Company, 50 17–20

American City Business Journals, Inc., 110 18–21

American Civil Liberties Union (ACLU), 60 28–31

American Classic Voyages Company, 27 34–37

American Coin Merchandising, Inc., 28 15–17; 74 13–16 (upd.)

American Colloid Co., 13 32–35 see AMCOL International Corp.

American Commercial Lines Inc., 99 31–34

American Cotton Growers Association see Plains Cotton Cooperative Association.

American Crystal Sugar Company, 11 13–15; 32 29–33 (upd.)

American Cyanamid, I 300–02; 8 24–26 (upd.)

American Diabetes Association, 109 31–35

American Eagle Outfitters, Inc., 24 26–28; 55 21–24 (upd.)

American Ecology Corporation, 77 36–39

American Electric Power Company, V 546–49; 45 17–21 (upd.)

American Equipment Company, Inc., 104 14–17

American Express Company, II 395–99; 10 59–64 (upd.); 38 42–48 (upd.)

American Family Corporation, III 187–89 see also AFLAC Inc.

American Family Insurance Group, 116 25–30

American Financial Group Inc., III 190–92; 48 6–10 (upd.)

American Foods Group, 43 23–27

American Furniture Company, Inc., 21 32–34

American General Corporation, III 193–94; 10 65–67 (upd.); 46 20–23 (upd.)

American General Finance Corp., 11 16–17

American Girl, Inc., 69 16–19 (upd)

American Golf Corporation, 45 22–24

American Gramaphone LLC, 52 18–20

American Greetings Corporation, 7 23–25; 22 33–36 (upd.); 59 34–39 (upd.)

American Healthways, Inc., 65 40–42

American Heart Association, Inc., 114 28–31

American Home Mortgage Holdings, Inc., 46 24–26

American Home Products, I 622–24; 10 68–70 (upd.) see also Wyeth.

American Homestar Corporation, 18 26–29; 41 17–20 (upd.)

American Institute of Certified Public Accountants (AICPA), 44 27–30

American International Group Inc., III 195–98; 15 15–19 (upd.); 47 13–19 (upd.); 109 36–45 (upd.)

American Italian Pasta Company, 27 38–40; 76 18–21 (upd.)

American Kennel Club, Inc., 74 17–19

American Lawyer Media Holdings, Inc., 32 34–37

American Library Association, 86 15–19

American Licorice Company, 86 20–23

American Locker Group Incorporated, 34 19–21

American Lung Association, 48 11–14

American Machine and Metals see AMETEK, Inc.

American Maize-Products Co., 14 17–20

American Management Association, 76 22–25

American Management Systems, Inc., 11 18–20

American Media, Inc., 27 41–44; 82 10–15 (upd.)

American Medical Alert Corporation, 103 15–18

American Medical Association, 39 15–18

American Medical International, Inc., III 73–75

American Medical Response, Inc., 39 19–22

American Metals Corporation see Reliance Steel & Aluminum Co.

American Modern Insurance Group see The Midland Co.

American Motors Corp., I 135–37 see also DaimlerChrysler AG.

American MSI Corporation see Moldflow Corp.

American National Insurance Company, 8 27–29; 27 45–48 (upd.)

American Nurses Association Inc., 102 11–15

American Olean Tile Company see Armstrong Holdings, Inc.

American Oriental Bioengineering Inc., 93 45–48

American Pad & Paper Company, 20 18–21

American Pfauter see Gleason Corp.

American Pharmaceutical Partners, Inc., 69 20–22

American Physicians Service Group, Inc., 114 32–36

American Pop Corn Company, 59 40–43

American Power Conversion Corporation, 24 29–31; 67 18–20 (upd.)

American Premier Underwriters, Inc., 10 71–74

American President Companies Ltd., 6 353–55 see also APL Ltd.

American Printing House for the Blind, 26 13–15

American Public Education, Inc., 108 49–52

American Re Corporation, 10 75–77; 35 34–37 (upd.)

American Red Cross, 40 26–29; 112 17–24 (upd.)

American Reprographics Company, 75 24–26

American Residential Mortgage Corporation, 8 30–31

American Restaurant Partners, L.P., 93 49–52

American Retirement Corporation, 42 9–12 *see also* Brookdale Senior Living.

American Rice, Inc., 33 30–33

American Rug Craftsmen *see* Mohawk Industries, Inc.

American Safety Razor Company, 20 22–24

American Savings Bank *see* Hawaiian Electric Industries, Inc.

American Science & Engineering, Inc., 81 22–25

American Seating Company, 78 7–11

American Skiing Company, 28 18–21

American Society for the Prevention of Cruelty to Animals (ASPCA), 68 19–22

The American Society of Composers, Authors and Publishers (ASCAP), 29 21–24

American Software Inc., 22 214; 25 20–22

American Standard Companies Inc., III 663–65; 30 46–50 (upd.)

American States Water Company, 46 27–30

American Steamship Company *see* GATX.

American Stores Company, II 604–06; 22 37–40 (upd.) *see also* Albertson's, Inc.

American Superconductor Corporation, 97 32–36

American Technical Ceramics Corp., 67 21–23

American Technology Corporation, 103 19–22

American Telephone and Telegraph Company *see* AT&T.

American Tire Distributors Holdings, Inc., 117 14–17

American Tobacco Co. *see* B.A.T. Industries PLC.; Fortune Brands, Inc.

American Tourister, Inc., 16 19–21 *see also* Samsonite Corp.

American Tower Corporation, 33 34–38

American Vanguard Corporation, 47 20–22

American Water Works Company, Inc., 6 443–45; 38 49–52 (upd.)

American Woodmark Corporation, 31 13–16

American Yearbook Company *see* Jostens, Inc.

AmeriCares Foundation, Inc., 87 23–28

America's Car-Mart, Inc., 64 19–21

America's Favorite Chicken Company, Inc., 7 26–28 *see also* AFC Enterprises, Inc.

Amerigon Incorporated, 97 37–40

AMERIGROUP Corporation, 69 23–26

Amerihost Properties, Inc., 30 51–53

Ameriprise Financial, Inc., 116 31–35

AmeriSource Health Corporation, 37 9–11 (upd.)

AmerisourceBergen Corporation, 64 22–28 (upd.)

Ameristar Casinos, Inc., 33 39–42; 69 27–31 (upd.)

Ameritech Corporation, V 265–68; 18 30–34 (upd.) *see also* AT&T Corp.

Ameritrade Holding Corporation, 34 27–30

Ameriwood Industries International Corp., 17 15–17 *see also* Dorel Industries Inc.

Amerock Corporation, 53 37–40

Ameron International Corporation, 67 24–26

Amersham PLC, 50 21–25

Ames Department Stores, Inc., 9 20–22; 30 54–57 (upd.)

AMETEK, Inc., 9 23–25; 114 37–42 (upd.)

N.V. Amev, III 199–202 *see also* Fortis, Inc.

Amey Plc, 47 23–25

AMF Bowling, Inc., 40 30–33

Amfac/JMB Hawaii L.L.C., I 417–18; 24 32–35 (upd.)

Amgen, Inc., 10 78–81; 30 58–61 (upd.); 89 51–57 (upd.)

AMI Metals, Inc. *see* Reliance Steel & Aluminum Co.

AMICAS, Inc., 69 32–34

Amil Participações S.A., 105 17–20

Amkor Technology, Inc., 69 35–37

Ammirati Puris Lintas *see* Interpublic Group of Companies, Inc.

Amnesty International, 50 26–29

Amoco Corporation, IV 368–71; 14 21–25 (upd.) *see also* BP p.l.c.

Amoskeag Company, 8 32–33 *see also* Fieldcrest Cannon, Inc.

AMP, Inc., II 7–8; 14 26–28 (upd.)

Ampacet Corporation, 67 27–29

Ampco-Pittsburgh Corporation, 79 26–29

Ampex Corporation, 17 18–20

Amphenol Corporation, 40 34–37

AMR *see* American Medical Response, Inc.

AMR Corporation, 28 22–26 (upd.); 52 21–26 (upd.)

AMREP Corporation, 21 35–37

AMS *see* Advanced Marketing Services, Inc.

Amscan Holdings, Inc., 61 24–26

AmSouth Bancorporation, 12 15–17; 48 15–18 (upd.)

Amsted Industries Incorporated, 7 29–31

Amsterdam-Rotterdam Bank N.V., II 185–86

Amstrad plc, III 112–14; 48 19–23 (upd.)

AmSurg Corporation, 48 24–27

Amtech *see* American Building Maintenance Industries, Inc.; ABM Industries Inc.

Amtrak *see* The National Railroad Passenger Corp.

Amtran, Inc., 34 31–33

AMVESCAP PLC, 65 43–45

Amway Corporation, III 11–14; 13 36–39 (upd.); 30 62–66 (upd.) *see also* Alticor Inc.

Amylin Pharmaceuticals, Inc., 67 30–32

Amy's Kitchen Inc., 76 26–28

ANA *see* All Nippon Airways Co., Ltd.

Anacomp, Inc., 94 30–34

Anadarko Petroleum Corporation, 10 82–84; 52 27–30 (upd.); 106 38–43 (upd.)

Anadolu Efes Biracilik ve Malt Sanayii A.S., 95 28–31

Anaheim Angels Baseball Club, Inc., 53 41–44

Analex Corporation, 74 20–22

Analog Devices, Inc., 10 85–87

Analogic Corporation, 23 13–16

Analysts International Corporation, 36 40–42

Analytic Sciences Corporation, 10 88–90

Analytical Surveys, Inc., 33 43–45

Anam Group, 23 17–19

Anaren Microwave, Inc., 33 46–48

Ancestry.com Inc., 116 36–39

Anchor Bancorp, Inc., 10 91–93

Anchor BanCorp Wisconsin, Inc., 101 27–30

Anchor Brewing Company, 47 26–28

Anchor Gaming, 24 36–39

Anchor Hocking Glassware, 13 40–42

Andersen, 10 94–95; 29 25–28 (upd.); 68 23–27 (upd.)

The Anderson-DuBose Company, 60 32–34

Anderson Trucking Service, Inc., 75 27–29

The Andersons, Inc., 31 17–21

Andin International, Inc., 100 11–14

Andis Company, Inc., 85 6–9

Andrade Gutierrez S.A., 102 16–19

Andreas Stihl AG & Co. KG, 16 22–24; 59 44–47 (upd.)

Andretti Green Racing, 106 44–48

Andrew Corporation, 10 96–98; 32 38–41 (upd.)

Andrew Peller Ltd., 101 31–34

The Andrews Institute, 99 35–38

Andrews Kurth, LLP, 71 31–34

Andrews McMeel Universal, 40 38–41

Andritz AG, 51 24–26

Andronico's Market, 70 10–13

Andrx Corporation, 55 25–27

Angang Steel Company Ltd., 117 18–22

Angelica Corporation, 15 20–22; 43 28–31 (upd.)

Angelini SpA, 100 15–18

AngioDynamics, Inc., 81 26–29

Angliss International Group *see* Vestey Group Ltd.

Anglo-Abrasives Ltd. *see* Carbo PLC.

Anglo American PLC, IV 20–23; 16 25–30 (upd.); 50 30–36 (upd.)

Angostura Holdings Ltd., 114 43–47

The Atlantic Group, 23 31–33
Atlantic Premium Brands, Ltd., 57 56–58
Atlantic Richfield Company, IV 375–77; 31 31–34 (upd.)
Atlantic Southeast Airlines, Inc., 47 29–31
Atlantis Plastics, Inc., 85 14–17
Atlas Air, Inc., 39 33–35
Atlas Bolt & Screw Company *see* The Marmon Group, Inc.
Atlas Copco AB, III 425–27; 28 37–41 (upd.); 85 18–24 (upd.)
Atlas Tag & Label *see* BISSELL, Inc.
Atlas Van Lines Inc., 14 37–39; 106 49–53 (upd.)
Atmel Corporation, 17 32–34
ATMI, Inc., 93 61–64
Atmos Energy Corporation, 43 56–58
Atochem S.A., I 303–04, 676 *see also* Total-Fina-Elf.
Atos Origin S.A., 69 45–47
Atrix Laboratories, Inc. *see* QLT Inc.
Attachmate Corporation, 56 19–21
Attica Enterprises S.A., 64 43–45
Atwood Mobil Products, 53 52–55
Atwood Oceanics, Inc., 100 40–43
Au Bon Pain Co., Inc., 18 35–38 *see also* ABP Corp.
AU Optronics Corporation, 67 38–40
Au Printemps S.A., V 9–11 *see also* Pinault-Printemps-Redoute S.A.
Aubert & Duval S.A.S., 107 24–27
Auchan Group, 37 22–24; 116 56–60 (upd.)
The Auchter Company, 78 21–24
Audible Inc., 79 42–45
Audio King Corporation, 24 52–54
Audiovox Corporation, 34 48–50; 90 35–39 (upd.)
August Schell Brewing Company Inc., 59 66–69
August Storck KG, 66 21–23
Augusta National Inc., 115 40–43
Ault Incorporated, 34 51–54
Auntie Anne's, Inc., 35 55–57; 102 29–33 (upd.)
Aurea Concesiones de Infraestructuras SA *see* Abertis Infraestructuras, S.A.
Aurora Casket Company, Inc., 56 22–24
Aurora Foods Inc., 32 67–69
Austal Limited, 75 36–39
The Austin Company, 8 41–44; 72 14–18 (upd.)
Austin Nichols *see* Pernod Ricard S.A.
Austin Powder Company, 76 32–35
Australia and New Zealand Banking Group Limited, II 187–90; 52 35–40 (upd.)
Australian Wheat Board *see* AWB Ltd.
Austrian Airlines AG (Österreichische Luftverkehrs AG), 33 49–52
Authentic Fitness Corp., 20 41–43; 51 30–33 (upd.)
Auto Value Associates, Inc., 25 26–28
Autobacs Seven Company Ltd., 76 36–38
Autobytel Inc., 47 32–34

Autocam Corporation, 51 34–36
Autodesk, Inc., 10 118–20; 89 78–82 (upd.)
Autogrill SpA, 49 31–33
Autoliv, Inc., 65 53–55
Autologic Information International, Inc., 20 44–46
Automated Sciences Group, Inc. *see* CACI International Inc.
Automatic Data Processing, Inc., III 117–19; 9 48–51 (upd.); 47 35–39 (upd.)
Automobiles Citroën, 7 35–38
Automobili Lamborghini Holding S.p.A., 13 60–62; 34 55–58 (upd.); 91 25–30 (upd.)
AutoNation, Inc., 50 61–64; 114 62–66 (upd.)
Autoridad del Canal de Panamá, 94 45–48
Autoroutes du Sud de la France SA, 55 38–40
Autostrada Torino-Milano S.p.A., 101 47–50
Autotote Corporation, 20 47–49 *see also* Scientific Games Corp.
AutoTrader.com, L.L.C., 91 31–34
AutoZone, Inc., 9 52–54; 31 35–38 (upd.); 110 28–33 (upd.)
Auvil Fruit Company, Inc., 95 32–35
AVA AG (Allgemeine Handelsgesellschaft der Verbraucher AG), 33 53–56
Avado Brands, Inc., 31 39–42
Avalon Correctional Services, Inc., 75 40–43
AvalonBay Communities, Inc., 58 11–13
Avantium Technologies BV, 79 46–49
Avaya Inc., 104 22–25
Avco Financial Services Inc., 13 63–65 *see also* Citigroup Inc.
Avecia Group PLC, 63 49–51
Aveda Corporation, 24 55–57
Avedis Zildjian Co., 38 66–68
Avendt Group, Inc. *see* Marmon Group, Inc.
Aventine Renewable Energy Holdings, Inc., 89 83–86
Avery Dennison Corporation, IV 251–54; 17 27–31 (upd.); 49 34–40 (upd.); 110 34–42 (upd.)
Aviacionny Nauchno-Tehnicheskii Komplex im. A.N. Tupoleva, 24 58–60
Aviacsa *see* Consorcio Aviacsa, S.A. de C.V.
Aviall, Inc., 73 42–45
Avianca Aerovías Nacionales de Colombia SA, 36 52–55
Aviation Sales Company, 41 37–39
Avid Technology Inc., 38 69–73
Avionics Specialties Inc. *see* Aerosonic Corp.
Avions Marcel Dassault-Breguet Aviation, I 44–46 *see also* Groupe Dassault Aviation SA.

Avis Group Holdings, Inc., 6 356–58; 22 54–57 (upd.); 75 44–49 (upd.)
Avista Corporation, 69 48–50 (upd.)
Aviva PLC, 50 65–68 (upd.)
Avnet, Inc., 9 55–57; 111 6–11 (upd.)
Avocent Corporation, 65 56–58
Avon Products, Inc., III 15–16; 19 26–29 (upd.); 46 43–46 (upd.); 109 50–56 (upd.)
Avon Rubber p.l.c., 108 65–69
Avondale Industries, Inc., 7 39–41; 41 40–43 (upd.)
AVTOVAZ Joint Stock Company, 65 59–62
AVX Corporation, 67 41–43
AWA *see* America West Holdings Corp.
AWB Ltd., 56 25–27
Awrey Bakeries, Inc., 56 28–30
AXA Colonia Konzern AG, III 210–12; 49 41–45 (upd.)
AXA Equitable Life Insurance Company, 105 21–27 (upd.)
AXA Group, 114 67–72 (upd.)
Axcan Pharma Inc., 85 25–28
Axcelis Technologies, Inc., 95 36–39
Axel Johnson Group, I 553–55
Axel Springer Verlag AG, IV 589–91; 20 50–53 (upd.)
Axsys Technologies, Inc., 93 65–68
Aydin Corp., 19 30–32
Aynsley China Ltd. *see* Belleek Pottery Ltd.
Azcon Corporation, 23 34–36
Azelis Group, 100 44–47
Azerbaijan Airlines, 77 46–49
Azienda Generale Italiana Petroli *see* ENI S.p.A.
Aztar Corporation, 13 66–68; 71 41–45 (upd.)
AZZ Incorporated, 93 69–72

B

B&G Foods, Inc., 40 51–54
B&J Music Ltd. *see* Kaman Music Corp.
B&Q plc *see* Kingfisher plc.
B.A.T. Industries PLC, 22 70–73 (upd.) *see also* Brown and Williamson Tobacco Corporation
B. Braun Medical Inc., 113 25–28
B. Dalton Bookseller Inc., 25 29–31 *see also* Barnes & Noble, Inc.
B/E Aerospace, Inc., 30 72–74
B.F. Goodrich Co. *see* The BFGoodrich Co.
B.J. Alan Co., Inc., 67 44–46
The B. Manischewitz Company, LLC, 31 43–46
B.R. Guest Inc., 87 43–46
B.W. Rogers Company, 94 49–52
B2W Companhia Global do Varejo, 117 27–30
BA *see* British Airways plc.
BAA plc, 10 121–23; 33 57–61 (upd.)
Baan Company, 25 32–34
Babbage's, Inc., 10 124–25 *see also* GameStop Corp.
The Babcock & Wilcox Company, 82 26–30

Barclays PLC, II 235–37; 20 57–60
  (upd.); 64 46–50 (upd.)
BarclaysAmerican Mortgage
  Corporation, 11 29–30
Barco NV, 44 42–45
Barden Companies, Inc., 76 42–45
Bardwil Industries Inc., 98 15–18
Bare Escentuals, Inc., 91 48–52
Barilla G. e R. Fratelli S.p.A., 17 35–37;
  50 77–80 (upd.)
Barings PLC, 14 45–47
Barloworld Ltd., I 422–24; 109 57–62
  (upd.)
Barmag AG, 39 39–42
Barnes & Noble, Inc., 10 135–37; 30
  67–71 (upd.); 75 50–55 (upd.)
Barnes & Noble College Booksellers,
  Inc., 115 44–46
Barnes Group, Inc., 13 72–74; 69
  58–62 (upd.)
Barnett Banks, Inc., 9 58–60 *see also*
  Bank of America Corp.
Barnett Inc., 28 50–52
Barneys New York Inc., 28 53–55; 104
  26–30 (upd.)
Baron de Ley S.A., 74 27–29
Baron Philippe de Rothschild S.A., 39
  43–46
Barr *see* AG Barr plc.
Barr Pharmaceuticals, Inc., 26 29–31;
  68 46–49 (upd.)
Barratt Developments plc, I 556–57; 56
  31–33 (upd.)
Barrett Business Services, Inc., 16
  48–50
Barrett-Jackson Auction Company
  L.L.C., 88 25–28
Barrick Gold Corporation, 34 62–65;
  112 38–44 (upd.)
Barrière *see* Groupe Lucien Barrière S.A.S.
Barry Callebaut AG, 29 46–48; 71
  46–49 (upd.)
Barry-Wehmiller Companies, Inc., 90
  40–43
The Bartell Drug Company, 94 62–65
Barton Malow Company, 51 40–43
Barton Protective Services Inc., 53
  56–58
The Baseball Club of Seattle, LP, 50
  81–85
BASF SE, I 305–08; 18 47–51 (upd.);
  50 86–92 (upd.); 108 85–94 (upd.)
Bashas' Inc., 33 62–64; 80 17–21 (upd.)
Basic Earth Science Systems, Inc., 101
  65–68
Basin Electric Power Cooperative, 103
  43–46
The Basketball Club of Seattle, LLC, 50
  93–97
Basketville, Inc., 117 31–34
Bass PLC, I 222–24; 15 44–47 (upd.);
  38 74–78 (upd.)
Bass Pro Shops, Inc., 42 27–30
Bassett Furniture Industries, Inc., 18
  52–55; 95 44–50 (upd.)
BAT Industries plc, I 425–27 *see also*
  British American Tobacco PLC.
Bata Ltd., 62 27–30

Bates Worldwide, Inc., 14 48–51; 33
  65–69 (upd.)
Bath Iron Works Corporation, 12
  27–29; 36 76–79 (upd.)
Battelle Memorial Institute, Inc., 10
  138–40
Batten Barton Durstine & Osborn *see*
  Omnicom Group Inc.
Battle Mountain Gold Company, 23
  40–42 *see also* Newmont Mining Corp.
Bauer Hockey, Inc., 104 31–34
Bauer Publishing Group, 7 42–43
Bauerly Companies, 61 31–33
Baugur Group hf, 81 45–49
Baumax AG, 75 56–58
Bausch & Lomb Inc., 7 44–47; 25
  53–57 (upd.); 96 20–26 (upd.)
Bavaria S.A., 90 44–47
Baxi Group Ltd., 96 27–30
Baxter International Inc., I 627–29; 10
  141–43 (upd.); 116 74–78 (upd.)
Baxters Food Group Ltd., 99 47–50
The Bay *see* The Hudson's Bay Co.
Bay State Gas Company, 38 79–82
Bayard SA, 49 46–49
BayBanks, Inc., 12 30–32
Bayer A.G., I 309–11; 13 75–77 (upd.);
  41 44–48 (upd.)
Bayerische Hypotheken- und
  Wechsel-Bank AG, II 238–40 *see also*
  HVB Group.
Bayerische Landesbank, 116 79–82
Bayerische Motoren Werke AG, I
  138–40; 11 31–33 (upd.); 38 83–87
  (upd.); 108 95–101 (upd.)
Bayerische Vereinsbank A.G., II 241–43
  see also HVB Group.
Bayernwerk AG, V 555–58; 23 43–47
  (upd.) *see also* E.On AG.
Bayou Steel Corporation, 31 47–49
BayWa AG, 112 45–49
BB&T Corporation, 79 57–61
BB Holdings Limited, 77 50–53
BBA *see* Bush Boake Allen Inc.
BBA Aviation plc, 90 48–52
BBAG Osterreichische
  Brau-Beteiligungs-AG, 38 88–90
BBC *see* British Broadcasting Corp.
BBDO Worldwide *see* Omnicom Group
  Inc.
BBGI *see* Beasley Broadcast Group, Inc.
BBN Corp., 19 39–42
BBVA *see* Banco Bilbao Vizcaya Argentaria
  S.A.
BCE, Inc., V 269–71; 44 46–50 (upd.)
Bci, 99 51–54
BDO Seidman LLP, 96 31–34
BE&K, Inc., 73 57–59
BEA *see* Bank of East Asia Ltd.
BEA Systems, Inc., 36 80–83
Beacon Roofing Supply, Inc., 75 59–61
Beall's, Inc., 113 37–40
Bear Creek Corporation, 38 91–94
Bear Stearns Companies, Inc., II
  400–01; 10 144–45 (upd.); 52 41–44
  (upd.)
Bearings, Inc., 13 78–80

Beasley Broadcast Group, Inc., 51
  44–46
Beate Uhse AG, 96 35–39
Beatrice Company, II 467–69 *see also*
  TLC Beatrice International Holdings,
  Inc.
BeautiControl Cosmetics, Inc., 21
  49–52
Beazer Homes USA, Inc., 17 38–41
bebe stores, inc., 31 50–52; 103 47–51
  (upd.)
Bechtel Corporation, I 558–59; 24
  64–67 (upd.); 99 55–60 (upd.)
Beckett Papers, 23 48–50
Beckman Coulter, Inc., 22 74–77
Beckman Instruments, Inc., 14 52–54
Becton, Dickinson and Company, I
  630–31; 11 34–36 (upd.); 36 84–89
  (upd.); 101 69–77 (upd.)
Bed Bath & Beyond Inc., 13 81–83; 41
  49–52 (upd.); 109 63–70 (upd.)
Beech Aircraft Corporation, 8 49–52 *see
  also* Raytheon Aircraft Holdings Inc.
Beech-Nut Nutrition Corporation, 21
  53–56; 51 47–51 (upd.)
Beef O'Brady's *see* Family Sports
  Concepts, Inc.
Beer Nuts, Inc., 86 30–33
Beggars Group Ltd., 99 61–65
Behr GmbH & Co. KG, 72 22–25
Behr Process Corporation, 115 47–49
Behring Diagnostics *see* Dade Behring
  Holdings Inc.
BEI Technologies, Inc., 65 74–76
Beiersdorf AG, 29 49–53
Bekaert S.A./N.V., 90 53–57
Bekins Company, 15 48–50
Bel *see* Fromageries Bel.
Bel-Art Products Inc., 117 35–38
Bel Fuse, Inc., 53 59–62
Bel/Kaukauna USA, 76 46–48
Belco Oil & Gas Corp., 40 63–65
Belden CDT Inc., 19 43–45; 76 49–52
  (upd.)
Belgacom, 6 302–04
Belk, Inc., V 12–13; 19 46–48 (upd.);
  72 26–29 (upd.)
Bell and Howell Company, 9 61–64; 29
  54–58 (upd.)
Bell Atlantic Corporation, V 272–74; 25
  58–62 (upd.) *see also* Verizon
  Communications.
Bell Canada Enterprises Inc. *see* BCE, Inc.
Bell Canada International, Inc., 6
  305–08
Bell Helicopter Textron Inc., 46 64–67
Bell Industries, Inc., 47 40–43
Bell Resources *see* TPG NV.
Bell Sports Corporation, 16 51–53; 44
  51–54 (upd.)
Bell's Brewery, Inc., 117 39–42
Bellcore *see* Telcordia Technologies, Inc.
Belleek Pottery Ltd., 71 50–53
Belleville Shoe Manufacturing
  Company, 92 17–20
Bellisio Foods, Inc., 95 51–54
BellSouth Corporation, V 276–78; 29
  59–62 (upd.) *see also* AT&T Corp.

The British United Provident Association Limited, 79 81–84

British Vita plc, 9 92–93; 33 77–79 (upd.)

British World Airlines Ltd., 18 78–80

Britvic Soft Drinks Limited *see* Britannia Soft Drinks Ltd. (Britvic)

Broadcast Music Inc., 23 74–77; 90 74–79 (upd.)

Broadcom Corporation, 34 76–79; 90 80–85 (upd.)

The Broadmoor Hotel, 30 82–85

Broadway Video Entertainment, 112 73–76

Broadwing Corporation, 70 29–32

Broan-NuTone LLC, 104 43–46

Brobeck, Phleger & Harrison, LLP, 31 74–76

Brocade Communications Systems Inc., 106 75–81

The Brock Group of Companies, 114 96–99

Brockhaus *see* Bibliographisches Institut & F.A. Brockhaus AG.

Brodart Company, 84 30–33

Broder Bros. Co., 38 107–09

Broderbund Software, Inc., 13 113–16; 29 74–78 (upd.)

Broken Hill Proprietary Company Ltd., IV 44–47; 22 103–08 (upd.) *see also* BHP Billiton.

Bronco Drilling Company, Inc., 89 118–21

Bronco Wine Company, 101 96–99

Bronner Brothers Inc., 92 29–32

Bronner Display & Sign Advertising, Inc., 82 53–57

Brookdale Senior Living, 91 69–73

Brooke Group Ltd., 15 71–73 *see also* Vector Group Ltd.

Brookfield Properties Corporation, 89 122–25

The Brooklyn Brewery, 109 82–86

Brooklyn Union Gas, 6 455–57 *see also* KeySpan Energy Co.

Brooks Brothers Inc., 22 109–12; 115 75–80 (upd.)

Brooks Sports Inc., 32 98–101

Brookshire Grocery Company, 16 63–66; 74 50–53 (upd.)

Brookstone, Inc., 18 81–83

Brose Fahrzeugteile GmbH & Company KG, 84 34–38

Brossard S.A., 102 61–64

Brother Industries, Ltd., 14 75–76

Brother's Brother Foundation, 93 100–04

Brothers Gourmet Coffees, Inc., 20 82–85 *see also* The Procter & Gamble Co.

Broughton Foods Co., 17 55–57 *see also* Suiza Foods Corp.

Brouwerijen Alken-Maes N.V., 86 47–51

Brown & Brown, Inc., 41 63–66

Brown & Haley, 23 78–80

Brown & Root, Inc., 13 117–19 *see also* Kellogg Brown & Root Inc.

Brown & Sharpe Manufacturing Co., 23 81–84

Brown and Williamson Tobacco Corporation, 14 77–79; 33 80–83 (upd.)

Brown Brothers Harriman & Co., 45 64–67

Brown-Forman Corporation, 114 100–07 (upd.)

Brown-Forman Corporation, I 225–27; 10 179–82 (upd.); 38 110–14 (upd.)

Brown Group, Inc., V 351–53; 20 86–89 (upd.) *see also* Brown Shoe Company, Inc.

Brown Jordan International Inc., 74 54–57

Brown Printing Company, 26 43–45

Brown Shoe Company, Inc., 68 65–69 (upd.)

Browning-Ferris Industries, Inc., V 749–53; 20 90–93 (upd.)

Broyhill Furniture Industries, Inc., 10 183–85

Bruce Foods Corporation, 39 67–69

Bruce Oakley, Inc., 107 61–64

Bruegger's Corporation, 63 79–82

Bruker Corporation, 113 62–65

Bruno's Supermarkets, Inc., 7 60–62; 26 46–48 (upd.); 68 70–73 (upd.)

Brunschwig & Fils Inc., 96 62–65

Brunswick Corporation, III 442–44; 22 113–17 (upd.); 77 68–75 (upd.)

Brush Engineered Materials Inc., 67 77–79

Brush Wellman Inc., 14 80–82

Bruster's Real Ice Cream, Inc., 80 51–54

Bryce Corporation, 100 80–83

BSA *see* The Boy Scouts of America.

BSC *see* Birmingham Steel Corporation

BSH Bosch und Siemens Hausgeräte GmbH, 67 80–84

BSN Groupe S.A., II 474–75 *see also* Groupe Danone

BT Group plc, 49 69–74 (upd.); 114 108–16 (upd.)

BTG, Inc., 45 68–70

BTG Plc, 87 80–83

BTR plc, I 428–30

BTR Siebe plc, 27 79–81 *see also* Invensys PLC.

Bubba Gump Shrimp Co. Restaurants, Inc., 108 128–31

Buca, Inc., 38 115–17

Buck Consultants, Inc., 55 71–73

Buck Knives Inc., 48 71–74

Buckeye Partners, L.P., 70 33–36

Buckeye Technologies, Inc., 42 51–54

Buckhead Life Restaurant Group, Inc., 100 84–87

The Buckle, Inc., 18 84–86; 115 81–84 (upd.)

Bucyrus International, Inc., 17 58–61; 103 80–87 (upd.)

The Budd Company, 8 74–76 *see also* ThyssenKrupp AG.

Buderus AG, 37 46–49

Budgens Ltd., 59 93–96

Budget Group, Inc., 25 92–94 *see also* Cendant Corp.

Budget Rent a Car Corporation, 9 94–95

Budweiser Budvar, National Corporation, 59 97–100

Buena Vista Home Video *see* The Walt Disney Co.

Bufete Industrial, S.A. de C.V., 34 80–82

Buffalo Grill S.A., 94 87–90

Buffalo Wild Wings, Inc., 56 41–43

Buffets Holdings, Inc., 10 186–87; 32 102–04 (upd.); 93 105–09 (upd.)

Bugatti Automobiles S.A.S., 94 91–94

Bugle Boy Industries, Inc., 18 87–88

Buhrmann NV, 41 67–69

Buick Motor Co. *see* General Motors Corp.

Build-A-Bear Workshop Inc., 62 45–48

Building Materials Holding Corporation, 52 53–55

Bulgari S.p.A., 20 94–97; 106 82–87 (upd.)

Bull *see* Compagnie des Machines Bull S.A.

Bull S.A., 43 89–91 (upd.)

Bulley & Andrews, LLC, 55 74–76

Bulova Corporation, 13 120–22; 41 70–73 (upd.)

Bumble Bee Seafoods L.L.C., 64 59–61

Bundy Corporation, 17 62–65

Bunge Ltd., 62 49–51

Bunzl plc, IV 260–62; 31 77–80 (upd.)

Burberry Group plc, 17 66–68; 41 74–76 (upd.); 92 33–37 (upd.)

Burda Holding GmbH. & Co., 23 85–89

Burdines, Inc., 60 70–73

The Bureau of National Affairs, Inc., 23 90–93

Bureau Veritas SA, 55 77–79

Burelle S.A., 23 94–96

Burger King Corporation, II 613–15; 17 69–72 (upd.); 56 44–48 (upd.); 115 85–92 (upd.)

Burgett, Inc., 97 88–91

Burke, Inc., 88 39–42

Burke Mills, Inc., 66 41–43

Burlington Coat Factory Warehouse Corporation, 10 188–89; 60 74–76 (upd.)

Burlington Industries, Inc., V 354–55; 17 73–76 (upd.)

Burlington Northern Santa Fe Corporation, V 425–28; 27 82–89 (upd.); 111 55–65 (upd.)

Burlington Resources Inc., 10 190–92 *see also* ConocoPhillips.

Burmah Castrol PLC, IV 381–84; 30 86–91 (upd.) *see also* BP p.l.c.

Burns International Security Services, 13 123–25 *see also* Securitas AB.

Burns International Services Corporation, 41 77–80 (upd.)

Burns, Philp & Company Ltd., 63 83–86

Burpee & Co. *see* W. Atlee Burpee & Co.

Canadian Pacific Railway Limited, V 429–31; 45 78–83 (upd.); 95 71–80 (upd.)

Canadian Solar Inc., 105 72–76

Canadian Tire Corporation, Limited, 71 89–93 (upd.)

Canadian Utilities Limited, 13 130–32; 56 53–56 (upd.)

Canal Plus, 10 195–97; 34 83–86 (upd.)

Canam Group Inc., 114 121–24

Canandaigua Brands, Inc., 13 133–35; 34 87–91 (upd.) *see also* Constellation Brands, Inc.

Canary Wharf Group Plc, 30 107–09

Cancer Treatment Centers of America, Inc., 85 45–48

Candela Corporation, 48 87–89

Candie's, Inc., 31 81–84

Candle Corporation, 64 62–65

Candlewood Hotel Company, Inc., 41 81–83

Canfor Corporation, 42 59–61

Canlan Ice Sports Corp., 105 77–81

Cannon Design, 63 90–92

Cannon Express, Inc., 53 80–82

Cannondale Corporation, 21 88–90

Cano Petroleum Inc., 97 92–95

Canon Inc., III 120–21; 18 92–95 (upd.); 79 89–95 (upd.)

Canstar Sports Inc., 16 79–81 *see also* NIKE, Inc.

Cantel Medical Corporation, 80 55–58

Canterbury Park Holding Corporation, 42 62–65

Cantine Cooperative Riunite *see* Banfi Products Corp.

Cantine Giorgio Lungarotti S.R.L., 67 88–90

Cantor Fitzgerald, L.P., 92 38–42

CanWest Global Communications Corporation, 35 67–703

Cap Gemini Ernst & Young, 37 59–61

Cap Rock Energy Corporation, 46 78–81

Capario, 104 55–58

Caparo Group Ltd., 90 102–06

Capcom Company Ltd., 83 50–53

Cape Cod Potato Chip Company, 90 107–10

Capel Incorporated, 45 84–86

Capella Education Company, 109 101–05

Capezio/Ballet Makers Inc., 62 57–59

Capita Group PLC, 69 79–81

Capital Cities/ABC Inc., II 129–31 *see also* Disney/ABC Television Group.

Capital City Bank Group, Inc., 105 82–85

Capital Group Companies, Inc., 115 105–08

Capital Holding Corporation, III 216–19 *see also* Providian Financial Corp.

Capital One Financial Corporation, 52 60–63

Capital Radio plc, 35 71–73

Capital Senior Living Corporation, 75 80–82

Capitalia S.p.A., 65 86–89

Capitol Records, Inc., 90 111–16

CapStar Hotel Company, 21 91–93

Capstone Turbine Corporation, 75 83–85

Captain D's, LLC, 59 104–06

Captaris, Inc., 89 126–29

Car Toys, Inc., 67 91–93

Caradon plc, 20 108–12 (upd.) *see also* Novar plc.

Caraustar Industries, Inc., 19 76–78; 44 63–67 (upd.)

The Carbide/Graphite Group, Inc., 40 82–84

CARBO Ceramics, Inc., 108 132–36

Carbo PLC, 67 94–96 (upd.)

Carbone Lorraine S.A., 33 88–90

Carborundum Company, 15 80–82 *see also* Carbo PLC.

Cardinal Health, Inc., 18 96–98; 50 120–23 (upd.); 115 109–15 (upd.)

Cardo AB, 53 83–85

Cardone Industries Inc., 92 43–47

Cardtronics, Inc., 93 119–23

Career Education Corporation, 45 87–89

CareerBuilder, Inc., 93 124–27

Caremark Rx, Inc., 10 198–200; 54 42–45 (upd.)

Carey International, Inc., 26 60–63

Cargill, Incorporated, II 616–18; 13 136–38 (upd.); 40 85–90 (upd.); 89 130–39 (upd.)

Cargolux Airlines International S.A., 49 80–82

Carhartt, Inc., 30 110–12; 77 88–92 (upd.)

Caribiner International, Inc., 24 94–97

Caribou Coffee Company, Inc., 28 62–65; 97 96–102 (upd.)

Caritas Internationalis, 72 57–59

Carl Allers Etablissement A/S, 72 60–62

Carl Kühne KG (GmbH & Co.), 94 101–05

Carl Zeiss AG, III 445–47; 34 92–97 (upd.); 91 85–92 (upd.)

Carlisle Companies Inc., 8 80–82; 82 58–62 (upd.)

Carl's Jr. *see* CKE Restaurants, Inc.

Carlsberg A/S, 9 99–101; 29 83–85 (upd.); 36 40 (upd.)

Carlson Companies, Inc., 6 363–66; 22 125–29 (upd.); 87 88–95 (upd.)

Carlson Restaurants Worldwide, 69 82–85

Carlson Wagonlit Travel, 55 89–92

Carlton and United Breweries Ltd., I 228–29 *see also* Foster's Group Limited

Carlton Communications plc, 15 83–85; 50 124–27 (upd.) *see also* ITV pcl.

Carma Laboratories, Inc., 60 80–82

CarMax, Inc., 55 93–95

Carmichael Lynch Inc., 28 66–68

Carmike Cinemas, Inc., 14 86–88; 37 62–65 (upd.); 74 64–67 (upd.)

Carnation Company, II 486–89 *see also* Nestlé S.A.

Carnegie Corporation of New York, 35 74–77

The Carnegie Hall Corporation, 101 100–04

Carnival Corporation, 6 367–68; 27 90–92 (upd.); 78 65–69 (upd.)

Carolina First Corporation, 31 85–87

Carolina Freight Corporation, 6 369–72

Carolina Pad and Paper Company *see* CPP International, LLC

Carolina Power & Light Company, V 564–66; 23 104–07 (upd.) *see also* Progress Energy, Inc.

Carolina Telephone and Telegraph Company, 10 201–03

Carpenter Co., 109 106–10

Carpenter Technology Corporation, 13 139–41; 95 81–86 (upd.)

The Carphone Warehouse Group PLC, 83 54–57

CARQUEST Corporation, 29 86–89

Carr-Gottstein Foods Co., 17 77–80

Carrabba's Italian Grill *see* Outback Steakhouse, Inc.

CarrAmerica Realty Corporation, 56 57–59

Carrefour SA, 10 204–06; 27 93–96 (upd.); 64 66–69 (upd.)

Carrere Group S.A., 104 59–63

The Carriage House Companies, Inc., 55 96–98

Carriage Services, Inc., 37 66–68

Carrier Access Corporation, 44 68–73

Carrier Corporation, 7 70–73; 69 86–91 (upd.)

Carrizo Oil & Gas, Inc., 97 103–06

Carroll's Foods, Inc., 46 82–85

Carrols Restaurant Group, Inc., 92 48–51

Carr's Milling Industries PLC, 108 137–41

The Carsey-Werner Company, L.L.C., 37 69–72

Carson, Inc., 31 88–90

Carson Pirie Scott & Company, 15 86–88

CART *see* Championship Auto Racing Teams, Inc.

Carter Hawley Hale Stores, V 29–32

Carter Holt Harvey Ltd., 70 41–44

Carter Lumber Company, 45 90–92

Carter-Wallace, Inc., 8 83–86; 38 122–26 (upd.)

Cartier Monde, 29 90–92

Carus Publishing Company, 93 128–32

Carvel Corporation, 35 78–81

Carver Bancorp, Inc., 94 106–10

Carver Boat Corporation LLC, 88 43–46

Carvin Corp., 89 140–43

Casa Bancária Almeida e Companhia *see* Banco Bradesco S.A.

Casa Cuervo, S.A. de C.V., 31 91–93

Casa Herradura *see* Grupo Industrial Herradura, S.A. de C.V.

CeWe Color Holding AG, 76 85–88

ČEZ a. s., 97 112–15

CF Industries Holdings, Inc., 99 89–93

CG&E *see* Cincinnati Gas & Electric Co.

CGM *see* Compagnie Générale Maritime.

CH2M HILL Companies Ltd., 22 136–38; 96 72–77 (upd.)

Chadbourne & Parke, 36 109–12

Chadwick's of Boston, Ltd., 29 106–08 *see also* Boston Apparel Group.

Chalk's Ocean Airways *see* Flying Boat, Inc.

The Chalone Wine Group, Ltd., 36 113–16

Champagne Bollinger S.A., 114 125–28

Champion Enterprises, Inc., 17 81–84

Champion Industries, Inc., 28 74–76

Champion International Corporation, IV 263–65; 20 127–30 (upd.) *see also* International Paper Co.

Championship Auto Racing Teams, Inc., 37 73–75

Chancellor Beacon Academies, Inc., 53 94–97

Chancellor Media Corporation, 24 106–10

Chanel SA, 12 57–59; 49 83–86 (upd.)

Channel Four Television Corporation, 93 141–44

Chantiers Jeanneau S.A., 96 78–81

Chaoda Modern Agriculture (Holdings) Ltd., 87 96–99

Chaparral Steel Co., 13 142–44

Charal S.A., 90 117–20

Chargeurs International, 6 373–75; 21 103–06 (upd.)

Charisma Brands LLC, 74 75–78

Charles M. Schulz Creative Associates, 114 129–33

The Charles Machine Works, Inc., 64 74–76

Charles River Laboratories International, Inc., 42 66–69

The Charles Schwab Corporation, 8 94–96; 26 64–67 (upd.); 81 62–68 (upd.)

The Charles Stark Draper Laboratory, Inc., 35 90–92

Charles Vögele Holding AG, 82 63–66

Charlotte Russe Holding, Inc., 35 93–96; 90 121–25 (upd.)

The Charmer Sunbelt Group, 95 91–94

Charming Shoppes, Inc., 8 97–98; 38 127–29 (upd.)

Charoen Pokphand Group, 62 60–63

Chart House Enterprises, Inc., 17 85–88; 96 82–86 (upd.)

Chart Industries, Inc., 21 107–09

Charter Communications, Inc., 33 91–94; 116 100–05 (upd.)

Charter Financial Corporation, 103 96–99

Charter Manufacturing Company, Inc., 103 100–03

ChartHouse International Learning Corporation, 49 87–89

Chas. Levy Company LLC, 60 83–85

Chase General Corporation, 91 102–05

The Chase Manhattan Corporation, II 247–49; 13 145–48 (upd.) *see also* JPMorgan Chase & Co.

Chateau Communities, Inc., 37 76–79

Chattanooga Bakery, Inc., 86 75–78

Chattem, Inc., 17 89–92; 88 47–52 (upd.)

Chautauqua Airlines, Inc., 38 130–32

CHC Helicopter Corporation, 67 101–03

Check Into Cash, Inc., 105 90–93

Checker Motors Corp., 89 144–48

Checkers Drive-In Restaurants, Inc., 16 95–98; 74 79–83 (upd.)

CheckFree Corporation, 81 69–72

Checkpoint Systems, Inc., 39 77–80

Chedraui *see* Grupo Comercial Chedraui S.A. de C.V.

The Cheesecake Factory Inc., 17 93–96; 100 100–05 (upd.)

Chef Solutions, Inc., 89 149–52

Chello Zone Ltd., 93 145–48

Chelsea Ltd., 102 74–79

Chelsea Milling Company, 29 109–11

Chelsea Piers Management Inc., 86 79–82

Chelsfield PLC, 67 104–06

Cheltenham & Gloucester PLC, 61 60–62

Chemcentral Corporation, 8 99–101

Chemed Corporation, 13 149–50

Chemfab Corporation, 35 97–101

Chemi-Trol Chemical Co., 16 99–101

Chemical Banking Corporation, II 250–52; 14 101–04 (upd.)

Chemical Waste Management, Inc., 9 108–10

Chemring Group plc, 113 75–79

Chemtura Corporation, 91 106–20 (upd.)

CHEP Pty. Ltd., 80 63–66

Cherokee Inc., 18 106–09

Cherry Brothers LLC, 105 94–97

Cherry Lane Music Publishing Company, Inc., 62 64–67

Chesapeake Corporation, 8 102–04; 30 117–20 (upd.); 93 149–55 (upd.)

Chesapeake Utilities Corporation, 56 60–62

Chesebrough-Pond's USA, Inc., 8 105–07

Cheshire Building Society, 74 84–87

Cheung Kong (Holdings) Ltd., IV 693–95; 20 131–34 (upd.); 94 117–24 (upd.)

Chevron Corporation, IV 385–87; 19 82–85 (upd.); 47 70–76 (upd.); 103 104–14 (upd.)

Cheyenne Software, Inc., 12 60–62

CHF Industries, Inc., 84 47–50

CHHJ Franchising LLC, 105 98–101

Chi-Chi's Inc., 13 151–53; 51 70–73 (upd.)

Chi Mei Optoelectronics Corporation, 75 93–95

Chiasso Inc., 53 98–100

Chiat/Day Inc. Advertising, 11 49–52 *see also* TBWA/Chiat/Day.

Chibu Electric Power Company, Incorporated, V 571–73

Chic by H.I.S, Inc., 20 135–37 *see also* VF Corp.

Chicago and North Western Holdings Corporation, 6 376–78 *see also* Union Pacific Corp.

Chicago Bears Football Club, Inc., 33 95–97

Chicago Blackhawk Hockey Team, Inc. *see* Wirtz Corp.

Chicago Board of Trade, 41 84–87

Chicago Bridge & Iron Company N.V., 82 67–73 (upd.)

Chicago Mercantile Exchange Holdings Inc., 75 96–99

Chicago National League Ball Club, Inc., 66 52–55

Chicago Pizza & Brewery, Inc., 44 85–88

Chicago Review Press Inc., 84 51–54

Chicago Symphony Orchestra, 106 105–09

Chicago Transit Authority, 108 147–50

Chicago Tribune *see* Tribune Co.

Chick-fil-A Inc., 23 115–18; 90 126–31 (upd.)

Chicken of the Sea International, 24 114–16 (upd.); 106 110–13 (upd.)

Chico's FAS, Inc., 45 97–99

ChildFund International, 106 114–17

ChildrenFirst, Inc., 59 117–20

Children's Comprehensive Services, Inc., 42 70–72

Children's Healthcare of Atlanta Inc., 101 105–09

Children's Hospitals and Clinics, Inc., 54 64–67

The Children's Place Retail Stores, Inc., 37 80–82; 86 83–87 (upd.)

Childtime Learning Centers, Inc., 34 103–06 *see also* Learning Care Group, Inc.

Chiles Offshore Corporation, 9 111–13

China Airlines, 34 107–10

China Automotive Systems Inc., 87 100–103

China Construction Bank Corp., 79 101–04

China Eastern Airlines Corporation Limited, 31 102–04; 108 151–55 (upd.)

China FAW Group Corporation, 105 102–07

China Life Insurance Company Limited, 65 103–05

China Merchants International Holdings Co., Ltd., 52 79–82

China Mobile Ltd., 108 156–59

China National Cereals, Oils and Foodstuffs Import and Export Corporation (COFCO), 76 89–91

China National Petroleum Corporation, 46 86–89; 108 160–65 (upd.)

China Nepstar Chain Drugstore Ltd., 97 116–19

China Netcom Group Corporation (Hong Kong) Limited, 73 80–83

I

Metropolitan Transportation Authority, 35 290–92

Metsä-Serla Oy, IV 314–16 *see also* M-real Oyj.

Metso Corporation, 30 321–25 (upd.); 85 269–77 (upd.)

Mettler-Toledo International Inc., 30 326–28; 108 342–47 (upd.)

Mexican Restaurants, Inc., 41 269–71

Mexichem, S.A.B. de C.V., 99 286–290

Meyer International Holdings, Ltd., 87 312–315

Meyer Natural Angus L.L.C., 112 272–75

MFS Communications Company, Inc., 11 301–03 *see also* MCI WorldCom, Inc.

MG&E *see* Madison Gas and Electric.

MGA Entertainment, Inc., 95 279–82

MGIC Investment Corp., 52 242–44

MGM MIRAGE, 17 316–19; 98 237–42 (upd.)

MGM/UA Communications Company, II 146–50 *see also* Metro-Goldwyn-Mayer Inc.

MGN *see* Mirror Group Newspapers Ltd.

Miami Herald Media Company, 92 251–55

Miami Subs Corporation, 108 348–52

Michael Anthony Jewelers, Inc., 24 334–36

Michael Baker Corporation, 14 333–35; 51 245–48 (upd.)

Michael C. Fina Co., Inc., 52 245–47

Michael Foods, Inc., 25 331–34

Michael Page International plc, 45 272–74

Michaels Stores, Inc., 17 320–22; 71 226–30 (upd.)

Michelin *see* Compagnie Générale des Établissements Michelin.

Michigan Bell Telephone Co., 14 336–38

Michigan National Corporation, 11 304–06 *see also* ABN AMRO Holding, N.V.

Michigan Sporting Goods Distributors, Inc., 72 228–30

Michigan Turkey Producers Co-op, Inc., 115 336–39

Micrel, Incorporated, 77 276–79

Micro Warehouse, Inc., 16 371–73

MicroAge, Inc., 16 367–70

Microdot Inc., 8 365–68

Micron Technology, Inc., 11 307–09; 29 323–26 (upd.); 116 340–45 (upd.)

Micros Systems, Inc., 18 335–38

Microsemi Corporation, 94 311–14

Microsoft Corporation, 6 257–60; 27 319–23 (upd.); 63 293–97 (upd.)

MicroStrategy Incorporated, 87 316–320

Mid-America Apartment Communities, Inc., 85 278–81

Mid-America Dairymen, Inc., 7 338–40

Midas Inc., 10 414–15; 56 228–31 (upd.)

Middle East Airlines - Air Liban S.A.L., 79 251–54

The Middleby Corporation, 22 352–55; 104 315–20 (upd.)

Middlesex Water Company, 45 275–78

The Middleton Doll Company, 53 222–25

Midland Bank plc, II 318–20; 17 323–26 (upd.) *see also* HSBC Holdings plc.

The Midland Company, 65 233–35

Midway Airlines Corporation, 33 301–03

Midway Games, Inc., 25 335–38; 102 267–73 (upd.)

Midwest Air Group, Inc., 35 293–95; 85 282–86 (upd.)

Midwest Grain Products, Inc., 49 261–63

Midwest Resources Inc., 6 523–25

Miele & Cie. KG, 56 232–35

MiG *see* Russian Aircraft Corporation (MiG).

Migros-Genossenschafts-Bund, 68 252–55

MIH Limited, 31 329–32

Mikasa, Inc., 28 268–70

Mike-Sell's Inc., 15 298–300

Mikohn Gaming Corporation, 39 276–79

Milacron, Inc., 53 226–30 (upd.)

Milan AC S.p.A., 79 255–58

Milbank, Tweed, Hadley & McCloy, 27 324–27

Miles Laboratories, I 653–55 *see also* Bayer A.G.

Millea Holdings Inc., 64 276–81 (upd.)

Millennium & Copthorne Hotels plc, 71 231–33

Millennium Pharmaceuticals, Inc., 47 249–52

Miller Brewing Company, I 269–70; 12 337–39 (upd.) *see also* SABMiller plc.

Miller Industries, Inc., 26 293–95

Miller Publishing Group, LLC, 57 242–44

Millicom International Cellular S.A., 115 340–43

Milliken & Co., V 366–68; 17 327–30 (upd.); 82 235–39 (upd.)

Milliman USA, 66 223–26

Millipore Corporation, 25 339–43; 84 271–276 (upd.)

The Mills Corporation, 77 280–83

Milnot Company, 46 289–91

Milton Bradley Company, 21 372–75

Milton CAT, Inc., 86 268–71

Milwaukee Brewers Baseball Club, 37 247–49

Mine Safety Appliances Company, 31 333–35

Minebea Co., Ltd., 90 298–302

The Miner Group International, 22 356–58

Minera Escondida Ltda., 100 293–96

Minerals & Metals Trading Corporation of India Ltd., IV 143–44

Minerals Technologies Inc., 11 310–12; 52 248–51 (upd.)

Minnesota Mining & Manufacturing Company, I 499–501; 8 369–71 (upd.); 26 296–99 (upd.) *see also* 3M Co.

Minnesota Power, Inc., 11 313–16; 34 286–91 (upd.)

Minnesota Twins, 112 276–80

Minntech Corporation, 22 359–61

Minolta Co., Ltd., III 574–76; 18 339–42 (upd.); 43 281–85 (upd.)

The Minute Maid Company, 28 271–74

Minuteman International Inc., 46 292–95

Minyard Food Stores, Inc., 33 304–07; 86 272–77 (upd.)

Miquel y Costas Miquel S.A., 68 256–58

Mirage Resorts, Incorporated, 6 209–12; 28 275–79 (upd.) *see also* MGM MIRAGE.

Miramax Film Corporation, 64 282–85

Mirant Corporation, 98 243–47

Miroglio SpA, 86 278–81

Mirror Group Newspapers plc, 7 341–43; 23 348–51 (upd.)

Misonix, Inc., 80 248–51

Mississippi Chemical Corporation, 39 280–83

Mississippi Power Company, 110 315–19

Misys PLC, 45 279–81; 46 296–99

Mitchell Energy and Development Corporation, 7 344–46 *see also* Devon Energy Corp.

Mitchells & Butlers PLC, 59 296–99

Mitel Corporation, 18 343–46

MITRE Corporation, 26 300–02; 107 269–72 (upd.)

MITROPA AG, 37 250–53

Mitsubishi Bank, Ltd., II 321–22 *see also* Bank of Tokyo-Mitsubishi Ltd.

Mitsubishi Chemical Corporation, I 363–64; 56 236–38 (upd.)

Mitsubishi Corporation, I 502–04; 12 340–43 (upd.); 116 346–52 (upd.)

Mitsubishi Electric Corporation, II 57–59; 44 283–87 (upd.); 117 263–69 (upd.)

Mitsubishi Estate Company, Limited, IV 713–14; 61 215–18 (upd.)

Mitsubishi Heavy Industries, Ltd., III 577–79; 7 347–50 (upd.); 40 324–28 (upd.)

Mitsubishi Materials Corporation, III 712–13

Mitsubishi Motors Corporation, 9 349–51; 23 352–55 (upd.); 57 245–49 (upd.)

Mitsubishi Oil Co., Ltd., IV 460–62 *see also* Nippon Mitsubishi Oil Corp.

Mitsubishi Rayon Co. Ltd., V 369–71

Mitsubishi Trust & Banking Corporation, II 323–24

Mitsubishi UFJ Financial Group, Inc., 99 291–296 (upd.)

Mövenpick Holding, 104 328–32
Movie Gallery, Inc., 31 339–41
Movie Star Inc., 17 337–39
Moy Park Ltd., 78 228–31
Mozilla Foundation, 106 299–303
MPI *see* Michael Page International plc.
MPRG *see* Matt Prentice Restaurant Group.
MPS Group, Inc., 49 264–67
MPW Industrial Services Group, Inc., 53 231–33
Mr. Bricolage S.A., 37 258–60
Mr. Coffee, Inc., 15 307–09
Mr. Gasket Inc., 15 310–12
Mr. Gatti's, LP, 87 321–324
Mrchocolate.com LLC, 105 309–12
Mrs. Baird's Bakeries, 29 338–41
Mrs. Fields' Original Cookies, Inc., 27 331–35; 104 333–39 (upd.)
Mrs. Grossman's Paper Company Inc., 84 277–280
MS&L *see* Manning Selvage & Lee.
MSC *see* Material Sciences Corp.
MSC Industrial Direct Co., Inc., 71 234–36
MSE, Inc., 113 261–64
MSWG, LLC, 105 313–16
Mt. *see also* Mount.
Mt. Olive Pickle Company, Inc., 44 293–95
MTA *see* Metropolitan Transportation Authority.
MTC *see* Management and Training Corp.
MTD Products Inc., 107 279–82
MTel *see* Mobile Telecommunications Technologies Corp.
MTG *see* Modern Times Group AB.
MTI Enterprises Inc., 102 279–82
MTN Group Ltd., 106 304–07
MTR Foods Ltd., 55 271–73
MTR Gaming Group, Inc., 75 265–67
MTS *see* Mobile TeleSystems.
MTS Inc., 37 261–64
Mueller Industries, Inc., 7 359–61; 52 256–60 (upd.)
Mueller Sports Medicine, Inc., 102 283–86
Mueller Water Products, Inc., 113 265–68
Mulberry Group PLC, 71 237–39
Mullen Advertising Inc., 51 259–61
Multi-Color Corporation, 53 234–36
Multimedia Games, Inc., 41 272–76
Multimedia, Inc., 11 330–32
Munich Re (Münchener Rückversicherungs-Gesellschaft Aktiengesellschaft in München), III 299–301; 46 303–07 (upd.)
Munir Sukhtian Group, 104 340–44
Muralo Company Inc., 117 270–73
Murdock Madaus Schwabe, 26 315–19
Murphy Family Farms Inc., 22 366–68 *see also* Smithfield Foods, Inc.
Murphy Oil Corporation, 7 362–64; 32 338–41 (upd.); 95 283–89 (upd.)
Murphy's Pizza *see* Papa Murphy's International, Inc.

The Musco Family Olive Co., 91 334–37
Musco Lighting, 83 276–279
Museum of Modern Art, 106 308–12
Musgrave Group Plc, 57 254–57
Music Corporation of America *see* MCA Inc.
Musicland Stores Corporation, 9 360–62; 38 313–17 (upd.)
Mutual Benefit Life Insurance Company, III 302–04
Mutual Life Insurance Company of New York, III 305–07
The Mutual of Omaha Companies, 98 248–52
Mutuelle Assurance des Commerçants et Industriels de France (Macif), 107 283–86
Muzak, Inc., 18 353–56
MWA *see* Modern Woodmen of America.
MWH Preservation Limited Partnership, 65 245–48
MWI Veterinary Supply, Inc., 80 265–68
Mycogen Corporation, 21 385–87 *see also* Dow Chemical Co.
Myers Industries, Inc., 19 277–79; 96 293–97 (upd.)
Mylan Laboratories Inc., I 656–57; 20 380–82 (upd.); 59 304–08 (upd.)
Myllykoski Oyj, 117 274–78
MYOB Ltd., 86 286–90
Myriad Genetics, Inc., 95 290–95
Myriad Restaurant Group, Inc., 87 328–331
MySpace.com *see* Intermix Media, Inc.

N

N.F. Smith & Associates LP, 70 199–202
N M Rothschild & Sons Limited, 39 293–95
N.V. *see under first word of company name*
NAACP *see* National Association for the Advancement of Colored People.
Naamloze Vennootschap tot Exploitatie van het Café Krasnapolsky *see* Grand Hotel Krasnapolsky N.V.
Nabisco Brands, Inc., II 542–44 *see also* RJR Nabisco.
Nabisco Foods Group, 7 365–68 (upd.) *see also* Kraft Foods Inc.
Nabors Industries Ltd., 9 363–65; 91 338–44 (upd.)
NACCO Industries, Inc., 7 369–71; 78 232–36 (upd.)
Nadro S.A. de C.V., 86 291–94
Naf Naf SA, 44 296–98
Nagasakiya Co., Ltd., V 149–51; 69 259–62 (upd.)
Nagase & Co., Ltd., 8 376–78; 61 226–30 (upd.)
NAI *see* Natural Alternatives International, Inc.; Network Associates, Inc.
Naked Juice Company, 107 287–90
Nalco Holding Company, I 373–75; 12 346–48 (upd.); 89 324–30 (upd.)
Nam Tai Electronics, Inc., 61 231–34

Namco Bandai Holdings Inc., 106 313–19 (upd.)
Nantucket Allserve, Inc., 22 369–71
Napster, Inc., 69 263–66
Narodowy Bank Polski, 100 297–300
NAS *see* National Audubon Society.
NASCAR *see* National Association for Stock Car Auto Racing.
NASD, 54 242–46 (upd.)
The NASDAQ Stock Market, Inc., 92 256–60
Nash Finch Company, 8 379–81; 23 356–58 (upd.); 65 249–53 (upd.)
Nashua Corporation, 8 382–84
Naspers Ltd., 66 230–32
Nastech Pharmaceutical Company Inc., 79 259–62
Nathan's Famous, Inc., 29 342–44
Nation Media Group, 116 357–61
National Amusements Inc., 28 295–97
National Aquarium in Baltimore, Inc., 74 198–200
National Association for Stock Car Auto Racing, 32 342–44
National Association for the Advancement of Colored People, 109 404–07
National Association of Securities Dealers, Inc., 10 416–18 *see also* NASD.
National Audubon Society, 26 320–23
National Australia Bank Ltd., 111 315–19
National Auto Credit, Inc., 16 379–81
National Bank of Canada, 85 291–94
National Bank of Greece, 41 277–79
The National Bank of South Carolina, 76 278–80
National Bank of Ukraine, 102 287–90
National Beverage Corporation, 26 324–26; 88 267–71 (upd.)
National Broadcasting Company, Inc., II 151–53; 6 164–66 (upd.); 28 298–301 (upd.) *see also* General Electric Co.
National Can Corp., I 607–08
National Car Rental System, Inc., 10 419–20 *see also* Republic Industries, Inc.
Nationa CineMedia, Inc., 103 266–70
National City Corporation, 15 313–16; 97 294–302 (upd.)
National Collegiate Athletic Association, 96 298–302
National Convenience Stores Incorporated, 7 372–75
National Council of La Raza, 106 320–23
National Discount Brokers Group, Inc., 28 302–04 *see also* Deutsche Bank A.G.
National Distillers and Chemical Corporation, I 376–78 *see also* Quantum Chemical Corp.
National Educational Music Co. Ltd., 47 256–58
National Enquirer see American Media, Inc.

Overstock.com, Inc., 75 307–09
Owens & Minor, Inc., 16 398–401; 68 282–85 (upd.)
Owens Corning, III 720–23; 20 413–17 (upd.); 98 285–91 (upd.)
Owens-Illinois, Inc., I 609–11; 26 350–53 (upd.); 85 311–18 (upd.)
Owosso Corporation, 29 366–68
Oxfam GB, 87 359–362
Oxford Health Plans, Inc., 16 402–04
Oxford Industries, Inc., 8 406–08; 84 290–296 (upd.)

P

P&C Foods Inc., 8 409–11
P & F Industries, Inc., 45 327–29
P&G *see* Procter & Gamble Co.
P&H *see* Palmer and Harvey Group PLC.
P.C. Richard & Son Corp., 23 372–74
P.F. Chang's China Bistro, Inc., 37 297–99; 86 317–21 (upd.)
P.H. Glatfelter Company, 8 412–14; 30 349–52 (upd.); 83 291–297 (upd.)
P.W. Minor and Son, Inc., 100 321–24
PACCAR Inc., I 185–86; 26 354–56 (upd.); 111 380–84 (upd.)
Pacer International, Inc., 54 274–76
Pacer Technology, 40 347–49
Pacific Basin Shipping Ltd., 86 322–26
Pacific Clay Products Inc., 88 292–95
Pacific Coast Building Products, Inc., 94 338–41
Pacific Coast Feather Company, 67 294–96
Pacific Coast Restaurants, Inc., 90 318–21
Pacific Continental Corporation, 114 320–23
Pacific Dunlop Limited, 10 444–46 *see also* Ansell Ltd.
Pacific Enterprises, V 682–84 *see also* Sempra Energy.
Pacific Ethanol, Inc., 81 269–72
Pacific Gas and Electric Company, V 685–87 *see also* PG&E Corp.
Pacific Internet Limited, 87 363–366
Pacific Mutual Holding Company, 98 292–96
Pacific Sunwear of California, Inc., 28 343–45; 104 363–67 (upd.)
Pacific Telecom, Inc., 6 325–28
Pacific Telesis Group, V 318–20 *see also* SBC Communications.
PacifiCare Health Systems, Inc., 11 378–80
PacifiCorp, Inc., V 688–90; 26 357–60 (upd.)
Packaging Corporation of America, 12 376–78; 51 282–85 (upd.)
Packard Bell Electronics, Inc., 13 387–89
Packeteer, Inc., 81 273–76
PacketVideo Corporation, 112 303–06
Paddock Publications, Inc., 53 263–65
Paddy Power plc, 98 297–300
PagesJaunes Groupe SA, 79 306–09
Paging Network Inc., 11 381–83
Pagnossin S.p.A., 73 248–50

PaineWebber Group Inc., II 444–46; 22 404–07 (upd.) *see also* UBS AG.
Paiste AG, 115 379–82
Pakistan International Airlines Corporation, 46 323–26
Pakistan State Oil Company Ltd., 81 277–80
PAL *see* Philippine Airlines, Inc.
Palace Sports & Entertainment, Inc., 97 320–25
Palfinger AG, 100 325–28
PALIC *see* Pan-American Life Insurance Co.
Pall Corporation, 9 396–98; 72 263–66 (upd.)
Palm Breweries NV, 113 296–99
Palm Harbor Homes, Inc., 39 316–18
Palm, Inc., 36 355–57; 75 310–14 (upd.)
Palm Management Corporation, 71 265–68
Palmer & Cay, Inc., 69 285–87
Palmer and Harvey Group PLC, 114 324–28
Palmer Candy Company, 80 277–81
Palmer Co. *see* R. M. Palmer Co.
Paloma Industries Ltd., 71 269–71
Palomar Medical Technologies, Inc., 22 408–10
Pamida Holdings Corporation, 15 341–43
The Pampered Chef Ltd., 18 406–08; 78 292–96 (upd.)
Pamplin Corp. *see* R.B. Pamplin Corp.
Pan-American Life Insurance Company, 48 311–13
Pan American World Airways, Inc., I 115–16; 12 379–81 (upd.)
Panalpina World Transport (Holding) Ltd., 47 286–88
Panamerican Beverages, Inc., 47 289–91; 54 74
PanAmSat Corporation, 46 327–29
Panattoni Development Company, Inc., 99 327–330
Panavision Inc., 24 372–74; 107 340–44 (upd.)
Pancho's Mexican Buffet, Inc., 46 330–32
Panda Restaurant Group, Inc., 35 327–29; 97 326–30 (upd.)
Panera Bread Company, 44 327–29
Panhandle Eastern Corporation, V 691–92 *see also* CMS Energy Corp.
Pantone Inc., 53 266–69
The Pantry, Inc., 36 358–60
Panzani, 84 297–300
Papa Gino's Holdings Corporation, Inc., 86 327–30
Papa John's International, Inc., 15 344–46; 71 272–76 (upd.)
Papa Murphy's International, Inc., 54 277–79
Papeteries de Lancey, 23 366–68
Papetti's Hygrade Egg Products, Inc., 39 319–21
Pappas Restaurants, Inc., 76 302–04

Par Pharmaceutical Companies, Inc., 65 286–88
The Paradies Shops, Inc., 88 296–99
Paradise Music & Entertainment, Inc., 42 271–74
Paradores de Turismo de Espana S.A., 73 251–53
Parallel Petroleum Corporation, 101 400–03
Parametric Technology Corp., 16 405–07
Paramount Pictures Corporation, II 154–56; 94 342–47 (upd.)
Paramount Resources Ltd., 87 367–370
PAREXEL International Corporation, 84 301–304
Parfums Givenchy S.A., 100 329–32
Paribas *see* BNP Paribas Group.
Paris Corporation, 22 411–13
Parisian, Inc., 14 374–76 *see also* Belk, Inc.
Park Corp., 22 414–16
Park-Ohio Holdings Corp., 17 371–73; 85 319–23 (upd.)
Parker Drilling Company, 28 346–48
Parker-Hannifin Corporation, III 601–03; 24 375–78 (upd.); 99 331–337 (upd.)
Parlex Corporation, 61 279–81
Parmalat Finanziaria SpA, 50 343–46
Parque Arauco S.A., 72 267–69
Parras *see* Compañia Industrial de Parras, S.A. de C.V. (CIPSA).
Parsons Brinckerhoff Inc., 34 333–36; 104 368–72 (upd.)
The Parsons Corporation, 8 415–17; 56 263–67 (upd.)
PartnerRe Ltd., 83 298–301
Partouche SA *see* Groupe Partouche SA.
Party City Corporation, 54 280–82
Patch Products Inc., 105 340–44
Pathé SA, 29 369–71 *see also* Chargeurs International.
Pathmark Stores, Inc., 23 369–71; 101 404–08 (upd.)
Patina Oil & Gas Corporation, 24 379–81
Patrick Cudahy Inc., 102 321–25
Patrick Industries, Inc., 30 342–45
Patriot Transportation Holding, Inc., 91 371–74
Patterson Dental Co., 19 289–91
Patterson-UTI Energy, Inc., 55 293–95
Patton Boggs LLP, 71 277–79
Paul Harris Stores, Inc., 18 409–12
Paul, Hastings, Janofsky & Walker LLP, 27 357–59
Paul Mueller Company, 65 289–91
Paul Reed Smith Guitar Company, 89 345–48
The Paul Revere Corporation, 12 382–83
Paul-Son Gaming Corporation, 66 249–51
Paul Stuart Inc., 109 437–40
Paul, Weiss, Rifkind, Wharton & Garrison, 47 292–94

ScanSource, Inc., 29 413–15; 74 295–98 (upd.)

Scarborough Public Utilities Commission, 9 461–62

SCB Computer Technology, Inc., 29 416–18

SCEcorp, V 715–17 *see also* Edison International.

Schaeffler KG, 110 412–17

Schawk, Inc., 24 424–26

Scheels All Sports Inc., 63 348–50

Scheid Vineyards Inc., 66 276–78

Schell Brewing *see* August Schell Brewing Company Inc.

Schenck Business Solutions, 88 349–53

Schenker-Rhenus Ag, 6 424–26

Scherer *see* R.P. Scherer.

Scherer Brothers Lumber Company, 94 379–83

Schering A.G., I 681–82; 50 418–22 (upd.)

Schering-Plough Corporation, I 683–85; 14 422–25 (upd.); 49 356–62 (upd.); 99 404–414 (upd.)

Schibsted ASA, 31 401–05

Schieffelin & Somerset Co., 61 323–25

Schincariol Participaçoces e Representações S.A., 102 372–75

Schindler Holding AG, 29 419–22

Schlage Lock Company, 82 330–34

Schlecker *see* Anton Schlecker.

Schlotzsky's, Inc., 36 408–10

Schlumberger Limited, III 616–18; 17 416–19 (upd.); 59 366–71 (upd.)

Schmitt Music Company, 40 388–90

Schmolz + Bickenbach AG, 104 408–13

Schneider Electric SA, II 93–94; 18 471–74 (upd.); 108 441–47 (upd.)

Schneider National, Inc., 36 411–13; 77 374–78 (upd.)

Schneiderman's Furniture Inc., 28 405–08

Schneidersöhne Deutschland GmbH & Co. KG, 100 377–81

Schnitzer Steel Industries, Inc., 19 380–82

Scholastic Corporation, 10 479–81; 29 423–27 (upd.)

Scholle Corporation, 96 370–73

School Specialty, Inc., 68 335–37

School-Tech, Inc., 62 318–20

Schott Brothers, Inc., 67 337–39

Schott Corporation, 53 296–98

Schottenstein Stores Corporation, 14 426–28 ; 117 377–80 (upd.)

Schouw & Company A/S, 94 384–87

Schreiber Foods, Inc., 72 303–06

Schroders plc, 42 332–35; 112 348–52 (upd.)

Schuff Steel Company, 26 431–34

Schultz Sav-O Stores, Inc., 21 454–56; 31 406–08 (upd.)

Schurz Communications, Inc., 98 345–49

The Schwan Food Company, 7 468–70; 26 435–38 (upd.); 83 340–346 (upd.)

The Schwarz Group, 100 382–87

Schwebel Baking Company, 72 307–09

Schweitzer-Mauduit International, Inc., 52 300–02

Schweizerische Post-, Telefon- und Telegrafen-Betriebe, V 321–24

Schweppes Ltd. *see* Cadbury Schweppes PLC.

Schwinn Cycle and Fitness L.P., 19 383–85 *see also* Huffy Corp.

SCI *see* Service Corporation International.

SCI Systems, Inc., 9 463–64 *see also* Sanmina-SCI Corporation.

Science Applications International Corporation, 15 438–40; 109 487–91 (upd.)

Scientific-Atlanta, Inc., 6 335–37; 45 371–75 (upd.)

Scientific Games Corporation, 64 343–46 (upd.)

Scientific Learning Corporation, 95 374–77

Scitex Corporation Ltd., 24 427–32

SCO *see* Santa Cruz Operation, Inc.

The SCO Group Inc., 78 333–37

Scolari's Food and Drug Company, 102 376–79

Scope Products, Inc., 94 388–91

SCOR S.A., 20 464–66

The Score Board, Inc., 19 386–88

Scotiabank *see* The Bank of Nova Scotia.

Scotsman Industries, Inc., 20 467–69

Scott Fetzer Company, 12 435–37; 80 339–43 (upd.)

Scott Paper Company, IV 329–31; 31 409–12 (upd.)

Scottish & Newcastle plc, 15 441–44; 35 394–97 (upd.)

Scottish and Southern Energy plc, 13 457–59; 66 279–84 (upd.)

Scottish Media Group plc, 32 404–06; 41 350–52

Scottish Power plc, 49 363–66 (upd.)

Scottish Radio Holding plc, 41 350–52

ScottishPower plc, 19 389–91

Scottrade, Inc., 85 374–77

The Scotts Company, 22 474–76

Scotty's, Inc., 22 477–80

The Scoular Company, 77 379–82

Scovill Fasteners Inc., 24 433–36

SCP Pool Corporation, 39 358–60

Screen Actors Guild, 72 310–13

The Scripps Research Institute, 76 323–25

SDGE *see* San Diego Gas & Electric Co.

SDL PLC, 67 340–42

Sea Containers Ltd., 29 428–31

Seaboard Corporation, 36 414–16; 85 378–82 (upd.)

SeaChange International, Inc., 79 374–78

SEACOR Holdings Inc., 83 347–350

Seagate Technology, 8 466–68; 34 400–04 (upd.); 105 382–90 (upd.)

The Seagram Company Ltd., I 284–86; 25 408–12 (upd.)

Seagull Energy Corporation, 11 440–42

Sealaska Corporation, 60 261–64

Sealed Air Corporation, 14 429–31; 57 313–17 (upd.)

Sealed Power Corporation, I 199–200 *see also* SPX Corp.

Sealright Co., Inc., 17 420–23

Sealy Corporation, 12 438–40; 112 353–57 (upd.)

Seaman Furniture Company, Inc., 32 407–09

Sean John Clothing, Inc., 70 288–90

SeaRay Boats Inc., 96 374–77

Sears plc, V 177–79

Sears Roebuck de México, S.A. de C.V., 20 470–72

Sears, Roebuck and Co., V 180–83; 18 475–79 (upd.); 56 309–14 (upd.)

Seat Pagine Gialle S.p.A., 47 345–47

Seattle City Light, 50 423–26

Seattle FilmWorks, Inc., 20 473–75

Seattle First National Bank Inc., 8 469–71 *see also* Bank of America Corp.

Seattle Lighting Fixture Company, 92 331–34

Seattle Pacific Industries, Inc., 92 335–38

Seattle Seahawks, Inc., 92 339–43

Seattle Times Company, 15 445–47

Seaway Food Town, Inc., 15 448–50 *see also* Spartan Stores Inc.

SEB Group *see* Skandinaviska Enskilda Banken AB.

SEB S.A. *see* Groupe SEB.

Sebastiani Vineyards, Inc., 28 413–15; 117 381–85 (upd.)

The Second City, Inc., 88 354–58

Second Harvest, 29 432–34

Securicor Plc, 45 376–79

Securitas AB, 42 336–39; 112 358–63 (upd.)

Security Capital Corporation, 17 424–27

Security Pacific Corporation, II 349–50

SED International Holdings, Inc., 43 367–69

La Seda de Barcelona S.A., 100 260–63

Seddon Group Ltd., 67 343–45

SEGA Corporation, 73 290–93

Sega of America, Inc., 10 482–85

Segway LLC, 48 355–57

SEI Investments Company, 96 378–82

Seibu Department Stores, Ltd., V 184–86; 42 340–43 (upd.)

Seibu Railway Company Ltd., V 510–11; 74 299–301 (upd.)

Seigle's Home and Building Centers, Inc., 41 353–55

Seiko Corporation, III 619–21; 17 428–31 (upd.); 72 314–18 (upd.)

Seino Transportation Company, Ltd., 6 427–29

Seita, 23 424–27 *see also* Altadis S.A.

Seitel, Inc., 47 348–50

The Seiyu, Ltd., V 187–89; 36 417–21 (upd.)

Sekisui Chemical Co., Ltd., III 741–43; 72 319–22 (upd.)

Select Comfort Corporation, 34 405–08

Select Medical Corporation, 65 306–08

Siltronic AG, 90 374–77

Silver Lake Cookie Company Inc., 95 378–81

Silver Wheaton Corp., 95 382–85

SilverPlatter Information Inc., 23 440–43

Silverstar Holdings, Ltd., 99 415–418

Silverstein Properties, Inc., 47 358–60

Simba Dickie Group KG, 105 404–07

Simco S.A., 37 357–59

Sime Darby Berhad, 14 448–50; 36 433–36 (upd.)

Simmons Company, 47 361–64

Simon & Schuster Inc., IV 671–72; 19 403–05 (upd.); 100 393–97 (upd.)

Simon Property Group Inc., 27 399–402; 84 350–355 (upd.)

Simon Transportation Services Inc., 27 403–06

Simplex Technologies Inc., 21 460–63

Simplicity Manufacturing, Inc., 64 353–56

Simpson Investment Company, 17 438–41

Simpson Thacher & Bartlett, 39 365–68

Sims Metal Management, Ltd., 109 503–07

Simula, Inc., 41 368–70

SINA Corporation, 69 324–27

Sinclair Broadcast Group, Inc., 25 417–19; 109 508–13 (upd.)

Sinclair Oil Corporation, 111 432–36

Sine Qua Non, 99 419–422

Singapore Airlines Limited, 6 117–18; 27 407–09 (upd.); 83 355–359 (upd.)

Singapore Press Holdings Limited, 85 391–95

Singapore Telecommunications Limited, 111 437–41

Singer & Friedlander Group plc, 41 371–73

The Singer Company N.V., 30 417–20 (upd.)

The Singing Machine Company, Inc., 60 277–80

SingTel *see* Singapore Telecommunications Limited

Sir Speedy, Inc., 16 448–50

Sirius Satellite Radio, Inc., 69 328–31

Sirona Dental Systems, Inc., 117 392–96

Sirti S.p.A., 76 326–28

Siskin Steel & Supply Company, 70 294–96

Sistema JSFC, 73 303–05

Sisters of Charity of Leavenworth Health System, 105 408–12

Six Flags, Inc., 17 442–44; 54 333–40 (upd.)

Sixt AG, 39 369–72

SJM Holdings Ltd., 105 413–17

SJW Corporation, 70 297–99

SK Group, 88 363–67

Skadden, Arps, Slate, Meagher & Flom, 18 486–88

Skalli Group, 67 349–51

Skandia Insurance Company, Ltd., 50 431–34

Skandinaviska Enskilda Banken AB, II 351–53; 56 326–29 (upd.)

Skanska AB, 38 435–38; 110 422–26 (upd.)

Skechers U.S.A. Inc., 31 413–15; 88 368–72 (upd.)

Skeeter Products Inc., 96 391–94

SKF *see* Aktiebolaget SKF.

Skidmore, Owings & Merrill LLP, 13 475–76; 69 332–35 (upd.)

SkillSoft Public Limited Company, 81 371–74

skinnyCorp, LLC, 97 374–77

Skipton Building Society, 80 344–47

Skis Rossignol S.A., 15 460–62; 43 373–76 (upd.)

Skoda Auto a.s., 39 373–75

Skyline Chili, Inc., 62 325–28

Skyline Corporation, 30 421–23

SkyMall, Inc., 26 439–41

Skype Technologies S.A., 108 452–55

SkyWest, Inc., 25 420–24

Skyy Spirits LLC, 78 348–51

SL Green Realty Corporation, 44 383–85

SL Industries, Inc., 77 383–86

Slaughter and May, 112 376–79

SLC Participaçoes S.A., 111 442–45

Sleeman Breweries Ltd., 74 305–08

Sleepy's Inc., 32 426–28

SLI, Inc., 48 358–61

Slim-Fast Foods Company, 18 489–91; 66 296–98 (upd.)

Sling Media, Inc., 112 380–83

Slinky, Inc. *see* Poof-Slinky, Inc.

SLM Corp., 25 425–28 (upd.); 116 441–46 (upd.)

Slough Estates PLC, IV 722–25; 50 435–40 (upd.)

Small Planet Foods, Inc., 89 410–14

Small World Toys, 115 429–32

Smart & Final LLC, 16 451–53; 94 392–96 (upd.)

Smart Balance, Inc., 100 398–401

SMART Modular Technologies, Inc., 86 361–64

SmartForce PLC, 43 377–80

Smarties *see* Ce De Candy Inc.

SMBC *see* Sumitomo Mitsui Banking Corp.

Smead Manufacturing Co., 17 445–48

SMG *see* Scottish Media Group.

SMH *see* Sanders Morris Harris Group Inc.; The Swatch Group SA.

Smith & Hawken, Ltd., 68 343–45

Smith & Nephew plc, 17 449–52; 41 374–78 (upd.)

Smith & Wesson Corp., 30 424–27; 73 306–11 (upd.)

The Smith & Wollensky Restaurant Group, Inc., 105 418–22

Smith Barney Inc., 15 463–65 *see also* Citigroup Inc.

Smith Corona Corp., 13 477–80

Smith International, Inc., 15 466–68; 59 376–80 (upd.)

Smith Micro Software, Inc., 112 384–87

Smith-Midland Corporation, 56 330–32

Smithfield Foods, Inc., 7 477–78; 43 381–84 (upd.); 114 384–89 (upd.)

SmithKline Beckman Corporation, I 692–94 *see also* GlaxoSmithKline plc.

SmithKline Beecham plc, III 65–67; 32 429–34 (upd.) *see also* GlaxoSmithKline plc.

Smith's Food & Drug Centers, Inc., 8 472–74; 57 324–27 (upd.)

Smiths Group plc, 25 429–31; 107 406–10 (upd.)

Smithsonian Institution, 27 410–13

Smithway Motor Xpress Corporation, 39 376–79

Smoby International SA, 56 333–35

Smorgon Steel Group Ltd., 62 329–32

Smucker's *see* The J.M. Smucker Co.

Smurfit Kappa Group plc, 26 442–46 (upd.) ; 83 360–368 (upd.)112 388–95 (upd.)

Snap-On, Incorporated, 7 479–80; 27 414–16 (upd.); 105 423–28 (upd.)

Snapfish, 83 369–372

Snapple Beverage Corporation, 11 449–51

SNC-Lavalin Group Inc., 72 330–33

SNCF *see* Société Nationale des Chemins de Fer Français.

SNEA *see* Société Nationale Elf Aquitaine.

Snecma Group, 46 369–72 *see also* SAFRAN.

Snell & Wilmer L.L.P., 28 425–28

SNET *see* Southern New England Telecommunications Corp.

Snow Brand Milk Products Company, Ltd., II 574–75; 48 362–65 (upd.)

Soap Opera Magazine see American Media, Inc.

Sobeys Inc., 80 348–51

Socata *see* EADS SOCATA.

Sociedad Química y Minera de Chile S.A., 103 382–85

Sociedade de Jogos de Macau, S.A. *see* SJM Holdings Ltd.

Società Finanziaria Telefonica per Azioni, V 325–27

Società Sportiva Lazio SpA, 44 386–88

Société Air France, 27 417–20 (upd.) *see also* Air France–KLM.

Société BIC S.A., 73 312–15

Societe des Produits Marnier-Lapostolle S.A., 88 373–76

Société d'Exploitation AOM Air Liberté SA (AirLib), 53 305–07

Société du Figaro S.A., 60 281–84

Société du Louvre, 27 421–23

Société Générale, II 354–56; 42 347–51 (upd.)

Société Industrielle Lesaffre, 84 356–359

Société Luxembourgeoise de Navigation Aérienne S.A., 64 357–59

Société Nationale des Chemins de Fer Français, V 512–15; 57 328–32 (upd.)

Société Nationale Elf Aquitaine, IV 544–47; 7 481–85 (upd.)

The Sunrider Corporation, 26 470–74
Sunrise Greetings, 88 385–88
Sunrise Medical Inc., 11 486–88
Sunrise Senior Living, Inc., 81 380–83
Sunshine Village Corporation, 103 415–18
Sunsweet Growers *see* Diamond of California.
Suntech Power Holdings Company Ltd., 89 432–35
Sunterra Corporation, 75 354–56
Suntory Ltd., 65 328–31
Suntron Corporation, 107 421–24
SunTrust Banks Inc., 23 455–58; 101 458–64 (upd.)
SunWize Technologies, Inc., 114 398–402
Super 8 Motels, Inc., 83 381–385
Super Food Services, Inc., 15 479–81
Supercuts Inc., 26 475–78
Superdrug Stores PLC, 95 390–93
Superior Energy Services, Inc., 65 332–34
Superior Essex Inc., 80 364–68
Superior Industries International, Inc., 8 505–07
Superior Uniform Group, Inc., 30 455–57
Supermarkets General Holdings Corporation, II 672–74 *see also* Pathmark Stores, Inc.
SUPERVALU INC., II 668–71; 18 503–08 (upd.); 50 453–59 (upd.); 114 403–12 (upd.)
Suprema Specialties, Inc., 27 440–42
Supreme International Corporation, 27 443–46 *see also* Perry Ellis International Inc.
Suramericana de Inversiones S.A., 88 389–92
Surrey Satellite Technology Limited, 83 386–390
The Susan G. Komen Breast CancerFoundation, 78 373–76
Susquehanna Pfaltzgraff Company, 8 508–10
Susser Holdings Corporation, 114 413–16
Sutherland Lumber Company, L.P., 99 431–434
Sutter Home Winery Inc., 16 476–78 *see also* Trinchero Family Estates.
Suzano *see* Companhia Suzano de Papel e Celulose S.A.
Suzuki Motor Corporation, 9 487–89; 23 459–62 (upd.); 59 393–98 (upd.)
SVB Financial Group, 109 521–25
Sveaskog AB, 93 430–33
Svenska Cellulosa Aktiebolaget SCA, IV 338–40; 28 443–46 (upd.); 85 413–20 (upd.)
Svenska Handelsbanken AB, II 365–67; 50 460–63 (upd.)
Svenska Spel AB, 107 425–28
Sverdrup Corporation, 14 475–78 *see also* Jacobs Engineering Group Inc.
Sveriges Riksbank, 96 418–22
SVP Worldwide LLC, 113 384–89

SWA *see* Southwest Airlines.
SWALEC *see* Scottish and Southern Energy plc.
Swales & Associates, Inc., 69 336–38
Swank, Inc., 17 464–66; 84 380–384 (upd.)
Swarovski International Holding AG, 40 422–25 *see also* D. Swarovski & Co.
The Swatch Group Ltd., 26 479–81; 107 429–33 (upd.)
Swedish Match AB, 12 462–64; 39 387–90 (upd.); 92 349–55 (upd.)
Swedish Telecom, V 331–33
SwedishAmerican Health System, 51 363–66
Sweet Candy Company, 60 295–97
Sweetbay Supermarket, 103 419–24 (upd.)
Sweetheart Cup Company, Inc., 36 460–64
The Swett & Crawford Group Inc., 84 385–389
SWH Corporation, 70 307–09
Swift & Company, 55 364–67
Swift Energy Company, 63 364–66
Swift Transportation Co., Inc., 42 363–66
Swinerton Inc., 43 397–400
Swire Pacific Ltd., I 521–22; 16 479–81 (upd.); 57 348–53 (upd.)
Swisher International Group Inc., 23 463–65
Swiss Air Transport Company Ltd., I 121–22
Swiss Army Brands, Inc. *see* Victorinox AG.
Swiss Bank Corporation, II 368–70 *see also* UBS AG.
The Swiss Colony, Inc., 97 395–98
Swiss Federal Railways (Schweizerische Bundesbahnen), V 519–22
Swiss International Air Lines Ltd., 48 379–81
Swiss Reinsurance Company (Schweizerische Rückversicherungs-Gesellschaft), III 375–78; 46 380–84 (upd.)
Swiss Valley Farms Company, 90 400–03
Swisscom AG, 58 336–39
Swissport International Ltd., 70 310–12
Sybase, Inc., 10 504–06; 27 447–50 (upd.)
Sybron International Corp., 14 479–81
Sycamore Networks, Inc., 45 388–91
Sykes Enterprises, Inc., 45 392–95
Sylvan, Inc., 22 496–99
Sylvan Learning Systems, Inc., 35 408–11 *see also* Educate Inc.
Symantec Corporation, 10 507–09; 82 372–77 (upd.)
Symbol Technologies, Inc., 15 482–84 *see also* Motorola, Inc.
Symrise GmbH and Company KG, 89 436–40
Syms Corporation, 29 456–58; 74 327–30 (upd.)
Symyx Technologies, Inc., 77 420–23

Synaptics Incorporated, 95 394–98
Synchronoss Technologies, Inc., 95 399–402
Syneron Medical Ltd., 91 471–74
Syngenta International AG, 83 391–394
Syniverse Holdings Inc., 97 399–402
SYNNEX Corporation, 73 328–30
Synopsys, Inc., 11 489–92; 69 339–43 (upd.)
SynOptics Communications, Inc., 10 510–12
Synovus Financial Corp., 12 465–67; 52 336–40 (upd.)
Syntax-Brillian Corporation, 102 405–09
Syntel, Inc., 92 356–60
Syntex Corporation, I 701–03
Synthes, Inc., 93 434–37
Sypris Solutions, Inc., 85 421–25
SyQuest Technology, Inc., 18 509–12
Syral S.A.S., 113 390–93
Syratech Corp., 14 482–84
SYSCO Corporation, II 675–76; 24 470–72 (upd.); 75 357–60 (upd.)
System Software Associates, Inc., 10 513–14
Systemax, Inc., 52 341–44
Systembolaget AB, 113 394–98
Systems & Computer Technology Corp., 19 437–39
Sytner Group plc, 45 396–98
Szerencsejáték Zrt., 113 399–402

T

T&D Holdings Inc., 114 417–21
T-Netix, Inc., 46 385–88
T-Online International AG, 61 349–51
T.J. Maxx *see* The TJX Companies, Inc.
T. Marzetti Company, 57 354–56
T. Rowe Price Associates, Inc., 11 493–96; 34 423–27 (upd.)
TA Triumph-Adler AG, 48 382–85
TAB Products Co., 17 467–69
Tabacalera, S.A., V 414–16; 17 470–73 (upd.) *see also* Altadis S.A.
TABCORP Holdings Limited, 44 407–10
TACA *see* Grupo TACA.
Taco Bell Corporation, 7 505–07; 21 485–88 (upd.); 74 331–34 (upd.)
Taco Cabana, Inc., 23 466–68; 72 344–47 (upd.)
Taco John's International Inc., 15 485–87; 63 367–70 (upd.)
Tacony Corporation, 70 313–15
TAG Heuer S.A., 25 459–61; 77 424–28 (upd.)
Tag-It Pacific, Inc., 85 426–29
Taiheiyo Cement Corporation, 60 298–301
Taittinger S.A., 43 401–05
Taiwan Semiconductor Manufacturing Company Ltd., 47 383–87
Taiwan Tobacco & Liquor Corporation, 75 361–63
Taiyo Fishery Company, Limited, II 578–79 *see also* Maruha Group Inc.
Taiyo Kobe Bank, Ltd., II 371–72

Takara Holdings Inc., 62 345–47

Takashimaya Company, Limited, V
193–96; 47 388–92 (upd.)

Take-Two Interactive Software, Inc., 46
389–91

Takeda Pharmaceutical Company
Limited, I 704–06; 46 392–95 (upd.);
115 437–42 (upd.)

The Talbots, Inc., 11 497–99; 31
429–32 (upd.); 88 393–98 (upd.)

Talecris Biotherapeutics Holdings Corp.,
114 422–25

Talisman Energy Inc., 9 490–93; 47
393–98 (upd.); 103 425–34 (upd.)

Talk America Holdings, Inc., 70 316–19

Talley Industries, Inc., 16 482–85

TALX Corporation, 92 361–64

TAM Linhas Aéreas S.A., 68 363–65

Tambrands Inc., 8 511–13 *see also*
Procter & Gamble Co.

TAME (Transportes Aéreos Militares
Ecuatorianos), 100 407–10

Tamedia AG, 53 323–26

Tamfelt Oyj Abp, 62 348–50

Tamron Company Ltd., 82 378–81

TAMSA *see* Tubos de Acero de Mexico,
S.A.

Tandem Computers, Inc., 6 278–80 *see
also* Hewlett-Packard Co.

Tandy Corporation, II 106–08; 12
468–70 (upd.) *see also* RadioShack
Corp.

Tandycrafts, Inc., 31 433–37

Tanger Factory Outlet Centers, Inc., 49
386–89

Tanimura & Antle Fresh Foods, Inc., 98
379–83

Tanox, Inc., 77 429–32

TAP—Air Portugal Transportes Aéreos
Portugueses S.A., 46 396–99 (upd.)

Tapemark Company Inc., 64 373–75

TAQA North Ltd., 95 403–06

Target Corporation, 10 515–17; 27
451–54 (upd.); 61 352–56 (upd.)

Targetti Sankey SpA, 86 385–88

Tarkett Sommer AG, 25 462–64

Tarmac Limited, III 751–54; 28 447–51
(upd.); 95 407–14 (upd.)

Taro Pharmaceutical Industries Ltd., 65
335–37

TAROM S.A., 64 376–78

Tarragon Realty Investors, Inc., 45
399–402

Tarrant Apparel Group, 62 351–53

Taschen GmbH, 101 465–68

Taser International, Inc., 62 354–57

Tastefully Simple Inc., 100 411–14

Tasty Baking Company, 14 485–87; 35
412–16 (upd.)

Tata Motors, Ltd., 109 526–30

Tata Steel Ltd., IV 217–19; 44 411–15
(upd.); 109 531–38 (upd.)

Tata Tea Ltd., 76 339–41

Tate & Lyle PLC, II 580–83; 42 367–72
(upd.); 101 469–77 (upd.)

Tati SA, 25 465–67

Tatneft *see* OAO Tatneft.

Tattered Cover Book Store, 43 406–09

Tatung Co., 23 469–71

Taubman Centers, Inc., 75 364–66

TaurusHolding GmbH & Co. KG, 46
400–03

Taylor & Francis Group plc, 44 416–19

Taylor Corporation, 36 465–67

Taylor Devices, Inc., 97 403–06

Taylor Guitars, 48 386–89

Taylor Made Group Inc., 98 384–87

Taylor Nelson Sofres plc, 34 428–30

Taylor Publishing Company, 12
471–73; 36 468–71 (upd.)

Taylor Wimpey PLC, 115 443–47
(upd.)

Taylor Woodrow plc, I 590–91; 38
450–53 (upd.)

TaylorMade-adidas Golf, 23 472–74; 96
423–28 (upd.)

TB Wood's Corporation, 56 355–58

TBA Global, LLC, 99 435–438

TBS *see* Turner Broadcasting System, Inc.

TBWA/Chiat/Day, 6 47–49; 43 410–14
(upd.) *see also* Omnicom Group Inc.

TC Advertising *see* Treasure Chest
Advertising, Inc.

TCBY Systems LLC, 17 474–76; 98
388–92 (upd.)

TCF Financial Corporation, 47
399–402; 103 435–41 (upd.)

Tchibo GmbH, 82 382–85

TCI *see* Tele-Communications, Inc.

TCO *see* Taubman Centers, Inc.

TD Bank *see* The Toronto-Dominion
Bank.

TDC A/S, 63 371–74

TDK Corporation, II 109–11; 17
477–79 (upd.); 49 390–94 (upd.);
114 426–32 (upd.)

TDL Group Ltd., 46 404–06 *see also*
Tim Hortons Inc.

TDS *see* Telephone and Data Systems,
Inc.

TEAC Corporation, 78 377–80

Teachers Insurance and Annuity
Association-College Retirement
Equities Fund, III 379–82; 45
403–07 (upd.)

Teamsters Union *see* International
Brotherhood of Teamsters.

TearDrop Golf Company, 32 445–48

Tech Data Corporation, 10 518–19; 74
335–38 (upd.)

Tech-Sym Corporation, 18 513–15; 44
420–23 (upd.)

TechBooks Inc., 84 390–393

TECHNE Corporation, 52 345–48

Technical Olympic USA, Inc., 75
367–69

Technip, 78 381–84

Technitrol, Inc., 29 459–62

Technology Research Corporation, 94
411–14

Technology Solutions Company, 94
415–19

Technotrans AG, 113 403–07

TechTarget, Inc., 99 439–443

Techtronic Industries Company Ltd., 73
331–34

Teck Resources Limited, 27 455–58;
112 401–06 (upd.)

Tecmo Koei Holdings Company Ltd.,
106 456–59

TECO Energy, Inc., 6 582–84

Tecumseh Products Company, 8
514–16; 71 351–55 (upd.)

Ted Baker plc, 86 389–92

Tee Vee Toons, Inc., 57 357–60

Teekay Shipping Corporation, 25
468–71; 82 386–91 (upd.)

Teijin Limited, V 380–82; 61 357–61
(upd.)

Tejon Ranch Company, 35 417–20

Tekelec, 83 395–399

Teknion Corporation, 114 433–36

Teknor Apex Company, 97 407–10

Tektronix, Inc., 8 517–21; 78 385–91
(upd.)

Telcordia Technologies, Inc., 59
399–401

Tele-Communications, Inc., II 160–62

Tele Norte Leste Participações S.A., 80
369–72

Tele2 AB, 115 448–52 (upd.)

Telecom Argentina S.A., 63 375–77

Telecom Australia, 6 341–42 *see also*
Telstra Corp. Ltd.

Telecom Corporation of New Zealand
Limited, 54 355–58

Telecom Eireann, 7 508–10 *see also*
eircom plc.

Telecom Italia Mobile S.p.A., 63 378–80

Telecom Italia S.p.A., 43 415–19

Teledyne Brown Engineering, Inc., 110
455–58

Teledyne Technologies Inc., I 523–25;
10 520–22 (upd.); 62 358–62 (upd.)

Telefonaktiebolaget LM Ericsson, V
334–36; 46 407–11 (upd.)

Telefónica de Argentina S.A., 61 362–64

Telefónica S.A., V 337–40; 46 412–17
(upd.); 108 475–82 (upd.)

Telefonos de Mexico S.A. de C.V., 14
488–90; 63 381–84 (upd.)

Telegraaf Media Groep N.V., 98 393–97
(upd.)

Telekom Austria AG, 115 453–57 (upd.)

Telekom Malaysia Bhd, 76 342–44

Telekomunikacja Polska SA, 50 464–68

Telenor ASA, 69 344–46

Telephone and Data Systems, Inc., 9
494–96

TelePizza S.A., 33 387–89

Television de Mexico, S.A. *see* Grupo
Televisa, S.A.

Television Española, S.A., 7 511–12

Télévision Française 1, 23 475–77

TeliaSonera AB, 57 361–65 (upd.)

Telkom S.A. Ltd., 106 460–64

Tellabs, Inc., 11 500–01; 40 426–29
(upd.)

Telsmith Inc., 96 429–33

Telstra Corporation Limited, 50 469–72

TELUS Corporation, 114 437–41
(upd.)

Telxon Corporation, 10 523–25

Tembec Inc., 66 322–24

Temple-Inland Inc., IV 341–43; 31 438–42 (upd.); 102 410–16 (upd.)

Tempur-Pedic Inc., 54 359–61

Ten Cate *see* Royal Ten Cate N.V.

Ten Thousand Villages U.S., 108 483–86

Tenaris SA, 63 385–88

Tenedora Nemak, S.A. de C.V., 102 417–20

Tenet Healthcare Corporation, 55 368–71 (upd.); 112 407–13 (upd.)

TenFold Corporation, 35 421–23

Tengasco, Inc., 99 444–447

Tengelmann Group, 27 459–62

Tennant Company, 13 499–501; 33 390–93 (upd.); 95 415–20 (upd.)

Tenneco Inc., I 526–28; 10 526–28 (upd.); 113 408–13 (upd.)

Tennessee Valley Authority, 50 473–77

TenneT B.V., 78 392–95

TEP *see* Tucson Electric Power Co.

TEPPCO Partners, L.P., 73 335–37

Tequila Herradura *see* Grupo Industrial Herradura, S.A. de C.V.

Ter Beke NV, 103 442–45

Teradyne, Inc., 11 502–04; 98 398–403 (upd.)

Terex Corporation, 7 513–15; 40 430–34 (upd.); 91 475–82 (upd.)

Tergal Industries S.A.S., 102 421–25

The Terlato Wine Group, 48 390–92

Terra Industries, Inc., 13 502–04; 94 420–24 (upd.)

Terra Lycos, Inc., 43 420–25

Terremark Worldwide, Inc., 99 448–452

Terrena L'Union CANA CAVAL, 70 320–22

Terumo Corporation, 48 393–95

Tesco plc, II 677–78; 24 473–76 (upd.); 68 366–70 (upd.)

Tesoro Corporation, 7 516–19; 45 408–13 (upd.); 97 411–19 (upd.)

Tessenderlo Group, 76 345–48

The Testor Corporation, 51 367–70

Tetley USA Inc., 88 399–402

Teton Energy Corporation, 97 420–23

Tetra Pak International SA, 53 327–29

Tetra Tech, Inc., 29 463–65

Teva Pharmaceutical Industries Ltd., 22 500–03; 54 362–65 (upd.); 112 414–19 (upd.)

Texaco Inc., IV 551–53; 14 491–94 (upd.); 41 391–96 (upd.) *see also* Chevron Corp.

Texas Air Corporation, I 123–24

Texas Industries, Inc., 8 522–24

Texas Instruments Incorporated, II 112–15; 11 505–08 (upd.); 46 418–23 (upd.)

Texas Pacific Group Inc., 36 472–74

Texas Rangers Baseball, 51 371–74

Texas Roadhouse, Inc., 69 347–49

Texas Utilities Company, V 724–25; 25 472–74 (upd.)

Textron Inc., I 529–30; 34 431–34 (upd.); 88 403–07 (upd.)

Textron Lycoming Turbine Engine, 9 497–99

TF1 *see* Télévision Française 1

TFM *see* Grupo Transportación Ferroviaria Mexicana, S.A. de C.V.

Tha Row Records, 69 350–52 (upd.)

Thai Airways International Public Company Limited, 6 122–24; 27 463–66 (upd.)

Thai Union Frozen Products PCL, 75 370–72

Thales S.A., 42 373–76

Thames Water plc, 11 509–11; 90 404–08 (upd.)

Thane International, Inc., 84 394–397

Thanulux Public Company Limited, 86 393–96

Theatre Development Fund, Inc., 109 539–42

Thermadyne Holding Corporation, 19 440–43

Thermo BioAnalysis Corp., 25 475–78

Thermo Electron Corporation, 7 520–22

Thermo Fibertek, Inc., 24 477–79 *see also* Kadant Inc.

Thermo Fisher Scientific Inc., 105 443–54 (upd.)

Thermo Instrument Systems Inc., 11 512–14

Thermo King Corporation, 13 505–07 *see also* Ingersoll-Rand Company Ltd.

Thermos Company, 16 486–88

Thermotech, 113 414–17

Things Remembered, Inc., 84 398–401

Thiokol Corporation, 9 500–02 (upd.); 22 504–07 (upd.)

Thistle Hotels PLC, 54 366–69

Thomas & Betts Corporation, 11 515–17; 54 370–74 (upd.); 114 442–48 (upd.)

Thomas & Howard Company, Inc., 90 409–12

Thomas Cook Travel Inc., 9 503–05; 33 394–96 (upd.)

Thomas Crosbie Holdings Limited, 81 384–87

Thomas H. Lee Co., 24 480–83

Thomas Industries Inc., 29 466–69

Thomas J. Lipton Company, 14 495–97

Thomas Nelson Inc., 14 498–99; 38 454–57 (upd.)

Thomas Publishing Company, 26 482–85

Thomaston Mills, Inc., 27 467–70

Thomasville Furniture Industries, Inc., 12 474–76; 74 339–42 (upd.)

Thomsen Greenhouses and Garden Center, Incorporated, 65 338–40

The Thomson Corporation, 8 525–28; 34 435–40 (upd.); 77 433–39 (upd.)

THOMSON multimedia S.A., II 116–17; 42 377–80 (upd.)

Thor Equities, LLC, 108 487–90

Thor Industries Inc., 39 391–94; 92 365–370 (upd.)

Thorn Apple Valley, Inc., 7 523–25; 22 508–11 (upd.)

Thorn EMI plc, I 531–32 *see also* EMI plc; Thorn plc.

Thorn plc, 24 484–87

Thorntons plc, 46 424–26

Thos. Moser Cabinetmakers Inc., 117 403–06

ThoughtWorks Inc., 90 413–16

Thousand Trails Inc., 33 397–99; 113 418–22 (upd.)

THQ, Inc., 39 395–97; 92 371–375 (upd.)

Threadless.com *see* skinnyCorp, LLC.

365 Media Group plc, 89 441–44

3Com Corporation, 11 518–21; 34 441–45 (upd.); 106 465–72 (upd.)

The 3DO Company, 43 426–30

3i Group PLC, 73 338–40

3M Company, 61 365–70 (upd.)

Thrifty PayLess, Inc., 12 477–79 *see also* Rite Aid Corp.

Thrivent Financial for Lutherans, 111 452–59 (upd.)

Thumann Inc., 104 442–45

ThyssenKrupp AG, IV 221–23; 28 452–60 (upd.); 87 425–438 (upd.)

TI Group plc, 17 480–83

TIAA-CREF *see* Teachers Insurance and Annuity Association-College Retirement Equities Fund.

Tianjin Flying Pigeon Bicycle Co., Ltd., 95 421–24

Tibbett & Britten Group plc, 32 449–52

TIBCO Software Inc., 79 411–14

TIC Holdings Inc., 92 376–379

Ticketmaster, 13 508–10; 37 381–84 (upd.); 76 349–53 (upd.)

Tidewater Inc., 11 522–24; 37 385–88 (upd.)

Tieto Oyj, 117 407–11

Tiffany & Co., 14 500–03; 78 396–401 (upd.)

TIG Holdings, Inc., 26 486–88

Tiger Aspect Productions Ltd., 72 348–50

Tiger Brands Limited, 112 420–24

Tigre S.A. Tubos e Conexões, 104 446–49

Tilcon-Connecticut Inc., 80 373–76

Tilia Inc., 62 363–65

Tillamook County Creamery Association, 111 460–63

Tilley Endurables, Inc., 67 364–66

Tillotson Corp., 15 488–90

TIM *see* Telecom Italia Mobile S.p.A.

Tim-Bar Corporation, 110 459–62

Tim Hortons Inc., 109 543–47 (upd.)

Timber Lodge Steakhouse, Inc., 73 341–43

The Timberland Company, 13 511–14; 54 375–79 (upd.); 111 464–70 (upd.)

Timberline Software Corporation, 15 491–93

TimberWest Forest Corp., 114 449–52

Time Out Group Ltd., 68 371–73

Time Warner Inc., IV 673–76; 7 526–30 (upd.) ; 109 548–58 (upd.)

The Times Mirror Company, IV 677–78; 17 484–86 (upd.) *see also* Tribune Co.

Trammell Crow Company, 8 532–34; 57 383–87 (upd.)

Trane, 78 402–05

Trans-Lux Corporation, 51 380–83

Trans World Airlines, Inc., I 125–27; 12 487–90 (upd.); 35 424–29 (upd.)

Trans World Entertainment Corporation, 24 501–03; 68 374–77 (upd.)

Transaction Systems Architects, Inc., 29 477–79; 82 397–402 (upd.)

TransAlta Utilities Corporation, 6 585–87

Transamerica—An AEGON Company, I 536–38; 13 528–30 (upd.); 41 400–03 (upd.)

Transammonia Group, 95 425–28

Transatlantic Holdings, Inc., 11 532–33

TransBrasil S/A Linhas Aéreas, 31 443–45

TransCanada Corporation, V 737–38; 93 438–45 (upd.)

Transco Energy Company, V 739–40 *see also* The Williams Companies.

Transiciel SA, 48 400–02

Transitions Optical, Inc., 83 411–415

Transmedia Network Inc., 20 494–97 *see also* Rewards Network Inc.

TransMontaigne Inc., 28 470–72

Transneft *see* Oil Transporting Joint Stock Company Transneft

Transnet Ltd., 6 433–35

Transocean Sedco Forex Inc., 45 417–19

Transport Corporation of America, Inc., 49 400–03

Transportes Aéreas Centro-Americanos *see* Grupo TACA.

Transportes Aéreos Militares Ecuatorianos *see* TAME (Transportes Aéreos Militares Ecuatorianos)

Transportes Aereos Portugueses, S.A., 6 125–27 *see also* TAP—Air Portugal Transportes Aéreos Portugueses S.A.

TransPro, Inc., 71 356–59

The Tranzonic Companies, 15 500–02; 37 392–95 (upd.)

Travel Ports of America, Inc., 17 493–95

TravelCenters of America LLC, 108 496–500

Travelers Corporation, III 387–90 *see also* Citigroup Inc.

Travelocity.com LP, 46 434–37; 113 438–42 (upd.)

Travelzoo Inc., 79 419–22

Travis Boats & Motors, Inc., 37 396–98

Travis Perkins plc, 34 450–52

TRC Companies, Inc., 32 461–64

Treadco, Inc., 19 454–56

Treasure Chest Advertising Company, Inc., 32 465–67

Tredegar Corporation, 52 349–51

Tree of Life, Inc., 29 480–82; 107 441–44 (upd.)

Tree Top, Inc., 76 357–59

TreeHouse Foods, Inc., 79 423–26

Trek Bicycle Corporation, 16 493–95; 78 406–10 (upd.)

Trelleborg AB, 93 455–64

Trend-Lines, Inc., 22 516–18

Trend Micro Inc., 97 429–32

Trendwest Resorts, Inc., 33 409–11 *see also* Jeld-Wen, Inc.

Trex Company, Inc., 71 360–62

Tri-State Generation and Transmission Association, Inc., 103 455–59

Tri Valley Growers, 32 468–71

Triarc Companies, Inc., 8 535–37; 34 453–57 (upd.)

Tribune Company, IV 682–84; 22 519–23 (upd.); 63 389–95 (upd.)

Trico Marine Services, Inc., 89 450–53

Trico Products Corporation, 15 503–05

Tridel Enterprises Inc., 9 512–13

Trident Seafoods Corporation, 56 359–61

Trigano S.A., 102 426–29

Trigen Energy Corporation, 42 386–89

Trilon Financial Corporation, II 456–57

TriMas Corp., 11 534–36

Trimble Navigation Limited, 40 441–43

Trina Solar Limited, 103 460–64

Trinchero Family Estates, 107 445–50 (upd.)

Třinecké Železárny A.S., 92 384–87

Trinity Industries, Incorporated, 7 540–41

Trinity Mirror plc, 49 404–10 (upd.)

TRINOVA Corporation, III 640–42

TriPath Imaging, Inc., 77 446–49

Triple Five Group Ltd., 49 411–15

Triple P N.V., 26 496–99

Tripwire, Inc., 97 433–36

TriQuint Semiconductor, Inc., 63 396–99

Trisko Jewelry Sculptures, Ltd., 57 388–90

Triton Energy Corporation, 11 537–39

Triumph-Adler *see* TA Triumph-Adler AG.

Triumph Group, Inc., 31 446–48

Triumph Motorcycles Ltd., 53 334–37

Trizec Corporation Ltd., 10 529–32

The TriZetto Group, Inc., 83 416–419

TRM Copy Centers Corporation, 18 526–28 *see also* Access to Money, Inc.

Tropicana Products, Inc., 28 473–77; 73 344–49 (upd.)

Troutman Sanders L.L.P., 79 427–30

True North Communications Inc., 23 478–80 *see also* Foote, Cone & Belding Worldwide.

True Religion Apparel, Inc., 79 431–34

True Temper Sports, Inc., 95 429–32

True Value Company, 74 353–57 (upd.)

TruFoods LLC, 114 457–60

Truman Arnold Companies, Inc., 114 461–64

Trump Organization, 23 481–84; 64 392–97 (upd.)

TRUMPF GmbH + Co. KG, 86 397–02

TruServ Corporation, 24 504–07 *see* True Value Co.

Trusthouse Forte PLC, III 104–06

Trustmark Corporation, 106 473–76

Truworths International Ltd., 107 451–54

TRW Automotive Holdings Corp., I 539–41; 11 540–42 (upd.); 14 510–13 (upd.); 75 376–82 (upd.)

TSA *see* Transaction Systems Architects, Inc.

Tsakos Energy Navigation Ltd., 91 483–86

TSB Group plc, 12 491–93

TSC *see* Tractor Supply Co.

Tsingtao Brewery Group, 49 416–20

TSMC *see* Taiwan Semiconductor Manufacturing Company Ltd.

TSYS *see* Total System Services, Inc.

TT electronics plc, 111 482–86

TTL *see* Taiwan Tobacco & Liquor Corp.

TTX Company, 6 436–37; 66 328–30 (upd.)

Tubby's, Inc., 53 338–40

Tubos de Acero de Mexico, S.A. (TAMSA), 41 404–06

Tucows Inc., 78 411–14

Tucson Electric Power Company, 6 588–91

Tuesday Morning Corporation, 18 529–31; 70 331–33 (upd.)

TUF *see* Thai Union Frozen Products PCL.

TUI *see* Touristik Union International GmbH. and Company K.G.

TUI Group GmbH, 42 283; 44 432–35

Tulikivi Corporation, 114 265–69

Tulip Ltd., 89 454–57

Tullow Oil plc, 83 420–423

Tully Construction Co. Inc., 114 470–73

Tully's Coffee Corporation, 51 384–86

Tultex Corporation, 13 531–33

Tumaro's Gourmet Tortillas, 85 430–33

Tumbleweed, Inc., 33 412–14; 80 377–81 (upd.)

Tumi, Inc., 112 439–42

Tunisair *see* Société Tunisienne de l'Air-Tunisair.

Tupolev Aviation and Scientific Technical Complex, 24 58–60

Tupperware Brands Corporation, 28 478–81; 78 415–20 (upd.)

Tupy S.A., 111 487–90

TurboChef Technologies, Inc., 83 424–427

Turbomeca S.A., 102 430–34

Turkish Airlines Inc. (Türk Hava Yollari A.O.), 72 351–53

Turkiye Is Bankasi A.S., 61 377–80

Türkiye Petrolleri Anonim Ortaklığı, IV 562–64

Turner Broadcasting System, Inc., II 166–68; 6 171–73 (upd.); 66 331–34 (upd.)

Turner Construction Company, 66 335–38

The Turner Corporation, 8 538–40; 23 485–88 (upd.)

Turtle Wax, Inc., 15 506–09; 93 465–70 (upd.)

Tuscarora Inc., 29 483–85

United Dominion Industries Limited, 8 544–46; 16 499–502 (upd.)

United Dominion Realty Trust, Inc., 52 369–71

United Farm Workers of America, 88 418–22

United Foods, Inc., 21 508–11

United HealthCare Corporation, 9 524–26 *see also* Humana Inc.

The United Illuminating Company, 21 512–14

United Industrial Corporation, 37 399–402

United Industries Corporation, 68 385–87

United Internet AG, 99 466–469

United Jewish Communities, 33 422–25

United Merchants & Manufacturers, Inc., 13 534–37

United Microelectronics Corporation, 98 421–24

United National Group, Ltd., 63 410–13

United Nations International Children's Emergency Fund (UNICEF), 58 349–52

United Natural Foods, Inc., 32 479–82; 76 360–63 (upd.)

United Negro College Fund, Inc., 79 447–50

United News & Media plc, 28 501–05 (upd.) *see also* United Business Media plc.

United Newspapers plc, IV 685–87 *see also* United Business Media plc.

United Online, Inc., 71 372–77 (upd.)

United Overseas Bank Ltd., 56 362–64

United Pan-Europe Communications NV, 47 414–17

United Paper Mills Ltd., IV 347–50 *see also* UPM-Kymmene Corp.

United Parcel Service, Inc., V 533–35; 17 503–06 (upd.); 63 414–19; 94 425–30 (upd.)

United Plantations Bhd., 117 427–30

United Press International, Inc., 25 506–09; 73 354–57 (upd.)

United Rentals, Inc., 34 466–69

United Retail Group Inc., 33 426–28

United Road Services, Inc., 69 360–62

United Service Organizations, 60 308–11

United Services Automobile Association, 109 559–65 (upd.)

United States Cellular Corporation, 9 527–29 *see also* U.S. Cellular Corp.

United States Filter Corporation, 20 501–04 *see also* Siemens AG.

United States Health Care Systems, Inc. *see* U.S. Healthcare, Inc.

United States Pipe and Foundry Company, 62 377–80

United States Playing Card Company, 62 381–84

United States Postal Service, 14 517–20; 34 470–75 (upd.); 108 516–24 (upd.)

United States Shoe Corporation, V 207–08

United States Soccer Federation, 108 525–28

United States Steel Corporation, 50 500–04 (upd.); 114 494–500 (upd.)

United States Sugar Corporation, 115 465–68

United States Surgical Corporation, 10 533–35; 34 476–80 (upd.)

United States Tennis Association, 111 503–06

United Stationers Inc., 14 521–23; 117 431–36 (upd.)

United Talent Agency, Inc., 80 392–96

United Technologies Automotive Inc., 15 513–15

United Technologies Corporation, I 84–86; 10 536–38 (upd.); 34 481–85 (upd.); 105 455–61 (upd.)

United Telecommunications, Inc., V 344–47 *see also* Sprint Corp.

United Utilities PLC, 52 372–75 (upd.)

United Video Satellite Group, 18 535–37 *see also* TV Guide, Inc.

United Water Resources, Inc., 40 447–50; 45 277

United Way Worldwide, 36 485–88; 112 451–56 (upd.)

UnitedHealth Group Incorporated, 103 476–84 (upd.)

Unitika Ltd., V 387–89; 53 341–44 (upd.)

Unitil Corporation, 37 403–06

Unitog Co., 19 457–60 *see also* Cintas Corp.

Unitrin Inc., 16 503–05; 78 427–31 (upd.)

Unitymedia GmbH, 115 469–72

Univar Corporation, 9 530–32

Universal American Corp., 111 507–10

Universal Compression, Inc., 59 402–04

Universal Corporation, V 417–18; 48 403–06 (upd.)

Universal Electronics Inc., 39 405–08

Universal Foods Corporation, 7 546–48 *see also* Sensient Technologies Corp.

Universal Forest Products, Inc., 10 539–40; 59 405–09 (upd.)

Universal Health Services, Inc., 6 191–93

Universal International, Inc., 25 510–11

Universal Manufacturing Company, 88 423–26

Universal Security Instruments, Inc., 96 434–37

Universal Stainless & Alloy Products, Inc., 75 386–88

Universal Studios, Inc., 33 429–33; 100 423–29 (upd.)

Universal Technical Institute, Inc., 81 396–99

Universal Truckload Services, Inc., 111 511–14

The University of Chicago Press, 79 451–55

University of Phoenix *see* Apollo Group, Inc.

Univision Communications Inc., 24 515–18; 83 434–439 (upd.)

UNM *see* United News & Media plc.

Uno Restaurant Holdings Corporation, 18 538–40; 70 334–37 (upd.)

Unocal Corporation, IV 569–71; 24 519–23 (upd.); 71 378–84 (upd.)

UNUM Corp., 13 538–40

UnumProvident Corporation, 52 376–83 (upd.)

Uny Co., Ltd., V 209–10; 49 425–28 (upd.)

UOB *see* United Overseas Bank Ltd.

UPC *see* United Pan-Europe Communications NV.

UPI *see* United Press International.

Upjohn Company, I 707–09; 8 547–49 (upd.) *see also* Pharmacia & Upjohn Inc.; Pfizer Inc.

UPM-Kymmene Corporation, 19 461–65; 50 505–11 (upd.)

The Upper Deck Company, LLC, 105 462–66

UPS *see* United Parcel Service, Inc.

Uralita S.A., 96 438–41

Uranium One Inc., 111 515–18

Urban Engineers, Inc., 102 435–38

Urban Outfitters, Inc., 14 524–26; 74 367–70 (upd.)

Urbi Desarrollos Urbanos, S.A. de C.V., 81 400–03

Urbium PLC, 75 389–91

URS Corporation, 45 420–23; 80 397–400 (upd.)

URSI *see* United Road Services, Inc.

US *see also* U.S.

US Airways Group, Inc., I 131–32; 6 131–32 (upd.); 28 506–09 (upd.); 52 384–88 (upd.); 110 472–78 (upd.)

US 1 Industries, Inc., 89 475–78

USA Interactive, Inc., 47 418–22 (upd.)

USA Mobility Inc., 97 437–40 (upd.)

USA Truck, Inc., 42 410–13

USAA, 10 541–43; 62 385–88 (upd.) *see also* United Services Automobile Association.

USANA, Inc., 29 491–93

USCC *see* United States Cellular Corp.

USF&G Corporation, III 395–98 *see also* The St. Paul Companies.

USG Corporation, III 762–64; 26 507–10 (upd.); 81 404–10 (upd.)

Ushio Inc., 91 496–99

Usinas Siderúrgicas de Minas Gerais S.A., 77 454–57

Usinger's Famous Sausage *see* Fred Usinger Inc.

Usinor SA, IV 226–28; 42 414–17 (upd.)

USO *see* United Service Organizations.

USPS *see* United States Postal Service.

USSC *see* United States Surgical Corp.

UST Inc., 9 533–35; 50 512–17 (upd.)

USTA *see* United States Tennis Association

USX Corporation, IV 572–74; 7 549–52 (upd.) *see also* United States Steel Corp.

Utah Medical Products, Inc., 36 496–99

Utah Power and Light Company, 27 483–86 *see also* PacifiCorp.

UTG Inc., 100 430–33

Utilicorp United Inc., 6 592–94 *see also*
Aquilla, Inc.
UTStarcom, Inc., 77 458–61
UTV *see* Ulster Television PLC.
Utz Quality Foods, Inc., 72 358–60
UUNET, 38 468–72
Uwajimaya, Inc., 60 312–14
Uzbekistan Airways National Air
Company, 99 470–473

V

V&S Vin & Sprit AB, 91 504–11 (upd.)
VA TECH ELIN EBG GmbH, 49
429–31
Vail Resorts, Inc., 11 543–46; 43
435–39 (upd.)
Vaillant GmbH, 44 436–39
Vaisala Oyj, 104 459–63
Valassis Communications, Inc., 8
550–51; 37 407–10 (upd.); 76
364–67 (upd.)
Vale S.A., 117 437–42 (upd.)
Valeo, 23 492–94; 66 350–53 (upd.)
Valero Energy Corporation, 7 553–55;
71 385–90 (upd.)
Valhi, Inc., 19 466–68; 94 431–35
(upd.)
Valio Oy, 117 443–47
Vallen Corporation, 45 424–26
Valley Media Inc., 35 430–33
Valley National Gases, Inc., 85 434–37
Valley Proteins, Inc., 91 500–03
ValleyCrest Companies, 81 411–14
(upd.)
Vallourec SA, 54 391–94
Valmet Oy, III 647–49 *see also* Metso
Corp.
Valmont Industries, Inc., 19 469–72
Valora Holding AG, 98 425–28
Valorem S.A., 88 427–30
Valores Industriales S.A., 19 473–75
The Valspar Corporation, 8 552–54; 32
483–86 (upd.); 77 462–68 (upd.)
Value City Department Stores, Inc., 38
473–75 *see also* Retail Ventures, Inc.
Value Line, Inc., 16 506–08; 73 358–61
(upd.)
Value Merchants Inc., 13 541–43
ValueClick, Inc., 49 432–34
ValueVision International, Inc., 22
534–36
Valve Corporation, 101 483–86
Van Camp Seafood Company, Inc., 7
556–57 *see also* Chicken of the Sea
International.
Van de Velde S.A./NV, 102 439–43
Van Hool S.A./NV, 96 442–45
Van Houtte Inc., 39 409–11
Van Lanschot NV, 79 456–59
Van Leer N.V. *see* Royal Packaging
Industries Van Leer N.V.; Greif Inc.
Vance Publishing Corporation, 64
398–401
Vandemoortele S.A./NV, 113 443–46
Vanderbilt *see* R.T. Vanderbilt Company,
Inc.
Vanderbilt University Medical Center,
99 474–477

The Vanguard Group, Inc., 14 530–32;
34 486–89 (upd.)
Vanguard Health Systems Inc., 70
338–40
Vann's Inc., 105 467–70
Van's Aircraft, Inc., 65 349–51
Vans, Inc., 16 509–11; 47 423–26
(upd.)
Vapores *see* Compañia Sud Americana de
Vapores S.A.
Varco International, Inc., 42 418–20
Vari-Lite International, Inc., 35 434–36
Varian Associates Inc., 12 504–06
Varian, Inc., 48 407–11 (upd.)
Variety Wholesalers, Inc., 73 362–64
Variflex, Inc., 51 391–93
VARIG S.A. (Viação Aérea
Rio-Grandense), 6 133–35; 29
494–97 (upd.)
Varity Corporation, III 650–52 *see also*
AGCO Corp.
Varlen Corporation, 16 512–14
Varsity Brands, Inc., 15 516–18; 94
436–40 (upd.)
Varta AG, 23 495–99
VASCO Data Security International,
Inc., 79 460–63
Vastar Resources, Inc., 24 524–26
Vattenfall AB, 57 395–98
Vaughan Foods, Inc., 105 471–74
Vauxhall Motors Limited, 73 365–69
VBA - Bloemenveiling Aalsmeer, 88
431–34
VCA Antech, Inc., 58 353–55
VDL Groep B.V., 113 447–50
Veba A.G., I 542–43; 15 519–21 (upd.)
see also E.On AG.
Vebego International BV, 49 435–37
Vecellio Group, Inc., 113 451–54
VECO International, Inc., 7 558–59 *see
also* CH2M Hill Ltd.
Vector Aerospace Corporation, 97
441–44
Vector Group Ltd., 35 437–40 (upd.)
Vectren Corporation, 98 429–36 (upd.)
Vedanta Resources plc, 112 457–61
Vedior NV, 35 441–43
Veeco Instruments Inc., 32 487–90
Veidekke ASA, 98 437–40
Veit Companies, 43 440–42; 92
398–402 (upd.)
Velcro Industries N.V., 19 476–78; 72
361–64 (upd.)
Velocity Express Corporation, 49
438–41; 94 441–46 (upd.)
Velux A/S, 86 412–15
Venator Group Inc., 35 444–49 (upd.)
see also Foot Locker Inc.
Vencor, Inc., 16 515–17
Vendex International N.V., 13 544–46
see also Koninklijke Vendex KBB N.V.
(Royal Vendex KBB N.V.).
Vendôme Luxury Group plc, 27 487–89
Venetian Casino Resort, LLC, 47
427–29
Ventana Medical Systems, Inc., 75
392–94
Ventura Foods LLC, 90 420–23

Venture Stores Inc., 12 507–09
Veolia Environnement, SA, 109 566–71
VeraSun Energy Corporation, 87
447–450
Verband der Vereine Creditreform e. V.,
117 448–52
Verbatim Corporation, 14 533–35; 74
371–74 (upd.)
Vereinigte Elektrizitätswerke Westfalen
AG, IV V 744–47
Veridian Corporation, 54 395–97
VeriFone, Inc., 18 541–44; 76 368–71
(upd.)
Verint Systems Inc., 73 370–72
VeriSign, Inc., 47 430–34
Veritas Software Corporation, 45
427–31
Verity Inc., 68 388–91
Verizon Communications Inc., 43
443–49 (upd.); 78 432–40 (upd.)
Verlagsgruppe Georg von Holtzbrinck
GmbH, 35 450–53
Verlagsgruppe Weltbild GmbH, 98
441–46
Vermeer Manufacturing Company, 17
507–10
The Vermont Country Store, 93 478–82
Vermont Pure Holdings, Ltd., 51
394–96
The Vermont Teddy Bear Co., Inc., 36
500–02
Versace *see* Gianni Versace SpA.
Vertex Pharmaceuticals Incorporated, 83
440–443
Vertis Communications, 84 418–421
Vertrue Inc., 77 469–72
Vestas Wind Systems A/S, 73 373–75
Vestey Group Ltd., 95 433–37
Veuve Clicquot Ponsardin SCS, 98
447–51
VEW AG, 39 412–15
VF Corporation, V 390–92; 17 511–14
(upd.); 54 398–404 (upd.)
VHA Inc., 53 345–47
Viacom Inc., 7 560–62; 23 500–03
(upd.); 67 367–71 (upd.) *see also*
Paramount Pictures Corp.
Viad Corp., 73 376–78
Viag AG, IV 229–32 *see also* E.On AG.
ViaSat, Inc., 54 405–08
Viasoft Inc., 27 490–93; 59 27
VIASYS Healthcare, Inc., 52 389–91
Viasystems Group, Inc., 67 372–74
Viatech Continental Can Company,
Inc., 25 512–15 (upd.)
Vicarious Visions, Inc., 108 529–32
Vicat S.A., 70 341–43
Vickers plc, 27 494–97
Vicon Industries, Inc., 44 440–42
VICORP Restaurants, Inc., 12 510–12;
48 412–15 (upd.)
Victor Company of Japan, Limited, II
118–19; 26 511–13 (upd.); 83
444–449 (upd.)
Victoria Coach Station Ltd. *see* London
Regional Transport.
Victoria Group, III 399–401; 44
443–46 (upd.)

Victorinox AG, 21 515–17; 74 375–78 (upd.)
Victory Refrigeration, Inc., 82 403–06
Vicunha Têxtil S.A., 78 441–44
Videojet Technologies, Inc., 90 424–27
Vidrala S.A., 67 375–77
Viel & Cie, 76 372–74
Vienna Sausage Manufacturing Co., 14 536–37
Viessmann Werke GmbH & Co., 37 411–14
Viewpoint International, Inc., 66 354–56
ViewSonic Corporation, 72 365–67
Viking Office Products, Inc., 10 544–46 *see also* Office Depot, Inc.
Viking Range Corporation, 66 357–59
Viking Yacht Company, 96 446–49
Village Roadshow Ltd., 58 356–59
Village Super Market, Inc., 7 563–64
Village Voice Media, Inc., 38 476–79
Villeroy & Boch AG, 37 415–18
Vilmorin Clause et Cie, 70 344–46
Vilter Manufacturing, LLC, 105 475–79
Vin & Spirit AB, 31 458–61 *see also* V&S Vin & Sprit AB.
Viña Concha y Toro S.A., 45 432–34
Vinci S.A., 27 54; 43 450–52; 113 455–59 (upd.)
Vincor International Inc., 50 518–21
Vinmonopolet A/S, 100 434–37
Vinson & Elkins L.L.P., 30 481–83
Vintage Petroleum, Inc., 42 421–23
Vinton Studios, 63 420–22
Vion Food Group NV, 85 438–41
Virbac Corporation, 74 379–81
Virco Manufacturing Corporation, 17 515–17
Virgin Group Ltd., 12 513–15; 32 491–96 (upd.); 89 479–86 (upd.)
Virginia Dare Extract Company, Inc., 94 447–50
Viridian Group plc, 64 402–04
Visa Inc., 9 536–38; 26 514–17 (upd.); 104 464–69 (upd.)
Viscofan S.A., 70 347–49
Vishay Intertechnology, Inc., 21 518–21; 80 401–06 (upd.)
Vision Service Plan Inc., 77 473–76
Viskase Companies, Inc., 55 379–81
Vista Bakery, Inc., 56 365–68
Vista Chemical Company, I 402–03
Vistana, Inc., 22 537–39
VistaPrint Limited, 87 451–454
Visteon Corporation, 109 572–76
VISX, Incorporated, 30 484–86
Vita Food Products Inc., 99 478–481
Vita Plus Corporation, 60 315–17
Vitacost.com Inc., 116 455–58
Vital Images, Inc., 85 442–45
Vitalink Pharmacy Services, Inc., 15 522–24
Vitamin Shoppe Industries, Inc., 60 318–20
Vitasoy International Holdings Ltd., 94 451–54
Viterra Inc., 105 480–83

Vitesse Semiconductor Corporation, 32 497–500
Vitro Corp., 10 547–48
Vitro Corporativo S.A. de C.V., 34 490–92
Vivarte SA, 54 409–12 (upd.)
Vivartia S.A., 82 407–10
Vivendi, 46 438–41 (upd.); 112 462–68 (upd.)
Vivra, Inc., 18 545–47 *see also* Gambro AB.
Vizio, Inc., 100 438–41
Vlasic Foods International Inc., 25 516–19
VLSI Technology, Inc., 16 518–20
VMware, Inc., 90 428–31
VNU N.V., 27 498–501
VNUS Medical Technologies, Inc., 103 485–88
Vocento, 94 455–58
Vodacom Group Pty. Ltd., 106 481–85
Vodafone Group Plc, 11 547–48; 36 503–06 (upd.); 75 395–99 (upd.)
voestalpine AG, IV 233–35; 57 399–403 (upd.); 115 473–78 (upd.)
Voith Sulzer Papiermaschinen GmbH *see* J.M. Voith AG.
Volcan Compañia Minera S.A.A., 92 403–06
Volcom, Inc., 77 477–80
Volga-Dnepr Group, 82 411–14
Volkert and Associates, Inc., 98 452–55
Volkswagen Aktiengesellschaft, I 206–08; 11 549–51 (upd.); 32 501–05 (upd.); 111 519–25 (upd.)
Volt Information Sciences Inc., 26 518–21
Volunteers of America, Inc., 66 360–62
Von Maur Inc., 64 405–08
Vonage Holdings Corp., 81 415–18
The Vons Companies, Inc., 7 569–71; 28 510–13 (upd.); 103 489–95 (upd.)
Vontobel Holding AG, 96 450–53
Voortman Cookies Limited, 103 496–99
Vornado Realty Trust, 20 508–10; 112 469–74 (upd.)
Vorwerk & Co. KG, 27 502–04; 112 475–79 (upd.)
Vosper Thornycroft Holding plc, 41 410–12
Vossloh AG, 53 348–52
Votorantim Participações S.A., 76 375–78
Vought Aircraft Industries, Inc., 49 442–45
Vranken Pommery Monopole S.A., 114 501–05
VSE Corporation, 108 533–36
VSM *see* Village Super Market, Inc.
VTech Holdings Ltd., 77 481–84
Vueling Airlines S.A., 97 445–48
Vulcabras S.A., 103 500–04
Vulcan Materials Company, 7 572–75; 52 392–96 (upd.)

W

W + K *see* Wieden + Kennedy.
W.A. Whitney Company, 53 353–56

W. Atlee Burpee & Co., 27 505–08
W.B Doner & Co., 56 369–72
W.B. Mason Company, 98 456–59
W.C. Bradley Co., 69 363–65
W.H. Brady Co., 16 518–21 *see also* Brady Corp.
W. H. Braum, Inc., 80 407–10
W H Smith Group PLC, V 211–13
W Jordan (Cereals) Ltd., 74 382–84
W.L. Gore & Associates, Inc., 14 538–40; 60 321–24 (upd.)
W.P. Carey & Co. LLC, 49 446–48
W.R. Berkley Corporation, 15 525–27; 74 385–88 (upd.)
W.R. Grace & Company, I 547–50; 50 522–29 (upd.)
W.S. Badcock Corporation, 107 461–64
W.W. Grainger, Inc., V 214–15; 26 537–39 (upd.); 68 392–95 (upd.)
W.W. Norton & Company, Inc., 28 518–20
Waban Inc., 13 547–49 *see also* HomeBase, Inc.
Wabash National Corp., 13 550–52
Wabtec Corporation, 40 451–54
Wachovia Bank of Georgia, N.A., 16 521–23
Wachovia Bank of South Carolina, N.A., 16 524–26
Wachovia Corporation, 12 516–20; 46 442–49 (upd.)
Wachtell, Lipton, Rosen & Katz, 47 435–38
The Wackenhut Corporation, 14 541–43; 63 423–26 (upd.)
Wacker-Chemie AG, 35 454–58; 112 480–85 (upd.)
Wacker Construction Equipment AG, 95 438–41
Wacoal Corp., 25 520–24
Waddell & Reed, Inc., 22 540–43
Waffle House Inc., 14 544–45; 60 325–27 (upd.)
Wagers Inc. (Idaho Candy Company), 86 416–19
Waggener Edstrom, 42 424–26
Wagon plc, 92 407–10
Wah Chang, 82 415–18
Wahl Clipper Corporation, 86 420–23
Wahoo's Fish Taco, 96 454–57
Wakefern Food Corporation, 33 434–37; 107 465–69 (upd.)
Wal-Mart de Mexico, S.A. de C.V., 35 459–61 (upd.)
Wal-Mart Stores, Inc., V 216–17; 8 555–57 (upd.); 26 522–26 (upd.); 63 427–32 (upd.)
Walbridge Aldinger Co., 38 480–82
Walbro Corporation, 13 553–55
Waldbaum, Inc., 19 479–81
Waldenbooks, 17 522–24; 86 424–28 (upd.)
Walgreen Co., V 218–20; 20 511–13 (upd.); 65 352–56 (upd.)
Walker Manufacturing Company, 19 482–84
Walkers Shortbread Ltd., 79 464–67
Walkers Snack Foods Ltd., 70 350–52

WestCoast Hospitality Corporation, 59 410–13
Westcon Group, Inc., 67 392–94
Westdeutsche Landesbank Girozentrale, II 385–87; 46 458–61 (upd.)
Westell Technologies, Inc., 57 408–10
Western Atlas Inc., 12 538–40
Western Beef, Inc., 22 548–50
Western Company of North America, 15 534–36
Western Digital Corporation, 25 530–32; 92 411–15 (upd.)
Western Gas Resources, Inc., 45 435–37
Western Oil Sands Inc., 85 454–57
Western Publishing Group, Inc., 13 559–61 *see also* Thomson Corp.
Western Refining Inc., 109 596–99
Western Resources, Inc., 12 541–43
The WesterN SizzliN Corporation, 60 335–37
Western Union Company, 54 413–16; 112 492–96 (upd.)
Western Wireless Corporation, 36 514–16
Westfield Group, 69 366–69
Westin Hotels and Resorts Worldwide, 9 547–49; 29 505–08 (upd.)
Westinghouse Air Brake Technologies Corporation, 116 463–66
Westinghouse Electric Corporation, II 120–22; 12 544–47 (upd.) *see also* CBS Radio Group.
WestJet Airlines Ltd., 38 493–95; 115 488–92 (upd.)
Westmoreland Coal Company, 7 582–85
Weston Foods Inc. *see* George Weston Ltd.
Westpac Banking Corporation, II 388–90; 48 424–27 (upd.)
WestPoint Stevens Inc., 16 533–36 *see also* JPS Textile Group, Inc.
Westport Resources Corporation, 63 439–41
Westvaco Corporation, IV 351–54; 19 495–99 (upd.) *see also* MeadWestvaco Corp.
Westwood One Inc., 23 508–11; 106 490–96 (upd.)
The Wet Seal, Inc., 18 562–64; 70 353–57 (upd.)
Wetterau Incorporated, II 681–82 *see also* Supervalu Inc.
Weyco Group, Incorporated, 32 510–13
Weyerhaeuser Company, IV 355–56; 9 550–52 (upd.); 28 514–17 (upd.); 83 454–461 (upd.)
WFS Financial Inc., 70 358–60
WFSC *see* World Fuel Services Corp.
WGBH Educational Foundation, 66 366–68
WH Smith PLC, 42 442–47 (upd.)
Wham-O, Inc., 61 390–93
Whataburger Restaurants LP, 105 493–97
Whatman plc, 46 462–65
Wheaton Industries, 8 570–73

Wheaton Science Products, 60 338–42 (upd.)
Wheelabrator Technologies, Inc., 6 599–600; 60 343–45 (upd.)
Wheeling-Pittsburgh Corporation, 7 586–88; 58 360–64 (upd.)
Wheels Inc., 96 458–61
Wherehouse Entertainment Incorporated, 11 556–58
Whirlpool Corporation, III 653–55; 12 548–50 (upd.); 59 414–19 (upd.)
Whitbread PLC, I 293–94; 20 519–22 (upd.); 52 412–17 (upd.); 97 468–76 (upd.)
White & Case LLP, 35 466–69
White Castle Management Company, 12 551–53; 36 517–20 (upd.); 85 458–64 (upd.)
White Consolidated Industries Inc., 13 562–64 *see also* Electrolux.
The White House, Inc., 60 346–48
White Lily Foods Company, 88 435–38
White Martins Gases Industriais Ltda., 111 526–29
White Mountains Insurance Group, Ltd., 48 428–31
White Rose, Inc., 24 527–29
White Wave, 43 462–64
Whitehall Jewellers, Inc., 82 429–34 (upd.)
Whiting Petroleum Corporation, 81 424–27
Whiting-Turner Contracting Company, 95 446–49
Whitman Corporation, 10 553–55 (upd.) *see also* PepsiAmericas, Inc.
Whitman Education Group, Inc., 41 419–21
Whitney Holding Corporation, 21 522–24
Whittaker Corporation, I 544–46; 48 432–35 (upd.)
Whittard of Chelsea Plc, 61 394–97
Whole Foods Market, Inc., 20 523–27; 50 530–34 (upd.); 110 479–86 (upd.)
WHX Corporation, 98 464–67
Wickes Inc., V 221–23; 25 533–36 (upd.)
Widmer Brothers Brewing Company, 76 379–82
Wieden + Kennedy, 75 403–05
Wienerberger AG, 70 361–63
Wikimedia Foundation, Inc., 91 523–26
Wilbert, Inc., 56 377–80
Wilbur Chocolate Company, 66 369–71
Wilbur-Ellis Company, 114 511–14
Wilco Farm Stores, 93 490–93
Wild Oats Markets, Inc., 19 500–02; 41 422–25 (upd.)
Wildlife Conservation Society, 31 462–64
Wilh. Werhahn KG, 101 491–94
Wilh. Wilhelmsen ASA, 94 459–62
Wilhelm Karmann GmbH, 94 463–68
Wilkinson Hardware Stores Ltd., 80 416–18
Wilkinson Sword Ltd., 60 349–52

Willamette Industries, Inc., IV 357–59; 31 465–68 (upd.) *see also* Weyerhaeuser Co.
Willamette Valley Vineyards, Inc., 85 465–69
Willbros Group, Inc., 56 381–83
William Grant & Sons Ltd., 60 353–55
William Hill Organization Limited, 49 449–52
William Jackson & Son Ltd., 101 495–99
William L. Bonnell Company, Inc., 66 372–74
William Lyon Homes, 59 420–22
William Morris Agency, Inc., 23 512–14; 102 448–52 (upd.)
William Reed Publishing Ltd., 78 467–70
William Zinsser & Company, Inc., 58 365–67
Williams & Connolly LLP, 47 445–48
Williams Communications Group, Inc., 34 507–10
The Williams Companies, Inc., IV 575–76; 31 469–72 (upd.)
Williams Scotsman, Inc., 65 361–64
Williams-Sonoma, Inc., 17 548–50; 44 447–50 (upd.); 103 515–20 (upd.)
Williamson-Dickie Manufacturing Company, 14 549–50; 45 438–41 (upd.)
Willis Group Holdings Ltd., 25 537–39; 100 456–60 (upd.)
Willkie Farr & Gallagher LLPLP, 95 450–53
Willow Run Foods, Inc., 100 461–64
Wilmar International Ltd., 108 537–41
Wilmer Cutler Pickering Hale and Dorr L.L.P., 109 600–04
Wilmington Trust Corporation, 25 540–43
Wilson Bowden Plc, 45 442–44
Wilson Sonsini Goodrich & Rosati, 34 511–13
Wilson Sporting Goods Company, 24 530–32; 84 431–436 (upd.)
Wilsons The Leather Experts Inc., 21 525–27; 58 368–71 (upd.)
Wilton Products, Inc., 97 477–80
Winbond Electronics Corporation, 74 389–91
Wincanton plc, 52 418–20
Winchell's Donut Houses Operating Company, L.P., 60 356–59
WinCo Foods Inc., 60 360–63
Wincor Nixdorf Holding GmbH, 69 370–73 (upd.)
Wind River Systems, Inc., 37 419–22
Windmere Corporation, 16 537–39 *see also* Applica Inc.
Windstream Corporation, 83 462–465
Windswept Environmental Group, Inc., 62 389–92
The Wine Group, Inc., 39 419–21; 114 515–18 (upd.)
Winegard Company, 56 384–87
Winmark Corporation, 74 392–95

Index to Industries

Accounting

American Institute of Certified Public Accountants (AICPA), 44
Andersen, 29 (upd.); 68 (upd.)
Automatic Data Processing, Inc., III; 9 (upd.); 47 (upd.)
BDO Seidman LLP, 96
BKD LLP, 96
CPP International, LLC, 103
CROSSMARK, 79
Deloitte Touche Tohmatsu International, 9; 29 (upd.)
Ernst & Young Global Limited, 9; 29 (upd.); 108 (upd.)
FTI Consulting, Inc., 77
Grant Thornton International, 57
Huron Consulting Group Inc., 87
JKH Holding Co. LLC, 105
KPMG International, 33 (upd.); 108 (upd.)
L.S. Starrett Co., 13
McLane Company, Inc., 13
NCO Group, Inc., 42
Paychex, Inc., 15; 46 (upd.)
PKF International, 78
Plante & Moran, LLP, 71
PRG-Schultz International, Inc., 73
PricewaterhouseCoopers International Limited, 9; 29 (upd.); 111 (upd.)
Resources Connection, Inc., 81
Robert Wood Johnson Foundation, 35
RSM McGladrey Business Services Inc., 98
Saffery Champness, 80
Sanders\Wingo, 99
Schenck Business Solutions, 88
StarTek, Inc., 79
Travelzoo Inc., 79

Univision Communications Inc., 24; 83 (upd.)

Advertising & Business Services

ABM Industries Incorporated, 25 (upd.)
Abt Associates Inc., 95
Accenture Ltd., 108 (upd.)
AchieveGlobal Inc., 90
Ackerley Communications, Inc., 9
ACNielsen Corporation, 13; 38 (upd.)
Acosta Sales and Marketing Company, Inc., 77
Acsys, Inc., 44
Adecco S.A., 36 (upd.); 116 (upd.)
Adelman Travel Group, 105
Adia S.A., 6
Administaff, Inc., 52
The Advertising Council, Inc., 76
The Advisory Board Company, 80
Advo, Inc., 6; 53 (upd.)
Aegis Group plc, 6
Affiliated Computer Services, Inc., 61
AHL Services, Inc., 27
Allegis Group, Inc., 95
Alloy, Inc., 55
Amdocs Ltd., 47
American Building Maintenance Industries, Inc., 6
Amey Plc, 47
Analysts International Corporation, 36
aQuantive, Inc., 81
The Arbitron Company, 38
Ariba, Inc., 57
Armor Holdings, Inc., 27
Asatsu-DK Inc., 82
Ashtead Group plc, 34
Avalon Correctional Services, Inc., 75

Bain & Company, 55
Barrett Business Services, Inc., 16
Barton Protective Services Inc., 53
Bates Worldwide, Inc., 14; 33 (upd.)
Bearings, Inc., 13
Berlitz International, Inc., 13; 39 (upd.)
Bernard Hodes Group Inc., 86
Bernstein-Rein, 92
Big Flower Press Holdings, Inc., 21
Billing Concepts, Inc., 26; 72 (upd.)
Billing Services Group Ltd., 102
The BISYS Group, Inc., 73
Booz Allen Hamilton Inc., 10; 101 (upd.)
Boron, LePore & Associates, Inc., 45
The Boston Consulting Group, 58
Bozell Worldwide Inc., 25
BrandPartners Group, Inc., 58
Bright Horizons Family Solutions, Inc., 31
Broadcast Music Inc., 23; 90 (upd.)
Bronner Display & Sign Advertising, Inc., 82
Buck Consultants, Inc., 55
Bureau Veritas SA, 55
Burke, Inc., 88
Burns International Services Corporation, 13; 41 (upd.)
Cambridge Technology Partners, Inc., 36
Campbell-Ewald Advertising, 86
Campbell-Mithun-Esty, Inc., 16
Cannon Design, 63
Capario, 104
Capita Group PLC, 69
Cardtronics, Inc., 93
Carmichael Lynch Inc., 28
Cash Systems, Inc., 93
Cazenove Group plc, 72
CCC Information Services Group Inc., 74
CDI Corporation, 6; 54 (upd.)
Cegedim S.A., 104

Aerospace

Agribusiness & Farming

Airlines

Flying Boat, Inc. (Chalk's Ocean
Airways), 56
Frontier Airlines Holdings Inc., 22; 84
(upd.)
Garuda Indonesia, 6
Gol Linhas Aéreas Inteligentes S.A., 73
Groupe Air France, 6
Grupo Aeroportuario del Pacífico, S.A. de
C.V., 85
Grupo TACA, 38
Gulf Air Company, 56
Hawaiian Holdings, Inc., 9; 22 (upd.); 96
(upd.)
Hawker Siddeley Group Public Limited
Company, III
Hong Kong Dragon Airlines Ltd., 66
Iberia Líneas Aéreas de España S.A., 6; 36
(upd.); 91 (upd.)
Icelandair, 52
Indian Airlines Ltd., 46
International Airline Support Group, Inc.,
55
IranAir, 81
Japan Airlines Corporation, I; 32 (upd.);
110 (upd.)
Jersey European Airways (UK) Ltd., 61
Jet Airways (India) Private Limited, 65
JetBlue Airways Corporation, 44
Kenmore Air Harbor Inc., 65
Kenya Airways Limited, 89
Kitty Hawk, Inc., 22
Kiwi International Airlines Inc., 20
KLM Royal Dutch Airlines, 104 (upd.)
Koninklijke Luchtvaart Maatschappij,
N.V. (KLM Royal Dutch Airlines), I;
28 (upd.)
Korean Air Lines Co., Ltd., 6; 27 (upd.);
114 (upd.)
Kuwait Airways Corporation, 68
Lan Chile S.A., 31
Lauda Air Luftfahrt AG, 48
Lloyd Aéreo Boliviano S.A., 95
Loganair Ltd., 68
LOT Polish Airlines (Polskie Linie
Lotnicze S.A.), 33
LTU Group Holding GmbH, 37
Malaysian Airlines System Berhad, 6; 29
(upd.); 97 (upd.)
Malév Plc, 24
Mesa Air Group, Inc., 11; 32 (upd.); 77
(upd.)
Mesaba Holdings, Inc., 28
Middle East Airlines - Air Liban S.A.L.,
79
Midway Airlines Corporation, 33
Midwest Air Group, Inc., 35; 85 (upd.)
MN Airlines LLC, 104
NetJets Inc., 96 (upd.)
Northwest Airlines Corporation, I; 6
(upd.); 26 (upd.); 74 (upd.)
Offshore Logistics, Inc., 37
Pakistan International Airlines
Corporation, 46
Pan American World Airways, Inc., I; 12
(upd.)
Panalpina World Transport (Holding)
Ltd., 47
People Express Airlines, Inc., I

Petroleum Helicopters, Inc., 35
PHI, Inc., 80 (upd.)
Philippine Airlines, Inc., 6; 23 (upd.)
Pinnacle Airlines Corp., 73
Preussag AG, 42 (upd.)
Qantas Airways Ltd., 6; 24 (upd.); 68
(upd.)
Qatar Airways Company Q.C.S.C., 87
Reno Air Inc., 23
Royal Brunei Airlines Sdn Bhd, 99
Royal Nepal Airline Corporation, 41
Ryanair Holdings plc, 35
SAA (Pty) Ltd., 28
Sabena S.A./N.V., 33
The SAS Group, 34 (upd.)
Saudi Arabian Airlines, 6; 27 (upd.)
Scandinavian Airlines System, I
Sikorsky Aircraft Corporation, 24; 104
(upd.)
Singapore Airlines Limited, 6; 27 (upd.);
83 (upd.)
SkyWest, Inc., 25
Société d'Exploitation AOM Air Liberté
SA (AirLib), 53
Société Luxembourgeoise de Navigation
Aérienne S.A., 64
Société Tunisienne de l'Air-Tunisair, 49
Southwest Airlines Co., 6; 24 (upd.); 71
(upd.)
Spirit Airlines, Inc., 31
Sterling European Airlines A/S, 70
Sun Country Airlines, 30
Swiss Air Transport Company, Ltd., I
Swiss International Air Lines Ltd., 48
TAM Linhas Aéreas S.A., 68
TAME (Transportes Aéreos Militares
Ecuatorianos), 100
TAP—Air Portugal Transportes Aéreos
Portugueses S.A., 46
TAROM S.A., 64
Texas Air Corporation, I
Thai Airways International Public
Company Limited, 6; 27 (upd.)
Tower Air, Inc., 28
Trans World Airlines, Inc., I; 12 (upd.);
35 (upd.)
TransBrasil S/A Linhas Aéreas, 31
Transportes Aereos Portugueses, S.A., 6
Turkish Airlines Inc. (Türk Hava Yollari
A.O.), 72
UAL Corporation, 34 (upd.); 107 (upd.)
United Airlines, I; 6 (upd.)
US Airways Group, Inc., I; 6 (upd.); 28
(upd.); 52 (upd.); 110 (upd.)
Uzbekistan Airways National Air
Company, 99
VARIG S.A. (Viação Aérea
Rio-Grandense), 6; 29 (upd.)
Virgin Group Ltd., 12; 32 (upd.); 89
(upd.)
Volga-Dnepr Group, 82
Vueling Airlines S.A., 97
WestJet Airlines Ltd., 38; 115 (upd.)

Automotive

AB Volvo, I; 7 (upd.); 26 (upd.); 67
(upd.)
Accubuilt, Inc., 74

Actia Group S.A., 107
Adam Opel AG, 7; 21 (upd.); 61 (upd.)
ADESA, Inc., 71
Advance Auto Parts, Inc., 57
Aftermarket Technology Corp., 83
Aisin Seiki Co., Ltd., III; 48 (upd.)
Alamo Rent A Car, Inc., 6; 24 (upd.); 84
(upd.)
Alfa Romeo, 13; 36 (upd.)
Alvis Plc, 47
American Axle & Manufacturing
Holdings, Inc., 67
American Motors Corporation, I
America's Car-Mart, Inc., 64
Amerigon Incorporated, 97
Andretti Green Racing, 106
Applied Power Inc., 9; 32 (upd.)
Arnold Clark Automobiles Ltd., 60
ArvinMeritor, Inc., 8; 54 (upd.)
Asbury Automotive Group Inc., 60
ASC, Inc., 55
Autobacs Seven Company Ltd., 76
Autocam Corporation, 51
Autoliv, Inc., 65
Automobiles Citroen, 7
Automobili Lamborghini Holding S.p.A.,
13; 34 (upd.); 91 (upd.)
AutoNation, Inc., 50
AutoTrader.com, L.L.C., 91
AVTOVAZ Joint Stock Company, 65
Bajaj Auto Limited, 39
Bayerische Motoren Werke AG, I; 11
(upd.); 38 (upd.); 108 (upd.)
Behr GmbH & Co. KG, 72
Belron International Ltd., 76
Bendix Corporation, I
Blue Bird Corporation, 35
BorgWarner Inc., III; 14; 32 (upd.); 85
(upd.)
Brose Fahrzeugteile GmbH & Company
KG, 84
The Budd Company, 8
Bugatti Automobiles S.A.S., 94
BYD Company Limited, 115
Caffyns PLC, 105
Canadian Tire Corporation, Limited, 71
(upd.)
Cardone Industries Inc., 92
CarMax, Inc., 55
CARQUEST Corporation, 29
Caterpillar Inc., III; 15 (upd.); 63 (upd.)
Checker Motors Corp., 89
China Automotive Systems Inc., 87
China FAW Group Corporation, 105
Chrysler Corporation, I; 11 (upd.)
CJSC Transmash Holding, 93
CNH Global N.V., 38 (upd.); 99 (upd.)
Collins Industries, Inc., 33
Commercial Vehicle Group, Inc., 81
Consorcio G Grupo Dina, S.A. de C.V.,
36
Crown Equipment Corporation, 15; 93
(upd.)
CSK Auto Corporation, 38
Cummins Engine Company, Inc., I; 12
(upd.); 40 (upd.)
Custom Chrome, Inc., 16; 74 (upd.)

TRW Automotive Holdings Corp., 75 (upd.)
TRW Inc., 14 (upd.)
Ugly Duckling Corporation, 22
United Auto Group, Inc., 26; 68 (upd.)
United Technologies Automotive Inc., 15
Universal Technical Institute, Inc., 81
Valeo, 23; 66 (upd.)
Van Hool S.A./NV, 96
Vauxhall Motors Limited, 73
Visteon Corporation, 109
Volkswagen Aktiengesellschaft, I; 11 (upd.); 32 (upd.); 111 (upd.)
Wagon plc, 92
Walker Manufacturing Company, 19
Webasto Roof Systems Inc., 97
Wilhelm Karmann GmbH, 94
Winnebago Industries, Inc., 7; 27 (upd.); 96 (upd.)
Woodward Governor Company, 13; 49 (upd.); 105 (upd.)
Yokohama Rubber Company, Limited, The, V; 19 (upd.); 91 (upd.)
ZF Friedrichshafen AG, 48
Ziebart International Corporation, 30; 66 (upd.)

Beverages

A & W Brands, Inc., 25
A. Smith Bowman Distillery, Inc., 104
Adolph Coors Company, I; 13 (upd.); 36 (upd.)
AG Barr plc, 64
Ajegroup S.A., 92
Ale-8-One Company Bottling Company, Inc., 117
Allied Domecq PLC, 29
Allied-Lyons PLC, I
Anadolu Efes Biracilik ve Malt Sanayii A.S., 95
Anchor Brewing Company, 47
Andrew Peller Ltd., 101
Angostura Holdings Ltd., 114
Anheuser-Busch InBev, I; 10 (upd.); 34 (upd.); 100 (upd.)
Apple & Eve L.L.C., 92
Asahi Breweries, Ltd., I; 20 (upd.); 52 (upd.); 108 (upd.)
Asia Pacific Breweries Limited, 59
August Schell Brewing Company Inc., 59
Bacardi & Company Ltd., 18; 82 (upd.)
Baltika Brewery Joint Stock Company, 65
Banfi Products Corp., 36; 114 (upd.)
Baron de Ley S.A., 74
Baron Philippe de Rothschild S.A., 39
Bass PLC, I; 15 (upd.); 38 (upd.)
Bavaria S.A., 90
BBAG Osterreichische Brau-Beteiligungs-AG, 38
Bell's Brewery, Inc., 117
Belvedere S.A., 93
Ben Hill Griffin, Inc., 110
Berentzen-Gruppe AG, 113
Beringer Blass Wine Estates Ltd., 22; 66 (upd.)
Bernick Companies, The, 75
Bitburger Braugruppe GmbH, 110
Blue Ridge Beverage Company Inc., 82

Boizel Chanoine Champagne S.A., 94
Bols Distilleries NV, 74
Boston Beer Company, Inc., The, 18; 50 (upd.); 108 (upd.)
Brauerei Beck & Co., 9; 33 (upd.)
Britannia Soft Drinks Ltd. (Britvic), 71
Bronco Wine Company, 101
Brooklyn Brewery, The, 109
Brouwerijen Alken-Maes N.V., 86
Brown-Forman Corporation, I; 10 (upd.); 38 (upd.); 114 (upd.)
Budweiser Budvar, National Corporation, 59
Cadbury Schweppes PLC, 49 (upd.)
Cains Beer Company PLC, 99
California Dairies Inc., 111
Cameron Hughes Wine, 103
Canandaigua Brands, Inc., 13; 34 (upd.)
Cantine Giorgio Lungarotti S.R.L., 67
Caribou Coffee Company, Inc., 28; 97 (upd.)
Carlsberg A/S, 9; 29 (upd.); 98 (upd.)
Carlton and United Breweries Ltd., I
Casa Cuervo, S.A. de C.V., 31
Central European Distribution Corporation, 75
Cerveceria Polar, I
Chalone Wine Group, Ltd., The, 36
Champagne Bollinger S.A., 114
Charmer Sunbelt Group, The, 95
City Brewing Company LLC, 73
Clearly Canadian Beverage Corporation, 48
Clement Pappas & Company, Inc., 92
Click Wine Group, 68
Coca Cola Bottling Co. Consolidated, 10
Coca-Cola Company, The, I; 10 (upd.); 32 (upd.); 67 (upd.)
Coffee Holding Co., Inc., 95
Companhia de Bebidas das Américas, 57
Compania Cervecerias Unidas S.A., 70
Constellation Brands, Inc., 68 (upd.)
Corby Distilleries Limited, 14
Cott Corporation, 52
D.G. Yuengling & Son, Inc., 38
Dairylea Cooperative Inc., 111
Dallis Coffee, Inc., 86
Daniel Thwaites Plc, 95
Davide Campari-Milano S.p.A., 57
Dean Foods Company, 21 (upd.)
Delicato Vineyards, Inc., 50
Deschutes Brewery, Inc., 57
Desnoes and Geddes Limited, 79
Diageo plc, 79 (upd.)
Direct Wines Ltd., 84
Distillers Company PLC, I
Double-Cola Co.-USA, 70
Dr Pepper/Seven Up, Inc., 9; 32 (upd.)
Drie Mollen Holding B.V., 99
Drinks Americas Holdings, LTD., 105
E. & J. Gallo Winery, I; 7 (upd.); 28 (upd.); 104 (upd.)
East Africa Breweries Limited, 116
Eckes AG, 56
Edrington Group Ltd., The, 88
Embotelladora Andina S.A., 71
Empresas Polar SA, 55 (upd.)
Energy Brands Inc., 88

F. Korbel & Bros. Inc., 68
Faygo Beverages Inc., 55
Federico Paternina S.A., 69
Ferolito, Vultaggio & Sons, 27; 100 (upd.)
Fiji Water LLC, 74
Florida's Natural Growers, 45
Foster's Group Limited, 7; 21 (upd.); 50 (upd.); 111 (upd.)
Freixenet S.A., 71
Frucor Beverages Group Ltd., 96
Fuller Smith & Turner P.L.C., 38
G. Heileman Brewing Company Inc., I
Gambrinus Company, The, 40
Gano Excel Enterprise Sdn. Bhd., 89
Gatorade Company, The, 82
Geerlings & Wade, Inc., 45
General Cinema Corporation, I
Glazer's Wholesale Drug Company, Inc., 82
Gluek Brewing Company, 75
Golden State Vintners, Inc., 33
Gosling Brothers Ltd., 82
Grand Metropolitan PLC, I
Grands Vins Jean-Claude Boisset S.A., 98
Green Mountain Coffee Roasters, Inc., 31; 107 (upd.)
Greenalls Group PLC, The, 21
Greene King plc, 31
Groupe Danone, 32 (upd.); 93 (upd.)
Grupo Industrial Herradura, S.A. de C.V., 83
Grupo Modelo, S.A. de C.V., 29
Gruppo Italiano Vini, 111
Guinness/UDV, I; 43 (upd.)
Hain Celestial Group, Inc., The, 43 (upd.)
Hansen Natural Corporation, 31; 76 (upd.)
Heineken N.V, I; 13 (upd.); 34 (upd.); 90 (upd.)
Heublein, Inc., I
High Falls Brewing Company LLC, 74
Hindustan Lever Limited, 79
Hiram Walker Resources, Ltd., I
Hite Brewery Company Ltd., 97
illycaffè S.p.A., 50; 110 (upd.)
Imagine Foods, Inc., 50
Interbrew S.A., 17; 50 (upd.)
Irish Distillers Group, 96
Ito En Ltd., 101
J.J. Darboven GmbH & Co. KG, 96
J. Lohr Winery Corporation, 99
Jacob Leinenkugel Brewing Company, 28
JD Wetherspoon plc, 30
Jim Beam Brands Worldwide, Inc., 58 (upd.)
John Dewar & Sons, Ltd., 82
Jones Soda Co., 69
Jugos del Valle, S.A. de C.V., 85
Karlsberg Brauerei GmbH & Co KG, 41
Kemps LLC, 103
Kendall-Jackson Winery, Ltd., 28
Kikkoman Corporation, 14
Kirin Brewery Company, Limited, I; 21 (upd.); 63 (upd.)
Kobrand Corporation, 82

Bio-Technology

Incyte Genomics, Inc., 52
Inverness Medical Innovations, Inc., 63
Invitrogen Corporation, 52
Judge Group, Inc., The, 51
Kendle International Inc., 87
Landec Corporation, 95
Life Technologies, Inc., 17
LifeCell Corporation, 77
Lonza Group Ltd., 73
Martek Biosciences Corporation, 65
Medarex, Inc., 85
Medtronic, Inc., 8; 30 (upd.); 67 (upd.)
Meridian Bioscience, Inc., 115
Millipore Corporation, 25; 84 (upd.)
Minntech Corporation, 22
Mycogen Corporation, 21
Nektar Therapeutics, 91
New Brunswick Scientific Co., Inc., 45
Omrix Biopharmaceuticals, Inc., 95
Pacific Ethanol, Inc., 81
Pharmion Corporation, 91
Qiagen N.V., 39
Quintiles Transnational Corporation, 21
RTI Biologics, Inc., 96
Seminis, Inc., 29
Senomyx, Inc., 83
Serologicals Corporation, 63
Sigma-Aldrich Corporation, I; 36 (upd.);
    93 (upd.)
Starkey Laboratories, Inc., 52
STERIS Corporation, 29
Stratagene Corporation, 70
Talecris Biotherapeutics Holdings Corp.,
    114
Tanox, Inc., 77
TECHNE Corporation, 52
TriPath Imaging, Inc., 77
Viterra Inc., 105
Waters Corporation, 43
Whatman plc, 46
Wilmar International Ltd., 108
Wisconsin Alumni Research Foundation,
    65
Wyeth, 50 (upd.)

Chemicals

A. Schulman, Inc., 8; 49 (upd.)
Aceto Corp., 38
Air Products and Chemicals, Inc., I; 10
    (upd.); 74 (upd.)
Airgas, Inc., 54
Akzo Nobel N.V., 13; 41 (upd.); 112
    (upd.)
Albaugh, Inc., 105
Albemarle Corporation, 59
AlliedSignal Inc., 9; 22 (upd.)
ALTANA AG, 87
American Cyanamid, I; 8 (upd.)
American Vanguard Corporation, 47
Arab Potash Company, 85
Arch Chemicals Inc., 78
ARCO Chemical Company, 10
Arkema S.A., 100
Asahi Denka Kogyo KK, 64
Atanor S.A., 62
Atochem S.A., I
Avantium Technologies BV, 79
Avecia Group PLC, 63

Azelis Group, 100
Baker Hughes Incorporated, III; 22
    (upd.); 57 (upd.)
Balchem Corporation, 42
BASF SE, I; 18 (upd.); 50 (upd.); 108
    (upd.)
Bayer A.G., I; 13 (upd.); 41 (upd.)
Betz Laboratories, Inc., I; 10 (upd.)
BFGoodrich Company, The, 19 (upd.)
BOC Group plc, I; 25 (upd.); 78 (upd.)
BorsodChem Zrt., 113
Braskem S.A., 108
Brenntag Holding GmbH & Co. KG, 8;
    23 (upd.); 101 (upd.)
Burmah Castrol PLC, 30 (upd.)
Cabot Corporation, 8; 29 (upd.); 91
    (upd.)
Calgon Carbon Corporation, 73
Caliper Life Sciences, Inc., 70
Calumet Specialty Products Partners, L.P.,
    106
Cambrex Corporation, 16
Campbell Brothers Limited, 115
Catalytica Energy Systems, Inc., 44
Celanese Corporation, I; 109 (upd.)
Celanese Mexicana, S.A. de C.V., 54
CF Industries Holdings, Inc., 99
Chemcentral Corporation, 8
Chemi-Trol Chemical Co., 16
Chemtura Corporation, 91 (upd.)
China Petroleum & Chemical
    Corporation (Sinopec Corp.), 109
Church & Dwight Co., Inc., 29
Ciba-Geigy Ltd., I; 8 (upd.)
Clorox Company, The, III; 22 (upd.); 81
    (upd.)
Croda International Plc, 45
Crompton Corporation, 9; 36 (upd.)
CVR Energy Corporation, 116
Cytec Industries Inc., 27
Degussa-Hüls AG, 32 (upd.)
DeKalb Genetics Corporation, 17
Dexter Corporation, The, I; 12 (upd.)
Dionex Corporation, 46
Dow Chemical Company, The, I; 8
    (upd.); 50 (upd.); 114 (upd.)
DSM N.V., I; 56 (upd.)
Dynaction S.A., 67
E.I. du Pont de Nemours & Company, I;
    8 (upd.); 26 (upd.); 73 (upd.)
Eastman Chemical Company, 14; 38
    (upd.); 116 (upd.)
Ecolab Inc., I; 13 (upd.); 34 (upd.); 85
    (upd.)
Eka Chemicals AB, 92
Elementis plc, 40 (upd.)
Engelhard Corporation, 72 (upd.)
English China Clays Ltd., 15 (upd.); 40
    (upd.)
Enterprise Rent-A-Car Company, 69
    (upd.)
Equistar Chemicals, LP, 71
Ercros S.A., 80
ERLY Industries Inc., 17
Ethyl Corporation, I; 10 (upd.)
Evonik Industries AG, 111 (upd.)
Ferro Corporation, 8; 56 (upd.)
Firmenich International S.A., 60

First Mississippi Corporation, 8
FMC Corporation, 89 (upd.)
Formosa Plastics Corporation, 14; 58
    (upd.)
Fort James Corporation, 22 (upd.)
Fuchs Petrolub AG, 102
G.A.F., I
General Chemical Group Inc., The, 37
Georgia Gulf Corporation, 9; 61 (upd.)
Givaudan SA, 43
Great Lakes Chemical Corporation, I; 14
    (upd.)
GROWMARK, Inc., 88
Grupo Comex, 115
Guerbet Group, 46
H.B. Fuller Company, 8; 32 (upd.); 75
    (upd.)
Hauser, Inc., 46
Hawkins Chemical, Inc., 16
Henkel KGaA, III; 34 (upd.); 95 (upd.)
Hercules Inc., I; 22 (upd.); 66 (upd.)
Hexion Specialty Chemicals, Inc., 116
Hillyard, Inc., 114
Hoechst A.G., I; 18 (upd.)
Hoechst Celanese Corporation, 13
Huls A.G., I
Huntsman Corporation, 8; 98 (upd.)
Ikonics Corporation, 99
IMC Fertilizer Group, Inc., 8
Imperial Chemical Industries PLC, I; 50
    (upd.)
Inergy L.P., 110
International Flavors & Fragrances Inc., 9;
    38 (upd.)
Israel Chemicals Ltd., 55
KBR Inc., 106 (upd.)
Kemira Oyj, 70
KMG Chemicals, Inc., 101
Koppers Industries, Inc., I; 26 (upd.)
Kwizda Holding GmbH, 102 (upd.)
L'Air Liquide SA, I; 47 (upd.)
Lawter International Inc., 14
LeaRonal, Inc., 23
Loctite Corporation, 30 (upd.)
Lonza Group Ltd., 73
Loos & Dilworth, Inc., 100
Lubrizol Corporation, The, I; 30 (upd.);
    83 (upd.)
LyondellBasell Industries Holdings N.V.,
    45 (upd.); 109 (upd.)
M.A. Hanna Company, 8
MacDermid Incorporated, 32
Makhteshim-Agan Industries Ltd., 85
Mallinckrodt Group Inc., 19
MBC Holding Company, 40
Melamine Chemicals, Inc., 27
Methanex Corporation, 40
Mexichem, S.A.B. de C.V., 99
Minerals Technologies Inc., 52 (upd.)
Mississippi Chemical Corporation, 39
Mitsubishi Chemical Corporation, I; 56
    (upd.)
Mitsui Petrochemical Industries, Ltd., 9
Monsanto Company, I; 9 (upd.); 29
    (upd.)
Montedison SpA, I
Morton International Inc., I; 9 (upd.); 80
    (upd.)

Construction

John Laing plc, I; 51 (upd.)
John W. Danforth Company, 48
Kajima Corporation, I; 51 (upd.); 117 (upd.)
Kaufman and Broad Home Corporation, 8
KB Home, 45 (upd.)
KBR Inc., 106 (upd.)
Kellogg Brown & Root, Inc., 62 (upd.)
Kiewit Corporation, 116 (upd.)
Kitchell Corporation, 14
Koll Company, The, 8
Komatsu Ltd., III; 16 (upd.); 52 (upd.)
Kraus-Anderson Companies, Inc., 36; 83 (upd.)
Kuhlman Corporation, 20
Kumagai Gumi Company, Ltd., I
Laing O'Rourke PLC, 93 (upd.)
Land and Houses PCL, 104
Larsen and Toubro Ltd., 117
Ledcor Industries Limited, 46
Lennar Corporation, 11
L'Entreprise Jean Lefebvre, 23
Lincoln Property Company, 8
Lindal Cedar Homes, Inc., 29
Linde A.G., I
M. A. Mortenson Company, 115
Manitowoc Company, Inc., The, 18; 59 (upd.)
MasTec, Inc., 55
Matrix Service Company, 65
May Gurney Integrated Services PLC, 95
McCarthy Building Companies, Inc., 48
MDU Resources Group, Inc., 114 (upd.)
Mellon-Stuart Company, I
Michael Baker Corp., 14
Modtech Holdings, Inc., 77
Morrison Knudsen Corporation, 7; 28 (upd.)
Morrow Equipment Co. L.L.C., 87
Mota-Engil, SGPS, S.A., 97
New Holland N.V., 22
Newpark Resources, Inc., 63
Nortek, Inc., 34
NVR Inc., 8; 70 (upd.)
Obayashi Corporation, 78
Obrascon Huarte Lain S.A., 76
O'Connell Companies Inc., The, 100
Ohbayashi Corporation, I
Opus Corporation, 34; 101 (upd.)
Orascom Construction Industries S.A.E., 87
Orleans Homebuilders, Inc., 62
Panattoni Development Company, Inc., 99
Parsons Brinckerhoff Inc., 34; 104 (upd.)
Parsons Corporation, The, 8; 56 (upd.)
PCL Construction Group Inc., 50
Peninsular & Oriental Steam Navigation Company (Bovis Division), The, I
Pepper Construction Group, LLC, The, 111
Perini Corporation, 8; 82 (upd.)
Peter Kiewit Sons' Inc., 8
Philipp Holzmann AG, 17
Pinguely-Haulotte SA, 51
Plaza Construction Corporation, 117
Post Properties, Inc., 26

Pulte Homes, Inc., 8; 42 (upd.); 113 (upd.)
Pyramid Companies, 54
Redrow Group plc, 31
Rinker Group Ltd., 65
RMC Group p.l.c., III; 34 (upd.)
Robertson-Ceco Corporation, 19
Rooney Brothers Co., 25
Rottlund Company, Inc., The, 28
Roy Anderson Corporation, 75
Ryan Companies US, Inc., 99
Ryland Group, Inc., The, 8; 37 (upd.); 107 (upd.)
Sandvik AB, IV; 32 (upd.); 77 (upd.)
Schuff Steel Company, 26
Seddon Group Ltd., 67
Servidyne Inc., 100 (upd.)
Shimizu Corporation, 109
Shorewood Packaging Corporation, 28
Simon Property Group Inc., 27; 84 (upd.)
Skanska AB, 38; 110 (upd.)
Skidmore, Owings & Merrill LLP, 69 (upd.)
SNC-Lavalin Group Inc., 72
Speedy Hire plc, 84
Stabler Companies Inc., 78
Standard Pacific Corporation, 52
Stone & Webster, Inc., 64 (upd.)
Strabag SE, 113
Structure Tone Organization, The, 99
Suffolk Construction Company, Inc., 114
Sundt Corp., 24
Swinerton Inc., 43
Tarmac Limited, III, 28 (upd.); 95 (upd.)
Taylor Wimpey PLC, I; 38 (upd.); 115 (upd.)
Technical Olympic USA, Inc., 75
Terex Corporation, 7; 40 (upd.); 91 (upd.)
ThyssenKrupp AG, IV; 28 (upd.); 87 (upd.)
TIC Holdings Inc., 92
Tishman Construction Company, 112
Toll Brothers Inc., 15; 70 (upd.)
Trammell Crow Company, 8
Tridel Enterprises Inc., 9
Tully Construction Co. Inc., 114
Turner Construction Company, 66
Turner Corporation, The, 8; 23 (upd.)
U.S. Aggregates, Inc., 42
U.S. Home Corporation, 8; 78 (upd.)
Urban Engineers, Inc., 102
Urbi Desarrollos Urbanos, S.A. de C.V., 81
VA TECH ELIN EBG GmbH, 49
Vecellio Group, Inc., 113
Veidekke ASA, 98
Veit Companies, 43; 92 (upd.)
Vinci S.A., 113 (upd.)
Wacker Construction Equipment AG, 95
Walbridge Aldinger Co., 38
Walter Industries, Inc., III; 22 (upd.); 72 (upd.)
Weitz Company, Inc., The, 42
Whiting-Turner Contracting Company, 95
Willbros Group, Inc., 56
William Lyon Homes, 59
Wilson Bowden Plc, 45

Wood Hall Trust PLC, I
WorleyParsons Ltd., 115
Yates Companies, Inc., The, 62
Zachry Group, Inc., 95

Containers

Ball Corporation, I; 10 (upd.); 78 (upd.)
BWAY Corporation, 24
Chesapeake Corporation, 8; 30 (upd.); 93 (upd.)
CLARCOR Inc., 17; 61 (upd.)
Constar International Inc., 64
Continental Can Co., Inc., 15
Continental Group Company, I
Crown Cork & Seal Company, Inc., I; 13 (upd.); 32 (upd.)
Crown Holdings, Inc., 83 (upd.)
DIC Corporation, 115
Gaylord Container Corporation, 8
Golden Belt Manufacturing Co., 16
Graham Packaging Holdings Company, 87
Greif Inc., 15; 66 (upd.)
Grupo Industrial Durango, S.A. de C.V., 37
Hanjin Shipping Co., Ltd., 50
Heekin Can Inc., 13
Inland Container Corporation, 8
Interpool, Inc., 92
Kerr Group Inc., 24
Keyes Fibre Company, 9
Libbey Inc., 49
Liqui-Box Corporation, 16
Longaberger Company, The, 12
Longview Fibre Company, 8
Mead Corporation, The, 19 (upd.)
Metal Box PLC, I
Mobile Mini, Inc., 58
Molins plc, 51
National Can Corporation, I
Owens-Illinois, Inc., I; 26 (upd.); 85 (upd.)
Packaging Corporation of America, 51 (upd.)
Pochet SA, 55
Primerica Corporation, I
Printpack, Inc., 68
PVC Container Corporation, 67
Rexam PLC, 32 (upd.); 85 (upd.)
Reynolds Metals Company, 19 (upd.)
Royal Packaging Industries Van Leer N.V., 30
RPC Group PLC, 81
Sealright Co., Inc., 17
Shurgard Storage Centers, Inc., 52
Smurfit Kappa Group plc, 112 (upd.)
Smurfit-Stone Container Corporation, 26 (upd.); 83 (upd.)
Sonoco Products Company, 8; 89 (upd.)
Thermos Company, 16
Tim-Bar Corporation, 110
Toyo Seikan Kaisha, Ltd., I
U.S. Can Corporation, 30
Ultra Pac, Inc., 24
Viatech Continental Can Company, Inc., 25 (upd.)
Vidrala S.A., 67
Vitro Corporativo S.A. de C.V., 34

Drugs & Pharmaceuticals

Varian, Inc., 12; 48 (upd.)
Veeco Instruments Inc., 32
VIASYS Healthcare, Inc., 52
Viasystems Group, Inc., 67
Vicon Industries, Inc., 44
Victor Company of Japan, Limited, II; 26 (upd.); 83 (upd.)
Vishay Intertechnology, Inc., 21; 80 (upd.)
Vitesse Semiconductor Corporation, 32
Vitro Corp., 10
Vizio, Inc., 100
VLSI Technology, Inc., 16
Vorwerk & Co. KG, 112 (upd.)
VTech Holdings Ltd., 77
Wells-Gardner Electronics Corporation, 43
WESCO International, Inc., 116
Westinghouse Electric Corporation, II; 12 (upd.)
Winbond Electronics Corporation, 74
Wincor Nixdorf Holding GmbH, 69 (upd.)
WuXi AppTec Company Ltd., 103
Wyle Electronics, 14
Xantrex Technology Inc., 97
Xerox Corporation, III; 6 (upd.); 26 (upd.); 69 (upd.)
Yageo Corporation, 16; 98 (upd.)
York Research Corporation, 35
Zenith Data Systems, Inc., 10
Zenith Electronics Corporation, II; 13 (upd.); 34 (upd.); 89 (upd.)
Zoom Telephonics, Inc., 18
Zoran Corporation, 77
Zumtobel AG, 50
Zytec Corporation, 19

Engineering & Management Services

AAON, Inc., 22
Aavid Thermal Technologies, Inc., 29
Acergy SA, 97
AECOM Technology Corporation, 79
Alliant Techsystems Inc., 30 (upd.)
Altran Technologies, 51
AMEC plc, 112
American Science & Engineering, Inc., 81
Amey Plc, 47
Analytic Sciences Corporation, 10
Arcadis NV, 26
Arthur D. Little, Inc., 35
Austin Company, The, 8; 72 (upd.)
Autostrada Torino-Milano S.p.A., 101
Babcock International Group PLC, 69
Balfour Beatty plc, 36 (upd.)
BE&K, Inc., 73
Bechtel Corporation, I; 24 (upd.); 99 (upd.)
Birse Group PLC, 77
Bowen Engineering Corporation, 105
Brock Group of Companies, The, 114
Brown & Root, Inc., 13
Bufete Industrial, S.A. de C.V., 34
C.H. Heist Corporation, 24
Camp Dresser & McKee Inc., 104
CDI Corporation, 6; 54 (upd.)

CH2M HILL Companies Ltd., 22; 96 (upd.)
Charles Stark Draper Laboratory, Inc., The, 35
Coflexip S.A., 25
CompuDyne Corporation, 51
Cornell Companies, Inc., 112
Corrections Corporation of America, 23
CRSS Inc., 6
Dames & Moore, Inc., 25
DAW Technologies, Inc., 25
Day & Zimmermann Inc., 9; 31 (upd.)
Donaldson Company, Inc., 16; 49 (upd.); 108 (upd.)
Doosan Heavy Industries and Construction Company Ltd., 108
Dycom Industries, Inc., 57
Edwards and Kelcey, 70
EG&G Incorporated, 8; 29 (upd.)
Eiffage S.A., 27; 117 (upd.)
Elliott-Lewis Corporation, 100
Essef Corporation, 18
Exponent, Inc., 95
FKI Plc, 57
Fluor Corporation, 34 (upd.); 112 (upd.)
Forest City Enterprises, Inc., 52 (upd.)
Foster Wheeler Ltd., 6; 23 (upd.); 76 (upd.)
Framatome SA, 19
Fraport AG Frankfurt Airport Services Worldwide, 90
Freese and Nichols, Inc., 107
Fugro N.V., 98
Gale International Llc, 93
Georg Fischer AG Schaffhausen, 61
Gilbane, Inc., 34
Great Lakes Dredge & Dock Company, 69
Grontmij N.V., 110
Grupo Dragados SA, 55
Halliburton Company, III; 25 (upd.); 55 (upd.)
Halma plc, 104
Harding Lawson Associates Group, Inc., 16
Harley Ellis Devereaux Corporation, 101
Harza Engineering Company, 14
HDR Inc., 48
Hittite Microwave Corporation, 106
HOK Group, Inc., 59
ICF Kaiser International, Inc., 28
IHC Caland N.V., 71
Invensys PLC, 50 (upd.)
Jacobs Engineering Group Inc., 6; 26 (upd.); 106 (upd.)
Jacques Whitford, 92
Jaiprakash Associates Limited, 101
Judge Group, Inc., The, 51
JWP Inc., 9
KBR Inc., 106 (upd.)
Keith Companies Inc., The, 54
Keller Group PLC, 95
Klöckner-Werke AG, 58 (upd.)
Kvaerner ASA, 36
Layne Christensen Company, 19
Louis Berger Group, Inc., The, 104
MacNeal-Schwendler Corporation, The, 25

Malcolm Pirnie, Inc., 42
Mason & Hanger Group Inc., 110
McDermott International, Inc., III; 37 (upd.)
McKinsey & Company, Inc., 9
Mead & Hunt Inc., 113
Michael Baker Corporation, 51 (upd.)
Mota-Engil, SGPS, S.A., 97
MSE, Inc., 113
National Technical Systems, Inc., 111
NBBJ, 111
Nooter Corporation, 61
NTD Architecture, 101
Oceaneering International, Inc., 63
Odebrecht S.A., 73
Ogden Corporation, 6
Opus Corporation, 34; 101 (upd.)
PAREXEL International Corporation, 84
Parsons Brinckerhoff Inc., 34; 104 (upd.)
Parsons Corporation, The, 8; 56 (upd.)
PBSJ Corporation, The, 82
Petrofac Ltd., 95
Quanta Services, Inc., 79
RCM Technologies, Inc., 34
Renishaw plc, 46
Ricardo plc, 90
Rosemount Inc., 15
Roy F. Weston, Inc., 33
Royal Vopak NV, 41
Rust International Inc., 11
Sandia National Laboratories, 49
Sandvik AB, IV; 32 (upd.); 77 (upd.)
Sarnoff Corporation, 57
Science Applications International Corporation, 15; 109 (upd.)
SENTEL Corporation, 106
Serco Group plc, 47
Siegel & Gale, 64
Siemens AG, 57 (upd.)
SRI International, Inc., 57
SSOE Inc., 76
Stone & Webster, Inc., 13; 64 (upd.)
Sulzer Ltd., III; 68 (upd.)
Susquehanna Pfaltzgraff Company, 8
Sverdrup Corporation, 14
Technip, 78
Tech-Sym Corporation, 44 (upd.)
Teledyne Brown Engineering, Inc., 110
Tetra Tech, Inc., 29
ThyssenKrupp AG, IV; 28 (upd.); 87 (upd.)
Towers Perrin, 32
Tracor Inc., 17
TRC Companies, Inc., 32
U.S. Army Corps of Engineers, 91
Underwriters Laboratories, Inc., 30
United Dominion Industries Limited, 8; 16 (upd.)
URS Corporation, 45; 80 (upd.)
VA TECH ELIN EBG GmbH, 49
VECO International, Inc., 7
Vinci, 43
Volkert and Associates, Inc., 98
VSE Corporation, 108
Weir Group PLC, The, 85
Willbros Group, Inc., 56
WS Atkins Plc, 45

Entertainment & Leisure

Financial Services: Banks

Financial Services: Excluding Banks

Food Products

Madrange SA, 58
Magic Seasoning Blends Inc. , 109
Maïsadour S.C.A., 107
Malt-O-Meal Company, 22; 63 (upd.)
Manna Pro Products, LLC, 107
Maple Grove Farms of Vermont, 88
Maple Leaf Foods Inc., 41; 108 (upd.)
Marble Slab Creamery, Inc., 87
Mars, Incorporated, 7; 40 (upd.); 114
  (upd.)
Mars Petcare US Inc., 96
Martha White Foods Inc., 104
Maruha Group Inc., 75 (upd.)
Maryland & Virginia Milk Producers
  Cooperative Association, Inc., 80
Maschhoffs, Inc., The, 82
Mastellone Hermanos S.A., 101
Maui Land & Pineapple Company, Inc.,
  29; 100 (upd.)
Mauna Loa Macadamia Nut Corporation,
  64
Maverick Ranch Association, Inc., 88
McCain Foods Limited, 77
McCormick & Company, Incorporated, 7;
  27 (upd.)
McIlhenny Company, 20
McKee Foods Corporation, 7; 27 (upd.);
  117 (upd.)
Mead Johnson & Company, 84
Medifast, Inc., 97
Meiji Dairies Corporation, II; 82 (upd.)
Meiji Seika Kaisha, Ltd., II; 64 (upd.)
Merisant Worldwide, Inc., 70
Meyer Natural Angus L.L.C., 112
Michael Foods, Inc., 25
Michigan Turkey Producers Co-op, Inc.,
  115
Mid-America Dairymen, Inc., 7
Midwest Grain Products, Inc., 49
Mike-Sell's Inc., 15
Milnot Company, 46
Molinos Río de la Plata S.A., 61
Monfort, Inc., 13
Morinaga & Co. Ltd., 61
Morinda Holdings, Inc., 82
Mountaire Corp., 113
Moy Park Ltd., 78
Mrchocolate.com LLC, 105
Mrs. Baird's Bakeries, 29
Mrs. Fields' Original Cookies, Inc., 27;
  104 (upd.)
Mt. Olive Pickle Company, Inc., 44
MTR Foods Ltd., 55
Murphy Family Farms Inc., 22
Musco Family Olive Co., The, 91
Nabisco Foods Group, II; 7 (upd.)
Nantucket Allserve, Inc., 22
Nathan's Famous, Inc., 29
National Presto Industries, Inc., 43 (upd.)
National Sea Products Ltd., 14
Natural Ovens Bakery, Inc., 72
Natural Selection Foods, 54
Naturally Fresh, Inc., 88
Nature's Path Foods, Inc., 87
Nature's Sunshine Products, Inc., 15; 102
  (upd.)
Naumes, Inc., 81

Nestlé S.A., II; 7 (upd.); 28 (upd.); 71
  (upd.)
New England Confectionery Co., 15
New World Pasta Company, 53
Newhall Land and Farming Company, 14
Newly Weds Foods, Inc., 74
Newman's Own, Inc., 37
Nichiro Corporation, 86
Niman Ranch, Inc., 67
Nippon Meat Packers, Inc., II; 78 (upd.)
Nippon Suisan Kaisha, Ltd., II; 92 (upd.)
Nisshin Seifun Group Inc., II; 66 (upd.)
Nissin Food Products Company Ltd., 75
Northern Foods plc, 10; 61 (upd.)
Northland Cranberries, Inc., 38
Nutraceutical International Corporation,
  37
NutraSweet Company, The, 8; 107 (upd.)
Nutreco Holding N.V., 56
Nutrexpa S.A., 92
NutriSystem, Inc., 71
Oakhurst Dairy, 60
Oberto Sausage Company, Inc., 92
Ocean Beauty Seafoods, Inc., 74
Ocean Spray Cranberries, Inc., 7; 25
  (upd.); 83 (upd.)
Odwalla Inc., 31; 104 (upd.)
OJSC Wimm-Bill-Dann Foods, 48
Olga's Kitchen, Inc., 80
Omaha Steaks International Inc., 62
Omega Protein Corporation, 99
Oregon Freeze Dry, Inc., 74
Ore-Ida Foods Inc., 13; 78 (upd.)
Organic To Go Food Corporation, 99
Organic Valley (Coulee Region Organic
  Produce Pool), 53
Orkla ASA, 18; 82 (upd.)
Oscar Mayer Foods Corp., 12
Otis Spunkmeyer, Inc., 28
Overhill Corporation, 51
Palmer Candy Company, 80
Panzani, 84
Papetti's Hygrade Egg Products, Inc., 39
Parmalat Finanziaria SpA, 50
Patrick Cudahy Inc., 102
Pendleton Grain Growers Inc., 64
Penford Corporation, 55
Penzeys Spices, Inc., 79
Pepperidge Farm, Incorporated, 81
PepsiCo, Inc., I; 10 (upd.); 38 (upd.); 93
  (upd.)
Perdigao SA, 52
Perdue Farms Inc., 7; 23 (upd.)
Perfetti Van Melle S.p.A., 72
Performance Food Group, 96 (upd.)
Perkins Foods Holdings Ltd., 87
Perry's Ice Cream Company Inc., 90
Pescanova S.A., 81
Pet Incorporated, 7
Petrossian Inc., 54
Pez Candy, Inc., 38
Philip Morris Companies Inc., 18 (upd.)
Phillips Foods, Inc., 63
Phillips Foods, Inc., 90 (upd.)
PIC International Group PLC, 24 (upd.)
Pilgrim's Pride Corporation, 7; 23 (upd.);
  90 (upd.)

Pillsbury Company, The, II; 13 (upd.); 62
  (upd.)
Pioneer Hi-Bred International, Inc., 9
Pizza Inn, Inc., 46
Poore Brothers, Inc., 44
PowerBar Inc., 44
Prairie Farms Dairy, Inc., 47
Premium Brands Holdings Corporation,
  114
Premium Standard Farms, Inc., 30
Princes Ltd., 76
Procter & Gamble Company, The, III; 8
  (upd.); 26 (upd.); 67 (upd.)
Prosper De Mulder Limited, 111
Provimi S.A., 80
Punch Taverns plc, 70
Puratos S.A./NV, 92
Purina Mills, Inc., 32
Quaker Foods North America, 73 (upd.)
Quaker Oats Company, II; 12 (upd.); 34
  (upd.)
Quality Chekd Dairies, Inc., 48
R. M. Palmer Co., 89
Raisio PLC, 99
Ralston Purina Company, II; 13 (upd.)
Ranks Hovis McDougall Limited, II; 28
  (upd.)
Real Good Food Company plc, The, 99
Reckitt Benckiser plc, II; 42 (upd.); 91
  (upd.)
Reddy Ice Holdings, Inc., 80
Reser's Fine Foods, Inc., 81
Rica Foods, Inc., 41
Rich Products Corporation, 7; 38 (upd.);
  93 (upd.)
Richtree Inc., 63
Ricola Ltd., 62
Ridley Corporation Ltd., 62
River Ranch Fresh Foods LLC, 88
Riviana Foods Inc., 27; 107 (upd.)
Roberts Dairy Company, 103
Rocky Mountain Chocolate Factory, Inc.,
  73
Roland Murten A.G., 7
Roman Meal Company, 84
Rose Acre Farms, Inc., 60
Rowntree Mackintosh, II
Royal Numico N.V., 37
Ruiz Food Products, Inc., 53
Russell Stover Candies Inc., 12; 91 (upd.)
Saarioinen Oy, 117
Sadia S.A., 59
SanCor Cooperativas Unidas Ltda., 101
Sanderson Farms, Inc., 15
Saputo Inc., 59
Sara Lee Corporation, II; 15 (upd.); 54
  (upd.); 99 (upd.)
Sarris Candies Inc., 86
Savannah Foods & Industries, Inc., 7
Schlotzsky's, Inc., 36
Schreiber Foods, Inc., 72
Schwan Food Company, The, 7; 26
  (upd.); 83 (upd.)
Schwebel Baking Company, 72
Seaboard Corporation, 36; 85 (upd.)
See's Candies, Inc., 30
Seminis, Inc., 29
Seneca Foods Corporation, 60 (upd.)

Food Services, Retailers, & Restaurants

Health Care Services

UnitedHealth Group Incorporated, 9; 103 (upd.)
Universal Health Services, Inc., 6
Vanderbilt University Medical Center, 99
Vanguard Health Systems Inc., 70
VCA Antech, Inc., 58
Vencor, Inc., 16
VISX, Incorporated, 30
Vivra, Inc., 18
WellPoint, Inc., 25; 103 (upd.)

Health, Personal & Medical Care Products

A-dec, Inc., 53
Abaxis, Inc., 83
Abbott Laboratories, I; 11 (upd.); 40 (upd.); 93 (upd.)
Abiomed, Inc., 47
Accuray Incorporated, 95
Acuson Corporation, 10; 36 (upd.)
Advanced Medical Optics, Inc., 79
Advanced Neuromodulation Systems, Inc., 73
Akorn, Inc., 32
ALARIS Medical Systems, Inc., 65
Alberto-Culver Company, 8; 36 (upd.); 91 (upd.)
Alco Health Services Corporation, III
Alès Groupe, 81
Allergan, Inc., 10; 30 (upd.); 77 (upd.)
American Medical Alert Corporation, 103
American Oriental Bioengineering Inc., 93
American Safety Razor Company, 20
American Stores Company, II; 22 (upd.)
Amway Corporation, III; 13 (upd.)
Andis Company, Inc., 85
AngioDynamics, Inc., 81
Ansell Ltd., 60 (upd.)
ArthroCare Corporation, 73
Artsana SpA, 92
Ascendia Brands, Inc., 97
Atkins Nutritionals, Inc., 58
Aveda Corporation, 24
Avon Products, Inc., III; 19 (upd.); 46 (upd.); 109 (upd.)
Ballard Medical Products, 21
Bally Total Fitness Holding Corp., 25
Bare Escentuals, Inc., 91
Bausch & Lomb Inc., 7; 25 (upd.); 96 (upd.)
Baxter International Inc., I; 10 (upd.); 116 (upd.)
BeautiControl Cosmetics, Inc., 21
Becton, Dickinson and Company, I; 11 (upd.); 36 (upd.); 101 (upd.)
Beiersdorf AG, 29
Big B, Inc., 17
Bindley Western Industries, Inc., 9
Biolase Technology, Inc., 87
Biomet, Inc., 10; 93 (upd.)
BioScrip Inc., 98
Biosite Incorporated, 73
Block Drug Company, Inc., 8; 27 (upd.)
Body Shop International plc, The, 11; 53 (upd.)
Boiron S.A., 73
Bolton Group B.V., 86
Borghese Inc., 107

Bristol-Myers Squibb Company, III; 9 (upd.)
Bronner Brothers Inc., 92
Burt's Bees, Inc., 58
C.O. Bigelow Chemists, Inc., 114
C.R. Bard Inc., 9; 65 (upd.)
Candela Corporation, 48
Cantel Medical Corporation, 80
Cardinal Health, Inc., 18; 50 (upd.); 115 (upd.)
Carl Zeiss AG, III; 34 (upd.); 91 (upd.)
Carma Laboratories, Inc., 60
Carson, Inc., 31
Carter-Wallace, Inc., 8
Caswell-Massey Co. Ltd., 51
CCA Industries, Inc., 53
Chanel SA, 12; 49 (upd.)
Chattem, Inc., 17; 88 (upd.)
Chesebrough-Pond's USA, Inc., 8
Chindex International, Inc., 101
Chronimed Inc., 26
Church & Dwight Co., Inc., 68 (upd.)
Cintas Corporation, 51 (upd.)
Clorox Company, The, III; 22 (upd.); 81 (upd.)
CNS, Inc., 20
COBE Cardiovascular, Inc., 61
Cochlear Ltd., 77
Colgate-Palmolive Company, III; 14 (upd.); 35 (upd.)
Combe Inc., 72
Conair Corporation, 17; 69 (upd.)
CONMED Corporation, 87
Connetics Corporation, 70
Cook Group Inc., 102
Cooper Companies, Inc., The, 39
Cordis Corporation, 19; 46 (upd.); 112 (upd.)
Cosmair, Inc., 8
Cosmolab Inc., 96
Coty Inc., 36; 115 (upd.)
Covidien Ltd., 91
Cyberonics, Inc., 79
Cybex International, Inc., 49
Cytyc Corporation, 69
Dade Behring Holdings Inc., 71
Dalli-Werke GmbH & Co. KG, 86
Datascope Corporation, 39
Del Laboratories, Inc., 28
Deltec, Inc., 56
Dentsply International Inc., 10; 109 (upd.)
DEP Corporation, 20
DePuy Inc., 30; 37 (upd.)
DHB Industries Inc., 85
Diagnostic Products Corporation, 73
Dial Corp., The, 23 (upd.)
Direct Focus, Inc., 47
Drackett Professional Products, 12
Drägerwerk AG, 83
drugstore.com, inc., 109
Drypers Corporation, 18
Duane Reade Holdings Inc., 109 (upd.)
Dynatronics Corporation, 99
DynaVox, Inc., 116
Edwards Lifesciences LLC, 112
Elizabeth Arden, Inc., 8; 40 (upd.)
Elscint Ltd., 20

Emerging Vision, Inc., 115
Empi, Inc., 26
Enrich International, Inc., 33
Essie Cosmetics, Ltd., 102
Essilor International, 21
Estée Lauder Companies Inc., The, 9; 30 (upd.); 93 (upd.)
Ethicon, Inc., 23
Exactech, Inc., 101
E-Z-EM Inc., 89
Farnam Companies, Inc., 107
Farouk Systems Inc., 78
Forest Laboratories, Inc., 11
Forever Living Products International Inc., 17
FoxHollow Technologies, Inc., 85
Franz Haniel & Cie. GmbH, 109
French Fragrances, Inc., 22
G&K Holding S.A., 95
Gambro AB, 49
General Nutrition Companies, Inc., 11; 29 (upd.)
Genzyme Corporation, 13; 77 (upd.)
GF Health Products, Inc., 82
Gillette Company, The, III; 20 (upd.); 68 (upd.)
Given Imaging Ltd., 83
GN ReSound A/S, 103
GNC Corporation, 98 (upd.)
Golden Neo-Life Diamite International, Inc., 100
Goody Products, Inc., 12
Groupe Yves Saint Laurent, 23
Grupo Omnilife S.A. de C.V., 88
Guerlain, 23
Guest Supply, Inc., 18
Guidant Corporation, 58
Guinot Paris S.A., 82
Hanger Orthopedic Group, Inc., 41
Health O Meter Products Inc., 14
Helen of Troy Corporation, 18
Helene Curtis Industries, Inc., 8; 28 (upd.)
Henkel KGaA, III; 34 (upd.); 95 (upd.)
Henry Schein, Inc., 31; 70 (upd.)
Herbalife Ltd., 17; 41 (upd.); 92 (upd.)
Huntleigh Technology PLC, 77
ICON Health & Fitness, Inc., 38; 102 (upd.)
Immucor, Inc., 81
Inamed Corporation, 79
Integra LifeSciences Holdings Corporation, 87
Integrated BioPharma, Inc., 83
Inter Parfums Inc., 35; 86 (upd.)
Intuitive Surgical, Inc., 79
Invacare Corporation, 11; 47 (upd.)
Invivo Corporation, 52
IRIS International, Inc., 101
IVAX Corporation, 11
IVC Industries, Inc., 45
Jean Coutu Group (PJC) Inc., The, 46
John Frieda Professional Hair Care Inc., 70
John Paul Mitchell Systems, 24; 112 (upd.)
Johnson & Johnson, III; 8 (upd.); 36 (upd.); 75 (upd.)

Hotels

Information Technology

Insurance

Legal Services

Manufacturing

Materials

Mining & Metals

Nonprofit & Philanthropic Organizations

Paper & Forestry

Personal Services

Petroleum

Harcourt General, Inc., 20 (upd.)
Harlequin Enterprises Limited, 52
HarperCollins Publishers, 15
Harris Interactive Inc., 41; 92 (upd.)
Harry N. Abrams, Inc., 58
Harte-Hanks Communications, Inc., 17
Havas SA, 10; 33 (upd.)
Hay House, Inc., 93
Haynes Publishing Group P.L.C., 71
Hazelden Foundation, 28
Health Communications, Inc., 72
Hearst Corporation, The, IV; 19 (upd.);
  46 (upd.)
Heidelberger Druckmaschinen AG, 40
Her Majesty's Stationery Office, 7
Herald Media, Inc., 91
Highlights for Children, Inc., 95
Hollinger International Inc., 24; 62 (upd.)
Hoover's, Inc., 108
HOP, LLC, 80
Houghton Mifflin Company, 10; 36
  (upd.)
HuffingtonPost.com, Inc., 111
IDG Books Worldwide, Inc., 27
IHS Inc., 78
Independent News & Media PLC, 61
Informa Group plc, 58
Information Holdings Inc., 47
International Data Group, Inc., 7; 25
  (upd.)
IPC Magazines Limited, 7
J.J. Keller & Associates, Inc., 81
Jeppesen Sanderson, Inc., 92
John Fairfax Holdings Limited, 7
John H. Harland Company, 17
John Wiley & Sons, Inc., 17; 65 (upd.)
Johnson Publishing Company, Inc., 28;
  72 (upd.)
Johnston Press plc, 35
Jostens, Inc., 25 (upd.); 73 (upd.)
Journal Communications, Inc., 86
Journal Register Company, 29
Jupitermedia Corporation, 75
Kable Media Services, Inc., 115
Kaplan, Inc., 42
Kelley Blue Book Company, Inc., 84
Kensington Publishing Corporation, 84
Kinko's, Inc., 43 (upd.)
Knight Ridder, Inc., 67 (upd.)
Knight-Ridder, Inc., IV; 15 (upd.)
Kodansha Ltd., IV; 38 (upd.)
Koenig & Bauer AG, 64
Krause Publications, Inc., 35
Lagardère SCA, 112
Landmark Communications, Inc., 12; 55
  (upd.)
Larry Flynt Publishing Inc., 31
Le Monde S.A., 33
Lebhar-Friedman, Inc., 55
Lee Enterprises Inc., 11; 64 (upd.)
LEXIS-NEXIS Group, 33
Lonely Planet Publications Pty Ltd., 55
M. DuMont Schauberg GmbH & Co.
  KG, 92
M. Shanken Communications, Inc., 50
Maclean Hunter Publishing Limited, IV;
  26 (upd.)
Macmillan, Inc., 7

Martha Stewart Living Omnimedia, Inc.,
  24; 73 (upd.)
Marvel Entertainment Inc., 10; 78 (upd.)
Matra-Hachette S.A., 15 (upd.)
Maxwell Communication Corporation plc,
  IV; 7 (upd.)
McClatchy Company, The, 23; 92 (upd.)
The McGraw-Hill Companies, Inc., IV;
  18 (upd.); 51 (upd.); 115 (upd.)
McMurry, Inc., 105
Mecklermedia Corporation, 24
Media General, Inc., 38 (upd.)
MediaNews Group, Inc., 70
Menasha Corporation, 8; 59 (upd.)
Meredith Corporation, 11; 29 (upd.); 74
  (upd.)
Merriam-Webster Inc., 70
Merrill Corporation, 18; 47 (upd.)
Metro International S.A., 93
Miami Herald Media Company, 92
Miller Publishing Group, LLC, 57
Miner Group International, The, 22
Mirror Group Newspapers plc, 7; 23
  (upd.)
Moore Corporation Limited, IV
Morris Communications Corporation, 36
Mrs. Grossman's Paper Company Inc., 84
MTI Enterprises Inc., 102
Multimedia, Inc., 11
MYOB Ltd., 86
N.V. Holdingmaatschappij De Telegraaf,
  23
Nashua Corporation, 8
Naspers Ltd., 66
Nation Media Group, 116
National Audubon Society, 26
National Geographic Society, 9; 30 (upd.);
  79 (upd.)
National Journal Group Inc., 67
National Wildlife Federation, 103
New Chapter Inc., 96
New Times, Inc., 45
New York Daily News, 32
New York Times Company, The, IV; 19
  (upd.); 61 (upd.)
News America Publishing Inc., 12
News Communications, Inc., 103
News Corporation, IV; 7 (upd.); 109
  (upd.)
Newsday Media Group, 103
Newsquest plc, 32
Next Media Ltd., 61
Nielsen Business Media, Inc., 98
Nihon Keizai Shimbun, Inc., IV
Nolo.com, Inc., 49
Northern and Shell Network plc, 87
Oberthur Technologies S.A., 113
Oji Paper Co., Ltd., 57 (upd.)
Onion, Inc., 69
O'Reilly Media, Inc., 99
Ottaway Newspapers, Inc., 15
Outlook Group Corporation, 37
PagesJaunes Groupe SA, 79
Pantone Inc., 53
PCM Uitgevers NV, 53
Pearson plc, IV; 46 (upd.); 103 (upd.)
Penguin Group, The, 100
PennWell Corporation, 55

Penton Media, Inc., 27
Perseus Books Group, The, 91
Petersen Publishing Company, 21
Phaidon Press Ltd., 98
Philadelphia Media Holdings LLC, 92
Phoenix Media/Communications Group,
  The, 91
Plain Dealer Publishing Company, 92
Playboy Enterprises, Inc., 18
Pleasant Company, 27
PMP Ltd., 72
PR Newswire, 35
Presstek, Inc., 33
Primedia Inc., 22
Progressive Inc., The, 110
Providence Journal Company, The, 28
Publishers Group, Inc., 35
Publishing and Broadcasting Limited, 54
Pulitzer Inc., 15; 58 (upd.)
Quad/Graphics, Inc., 19
Quebecor Inc., 12; 47 (upd.)
R.L. Polk & Co., 10
R.R. Bowker LLC, 100
R.R. Donnelley & Sons Co., IV; 9 (upd.);
  38 (upd.); 113 (upd.)
Rand McNally & Company, 28
Random House Inc., 13; 31 (upd.); 106
  (upd.)
Ravensburger AG, 64
RCS MediaGroup S.p.A., 96
Reader's Digest Association, Inc., The, IV;
  17 (upd.); 71 (upd.)
Real Times, Inc., 66
Recycled Paper Greetings, Inc., 21
Reed Elsevier plc, IV; 17 (upd.); 31 (upd.)
Reuters Group PLC, IV; 22 (upd.); 63
  (upd.)
Rodale, Inc., 23; 47 (upd.)
Rogers Communications Inc., 30 (upd.)
Rowohlt Verlag GmbH, The, 96
Rural Press Ltd., 74
St Ives plc, 34
Salem Communications Corporation, 97
Sanborn Map Company Inc., 82
SanomaWSOY Corporation, 51
Schawk, Inc., 24
Schibsted ASA, 31
Scholastic Corporation, 10; 29 (upd.)
Schurz Communications, Inc., 98
Scott Fetzer Company, 12; 80 (upd.)
Scottish Media Group plc, 32
Seat Pagine Gialle S.p.A., 47
Seattle Times Company, 15
Sheridan Group, Inc., The, 86
Sierra Club, The, 28
Simon & Schuster Inc., IV; 19 (upd.);
  100 (upd.)
Singapore Press Holdings Limited, 85
Sir Speedy, Inc., 16
SkyMall, Inc., 26
Société du Figaro S.A., 60
Softbank Corp., 13
Source Enterprises, Inc., The, 65
Southam Inc., 7
Southern Progress Corporation, 102
SPIEGEL-Verlag Rudolf Augstein GmbH
  & Co. KG, 44

Retail & Wholesale

Rubber & Tires

Cooper Tire & Rubber Company, 8; 23
(upd.)
Day International, Inc., 84
Elementis plc, 40 (upd.)
General Tire, Inc., 8
Goodyear Tire & Rubber Company, The,
V; 20 (upd.); 75 (upd.)
Hankook Tire Company Ltd., 105
Kelly-Springfield Tire Company, The, 8
Kumho Tire Company Ltd., 105
Les Schwab Tire Centers, 50; 117 (upd.)
Myers Industries, Inc., 19; 96 (upd.)
Pirelli S.p.A., V; 15 (upd.)
Safeskin Corporation, 18
Sumitomo Rubber Industries, Ltd., V; 107
(upd.)
Tillotson Corp., 15
Treadco, Inc., 19
Trelleborg AB, 93
Ube Industries, Ltd., III; 38 (upd.)
Yokohama Rubber Company, Limited,
The, V; 19 (upd.); 91 (upd.)

Telecommunications

A.S. Eesti Mobiltelefon, 117
A.H. Belo Corporation, 30 (upd.)
Abertis Infraestructuras, S.A., 65
Abril S.A., 95
Acme-Cleveland Corp., 13
ADC Telecommunications, Inc., 10; 89
(upd.)
Adelphia Communications Corporation,
17; 52 (upd.)
Adtran Inc., 22
Advanced Fibre Communications, Inc., 63
AEI Music Network Inc., 35
AirTouch Communications, 11
Alaska Communications Systems Group,
Inc., 89
Albtelecom Sh. a, 111
Alcatel S.A., 36 (upd.)
Alcatel-Lucent, 109 (upd.)
Allbritton Communications Company,
105
Alliance Atlantis Communications Inc., 39
ALLTEL Corporation, 6; 46 (upd.)
América Móvil, S.A. de C.V., 80
American Tower Corporation, 33
Ameritech Corporation, V; 18 (upd.)
Amstrad plc, 48 (upd.)
AO VimpelCom, 48
AOL Time Warner Inc., 57 (upd.)
Arch Wireless, Inc., 39
ARD, 41
ARINC Inc., 98
ARRIS Group, Inc., 89
Ascent Media Corporation, 107
Ascom AG, 9
Aspect Telecommunications Corporation,
22
Asurion Corporation, 83
AT&T Bell Laboratories, Inc., 13
AT&T Corporation, V; 29 (upd.); 68
(upd.)
AT&T Wireless Services, Inc., 54 (upd.)
Avaya Inc., 104
Basin Electric Power Cooperative, 103
BCE Inc., V; 44 (upd.)

Beasley Broadcast Group, Inc., 51
Belgacom, 6
Bell Atlantic Corporation, V; 25 (upd.)
Bell Canada, 6
BellSouth Corporation, V; 29 (upd.)
Belo Corporation, 98 (upd.)
Bertelsmann A.G., IV; 15 (upd.); 43
(upd.); 91 (upd.)
BET Holdings, Inc., 18
Bharti Tele-Ventures Limited, 75
BHC Communications, Inc., 26
Blackfoot Telecommunications Group, 60
Bonneville International Corporation, 29
Bouygues S.A., I; 24 (upd.); 97 (upd.)
Brasil Telecom Participaçoes S.A., 57
Brightpoint Inc., 18; 106 (upd.)
Brite Voice Systems, Inc., 20
British Broadcasting Corporation Ltd., 7;
21 (upd.); 89 (upd.)
British Columbia Telephone Company, 6
British Telecommunications plc, V; 15
(upd.)
Broadwing Corporation, 70
BT Group plc, 49 (upd.); 114 (upd.)
Cable & Wireless HKT, 30 (upd.)
Cable and Wireless plc, V; 25 (upd.)
Cablevision Systems Corporation, 7; 30
(upd.); 109 (upd.)
CalAmp Corp., 87
Canadian Broadcasting Corporation
(CBC), The, 37
Canal Plus, 10; 34 (upd.)
CanWest Global Communications
Corporation, 35
Capital Radio plc, 35
Carlton Communications PLC, 15; 50
(upd.)
Carolina Telephone and Telegraph
Company, 10
Carphone Warehouse Group PLC, The,
83
Carrier Access Corporation, 44
CBS Corporation, 28 (upd.)
CBS Television Network, 66 (upd.)
C-COR.net Corp., 38
Centel Corporation, 6
Centennial Communications Corporation,
39
Central European Media Enterprises Ltd.,
61
Century Communications Corp., 10
Century Telephone Enterprises, Inc., 9; 54
(upd.)
Cesky Telecom, a.s., 64
Chancellor Media Corporation, 24
Channel Four Television Corporation, 93
Charter Communications, Inc., 33; 116
(upd.)
Chello Zone Ltd., 93
China Mobile Ltd., 108
China Netcom Group Corporation (Hong
Kong) Limited, 73
China Telecom, 50
Chris-Craft Corporation, 9, 31 (upd.); 80
(upd.)
Christian Broadcasting Network, Inc.,
The, 52
Chrysalis Group plc, 40

Chugach Alaska Corporation, 60
Chunghwa Telecom Co., Ltd., 101 (upd.)
CIENA Corporation, 54
Cincinnati Bell, Inc., 6; 105 (upd.)
Citadel Communications Corporation, 35
Citizens Communications Company, 79
(upd.)
Clear Channel Communications, Inc., 23;
116 (upd.)
Clearwire, Inc., 69
Cogent Communications Group, Inc., 55
COLT Telecom Group plc, 41
Comcast Corporation, 24 (upd.); 112
(upd.)
Comdial Corporation, 21
Commonwealth Telephone Enterprises,
Inc., 25
CommScope, Inc., 77
Comsat Corporation, 23
Comtech Telecommunications Corp., 75
Comverse Technology, Inc., 15; 43 (upd.)
Corning Inc., III; 44 (upd.); 90 (upd.)
Corporation for Public Broadcasting, 14;
89 (upd.)
Cox Radio, Inc., 89
Craftmade International, Inc., 44
Cumulus Media Inc., 37
DDI Corporation, 7
Deutsche Telekom AG, V; 48 (upd.); 108
(upd.)
Dialogic Corporation, 18
Digital Angel Corporation, 106
Directorate General of
Telecommunications, 7
DIRECTV, Inc., 38; 75 (upd.)
Discovery Communications, Inc., 42
DISH Network Corporation, 112
Dobson Communications Corporation, 63
DSC Communications Corporation, 12
EchoStar Corporation, 35; 112 (upd.)
ECI Telecom Ltd., 18
Egmont Group, 93
eircom plc, 31 (upd.)
Electric Lightwave, Inc., 37
Electromagnetic Sciences Inc., 21
EMBARQ Corporation, 83
Emmis Communications Corporation, 47
Empresas Públicas de Medellín S.A.E.S.P.,
91
Energis plc, 47
Entercom Communications Corporation,
58
Entravision Communications Corporation,
41
Equant N.V., 52
Eschelon Telecom, Inc., 72
ESPN, Inc., 56
Eternal Word Television Network, Inc., 57
Eutelsat S.A., 114
EXCEL Communications Inc., 18
Executone Information Systems, Inc., 13
Expand SA, 48
Facebook, Inc., 90
FASTWEB S.p.A., 83
Fisher Communications, Inc., 99
4Kids Entertainment Inc., 59
Fox Family Worldwide, Inc., 24

Textiles & Apparel

Red Wing Shoe Company, Inc., 9; 30
(upd.); 83 (upd.)
Reebok International Ltd., V; 9 (upd.); 26
(upd.)
Reliance Industries Ltd., 81
Renfro Corporation, 99
Rieter Holding AG, 42
Robert Talbott Inc., 88
Rocawear Apparel LLC, 77
Rocky Brands, Inc., 102 (upd.)
Rollerblade, Inc., 15; 34 (upd.)
Royal Ten Cate N.V., 68
rue21, Inc., 116
Russell Corporation, 8; 30 (upd.); 82
(upd.)
Rusty, Inc., 95
St. John Knits, Inc., 14
Salant Corporation, 12; 51 (upd.)
Salvatore Ferragamo Italia S.p.A., 62
Sao Paulo Alpargatas S.A., 75
Saucony Inc., 35; 86 (upd.)
Schott Brothers, Inc., 67
Sealy Corporation, 112 (upd.)
Seattle Pacific Industries, Inc., 92
Shaw Industries, Inc., 40 (upd.)
Shelby Williams Industries, Inc., 14
Shoe Pavilion, Inc., 84
Skechers U.S.A. Inc., 31; 88 (upd.)
skinnyCorp, LLC, 97
Sole Technology Inc., 93
Sophus Berendsen A/S, 49
Spanx, Inc., 89
Speizman Industries, Inc., 44
Springs Global US, Inc., V; 19 (upd.); 90
(upd.)
Starter Corp., 12
Stefanel SpA, 63
Steiner Corporation (Alsco), 53
Steven Madden, Ltd., 37
Stirling Group plc, 62
Stoddard International plc, 72
Stone Manufacturing Company, 14; 43
(upd.)
Stride Rite Corporation, 8; 37 (upd.); 86
(upd.)
Stussy, Inc., 55
Sun Sportswear, Inc., 17
Superior Uniform Group, Inc., 30
Swank, Inc., 17; 84 (upd.)
Tag-It Pacific, Inc., 85
Talbots, Inc., The, 11; 31 (upd.); 88
(upd.)
Tamfelt Oyj Abp, 62
Tarrant Apparel Group, 62
Ted Baker plc, 86
Teijin Limited, V
Thanulux Public Company Limited, 86
Thomaston Mills, Inc., 27
Tilley Endurables, Inc., 67
Timberland Company, The, 13; 54 (upd.);
111 (upd.)
Tommy Bahama Group, Inc., 108
Tommy Hilfiger Corporation, 20; 53
(upd.)
Too, Inc., 61
Toray Industries, Inc., V; 51 (upd.)
True Religion Apparel, Inc., 79
Truworths International Ltd., 107

Tultex Corporation, 13
Tumi, Inc., 112
Umbro plc, 88
Under Armour Performance Apparel, 61
Unifi, Inc., 12; 62 (upd.)
United Merchants & Manufacturers, Inc.,
13
United Retail Group Inc., 33
Unitika Ltd., V; 53 (upd.)
Van de Velde S.A./NV, 102
Vans, Inc., 16; 47 (upd.)
Varsity Spirit Corp., 15
VF Corporation, V; 17 (upd.); 54 (upd.)
Vicunha Têxtil S.A., 78
Volcom, Inc., 77
Vulcabras S.A., 103
Walton Monroe Mills, Inc., 8
Warnaco Group Inc., The, 12; 46 (upd.)
Wellco Enterprises, Inc., 84
Wellman, Inc., 8; 52 (upd.)
West Point-Pepperell, Inc., 8
WestPoint Stevens Inc., 16
Weyco Group, Incorporated, 32
Williamson-Dickie Manufacturing
Company, 14; 45 (upd.)
Wolverine World Wide, Inc., 16; 59
(upd.)
Woolrich Inc., 62
Zara International, Inc., 83

Tobacco

Altadis S.A., 72 (upd.)
Altria Group Inc., 109 (upd.)
American Brands, Inc., V
B.A.T. Industries PLC, 22 (upd.)
British American Tobacco PLC, 50 (upd.);
114 (upd.)
Brooke Group Ltd., 15
Brown & Williamson Tobacco
Corporation, 14; 33 (upd.)
Culbro Corporation, 15
Dibrell Brothers, Incorporated, 12
DIMON Inc., 27
800-JR Cigar, Inc., 27
Gallaher Group Plc, V; 19 (upd.); 49
(upd.)
General Cigar Holdings, Inc., 66 (upd.)
Holt's Cigar Holdings, Inc., 42
House of Prince A/S, 80
Imasco Limited, V
Imperial Tobacco Group PLC, 50
Japan Tobacco Inc., V; 46 (upd.)
KT&G Corporation, 62
Lorillard, Inc., 112
Nobleza Piccardo SAICF, 64
North Atlantic Trading Company Inc., 65
Philip Morris Companies Inc., V; 18
(upd.)
PT Gudang Garam Tbk, 103
R.J. Reynolds Tobacco Holdings, Inc., 30
(upd.)
RJR Nabisco Holdings Corp., V
Rothmans UK Holdings Limited, V; 19
(upd.)
Seita, 23
Souza Cruz S.A., 65
Standard Commercial Corporation, 13; 62
(upd.)

Swedish Match AB, 12; 39 (upd.); 92
(upd.)
Swisher International Group Inc., 23
Tabacalera, S.A., V; 17 (upd.)
Taiwan Tobacco & Liquor Corporation,
75
Universal Corporation, V; 48 (upd.)
UST Inc., 9; 50 (upd.)
Vector Group Ltd., 35 (upd.)

Transport Services

ABC Rail Products Corporation, 18
Abertis Infraestructuras, S.A., 65
Adams Express Company, The, 86
Aegean Marine Petroleum Network Inc.,
89
Aéroports de Paris, 33
Air Express International Corporation, 13
Air Partner PLC, 93
Air T, Inc., 86
Airborne Freight Corporation, 6; 34
(upd.)
Alamo Rent A Car, Inc., 6; 24 (upd.); 84
(upd.)
Alaska Railroad Corporation, 60
Alexander & Baldwin, Inc., 10, 40 (upd.)
Allied Worldwide, Inc., 49
AMCOL International Corporation, 59
(upd.)
AMERCO, 6; 67 (upd.)
American Classic Voyages Company, 27
American Commercial Lines Inc., 99
American President Companies Ltd., 6
Anderson Trucking Service, Inc., 75
Anschutz Corp., 12
APL Limited, 61 (upd.)
Aqua Alliance Inc., 32 (upd.)
Arlington Tankers Ltd., 101
Arriva PLC, 69
Atlas Van Lines Inc., 14; 106 (upd.)
Attica Enterprises S.A., 64
Austal Limited, 75
Avis Group Holdings, Inc., 75 (upd.)
Avis Rent A Car, Inc., 6; 22 (upd.)
Avondale Industries, 7; 41 (upd.)
BAA plc, 10
BAE Systems Ship Repair, 73
Bekins Company, 15
Belships ASA, 113
Bénéteau SA, 55
Berliner Verkehrsbetriebe (BVG), 58
Bollinger Shipyards, Inc., 61
Boyd Bros. Transportation Inc., 39
Brambles Industries Limited, 42
Brink's Company, The, 58 (upd.)
British Railways Board, V
Broken Hill Proprietary Company Ltd.,
22 (upd.)
Buckeye Partners, L.P., 70
Budget Group, Inc., 25
Budget Rent a Car Corporation, 9
Burlington Northern Santa Fe
Corporation, V; 27 (upd.); 111 (upd.)
C.H. Robinson Worldwide, Inc., 40
(upd.); 116 (upd.)
Canadian National Railway Company, 71
(upd.)
Canadian National Railway System, 6

Utilities

Waste Services

Geographic Index

France

Baltimore Technologies Plc, 42
Bank of Ireland, 50
Cahill May Roberts Group Ltd., 112
CRH plc, 64
CryptoLogic Limited, 106
DCC plc, 115
DEPFA BANK PLC, 69
Dunnes Stores Ltd., 58
eircom plc, 31 (upd.)
Elan Corporation PLC, 63
Fyffes PLC, 38; 106 (upd.)
Glanbia plc, 59
Glen Dimplex, 78
Grafton Group plc, 104
Greencore Group plc, 98
Harland and Wolff Holdings plc, 19
IAWS Group plc, 49
Independent News & Media PLC, 61
Ingersoll-Rand PLC, 115 (upd.)
IONA Technologies plc, 43
Irish Distillers Group, 96
Irish Food Processors Ltd., 111
Irish Life & Permanent Plc, 59
Jefferson Smurfit Group plc, IV; 19
  (upd.); 49 (upd.)
Jurys Doyle Hotel Group plc, 64
Kerry Group plc, 27; 87 (upd.)
Musgrave Group Plc, 57
Paddy Power plc, 98
Ryanair Holdings plc, 35
Shannon Aerospace Ltd., 36
Shire PLC, 109
SkillSoft Public Limited Company, 81
Smurfit Kappa Group plc, 112 (upd.)
Stafford Group, 110
Telecom Eireann, 7
Thomas Crosbie Holdings Limited, 81
Waterford Wedgwood plc, 34 (upd.)
WPP Group plc, 112 (upd.)

Israel

Aladdin Knowledge Systems Ltd., 101
Alon Israel Oil Company Ltd., 104
Amdocs Ltd., 47
Bank Hapoalim B.M., II; 54 (upd.)
Bank Leumi le-Israel B.M., 60
Blue Square Israel Ltd., 41
BVR Systems (1998) Ltd., 93
Castro Model Ltd., 86
ECI Telecom Ltd., 18
EL AL Israel Airlines Ltd., 23; 107 (upd.)
Elscint Ltd., 20
Emblaze Ltd., 117
EZchip Semiconductor Ltd., 106
Galtronics Ltd., 100
Given Imaging Ltd., 83
IDB Holding Corporation Ltd., 97
Israel Aircraft Industries Ltd., 69
Israel Chemicals Ltd., 55
Israel Corporation Ltd., 108
Koor Industries Ltd., II; 25 (upd.); 68
  (upd.)
Lipman Electronic Engineering Ltd., 81
Makhteshim-Agan Industries Ltd., 85
NICE Systems Ltd., 83
Orbotech Ltd., 75
Scitex Corporation Ltd., 24
Strauss-Elite Group, 68

Syneron Medical Ltd., 91
Taro Pharmaceutical Industries Ltd., 65
Teva Pharmaceutical Industries Ltd., 22;
  54 (upd.); 112 (upd.)
Tnuva Food Industries Ltd., 111

Italy

ACEA S.p.A., 115
AgustaWestland N.V., 75
Alfa Romeo, 13; 36 (upd.)
Alitalia—Linee Aeree Italiana, S.p.A., 6;
  29 (upd.); 97 (upd.)
Alleanza Assicurazioni S.p.A., 65
Angelini SpA, 100
Aprilia SpA, 17
Arnoldo Mondadori Editore S.p.A., IV;
  19 (upd.); 54 (upd.)
Artsana SpA, 92
Assicurazioni Generali S.p.A., III; 15
  (upd.); 103 (upd.)
Autogrill SpA, 49
Automobili Lamborghini Holding S.p.A.,
  13; 34 (upd.); 91 (upd.)
Autostrada Torino-Milano S.p.A., 101
Azelis Group, 100
Banca Commerciale Italiana SpA, II
Banca Fideuram SpA, 63
Banca Intesa SpA, 65
Banca Monte dei Paschi di Siena SpA, 65
Banca Nazionale del Lavoro SpA, 72
Barilla G. e R. Fratelli S.p.A., 17; 50
  (upd.)
Benetton Group S.p.A., 10; 67 (upd.)
Brioni Roman Style S.p.A., 67
Bulgari S.p.A., 20; 106 (upd.)
Cantine Giorgio Lungarotti S.R.L., 67
Capitalia S.p.A., 65
Cinemeccanica SpA
Compagnia Italiana dei Jolly Hotels
  S.p.A., 71
Credito Italiano, II
Cremonini S.p.A., 57
Davide Campari-Milano S.p.A., 57
De Agostini Editore S.p.A., 103
De Rigo S.p.A., 104
De'Longhi S.p.A., 66
Diadora SpA, 86
Diesel SpA, 40
Dolce & Gabbana SpA, 62
Ducati Motor Holding SpA, 30; 86 (upd.)
Enel S.p.A., 108 (upd.)
ENI S.p.A., 69 (upd.)
Ente Nazionale Idrocarburi, IV
Ente Nazionale per L'Energia Elettrica, V
Ermenegildo Zegna SpA, 63
Fabbrica D' Armi Pietro Beretta S.p.A., 39
FASTWEB, 83
Ferrari S.p.A., 13; 36 (upd.)
Ferrero SpA, 54
Ferretti Group SpA, 90
Ferrovie Dello Stato Societa Di Trasporti e
  Servizi S.p.A., 105
Fiat SpA, I; 11 (upd.); 50 (upd.)
Fila Holding S.p.A., 20; 52 (upd.)
Finarte Casa d'Aste S.p.A., 93
Finmeccanica S.p.A., 84
Gianni Versace S.p.A., 22; 106 (upd.)
Giorgio Armani S.p.A., 45

Gruppo Coin S.p.A., 41
Gruppo Italiano Vini, 111
Gruppo Riva Fire SpA, 88
Guccio Gucci, S.p.A., 15
I Grandi Viaggi S.p.A., 105
illycaffè S.p.A., 50; 110 (upd.)
Industrie Natuzzi S.p.A., 18
Industrie Zignago Santa Margherita
  S.p.A., 67
Ing. C. Olivetti & C., S.p.a., III
Istituto per la Ricostruzione Industriale
  S.p.A., I; 11
Juventus F.C. S.p.A., 53
La Doria S.p.A., 101
Luxottica SpA, 17; 52 (upd.)
Magneti Marelli Holding SpA, 90
Marchesi Antinori SRL, 42
Marcolin S.p.A., 61
Mariella Burani Fashion Group, 92
Martini & Rossi SpA, 63
Marzotto S.p.A., 20; 67 (upd.)
Mediaset SpA, 50
Mediolanum S.p.A., 65
Milan AC, S.p.A. 79
Miroglio SpA, 86
Montedison SpA, I; 24 (upd.)
Officine Alfieri Maserati S.p.A., 13
Olivetti S.p.A., 34 (upd.)
Pagnossin S.p.A., 73
Parmalat Finanziaria SpA, 50
Peg Perego SpA, 88
Perfetti Van Melle S.p.A., 72
Piaggio & C. S.p.A., 20; 100 (upd.)
Pirelli & C. S.p.A., 75 (upd.)
Pirelli S.p.A., V; 15 (upd.)
Poste Italiane S.p.A., 108
RCS MediaGroup S.p.A., 96
Recordati Industria Chimica e
  Farmaceutica S.p.A., 105
Reno de Medici S.p.A., 41
Rinascente S.p.A., 71
Riunione Adriatica di Sicurtè SpA, III
Safilo SpA, 54
Salvatore Ferragamo Italia S.p.A., 62
Sanpaolo IMI S.p.A., 50
Seat Pagine Gialle S.p.A., 47
Sirti S.p.A., 76
Società Finanziaria Telefonica per Azioni,
  V
Società Sportiva Lazio SpA, 44
Stefanel SpA, 63
Targetti Sankey SpA, 86
Telecom Italia Mobile S.p.A., 63
Telecom Italia S.p.A., 43
Tiscali SpA, 48
UniCredit S.p.A., 108 (upd.)

Jamaica
Air Jamaica Limited, 54
Desnoes and Geddes Limited 79
GraceKennedy Ltd., 92
Wray & Nephew Group Ltd., 98

Japan
AEON Co., Ltd., 68 (upd.)
Aisin Seiki Co., Ltd., III; 48 (upd.)
Aiwa Co., Ltd., 30
Ajinomoto Co., Inc., II; 28 (upd.); 108
  (upd.)

Mitsubishi Electric Corporation, II; 44 (upd.); 117 (upd.)

Mitsubishi Estate Company, Limited, IV; 61 (upd.)

Mitsubishi Heavy Industries, Ltd., III; 7 (upd.); 40 (upd.)

Mitsubishi Materials Corporation, III

Mitsubishi Motors Corporation, 9; 23 (upd.); 57 (upd.)

Mitsubishi Oil Co., Ltd., IV

Mitsubishi Rayon Co., Ltd., V

Mitsubishi Trust & Banking Corporation, The, II

Mitsubishi UFJ Financial Group, Inc., 99 (upd.)

Mitsui & Co., Ltd., I; 28 (upd.); 110 (upd.)

Mitsui Bank, Ltd., The, II

Mitsui Marine and Fire Insurance Company, Limited, III

Mitsui Mining & Smelting Company, Ltd., IV; 102 (upd.)

Mitsui Mining Company, Limited, IV

Mitsui Mutual Life Insurance Company, III; 39 (upd.)

Mitsui O.S.K. Lines, Ltd., V; 96 (upd.)

Mitsui Petrochemical Industries, Ltd., 9

Mitsui Real Estate Development Co., Ltd., IV

Mitsui Trust & Banking Company, Ltd., The, II

Mitsukoshi Ltd., V; 56 (upd.)

Mizuho Financial Group Inc., 58 (upd.)

Mizuno Corporation, 25

Morinaga & Co. Ltd., 61

Nagasakiya Co., Ltd., V; 69 (upd.)

Nagase & Co., Ltd., 8; 61 (upd.)

Namco Bandai Holdings Inc., 106 (upd.)

NEC Corporation, II; 21 (upd.); 57 (upd.)

NGK Insulators Ltd., 67

NHK, III; 115 (upd.)

Nichii Co., Ltd., V

Nichimen Corporation, IV; 24 (upd.)

Nichirei Corporation, 70

Nichiro Corporation, 86

Nidec Corporation, 59

Nihon Keizai Shimbun, Inc., IV

Nikko Securities Company Limited, The, II; 9 (upd.)

Nikon Corporation, III; 48 (upd.)

Nintendo Co., Ltd., III; 7 (upd.); 28 (upd.); 67 (upd.)

Nippon Credit Bank, II

Nippon Electric Glass Co. Ltd., 95

Nippon Express Company, Ltd., V; 64 (upd.)

Nippon Life Insurance Company, III; 60 (upd.)

Nippon Light Metal Company, Ltd., IV

Nippon Meat Packers Inc., II; 78 (upd.)

Nippon Mining Holdings Inc., 102 (upd.)

Nippon Oil Corporation, IV; 63 (upd.)

Nippon Paint Company Ltd., 115

Nippon Seiko K.K., III

Nippon Sheet Glass Company, Limited, III

Nippon Shinpan Co., Ltd., II; 61 (upd.)

Nippon Soda Co., Ltd., 85

Nippon Steel Corporation, IV; 17 (upd.); 96 (upd.)

Nippon Suisan Kaisha, Ltd., II; 92 (upd.)

Nippon Telegraph and Telephone Corporation, V; 51 (upd.); 117 (upd.)

Nippon Yusen Kabushiki Kaisha (NYK), V; 72 (upd.)

Nippondenso Co., Ltd., III

Nissan Motor Company Ltd., I; 11 (upd.); 34 (upd.); 92 (upd.)

Nisshin Seifun Group Inc., II; 66 (upd.)

Nisshin Steel Co., Ltd., IV

Nissho Iwai K.K., I

Nissin Food Products Company Ltd., 75

NKK Corporation, IV; 28 (upd.)

NOF Corporation, 72

Nomura Securities Company, Limited, II; 9 (upd.)

Norinchukin Bank, II

NTN Corporation, III; 47 (upd.)

Obayashi Corporation, 78

Odakyu Electric Railway Co., Ltd., V; 68 (upd.)

Ohbayashi Corporation, I

Oji Paper Co., Ltd., IV; 57 (upd.)

Oki Electric Industry Company, Limited, II

Okuma Holdings Inc., 74

Okura & Co., Ltd., IV

Olympus Corporation, 106

Omron Corporation, II; 28 (upd.); 115 (upd.)

Onoda Cement Co., Ltd., III

Onoken Company Ltd., 110

ORIX Corporation, II; 44 (upd.); 104 (upd.)

Osaka Gas Company, Ltd., V; 60 (upd.)

Otari Inc., 89

Paloma Industries Ltd., 71

Pearl Corporation, 78

Pentax Corporation, 78

Pioneer Electronic Corporation, III; 28 (upd.)

Rengo Co., Ltd., IV

Ricoh Company, Ltd., III; 36 (upd.); 108 (upd.)

Roland Corporation, 38

Ryoshoku Ltd., 72

Sankyo Company, Ltd., I; 56 (upd.)

Sanrio Company, Ltd., 38; 104 (upd.)

Sanwa Bank, Ltd., The, II; 15 (upd.)

SANYO Electric Co., Ltd., II; 36 (upd.); 95 (upd.)

Sanyo-Kokusaku Pulp Co., Ltd., IV

Sapporo Holdings Limited, I; 13 (upd.); 36 (upd.); 97 (upd.)

SEGA Corporation, 73

Seibu Department Stores, Ltd., V; 42 (upd.)

Seibu Railway Company Ltd., V; 74 (upd.)

Seiko Corporation, III; 17 (upd.); 72 (upd.)

Seino Transportation Company, Ltd., 6

Seiyu, Ltd., The, V; 36 (upd.)

Sekisui Chemical Co., Ltd., III; 72 (upd.)

Sharp Corporation, II; 12 (upd.); 40 (upd.); 114 (upd.)

Shikoku Electric Power Company, Inc., V; 60 (upd.)

Shimano Inc., 64

Shimizu Corporation, 109

Shionogi & Co., Ltd., III; 17 (upd.); 98 (upd.)

Shiseido Company, Limited, III; 22 (upd.), 81 (upd.)

Shochiku Company Ltd., 74

Showa Shell Sekiyu K.K., IV; 59 (upd.)

Snow Brand Milk Products Company, Ltd., II; 48 (upd.)

Softbank Corp., 13; 38 (upd.)

Sojitz Corporation, 96 (upd.)

Sompo Japan Insurance, Inc., 98 (upd.)

Sony Corporation, II; 12 (upd.); 40 (upd.); 108 (upd.)

Square Enix Holdings Co., Ltd., 101

Sumitomo Bank, Limited, The, II; 26 (upd.)

Sumitomo Chemical Company Ltd., I; 98 (upd.)

Sumitomo Corporation, I; 11 (upd.); 102 (upd.)

Sumitomo Electric Industries, Ltd., II

Sumitomo Heavy Industries, Ltd., III; 42 (upd.)

Sumitomo Life Insurance Company, III; 60 (upd.)

Sumitomo Marine and Fire Insurance Company, Limited, The, III

Sumitomo Metal Industries Ltd., IV; 82 (upd.)

Sumitomo Metal Mining Co., Ltd., IV

Sumitomo Mitsui Banking Corporation, 51 (upd.)

Sumitomo Realty & Development Co., Ltd., IV

Sumitomo Rubber Industries, Ltd., V; 107 (upd.)

Sumitomo Trust & Banking Company, Ltd., The, II; 53 (upd.)

Suntory Ltd., 65

Suzuki Motor Corporation, 9; 23 (upd.); 59 (upd.)

T&D Holdings Inc., 114

Taiheiyo Cement Corporation, 60 (upd.)

Taiyo Fishery Company, Limited, II

Taiyo Kobe Bank, Ltd., The, II

Takara Holdings Inc., 62

Takashimaya Company, Limited, V; 47 (upd.)

Takeda Pharmaceutical Company Limited, I; 46 (upd.); 115 (upd.)

Tamron Company Ltd., 82

TDK Corporation, II; 17 (upd.); 49 (upd.); 114 (upd.)

TEAC Corporation, 78

Tecmo Koei Holdings Company Ltd., 106

Teijin Limited, V; 61 (upd.)

Terumo Corporation, 48

Tobu Railway Company Ltd., 6; 98 (upd.)

Tohan Corporation, 84

Toho Co., Ltd., 28

Tohoku Electric Power Company, Inc., V

United States

AAF-McQuay Incorporated, 26
AAON, Inc., 22
AAR Corp., 28
Aaron Rents, Inc., 14; 35 (upd.)
Aaron's, Inc., 114 (upd.)
AARP, 27
Aavid Thermal Technologies, Inc., 29
ABARTA, Inc., 100
Abatix Corp., 57
Abaxis, Inc., 83
Abbott Laboratories, I; 11 (upd.); 40
   (upd.); 93 (upd.)
ABC Appliance, Inc., 10
ABC Carpet & Home Co. Inc., 26
ABC Family Worldwide, Inc., 52
ABC Rail Products Corporation, 18
ABC Supply Co., Inc., 22
Abercrombie & Fitch Company, 15; 35
   (upd.); 75 (upd.)
Abigail Adams National Bancorp, Inc., 23
Abiomed, Inc., 47
ABM Industries Incorporated, 25 (upd.)
ABP Corporation, 108
Abrams Industries Inc., 23
Abraxas Petroleum Corporation, 89
Abt Associates Inc., 95
Academy of Television Arts & Sciences,
   Inc., 55
Academy Sports & Outdoors, 27
Acadia Realty Trust, 106
Acadian Ambulance & Air Med Services,
   Inc., 39
Access to Money, Inc., 108 (upd.)
ACCION International, 87
Acclaim Entertainment Inc., 24
ACCO World Corporation, 7; 51 (upd.)
Accredited Home Lenders Holding Co.,
   91
Accubuilt, Inc., 74
Accuray Incorporated, 95
AccuWeather, Inc., 73
ACE Cash Express, Inc., 33
Ace Hardware Corporation, 12; 35 (upd.)
Aceto Corp., 38
AchieveGlobal Inc., 90
Ackerley Communications, Inc., 9
Acme United Corporation, 70
Acme-Cleveland Corp., 13
ACNielsen Corporation, 13; 38 (upd.)
Acorn Products, Inc., 55
Acosta Sales and Marketing Company,
   Inc., 77
Acsys, Inc., 44
ACT, Inc., 114
Action Performance Companies, Inc., 27
Activision, Inc., 32; 89 (upd.)
Actuant Corporation, 94 (upd.)
Acuity Brands, Inc., 90
Acushnet Company, 64
Acuson Corporation, 10; 36 (upd.)
Acxiom Corporation, 35
Adams Express Company, The, 86
Adams Golf, Inc., 37
Adaptec, Inc., 31
ADC Telecommunications, Inc., 10; 30
   (upd.); 89 (upd.)
A-dec, Inc., 53
Adelman Travel Group, 105

Adelphia Communications Corporation,
   17; 52 (upd.)
ADESA, Inc., 71
Administaff, Inc., 52
Adobe Systems Inc., 10; 33 (upd.); 106
   (upd.)
Adolor Corporation, 101
Adolph Coors Company, I; 13 (upd.); 36
   (upd.)
ADT Security Services, Inc., 12; 44 (upd.)
Adtran Inc., 22
Advance Auto Parts, Inc., 57
Advance Publications Inc., IV; 19 (upd.);
   96 (upd.)
Advanced Circuits Inc., 67
Advanced Fibre Communications, Inc., 63
Advanced Marketing Services, Inc., 34
Advanced Medical Optics, Inc. 79
Advanced Micro Devices, Inc., 6; 30
   (upd.); 99 (upd.)
Advanced Neuromodulation Systems, Inc.,
   73
Advanced Technology Laboratories, Inc., 9
Advanstar Communications, Inc., 57
Advanta Corporation, 8; 38 (upd.)
Advantica Restaurant Group, Inc., 27
   (upd.)
Adventist Health, 53
Advertising Council, Inc., The, 76
Advisory Board Company, The, 80
Advo, Inc., 6; 53 (upd.)
Advocat Inc., 46
AECOM Technology Corporation 79
AEI Music Network Inc., 35
AEP Industries, Inc., 36
AeroGrow International, Inc., 95
Aerojet-General Corp., 63
Aeronca Inc., 46
Aeroquip Corporation, 16
Aerosonic Corporation, 69
AeroVironment, Inc., 97
AES Corporation, The, 10; 13 (upd.); 53
   (upd.)
Aetna Inc., III; 21 (upd.); 63 (upd.)
AFC Enterprises, Inc., 32; 83 (upd.)
Affiliated Computer Services, Inc., 61
Affiliated Foods Inc., 53
Affiliated Managers Group, Inc. 79
Affiliated Publications, Inc., 7
Affinity Group Holding Inc., 56
Affymetrix Inc., 106
Aflac Incorporated, 10 (upd.); 38 (upd.);
   109 (upd)
Africare, 59
After Hours Formalwear Inc., 60
Aftermarket Technology Corp., 83
Ag Services of America, Inc., 59
Ag-Chem Equipment Company, Inc., 17
AGCO Corporation, 13; 67 (upd.)
Agere Systems Inc., 61
Agilent Technologies Inc., 38; 93 (upd.)
Agilysys Inc., 76 (upd.)
AGL Resources Inc., 116
Agland, Inc., 110
Agri Beef Company, 81
Agway, Inc., 7; 21 (upd.)
AHL Services, Inc., 27
Air & Water Technologies Corporation, 6

Air Express International Corporation, 13
Air Methods Corporation, 53
Air Products and Chemicals, Inc., I; 10
   (upd.); 74 (upd.)
Air T, Inc., 86
Air Wisconsin Airlines Corporation, 55
Airborne Freight Corporation, 6; 34
   (upd.)
Airborne Systems Group, 89
Airgas, Inc., 54
AirTouch Communications, 11
AirTran Holdings, Inc., 22
AK Steel Holding Corporation, 19; 41
   (upd.)
Akamai Technologies, Inc., 71
Akeena Solar, Inc., 103
Akin, Gump, Strauss, Hauer & Feld,
   L.L.P., 33
Akorn, Inc., 32
Alabama Farmers Cooperative, Inc., 63
Alabama National BanCorporation, 75
Alamo Group Inc., 32
Alamo Rent A Car, 6; 24 (upd.); 84
   (upd.)
ALARIS Medical Systems, Inc., 65
Alaska Air Group, Inc., 6; 29 (upd.)
Alaska Communications Systems Group,
   Inc., 89
Alaska Railroad Corporation, 60
Albany International Corporation, 8; 51
   (upd.)
Albany Molecular Research, Inc., 77
Albaugh, Inc., 105
Alba-Waldensian, Inc., 30
Albemarle Corporation, 59
Alberici Corporation, 76
Albert Trostel and Sons Company, 113
Albert's Organics, Inc., 110
Alberto-Culver Company, 8; 36 (upd.); 91
   (upd.)
Albertson's, Inc., II; 7 (upd.); 30 (upd.);
   65 (upd.)
Alco Health Services Corporation, III
Alco Standard Corporation, I
Alcoa Inc., 56 (upd.)
Aldila Inc., 46
Aldus Corporation, 10
Ale-8-One Company Bottling Company,
   Inc., 117
Aleris International, Inc., 110
Alex Lee Inc., 18; 44 (upd.)
Alexander & Alexander Services Inc., 10
Alexander & Baldwin, Inc., 10; 40 (upd.)
Alexander's, Inc., 45
Alexandria Real Estate Equities, Inc., 101
Alfa Corporation, 60
Alico, Inc., 63
Alienware Corporation, 81
Align Technology, Inc., 94
All American Communications Inc., 20
Allbritton Communications Company,
   105
Alleghany Corporation, 10; 60 (upd.)
Allegheny Energy, Inc., 38 (upd.)
Allegheny Ludlum Corporation, 8
Allegheny Power System, Inc., V
Allegheny Technologies Incorporated, 112
   (upd.)

Brother's Brother Foundation, 93
Brothers Gourmet Coffees, Inc., 20
Broughton Foods Co., 17
Brown & Brown, Inc., 41
Brown & Haley, 23
Brown & Root, Inc., 13
Brown & Sharpe Manufacturing Co., 23
Brown & Williamson Tobacco
 Corporation, 14; 33 (upd.)
Brown Brothers Harriman & Co., 45
Brown Jordan International Inc., 74
 (upd.)
Brown Printing Company, 26
Brown Shoe Company, Inc., V; 20 (upd.);
 68 (upd.)
Brown-Forman Corporation, I; 10 (upd.);
 38 (upd.); 114 (upd.)
Browning-Ferris Industries, Inc., V; 20
 (upd.)
Broyhill Furniture Industries, Inc., 10
Bruce Foods Corporation, 39
Bruce Oakley, Inc., 107
Bruegger's Corporation, 63
Bruker Corporation, 113
Bruno's Supermarkets, Inc., 7; 26 (upd.);
 68 (upd.)
Brunschwig & Fils Inc., 96
Brunswick Corporation, III; 22 (upd.); 77
 (upd.)
Brush Engineered Materials Inc., 67
Brush Wellman Inc., 14
Bruster's Real Ice Cream, Inc., 80
Bryce Corporation, 100
BTG, Inc., 45
Bubba Gump Shrimp Co. Restaurants,
 Inc., 108
Buca, Inc., 38
Buck Consultants, Inc., 55
Buck Knives Inc., 48
Buckeye Partners, L.P., 70
Buckeye Technologies, Inc., 42
Buckhead Life Restaurant Group, Inc.,
 100
Buckle, Inc., The, 18; 115 (upd.)
Bucyrus International, Inc., 17; 103
 (upd.)
Budd Company, The, 8
Budget Group, Inc., 25
Budget Rent a Car Corporation, 9
Buffalo Wild Wings, Inc., 56
Buffets Holdings, Inc., 10; 32 (upd.); 93
 (upd.)
Bugle Boy Industries, Inc., 18
Build-A-Bear Workshop Inc., 62
Building Materials Holding Corporation,
 52
Bulley & Andrews, LLC, 55
Bulova Corporation, 13; 41 (upd.)
Bumble Bee Seafoods L.L.C., 64
Bundy Corporation, 17
Bunge Ltd., 62
Burdines, Inc., 60
Bureau of National Affairs, Inc., The, 23
Burger King Corporation, II; 17 (upd.);
 56 (upd.); 115 (upd.)
Burgett, Inc., 97
Burke Mills, Inc., 66
Burke, Inc., 88

Burlington Coat Factory Warehouse
 Corporation, 10; 60 (upd.)
Burlington Industries, Inc., V; 17 (upd.)
Burlington Northern Santa Fe
 Corporation, V; 27 (upd.); 111 (upd.)
Burlington Resources Inc., 10
Burns International Services Corporation,
 13; 41 (upd.)
Burr-Brown Corporation, 19
Burroughs & Chapin Company, Inc., 86
Burt's Bees, Inc., 58
Burton Corporation, The, 22; 94 (upd.)
Busch Entertainment Corporation, 73
Bush Boake Allen Inc., 30
Bush Brothers & Company, 45
Bush Industries, Inc., 20
Business Men's Assurance Company of
 America, 14
Butler Manufacturing Company, 12; 62
 (upd.)
Butterick Co., Inc., 23
Buttrey Food & Drug Stores Co., 18
buy.com, Inc., 46
BWAY Corporation, 24
C & S Wholesale Grocers, Inc., 55
C&K Market, Inc., 81
C.F. Martin & Co., Inc., 42
C.F. Sauer Company, The, 90
C.H. Guenther & Son, Inc., 84
C.H. Heist Corporation, 24
C.H. Robinson Worldwide, Inc., 11; 40
 (upd.); 116 (upd.)
C.O. Bigelow Chemists, Inc., 114
C.R. Bard, Inc., 9; 65 (upd.)
C.R. Meyer and Sons Company, 74
CA Inc., 116
Cabela's Inc., 26; 68 (upd.)
Cabletron Systems, Inc., 10
Cablevision Electronic Instruments, Inc.,
 32
Cablevision Systems Corporation, 7; 30
 (upd.); 109 (upd.)
Cabot Corporation, 8; 29 (upd.); 91
 (upd.)
Cabot Creamery Cooperative, Inc., 102
Cache Incorporated, 30
CACI International Inc., 21; 72 (upd.)
Cactus Feeders, Inc., 91
Cadence Design Systems, Inc., 11; 48
 (upd.)
Cadence Financial Corporation, 106
Cadmus Communications Corporation,
 23
Cadwalader, Wickersham & Taft, 32
CAE USA Inc., 48
Caere Corporation, 20
Caesars World, Inc., 6
Cagle's, Inc., 20
Cahners Business Information, 43
CalAmp Corp., 87
Calavo Growers, Inc., 47
CalComp Inc., 13
Calcot Ltd., 33
Caldor Inc., 12
Calgon Carbon Corporation, 73
California Cedar Products Company, 58
California Dairies Inc., 111

California Pizza Kitchen Inc., 15; 74
 (upd.)
California Sports, Inc., 56
California Steel Industries, Inc., 67
California Water Service Group 79
Caliper Life Sciences, Inc., 70
Callanan Industries, Inc., 60
Callard and Bowser-Suchard Inc., 84
Callaway Golf Company, 15; 45 (upd.);
 112 (upd.)
Callon Petroleum Company, 47
Calloway's Nursery, Inc., 51
Cal-Maine Foods, Inc., 69
CalMat Co., 19
Calpine Corporation, 36; 113 (upd.)
Caltex Petroleum Corporation, 19
Calumet Specialty Products Partners, L.P.,
 106
Calvin Klein, Inc., 22; 55 (upd.)
CAMAC International Corporation, 106
Cambrex Corporation, 16; 44 (upd.)
Cambridge SoundWorks, Inc., 48
Cambridge Technology Partners, Inc., 36
Camden Property Trust, 77
Camelot Music, Inc., 26
Cameron & Barkley Company, 28
Cameron Hughes Wine, 103
Cameron International Corporation, 110
Camp Dresser & McKee Inc., 104
Campagna-Turano Bakery, Inc., 99
Campbell Hausfeld, 115
Campbell Scientific, Inc., 51
Campbell Soup Company, II; 7 (upd.); 26
 (upd.); 71 (upd.)
Campbell-Ewald Advertising, 86
Campbell-Mithun-Esty, Inc., 16
Campmor, Inc., 104
Campo Electronics, Appliances &
 Computers, Inc., 16
Canandaigua Brands, Inc., 13; 34 (upd.)
Cancer Treatment Centers of America,
 Inc., 85
Candela Corporation, 48
Candie's, Inc., 31
Candle Corporation, 64
Candlewood Hotel Company, Inc., 41
Cannon Design, 63
Cannon Express, Inc., 53
Cannondale Corporation, 21
Cano Petroleum Inc., 97
Cantel Medical Corporation, 80
Canterbury Park Holding Corporation, 42
Cantor Fitzgerald, L.P., 92
Cap Rock Energy Corporation, 46
Capario, 104
Cape Cod Potato Chip Company, 90
Capel Incorporated, 45
Capella Education Company, 109
Capezio/Ballet Makers Inc., 62
Capital Cities/ABC Inc., II
Capital City Bank Group, Inc., 105
Capital Group Companies, Inc., 115
Capital Holding Corporation, III
Capital One Financial Corporation, 52
Capital Senior Living Corporation, 75
Capitol Records, Inc., 90
CapStar Hotel Company, 21
Capstone Turbine Corporation, 75

Corbis Corporation, 31

Corcoran Group, Inc., The, 58

Cordis Corporation, 19; 46 (upd.); 112 (upd.)

CoreStates Financial Corp, 17

Corinthian Colleges, Inc., 39; 92 (upd.)

Corky McMillin Companies, The, 98

Corn Products International, Inc., 116

Cornell Companies, Inc., 112

Corning Inc., III; 44 (upd.); 90 (upd.)

Corporate Executive Board Company, The, 89

Corporate Express, Inc., 22; 47 (upd.)

Corporate Software Inc., 9

Corporation for Public Broadcasting, 14; 89 (upd.)

Correctional Services Corporation, 30

Corrections Corporation of America, 23

Corrpro Companies, Inc., 20

CORT Business Services Corporation, 26

Corus Bankshares, Inc., 75

Cosi, Inc., 53

Cosmair, Inc., 8

Cosmetic Center, Inc., The, 22

Cosmolab Inc., 96

Cost Plus, Inc., 27; 107 (upd.)

CoStar Group, Inc., 73

Costco Wholesale Corporation, V; 43 (upd.); 105 (upd.)

Cost-U-Less, Inc., 51

Cotter & Company, V

Cotton Incorporated, 46

Coty Inc., 36; 115 (upd.)

Coudert Brothers, 30

Council on International Educational Exchange Inc., 81

Country Kitchen International, Inc., 76

Countrywide Financial, 16; 100 (upd.)

County Seat Stores Inc., 9

Courier Corporation, 41

Cousins Properties Incorporated, 65

Covance Inc., 30; 98 (upd.)

Covanta Energy Corporation, 64 (upd.)

Coventry Health Care, Inc., 59

Covington & Burling, 40

Cowen Group, Inc., 92

Cowles Media Company, 23

Cox Enterprises, Inc., IV; 22 (upd.); 67 (upd.)

Cox Radio, Inc., 89

CPAC, Inc., 86

CPC International Inc., II

CPI Aerostructures, Inc., 75

CPI Corp., 38

CPP International, LLC, 103

CR England, Inc., 63

CRA International, Inc., 93

Cracker Barrel Old Country Store, Inc., 10

Craftmade International, Inc., 44

Craftmatic Organization Inc., 117

Craig Hospital, 99

craigslist, inc., 89

Crain Communications, Inc., 12; 35 (upd.)

Cramer, Berkowitz & Co., 34

Cramer-Krasselt Company, 104

Crane & Co., Inc., 26; 103 (upd.)

Crane Co., 8; 30 (upd.); 101 (upd.)

Cranium, Inc., 69

Crate and Barrel, 9

Cravath, Swaine & Moore, 43

Crawford & Company, 87

Cray Inc., 75 (upd.)

Cray Research, Inc., III; 16 (upd.)

Crayola LLC, 115 (upd.)

Creative Artists Agency LLC, 38

Credence Systems Corporation, 90

Credit Acceptance Corporation, 18

Cree Inc., 53

Crete Carrier Corporation, 95

Crimson Exploration Inc., 116

Crispin Porter + Bogusky, 83

Crocs, Inc., 80

Crompton Corporation, 9; 36 (upd.)

Croscill, Inc., 42

Crosman Corporation, 62

Cross Country Healthcare, Inc., 105

CROSSMARK 79

Crosstex Energy Inc., 107

Crowley Maritime Corporation, 6; 28 (upd.)

Crowley, Milner & Company, 19

Crown Books Corporation, 21

Crown Central Petroleum Corporation, 7

Crown Crafts, Inc., 16

Crown Equipment Corporation, 15; 93 (upd.)

Crown Holdings, Inc., 83 (upd.)

Crown Media Holdings, Inc., 45

Crown Vantage Inc., 29

Crown, Cork & Seal Company, Inc., I; 13; 32 (upd.)

CRSS Inc., 6

Cruise America Inc., 21

Crum & Forster Holdings Corporation, 104

CryoLife, Inc., 46

Crystal Brands, Inc., 9

CS First Boston Inc., II

CSG Systems International, Inc., 75

CSK Auto Corporation, 38

CSN Stores LLC, 116

CSS Industries, Inc., 35

CSX Corporation, V; 22 (upd.); 79 (upd.)

CTB International Corporation, 43 (upd.)

C-Tech Industries Inc., 90

CTG, Inc., 11

CTS Corporation, 39

Cubic Corporation, 19; 98 (upd.)

CUC International Inc., 16

Cuisinart Corporation, 24

Cuisine Solutions Inc., 84

Culbro Corporation, 15

CulinArt, Inc., 92

Cullen/Frost Bankers, Inc., 25; 111 (upd.)

Culligan Water Technologies, Inc., 12; 38 (upd.)

Culp, Inc., 29

Culver Franchising System, Inc., 58

Cumberland Farms, Inc., 17; 84 (upd.)

Cumberland Packing Corporation, 26

Cummins Engine Company, Inc., I; 12 (upd.); 40 (upd.)

Cumulus Media Inc., 37

CUNA Mutual Group, 62

Cunard Line Ltd., 23

CUNO Incorporated, 57

Current, Inc., 37

Curtice-Burns Foods, Inc., 7; 21 (upd.)

Curtiss-Wright Corporation, 10; 35 (upd.)

Curves International, Inc., 54

Cushman & Wakefield, Inc., 86

Custom Chrome, Inc., 16; 74 (upd.)

Cutera, Inc., 84

Cutter & Buck Inc., 27

CVR Energy Corporation, 116

CVS Caremark Corporation, 45 (upd.); 108 (upd.)

Cyan Worlds Inc., 101

Cybermedia, Inc., 25

Cyberonics, Inc. 79

Cybex International, Inc., 49

Cygne Designs, Inc., 25

Cygnus Business Media, Inc., 56

Cymer, Inc., 77

Cypress Semiconductor Corporation, 20; 48 (upd.)

Cyprus Amax Minerals Company, 21

Cyprus Minerals Company, 7

Cyrk Inc., 19

Cystic Fibrosis Foundation, 93

Cytec Industries Inc., 27

Cytyc Corporation, 69

Czarnikow-Rionda Company, Inc., 32

D&H Distributing Co., 95

D&K Wholesale Drug, 14

D'Agostino Supermarkets Inc., 19

D'Arcy Masius Benton & Bowles, Inc., VI; 32 (upd.)

D.A. Davidson & Company, 106

D.F. Stauffer Biscuit Company, 82

D.G. Yuengling & Son, Inc., 38

D.R. Horton, Inc., 58

Dade Behring Holdings Inc., 71

Daffy's Inc., 26

Daily Journal Corporation, 101

Dain Rauscher Corporation, 35 (upd.)

Dairy Farmers of America, Inc., 94

Dairy Mart Convenience Stores, Inc., 7; 25 (upd.)

Dairyland Healthcare Solutions, 73

Dairylea Cooperative Inc., 111

Daisy Outdoor Products Inc., 58

Daisytek International Corporation, 18

Daktronics, Inc., 32; 107 (upd.)

Dale and Thomas Popcorn LLC, 100

Dale Carnegie & Associates Inc. 28; 78 (upd.)

Dallas Cowboys Football Club, Ltd., 33; 115 (upd.)

Dallas Semiconductor Corporation, 13; 31 (upd.)

Dallis Coffee, Inc., 86

Dal-Tile International Inc., 22

Damark International, Inc., 18

Dames & Moore, Inc., 25

Dan River Inc., 35; 86 (upd.)

Dana Holding Corporation, I; 10 (upd.); 99 (upd.)

Danaher Corporation, 7; 77 (upd.)

Daniel Industries, Inc., 16

Daniel Measurement and Control, Inc., 74 (upd.)

Uruguay